Manchester City Battalions

The Right Hon. the EARL OF DERBY, K.G., P.C.

Manchester City Battalions

OF THE

90th & 91st INFANTRY BRIGADES

BOOK OF HONOUR

EDITED BY

BRIGADIER-GENERAL F. KEMPSTER, D.S.O., &
BRIGADIER-GENERAL H. C. E. WESTROPP

The Naval & Military Press Ltd

Published by

The Naval & Military Press Ltd
Unit 5 Riverside, Brambleside
Bellbrook Industrial Estate
Uckfield, East Sussex
TN22 1QQ England

Tel: +44 (0)1825 749494

www.naval-military-press.com
www.nmarchive.com

In reprinting in facsimile from the original, any imperfections are inevitably reproduced and the quality may fall short of modern type and cartographic standards.

FOREWORD

BY

The Right Hon. the EARL OF DERBY, K.G., P.C.

Derby House,
Stratford Place, W.,
24 July, 1916.

I commend this book to the people of Manchester and the surrounding district. It is a fitting record of the magnificent patriotism which has inspired that area since the beginning of the War, and it is well that people should realise how splendid was the response when the City Battalions were formed.

Since the book has been compiled there will be many names figuring in it which will have been added to another Roll of Honour—the roll of those who have laid down their lives for their Country.

Together with their friends the Liverpool City Battalions, the County Palatine Artillery, and St. Helens Battalion of the South Lancashire Regiment, which has been formed into a Pioneer Battalion, the City of Manchester Battalions have helped to form a Division which has won for itself unfading glory and has shown that new Battalions formed under the stress of War can nobly uphold the traditions of their older regular battalions.

Manchester has every reason to be proud of its sons, and I am glad to think that this record will remain, not only for those of this generation but a succeeding generation, to show how the call of duty was answered by the City.

Derby

Contents

Portrait of the Rt. Hon. the Earl of DERBY, K.G., P.C.	*Frontispiece*
	PAGE
Photographic Group of Organising Committee	x
A Record of the Manchester City Battalions by A. HERBERT DIXON, Esq. and E. TOOTAL BROADHURST, Esq.	xi
List of Guarantors	xix
Clothing and Equipment Band of Workers	xxiv
View of Depôt Goods Store	xxiv
Views of the lines at Heaton Park	xxiii and xxvi
A Short History of the Manchester Regiment, by Brigadier-General H. C. E. WESTROPP	xxvii

90th Infantry Brigade.

16th Service Battalion:—Headquarters Staff	1
Officers	4
Non-Commissioned Officers (Sergeants)	6
Bugle Band	8
A. Company, Platoons I—IV; B. Company, Platoons V—VIII; C. Company, Platoons IX—XII; D. Company, Platoons XIII—XVI; E. Company, Platoons XVII—XX	10—50
17th Service Battalion:—Officers	52
Non-Commissioned Officers (Sergeants)	54
Bugle Band	56
A. Company, Platoons I—IV; B. Company, Platoons V—VIII; C. Company, Platoons IX—XII; D. Company, Platoons XIII—XVI; E. Company, Platoons XVII—XX	58—99
18th Service Battalion:—Officers	102
Non-Commissioned Officers (Sergeants)	104
Bugle Band	106
A. Company, Platoons I—IV; B. Company, Platoons V—VIII; C. Company, Platoons IX—XII; D. Company, Platoons XIII—XVI; E. Company, Platoons XVII—XX	108—153
19th Service Battalion:—Officers	156
Non-Commissioned Officers (Sergeants)	158
Bugle Band	160
A. Company, Platoons I—IV; B. Company, Platoons V—VIII; C. Company, Platoons IX—XII; D. Company, Platoons XIII—XVI; E. Company, Platoons XVII—XX	162—201

Contents

	PAGE
91st Infantry Brigade.	
20th Service Battalion :—Headquarters Staff	205
Officers	208
Non-Commissioned Officers (Sergeants)	210
Bugle Band	212
A. Company, Platoons I—IV ; B. Company, Platoons V—VIII ; C. Company, Platoons IX—XII ; D. Company, Platoons XIII—XVI ; E. Company, Platoons XVII—XX	214—254
21st Service Battalion :—Officers	256
Non-Commissioned Officers (Sergeants)	258
Bugle Band	260
A. Company, Platoons I—IV ; B. Company, Platoons V—VIII ; C. Company, Platoons IX—XII ; D. Company, Platoons XIII—XVI ; E. Company, Platoons XVII—XX	262—300
22nd Service Battalion :—Officers	304
Non-Commissioned Officers (Sergeants)	306
Bugle Band	308
A. Company, Platoons I—IV ; B. Company, Platoons V—VIII ; C. Company, Platoons IX—XII ; D. Company, Platoons XIII—XVI ; E. Company, Platoons XVII—XX	310—348
23rd Service Battalion :—Officers	350
Non-Commissioned Officers (Sergeants)	352
Bugle Band	354
A. Company, Platoons I—IV ; B. Company, Platoons V—VIII ; C. Company, Platoons IX—XII ; D. Company, Platoons XIII—XVI ; E. Company, Platoons XVII—XX	356—396
91st Infantry Brigade Depot Officers and Supernumerary Officers	400

Index of Rolls of Honour and Attested Men.

	Page in Roll of Honour	Attested List
Adams & Co. Ltd.	405	
Affleck & Brown Ltd. & Brown Bros. Ltd.	406—407	1
Agnew (J. H.) & Bro.	761	49
Aitken, Campbell & Co. Ltd.		1
Anglo-Syrian Trading Co. Ltd.	413	1
Armitage (Sir Elkanah) & Sons Ltd.	408	
Armitage & Rigby Ltd.	656, 657	1
Armstrong (Sir W. G.), Whitworth & Co. Ltd.	409—412	
Arning & Co.	413	1
Ascoli (E.) & Son	658	1
Ashton & Co. Ltd.	658	1
Associated Newspapers Ltd.	747	49
Baerlein & Sons and Baerlein Bros.	421	1
Bannerman (Henry) & Sons Ltd.	414	2
Barber & Colman Ltd.	659	2
Barber (James) & Co. Ltd.	659	2
Barclay (Robert) & Co.	710	2
Barlow & Jones Ltd.	416—417	2
Barnes (James) Ltd.	415	2
Baxendale & Co. Ltd.	418a	3
Baxter, Woodhouse & Taylor Ltd.	454	
Beaty Bros. (Mcr.) Ltd.	418	2
Beatty, Altgeldt & Co.	662	2
Beith, Stevenson & Co. Limited	420	
Bellhouse (John & William) Ltd.	661	3
Belsize Motors Ltd.	422—423	
Benton (C.)	754	
Sir Jacob Behrens & Sons	419	2
Behrens (Louis) & Sons	454	3
Behrens (S. L.) (Manchester) Ltd.	660	3
Berisford (S. & W.) Ltd.	455	3
Binks (C.) Ltd.	662	3
Blakeley & Beving Ltd.	663	3
Black & Green Ltd.	730	
Blair (James S.) & Son	749	
Bles (S. D.) & Sons	424	3
Blyton, Astley & Co.	664	
Bolton (John) & Co.	455	3
Bond (Henry) & Co. Ltd.	762	49
Booth (Isaac) & Son	752	
Booth (John) & Co. Ltd.	764	
Bothamley (Wilson) & Son	652	48
Bowen (Herbert B.)	664	
Bradford Collieries	511—514	
Bradford Dyers' Association Ltd.	425—440	4
Brandt (H. O.) & Co.	665	10
Brayshay (Thomas) & Sons	665	10
Briggs (Thomas) (Manchester) Ltd.	441	
Briggs (Wm.) & Co. Ltd.	442	10
Brine (Fredk.) & Co.	666	
Brisbane, Jones & Co. Ltd.	666	11
British Cotton & Wool Dyers' Assoc. Ltd.	443—446	8
British Reinforced Concrete Engineering Co. Ltd.	447	11
Britton (C. H.) & Sons	456	10
Brookfield, Aitchison & Co. Ltd.	448	
Broome & Foster Ltd.	449	11
Broughton Copper Co. Ltd.	450—451	10
Brown & Forth	667	10
Buck (Edward R.) & Sons	456	11
Burgess, Ledward & Co. Ltd.	452—453	11
Burgon (A.) & Co. Ltd.	667	11
Bury (Isaac) Ltd.	668	3
Calico Printers' Association Ltd.	772—786	
Casdagli (E.) & Sons	669	12
Champness (William) & Sons	669	12
Chorlton Brothers Ltd.	457	11
Churchill Machine Tool Co. Ltd.	670	11

Contents

Name	Page in Roll of Honour	Page in Attested List
Claus & Co. Limited	480	11
Clayton Aniline Co. Ltd.	458	12
Coates, Wilson & Co.	671	
Cooper (I. J. & G.) Ltd.	459—461	12
Co-operative Wholesale Soc. Ltd.	462—476	12
Crossley Bros. Ltd.	477—478	
Crossley Motors Ltd.	479	19
Currie (Donald) & Co.	480	20
"Daily News" Ltd.	758	49
Daniels (Harold) & Co.	671	20
Dean (F. A.)	672	20
Decorators' Supply Co. Ltd.		20
Dehn & Co.	486	20
Denman (Jas. L.) & Co. Ltd.	486	
Dewhurst (Geo. & Co.) Ltd.	481—484	20
Ditchfield (John)	730	49
Dugdale, Everton & Co.	485	
Duncan, Fox & Co.	484a	20
Dunkerley (C. C.) & Co.	672	21
Dyson (A. K.) & Co. Ltd.	673	21
Eadie Bros. & Co. Ltd.	493	
East Lancashire Mills Co. Ltd.	493	
Eckstein, Heap & Co. Ltd.	487	21
Edwards, Cunliffe & Co. Ltd.	673	21
Ehrenbach, Brumm & Co.	674	
Elson & Neill	674	21
English Sewing Cotton Co. Ltd.	488—489	21
English Velvet & Cord Dyers' Assoc. Ltd.	490—492	
Etchells, Congdon & Muir Ltd.	675	
Falk, Stadelmann & Co. Ltd.	753	49
Farmer (Sir James) & Sons Ltd.	494	22
Felber, Jucker & Co. Ltd.	521	25
Fine Cotton Spinners' and Doublers' Association Ltd.	495—510	22
Finnigans Limited	515	26
Finlay, Campbell & Co. Ltd.	520	25
Fisher Renwick Manchester—London Steamers Ltd.	748	49
Fletcher, Arthur & Co.	675	
Forbes & Co.	520	
Fothergill & Harvey Ltd.	676	
Frankenburg (I.) & Sons Ltd.	516—518	26
Frankenstein (P.) & Sons Ltd.	519	22
Gatley, Vickers & Co.	677	26
Gaddum (H. T.) & Co.	525	26
Goldschmidt, Hahlo & Co.	524	27
Goodair (Richard) Ltd.	523	26
Goodwin (G. W.) & Son	522	26
Gottschalck (G.) & Co.	521	26
Graham (William) & Co.	712	50
Grandage & Co.	752	50
Greg Bros. & Co.	525	27
Groves & Whitnall Ltd.	678	27
Hall, Higham & Co.	526	27
Hall and Pickles	527	27
Hall (John) Ltd.	544	
Hardman & Holden Ltd.	528	
Haugk, von Zabern & Co.	679	27
Haworth (Richard) & Co. Ltd.	529—531	28
Heginbottom (Samuel) & Sons Ltd.	759	
Hertz (M.) & Co. Ltd.	532	27
Heyn Franc & Co.	533	27
Heynssen, Martienssen & Co.	680	27
Heywood (John) Ltd.	744, 745	50
Hill (Thos. G.) & Co. Ltd.	681	27
Hiltermann Brothers	544	27
Hinrichsen (S.) & Co.	679	27
Hogg & Mitchell	538	27
Hollins Mills Co. Ltd.	534, 535	27
Hollings (E. H.) & Sons	714	50
Holmes, Terry & Co. Ltd.	536, 537	
Horrockses, Crewdson & Co.	539	28
Household Stores Association Ltd.	541	
Hough, Hoseason & Co.	545	28
Hoyle (Joshua) & Sons Ltd.	540	28
Hudson (Sydney) Ltd.	542	28
Hulme (Alfred) Ltd.	545	28
Hulton (E.) & Co. Ltd.	723—725	50
Hutton (James F.) & Co. Ltd.	543	28
Irwell & Eastern Rubber Co. Ltd.	546	28
Jersey (de) & Co.	726	
Johnson (Jabez), Hodgkinson & Pearson Ltd.	552, 553	28
Johnson (Richard) & Nephew Ltd.	547—549	
Johnson (Rd.), Clapham & Morris Ltd.	550, 551	29
Johnson (R.) & Sons Ltd.	728	50
Jones Brothers Ltd.	554	29
Jones (W. W.), Dooly & Co.	555	29
Kay & Lee Ltd.	682	29
Kendal, Milne & Co.	556	29
Kessler & Co. Ltd.	555	
Kidsons, Taylor & Co.	684	29
Kriegsfeld (I.)	683	29
Lancashire & Yorkshire Bank Ltd.	558, 559	
Langworthy Bros. & Co. Ltd.	557	30
Latham (J. O.) & Co.	563	
Lawton & Stevenson Ltd.	722	50
Lea, (R. J.) Ltd.	563	30
Leek (George) & Sons Ltd.	684	30
Lenthall (George) & Sons	561	30
Levinstein Limited	560	30
Lewis (John T.) & Sons Ltd.	561	30
Lichtenstein (J. & E.) Ltd.	685	30
Liepmann (Julius) & Co.'s Succrs.	562	30
Linotype & Machinery Ltd.	766—769	
Liotard (J.) & Sestier	562	30

Contents

	Page in Roll of Honour	Attested List
Livesey (Thos.) & Son	685	30
Luke (Sam)	564	30
Lowthian, Drake & Co.	564	31
McDougall (Arthur) Ltd.	579	37
Mabbott & Co. Limited	565	37
Macintosh (Chas.) & Co. Ltd.	566—568	36
Manchester Corporation	404a	31
Manchester Education Committee	404b	32
Manchester Grammar School	404c	
"Manchester Guardian"	757	
Manchester Ship Canal	404d	32
Manchester Liners Ltd.	578	37
Manchester Evening News	711	
Manchester Steam Users' Association	714	52
Manchester Stock Exchange	739—741	50
Mandleberg (J.) & Co. Ltd.	770, 771	51
Marchington (Henry)	686	37
Mason, Scheidler & Co. Ltd.	578	37
Mather & Platt Ltd.	731—738	
Mead (T. Seymour) & Co. Ltd.	569, 570	37
Merttens & Co. Ltd.	579	38
Middleton, Jones & Co. Ltd.	570a	38
Midgley (David) & Sons Ltd.	571	38
Milner (John) Ltd.	721	
Möller (Ricardo)	753	50
Moorhouse (James) & Son Ltd.	572	38
Morris & Jones Ltd.	574	38
Morris (H. N.) & Co. Ltd.	715	51
Morreau, Spiegelberg & Co.	573	38
Moseley (David) & Sons Ltd.	575—577	38
Muratti (B.), Sons & Co. Ltd.	686	
Myrtle, Burt & Co.	750	52
Nasmyth, Wilson & Co. Ltd.	687, 688	
Nathan's (N. P.) Sons	580	38
O'Hanlon (Wm.) & Co. Ltd.	582	39
"Oak Tree" Hosiery Co. Ltd.	581	38
Ogden (Jas. E.) & Sons Ltd.	689	39
Ollivant (G. B.) & Co. Ltd.	689	39
Owen (Geo.) & Co.	583	39
Oxendale & Co.	583	39
Paterson, Zochonis & Co.	690	40
Paulsen, Koedt & Co.	690	39
Peak (George) & Co. Ltd.	584	
Peel, Watson & Co. Ltd.	585	39
Phethean (John) & Co. Ltd.	765	
Phillips (F.) & Co.	709	52
Philips (J. & N.) & Co.	586—589	39
Pickard & Daine		39
Pochin (H. D.) & Co. Ltd.	742, 743	52
Pownall (W. & H.) Ltd.	590	
Premier Waterproof & Rubber Co. Ltd.	591	39
Prestwich (A.) & Co. Ltd.	716	
Pugh, Davies & Co. Ltd.	717	52
Ralli Brothers	592	40
Reddaway (F.) & Co. Ltd.	594, 595	
Redpath, Brown & Co. Ltd.	692—695	40
Refuge Assurance Co. Ltd.	596, 597	40
Reiss Brothers	593	40
Renshaw & Barrow	697	
Ritchie & Eason	696	40
Roberts (J. F. & H.) Ltd.	599	40
Robinson (George) & Co.	598	40
Roe (A. V.) & Co. Ltd.	727	52
Rose, Hewitt & Co.	600	41
Roskill (G.) & Co.	697	
Rothwell (E.) & Sons	601	41
Royce Ltd.	691	41
Rylands & Sons Ltd.	602—605	41
Samuels (C. E.) & Co.	699	42
Sassoon (E. D.) & Co.	751	53
Schill Bros. Ltd.	608	42
Schmidt's Superheating Co. (1910) Ltd.	720	53
Scott (Robert) & Co.	610	42
Scottish Widows' Fund & Life Assurance Society	606, 607	43
Sherratt & Hughes	718	53
Shrewsbury & Challiner Tyre Co. Ltd.	719	43
Sidebottom (G. I.) & Co.	698	42
Simon, Son & Co.	610	43
Simon (Henry) Ltd.	611	43
Simon-Carves Ltd.	609	
Simpson & Godlee Ltd.	612, 613	43
Sivewright, Bacon & Company	614	43
Slater (Henry & Leigh) Ltd.	615	43
Smedley (J.) & Co. Ltd.	619	
Smethurst & Holden Ltd.	755	53
Smith & Coventry Ltd.	617	43
Smith (J. T.) & J. E. Jones Ltd.	616	43
Smith (Joshua) (1908) Ltd.	618	43
Southern Cotton Oil Co. of Great Britain Ltd.	620, 621	44
Sparrow Hardwick & Co.	622, 623	44
Spence (Peter) & Sons Ltd.	624	44
Spencer (Robert) & Nephews Ltd.	619	44
Spurrier, Glazebrook & Co. Ltd.	722	54
Stadelbauer & Co.	625	44
Steinthal & Co.	754	53
Stevenson (Hugh) & Sons Ltd.	626, 627	44
Stewart, Thomson & Co. Ltd.	628	44
Stott & Smith Ltd.	629	45
Stott (Louis)		45
Stubbs (Joseph) Ltd.	630	45
Susmann (Paul) & Co.	699	
Sutcliffe (W.) & Son	700	44
Sutcliffe & Bingham Ltd.	700	44

Contents

	Page in Roll of Honour	Attested List		Page in Roll of Honour	Attested List
Taylor (Fred.) & Sons	756		Watts (S. & J.) & Co.	644, 645	47
Taylor (T.) Ltd.	763		Watson (George) & Co.		48
Tennants (Lancashire) Ltd.	639	45	Watson (Herbert) & Co.	647	
Tetlow (Henry) & Sons	631		Wheeldon (James) & Sons Ltd.	707	48
Thomas (Bertram)	639	45	Whitehead (G. & G.) Ltd.	705	
Threlfall's Brewery Co. Ltd.	701		Whitworth (Herbert) Ltd.	746	
Thrutchley & Co. Ltd.	702	45	Whitworth & Mitchell Ltd.	708	48
Tootal Broadhurst Lee Co. Ltd.	632—638	46	Widdowson (John H.)	708	
Tutton (W. H.) & Co. Ltd.	702	45	Williams (J. D.) & Co.	654	48
Turnbull (Henry) & Co. Ltd.	703	45	Wilson Bothamley & Son	652	48
Union Bank of Manchester Ltd.	640—642	46	Wilson, Knowles & Co.	709	48
Union Mills Co.	704	46	Wilson, Latham & Co.	652	
United Yeast Co. Ltd.	643	47	Wilson (H. White) & Co.	654	47
Vickers (Thomas) & Sons Ltd.	705	47	Wood (Edward) & Co. Ltd.	648, 649	48
Walker & Homfrays Ltd.	646	54	Woolley (James), Sons & Co. Ltd.	650, 651	48
Walker (Geo. H.) & Son	729	54	Woodhouse, Hambly & Co.	653	48
Wallpaper Manufacturers Ltd.	706	48	Wright & Green Ltd.	713	
Welsh, Warburton & Co.	647		Young (Alfred) & Co. Ltd.	653	48
Wallwork (H.) & Co. Ltd.	760	54	Ziegler (Ph.) & Co.	718	54

A Record of the Manchester City Battalions

BY

A. HERBERT DIXON, Esq.,
Chairman of the Organising Committee,

AND

E. TOOTAL BROADHURST, Esq.

THE COMMITTEE.

A. E. PIGGOTT, Esq.,   Sir DANIEL McCABE, J.P.,   E. TOOTAL BROADHURST, Esq., J.P.   KENNETH LEE, Esq.   Staff Captain
Financial Secretary.   *Lord Mayor of Manchester.*   EDWARD M. PHILLIPS, Esq.   ARTHUR TAYLOR.
         VERNON BELLHOUSE, Esq.   A. HERBERT DIXON, Esq., *Chairman.*

A Record of the Manchester City Battalions

BY

A. HERBERT DIXON, Esq.,

AND

E. TOOTAL BROADHURST, Esq.

24th April 1915.

At the moment when the last drum is sounding and the last cheer is wafted towards the fast departing train, it is very fitting to turn our thoughts to the conception and eventual fulfilment of the movement in Manchester to raise and equip a battalion of their own as part of their contribution to the country in this hour of dire need.

To-day Manchester sent away 4,400 men constituting the 90th Brigade, consisting of the 16th, 17th, 18th and 19th Battalions of the Manchester Regiment trained in Heaton Park, men in the zenith of their youth and strength, men who had enthusiastically and voluntarily responded to the call of arms, and men of whom Manchester indeed may be justly proud; and within a few days this splendid contingent will be followed by their fellow soldiers from Morecambe, constituting the 91st Brigade, and this will give to the country some 9,000 men, irrespective of the 2,000 men left behind to form the depot companies for these two Brigades, who will be a constant source of supply in case of attrition either through losses or any other causes which may arise.

When one reflects upon the origin of this movement, which started only with the hope of raising one Battalion—1,100 strong—and realises that it has now completed eight Battalions of 1,320 men each, or in all a total of 10,560 men, it will indeed be seen that Manchester has more than risen to her responsibilities, and has beyond a doubt proved to the world her loyalty to the Empire and the real grit that has always been passively acknowledged by the country in general.

It would be an omission at this point if it were not recognised that the real inception of the whole of this movement came from the Earl of Derby, and no one can adequately convey to the public how much of the success which has ensued is due to his Lordship's keen enthusiasm and tremendously energetic support, which has never been refused even in the midst of the many and great duties which he has personally taken upon himself during the present crisis.

Originally starting in Liverpool with what he elected to call a "Pals' Battalion," it was not long before Manchester, with that friendly rivalry that has always existed between the two cities, thought she ought not to lag behind. A suggestion had been made at a meeting of the Home Trade Association held on Monday, 24th August, that many recruits would be found in the warehouses and offices of Manchester, and it was urged at that meeting that every employer ought to agree to pay during service half salaries and wages of married men, and something to the real dependents of single men who enlisted, and to guarantee re-instatement at the close of the War.

A few days later, on Friday, 28th August, under the auspices and hospitality of the Lord Mayor, an influential body of employers met at the Town Hall, when it was resolved to raise and equip a battalion from the warehouses and offices of Manchester, and to ask all employers to agree to the following conditions:—

PROPOSED BATTALION

OF

MANCHESTER CLERKS AND WAREHOUSEMEN.

A BATTALION is being raised composed entirely of employees in Manchester offices and warehouses upon the ordinary conditions of enlistment in Lord Kitchener's army, namely, for three years, or the duration of the War. The Battalion will be clothed and equipped (excepting arms) by a fund being raised for the purpose.

We therefore desire to call the attention of all our employees between the ages of 19 and 35 years to the call of Lord Kitchener, which was emphasized by the Prime Minister in the House of

Commons, for further recruits, and, in order to encourage enlistment, we are prepared to offer to all employees enlisting within the next two weeks the following conditions:—

(1) Four weeks' full wages from date of leaving.

(2) Re-engagement on discharge from service guaranteed.

(3) Half-pay during absence on duty for married men from the date that full-pay ceases, to be paid to the wife.

(4) Special arrangements made for single men who have relatives entirely dependent on them.

(5) The above payments only apply to those enlisting in the Ranks, and not to anyone who may obtain a commission otherwise than by promotion from the Ranks, but each case (if any) of those obtaining a commission, will be treated on its merits.

(6) The above offer is for voluntary service only, and should the Government decide on compulsory training later, the offer will not apply to those affected by such compulsion.

Names should be sent in to your employer.

From this small beginning emanated the movement which has become of such great importance. When we say "small beginning," it is perhaps hardly a fair expression, seeing that in the room the greatest enthusiasm prevailed, and before the meeting separated a Guarantee Fund amounting to some £15,000 had already been voted by the members present, and a decision arrived at to wire to the War Office offering on behalf of Manchester to raise, equip and clothe one battalion 1,100 strong of Manchester citizens, entirely at the expense of Manchester men. A committee was formed and instructed to take all necessary steps to recruit these men, who immediately on recruitment were to be handed over to the military authorities.

This would be an ungrateful history if it did not record that at the head of the guarantors were the civic authorities in the shape of the Gas Committee, who promptly guaranteed the sum of £7,000 out of a special reserve fund in their control. Indeed, the civic authorities from the highest to the lowest have throughout vied with one another in assisting the Committee in their work, and splendid services have been rendered, not only by the Lord Mayor himself, who has taken the most prominent and active interest in the movement, but also by the heads and members of the various important city departments, amongst which we may especially mention the Parks Committee, the Tramways Committee, the Waterworks Committee, the Gas and Sanitary Committees. It would also be difficult to duly acknowledge the help and services, always most readily given, of the Chief Constable and those under him.

In due course the consent of the War Office was obtained, but with a very large, and, looking back now it must be owned, a very proper proviso, namely, that although the absolute control of the new Battalions, and the work of clothing, equipping, billetting, hutting, etc., etc., was to be entirely in the hands of the Committee, yet they (the War Office) would not allow any private individuals to actually pay the first cost of the above expenditure, on the ground, it is believed, that it might lead to invidious comparisons. This meant that a certain amount per head was allowed for every man recruited, both for clothing, equipping, hutting, etc., but, at the same time, many extra things were required and large expenses eventually necessary in order, not only to properly advertise the requirements of Manchester, but also to give to her soldiers certain articles not coming under the War Office schedule; and the fact of having a Guarantee Fund enabled the Committee to work with much better results than could otherwise have been the case.

It is impossible to realise unless one was in the thick of it, the extraordinary enthusiasm and the ready response to the first appeal. Within twenty-four hours the ordinary channels of recruiting were blocked, and Albert Square was crowded by a band of keen young men all asking to be taken on, and all dissatisfied at the necessarily slow process. Prompt steps were taken, the Free Trade Hall was secured, and thanks to the Rev. S. F. Collier and his staff, most efficient accommodation was also found at the Albert Hall immediately opposite. The men assembled in the gallery of the Free Trade Hall and were marched in companies of 50 across to the Albert Hall, where the medical examination and enrolment took place. In this arrangement the Committee received the greatest assistance from a number of the City Police of the A Division under Inspector Bairstow. The medical world rushed to the assistance of the Committee; magistrates attended at all hours for the purposes of swearing in; and volunteers of every kind were forthcoming, and thus in a day or two everything had changed. The first Battalion was full, consent had been given for the second, and day after day this enthusiasm still maintained itself until a Brigade was recruited instead of the original proposed Battalion. Some little pause took place at this time, partially owing to the idea that possibly enough men had been obtained, when suddenly the cry came that more men were wanted, and still more. This time the Town Hall was thrown open; drums were beaten, once more willing voluntary help was forthcoming, and again a steady stream of Manchester's youngest and best blood flowed on with only one idea, namely, to do their little bit. Men from the existing Battalions went out far and wide and pulled in their friends. Meetings were held all over and the position put before willing ears. Every possible encouragement was given by employers in Manchester, often very much to their detriment, and almost like magic three more Battalions were formed. With seven Battalions filled it was thought desirable to complete a second Brigade, and recruiting was opened for a Battalion of Bantams, who flocked at once to the standard, and in a very short space of time this 23rd City Battalion was full up of men who, though short in stature, are of excellent physique, and who will, when their turn comes, do credit, not only to their regiment, but also to the City of Manchester itself.

It will be readily understood that a real difficulty arose in the organisation and management of numbers of new recruits before they were taken over by the commanding officers sent down by the Military

Authorities; but here again Manchester citizens came to the rescue, and no one can adequately acknowledge the services rendered by Colonel F. R. McConnel, Major Sington, and others, who took each lot in hand and put them through their initial stages.

Turning to another side of the question equally important perhaps in its way, we cannot but refer to the band of workers who have so admirably succeeded in clothing and equipping this large number of men. It has been no mean task when one considers that each soldier requires very nearly fifty different articles, either of clothing or equipment, every one of which articles has to be up to a certain standard according to War Office requirements; and when you add to this the undeniable difficulty of securing anything whatsoever in a market which was under the control of the War Office, with very proper power of commandeering at a moment's notice any article about to be delivered to local battalions, it will be seen that the task presented many difficulties; and one cannot pass over without record the splendid work put in by the various members of the staff who worked so ably under the Committee, and who can indeed in time to come feel and say that they did their very best.

One of the many difficulties encountered by the Committee was the responsibility with regard to each article of clothing and equipment being fully up to the standard demanded by the Authorities, but all trouble was taken off their shoulders by the action of the Manchester Testing House, who placed the whole of their experience and appliances entirely at the disposal of the Committee, with the result that every article of clothing and equipment was checked by them and passed as correct before distribution to the men.

The original uniform was blue with the well known dark grey overcoat, and very serviceable it looked; but still there was a feeling that these Battalions would never consider themselves real soldiers until they donned the universal khaki. Needless to say they would have been promptly put into khaki had it not been forbidden by the War Office, who required at that time every yard they could obtain, and it was only on the discovery of a private source from which the Government were not drawing that the Committee decided to have the second suit a khaki, and thus the Brigades which Manchester sends forth to-day are all clothed in this uniform.

Another side to the work, and a very important one, was the question of hutting. Here again the matter was left entirely in the hands of the Committee, who had, however, to work to specifications sent down by the War Office, and to a figure definitely stated by the Authorities. Anyone who visits Heaton Park will admit—as has already been admitted by the highest military authorities—that this part of the work could hardly have been improved upon, and here once again it is only fair to place on record the extraordinarily good work done by those men who, for months and months, gladly and voluntarily gave their services whilst the work proceeded. Nor can it ever be forgotten how very splendidly the Committee were backed up in this section of the work by the Civic Authorities.

The 91st Brigade, having been formed later than the 90th, have been billetted at Morecambe, it having been thought that by so doing it would not only save the very large cost involved in building another camp elsewhere, which possibly would not be used for more than six weeks to two months, but also might be of assistance to a Lancashire seaside town, which possibly might be rather hard hit owing to the war. All arrangements were made by the Military Authorities at Morecambe, and have worked out to the satisfaction of everyone.

So far we have only spoken of the work that Manchester has done to recruit and handle these men; but what of the men themselves? It is not too much to say that these men leave us to-day infinitely better men physically and from a disciplinarian point of view than they were when they first recruited. It is tremendously to their credit that they rallied round the banner without delay, and with the splendid enthusiasm that augurs well for the future. They are now on leaving Manchester in the very finest condition physically, and eagerly anticipate the last two or three months of musketry instruction which we hope is ready for them at Grantham. Their training has been no feather bed for any of them. The stern necessity of getting them really fit and well, and the somewhat difficult feeling of discipline and restraint which had to be imbued into them, constant calls to exercise and to work from early dawn to dewy eve made upon them by their leaders, have been met cheerfully and willingly by one and all. It is not too much to say that they have conducted themselves like men throughout the whole of this trying period. Their reward is in the first place the happy feeling that they have done and are doing their duty, and in the second, no one can doubt but that they have to-day that inestimable blessing, a feeling of perfect health and strength. It will gratify them to know that when they marched past Lord Kitchener on the eventful Sunday of a few weeks ago, they met with his unqualified approval. Should this war continue, as it probably will continue, beyond the next two or three months, these soldier citizens of Manchester will undoubtedly find themselves at the front side by side, not only with their own glorious regiment, but with other regulars and comrades in arms; and in saying farewell to them to-day we one and all can only feel proud of them, for they leave behind a firm conviction that, come what may, they will do credit to their regiment and their country. Officered by men of the highest military efficiency and with juniors whose experience is to a large extent out-balanced by their sense of responsibility and their keenness to serve their country, one can indeed bid them God-speed on their way with every sense of security and satisfaction.

List of Guarantors.

	£	s.	d.
Gas Department, Manchester Corporation	7000	0	0
C. Roskill	2000	0	0
E. Tootal Broadhurst	1000	0	0
Fine Cotton Spinners	1000	0	0
Horrockses, Crewdson & Co., Ltd.	1000	0	0
Arnold Seymour Mead	1000	0	0
Stock Exchange	1000	0	0
Calico Printers' Association	700	0	0
Holmes, Terry & Co.	500	0	0
Co-operative Wholesale Society, Ltd.	500	0	0
Gerard P. Dewhurst, Ltd.	500	0	0
English Sewing Cotton Co., Ltd.	500	0	0
J. & N. Philips & Co. and Staff	500	0	0
S. & J. Watts & Co.	500	0	0
E. D. Sassoon & Co.	300	0	0
Brunner, Mond & Co.	259	0	0
Barlow & Jones, Ltd.	250	0	0
R. H. Brookes (for I. J. & G. Cooper, Ltd.)	250	0	0
Finnigan's, Ltd.	250	0	0
A. & S. Henry & Co.	250	0	0
Jabez Johnson, Hodgkinson, & Pearson, Ltd.	250	0	0
The Hollins Mill Co., Ltd.	200	0	0
Haslams, Ltd.	200	0	0
Henry Bannerman & Sons, Ltd.	200	0	0
Kendal, Milne & Co.	200	0	0
Baxendale & Co., Ltd.	200	0	0
Richard Haworth & Co., Ltd.	200	0	0
Peel, Watson & Co.	150	0	0
The Employees of Rd. Haworth & Co., Ltd.	111	8	9
Sir Jacob Behrens & Sons	100	0	0
The Irkdale Printing Co. (G. N. & T. C. Midwood)	100	0	0
James Greaves	100	0	0
"The Manchester Evening News" (William Evans & Co.)	100	0	0
John Williams & Sons, Ltd.	100	0	0
William Mothersill & Co.	100	0	0
Robert Barclay & Co.	100	0	0
David Midgley & Sons, Ltd.	100	0	0
Refuge Assurance Co., Ltd.	100	0	0
Arning & Co.	100	0	0
E. H. Broadhurst	100	0	0
T. Collier & Co., Ltd.	100	0	0
Jones Bros., Ltd.	100	0	0
Lewis B. Kendal	100	0	0
Arthur McDougall, Ltd.	100	0	0
William Sutcliffe	100	0	0

	£	s.	d.
J. F. & H. Roberts, Ltd.	100	0	0
Hans Renold, Ltd.	100	0	0
Sparrow, Hardwick & Co.	100	0	0
Fred Taylor & Sons	100	0	0
Julius Lieppmann & Co.'s Successors	100	0	0
George Fraser, Son & Co., Ltd.	100	0	0
Sutton & Co.	100	0	0
J. D. Williams	100	0	0
W. Graham & Co.	100	0	0
Joshua Hoyle & Sons, Ltd.	100	0	0
Stott & Smith	100	0	0
John Ashworth, Ltd.	100	0	0
John Heywood, Ltd.	100	0	0
Wilson Bothamley & Son	60	0	0
Rd. Johnson, Clapham & Morris, Ltd.	55	0	0
Geo. Peak & Co.	52	10	0
Palatine Bank, Ltd.	50	0	0
Eadie Bros. & Co., Ltd.	50	0	0
Heyn Franc & Co.	50	0	0
Simpson & Godlee, Ltd.	50	0	0
Smethurst & Holden, Ltd.	50	0	0
John Peel & Co.	50	0	0
Ashton Bros. & Co., Ltd.	50	0	0
Commercial Estates, Ltd.	50	0	0
Grandage & Co.	50	0	0
J. K. W. Hesketh	50	0	0
Ogdens & Madeleys, Ltd.	50	0	0
George Robinson & Co.	50	0	0
Richard Goodair, Ltd.	50	0	0
John Munn & Co.	50	0	0
J. Thomas & Co.	50	0	0
Jaffé & Sons	50	0	0
Pugh, Davies & Co.	50	0	0
Welsh, Warburton & Co.	50	0	0
Peter Spence & Sons, Ltd.	50	0	0
The Southern Cotton Oil Co., Ltd.	50	0	0
McIntyre, Hogg, Marsh & Co., Ltd.	50	0	0
The Premier Waterproof & Rubber Co., Ltd.	50	0	0
Lomnitz & Duxbury, Ltd.	50	0	0
Hall, Higham & Co.	50	0	0
Hickson, Lloyd & King	50	0	0
Exors. of Thomas Hudson	50	0	0
C. H. Britton & Co.	40	0	0
Henry Vollmer Ltd.	40	0	0
Beaty Bros., Ltd.	40	0	0
W. & H. Pownall	35	0	0
Finlay, Campbell & Co., Ltd.	30	0	0
Smith, Garnett & Co.	26	5	0
John Bolton & Co.	25	0	0
Miss Hurst	25	0	0

	£	s.	d.
F. J. Hayes	25	0	0
William Marsden	25	0	0
Sidebottom & Hardie	25	0	0
The Unbreakable Pulley Co., Ltd.	25	0	0
H. Walkden	25	0	0
William Timpson, Ltd.	25	0	0
Exors. of Samuel Pitts	25	0	0
J. Liotard & Sestier	25	0	0
Thrutchley & Co., Ltd.	25	0	0
Manchester & Salford Equitable Co-operative Soc., Ltd.	25	0	0
John Royle & Co., Ltd.	25	0	0
Reid, Waters & Co.	25	0	0
Wilson, Latham & Co.	25	0	0
Manchester Velvet Co.	25	0	0
Alen G. Hogg	25	0	0
Herbert Watson & Co.	25	0	0
E. Rothwell & Sons	25	0	0
London City & Midland Bank Ltd.	25	0	0
Greg Bros. & Co.	21	0	0
Rose, Hewitt & Co.	21	0	0
James Barnes, Ltd.	20	0	0
Joseph Bridge & Co., Ltd.	20	0	0
E. S. David, Sons & Co.	20	0	0
Forbes & Co.	20	0	0
Frank Merriman	20	0	0
Rigby, Wainwright & Co.	20	0	0
Robert, Williams & Sons (Gorton), Ltd.	20	0	0
Adolphus Sington & Co.	20	0	0
Henry & Leigh Slater, Ltd.	20	0	0
Henry Blacklock & Co., Ltd.	20	0	0
Mabbott & Co.	20	0	0
James L. Denman & Co., Ltd.	20	0	0
S. Heginbottom & Sons, Ltd.	15	0	0
Manchester Billposting Co., Ltd.	14	13	0
The United Theatres Co., Ltd.	10	10	0
Chas. Scheerbart	10	10	0
Hughes & Young, Ltd.	10	0	0
W. H. Pennington	10	0	0
Arthur Foote	10	0	0
Hall & Pickles	10	0	0
Felber, Jucker & Co., Ltd.	10	0	0
East Lancashire Mills Co., Ltd.	10	0	0
John Hall, Ltd.	10	0	0
Fred. W. Millington, Ltd.	10	0	0
Heycock & Co.	10	0	0
Kidsons, Taylor & Co.	10	0	0
Sutcliffe & Bingham	10	0	0
F. H. Sugden	10	0	0
Robert Scott & Co.	10	0	0
John Worrall	10	0	0

	£	s.	d.
Simon, Son & Co.	10	0	0
Batho, Taylor, & Ogden, Ltd.	10	0	0
Robert Spencer & Nephews, Ltd.	10	0	0
W. W. Jones, Dooly & Co.	10	0	0
Furness & Goodwin	10	0	0
Edwin Collier & Co.	10	0	0
James Moorhouse & Sons, Ltd.	10	0	0
Armitage & Rigby, Ltd.	10	0	0
E. R. Buck & Sons	10	0	0
John S. Morris & Sons (Oils), Ltd.	10	0	0
Marshall & Crossland	10	0	0
Mrs. Lucy Peters	7	0	0
Smith & Brooks	5	0	0
William Lindop	5	0	0
Orford & Sons	5	0	0
Harold Hope	5	0	0
W. Gould	5	0	0
H. O. Thistleton & Son	5	0	0
Winnington District Co-operative Society	5	0	0
Joseph J. Hewitt	3	3	0
The Crescent Waterproof Co., Ltd.	3	0	0
H. Luke, Ltd.	3	0	0
Stroeger & Co. (George Watson, Successor)	2	2	0
Cuthbert B. Leeming	2	1	0
William Shufflebottom	2	0	0
Robert Brierley	2	0	0
J. Mottershead	2	0	0
D. Jessop & Son	1	1	0
A Well-Wisher	1	1	0
Thomas Briggs, Ltd.	1	0	0
W. Brownhall, Junr.	0	5	0
Total Amount Guaranteed	£26,701	9	9

ARTHUR E. PIGGOTT,
Financial Secretary.

List of Gifts.

Messrs. A. G. Bateman & Co.—Made up free of charge 6,000 Flannel Shirts.
Messrs. Chorlton Bros. Ltd.—4,000 pairs of Putties.
Messrs. Kay & Lee, Ltd.—4,000 Holdalls.
Messrs. Henry Cardwell & Co.—A "Tug-of-War" Rope, &c.
The Manchester Chamber of Commerce Testing House.—Free Testing of Cloth, &c., &c.
Mr. Luke O'Reilly.—Empty Barrels.
Mr. H. H. Leeming of John A. Bremmer & Co.—Empty Barrels.
Messrs. Ralli Bros.—Free use of their old warehouse in Peter Street, for Brigade Stores.

THE LINES AT HEATON PARK.

16th BATTALION.

17th BATTALION.

CLOTHING AND EQUIPMENT BAND OF WORKERS.

W. H. Silcock.   C. Watkins.   A. Eastwood.
J. Kennerdell.

H. S. Porter,   W. S. Mason,   J. Cunningham,
Architect of Hutments.   *Equipment Secretary.*   *Storekeeper.*

THE STORES (Section only).

A Short History of the Manchester Regiment

BY

BRIGADIER-GENERAL H. C. E. WESTROPP

THE LINES AT HEATON PARK.

18th BATTALION.

19th BATTALION.

A Short History of the Manchester Regiment

BY

BRIGADIER-GENERAL H. C. E. WESTROPP

[Being Extracts from an Address to the First City Brigade Manchester Regiment in the Free Trade Hall, Manchester, 8th January, 1915].

"It is the History of Regiments—it is their pride, and it is their traditions, which make a Regiment illustrious, which make it formidable in the field, and when weapons and numbers alone will not avail, they give the Regiment its glory and its confidence."

You will find in the preface of the small book of Records of the 2nd Battalion Manchester Regiment, the 96th of the Line, the following words:—

"The British soldier, if not always invincible, is dauntless in battle, and it is to the valour of the rank and file, as much as anything else, that England owes her vast Empire."

And again:—

"Be proud of your Regiment, and your uniform, and remember that the men who served in the Regiment before you helped to build up the present British Empire, the finest the World has ever seen, and whose glory it is your duty to maintain."

About three years ago I went to Ashton, to hand over the old Colours of the 2nd Battalion to be cared for in the Parish Church, and a most beautiful old Church it is. The Service was most solemn and impressive, and the greatest public interest was taken in the ceremony. Afterwards, at a luncheon given by the Mayor of Ashton, who was so interested in this Regiment for which I had the honour to speak, I gave a short account of the Services rendered by both Regular Battalions, and I propose to repeat my remarks, with some additions and omissions.

The First Battalion of the Manchester Regiment was formerly known as the 63rd Regiment, having been constituted by King George III on 9th May, 1758, out of the Second Battalion of General Wolfe's 8th Foot.

The Second Battalion Manchester Regiment was originally raised in January 1824, as the 96th Foot, by command of King George IV, by Major-General Fuller at Manchester. It inherited the honours of former regiments bearing the same number, as shown later on.

The following are the Honours borne on the Colours:—

    Egmont-op-Zee, 63rd.
    Martinique, 63rd and 96th.
    Guadaloupe, 63rd and 96th.
    Peninsula, 96th.
    Alma, 63rd.
    Inkerman, 63rd.
    Sebastopol, 63rd.
    New Zealand, 96th.
    Afghanistan, 1879—1880, 63rd.
    Egypt 1882, 63rd and 96th.
    South Africa 1899—1902, 63rd and 96th.
    Defence of Ladysmith, 63rd.

That in itself is a fine list of Battle Honours for the Colours, but besides these is a long list of Battles, Expeditions, etc., which show what distinguished services the old First Battalion, 63rd Regiment, has handed down to us. The list includes all the main actions in which the First Battalion has taken part.

Manchester Regiment

Statement showing Battles, Campaigns, and Expeditions, etc., in which the 1st Battalion Manchester Regiment (late 63rd) has taken part—from 1755 to 1913.

DATES	COLONEL	LIEUT. COLONEL	BATTLES, CAMPAIGNS, ETC.	GENERALS IN COMMAND
24 January, 1759	D. Watson	P. Desbuay	Guadaloupe	Barrington
17 January, 1775	F. Grant	L. Paterson	Bunker's Hill	Gage
27 August, 1776	,,	,,	Brooklyn	Sir H. Clinton
11 September, 1777	,,	,,	Brandywine	,,
6 October, 1777	,,	,,	Fort Clinton	,,
31 May, 1779	,,	,,	Stony Point	Vaughan
12 May, 1780	,,	,,	Charleston	Sir H. Clinton
9 September, 1780	,,	,,	Fish Dam	Major Wemyss
20 November, 1780	,,	,,	Blackstock Hill	Col. Tarleton
25 April, 1781	,,	,,	Hobskirk Hill	Lord Rawdon
8 September, 1781	,,	,,	Ecctaw Springs	Col. Stewart
4 November, 1794	Earl Balcarres	Levison Gower	Nimeguen	Duke of York
31 December, 1794	,,	,,	Bommel	,,
4 January, 1795	,,	,,	Geldermalsen	,,
24 March, 1796	,,	,,	Port Royal	R. A. Abercrombie
1 May, 1796	,,	,,	St. Lucia	,,
10 June, 1796	,,	,,	St. Vincent	,,
July—October, 1796	,,	,,	Charib War	P. Hunter
August, 1798	,,	H. Brereton	Honduras	,,
27 August, 1799	,,	,,	Helder	Sir R. A. Abercrombie
11 Setpember, 1799	,,	,,	Juyp	Duke of York
19 September, 1799	,,	,,	Schagen Burg	,,
2 October, 1799	,,	,,	Egmont-op-Zee	,,
6 October, 1799	,,	,,	Alkmaar	,,
25 June, 1800	,,	,,	Coast of France	Sir J. Pulteney
August, 1800	,,	,,	Ferrol	,,
24 December, 1807	,,	D. Boswell	Madeira	Lord Beresford
8 February, 1809	,,	S. Fairtlough	Martinique	Col. Barnes
8—15 August, 1809	,,	Cosmo Gordon	Flushing	Earl of Chatham

2nd Bn. 63rd.
(afterwards disbanded).

DATES	COLONEL	LIEUT. COLONEL	BATTLES, CAMPAIGNS, ETC.	GENERALS IN COMMAND
6 February, 1810	,,	S. Fairtlough	Guadaloupe	Sir G. Beckwith
8, 9, 10 August, 1815	,,	D. Rattray	,,	Sir J. Leith
1 January, 1827	William Dyott	E. Burke	Portugal	Sir W. Clinton
20 September, 1854	Thomas Kenah	E. S. T. Swyny	Alma	Lord Raglan
25 October, 1854	,,	,,	Balaklava	,,
5 November, 1854	,,	,,	Inkerman	,,
31 May, 1855	,,	Hon. R. A. G. Dalzell	Kertch	Sir G. Brown
18 June, 1855	,,	P. Lindesey	Redan	Lord Raglan
8 September, 1855	,,	,,	Sebastopol	J. Simpson
4 October, 1855	,,	,,	Kinburn	Hon. A. Spencer
12 August, 1880	Sir R. Waddy	W. L. Auchinleck	Afghanistan	R. Phayre
14 October, 1881	,,	,,	Kandahar	H. H. James
10 July, 1882	E. R. Jeffrey	,,	Egypt	Sir G. Wolseley
1899-1902	V. H. Bowles	A. E. R. Curran	South Africa Defence of Ladysmith	{ Sir G. White Sir R. Buller Lord Roberts

A Short History of the

SERVICES OF THE 2ND BATTALION MANCHESTER REGIMENT, LATE 96TH.

The 96th, like other Regiments which have borne high numbers, has been raised and disbanded on several occasions.

The first 96th was raised in 1760 for service in Southern India under Clive, and saw much fighting in the Carnatic against the French and their native allies.

The second 96th was raised in the American War of Independence, and was disbanded in the Channel Islands 1783.

The Third 96th was raised at the time of the French Revolution (1793), served in the West Indies, and was broken up at Halifax, Nova Scotia, 1797.

The fourth 96th was raised from the 52nd Foot in 1803, and had two Battalions, the first of which served in the West Indies, and a portion was present at the capture of Guadaloupe. But in 1815, when the 95th (Rifle Brigade) was taken out of the line, it was renumbered 95th and disbanded in 1818.

After the capture of Minorca by Sir John Stuart a Regiment was raised in that island, and in 1800 joined the expedition under Sir Ralph Abercrombie against the French in Egypt. Took part in the Battle of Alexandria, and captured a French Colour now at the Royal Hospital, Chelsea. It served under the Duke of Wellington in the Peninsula, repulsed the French at the point of the bayonet at Vimiera, and was present at Talavera and Busaco. It appears in the Army List of 1816 as the 96th (Queen's Own) Regiment. Disbanded at Limerick 1818.

The sixth 96th Regiment (the present 2nd Battalion Manchester Regiment). After "Stuart's Regiment," 96th, was disbanded in 1818, its place remained vacant on the Army List for six years until 1824, when the present Battalion was raised and numbered 96th by the King's command, by Major-General L. Fuller, curiously enough at Manchester, the name conferred upon it fifty-seven years later (1881), when the 63rd West Suffolk Regiment and the 96th became the 1st and 2nd Battalions of "The Manchester Regiment." This, the sixth, and last Regiment raised under the number 96, carried the honours of

Stuart's Regiment: Sphinx—Egypt—Peninsula, and took part in the New Zealand War in 1845, and were engaged in the Bay of Islands twice and at Hekies Pah. As the 2nd Manchester Regiment: in the Egyptian War 1882, the Miranzai Expedition 1891, and in the South African War.

The following is a list of the Colours which have been presented to the 96th and 2nd Battalion:—

In 1779.—To the second Regiment raised and numbered 96. These Colours are still in the Officers' Mess 2nd Batt., and were carried in the Army Pageant in London about four years ago.

In 1824.—New Colours were taken into use but not presented until the following year, when they were consecrated at Halifax, Nova Scotia, by order of Major-General Sir Howard Douglas, and presented by Lady Lumley, and were carried until 1861, and are now in the Manchester Cathedral.

In 1861.—Colours were presented by Major-General Shirley, commanding troops at the Curragh. Carried until 1886, and are now in the Manchester Cathedral.

In 1886.—Colours were presented by the Commander-in-Chief in India, Sir Frederick, afterwards Lord, Roberts, which were placed recently in the Parish Church at Ashton-under-Lyne.

In 1911.—Colours were presented by His Majesty King George V in the Phœnix Park, Dublin, and are now carried. The following is the message to the Battalion handed to me by the King:—

"To take part in the ceremony of the presentation of new Colours is an occasion which must appeal, not only to the Regiment, but to all who are imbued with the true military spirit. It is the commencement of a new chapter in the life of the Regiment, when all Ranks—and especially the young soldiers—should remember those names and mottoes borne on its Colours, recalling as they do the history of the Regiment, its victories, its leaders, and those who in the past have fought and died on the field of battle.

"Your Battalion has seen service in New Zealand, Egypt, India, and South Africa, and I know you will always be ready to obey the call of duty.

"Though no longer led to the attack by your Colours, their consecration to-day will remind you that God's blessing is not denied to those who give their lives for their country, and its freedom. Every man knows that he has them in his special keeping, and by his action he can secure to them new lustre.

"With such feelings, I have much pleasure in confiding these Colours to your charge.

11th July, 1911.   (Sig.)   GEORGE R.I."

His Majesty's words are not yet four years old, and we know, and history will show, how so many who listened to them have given their lives for their country and its freedom, and by their action have added new lustre to the Regiment, which, in this city, is deservedly held in such high honour. Every man in that Battalion knew, and every man in all Battalions of this Regiment knows, that he holds the honour of this city, and of the old Regiments which brought here their fighting history and traditions, in the hollow of his hand—that is a noble responsibility.

Believe me it is no light one. It is no exaggeration to say that the recent services of the gallant Regiments in Sir John French's Army (including our 1st and 2nd Battalions) against tremendous odds, have been the admiration of all unprejudiced people in the world. This is the standard of soldiering which we must all endeavour to sustain.

Now a few brief extracts regarding the Services of our 1st Battalion, the old 63rd of the Line, which has been in most quarters of the Globe. In Holland, France, America, Canada, the West Indies, Spain, Portugal, Madeira, the Crimea, Egypt, South Africa, India, Afghanistan, Australia, and is now at the Front.

Bunker's Hill (1775). "Tested the mettle of the Regiment. Twice it was stopped and twice it returned to the charge, in the middle of a hot summer's day, encumbered with three days' provisions and with their knapsacks on their backs, which, with cartouche box, ammunition, and firelock, weighed altogether about 125 pounds, with a steep hill to climb, intersected with walls and fences, in the face of a hot and well directed fire, it gained a complete victory over three times their number of the enemy, strongly posted."

An extract from the " History of the War in the Crimea :—

" Battle of Inkerman, 1854, which lasted without a moment's pause from daylight on Sunday, 5th November, till about half-past two in the afternoon. The Generals of the Fourth Division being all killed or wounded, Brigadier-General Pennefather of the 2nd Division rode up to Colonel Swyny and said : ' Let us see what metal the 63rd is made of. The enemy will be soon upon you, be ready to give him a volley, and charge.' The Regiment was lying down in line under heavy artillery fire and the enemy advanced in columns. The Colonel gave the order, a volley was fired and the Regiment with its usual cheer charged with the bayonet and drove the Russians down the Barrier. They, however, disputed every inch of ground with incredible fury and determination. The conflicts were of the most deadly character. The colonel and officers carrying the Colours, and many others were killed."

Some years ago I was sent the following account of the death of Ensign Clutterbuck, 63rd Regiment :—

" James Hutton Clutterbuck was the son of Robert Clutterbuck of Watford, Herts., and grandson of the author of the ' History of Hertfordshire.' This youth had not attained his twentieth year when he died at Inkerman, having received a bullet in the neck which descended to the chest and pierced the lungs. He had been in the Army only sixteen months. How he fought and died has been well described by an humble soldier, of his Regiment, in the following letter :—' The Regiment, with the 21st, formed line. We charged gloriously; we routed thousands, and as fast as we could run in pursuit, and load our pieces, they fell. We could not miss them, they were so thick. We chased them for the best part of a mile, past their own entrenchments, and beyond that. In the thick of the whole of it fell poor Mr. Clutterbuck, who was carrying the Queen's Colour, and cheering on the men—I think the last words he said were, " Come on 63rd "—when he received a shot right through the neck which killed him instantly. He died gloriously. I never saw a braver man than him on the field that day, although it is with sorrow I have to record his death. I was by his side the whole of the time. It was between eight and nine in the morning of the 5th that he received his death wound. After the fight was over I went to him and had his remains removed to camp. I took a small piece of his hair, which I send to you to give to his respected friends. His disconsolate father may well be proud of having such a son, for he fought and died bravely, with the Queen's Colour of the 63rd in his hand. We lost General Cathcart, and Colonel Seymour, Adjutant-General. Mr. Clutterbuck was laid alongside of them.' Lieut. H. T. Twysden, who was carrying the Regimental Colour, was mortally wounded and died on the 9th November in the camp."

To pass over many years Field Marshal Sir George White, speaking to a large and representative gathering at Capetown after the South African War, amongst other remarks said:—

" During the attack on Cæsar's Camp (at Ladysmith) a remote corner was held by sixteen of the Manchester Regiment, who fought from three in the morning until dusk, when the Devonshires reinforced them. Fourteen of the little band lay dead, and of the two survivors one was wounded, but they still held their position, and got V.C.'s."

When the monument was unveiled here, 26th October, 1908, after the South African War, Sir George wrote:—

" The steadfastness of devotion with which a detachment of the Manchester Regiment held a position at Cæsar's Camp, during the

Boer attack on Ladysmith on the 6th January, 1900, was worthy of the best records of the British Army, and the City of Manchester does well to perpetuate it as an example of patriotism to her citizens *and as an imperishable memory.*"

And Sir Ian Hamilton, on the same occasion, when he unveiled the statue, said :—

"They fought against starvation on the morning of the 6th January till 5-30 in the evening. These starving, ragged lads kept back the Boers from the vitals of the town . . . . We lament their loss, but we do not in lamenting *forget,* that Manchester has also cause for deep pride and thankfulness, *at the thought that she could, were it needed, call up battalion after battalion to fight in a just cause—battalions who would be inspired by the memory and example of these heroic comrades of theirs who have gone on before.* Yes, Manchester laments her dead, but accepts their gifts of love and life. She would have it no otherwise, and would not, if she *might,* take again the purple of their blood out of the Cross on the breast-plate of England."

To come almost to the present moment. We heard a few days ago an account of what was thought and said concerning a terrific fight in which our *First* Battalion has been engaged.

Believe me when the history of this war comes to light, in due course, when names of places and people can be mentioned without detriment to present operations, you will indeed have cause for thankfulness that this city can produce such brave men, who have increased the reputation of the British soldier as a fighting man by a magnificent piece of work which will live long in the annals of our oldest Battalion, and in those of this city, I trust. Is it to be wondered at that we Regular Officers take so much interest in the history and traditions of this Regiment, both before and after its connection with this city? Is it to be wondered at that all soldiers, who have served for any time, recognise the value of *esprit de corps?* Is it to be wondered at that the noble and heroic deeds of our predecessors, and our present comrades, fill us with a sense of the duty we owe, in times of stress, to Old England? Is it to be wondered at that the British soldier, with such predecessors and comrades, is not down-hearted, and is ready cheerfully to hold his own against any odds?

The history of both Battalions makes a fine record. It is the history of the combined doings of Colonels and Officers, and rank and file. The history of Services under past conditions, and of that glorious pride, which makes the British Regiment what it is, and which is passed down from one generation to another, lest any should forget the traditions which must be maintained, or the confidence the record engenders. Well, so much for the record, in brief, which has been well, aye more than well, maintained, since the Regiment has derived its supply of men from this city and this district.

For many years it has been my privilege, in one capacity or another, to have been commanding Lancashire men, and I have never had the slightest doubt that any Battalion composed of them, *if properly trained and disciplined*, could possibly fail in the field. In bidding farewell to the 2nd Battalion I used, amongst others, the following words: " I sincerely hope that the old-fashioned Lancashire lads, with grit, and a fighting spirit, may for years to come join a Regiment, in ever increasing numbers, in which they are appreciated and understood." Every man, of whatever rank, who has served or will serve for any considerable period of years in this Regiment, will *find* that there is slowly but certainly, perhaps at first even without his knowledge, being woven round his heart a sensitive belt, which works and palpitates with the feelings of those around him, directly the honour or success of his Regiment is concerned in peace, or war, which does not slacken but grows more closely as the years roll on, and when he comes to say " Good-bye " to his comrades, is at its greatest tension. Tactics, drill, musketry, field training, etc., etc., may change and change again, but the rules of friendship, of mutual support, of *esprit de corps* never change, and will continue until Regiments, Brigades, and Armies have ceased to be. One individual supporting another. One Section supporting the next. Platoon supporting platoon. Battalion supporting Battalion. The guns supporting the infantry. In fact all arms combining together, concentrated mutual trained effort, and *esprit de corps* which make up the total morale of an army in the field, on which the Commander-in-Chief can rely.

Life is short, each one of us holds the honour of the Regiment in his hand for a span of years with the Colours, and indeed cherishes it, having been one of " ours " always in civil life afterwards. The older one grows the quicker time passes. The older one grows the more one regrets if the best use has not been made of it. The longer one serves the more one realizes how necessary it is to make every man in this Regiment remember that he is one who has to carry on the fine traditions of the old Battalions, who has to represent the city, after which the Regiment is named—one of the first commercial cities in the Empire—and that he serves the King, the Duke of Lancaster, who represents not only Old England but also that Empire which our predecessors have done so much to build up, and which we, and our sons after us, have to uphold and maintain against all enemies, however powerful.

This Brigade, raised under the auspices of the Earl of Derby, K.G., and the Lord Mayor of Manchester, and with the aid of the excellent and hardworking Committee, indeed represents this city, which has responded so nobly to the call to arms as much at least as any force that has ever been raised in it, and starts with the fine traditions of hard work, grit, and self-sacrifice for the common good which, we all know, have so long been connected with the inhabitants of this city and county. A lucky Brigade, indeed, to start under such circumstances, and in addition equally lucky to form new Battalions to the Line Battalions second to none in a fighting sense in our Army. From your willingness to join the Colours, from your keenness to excel in training, from your behaviour, I am certain that a good honest healthy discipline will prevail under all circumstances, hard or easy. You know, as well as I do, that a Regiment without discipline in our Army is impossible, it would not be fit to live in. In fact it would cease to be a Regiment in the best sense, and become a disgrace to one of the smallest but, I believe, the best fighting armies in the world. One thing discipline teaches, and that is, consideration for others, for those above, for those below, and from the junior ranks for the senior. Support your Commanding and other Officers and N.C.O.'s up to the hilt, and they will jump to it and work all the more earnestly for the Regimental good.

Believe me, every man living, however clever, however independent, however rich, however poor, wants support, and plenty of it at times from the cradle to " lights out," from the senior officer present to the smallest youngster here straight from school. Well, that is what is necessary, and which I was lucky enough to find existing in our Regular Battalions when I joined about thirty-two years ago, and which has been in strong evidence ever since. Many of us have known Officers and Non-Commissioned Officers of whom it was said the men would do anything for, because they worked in a cheerful way, with all their capacity, for the general good of the Regiment. Lucky men, who used the powers all, more or less, possess of influence, of sympathy, and leadership. Simple virtues, perhaps, but ones which spring from a very valuable old-fashioned motor, the heart, which helps a properly tuned brain to give off those positive wireless sparks which make others think, feel, and act with it, and keeps alight that lamp of Regimental spirit, which has never yet flickered, much less gone out. I finish as I commenced, with a quotation from Lord Rosebery:—

" It is the history of Regiments, it is their pride and their traditions which make a Regiment illustrious, and formidable in the field, and when weapons and numbers alone will not avail they give the Regiment its glory, and its *confidence*."

Manchester City Battalions
OF THE
90th Infantry Brigade

90TH INFANTRY BRIGADE

Headquarters' Staff.

* * *

Front Row (Left to Right).

    Rev. R. W. BALLEINE
        (Brigade Chaplain).

    Brigadier-General H. C. E. WESTROPP
        (Commanding 90th Brigade).

    Major C. L. R. PETRIE, D.S.O.
        (Brigade Major).

    Captain ARTHUR TAYLOR
        (Acting Staff Captain).

Back Row (Left to Right).

    Corporal MITCHELL
        (Second Clerk).

    Lance-Corporal R. T. LOMAX
        (Orderly).

    Brigade Q.M.-Sergt. C. E. STEWART
        (Brigade Clerk).

    Private J. FIELDING (Orderly).

    Lance-Corporal A. J. TYLDESLEY
        (Dispatch Rider).

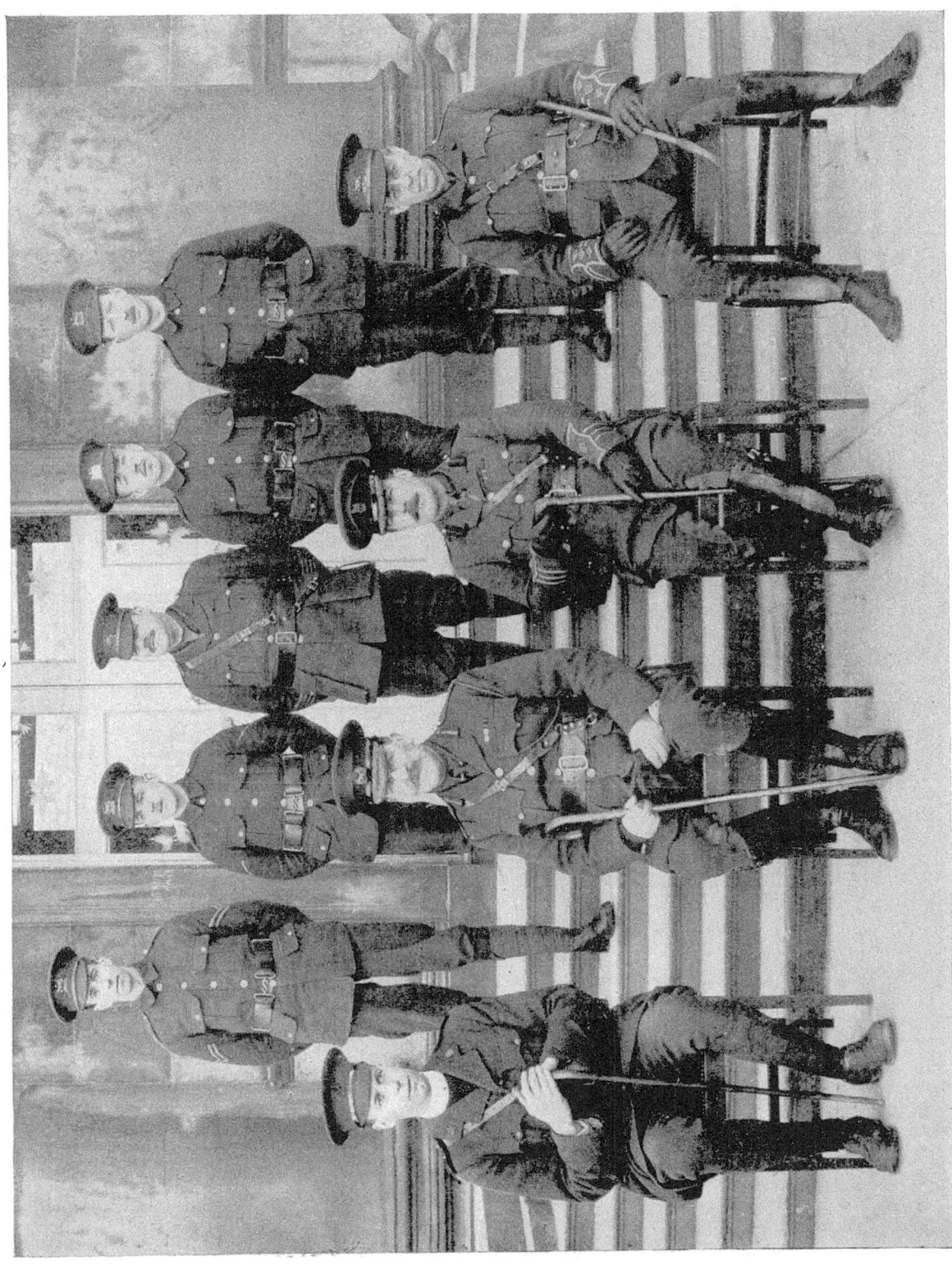

16th (Service) Battalion

16th (Service) Battalion Manchester Regiment.

Roll of Officers.

Lieut.-Col.	Crawford, J. C.	2nd Lieut.	Philips, R. O.
Major	Comyn, D. C. E. ff.	,,	Megson, R. H.
Capt. & Adjt.	Sotham, E. G.	,,	Rhodes, E. L.
Captain	Greg, H. S.	,,	Percy, J. E. G.
,,	Wheatley-Crowe, H. S.	,,	Henriques, G. L. Q.
,,	Roberts, R. E.	,,	Knowles, R. K.
,,	Walker, F.	,,	Hook, C. W. K.
,,	Patey, M. H. R.	,,	Mead, P. J.
,,	Payne, J. J.	,,	Clarke, W. F.
,,	Worthington, J. H.	,,	Hayward-Browne, I. W.
,,	Geary, Sir W. N. M., Bart.	,,	Dyer, H. de D.
,,	Taylor, A.	,,	Gibbon, R.
,,	Johnson, W. M.	,,	Prestwich, E.
,,	Elstob, W.	,,	Bles, G. M.
Lieutenant	Behrens, F. E.	,,	Barber, G. A.
,,	Wilson, L. F.	,,	Allen, S. R.
,,	Oliver, J. M.	,,	Slack, E. S.
,,	Dalgliesh, A. B.	Lieut. & Q.M.	Ball, J. T.
,,	Davidson, W. S.	Lieutenant	Fletcher, F. S. (Med. Off.)
,,	Sington, A. J. C.		*Attached.*
,,	Morris, G. P.	Lieut.-Col.	Ledward, H.
		Captain	Cunliffe, H. H.

Brigadier-General Westropp, Major Petrie, D.S.O., and the Chaplain (Rev. W. R. Balleine) also appear on the Photograph.

The following were not present when the Photograph was taken :—

2nd Lieut.	Clayton, E. G.	2nd Lieut.	O'Connel de Courcy Macdonnel, J. P.
,,	Day, C. E.	,,	Nash, T. A. H.

16th (Service) Battalion Manchester Regiment.

Non-Commissioned Officers' (Sergeants) Roll.

Warrant Officer.
6224 R.S.M. CHEETHAM, R.

7152 B.Q.M.S. STEWART, C. E.
6993 R.Q.M.S. GUINAN, T.
7281 R.O.R.S. LYON, W. F.

Roll No.	Rank and Name.		Roll No.	Rank and Name.	
6242	C.S.M.	FARRELL, J. F.	6571	Sergeant	WHARTON, D.
6516	,,	KENNELLY, J. G.	6702	,,	WINNING, T. A.
6824	,,	CLARKE, J.	6551	,,	MASON, W. A.
7045	,,	REDDY, J.	6345	,,	BROCKLEHURST, J.
6574	,,	BLAKELEY, J. H.	6884	,,	HIGGS, J. A.
6366	C.Q.M.S.	DARLINGTON, P.	6900	,,	LINGARD, H.
6512	,,	JOYCE, T.	6737	,,	EDGAR, J. V.
7179	,,	DEWAN, T.	6563	,,	THOMAS, E.
6312	,,	STURGESS, F.	7138	,,	PALIN, H.
7090	Sgt. Cook	CARR, S.	6987	,,	FINAN, G.
6850	Pion. Sgt.	CLIFFE, R.	7115	,,	HAWXBY, H.
6794	M.G.Sgt.	RALPHS, T.	7266	,,	TURNER, F. H.
6343	Trns. Sgt.	BROADBENT, G.	6955	,,	BARKER, C.
7171	Sergeant	BURKE, T.	7189	,,	BAKER, G.
6239	,,	DUNKLEY, F.	6214	,,	BEAN, T. W.
6320	,,	WELSH, T. E.	6310	,,	PAYNE, J.
6244	,,	FARR, A. W.	7323	,,	MILLER, J.
6216	,,	BIRCH, F. J.	6206	,,	ARCHER, W.
6201	,,	ADAMSON, J.	6359	,,	COCHRANE, F.
6407	,,	MILES, M. V.	7472	,,	CONNELL, W.
6324	,,	WILLIAMS, J. C.	7471	,,	HICKIN, T.
6485	,,	DEANE, G. S.	6840	,,	BRAMHALL, G. T.
6623	,,	HASLAM, E.	6352	L.-Sergt.	BUSH, C. E.
6506	,,	HOLMES, J.	6315	,,	SUTTON, P.
6633	,,	HUNT, E.	7218	,,	FORSYTH, E. C.
6669	,,	REYNOLDS, F.	6640	,,	LEIGH, C.
6680	,,	SMITH, E.	6643	,,	LUCKMAN, F. A.
6745	,,	GORTON, A.	7010	,,	IRLAM, G. A.

Also on the Photograph : Lieut.-Col. CRAWFORD and Capt. and Adjt. SOTHAM.

The following were not present when the Photograph was taken, but see Supplementary Photograph on p. 50.

7441	C.Q.M.S.	LAMBOURN, A.	7092	M.G.Sgt.	COSGROVE, J.
6522	Sergeant	MCWILLIAMS, J. L.	6555	L.-Sergt.	SEERS, A. H. J.
6969	,,	CHEETHAM, S.	6355	,,	CAPPER.
6723	,,	BROWN, F. J. M.	6230	,,	CUNNINGHAM.
7003	,,	HINCE, R.	7169	,,	JACQUES, J.

16th (Service) Battalion Manchester Regiment.

Bugle Band.

Roll No.	Rank and Name.		Roll No.	Rank and Name.	
7171	Sergeant	BURKE, T.	6929	Drummer	SLATER.
6327	L.-Corpl.	WILLIAMSON, H.	6870	,,	FOSTER.
6459	,,	BARLOW, P.	7176	,,	DUNBAR, D. H.
6446	Drummer	WHITE, J.	7112	,,	GOODSON, F. O.
6329	,,	WILSON, W.	7183	,,	MIDDLEMISS, C. E.
6334	,,	BROWN, J.	7035	,,	MORRIS, S.
6431	,,	RUSSELL, A.	7184	,,	WATERHOUSE, H.
7278	,,	HUGHES, T.	7072	,,	HARROP, G.
6330	,,	WOMBY, T.	6432	,,	SHARPLES, J.
7217	,,	EDGE, W. H.	7084	,,	BROOKES, S.
6502	,,	HIGGINBOTTOM, A. W.	7185	,,	COOKE, T. H.
6641	,,	LEONARD, H.	7170	,,	PENNY, J.
6684	,,	SMITH, W.	7087	,,	PITT, J. H.
7280	,,	JONES, G.			

Also on the Photograph : Capt. and Adjt. E. G. SOTHAM.

The following were not present when the Photograph was taken, but see Supplementary Photograph on p. 50.

6313 Private STARKIE, W. 7225 Private BARBER, I.

B 2

16th (Service) Battalion Manchester Regiment.
"A" COMPANY.

Officer Commanding Company - Capt. J. H. Worthington.*
Second in Command - - - Capt. W. Elstob.*
Company Sergeant Major - - Farrell, J. T.
Company Quartermaster Sergeant - Darlington, P.†

PLATOON NO. I.

Platoon Commander - - - 2nd Lieut. G. L. Q. Henriques.
Platoon Sergeant - - - Dunkley, F.

Roll No.	Rank and Name.		Roll No.	Rank and Name.	
6224	R.S.M.	Cheetham, R.	24 6226	Private	Clegg, J. 9/7/16 killed
7281	R.Q.M.S.	Lyon, W. F.	6264	,,	Jones, P.
6310	Sergeant	Payne, J. A.	6229	,,	Crompton, F.
6320	,,	Welsh, T. E.	6291	,,	Palmer, F. S.
age 26. 6322	Corporal	Whitehead, L. 30/7/16 killed Sgt	6262	,,	Jenkins, W.
22 6240	,,	Edge, G. 3/7/16 died.	6319	,,	Warwick, H.
6321	L.-Corpl.	Whitaker, J. F.	25 6270	,,	Leather, A. 1/7/16
6327	,,	Williamson, H.	6204	,,	Akister, F.
age 21 6317	,,	Thomas, W. N. 1/7/16 killed	7205	,,	Burton, W.
6222	,,	Cartman, T.	6313	,,	Starkie, W.
6326	,,	Williams, W. ... died.	6276	,,	Mason, C.
6259	,,	Ingham, S.	6331	,,	Wood, W.
6243	,,	Fisher, J.	7193	,,	Anderson, J.
6248	Private	Garstang, T. E.	6309	,,	Smith, H.
6215	,,	Bennett, P.	6304	,,	Shaw, P.
6275	,,	Mather, L. 9/7/16 killed	6277	,,	Mason, A.
6311	,,	Smith, W. G.	6286	,,	Ogden, F. 1/7/16
6227	,,	Clegg, G. R.	6211	,,	Barber, A. J.
7192	,,	Adshead, T.	6299	,,	Robinson, H.
6258	,,	Howman, A. E.	6293	,,	Parkes, J.
6282	,,	Neild, F.	6212	,,	Barlow, H.
6316	,,	Thomas, R. G.	6283	,,	Nugent, J.
7201	,,	Broady, G.	6285	,,	Nuttall, S. W.
6333	,,	Wynn, W.	6302	,,	Ryder, H.
7202	,,	Broady, J.	6209	,,	Ashworth, F. E.
6318	,,	Titterington, J.	6232	,,	Dawson, H.
age 19. 6208	,,	Aston, L. 1/7/16 killed	6217	,,	Blunt, T.
7194	,,	Arrandale, S. R.	6220	,,	Bridge, J.
6221	,,	Burgess, C.	29 6303	,,	Scowcroft, J. 1/7/16
6325	,,	Williams, S. R.	6261	,,	James, H.

* For portrait, see Officers' Group, p. 5.   † For portrait, see Sergeants' Group, p. 7.

The following were not present when the Platoon Photograph was taken,
but see Supplementary Photograph on p. 50.

6236	Corporal	Denny, A.	6241	Private	Edge, H.
6203	Private	Aldcroft, E.	6253	,,	Hayes, H.
7199	,,	Bennett, R.	6290	,,	Owen, S.
6237	,,	Dickinson, J. T.	6295	,,	Ramsbottom, S. W.

16th (Service) Battalion Manchester Regiment.

"A" COMPANY.

Officer Commanding Company - Capt. J. H. WORTHINGTON.*
Second in Command - - - Capt. W. ELSTOB.*
Company Sergeant Major - - FARRELL, J. T.†
Company Quartermaster Sergeant - DARLINGTON, P.†

PLATOON NO. II.

Platoon Commander - - - 2nd Lieut. R. O. PHILLIPS.
Platoon Sergeant - - - - FARR, A. W.

Roll No.	Rank and Name.		Roll No.	Rank and Name.	
6214	Sergeant	BEAN, W.	6332	Private	WOODBURN, G.
6230	L.-Sergt.	CUNNINGHAM, D.	6223	,,	CAVANAGH, W.
6315	,,	SUTTON, P.	6228	,,	COWSILL, A.
6294	L.-Corpl.	RACK, R.	6246	,,	FROOD, T.
6287	,,	ORMEROD, A. E.	6266	,,	KELLY, C. H.
6225	,,	CLAYTON, H.	6257	,,	HOLLIDAY, W.
6284	,,	NUTTALL, O.	6200	,,	ACKRILL, J. F.
7207	,,	CIRCUIT, C.	6213	,,	BARRETT, H.
6271	Private	LEATHER, H.	6235	,,	DEAVILLE, A.
6268	,,	KING, G.	6301	,,	ROYLE, T. R.
6278	,,	MAYER, J.	6250	,,	GRESTY, W.
6232	,,	DAWSON, J. T.	6281	,,	MORTON, S. G.
6269	,,	LAMBERT, J. *killed - Somme*	7203	,,	BRADY, J. F.
6292	,,	PARK, J. H.	6298	,,	ROBERTS, E. W.
6273	,,	LITTLER, F.	6296	,,	REES, A. F.
6260	,,	ISLIP, A. W.	7195	,,	BALLANTYNE, C.
6297	,,	REID, N. T.	30 6202	,,	ALBAN, L. *1/7/0*
7211	,,	DOHERTY, J. T.	6218	,,	BOND, C.
6265	,,	KAYE, C.	6249	,,	GRAHAM, W.
6234	,,	DEARNE, P.	6323	,,	WHITEHURST, E.
6306	,,	SMITH, F. C.	22 7204	,,	BUCKLEY, J. A. *?/7/16*
7213	,,	DERVIN, J.	6252	,,	HAWLEY, A. J.
6263	,,	JOHNSTONE, C. S.	6330	,,	WOMBY, T.
6267	,,	KERSHAW, G. A.	6328	,,	WILLIAMSON, J.
6437	,,	SMITH, H.	6255	,,	HILL, F. W.
33 6245	,,	FLETCHER, J. *1/7/16 killed*	6210	,,	AUKLAND, W.
6280	,,	MILLS, E.	7206	,,	CHANCE, A.
7210	,,	COWDEN, D.	6254	,,	HEATON, C.
6231	,,	DART, F.			

* For portrait, see Officers' Group, p. 5. † For portrait, see Sergeants' Group, p. 7.

The following were not present when the Platoon Photograph was taken, but see Supplementary Photograph on p. 50.

6216	Sergeant	BIRCH, F. J.	6256	Private	HODGE, H.
6207	Private	ARNFIELD, T.	6288	,,	ORMSON, W.
6247	,,	FURNISS, T.	6329	,,	WILSON, W.

16th (Service) Battalion Manchester Regiment.
"A" COMPANY.

Officer Commanding Company - Capt. J. H. WORTHINGTON.*
Second in Command - - - Capt. W. ELSTOB.*
Company Sergeant Major - - FARRELL, J. T.†
Company Quartermaster Sergeant - DARLINGTON, P.†

PLATOON NO. III.

Platoon Commander - - - 2nd Lieut. C. W. K. HOOK.*
Platoon Sergeant - - - - ADAMSON, J.

Roll No.	Rank and Name.		Roll No.	Rank and Name.	
6407	Sergeant	MILES, M. V.	7208	Private	CARTER, J.
6355	L.-Sergt.	CAPPER, A.	6395	,,	KELLY, J. H.
6369	Corporal	DIXON, T. J.	6370	,,	DOOLEY, E.
6420	,,	PILOT, R.	7200	,,	BLAKELEY, J.
6444	L.-Corpl.	WARREN, C. F.	6415	,,	PERRY, A. E.
6449	,,	WILSON, H.	6367	,,	DALTON, S.
6347	,,	BOOTHMAN, H.	6413	,,	RATCHFORD, G.
6372	,,	DURRAD, W. E.	6388	,,	HOWELL, H.
6451	,,	WILSON, R.	6428	,,	ROBINSON, H.
6891	,,	BRADLEY, T.	6393	,,	JONES, T.
6378	,,	GAMMOND, T.	7196	,,	BARBER, C. P.
6448	Private	WILKINSON, A.	6361	,,	COVENTRY, J.
6335	,,	ATHERTON, H.	6363	,,	CROSS, G.
6381	,,	HARRISON, A.	6357	,,	CHEETHAM, H.
6308	,,	SMITH, H. N.	6373	,,	EACHUS. D.
6340	,,	BELL, A.	7197	,,	BARRETT, H.
6392	,,	JEPSON, G.	6418	,,	PICKERING, H.
6441	,,	TWIGGS, W.	6419	,,	PICKERING, R.
6362	,,	COATES, T.	6385	,,	HOUGHTON, G.
6377	,,	FROST, G.	6438	,,	STARKEY, G.
6387	,,	HOUSLEY, C. A.	6380	,,	HAZELHURST, J. W.
6424	,,	RIDDICK, W.	6341	,,	BENTLEY, F.
6433	,,	SCOTT, H.	6446	,,	WHITE, J.
6400	,,	LITTLER, J. L.	6402	,,	MACKEREL, J.
6425	,,	RIGBY, S.	6354	,,	CAPPER, E. L.
6408	,,	MITCHELL, T.	6409	,,	MOLYNEAUX, G.
6411	,,	MYERS, E. W.	6429	,,	ROBINSON, R.
7209	,,	CHAMLEY, J.	6422	,,	PRESTON, J.
6450	,,	WILSON, J.	6350	,,	BURKE, U.
6358	,,	CLARKE, J.			

Also on the Photograph : M.G.O. Lieut. G. P. Morris (attached).

* For portrait, see Officers' Group, p. 5.   † For portrait, see Sergeants' Group, p. 7.

The following were not present when the Platoon Photograph was taken, but see Supplementary Photograph on p. 50.

| 6414 | L.-Corpl. | PARKER, T. | 6399 | Private | LEWIS, J. L. |
| 6360 | Private | COOPER, H. | | | |

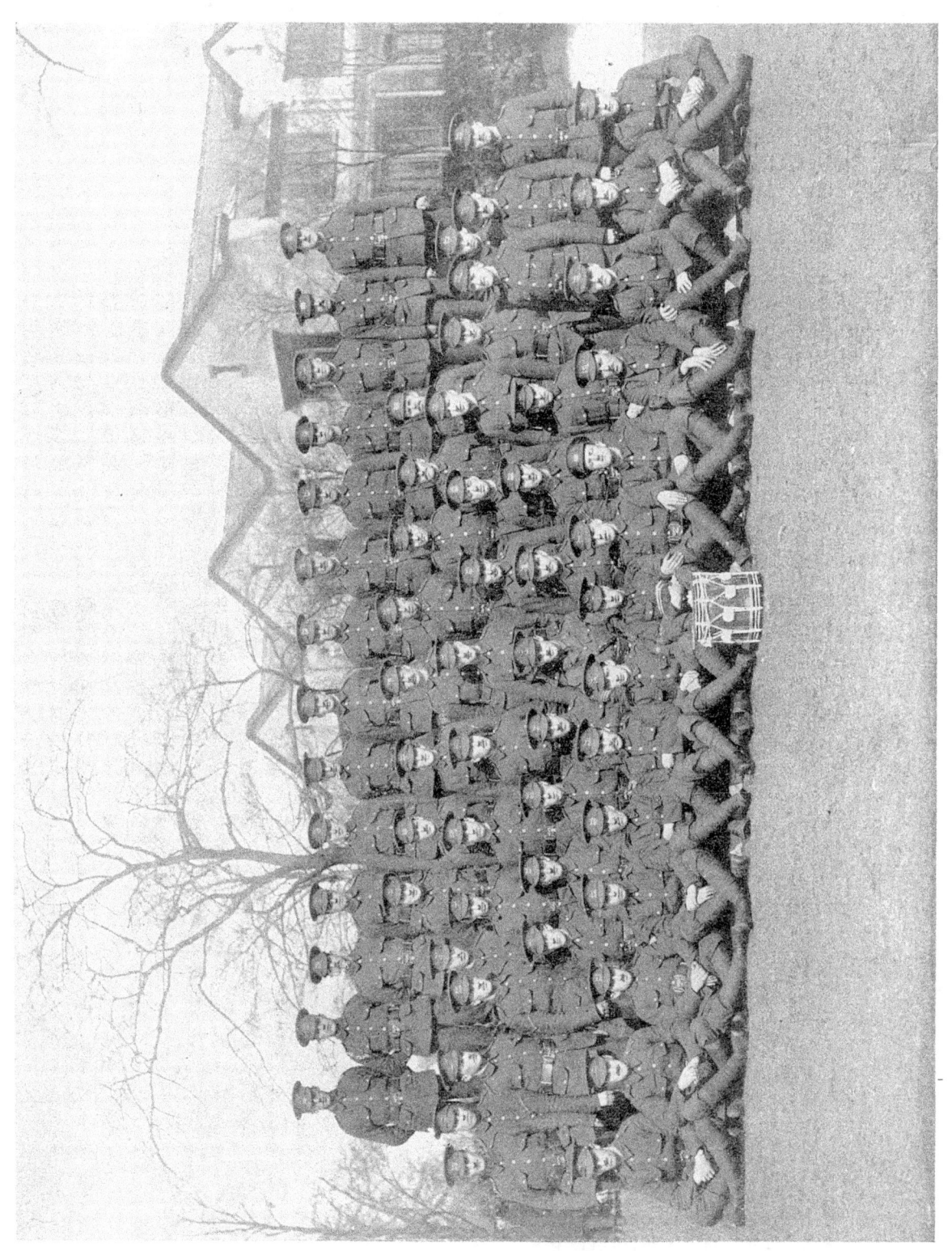

16th (Service) Battalion Manchester Regiment.

"A" COMPANY.

Officer Commanding Company - Capt. J. H. WORTHINGTON.*
Second in Command - - - Capt. W. ELSTOB.
Company Sergeant Major - - FARRELL, J. T.†
Company Quartermaster Sergeant - DARLINGTON, P.†

PLATOON NO. IV.

Platoon Commander - - - 2nd Lieut. P. J. MEAD.*
Platoon Sergeant - - - - WILLIAMS, J. C.

Roll No.	Rank and Name.		Roll No.	Rank and Name.	
6345	Sergeant	BROCKLEHURST, J.	6334	Private	AIDLEY, J. J.
6343	,,	BROADBENT, G.	6238	,,	DUCKWORTH, H.
6352	L.-Sergt.	BUSH, C. E.	6336	,,	ARMSTRONG, F.
6423	Corporal	RAYNER, J.	6351	,,	BUCKLEY, A. J.
6365	,,	CRAWFORD, F.	6442	,,	WALKER, A.
6348	,,	BRUCE, J. P.	6339	,,	BEEVER, C. P.
6397	L.-Corpl.	LEATHER, J. P.	6348	,,	BRUCE, G. H.
6219	,,	BROWN, W. I.	6368	,,	DAWSON, S. P.
6398	,,	LEESON, A. E.	6445	,,	WAYNE, F.
6356	,,	CHALLINOR, R.	6430	,,	ROBINSON, T. W.
6426	Private	ROBERTS, C.	6436	,,	SINGLETON, J.
6427	,,	ROBINSON, A.	6374	,,	ECCLESTON, W.
6389	,,	HOBSON, F. H.	6440	,,	TOWERS, W.
6439	,,	TOLLETT, H.	6346	,,	BROUGHTON, A.
7074	,,	ASHTON, C. E.	6447	,,	WHITLEY, C. A.
6452	,,	YARWOOD, H. C.	6274	,,	LOCKWOOD, C. D.
6394	,,	JONES, M. A.	6305	,,	SHERRING, F.
6272	,,	LESTER, S. N.	6364	,,	CROFT, G. W.
6353	,,	CALDWELL, L. G.	6406	,,	MERRILL, T. E.
6405	,,	MAHER, J.	6417	,,	PETERS, A. E.
6376	,,	EVANS, T.	6403	,,	MAYORS, J.
6443	,,	WARD, W. N.	6379	,,	GAFFNEY, W.
6300	,,	ROBINSON, K.	6431	,,	RUSSELL, A.
6307	,,	SMITH, F. R.	6219	,,	BROWN, J.
6435	,,	SEIPEN, J. A.	6689	,,	TATTERSALL, A.
6347	,,	BRIGGS, J.	6391	,,	JACKSON, F.
7198	,,	BARNES, J.	6410	,,	MURRAY, J.
7212	,,	DELANEY, J.	6421	,,	PLANT, L.
6384	,,	HEYWOOD, J. H.	6390	,,	HULL, G.
6386	,,	HORFORD, T.	6396	,,	KEACH, T. J.
6404	,,	MARRIOTT, G.			

* For portrait, see Officers' Group, p. 5.   † For portrait, see Sergeants' Group, p. 7.

The following were not present when the Platoon Photograph was taken, but see Supplementary Photograph on p. 50.

6337	Private	BARLOW, H.	6382	Private	HARRISON, J.
6375	,,	EDMUNDS, G. F.	7278	,,	HUGHES, T.

16th (Service) Battalion Manchester Regiment.

"B" COMPANY.

Officer Commanding Company - Capt. M. H. R. Patey.*
Second in Command - - - Lieut. F. E. Behrens.
Company Sergeant Major - - Kennelly, J. G.
Company Quartermaster Sergeant - Joyce, T.

PLATOON NO. V.

Platoon Commander - - - Lieut. F. E. Behrens.
Platoon Sergeant - - - - Haslam, E.

Roll No.	Rank and Name.		Roll No.	Rank and Name.	
6522	Sergeant	McWilliams, J. L.	6496	Private	Hadfield, D. D.
6571	,,	Wharton, G.	6502	,,	Higginbottom, A. W.
6555	L.-Sergt.	Seers, A. H. J.	6508	,,	Howatson, A.
6556	Corporal	Singleton, A.	6509	,,	Hughes, F.
6463	L.-Corpl.	Bennett, F.	6513	,,	Kay, E.
6493	,,	Gudgeon, F.	6514	,,	Kay, Harold.
6503	,,	Hill, R.	6519	,,	Levey, J.
6543	,,	Pollitt, G. S.	6523	,,	Maher, N.
6546	,,	Proffitt, W.	6525	,,	Matthews, H. G.
6455	Private	Armstrong, W. F.	6526	,,	Meikle, J.
6457	,,	Bailey, A.	6527	,,	Mein, W.
6582	,,	Bentley, C.	6535	,,	Ogden, T.
6469	,,	Bonner, E. A.	6537	,,	Onley, J.
6467	,,	Bonney, H. F.	6663	,,	Owen, G. T.
6468	,,	Bowler, C.	6541	,,	Pearson, G.
6473	,,	Campbell, W. R.	6542	,,	Pickup, A.
6476	,,	Chadwick, A.	6544	,,	Potter, F. W.
6483	,,	Crosby, J.	6545	,,	Proffitt, A.
7215	,,	Dawson, J.	6547	,,	Read, E.
6488	,,	Entwistle, J. S.	6549	,,	Reilly, E. J.
6489	,,	Evered, R.	6550	,,	Richardson, F.
6492	,,	Grierson, S.	6553	,,	Rushton, A.
7221	,,	Griffin, M.	6554	,,	Scrymgeour, J.
6495	,,	Hackett, W.	6675	,,	Sharp, J. A.
6498	,,	Hart, C. R.	6557	,,	Smith, J.
6499	,,	Hart, E.	6559	,,	Speed, E.

* For portrait, see Officers' Group, p. 5.

The following were not present when the Platoon Photograph was taken, but see Supplementary Photograph on p. 50.

6458	Private	Balfe, F.	7235	Private	Loxley, W. F.
6475	,,	Catlow, J. R.	6565	,,	Towers, J.
7223	,,	Hull, R. J.			

16th (Service) Battalion Manchester Regiment.

"B" COMPANY.

Officer Commanding Company - Capt. M. H. R. Patey.*
Second in Command - - - Lieut. F. E. Behrens.*
Company Sergeant Major - - Kennelly, J. G.†
Company Quartermaster Sergeant - Joyce, T.†

PLATOON NO. VI.

Platoon Commander - - - 2nd Lieut. J. E. G. Percy.
Platoon Sergeant - - - - Smith, E.

Roll No.	Rank and Name.		Roll No.	Rank and Name.	
6669	Sergeant	Reynolds, F.	6625	Private	Henderson, F.
6472	Corporal	Campbell, A. G.	6504	,,	Holden, N.
6524	,,	Martin, F.	6505	,,	Holland, J.
6536	,,	Oldham, W.	6510	,,	Jenkinson, F. R.
6459	L.-Corpl.	Barlow, P.	6511	,,	Johnson, B.
6465	,,	Beswick, H. B.	6515	,,	Kay, Harry.
6482	,,	Cressy, R.	6517	,,	Kilding, A.
6532	,,	Moffatt, L.	6518	,,	Lawrenson, J. H.
6561	,,	Stoddard, R.	6520	,,	Lomax, S.
6560	,,	Stafford, W.	6521	,,	McMahon, J.
6562	,,	Storey, J.	6650	,,	Marsland, H. K.
6568	,,	Waldron, B.	6653	,,	Meisenheimer, H. G.
6570	,,	Watson, A.	6530	,,	Mellalieu, H.
6453	Private	Anderson, A. F.	6528	,,	Minns, H.
6460	,,	Barnes, W.	6531	,,	Moffatt, C.
6461	,,	Battell, F.	6658	,,	Monks, A.
6462	,,	Beever, G.	6533	,,	Moore, J.
6464	,,	Bellamy, H. B.	6534	,,	Morris, W.
6470	,,	Briggs, A.	6539	,,	Park, W.
6471	,,	Briggs, V. J.	6540	,,	Patrick, G.
6474	,,	Carr, G. L.	6666	,,	Pike, S. R.
6478	,,	Cocks, B. C.	6548	,,	Rear, A. F.
6479	,,	Collins, F.	6551	,,	Rigby, H.
6480	,,	Cooper, N.	6676	,,	Sheard, G.
6606	,,	Edwards, J. L.	6677	,,	Sinclair, J. E.
6487	,,	Ellor, V.	6558	,,	Smith, W. V.
6490	,,	Feay, L.	6566	,,	Travis, J.
6491	,,	Gosling, A.	6567	,,	Turner, W. B.
6497	,,	Hallett, E.	6569	,,	Watson, A. G.
6500	,,	Hawker, F.	6825	,,	Woodward, L. E.

* For portrait, see Officers' Group, p. 5.   † For portrait, see Sergeants' Group, p. 7.

The following were not present when the Platoon Photograph was taken, but see Supplementary Photograph on p. 50.

6456	Private	Atkinson, T. A.	6690	Private	Taylor, P. E.
6481	,,	Crabtree, F.			

16th (Service) Battalion Manchester Regiment.

"B" COMPANY.

Officer Commanding Company - Capt. M. H. R. Patey.*
Second in Command - - - Lieut. F. E. Behrens.*
Company Sergeant Major - - Kennelly, J. G.†
Company Quartermaster Sergeant - Joyce, T.†

PLATOON NO. VII.

Platoon Commander - - - Lieut. J. M. Oliver.
Platoon Sergeant - - - - Winning, T. A.

Roll No.	Rank and Name.		Roll No.	Rank and Name.	
6485	Sergeant	Deane, G. S.	6609	Private	Evans, H. C.
6640	L.-Sergt.	Leigh, C.	6622	,,	Hardy, L.
6596	L.-Corpl.	Corkhill, J. R.	6624	,,	Helsby, H.
6642	,,	Lomas, W.	6627	,,	Hewitt, C.
6644	,,	McCaw, F.	6628	,,	Hill, R.
6645	,,	McMillan, A. J.	7230	,,	Houldsworth, T.
6672	,,	Roberts, T. H.	6630	,,	Hoye, A.
6681	,,	Smith, J. F.	6632	,,	Hulme, J.
6698	,,	Wightman, A. B.	6635	,,	Jolly, G. H.
6575	Private	Airey, T.	7233	,,	Jones, E.
6577	,,	Allen, H.	6636	,,	Jowle, R.
7225	,,	Barber, I.	6638	,,	Keeling, S.
6587	,,	Batson, W.	7234	,,	Kelly, H.
6581	,,	Bell, F. J.	6641	,,	Leonard, H.
6584	,,	Billsborough, H.	6646	,,	McMinn, W. J.
6585	,,	Blears, F. E.	6647	,,	Maddocks, J.
6586	,,	Bond, J.	6656	,,	Minor, H.
6590	,,	Caiger, B.	6657	,,	Moffatt, S.
6591	,,	Cattrall, H. W.	6659	,,	Naylor, C. D.
6594	,,	Cohen, S.	6660	,,	Naylor, H.
6598	,,	Dakin, E. F.	6664	,,	Parker, C. W.
6600	,,	Dean, H.	6668	,,	Pollard, R.
6601	,,	Dean, T.	6671	,,	Roberts, C. R.
7216	,,	Dixon, J.	6678	,,	Slater, A.
7214	,,	Doherty, J.	6686	,,	Stanley, H.
6602	,,	Drummond, A.	6695	,,	Wallis, G. H.
6604	,,	Eccles, R.	6696	,,	Walton, A.
7217	,,	Edge, W. H.	6699	,,	Whaling, J. D.
6612	,,	Francis, D. E.	6700	,,	Whittenbury, H. A.

* For portrait, see Officers' Group, p. 5. † For portrait, see Sergeants' Group, p. 7.

The following were not present when the Platoon Photograph was taken,
but see Supplementary Photograph on p. 50.

6643	L.-Sergt.	Luckman, F. A.	6684	Private	Smith, W.
6578	Private	Andrews, J.			

16th (Service) Battalion Manchester Regiment.

"B" COMPANY.

Officer Commanding Company - Capt. M. H. R. Patey.*
Second in Command - - - Lieut. F. E. Behrens.*
Company Sergeant Major - - Kennelly, J. G.†
Company Quartermaster Sergeant - Joyce, T.†

PLATOON NO. VIII.

Platoon Commander - - - 2nd Lieut. E. L. Rhodes.
Platoon Sergeant - - - Holmes, J.

Roll No.	Rank and Name.		Roll No.	Rank	Name.
6633	Sergeant	Hunt, E.	6614	Private	Furnifer, W.
6651	,,	Mason, W. A.	6616	,,	Gibson, J. H.
7218	L.-Sergt.	Forsyth, E. C.	6617	,,	Gosling, H.
6620	Corporal	Halliday, R.	7220	,,	Grayston, F.
6626	,,	Henderson, W.	6494	,,	Hackett, M. F.
6588	L.-Corpl.	Buckland, F.	6621	,,	Halsall, S. A.
6593	,,	Clayton, W. G.	6501	,,	Hayes, H. G.
6597	,,	Coxon, W. H.	6629	,,	Howarth, W.
6683	,,	Smith, R.	6631	,,	Hoyle, J.
6691	,,	Thomas, F.	7231	,,	Johnson, H.
6692	,,	Thompson, R.	6637	,,	Jupp, F.
6576	Private	Aldred, T.	6648	,,	Mallard, J. E.
6579	,,	Austin, W. E.	6655	,,	Mills, W.
7226	,,	Broady, G.	6654	,,	Milsom, H. J.
6589	,,	Butterworth, D.	6661	,,	Newton, B.
6592	,,	Clark, E. C.	6665	,,	Pickford, M.
6595	,,	Conway, J.	6670	,,	Richardson, W.
3895	,,	Connolly, T.	6552	,,	Rosenberg, E.
6603	,,	Eavis, W.	6673	,,	Rowland, P.
6605	,,	Edwards, E.	6682	,,	Smith, R. W.
6607	,,	Elliott, C.	6685	,,	Sootheren, J. C.
6608	,,	Ellis, H.	6687	,,	Stevenson, J.
6610	,,	Findlater, N.	6693	,,	Thorley, G.
6611	,,	Fisher, T.	6703	,,	Williams, A.
6613	,,	Fraser, H. C.	6706	,,	Wood, P. H.
6573	,,	Frith, J.	6708	,,	Yates, A.
7222	,,	Garner, J. H.			

* For portrait, see Officers' Group, p. 5. † For portrait, see Sergeants' Group, p. 7.

The following were not present when the Platoon Photograph was taken, but see Supplementary Photograph on p. 50.

Roll No.	Rank	Name	Roll No.	Rank	Name
6634	L.-Corpl.	Jackson, A. H.	6639	Private	Lawson, J.
6694	,,	Tyldesley, A. J.	6649	,,	Maloney, H.
4358	Private	Bridson, H.	6679	,,	Smethurst, S. R.
6615	,,	Gee, A.	6709	,,	Yates, J.
7219	,,	Gibson, H.			

16th (Service) Battalion Manchester Regiment.

"C" COMPANY.

Officer Commanding Company	Capt. F. WALKER.*
Second in Command	Capt. W. M. JOHNSON.
Company Sergeant Major	CLARKE, J.
Company Quartermaster Sergeant	DEWAN, T.

PLATOON NO. IX.

Platoon Commander	2nd Lieut. R. GIBBON.*
Platoon Sergeant	BROWN, J. F. M.

Roll No.	Rank and Name.		Roll No.	Rank and Name.	
6737	Sergeant	EDGAR, J. V.	6746	Private	GOSLING, F.
6719	L.-Corpl.	BRADLEY, J. W.	6758	,,	HOLMES, J. P.
6717	,,	BERRY, F.	6761	,,	HUTTON, E.
6722	,,	BROCK, W. P.	7280	,,	JONES, C.
7252	,,	RAVENSCROFT, S.	6769	,,	LAWRENSON, S.
6798	,,	ROBINSON, J.	6780	,,	McKENNA, J.
6711	Private	ALDOUS, H. F.	6781	,,	McSPIRIT, J.
6714	,,	BANCROFT, J.	6775	,,	MALEY, T.
6715	,,	BELLFIELD, G. H.	6787	,,	NORBURY, F.
6716	,,	BELL, A.	6788	,,	PARRY, T.
6718	,,	BILLINGE, T.	6789	,,	PEARSON, W.
6973	,,	BUCKLEY, W. E.	6791	,,	PINKERTON, N.
6726	,,	BURTON, F.	7251	,,	RANKIN, W.
6720	,,	BRISTER, J. C.	6770	,,	LAWSON, S.
6724	,,	BRUNTON, R. E.	6795	,,	RICHARDSON, F.
6721	,,	BROADHURST, R.	7253	,,	REID, R.
6727	,,	CAMERON, A. E.	7255	,,	ROBERTS, W.
6732	,,	COLLINS, D.	6799	,,	ROWBOTTOM, J.
6733	,,	CULLERNE, L.	7256	,,	ROYLE, W.
6734	,,	DAVIES, H.	6803	,,	SCOTT, A. E.
6371	,,	DOVESTON, A.	6808	,,	STONEHEWER, H. B.
6738	,,	EGDEN, J.	6809	,,	SWANWICK, R.
6739	,,	EVANS, W.	6812	,,	TAYLOR, R.
6741	,,	FINNIGAN, J.	6813	,,	TWIGG, R.
6848	,,	GUBBINS, J.	6815	,,	WARD, E. N.
6744	,,	GLEAVE, W. B.	6817	,,	WARRINGTON, S. T.
6750	,,	HARLING, J. T.	6821	,,	WOODGATE, H.
6751	,,	HAWLEY, H.	6779	,,	McDONOUGH, J. J.

* For portrait, see Officers' Group, p. 5.

The following were not present when the Platoon Photograph was taken, but see Supplementary Photograph on p. 50.

Roll No.	Rank	Name	Roll No.	Rank	Name
6814	Corporal	WALKER, T.	6760	Private	HUGHES, J.
6831	L.-Corpl.	BARROW, G.	6801	,,	SCALE, J. C.
6710	Private	ALDERSON, R.	7257	,,	SHOTTON, S.
6753	,,	HETHERINGTON, H.			

16th (Service) Battalion Manchester Regiment.

"C" COMPANY.

Officer Commanding Company	Capt. F. Walker.*
Second in Command	Capt. W. M. Johnson.*
Company Sergeant Major	Clarke, J.†
Company Quartermaster Sergeant	Dewan, T.†

PLATOON NO. X.

Platoon Commander	2nd Lieut. R. K. Knowles.
Platoon Sergeant	Thomas, E.

Roll No.	Rank and Name.		Roll No.	Rank and Name.	
6800	L.-Sergt.	Royle, H. V.	7238	Private	Lord, J.
6712	Corporal	Allen, H.	6776	,,	McCracken, F. W.
6757	,,	Hollingsworth, J. E.	6777	,,	McElliney, J.
6796	L.-Corpl.	Robinson, F.	6778	,,	McGow, J. G.
6771	,,	Leaver, R.	7243	,,	McDowell, J.
6774	,,	Maher, D.	6784	,,	Moore, G. H.
6893	,,	Hughes, W. J.	6786	,,	Neill, W.
6831	,,	Barrow, G.	6792	,,	Plummer, W. H.
6713	Private	Ashton, R. O.	6793	,,	Pointon, T.
6725	,,	Burns, G. C.	7249	,,	Ratcliffe, J. F.
6728	,,	Chapman, J. W.	7250	,,	Ratcliffe, W.
6729	,,	Chapman, W.	6797	,,	Robinson, H.
6731	,,	Clifford, G. J.	6802	,,	Schaefer, G.
6735	,,	Dickenson, S. C.	6805	,,	South, H.
6736	,,	Eaton, N.	6806	,,	South, P.
6740	,,	Fenlon, W.	6807	,,	Stevens, R.
6742	,,	Fitton, W.	6810	,,	Taylor, A. B.
6747	,,	Greenhalgh, R.	6811	,,	Taylor, A. C.
6619	,,	Halliday, W.	6816	,,	Watson, F.
6752	,,	Hebron, E.	6818	,,	Williams, E.
6755	,,	Higginson, J.	6819	,,	Wilson, N. F.
6756	,,	Holland, H. R.	6820	,,	Wilson, R.
6759	,,	Hopewell, C.	6823	,,	Worrall, F.
6762	,,	Irlam, S. D.	6743	,,	Fosbrooke, J. J.
6763	,,	Jackson, S. A.	6727	,,	Almond, A.
6764	,,	Jones, A.	6830	,,	Barlow, M.
6766	,,	Jones, R. V.	6836	,,	Billam, H.
6768	,,	Knowles, E.	6873	,,	Gibbons, J.
6772	,,	Littlejohn, J.	6749	,,	Clarke, J.
6773	,,	Lomas, M.			

* For portrait, see Officers' Group, p. 5.   † For portrait, see Sergeants' Group, p. 7.

The following were not present when the Platoon Photograph was taken, but see Supplementary Photograph on p. 50.

6730	Private	Clarke, A. G.	6767	Private	Kinder, L.

16th (Service) Battalion Manchester Regiment.

"C" COMPANY.

Officer Commanding Company	Capt. F. WALKER.*
Second in Command	Capt. W. M. JOHNSON.*
Company Sergeant Major	CLARKE, J.†
Company Quartermaster Sergeant	DEWAN, T.†

PLATOON NO. XI.

Platoon Commander	2nd Lieut. W. F. CLARKE.
Platoon Sergeant	GORTON, A.

Roll No.	Rank and Name.		Roll No.	Rank and Name.	
6884	Sergeant	HIGGS, J. A.	6876	Private	GREEN, G.
6794	,,	RALPHS, T.	6883	,,	HEALEY, G.
6850	Corporal	CLIFFE, R.	6888	,,	HOLT, S. H.
6872	,,	GARSIDE, F.	6890	,,	HOWARD, S.
6832	L.-Corpl.	BARTON, H.	6896	,,	KIRKHAM, S. A.
6849	,,	CLARKE, G.	6899	,,	LEATER, H.
6834	,,	BERRA, N. E.	7236	,,	LOMAX, W.
6879	,,	GRIFFITH, J. M.	7239	,,	LOWE, G.
6870	Private	FOSTER, F.	6908	,,	MARSDEN, R. K.
6714	,,	BANCROFT, S. A.	6902	,,	McFARLANE, H.
6833	,,	BATES, T.	6911	,,	MITCHELL, R. H.
6835	,,	BERRESFORD, R.	6913	,,	MOTTRAM, F.
6838	,,	BOWLES, E.	6914	,,	MYERS, T.
6839	,,	BOWLES, F.	6904	,,	McLOUGHLIN, J.
6841	,,	BRITTAIN, H. F.	6915	,,	NEWTON, H. A.
6842	,,	BROADBENT, S.	6916	,,	NORRIS, J.
6844	,,	BROWN, H.	6917	,,	OLDFIELD, W.
6845	,,	BROWN, F.	6790	,,	PEERS, A.
6847	,,	CARTLEDGE, J.	6925	,,	ROSS, H.
6852	,,	COOKE, J. H.	6932	,,	STEVENS, W. J.
6854	,,	CROSSLEY, R.	6939	,,	TOLE, J. F.
6856	,,	DAVIES, F. J.	7282	,,	TRAFFORD, T. R.
6861	,,	DUNN, H.	6940	,,	TRAVIS, P.
6863	,,	EXELBY, E. J.	6941	,,	WARREN, A.
6867	,,	FIELDING, J.	6942	,,	WARREN, N.
6865	,,	FINDLOW, H.	6943	,,	WIGGINS, F.
6869	,,	FORDE, J.	6822	,,	WORDSWORTH, G.
6874	,,	GOOCH, J.	6910	,,	MILLWARD, A.

* For portrait, see Officers' Group, p. 5. † For portrait, see Sergeants' Group, p. 7.

The following were not present when the Platoon Photograph was taken, but see Supplementary Photograph on p. 50.

Roll No.	Rank	Name	Roll No.	Rank	Name
6864	Corporal	FAIRBANK, O.	7237	Private	JOHNSON, S.
6843	L.-Corpl.	BROOMER, H.	6930	,,	SPARROW, J.
6828	Private	BAINES, G.			

16th (Service) Battalion Manchester Regiment.

"C" COMPANY.

Officer Commanding Company	- Capt. F. Walker.*
Second in Command - -	- Capt. W. M. Johnson.*
Company Sergeant Major -	- Clarke, J.†
Company Quartermaster Sergeant -	Dewan, T.†

PLATOON NO. XII.

Platoon Commander - -	- Lieut. W. S. Davidson.
Platoon Sergeant - - -	- Lingard, H.

Roll No.	Rank and Name.		Roll No.	Rank and Name.	
6840	Sergeant	Bramhall, G. T.	6889	Private	Hopton, J.
6826	Corporal	Acheson, S.	6892	,,	Howell, J.
6923	,,	Redford, W.	7246	,,	Johnson, T.
6903	L.-Corpl.	McKenzie, J.	6897	,,	Kitching, L. A.
6912	,,	Montgomery, H. W.	6895	,,	Kelsey, W. J.
6837	,,	Bottrill, C. T.	6898	,,	Knowles, A.
7244	,,	Murray, T.	6901	,,	Lynch, J.
6929	Private	Slater, F.	6907	,,	Marginson, F.
6851	,,	Cohen, M.	7242	,,	Mather, A.
6853	,,	Corley, E.	6905	,,	McMaster, J.
6855	,,	Crompton, S.	6919	,,	Owen, T. J.
6857	,,	Davies, S.	7248	,,	Pearson, A. J.
6859	,,	Dewhurst, H.	6921	,,	Pollitt, G.
6860	,,	Donbavand, R. J.	7247	,,	Peduzzi, J.
6862	,,	Eardley, C.	6922	,,	Railton, D.
6866	,,	Fish, H.	6924	,,	Roberts, E. E.
6868	,,	Fitters, H.	6928	,,	Shaw, A. E.
6871	,,	Francis, H.	6933	,,	Taylor, G. A.
6875	,,	Goulden, W.	6934	,,	Taylor, M.
6877	,,	Green, S. E.	6935	,,	Taylor, S.
6878	,,	Griffith, E. E.	6938	,,	Thorniley, M.
6882	,,	Hardcastle,	6974	,,	Wood, E. H.
6881	,,	Hart, J. W.	6944	,,	Worral, W.
6886	,,	Hill, G.	6945	,,	Wright, C. T.
6887	,,	Hitchcock, F.	6848	,,	Chadwick, F.

* For portrait, see Officers' Group, p. 5.   † For portrait, see Sergeants' Group, p. 7.

The following were not present when the Platoon Photograph was taken, but see Supplementary Photograph on p. 50.

Roll No.	Rank	Name	Roll No.	Rank	Name
6885	Private	Hegson, E. J.	6926	Private	Scholes, W.
6894	,,	Jackman, H.	6931	,,	Sternes, W. K.
7245	,,	Mathews, J. W.	6936	,,	Teasdale, G. E.
6918	,,	Oldham, J.	6937	,,	Thomas, W. E.
6920	,,	Perkin, F.	7241	,,	Lloyd, J. F.

16th (Service) Battalion Manchester Regiment.

"D" COMPANY.

Officer Commanding Company - Capt. M. S. Greg.*
Second in Command - - - Capt. J. J. Payne.*
Company Sergeant Major - - Reddy, J.
Company Quartermaster Sergeant - Lambourn, A.†

PLATOON NO. XIII.

Platoon Commander - - - Lieut. A. B. Dalgleish.
Platoon Sergeant - - - - Hince, R.

Roll No.	Rank and Name.		Roll No.	Rank and Name.	
7006	Corporal	Hughes, Rhys.	7002	Private	Hince, C.
7028	,,	Mitchell, J.	7012	,,	Jepson, J.
7259	,,	Simpson, T. E.	7013	,,	Jessop, C. O.
7182	L.-Corpl.	Eastwood, J. E.	7016	,,	Johnson, J.
7004	,,	Holmes, A. C.	7269	,,	Jones, J.
7030	,,	Monnington, F. G.	7118	,,	Kirkley, G. H.
6949	Private	Atkinson, G.	7025	,,	Lucas, H. J.
6205	,,	Anderson, W.	7132	,,	McHugh, J. R.
6956	,,	Barker, N. A.	7029	,,	Malpass, J. E. S.
6952	,,	Barnes, R. A.	7031	,,	Moss, J. W.
6954	,,	Batley, H.	7032	,,	Nichol, W.
6957	,,	Bell, F. J.	7033	,,	Nicholson, G. M.
6960	,,	Broadbent, T.	7041	,,	Pilling, F. K.
6961	,,	Brookes, R.	7180	,,	Price, C. T. F.
6965	,,	Caine, O. H.	7049	,,	Roe, P. T.
6967	,,	Casson, S. W.	7056	,,	Smith, H. F.
6968	,,	Chaters, J. C.	7260	,,	Smith, J. G.
6972	,,	Cooper, C.	6432	,,	Sharples, J.
6980	,,	Drabble, A.	7061	,,	Thompson, E. J.
6984	,,	Elliott, T.	7263	,,	Thorniley, T. E.
6985	,,	Ellison, C. H.	7062	,,	Tootill, E.
6994	,,	Guntrip, H.	7063	,,	Turner, F. H.
7072	,,	Harrop, G.	7064	,,	Tysoe, G.
7000	,,	Hawthorn, H.	7066	,,	Wheeldon, S.
7001	,,	Henry, E.	7067	,,	Willcox, D.
7284	,,	Helsby, E. A.	7068	,,	Willis, A.
7011	,,	Jelly, J.	7178	,,	Foster, F.

* For portrait, see Officers' Group, p. 5. † For portrait, see Sergeants' Group, p. 7.

The following were not present when the Platoon Photograph was taken, but see Supplementary Photograph on p. 50.

6973	Sergeant	Carter, T.	7014	Private	Johnston, A.
7010	L.-Sergt.	Irlam, G. A.	7036	,,	Owen, A. H.
6950	Private	Austin, T. S.	7069	,,	Wilson, T. L.
6975	,,	Coppock, R. L.			

16th (Service) Battalion Manchester Regiment.

"D" COMPANY.

Officer Commanding Company	Capt. M. S. Greg.*
Second in Command	Capt. J. J. Payne.*
Company Sergeant Major	Reddy, J.†
Company Quartermaster Sergeant	Lambourn, A.†

PLATOON NO. XIV.

Platoon Commander	2nd Lieut. S. R. Allen.*
Platoon Sergeant	Finan, G.†

Roll No.	Rank and Name.		Roll No.	Rank and Name.	
6955	Sergeant	Barker, C.	7024	Private	Lindsay, J.
6948	L.-Corpl.	Ashcroft, H.	7026	,,	McNally, W. J.
6992	,,	Guilford, H. S.	7035	,,	Morris, S.
7020	,,	Lawton, R. G.	7136	,,	Nash, G. M.
7065	,,	Watkin, J.	7034	,,	Nickson, W. B.
6946	Private	Andrews, T.	7038	,,	Palmer, H.
6951	,,	Bailey, G. V.	7040	,,	Peel, H.
6953	,,	Barrington, H.	7042	,,	Poyser, E. C.
6958	,,	Bennett, N.	7043	,,	Pressler, G. H.
6962	,,	Brown, T.	7046	,,	Rhodes, E. A.
6964	,,	Buttle, W.	7047	,,	Rigby, R.
6968	,,	Coates, J. W.	7050	,,	Rothwell, W. H.
6971	,,	Cochrane, H.	7052	,,	Roughton, A.
6977	,,	Cowell, J.	7053	,,	Roughton, W. E.
6979	,,	Dolan, A. M.	7051	,,	Rowlinson, E.
6982	,,	England, R.	7055	,,	Simpson, G.
6986	,,	Enstone, C.	7057	,,	Stanway, R.
6988	,,	Foster, J.	7058	,,	Stoddard, S. W.
6991	,,	Griffiths, A.	7060	,,	Taylor, S.
6995	,,	Hallam, C. H.	7268	,,	Vernon, H.
7005	,,	Housley, R. D.	7270	,,	Wade, J. T.
7008	,,	Hyde, John.	7070	,,	Wilson, H. P.
7009	,,	Innes, J. E.	7272	,,	Williams, F. J.
7015	,,	Johnson, F.	7275	,,	Woods, E.
7265	,,	Johnstone, W. D.			

Also on Photograph : 2nd Lieut. R. Gibbon.

* For portrait, see Officers' Group, p. 5.   † For portrait, see Sergeants' Group, p. 7.

The following were not present when the Platoon Photograph was taken, but see Supplementary Photograph on p. 50.

6987	Sergeant	Finan, G.	6996	Private	Harrison, F.
6976	Corporal	Coward, L. C.	7023	,,	Little, W. G.
7021	L.-Corpl.	Lees, F. J.	7039	,,	Parker, H.
6966	Private	Campbell, T. S.			

16th (Service) Battalion Manchester Regiment.

"D" COMPANY.

Officer Commanding Company	Capt. M. S. GREG.*
Second in Command	Capt. J. J. PAYNE.*
Company Sergeant Major	REDDY, J.†
Company Quartermaster Sergeant	LAMBOURN, A.

PLATOON NO. XV.

Platoon Commander	Lieut. L. F. WILSON.
Platoon Sergeant	TURNER, F. H.

Roll No.	Rank and Name.	Roll No.	Rank and Name.
7152	B.Q.M.S. STEWART, C. E.	7168	Private HYDE, R.
6993	R.Q.M.S. GUINAN, T.	7129	,, KNOWLAND, G. H.
7171	Sergeant BURKE, T.	7130	,, LABREY, E. E.
7099	,, CARR, S.	7183	,, MIDDLEMISS, C. E.
7169	L.-Sergt. JACQUES, J.	7137	,, NAYLOR, W.
6529	Corporal MITCHELL, S.	7135	,, NIELD, J.
7059	,, SUMMERS, H. B.	7177	,, ORMROD, S. M.
7261	,, TATTERSALL, H. N.	7139	,, PENN, J.
7077	,, BINGHAM, J. A.	7142	,, REDFERN, J.
7088	L.-Corpl. BURROWS, T.	7143	,, ROE, G.
7075	Private BALLARD, H.	7144	,, RUSSELL, C. A.
7172	,, BARBER, J. H.	7147	,, SEDDON, H.
7078	,, BLANKENBERGER, O. P.	7145	,, SCHOFIELD, J.
7079	,, BOOTH, W.	7148	,, SHENTON, T.
7086	,, BURKE, J.	7258	,, SHANNON, H.
7095	,, CRAWFORD, H.	7157	,, TAYLOR, H. G.
7100	,, DILLON, J.	7158	,, TOFT, H. D.
7101	,, DOBSON, T.	7160	,, TURNER, W.
7097	,, DOLEMAN, A.	7262	,, TATE, G. H.
7103	,, DOVER, W.	7174	,, USHER, J.
7104	,, DOWLING, W.	7275	,, WALTON, J.
7105	,, DUDSON, S.	7162	,, WEBSTER, F.
7107	,, ELLISON, C.	7273	,, WILKINS, G.
7108	,, FORREST, A.	7274	,, WILSON, R.
7110	,, GARNER, C. A.	7164	,, WINDSOR, S.
7112	,, GOODSON, F. O.	7071	,, WYCHERLEY, H.
7111	,, GOWAN, H.	7277	,, YATES, H.
7121	,, HOWELLS, A.	7176	,, DUNBAR, D. H.
7125	,, KILPATRICK, H.	7178	,, HODGSON, J.

* For portrait, see Officers' Group, p. 5. † For portrait, see Sergeants' Group, p. 7.

The following were not present when the Platoon Photograph was taken, but see Supplementary Photograph on p. 50.

6981	Sergeant DUNSTAN, F. J.	7113	Private GREAVES, W.
7128	L.-Corpl. KIRKPATRICK, R.	7146	,, SCOTT, J.
7081	Private BRENNAN, P.		

16th (Service) Battalion Manchester Regiment.

"D" COMPANY.

Officer Commanding Company - Capt. M. S. Greg.*
Second in Command - - - Capt. J. J. Payne.*
Company Sergeant Major - - Reddy, J.†
Company Quartermaster Sergeant - Lambourn, A.†

PLATOON NO. XVI.

Platoon Commander - - - 2nd Lieut. R. H. Megson.
Platoon Sergeant - - - - Hawxby, H.

Roll No.	Rank and Name.		Roll No.	Rank and Name.	
7189	Sergeant	Baker, G.	7117	Private	Hill, F.
7138	,,	Palin, H.	7007	,,	Hughes, Robt.
7092	,,	Cosgrove, J.	7123	,,	Jones, E.
7085	Corporal	Burgess, H.	7127	,,	Kinsey, F.
7109	,,	Fowler, H.	7126	,,	Kirkland, H.
7027	,,	Marsden, A. W.	7133	,,	Martin, J.
7191	,,	Pennington, T. E.	7134	,,	Murphy, D.
7080	L.-Corpl.	Bottomley, F.	7170	,,	Penney, J.
6989	,,	Gosling, J.	7187	,,	Pitt, J. H.
6998	,,	Harrison, P. A.	7140	,,	Platford, H.
7122	,,	Johnson, B.	7141	,,	Ravenscroft, F.
7073	Private	Ashmore, G.	7044	,,	Read, R.
6947	,,	Astles, H.	7418	,,	Reddy, J.
7076	,,	Bamber, R.	7150	,,	Stenson, W.
7082	,,	Brennan, T.	7151	,,	Stevenson, K.
7083	,,	Brierley, T.	7154	,,	Stuttard, C. A.
7084	,,	Brookes, S.	7158	,,	Thompson, E.
7087	,,	Burrows, R.	7264	,,	Thacker, G.
7089	,,	Caldwell, W.	7156	,,	Taylor, H.
7190	,,	Chadwick, J. W.	7267	,,	Upton, W.
7091	,,	Coleman, A.	7161	,,	Upton, T. L.
7185	,,	Cooke, T. H.	7184	,,	Waterhouse, H.
7098	,,	Davies, F.	7163	,,	Wickman, W.
7102	,,	Dorrington, A.	7175	,,	Wilde, E.
6997	,,	Harrison, J. S.	7168	,,	Wilkinson, M.
7114	,,	Hatton, G.	7276	,,	Woodnett, H.
7116	,,	Hibbert, G. F.	7167	,,	Yarwood, T.

* For portrait, see Officers' Group, p. 5. † For portrait, see Sergeants' Group, p. 7.

The following were not present when the Platoon Photograph was taken, but see Supplementary Photograph on p. 50.

7186 Sergeant Redfern, J.　　　　　　7149 Private Smith, H.

16th (Service) Battalion Manchester Regiment.

"E" COMPANY.

Officer Commanding Company -	Capt. H. H. CUNLIFFE.*
Second in Command - -	Capt. Sir W. N. M. GEARY, Bart.*
Company Sergeant Major -	BLAKELEY, J.†
Company Quartermaster Sergeant -	STURGESS, F.†

PLATOON NO. XVII.

Platoon Commander - - -	2nd Lieut. P. J. MEAD.
Platoon Sergeant - - -	ARCHER, W.

Roll No.	Rank and Name.		Roll No.	Rank and Name.	
6359	Sergeant	COCHRANE, F.	7329	Private	JONES, R. R.
7010	,,	IRLAM, G. A.	7288	,,	HOWSE, W. A.
7424	Corporal	BAILEY, P. J.	7289	,,	HOWSE, H.
7423	,,	NORMAN, H. J.	7297	,,	CUMMINGS, F.
6572	,,	WILSON, H.	7286	,,	SIDDALL, J. E.
7382	L.-Corpl.	BRECKELL, H.	7305	,,	JOYNSON, W.
7368	,,	CHAPMAN, L.	7311	,,	NELSON, E.
7313	,,	GLENDENING, H.	7290	,,	ASHTON, H.
7314	,,	FULCHER, J.	7294	,,	FAGAN, J. H.
7397	,,	FOX, J.	7321	,,	ASHWORTH, R.
7315	,,	WATSON, T. P.	7340	,,	POTTER, W. E.
7399	,,	McLOUGHLIN, P. A.	7295	,,	STARKIE, H.
7309	,,	PICKSTOCK, E.	7367	,,	HORTON, F. L.
7366	,,	CAINE, W.	7401	,,	SENIOR, R.
7316	Private	BOYD, J.	7364	,,	BRANNAN, T.
7394	,,	WOOD, J. H.	7310	,,	TELFORD, P.
7320	,,	BROOKE, J.	7398	,,	BEVERLEY, A. E.
7300	,,	HOWARTH, A. E.	7331	,,	TIMPERLEY, W.
7306	,,	ROMER, J.	7326	,,	LIGHTFOOT, A.
7293	,,	WALKER, G. W.	7337	,,	CARTER, W. H.
7298	,,	CHAMLEY, A.	7099	,,	DAVIS, F. W.
7299	,,	CONCANNON, J.	7124	,,	KELLY, J.
7347	,,	ROBINSON, A.	7214	,,	FOSTER, F.
7291	,,	MURRAY, T. L.	7318	,,	MOONEY, W.
7301	,,	TIPLER, H.	7328	,,	BALL, A.
7317	,,	WOOD, J.	7296	,,	LENNON, J.
7287	,,	THOMPSON, R. S.	6983	,,	ELLIOTT, A.
7292	,,	BOSTWICK, W.			

* For portrait, see Officers' Group, p. 5. † For portrait, see Sergeants' Group, p. 7.

The following were not present when the Platoon Photograph was taken, but see Supplementary Photograph on p. 50.

Roll No.	Rank	Name	Roll No.	Rank	Name
7293	Private	WALKER, G. W.	7400	Private	SUTHERLAND, N.
7131	,,	LOCKWOOD, G.	7388	,,	KEELING, G.

16th (Service) Battalion Manchester Regiment.

"E" COMPANY.

Officer Commanding Company - Capt. H. H. CUNLIFFE.*
Second in Command - - - Capt. Sir W. N. M. GEARY, Bart.*
Company Sergeant Major - - BLAKELEY, J.†
Company Quartermaster Sergeant - STURGESS, F.

PLATOON NO. XVIII.

Platoon Commander - - - 2nd Lieut. C. W. K. HOOK.
Platoon Sergeant - - - - CHEETHAM, S.

Roll No.	Rank and Name.		Roll No.	Rank and Name.	
6701	Corporal	WILCOCKS, L.	7336	Private	WEILDING, C.
6619	,,	TATTERSALL, J.	7409	,,	LAWLEY, A.
6477	,,	CLARK, F. W.	7380	,,	SCHOFIELD, P. J.
7105	L.-Corpl.	FAIRBANK, C.	7322	,,	WALKER, J.
7265	,,	JONES, G.	7350	,,	KELLY, A.
7273	,,	BLOOMER, F.	7370	,,	ECKERSLEY, W. E.
7338	Private	POLLARD, W.	7373	,,	CLANCY, J.
7356	,,	BIRCH, J. C.	7361	,,	PARKER, A. E.
7355	,,	BELL, W.	7358	,,	FORGHAM, I. W.
7344	,,	SMITH, J.	7333	,,	ORD, W.
7324	,,	FITCHETT, J.	7346	,,	BURNS, J. A.
7372	,,	REGAN, M.	7376	,,	WATERS, G.
7373	,,	CLANCY, J.	7369	,,	COBB, H. G.
7353	,,	CONMEY, J.	7345	,,	ELSWORTH, H.
7381	,,	WARBURTON, A.	7383	,,	HOWARD, J. R.
7358	,,	FORGHAM, J. W.	7371	,,	BERRY, D.
7357	,,	E?WARDS, P.	7356	,,	BIRCH, J. C.
7342	,,	LORD, W.	7335	,,	FOX, P.
7351	,,	HULME, A.	7312	,,	MILWARD, G.
7404	,,	GOLDSMITH, W. H.	7396	,,	BANKS, S. S.
7377	,,	ADAMS, W.	7389	,,	ROBINSON, F.
7408	,,	MORBRAY, J.	7387	,,	DICKINSON, A.
7369	,,	COBB, H. G.	7379	,,	THOMSON, R. C.
7391	,,	HUGHES, H.	7349	,,	BROADBENT, T. H.
7385	,,	BAILEY, J.	7374	,,	GLEAVE, W.
7415	,,	PICKERSGILL, A.	7359	,,	GLEAVE, J. H.
7416	,,	WARD, L.	7393	,,	MALLALIEU, L. S.
7411	,,	BISHOP, S. M.	7354	,,	SIDDALL, J. W.
7432	,,	FORESTER, A.	7218	,,	KETTLEWELL, F.
7413	,,	KYNASTON, W.	7378	,,	POPPLEWELL, J.
7332	,,	MONKS, A.	7325	,,	DICKINSON, T.

* For portrait, see Officers' Group, p. 5.   † For portrait, see Sergeants' Group, p. 7.

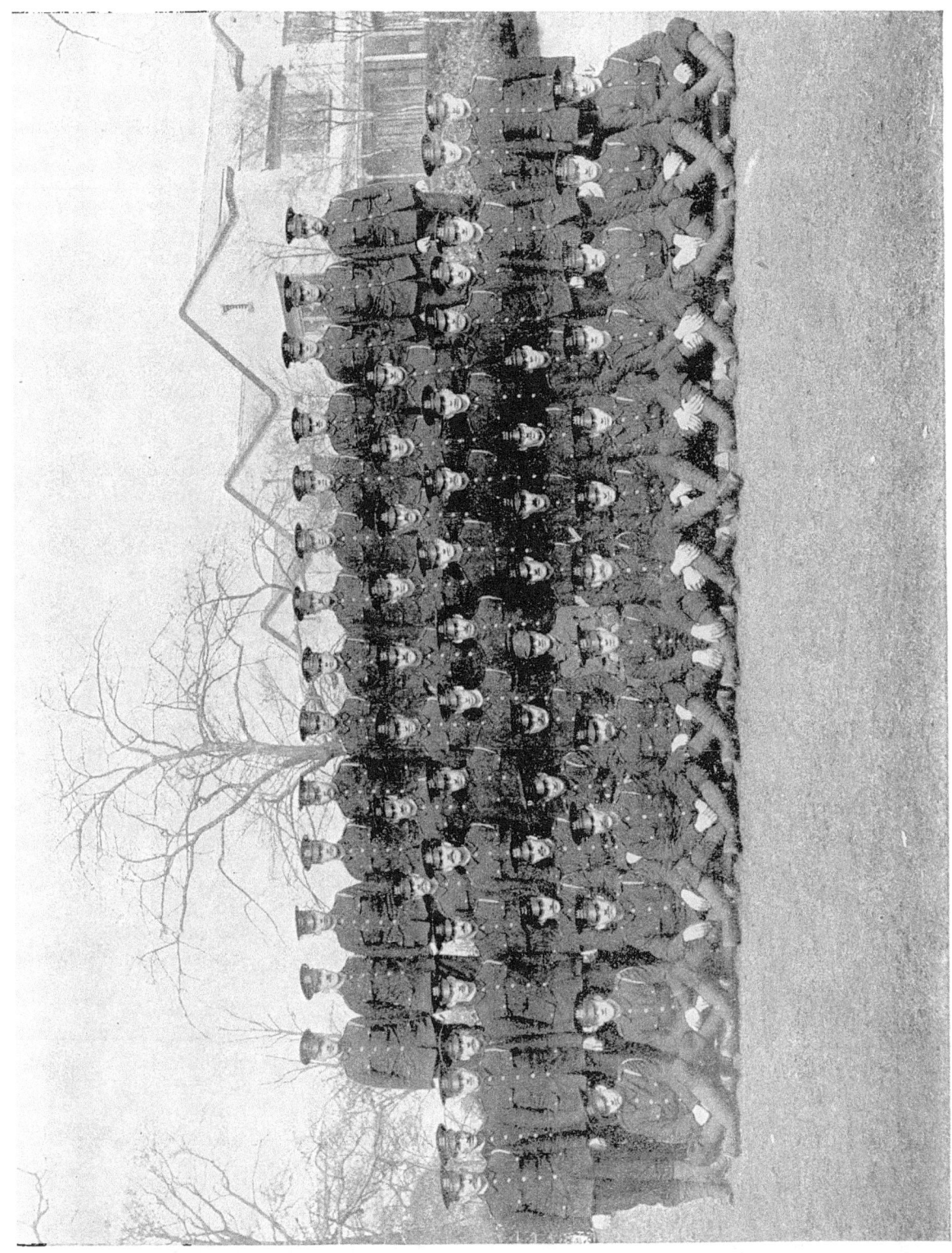

16th (Service) Battalion Manchester Regiment.

"E" COMPANY.

Officer Commanding Company	Capt. H. H. CUNLIFFE.*
Second in Command	Capt. Sir W. N. M. GEARY, Bart.*
Company Sergeant Major	BLAKELEY, J.†
Company Quartermaster Sergeant	STURGESS, F.

PLATOON NO. XIX.

Platoon Commander	2nd Lieut. I. W. HAYWARD-BROWNE.
Platoon Sergeant	CONNELL, W.

Roll No.	Rank and Name.		Roll No.	Rank and Name.	
6765	Corporal	JONES, E. W.	7477	Private	BROWN, F.
7054	L.-Corpl.	ROWSHAM, F.	7425	,,	POWNALL, F.
7433	Private	CLARE, A.	7438	,,	EVISON, M.
7352	,,	FAIRBROTHER, W. E.	7437	,,	DICKSON, W.
7340	,,	HALL, S.	7450	,,	GLEADALL, E.
7410	,,	WILD, J. W.	7443	,,	DELAUNEY, H.
7421	,,	PHILLIPS, W.	7449	,,	GRESTY, E.
7445	,,	FORTUNE, N.	7447	,,	AINSWORTH, R. W.
7426	,,	WEEKS, S. W.	7461	,,	WALTON, A.
7455	,,	FLINN, F.	7465	,,	HUGHES, R.
7431	,,	SLATER, J.	7456	,,	EDGE, E.
7414	,,	ALBINSON, G.	7448	,,	HAZELGROVE, V.
7422	,,	SMITH, N.	7428	,,	TILZEY, H.
7245	,,	MATTHEWS, J.	7453	,,	MASKEW, H.
7231	,,	SHORTON, S.	7434	,,	RAMSDEN, W.
7419	,,	VICKERS, C.	7435	,,	JOHNSON, H. H.
7303	,,	HEWITT, T. E.	7460	,,	WHEDDON, W. E.
7454	,,	MELLOR, S. J.	7458	,,	CHARLESWORTH, G. E.
7444	,,	BOARDMAN, E.	7459	,,	HITCHEN, F.
7466	,,	DEAKIN, J.	7420	,,	MEARS, S. F.
7442	,,	BROWN, G. D.	7384	,,	FLYNN, P.
7457	,,	RICHARDSON, E. W.	7402	,,	HILL, L.
7407	,,	HALLIWELL, H.	7360	,,	BENNETT, R.
7405	,,	ISHERWOOD, W.	7349	,,	ROGERS, G.
7386	,,	MARRIOTT, A.	6885	,,	HIGSON, W.
7363	,,	NORTON, J. H.	7365	,,	HUDSON, W.
7412	,,	CLARKSON, C. E.	7354	,,	SIDDALL, J. W.
7429	,,	THOMSON, W.	7470	,,	STEELE, E.
7446	,,	EVANS, P.	7348	,,	SOUTHWOOD, H.
7427	,,	TAYLOR, J.	7436	,,	BOARDMAN, E.

* For portrait, see Officers' Group, p. 5. † For portrait, see Sergeants' Group, p. 7.

The following were not present when the Platoon Photograph was taken, but see Supplementary Photograph on p. 50.

7362	Private	LENEGAN, W.	7439	Private	ROGERS, G.

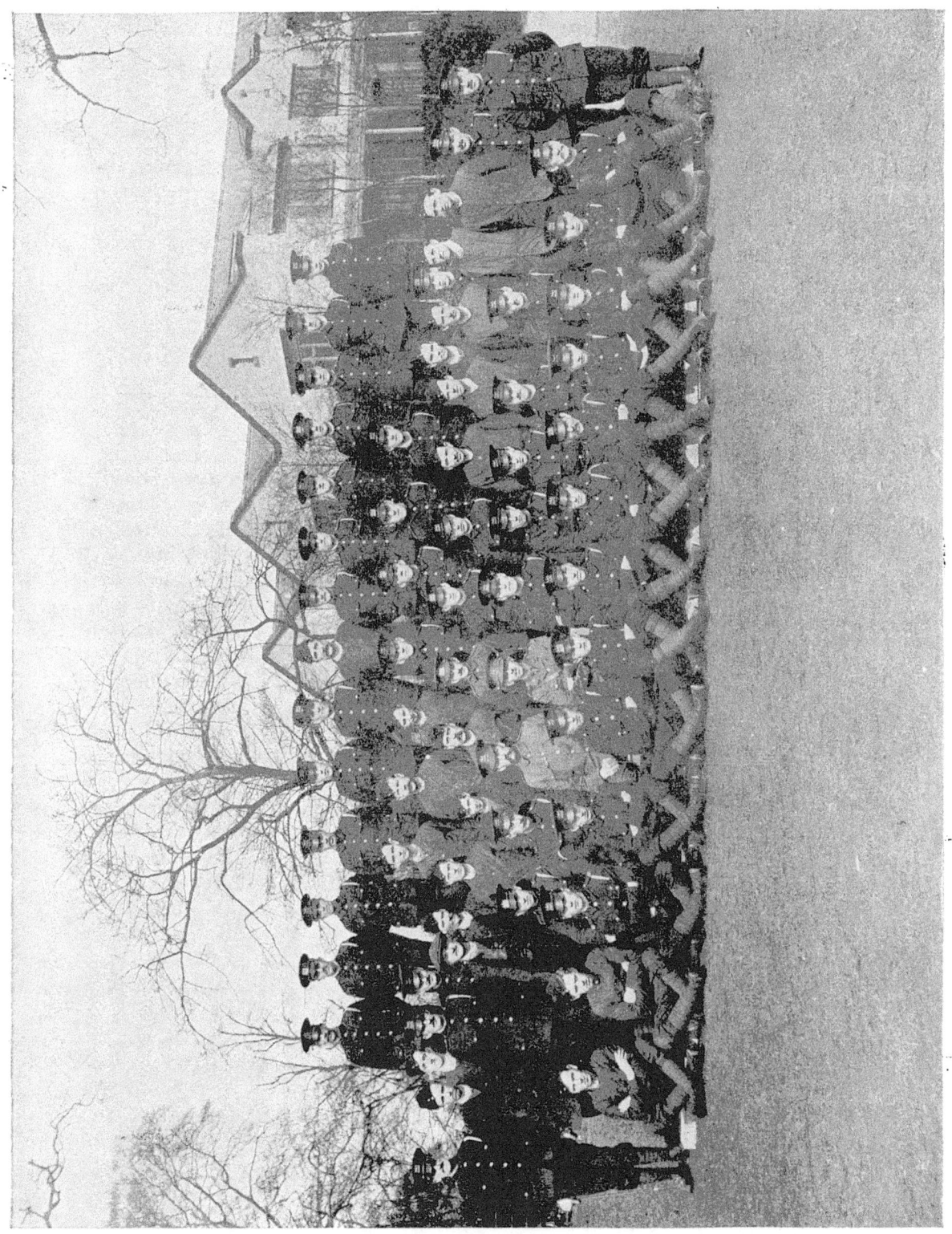

16th (Service) Battalion Manchester Regiment.

"E" COMPANY.

Officer Commanding Company - Capt. H. H. Cunliffe.*
Second in Command - - - Capt. Sir W. N. M. Geary, Bart.*
Company Sergeant Major - - Blakeley, J.†
Company Quartermaster Sergeant - Sturgess, F.

PLATOON NO. XX.

Platoon Commander - - - 2nd Lieut. E. Prestwich.
Platoon Sergeant - - - - Hickin, T.

Roll No.	Rank and Name.		Roll No.	Rank and Name.	
6909	L.-Corpl.	Massey, H.	7508	Private	Nash, T.
7526	Private	Brewer, J.	7484	,,	Barker, H.
7492	,,	Robinson, J.	7496	,,	Pimblett, C.
7501	,,	Goswell, G.	7468	,,	Maddaford, E.
7538	,,	Edwards, F.	7469	,,	Maddaford, P.
7486	,,	Hayes, S.	7452	,,	Callaghan, L.
7482	,,	Shenton, H.	7506	,,	Hargreaves, R. H.
7488	,,	Jones, P.	7304	,,	Richardson, H.
7512	,,	Tomlinson, A.	7473	,,	Higginson, J.
7505	,,	Shaw, J. H.	7464	,,	Jones, E.
7511	,,	O'Connell, D.	7522	,,	Higson, J.
7539	,,	Helsby, T.	7480	,,	Richardson, C. H.
7507	,,	Fletcher, W. R.	7451	,,	Dawson, L.
7527	,,	Greenwood, J. D.	7474	,,	Buck, H.
7502	,,	Goodwill, J. H.	7499	,,	Powell, F.
7516	,,	Mulleady, J.	7523	,,	Brady, A.
7524	,,	Huntbach, A.	7498	,,	Goldstone, A.
7500	,,	Swaithes, T.	7497	,,	Dawson, J. C.
7489	,,	Whitehead, H.	7494	,,	Russell, H. H.
7491	,,	Smith, P.	7365	,,	Hudson, W.
7533	,,	Taylor, C.	7483	,,	Wardle, P.
7536	,,	Abbott, J.	7515	,,	Richardson, C. C.
7535	,,	Mottershead, J. R.	7531	,,	Buckley, W. A.
7493	,,	Taylor, J.	7479	,,	Widdifield, F.
7517	,,	Harper, J.	7520	,,	Skippers, J.
7513	,,	Clarke, J.	7537	,,	Royle, E.
7540	,,	Stokes, C.	7503	,,	Lloyd, E. F.
7478	,,	Pennington, R.	7481	,,	Sanders, J.
7487	,,	Adshead, J.	7514	,,	Andrews, A.
7485	,,	Stabler, W. S.	7525	,,	Rankin, E.
7495	,,	Lawson, E.	7543	,,	Currie, J.

Also on the Photograph : 2nd Lieut. G. M. Bles.

* For portrait, see Officers' Group, p. 5.   † For portrait, see Sergeants' Group, p. 7.

16th BATTALION.—Supplementary Photo of men who were not present when the Platoon Photographs were taken. For names, see Platoon lists.

17th (Service) Battalion

17th (Service) Battalion Manchester Regiment.

Roll of Officers.

Colonel	Johnson, H. A.	Lieut.	Whittall, F. J. G.
Major	Casswell, F.	,,	Greg, A. H.
Capt. & Adj.	Larpent, L. de H	,,	Madden, J. G.
Captain	Aitken, J. K.	2nd Lieut.	Dawson, W. H. H.
,,	Whitehead, J. J.	,,	Potts, G. F.
,,	Lloyd, E.	,,	Wigley, E.
,,	Williams, J. V.	,,	Ward, G. F.
,,	Kenworthy, S.	,,	Holt, A. T. S.
,,	Fearenside, E.	,,	Humphreys, L. B.
,,	Macdonald, C. L.	,,	Tonge W. R.
,,	Ford, R. J.	,,	Hiller, A. H.
,,	Malim, E. J.	,,	Mansergh, R. F.
,,	Harrey, A.	,,	Kirkwood, J. D.
Chaplain	Balleine, Rev. W. R.	,,	Orford, W. K.
Lieut.	Heyworth, E. L.	,,	Dowling, B. B.
,,	Sidebotham, J. N. W.	,,	Cameron, A. G.
,,	Vaudrey, N.	,,	Elwell, E. E.
,,	Etchells, T.	Lt. & Q.M.	Yarwood, T. A.

2nd Lieut. K. A. Bowles was not present when the Photograph was taken.

17th (Service) Battalion Manchester Regiment.

Non-Commissioned Officers' (Sergeants) Roll.

Warrant Officer.
9369 R.S.M. COATES, H.

9050 R.Q.M.S. DALLEY, G. F. V.
9049 R.O.R.S. DEWHIRST, A. W.

Roll No.	Rank and Name.		Roll No.	Rank and Name.	
9070	C.S.M.	GREEN, J. H.	8903	Sergeant	TURNER, J.
9098	,,	HAYMES, A.	8291	,,	SYLVESTER, A.
9065	,,	BRADLEY, N.	8742	,,	MOXON, F. W.
9072	,,	FOSTER, W.	8337	,,	WILSON, H. J.
9073	,,	GALE, J.	8097	,,	COATES, H. K.
9348	C.Q.M.S.	WADDINGTON, H.	8357	,,	YEOMANS, F.
10311	,,	SHORT, T. J.	8579	,,	GOUGH, C.
9195	,,	JOHNSON, C.	9306	,,	BRUCKSHAW, G.
9044	,,	McKELLEN, P. J.	9221	,,	PUGH, J. O.
9056	Sgt. Cook	TOWNLEY, R.	9224	,,	CRICHTON, N. D.
9438	Pion. Sgt.	JONES, F. W.	9240	,,	BUTLER, H. J.
8336	M.G.S.	WILKINSON, F. A.	9244	,,	SUMMERSBY, A.
8290	,,	STREAT, A. N.	9225	,,	HARVEY, H.
9241	Trns. Sgt.	FREEMAN, W.	8762	,,	MILLWARD, B.
8269	Sig. Sgt.	PORTER, J. S.	8515	,,	DOBSON, H. M.
9055	Sergeant	STRAHAN, W. B.	9506	,,	GOULDER, E.
8087	,,	CHANDLER, F. E.	8067	,,	BOLTON, C.
8114	,,	COOKSON, A. E.	9513	,,	HULL, E. J.
8289	,,	STREAT, R.	8295	,,	SILCOCK, F. H.
8511	,,	DRAKE, H. H.	8253	,,	NORBURY, A.
8526	,,	DENNERLEY, H. F.	9021	L.-Sergt.	McCANN, T.
8540	,,	EVANS, H. R.	9237	,,	PICKLES, A.
8619	,,	HAM, E. N.	9238	,,	HARBURN, R.
8673	,,	JONES, P. H.	9243	,,	REYNOLDS, J.
8684	,,	JACQUES, F.	8865	,,	SIMPSON, P.
8730	,,	McMENEMY, J.	8353	,,	WILSON, E.
9813	,,	TOMKINSON, W. A.	8790	,,	PINDER, J. C.
9047	,,	MARSDEN, T. R.	9252	,,	GREENWOOD, E. G.
8066	,,	BINGHAM, H.	9054	,,	DIXON, H.
8213	,,	LINFOOT, H.	9231	,,	POWELL, E.
8396	,,	BAMFORD, G.		*Attached.*	
8925	,,	VICKERS, W.		Sgt. Ins.	YOUNG, G.
8140	,,	FOALE, E.		Sergeant	BOOTH, J.

Also on the Photograph: Col. H. A. JOHNSON and Capt. and Adjt. L. DE H. LARPENT.

The following were not present when the Photograph was taken, but see pp. 85, 89.

8351 C.Q.M.S. WOOD, J.   8890 Sergeant SANDERSON, R.
9010 Sergeant ILLINGWORTH, J.

17th (Service) Battalion Manchester Regiment.

Bugle Band.

Roll No.	Rank and Name.		Roll No.	Rank and Name.	
8180	L.-Corpl.	Hooley, A.	9481	Drummer	Thomas, E.
8254	Drummer	Norribottom, E.	8200	,,	Jones, A.
8969	,,	Watkins, S.	9087	,,	Rothwell, A.
8352	,,	Woolford, R.	9077	,,	Pollitt, E.
8948	,,	Waine, W.	8210	,,	Knight, A.
8456	,,	Blackburn, A.	8521	,,	Dunscombe, A.
9081	,,	Price, W.	8307	,,	Thornley, E.
8893	,,	Shore, J.	8550	,,	Froggatt, B. G.
8479	,,	Coase, J.	8949	,,	Waldron, H.
8316	,,	Viner, A.	8253	,,	Nixson, J. H.
9075	,,	Barratt, A.	8771	,,	Needham, T.
8905	,,	Taylor, G.	8711	,,	Laurie, D.
8625	,,	Hiley, E.	8478	,,	Clark, T.
8620	,,	Owens, E.	9084	,,	McCormick, T.
8351	,,	Wood, E.	9085	,,	Sowerbutts, W.

Also on the Photograph: Capt. Whitehead, 2nd Lieut. Mansergh and R.S.M. Coates.

The following were not present when the Photograph was taken, but see Supplementary Photographs on pp. 98, 99.

Roll No.	Rank and Name.		Roll No.	Rank and Name.	
9513	Sergeant	Hull, E. J.	9184	Drummer	Hawkesworth, A.
8323	L.-Corpl.	Wallwork, E.	9384	,,	Leach, J.
9500	Drummer	Bowers.	8746	,,	McKinley, W.
9512	,,	Bennett, W. R.	8743	,,	Maddock, H. T.
8490	,,	Crowder, R. C.	9485	,,	Newton, W.
8491	,,	Crowder, W. L.	9514	,,	Oven, W.
8529	,,	Daniels, J.	8990	,,	Williams, G.
9111	,,	Evans, F.	9344	,,	Thorley, R.
9395	,,	Hampson, W.	9324	,,	Chester, W.
8595	,,	Hawkins, T.	8339	,,	Windows, J.
9516	,,	Holbrook, J. H.			

17th (Service) Battalion Manchester Regiment.

"A" COMPANY.

Officer Commanding Company - Capt. E. Lloyd.*
Second in Command - - - Capt. E. Fearenside.*
Company Sergeant Major - - Green, J. H.
Company Quartermaster Sergeant - Waddington, H.†

PLATOON NO. I.

Platoon Commander - - - Lieut. J. N. W. Sidebotham.
Platoon Sergeant - - - - Linfoot, H.

Roll No.	Rank and Name.		Roll No.	Rank and Name.	
9369	R.S.-Maj.	Coates, H.	8934	Private	Wolstencroft, J. E. H.
8140	Sergeant	Foale, E.	8466	,,	Crowe, F. G.
8932	Corporal	Williams, P.	8855	,,	Scott, J.
8928	,,	Whatmough, T.	8316	,,	Viner, A.
8282	L.-Corpl.	Stableford, D. S.	8765	,,	North, J. H.
8668	,,	Jones, F. A.	8593	,,	Hampson, G. H.
9048	,,	Sharples, T.	9161	,,	Jones, J. E.
8374	,,	Barlow, A.	8687	,,	Kelly, S. H.
8567	Private	Gilbert, S.	8927	,,	Weldon, A.
8592	,,	Hampson, A.	8468	,,	Cadman, C.
8820	,,	Roberts, S.	8686	,,	Kay, A.
8663	,,	Ingle, E.	8533	,,	Ellison, J.
8273	,,	Remmos, A. A. O.	8381	,,	Bond, G. T.
8377	,,	Da. Bell, P.	8568	,,	Gosling, F. H.
8816	,,	Rain, R.	8380	,,	Blair, J.
9078	,,	Rothwell, A.	8936	,,	Worthington, P.
8375	,,	Barlow, C. F.	8153	,,	Hill, W. E.
8667	,,	Johnson, W. V.	8042	,,	Ashworth, A.
8202	,,	Kerr, R.	8164	,,	Hulme, A. L.
9159	,,	Camp, A.	8594	,,	Hayes, A.
8211	,,	Lear, F.	8376	,,	Barratt, N.
8789	,,	Parker, C.	8723	,,	Macauley, W.
8930	,,	Wilcox, J.	8212	,,	Linaker, A. B.
8767	,,	Newman, P.	8670	,,	Jackson, A.
8317	,,	Wade, P. J.	8669	,,	Jones, S.
8692	,,	Knowles, H.	8664	,,	Ingle, P.
9030	,,	Richards, W.	8162	,,	Headon, N.
8672	,,	Jones, A. W.	9026	,,	Hanley, J.
8567	,,	Grundy, S.			

* For portrait, see Officers' Group, p. 53.   † For portrait, see Sergeants' Group, p. 55.

The following were not present when the Platoon Photograph was taken, but see Supplementary Photographs on pp. 98, 99.

8245	L.-Sergt.	Norbury, A.	8817	Private	Ralston, A.
9008	L.-Corpl.	Halliwell, F. R.	8818	,,	Roberts, T.
8858	,,	Slack, J. F.	8792	,,	Platt, C.
8154	Private	Hampton, W.	8929	,,	Whyatt, A.
8361	,,	Alton, A.	8214	,,	Lomas, S.
8602	,,	Herbert, E.			

17th (Service) Battalion Manchester Regiment.

"A" COMPANY.

Officer Commanding Company - Capt. E. Lloyd.*
Second in Command - - - Capt. E. Fearenside.*
Company Sergeant Major - - Green, J. H.†
Company Quartermaster Sergeant - Waddington, H.

PLATOON NO. II.

Platoon Commander - - - 2nd Lieut. W. R. Tonge.
Platoon Sergeant - - - - McMenemy, J.

Roll No.	Rank	and Name.	Roll No.	Rank	and Name.
8579	Sergeant	Gough, C.	8287	Private	Spencer, U.
9238	L.-Sergt.	Harburn, R.	8727	,,	Marsden, S.
8534	L.-Corpl.	Ellison, T. A.	8548	,,	Fawcett, A.
9029	,,	Marshall, H.	8935	,,	Worthington, P. N.
8383	,,	Brown, F. H.	8681	,,	Jones, E.
8532	,,	Edwards, J. H.	8600	,,	Hopwood, H.
8782	,,	Ogden, C. H.	10462	,,	Tant, H.
8780	Private	Oldham, J.	8263	,,	Price, T.
8509	,,	Davies, H.	8203	,,	Knowles, S.
8571	,,	Gleave, J.	8725	,,	Mallalieu, J. P.
8702	,,	Lees, F. H.	10609	,,	Bernstein, B.
8382	,,	Bradshaw, E.	8666	,,	Jackson, W.
8137	,,	Fearn, H. L.	8161	,,	Hayes, J.
9067	,,	Bradley, T. J.	9126	,,	Blades, M.
9150	,,	Appleby, P. N.	8390	,,	Barlow, E.
8281	,,	Sharples, H.	8689	,,	Kelly, G.
8781	,,	Overton, C. E.	8599	,,	Holt, A.
8544	,,	Foden, A.	8688	,,	Knight, J.
8088	,,	Cowan, J.	8857	,,	Shaw, R. E.
8119	,,	Devany, H. L.	9149	,,	Ashworth, J.
9028	,,	Mallalieu, F.	9147	,,	McBride, E.
8379	,,	Bennett, H. B.	8054	,,	Buxton, A.
10332	,,	Allred, T.	8721	,,	McBride, A.
8947	,,	Williams, T.	8603	,,	Himsworth, J. W.
8463	,,	Coope, J. J.	8258	,,	O'Donnell, J.
8859	,,	Smith, F.	8322	,,	Adams, A. W.
8204	,,	Kelly, C.	8144	,,	Gouldsborough, W.
8783	,,	Ollerhead, F.	8462	,,	Clarke, F.

* For Officers' Group, see p. 53. † For Sergeants' Group, see p. 55.

The following were not present when the Platoon Photograph was taken, but see Supplementary Photographs on pp. 98, 99.

Roll No.	Rank	Name	Roll No.	Rank	Name
8860	L.-Corpl.	Stock, A.	8861	Private	Stockton, R.
9130	Private	Delaney, W.	8793	,,	Potts, C.
9133	,,	Hewitt, C. F.	10744	,,	Walton, F.
8510	,,	Derbyshire, J.	9068	,,	Wild, H.

17th (Service) Battalion Manchester Regiment.

"A" COMPANY.

Officer Commanding Company	Capt. E. Lloyd.*
Second in Command	Capt. E. Fearenside.*
Company Sergeant Major	Green, J. H.†
Company Quartermaster Sergeant	Waddington, H.†

PLATOON NO. III.

Platoon Commander	2nd Lieut. R. F. Mansergh.
Platoon Sergeant	Chandler, F. E.†

Roll No.	Rank and Name.		Roll No.	Rank and Name.	
8903	Sergeant	Turner, J.	9148	Private	Hawksworth, A.
9054	L.-Sergt.	Dixon, H.	9027	,,	Jones, C. G.
8047	Corporal	Amos, P. A.	9075	,,	Barrett, R.
8170	,,	Hare, S. B.	8604	,,	Hoyle, F.
8155	L.-Corpl.	Handley, F.	8856	,,	Scott, W.
9051	,,	Barton, H. F.	8943	,,	Wilkins, A.
8084	,,	Broadmeadow, S.	8055	,,	Bell, A. A.
8705	,,	Linney, L.	9143	,,	Conroy, E.
9045	,,	Brownjohn, L. C.	8547	,,	Forsyth, F.
8728	Private	McCaig, J. H.	8942	,,	White, H. G.
10772	,,	Gray, T.	8394	,,	Bretnall, H.
8227	,,	Moss, G. N.	8508	,,	Darnborough, L. J.
8933	,,	Williams, S.	8473	,,	Collier, A.
9162	,,	Lavin, T.	8823	,,	Roscoe, T. C.
8822	,,	Robinson, G. H.	8794	,,	Pemberton, B. W.
8461	,,	Chant, W.	9077	,,	Pollitt, C.
8595	,,	Hawkins, T.	8937	,,	Waller, H. G.
8388	,,	Bardsley, J.	8392	,,	Bennett, A. E.
8868	,,	Snowdon, L. L.	8469	,,	Carlin, J.
8364	,,	Ashton, W.	8726	,,	Murch, P.
8387	,,	Barnett, F.	8472	,,	Clark, J.
8190	,,	Jones, A.	9046	,,	Brown, T.
8941	,,	Watts, A.	8706	,,	Leach, J.
8869	,,	Stelfox, E.	8284	,,	Schofield, R.
8396	,,	Brumfitt, H.	8478	,,	Craig, H.
8378	,,	Bell, J.	8901	,,	Thomson, J.
8570	,,	Garbutt, G. S.	8703	,,	Law, J.

* For portrait, see Officers' Group, p. 53. † For portrait, see Sergeants' Group, p. 55.

The following were not present when the Platoon Photograph was taken, but see Supplementary Photographs on pp. 98, 99.

Roll No.	Rank	Name	Roll No.	Rank	Name
8087	Sergeant	Chandler, F. E.	8364	Private	Ashton, W.
9094	L.-Corpl.	Lucas, S.	9160	,,	Kemmery, E.
8693	,,	Kay, P. H.	9163	,,	Lancaster, G.

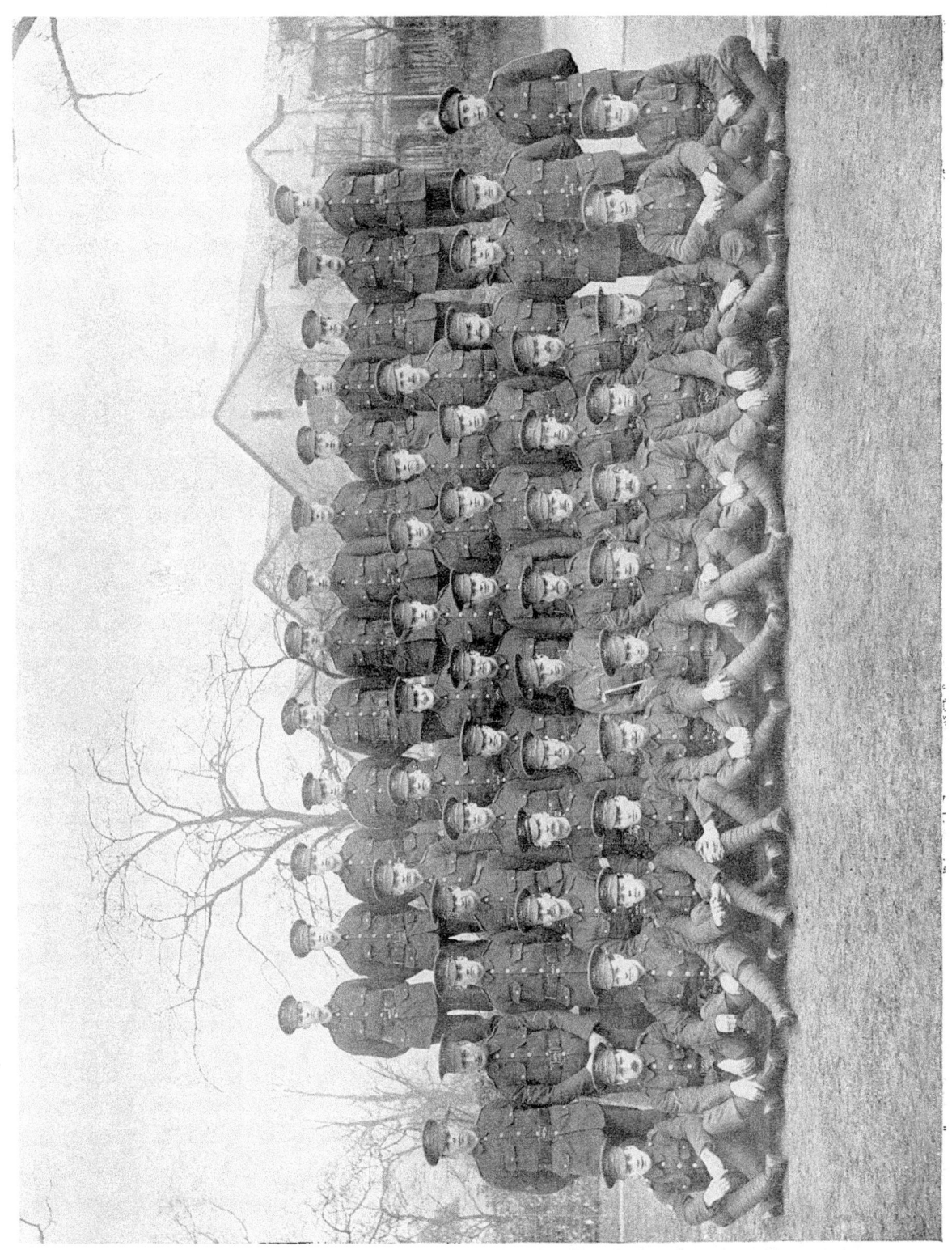

17th (Service) Battalion Manchester Regiment.

"A" COMPANY.

Officer Commanding Company -	Capt. E. Lloyd.*
Second in Command - - -	Capt. E. Fearenside.*
Company Sergeant Major -	Green, J. H.†
Company Quartermaster Sergeant -	Waddington, H.†

PLATOON NO. IV.

Platoon Commander - - -	2nd Lieut. J. D. Kirkwood.
Platoon Sergeant - - -	Drake, H. H.

Roll No.	Rank and Name.		Roll No.	Rank and Name.	
9242	Sergeant	Reynolds, J.	8724	Private	Morton, N.
9248	Corporal	Rowe, J.	9129	,,	Salt, F.
8403	,,	Bird, S.	10540	,,	Harper, T. W.
8536	L.-Corpl.	Evans, S.	8319	,,	Williams, E.
8940	,,	Watson, B.	8145	,,	Greenhill, J.
8156	,,	Hawkins, G.	9145	,,	Newman, E. T.
8391	,,	Barratt, A.	8704	,,	Leather, G.
8824	,,	Ryder, A.	8694	,,	Kinnimonth, S. G.
10337	Private	Atkinson, R.	8691	,,	Kemp, H.
8389	,,	Barlow, J. H.	8825	,,	Ryder, V.
8386	,,	Bailey, A. E.	8157	,,	Heaton, H.
8385	,,	Baguley, J.	8866	,,	Smith, G. W.
8397	,,	Bunting, F.	9142	,,	Monks, J. S.
8056	,,	Booth, B.	8956	,,	Hawkesworth, E.
8392	,,	Bennett, A. E.	8766	,,	Newland, W.
10361	,,	Clarke, C. S.	8946	,,	Wright, R.
8465	,,	Creighton, P.	8690	,,	Kelsall, C.
9146	,,	Davies, C. E.	8320	,,	Williams, F.
8537	,,	Evans, W.	8926	,,	Webb, J. S.
8545	,,	Faulkner, J.	8920	,,	Upton, W. H.
8158	,,	Hurst, C.	8821	,,	Robinson, F. G.
9099	,,	Neal, H.	8944	,,	Wilkinson, H.
8863	,,	Schofield, L.	8945	,,	Wilson, S. D.
8819	,,	Roberts, J. H.	8764	,,	Needham, N.
8938	,,	Ward, A.	8318	,,	Williams, A.
8939	,,	Ward, H.	8228	,,	McKenna, J.
8867	,,	Smith, J. G.	8160	,,	Howard, P.
8902	,,	Toft, L.	8321	,,	Wilson, G. S.
8286	,,	Shaw, A.	9140	,,	Maund, L.
8573	,,	Gurney, H. B.			

* For portrait, see Officers' Group, p. 53. † For portrait, see Sergeants' Group, p. 55.

The following were not present when the Platoon Photograph was taken, but see Supplementary Photographs on pp. 98, 99.

9097	L.-Corpl.	Coates, A. S.	8322	Private	Wilkinson, W.

D

17th (Service) Battalion Manchester Regiment.
"B" COMPANY.

Officer Commanding Company - Capt. J. J. WHITEHEAD.*
Second in Command - - Capt. J. V. WILLIAMS.*
Company Sergeant Major - HAYMES, A.
Company Quartermaster Sergeant - SHORT, T. J.†

PLATOON NO. V.

Platoon Commander - - - 2nd Lieut. W. H. H. DAWSON.
Platoon Sergeant - - - HAM, E. N.

Roll No.	Rank and Name.		Roll No.	Rank and Name.	
8357	Sergeant	YEOMANS, F.	8400	Private	BAMFORD, R.
9231	L.-Sergt.	POWELL, E.	8057	,,	BARRATT, A.
8418	Corporal	BUTTERWORTH, W. S.	8062	,,	BUTLER, C.
9239	,,	APPLEYARD, J.	8092	,,	CONSTANTINE, E.
8417	L.-Corpl.	BERRISFORD, C. W.	8090	,,	CASTLEDINE, C.
8109	,,	CUNNINGHAM, W. J.	8482	,,	CLUTTON, E.
8171	,,	HENSHALL, G.	8091	,,	COLBY, G. A.
8483	,,	CROASDALE, E. W.	8093	,,	CRAWSHAW, E. J.
8147	,,	GRINDROD, W. P.	8512	,,	DAVIDSON, J. E.
8618	,,	HALLSWORTH, W.	8513	,,	DAWSON, J.
8043	Private	AIKEN, J.	8514	,,	DENT, C.
8365	,,	ALLSOPP, F. G.	8120	,,	DOWNING, L.
8366	,,	ARMSTRONG, S.	8121	,,	DUNN, W.
8408	,,	BOLT, R.	8551	,,	FISHER, A. E.
8409	,,	BOLT, W. N.	8552	,,	FITTIS, A.
8399	,,	BAMFORD, H.	8553	,,	FROST, R.
8405	,,	BERLYN, C. S.	10639	,,	FURLONG, F. P.
8411	,,	BRADLEY, H. L.	8146	,,	GARVIN, H. C.
8402	,,	BATEY, T. W.	8574	,,	GARNER, A.
8410	,,	BRADFORD, L. J.	8576	,,	GILL, N.
8412	,,	BROOMFIELD, W.	8577	,,	GODFREY, G. W.
8413	,,	BROWN, H.	8578	,,	GRANT, J. C.
10623	,,	BROCKLEHURST, P.	8616	,,	HALL, A. E.
8414	,,	BOURNE, F.	8625	,,	HILEY, E.
8415	,,	BURN, R. A.	8617	,,	HALL, H. S.
8407	,,	BOWKER, N.	8615	,,	HAGUE, H.
8404	,,	BENNETT, W. E.	8168	,,	HALL, P.
8401	,,	BARNETT, G.	8620	,,	HARDMAN, S. J. T.
8060	,,	BROWN, HT.	8169	,,	HAMER, R.
8061	,,	BULL, A.	8963	,,	WINTERBURN, J.
8416	,,	BURNS, E.	9500	,,	BOWER, A.

* For portrait, see Officers' Group, p. 53.   † For portrait, see Sergeants' Group, p. 55.

The following were not present when the Platoon Photograph was taken, but see Supplementary Photographs on pp. 98, 99.

9049	Sergeant	DEWHIRST, A. W.	8481	Private	CALVERT, T. P.
8403	Private	BEDFORD, J.	8159	,,	HALL, A.
8058	,,	BARROW, T.			

17th (Service) Battalion Manchester Regiment.

"B" COMPANY.

Officer Commanding Company - Capt. J. J. WHITEHEAD.*
Second in Command - - Capt. J. V. WILLIAMS.*
Company Sergeant Major - - HAYMES, A.
Company Quartermaster Sergeant - SHORT, T. J.†

PLATOON NO. VI.

Platoon Commander - - Lieut. N. VAUDREY.
Platoon Sergeant - - - JONES, P. H.

Roll No.	Rank and Name.	Roll No.	Rank and Name.
9252	L.-Sergt. GREENWOOD, E. S.	9120	Private MANFORD, W.
8961	Corporal WILLIAMS, A.	8231	,, MERCHANT, H. E.
8993	L.-Corpl. WORRALL, A.	8736	,, MILLICHAP, T.
8074	,, BUCKLEY, H.	8247	,, NEWEY, T.
8833	,, ROEBUCK, J. B.	8769	,, NEWTON, J.
8832	,, ROBSON, A. S.	8249	,, NEWTON, J.
8622	,, HEARDMAN, F.	8255	,, NEWTON, A.
8876	,, SHERLOCK, J. S.	8251	,, NORBURY, B.
9115	Private BYRNE, T.	8250	,, NORMAN, G. A.
10642	,, FARNLEY, E.	8785	,, OVENS, W.
9152	,, GEE, J.	8795	,, PARKER, J. O.
8605	,, HARRIS, G. A.	8796	,, PEACOCK, H.
8621	,, HARRISON, L. W.	8797	,, PEARSON, A.
8623	,, HERBERT, H. F.	8798	,, POTTS, A.
8173	,, HOUGH, A.	8830	,, RAE, A.
8174	,, HYNCH, W.	8831	,, RAWLINSON, C.
8193	,, JONES, J. H.	8274	,, REDING, H.
8205	,, KENYON, W.	8875	,, SCHOLEY, C.
8711	,, LAURIE, D.	8906	,, TIGHE, J.
8216	,, LEE, W.	8304	,, TRENBATH, H. E.
8217	,, LLOYD, A. R.	8306	,, TRUEMAN, C.
8713	,, LLOYD, H.	8958	,, WALTON, W. E.
8230	,, MACKIE, A.	8959	,, WHATMOUGH, F.
8737	,, MACKINTOSH, W.	8329	,, WHITE, E. H.
8738	,, McLINDEN, H.	8960	,, WHITTAKER, J.
8739	,, McMAHON, J.	8330	,, WILSON, W.
8740	,, MADDOCKS, M.	8964	,, WOODALL, F.
9102	,, MALLINSON, D. W.	8965	,, WRIGHT, G.
8741	,, MARKS, F.		

* For portrait, see Officers' Group, p 53.   † For portrait, see Sergeants' Group, p. 55.

The following were not present when the Platoon Photograph was taken, but see Supplementary Photographs on pp. 98, 99.

Roll No.	Rank and Name.	Roll No.	Rank and Name.
8290	Sergeant STREAT, A. N.	8275	Private ROWBOTHAM, A. S.
8613	Corporal HOWE, H.	8904	,, TABBRON, A.
8770	L.-Corpl. NORTON, L.	8957	,, WALKER, T. C.
8624	,, HAY, D. F.		

17th (Service) Battalion Manchester Regiment.
"B" COMPANY.

Officer Commanding Company	Capt. J. J. WHITEHEAD.*
Second in Command	Capt. J. V. WILLIAMS.*
Company Sergeant Major	HAYMES, A.†
Company Quartermaster Sergeant	SHORT, T. J.

PLATOON NO. VII.

Platoon Commander	2nd Lieut. L. B. HUMPHREYS.
Platoon Sergeant	STREAT, R.

Roll No.	Rank and Name.		Roll No.	Rank and Name.	
9224	Sergeant	CRICHTON, N. D.	8122	Private	DEAKIN, A.
8292	Corporal	SOUTHWORTH, G.	8124	,,	DOWNES, J.
9264	,,	FOX, W.	8517	,,	DAWSON, G. L.
8421	,,	BENNINGTON, F. C.	8518	,,	DEWSBURY, H.
8095	L.-Corpl.	CHAPMAN, R. W.	8521	,,	DUNSCOMBE, A.
8520	,,	DEAN, F. H.	8519	,,	DENT, F. A. W.
8045	Private	ASHTON, F.	8516	,,	DAVIES, T.
8367	,,	ATKINSON, C.	8130	,,	ELLIS, J. H.
8429	,,	BRIERLEY, W.	8538	,,	ECKERSALL, H.
8423	,,	BERRISFORD, T.	9123	,,	FENTON, J. T.
8420	,,	BARTON, F.	8549	,,	FOSTER, G. L.
8430	,,	BROWN, H.	8550	,,	FROGGART, B. G.
9090	,,	BROWN, F.	8581	,,	GREGORY, W.
8063	,,	BROWN, P.	8148	,,	GOODIER, R.
8431	,,	BURNS, T.	8166	,,	HASSALL, F.
8425	,,	BOARDMAN, R.	8614	,,	HULTON, T.
8419	,,	BACON, D. R.	9131	,,	HEAP, A. E.
8422	,,	BENVILLE.	8165	,,	HALL, T.
9128	,,	BILLINGE, H.	8609	,,	HOLLINGSWORTH, H.
8096	,,	CLELAND, J.	8606	,,	HAYES, H.
8475	,,	CAMPKIN, C.	8608	,,	HOBSON, F.
8094	,,	CARLINE, R.	9103	,,	NOLAN, L.
8478	,,	CLARKE, T. H.	9132	,,	TAYLOR, A.
8476	,,	CARR, H.	9127	,,	WALROND, G. H.
8479	,,	COASE, J.			

* For portrait, see Officers' Group, p. 53.   † For portrait, see Sergeants' Group, p. 55.

The following were not present when the Platoon Photograph was taken, but see Supplementary Photographs on pp. 98, 99.

Roll No.	Rank and Name.		Roll No.	Rank and Name.	
8098	L.-Corpl.	CUBITT, W. W. G.	9222	Private	CALLOWAY, H. R.
8129	,,	EARLAM, E.	9223	,,	CLARKSON, H.
8283	,,	STANLEY, G.	9227	,,	GOODWIN, G. H.
8044	Private	ANNEQUIN, H	8607	,,	HEALEY, P.
8428	,,	BOWDEN, H.	8612	,,	HORAN, R. A.
8427	,,	BOTTOMLEY, W.	8610	,,	HOGAN, J.
8426	,,	BOOTH, U.	9218	,,	ROBERTS, M.
8123	,,	DICKENSON, R.	9100	,,	WHITEHEAD, M.

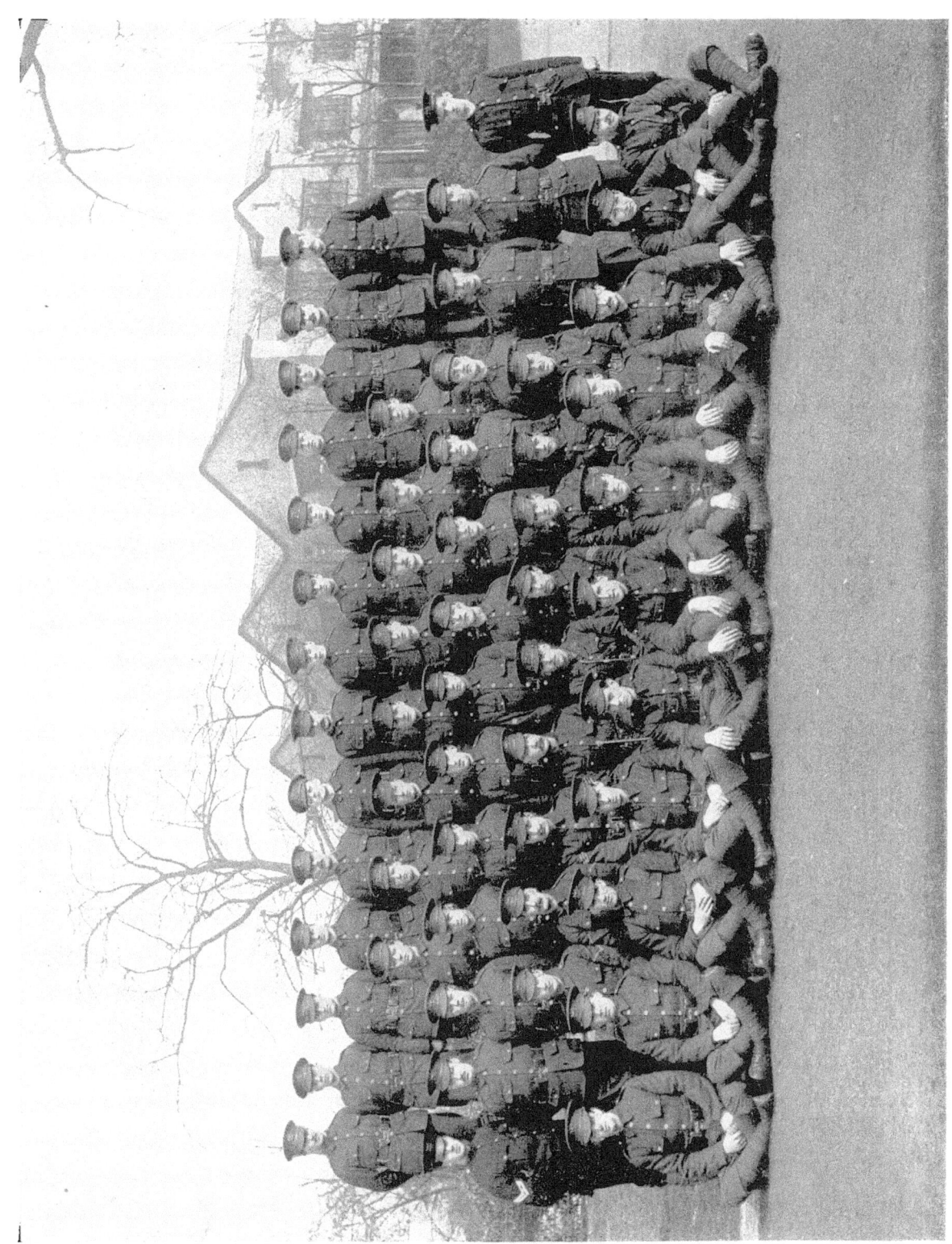

17th (Service) Battalion Manchester Regiment.
"B" COMPANY.

Officer Commanding Company - Capt. J. J. WHITEHEAD.*
Second in Command - - Capt. J. V. WILLIAMS.*
Company Sergeant Major - HAYMES, A.†
Company Quartermaster Sergeant - SHORT, T. J.†

PLATOON NO. VIII.

Platoon Commander - - Lieut. J. G. MADDEN.
Platoon Sergeant - - - BAMFORD, G.

Roll No.	Rank and Name.	Roll No.	Rank and Name.
8097	Sergeant COATES, H. K.	8359	Private MOORES, H.
8138	L.-Sergt. FARROW, J. W.	8734	,, MORRISEY, J.
8246	Corporal NEWMAN, J.	8233	,, MURPHY, L.
8735	L.-Corpl. MOTTASHED, W. W.	8771	,, NEEDHAM, T.
8709	,, LOWE, H.	8773	,, NIXON, C.
8772	,, NEWLOVE, F. W.	8774	,, NIXON, G. A.
8323	,, WALLWORK, E.	8799	,, PENNINGTON, H.
8324	,, WARBURTON, E. A.	8814	,, PREECE, W.
8955	,, WRIGHT, L. W.	9081	,, PRICE, W.
9155	Private BARRATT, A.	8826	,, ROGERS, A.
9153	,, FOSTER, R.	8827	,, ROGERS, H.
8192	,, JACKSON, E.	8829	,, ROYLE, E. C.
8675	,, JONES, H. H.	8288	,, SHEARER, W.
8676	,, JONES, J.	8870	,, SINGLETON, A.
8677	,, JONES, R.	8871	,, SNAPE, H.
8678	,, JOHNSON, T.	8872	,, SPEARS, R.
8695	,, KENT, L.	8873	,, STALEY, J.
8696	,, KING, C.	8874	,, SUMMERS, F.
8996	,, KING, J.	8305	,, TAYLOR, G.
8206	,, KNIGHT, A. H.	8923	,, VERNON, H. W.
8207	,, KNOWLSON, H.	8948	,, WAINE, W.
8712	,, LEDGER, L.	8949	,, WALDRON, H.
8707	,, LEEMING, T.	8325	,, WARBURTON, K.
8215	,, LIDGARD, C.	8326	,, WATSON, T.
9080	,, LINDSAY, F.	8951	,, WEBB, J. W.
8708	,, LOMAX, R.	8327	,, WHITEHEAD, G.
8710	,, LOWE, W. E.	8952	,, WHITTLE, H.
8731	,, McCLURE, W.	8328	,, WILLISON, P. J.
8232	,, MOORES, D.	8954	,, WRIGHT, C. F.

* For portrait, see Officers' Group, p. 53.   † For portrait, see Sergeants' Group, p. 55.

The following were not present when the Platoon Photograph was taken, but see Supplementary Photographs on pp. 98, 99.

Roll No.	Rank and Name.	Roll No.	Rank and Name.
9513	Sergeant HULL, E. J.	8264	Private PHILLIPS, W. J. H.
8355	L.-Corpl. WOLSTONCROFT, D.	8997	,, ROGERS, E.
8732	,, McCORMACK, T.	8828	,, ROSE, J.
8674	Private JONES, G. R.	8953	,, WILSON, H.
9154	,, KIRTON, A.		

17th (Service) Battalion Manchester Regiment.

"C" COMPANY.

Officer Commanding Company - Capt. S. Kenworthy.*
Second in Command - - - Capt. E. J. Malim.*
Company Sergeant Major - - Bradley, N.
Company Quartermaster Sergeant - Johnson, C.

PLATOON NO. IX.

Platoon Commander - - - Lieut. E. L. Heyworth.
Platoon Sergeant - - - - Dennerly, H. F.

Roll No.	Rank and Name.		Roll No.	Rank and Name.	
8336	Sergeant	Wilkinson, F. A.	8276	Private	Ridings, A.
9255	Corporal	Huddleston, F.	8340	,,	Withington, H.
8259	,,	O'Hara, J.	9032	,,	Bamford, S.
8632	L.-Corpl.	Helme, F. S.	8434	,,	Beasley, W.
9002	,,	Wilson, N.	8105	,,	Colquhoun, A.
8714	,,	Lancashire, J.	9033	,,	Edwards, E.
8435	Private	Bedford, F. G.	8150	,,	Gordon, F.
8436	,,	Bellamy, H. L.	8175	,,	Hands, C. C.
8444	,,	Bowman, C. H.	8236	,,	Mercer, H.
8554	,,	Falla, E.	8775	,,	Naylor, L.
8631	,,	Hatton, W.	8260	,,	Owens, E.
8745	,,	Martindale, H. O.	8807	,,	Prichard, G. H.
8237	,,	Moores, E.	8369	,,	Ashworth, E. R.
8278	,,	Robinson, S.	8050	,,	Atkinson, J. C.
8294	,,	Shufflebottom, O.	8064	,,	Bailey, A. J.
8296	,,	Simpson, H. J.	8073	,,	Buckley, A.
8309	,,	Thomas, G. H. G.	8102	,,	Clough, O.
8979	,,	Wilshaw, F. W.	8125	,,	Davis, A. W.
8338	,,	Wilson, J. T.	8177	,,	Hermon, H. G.
8524	,,	Day, F. J.	8637	,,	Holt, J.
8525	,,	Demaine, W.	8638	,,	Holt, J. P.
8135	,,	Evans, H. K.	9189	,,	Howe, S.
8630	,,	Harris, H. W.	8208	,,	Knaggs, E.
8194	,,	Jackson, A. E.	9187	,,	Judson, A.
10286	,,	Kenyon, J.	9034	,,	McEwan, W.
8219	,,	Lucas, F.	9001	,,	Westall, H.
8841	,,	Roberts, L. C.	9167	,,	Storer, E.
8911	,,	Thomas, W.			

* For portrait, see Officers' Group, p. 53.

The following were not present when the Platoon Photograph was taken, but see Supplementary Photographs on pp. 98, 99.

8438	L.-Corpl.	Bickerton, T. H.	8487	Private	Copsey, H.
8882	Private	Smethurst, F. J.	8584	,,	Godfrey, G. L.
8977	,,	Williams, E. H.	8100	,,	Carter, S.
8446	,,	Brown, E. H.			

17th (Service) Battalion Manchester Regiment.

"C" COMPANY.

Officer Commanding Company - Capt. S. Kenworthy.*
Second in Command - - - Capt. E. J. Malim.*
Company Sergeant Major - - Bradley, N.†
Company Quartermaster Sergeant - Johnson, C.†

PLATOON NO. X.

Platoon Commander - - - 2nd Lieut. G. F. Ward.
Platoon Sergeant - - - - Bingham, H.

Roll No.	Rank and Name.		Roll No.	Rank and Name.	
9241	Sergeant	Freeman, W.	8840	Private	Roberts, J.
9250	Corporal	Hobson, J. T.	8439	,,	Birchall, H.
8315	,,	Utting, R. A.	9052	,,	Bull, J.
8489	L.-Corpl.	Crossley, W.	8447	,,	Burke, S.
8180	,,	Hooley, A.	8107	,,	Craig, W.
8804	,,	Pickthall, H.	8104	,,	Coleman, J. E.
10478	,,	Worsdall, A.	8142	,,	Fitzpatrick, J.
8176	Private	Hayes, J. C.	8151	,,	Gordon, G.
8907	,,	Tatton, H.	8254	,,	Norrisbottom, E.
8837	,,	Riding, T.	8803	,,	Penny, W.
8980	,,	Wood, H.	8889	,,	Swindells, W.
8974	,,	Whelan, W.	8967	,,	Walker, H.
8972	,,	Westall, A.	8966	,,	Walker, J.
8046	,,	Ackerley, S.	8973	,,	Whaling, T.
8490	,,	Crowder, R. C.	9121	,,	Ankers, T.
8134	,,	Ellis, R.	8448	,,	Butler, T. A.
8235	,,	Mattock, H. N.	8749	,,	Morley, F.
10430	,,	Mottashed, H.	8238	,,	Mottram, F.
8746	,,	McKinley, W.	8748	,,	Moore, G. H.
8486	,,	Chapman, J. H.	8252	,,	Neil, G.
8491	,,	Crowder, W. L.	8776	,,	Neill, J. A.
8582	,,	Garlick, R.	8267	,,	Parrott, F.
8636	,,	Hole, W.	8839	,,	Riley, W. L.
8680	,,	Jamieson, W.	8333	,,	Wheeldon, A.
8743	,,	Maddock, H. T.	9122	,,	Kirwan, J.
8777	,,	Newton, F.	9191	,,	Turner, E. W.
8253	,,	Nixon, J. H.	9192	,,	Thornton, J.
8268	,,	Pearson, S.	9190	,,	Taylor, G. H.
8277	,,	Rimmer, A.	9193	,,	Huntbach, C.

* For portrait, see Officers' Group, p. 53. † For portrait, see Sergeants' Group, p. 55.

The following were not present when the Platoon Photograph was taken, but see Supplementary Photographs on pp. 98, 99.

8717	L.-Corpl.	Lyne, G.	8877	Private	Schofield, J.
8983	,,	Woolfenden, E.	8585	,,	Goodier, J. H.
8339	Private	Windows, J.	8834	,,	Ramsden, P. G.
9154	,,	Stocks, W.			

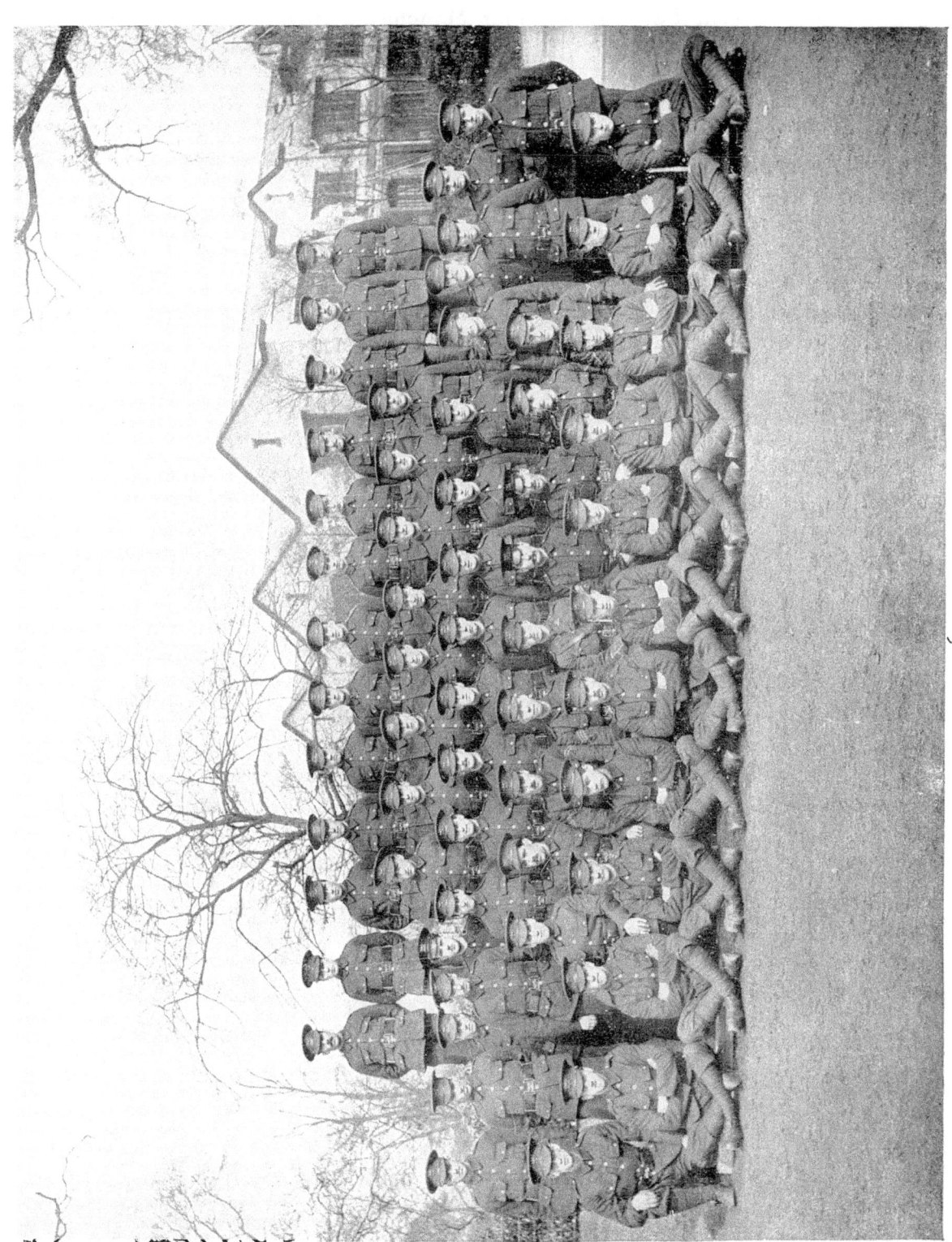

17th (Service) Battalion Manchester Regiment.

"C" COMPANY.

Officer Commanding Company	Capt. S. KENWORTHY.*
Second in Command	Capt. E. J. MALIM.*
Company Sergeant Major	BRADLEY, N.†
Company Quartermaster Sergeant	JOHNSON, C.†

PLATOON NO. XI.

Platoon Commander	2nd Lieut. E. E. ELWELL.
Platoon Sergeant	WILSON, H.

Roll No.	Rank and Name.			Roll No.	Rank and Name.	
8269	Sergeant	PORTER, J. S.		8433	Private	BAKER, P.
9221	,,	PUGH, J. O.		8522	,,	DALE, C.
9021	L.-Sergt.	McCANN, T.		8182	,,	HOUSEMAN, W.
8181	Corporal	HOUCHIN, B.		8629	,,	HARDING, S.
8971	,,	WEETMAN, T.		8633	,,	HILL, H. A.
8441	L.-Corpl.	BLACOW, E. M.		8801	,,	PARKER, H.
8075	,,	BURGESS, J.		8881	,,	SKINNER, W. O.
8716	,,	LOMAX, R. T.		8914	,,	TOWNLEY, S.
8335	,,	WILD, G.		8976	,,	WILKINSON, A.
8931	,,	WILLIAMS, D.		8981	,,	WOOD, R. M.
8838	,,	RILEY, E. H.		8978	,,	WILLIAMS, R. D.
8842	,,	ROWBOTHAM, S.		9116	,,	WRIGHT, W. J.
8332	,,	WARRINGTON, B.		8445	,,	BRADSHAW, R.
8069	Private	BRERETON, R. H.		8587	,,	GREEN, H.
8998	,,	CHAPMAN, L.		8179	,,	HILTON, H. A.
8101	,,	CLARKE, E.		8368	,,	ARMITAGE, J.
8132	,,	EDMONDSON, L. A.		8049	,,	ARNALL, H.
8555	,,	FARRELL, C. S.		8071	,,	BROOKES, T.
8586	,,	GREATOREX, F.		8099	,,	CANN, W.
8627	,,	HANCOCK, E.		8556	,,	FAULKNER, C.
8808	,,	PRITCHETT, A.		8583	,,	GLENNIE, D.
8297	,,	STEPTOE, F.		9110	,,	ASHWORTH, W.
8879	,,	SIDEBOTHAM, R. J.		9194	,,	DOUGHERTY, W.
8885	,,	SOUTHWORTH, F.		9195	,,	COTGRAVE, H.
8310	,,	TWIGG, F.		9196	,,	STANLEY, E.
9117	,,	HASSETT, P.		9197	,,	CASH, E. A.
8443	,,	BODDY, J. H.				

* For portrait, see Officers' Group, p. 53.   † For portrait, see Sergeants' Group, p. 55.

The following were not present when the Platoon Photograph was taken, but see Supplementary Photographs on pp. 98, 99.

Roll No.		Name		Roll No.		Name
8106	Private	COOPER, J. W. H.		8888	Private	STRINGER, W.
8887	,,	STREET, J.		8924	,,	VIPOND, A.
8485	,,	CARTER, I.		9139	,,	GREENHALGH, M.
8786	,,	ORR, W.		8999	,,	FLOWER, E.
8802	,,	PENDERGAST, L.		9119	,,	CORRIGAN, M.
8806	,,	POWER, F.		8715	,,	LANGSHAW, W.
8884	,,	SMITH, W. E. R.		8836	,,	RICHARDSON, C. K.
8566	,,	FULLER, E.				

17th (Service) Battalion Manchester Regiment.
"C" COMPANY.

Officer Commanding Company	- Capt. S. Kenworthy.*
Second in Command - -	Capt. E. J. Malim.*
Company Sergeant Major -	- Bradley, N.†
Company Quartermaster Sergeant -	Johnson, C.†

PLATOON NO. XII.

Platoon Commander - -	- 2nd Lieut. W. K. Orford.
Platoon Sergeant - - -	- Tomkinson, W. A.

Roll No.	Rank and Name.		Roll No.	Rank and Name.	
8540	Sergeant	Evans, H. R.	8183	Private	Hughes, H.
9237	„	Pickles, A.	8679	„	Jackson, F. A.
9254	Corporal	Bees, F. G.	8195	„	James, J. F. A.
8440	L.-Corpl.	Blackstock, W.	8682	„	Jones, L.
8070	„	Bridge, F.	8744	„	Marsh, T. H.
8133	„	Edwards, A.	8234	„	Mason, H.
8539	„	Eccles, W.	9084	„	McCormick, J.
8805	„	Podmore, A. B.	8747	„	Mills, W.
8835	„	Rhodes, A.	8750	„	Moss, H.
8298	„	Sturgeon, R.	8778	„	Nicholls, A.
8968	„	Wallwork, G.	9105	„	Ogden, S. H.
8975	„	Whittle, W.	8800	„	Page, T.
8048	Private	Archer, T.	8266	„	Parkin, T.
8437	„	Bennett, H.	9071	„	Powell, J.
8065	„	Beswick, J.	8878	„	Shelmerdine, E. S.
8442	„	Bloor, W.	8293	„	Sherwin, J. W.
8068	„	Brabin, C.	8883	„	Smith, H.
8460	„	Buckley, H.	9085	„	Sowerbutts, W. H.
8103	„	Coates, J.	9157	„	Shaw, J.
8498	„	Cotton, W.	8908	„	Taylor, P.
8126	„	Dawson, H. S.	9118	„	Thirlwall, F.
8528	„	Dunn, F.	8307	„	Thorniley, E.
9166	„	Elliott, C.	8912	„	Tomkinson, E.
8149	„	German, A.	8312	„	Toole, W.
8626	„	Hadcock, W. L.	8308	„	Turner, F. M.
8628	„	Hanly, J.	9198	„	Train, G. F.
8634	„	Hipworth, R.	8969	„	Watkins, S.
8635	„	Hodgson, J. R.	8970	„	Watkins, W.
8639	„	Howell, T.	8334	„	Whitehead, W.
8640	„	Howles, H.	8982	„	Woodvine, E.
8641	„	Hulme, J.			

* For portrait, see Officers' Group, p. 53. † For portrait, see Sergeants' Group, p. 55.

The following were not present when the Platoon Photograph was taken, but see Supplementary Photographs on pp. 98, 99.

Roll No.	Rank and Name.		Roll No.	Rank and Name.	
9259	Corporal	Wright, J.	9199	Private	Marchant, A. N.
8108	Private	Cuffwright, G.	8843	„	Russell, B. W.

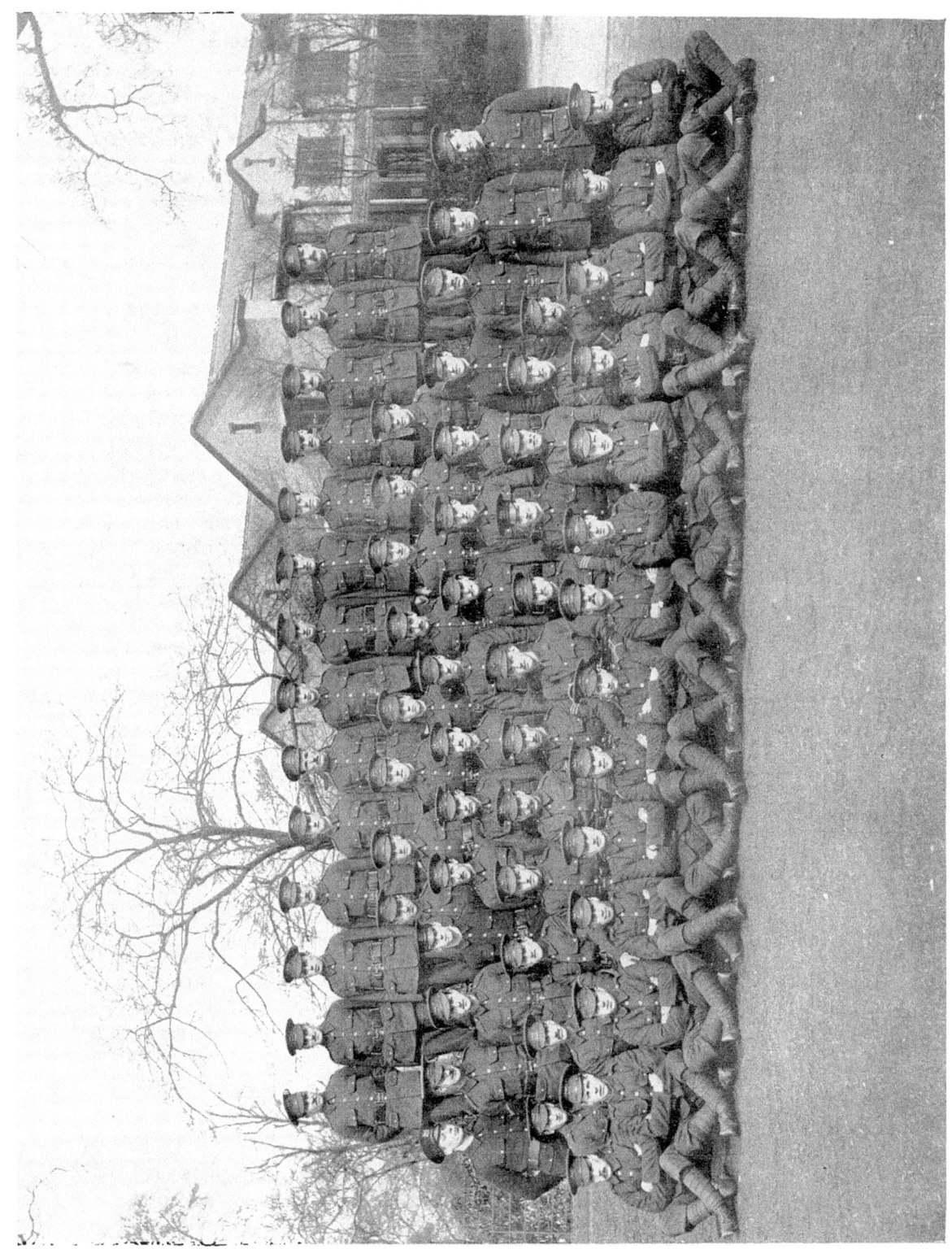

17th (Service) Battalion Manchester Regiment.

"D" COMPANY.

Officer Commanding Company - Capt. C. J. MACDONALD.*
Second in Command - - - Capt. H. HARREY.*
Company Sergeant Major - - FOSTER, W.†
Company Quartermaster Sergeant - WOOD, J.†

PLATOON NO. XIII.

Platoon Commander - - - 2nd Lieut. G. F. POTTS.
Platoon Sergeant - - - - MOXON, F. W.

Roll No.	Rank and Name.		Roll No.	Rank and Name.	
9006	Sergeant	BRUCKSHAW, G.	8272	Private	PRESTON, J. C.
9256	Corporal	BROSTER, A.	8314	,,	TRAVIS, W.
8523	,,	DAVIDSON, G. H.	8921	,,	UNSWORTH, W.
8661	,,	HUGHES, W.	8347	,,	WEBSTER, F.
8459	L.-Corpl.	BROWN, J.	9169	,,	JACOBS, T. G.
8454	,,	BERESFORD, W.	9173	,,	WILLIAMS, E.
8564	,,	FORREST, J.	9165	,,	BAILEY, A. A.
8685	,,	JOHNSTONE, A.	9174	,,	BOOTH, T. H.
9024	,,	LLOYD-BRYANT, R.	8112	,,	CLUBB, G. C.
8922	,,	UREN, P. D.	8561	,,	FERN, A.
8455	Private	BLACK, A.	8562	,,	FIDDLER, J. W.
9108	,,	CHARLES, J.	8188	,,	HOWE, T.
9091	,,	COWLEY, J.	8210	,,	KNIGHT, A.
8143	,,	FORSYTH, J.	8242	,,	MOTTRAM, A.
8590	,,	GORNER, F.	8243	,,	MURPHY, J.
8644	,,	HARDY, T.	8188	,,	OWEN, H.
8651	,,	HIGGINS, J.	9185	,,	HAMER, S.
8222	,,	LEE, G. B.	9156	,,	HILTON, R. T.
8752	,,	McCABE, W.	8053	,,	ASHLEY, G.
8756	,,	McDOWELL, N.	8083	,,	BRAY, S.
8893	,,	SHORE, J.	8086	,,	BROWN, T. G.
8341	,,	WALKER, A.	8530	,,	DERBYSHIRE, W.
9112	,,	SHENTON, H.	8642	,,	HAMMOND, F.
9164	,,	BUTTERWORTH, A.	8665	,,	IBBOTSON, C.
9134	,,	CLARKE, W.	9040	,,	IRLAM, W.
8128	,,	DENHAM, S.	8683	,,	JACKSON, R.
8136	,,	EDDLESTONE, J.	8220	,,	LAFFERTY, J.
9111	,,	EVANS, F.	8989	,,	WILLIAMS, E.
8652	,,	HILL, T.	8078	,,	BILLING, J.
8300	,,	SHIEL, J.			

* For portrait, see Officers' Group, p. 53.   † For portrait, see Sergeants' Group, p. 55.

The following were not present when the Platoon Photograph was taken, but see Supplementary Photographs on pp. 98, 99.

Roll No.	Rank	Name	Roll No.	Rank	Name
8850	L.-Corpl.	RONALD, F.	8646	Private	HEAP, J.
9268	Private	CRABTREE, B.	9180	,,	SHEEN, D.
8303	,,	STOTT, J. H. H.	8847	,,	REEDER, W.
9267	,,	PEMBERTON, A.			

17th (Service) Battalion Manchester Regiment.
"D" COMPANY.

Officer Commanding Company	Capt. C. J. MACDONALD.*
Second in Command	Capt. H. HARREY.*
Company Sergeant Major	FOSTER, W.
Company Quartermaster Sergeant	WOOD, J.†

PLATOON NO. XIV.

Platoon Commander	Lieut. F. J. G. WHITTALL.
Platoon Sergeant	JACQUES, F.

Roll. No.	Rank and Name.		Roll No.	Rank and Name.	
9010	Sergeant	ILLINGWORTH, J.	9014	Private	ROYLE, G.
9438	,,	JONES, F. W.	9063	,,	WRIGHTSON, A. W.
9056	,,	TOWNLEY.	9175	,,	BAYLEY, F.
8451	Corporal	BAILEY, R.	8496	,,	CHAMP, H.
8197	,,	JACKSON, M.	8152	,,	GALLIMORE, J. T.
8751	L.-Corpl.	MACDONALD, A.	8655	,,	HIRST, H.
9095	,,	MACDONALD, C. J.	8189	,,	HUBBARD, T.
8896	,,	SCHOFIELD, B.	8718	,,	LANDLESS, C.
8815	,,	QUINN, G.	8759	,,	MARTIN, H. F.
8846	,,	REDHEAD, D. A.	8757	,,	MCNALLY, W.
8457	Private	BOWES, P. A.	8763	,,	MITTON, C.
8085	,,	BROUGH, G.	8851	,,	ROTHWELL, C.
8653	,,	HILTON, O. T.	8854	,,	RUSSELL, A.
8657	,,	HOWARD J.	8915	,,	THOMAS, L.
8201	,,	JONES, O.	8918	,,	TUNNINGLEY, O.
8223	,,	LEWIS, J.	9181	,,	MASSEY, W. G.
8812	,,	PRICE, H.	9510	,,	BAYLEY, L.
8848	,,	RIDDELL, P.	8052	,,	ANDERTON, M.
8991	,,	WOOD, C.	8449	,,	BACKHOUSE, P.
9186	,,	ROBINSON, R.	8504	,,	CRUTCHLEY, T.
9176	,,	SPEAK, F.	8541	,,	EATON, C. W.
8051	,,	AINSWORTH, T.	9037	,,	HITCHEN, L. F.
8452	,,	BARNES, A. J.	8198	,,	JOHNSON, A.
8493	,,	CAMPBELL, S.	8698	,,	KAY, J. T.
8505	,,	CROSBY, G.	8813	,,	PUGH, P. W.
9036	,,	FAWKES, C.	8985	,,	WALTON, C. H.
8645	,,	HAYDOCK, T.	8345	,,	WARRINGTON, W. B.
8241	,,	MITCHELL, A.	8988	,,	WHITEHEAD, E.
8845	,,	RAYNOR, J.	8352	,,	WOOLFORD, R.
8916	,,	TOWER, P. K.			

* For portrait, see Officers' Group, p. 53.   † For portrait, see Sergeants' Group, p. 55.

The following were not present when the Platoon Photograph was taken, but see Supplementary Photographs on pp. 98, 99.

Roll No.	Rank	Name	Roll No.	Rank	Name
8697	L.-Corpl.	KAY, F. J.	8115	Private	COOPER, D.
8849	Private	ROGERS, W.	9251	,,	MEAKINS, F.
8342	,,	WALKER, W.	8502	,,	COX, A. E.
9265	,,	RIDINGS, G. H.	8987	,,	WAYGOOD, C. W
9233	,,	JENKINSON, A. W.	8588	,,	GARFT, G. W.
9262	,,	MACDONALD, A.	8184	,,	HANBY, F.
8255	,,	NEWTON, A.	8350	,,	WOOD, E.

17th (Service) Battalion Manchester Regiment.

"D" COMPANY.

Officer Commanding Company - Capt. C. J. MACDONALD.*
Second in Command - - - Capt. H. HARREY.*
Company Sergeant Major - - FOSTER, W.†
Company Quartermaster Sergeant - WOOD, J.†

PLATOON NO. XV.

Platoon Commander - - - 2nd Lieut. A. T. S. HOLT.
Platoon Sergeant - - - GOULDER, E.†

Roll No.	Rank and Name.	Roll No.	Rank and Name.
9055	Sergeant STRAHAN, W. B.	8591	Private GREENWOOD, N.
8114	,, COOKSON, A. E.	8720	,, LINNEY, A.
8353	L.-Sergt. WILSON, E.	9042	,, PATE, L. A.
9247	Corporal ROBINSON, P.	8372	,, ASHWORTH, A.
8649	L.-Corpl. HETHERINGTON, O. M.	8080	,, BLOUNT, H.
8699	,, KENYON, R.	8117	,, CROMPTON, P.
8700	,, KERSHAW, J.	9113	,, DODD, H.
9019	,, VALENTINE, A. G.	8542	,, EMERSON, J.
9003	Private ASPINALL, A.	8563	,, FODEN, H.
9004	,, BENNETT, T.	8844	,, RATCLIFFE, D.
9005	,, BLUNDELL, G.	8895	,, SHAW, C.
9022	,, BOARDMAN, J.	8313	,, TWEDDLE, C.
9023	,, ENSTONE, C.	8344	,, WARBURTON, J. W.
9011	,, MILLS, N. R.	9172	,, LIGHT, L.
9109	,, MONAGHAN, T.	9182	,, NIXON, T.
9012	,, O'DONOGHUE, T.	8076	,, BARNFIELD, T.
9013	,, OLIPHANT, J.	8501	,, COWMAN, J.
9015	,, STATHAM, J.	8529	,, DANIELS, J.
9018	,, TOWNLEY, G.	8565	,, FRITH, E.
9043	,, WALKDEN, R.	8589	,, GOODBRAND, G.
8760	,, MELIA, M.	8656	,, HOLMES, J.
9168	,, ARMSTRONG, A.	8754	,, McCARLEY, F.
8370	,, AIMSON, L.	8779	,, NORTON, W.
8453	,, BENNETT, J.	8897	,, SLIGHT, R.
8456	,, BLACKBURN, A.	8990	,, WILLIAMS, G.
8494	,, CARTER, W.	8992	,, WOOD, S. C.
8495	,, CARTWRIGHT, J. W.	9178	,, HAYTON, W.
9035	,, CORDT, J.	8163	,, HUDSON, H.
8118	,, CRUTCHLEY, F.	9179	,, MOORE, L.
9009	,, HEWIT, E. J.		

* For portrait, see Officers' Group, p. 53. † For portrait, see Sergeants' Group, p. 55.

The following were not present when the Platoon Photograph was taken, but see Supplementary Photographs on pp. 98, 99.

9506	Sergeant GOULDER, E.	9235	Private OWEN, R.
8295	L.-Sergt. SILCOCK, F. H.	8753	,, McCARDELL, P.
8852	L.-Corpl. ROYLE, G.	8758	,, MAFFIA, A.
8984	,, WALKER, J. L.	9384	,, LEACH, J.
9020	Private YATES, F. J.	9427	,, STANIFORTH, T.
9249	,, SHEPHERD, F.		

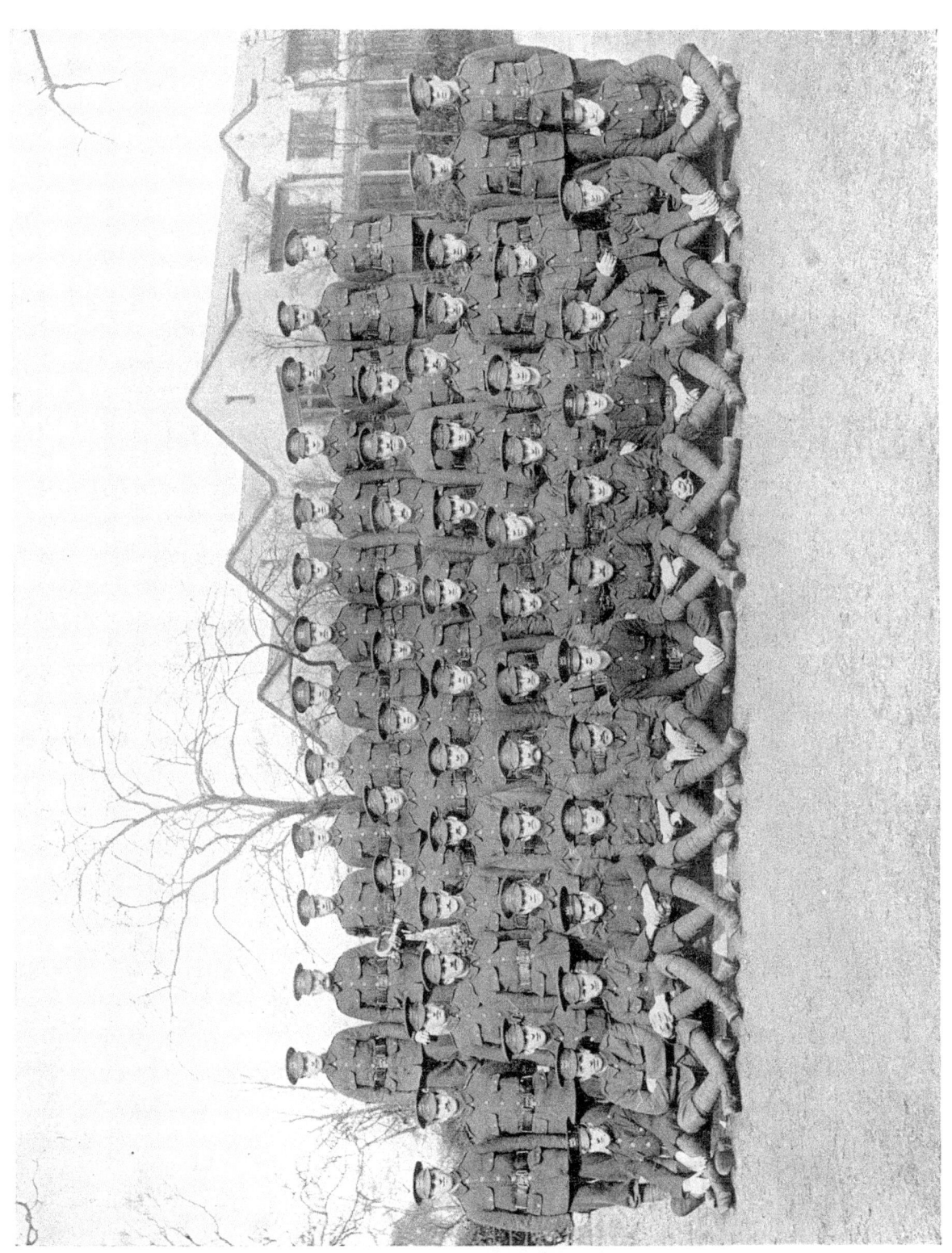

17th (Service) Battalion Manchester Regiment.

"D" COMPANY.

Officer Commanding Company - Capt. C. J. MACDONALD.*
Second in Command - - - Capt. H. HARREY.*
Company Sergeant Major - - FOSTER, W.†
Company Quartermaster Sergeant - WOOD, J.

PLATOON NO. XVI.

Platoon Commander - - - 2nd Lieut. E. WIGLEY.
Platoon Sergeant - - - MARSDEN, T. R.†

Roll No.	Rank and Name.		Roll No.	Rank and Name.	
8925	Sergeant	VICKERS, W.	8301	Private	SMITH, A.
9244	,,	SUMMERSBY, J.	8919	,,	TURNER, L.
8865	L.-Sergt.	SIMPSON, P.	9138	,,	YATES, H.
8265	Corporal	PALMER, H.	9184	,,	WILLIAMS, C.
8499	L.-Corpl.	COWAP, S.	8810	,,	PATEMAN, F. H.
8560	,,	FERGUSON, S. S.	8450	,,	BAILEY, D.
8898	,,	SMITH, W.	8506	,,	COUCHER, E. J.
8079	Private	BLAKELEY, F.	9039	,,	HUNTER, R.
8110	,,	CAWLEY, H.	8853	,,	RULE, F. R.
8643	,,	HARDING, F. S.	10324	,,	SMITH, S.
8650	,,	HIBBERT, W.	8899	,,	STEWART, R.
8654	,,	HILTON, W.	9017	,,	TAYLOR, S.
8658	,,	HOWARTH, H.	10875	,,	WALMSLEY, J.
8200	,,	JONES, A.	8343	,,	WARBURTON, A.
8239	,,	MCGRATH, A.	9025	,,	WRIGHT, F.
8257	,,	NUTTALL, F.	9041	,,	LINDSAY, G. D.
8256	,,	NUTTALL, A. E.	9183	,,	ROBERTSHAW, T. A.
8809	,,	PARTINGTON, J.	8371	,,	ALMOND, F.
8280	,,	ROSKELL, A.	8116	,,	CRITCHLOW, C.
8500	,,	COWELL, E.	8186	,,	HAZLEY, E.
8141	,,	FARRINGTON, C. M.	8648	,,	HESKETH, W.
8647	,,	HENDERSON, R.	8660	,,	HOWSE, F. R.
8659	,,	HOWARTH, J.	8209	,,	KERR, C.
9137	,,	HOULKER, G.	8224	,,	LITTLE, H.
8226	,,	LOWE, R.	8270	,,	PARSONAGE, G.
8240	,,	MENDES, N. E.	8891	,,	SEDGELEY, G. H.
8787	,,	OGDEN, F.	8354	,,	WRAY, W. L.

* For portrait, see Officers' Group, p. 53.   † For portrait, see Sergeants' Group, p. 55.

The following were not present when the Platoon Photograph was taken, but see Supplementary Photographs on pp. 98, 99.

Roll No.	Rank	Name	Roll No.	Rank	Name
8261	L.-Corpl.	PASS, E. L.	9234	Private	MCNEE, G.
8755	,,	MCGREGOR, R.	8225	,,	LOWE, D. C.
8302	Private	STOCKS, J.	9177	,,	CADMAN, E.
9465	,,	MARSHALL, C.	9260	,,	SMYTH, J. H.
9516	,,	HOLBROOK, J. H.	8187	,,	HEATON, H. V.
8077	,,	BERTENSHAW, R.	8199	,,	JOHNSTONE, J. R.
8082	,,	BRADBURY, B.	8356	,,	WRIGHT, A. E.

17th (Service) Battalion Manchester Regiment.

"E" COMPANY.

Officer Commanding Company	Capt. J. K. AITKEN.*
Second in Command	Capt. R. J. FORD,*
Company Sergeant Major	GALE, J.
Company Quartermaster Sergeant	McKELLEN, P. J.

PLATOON NO. XVII.

Platoon Commander	Lieut. T. ETCHELLS.
Platoon Sergeant	BUTLER, H. J.

Roll No.	Rank and Name.	Roll No.	Rank and Name.
8791	L.-Sergt. PINDER, J. C.	9171	Private SHEPHERD, H.
9242	Corporal WALKER, E.	9236	,, DOYLE, M.
8229	,, MATTHEWS, F.	9204	,, SINGLETON, J.
8531	L.-Corpl. EDGAR, W.	9260	,, SMYTH, C.
8701	,, LEACH, J.	9202	,, HARVEY, W.
8139	,, FARRINGTON, E.	9205	,, BROWN, J.
9261	Private CLARKE, W.	9203	,, WILSON, R.
9232	,, COLLIER, J.	9208	,, ELLISON, A.
9269	,, HATTON, F.	9210	,, BROUGH, T.
9272	,, HEAP, H.	9212	,, FLEMING, P.
9273	,, HARDMAN, P.	9201	,, KELLY, S.
9448	,, JERMYN, H.	9213	,, KNIGHT, W. B.
9263	,, MAUND, C.	9469	,, HOLLINGSWORTH, A.
9271	,, RHODES, C.	9214	,, FINNEY, F.
9228	,, CONROY, E.	9217	,, SANDERSON, E.
9262	,, McDONALD, A.	9219	,, COOPER, T. G.
9258	,, SHELDON, E.	9220	,, BROUGH, R.
9275	,, SMITH, A.	9223	,, CLARKSON, H.
9460	,, SUTTON, W. H.	9334	,, LONG, F. A.
9455	,, THOMAS, J. W.	9216	,, KAVENEY, J.
9274	,, WILLIAMSON, H.	9211	,, CALDWELL, C.
9251	,, MEAKINS, F.	9222	,, CALLAWAY, H. K.
9265	,, RIDINGS, G. H.	9227	,, GOODWIN, G. H.
9268	,, CRABTREE, B.	9234	,, McNEE, G.
9267	,, PEMBERTON, A.	9218	,, ROBERTS, M.

* For portrait, see Officers' Group, p. 53.

The following were not present when the Platoon Photograph was taken, but see Supplementary Photographs on pp. 98, 99.

Roll No.	Rank and Name.	Roll No.	Rank and Name.
8291	Sergeant SYLVESTER, A.	9462	Private BRETHERTON, E.
9257	Private KEMP, M.	9207	,, CAFFERY, D.
9209	,, TOWERS, W.	9499	,, GIBSON, W.
9226	,, KERSHAW, J.	9501	,, WALLS, L.

17th (Service) Battalion Manchester Regiment.

"E" COMPANY.

Officer Commanding Company - Capt. J. K. Aitken.*
Second in Command - - - Capt. R. J. Ford,*
Company Sergeant Major - - Gale, J.†
Company Quartermaster Sergeant - McKellen, P. J.†

PLATOON NO. XVIII.

Platoon Commander - - - 2nd Lieut. A. G. Cameron.
Platoon Sergeant - - - Millward, B.†

Roll No.	Rank and Name.		Roll No.	Rank and Name.	
8295	L.-Sergt.	Silcock, F. H.	9276	Private	Sanders, A. W.
8331	Corporal	Walker, T.	9309	,,	Willett, C.
8497	,,	Cooke, A.	9320	,,	Brogan, P.
8178	L.-Corpl.	Higgins, C.	9323	,,	Carter, C. F.
8467	,,	Culshaw, W.	9292	,,	Crompton, J.
8261	,,	Pass, E. L.	9422	,,	Cullum, S. W.
8697	,,	Kay, F. J.	9404	,,	Healey, J. W.
9321	Private	Butler, A. E.	9311	,,	Hurst, A.
9423	,,	Catlow, C.	9446	,,	Melton, F. W.
9312	,,	Fleming, J.	9314	,,	Owens, R.
9329	,,	Hanaby, H.	9304	,,	Reddington, W.
9298	,,	Hanbidge, A.	9355	,,	Stewart, A.
9444	,,	Hansell, A.	9288	,,	Baker, A.
9331	,,	Kay, A.	9291	,,	Brannan, F. G.
9315	,,	Sale, J.	9271	,,	Buckley, E. A.
9343	,,	Swain, G.	9350	,,	Day, C.
9489	,,	White, F.	9294	,,	Davies, A.
9287	,,	Ashton, E.	9283	,,	Goldstone, M.
9289	,,	Bailey, G.	9286	,,	Hodgson, A. C.
9290	,,	Bolton, W.	9281	,,	Jones, G.
9280	,,	Brooksbank, C.	9300	,,	Meadows, J.
9296	,,	Golding, J.	9307	,,	Steele, F.
9282	,,	Hardacre, H.	9285	,,	West, G.
9301	,,	Midgley, C. F.	9308	,,	Warren, H.
9303	,,	Reeves, F.	9310	,,	Young, G.

* For portrait, see Officers' Group, p. 53. † For portrait, see Sergeants' Group, p. 55.

The following were not present when the Platoon Photograph was taken, but see Supplementary Photographs on pp. 98, 99.

Roll No.	Rank	Name	Roll No.	Rank	Name
8762	Sergeant	Millward, B.	9313	Private	Farmer, J.
9295	Private	Davies, M.	9443	,,	McNicholls, L.
8754	,,	McCarley, F.	9342	,,	Schaw, S.
9471	,,	Griffiths, A. E.	9316	,,	Wright, J.
9279	,,	Merrill, H.	9511	,,	Rodger, G. W.
9498	,,	Ratcliffe, T. C.			

17th (Service) Battalion Manchester Regiment.

"E" COMPANY.

Officer Commanding Company - Capt. J. K. Aitken.*
Second in Command - - - Capt. R. J. Ford.*
Company Sergeant Major - - Gale, J.†
Company Quartermaster Sergeant - McKellen, P. J.†

PLATOON NO. XIX.

Platoon Commander - - - 2nd Lieut. B. B. Dowling.
Platoon Sergeant - - - - Goulder, E.

Roll No.	Rank and Name.		Roll No.	Rank and Name.	
9225	Sergeant	Harvey, H.	9382	Private	Black, R.
8662	Corporal	Hughes, S. A.	9400	,,	Stelfox, J.
9245	,,	Braznell, J.	9357	,,	Wright, P.
8283	L.-Corpl.	Stanley, G.	9497	,,	Appleyard, A.
8262	,,	Perkin, H.	9393	,,	Copeland, A.
9324	Private	Chester, W.	9399	,,	Power, J. E.
9347	,,	Freedman, A.	9381	,,	Newton, W.
9328	,,	Greenwood, C.	9364	,,	Casey, R.
9299	,,	Hudson, B.	9405	,,	Jibson, J.
9341	,,	Ralph, P.	9353	,,	Price, N.
9344	,,	Thorley, R.	9337	,,	Mathews, T.
9375	,,	Jones, L. E.	9372	,,	Howson, P.
9356	,,	Grundy, W.	9327	,,	Dean, G.
9467	,,	Morris, P.	9458	,,	Ratcliffe, T.
9379	,,	Preece, J.	9319	,,	Blakeway, F.
9481	,,	Thomas, E.	9346	,,	Wilson, J.
9330	,,	Jamieson, G.	9333	,,	Kimber, B. W.
9416	,,	Leech, G.	9484	,,	Hamilton, J.
9395	,,	Hampson, W.	9306	,,	Smith, W. E.
9401	,,	West, A. A.	9335	,,	Lundy, T.
9206	,,	Gething, S.	9345	,,	Tophill, T.
9358	,,	Pendlebury, P.	9351	,,	Walker, J.
9370	,,	Felton, T. R.	9340	,,	Morrell, A.
9398	,,	Morrow, F.	9354	,,	Rowbottom, A.
9368	,,	Brierley, J. M.	9454	,,	Fishwick, W.
9475	,,	Smith, W. F.	9352	,,	Hollingsworth, J.
9482	,,	Taylor, W.	9463	,,	Cragen, F.
9385	,,	Ryecroft, W.	9322	,,	Byrne, H.
9464	,,	Burns, H.	9470	,,	Kane, E.
9361	,,	Conley, H.			

* For portrait, see Officers' Group, p. 53.   † For portrait, see Sergeants' Group, p. 55.

The following were not present when the Platoon Photograph was taken, but see Supplementary Photographs on pp. 98, 99.

9496 Private Ogden, T.   9359 Private Purcell, J.

17th (Service) Battalion Manchester Regiment.

"E" COMPANY.

Officer Commanding Company	Capt. J. K. AITKEN.*
Second in Command	Capt. R. J. FORD,*
Company Sergeant Major	GALE, J.†
Company Quartermaster Sergeant	McKELLEN, P. J.†

PLATOON NO. XX.

Platoon Commander	2nd Lieut. A. H. HILLER.
Platoon Sergeant	MARSDEN, T. R.

Roll No.	Rank and Name.		Roll No.	Rank and Name.	
8515	Sergeant	DOBSON, H. M.	9427	Private	STANIFORTH, T.
9253	Corporal	SIDWELL, F. H.	9412	,,	HARDMAN, H. R.
9246	,,	BRIERLEY, J.	9483	,,	MADDEN, T.
8373	L.-Corpl.	ATKIN, C. H.	9494	,,	WELLS, J.
8129	,,	EARLAM, E.	9457	,,	VLIES, E. V.
9477	Private	BARRATT, H.	9451	,,	WALTON, R.
9406	,,	JOHNSON, F. W.	9492	,,	McCARTNEY, J.
9452	,,	JAMIESON, J. H.	9493	,,	THORNTON, J.
9403	,,	SHORE, A.	9472	,,	SCOTT, A.
9436	,,	LEE, P. G.	9368	,,	BRIERLEY, J.
9410	,,	HARRISON, A.	9367	,,	BENNETT, H.
9439	,,	GRUNDY, P.	9413	,,	CULLIS, W.
9384	,,	LEACH, J.	9478	,,	REED, G. W.
9456	,,	ELLERSHAW, E. J.	9397	,,	JACKSON, S.
9461	,,	DAWSON, W.	9374	,,	JONES, E.
9468	,,	ORMROD, J.	9420	,,	YOUNG, F.
9415	,,	ARCHER, A.	9430	,,	BURGESS, F. G.
9411	,,	CLAYTON, J. A.	9474	,,	HEWITT, A. B.
9491	,,	GAMBLE, D.	9387	,,	HOPKINSON, F.
9408	,,	GILBANKS, A.	9488	,,	WELTON, W.
9432	,,	HILTON, C. H.	9435	,,	GRIMSHAW, J.
9453	,,	JAMIESON, J.	9429	,,	PRIOR, F. M.
9414	,,	KEARSLEY, F.	9379	,,	STODDART, A.
9450	,,	LEA, D.	9476	,,	PRICE, G.
9417	,,	SCOTT, W.	9505	,,	SMITH, F. C.
9381	,,	NEWTON, W.	9486	,,	OWEN, T. W.
9449	,,	WOOLEY, W.			

* For portrait, see Officers' Group, p. 53. † For portrait, see Sergeants' Group, p. 55.

The following were not present when the Platoon Photograph was taken, but see Supplementary Photographs on pp. 98, 99.

Roll No.	Rank	Name	Roll No.	Rank	Name
9236	Private	DOYLE, M.	9466	Private	GRIFFITHS, W. P.
9495	,,	GRIMSHAW, J.	9419	,,	CANDLETT, J.
9507	,,	BURNS, J.	9493	,,	TAYLOR, P.
9378	,,	SQUIRES, J. H.	9508	,,	WHITTER, C. E.
9362	,,	STONES, A.	9440	,,	LEE, J.
9509	,,	MORREY, J.	9487	,,	PRITCHARD, J. E.

17th BATTALION.—Supplementary Photo of men of A and B Companies who were not present when the Platoon Photographs were taken. For names, see Platoon lists.

17th BATTALION.—Supplementary Photo of men of C and D Companies who were not present when the Platoon Photographs were taken. For names, see Platoon lists.

18th (Service) Battalion

18th (Service) Battalion Manchester Regiment.

Roll of Officers.

Lieut.-Col.	Fraser, W. A.	Lieut.	Knowles, W. P.
Major	Barkworth, H. A. S.	,,	Renshaw, L.
Capt. & Adjt.	Hoare, G. E.	,,	Blythe, P. A.
Capt.	Lupton, G.	,,	Watson, H. G.
,,	Fraser, G. J. R.	,,	Bower, H. G. S.
,,	Heathcote, G.	,,	Crawshaw, H. H.
,,	Payne, W.	,,	Kelly, T. J.
,,	Berry, D.	2nd Lieut.	England, R. S.
,,	Godlee, P.	,,	Beaumont, J. S.
,,	Wylde, C. H.	,,	Harrison, H. B.
,,	Lynde, G. S.	,,	Haworth, P. G.
,,	Penn-Gaskell, W.	,,	Nelson, J. L.
Chaplain	Balleine, Rev. R. W.	,,	Harris, A. A. F.
Lieut.	Henshall, C.	,,	Powell, H. A.
,,	Woollam, S. E.	,,	Wallwork, W.
,,	Cunliffe, J. G.	,,	Tavaré, B. T. N.
,,	Hobkirk, R.	Lt. & Q.M.	Pierce, T. C.

Lieut. T. J. J. Curran, R.A.M.C., Medical Officer.

The following were not present when the Photograph was taken, but see pp. 110, 142.

Major	Hodgson, T. G.	2nd Lieut.	Townsend, A. E.
Lieut.	Powell, F. J.	,,	Statham, A. J.
2nd Lieut.	Blenkiron, D.	,,	Brunton, M.

18th (Service) Battalion Manchester Regiment.

Non-Commissioned Officers' (Sergeants) Roll.

Warrant Officer.
10868 R.S.M. REYNOLDS, W.

10309 R.Q.M.S. STONES, C. G.
10364 R.O.R.S. CHILTON, E. S.

Roll No.	Rank and Name.		Roll No.	Rank and Name.	
10063	C.S.M.	MURNAGHAN, G. A. G.	10173	Sergeant	LEACH, R.
10308	,,	McCARTNEY, J	10569	,,	SMITH, G. H.
10061	,,	EVANS, W. L.	10398	,,	HOLT, G. W.
10869	,,	WAITE, G.	10565	,,	PEARSON, J. T.
10947	,,	EVANS, G.	11079	,,	DIXON, A.
10579	C.Q.M.S.	WADDICOR, W. N.	9890	,,	MAUDE, J. W.
10310	,,	JONES, W.	10081	,,	BLEASE, J.
10600	,,	BEATTIE, V.	10356	,,	BUCKLEY, H.
10866	,,	RALSTON, J.	10602	,,	AIRLEY, A. W.
10871	,,	HOUGH, W.	11078	,,	BENNETT, W. E.
10307	Sgt. Cook	BUZZA, J.	9944	,,	WATSON, A.
9877	Pion. Sgt.	JOHNSON, C. E.	10142	,,	HEATON, H. J.
9959	M.G.Sgt.	WILFORD, R. B.	10561	,,	NICHOLSON, J. M.
10835	,,	POTTS, F. W.	10818	,,	HILL, E. C.
11065	Trns. Sgt.	WILSON, L.	9901	,,	McMILLAN, B. T.
10122	Sig. Sgt.	GILL, C. W.	10181	,,	MIDGLEY, J. T.
10067	Sergeant	OGDEN, P.	10343	,,	BELL, S.
10896	,,	ASTLES, A.	10236	,,	BOWERS, A. H.
10263	,,	ROBINSON, H. H.	9937	,,	TIDSWELL, J.
10064	,,	FRIDAY, A. L.	9992	,,	REDFERN, A.
10267	,,	TODD, H. C.	10328	,,	SPINK, W.
10599	,,	SMITH, R. U.	9967	L.-Sergt.	BARROW, J.
10582	,,	STREDDAR, P. E.	10257	,,	NEILL, G. C.
10867	,,	CONNOR, J.	10704	,,	RIDGARD, H. G.
10872	,,	LEMAN, H.	10103	,,	DUNN, A.
10880	,,	MOSS, S. F.	10399	,,	DAVIES, W. B.
10416	,,	JONES, T.	10657	,,	HILL, J. A.
10106	,,	DOOTSON, R.	10427	,,	STALLARD, K.
10168	,,	LINDUP, J. E.		Staff-Sgt.	BEADON, J.
9957	,,	WILSON, F.			

Also on the Photograph: Lt.-Col. W. A. FRASER, Major H. A. S. BARKWORTH, Capt. and Adjt. G. E. HOARE, and Lt. and Qr.-Master T. C. PIERCE.

The following were not present when the Photograph was taken, but see Supplementary Photographs on pp. 148—153.

10894	Sergeant	PERKINS, P.	10608	Sergeant	BERRY, E. J.
10732	,,	VINE, T. C.	10331	L.-Sergt.	HEMSLEY, S. J.
11099	,,	MARSDEN, J.	10611	,,	BLACKBURN, E.
9801	,,	PARKES, B.			

E2

18th (Service) Battalion Manchester Regiment.

Bugle Band.

Roll No.	Rank and Name.		Roll No.	Rank and Name.	
10067	Sergeant	Ogden, P.	10111	Drummer	Etheridge, H. O.
10244	Corporal	Eastwood, H.	10810	,,	Empson, H.
10668	L.-Corpl.	Jackson, E.	10023	,,	Hollinworth, W.
10138	,,	Heslop, J.	9863	,,	Hayes, J. H.
10794	,,	Tatlock, T.	10824	,,	Johnson, H.
9964	Drummer	Atherley, G.	10153	,,	Knight, T.
10068	,,	Archer, J. E.	10549	,,	Kett, L.
10094	,,	Beresford, W.	10190	,,	Norris, A. G.
10084	,,	Bradley, A.	10694	,,	Penny, A.
10339	,,	Ball, W.	9923	,,	Reeves, F. W.
10801	,,	Briggs, F.	9920	,,	Radford, N.
10624	,,	Bramwell, T.	10218	,,	Street, H.
10079	,,	Billington, W.	10231	,,	Wilson, R. K.
10098	,,	Colbridge, G.	10897	,,	Wild, C. A.
10764	,,	Dauncey, F. G.			

Also on the Photograph : Major H. A. S. Barkworth.

The following were not present when the Photograph was taken, but see Supplementary Photographs on pp. 148—153.

10367	Drummer	Carter, G.	10136	Drummer	Hickes, W. H.
10651	,,	Evans, J.	10496	,,	Johnson, G. F.
10826	,,	Kennedy, P. J.	10420	,,	Lucey, F. G.

18th (Service) Battalion Manchester Regiment.

"A" COMPANY.

Officer Commanding Company	Captain C. H. Wylde.
Second in Command	Capt. D. Berry.*
Company Sergeant Major	Murnaghan, G. A. G.†
Company Quartermaster Sergeant	Waddicor, W. N.†

PLATOON NO. I.

Platoon Commander	Lieut. L. Renshaw.
Platoon Sergeant	Friday, A. L.

Roll No.	Rank and Name.		Roll No.	Rank and Name.	
10016	L.-Corpl.	Egan, F.	9906	Private	Nichol, G. T.
9936	,,	Stewart, J. A.	9943	,,	Whitworth, J. E.
10045	,,	Shirley, S. M.	10052	,,	Wood, J.
9872	,,	Hulton, O.	9970	,,	Clegg, H.
10517	,,	Webster, J.	9975	,,	Giblin, J.
9816	Private	Brooks, H.	9993	,,	Rowlinson, H.
10015	,,	Dawson, J.	9960	,,	Whitehead, R.
10032	,,	Lever, A.	10928	,,	Davies, R. G.
9955	,,	Wilkinson, P.	10930	,,	Parry, J.
10011	,,	Chambers, R.	10989	,,	Jones, E.
9828	,,	Charles, E. R.	9883	,,	Lunn, Len.
9839	,,	Dean, A. B.	9894	,,	Morrison, J.
10014	,,	Dixon, W. G.	10040	,,	Rowarth, L.
9845	,,	Edmundson, B. G.	11023	,,	Hanvey, D.
10017	,,	Elliott, G. V.			

* For portrait, see Officers' Group, p. 103.   † For portrait, see Sergeants' Group, p. 105.

The following were not present when the Platoon Photograph was taken, but see Supplementary Photographs on pp. 148—153.

Roll No.	Rank	Name	Roll No.	Rank	Name
11099	Sergeant	Marsden, J.	9897	Private	Mitchell, J.
9967	L.-Sergt.	Barrow, J.	10955	,,	Eastwood, W. P.
9802	Corporal	Lobb, W. H.	9912	,,	Payne, R. H.
9987	,,	Macpherson, J.	11029	,,	Haggis, H. W.
9893	L.-Corpl.	Mowbray, H.	9844	,,	Denton, B.
9991	,,	Roberts, T. O.	9836	,,	Davies, Albert.
9933	,,	Stewardson, R.	10021	,,	Greenhalgh, J. R.
10023	Private	Hollinworth, W.	9977	,,	Hearne, F. J.
9863	,,	Hayes, J. H.	11033	,,	Midgley, W. H.
9923	,,	Reeves, Fred.	9984	,,	Kirkley, E.
10012	,,	Connolley, A.	9908	,,	O'Neil, J. L.
10013	,,	Davies, J. W.	10058	,,	O'Brien, T.
9850	,,	Green, W.	10981	,,	Holgate, G.
10022	,,	Greenhalgh, W. A.	10950	,,	Southern, S.
9880	,,	Kettle, W.	10961	,,	Kennedy, W.
10037	,,	Mallinson, T.	10997	,,	Davies, R.
9986	,,	Morris, J. A.	11015	,,	Mosoph, W.
10039	,,	Poppleton, E.	10975	,,	Aikenhead, J.
10991	,,	Blain, R.			

18th (Service) Battalion Manchester Regiment.

"A" COMPANY.

Officer Commanding Company - Capt. C. H. WYLDE.*
Second in Command - - - Capt. D. BERRY.*
Company Sergeant Major - - MURNAGHAN, G. A. G.†
Company Quartermaster Sergeant - WADDICOR, W. N.

PLATOON NO. II.

Platoon Commander - - - 2nd Lieut. D. BLENKIRON.*
Platoon Sergeant - - - - WILFORD, R. B.

Roll No.	Rank and Name.		Roll No.	Rank and Name.	
9890	Sergeant	MAUDE, J. W.	10049	Private	WARD, A. E.
9907	Corporal	NEWTON, N. H.	9942	,,	WHITE, G. E.
9982	,,	JOYNT, E.	9958	,,	WHITNALL, A. V.
10030	,,	JOWETT, J.	10050	,,	WHITTAKER, F. G.
9971	L.-Corpl.	CHAPMAN, H.	10004	,,	ALLISON, F.
10029	,,	HUTCHINSON, R. H.	10009	,,	BUTTERWORTH, J.
9932	,,	SHEPLEY, G. B.	9966	,,	BOOTHAM, S.
9951	,,	WOOD, E. F.	9854	,,	GOODRICKE, A.
9949	,,	WOODWARD, R.	9980	,,	HARRISON, A.
9823	Private	BANNISTER, H. P.	10028	,,	HALLIWELL, J.
9851	,,	GRATRIX, F.	10033	,,	LOCKETT, S.
10020	,,	GUTHRIE, D.	10041	,,	SEATON, J.
9869	,,	HOLLAND, W. T.	9837	,,	DAVIES, ARTHUR.
9927	,,	SMITH, W.	9861	,,	HARWOOD, J. W.
9934	,,	SUMNER, J.	10038	,,	NORMINGTON, E.
9956	,,	WRIGHT, W.	10060	,,	NASH, W.
9824	,,	BRANT, R.	9884	,,	LIVESEY, R. C.
9979	,,	HUTTON, R. W.	10003	,,	WALKER, W.
9921	,,	RAVENSCROFT, H. V.	9945	,,	WATSON, H. A.
9892	,,	MASSEY, S.	9994	,,	ROYLE, E.
10005	,,	BATES, F.	9989	,,	PERCIVAL, F.
9911	,,	PLANT, F.	9832	,,	CARR, R.
9997	,,	SANT, H.			

Also on the Photograph : 2nd Lieut. H. B. HARRISON.

* For portrait, see Officers' Group, p. 103.   † For portrait, see Sergeants' Group, p. 105.

The following were not present when the Platoon Photograph was taken, but see Supplementary Photographs on pp. 148—153.

9849	L. Corpl.	GREENALL, E.	10010	Private	BUTLER, A.
10036	,,	MCCANN, W.	10956	,,	THORNTON, F.
10047	Private	TONGE, F.	9995	,,	STOTT, A.
9935	,,	STOTT, G. E.	10962	,,	WILSON, O.
9950	,,	WOOD, H.	9968	,,	CAROLAN, G.
10948	,,	LOWE, G.	10944	,,	DAVIES, F.
10968	,,	CASHION, J.	9822	,,	BARDSLEY, F.
9819	,,	BATES, W.	10945	,,	TIMES, W.
10027	,,	HOLT, J.	10957	,,	GOODYEAR, G. W.
10915	,,	MAGUIRE, C.	9807	,,	BERESFORD, W.

18th (Service) Battalion Manchester Regiment.

"A" COMPANY.

Officer Commanding Company - Capt. C. H. WYLDE.*
Second in Command - - - Capt. D. BERRY.*
Company Sergeant Major - - MURNAGHAN, G. A. G.†
Company Quartermaster Sergeant - WADDICOR, W. N.†

PLATOON NO. III.

Platoon Commander - - Lieut. H. G. S. BOWER.
Platoon Sergeant - - - WILSON, F.†

Roll No.	Rank and Name.		Roll No.	Rank and Name.	
10236	Sergeant	BOWERS, H.	9940	Private	WHITEHEAD, W.
10007	Corporal	BRANSTON, H.	10024	,,	HANCOCK, H.
10000	L.-Corpl.	WIGGANS, R.	9878	,,	JACKSON, H.
9963	Private	ANDERSON, L. S.	9919	,,	RUSHTON, A.
9809	,,	BROWN, A. E.	9918	,,	ROBERTSON, T.
10019	,,	FORRESTER, A.	10046	,,	TAYLOR, F. M.
9846	,,	FOGARTY, J.	9939	,,	TILSTON, E.
10025	,,	HULTON, D.	9812	,,	BAILEY, E.
9870	,,	HOLLINS, H.	9811	,,	BILLINGTON, H.
9840	,,	DOMNEY, W.	9965	,,	BURROWS, J.
9864	,,	HEPWOOD, W. F.	9972	,,	CHAPMAN, S.
9978	,,	HORNER, H.	9976	,,	GOWENLOCK, G.
9865	,,	HENDERSON, G.	9848	,,	GYVES, A. L.
9867	,,	HILL, J. W.	9868	,,	HODGKINSON, F.
9988	,,	OPIE, W.	9873	,,	HUNT, A.
9926	,,	SIMPKINS, R.	9947	,,	WHITWAM, B.
9929	,,	SMITH, A.	10001	,,	WILLIAMS, R. H.
10056	,,	WILLIAMS, H. W.	11032	,,	BARTON, F.
10048	,,	WORSLEY, W.			

* For portrait, see Officers' Group, p. 103. † For portrait, see Sergeants' Group, p. 105.

The following were not present when the Platoon Photograph was taken, but see Supplementary Photographs on pp. 148—153.

Roll No.	Rank and Name.		Roll No.	Rank and Name.	
9957	Sergeant	WILSON, F.	9985	Private	LINFORD, G.
9877	,,	JOHNSON, C. E.	10044	,,	SWINDELLS, P. R.
10042	Corporal	SAMPSON, S.	9952	,,	WOODWARD, C. G.
9842	,,	DEVEY, H. S.	9860	,,	HAMPTON, H.
9998	L.-Corpl.	THOMAS, W.	10026	,,	HARGREAVES, A.
9990	,,	PEARSON, G.	9875	,,	JOHNSON, H.
9983	,,	JOHNSON, J. H.	9885	,,	LENGDEN, J.
10034	,,	LEVER, J.	9889	,,	MADELEY, L.
9862	Private	HART, O.	9920	,,	RADFORD, N.
9909	,,	OGDEN, W.	10926	,,	PERKINS, C. H.
9913	,,	PARKER, P.	10903	,,	LEVER, G.
9925	,,	SCOTT, J.	10993	,,	HETHERINGTON, H.
9954	,,	WOOLRICH, S.	11018	,,	MARSHALL, A.
9948	,,	WEBB, A.	9803	,,	AMOS, J.
9904	,,	MELLOR, T. A.	9871	,,	HENSHALL, J.
			11017	,,	CAMMELL, T. E.

18th (Service) Battalion Manchester Regiment.

"A" COMPANY.

Officer Commanding Company	Capt. C. H. WYLDE.
Second in Command	Capt. D. BERRY.*
Company Sergeant Major	MURNAGHAN, G. A. G.
Company Quartermaster Sergeant	WADDICOR, W. N.

PLATOON NO. IV.

Platoon Commander	2nd Lieut. H. B. HARRISON.
Platoon Sergeant	WATSON, A.†

Roll No.	Rank and Name.	Roll No.	Rank and Name
9801	Sergeant PARKES, B.	11042	Private DAVIES, H.
10103	L.-Sergt. DUNN, A. C.	9805	,, ARMSTRONG, H.
10875	Corporal WALMESLEY, J.	9815	,, BAILEY, F.
9969	L.-Corpl. CHADWICK,	9857	,, HARRISON, F.
9973	,, DYSON, J.	9866	,, HEWITT, W.
9847	,, FOSTER, F. M.	9882	,, KERSHAW, J.
9830	Private CROFT, T.	9900	,, McCORMICK, H.
9841	,, DEAN, H.	9917	,, REEVES, F. W.
9805	,, ATKINSON, A. E.	9899	,, MARTIN, P. J.
9818	,, BERESFORD, C.	9928	,, SPACKMAN, A.
9831	,, COOPER, J.	10987	,, PRICE, J.
9827	,, COWX, W.	10970	,, TAYLOR, F.
9852	,, GARLICK, C.	9825	,, BROWN, F.
9876	,, JONES, C. T.	9826	,, BROWN, H.
9903	,, MILLWARD, A. P. N.	9888	,, McKAY, H. L.
9914	,, PAGE, W. C.	9898	,, MELLON, J.
9910	,, PERKINS, C. A.	9924	,, ROBINSON, F.
9915	,, PORTER, G. S.	9916	,, RUSHTON, R.
9931	,, SNELSON, T.	9953	,, WILKINSON, D.
10043	,, SWAIN, C. H. B.	10054	,, WILKS, E.
9946	,, WEBB, W. F.		

* For portrait, see Officers' Group, p. 103.　　† For portrait, see Sergeants' Group, p. 105.

The following were not present when the Platoon Photograph was taken, but see Supplementary Photographs on pp. 148—153.

9944	Sergeant WATSON, A.	9817	Private BRADBURY, J.
	Staff-Sgt. BEADON.	9808	,, BOULTON, G. R.
9838	L.-Corpl. DEAKIN, V. J.	9843	,, DONNON, J.
9895	,, MOORES, H.	9858	,, HANSON, W.
9964	,, ATHERLEY, G.	9981	,, HICKS, H.
9855	Private GIBSON, G. R.	9833	,, COGGER, J. J.
9881	,, KELLY, W.	9806	,, ANDERSON, T.
9821	,, BAILEY, J.	9813	,, BOTTOMLEY, J.
9891	,, MILLAR, A.	9905	,, MISKELLY, S.
11047	,, WILLCOCK, R. B.	9930	,, SMITH, J.
9814	,, BARDSLEY, H. T.	9938	,, TREANOR, A.
9896	,, MOLDEN, C.		

18th (Service) Battalion Manchester Regiment,

"B" COMPANY.

Officer Commanding Company - Capt. G. Lupton.
Second in Command - - - Capt. G. S. Lynde.*
Company Sergeant Major - - McCartney, J.
Company Quartermaster Sergeant - Jones, Wm.

PLATOON NO. V.

Platoon Commander - - - Lieut. W. P. Knowles.
Platoon Sergeant - - - - Dootson, R.

Roll No.	Rank and Name.		Roll No.	Rank and Name.	
10142	Sergeant	Heaton, H. J.	10167	Private	Lister, G. R.
10255	L.-Corpl.	Moody, T.	10317	,,	Whittaker, H.
10191	,,	Owens, F.	10292	,,	Wright, H. L.
10169	,,	Leslie, W.	10147	,,	Hay, F.
10208	Private	Seddon, A. J.	10197	,,	Pierce, B.
10280	,,	Hooley, J. W.	10227	,,	Warham, J.
10225	,,	Winsby, W. R.	10898	,,	Tomlinson, S.
10114	,,	Fallows, H. E.	10282	,,	Higginson, S.
10899	,,	King, F. C.	10296	,,	Allport, G.
10291	,,	Salthouse, J.	10158	,,	King, J. E.
10186	,,	McKeiver, J.	10287	,,	Orpwood, S.
10289	,,	Rafferty, P.	10293	,,	Wyatt, F. G.
10212	,,	Shandley, J.	10226	,,	Wood, F.
10093	,,	Cosgrove, D.	10197	,,	McNulty, W.
10273	,,	Logan, D.	10199	,,	Pearson, J.
10140	,,	Heath, G.	10281	,,	Hurst, J.
10256	,,	McCreery, W.	10145	,,	Haskell, S.
10165	,,	Llewellyn, J.	10895	,,	Thorpe, Rd.
10215	,,	Schofield, H.	11120	,,	McNulty, J.

* For portrait, see Officers' Group, p. 103.

The following were not present when the Platoon Photograph was taken, but see Supplementary Photographs on pp. 148—153.

Roll No.	Rank and Name.		Roll No.	Rank and Name.	
10251	Corporal	Hetherington.	10274	Private	Cartwright, A.
10177	L.-Corpl.	Millington, W. H.	10152	,,	Johnson, C. C.
10302	,,	Perkins, G. E.	10285	,,	Kay, L. L.
10537	,,	Fitzpatrick, J.	10087	,,	Barry, T. H.
10207	Private	Ryan, G.	10151	,,	Joyce, P.
10184	,,	Maxwell, R.	10206	,,	Richardson, H.
10211	,,	Shepherd, J.	10220	,,	Turner, C.
10120	,,	Fahy, M.	10192	,,	Orman, G.
10089	,,	Beckett, J. H.	10934	,,	Cooper, M.
10161	,,	Lomax, A.	10275	,,	Clarkson, W.
10132	,,	Hilton, S.	10154	,,	Kerrighan, J.
10271	,,	Allison, J.			

18th (Service) Battalion Manchester Regiment.

"B" COMPANY.

Officer Commanding Company - Capt. G. LUPTON.*
Second in Command - - - Capt. G. S. LYNDE.*
Company Sergeant Major - - MCCARTNEY, J.†
Company Quartermaster Sergeant - JONES, WM.†

PLATOON NO. VI.

Platoon Commander - - - 2nd Lieut. J. L. NELSON.
Platoon Sergeant - - - TODD, H.

Roll No.	Rank and Name.		Roll No.	Rank and Name.	
10307	Sgt.-Cook	BUZZA, J.	10182	Private	MIDDLETON, E.
10122	Sergeant	GILL, C. W.	10279	,,	GREEN, T.
10611	L.-Sergt.	BLACKBURN, E.	10196	,,	PERCIVAL, H.
10102	L.-Corpl.	CURRY, J.	10265	,,	SMITH, L.
10135	,,	HAYES, J. R.	10203	,,	ROSE, H. W.
10686	,,	MELLOR, S. G.	10918	,,	WEBSTER, J. W.
10230	,,	WADDICOR, G.	10118	,,	FIELDEN, T.
10113	Private	FARRINGTON, J.	10123	,,	GREEN, J. T.
10150	,,	INGHAM, A.	10134	,,	HOPKINS, O. H.
10254	,,	JONES, J. H.	10217	,,	SUTTON, J.
10198	,,	PURCELL, D.	10214	,,	SAUNDERS, A.
10115	,,	FRANKISH, J.	10290	,,	SNELSON, F.
10129	,,	HUNTER, W.	10223	,,	TOOLE, E.
10164	,,	LOUGHLER, H.			

* For portrait, see Officers' Group, p. 103. † For portrait, see Sergeants' Group, p. 105.

The following were not present when the Platoon Photograph was taken, but see Supplementary Photographs on pp. 148—153.

Roll No.	Rank	Name	Roll No.	Rank	Name
10204	L.-Corpl.	RAINSBURY, E.	10116	Private	FLEMMING, W.
10216	,,	STREET, J. A.	10288	,,	PARRY, R. E.
10070	Private	ALDRED, S.	10073	,,	ATKIN, H.
10109	,,	DUTTON, E.	10929	,,	MOODY, J.
10252	,,	HENSHAW, J.	10205	,,	ROGERSON, R. H.
10213	,,	SUTHERLAND, G.	10086	,,	BARLOW, J.
10222	,,	TILBURY, S.	10314	,,	WOOD, W. H.
10088	,,	BANKS, N.	10077	,,	BULLIMENT, A.
10938	,,	HIGGINS, C.	10262	,,	ROBERTS, G.
10294	,,	WOOD, FRED.	10094	,,	CARTER, F.
10105	,,	DAVIES, A.	10149	,,	HARDY, T.
10170	,,	LEWIS, T.	10072	,,	ASPIN, H.
10250	,,	HAYNES, E.	10082	,,	BIRCHALL, J.
10221	,,	TRUEMAN, H.	10125	,,	GRINROD, S.
10176	,,	MOORHOUSE, J.	10920	,,	CORKER, F.
10100	,,	COX, D.	11016	,,	MANUEL, C.
10131	,,	HIGGS, G. H.	10974	,,	SCOTT, A. O.

18th (Service) Battalion Manchester Regiment.

"B" COMPANY.

Officer Commanding Company - Capt. G. Lupton.
Second in Command - - - Capt. G. S. Lynde.*
Company Sergeant Major - McCartney, J.†
Company Quartermaster Sergeant - Jones, Wm.†

PLATOON NO. VII.

Platoon Commander - - - 2nd Lieut. J. S. Beaumont.
Platoon Sergeant - - - - Lindup, J.

Roll No.	Rank and Name.		Roll No.	Rank and Name.	
10263	Sergeant	Robinson, R. H.	10210	Private	Smith, S.
10704	L.-Sergt.	Ridgard, H. G.	10277	,,	Flanagan, T.
10194	Corporal	Parry, N. N.	10248	,,	Gibbon, G.
10074	L.-Corpl.	Ashcroft, J. H.	10137	,,	Heywood, A.
10108	,,	Daley, P.	10284	,,	Kettle, A.
10117	,,	Fletcher, A.	10310	,,	Roberts, A.
10305	,,	Lees, J. C.	10303	,,	Walton, W.
10104	Private	Downes, T.	10304	,,	Wilde, H.
10128	,,	Goddard, J.	10233	,,	Wightmore, J.
10143	,,	Holmes, J.	10095	,,	Catton, J. H.
10269	,,	Wrigley, E. H.	10124	,,	Green, T.
10101	,,	Cosgrove, T. J.	10127	,,	Graham, T.
10200	,,	Penkett, B.	10141	,,	Hart, W.
10224	,,	Vicker, E.	10195	,,	Parry, S. H.
10229	,,	Wrigley, H.	10315	,,	Webster, J. P.
10266	,,	Schofield, H.	10241	,,	Dobson, H.
10235	,,	Butterworth, A.			

* For portrait, see Officers' Group, p. 103.   † For portrait, see Sergeants' Group, p. 105.

The following were not present when the Platoon Photograph was taken, but see Supplementary Photographs on pp. 148—153.

Roll No.	Rank and Name.		Roll No.	Rank and Name.	
10173	Sergeant	Leach, R.	10174	Private	Lancaster, R.
10157	L.-Corpl.	Kelly, C.	10096	,,	Cookson, H.
10185	,,	Makin, E.	10139	,,	Hembry, J.
10121	Private	Gurling, W.	10188	,,	McCaslin, J. E.
10163	,,	Lovatt, E.	10228	,,	Wignall, H.
10175	,,	Mullin, J.	10268	,,	Wilson, F. C.
10219	,,	Snelson, S.	10953	,,	Farrand, C.
10232	,,	Wickman, W.	11013	,,	Hilton, J.
10193	,,	Oswald, C.	11010	,,	Turner, P.
10148	,,	Hooley, C.	10278	,,	Gilgryst, W.
10985	,,	Grange, H.	10133	,,	Hyde, F.
10977	,,	Robinson, T.	10261	,,	Quinn, N. W.
10071	,,	Andrews, J.	10975	,,	Kay, R.
10319	,,	Barklam, G.	10156	,,	Keogh, E.
10322	,,	Bowyer, J.			

18th (Service) Battalion Manchester Regiment.

"B" COMPANY.

Officer Commanding Company - Capt. G. Lupton.
Second in Command - - - Capt. G. S. Lynde.*
Company Sergeant Major - - McCartney, J.
Company Quartermaster Sergeant - Jones, Wm.

PLATOON NO. VIII.

Platoon Commander - - - 2nd Lieut. T. J. Kelly.
Platoon Sergeant - - - Dixon, A.

Roll No.	Rank and Name.		Roll No.	Rank and Name.	
10081	Sergeant	Blease, J. D.	10264	Private	Scholes, H.
10894	,,	Perkins, P.	10326	,,	Scholes, W.
10239	Corporal	Clegg, S.	10300	,,	White, F. H.
10298	,,	Fairhurst, F.	10183	,,	Mayho, T.
10144	,,	Holden, A.	10091	,,	Campbell, C.
10283	L.-Corpl.	Jones, E.	10330	,,	Spencer, H.
10166	,,	Leyland, C.	10202	,,	Royds, E.
10160	,,	Lockwood, R.	10201	,,	Peach, A. E.
10110	Private	Doyle, J.	10069	,,	Allen, P. R.
10246	,,	Farnsworth, B.	10092	,,	Chorlton, J.
10146	,,	Harrop, J.	10097	,,	Chorlton, C.
10180	,,	McMillan, D.	10130	,,	Higgins, L.
10260	,,	Priestner, W.	10240	,,	Cooper, E.
10323	,,	Burton, C.	10080	,,	Berry, J. R.
10238	,,	Craven, W.	10090	,,	Clay, H.
10242	,,	Dixon, J.	10112	,,	Evans, F.
10119	,,	Fergie, A. B.	10245	,,	Flaherty, W.
10258	,,	Oldroyd, R.	10172	,,	Larkin, F.
10276	,,	Farrelly, J.	10241	,,	Dobson, H.
10327	,,	Sparling, W.			

* For portrait, see Officers' Group, p. 103.

The following were not present when the Platoon Photograph was taken, but see Supplementary Photographs on pp. 148—153.

Roll No.	Rank and Name.		Roll No.	Rank and Name.	
10171	Corporal	Lamb, T.	10253	Private	Ingham, S.
10189	L.-Corpl.	Nuttall, F	10249	,,	Grundy, W.
10297	Private	Critchlow, J.	10234	,,	White, J. W.
10162	,,	Lunt, J.	10247	,,	Grundy, S.
10218	,,	Street, H.	10178	,,	Maher, T.
10942	,,	McGrath, J. W.	10187	,,	McCawley, A.
10933	,,	Sherratt, F.	10318	,,	Ashworth, J.
10917	,,	Ryde, F. E.	10984	,,	Tidswell, J.
11014	,,	Savage, R. W.	10964	,,	Burns, J.
10982	,,	Allen, W.	11064	,,	Costello, J.
11027	,,	Grange, A.	10990	,,	Cowen, J.
10881	,,	Brookes, A. F.	11021	,,	Turner, J. H.
10243	,,	Entwistle, J.	10978	,,	Bennett, W.
10325	,,	Smethurst, J.	10085	,,	Butterworth, T.

18th (Service) Battalion Manchester Regiment.

"C" COMPANY.

Officer Commanding Company - Capt. G. Heathcote.*
Second in Command - - - Capt. W. Penn-Gaskell.*
Company Sergeant Major - - Evans, W. L.
Company Quartermaster Sergeant - Beattie, V.†

PLATOON NO. IX.

Platoon Commander - - - Lieut. S. E. Woollam.
Platoon Sergeant - - - - Smith, G. H.

Roll No.	Rank and Name.		Roll No.	Rank and Name.	
10896	Sergeant	Astles, A.	10900	Private	Garside, A.
10331	L.-Sergt.	Hemsley.	10392	,,	Gibb, H.
10494	Corporal	Hodges, J. W.	10544	,,	Hall, F.
10553	,,	Latham, H.	10541	,,	Horton, T. C.
10520	,,	Wimbury, F.	10509	,,	Howard, H.
10537	L.-Corpl.	Fitzpatrick, J.	10408	,,	Hamer, T.
10575	,,	Whitworth, E. W.	10424	,,	Line, W.
10415	,,	Johnson, P.	10552	,,	Loynd, A.
10493	,,	Harper, C.	10559	,,	Moss, E. L.
10376	,,	Deakin, R.	10556	,,	Morris, W. H.
10333	Private	Ash, R.	10555	,,	McNamara, E.
10589	,,	Allen, R. H.	10557	,,	McLow, H. H.
10352	,,	Bratt, J. A.	10434	,,	Northend, W.
10353	,,	Broady, W.	10436	,,	Orton, E.
10355	,,	Bancroft, A.	10562	,,	Oldham, J.
10339	,,	Ball, W. R.	10438	,,	Prince, E.
10372	,,	Calvert, T. A.	10566	,,	Robinson, F.
10373	,,	Cooper, A. A.	10445	,,	Rushworth, H.
10530	,,	Cheetham, P.	10511	,,	Richards, W.
10371	,,	Coucill, J.	10456	,,	Sheppard, L.
10532	,,	Cragg, S.	10455	,,	Sheridan, P.
10360	,,	Chapman, J.	10460	,,	Tilley, A. L.
10533	,,	Davies, A.	10513	,,	Webb, A.
10484	,,	Delaney, G.	10475	,,	Wharton, F. L.
10385	,,	Elton, H.	10521	,,	Wilding, J. W.
10901	,,	Garside, J. A.			

* For portrait, see Officers' Group, p. 103.   † For portrait, see Sergeants' Group, p. 105.

The following were not present when the Platoon Photograph was taken, but see Supplementary Photographs on pp. 148—153.

Roll No.	Rank and Name.		Roll No.	Rank and Name.	
10364	C.Q.M.S.	Chilton, E. S.	10543	Private	Hughes, J. H.
10554	L.-Corpl.	Leech, H.	11031	,,	Howcroft, C.
10480	Private	Burgon, T.	10498	,,	Kirkland, S.
10338	,,	Bell, C. A.	10997	,,	Kirkham, J.
11020	,,	Darbyshire, W.	10996	,,	Podmore, J. T.
10995	,,	Davies, J. J.	10440	,,	Pickering, J.
11003	,,	Done, G.	10567	,,	Riley, W. H.
10387	,,	Earnshaw, J.	10459	,,	Seville, W.
10489	,,	Gamble, W. H.	10518	,,	Withers, A.

18th (Service) Battalion Manchester Regiment.

"C" COMPANY.

Officer Commanding Company - Capt. G. Heathcote.*
Second in Command - - - Capt. W. Penn-Gaskell.*
Company Sergeant Major - - Evans, W. L.†
Company Quartermaster Sergeant - Beattie, V.†

PLATOON NO. X.

Platoon Commander - - - Lieut. P. A. Blythe.
Platoon Sergeant - - - - Streddar, P. E.

Roll No.	Rank and Name.		Roll No.	Rank and Name.	
11078	Sergeant	Bennett, W. E.	10492	Private	Howarth, A.
10391	Corporal	Fisher, D. K.	10410	,,	Irlam, W.
10902	,,	Ingham, J. H.	10414	,,	Jones, A.
10272	L.-Corpl.	Brooke, A. J. B.	10550	,,	Livsey, F. L.
11060	,,	Bennett, H. G.	10421	,,	Lloyd, A.
10524	,,	Broughton, R. B.	10556	,,	Levings, S. A.
10351	,,	Bond, W.	10422	,,	Lamb, G.
10679	,,	Morris, F.	10425	,,	Moores, B.
10446	,,	Ringham, H. T.	10428	,,	Middleton, A. H.
10335	Private	Adams, F.	10505	,,	Mason, J. G.
10528	,,	Booth, A.	10441	,,	Plunkett, G. H.
10350	,,	Bayley, E.	10444	,,	Redford G.
10349	,,	Brereton, C. W.	10442	,,	Ryder, G.
10529	,,	Burnett, J. H.	10458	,,	Spenceley, W. H.
10348	,,	Broome, E.	10570	,,	Street, F.
10369	,,	Creswell, F. G.	10512	,,	Tierney, G.
10368	,,	Cragg, H.	10461	,,	Tomlinson, J.
10374	,,	Cope, C. W.	10583	,,	Thompson, W.
10592	,,	Dickson, R.	10578	,,	Woods, A. R.
10375	,,	Dodson, G. W.	10515	,,	Walton, E.
10380	,,	Doleman, S.	10476	,,	Wilson, F.
10378	,,	Dickenson, F.	10580	,,	Wardle, H.
11001	,,	Donaldson, J.	10479	,,	Young, A.
10546	,,	Hall, C.	10522	,,	Young, H.
10403	,,	Holliday, F.			

* For portrait, see Officers' Group, p. 103. † For portrait, see Sergeants' Group, p. 105.

The following were not present when the Platoon Photograph was taken, but see Supplementary Photographs on pp. 148—153.

Roll No.		Name	Roll No.		Name
10347	Private	Birchall, J. W.	10413	Private	Jones, E.
10234	,,	Bedford, H.	10994	,,	Marr, W.
10594	,,	Bolland, H.	10431	,,	Morris, H.
10370	,,	Curran, T.	10574	,,	Wright, J. C.
10486	,,	Davies R.	11043	,,	Williams, L.
10988	,,	Daniel, J.	10469	,,	Wignall, R. H.
10488	,,	Gate, K.	11228	,,	Wimbury, H.
11024	,,	Hunt, W.			

18th (Service) Battalion Manchester Regiment.

"C" COMPANY.

Officer Commanding Company - Capt. G. HEATHCOTE.
Second in Command - - - Capt. W. PENN-GASKELL.*
Company Sergeant Major - - EVANS, W. L.†
Company Quartermaster Sergeant - BEATTIE, V.†

PLATOON NO. XI.

Platoon Commander - - - Lieut. J. G. CUNLIFFE.*
Platoon Sergeant - - - HOLT, G. W.

Roll No.	Rank and Name.	Roll No.	Rank and Name.
10565	Sergeant PEARSON, J. T.	10395	Private GLEAVE, W. E.
10835	L.-Sergt. POTTS, F. W.	10586	,, GOUGH, J.
10426	Corporal McNAMARA, J.	10406	,, HILL, J. H.
10394	,, GREAVES, J.	10411	,, INGOE, H.
10363	L.-Corpl. COYLE, A.	10495	,, INGHAM, A.
10465	,, THOMPSON, J. H.	10419	,, KIRELLY, J.
10453	,, STANDEN, W.	10502	,, LONGSHAW, A.
10514	,, WHITTINGHAM, S.	10423	,, LAW, A.
10491	,, HIGSON, W. H.	10560	,, MARTIN, J. G.
10588	,, PAYNE, J.	10433	,, MOLLOY, C. E.
10464	,, TINKER, G. H.	10595	,, MOORES, H.
10597	Private ALMOND, J.	10435	,, NIGHTINGALE, H.
10336	,, ANDERSON, T.	10510	,, OGDEN, T.
10523	,, ANTWISS, J.	10437	,, OLIVER, F. S.
10341	,, BAKE, R.	10448	,, ROYLE, W.
10340	,, BOUCHER, H. C.	10447	,, ROBBINS, G.
10345	,, BIRDSALL, E.	10454	,, SILCOCK, F.
10342	,, BUTLER, W.	10452	,, STANDEN, E.
10366	,, CHAPMAN, W.	10463	,, THORNLEY, F.
10358	,, CONNOR, F.	10467	,, TILSTON, W. E.
10365	,, CONNOLLY, W.	10573	,, TUNSTALL, S. E.
10384	,, DAVIES, J. H.	10576	,, WEBB, W.
10485	,, DINWOODIE, N. S.	10474	,, WARK, G.
10388	,, EITE, R.	10519	,, WILSON, N.
10389	,, FENNA, S.	10473	,, WILSON, B.
10538	,, GEORGE, D.	10577	,, WOODALL, W. L.

* For portrait, see Officers' Group, p. 103.   † For portrait, see Sergeants' Group, p. 105.

The following were not present when the Platoon Photograph was taken,
but see Supplementary Photographs on pp. 148—153.

11028	Private	FOSTER, E.	10449 Private	RUSSELL, R.
11026	,,	CAMPBELL, J.	10952 ,,	SIMPSON, H.
11060	,,	FOSTER, W. H.	11009 ,,	SIMPSON, J. B.
10396	,,	GOULD, F. L.	10596 ,,	SPENSER, S. R.
10547	,,	HARRINGTON, J.	10466 ,,	TROTTER, J.

F

18th (Service) Battalion Manchester Regiment

"C" COMPANY

Officer Commanding Company -	Capt. G. Heathcote.*
Second in Command - - -	Capt. W. Penn-Gaskell.*
Company Sergeant Major - -	Evans, W. L.†
Company Quartermaster Sergeant -	Beattie, V.

PLATOON NO. XII.

Platoon Commander -	Lieut. H. H. Crawshaw.
Platoon Sergeant - - - -	Smith, R. U.

Roll No.	Rank and Name.		Roll No.	Rank and Name.	
10356	Sergeant	Buckley, H.	10400	Private	Howarth, E.
10561	,,	Nicholson, J. M.	10412	,,	Johnson, F. C.
10482	Corporal	Darbyshire, E.	10497	,,	Johnson, C. A.
10563	L.-Corpl.	Starkie, H.	10548	,,	Jarvis, T.
10584	,,	Atkinson, H.	10496	,,	Johnson, G. F.
10507	,,	Nixon, F.	10417	,,	Kelsall, E.
10490	,,	Hayes, G. W.	10549	,,	Kett, L.
10536	,,	Fanning, M. T.	10499	,,	Latham, W.
10531	,,	Carless, P.	10501	,,	Leigh, F.
10418	,,	Kay, C. P.	10420	,,	Lucey, T. G.
10439	,,	Parry, J.	10432	,,	Makinson, R.
10334	Private	Armstrong, W.	10503	,,	Melem, E.
10525	,,	Barker, G.	10504	,,	Miller, R.
10527	,,	Bradshaw, C.	10427	,,	Martin, R.
10339	,,	Ball, W. R.	10587	,,	Ormerod, J.
10481	,,	Cottrell, W.	10508	,,	Obbard, P.
10534	,,	Dakin, J. W.	10564	,,	Pritchard, A. E.
10383	,,	Done, R.	10443	,,	Royle, L.
10487	,,	Fiddes, R.	10450	,,	Smith, E.
10390	,,	Forster, S.	10451	,,	Schofield, P.
10539	,,	Gregory, S.	10571	,,	Thornley, A.
10393	,,	Godbert, W.	10572	,,	Towers, T.
10399	,,	Harvey, H.	10468	,,	Voinus, W. H.
10402	,,	Holt, H.	10472	,,	Wright, T. H.
10542	,,	Howarth, G. H.	10470	,,	Wood, A.
10407	,,	Hicks, D. M.	10516	,,	Whittaker, J.
10404	,,	Harding, R. D.	10471	,,	Watson, C.
10392	,,	Hughes, H. P.	10477	,,	Wolstencroft, E.

* For portrait, see Officers' Group, p. 103. † For portrait, see Sergeants' Group, p. 105.

The following were not present when the Platoon Photograph was taken, but see Supplementary Photographs on pp. 148—153.

Roll No.	Rank	Name	Roll No.	Rank	Name
10367	Private	Carter, G.	11008	Private	Hawkins, A. T.
10382	,,	Derwent, F. R.	10924	,,	Marsden, H.
10381	,,	Dodgson, A.	10951	,,	Pygott, T.
10386	,,	Ellison, A.	10943	,,	Walley, F.
10401	,,	Howell, C.			

18th (Service) Battalion Manchester Regiment.

"D" COMPANY.

Officer Commanding Company - Capt. C. J. R. Fraser.*
Second in Command - - - Capt. P. Godlee.*
Company Sergeant Major - - Waite, G.†
Company Quartermaster Sergeant - Ralston, J.

PLATOON NO. XIII.

Platoon Commander - - - 2nd Lieut. P. G. D. Haworth.
Platoon Sergeant - - - - Connor, J.

Roll No.	Rank and Name.		Roll No.	Rank and Name.	
10377	L.-Sergt.	Davies, W. B.	10740	Private	Warner, T. G.
10831	Corporal	Needham, T.	10707	,,	Royle, A.
10697	,,	Perkins, A.	10722	,,	Timperley, T.
10775	,,	Hicks, W.	10761	,,	Broomhead, J. W.
10721	,,	Tomlinson, F.	10767	,,	Castles, J.
10838	L.-Corpl.	Sedgwick, C.	10616	,,	Burkett, W.
10712	,,	Senior, P. S.	10695	,,	Pownall, E.
10650	,,	Holt, J. P.	10925	,,	Murphy, A.
10786	,,	Rylands, F.	10752	,,	Wardle, A.
10790	,,	Squibbs, F. L.	10765	,,	Curren, H.
10673	Private	Knowles, A.	10687	,,	McGrath, W.
10791	,,	Squibbs, G. L.	10842	,,	Stewart, E.
10874	,,	Randles, J.	10630	,,	Croker, A.
10764	,,	Booth, S. D.	10644	,,	Godley, R. E.
10725	,,	Tomkinson, F. J.	10788	,,	Rogerson, W. H.
10633	,,	Dutton, T.	10798	,,	Andrew, P.
10680	,,	Maybury, W.	10714	,,	Scott, Alb.
10727	,,	Trevelyan, J. H.	10703	,,	Riley, J. C.
10693	,,	Parsons, W.	10619	,,	Booth, S.
10618	,,	Beagley, C. P.	10671	,,	Kelly, W.
10785	,,	Rogerson, S.	10807	,,	Downhill, H.
10763	,,	Booth, A. E.	10789	,,	Stott, L. C.
10972	,,	Hewitson, J.	10615	,,	Baker, S.
10663	,,	Illingworth, C. H.	10850	,,	Tristram, S. H.
10778	,,	Hand, W. E.	10711	,,	Smith, W. E.
10739	,,	Whitehead, R.	10857	,,	Wright, J.
10784	,,	Owen, F.	10708	,,	Roberts, A.

* For portrait, see Officers' Group, p. 103. † For portrait, see Sergeants' Group, p. 105.

The following were not present when the Platoon Photograph was taken,
but see Supplementary Photographs on pp. 148—153.

10732	Sergeant	Vine, F. C.	10769	Private	Freeman, F. E.
10655	L.-Corpl.	Hancox, C.	10607	,,	Band, J.
10796	Private	Woodhead, J.	10776	,,	Heap, J.
10939	,,	Penny, R.			

18th (Service) Battalion Manchester Regiment.

"D" COMPANY.

Officer Commanding Company	Capt. C. J. R. Fraser.*
Second in Command	Capt. P. Godlee.*
Company Sergeant Major	Waite, G.
Company Quartermaster Sergeant	Ralston, J.†

PLATOON NO. XIV.

Platoon Commander	Lieut. H. G. Watson.
Platoon Sergeant	Bell, S.

Roll No.	Rank and Name.		Roll No.	Rank and Name.	
9901	Sergeant	McMillan, B. T.	10827	Private	Lyon, E.
10427	L.-Sergt.	Stallard, K.	10736	,,	Williams, E.
10689	Corporal	Newton, W.	10777	,,	Haworth, H.
10638	L.-Corpl.	Ferns, G. H.	10802	,,	Carter, S.
10692	,,	Pickard, B.	10702	,,	Ratcliffe, F.
10617	Private	Bagnall, J. W.	10793	,,	Tucker, H. A.
10815	,,	Green, F. B.	10840	,,	Siddall, J. H.
10730	,,	Thompson, A.	10766	,,	Cumpsty, C. P.
10731	,,	Thompson, Frank.	10803	,,	Clare, A.
10817	,,	Gargan, F. J.	10805	,,	Cowley, F.
10856	,,	Williams, T.	10613	,,	Burgess, S.
10724	,,	Thompson, J.	10626	,,	Crowe, W.
10854	,,	Webb, J.	10705	,,	Rourke, J.
10754	,,	Young, A. A.	10667	,,	Johnson, W.
10719	,,	Scholes, F.	10853	,,	Wardle, J.
10706	,,	Rhodes, S.	10636	,,	Dawson, A.
10688	,,	Minett, W. L.	10734	,,	Wrigley, J. A.
10658	,,	Hindley, F. S.	10678	,,	Mack, R. G.
10653	,,	Harper, H.	10821	,,	Howell, L. R.
10735	,,	Woodward, F. N.	10628	,,	Cornall, W. C.
10737	,,	Williams, L. R.	11007	,,	Booth, A.
10839	,,	Shedlock, A.	10999	,,	Griffin, T.
10612	,,	Brooke, C. E.	11005	,,	Browne, B.
10666	,,	Jones, H. L.	11030	,,	Baggoley, R.
10922	,,	Culpan, T.	10931	,,	Hollis, J.
10601	,,	Keenaghan, D.	11002	,,	McGowan, J.
10843	,,	Tanner, E.	10916	,,	Birch, F. R.

* For portrait, see Officers' Group, p. 103.   † For portrait, see Sergeants' Group, p. 105.

The following were not present when the Platoon Photograph was taken, but see Supplementary Photographs on pp. 148–153.

Roll No.	Rank	Name	Roll No.	Rank	Name
10716	L.-Corpl.	Sternshine, M.	10698	Private	Part, E.
10748	,,	Walker, S. F.	10819	,,	Holbrook, H.
10713	Private	Stahl, M.	10949	,,	Gray, J.
10844	,,	Taylor, S.	11035	,,	Foy, W. J.
10973	,,	Bryan, T.	11057	,,	Street, H.
10781	,,	Kirkham, H.			

18th (Service) Battalion Manchester Regiment.

"D" COMPANY.

Officer Commanding Company -	Capt. C. J. R. FRASER.*
Second in Command - - -	Capt. P. GODLEE.*
Company Sergeant Major -	WAITE, G.†
Company Quartermaster Sergeant -	RALSTON, J.

PLATOON NO. XV.

Platoon Commander - - -	Lieut. C. HENSHALL.*
Platoon Sergeant - - - -	LEMAN, H.

Roll No.	Rank and Name.		Roll No.	Rank and Name.	
10818	Sergeant	HILL, E. C.	10757	Private	ASHWORTH, A.
10605	L.-Corpl.	ASHES, W.	10756	,,	YOUNGHUSBAND, A.
10809	,,	ENTWISTLE, J. E.	10983	,,	ATKINSON, D.
10629	,,	CUMMINGS, J.	10729	,,	THOMPSON, FRED.
10649	,,	HOLLAND, T.	10811	,,	EDWARDS, R.
10751	,,	WILLIAMS, J.	10603	,,	AUSTIN, T. W. E.
10795	Private	WILKINSON, T.	10863	,,	ELIFFE, F.
10718	,,	SCOTT, ALF.	10826	,,	KENNEDY, P. J.
10720	,,	TAWN, A.	10800	,,	BOOTH, W.
10656	,,	HALL, P. E. R.	10760	,,	BAMFORD, W.
10654	,,	HARWOOD, T.	10787	,,	RUSHTON, R. W.
10622	,,	BROWN, F.	10681	,,	McDONALD, C.
10762	,,	BOWLES, H.	10806	,,	COYLE, J.
10699	,,	PANNIFER, W. N. S.	10723	,,	TAFT, F.
10675	,,	KILNER, S.	10858	,,	DELANEY, R. J.
10742	,,	WHITWORTH, W.	10865	,,	WOODALL, F.
10535	,,	ELLISON, W. H.	10691	,,	NAYLOR, W. T.
10804	,,	COOPE, W. E.	10755	,,	YATES, S.
10851	,,	WALKER, A. E.	10717	,,	STANSFIELD, H. N.
10620	,,	BUTLER, B. F.	10862	,,	ELIFFE, H.
10855	,,	WHITE, M.	10610	,,	BUTTRESS, J. A.
10841	,,	SMITH, A.	10780	,,	JONES, W. H.
10643	,,	GRIFFITH, J. W.	10832	,,	ORMEROD, A.
10738	,,	WEARING, C. E.	10813	,,	GRIFFIN, V.

Also on Photograph: 2nd Lieut. A. A. F. HARRIS.

* For portrait, see Officers' Group, p. 103.   † For portrait, see Sergeants' Group, p. 105.

The following were not present when the Platoon Photograph was taken, but see Supplementary Photographs on pp. 148—153.

Roll No.	Rank	Name	Roll No.	Rank	Name
10647	Corporal	GRATTIDGE, A.	10631	Private	CARTER, R. C.
10829	L.-Corpl.	McKELLON, I.	10733	,,	WATTERSON, E. S.
10864	Private	ENTWISTLE, W.	10859	,,	LOFTHOUSE, F. L.
10834	,,	PERKINS, ALEX.	10860	,,	TAWS, A. E.
10701	,,	RATCLIFFE, P.	10782	,,	LAKING, G. H.
10749	,,	WILSON, T.	10967	,,	CHEASE, W. E.
10770	,,	FOSTER, J.	11038	,,	PALIN, H. R.
10847	,,	THOMAS, W.	10041	,,	HICKS, H. V.
10635	,,	DINWOODIE, C. H.			

18th (Service) Battalion Manchester Regiment.

"D" COMPANY.

Officer Commanding Company	Capt. C. J. R. Fraser.*
Second in Command	Capt. P. Godlee.*
Company Sergeant Major	Waite, G.
Company Quartermaster Sergeant	Ralston, J.†

PLATOON NO. XVI.

Platoon Commander	Lieut. R. Hobkirk.
Platoon Sergeant	Moss, S. F.

Roll No.	Rank and Name.		Roll No.	Rank and Name.	
10602	Sergeant	Airley, A. W.	10783	Private	Murphy, J.
10684	Corporal	McCormick, J.	10677	,,	Lee, J.
10741	,,	Walker, C.	10797	,,	Aisthorpe, J. W.
10672	L.-Corpl.	Kerfoot, W.	10792	,,	Slinn, P.
10710	,,	Sutton, J.	10746	,,	Whiteley, E. A.
10651	,,	Honeyman, F.	10814	,,	Grimshaw, W.
10846	,,	Tattersall, N.	10670	,,	Kilbeg, J.
10685	,,	Makin, A.	10774	,,	Hill, J. R.
10830	Private	Marlor, N.	10876	,,	Smith, J. W.
10986	,,	Leonard, A. V.	10640	,,	Farrell, F.
11011	,,	Marriott, T. H.	10773	,,	Gilson, F.
10808	,,	Dyson, H.	10877	,,	Wright, T.
10825	,,	Kinsey, F.	10700	,,	Quick, F.
10822	,,	Hurst, A.	10632	,,	Cowgill, T.
10845	,,	Taylor, H.	10833	,,	Parker, H.
10660	,,	Harrison, J.	10634	,,	Denton, W.
10823	,,	Hurst, J. T.	10816	,,	Gorton, J.
10674	,,	Kendall, N.	10676	,,	Little, F.
10606	,,	Batwell, D.	10604	,,	Anyon, C. H.
10683	,,	Marsden, E.	10645	,,	Gregory, W. A. W.
10659	,,	Hopwood, H.	10627	,,	Crampton, G. B.

* For portrait, see Officers' Group, p. 103. † For portrait, see Sergeants' Group, p. 105.

The following were not present when the Platoon Photograph was taken, but see Supplementary Photographs on pp. 148—153.

Roll No.		Rank and Name.	Roll No.		Rank and Name.
10648	Private	Howarth, E.	10758	Private	Anyon, N. E.
10743	,,	Williams, F. C.	10662	,,	Heyworth, G.
10661	,,	Hill, S.	10812	,,	Foy, J.
10828	,,	Murch, A.	10669	,,	Jolley, L.
10726	,,	Turner, S.	10682	,,	Morrison, T.
10709	,,	Robinson, G. E.	10958	,,	Bell, W.
10779	,,	Hammond, A. F.	11048	,,	Walker, J. D.
10747	,,	Wood, T.	11056	,,	Entwistle, J.
10646	,,	Griffis, A.	10909	,,	Ansty, R.
10820	,,	Hamer, G. D.			

18th (Service) Battalion Manchester Regiment.

"E" COMPANY.

Officer Commanding Company - Capt. W. Payne.
Company Sergeant Major - Evans, G.
Company Quartermaster Sergeant - Hough, W.†

PLATOON NO. XVII.

Platoon Commander - - - 2nd Lieut. R. D. England.
Platoon Sergeant - - - Redfern, A.

Roll No.	Rank and Name.		Roll No.	Rank and Name.	
10181	Sergeant	Midgley, C. T.	10907	Private	Harper, A.
10608	,,	Berry, E. J.	11090	,,	Humphreys, W.
10328	,,	Spink, W.	10946	,,	Hardy, F.
9937	,,	Tidswell, J.	11041	,,	Hicks, H. V.
11095	Corporal	Sharrocks, W.	11061	,,	Harrop, J. A.
10321	,,	Bailey, W.	11087	,,	Kay, G. H.
10051	L.-Corpl.	Willshaw, H. C.	10963	,,	Lane, F.
9853	,,	Grundy, J.	11072	,,	Longbottom, W.
10954	,,	Stewart, A.	11107	,,	Moores, A.
10935	,,	Heald, W.	11052	,,	Melia, J. W.
10910	,,	Pearson, J. R.	11055	,,	Mackinson, F.
10923	,,	Wilkinson, J.	11074	,,	Napthali, R.
10919	,,	Travers, G.	11088	,,	O'Brien, J. P.
11104	Private	Aukland, S.	10910	,,	Philpott, F. A.
11022	,,	Barlow, R.	10914	,,	Rooke, J. C.
11062	,,	Bardsley, W.	11103	,,	Robinson, H.
11081	,,	Bridge, H. W.	11035	,,	Rushton, F. A.
11067	,,	Cooper, J. H.	11054	,,	Reeves, J. W.
10944	,,	Davies, F.	11108	,,	Sharp, P.
11050	,,	Dewsnip, F.	10936	,,	Taylor, B. L.
11092	,,	Dalton, R.	10962	,,	Wilson, O.
11117	,,	Ellis, J.	11025	,,	Waller, J. F.
11069	,,	Ellison, H.	11051	,,	Walkden, T.
11060	,,	Foster, W. H.	11053	,,	Wood, J. L.

† For portrait, see Sergeants' Group, p. 105.

18th (Service) Battalion Manchester Regiment.

"E" COMPANY.

Officer Commanding Company	-	Capt. W. PAYNE.*
Company Sergeant Major	-	EVANS, G.†
Company Quartermaster Sergeant	-	HOUGH, W.†

PLATOON NO. XVIII.

Platoon Commander	-	2nd Lieut. H. A. POWELL.
Platoon Sergeant	-	JONES, T.

Roll No.	Rank and Name.		Roll No.	Rank and Name.	
10657	Corporal	HILL, J. A.	11073	Private	ROONEY, C. W.
10998	L.-Corpl.	UPTON, J. S.	11076	,,	ROWLANDS, E. J.
11040	Private	ANDERSON, W.	11084	,,	ROBERTS, T.
11121	,,	BOHANNA, E.	11110	,,	SELLARS, A. H.
11071	,,	BROOKS, T. A.	11115	,,	SLACK, R.
10976	,,	CHESTERS, E.	11059	,,	STANLEY, W.
11080	,,	DAVIES, T. T.	11122	,,	SMITH, S.
11106	,,	DAWSON, E. J.	11070	,,	WARREN, J.
11094	,,	DORAN, J.	11083	,,	WHITBY, H. F.
11093	,,	DUNSCOMBE, H.	11085	,,	WHITBY, A.
11082	,,	FOWLER, C. H.	11091	,,	WILDING, T. W.
11109	,,	HALLIWELL, F.	11097	,,	WALKER, J. E.
11101	,,	HANDLEY, E. R.	11098	,,	WHITELEGG, R.
11123	,,	HOWARTH, W.	11119	,,	WRIGHT, J. A.
11096	,,	KENNY, I.	11118	,,	GROOM, W.
11089	,,	MAY, F. H.	11124	,,	RILEY, H.
11036	,,	MOORE, J. P.	11134	,,	SWANN, A.
11075	,,	McCULLAM, W.	11135	,,	HONEY, G.
11063	,,	O'MARA, A. G.	11148	,,	DAY, H.
11116	,,	PEARSON, W.			

* For portrait, see Officers' Group, p. 103. † For portrait, see Sergeants' Group, p. 105.

18th (Service) Battalion Manchester Regiment.

"E" COMPANY.

Officer Commanding Company - Capt. W. Payne.*
Company Sergeant Major - - Evans, G.†
Company Quartermaster Sergeant - Hough, W. †

PLATOON NO. XIX.

Platoon Commander - - - 2nd Lieut. R. Walwork.
Platoon Sergeant - - - Neill, G. C.

Roll No.	Rank and Name.		Roll No.	Rank and Name.	
10094	L.-Corpl.	Sears, J. L.	11153	Private	Vickers, W.
11105	Private	Kay, F.	11145	,,	Nicholson, G.
11125	,,	Longshaw, J.	11175	,,	Crompton, A.
11113	,,	Nuttall, H.	11179	,,	Patton, A.
11133	,,	Browne, G.	11177	,,	Crook, G.
11137	,,	Bray, S.	11216	,,	Gribbin, E.
11138	,,	O'Brien, J.	11197	,,	Hiles, L.
11139	,,	Gaynon, G.	11187	,,	Carr, J.
11157	,,	Jackson, F.	11142	,,	Brown, C. B.
11150	,,	Cassin, J.	11198	,,	Marsden, J. D.
11192	,,	Lawless, J.	11158	,,	Forrest, R.
11200	,,	Chadderton.	11102	,,	Dunn, W. B.
11149	,,	Beckett, N.	11172	,,	Colecliffe, E.
11191	,,	Hulmes, A.	11176	,,	May, W.
11152	,,	Armston, F.	11112	,,	Shillicorn, P.
11215	,,	Greatbanks, J.	11111	,,	Nuttall, F.

* For portrait, see Officers' Group, p. 103.   † For portrait, see Sergeants' Group, p. 105.

18th (Service) Battalion Manchester Regiment.

"E" COMPANY.

Officer Commanding Company - Capt. W. Payne.*
Company Sergeant Major - - Evans, G.†
Company Quartermaster Sergeant - Hough, W.†

PLATOON NO. XX.

Platoon Commander - - - 2nd Lieut. B. T. N. Tavaré.
Platoon Sergeant - - - - Cush, J.

Roll No.	Rank and Name.		Roll No.	Rank and Name.	
11118	Private	Marshall, A.	11147	Private	Owen, J.
11126	,,	Maycock, E.	11168	,,	Pasquill, J. A.
11127	,,	Chappell, A.	11185	,,	Cadman, T. H.
11128	,,	Hatfield, T. A.	11190	,,	Hickson, T., Junr
11129	,,	Fox, L.	11189	,,	Bond, J. R.
11131	,,	Carter, F.	11188	,,	Costigan, J.
11132	,,	Hickson, T., Senr.	11141	,,	Hill, W.
11136	,,	Meachin, W.	11143	,,	Groves, L.
11140	,,	Mabey, R. C.	11151	,,	Williams, W. T.
11165	,,	Elsby, J.	11186	,,	Frawley, J. C.
11170	,,	Eyre, R.	11154	,,	Hulston, J.
11156	,,	Mills, A.	11159	,,	Cox, N.
11144	,,	Benson, J.	11181	,,	Sharrock, S.
11184	,,	Burgess, G.		,,	Lumb, O. W. H.

* For portrait, see Officers' Group, p. 103.   † For portrait, see Sergeants' Group, p. 105.

18th BATTALION.—Supplementary Photo of men of A Company who were not present when the Platoon Photographs were taken. For names, see Platoon lists.

18th BATTALION.—Supplementary Photo of men of A Company who were not present when the Platoon Photographs were taken. For names, see Platoon lists.

18th BATTALION.—Supplementary Photo of men of B Company who were not present when the Platoon Photographs were taken. For names, see Platoon lists.

18th BATTALION.—Supplementary Photo of men of B Company who were not present when the Platoon Photographs were taken. For names, see Platoon lists.

18th BATTALION.—Supplementary Photo of men of C Company who were not present when the Platoon Photographs were taken. For names, see Platoon lists.

18th BATTALION.—Supplementary Photo of men of D Company who were not present when the Platoon Photographs were taken. For names, see Platoon lists.

19th (Service) Battalion

19th (Service) Battalion Manchester Regiment,

Roll of Officers.

Colonel	Kettlewell, E. A.	2nd Lieut.	Heywood, A. T.
L.-Col.	Lloyd, W. E.	,,	Turner, H. E.
Major	Howe, E. H.	,,	Foster, B. la T.
,,	Allen, R. J.	,,	Ince, N. S.
Capt. & Adjt.	Grounds, J. N. B.	,,	Solly, A. N.
Captain	Birley, H. K.	,,	Foster, P. la T.
,,	Cunliffe, W. S.	,,	Chadwick, L. A.
,,	Joyce, C.	,,	Henshall, F.
,,	Agnew, C. G.	,,	Swaine, G. R.
Chaplain	Balleine, Rev. W. R.	,,	Smith, W. R.
Lieut.	Royle F. W.	,,	Boxall, F. S.
,,	Hislop, J. A.	,,	Mawdsley, E. W.
,,	Myers, J. W.	,,	Atkinson, A. W.
,,	Clarke, W. M.	,,	Craston, N. H.
,,	Orr, W. M. B.	,,	Tidy, W. E.
,,	Owen, G. St. John	Lt.-Surg.	Stocks, A. V.
,,	Mather, R. C.	Lt. & Qr.	O'Malley, J. F.
,,	Higgins, J. B.		

The following were not present when the Photograph was taken :—

Lieut.	Towers, F.	2nd Lieut.	Caldwell, J. A.
,,	Leresche, G.	,,	Read, N.

19th (Service) Battalion Manchester Regiment.

Non-Commissioned Officers' (Sergeants) Roll.

Warrant Officer and R.S.M. (Acting).
11454 C.S.M. Wilkinson, W. H.

11453 R.Q.M.S. Maguire, J.
11452 R.O.R.S. Wookey, J.

Roll No.	Rank	and Name.	Roll No.	Rank	and Name.
11721	C.S.M.	Grayburn, A. H.	11937	Sergeant	Swindells, H. B.
12532	,,	Lane, T.	11804	,,	Entwistle, E. C.
11454	,,	Wilkinson, W. H.	12810	,,	Robertson, J. T.
11990	,,	Buchan, J. B.	11993	,,	Beswick, C.
12256	,,	Nuttall, F.	11994	,,	Spears, J.
11991	C.Q.M.S.	Charlton, T.	12075	,,	Evers, H. M.
12336	,,	Grimshaw, G. F.	12123	,,	Jones, J. A.
11798	,,	Duckworth, H. H.	12073	,,	Entwistle, J.
11723	,,	Bush, G. W.	12104	,,	Rosenberg, A.
11456	,,	Wall, J.	12255	,,	Almond, J.
12507	Sgt. Cook	Wilson, S.	12508	,,	Jutton, H. C.
11652	Pion. Sgt.	Nightingale, R.	12257	,,	Comstive, W. R.
12367	M.G.S.	Hubbard, H.	12281	,,	Bedford, P. W.
12688	Trns. Sgt.	Crosby, W.	12411	,,	Milner, A. B.
11992	Sig. Sgt.	Holborn, E.	12312	,,	Dear, S.
11459	Sergeant	Busby, W.	12468	,,	Thomas, A.
11565	,,	Hayes, H. S.	11457	,,	Mason, B.
11535	,,	Evans, H. A.	11544	,,	Fitch, H. E.
11682	,,	Rothwell, H.	11550	,,	Garner, F.
11568	,,	Hartt, H.	11772	,,	Cooke, H. E.
12529	,,	Joyce, E.	12517	,,	Walters, F.
11509	,,	Charnock, L.	11822	L.-Sergt.	Harrison, W. T.
11723	,,	Bush, G. W.	11857	,,	Hunter, C. A.
11964	,,	Wilson, L. E.	11873	,,	Lane, F. G.
12555	,,	Dickinson, W.	12033	,,	Carter, S.

Lt.-Col. W. E. Lloyd and Capt. and Adjt J. N. B. Grounds also appear on the Photograph.

The following were not present when the Photograph was taken :—

11892 Sergeant Morris, F.   12229 Sergeant Waddington, H.

19th (Service) Battalion Manchester Regiment.

Bugle Band.

Roll No.	Rank and Name.		Roll No.	Rank and Name.	
11829	L.-Sergt.	Harrison, W. H.	11814	Drummer	Gillbanks, W.
12500	L.-Corpl.	Wallwork, A.	12349	,,	Grisenthwaite, W.
12612	Drummer	Blaydon, C. B.	12357	,,	Hoskins, F.
12560	,,	Burrows, W. T.	12377	,,	Jameson, R. H.
11775	,,	Coombs, J. T.	12389	,,	Kellock, G.
11504	,,	Cassidy, W.	12153	,,	Moran, T.
12034	,,	Carter, W.	11886	,,	Mapley, G. E.
12505	,,	Crowther, W.	11941	,,	Shone, J. H.
11534	,,	Ellison, J. E.	12216	,,	Sutton, J.
11530	,,	Eddows, T.	12235	,,	Wareham, W.
12082	,,	Gilligan, J.	12586	,,	Wray, E.

The following were not present when the Photograph was taken, but see Supplementary Photographs on pp. 198—201.

11570	Drummer Harrison, P. L.	11976	Drummer Yates, F.
12774	,, Smith.		

G

19th (Service) Battalion Manchester Regiment.
"A" COMPANY.

Officer Commanding Company -	Capt. and Hon. Major E. H. Howe.*
Second in Command - - -	Lieut. J. W. Myers.*
Company Sergeant Major - -	Busby, W. J.†
Company Quartermaster Sergeant -	Wall, James.†

PLATOON NO. I.

Platoon Commander - - -	Lieut. F. Towers.*
Platoon Sergeant - - - -	Rothwell, H.

Roll No.	Rank and Name.		Roll No.	Rank and Name.	
11989	Corporal	Wallis, W. J.	11561	Private	Gray, J. L.
11502	L.-Corpl.	Carroll, A.	11711	,,	Grindrod, J.
11619	,,	Morrisey, J.	11581	,,	Hyde, G.
11506	,,	Chadwick, W. A.	11612	,,	Mellor, E.
11663	,,	Schofield, G.	11606	,,	Moe, H. F.
11464	Private	Baker, G. A.	11669	,,	Skeffington, D.
11471	,,	Bayley, W. A.	11697	,,	Wardle, J.
11475	,,	Birdsall, A.	11702	,,	Whittaker, F.
11474	,,	Bird, J.	11700	,,	Wilson, J.
11526	,,	Dobb, T.	12601	,,	Ogden, W.
11528	,,	Duckworth, A. C.	11468	,,	Barker, H.
11560	,,	Grinton, T. L.	11485	,,	Brereton, S.
11583	,,	Johnson, J. W.	11582	,,	Ibbotson, A.
11597	,,	Lowe, R. A.	11602	,,	McLeavy, R. E.
11609	,,	Maybury, H.	11623	,,	Newton, T.
11691	,,	Verity, J.	11654	,,	Ryder, N.
12512	,,	Appleyard, A. E.	11671	,,	Smith, J. W.
11482	,,	Bowes, F.	11699	,,	Wilson, W.
11538	,,	Feachnie, A. L.	12730	,,	Shevlin, J.
11567	,,	Hanney, E. B.	12608	,,	Tierney, W. E.
12516	,,	Holland, H.	12610	,,	Roberts, A.
11604	,,	Marsh, O. G.	12613	,,	Roberts, J. S.
11710	,,	Yuill, J. G.	11548	,,	Fitzsimons, S.
11647	,,	Riley, J.	12611	,,	Tomlinson, R.
11651	,,	Roberts, T.	12669	,,	Ball, J.
11655	,,	Rycroft, J. H.	12614	,,	Bailey, S. H.
12514	,,	Swainston, L.	12668	,,	Crawshaw, E.
11522	,,	Davenport, A. E.	12665	,,	O'Connor, T. P.
11556	,,	Goodhead, S. F.	12663	,,	Morton, T. B.

Also on the Photograph: 2nd Lieut. N. H. Craston.

* For portrait, see Officers' Group, p. 157.   † For Portrait, see Sergeants' Group, p. 159.

The following were not present when the Platoon Photograph was taken,
but see Supplementary Photographs on pp. 198—201.

11454	B.S.-Maj. Wilkinson, W. H.		11459	C.S.-Maj. Busby, W. J.	
11455	C.Q.M.S. Ryder, E.		12691	Corporal Taylor, W. H.	
11687	Pte. Tidswell, C.	11514 Pte. Cowen, A. G.		11580 Pte. Hudson, J.	
11505	,, Crowther, W.	12599 ,, White, M.		11631 ,, Pearson, G.	
12584	,, Smith, J.	11690 ,, Vernon, W.		11653 ,, Rushby, R.	
12583	,, Wain, W.	12600 ,, Williams, H.		11674 ,, Spencer, A.	
12515	,, Hooper, H.	11598 ,, Lowe, W.		11673 ,, Stephens, A. C.	
11594	,, Litt, J.	11608 ,, Manton, H.		12602 ,, Howarth, W.	
12513	,, McLaine, J.	11616 ,, Molland, F. L.		12604 ,, Maybury, G.	

19th (Service) Battalion Manchester Regiment.
"A" COMPANY.

Officer Commanding Company -	Capt. and Hon. Major E. H. HOWE.*
Second in Command - - -	Lieut. J. W. MYERS.
Company Sergeant Major - -	BUSBY, W. J.†
Company Quartermaster Sergeant -	WALL, JAMES.†

PLATOON NO. II.

Platoon Commander - - -	Lieut. F. S. BOXALL.
Platoon Sergeant - - - -	CHARNOCK, L.

Roll No.	Rank and Name.	Roll No.	Rank and Name.
11565	Pioneer-S. HAYES, H. G.	11677	Private SUGGETT, IRA.
11532	Corporal EDWARDS, W.	11460	,, ALLAN, F. R.
11713	,, WHITEHEAD, F. C.	11467	,, BARLASS, A.
11630	L.-Corpl. PARKER, F.	11539	,, FENTON, F.
11497	,, BURNS, J.	11562	,, GREENWOOD, J.
10491	,, BROOKES, W.	11629	,, PARTINGTON, H.
11503	Private CASEWELL, G.	11670	,, SKEET, H.
11527	,, DRUMMOND, W.	11686	,, TAYLOR, A. E.
11563	,, GREGORY, G.	11692	,, WATERS, J.
11596	,, LOFTUS, W.	11714	,, WHITER, J.
11634	,, PICKERING, E.	11706	,, WILLIAMS, T.
11635	,, POLLARD, H.	11705	,, WILLIAMS, R. H.
11642	,, RATCLIFFE, J. A.	11463	,, BAGULEY, J.
11641	,, RATCLIFFE, T.	11512	,, COX, G.
12606	,, DAVIES, T.	11577	,, HOPE, F.
12607	,, WATERS, A.	11566	,, HAIGH, W.
11498	,, BURTON, F.	11632	,, PILLING, J. E.
11524	,, DIGNAN, J. P.	11660	,, REEVES, D.
11559	,, GRAY, L.	11657	,, RILEY, T.
11571	,, HELICON, F.	11683	,, TAYLOR, J.
11600	,, LYONS, J.	11715	,, WOODFIN, H.
11676	,, STOTT, H.	12585	,, MELIA, R.

* For portrait, see Officers' Group, p. 157. † For Portrait, see Sergeants' Group, p. 159.

The following were not present when the Platoon Photograph was taken, but see Supplementary Photographs on pp. 198—201.

Roll No.	Rank and Name.	Roll No.	Rank and Name.
11638	L.-Corp. PRICKETT, R. T.	11645	Private REDFERN, E.
11557	,, GORTON, A. E.	12608	,, TIERNEY, W. E.
12500	,, WALLWORK, A.	12613	,, ROBERTS, J. S.
11510	,, CLIFFE, T.	11637	,, PRESTON, P.
11500	Private CARLEY, L.	12610	,, ROBERTS, A.
11618	,, MONAGHAN, J. F.	12611	,, TOMLINSON, R.
11504	,, CASSIDY, W.	11483	,, BOYLE, J.
12521	,, ASHWORTH, S.	11585	,, JOHNSTON, W.
11545	,, FLETCHER, T. A.	11605	,, MAHER, T.
11572	,, HIBBERT, W.	12668	,, CRAWSHAW, E.
11588	,, JONES, W. H.		

19th (Service) Battalion Manchester Regiment.
"A" COMPANY.

Officer Commanding Company -	Capt. and Hon. Major E. H. Howe.*
Second in Command - - -	Lieut. J. W. Myers.*
Company Sergeant Major - -	Busby, W. J.†
Company Quartermaster Sergeant -	Wall, James.†

PLATOON NO. III.

Platoon Commander - - -	Lieut. G. St. John Owen.
Platoon Sergeant - - -	Evans, H. A.

Roll No.	Rank and Name.		Roll No.	Rank and Name.	
12529	Sergeant	Joyce, E.	11656	Private	Redford, H.
11550	L.-Sergt.	Garner, F.	11688	,,	Thornley, A.
11614	Corporal	Mitchell, A.	11465	,,	Bamber, E.
11584	L.-Corpl.	Jackson, F.	11470	,,	Bate, C. C.
11599	,,	Lucas, A.	11469	,,	Bate, E. L.
11473	Private	Bickers, W.	11480	,,	Bott, J.
11495	,,	Burgess, J.	11661	,,	Senior, W.
11496	,,	Burgess, N.	11666	,,	Shaw, T.
11499	,,	Butler, J.	11707	,,	Wilkinson, J.
11533	,,	Ellis, E. A.	11701	,,	Wilson, J. B.
11546	,,	Fletcher, T. G.	11718	,,	Wood, G.
11610	,,	Marn, P.	11679	,,	Taylor, H. A.
11658	,,	Roberts, W. W.	11461	,,	Allonby, J. F.
11667	,,	Sheasby, J.	11494	,,	Burgess, H.
11708	,,	Wilkinson, A.	11508	,,	Chambers, D.
12656	,,	Lawton, W.	11523	,,	Devine, T. W.
11487	,,	Briggs, H.	11553	,,	Gibson, C.
11511	,,	Cooper, H.	11579	,,	Hough, W.
11536	,,	Fallows, W. H.	12518	,,	Jones, G.
11543	,,	Fitton, F.	11613	,,	Miller, A.
11573	,,	Hill, H.	11659	,,	Russell, R. B.
11574	,,	Hill, J. E.	11682	,,	Taylor, A. Y.
11587	,,	Jones, F.	11621	,,	Neill, T.
11589	,,	Kenyon, H.	11665	,,	Shatwell, J.
11622	,,	Newman, A.	11712	,,	Wright, G. F.
11685	,,	Taylor, J.			

* For portrait, see Officers' Group, p. 157.   † For Portrait, see Sergeants' Group, p. 159.

The following were not present when the Platoon Photograph was taken, but see Supplementary Photographs on pp. 198—201.

Roll No.	Rank	Name	Roll No.	Rank	Name
11505	Corporal	Chappell, S. R.	12662	Private	Donoghue, M. N.
11518	Private	Crook, W.	12663	,,	Morton, T. B.
11578	,,	Hopkins, J.	11472	,,	Benn, T.
11704	,,	Williams, A.	11534	,,	Ellison, J.
12614	,,	Bailey, G. H.	11636	,,	Preece, E. J.
12586	,,	Wray, E.	11693	,,	Warburton, T.
12634	,,	Sheldon, G.	12664	,,	Collinson, J. J.
11639	,,	Pugh, A.	12665	,,	O'Connor, T. P.
11531	,,	Edney, G. F.	11684	,,	Taylor, E. N.
11530	,,	Eddows, T.	12666	,,	Brown, J. E.
11620	,,	Morgan, G. H.	12686	,,	Hopkins, T. H.

19th (Service) Battalion Manchester Regiment,

"A" COMPANY.

Officer Commanding Company -	Capt. and Hon. Major E. H. Howe.*
Second in Command - - -	Lieut. J. W. Myers.*
Company Sergeant Major - -	Busby, W. J.†
Company Quartermaster Sergeant -	Wall, James.

PLATOON NO. IV.

Platoon Commander - - -	Lieut. W. M. Clarke.
Platoon Sergeant - - - -	Hartt, H.

Roll No.	Rank and Name.		Roll No.	Rank and Name.	
11625	Pioneer-S.	Nightingale, R.	11650	Private	Roberts, J.
11576	Corporal	Holding, H.	11662	,,	Seerey, O.
11648	,,	Riddell, R. R.	11672	,,	Southern, F.
11681	,,	Taylor, H. L.	11689	,,	Turner, F.
11680	,,	Taylor, L. W.	11695	,,	Walker, H.
11878	L.-Corpl.	Livesey, A.	11709	,,	Yates, P.
11575	,,	Hirst, A.	11484	,,	Bradley, J.
11466	Private	Banks, P. R.	11492	,,	Brown, J.
11720	,,	Birchall, H. L.	11517	,,	Crabtree, J.
11527	,,	Duckworth, W.	11521	,,	Daly, T. L.
11540	,,	Fish, A.	11537	,,	Fallows, S.
11541	,,	Fish, N.	11547	,,	Foy, F. H.
11555	,,	Glover, T.	11549	,,	Garner, H.
11591	,,	Knaggs, W. H.	11601	,,	Mackenzie, D.
11649	,,	Rogers, J.	11627	,,	Nickson, H. T.
11668	,,	Siddall, A.	11478	,,	Blomley, T.
11703	,,	Whittaker, J.	11479	,,	Bonney, W.
11716	,,	Wood, J.	11509	,,	Clowes, Jas.
11719	,,	Woodhead, W.	11542	,,	Fishwick, J. W.
11486	,,	Bridge, H.	11628	,,	Pedley, J. W.
11489	,,	Brooks, F.	11643	,,	Ramsbottom, W.
11516	,,	Crabtree, C. W.	11646	,,	Reid, J. A.
11558	,,	Gosling, J.	11675	,,	Stockton, E.

Also on the Photograph: 2nd Lieut. N. H. Craston.

* For portrait, see Officers' Group, p. 157.   † For Portrait, see Sergeants' Group, p. 159.

The following were not present when the Platoon Photograph was taken, but see Supplementary Photographs on pp. 198—201.

Roll No.	Rank	Name	Roll No.	Rank	Name
11521	L.-Corpl.	Dovey.	11698	Private	Weir, J.
11615	,,	Mitchell.	11525	,,	Dixon, H.
11592	Private	Langton, B.	11624	,,	Newbrook, F. A.
11626	,,	Neild, E.	12730	,,	Shevlin, J.
11570	,,	Harrison, P. L.	11462	,,	Ashton, F.
11519	,,	Cummings, C. E.	11501	,,	Cartledge, J. A.
11564	,,	Greenwood, G.	11644	,,	Ramsbottom, F.
11678	,,	Taylor, A.	12669	,,	Ball, Jas.
11481	,,	Bowling, F.			

19th (Service) Battalion Manchester Regiment.
"B" COMPANY.

Officer Commanding Company -	Capt. H. Kennedy Birley.*
Second in Command - - -	Capt. C. Joyce.*
Company Sergeant Major - -	Grayburn, A. H.†
Company Quartermaster Sergeant -	Bush, G. W.†

PLATOON NO. V.

Platoon Commander - - -	Lieut. W. Boyd Orr.
Platoon Sergeant - - - -	Walters, F.

Roll No.	Rank and Name.	Roll No.	Rank and Name.
11873	L.-Sergt. Lane, F. G.	12582	Private Garvey, H.
11799	Corporal Durandeaux, R. F.	12623	,, Ward, T.
11833	L.-Corpl. Higgins, J.	12618	,, Orme, H.
11883	,, McGrath, B.	11756	,, Brierley, A.
11792	,, Dickinson, E.	11762	,, Bryan, C.
11895	Private Mounsey, P.	12589	,, Collins, J. B.
11939	,, Southworth, A.	11783	,, Davenport, T.
11864	,, Jones, B.	11791	,, Dickinson, W.
11790	,, Dickinson, H.	11868	,, Keatinge, H.
11970	,, Wood, J.	11869	,, Kettle, A.
11859	,, Ingham, H.	11974	,, Wright, H. A.
11944	,, Thompson, J.	11930	,, Smith, H.
11914	,, Race, A.	11852	,, Howard, T. H.
11916	,, Rhodes, C.	11853	,, Howarth, C. A.
11750	,, Boulton, S. F.	11891	,, Morris, A.
11782	,, Curzon, G.	11898	,, Norris, E.
11777	,, Cornes, N.	11900	,, Orme, F.
11740	,, Bates, W.	11901	,, Parkinson, J. R.
11796	,, Mullineaux, E.	11902	,, Partington, T.
11850	,, Hulme, I. W.	12625	,, Arnold, E.
12690	,, Rowell, G.	11801	,, Ellis, A.
12591	,, Shelton, J. R.		

* For portrait, see Officers' Group, p. 157.   † For Portrait, see Sergeants' Group, p. 159.

The following were not present when the Platoon Photograph was taken, but see Supplementary Photographs on pp. 198—201.

Roll No.	Rank and Name.	Roll No.	Rank and Name.
11797	L.-Corpl. Dolphin, R.	11912	Private Proctor, F.
11819	,, Greaves, J.	11888	,, Mellor, J.
11814	Private Gillbanks, W.	11774	,, Cookson, F.
11982	,, Parker, L.	11976	,, Yates, F.
11922	,, Ryan, J.	11741	,, Batting, E. A.
11910	,, Pilkington, A.	11816	,, Godsall, E.
11744	,, Bennett, L.	11965	,, Wiggings, C. A.
11749	,, Bold, H.	11884	,, McLeavy, H.
11728	,, Allcock, W.	11919	,, Rowlinson, W.
11862	,, Johnson, H.	11940	,, Snelgrove, H.
11875	,, Lawton, A. W.	11812	,, Gavin, E.
11863	,, Jolley, R.	11831	,, Head, B.

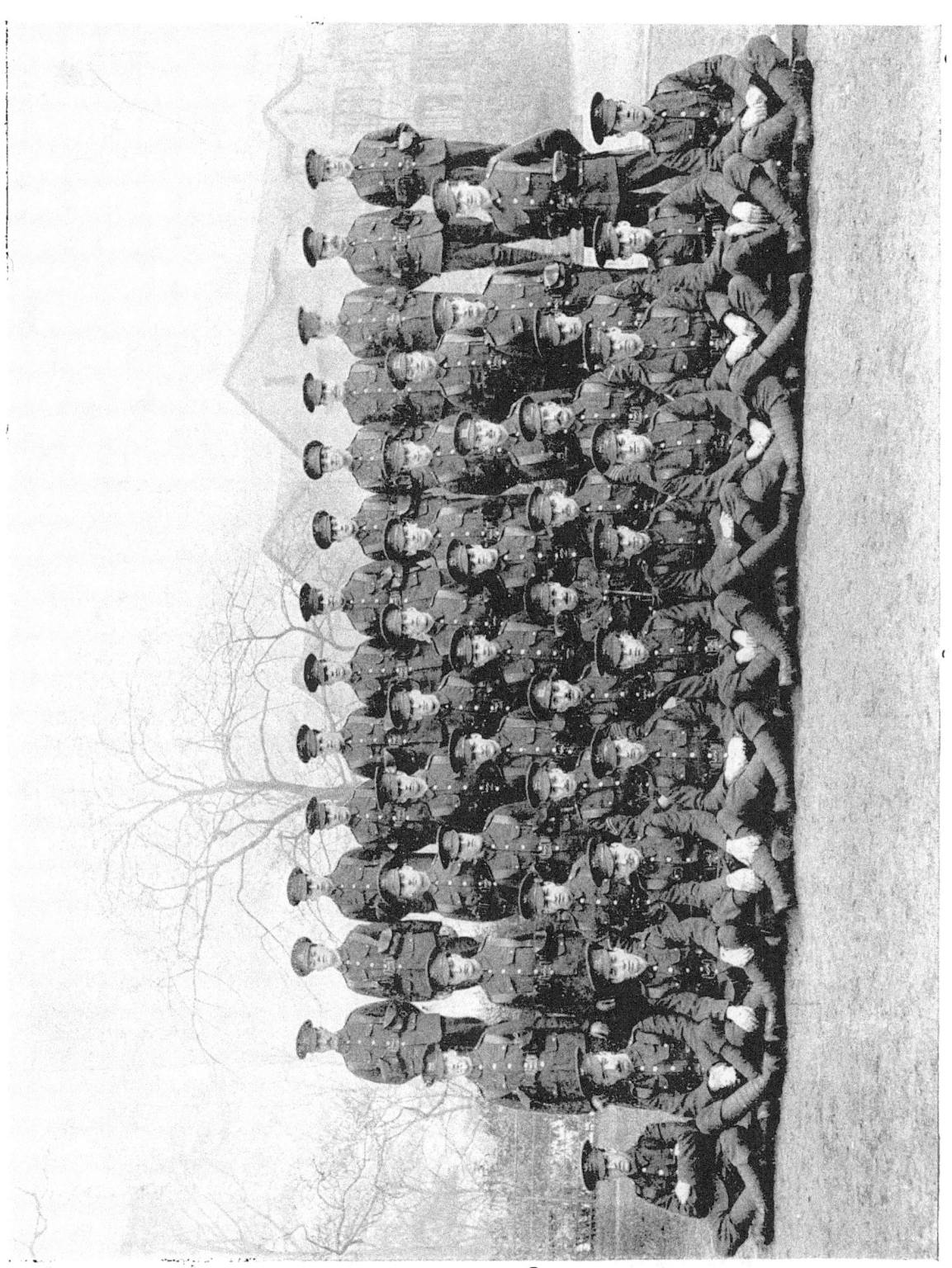

19th (Service) Battalion Manchester Regiment.

"B" COMPANY.

Officer Commanding Company	Capt. H. Kennedy Birley.*
Second in Command	Capt. C. Joyce.*
Company Sergeant Major	Grayburn, A. H.†
Company Quartermaster Sergeant	Bush, G. W.†

PLATOON NO. VI.

Platoon Commander	2nd Lieut. P. la T. Foster.
Platoon Sergeant	Entwistle, C. E.

Roll No.	Rank and Name.		Roll No.	Rank and Name.	
11979	Corporal	Ryder, T.	11849	Private	Horton, E.
11861	L.-Corpl.	Johnson, A.	11842	,,	Holland, H.
11784	,,	Davies, C.	11913	,,	Pugh, H.
11938	,,	Sutcliffe, R. H.	11933	,,	Smith, F.
12520	Private	Evans, R. L.	11918	,,	Robinson, L.
11806	,,	Finch, T.	11945	,,	Walker, O.
11830	,,	Haydock, H.	11948	,,	Warden, W. S.
11839	,,	Hiorns, A.	11953	,,	West, R.
11844	,,	Holmes, A. S.	11865	,,	Jones, E.
11920	,,	Rothwell, W.	12587	,,	Lippiett, J.
11921	,,	Rowbotham, J.	11882	,,	McGee, E.
11949	,,	Warren, D.	11787	,,	Dawson, W.
11957	,,	Whitehead, A.	11727	,,	Adshead, A.
11943	,,	Tench, W.	11761	,,	Bucklow, G. E.
11810	,,	Fury, J.	11788	,,	Derbyshire, J. C.
11858	,,	Hynes, J. J.	11817	,,	Gough, L.
11828	,,	Harrison, A.	11821	,,	Grimshaw, R. H.
11825	,,	Hall, W. H.	11887	,,	Meadows, S.
11820	,,	Griffiths, R.	11973	,,	Woore, P. E.
11771	,,	Chambers, A.	11897	,,	Newman, S.
11867	,,	Jones, J.	12530	,,	Statters, H.
11915	,,	Ratcliffe, H.	12528	,,	Travis, C.
11758	,,	Britton, J.	12616	,,	Kelly, A.
11778	,,	Cotton, W.	12620	,,	Murphy, F.
11789	,,	Derbyshire, L.	11766	,,	Burgess, C.

* For portrait, see Officers' Group, p. 157.   † For Portrait, see Sergeants' Group, p. 159.

Also on the Photograph : 2nd Lieut. N. H. Craston.
The following were not present when the Platoon Photograph was taken, but see Supplementary Photographs on pp. 198—201.

Roll No.	Rank and Name.		Roll No.	Rank and Name.	
12555	Sergeant	Dickenson, W.	11893	Private	Morrison, W.
11794	Private	Dixon, L. S.	11941	,,	Shone, J. H.
11785	,,	Davies, W.	11872	,,	Lambert, J.
11942	,,	Spence, J.	11960	,,	Williams, A.
11754	,,	Benson, J.	11730	,,	Andrews, R.

19th (Service) Battalion Manchester Regiment.

"B" COMPANY.

Officer Commanding Company -	Capt. H. Kennedy Birley.*
Second in Command - - -	Capt. C. Joyce.*
Company Sergeant Major - -	Grayburn, A. H.†
Company Quartermaster Sergeant -	Bush, G. W.†

PLATOON NO. VII.

Platoon Commander - - -	2nd Lieut. N. S. Ince.
Platoon Sergeant - - - -	Cooke, H. E.

Roll No.	Rank and Name.		Roll No.	Rank and Name.	
11937	Sergeant	Swindells, H. B.	11911	Private	Pollitt, O.
11739	Corporal	Barnes, B. M.	11980	,,	Robertshaw, A.
11907	,,	Perry, J. W.	11950	,,	Watson, G. E.
11880	,,	Loose, E. E.	11967	,,	Winterburn, C.
11733	L.-Corpl.	Ashburn, W. B.	12622	,,	Shaw, F. J.
11909	,,	Pilling, R.	11765	,,	Buerdsall, J. E.
11759	Private	Broadley, H.	11827	,,	Hargreave, A.
11811	,,	Garside, L.	12593	,,	Parkinson, E.
11846	,,	Holt, G.	11904	,,	Parsons, F. M.
11840	,,	Hobson, P.	11946	,,	Walker, L. S.
11860	,,	Jennings, F.	12592	,,	Wallis, G.
11908	,,	Pilkington, B. J.	11975	,,	Wynn, W. J.
11978	,,	Riley, H.	11732	,,	Armstrong, G. A.
11924	,,	Scholes, E.	11755	,,	Brady, G. A.
11929	,,	Smith, G. E.	11769	,,	Caldwell, C. W.
11968	,,	Woodings, E. J.	11773	,,	Cooke, W. H.
11969	,,	Woodruff, L.	11786	,,	Davies, E.
11986	,,	Thomas, G. W.	11826	,,	Hankey, T.
11987	,,	Thompson, H.	11841	,,	Holden, J.
11818	,,	Gough, Z.	11851	,,	Houghton, N.
11751	,,	Bottomley, J.	11855	,,	Hughes, W. C.
11780	,,	Crank, R. A.	11870	,,	Kirkham, H.
11815	,,	Gilman, J.	11885	,,	McWalter, W.
11835	,,	Hilditch, G.	11923	,,	Schofield, R.
11838	,,	Hipkins, H.	11928	,,	Smith, A.
11854	,,	Hughes, F.	11958	,,	Williamson, J. H.
11874	,,	Latham, C. W.	11988	,,	Sykes, E. C.
11881	,,	McDonald, F.	11746	,,	Billing, C. E.
11906	,,	Peers, A.			

* For portrait, see Officers' Group, p. 157. † For Portrait, see Sergeants' Group, p. 159.

The following were not present when the Platoon Photograph was taken, but see Supplementary Photographs on pp. 198—201.

Roll No.		Name	Roll No.		Name
11962	Private	Wilkinson, R. H.	11845	Private	Holt, J.
11770	,,	Cash, T. H.	11879	,,	Lomax, H.
11823	,,	Hall, L. G.	11934	,,	Street, A.

19th (Service) Battalion Manchester Regiment.

"B" COMPANY.

Officer Commanding Company -	Capt. H. Kennedy Birley.*
Second in Command - - -	Capt. C. Joyce.*
Company Sergeant Major - -	Grayburn, A. H.†
Company Quartermaster Sergeant -	Bush, G. W.

PLATOON NO. VIII.

Platoon Commander - - -	2nd Lieut. E. W. Mawdsley.
Platoon Sergeant - - - -	Wilson, L. E.

Roll No.	Rank and Name.	Roll No.	Rank and Name.
11857	L.-Sergt. Hunter, C. A.	11803	Private England, R. H.
11876	Corporal Leaver, H. C.	11869	,, Furness, R.
11569	L.-Corpl. Harmaman, J.	11813	,, Gibbons, W.
11754	,, Brandreth, Arthur.	11824	,, Hall, W.
11753	Private Brandreth, Albert.	11834	,, Highton, W.
11899	,, Andrews, A. W.	11832	,, Heywood, R.
11729	,, Allen, F.	11843	,, Hollos, F.
11737	,, Barlow, H.	12619	,, Hollos, E.
11742	,, Beckett, F.	11848	,, Hopwood, N.
11734	,, Baillie, W.	11836	,, Hilton, L.
11760	,, Brookes, W.	11847	,, Holt, J.
11805	,, Bagaley, E. G.	11871	,, Lamb, J. H.
11761	,, Brown, E.	11894	,, Morton, H. R.
11743	,, Bennett, F. H.	12526	,, McNicholl, J. W.
11738	,, Barnes, T.	12594	,, Mottershead, S. S.
11747	,, Binks, F. R.	11977	,, Nuttall, N.
12527	,, Brierley, J. H.	12525	,, Robinson, A.
11736	,, Barlow, H.	11925	,, Scholes, P.
11763	,, Bryce, F.	11935	,, Stromberg, H. C.
11768	,, Brownbill, R. H.	11926	,, Sidebottom, A.
11776	,, Cooper, F. G.	11984	,, Thorpe, H.
11781	,, Crooks, S.	11955	,, Whitfield, G.
11779	,, Cottam, A.	11981	,, Wheatcroft, F. H.
11805	,, Evans, F.	11954	,, Wheatcroft, S.
11802	,, Ellis, P. W.	11956	,, Whitehead, J.

* For portrait, see Officers' Group, p. 157. † For Portrait, see Sergeants' Group, p. 159.

The following were not present when the Platoon Photograph was taken, but see Supplementary Photographs on pp. 198—201.

Roll No.	Rank	Name	Roll No.	Rank	Name
11899	Corporal	Ollerenshaw, H.	11890	Private	Moran, J.
12596	Private	Brown, G. B.	12523	,,	Farrell, J. W.
11757	,,	Brindle, H.	11856	,,	Hulme, J. H.
11796	,,	Dolan, L.	11877	,,	Lingard, J. M.
11932	,,	Smith, H.			

19th (Service) Battalion Manchester Regiment.

"C" COMPANY.

Officer Commanding Company -	Capt. W. S. Cunliffe.*
Second in Command - - -	Lieut. G. Leresche.*
Company Sergeant Major - -	Buchan, J. B.†
Company Quartermaster Sergeant -	Charlton, T.

PLATOON NO. IX.

Platoon Commander - - -	2nd Lieut. F. Henshall.
Platoon Sergeant - - - -	Evers, H.

Roll No.	Rank and Name.	Roll No.	Rank and Name.
12194	Sergeant Rosenberg, A.	12089	Private Grierson, R.
12033	L.-Sergt. Carter, S.	12008	,, Bayout, H.
12103	Corporal Heywood, J.	12204	,, Singleton, H.
12227	L.-Corpl. Tyson, F.	12028	,, Burke, R.
12017	,, Bowen, T. A.	12208	,, Spence, S.
12162	,, Norbury, L.	12053	,, Crossley, W.
12091	Private Hall, W. E. J.	12055	,, Crowe, W.
12574	,, Fletcher, J. R.	12573	,, Brierley, W.
12012	,, Atkinson, W. P.	12016	,, Bootham, J.
12134	,, Lockwood, J.	12116	,, Hughes, W. L.
12120	,, Jay, J.	12224	,, Toole, W.
12056	,, Crowe, A. G.	12113	,, Hope, G. W.
12172	,, Parkin, L.	12171	,, Pattinson, E.
12585	,, Gardiner, F.	12598	,, Allen, E.
12100	,, Heaviside, A.	12182	,, Postles, H.
12148	,, Miller, A.	12575	,, Bonham, J.
12581	,, Broadhurst, W.	12108	,, Hodgkinson, H.
12249	,, Womack, F.	12659	,, Hodkinson, H.
12003	,, Atkinson, W.	12230	,, Walker, G.
12110	,, Holmes, H.	12169	,, Orr, F.
12112	,, Holt, E. J.	12102	,, Heywood, F. B.
12209	,, Spencer, R.	12092	,, Halstead, A.
12154	,, Morton, H.	12107	,, Hodgkinson, R. J.
12129	,, Knighton, R. D.	12231	,, Walker, H.
12043	,, Condcliffe, S.	12147	,, Miller, J.
12007	,, Bardsley, E.	12074	,, Evans, G. E.
12001	,, Amatt, A.	12228	,, Varley, A.
12654	,, Marshall, J. R.		

* For portrait, see Officers' Group, p. 157. † For Portrait, see Sergeants' Group, p. 159.

The following were not present when the Platoon Photograph was taken, but see Supplementary Photographs on pp. 198—201.

Roll No.	Rank and Name.	Roll No.	Rank and Name.
12185	L.-Corpl. Plant, H.	12128	Private Kennedy, G.
12000	Private Amatt, J. R.	12137	,, Lyth, L.
11998	,, Anderson, P.	12138	,, Marsden, B.
12075	,, Dale, C.	12200	,, Skeldon, H.
12118	,, Jackson, J.	12531	,, Thompson, E. R.

19th (Service) Battalion Manchester Regiment.

"C" COMPANY.

Officer Commanding Company -	Capt. W. S. CUNLIFFE.*
Second in Command - - -	Lieut. G. LERESCHE.*
Company Sergeant Major - -	BUCHAN, J. B.†
Company Quartermaster Sergeant -	CHARLTON, T.†

PLATOON NO. X.

Platoon Commander - - -	2nd Lieut. J. B. HIGGINS.
Platoon Sergeant - - - -	HOLBORN, E.

Roll No.	Rank and Name.		Roll No.	Rank and Name.	
12059	Corporal	DARBY, W.	12655	Private	MANSFIELD, W.
11996	,,	ALDCROFT, J.	11999	,,	ANDREWS, J.
12174	,,	PEARSON, J. C.	12186	,,	PRICE, G.
12099	L.-Corpl.	HEATON, M.	12177	,,	PHILLIPS, R.
12127	,,	JONES, W. A.	12253	,,	WYRILL, H. A.
12232	Private	WALKER, H.	12236	,,	WALSH, J.
12238	,,	WELBY, J.	12176	,,	PHILLIPS, R.
12605	,,	TAYLOR, F.	12197	,,	ROYSE, A.
12025	,,	BROWN, R.	12009	,,	BENSON, W.
12151	,,	MITCHELL, A.	12117	,,	IRWIN, A.
12139	,,	McDONALD, H.	12230	,,	TATTERSALL, J.
12206	,,	SMITH, A.	12246	,,	WILSON, C.
12136	,,	LYNCH, J.	12161	,,	NICHOLLS, F.
12154	,,	MIDDLETON, E.	12046	,,	COOTE, H. P.
12049	,,	COPE, R.	12109	,,	HOLDSWORTH, J.
12233	,,	WALKER, H.	12065	,,	DENTON, H.
12184	,,	POWNALL, W.	12079	,,	FOLEY, T.
12239	,,	WHITELEY, A.	12064	,,	DENT, A.
12093	,,	HARDING, W.	12051	,,	CROSS, F.
12202	,,	SHIERS, C. E.	12164	,,	OAKSWORTH, A.
12030	,,	CALVERLEY, F. H.	12188	,,	RATHBONE, T.
12543	,,	BURDEN, S. J.	12187	,,	RUMNEY, R.
12179	,,	PLATT, L.			

* For portrait, see Officers' Group, p. 157. † For Portrait, see Sergeants' Group, p. 159.

The following were not present when the Platoon Photograph was taken, but see Supplementary Photographs on pp. 198—201.

Roll No.	Rank	Name	Roll No.	Rank	Name
12022	Private	BRADBURY, F.	12101	Private	HEYWOOD, A.
12040	,,	CLEGG, A.	12105	,,	HILTON, S.
12034	,,	CARTER, W.	12132	,,	LEACH, G.
12031	,,	CARWARDINE, W.	12143	,,	McKIL, W. A.
12082	,,	GILLIGAN, J.	12153	,,	MORAN, T.
12084	,,	GLAZEBROOK, A.	12159	,,	MURRAY, A.
12197	,,	HEALD, G.	12221	,,	THISTLETHWAITE, E.

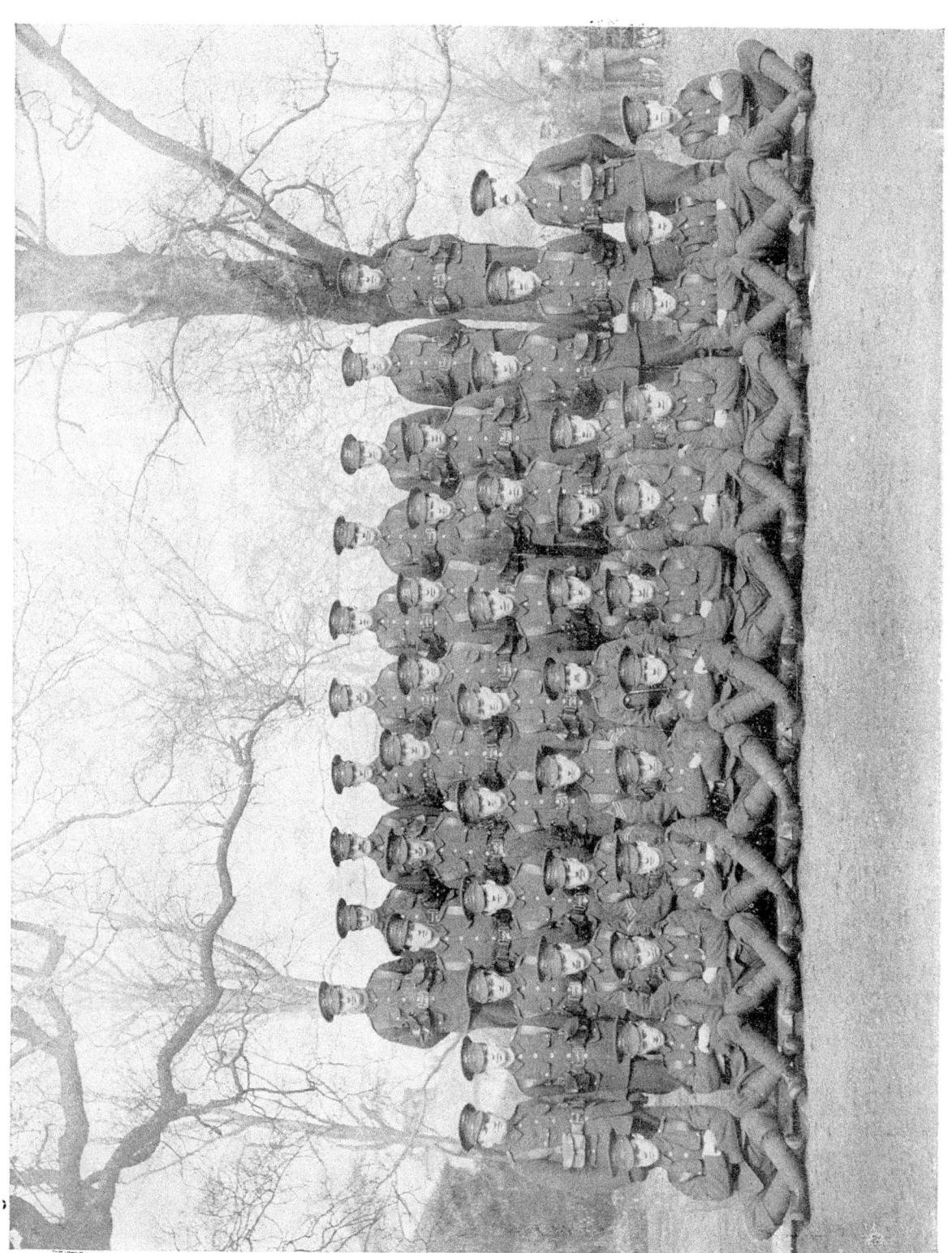

19th (Service) Battalion Manchester Regiment.

"C" COMPANY.

Officer Commanding Company - Capt. W. S. Cunliffe.*
Second in Command - - - Lieut. G. Leresche.*
Company Sergeant Major - - Buchan, J. B.†
Company Quartermaster Sergeant - Charlton, T.†

PLATOON NO. XI.

Platoon Commander - - - 2nd Lieut. A. W. Atkinson.
Platoon Sergeant - - - - Beswick, C.

Roll No.	Rank and Name.		Roll No.	Rank and Name.	
12123	Sergeant	Jones, J.	12063	Private	Dawes, N.
12018	Corporal	Bowman, T.	12215	,,	Stretch, T.
12029	L.-Corpl.	Burton, T.	12111	,,	Holt, G. L.
12180	,,	Poizer, S.	11679	,,	Airey, S.
12157	,,	Minor, F. D.	12085	,,	Goodfellow, S.
12226	Private	Turner, J. W.	12644	,,	Traynor, D.
12251	,,	Wroe, S.	12234	,,	Ward, T.
12250	,,	Wormold, A.	12038	,,	Chester, S.
12244	,,	Wilkinson, F.	12124	,,	Jones, E. E.
12454	,,	Sutton, W.	12090	,,	Hague, H.
11997	,,	Allen, A.	12023	,,	Broadhurst, J.
12087	,,	Gray, F. R.	12122	,,	Johnston, A.
12173	,,	Parker, F.	12533	,,	Johnson, A.
12077	,,	Fletcher, H.	12615	,,	Levitt, G.
12252	,,	Wright, C.	12069	,,	Duxbury, J.
12303	,,	Siddall, A. V.	12005	,,	Bannister, F.
12095	,,	Harrison, R.	12165	,,	Ogden, J. D.
12689	,,	Garvan, E.	12010	,,	Bibby, F.
12010	,,	Chapman, J.	12550	,,	Ogden, P.
12572	,,	Spear, C.	12072	,,	Evans, A.
12047	,,	Coop, J. W.	12046	,,	Coop, H. P.
12125	,,	Jones, G. E.	12060	,,	Davenport, C.
12024	,,	Blaydon, E.			

* For portrait, see Officers' Group, p. 157. † For Portrait, see Sergeants' Group, p. 159.

The following were not present when the Platoon Photograph was taken, but see Supplementary Photographs on pp. 198—201.

Roll No.	Rank	Name	Roll No.	Rank	Name
12190	Corporal	Rigg, R.	12192	Private	Roe, W.
12006	Private	Baldwin, A.	12196	,,	Rowbotham, W.
12068	,,	Duke, J. H.	12198	,,	Sands, W.
12140	,,	McEwen, J. A.	12218	,,	Tait, W.
12191	,,	Robinson, B.			

19th (Service) Battalion Manchester Regiment.
"C" COMPANY.

Officer Commanding Company -	Capt. W. S. Cunliffe.*
Second in Command - -	Lieut. G. Leresche.*
Company Sergeant Major -	Buchan, J. B.
Company Quartermaster Sergeant -	Charlton, T.†

PLATOON NO. XII.

Platoon Commander - - -	2nd Lieut. H. E. Turner.
Platoon Sergeant - - - -	Spears, J.

Roll No.	Rank and Name.		Roll No.	Rank and Name.	
12245	Corporal	Winnings, R. G.	12141	Private	McEwen, J. W.
12166	,,	Ogden, W. L.	12223	,,	Tommins, W.
12015	L.-Corpl.	Boon, H.	12210	,,	Stansby, W. W.
12152	,,	Montgomery, M.	12658	,,	Jackson, R. L.
12071	,,	Edwards, G. E.	12130	,,	Larmour, W.
12648	Private	McGhie, A.	12181	,,	Pollard, T.
12121	,,	Jay, J.	12058	,,	Dale, B.
12650	,,	Woolridge, G.	12115	,,	Hewes, W. C.
12032	,,	Carruthers, G.	12061	,,	Davies, J.
12080	,,	Foster, J. W.	12170	,,	Owen, J.
12160	,,	Mycock, J.	12615	,,	Levitt, G.
12240	,,	Whitehead, J.	12217	,,	Sweetman, H.
12114	,,	Hover, P.	12243	,,	Willcocks, C.
12135	,,	Lolley, J.	12035	,,	Carroll, P.
12078	,,	Flindle, H.	12657	,,	Dixon, A.
12158	,,	Muir, L.	12642	,,	Ferguson, C. D.
12578	,,	Green, J.	12627	,,	Savage, E.
12142	,,	McKail, D.	12193	,,	Ross, T.
12045	,,	Cooke, R.	12546	,,	Irwin, N.
12144	,,	McNamara, G.	12011	,,	Blaney, H.
12019	,,	Bradshaw, H. C.	12131	,,	Lawrence, J.
12205	,,	Slater, R.	12027	,,	Bunting, E.
12576	,,	Cliffe, G.	12076	,,	Fairclough, F.
12646	,,	Ross, T.	12004	,,	Bainbridge, A.
12213	,,	Stonehewer, J. H.			

* For portrait, see Officers' Group, p. 157.   † For Portrait, see Sergeants' Group, p. 159.

The following were not present when the Platoon Photograph was taken, but see Supplementary Photographs on pp. 198—201.

Roll No.	Rank	Name	Roll No.	Rank	Name
12073	Sergeant	Entwistle, J.	12155	Private	Moss, F.
12020	Private	Bray, J.	12199	,,	Sandford, G.
12577	,,	Brockbank, F.	12201	,,	Shephard, T.
12042	,,	Collinge, W.	12522	,,	Thompson, S.
12062	,,	Davies, E.	12222	,,	Thorp, F.
12066	,,	Dodd, E.	12248	,,	Woolley, J.
12603	,,	Haslam, F.	12242	,,	Whitfield, S.
12106	,,	Hirst, R.			

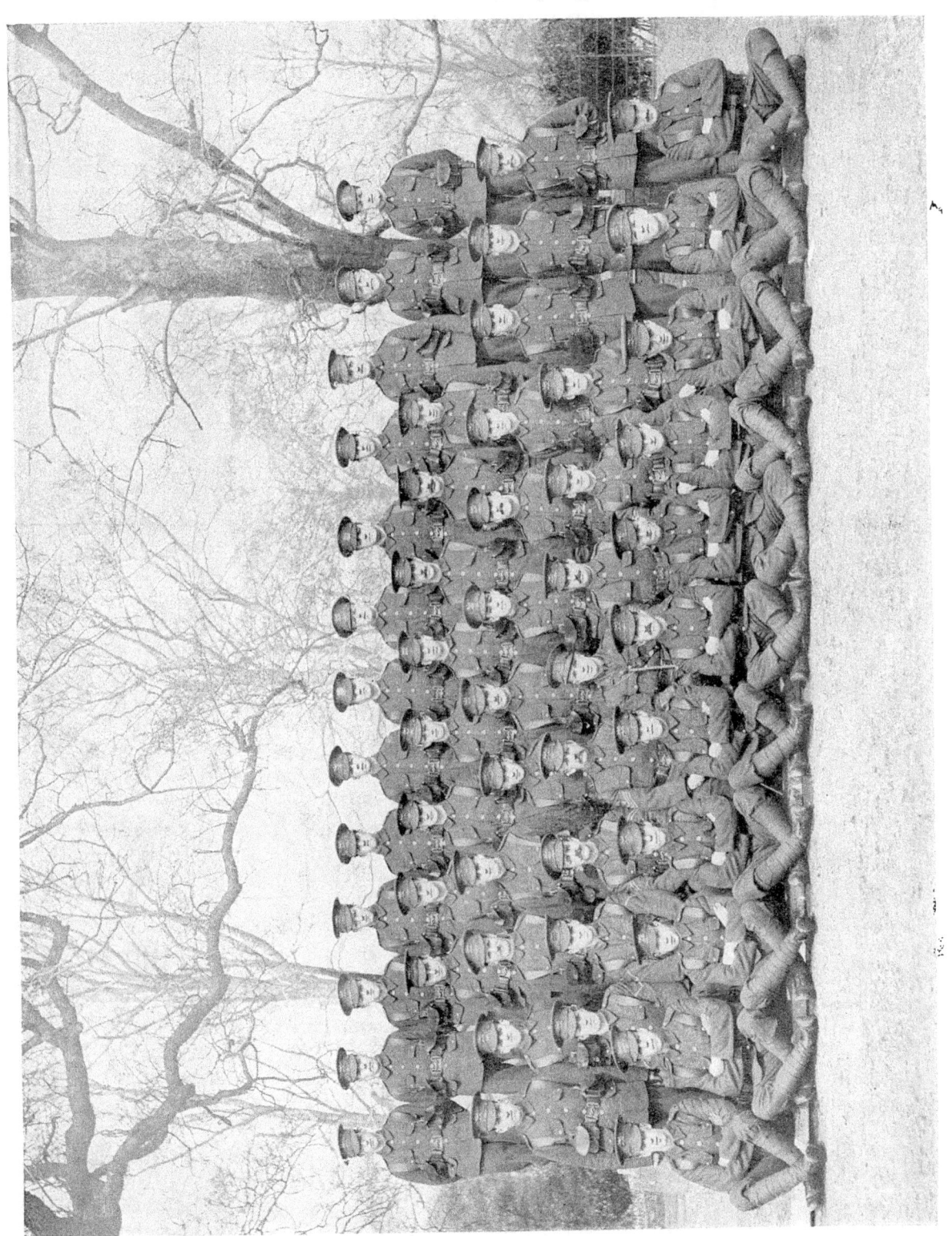

19th (Service) Battalion Manchester Regiment.
"D" COMPANY.

Officer Commanding Company -	Major R. J. Allen.*
Second in Command - - -	Lieut. F. W. Royle.*
Company Sergeant Major - -	Lane, T.†
Company Quartermaster Sergeant -	Grimshaw, G. F.†

PLATOON NO. XIII.

Platoon Commander - - -	2nd Lieut. A. N. Solly.
Platoon Sergeant - - - -	Comstive, W. R.

12281	Sergeant	Bedford, P. W.	12369	Private	Howarth, H.
12472	Corporal	Thackray, E. C.	12547	,,	Jackson, H.
12433	,,	Pearce, W. T.	12570	,,	Johnson, W. C.
12394	L.-Corpl.	Lea, P. H.	12565	,,	Jepson, S.
12348	,,	Griffiths, A.	12288	,,	Kirk, H.
12469	,,	Tomlinson, A. C.	12401	,,	Lambert, W.
12548	Private	Abbott, C.	12403	,,	Loynds, H.
12292	,,	Bomford, A. R.	12564	,,	Lord, H. J.
12291	,,	Bowker, J.	12400	,,	Lawson, A.
12289	,,	Brereton, W.	12414	,,	Moorhouse, E.
12305	,,	Connell, E.	12413	,,	Masters, A.
12309	,,	Calverley, J.	12435	,,	Powell, G. W.
12300	,,	Coupe, S.	12434	,,	Phillips, A.
12308	,,	Campion, W.	12443	,,	Read, H. E. M.
12304	,,	Cowburn, A. G.	12563	,,	Rodgers, A. E.
12307	,,	Clark, J.	12458	,,	Smith, H.
12320	,,	Davies, H. O.	12649	,,	Smethurst, C. W.
12318	,,	Dean, A.	12455	,,	Standring, W.
12321	,,	Dakin, W. S.	12621	,,	Sawyer, J.
12319	,,	Dawson, W.	12457	,,	Snow, T. W.
12326	,,	Ennever, H. W.	12626	,,	Spragg, W. T.
12624	,,	Gee, J.	12632	,,	Thornton, J. R.
12544	,,	Gregory, F.	12549	,,	Tomlinson, G.
12373	,,	Harper, H. H.	12475	,,	Unwin, H.
12368	,,	Harper, W. P.	12062	,,	Williams, G.
12562	,,	Hanvey, D.	12496	,,	Wood, W.
12371	,,	Hunt, E. H.	12492	,,	Watts, R.
12627	,,	Hill, S. H.	12494	,,	Wilson, J. L.
12370	,,	Hoffmann, W.	12628	,,	Webster, G.

* For portrait, see Officers' Group, p. 157. † For Portrait, see Sergeants' Group, p. 159.

The following were not present when the Platoon Photograph was taken, but see Supplementary Photographs on pp. 198—201.

12507	Sergeant	Wilson, S.	12491	Private	Watts, E. C.
11617	L.-Corpl.	Mowatt, H. M.	12495	,,	Woodyear, W. P.
12290	Private	Brookes, W.	12509	,,	Walker, A. C.
12347	,,	George, F. H.	12352	,,	Gunby, J.
12351	,,	Greener, W.	12412	,,	McClusky, W.
12379	,,	Jackson, J. A.	12349	,,	Grisenthwaite, W.
12380	,,	Jones, S.	12389	,,	Kellock, G.
12402	,,	Litherland, W.	12317	,,	Dugdale, D.
12420	,,	Oxley, G. A.			

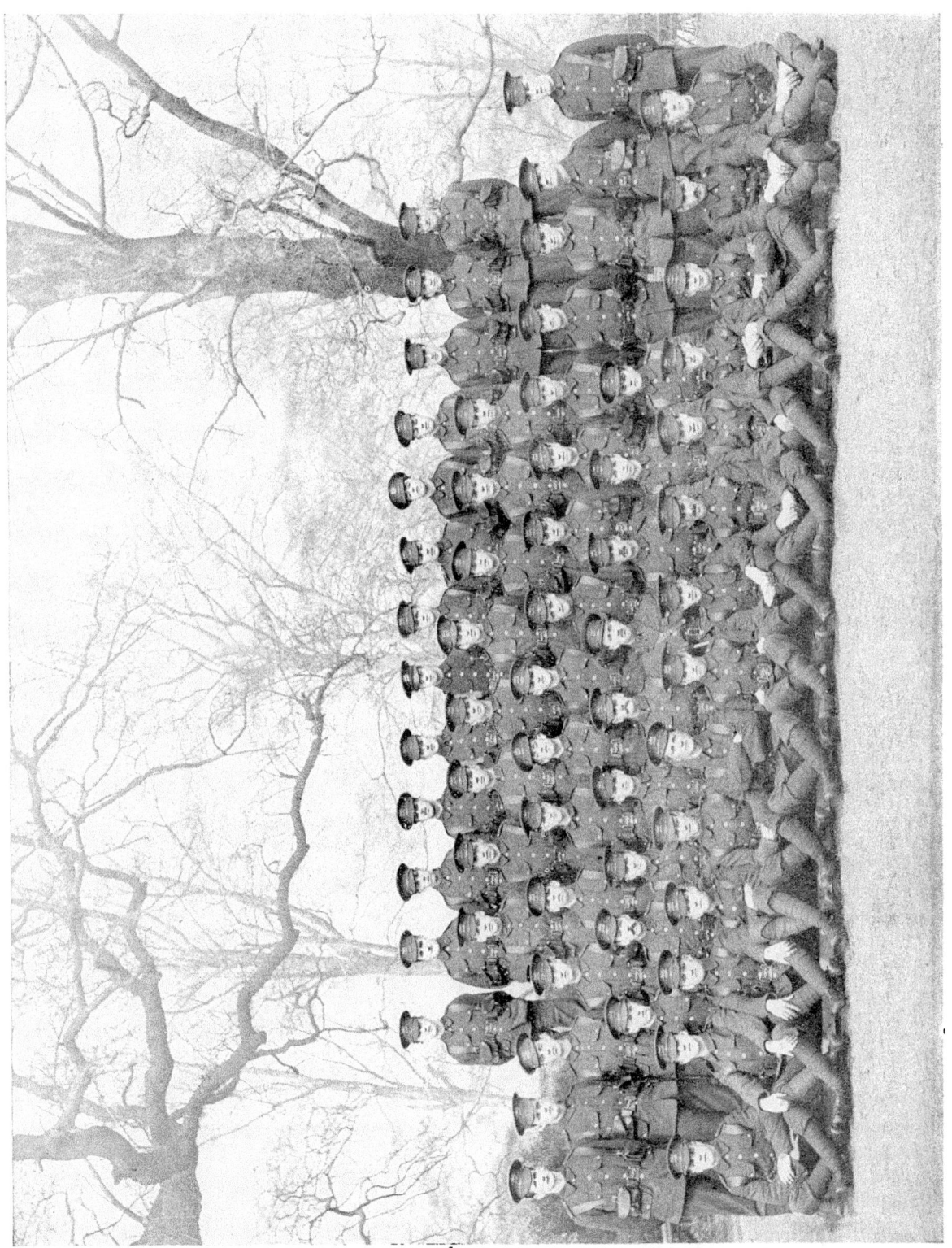

19th (Service) Battalion Manchester Regiment,

"D" COMPANY.

Officer Commanding Company -	Major R. J. Allen.
Second in Command - - -	Lieut. F. W. Royle.
Company Sergeant Major - -	Lane, T.
Company Quartermaster Sergeant -	Grimshaw, G. F.

PLATOON NO. XIV.

Platoon Commander - - -	Lieut. J. A. Caldwell.
Platoon Sergeant - - - -	Milner, A. B.

Roll No.	Rank and Name.		Roll No.	Rank and Name.	
12255	Sergeant	Almond, J.	12398	Private	Lomas, W.
12369	L.-Sergt.	Hubbard, H.	12396	,,	Lamb, W.
12397	Corporal	Lockyear, H. E.	12410	,,	Massey, S.
12364	L.-Corpl.	Harrop, S. M.	12385	,,	King, O.
12285	,,	Briggs, E.	12419	,,	Owen, C.
12259	Private	Armsby, E.	12556	,,	Parry, C. J.
12288	,,	Burgess, L. S.	12432	,,	Pilkington, L.
12283	,,	Blundell, F.	12431	,,	Parkinson, G.
12286	,,	Burke, W.	12446	,,	Royston, A.
12287	,,	Blears, F.	12445	,,	Rowe, A.
12284	,,	Booth, F.	12460	,,	Siddall, N.
12282	,,	Burrough, A.	12463	,,	Stoneheuer, A. J. R.
12301	,,	Coope, F.	12633	,,	Switzer, J. W.
12302	,,	Courtney, J.	12462	,,	Spink, E.
12303	,,	Cully, J.	12461	,,	Snowden, K.
12315	,,	Dawber, J. O. S.	12474	,,	Toft, W. S.
12620	,,	Duckworth, S.	12471	,,	Thacker, E.
12329	,,	Francis, W.	12484	,,	Ward, E. G.
12343	,,	Grant, H.	12490	,,	Wright, S.
12344	,,	Greaves, G.	12485	,,	Whitworth, P.
12345	,,	Gwyther, E.	12486	,,	Wilkinson, W.
12365	,,	Halstead, J.	12489	,,	Wright, J.
12366	,,	Heathergill, C.	12728	,,	Dewhurst, G. A.
12386	,,	Kinder, B. A.	12293	,,	Carr, J.
12399	,,	Looker, B.	12447	,,	Shoreman, J.

The following were not present when the Platoon Photograph was taken, but see Supplementary Photographs on pp. 198—201.

Roll No.	Rank and Name.		Roll No.	Rank and Name.	
12688	Sergeant	Crosby.	12387	Private	Knibbs, F.
12168	Corporal	Oldham, C.	12416	,,	Noble, B.
11696	L.-Corpl.	Warren, J.	12568	,,	Spurr, S. S.
12629	Private	Booth, W.	12470	,,	Taylor, F.
12560	,,	Burrow, W. T.	12488	,,	Woodcock, C. E.
12300	,,	Cook, E.	12483	,,	Ward, F.
12316	,,	Dilworth, E.	12559	,,	Walton, H.
12534	,,	Holt, G.	12487	,,	Wilson, E.

19th (Service) Battalion Manchester Regiment.

"D" COMPANY.

Officer Commanding Company	-	Major R. J. ALLEN.*
Second in Command	- -	Lieut. F. W. ROYLE.*
Company Sergeant Major	-	LANE, T.†
Company Quartermaster Sergeant	-	GRIMSHAW, G. F.†

PLATOON NO. XV.

Platoon Commander	- - -	2nd Lieut. W. R. SMITH.
Platoon Sergeant	- - -	THOMAS, A.

Roll No.	Rank and Name.		Roll No.	Rank and Name.	
12312	Sergeant	DEAR, S.	12358	Private	HIGGINBOTTOM, J. L.
12429	Corporal	PATERSON, F.	12376	,,	JEFFREYS, F.
12363	L.-Corpl.	HARRIS, J.	12383	,,	KETTLEWELL, F. J.
12506	Private	ASHTON, J. E.	12384	,,	KINDERS, C.
12269	,,	BYRNE, W. H.	12553	,,	LARKIN, J.
12567	,,	BAKER, R.	12395	,,	LAMBERT, L. N.
12258	,,	BELL, RD.	12392	,,	LOGAN, E. B.
12270	,,	BURTON, G.	12409	,,	McGLYNN, F.
12273	,,	BLAIR, W.	12545	,,	MIGHALL, HY.
12557	,,	COPESTAKE, W.	12407	,,	MACKCRETH, F.
12295	,,	CRAVEN, A. R.	12406	,,	MITCHELL, W.
12294	,,	CRAWSHAW, J.	12418	,,	OLDHAM, A.
12299	,,	CALDWELL, W. H.	12415	,,	NEFF, C.
12311	,,	DOWNING, G. W.	12428	,,	PEARSON, S. S.
12637	,,	DANIELS, F.	12427	,,	PENNY, H.
12314	,,	DAVIES, G.	12552	,,	PRICKETT, J. E. O.
12323	,,	ELSBY, W.	12441	,,	REGAN, W.
12322	,,	EDWARDS, N.	12439	,,	RUSSELL, M.
12327	,,	FRENCH, E.	12440	,,	ROWLEY, H. R.
12326	,,	FOX, M.	12442	,,	REID, A.
12328	,,	FENTON, E. S.	12538	,,	SHARPLES, W. B.
12341	,,	GATE, F.	12458	,,	SMITH, E.
12334	,,	GREAVES, H.	12453	,,	SALTER, F.
12337	,,	GREEN, C. B.	12467	,,	THOMAS, D.
12636	,,	GOADBY, C.	12479	,,	WOODRUFF, E. V.
12361	,,	HANCOCK, J.	12491	,,	WATTS, C.
12359	,,	HEALEY, C. W.	12480	,,	WILDGOOSE, J.
12362	,,	HAZE, G. A.	12477	,,	WILLIAMS, L.

* For portrait, see Officers' Group, p. 157.   † For Portrait, see Sergeants' Group, p. 159.

The following were not present when the Platoon Photograph was taken, but see Supplementary Photographs on pp. 198—201.

Roll No.	Rank	Name	Roll No.	Rank	Name
12276	Corporal	BELL, R.	12375	Private	JEVONS, R.
12277	L.-Corpl.	BATTELL, J. T.	12377	,,	JAMESON, R. W.
11493	,,	BRUCE, W. S.	12635	,,	KNOWLES, D.
12298	Private	CHALMERS, C.	12464	,,	TURNER, J. E.
12296	,,	CHADAWAY, G.	12478	,,	WILSON, W.
12340	,,	GAVIN, A.			

19th (Service) Battalion Manchester Regiment.
"D" COMPANY.

Officer Commanding Company -	Major R. J. Allen.*
Second in Command - - -	Lieut. F. W. Royle.*
Company Sergeant Major - -	Lane, T.†
Company Quartermaster Sergeant -	Grimshaw, G. F.†

PLATOON NO. XVI.

Platoon Commander - - -	2nd Lieut. B. La T. Foster.
Platoon Sergeant - - - -	Jutton, H. C.

Roll No.	Rank and Name.		Roll No.	Rank and Name.	
12457	Sergeant	Mason, B.	12641	Private	Jessop, F.
12260	Corporal	Andrews, J.	12374	,,	Jones, A.
12408	,,	Moreland, E. R.	12534	,,	Jones, A.
12353	,,	Hodges, J. W.	12639	,,	Kelly, T.
12279	,,	Backhouse, C. F.	12539	,,	Kirkman, J.
12278	Private	Batty, A.	12382	,,	Knowles, G.
12537	,,	Brown, J. L.	12390	,,	Lowry, W.
12264	,,	Blinkhorn, C. F.	12393	,,	Lidbetter, A. E.
12266	,,	Bryan, T. A.	12536	,,	Lucas, R.
12275	,,	Boyle, J. L.	12405	,,	McAvoy, W.
12272	,,	Buckley, R. L.	12423	,,	Poyser, C. A.
12271	,,	Burrow, T. H.	12424	,,	Parker, T.
12297	,,	Chadwick, C. S.	12569	,,	Purkis, M. J.
12313	,,	Dempsey, E. F.	12430	,,	Parker, S. E. C.
12310	,,	Diggle, H.	12437	,,	Roberts, S.
12324	,,	Eckersley, A. J.	12571	,,	Robinson, J. K.
12535	,,	Edwards, G.	12551	,,	Rowlinson, J. H.
12330	,,	Gabriel, R.	12542	,,	Radcliffe, E.
12339	,,	Gordon, P. N.	12450	,,	Seddon, J. H.
12342	,,	Gledhill, L. C.	12451	,,	Settle, F.
12333	,,	Glover, P.	12449	,,	Snelson, G.
12338	,,	Gorton, W.	12466	,,	Tinker, J.
12640	,,	Horrocks, F.	12638	,,	Webb, S. C.
12360	,,	Hatton, Hy.	12482	,,	Walker, H. H.
12710	,,	Holmes, P. H.	12497	,,	Yarwood, F.
12356	,,	Hodson, W.	12476	,,	Wollen, A. A.

* For portrait, see Officers' Group, p. 157.   † For Portrait, see Sergeants' Group, p. 159.

The following were not present when the Platoon Photograph was taken, but see Supplementary Photographs on pp. 198—201.

Roll No.	Rank	Name	Roll No.	Rank	Name
12265	L.-Corpl.	Birtles, O.	12378	Private	Jennings, W.
12261	Private	Ashworth, A.	12391	,,	Llewellyn, N.
12263	,,	Arnold, J. H.	12561	,,	Luzar, L.
12274	,,	Bogle, D.	12425	,,	Platt, H.
12498	,,	Dalton, J.	12438	,,	Ridgeway, W. R.
12540	,,	Doonan, W. J.	12541	,,	Roberts, S.
12335	,,	Garrard, E.	12436	,,	Rogers, W. H.
12332	,,	Glover, H. J.	12465	,,	Tate, C.
12355	,,	Hurdle, G.			

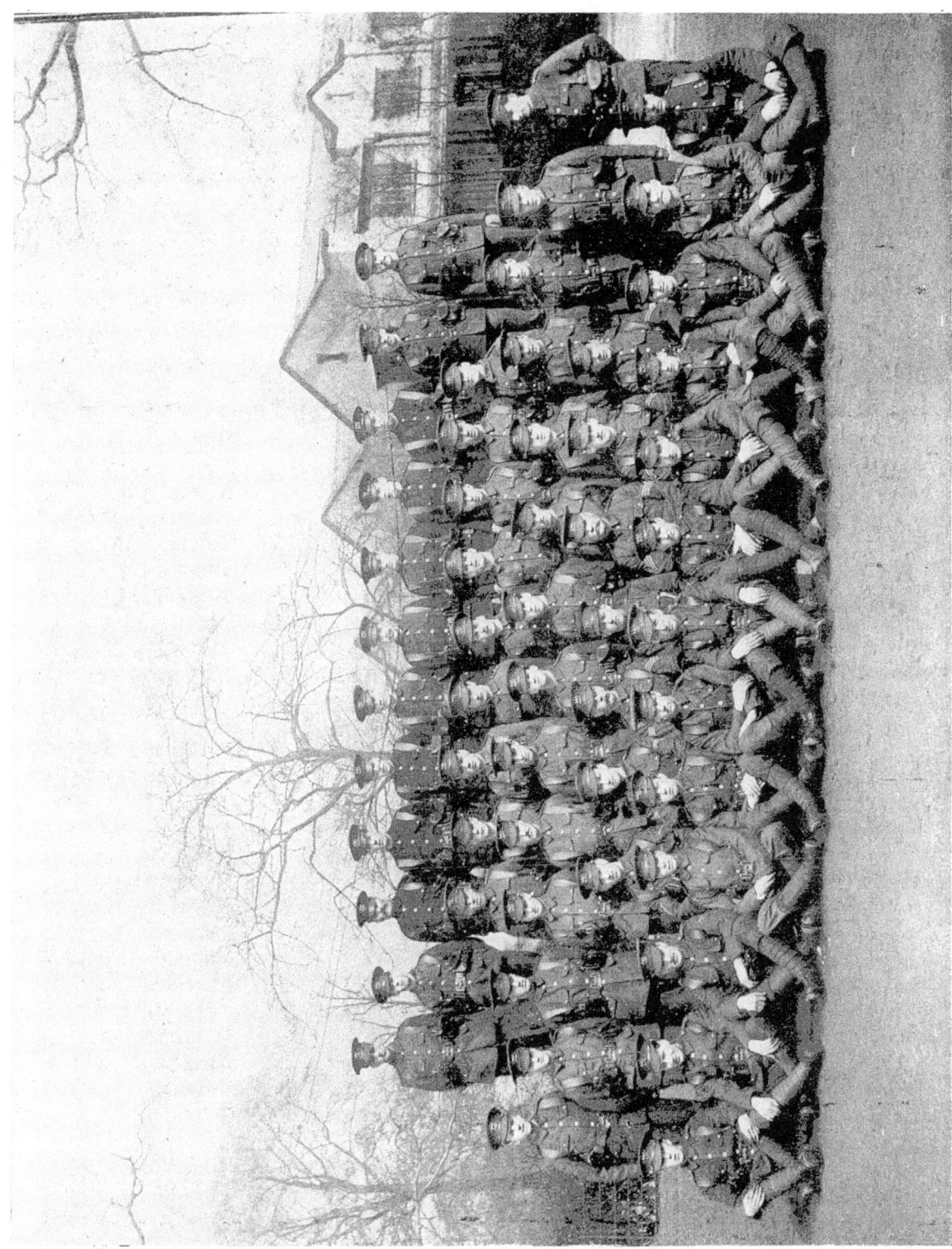

19th (Service) Battalion Manchester Regiment.
"E" COMPANY.

Officer Commanding Company - Capt. C. G. AGNEW.*
Company Sergeant Major - - NUTTALL, F.
Company Quartermaster Sergeant - DUCKWORTH, H. H.†

PLATOON NO. XVII.

Platoon Commander - - - 2nd Lieut. L. A. CHADWICK.

Roll No.	Rank and Name.		Roll No.	Rank and Name.	
12098	L.-Corpl.	HEALEY, R.	12757	Private	TITLEY, F.
12758	Private	CONROY, J.	12765	,,	CARNEY, E.
12683	,,	WILKINSON, J.	12788	,,	WARD, J. C.
12759	,,	SEVILLE, J.	12797	,,	BANNERMAN, C.
12833	,,	WOOD, W.	12793	,,	BUTLER, W.
12762	,,	BRIGGS, W.	12777	,,	BEAMISH, J.
12748	,,	KILROY, D.	12787	,,	BUCKLEY, J.
12828	,,	HANNABY.	12781	,,	MOLLOY, J.
12696	,,	SELBY.	12680	,,	WRIGHT.
12747	,,	RODGERS, G.	12774	,,	SMITH, T.
12686	,,	HOPKINS, T.	12760	,,	CLAYTON, A.
12785	,,	WILLIAMS, P.	12673	,,	SMITH.
12773	,,	ASQUITH, A.	12672	,,	CHARLTON, W.
12780	,,	LYON, A.	12753	,,	SKINKIS, S.
12837	,,	WELSH, J.	12771	,,	TAYLOR, F.
12792	,,	HUDSON, J.	12756	,,	HUGHES, J.
12783	,,	TURNER, N.	12736	,,	JONES, R.
12519	,,	LIVESEY, A.	12732	,,	BELLFIELD, R.
12211	,,	STANWAY, B.	12745	,,	JOHNSON, B.
11985	,,	TIVEY, J. C.	12791	,,	DEARDEN, J.
12590	,,	DAVIES, T. H.	12685	,,	PICKERING, J. J.
12026	,,	BULCOCK, H.	12776	,,	LESTER, R.
11800	,,	DYER, W.	12777	,,	BEAMISH, J.
12675	,,	HIBBERT.	12789	,,	WARD, S.
12676	,,	WILDE, C.	12746	,,	BUTLER, H.
12674	,,	MANNION, J.	12798	,,	SMITH, J.
12770	,,	JOHNSTON, H.	12769	,,	OATES, J.
12671	,,	SHEPHERD, J.	12752	,,	GRIFFITHS, H.
12755	,,	JOHNSON, G.	12790	,,	PINKSTONE, W. H.
12766	,,	HENDERSON, E.	12764	,,	TUDGE, E.

* For portrait, see Officers' Group, p. 157.   † For Portrait, see Sergeants' Group, p. 159.

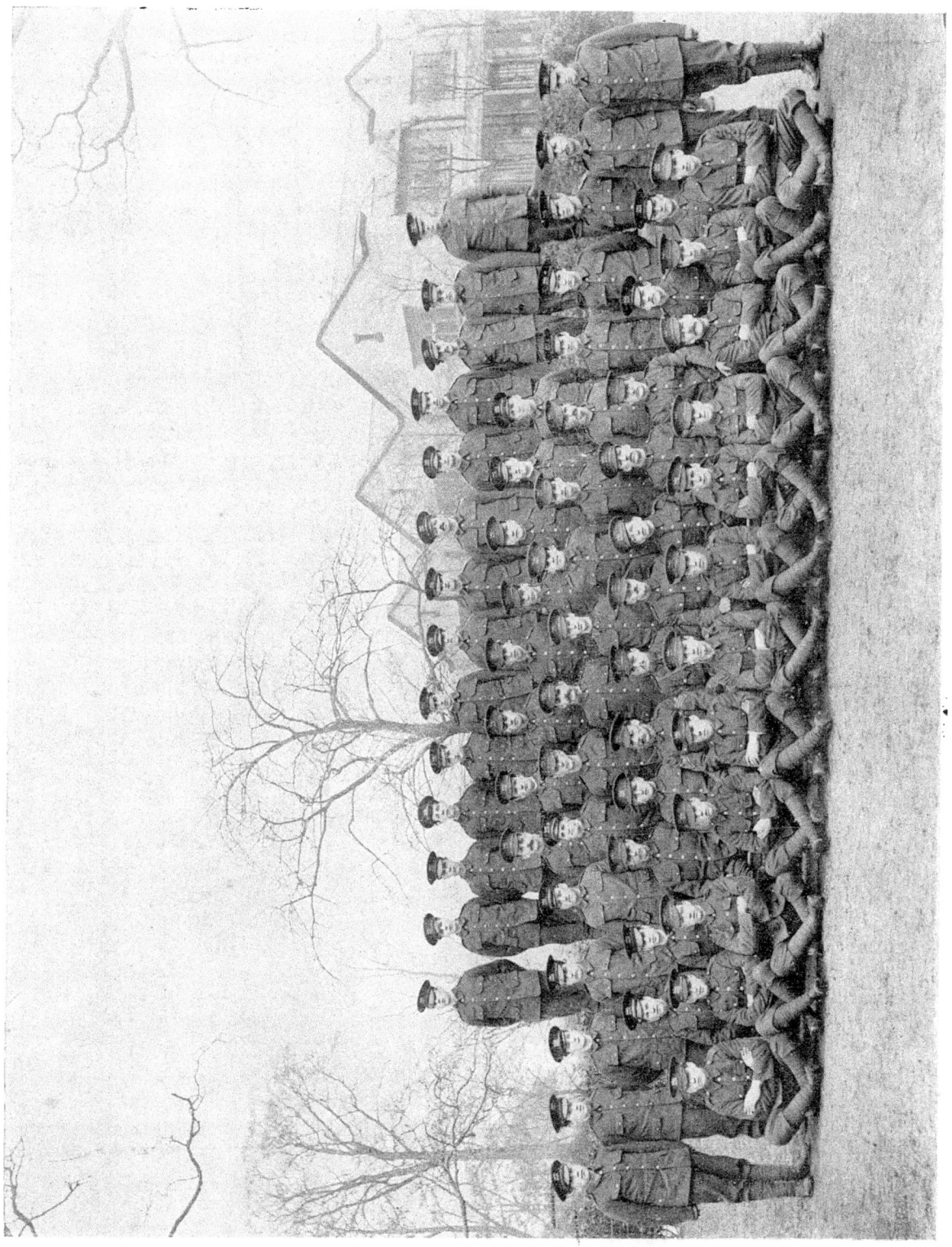

19th (Service) Battalion Manchester Regiment.

"E" COMPANY.

Officer Commanding Company - Capt. C. G. AGNEW.*
Company Sergeant Major - - NUTTALL, F.†
Company Quartermaster Sergeant - DUCKWORTH, H. H.

PLATOON NO. XVIII.

Roll No.	Rank and Name.		Roll No.	Rank and Name.	
12700	Private	WALKER, C. E.	12677	Private	BRIDGE, C.
12749	,,	ROBERTS, G.	12708	,,	SIMPSON, H.
12763	,,	TORKINGTON, H.	12262	,,	ASPELL, J. T.
11808	,,	FOX, J.	12096	,,	HARRISON, T. H.
12725	,,	HARDMAN, I.	11518	,,	CROOK, W.
12783	,,	TURNER, N.	12643	,,	STROWGER, L.
12703	,,	TAYLOR, T.	12488	,,	WOODCOCK, C.
12682	,,	RICHARDSON, F.	12084	,,	GLAZEBROOK, A.
12697	,,	LAWLESS, G.	12290	,,	BROOKS, W.
12754	,,	DANCE, E.	12225	,,	THORNHILL, C.
12693	,,	BUCKLEY, J.	12054	,,	CROWTHER, S.
11952	,,	WARBURTON, W. B.	11972	,,	WOOLFENDEN, R.
12695	,,	SWETNAM, A.	12833	,,	WOOD, W.
12421	,,	PENN, A.	12793	,,	BUTLER, W.
12280	,,	BAXTER, F.	12727	,,	SIMPSON, R.
12744	,,	REDFERN, W. H.	12743	,,	REED, T.
12713	,,	LEAK, H.	12726	,,	PAINE, H. E.
12720	,,	BENNETT, W. E.	12775	,,	McNAMARA, T.
12372	,,	HUTCHINSON, A.	12718	,,	BARNETT, S.
12712	,,	HADFIELD, J.	12738	,,	PRUNTY, P.
12750	,,	ELLIOTT, H.	12741	,,	MORRIS, E.
12714	,,	LLOYD, J. T.	12751	,,	DOLAN, J.
12721	,,	MOYES, S.	12724	,,	GILCHRIST, J.
12711	,,	McDERMOTT, M.	12734	,,	IBBOTSON, R.
12717	,,	STEWART, N.	12729	,,	FARNWORTH, F.
12709	,,	McMANUS, W.	12723	,,	THEOBALD, F.
12718	,,	BARNETT, S.	12722	,,	JONES, O. J.
12715	,,	SMITH, R.	12733	,,	FREER, S.
12716	,,	MADDERS, S.	12795	,,	STERNBERG, F.
12707	,,	RAMSBOTTOM, G. H.	12744	,,	GEORGE, R.

* For portrait, see Officers' Group, p. 157. † For Portrait, see Sergeants' Group, p. 159.

19th BATTALION.—Supplementary Photo of men of A Company who were not present when the Platoon Photographs were taken. For names, see Platoon lists.

19th BATTALION.—Supplementary Photo of men of B Company who were not present when the Platoon Photographs were taken. For names, see Platoon lists.

19th BATTALION.—Supplementary Photo of men of C Company who were not present when the Platoon Photographs were taken. For names, see Platoon lists.

19th BATTALION.—Supplementary Photo of men of D Company who were not present when the Platoon Photographs were taken. For names, see Platoon lists.

Manchester City Battalions
OF THE
91st Infantry Brigade

91st INFANTRY BRIGADE

Headquarters' Staff.

* * *

Front Row (Left to Right).
    Captain A. K. GRANT
        (Brigade Major).

    Brigadier-General F. J. KEMPSTER, D.S.O.
        (Commanding 91st Brigade).

    Captain H. V. R. HODSON
        (Acting Staff Captain).

Back Row (Left to Right).
    Sergeant S. G. BISHOP
        (Brigade Clerk).

    Private J. HOOPER (Orderly).

    Sergeant W. HEAP
        (Acting Quartermaster Sergeant).

20th (Service) Battalion

20th (Service) Battalion Manchester Regiment.

Roll of Officers.

Colonel	ARNOLD, A. J., D.S.O.	Lieutenant	NICHOLLS, F.
Maj. & Hon. Lt.-Col.	GOLDSCHMIDT, SIDNEY G.	,,	COOPER, W. C.
		,,	BAGSHAW, W. B.
Major	SMALLEY, E.	,,	SHEPHERD, C. H. B.
,,	MERRIMAN, F. B.	2nd-Lieut.	EATON, J. W.
Capt. & Adj.	BRYANT, F.	,,	BROOKS, F. S.
Captain	KNIGHT, H. J., V.C.	,,	DIXEY, A. G.
,,	HARFORD, J. F.	,,	BINNING, K. R.
,,	McNULTY, E. J.	,,	AGNEW, E. K.
Lieutenant	WHITE, J. V.	,,	JAMES, F.
,,	GEMMELL, J. S.	,,	HODGSON, C. B. V.
,,	LAITHWAITE, J.	,,	BAGSHAW, H. S.
,,	RAMSBOTTOM, J. W.	,,	ROSS, F. G.
,,	WATTS, S.	,,	CLEGG, T. H.
,,	MILNE, D. F.	,,	GIFFARD, J. S.
,,	CREWDSON, T. W.	,,	GIFFARD, G. G.

The following were not present when the Photograph was taken:—

Captain	DEAN-WILLCOCKS, A.	2nd-Lieut.	SMITH, C. L.
,,	GALLOWAY, J.	Lt. & Q.M.	CAIN, A. A.

For Officers of the Depot Companies, see Photograph on p. 401.

20th (Service) Battalion Manchester Regiment.

Non-Commissioned Officers' (Sergeants) Roll.

Warrant Officer.
6516   R.S.M.   Kennelly, J. G.

17730   R.Q.M.S. Pittam, J. W. P.
17566   R.O.R.S. Brigham, H. A.

Roll No.	Rank	and Name.	Roll No.	Rank	and Name.
10879	C.S.M.	Malley, T.	17494	Sergeant	Stewart, J. A
17436	,,	Myatt, A.	17308	,,	Cain, W.
17038	,,	Carberry, J.	17604	,,	Dickinson, T.
18386	,,	Amor, A. H.	17617	,,	Eyre, E.
17418	C.Q.M.S.	Lyons, C. W.	17658	,,	Hornsby, W. E.
17838	,,	Brown, A. H.	17430	,,	Meadows, J.
17056	,,	Cottrell, C. O.	17740	,,	Robertshaw, H.
17195	,,	Phippen, A. E.	17277	,,	Adamson, J.
17813	Sgt. Cook	Bain, A. A.	17295	,,	Beswick, E.
17193	Pion. Sgt.	Payne, A. P.	17880	,,	Edwards, J.
17787	M.G. Sgt.	Walker, R.	17892	,,	Ford, J. S.
18156	Trns. Sgt.	Straiton, J.	17898	,,	George, E.
18046	Sig. Sgt.	Wagster, S.	17950	,,	Knight, H.
17014	Sgt. Dr.	Blacklock, J.	18021	,,	Rocca, F.
17340	Sgt. Smr.	Dunn, S.	17208	,,	Roberts, A
17355	Sgt. Tlr.	Gilbert, A. J.	17137	L.-Sergt.	Kean, F. W.
17850	Sgt. Prov.	Chapman, J.	17116	,,	Heywood, C. S.
17152	Sergeant	McCulloch, W.	17034	,,	Bury, J. W.
17230	,,	Sutton, R. C.	17298	,,	Booth, O.
17065	,,	Daniels, W. J.	17314	,,	Clark, W.
17156	,,	Maguire, W.	17466	,,	Ramsden, W. H.
17117	,,	Higginbottom, J.	18359	,,	Ogden, J. M.
17445	,,	Nowell, L.	18357	,,	Porter, E.
17058	,,	Crompton, G.	17606	,,	Dixon, A.
17305	,,	Burgoyne, J.	18125	,,	Darlington, T.
17323	,,	Cox, W. H.	17633	,,	Gill, G. B.
18416	,,	Dow, R. G. C.	17780	,,	Twittey, C. E.
17448	,,	Oldham, C.	18360	,,	Chard, H. A. J.
18358	,,	Irving, G.	17868	,,	Davies, H.
17577	,,	Byway, M. A.	17980	,,	Mills, A.

Also on the Photograph: Major and Hon. Lieut.-Col. S. G. Goldschmidt, Capt. and Adjt. F. Bryant.

The following were not present when the Photograph was taken:—

17495	Sergeant	Stirling, D.	17492	L.-Sergt.	Stacey, F. W.
17626	,,	Forsyth, C. A.			

20th (Service) Battalion Manchester Regiment.

Bugle Band.

Roll No.	Rank and Name.		Roll No.	Rank and Name.	
17014	Sergeant	BLACKLOCK, J.	17940	Drummer	JACOBS, G. F.
17031	Corporal	BURKE, A.	17159	,,	MARSHALL, T.
17321	Drummer	COWLEY, A.	18132	,,	MARSHALL, S.
17579	,,	CAUFIELD, H. A.	17154	,,	MCLORNON, W.
17588	,,	CLEGG, H.	17435	,,	MOSSDALE, S.
17310	,,	CHARNLEY, W. J.	17196	,,	PIMBLETT, H.
17330	,,	DARGAN, J.	17472	,,	ROBERTS, R.
17877	,,	DRINKWATER, C.	17742	,,	ROUGHSEDGE, H.
17360	,,	GRIMSHAW, W.	17221	,,	SMITH, A. W.
18086	,,	GREEN, F.	18295	,,	SOUTHERN, T.
17105	,,	HALLOWS, J.	13604	,,	TAYLOR, J.
17920	,,	HEYWOOD, F.	17530	,,	WILKINSON, F.
17392	,,	JONES, A.			

The following were not present when the Photograph was taken:—

Roll No.	Rank and Name.		Roll No.	Rank and Name.	
17623	Drummer	FLETCHER, G.	18299	Drummer	HILL, W.
17631	,,	GARVEY, F.	17409	,,	HALL, P.
17776	,,	TONGE, H.			

20th (Service) Battalion Manchester Regiment.

"A" COMPANY.

Officer Commanding Company	Capt. H. J. Knight, V.C.*
Second in Command	Capt. E. J. McNulty.*
Company Sergeant Major	Carberry, J.†
Company Quartermaster Sergeant	Cottrell, C. O.†

PLATOON NO. I.

Platoon Commander	2nd Lieut. F. James.
Platoon Sergeant	McCulloch, W.

Roll No.	Rank and Name.		Roll No.	Rank and Name.	
17193	Sergeant	Payne, A. B.	17105	Private	Hallows, J.
17230	,,	Sutton, R. C.	17128	,,	Hurst, J.
17137	L.-Sergt.	Kean, F. W.	17109	,,	Hardy, J.
17867	Corporal	Dalton, J. W.	17133	,,	Jackson, S.
17024	L.-Corpl.	Broadsmith, R. J.	17141	,,	Kirby, H.
18384	,,	Dale, M.	17143	,,	Knowles, S. F.
17107	,,	Hannible, J.	17148	,,	Lees, T.
17177	,,	Mulelly, T. H.	17173	,,	Morgan, H.
17198	,,	Potts, J.	17159	,,	Marshall, T.
17002	Private	Ainsworth, W.	17172	,,	Moores, W.
18133	,,	Bowers, W.	17182	,,	Nield, F.
17016	,,	Booth, C.	17183	,,	Oldham, J.
17022	,,	Bramhall, T.	17190	,,	Parkinson, H.
17012	,,	Bennett, A.	17191	,,	Parrot, O.
17005	,,	Bannister, W. J.	17201	,,	Pritchard, R.
17020	,,	Booth, W. H.	17196	,,	Pimblett, H.
18115	,,	Bottoms, W.	17211	,,	Rowland, G. H.
17008	,,	Barrow, G.	17204	,,	Rickson, R.
17006	,,	Barnshaw, J. J.	17212	,,	Rowland, H. F.
17042	,,	Charlesworth, J.	17207	,,	Robbins, F.
17040	,,	Cass, J.	17210	,,	Rogers, M.
17053	,,	Coombs, W. J.	17217	,,	Shaw, A.
18145	,,	Clarke, H.	17234	,,	Tattersall, N.
17071	,,	Dimelow, W.	17237	,,	Taylor, J.
18385	,,	Duff, J. J.	17238	,,	Taylor, T.
17077	,,	Eadsforth, G.	17232	,,	Tattersall, A.
17085	,,	Finch, W.	17233	,,	Tattersall, J.
17100	,,	Gowen, R. G.	17255	,,	Wilde, A.

* For portrait, see Officers' Group, p. 209. † For portrait, see Sergeants' Group, p. 211.

The following were not present when the Platoon Photograph was taken:—

Roll No.	Rank	Name	Roll No.	Rank	Name
17057	L.-Corpl.	Crawshaw, S.	17131	Private	Ingleson, H.
17036	Private	Butters, S.	17151	,,	Livett, W.
17118	,,	Higgins, A.	18313	,,	Lyons, A.
17030	,,	Burgess, S.	17221	,,	Smith, A. W.
17110	,,	Harrison, A.			

20th (Service) Battalion Manchester Regiment.

"A" COMPANY.

Officer Commanding Company - Capt. H. J. Knight, V.C.*
Second in Command - - Capt. E. J. McNulty.*
Company Sergeant Major - - Carberry, J.†
Company Quartermaster Sergeant - Cottrell, C. O.

PLATOON NO. II.

Platoon Commander - - - 2nd Lieut. J. W. Eaton.
Platoon Sergeant - - - Maguire, W.

Roll No.	Rank and Name.		Roll No.	Rank and Name.	
17014	Sergeant	Blacklock, J.	17127	Private	Hunt, W.
17209	Corporal	Robinson, F.	17139	,,	Kelshaw, H.
17185	L.-Corpl.	Owen, A.	17138	,,	Kennion, W.
17216	,,	Seddon, W. H.	17150	,,	Lever, F. J.
18383	,,	Wain, G. L.	18196	,,	Lewsey, A. W.
17249	,,	Warburton, T.	17165	,,	Meacock, E.
18119	Private	Adamson, L.	17163	,,	Massey, H.
18139	,,	Atherton, W.	17153	,,	McKnight, T. H.
18175	,,	Ashton, W.	17169	,,	Mellor, J.
18081	,,	Bowyer, E.	17186	,,	Owen, S.
17026	,,	Broughton, J.	17184	,,	Oldham, W.
17013	,,	Bent, J. A.	17187	,,	Painter, J. F.
17052	,,	Cooke, T.	17219	,,	Sheehan, B.
17050	,,	Colwell, J.	17231	,,	Swain, T.
17074	,,	Doyle, A.	17222	,,	Smith, E.
18314	,,	Davies, E.	17227	,,	Stansfield, G. D.
17088	,,	Franks, J. E.	17218	,,	Sharp, C.
17087	,,	Foden, G.	18174	,,	Sugden, A.
17001	,,	Green, S.	17236	,,	Taylor, H. J.
17099	,,	Goss, V.	17242	,,	Thornycroft, T.
17095	,,	Glover, J. S.	17244	,,	Valentine, I.
17122	,,	Howard, F. L.	17260	,,	Wilkinson, J. A.
17125	,,	Hughes, J.	17272	,,	Woodhead, E. J.
17104	,,	Hall, R. A.	17248	,,	Walton, J.
17126	,,	Hulme, P. J.	17263	,,	Williams, H.
17384	,,	Horridge, A.	17258	,,	Wilkinson, C. L.
17142	,,	Knight, F. S. J.			

* For portrait, see Officers' Group, p. 209. † For portrait, see Sergeants' Group, p. 211.

The following were not present when the Platoon Photograph was taken:—

17065	Sergeant	Daniels, W. J.	17111	Private	Healey, F.
17031	Corporal	Burke, A.	17161	,,	Mason, W.
17214	,,	Sanford, C. R.	17154	,,	McLornon, W.
17262	,,	Williams, A.	17164	,,	Matthews, F. J.
17096	Private	Gornall, A. H.	17245	,,	Valentine, R.
17091	,,	Garner, A.	17259	,,	Wilkinson, H.
17121	,,	Holmes, J.			

20th (Service) Battalion Manchester Regiment.
"A" COMPANY.

Officer Commanding Company	Capt. H. J. Knight, V.C.*
Second in Command	Capt. E. J. McNulty.*
Company Sergeant Major	Carberry, J.†
Company Quartermaster Sergeant	Cottrell, C. O.†

PLATOON NO. III.

Platoon Commander	Lieut. D. F. Milne.
Platoon Sergeant	Higginbottom, J.

Roll No.	Rank and Name.		Roll No.	Rank and Name.	
17445	Sergeant	Nowell, L.	18326	Private	Dickenson, W.
17034	L.-Sergt.	Bury, J. W.	17093	,,	Gilligan, W.
17395	Corporal	Jones, J. F.	17094	,,	Glew, W.
17442	,,	Nicholson, T.	17120	,,	Hill, F.
17084	L.-Corpl.	Fender, J.	17155	,,	Hewison, L.
17103	,,	Hague, A. B.	18130	,,	Hughes, C.
17147	,,	Lees, S. S.	17132	,,	Jackson, C.
17158	,,	Marginson, H.	17140	,,	King, E.
17166	,,	Meadowcroft, H. C.	17145	,,	Leach, E.
17261	,,	Wilkinson, R. M.	18190	,,	Lawson, H. R.
17009	Private	Baume, H.	17155	,,	McWhirter, F.
17032	,,	Burke, A. P.	17170	,,	Minton, L.
17029	,,	Buckright, G.	18333	,,	Miller, A.
17275	,,	Bradshaw, J.	17131	,,	Nicholls, E. J.
18336	,,	Bull, A.	17197	,,	Plover, G.
17276	,,	Conville, J.	18302	,,	Penny, R.
17062	,,	Cummings, J. W.	17203	,,	Rayner, J.
17063	,,	Cummins, J.	17228	,,	Stevenson, T. E.
17039	,,	Carruthers, J.	17226	,,	Stansby, T. A.
17049	,,	Collins, J. P.	18222	,,	Sherborne, R. W.
17048	,,	Coleman, A.	17223	,,	Southern, R.
17041	,,	Chance, F. W.	17270	,,	Wood, H. C.
17067	,,	Davies, E.	17207	,,	Wilson, H.
17070	,,	Diaper, J. B.	17254	,,	Wiggins, R.
17073	,,	Dodd, F.	17271	,,	Wood, T.
17064	,,	Dance, J.	17266	,,	Williamson, J. N.
18189	,,	Dillon, E.	17273	,,	Yates, H.
18223	,,	France, A.			

* For portrait, see Officers' Group, p. 209.   † For portrait, see Sergeants' Group, p. 211.

The following were not present when the Platoon Photograph was taken:—

Roll No.	Rank	Name	Roll No.	Rank	Name
11554	Private	Glew, F. G.	17269	Private	Withington, W. H.
17027	,,	Barrick, W. J.	17097	,,	Gorton, A.
17061	,,	Cryan, D.	18372	,,	Lee, A.
17405	,,	Chesworth, H.	17157	,,	Maloney, E.
17075	,,	Dudley, W.	17213	,,	Ryan, T.
17076	,,	Dunn, F.			

20th (Service) Battalion Manchester Regiment.
"A" COMPANY.

Officer Commanding Company	Capt. H. J. Knight, V.C.*
Second in Command	Capt. E. J. McNulty.*
Company Sergeant Major	Carberry, J.
Company Quartermaster Sergeant	Cottrell, C. O.†

PLATOON NO. IV.

Platoon Commander	2nd Lieut. T. H. Clegg.
Platoon Sergeant	Crompton, G.

Roll No.	Rank and Name.		Roll No	Rank and Name.	
17208	Sergeant	Roberts, A.	17124	Private	Hughes, H.
17119	Corporal	Preston, P.	17122	,,	Heaton, A.
17264	,,	Williams, H. G.	17129	,,	Huxley, F.
17021	L.-Corpl.	Brady, G.	17130	,,	Illingworth, A.
17092	,,	Giles, R.	17135	,,	Jones, E. W.
17089	,,	Frost, H.	17144	,,	Knowles, J. F.
17220	,,	Smith, A.	17149	,,	Lennox, H.
17265	,,	Williamson, E.	17175	,,	Morrison, W.
17001	Private	Ackers, S.	71162	,,	Massey, C.
17033	,,	Burns, J.	17171	,,	Moore, J. E.
17015	,,	Blackwell, C. E.	17174	,,	Morris, J. B.
17028	,,	Buckley, C.	17188	,,	Palmer, A.
17131	,,	Buckley, E. S.	17189	,,	Parkin, H.
17023	,,	Brierley, H.	17192	,,	Partington, C.
17011	,,	Bednall, R. D.	17202	,,	Ravenscroft, J.
17019	,,	Booth, S.	3606	,,	Roberts, W.
17025	,,	Brockley, S.	17748	,,	Sewell, A.
17054	,,	Coppock, W.	17225	,,	Stanley, J.
17060	,,	Crowther, W.	17224	,,	Spratt, G. H.
17051	,,	Cooke, A.	17229	,,	Stock, W.
17055	,,	Cornes, H.	17241	,,	Thomas, J.
17068	,,	Delph, T.	17243	,,	Tonge, H.
17066	,,	Davies, E.	17246	,,	Venables, G. A.
17080	,,	Edmundson, S.	17247	,,	Waite, W.
17081	,,	Edwards, J.	17251	,,	West, F. J.
17090	,,	Furby, F. C.	17268	,,	Withington, J. W.
17102	,,	Griffiths, D.	17274	,,	Young, W.
17106	,,	Hammersley, A.		,,	Wilde, S. E.
17114	,,	Heslop, A.			

* For portrait, see Officers' Group, p. 209. † For portrait, see Sergeants' Group, p. 211.

The following were not present when the Platoon Photograph was taken:—

Roll No.	Rank	Name	Roll No.	Rank	Name
17116	L.-Sergt.	Heywood, C. S.	17136	Private	Jones, J. C.
17035	Private	Butler, L.	17146	,,	Lees, F.
17047	,,	Cleasby, J.	17178	,,	Murdock, T. G.
17069	,,	Derbyshire,	17160	,,	Martin, W. H.
17083	,,	Farrell, J. W.	17179	,,	Nevin, J. E.
17119	,,	Higginson,			

20th (Service) Battalion Manchester Regiment.
"B" COMPANY.

Officer Commanding Company - Major E. Smalley.*
Second in Command - - Capt. J. Galloway
Company Sergeant Major - Malley, T.†
Company Quartermaster Sergeant - Lyons, C. W.

PLATOON NO. V.

Platoon Commander - - - 2nd Lieut. H. S. Bagshaw.
Platoon Sergeant - - - Stirling, D.

Roll No.	Rank and Name.		Roll No.	Rank and Name.	
17340	Sergeant	Dunn, S.	17400	Private	Kelley, H.
17314	L.-Sergt.	Clarke, W.	17431	,,	Millington, F.
17416	Corporal	Ludgate, F.	17425	,,	McBride, T.
17338	L.-Corpl.	Dow, J. F.	17443	,,	Neild, R.
17406	,,	Leicester, B.	18335	,,	Nightingale, J.
17412	,,	Llanwarne, L.	17438	,,	Nancollas, J.
17429	,,	McVie, J.	18181	,,	O'Neill, P.
17773	,,	Todd, J. E.	17462	,,	Pomfret, J. W.
17283	Private	Ardron, A.	17460	,,	Petto, J.
18417	,,	Barnes, F.	18251	,,	Robinson, J.
18338	,,	Baker, H.	17473	,,	Rogerson, A.
17287	,,	Barber, W.	17493	,,	Stanton, E.
17303	,,	Bullock, H.	17498	,,	Sutton, J. B.
18146	,,	Collins, E.	18388	,,	Sutton, S.
17326	,,	Coyle, J.	17479	,,	Scott, G.
18221	,,	Deering, T.	17512	,,	Townsend, E.
17339	,,	Drinkwater, T.	17503	,,	Taylor, J.
18084	,,	Dando, N.	13604	,,	Taylor, J. J.
17351	,,	Furness, W.	18349	,,	Turner, W.
17360	,,	Grimshaw, W.	17508	,,	Tomkinson, I.
17367	,,	Hardman, J.	17502	,,	Taylor, H.
17362	,,	Haigh, S. B.	17531	,,	Wilkinson, F.
18165	,,	Hawes, H.	18160	,,	Wainwright, J.
17382	,,	Holgate, E.	17519	,,	Wales, C. H.
17385	,,	Hughes, S.	17522	,,	Walton, J.
17387	,,	Ingle, F.	17535	,,	Wood, A.
17390	,,	Jackson, R. M.	18282	,,	Wallwork, H. N.
17399	,,	Kelly, E.	17520	,,	Walker, A.
17419	,,	Mancer, W.			

Also on the Photograph: Lieut. W. C. Cooper.

* For portrait, see Officers' Group, p. 209. † For portrait, see Sergeants' Group, p. 211.

The following were not present when the Platoon Photograph was taken:—

18380	L.-Corpl.	Hamilton, G. L.	17424	Private	May, S.
18278	Private	Beasley, W.	17354	,,	Garnett, A.
17327	,,	Cross, J.	17440	,,	Newlands, A.
18369	,,	Dakin, T.	18168	,,	Shea, J.
17350	,,	Frost, V.	17509	,,	Tomlinson, H.

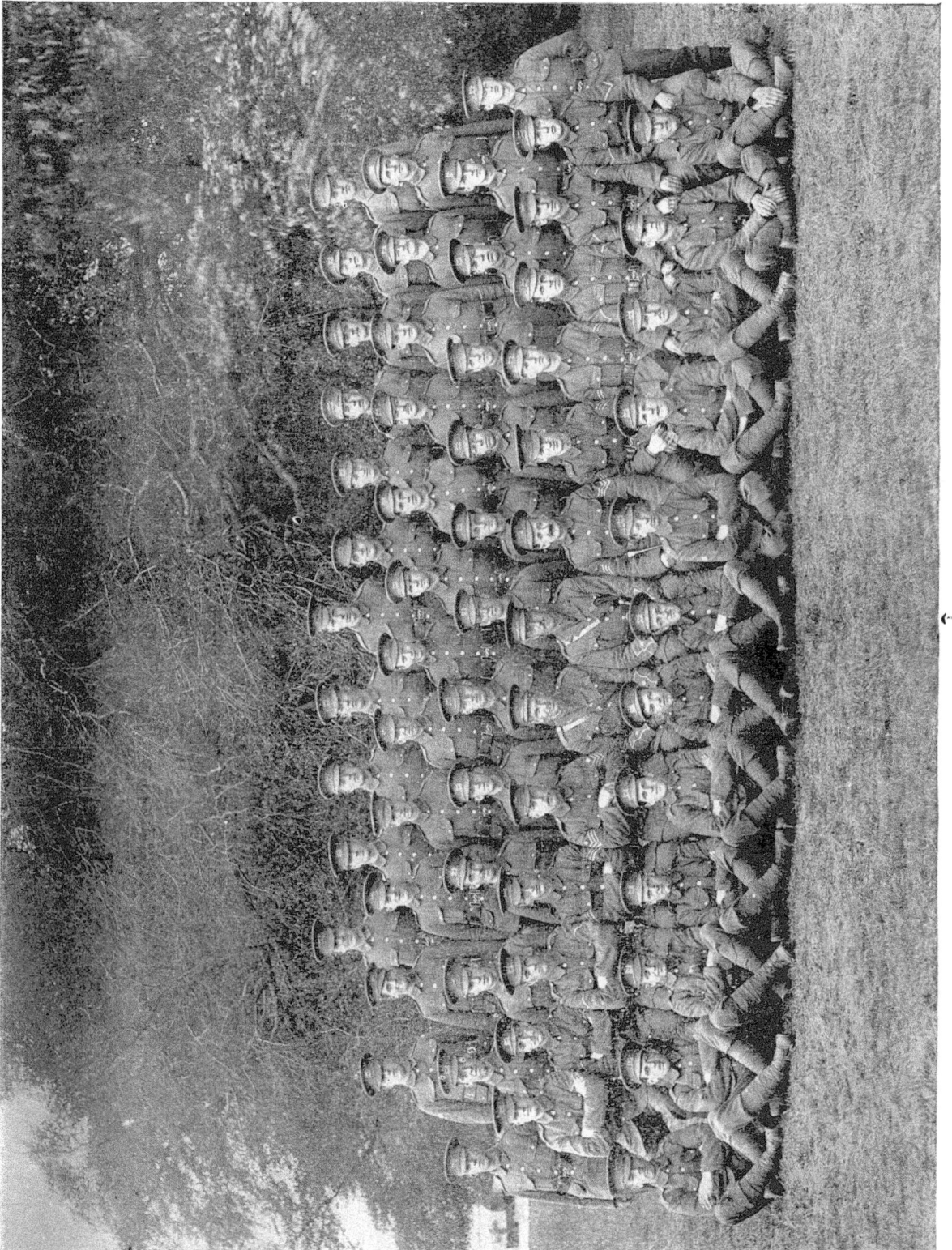

20th (Service) Battalion Manchester Regiment.

"B" COMPANY.

Officer Commanding Company - Major E. SMALLEY.*
Second in Command - - - Capt. J. GALLOWAY.
Company Sergeant Major - - MALLEY, T.†
Company Quartermaster Sergeant - LYONS, C. W.†

PLATOON NO. VI.

Platoon Commander - - - 2nd Lieut. K. R. BINNING.
Platoon Sergeant - - - - COX, W. H.

Roll No.	Rank and Name.		Roll No.	Rank and Name.	
17305	Sergeant	BURGOYNE, J.	17378	Private	HERON, J.
17312	Corporal	CLARKE, F. H.	17389	,,	JACKSON, N.
18381	,,	HELLAWELL, J.	17398	,,	KEATES, A.
17304	L.-Corpl.	BURGOYNE, J. A.	17410	,,	LEYBOURNE, P.
17793	,,	WEBB, C.	17414	,,	LOWE, J. F.
17282	Private	ANTHONY, E.	17408	,,	LENG, F.
17307	,,	BUSH, H.	17403	,,	LEAR, E.
17297	,,	BOOR, B.	17435	,,	MOSDALE, S.
17289	,,	BATE, J.	18096	,,	MCRAE, J.
17316	,,	COLEMAN, F.	17439	,,	NEEDHAM, S.
17320	,,	COTTON, J.	18180	,,	NICHOLSON, B.
17326	,,	CROMPTON, J. B.	17449	,,	OSWELL, O.
17311	,,	CHORLTON, F.	17464	,,	POOLE, J.
17337	,,	DODGE, R.	17451	,,	PALMER, H.
17332	,,	DENT, W.	17463	,,	POOLE, A.
17329	,,	DADY, J.	17472	,,	ROBERTS, R.
17345	,,	EXTON, H. B.	17468	,,	READ, P.
17344	,,	EVERETT, S. E.	17477	,,	SAWYER, E.
17341	,,	EATON, A.	17488	,,	SMITH, F.
18219	,,	GEE, J.	18337	,,	SMITH, J.
17361	,,	GRUMMITT, N.	17483	,,	SHIRES, W.
17364	,,	HALL, E.	17515	,,	TREES, V.
17368	,,	HARE, L. A.	17514	,,	TREES, C.
18143	,,	HILL, C.	17513	,,	TOZER, F. J.
18308	,,	HOLDEN, N.	17536	,,	WOOD, F.
17377	,,	HENSON, H.	17523	,,	WARD, C. H.
17379	,,	HIGSON, W. F.			

* For portrait, see Officers Group, p. 209.   † For portrait, see Sergeants' Group, p. 211.

The following were not present when the Platoon Photograph was taken:—

17492	L.-Sergt.	STACEY, F. W.	18176	Private	FRANCIS, A.
17396	L.-Corpl.	JONES, R.	17363	,,	HALL, C.
17310	Private	CHARNLEY, W. J.	17484	,,	SINGLETON, S.
17302	,,	BUCKLEY, W.	18232	,,	TITTERINGTON, W.
17333	,,	DIGGLE, T.	17517	,,	UPTON, A.
18142	,,	DALY, J.	17529	,,	WHITTLE, W.
17330	,,	DARGAN, J.			

20th (Service) Battalion Manchester Regiment.
"B" COMPANY.

Officer Commanding Company - Major E. Smalley.*
Second in Command - - - Capt. J. Galloway.
Company Sergeant Major - - Malley, T.†
Company Quartermaster Sergeant - Lyons, C. W.†

PLATOON NO. VII.

Platoon Commander - - - Lieut. S. Watts.
Platoon Sergeant - - - Oldham, C.

Roll No.	Rank and Name.	Roll No.	Rank and Name.
18416	Sergeant Dow, R.	18116	Private Griffiths, J. W.
17466	L.-Sergt. Ramsden, W. H.	17358	,, Gough, H.
17510	Corporal Toogood, M.	18089	,, Hill, A.
17342	L.-Corpl. Eaves, J. J.	18088	,, Hughes, P.
17405	,, Lee, F.	17373	,, Heald, G. N.
17476	,, Savage, A. E.	17374	,, Heald, H.
17526	,, Welbourn, F. B.	17380	,, Hill, W. L.
17279	Private Aldous, P.	17386	,, Hempsall, C.
17280	,, Allen, J.	18220	,, Harris, A. W.
17301	,, Brown, R.	17372	,, Hayes, F.
17290	,, Batterby, G.	18090	,, Kirkham, J.
18079	,, Brown, J. W.	18351	,, Lee, A.
17292	,, Berry, L.	17402	,, Law, W. H.
18354	,, Birch, J.	18153	,, Madden, H.
17293	,, Bertenshaw, A.	18347	,, Murphy, J.
18082	,, Bryan, J.	17421	,, Mather, W.
18147	,, Chamberlain, F.	17446	,, Oakes, G. S.
17328	,, Cunliffe, J. P.	17456	,, Patterson, W. A.
18238	,, Corbett, H.	17475	,, Rowland, H.
18237	,, Cliffe, R.	17480	,, Scott, W.
17234	,, Coxon, H.	17499	,, Swettenham, W. H.
18352	,, Chadwick, F.	17511	,, Toole, J.
17321	,, Cowley, A.	17587	,, Tobin, P.
17336	,, Dodd, T.	17527	,, Welbourn, J.
17335	,, Dixon, C. B.	17537	,, Wood, G. F.
17346	,, Farr, W.	17538	,, Worsley, H.
17348	,, Fitzpatrick, F.	17539	,, Worth, H.
18085	,, Green, J. H.	17524	,, Worland, H. T.
17356	,, Gorton, W.		

* For portrait, see Officers' Group, p. 209.   † For portrait, see Sergeants' Group, p. 211.

Also on the Photograph: 2nd Lieut. F. G. Ross.

The following were not present when the Platoon Photograph was taken:—

17281	Private Andrews, B.	17411	Private Lillie, L.
17299	,, Boothroyd, R. H.	17406	,, Lemon, G.
17331	,, Dennington, J. H.	17433	,, Moran, J.
17383	,, Horan, T.	17540	,, Wroe, S.
17409	,, Hall, P.		

20th (Service) Battalion Manchester Regiment.
"B" COMPANY.

Officer Commanding Company	Major E. SMALLEY.*
Second in Command	Capt. J. GALLOWAY.
Company Sergeant Major	MALLEY, T.†
Company Quartermaster Sergeant	LYONS, C. W.†

PLATOON NO. VIII.

Platoon Commander	2nd Lieut. A. G. DIXEY.
Platoon Sergeant	STEWART, J. A.

Roll No.	Rank and Name.		Roll No.	Rank and Name.	
17355	Sergeant	GILBERT, J. A.	17386	Private	HUMPHREYS, A.
18358	,,	IRVING, G.	17401	,,	KEMPSTER, W.
17413	Corporal	LONGSON, A.	17404	,,	LEARY, T.
17459	,,	PERRY, H.	17417	,,	LUND, E.
17322	L.-Corpl.	COX, A. R.	17422	,,	MAXWELL, S.
18345	,,	PEERS, A.	17426	,,	McCORD, D.
17533	,,	WILLIAMS, C. M.	17432	,,	MITCHELL, W.
17284	Private	ASHTON, H.	17437	,,	MYLES, W. O. A.
17285	,,	ASPINALL, J.	17447	,,	OLDHAM, A.
17286	,,	AUSTIN, H.	17453	,,	PARKER, A. E.
17288	,,	BARLOW, S. H.	17454	,,	PARKER, F.
17291	,,	BELLIS, J.	17455	,,	PARNELL, H.
17294	,,	BESSEL, H.	17457	,,	PEARSON, J.
17296	,,	BIRD, D.	17465	,,	PYBUS, B.
18340	,,	BOSTOCK,	17467	,,	RAWSON, J.
17309	,,	CAIN, T. S.	17474	,,	ROTHWELL, A.
17317	,,	COLLEY, J.	17482	,,	SHAW, H.
17318	,,	COLLINGE, T. J.	17486	,,	SLATER, H.
17347	,,	FIRTH, E. A.	17501	,,	TASKER, J. J.
17353	,,	GARLAND, J. G.	17506	,,	THORNLEY, E.
17357	,,	GOSPEL, F.	17528	,,	WHITE, S.
17359	,,	GRACE, J.	17532	,,	WILLIAMS, A.
17366	,,	HAMMOND, J. E.	17534	,,	WINDLE, F.
18090	,,	HEYWOOD, A.	18127	,,	WALKER, G.
17397	,,	KANARD, J.			

* For portrait, see Officers' Group, p. 209. † For portrait, see Sergeants' Group, p. 211.

The following were not present when the Platoon Photograph was taken:—

Roll No.		Name	Roll No.		Name
17278	Private	AINSWORTH, E.	17428	Private	McLOUGHLIN, C.
17365	,,	HALL, J. H.	18286	,,	JONES, C. A.
18120	,,	HARGREAVES, G.	17461	,,	PILLING, T.
17370	,,	HATON, J.	17470	,,	RIDDLE, A. H.
18164	,,	HAYES, C.	17485	,,	SLATER, E.
18087	,,	HALLIWELL, T. E.	17490	,,	SMITH, R.
17371	,,	HOWARTH, J. H.	17500	,,	TASKER, H.
17391	,,	JOHNSON, A.	17505	,,	TERRY, F.
17392	,,	JONES, A.	17531	,,	WILKINSON, F.

20th (Service) Battalion Manchester Regiment.
"C" COMPANY.

Officer Commanding Company	Major F. B. Merriman.*
Second in Command	Lieut. J. V. White.*
Company Sergeant Major	Amor, A. H.
Company Quartermaster Sergeant	Phippen, A. E.

PLATOON NO. IX.

Platoon Commander	2nd Lieut. C. L. Smith
Platoon Sergeant	Robertshaw, H.

Roll No.	Rank and Name.		Roll No.	Rank and Name.	
17730	R.Q.M.S.	Pittam, J. W.	17696	Private	McWilliams, J.
18359	L.-Sergt.	Ogden, J. M.	17710	,,	Murphy, A.
17780	,,	Twitty, C. E.	17711	,,	Murphy, S.
18373	Corporal	Lloyd, J. R.	18126	,,	Musgrave, A.
17702	,,	Medcalf, J.	17715	,,	Newton, L.
18124	L.-Corpl.	Darlington, H.	18134	,,	Nutter, J.
17632	,,	Gaunt, A.	17721	,,	Oswald, A.
17668	,,	Jones, H.	18100	,,	Platt, H.
17546	Private	Atkinson, J. E.	18098	,,	Pedley, J.
17545	,,	Atkinson, E.	17735	,,	Pyatt, R.
17557	,,	Blair, A.	18428	,,	Pittam, E.
17564	,,	Brett, H.	17738	,,	Riley, J. A.
17559	,,	Bonehill, C.	17742	,,	Roughsedge, H.
17595	,,	Cross, J.	17741	,,	Rosenberg, H. H.
17608	,,	Done, T.	17743	,,	Royle, H.
17623	,,	Fletcher, G.	17755	,,	Simpson, R.
17625	,,	Forster, H.	17776	,,	Tonge, H.
17631	,,	Garvey, F.	17774	,,	Tompkinson, H. S. C.
17639	,,	Guntrip, P.	17777	,,	Topper, H. S.
17638	,,	Guard, P. B.	17768	,,	Taylor, A. E.
17650	,,	Hinde, L.	17795	,,	Westerman, H. A.
17642	,,	Halpin, A.	17804	,,	Wilson, J.
17643	,,	Hammond, R.	17806	,,	Wright, C. S.
17673	,,	Kempster, F.	17802	,,	Wilding, W.
17690	,,	Lucas, H.	17803	,,	Wilkes, A.
17689	,,	Loynton, H. W.	17785	,,	Walker, G. E.
17701	,,	Meadon, P.	17805	,,	Wood, A.

* For portrait, see Officers' Group, p. 209.

Also on the Photograph: Lieut. C. H. B. Shepherd.

The following were not present when the Platoon Photograph was taken, but see Supplementary Photograph on p. 254.

Roll No.	Rank	Name	Roll No.	Rank	Name
17626	Sergeant	Forsyth, C. A.	18363	Private	O'Neill, J. F.
17588	Private	Clegg, H.	17761	,,	Starkie, E.
17620	,,	Finn, J.	17763	,,	Stinton, S.
17688	,,	Lord, A.	17775	,,	Tonge, E. S.
17744	,,	Royle, W.			

20th (Service) Battalion Manchester Regiment.
"C" COMPANY.

Officer Commanding Company - Major F. B. MERRIMAN.*
Second in Command - - - Lieut. J. V. WHITE.
Company Sergeant Major - - AMOR, A. H.†
Company Quartermaster Sergeant - PHIPPEN, A. E.†

PLATOON NO. X.

Platoon Commander - - - Lieut. F. NICHOLLS.
Platoon Sergeant - - - - DICKINSON, T.

Roll No.	Rank and Name.		Roll No.	Rank and Name.	
17308	Sergeant	CAIN, W.	17665	Private	HUTCHINSON, F.
17658	„	HORNSBY, W. E.	17108	„	HANSON, G.
17037	Corporal	CAMPBELL, R. A.	17675	„	KENYON, J. W.
17599	L.-Corpl.	DALE, E.	17670	„	KEEGAN, J.
17598	„	DAVIES, S.	17685	„	LIGHTBOWNE, G.
17694	„	MACHIN, J.	18290	„	LAW, H.
17757	„	SMITH, J. F.	17700	„	MAUGHAN, T.
17771	„	TERRELL, G. A.	18178	„	MOREWOOD, J.
18293	Private	ASTEN, J.	17713	„	NEEDHAM, A.
17548	„	BAILEY, J. S.	18362	„	NORREY, E.
17576	„	BUTLER, H. C.	18321	„	ORMSBY, J.
17567	„	BROWN, D.	17728	„	PEARSON, M.
17569	„	BROWN, E.	17727	„	PEAKE, F. E.
17552	„	BATTEY, W. H.	18216	„	PUGH, H.
17574	„	BURKE, J. T.	18099	„	PEAT, J.
18370	„	BRERETON, S.	18182	„	PHILLIPS, J.
17590	„	COATES, R.	17766	„	SWINDELLS, P.
17592	„	COOPER, S.	17752	„	SHELTON, A.
17587	„	CHRISTIAN, M. R.	17758	„	SMITH, S.
18346	„	COLLINSON, F.	17759	„	STANLEY, J.
17600	„	DEAN, R. P.	17747	„	SECCOMBE, J.
17605	„	DILLON, G. F.	17764	„	SUMMERS, T.
17616	„	EVES, S. H.	17772	„	THOMPSON, J.
17629	„	FURPHY, D.	17782	„	VANCE, J.
17627	„	FOULKES, J.	17786	„	WALKER, J.
17624	„	FIRTH, A.	17798	„	WHITEHEAD, W.
17622	„	FISHER, G. J.	17794	„	WELSH, A.
17635	„	GRAINGER, W. E.	17792	„	WARREN, H.
17641	„	HALLIHAN, J. W.	17789	„	WALLACE, S.
17648	„	HILL, J.	18218	„	YATES, W.

* For portrait, see Officers' Group, p. 209.   † For portrait, see Sergeants' Group, p. 211.

The following were not present when the Platoon Photograph was taken,
but see Supplementary Photograph on p. 254.

17239	Sergeant	TAYLOR, W. A.	18243	Private	OWEN, J.
18187	Private	BRADLEY, H.	18012	„	PITT, J.
17634	„	GLOVER, J.	17760	„	STANTON, A.
17698	„	MARTINDALE, H.	17796	„	WHALLEY, G.
17695	„	MCPHEE, A.			

20th (Service) Battalion Manchester Regiment.

"C" COMPANY.

Officer Commanding Company - Major F. B. Merriman.*
Second in Command - - - Lieut. J. V. White.*
Company Sergeant Major - - Amor, A. H.†
Company Quartermaster Sergeant - Phippen, A. E.†

PLATOON NO. XI.

Platoon Commander - - - 2nd Lieut. C. B. V. Hodgson.
Platoon Sergeant - - - Byway, M. A.

Roll No.	Rank and Name.		Roll No.	Rank and Name.	
17430	Sergeant	Meadows, J. R.	17666	Private	Ireland, A.
18125	L.-Sergt.	Darlington, T.	17686	,,	Lilly, T. S.
17633	,,	Gill, G.	17679	,,	Lawson, L.
17585	L.-Corpl.	Cheetham, W.	18132	,,	Marshall, S. M.
17637	,,	Grocott, J.	17706	,,	Morrow, A.
17683	,,	Leeson, G.	17705	,,	Morris, H.
18375	,,	Sladen, J.	17720	,,	Osborne, A. E.
17556	Private	Blagden, J.	17723	,,	Parker, W.
17562	,,	Bradley, T.	17731	,,	Porter, R. S.
17558	,,	Blewitt, S.	18270	,,	Parker, W. J.
17573	,,	Burgess, J.	18246	,,	Rorke, S.
17565	,,	Bridge, C.	18244	,,	Redford, S.
17570	,,	Brown, L.	18364	,,	Slater, A.
17553	,,	Batty, H.	17756	,,	Smith, J.
17586	,,	Chisnall, J.	18284	,,	Sibbles, J.
17583	,,	Charlton, J.	17767	,,	Swindells, M.
17584	,,	Chase, W.	17779	,,	Turner, S.
17596	,,	Cuffwright, W.	17781	,,	Valentine, A.
17603	,,	Dickinson, W.	18248	,,	Wall, J.
17618	,,	Faragher, E.	17800	,,	Whitton, J. H.
17640	,,	Hall, E.	18389	,,	Whittan, R.
17660	,,	Howarth, J.	17807	,,	Wright, F.
17669	,,	Jones, R.	18234	,,	Yates, A.
17667	,,	Johnson, J.			

* For portrait, see Officers' Group, p. 209. † For portrait, see Sergeants' Group, p. 211.

The following were not present when the Platoon Photograph was taken, but see Supplementary Photograph on p. 254.

Roll No.	Rank	Name	Roll No.	Rank	Name
17778	L.-Corpl.	Townshend, H. E	18264	Private	Heald, W.
17580	Private	Carrington, J.	17655	,,	Hollins, W.
17624	,,	Foley, J.	18269	,,	Hollidge, A.
18262	,,	Gregory, W.	17712	,,	Naylor, J.
17663	,,	Hulme, A.	17732	,,	Potter, F.
17657	,,	Hooper, J.	17797	,,	Wheatley, J.
17659	,,	Howard, R.			

20th (Service) Battalion Manchester Regiment.
"C" COMPANY.

Officer Commanding Company	Major F. B. MERRIMAN.*
Second in Command	Lieut. J. V. WHITE.*
Company Sergeant Major	AMOR, A. H.†
Company Quartermaster Sergeant	PHIPPEN, A. E.†

PLATOON NO. XII.

Platoon Commander	Lieut. J. LAITHWAITE.
Platoon Sergeant	EYRE, E.

Roll No.	Rank and Name.		Roll No.	Rank and Name.	
17566	R.Q.M.S.	BRIGHAM, H. A.	18325	Private	HOBSON, A.
17787	,,	WALKER, R.	17684	,,	LETHBRIDGE, T.
17606	L.-Sergt.	DIXON, A.	17699	,,	MAUDSLEY, R.
18357	,,	PORTER, E.	17707	,,	MOUNTAIN, E.
17423	Corporal	MAY, E.	17708	,,	MOUNTAIN, H.
17614	L.-Corpl.	ELLISON, S.	17978	,,	MILLINGTON, G.
17671	,,	KELLY, T.	18331	,,	MERRIMAN, W.
17677	,,	LAMB, J.	18332	,,	MADDOCKS, W.
17676	,,	LAMBERT, H.	17714	,,	NELSON, J. E.
17680	,,	LEATHER, J. N.	17718	,,	ORME, J. L.
17549	Private	BARDSLEY, J. A.	17719	,,	ORRELL, H.
17547	,,	BAGLEY, W.	17722	,,	OWEN, A. E.
17579	,,	CAUFIELD, H. A.	17724	,,	PARKYN, J. R.
17592	,,	CHAMBERS, F.	17725	,,	PASS, W. A.
17589	,,	CLULOW, J. W.	18263	,,	PEARSON, J.
17609	,,	DOWNWARD, J.	17736	,,	QUARTON, J.
17615	,,	ENTWISTLE, W.	18247	,,	ROWLAND, E.
17645	,,	HEALD, G. F.	17746	,,	SANDERSON, G.
17646	,,	HEALD, H.	17753	,,	SHIELS, R.
17664	,,	HUNT, W.	18315	,,	SLATER, F.
17647	,,	HESKETH, J.	17769	,,	TAYLOR, A.
17654	,,	HOLLAND, P.	17783	,,	WAGSTAFF, A. C.
17652	,,	HOCKADAY, F. L.	17790	,,	WALSH, R.
17946	,,	JONES, G.	17791	,,	WARDROP, V. M.
17682	,,	LEE, J.			

* For portrait, see Officers' Group, p. 209. † For portrait, see Sergeants' Group, p. 211.

The following were not present when the Platoon Photograph was taken, but see Supplementary Photograph on p. 254.

Roll No.	Rank	Name	Roll No.	Rank	Name
17593	L.-Corpl.	COWBURN, A.	17611	Private	EATON, H.
17628	,,	FRODSHAM, J. C.	17601	,,	DICKENSON, J. E.
17543	Private	ARMISTEAD, J.	18204	,,	DRABBLE, J.
17560	,,	BOYLE, A.	17612	,,	ECKERSLEY, R.
17553	,,	BERRY, J.	18259	,,	FIELD, F.
17563	,,	BRASSINGTON, S.	17649	,,	HILL, W.
17572	,,	BUCKLAND, F. E.	17653	,,	HOLLAND, J.
17594	,,	CROMPTON, W.	17674	,,	KENYON, J.
17591	,,	COOK, H. S.	17709	,,	MUNRO, A.
17578	,,	CALDWELL, H.	17751	,,	SHELDON, A.

20th (Service) Battalion Manchester Regiment.

"D" COMPANY.

Officer Commanding Company - Capt. A. Dean-Willcocks.
Second in Command - - - Lieut. J. S. Gemmell.*
Company Sergeant Major - - Myatt, A.
Company Quartermaster Sergeant - Brown, A. H.

PLATOON NO. XIII.

Platoon Commander - - - Lieut. J. W. Ramsbottom.
Platoon Sergeant - - - - George, E.

Roll No.	Rank and Name.		Roll No.	Rank and Name.	
17980	L.-Sergt.	Mills, A.	17896	Private	Gadsby, T.
17808	Corporal	Adshead, R. W.	17887	,,	Fittis, A. E.
17974	,,	Mellor, T.	17900	,,	Gibson, E.
17842	L.-Corpl.	Cadman, H.	17917	,,	Hardman, S. H.
17848	,,	Chadwick, R.	17915	,,	Hayman, F.
17942	,,	Jenkins, A.	17924	,,	Hill, A. J.
17948	,,	Keggen, H.	17923	,,	Higgins, H.
18376	,,	Sloane, W. H.	17930	,,	Howard, H.
17827	Private	Boardman, C. B.	17927	,,	Holme, E. H.
17821	,,	Barton, J. H.	17922	,,	Higginbottom, E. H.
17836	,,	Brierley, S.	17958	,,	Lawton, R. A.
17820	,,	Bartlett, W. H.	17981	,,	Milner, H.
17824	,,	Bebbington, F. B.	17965	,,	McCormack, W. M.
17826	,,	Berry, J. H.	18001	,,	O'Laughlin, P.
17833	,,	Brady, A.	18013	,,	Preece, R.
17862	,,	Craig, S.	18016	,,	Ritchie, J.
17853	,,	Clegg, F.	18029	,,	Simons, N.
17843	,,	Carpenter, F. H.	18036	,,	Sproston, G.
17857	,,	Coogan, H.	18040	,,	Thomas, A.
17845	,,	Carroll, S.	18004	,,	Tipton, H.
17870	,,	Derbyshire, W.	18047	,,	Wainwright, J.
17876	,,	Doyle, J.	18064	,,	Wilkinson, A.
17882	,,	Entwistle, A. S.	18067	,,	Williams, G. H.
17883	,,	Eyre, H. E.	18063	,,	Wilkins, J.
17889	,,	Foley, W.	18161	,,	Withington, F.
17893	,,	Fox, T.	17541	,,	Wylie, J.

* For portrait, see Officers' Group, p. 209.

The following were not present when the Platoon Photograph was taken:—

Roll No.	Rank	Name	Roll No.	Rank	Name
17817	Private	Barlow, F. H.	18297	Private	Jones, R.
17822	,,	Bateson, J.	17987	,,	Morris, J.
17861	,,	Cowburn, J.	18026	,,	Rutley, L.
17907	,,	Gregg, A.	18169	,,	Taylor, J.
18086	,,	Green, F.	18059	,,	White, T.
18295	,,	Southern, T.			

20th (Service) Battalion Manchester Regiment.
"D" COMPANY.

Officer Commanding Company - Capt. A. Dean-Willcocks.
Second in Command - - - Lieut. J. S. Gemmell.*
Company Sergeant Major - - Myatt, A.†
Company Quartermaster Sergeant - Brown, A. H.†

PLATOON NO. XIV.

Platoon Commander - - - 2nd Lieut. F. S. Brooks.
Platoon Sergeant - - - - Knight, H.

Roll No.	Rank and Name.		Roll No.	Rank and Name.	
17813	Sergeant	Bain, A. A.	17912	Private	Hall, J.
17295	,,	Beswick, E.	17914	,,	Hall, W.
17850	,,	Chapman, J. H.	17918	,,	Haynes, S.
17889	Corporal	Flynn, P.	17913	,,	Hall, W.
17944	,,	Jones, E.	17932	,,	Hudson, R. H.
18377	,,	Threlfall, N.	17943	,,	Jennings, C.
17947	L.-Corpl.	Joyce, H.	17951	,,	Kilvert, J. H.
17989	,,	Mott, J. W.	17960	,,	Lowe, C. W.
17997	,,	Nicholson, C. H.	17990	,,	Mowatt, S. B.
18039	,,	Taylor, W. H.	18397	,,	Mowatt, W.
17809	Private	Agnew, E.	17985	,,	Morgan, T.
17810	,,	Astley, T.	17971	,,	Matkin, J.
17811	,,	Bailey, J.	17999	,,	Nuttall, W.
17839	,,	Burke, T. H.	18014	,,	Prestwich, T.
17828	,,	Booth, T.	18003	,,	Page, H.
17815	,,	Banks, J.	18019	,,	Robinson, A.
17878	,,	Dudley, W.	18245	,,	Richmond, A.
17873	,,	Domican, A.	18030	,,	Slater, J.
17871	,,	Dixon, E.	18035	,,	Spiller, P.
17879	,,	Duffy, W. F.	18038	,,	Stevenson, J.
17874	,,	Downhill, F.	18027	,,	Sandham, T.
17885	,,	Fallowfield, H.	18163	,,	Shelmerdine, A.
17886	,,	Fawkes, E. J.	18065	,,	Wilkinson, H.
17904	,,	Gough, F.	18058	,,	Whetton, T.
17906	,,	Green, S.	18074	,,	Worrall, A. E.
17925	,,	Hindley, G. J.	18054	,,	Wardle, F. W.
17916	,,	Harrison, H.	18048	,,	Walker, A.
17936	,,	Humphries, G. W.	18118	,,	Widdeson, W.
17909	,,	Hackett, F.	18108	,,	Wood, W.
17937	,,	Hyde, F.	18076	,,	Yates, J.

* For portrait, see Officers' Group, p. 209. † For portrait, see Sergeants' Group, p. 211.

The following were not present when the Platoon Photograph was taken :—

Roll No.	Rank	Name	Roll No.	Rank	Name
17910	Sergeant	Halcrow, F. C.	17977	Private	Millington, F. W.
18257	Private	Booth, J.	17994	,,	Neiles, H.
17825	,,	Bebbington, J. H.	18306	,,	Richards, F.
18197	,,	Delany, E. L.	18032	,,	Southern, A.
17881	,,	Egan, F.	18049	,,	Walker, H.
17945	,,	Jones, F.	18212	,,	Wall, F.
17967	,,	McGuinness, B.	18303	,,	Whittaker, J. W.

20th (Service) Battalion Manchester Regiment.

"D" COMPANY.

Officer Commanding Company - Capt. A. Dean-Willcocks.
Second in Command - - - Lieut. J. S. Gemmell.*
Company Sergeant Major - - Myatt, A.†
Company Quartermaster Sergeant - Brown, A. H.†

PLATOON NO. XV.

Platoon Commander - - - Lieut. W. B. Bagshaw.
Platoon Sergeant - - - - Edwards, J.

Roll No.	Rank and Name.		Roll No.	Rank and Name.	
18021	Sergeant	Rocca, F.	17988	Private	Moss, A.
18360	L.-Sergt.	Chard, H. A. J.	17983	,,	Moore, J. H.
17839	L.-Corpl.	Burke, T.	17976	,,	Merron, E.
17834	,,	Brereton, N.	17984	,,	Moran, T.
17866	,,	Cuss, C.	17986	,,	Morrey, W. J.
17884	,,	Fairhurst, W.	18320	,,	Massey, W.
18009	,,	Pawley, E.	17998	,,	Norton, H.
17830	Private	Boyer, R.	17996	,,	Newey, E. H.
17829	,,	Bown, F.	17992	,,	Naylor, H.
17832	,,	Bradshaw, A.	17993	,,	Naylor, J. W.
17818	,,	Barnett, G. A.	18000	,,	Ogden, E.
17831	,,	Bradbury, A.	18011	,,	Pilkington, N.
17844	,,	Carr, J.	18006	,,	Parker, A.
17849	,,	Chapman, E.	18020	,,	Robinson, S.
17852	,,	Clayton, H.	18022	,,	Rogerson, D. H.
17856	,,	Connors, H.	18158	,,	Richardson, H.
17859	,,	Cooper, A.	18034	,,	Speed, F.
17875	,,	Downs, T.	18012	,,	Shaw, J.
17891	,,	Ford, F.	18041	,,	Thomas, A.
17897	,,	Gale, N.	18157	,,	Thornley, J.
17899	,,	Gibbons, T.	18104	,,	Trigg, A.
17903	,,	Gothard, W. J.	18155	,,	Taylor, R.
17926	,,	Hoffman, W. J.	18055	,,	Wass, W.
17933	,,	Hughes, W.	18072	,,	Windridge, W.
17952	,,	Kirby, A.	18066	,,	Wilkinson, J.
17961	,,	Lowe, P.	18141	,,	Windsor, W. E.
17957	,,	Lamb, H.	18341	,,	Walmsley, J. T.
17982	,,	Milns, F.	18107	,,	Walker, R.

* For portrait, see Officers' Group, p. 209.   † For portrait, see Sergeants' Group, p. 211.

The following were not present when the Platoon Photograph was taken:—

Roll No.	Rank	Name	Roll No.	Rank	Name
18046	Sergeant	Wagster, S.	18334	Private	Hambleton, P.
17864	Private	Croker, J.	17869	,,	Delany, C.
17855	,,	Coles, F.	18371	,,	Dale, L.
17911	,,	Hall, G.	18042	,,	Thompson, F.
17970	,,	Massie, C.	18070	,,	Willoughby, C. W.

20th (Service) Battalion Manchester Regiment.

"D" COMPANY.

Officer Commanding Company - Capt. A. Dean-Willcocks.
Second in Command - - - Lieut. J. S. Gemmell.*
Company Sergeant Major - - Myatt, A.†
Company Quartermaster Sergeant - Brown, A. H.†

PLATOON NO. XVI.

Platoon Commander - - - 2nd Lieut. E. K. Agnew.
Platoon Sergeant - - - - Ford, J. S.

Roll No.	Rank and Name.		Roll No.	Rank and Name.	
17277	Sergeant	Adamson, J.	17953	Private	Kirk, J.
17868	L.-Sergt.	Davies, H.	17950	,,	Kershaw, C. H.
17814	Corporal	Baker, C.	17949	,,	Kelsall, J. W.
18017	,,	Robbins, J. T.	17959	,,	Leather, D.
17972	L.-Corpl.	Matthew, A.	17963	,,	Lyon, A.
18056	,,	Watkins, J.	17962	,,	Luttmann, G.
17860	,,	Corns, W.	17956	,,	Ladkin, T. G.
17841	Private	Burrows, S.	17973	,,	Matthews, E.
17812	,,	Bailey, R.	17968	,,	Mason, A.
17823	,,	Beattie, H. B.	17971	,,	Muchan, F.
17865	,,	Curvis, W.	17995	,,	Nelson, W.
17847	,,	Chadwick, G. T.	18037	,,	Stephen, L.
17851	,,	Chisholm, W.	18028	,,	Shannon, R.
18083	,,	Chadwick, E.	18031	,,	Smith, R. S.
17872	,,	Dolan, T.	18135	,,	Shaw, W.
17888	,,	Flemming, M. M.	18154	,,	Sidebottom, H.
17895	,,	Frizzell, T.	18121	,,	Sidebottom, S.
17901	,,	Goddard, L.	18043	,,	Timms, F.
17908	,,	Guthrie, C. S.	18053	,,	Ward, F.
17902	,,	Gordon, J.	18061	,,	Whitlam, W. J.
17919	,,	Hesford, B.	18068	,,	Williams, A.
17931	,,	Howard, B.	18073	,,	Woolley, W.
17935	,,	Hulse, G.	18052	,,	Ward, R. R.
17928	,,	Holt, A. E.	18060	,,	Whitehouse, J.
17934	,,	Hulme, J.	18057	,,	Whalley, P.

Also on the Photograph: 2nd Lieut. G. G. Giffard.

* For portrait, see Officers' Group, p. 209. † For portrait, see Sergeants' Group, p. 211.

The following were not present when the Platoon Photograph was taken:—

18002	L.-Corpl.	Owen, R. G.	18008	Private	Parsonage, A.
18024	,,	Rowen, E.	17846	,,	Chadwick, E.
17816	Private	Barber, H.	17877	,,	Drinkwater, C.
17894	,,	France, J.	17921	,,	Heywood, T.
17941	,,	Jacob, J. E.	17920	,,	Heywood, F.
18033	,,	Speakman, J. H.	17940	,,	Jacob, G. F.
18048	,,	Walker, H.	17939	,,	Jacob, A.
18062	,,	Wilcock, G. H.	18007	,,	Parker, W. E.

20th (Service) Battalion Manchester Regiment.

"E" COMPANY.

Officer Commanding Company	Capt. G. B. Sayce.
Second in Command	Capt. T. A. Harris.
Company Sergeant Major	Clarke, T
Company Quartermaster Sergeant	Howard, R.

PLATOON NO. XVII.

Platoon Commander	Lieut. H. Lomas.
Platoon Sergeant	Browne, F.

Roll No.	Rank and Name.		Roll No.	Rank and Name.	
18374	Corporal	Paynting, J. H.	18215	Private	Taylor, F.
18316	,,	Osborne, H.	26004	,,	Cooper, T. L.
18151	L.-Corpl.	Horsfall, H.	26082	,,	Longden, M.
17334	,,	Dinning, J.	26066	,,	Norbury, J. C.
18227	Private	Connor, E.	18393	,,	Watkins, W. R.
18214	,,	Hallewell, F.	18493	,,	Young, W. H.
18400	,,	Bradbury, J.	18200	,,	Froggatt, W.
18390	,,	Cross, C. H.	18500	,,	Hamilton, E.
18209	,,	Harbottle, F.	18481	,,	Murphy, J.
18232	,,	Wolstencroft, D.	26098	,,	Morris, R.
18391	,,	Horrocks, A.	18477	,,	Russell, G.
18395	,,	Boardman, A.	26071	,,	Broadbent, F.
18392	,,	White, W.	18106	,,	Ward, H.
18435	,,	Rigby, H.	18457	,,	Sainter, A. E.
26042	,,	Brown, R. J.	18418	,,	Hollows, R.
26024	,,	Caudwell, E.	26086	,,	Thomas, F.
26054	,,	Hunt, H.	18242	,,	Johnson, W.
26012	,,	Roberts, A. E.	18434	,,	Potter, J. E.
26050	,,	Unsworth, H.	18473	,,	Mortique, W. M.
26038	,,	Toole, J.	26090	,,	Jones, H.
26032	,,	Gilliver, A.	26078	,,	Hibbert, H.
26046	,,	Kay, E.	18399	,,	Taylor, R.
26058	,,	Corless, J.	18441	,,	Hardman, F.
26028	,,	Edwards, H.	18461	,,	Houghton, H. C.
18401	,,	Lloyd, J.	18185	,,	Atkinson, W.
18485	,,	McAndrew, P.	26008	,,	Williams, G.
18394	,,	Douglas, A.	18445	,,	Hardy, J.
18402	,,	Whitworth, S. W.	18250	,,	Worthington, P.
18228	,,	Stansfield, T.			

20th (Service) Battalion Manchester Regiment.

"E" COMPANY.

Officer Commanding Company - Capt. G. B. SAYCE.*
Second in Command - - - Capt. T. A. HARRIS.*
Company Sergeant Major - - CLARKE, T.*
Company Quartermaster Sergeant - HOWARD, R.*

PLATOON NO. XVIII.

Platoon Commander - - - Lieut. B. DENTON-THOMPSON.
Platoon Sergeant - - - WORSLEY, F. H.

Roll No.	Rank and Name.		Roll No.	Rank and Name.	
18161	Corporal	ROWAN, W.	18225	Private	MATHER, E.
18078	,,	ARNISON, J.	17750	,,	SHARPLES, R.
17630	L.-Corpl.	GANNON, J.	18224	,,	THOMAS, J.
18179	,,	MILLS, A. F.	18253	,,	LAMBERT, J.
17481	,,	SEMARK, F. G.	26055	,,	KENNEDY, J.
18271	,,	KELLY, P.	26083	,,	BATES, W.
18307	,,	SLIM, J.	18463	,,	RENSHAW, H.
18326	Private	SCOTT, F.	26039	,,	KAY, A.
18287	,,	BURKE, T.	26063	,,	TUKE, T.
18430	,,	CONQUEST, W. A.	26013	,,	HARDY, F.
18231	,,	MURPHY, L.	26029	,,	ARROWSMITH, E.
26092	,,	HENLEY, D.	18438	,,	GREENWOOD, J.
26075	,,	OLDHAM, W.	18442	,,	PARKINSON, C. H.
26035	,,	WALKER, F.	18446	,,	PENDLEBURY, J.
18255	,,	HENNESSY, J.	18480	,,	DAVIES, F.
18319	,,	MELLARD, G. A. T.	18454	,,	ROBERTS, J.
26047	,,	PICKFORD, R.	18490	,,	ABBOTT, J.
18172	,,	DIXON, G.	18458	,,	WILKINSON, S. B.
26087	,,	FOX, T.	18462	,,	SHARPLES, R.
17554	,,	BAYES, A.	18466	,,	MOORES, N.
18406	,,	PLANT, S. C.	18470	,,	GUEST, E. S.
18405	,,	CRESSWELL, A.	18474	,,	STEVENSON, T. S.
26043	,,	BUTLER, W.	18478	,,	SMETHURST, C.
17597	,,	DAVIES, E.	18497	,,	BUTLER, C.
17854	,,	COE, C.	26001	,,	ALLEN, W. J.
26025	,,	CUSHION, A.	26005	,,	PAUL, E.
18252	,,	HAUGHTON, F.	26009	,,	PARR, J. R.
26051	,,	RHODES, J.	18282	,,	JACKSON, S.
26017	,,	SIDEBOTTOM, W.	26091	,,	ASHWORTH, J.
18691	,,	McDONOUGH, J.			

* For portrait, see Platoon XVII, p. 247.

20th (Service) Battalion Manchester Regiment.

"E" COMPANY.

Officer Commanding Company - Capt. G. B. Sayce.*
Second in Command - - - Capt. T. A. Harris.*
Company Sergeant Major - - Clarke, T.*
Company Quartermaster Sergeant - Howard, R.*

PLATOON NO. XIX.

Platoon Commander - - - Lieut. R. L. Hartley.
Platoon Sergeant - - - West, S. W.

Roll No.	Rank and Name.		Roll No.	Rank and Name.	
18382	L.-Sergt.	Mayer, A. G.	18439	Private	Thompson, H.
18018	L.-Corpl.	Roberts, A.	18422	,,	Williams, E. E.
18268	,,	Griffiths, T. S.	18431	,,	Morritt, W.
18261	,,	Walsh, J.	18437	,,	Ellison, F.
18162	,,	Brown, J.	18443	,,	Jepson, W. E.
18292	,,	Catlin, W.	18447	,,	Tevnan, E.
17059	,,	Crook, W.	18451	,,	Hancock, F.
17306	Private	Burnett, A.	18455	,,	Seddon, A. P.
17010	,,	Beard, G.	18459	,,	Sproson, T.
18352	,,	Connolly, W. H.	18463	,,	Angus, A. H.
18241	,,	Harley, W. H.	18491	,,	Hughes, D.
18285	,,	Hogg, J.	18494	,,	Jackson, B.
17964	,,	Lyst, H.	18498	,,	Greaves, E.
18294	,,	McDermott, J. F.	26002	,,	Rowe, W. H.
18312	,,	McComish, J.	26006	,,	Armstrong, W.
18427	,,	McLeavy, J.	26010	,,	Pearson, A.
18344	,,	Ogden, D.	26014	,,	Jackson, L. J.
18328	,,	Oldfield, J.	26018	,,	Cockin, J.
18191	,,	Ridgard, J. W.	26022	,,	Mulkerns, M.
18256	,,	Richardson, J.	26026	,,	Donley, A.
17235	,,	Taylor, C.	26036	,,	Price, J.
17521	,,	Walsh, T.	26042	,,	Garnett, F.
18110	,,	Wolstenholme, G.	18467	,,	Seddon, E.
18403	,,	Bradwell, F.	26044	,,	Byrne, J.
18423	,,	Griffiths, H.	26052	,,	Ogden, S. H.
18424	,,	Kirby, T.	26060	,,	Cole, E. B.
18412	,,	Miller, W.	26056	,,	Hall, H.
18414	,,	Platt, J.	26072	,,	Royle, T.
18421	,,	Settle, R. J.	26088	,,	Page, T.

* For portrait, see Platoon XVII, p. 247.

20th (Service) Battalion Manchester Regiment.

"E" COMPANY.

Officer Commanding Company - Capt. G. B. SAYCE.*
Second in Command - - - Capt. T. A. HARRIS.*
Company Sergeant Major - - CLARKE, T.*
Company Quartermaster Sergeant - HOWARD, R.*

PLATOON NO. XX.

Platoon Commander - - - 2nd Lieut. C. K. HALDANE.
Platoon Sergeant - - - SHOESMITH, W.

Roll No.	Rank and Name.		Roll No.	Rank and Name.	
17313	Sergeant	CLARKE, H.	18368	Private	WAITE, T.
18378	Corporal	WILSON, D. A.	18472	,,	FERNS, J. E.
18129	L.-Corpl.	TOLAN, S.	26015	,,	LYNCH, P.
18159	,,	WARBURTON, A.	18499	,,	BOYD, E.
18280	,,	COLLINS, R. W.	26011	,,	MASSEY, C.
18460	Private	LUCAS, A. R.	18480	,,	BRIERLEY, F.
18411	,,	JACKSON, T.	18322	,,	LITH, G.
18407	,,	HORRIDGE, H.	18342	,,	HOLT, F.
18406	,,	HOUGHTON, H.	18305	,,	SKADE, H.
26073	,,	ROBERTS, E.	26085	,,	ROOD, T.
18409	,,	BURGESS, C.	26007	,,	COOKE, M.
18413	,,	ATHERTON, H.	18440	,,	PICKLES, W.
17319	,,	COPELAND, T.	18410	,,	BENNETT, H. J.
18408	,,	WREN, J.	18484	,,	HUDSON, T. W.
17843	,,	CARPENTER, F. H.	18488	,,	LEECH, W.
17352	,,	FUTVOYE, G. F.	18112	,,	TAYLOR, T.
17487	,,	SMITH, A. R.	18448	,,	WEBBER, S.
26057	,,	DANBY, G. H.	18432	,,	THOMPSON, S.
17086	,,	FITZGERALD, T.	26065	,,	PRINCE, J.
18415	,,	SENIOR, T.	26061	,,	PARKINSON, E.
26023	,,	ISHERWOOD, J.	18419	,,	REDING, J.

* For portrait, see Platoon XVII, p. 247.

20th Battalion.—Supplementary Photo.

21st (Service) Battalion

21st (Service) Battalion Manchester Regiment.

Roll of Officers.

Colonel	Norman, W. W.	Lieutenant	Langdon, G.
Major	Moore, H.	,,	Gilmore, E. F.
,,	Ommanney, F. F.	,,	Taylor, F. T.
,,	Logan, J. R.	,,	Scott, H. E.
Capt. & Adjt.	Brooks, H. J.	,,	Walker, H. W.
Captain	Wilson, T. I. W.	,,	Carstairs, N. M.
,,	Hobson, C. J. M.	2nd Lieut.	Lillie, A. P.
,,	Fitzpatrick, J.	,,	Harris, A.
,,	Parker, R. F.	,,	Lee-Evans, G.
,,	Swallow, H. B.	,,	Russell, A. S.
,,	Plummer, N.	,,	Smith, H. C.
Lieutenant	Chapman, J.	,,	Simpson, E. T.
,,	Chapman, J.	,,	Hirst, H. H.
,,	Cunliffe, J. L.	,,	Scrutton, F. S.
,,	Thorniley, P. A. H.	Lt. & Q.M.	Waterhouse, R.

For Officers of the Depot Companies, see Photograph on p. 401.

21st (Service) Battalion Manchester Regiment.

Non-Commissioned Officers' (Sergeants) Roll.

Warrant Officer.
4/2952 R.S.M. WADE, E.

19637 R.Q.M.S. CUNLIFFE, L.
19162 R.O.R.S. JENKINS, P. E.

Roll No.	Rank and Name.		Roll No.	Rank and Name.	
18504	C.S.M.	GIBBS, C.	18965	Sergeant	OWEN, A.
19319	"	BARLOW, F.	18827	"	COLES, G. S.
19045	"	TURNER, T.	19168	"	JULIAN, H.
18775	C.Q.M.S.	STANSFIELD, J.	19383	"	FITZHUGH, T.
19046	"	SUTER, E. A.	19482	"	PARKES, D.
19313	"	STOCKTON, W.	19480	"	PERFITT, W. F.
19066	Pion. Sgt.	BITHELL, C. F.	19486	"	PALMER, W. O.
18624	Trns. Sgt.	ISHERWOOD, D.	19104	"	DONALDSON, W. J.
19044	Sig. Sgt.	AITKEN, J.	19008	"	SPROUT, H.
19872	Sergeant	MOORE, H. L.	19020	"	TURNER, J.
16219	"	SLATER, J. F.	19179	"	LEE, A.
19039	"	YEARSLEY, C.	19145	"	HENSHAW, R.
18502	"	ROWBOTHAM, A.	18910	"	HAWORTH, J.
18545	"	CAPPER, W.	19220	"	NICHOL, T. C.
18604	"	HART, J. W.	19837	"	REEVES, R.
18729	"	SMITH, J. B.	18707	L.-Sergt.	ROGERSON, A.
18553	"	COLLINS, T.	18727	"	SMITH, H.
18815	"	BERRY, W.	19034	"	WILSON, W. A.
19037	"	WALKER, H.	18912	"	HAYWARD, J. T.
19056	"	BARKER, H.	18977	"	PRATT, J.
18855	"	DOWNS, T. E.	19430	"	LAMBERT, F.
18797	"	BURGESS, F.	19315	"	ADSHEAD, J.
18848	"	DUTSON, S.	19126	"	GOVER, H.
18823	"	BROWNSON, H.	19226	"	PALIN, J.
18609	"	HEAP, J.			

Also on the Photograph: Col. W. W. NORMAN, Maj. H. MOORE, Capt. & Adj. H. J. BROOKS, and Lt. & Q.Mr. R. WATERHOUSE.

The following were not present when the Photograph was taken:—

19312	C.S.M.	COLBERT, J. T.	18751	Sergeant	WARD, J. B.
18501	C.Q.M.S.	HARVEY, W. J.	18886	"	GREENHALGH, W. M.
19833	Sgt. Cook	LITTLEWOOD, F.			

21st (Service) Battalion Manchester Regiment.

Bugle Band.

Roll No.	Rank and Name.		Roll No.	Rank and Name.	
19039	Sergeant	YEARSLEY, C.	19626	Drummer	WOOD, P.
18684	L.-Corpl.	PERCIVAL, H.	19505	,,	SAYER, H.
18694	Drummer	RAWLINSON, B.	19743	,,	WALKER, H.
18708	,,	ROYLE, A.	18592	,,	GREEN, J.
18836	,,	CLARKE, J.	18562	,,	DAVENPORT, R.
18925	,,	JOHNSTON, F.	19079	,,	CHATTERTON, S. B.
19014	,,	TRAVIS, E.	19713	,,	MASSEY, J.
18980	,,	REVETT, W.	19799	,,	ATKINS, H.
19174	,,	KNEALE, S.	19062	,,	BERRY, G. C.
19182	,,	LINDSAY, J.	19250	,,	SELLARS, C.
19223	,,	NUGENT, J.	19503	,,	SALE, E.
19764	,,	GILBERT, E.	19752	,,	GALLEYMORE, J. W.
19591	,,	SPELLMAN, J.			

The following were not present when the Photograph was taken :—

| 18720 | Drummer SHAW, W. | 18943 | Drummer LEES, J. J. |

21st (Service) Battalion Manchester Regiment.

"A" COMPANY.

Officer Commanding Company - Major R. J. LOGAN.*
Second in Command - - - Capt. N. PLUMMER.*
Company Sergeant Major - - GIBBS, C.
Company Quartermaster Sergeant - HARVEY, W. J.

PLATOON NO. I.

Platoon Commander - - - Lieut. J. L. CUNLIFFE.
Platoon Sergeant - - - - ROWBOTHAM, A.

Roll No.	Rank and Name.	Roll No.	Rank and Name
18681	Corporal PEART, H.	19614	Private PLEVIN, J.
18688	,, PLANT, W.	18713	,, RYLANDS, F.
18639	L.-Corpl. KILNER, I. C.	18716	,, SCOBLE, H.
18709	,, ROYLE, R.	18723	,, SIMMONS, A.
18594	,, GREENOUGH, W.	18750	,, WARD, F.
19031	,, WILLIS, H.	19689	,, WATERHOUSE, H.
18722	,, SIEPEN, A.	18539	,, BURNHAM, J.
18617	,, HOLTUM, C.	18635	,, JONES, C.
18662	Private McHUGH, M.	18600	,, HARRISON, G. W.
18669	,, MOSLEY, F. S.	18525	,, BERRY, J.
18621	,, HAWORTH, J.	18576	,, FLINT, A.
18644	,, LEIGH, H.	18620	,, HOUGHTON, J.
18699	,, RICHARDSON, W.	18725	,, SHELTON, J.
18593	,, GREEN, J.	18701	,, REILLY, J.
18605	,, HUXLEY, A.	18515	,, BARNES, W.
18749	,, WATERS, J.	18618	,, HOPKINS, C.
19755	,, NICHOLLS, C.	18613	,, HEYDEN, F.
18677	,, PARKER, R.	19596	,, WRIGHT, A.
19816	,, TATLER, J.	18591	,, GREEN, F.
18647	,, LEWIS, S.	18641	,, KNOWLES, A.
18571	,, ELLIS, T.	19597	,, McDONALD, B.
18548	,, CASANOVE, M.	19636	,, DUFFY, M.
18554	,, COLTON, E.	19635	,, WHITE, H.
18558	,, CROSBIE, J.	18563	,, DAVIES, B.
18569	,, DRANSFIELD, C.	18654	,, MARSDEN, J. W.
18619	,, HOUGH, H.	19621	,, RYDEHEARD, T.
19595	,, IDDLES, W.	19672	,, HUMPHREYS, H. D.
18663	,, McMAHON, A.	19697	,, TAYLOR, J.

* For portrait, see Officers' Group, p. 257.

21st (Service) Battalion Manchester Regiment.
"A" COMPANY.

Officer Commanding Company - Major R. J. Logan.*
Second in Command - - - Capt. N. Plummer.*
Company Sergeant Major - - Gibbs, C.†
Company Quartermaster Sergeant - Harvey, W. J.

PLATOON NO. II.

Platoon Commander - - - 2nd Lieut. E. T. Simpson.
Platoon Sergeant - - - - Barker, F.

Roll No.	Rank and Name.		Roll No.	Rank and Name.	
18728	Sergeant	Smith, J. B.	18767	Private	Wisdom, A.
18727	L.-Sergt.	Smith, H.	18687	,,	Pittpladdy, R.
18660	Corporal	McGreaves, H. C.	18768	,,	Wood, F.
18666	,,	Mollard, A. E.	18531	,,	Boothman, H.
18612	L.-Corpl.	Hestford, A.	18566	,,	Dobson, W.
18519	,,	Bann, F.	18601	,,	Harrison, J.
18536	,,	Brook, H.	18528	,,	Blackwood, F.
18556	,,	Court, L.	18511	,,	Ball, R.
18719	,,	Shaw, A.	18565	,,	Diamond, W.
18575	Private	Fitzpatrick, J.	18616	,,	Holt, G. T.
18759	,,	Whittaker, J. F.	18682	,,	Peers, W. J.
18733	,,	Swinburn, E.	18550	,,	Chesworth, H.
18622	,,	Howlett, T.	18602	,,	Harrison, W. B.
18761	,,	Whyatt, H.	18597	,,	Hampson, F.
18625	,,	Isherwood, J.	18732	,,	Sutton, T.
18664	,,	Meehan, J.	18672	,,	Naughton, J.
18734	,,	Taylor, R.	18721	,,	Sidebotham, H.
18670	,,	Mullard, H.	18747	,,	Walker, H.
18522	,,	Beaumont, H.	19785	,,	Yates, H. W.
18510	,,	Bailey, R.	19809	,,	Holland, A.
18527	,,	Black, A. E.	19084	,,	Conway, J.
18564	,,	Densley, J.	19810	,,	Jaques, H. W.
18579	,,	Foley, J.	19766	,,	Nicholls, A.
18588	,,	Grainger, G. E.	19812	,,	Norris, Z.
18595	,,	Groom, T.			
18598	,,	Hampton, F.		*Attached.*	
18561	,,	Daniels, F.	18553	Sergeant	Collins, T.
18742	,,	Turner, R. S.			

* For portrait, see Officers' Group, p. 257.   † For portrait, see Sergeants' Group, p. 259.

The following were not present when the Platoon Photograph was taken :—

18610	Sergeant	Heap, W.	18695	Private	Read, A.
18653	Private	Marran, M.	18743	,,	Twitty, G. B.
18517	,,	Battersby, J.	18730	,,	Sparling, W.
18567	,,	Dolman, T. W.	18629	,,	James, G. F.
18744	,,	Vaughan, W.	18520	,,	Baxter, B.
18562	,,	Davenport, R.	18694	,,	Rawlinson, B.
18715	,,	Sarsfield, R.			

21st (Service) Battalion Manchester Regiment.

"A" COMPANY.

Officer Commanding Company - Major R. J. Logan.*
Second in Command - - - Capt. N. Plummer.*
Company Sergeant Major - - Gibbs, C.†
Company Quartermaster Sergeant - Harvey, W. J.

PLATOON NO. III.

Platoon Commander - - - 2nd Lieut. A. Harris.
Platoon Sergeant - - - - Capper, W.

Roll No.	Rank and Name.		Roll No.	Rank and Name.	
18559	Corporal	Crossland, A. E.	18748	Private	Wall, W. E.
18652	L.-Corpl.	Madden, F. J.	18674	,,	Osborne, W.
18756	,,	White, A.	18656	,,	Martin, C. H.
18573	,,	Fenn, E.	18572	,,	Ellor, S.
18570	,,	Elliott, H.	18680	,,	Pearson, A. E.
18714	Private	Sandall, H.	18642	,,	Lane, A.
18746	,,	Waggett, F.	18532	,,	Boyes, R.
18758	,,	Whitehead, A.	18762	,,	Wild, J.
18603	,,	Hart, F.	19762	,,	Collins, W.
18766	,,	Wilson, A.	19744	,,	Hudson, T.
19869	,,	Osborne, J.	19767	,,	Holliday, M.
18709	,,	Tomlinson, J.	19733	,,	Suddons, T.
18741	,,	Turner, G. E.	19654	,,	Smith, W.
18773	,,	Young, W. J.	19655	,,	Greenwood, C.
19731	,,	Dutton, F.	19687	,,	Daniels, F.
19790	,,	Holme, G.	18671	,,	Mycock, A.
19899	,,	Waggett, W.	18740	,,	Toole, A.
18537	,,	Brooks, R.	18630	,,	Jenkins, A.
18530	,,	Bolland, J.	18540	,,	Burt, S.
18513	,,	Bardsley, T.	18737	,,	Thompson, A.
18552	,,	Cockcroft, L.	19775	,,	Sherry, S.
18590	,,	Green, E.	18703	,,	Rippingham, S.
18631	,,	Johnson, C.	18685	,,	Petrie, C.
18712	,,	Rider, W.	18760	,,	Whewell, T.
18547	,,	Carroll, W.	19910	,,	Crossland, J. W.
18544	,,	Cannell, W.	18667	,,	Moreton, T.

* For portrait, see Officers' Group, p. 257. † For portrait, see Sergeants' Group, p. 259.

The following were not present when the Platoon Photograph was taken:—

18587	Corporal	Goodman, W.	18632	Private	Johnson, T.
18551	Private	Clayton, H.	19804	,,	Dunn, W.
18592	,,	Green, J.	19787	,,	Wilson, F.
18538	,,	Bunting, G.	18611	,,	Henshaw, T.
18650	,,	Lucas, F.	19079	,,	Chatterton, S. B.

21st (Service) Battalion Manchester Regiment.

"A" COMPANY.

Officer Commanding Company - Major R. J. LOGAN.*
Second in Command - - - Capt. N. PLUMMER.*
Company Sergeant Major - - GIBBS, C.†
Company Quartermaster Sergeant - HARVEY, W. J.

PLATOON NO. IV.

Platoon Commander - - - Lieut. E. F. GILMORE.
Platoon Sergeant - - - HART, J. W.†

Roll No.	Rank	and Name.	Roll No.	Rank	and Name.
18707	Sergeant	ROGERSON, A.	18770	Private	WORTHINGTON, A.
19872	,,	MOORE, H. L.	18698	,,	RICHARDSON, L.
19518	Corporal	SODEN, P.	18679	,,	PARTRIDGE, C. C.
18931	,,	KENWORTHY.	19800	,,	CAPPER, H.
18769	L.-Corpl.	WOOLER, T.	18634	,,	JONES, A.
18529	,,	BODEN, R. G.	18507	,,	ALLCOCK, J.
18696	,,	REDMAN, W.	18555	,,	COOPER, H.
18608	,,	HAYWARD, E.	18582	,,	FERNIFER, J.
18508	Private	APPLETON, J.	18614	,,	HOLMES, J.
18523	,,	BEESLEY, A.	18627	,,	JACKSON, W.
18541	,,	BUSHELL, C.	18582	,,	GARSIDE, P.
18615	,,	HOLT, F.	18583	,,	GABITIS, G.
18596	,,	HALL, J.	18675	,,	PACEY, J. H.
18640	,,	KIRKMAN, W.	18658	,,	MASON, T.
18643	,,	LEES, T.	18581	,,	FRASER, A.
18655	,,	MARSHALL, C.	19765	,,	GIFFORD, G. W.
18693	,,	RALPHS, W.	18696	,,	RENSHAW, E.
18710	,,	RYAN, J.	18648	,,	LEWTAS, E.
18523	,,	BENNETT, S.	18659	,,	MCCARTHY, M.
19704	,,	BILLINGTON, H.	18514	,,	BARLOW, F. S.
18533	,,	BRADLEY, E.	18542	,,	BUTTERFIELD, J.
18607	,,	HAYES, H.	18546	,,	CORNES, J. W.
18633	,,	JOLLY, R.	18509	,,	AYLOTT, J.
18636	,,	JONES, H.	18560	,,	CROSSLEY, H.
18689	,,	PLAYFOOT, E.	18711	,,	RYDER, J. W.
18718	,,	SCOTT, W.	19693	,,	DAVIES, F.
18717	,,	SCOTT, J.	19708	,,	CROMBLEHOLME, D.
18735	,,	TAYLOR, R. C.	19679	,,	KELLY, W.
18753	,,	WEBB, F.	19688	,,	MAHER, T.
18755	,,	WESTMACOTT, A. J.	19723	,,	TERRY, R. H.

* For portrait, see Officers' Group, p. 257. † For portrait, see Sergeants' Group, p. 259.

The following were not present when the Platoon Photograph was taken:—

| 18689 | L.-Corpl | PERCIVAL, H. | 18668 | Private | MORRIS, J. |
| 18690 | Private | POPPLEWELL, F. | 18708 | ,, | ROYLE, A. |

21st (Service) Battalion Manchester Regiment.

"B" COMPANY.

Officer Commanding Company - Capt. C. J. M. Hobson.*
Second in Command - - - Capt. J. Fitzpatrick.*
Company Sergeant Major - - Barlow, F.†
Company Quartermaster Sergeant - Stansfield, J.†

PLATOON NO. V.

Platoon Commander - - - Lieut. H. B. Swallow.
Platoon Sergeant - - - - Downs, T.

Roll No.	Rank and Name.		Roll No.	Rank and Name.	
19044	Sergeant	Aitken, J.	18890	Private	Hill, J.
18848	,,	Dutson, S.	18889	,,	Harratt, J.
18912	L.-Sergt.	Hayward, J. T.	18894	,,	Hutchinson, J. S.
19588	Corporal	Downs, A. H.	18929	,,	Kenny, L.
18968	,,	Pearson, C.	18945	,,	McCourt, M.
18989	L.-Corpl.	Robinson, J.	18953	,,	Malley, E.
18967	,,	Pawsey, C.	18961	,,	Nuttall, E.
18928	,,	Kennedy, P. J.	18971	,,	Price, T.
18780	Private	Ashworth, A.	18969	,,	Price, E.
18788	,,	Barlow, R.	18966	,,	Pattison, J.
18795	,,	Booth, J.	18983	,,	Russell, E.
19040	,,	Butler, L.	18984	,,	Ryder, T.
18792	,,	Birchall, R.	18980	,,	Revett, W.
18791	,,	Blakeley, J.	18982	,,	Rowles, J.
18794	,,	Bruce, E.	18981	,,	Rowles, E.
19042	,,	Brunt, J.	19016	,,	Tomlinson, W.
18826	,,	Clayton, W.	19017	,,	Toole, P.
18828	,,	Corcoran, J.	19015	,,	Terry, E.
18830	,,	Cox, W.	19029	,,	Wright, J.
18829	,,	Courtney, T.	19026	,,	Wickham, J.
18846	,,	Darbyshire, E.	19024	,,	Wain, J.
18847	,,	Dobson, W.	19014	,,	Travis, E.
18860	,,	Farnworth, W.	19030	,,	Woodhouse, F.
18859	,,	Farrand, H.	19027	,,	Wilkinson, J.
18861	,,	Fitzgerald, R.	19029	,,	Wolstenholme, J.
18862	,,	Flanagan, J.	19742	,,	Timmis, W.
18864	,,	Greenhalgh, G.	19613	,,	Lewis, W.
18863	,,	Graham, A.	19713	,,	Massey, J.
18888	,,	Harper, W.	19827	,,	Steele, A.
18891	,,	Hinchley, L.	19805	,,	Ennis, M.
18893	,,	Huddart, J.	18949	,,	Elliott, G.
18887	,,	Hall, T.	18904	,,	Harrison, R.

* For portrait, see Officers' Group, p. 257.   † For portrait, see Sergeants' Group, p. 259.

21st (Service) Battalion Manchester Regiment.

"B" COMPANY.

Officer Commanding Company - Capt. C. J. M. Hobson.*
Second in Command - - - Capt. J. Fitzpatrick.*
Company Sergeant Major - - Barlow, F.
Company Quartermaster Sergeant - Stansfield, J.†

PLATOON NO. VI.

Platoon Commander - - - 2nd Lieut. H. C. Smith.
Platoon Sergeant - - - - Berry, W.

Roll No.	Rank and Name.		Roll No.	Rank and Name.	
18965	Sergeant	Owen, A.	18877	Private	Grant, A.
19034	L.-Sergt.	Wilson, W. A.	18878	,,	Greenwood, J.
18993	Corporal	Rigby, W.	18906	,,	Haigh, J.
18913	,,	Humphries, W.	18905	,,	Hammond, J.
18790	L.-Corpl.	Bardsley, J. H.	18914	,,	Hibbert, W.
19845	,,	Walker, G.	19662	,,	Hicklin, J.
19033	,,	White, G. W.	18908	,,	Higgins, P.
18776	Private	Adams, A.	18907	,,	Hulme, T.
19630	,,	Adams, A.	18922	,,	Jones, E.
18782	,,	Astley, W.	18923	,,	Jones, E.
18809	,,	Bardsley, E.	18954	,,	Mayers, H. W.
18812	,,	Barnes, H.	18950	,,	Molloy, W. H.
18813	,,	Breakey, H.	18951	,,	McCormack, F.
18789	,,	Brooks, H.	19711	,,	McCreery, P. M.
18814	,,	Burgess, G. E.	18952	,,	McNeill, J.
18810	,,	Buckley, J.	18964	,,	O'Neill, T.
18811	,,	Buckley, P.	18974	,,	Parkin, J.
18808	,,	Byrne, W.	18975	,,	Pickup, N.
18840	,,	Callaghan, T.	19795	,,	Poulton, E. P.
18843	,,	Connor, W.	18992	,,	Rodway, J.
18841	,,	Coulson, J. S.	18990	,,	Rose, T.
18838	,,	Crane, T. A.	18994	,,	Rowark, J. E.
18852	,,	Davies, E.	18991	,,	Ryder, F.
19734	,,	Dearden, F.	19009	,,	Saxon, W.
18856	,,	Dickinson, P.	19001	,,	Smith, R.
18867	,,	Flatterly, F.	19736	,,	Swain, F.
19648	,,	Fletcher, H.	19038	,,	Yates, W.
18880	,,	Gathrick, A.	18870	,,	Fox, E.
18876	,,	Grant, H.			

* For portrait, see Officers' Group, p. 257. † For portrait, see Sergeants' Group, p. 259.

The following were not present when the Platoon Photograph was taken:—

| 18692 | Private | Rabone, A. | 18853 | Private | Donoghue, P. J. |
| 19010 | ,, | Stubbs, F. P. | 18868 | ,, | Fletcher, J. |

21st (Service) Battalion Manchester Regiment.
"B" COMPANY.

Officer Commanding Company	Capt. C. J. M. Hobson.*
Second in Command	Capt. J. Fitzpatrick.*
Company Sergeant Major	Barlow, F.†
Company Quartermaster Sergeant	Stansfield, J.

PLATOON NO. VII.

Platoon Commander	Lieut. N. M. Carstairs.
Platoon Sergeant	Walker, H.

Roll No.	Rank and Name.	Roll No.	Rank and Name.
18797	Sergeant Burgess, F.	18927	Private Jagger, H.
18777	Corporal Ainscough, J.	19843	,, Crane, J.
18819	,, Barrie, L.	19737	,, Morris, T.
18939	L.-Corpl. Lunt, H.	19680	,, Liggett, C.
19617	,, Stevenson, L.	18884	,, Greenup, J.
18942	,, Lees, W.	18932	,, Kerrigan, J.
18940	,, Lunt, G.	18871	,, Fitzpatrick, F.
18944	,, Leonard, J.	18996	,, Rochcliffe, F.
18924	Private Johnson, J.	18820	,, Berisford, J.
18976	,, Palmer, J.	18817	,, Bates, S.
19615	,, Barlow, J.	18917	,, Handley, G.
19600	,, Wheeler, A.	19727	,, Bray, T.
19012	,, Shaw, J.	19746	,, Brown, G.
18978	,, Parkington, J.	19750	,, Swift, H.
18784	,, Andrew, F.	18824	,, Brentnall, S.
18919	,, Hodgson, T.	18816	,, Bashall, H.
18882	,, Gill, S.	18959	,, Morris, L.
18785	,, Austin, A.	19011	,, Starr, J.
18956	,, Mayo, P.	19022	,, Taft, R.
19023	,, Venables, W.	19036	,, Whitmore, R.
18955	,, Mannion, J.	19035	,, Wilson, F.
18938	,, Lowe, S.	18787	,, Aston, S.
18916	,, Hassall, H.	19690	,, Baggs, J.
19599	,, Perrin, W.	19761	,, Steele, J.
19602	,, Sullivan, J.	18957	,, Moss, J.
19768	,, Collins, C.	18933	,, Kearney, E.
18879	,, Gatenby, A.	19674	,, Holden, T.

* For portrait, see Officers' Group, p. 257.   † For portrait, see Sergeants' Group, p. 259.

The following were not present when the Platoon Photograph was taken:—

Roll No.	Rank and Name.	Roll No.	Rank and Name.
18937	Corporal Lewis, H.	18941	Private Lythgoe, T.
19678	Private Kirkham, J.	19746	,, Brown, G.
19753	,, Thornley, T.	18920	,, Honeysett, R.
18918	,, Hinds, R.	18854	,, Demet, L.
18997	,, Ramshaw, J.	18821	,, Beven, S.
19732	,, Mortimore, G.	18925	,, Johnson, F.
19647	,, Fazackerley, Z.	19013	,, Sutherland, T.
19695	,, Booth, A.	18885	,, Gage, W.
18943	,, Lees, J.		

21st (Service) Battalion Manchester Regiment,

"B" COMPANY.

Officer Commanding Company	Capt. C. J. M. Hobson.*
Second in Command	Capt. J. Fitzpatrick.*
Company Sergeant Major	Barlow, F.†
Company Quartermaster Sergeant	Stansfield, J.†

PLATOON NO. VIII.

Platoon Commander	Lieut. H. E. Scott.
Platoon Sergeant	Greenhalgh, W. M.

Roll No.	Rank and Name.		Roll No.	Rank and Name.	
18977	L.-Sergt.	Pratt, J.	18902	Private	Hewitt, J.
18842	Corporal	Cotgrave, J. E.	18901	"	Hewitt, A.
18834	L.-Corpl.	Canning, H.	18899	"	Hill, H.
19004	"	Stevenson, A.	18895	"	Horford, J.
19587	"	Jones, R.	18897	"	Heywood, J. H.
18778	Private	Allen, F.	18896	"	Heron, S.
19798	"	Alton, B.	18903	"	Hayes, T.
18978	"	Basnett, W. F.	18898	"	Hodgson, A.
19832	"	Brown, G.	18926	"	Jeffs, A.
19663	"	Boyle, W. H.	18921	"	Johnson, R.
18802	"	Bailey, H.	18930	"	Kirven, J. E.
18801	"	Butterworth, J.	19728	"	Minister, A.
18800	"	Bennett, H.	18936	"	Livseley, G. H.
18807	"	Brentnall, N.	18949	"	Mansfield, J.
18804	"	Braddock, J. H.	18900	"	Nuttall, T. H.
18802	"	Beard, J.	18963	"	Ollerenshaw, W.
18836	"	Clarke, J.	18913	"	Parry, O.
18833	"	Chadwick, A.	18986	"	Roberts, A.
19869	"	Charnock, A.	18985	"	Reddish, P.
18851	"	Davies, J.	18987	"	Rogers, J.
18849	"	Dawson, C.	18988	"	Rutter, A.
18850	"	Doherty, J. W.	19006	"	Simpson, T.
18866	"	Featherstone, A.	19005	"	Slater, G.
18857	"	Earnshaw, F.	19002	"	Shufflebottom, C.
18865	"	Firth, D.	19003	"	Spurr, G.
18872	"	Garnett, J.	19007	"	Steel, J.
18875	"	Gledhill, T.	19018	"	Taylor, B. H.
19752	"	Gallimore, W.	19032	"	Wilson, H. R.
18873	"	Gibbons, T.	19031	"	Willis, J.
18900	"	Higginbottom, H.	19616	"	Pratt, R.

* For portrait, see Officers' Group, p. 257. † For portrait, see Sergeants' Group, p. 259.

The following were not present when the Platoon Photograph was taken:—

19039	Sergeant	Yearsley, C.	18871	Private	Ashworth, P.
18779	Private	Allen, J. E.	18962	"	Ogden, T.

21st (Service) Battalion Manchester Regiment.

"C" COMPANY.

Officer Commanding Company - Capt. T. I. W. Wilson.*
Second in Command - - Capt. R. F. Parker.
Company Sergeant Major - - Turner, T.†
Company Quartermaster Sergeant - Suter, E. A.†

PLATOON NO. IX.

Platoon Commander - - - 2nd Lieut. W. B. Purvis.
Platoon Sergeant - - - Henshaw, R.

Roll No.	Rank and Name.		Roll No	Rank and Name.	
19837	Sergeant	Reeves, R.	19264	Private	Smith, W.
19169	Corporal	Kearney, P.	19102	,,	Dickens, J.
19091	,,	Courtney, J.	19116	,,	Freeman, G. H.
19188	L.-Corpl.	McCormick, J.	19135	,,	Hall, W.
19096	,,	Davies, B.	19242	,,	Robinson, H.
19075	,,	Bury, J. H.	19279	,,	Taylor, A.
19310	Private	Wrigley, H.	19296	,,	Wilkinson, A.
19138	,,	Hannah, H.	19292	,,	Walworth, J. J.
19270	,,	Stead, J.	19058	,,	Bates, J. W.
19273	,,	Stringer, R.	19131	,,	Griffiths, W.
19257	,,	Smith, A.	19272	,,	Stevens, W.
19099	,,	Dawson, D.	19184	,,	Lomax, P.
19703	,,	Elkes, J.	19665	,,	Dashwood, C.
19194	,,	Maguire, A.	19707	,,	Seddon, H.
19605	,,	Hughes, J. A.	19216	,,	Mottram, H.
19052	,,	Ashcroft, L.	19248	,,	Savage, H.
19081	,,	Clarkson, F.	19306	,,	Wood, A.
19299	,,	Wilkinson, J.	19160	,,	Hurst, H.
19121	,,	Gavan, J. F.	19215	,,	Morris, S.
19146	,,	Herd, R.	19214	,,	Morgan, E. T.
19277	,,	Stenson, J.	19263	,,	Smith, T. H.
19203	,,	Massey, T.	19218	,,	Murtough, J.
19151	,,	Holt, E. C.	19221	,,	Nicholson, T.
19191	,,	Macfarlane, W.	19251	,,	Short, W.
19258	,,	Smith, A.	19604	,,	Thorneycroft, J.
19309	,,	Wright, J.	19729	,,	Schofield, A.
19130	,,	Greenwood, J.	19236	,,	Powell, E.
19294	,,	Whork, J.	19788	,,	Crichton, A.
19159	,,	Hurst, A.	19078	,,	Chadwick, F.

* For portrait, see Officers' Group, p. 257. † For portrait, see Sergeants' Group, p. 259.

The following were not present when the Platoon Photograph was taken:—

19074	Private	Bulcock, J.	19259	Private	Smith, C. E.
19223	,,	Nugent, J.	19165	,,	Johnson, J.
19154	,,	Howarth, S. H.	19161	,,	Jackson, S.

21st (Service) Battalion Manchester Regiment.

"C" COMPANY.

Officer Commanding Company -	Capt. T. I. W. Wilson.*
Second in Command - - -	Capt. R. F. Parker.*
Company Sergeant Major -	Turner, T.
Company Quartermaster Sergeant -	Suter, E. A.†

PLATOON NO. X.

Platoon Commander - - -	Lieut. P. A. H. Thorniley.
Platoon Sergeant - - - -	Haworth, J.

Roll No.	Rank and Name.	Roll No.	Rank and Name.
19162	R.O.R.S. Jenkins, P.	19173	Private Kingston, J. A.
19220	Sergeant Nichol, T. C.	19171	,, Kelly, J.
19126	L.-Sergt. Gover, H.	19172	,, Kemp, H. R.
19125	Corporal Goodyear, H. K.	19181	,, Lennon, C.
19180	,, Lee, P. G.	19177	,, Latham, T.
19105	L.-Corpl. Dove, R.	19199	,, Mason, G. H.
19152	,, Holt, L.	19190	,, McDermott, T.
19239	,, Richards, H.	19208	,, Middleton, P.
19253	,, Silvester, H.	19210	,, Miller, A.
19051	Private Andrews, J.	19197	,, Martin, J.
19211	,, Billington, J.	19222	,, Nixon, R.
19072	,, Brown, N.	19229	,, Palyn, L.
19073	,, Bruce, J. A.	19238	,, Quinn, W.
19064	,, Birkby, E.	19241	,, Roberts, T.
19092	,, Cousins, F.	19246	,, Ryan, C.
19086	,, Cooper, S.	19252	,, Shoreman, R.
19097	,, Davies, F.	19277	,, Sykes, G. W.
19101	,, Dennerley, W.	19631	,, Stewart, J.
19100	,, Deakin, J.	19650	,, Stocks, R.
19111	,, Evans, H.	19724	,, Tomlinson, W.
19114	,, Fitton, A.	19295	,, Whittingham, J.
19115	,, Flood, J.	19287	,, Walker, J. H.
19123	,, Goodall, A.	19301	,, Wilson, R.
19128	,, Green, R.	19710	,, Whitehead, J.
19119	,, Gaitskell, R. W.	19286	,, Watson, H.
19153	,, Horridge, W.	19059	,, Beech, A.
19673	,, Horton, H.	19147	,, Hewitt, F.
19783	,, Harty, G.		

* For portrait, see Officers' Group, p. 257.   † For portrait, see Sergeants' Group, p. 259.

The following were not present when the Platoon Photograph was taken:—

Roll No.	Rank	Name	Roll No.	Rank	Name
19061	Private	Beeston, F. J.	19142	Private	Haslam, J.
19059	,,	Blenkinsop, H.	19196	,,	Markham, J. T.
19764	,,	Gilbert, E.	19166	,,	Jones, C. W.
19155	,,	Howarth, S.	19780	,,	Lawrence, W.
19164	,,	Johnson, H.	19195	,,	Makin, F.

21st (Service) Battalion Manchester Regiment,

"C" COMPANY.

Officer Commanding Company	Capt. T. I. W. Wilson.*
Second in Command	Capt. R. F. Parker.*
Company Sergeant Major	Turner, T.†
Company Quartermaster Sergeant	Suter, E. A.

PLATOON NO. XI.

Platoon Commander	Lieut. H. W. Walker.
Platoon Sergeant	Sprout, H.

Roll No.	Rank and Name.	Roll No.	Rank and Name.
16219	Sergeant Slater, J. F.	19185	Private Lovatt, H.
19179	,, Lee, A.	19187	,, Mackey, W.
19226	L. Sergt. Palin, J.	19628	,, Markham, E.
19234	Corporal Porter, W. H.	19193	,, Maddison, E.
19293	,, Webster, E.	19186	,, Mackenzie, G.
19281	L.-Corpl. Thomas, S.	19198	,, Marsland, F.
19064	,, Birmingham, J.	19200	,, Maskrey, E. J.
19050	Private Allsop, S.	19192	,, McRoy, W.
19048	,, Aldcroft, J.	19206	,, Makin, F.
19057	,, Barnes, F.	19201	,, Massey, W. R.
19070	,, Bond, S. R.	19781	,, McGarva, A.
19067	,, Brownlow, W. H.	19209	,, Middlebrooke, E.
19068	,, Blair, D.	19589	,, Oldham, A.
19089	,, Catterall, B.	19610	,, Perrigo, H.
19080	,, Clare, S.	19225	,, Painter, R. H.
19090	,, Coulson, B.	19243	,, Rodgers, P. H.
19098	,, Davies, J. G.	19240	,, Riley, W.
19110	,, Evans, F.	19260	,, Smith, C.
19122	,, Goldburn, F.	19274	,, Strutt, H.
19127	,, Green, F.	19284	,, Tynan, J.
19137	,, Hampson, P.	19311	,, Vout, W.
19157	,, Huntington, C.	19302	,, Williams, A.
19144	,, Henry, J.	19303	,, Williams, J.
19158	,, Hurd, T.	19307	,, Wood, A.
19139	,, Hardie, H.	19300	,, Wilkinson, T.
19606	,, Larrard, J. W.	19305	,, Wild, J. A. L.
19178	,, Leaver, S.		

* For portrait, see Officers' Group, p. 257.   † For portrait, see Sergeants' Group, p. 259.

The following were not present when the Platoon Photograph was taken:—

Roll No.	Rank and Name.	Roll No.	Rank and Name.
19049	Private Allen, T.	19174	Private Kneale, S.
19627	,, Brown, W.	19182	,, Lindsay, J. A.
19077	,, Carlton, W.	19250	,, Sellars, C.
19106	,, Ducker, E.	19282	,, Treacher, H.
19112	,, Evans, J.	19656	,, Wotherspoon, J.
19120	,, Gaskell, H.		

21st (Service) Battalion Manchester Regiment.

"C" COMPANY.

Officer Commanding Company - Capt. T. I. W. Wilson.*
Second in Command - - - Capt. R. F. Parker.*
Company Sergeant Major - - Turner, T.†
Company Quartermaster Sergeant - Suter, E. A.†

PLATOON NO. XII.

Platoon Commander - - - 2nd Lieut. A. S. Russell.
Platoon Sergeant - - - Turner, J.

Roll No.	Rank and Name.		Roll No.	Rank and Name.	
19104	Sergeant	Donaldson, W. J.	19175	Private	Lamb, G.
19066	,,	Bithell, C. F.	19276	,,	Sutton, G.
18678	Corporal	Parkinson, F.	19730	,,	Trowbridge, F.
18764	,,	Williamson, E.	18745	,,	Vickers, W.
19054	L.-Corpl.	Atherton, S. B.	19183	,,	Lloyd, G. H.
19280	,,	Taylor, J.	19269	,,	Southern, A.
19204	,,	Massey, A.	19087	,,	Corrie, F.
19289	Private	Ward, A.	19254	,,	Simpson, A.
19060	,,	Beesley, W.	19134	,,	Hall, A.
19232	,,	Penkethman, J.	19062	,,	Berry, G. C.
19297	,,	Wilkinson, C.	19071	,,	Bowker, H.
19298	,,	Wilkinson, E.	19149	,,	Hibbert, F.
19150	,,	Hodges, H.	19148	,,	Hewitson, J.
19093	,,	Coxey, W.	19113	,,	Ferrier, A.
19304	,,	Williams, L. C.	19224	,,	O'Connor, P.
19291	,,	Welsh, C.	19088	,,	Cosgrove, C.
19067	,,	Bithell, J.	19132	,,	Guerden, H.
19124	,,	Goodier, J.	19133	,,	Guerden, M.
19769	,,	Rothwell, J. H.	19278	,,	Taylor, D.
19176	,,	Langhorn, J.	19140	,,	Harrison, F.
19053	,,	Ashworth, L.	19285	,,	Unsworth, F.
19095	,,	Davies, H.	19262	,,	Smith, J.
19108	,,	Dutton, S.	19256	,,	Smethurst, T.
19118	,,	Frobisher, J.	19692	,,	MacNiece, J.
19219	,,	Mytton, R.	19245	,,	Royle, A.
19265	,,	Smith, W.	19653	,,	Rawsterne, J.
19275	,,	Sutcliffe, J.			

* For portrait, see Officers' Group, p. 257. † For portrait, see Sergeants' Group, p. 259.

The following were not present when the Platoon Photograph was taken:—

19141	L.-Corpl.	Hart, L.	19085	Private	Conway, J.
19094	Private	Coxey, G.	19701	,,	Rutter, J.
19228	,,	Palmer, T.	19205	,,	Mather, W.
19233	,,	Pickering, J.	19047	,,	Abbott, J.
19249	,,	Seddon, S.	19129	,,	Greaves, R.
19103	,,	Dillon, J.			

21st (Service) Battalion Manchester Regiment.

"D" COMPANY.

Officer Commanding Company	- Major F. F. OMMANNEY.*
Second in Command	- - - Lieut. J. CHAPMAN.*
Company Sergeant Major	- - COLBERT, J. T.
Company Quartermaster Sergeant	- STOCKTON, W.†

PLATOON NO. XIII.

Platoon Commander	- - 2nd Lieut. F. S. SCRUTTON.
Platoon Sergeant	- - - - JULIAN, H.

Roll No.	Rank and Name.		Roll No.	Rank and Name.	
19482	Sergeant	PARKES, D.	19388	Private	FRASER, J. E.
19430	L.-Sergt.	LAMBERT, F.	19368	,,	DAVIES, J. W.
19443	Corporal	MAKIN, F. O.	19403	,,	HARTLEY, J. W.
19519	L.-Corpl.	STANLEY, W. E.	19493	,,	RATHBONE, A.
19747	,,	TURNER, F.	19557	,,	WRIGHT, J.
19422	Private	KEATING, J.	19344	,,	BURROWS, J. H.
19329	,,	BOOTH, F. A.	19537	,,	WARBURTON, J.
19435	,,	LEIGH, W. A.	19528	,,	THORNHILL, W.
19531	,,	VASEY, S.	19495	,,	PRITCHARD, P. W.
19448	,,	McCANN, R.	19516	,,	SMITH, W.
19457	,,	MEADOWS, C. A.	19362	,,	DARBYSHIRE, W.
19324	,,	BENNION, O.	19400	,,	HALLAM, L.
19504	,,	SAWTRIDGE, W. C.	19323	,,	BEECH, T.
19539	,,	WATSON, G. W.	19512	,,	SMITH, C.
19442	,,	LUCY, J.	19513	,,	SMITH, J. F.
19376	,,	EDGE, A.	19429	,,	LAMBERT, A.
19509	,,	SHAW, GEO.	19399	,,	GROVES, T.
19530	,,	VARDON, H. O.	19409	,,	HIGHFIELD, W. E.
19363	,,	DAVIES, G.	19473	,,	NEWHAM, J. W.
19552	,,	WILSON, A.	19611	,,	LEECH, T.
19342	,,	BURGESS, S.	19609	,,	HOWARD, F.
19432	,,	LAWTON, S. H.	19568	,,	BARON, W.
19494	,,	READY, G.	19638	,,	RENSHAW, J.
19330	,,	BOOTH, H. A.	19566	,,	THOMASON, E.
19469	,,	MORLEY, J. B.	19714	,,	WILKINSON, G.
19522	,,	SUTCLIFFE, H.	19669	,,	HOWARD, J.
19532	,,	WADE, B.	19668	,,	HOWARD, C.
19477	,,	OGDEN, A.	19590	,,	OGDEN, J. T.
19387	,,	FOULKES, C. E.	19374	,,	EASDALE, S.

* For portrait, see Officers' Group, p. 257.   † For portrait, see Sergeants' Group, p. 259.

The following were not present when the Platoon Photograph was taken :—

19503	Private	SALE, E.	19754	Private	QUINN, J.
19440	,,	LITSTER, A.	19591	,,	SPELMAN, J.
19472	,,	NELSON, O.	19885	,,	BARON, M.
19544	,,	WHITEHOUSE, A.	19856	,,	FAIRBROTHER, H.

21st (Service) Battalion Manchester Regiment.

"D" COMPANY.

Officer Commanding Company	- Major F. F. Ommanney.*
Second in Command - -	- Lieut. J. Chapman.*
Company Sergeant Major -	- Colbert, J. T.
Company Quartermaster Sergeant -	Stockton, W.†

PLATOON NO. XIV.

Platoon Commander - -	- 2nd Lieut. G. Lee-Evans.
Platoon Sergeant - - -	- Fitzhugh, T.

Roll No.	Rank and Name.	Roll No.	Rank and Name.
19486	Sergeant Perfitt, W.	19407	Private Hibbs, A.
19739	Corporal Beamish, A.	19406	,, Hewitt, F.
19506	,, Seal, J. H.	19414	,, Hughes, T.
19370	L.-Corpl. Dowley, J. E.	19670	,, Howard, H.
19340	,, Brown, G.	19677	,, Johnson, C.
19847	,, Thorley, C. H.	19425	,, Kennedy, J.
19317	Private Athay, P.	19459	,, Meehan, W.
19585	,, Beardmore, F.	19463	,, Mills, R.
19333	,, Bower, E.	19792	,, McGinn, E.
19332	,, Bosley, J.	19451	,, McIntyre, S.
19336	,, Bradley, E.	19452	,, McKellor, J.
19341	,, Bruce, A.	19474	,, Newman, J.
19343	,, Burgoyne, E.	19813	,, Oldham, J. W.
19354	,, Cole, H.	19620	,, Peacock, E. H.
19353	,, Cole, F. K.	19497	,, Roberts, S.
19355	,, Cole, R. A.	19498	,, Roberts, W. H.
19360	,, Cox, G.	19499	,, Robinson, W.
19358	,, Cook, T.	19510	,, Shedwick, A.
19357	,, Collins, R.	19523	,, Tansey, J.
19356	,, Cotgreave, I.	19526	,, Thistlewhaite, P.
19659	,, Clayten, C. A.	19718	,, Towers, G.
19364	,, Davies, P.	19537	,, Walsh, J.
19365	,, Daw, J.	19545	,, Whitham, J.
19807	,, Ewart, J. G.	19543	,, Wheatley, F.
19720	,, Ewart, A.	19634	,, Wilson, R.
19660	,, Flavell, J.	19554	,, Wolstencroft, W.
19386	,, Fordsman, S.	18752	,, Warnes, E.
19392	,, Gilligan, J.	19829	,, Wilcock, R.
19395	,, Gough, J.	19556	,, Wright, H.
19401	,, Harper, E.	18757	,, White, J.
19836	,, Hawes, A.	19490	,, Pollitt, W.

* For portrait, see Officers' Group, p. 257. † For portrait, see Sergeants' Group, p. 259.

The following were not present when the Platoon Photograph was taken :—

Roll No.	Rank and Name.	Roll No.	Rank and Name.
19345	Private Butterworth, A.	19520	Private Stokes, W. H.
18705	,, Robinson, J.	19725	,, Taylor, A.
19757	,, Shindler, L.	19702	,, Woods, S. H.

K

21st (Service) Battalion Manchester Regiment.

"D" COMPANY.

Officer Commanding Company	Major F. F. Ommanney.*
Second in Command	Lieut. J. Chapman.*
Company Sergeant Major	Colbert, J. T.
Company Quartermaster Sergeant	Stockton, W.

PLATOON NO. XV.

Platoon Commander	Lieut. G. Langdon.
Platoon Sergeant	Coles, G. S.

Roll No.	Rank and Name.		Roll No.	Rank and Name.	
19480	Sergeant	Palmer, W. O.	19318	Private	Bamber, R.
19842	Corporal	Clements, G. W.	19441	,,	Lloyd, W.
19479	,,	Owen, J.	19445	,,	Matthews, W.
19321	L.-Corpl.	Barrow, J.	19511	,,	Sherratt, E.
19381	,,	Farran, R.	19508	,,	Shatwell, W.
19372	,,	Duerden, F.	19571	,,	Ellis, G.
19410	Private	Holden, S.	19576	,,	Kershaw, G.
19380	,,	Farragher, D.	19585	,,	Hartley, J. R.
19359	,,	Cornick, S.	19327	,,	Blake, T.
19464	,,	Minshall, B.	19657	,,	Bennett, S.
19450	,,	McGrath, J.	19715	,,	Bennett, H. S.
19314	,,	Adams, J.	19623	,,	Rowe, V.
19417	,,	Jackson, C. A.	19570	,,	Dolan, T.
19574	,,	Hall, R.	19351	,,	Clark, T.
19334	,,	Bowyer, S.	19350	,,	Clark, J.
19631	,,	Lepp, E.	19439	,,	Linney, T.
19726	,,	Partington, J.	19426	,,	Kitchen, W.
19488	,,	Prior, P.	19438	,,	Levis, A.
19437	,,	Lester, F.	19371	,,	Draper, W.
19369	,,	Dodd, E.	19411	,,	Hilton, A.
19423	,,	Kelly, C.	19436	,,	Leigh, T.
19536	,,	Walsh, J.	19316	,,	Aspinall, T.
19373	,,	Dunbar, W.	19772	,,	Briggs, H.
19618	,,	Harrison, T.	19646	,,	Flanagan, A.
19748	,,	Simmonds, A.	19758	,,	Tabner, W.
19657	,,	Bennett, J.	19756	,,	Davies, G.
19424	,,	Kelly, G. W.	19793	,,	Moores, T.
19500	,,	Rogers, W.	19683	,,	Rigg, T.

* For portrait, see Officers' Group, p. 257.

The following were not present when the Platoon Photograph was taken:—

19434	Corporal	Leman, L. P.	19641	Private	Crompton, J.
19575	L.-Corpl.	Higson, F.	19578	,,	Painter, T. W.
19325	Private	Berry, R.	19784	,,	Harper, G.
19572	,,	Knowles, T.	19808	,,	Hindley, R.
19626	,,	Wood, P.	19505	,,	Sayer, H.
19743	,,	Walker, H.	19462	,,	Miles, E.
19550	,,	Willingham, G.			

21st (Service) Battalion Manchester Regiment.

"D" COMPANY.

Officer Commanding Company - Major F. F. OMMANNEY.
Second in Command - - - Lieut. J. CHAPMAN.
Company Sergeant Major - - COLBERT, J. T.
Company Quartermaster Sergeant - STOCKTON, W.†

PLATOON NO. XVI.

Platoon Commander - - - 2nd Lieut. A. P. LILLIE.
Platoon Sergeant - - - - BROWNSON, H.

Roll No.	Rank and Name.		Roll No.	Rank and Name.	
18609	Sergeant	HEAP, J. D. P.	19507	Private	SEDGWICK, E.
19315	L.-Sergt.	ADSHEAD, J.	19534	,,	WALSH, H.
19347	Corporal	CAVE, F. J.	19352	,,	CLOUDSDALE, F.
19553	,,	WINDSOR, S.	19582	,,	CALADINE, F.
19378	L.-Corpl.	FAIRCLOUGH, E.	19394	,,	GORDON, C.
19592	,,	BEDDOW, R.	19446	,,	MOODY, H.
19779	,,	SWALE, T.	19398	,,	HAGAN, C.
19338	Private	BRERETON, S. W.	19322	,,	BASTABLE, A. E.
19481	,,	PARISH, J. H.	19555	,,	WOOD, C.
19384	,,	FORGARTY, J.	19379	,,	FALLOWS, H.
19547	,,	WILKS, J. W.	19456	,,	MEACHEN, A.
19331	,,	BOOTH, J.	19412	,,	HOUGHTON, E.
19458	,,	MEE, H. B.	19455	,,	McGLYNN, A.
19382	,,	FISHER, G.	19549	,,	WILLIAMS, T.
19335	,,	BOYLIN, C. A.	19405	,,	HESFORD, V.
19348	,,	CLARKE, A.	19478	,,	OSBORNE, W. H.
19396	,,	GREEN, J.	19399	,,	HANRAHAN, J.
19475	,,	O'BRIEN, T.	19390	,,	GERAGHTY, J.
19418	,,	JENKINSON, R. A.	19745	,,	TOMLINSON, E.
19452	,,	McKEAND, W.	19419	,,	JONES, S.
19820	,,	COOPER, R. W.	19517	,,	SMYTHE, T. H.
19346	,,	CARTWRIGHT, A.	19444	,,	MASON, G. H.
19361	,,	DALE, A.	19391	,,	GIBBONS, G.
19427	,,	KNOWLES, W.	19404	,,	HELME, J.
19431	,,	LANG, J.	19461	,,	MELMORE, D.
19428	,,	LACEY, J. P.	19467	,,	MOORE, W.
19447	,,	MAWSON, H.	19468	,,	MORLEY, J. H.
19446	,,	MAWSON, F.	19421	,,	KEELAN, J.
19501	,,	ROYLE, F.	19622	,,	CLOWES, J.
19649	,,	ADSHEAD, W.			

† For portrait, see Sergeants' Group, p. 259.

The following were not present when the Platoon Photograph was taken:—

19393	Private	GODFREY, J. E.	19799	Private	ATKINS, H.
19583	,,	COOPER, H.	18592	,,	GREEN, J.
19538	,,	WARD, J.	19629	,,	MERRICK, G.

21st (Service) Battalion Manchester Regiment.

"E" COMPANY.

Officer Commanding Company - Capt. W. M. Marsden.
Second in Command - - Lieut. G. H. Harris.
Company Sergeant Major - - Cassin, P.
Company Quartermaster Sergeant - Grimshaw, J. W

PLATOON NO. XVII.

Platoon Commander - - 2nd Lieut. W. B. Purvis.
Platoon Sergeant - - Johnson, F.

Roll No.	Rank and Name.		Roll No.	Rank and Name.	
18657	Corporal	Jones, J.	19823	Private	Jones, R. H.
19485	,,	Pearson, H.	19420	,,	Jones, W.
18599	,,	Harling, J.	19740	,,	Lewis, A.
18731	L.-Corpl.	Stanway, H.	19811	,,	Leatherbarrow, T.
19900	,,	Haworth, H. P.	19700	,,	Marland, W.
19757	,,	Wilkinson, A.	19759	,,	McGinty, J.
19716	,,	McAleece, J.	19449	,,	McCoy, R.
19831	Private	Birtles, H.	19217	,,	Murphy, H.
18818	,,	Burgoin, E.	18661	,,	McGuire, J.
19712	,,	Bradshaw, G.	19454	,,	McKeown, T.
19640	,,	Dewhurst, F.	19770	,,	Naylor, J.
19568	,,	Doody, J.	18691	,,	Pyatt, P.
19834	,,	Elder, A. J.	19825	,,	Procter, W.
19698	,,	Ellis, E.	19632	,,	Scholes, J. W.
19806	,,	Evans, A.	19699	,,	Smith, J.
18578	,,	Ford, J.	19719	,,	Smith, W.
19835	,,	Fryer, A.	19593	,,	Smith, W.
18586	,,	Gee, J.	19760	,,	Shannon, H.
19651	,,	Hulme, J.	19255	,,	Singleton, T.
19771	,,	Hunt, J.	19154	,,	Smith, J. W.
19794	,,	Hill, J. N.	19686	,,	Turner, E.
19789	,,	Harrison, R.	19683	,,	Peers, W. J.
19598	,,	Hewitt, J.	19685	,,	Studdart, H.
19416	,,	Janson, T.		,,	Johnson, T. R.

Attached.

19971 Private Cooper, W. H.   Private Roberts.

The following were not present when the Platoon Photograph was taken:—

19840 Sergeant Woods, G.   19824 Private Jones, R.
19326 Private Blain, A.   19844 ,, Woodbine, C.
19625 ,, Cragg, W.

21st (Service) Battalion Manchester Regiment.
"E" COMPANY.

Officer Commanding Company - Capt. W. M. MARSDEN.*
Second in Command - - - Lieut. G. H. HARRIS.
Company Sergeant Major - - CASSIN, P.*
Company Quartermaster Sergeant - GRIMSHAW, J. W.*

PLATOON NO. XVIII.

Platoon Commander - - 2nd Lieut. G. G. L. CRUICKSHANK.
Platoon Sergeant - - - - BIRTWISLE, C.

Roll No.	Rank and Name.		Roll No.	Rank and Name.	
18979	L.-Sergt.	PARKER, B.	19527	Private	THOMPSON, J. A.
19567	Corporal	SHUTTLEWORTH, J. H.	19235	,,	POTTER, E. A.
19705	L.-Corpl.	ELLIS, J. A.	19369	,,	DODD, E. F.
19846	,,	WALLACE, J.	19055	,,	BALL, J. H.
19815	,,	RUMNEY, J.	19893	,,	BARNETT, F. V.
19749	Private	ASHTON, H.	19337	,,	BRADLEY, J. A.
19880	,,	BAILEY, S.	19339	,,	BRIERLEY, W.
19894	,,	BULL, F. P.	19889	,,	BROWNHILL, W. L.
19870	,,	COWLEY, C.	18535	,,	BRITLAND, G.
19881	,,	FIELDS, W. H.	19349	,,	CLARKE, E.
19858	,,	EAST, F.	18837	,,	CHAMBERLAIN, E.
19887	,,	FIRBY, G.	19107	,,	DUCKER, B
19874	,,	GRESTY, C.	19375	,,	ECKERSLEY, A.
19882	,,	HOULDSWORTH, A.	18871	,,	FITZPATRICK, F.
19879	,,	JOHNSON, J.	19851	,,	GOSNALL, C.
18934	,,	LAWSON, W.	19860	,,	HARRIS, J. H.
19776	,,	PEARLMAN, J.	19136	,,	HANRAHAN, T.
19873	,,	RISBY, T.	19413	,,	HUGGINS, G.
19874	,,	RYLANCE, R.	19415	,,	HUNTINGTON, C.
19491	,,	RAINFORD, P.	19207	,,	MELLOR, W.
19502	,,	RUSSELL, W.	19189	,,	McCAFFREY, W.
19883	,,	SMITH, W. H.	19213	,,	MORGAN, A.
19741	,,	SYNOTT, M.	19488	,,	PRIOR, P.
19267	,,	SNAPE, H.	19858	,,	STOTT, J.
19875	,,	TIMPERLEY, M.	19542	,,	WELCH, A.
19872	,,	THOMPSON, S.	18772	,,	YATES, J.

Attached.

19777	Private	ALLISON, J.		Private	BRIGGS.
19839	,,	STANSFIELD,			

Also on the Photograph: 2nd Lieut. C. G. YEANDLE.

The following were not present when the Platoon Photograph was taken :—

19888	Private	KEHOE, J.	19884	Private	ATHERTON, J.
19876	,,	MELLOR, H.	19608	,,	BYRNE, G.
19266	,,	SMITH, H.	19866	,,	PICKSTONE, J.
19476	,,	O'BRIEN, W.	19862	,,	WEATHERBY, J.
19857	,,	ALDRED, S.			

* For portrait, see Platoon XVII, p. 295.

K 2

21st (Service) Battalion Manchester Regiment.

"E" COMPANY.

Officer Commanding Company - Capt. W. M. Marsden.*
Second in Command - - Lieut. G. H. Harris.
Company Sergeant Major - - Cassin, P.*
Company Quartermaster Sergeant - Grimshaw, J. W.*

PLATOON NO. XIX.

Platoon Commander - - - 2nd Lieut. G. Coatman.
Platoon Sergeants - - - - Houghton and Brunskill.

Roll No.	Rank and Name.		Roll No.	Rank and Name.	
19389	Corporal	Garlick, J.	19927	Private	McBride, C. E.
19170	,,	Keightley, T.	19944	,,	McEvilly, R. C.
18673	L.-Corpl.	Oliver, J.	19981	,,	Reid, J.
19639	,,	Underhill, S.	19949	,,	Rough, J.
19941	Private	Bushell, B.	19983	,,	Robinson, J.
19916	,,	Batty, J. W.	19898	,,	Ramsden, M. J.
19897	,,	Barnes, P.	19909	,,	Robinson, J.
19913	,,	Collins, W. C.	19931	,,	Shaw, T.
19964	,,	Clayton, P.	19930	,,	Sandland, J.
19971	,,	Cooper, W. H.	19932	,,	Smith, W. H.
19972	,,	Dawson, T.	19984	,,	Steward, H.
19902	,,	Elford, V. H.	19891	,,	Smith, W.
19973	,,	Fieldhouse, W.	19986	,,	Tidswell, H.
19958	,,	Henshaw, F.	19955	,,	Truelock, T. H.
19995	,,	Herbert, M.	19899	,,	Thompson, B.
19975	,,	Harkins, J.	19895	,,	Tottey, G.
19890	,,	Jubbs, J.	19896	,,	Townsend, W. H.
19947	,,	Lord, J. P.	19987	,,	Vollborth, H.
19905	,,	Leighton, J.	19988	,,	Wells, H.
19903	,,	Main, A.	19937	,,	Whitehouse, F.
19907	,,	McNeeney, J.	19892	,,	Williamson, A. H.
19978	,,	Moores, J.			

* For portrait, see Platoon XVII, p. 295.

Attached.

19844	L.-Corpl.	Fox.	19830	Private	Bighland.
19818	,,	Bardsley, H.	19822	,,	Finn, M.
			19865	,,	Calvert.

The following were not present when the Platoon Photograph was taken:—

19966	Private	Arnott, J.	19953	Private	Jackson, J. W.
19990	,,	Bennett, A.	19980	,,	Murphy, J.
19968	,,	Bradbury, A.	19992	,,	O'Brien, M. G.
19965	,,	Cassin, J.	19959	,,	Royle, J.
19921	,,	Devaney, W.	19963	,,	Swift, T.
19974	,,	Hall, G.	19994	,,	Weston, A. J.
19852	,,	Hodcroft, A.	19639	,,	Underhill, S.

21st (Service) Battalion Manchester Regiment.

"E" COMPANY.

Officer Commanding Company	Capt. W. M. Marsden.*
Second in Command	Lieut. G. H. Harris.
Company Sergeant Major	Cassin, P.*
Company Quartermaster Sergeant	Grimshaw, J. W.*

PLATOON NO. XX.

Platoon Commander	2nd Lieut. H. Bentley.
Platoon Sergeant	Fish, J.

Roll No.	Rank and Name.		Roll No.	Rank and Name.	
18518	Corporal	Battersby, J.	19572	Private	Keating, J.
19841	,,	Chidley, A.	19934	,,	Lawlor, S.
19541	,,	Watts, W. H.	26573	,,	Lamb, D.
19915	Private	Arden, P.	26754	,,	Logan, W.
19916	,,	Beswick, C.	26768	,,	Laythorne, H.
19997	,,	Black, J.	19759	,,	McFarland, S.
19917	,,	Berriman, P.	26765	,,	Millington, H.
19886	,,	Bostock, C.	19938	,,	Peers, W. J.
19951	,,	Coultis, W. H.	26763	,,	Royal, J.
19946	,,	Davies, W.	19933	,,	Smith, J.
19999	,,	Farrell, J.	26761	,,	Taylor, F.
19925	,,	Horne, J.	26762	,,	Towers, J. M.
20000	,,	Hinson, H.	26764	,,	Unsworth, W. E.
19977	,,	Holland, K.	26765	,,	Worthington, W.
19923	,,	Haig, G.	19955	,,	Wilson, G.
19924	,,	Holt, J. T.	19936	,,	Waddington, J. W.
26769	,,	Herbert, J.	18946	,,	Mullen.
19758	,,	Johnson, J.			

Attached.

3088	Sergeant	Goodman, J.	3406	Sergeant	Farrell, T.

* For portrait, see Platoon XVII, p. 295.

The following were not present when the Platoon Photograph was taken:—

19156	Corporal	Hughes, R.	26766	Private	Pratt, J.
19956	Private	Garnett, J.	26760	,,	Sandiford, J.

22nd (Service) Battalion

22nd (Service) Battalion Manchester Regiment.

Roll of Officers.

Lieut.-Col.	ETHERIDGE, C. DE C., D.S.O.	Lieutenant	OLDHAM, E.
Major	TAYLEUR, W.	”	MURRAY, D. S.
Capt. & Adjt.	TOWNSEND, J. E.	”	BURCHILL, V.
Captain	EARLES, F. J.	1894 ”	GOMERSALL, W. E. 1/7/16
”	MURRAY, D.	2nd Lieut.	STATHAM, H. R.
1888 ”	MAY, C. C. 1/7/16	”	SHELMERDINE, J. A.
”	BLAND, A. E.	”	HARRISON, F. A.
”	WORTHINGTON, T. R.	”	REID, W. M.
”	RAMSBOTTOM, G. O.	”	WICKS, F. C.
”	BOWLY, R. W.	”	ROSE, H.
Lieutenant	PRINCE, J. F.	”	RILEY, E. L.
”	MELLOR, ROY.	”	KNUDSON, O. J.
”	CUSHION, W. B.	Lieut. & M.O.	MACGREGOR, G. B.
		Lieut. & Q.M.	MAIDEN, E. L.

2nd Lieut. J. P. H. WOOD was not present when the Photograph was taken.

For Officers of the Depot Companies, see Photograph on p. 401.

22nd (Service) Battalion Manchester Regiment.

Non-Commissioned Officers' (Sergeants) Roll.

Warrant Officer.
17662   R.S.M.   Hughes, J.

21088   R.Q.M.S. Barker, F.
21394   R.O.R.S. McSweeny, D.

Roll No.	Rank and Name.		Roll No.	Rank and Name.	
21046	C.S.M.	Burgess, G.	20310	Sergeant	McCoy, J. W.
21402	,,	Vaughan, G.	21030	,,	Wagstaffe, A.
21403	,,	Knowles, F. C.	20413	,,	Bradley, J.
21404	,,	Cunningham, J.	20823	,,	Wilson, W.
20733	C.Q.M.S.	Till, L. O.	21039	,,	Dyson, J. P.
20283	,,	Garside, R. T.	20674	,,	Barber, F.
20434	,,	Howard, H.	20541	,,	Anderson, S.
20266	,,	Wilcox, H.	20634	,,	Hart, F. H.
21266	Sgt. Cook	Lewtas, T.	20104	,,	Lumby, H.
21169	M.G. Sgt.	Allen, J.	20926	,,	Hannah, W. G.
20097	Sig. Sgt.	Jackson, T. H.	20703	,,	Jones, J.
20533	Sergeant	Talbot, J.	21386	,,	Taylor, A. E.
20009	,,	Curtin, M.	21378	,,	Davis, F.
20316	,,	Rimmer, F.	21380	,,	Hargreaves, J.
20598	,,	Treasure, H. H.	20128	,,	Whitworth, H.
20942	,,	Lancaster, H.	20870	,,	Mottershead, A.
20400	,,	Whitelegge, E.	20919	L.-Sergt.	Grindrod, J.
20543	,,	Booth, T.	20780	,,	Clarke, J. T.
20810	,,	Pye, T.	21005	,,	Machin, W. A.
20010	,,	Clayton, W.	20431	,,	Heywood, E.
20177	,,	Nelson, J.	20488	,,	Dearden, G.
20344	,,	Corless, T.	20750	,,	Jolly, A.
20766	,,	Aldcroft, S.		*Gym. Staff.*	
20155	,,	Hodcroft, H.		Staff. Sgt.	Hook.
20055	,,	Scruton, W.		Sgt. Dr.	Hunter.

Also on the Photograph: Lt.-Col. C. de C. Etheridge, *D.S.O.*, Capt. & Adj. J. E. Townsend, and Lt. & Qr.Master E. L. Maiden.

The following were not present when the Photograph was taken:—

20592	Sergeant	Oley, J. C.	20761	Sergeant	Hill, A.
20249	,,	Platt, H.	21001	,,	Knox, T.
20921	,,	Greenwood, W. A.	20446	,,	Leavey, G. R.

22nd (Service) Battalion Manchester Regiment.

Bugle Band.

Roll No.	Rank and Name.		Roll No.	Rank and Name.	
7332	Sergeant	Hunter, T. W.	20442	Drummer	Jackson, E.
20025	Corporal	Flaherty, T.	20974	,,	Birch, W. R.
20251	,,	Pinder, A.	21045	,,	Birch, C. A.
20036	Drummer	Johnson, P.	20763	,,	Spandley, R.
20151	,,	Crowe, W.	20667	,,	Sterling, W.
20197	,,	Wild, J.	20606	,,	Anderson, J. S.
20247	,,	Oldham, E.	20752	,,	Morgan, J.
20222	,,	Fox, A.	20584	,,	Lynch, J.
20252	,,	Prince, A.	20740	,,	Adams, S.
20368	,,	Keyworth, J.	20754	,,	Newcombe, A. A.
20335	,,	Whitehead, J.	20749	,,	Jackson, W.
20334	,,	Whitehead, W. H.	20968	,,	Booth, C. L.
20426	,,	Grimrod, H.	20807	,,	Nolan, J. M.
20330	,,	Timperley, E.	21374	,,	Jones, E.
21091	,,	Harwood, F.	20422	,,	Freeman, R.

Also on the Photograph: Capt. D. Murray and R.S.M. Hughes, J.

22nd (Service) Battalion Manchester Regiment.

"A" COMPANY.

Officer Commanding Company - Capt. C. C. May.*
Second in Command - - - Capt. R. W. Bowly.*
Company Sergeant Major - - Burgess, G.
Company Quartermaster Sergeant - Howard, H.†

PLATOON NO. I.

Platoon Commander - - - Lieut. E. Oldham.
Platoon Sergeant - - - - Hodcroft, H.

Roll No.	Rank and Name.		Roll No.	Rank and Name.	
21394	R.Q.M.S.	McSweeney, D.	20033	Private	Hinde, R.
20009	Sergeant	Curtain, M.	20034	,,	Harvey, H.
20055	,,	Scrutton, W.	21148	,,	Jones, H.
20005	Corporal	Briggs, H.	20036	,,	Johnson, P.
20156	,,	Hatch, W.	21263	,,	Kimber, J. C.
20025	,,	Flaherty.	20040	,,	McMillan, H.
20058	L.-Corpl.	Stapleton, S.	20042	,,	Morris, E.
20019	,,	Davies, W. H.	21116	,,	Newton, F.
20051	Private	Ackers, J.	21132	,,	O'Hara, D.
21232	,,	Brown, W.	21144	,,	Purcell, W. R.
21400	,,	Beswick, R.	20047	,,	Ryder, F.
21211	,,	Yarwood, F.	21283	,,	Rogerson, J.
21223	,,	Barlow, F. B.	20114	,,	Ratcliffe.
21090	,,	Bunting, A.	20049	,,	Rooney, M.
21311	,,	Butterfield, C.	20050	,,	Roach, T.
20006	,,	Crowther, E. W.	21372	,,	Sharp, G.
21312	,,	Cassell, F.	20053	,,	Standing, F.
20012	,,	Conolly, R.	20056	,,	Schofield, P.
20013	,,	Curry, R.	20057	,,	Smith, R.
20016	,,	Chambers, W.	20060	,,	Stelfox, W. H.
20018	,,	Davison, T.	20061	,,	Siddall, J.
20024	,,	Ferns, T.	21206	,,	Sullivan, A.
20026	,,	Fox, W. D.	21321	,,	Sankey, E.
21393	,,	Flood, S.	21186	,,	Stevens, J.
20023	,,	Grayson, S. W.	20062	,,	Taylor, V.
20357	,,	Grundy, J. H.	20064	,,	Tarpey, T.
20029	,,	Harrop, W.	20063	,,	Tebay, J.
20030	,,	Holt, R.	21397	,,	Williams, J.
20031	,,	Hogan, J.	21392	,,	Wilson, A.
20066	,,	Wallwork, A.	20065	,,	Whitworth, H.
20127	,,	Wolstencroft, H.	20067	,,	Young, F. T.
20032	,,	Horrocks, J.			

* For portrait, see Officers' Group, p. 305. † For portrait, see Sergeants' Group, p. 307.

The following were not present when the Platoon Photograph was taken:—

| 20015 | Private | Cohen, A. | 21370 | Private | Bergemier, C. E. |
| 20037 | ,, | Jacobs, R. | | | |

22nd (Service) Battalion Manchester Regiment.

"A" COMPANY.

Officer Commanding Company - Capt. C. C. May.*
Second in Command - - - Capt. R. W. Bowly.*
Company Sergeant Major - - Burgess, G.†
Company Quartermaster Sergeant - Howard, H.†

PLATOON NO. II.

Platoon Commander - - - 2nd Lieut. H. Rose.
Platoon Sergeant - - - - Clayton, W.

Roll No.	Rank and Name.	Roll No.	Rank and Name.
20104	Sergeant Lumby, H.	20105	Private Maher, H.
20122	Corporal Thompson, W. R.	20106	,, Mason, J.
20035	,, Hay, W.	20107	,, Martin, F.
20133	L.-Corpl. Weekes, T.	21273	,, Mitchell, E.
20039	,, Brocklehurst, W.	21272	,, Massey, J.
20068	Private Anderson, H.	20108	,, Neighbour, T.
20071	,, Bradshaw, F.	21121	,, Pardoe, E. A.
20074	,, Bailey, W.	21184	,, Pritchard, E.
20075	,, Burke, L.	20110	,, Richards, E.
20076	,, Bailey, W.	20112	,, Renshaw, J.
20070	,, Broome, W.	20113	,, Ravenscroft, J.
21197	,, Baguley, J.	20121	,, Shaw, W.
20072	,, Bayliss, L.	20115	,, Spencer, E.
20080	,, Dawson, H.	20120	,, Stubbs, W.
20078	,, Deakin, J.	20119	,, Sykes, H. O.
20151	,, Crowe, W.	21355	,, Schofield, J.
21107	,, Calvert, A.	21294	,, Sutton, H.
21108	,, Cockcroft, J. A.	21207	,, Speet, W.
20081	,, Everett, C.	20123	,, Toole, W.
20086	,, Graney, J.	20124	,, Taylor, T.
21252	,, Gaskell, T.	20125	,, Verdon, J.
20089	,, Holt, J.	20126	,, Vickers, A. L.
20090	,, Healey, J. H.	20129	,, Wolstenholme, E.
21337	,, Hodgert, W.	20131	,, Wall, R.
20092	,, Hill, J. W.	20132	,, Wilkinson, W.
20093	,, Harrison, J. A.	20134	,, Woolley, J.
21212	,, Hill, H.	21210	,, Watkins, A. E.
20095	,, Icke, E. W.	21195	,, Wilson, A.
20098	,, Jones, W.	20075	,, Bailey, Wm.
20099	,, Kennedy, E. A.	21200	,, Hall, J.
20103	,, Lawson, T.	21146	,, Finch, H.

* For portrait, see Officers' Group, p. 305.   † For portrait, see Sergeants' Group, p. 307.

The following were not present when the Platoon Photograph was taken:—

20088	L.-Corpl. Halpern, B.	20082	Private Fuller, F.
20100	,, Layland, A.	20117	,, Shipper, L.
20094	Private Hill, S.		

22nd (Service) Battalion Manchester Regiment.

"A" COMPANY.

Officer Commanding Company - Capt. C. C. May.*
Second in Command - - - Capt. R. W. Bowly.*
Company Sergeant Major - - Burgess, G.†
Company Quartermaster Sergeant - Howard, H.†

PLATOON NO. III.

Platoon Commander - - - 2nd Lieut. E. L. Riley.
Platoon Sergeant - - - Nelson, J.

Roll No.	Rank and Name.		Roll No.	Rank and Name.	
20128	Sergeant	Whitworth, H.	20163	Private	Houghton, D. B.
21380	,,	Hargreaves, J.	20168	,,	Jackson, F.
20141	Corporal	Baines, W.	20096	,,	Jones, E.
20167	,,	Jones, H. C.	20170	,,	Kenyon, C.
21377	L.-Corpl.	Caine, T. H.	20171	,,	Kennedy, J.
20166	,,	Jackson, C. A.	20172	,,	Leech, C.
21192	Private	Armstrong, J.	20173	,,	Lawe, T.
20135	,,	Atkinson, H.	20175	,,	Millward, S.
20137	,,	Blease, H.	20176	,,	Morris, A.
20138	,,	Borthwick, J.	20202	,,	Millward, J. H. L.
20140	,,	Baker, J.	20201	,,	Oliver, J.
20142	,,	Booth, H.	21193	,,	Poyser, C.
21196	,,	Briggs, J.	20179	,,	Poole, W.
21115	,,	Byrne, J.	21280	,,	Poole, W.
20143	,,	Brown, J.	20180	,,	Parry, T.
21329	,,	Brotherton, J.	21282	,,	Rigby, H.
20144	,,	Brogan, J.	20181	,,	Rhodes, H.
20146	,,	Bailey, T. A.	21284	,,	Rogers, H.
20145	,,	Boardman, J.	20183	,,	Rigg, T.
20152	,,	Cliffe, J.	20185	,,	Sowter, J.
21244	,,	Donlan, T.	20187	,,	Shaw, C.
21153	,,	Diamond, A.	20190	,,	Shaw, R.
20154	,,	Sutton, J.	21288	,,	Shelley, J.
21143	,,	Duffy, P.	20191	,,	Taylor, W.
20200	,,	Franklin, J.	20192	,,	Tomkinson, C.
21219	,,	Green.	21208	,,	Vickerman, J.
20157	,,	Hulme, J.	20195	,,	Wilson, J.
20158	,,	Hammond, J.	20196	,,	Wilde, F.
20159	,,	Heapes, A.	20197	,,	Wilde, J.
20161	,,	Ham, J.	21298	,,	Whitehead, S.
20162	,,	Hornby, W.	20198	,,	Young, W.
20164	,,	Heath, A.			

* For portrait, see Officers' Group, p. 305. † For portrait, see Sergeants' Group, p. 307.

The following were not present when the Platoon Photograph was taken:—

20184 L.-Corpl. Sandham, J. M.   20194 Private Tierney, J.

22nd (Service) Battalion Manchester Regiment.

"A" COMPANY.

Officer Commanding Company - Capt. C. C. May.*
Second in Command - - - Capt. R. W. Bowly.*
Company Sergeant Major - - Burgess, G.†
Company Quartermaster Sergeant - Howard, H.

PLATOON NO. IV.

Platoon Commander - - - 2nd Lieut. F. A. Harrison.
Platoon Sergeant - - - Platt, H.

Roll No.	Rank and Name.		Roll No.	Rank and Name.	
21088	R.Q.M.S.	Barker, F.	20234	Private	Jones, E.
20130	Sergeant	Wagstaffe, H.	20235	,,	Kershaw, R.
20262	Corporal	Vickers, L.	20237	,,	Layland, W.
20217	L.-Corpl.	Crosfield, G.	20238	,,	Lever, H.
20211	,,	Brown, W.	20239	,,	Lounsbach, H.
21064	,,	Smith, T. W.	20240	,,	Leonard, P.
21218	,,	Taylor, C. H.	20242	,,	Mitchell, E.
20203	Private	Allen, A.	20243	,,	Mooney, M.
20205	,,	Binns, W.	20244	,,	Mitchell, W.
20206	,,	Brookes, W.	20245	,,	Mitchell, W.
20209	,,	Byatt, J.	20246	,,	Neaves, J.
20210	,,	Broyden, W.	20247	,,	Oldham, E.
20211	,,	Blackshaw, A. H.	20250	,,	Potts, E.
20213	,,	Baugh, W.	20255	,,	Radford, W.
20214	,,	Bennett, W.	20252	,,	Prince, A.
20212	,,	Bently, R.	20253	,,	Parry, A.
20215	,,	Collett, J.	20254	,,	Ryan, J.
20216	,,	Collinge, G.	20256	,,	Richardson, E.
20218	,,	Davies, J.	20257	,,	Roper, W.
20219	,,	Dexter, W.	20260	,,	Stott, J.
20220	,,	Delaney, J.	20261	,,	Stawler, J.
20222	,,	Fox, A.	20263	,,	Warburton, W.
20223	,,	Gibson, A.	20264	,,	Woodcroft, F.
20224	,,	Hendrick, E.	20265	,,	Wright, A.
20227	,,	Hickson, C.	20267	,,	Worsley, H.
20228	,,	Highland, E.	20269	,,	Wear, R.
20229	,,	Holland, R. H.	21302	,,	Wood, F.
20230	,,	Hargreaves, R.	21168	,,	Walker, J.
20231	,,	Horrox, F.	21153	,,	Hopkinson, S.
20232	,,	Hinde, J. T.	21250	,,	Garner, A.
20233	,,	Hallam, G.	20110	,,	Pardoe, H.
20226	,,	Healey, H.	20676	,,	Bleackley, C.
20236	,,	Loundes, J.			

* For portrait, see Officers' Group, p. 305. † For portrait, see Sergeants' Group, p. 307.

The following were not present when the Platoon Photograph was taken:—
20116 Corporal Stahl, J.   20241 Private McKeown, J.

22nd (Service) Battalion Manchester Regiment

"B" COMPANY.

Officer Commanding Company	Capt. D. MURRAY.*
Second in Command	Capt. A. E. BLAND.*
Company Sergeant Major	KNOWLES, F.
Company Quartermaster Sergeant	GARSIDE, R.†

PLATOON NO. V.

Platoon Commander	2nd Lieut. J. A. SHELMERDINE.
Platoon Sergeant	MCCOY, J.

Roll No.	Rank and Name.		Roll No.	Rank and Name.	
20533	Sergeant	TALBOT, J.	20306	Private	LOWE, J. W.
20297	Corporal	HARWOOD, B.	20273	,,	PLANT, W.
20328	,,	TAWNEY, R. H.	20319	,,	RAVENSCROFT, W.
20414	,,	BROWN, M.	20321	,,	RIDGWAY, J. G.
20315	L.-Corpl.	LEE, G.	20327	,,	TOWNSEND, A.
20331	,,	WHITEHEAD, W.	20276	,,	BOOTH, F.
20272	Private	BIRTLES, T.	20318	,,	ROWE, A.
21091	,,	HARWOOD, F.	20317	,,	ROWE, S.
20334	,,	WHITEHEAD, W. H.	20274	,,	BUMBY, W.
20335	,,	WHITEHEAD, J.	20288	,,	GASKELL, F. A.
20278	,,	BONE, S.	20286	,,	FAULKNER, S.
20279	,,	CARROLL, T.	20308	,,	MAWSON, H.
20282	,,	CORNALL, S. W.	20271	,,	ASHWORTH, W.
20301	,,	KNOWLSON, W.	20329	,,	TOWNSEND, J.
20307	,,	MIDDLETON, E.	20280	,,	CRAVEN, S.
20311	,,	PICKSTONE, H.	20325	,,	SHEPHERD, A.
20312	,,	PILLING, J.	20294	,,	HORROCKS, G.
20324	,,	SHEASBY, L. C.	21124	,,	JOHNSTONE, A.
20322	,,	SMITH, J.	20314	,,	PINNINGTON, V.
20323	,,	STAFFORD, H.	20333	,,	WOOLLEY, W.
20336	,,	VARAH, G. E.	20332	,,	WOOLLEY, J.
20359	,,	GRALEY, P.	20285	,,	EVANS, W. J.
21188	,,	WORTHINGTON, W.	20298	,,	JOHNSON, J.
21104	,,	BLOMILY, J. B.	20281	,,	CROSSLEY, H.
20273	,,	BROWN, J.	20300	,,	JONES, S.
20277	,,	BULL, W.	20320	,,	RAWSON, H.
20293	,,	HART, E.	20284	,,	DEAN, W.
20296	,,	HARTLEY, I.	20313	,,	PENNY, W.
20292	,,	HIBBERT, W.	20303	,,	KELLY, D.
21072	,,	HEAP, J. T.	20315	,,	PARKER, R.
20304	,,	JENKINS, W. H.	21230	,,	BRANDWOOD, F.
20299	,,	JOHNSTONE, S.	21317	,,	KAY, A.

* For portrait, see Officers' Group, p. 305. † For portrait, see Sergeants' Group, p. 307.

20917 Private GLOVER, E., was not present when the Platoon Photograph was taken.

22nd (Service) Battalion Manchester Regiment.

"B" COMPANY.

Officer Commanding Company	Capt. D. Murray.*
Second in Command	Capt. A. E. Bland.*
Company Sergeant Major	Knowles, F.
Company Quartermaster Sergeant	Garside, R.†

PLATOON NO. VI.

Platoon Commander	Lieut. J. F. Prince.
Platoon Sergeant	Whitelegge, E.

Roll No.	Rank and Name.		Roll No.	Rank and Name.	
21169	Sergeant	Allen, J.	20362	Private	Hudson, H.
20295	Corporal	Hargreaves, A.	20365	,,	Jubb, E. H.
20378	,,	Mitchell, T.	20371	,,	King, W.
20372	L.-Corpl.	Lennon, D.	20375	,,	Keyworth, J.
20387	,,	Powner, C.	21221	,,	Knowles, A.
20354	,,	Fisher, F.	21264	,,	Kavanagh, D.
20338	,,	Bradshaw, A.	20374	,,	Lee, S.
21239	Private	Corless, W.	21371	,,	McCoy, S.
21141	,,	Allott, A.	21118	,,	Mason, T.
20342	,,	Brockbank, T.	20382	,,	Monaghan, H.
20341	,,	Bramhall, H.	20379	,,	Moran, W. P.
21308	,,	Beck, J.	20383	,,	Nuttall, A.
21175	,,	Beech, J.	21274	,,	Neill, W. M.
21389	,,	Bruton, W. E.	20384	,,	O'Neill, W. E.
20343	,,	Blow, R.	20388	,,	Powner, G.
21128	,,	Booth, F.	21129	,,	Phillips, H.
20348	,,	Clarke, J. A.	20385	,,	Poole, F.
21240	,,	Coyne, T.	21389	,,	Pimblott, T.
20345	,,	Clayton, F.	20654	,,	Priest, C. W.
20350	,,	Dixon, A.	20375	,,	Rathbone, F.
20351	,,	Daniels, H.	21320	,,	Ryan, E.
20352	,,	Dinsdale, J. E.	21163	,,	Smith, G.
20355	,,	Frobisher, W.	21322	,,	Smith, J.
20353	,,	Flanagan, W.	21286	,,	Schnelle, R. H.
20358	,,	Grant, J.	21289	,,	Smith, J.
20360	,,	Garside, J.	20397	,,	Thompson, J.
21147	,,	Gleave, X.	21109	,,	Taylor, R.
21336	,,	Gibson, R. W.	21358	,,	Vernon, G.
20356	,,	Grady, F.	21125	,,	Williamson, J.
20364	,,	Hills, W.	21360	,,	Wilson, J.
21314	,,	Haslam, W.	21325	,,	Willis, F.
20402	,,	Williamson, J.	21368	,,	Wroe, J. R.
20404	,,	Walker, G.	20401	,,	Walsh, J.

* For portrait, see Officers' Group, p. 305. † For portrait, see Sergeants' Group, p. 307.

I.

22nd (Service) Battalion Manchester Regiment.

"B" COMPANY.

Officer Commanding Company	Capt. D. Murray.*
Second in Command	Capt. A. E. Bland.*
Company Sergeant Major	Knowles, F.†
Company Quartermaster Sergeant	Garside, R.

PLATOON NO. VII.

Platoon Commander	2nd Lieut. W. M. Reid.
Platoon Sergeant	Rimmer, F.

Roll No.	Rank and Name.		Roll No.	Rank and Name.	
20413	Sergeant	Bradley, J.	20418	Private	Dawson, F.
20087	Corporal	Hall, G.	20426	,,	Grindrod, H.
20427	,,	Gresty, G. K.	21233	,,	Broadhurst, J.
20291	,,	Gee, W.	21140	,,	Woods, J.
20469	L.-Corpl.	Winterbottom, S.	21296	,,	Yates, A. H.
21318	,,	Lindley, T.	20405	,,	Adams, J.
21376	,,	Cobham, G.	20411	,,	Bleakley, E.
20455	,,	Naylor, P.	20471	,,	Calvert, T. W.
21385	Private	Townson, H.	20424	,,	Fairbrother, J. W.
20441	,,	Irving, H.	20438	,,	Hill, E.
21259	,,	Irving, C.	20448	,,	Mather, F.
20440	,,	Heywood, W.	20453	,,	Murray, L.
20447	,,	Ludlow, W.	20456	,,	Pomfret, J.
20443	,,	Jackson, T. H.	20465	,,	Tatman, G.
21187	,,	Tetlow, A.	21165	,,	Tracy, W.
20430	,,	Howarth, R.	20470	,,	Whetnall, W.
20432	,,	Howarth, J.	21269	,,	Lounsbach, J.
20467	,,	Wray, A.	21396	,,	Jay, J.
21291	,,	Southworth, S.	21295	,,	Fortune, J.
21202	,,	Lamb, J.	21306	,,	Barker, J. R.
20465	,,	Stevenson, M.	20408	,,	Beckett, H.
21375	,,	Broome, R.	21106	,,	Bullen, S.
20415	,,	Carrington, J.	21238	,,	Clayton, T.
21234	,,	Broome, A.	20421	,,	Edwards, J. C.
20425	,,	Freeman, G.	20428	,,	Griffiths, G.
20462	,,	Redfern, W.	20429	,,	Heywood, A.
20439	,,	Hawkins, W.	20449	,,	Mills, F.
20412	,,	Barlow, A.	20459	,,	Parrish, W.
20406	,,	Austin, G.	21279	,,	Place, E.
20444	,,	Kewley, L. F.	20418	,,	Potts, E.
20460	,,	Plimmer, J.	20466	,,	Taylor, W.
20454	,,	Murray, W.	20464	,,	Todkill, G.
20461	,,	Rodman, G. W.	21300	,,	Wild, D.
20450	,,	Murray, J. W.	20422	,,	Jackson, E.

* For portrait, see Officers' Group, p. 305.   † For portrait, see Sergeants' Group, p. 307.

22nd (Service) Battalion Manchester Regiment.

"B" COMPANY.

Officer Commanding Company - Capt. D. Murray.
Second in Command - - - Capt. A. E. Bland.
Company Sergeant Major - - Knowles, F.†
Company Quartermaster Sergeant - Garside, R.†

PLATOON NO. VIII.

Platoon Commander - - - Lieut. D. S. Murray.
Platoon Sergeant - - - - Davies, F.

Roll No.	Rank and Name.		Roll No.	Rank and Name.	
20488	L.-Sergt.	Dearden, G.	21126	Private	Dinsdale, R.
20498	Corporal	Hadfield, H.	20487	,,	Dransfield, A.
20538	L.-Corpl.	Woodcock, W. H.	21096	,,	Grimsley, J.
20507	,,	Knight, W.	21333	,,	Greenhalgh, T.
21391	,,	Ellershaw, A.	20500	,,	Hindson, H.
21100	Private	Bannister, H.	21366	,,	Jepson, T.
20480	,,	Corrigan, C.	20381	,,	Magee, T.
21247	,,	Fenna, T.	20518	,,	Mahon, D.
20495	,,	Hilton, F.	20514	,,	Morris, F.
20503	,,	Jones, A.	21319	,,	Roberts, J.
20302	,,	Knowles, J.	20537	,,	Widdows, W.
20579	,,	Mahon, J.	21304	,,	Allman, A.
20512	,,	Middleton, T.	20474	,,	Bell, A.
20528	,,	Shann, W.	20473	,,	Beswick, J.
20525	,,	Sills, H.	20483	,,	Clarke, E.
20529	,,	Stringer, F.	20486	,,	Daley, J.
20527	,,	Shann, R.	20499	,,	Hampson, J. H.
20479	,,	Bell, B.	20516	,,	Mather, W. E.
20478	,,	Barton, A.	20517	,,	Mellor, A.
21110	,,	Davies, J.	20520	,,	Partington, F.
20491	,,	Flannagan, L.	20524	,,	Skinner, G.
20490	,,	Forrest, J. R.	20535	,,	Whitehead, R.
20496	,,	Huddert, R.	20645	,,	Lear, J.
20501	,,	Jackson, J.	20511	,,	Lees, J.
20534	,,	Taylor, W.	20515	,,	Martin, P.
20531	,,	Taylor, A.	20670	,,	Wright, W.
20530	,,	Turner, H.	20493	,,	Grindrick, J.
20330	,,	Timperly, E.	20477	,,	Butcher, J.
21327	,,	Wolstenholme, J.	20709	,,	McWhirter, A.
21328	,,	Wolstenholme, W.	20536	,,	Wheelhouse, J.
20485	,,	Daley, G.			

† For portrait, see Sergeants' Group, p. 307.

22nd (Service) Battalion Manchester Regiment.

"C" COMPANY.

Officer Commanding Company - Capt. G. O. Ramsbottom.
Second in Command - - - Capt. T. R. Worthington.*
Company Sergeant Major - - Vaughan, G.†
Company Quartermaster Sergeant - Till, L. O.†

PLATOON NO. IX.

Platoon Commander - - - Lieut. W. B. Cushion.
Platoon Sergeant - - - - Hart, F.

Roll No.	Rank and Name.		Roll No.	Rank and Name.	
20750	L.-Sergt.	Jolley, A.	20568	Private	Hill, M.
20599	Corporal	Torkington, F.	21179	,,	Gough, S.
20560	L.-Corpl.	Fouchard, G. E.	20569	,,	Hesford, S.
20744	,,	Cordey, W.	20570	,,	Holbrook, H.
20650	,,	Northgraves, D.	20573	,,	Holland, E.
20725	,,	Starbuck, A.	20572	,,	Horrocks, W.
20540	Private	Arnold, J. W.	20574	,,	Irlam, J.
20545	,,	Buss, H.	20575	,,	Jones, R.
20542	,,	Bowden, J.	20576	,,	Jones, A.
20546	,,	Biddleston, W. H.	21105	,,	Jones, J. H.
20547	,,	Brodrick, A. E.	20577	,,	Jackson, A.
20548	,,	Bebbington, A.	20578	,,	Jones, S.
20549	,,	Brown, W. E.	20579	,,	Kirk, W. H.
20550	,,	Buckley, A. J.	20581	,,	Kenny, P.
21309	,,	Brooks, E.	20584	,,	Lynch, J.
20551	,,	Cooke, R.	20585	,,	Lewis, G.
20552	,,	Crompton, J. E.	20586	,,	Little, D.
20553	,,	Conway, T.	20587	,,	Lomas, D. Mc L.
20554	,,	Cheetham, W.	20588	,,	Mitchell, G. E.
20555	,,	Cooper, R.	20589	,,	McCartney, T.
20556	,,	Cash, J. E.	21346	,,	McCairn, J.
20605	,,	Coope, C. M.	20590	,,	Musgrave, F. W.
21352	,,	Crossley, S.	20591	,,	Musgrove, S.
20557	,,	Davies, C.	21055	,,	Murphy, J.
20559	,,	Evans, E.	20593	,,	Park, W. H.
20561	,,	Franks, W.	20595	,,	Smith, S.
20563	,,	Furphey, H.	20597	,,	Styles, T.
21097	,,	France, W.	20600	,,	Taylor, W.
21083	,,	Farley, J.	20601	,,	Whitworth, C.
20564	,,	Garside, H. R.	20602	,,	Webb, H. W.
20565	,,	Gaskell, A.	21191	,,	Ward, T.
20566	,,	Gibson, G.	21167	,,	Walton, W.

* For portrait, see Officers' Group, p. 305.   † For portrait, see Sergeants' Group, p. 307.

20592 Sergeant Oley, J. C., was not present when the Platoon Photograph was taken.

22nd (Service) Battalion Manchester Regiment.

"C" COMPANY.

Officer Commanding Company	Capt. G. C. Ramsbottom.*
Second in Command	Capt. T. R. Worthington.*
Company Sergeant Major	Vaughan, G.
Company Quartermaster Sergeant	Till, L. O.†

PLATOON NO. X.

Roll No.	Rank and Name.		Roll No.	Rank and Name.	
	Platoon Commander	-	2nd Lieut. J. P. H. Wood.		
	Platoon Sergeant	-	Booth, T.		
20761	Sergeant	Hill, A.	20641	Private	Hurst, E.
20431	L.-Sergt.	Heywood, E.	20642	,,	Lupton, A.
20619	Corporal	Critchlow, W. H.	20644	,,	Littler, J.
20640	,,	Hartley, A.	20582	,,	Leek, J.
21172	L.-Corpl.	Browne, B.	20583	,,	Leek, H.
20624	,,	Dyson, J. E.	20646	,,	Leigh, W.
20627	,,	Everett, S.	20647	,,	McLintock, G.
20606	Private	Anderson, J. S.	20648	,,	Murray, J.
20607	,,	Airey, R.	20649	,,	May, W.
20609	,,	Adshead, R.	20651	,,	Morris, T. E.
20544	,,	Birchall, A.	21181	,,	Middleton, F. A.
20611	,,	Beard, J. C.	20653	,,	Ostell, S.
20612	,,	Bradley, J.	20652	,,	Owens, S.
20613	,,	Burgess, F.	20655	,,	Ridgway, W. F.
20614	,,	Bartram, D.	20657	,,	Robinson, A.
20616	,,	Bould, T.	20658	,,	Riley, J.
20617	,,	Bloomfield, J. W.	20660	,,	Rodgers, W. H.
20618	,,	Carroll, T.	20661	,,	Smith, C. F.
20621	,,	Dale, E.	20662	,,	Smith, J. E.
20622	,,	Davidson, R.	20663	,,	Smirthwaite, G.
20623	,,	Davis, T. R.	20664	,,	Shrimpton, H. F.
20626	,,	Davey, A.	20665	,,	Skelley, R. C.
20628	,,	Fitzsimmons, J.	20666	,,	Stringfellow, T.
21243	,,	Doyle, J.	20667	,,	Stirling, W.
21245	,,	Draper, G. H.	20668	,,	Stott, W.
20629	,,	Goodbrand, H.	21383	,,	Sharples, E.
20630	,,	Gibbons, H. S.	21354	,,	Sweatman, W.
20632	,,	Higgins, T.	20671	,,	Wood, G.
20631	,,	Gaskell, J. R.	21190	,,	Ward, F.
20636	,,	Holden, G.	20672	,,	Young, A.
20635	,,	Horne, W.	21295	,,	Thornbury, J.
20637	,,	Holden, J.	21338	,,	Haigh, E.
20639	,,	Hilton, F.			

* For portrait, see Officers' Group, p. 305. † For portrait, see Sergeants' Group, p. 307.

20638 Private Height, J. H., was not present when the Platoon Photograph was taken.

22nd (Service) Battalion Manchester Regiment.

"C" COMPANY.

Officer Commanding Company - Capt. G. O. Ramsbottom.*
Second in Command - - - Capt. T. R. Worthington.
Company Sergeant Major - - Vaughan, G.†
Company Quartermaster Sergeant - Till, L. O.

PLATOON NO. XI.

Platoon Commander - - - 2nd Lieut. O. J. Knudson.
Platoon Sergeant - - - - Treasure, H.

Roll No.	Rank and Name.		Roll No.	Rank and Name.	
20703	Sergeant	Jones, J. E.	21343	Private	Jones, T.
20603	Corporal	Wootton, T.	20702	,,	Harrison, T.
20594	,,	Sharpley, R.	21257	,,	Harrison, J.
21382	L.-Corpl.	Salisbury, W.	21258	,,	Heywood, J. H.
20706	,,	Killeen, J.	21262	,,	Kitson, G.
20680	,,	Bates, R.	20705	,,	Kirkwood, A.
20673	Private	Ashworth, H. A.	21183	,,	Maden, J.
20139	,,	Buckley, J. A.	20707	,,	McNally, P.
20678	,,	Bourne, E. J.	21271	,,	Mason, H.
20677	,,	Boothman, R.	20710	,,	Noblett, J.
21094	,,	Barlow, J.	21158	,,	Perrins, E.
21305	,,	Ball, J.	20711	,,	Preston, H.
20675	,,	Bailey, J.	20712	,,	Parkington, G.
21229	,,	Brade, W.	20715	,,	Potter, J. E.
20684	,,	Clowes, J.	20714	,,	Philipson, H.
20683	,,	Corbett, W.	20713	,,	Proctor, C.
20681	,,	Collinge, F.	20720	,,	Richardson, R.
20682	,,	Cotton, A.	20718	,,	Richardson, E.
20685	,,	Dunn, L. A.	20719	,,	Raine, J.
20686	,,	Dunn, W.	20723	,,	Shorrocks, J.
20689	,,	Finlow, H.	20726	,,	Stevens, H.
20690	,,	Fox, C. W.	21185	,,	Stanworth, J.
21255	,,	Green, S.	20734	,,	Taylor, W. G.
20691	,,	Gilbert, J. B.	20729	,,	Taylor, J. R.
20692	,,	Goode, O.	20730	,,	Thomason, E.
21217	,,	Greenwood, W.	20736	,,	Thorpe, W.
20694	,,	Goulding, T.	20735	,,	Turner, R.
21357	,,	Hillen, T.	20728	,,	Townley, S.
20697	,,	Heaps, G.	20731	,,	Todman, J.
20696	,,	Hurst, J. A.	20739	,,	Walton, W. L.
20700	,,	Ineson, R.	20737	,,	Welch, J.
20701	,,	Jacques, H.	20738	,,	Warburton, J.
20704	,,	Jones, C. T.			

* For portrait, see Officers' Group, p. 305. † For portrait, see Sergeants' Group, p. 307.

Also on this Photograph : Lieut. D. S. Murray.

20724 Private Stockton, C., was not present when the Platoon Photograph was taken.

22nd (Service) Battalion Manchester Regiment.

"C" COMPANY.

Officer Commanding Company	Capt. G. O. RAMSBOTTOM.*
Second in Command	Capt. T. R. WORTHINGTON.
Company Sergeant Major	VAUGHAN, G.†
Company Quartermaster Sergeant	TILL, L. O.†

PLATOON NO. XII.

Platoon Commander	2nd Lieut. O. J. KNUDSON.*
Platoon Sergeant	BARBER, F.

Roll No.	Rank and Name.		Roll No.	Rank and Name.
20541	Sergeant ANDERSON, S.	25	20751	Private HAITH, W. 1/7/16.
21368	L.-Sergt. TAYLOR, R.		21077	" HOUGHTON, R.
20562	Corporal FORD, M.		21040	" HIGGINS, H.
21231	" BRANTINGHAM.		21256	" HENNESEY, F.
21099	L.-Corpl. HARRISON, G.		21316	" HODGSON, H.
20758	" PHILLIPS, H. J.		21119	" LONG, G. A.
21068	" THORPE, J.		20752	" MORGAN, J.
20740	Private ADAMS, S.		20753	" MOFFATT, J. A.
20742	" BRUNT, W. killed.		20754	" NEWCOMB, A.
20741	" BLACKIE, G.		20755	" OUSBEY, G.
21085	" BRADSHAW, J. killed		21275	" OATWAY, H.
21045	" BIRCH, C. A.		21277	" OLDHAM, S.
20974	" BIRCH, W. R.		20756	" PLACE, F.
21307	" BARNSLEY, M.		20757	" POTTS, H.
20743	" CARR, G.		20759	" POLLARD, L.
21084	" CHEADLE, F.		21057	" PREDHUMEAU, L.
21198	" CRAGGS, C.		21061	" POWELL, R. 1/7/16
20747	" DUGDALE, W. G.		20760	" ROBERTS, F.
21076	" DUFFY, J.		21043	" RODGERS, T. B.
21038	" DOXEY, W. H.		20762	" SKEWES, F. W.
21313	" DALE, J.		20763	" SPANDLEY, R.
21113	" EATON, W.		20764	" SMITH, P. 9/7/16
20746	" FORSTER, H.		21066	" STUBBS, L.
20748	" GIBSON, H. A.		21071	" SMITH, W.
21064	" GREENHALGH, F. H.		21164	" SWIFT, H.
21405	" GODWIN, E.		21044	" THOMAS, J.
21251	" GALLOWAY, J.		21299	" URMSTON, A.
21334	" GREENHALGH, S. W.		21065	" WHEIGHTMAN, J.
21081	" HARRISON, W.		21056	" WRIGHTAM, G.
21082	" HARRISON, T.		21069	" WHIPP, A. killed.
21092	" HEATH, A. 1/7/16 killed		21070	" WOLSTENCROFT, E.
21095	" HOWDEN, J. T.		21258	" HEYWOOD, J. H.

* For portrait, see Officers' Group, p. 305.   † For portrait, see Sergeants' Group, p. 307.

21041 Private JENNINGS, J., was not present when the Platoon Photograph was taken.

22nd (Service) Battalion Manchester Regiment.

"D" COMPANY.

Officer Commanding Company - Capt. F. J. Earles.
Second in Command - - 2nd Lieut. W. J. Cowan.
Company Sergeant Major - - Cunningham, J.†
Company Quartermaster Sergeant - Wilcox, H.†

PLATOON NO. XIII.

Platoon Commander - - Lieut. Roy Mellor.
Platoon Sergeant - - - Pye, T.

Roll No.	Rank	and Name.	Roll No.	Rank	and Name.
20114	R.S.M.	Hughes, J.	20808	Private	Pickersgill, S.
20823	Sergeant	Wilson, W.	20812	,,	Page, J. E.
21386	,,	Taylor, E. A.	20817	,,	Smith, P.
20097	,,	Jackson, T.	20828	,,	Yates, H.
20780	L.-Sergt.	Clarke, J. T.	20770	,,	Ball, J. E.
21379	Corporal	Gourlay, A.	20775	,,	Craven, E.
20798	L.-Corpl.	Kenny, E.	20774	,,	Conway, J. L.
20806	,,	Nuttall, J.	20776	,,	Coard, W. V.
20830	,,	Jones, J.	21103	,,	Derbyshire, H.
20778	,,	Cain, T.	20784	,,	Fenton, T. A.
20787	,,	Hopkinson, W.	20799	,,	Lomax, A.
20825	,,	Whitehead, H.	20809	,,	Powell, W.
20814	,,	Rossbottom, R.	20820	,,	Thompson, S.
20769	Private	Bell, A.	20826	,,	Worthington, G.
20807	,,	Nolan, J.	20822	,,	Wood, J.
20771	,,	Bell, A.	20811	,,	Pyke, H.
20779	,,	Connor, H.	21398	,,	Harrington, T.
20781	,,	Chapman, L.	20832	,,	Buller, F.
20785	,,	Gee, R.	20791	,,	Herberts, G.
20790	,,	Howard, J.	20792	,,	Hall, G.
20793	,,	Heys, H.	20831	,,	Jenkins, L.
20796	,,	Jackson, W.	20797	,,	Kimmings, W.
20801	,,	Mullin, T.	20800	,,	Lister, T.
20804	,,	Meehan, J.	20829	,,	Rossbottom, H.
20824	,,	Wilson, J.	20815	,,	Stevenson, J. A.
20827	,,	Welsby, C.	20816	,,	Shatwell, S.
20772	,,	Brown, G.	20819	,,	Taylor, C.
20795	,,	Holt, B.	20821	,,	Virgin, B.
20788	,,	Hartley, G.	21384	,,	Skarratt, J.
20805	,,	McGannity, W.	21216	,,	Furness.
20802	,,	McKee, T.	21201	,,	Howarth, J.
20803	,,	Murphy, A.	20818	,,	Smith, A.

† For portrait, see Sergeants' Group, p. 307.

The following were not present when the Platoon Photograph was taken:—

| 20767 | Private | Armstrong, M. | 20777 | Private | Crawford, R. |
| 21131 | ,, | Bailey, J. | | | |

22nd (Service) Battalion Manchester Regiment.

"D" COMPANY.

Officer Commanding Company - Capt. F. J. Earles.*
Second in Command - - 2nd Lieut. W. J. Cowan.
Company Sergeant Major - Cunningham, J.
Company Quartermaster Sergeant - Wilcox, H.†

PLATOON NO. XIV.

Platoon Commander - - 2nd Lieut. F. C. Wicks.
Platoon Sergeant - - Alcroft, S.

Roll No.	Rank and Name.		Roll No.	Rank and Name.	
20780	Sergeant	Mottershead, A.	20868	Private	Leigh, W.
21128	Corporal	Hinsley, H.	20869	,,	Morris, E. R.
20862	,,	Johnson, G.	20871	,,	Morrison, M. J.
20251	,,	Pinder, A.	20872	,,	Morris, J.
20958	L.-Corpl.	Treece, W. E.	20873	,,	Medley, G.
20879	,,	Neild, A.	20874	,,	Meek, F.
20842	,,	Calderbank, S.	20875	,,	Mooney, J.
20833	Private	Atkin, S. E.	20866	,,	McShane, A.
20834	,,	Bellfield, J.	20877	,,	McConn, R.
20835	,,	Burrows, V.	20878	,,	Norbury, G.
20836	,,	Barnes, A.	20880	,,	Oldham, R.
20837	,,	Birch, F.	20881	,,	Parry, W.
20838	,,	Barlow, C. H.	20882	,,	Pollitt, G.
20839	,,	Burrage, G.	20883	,,	Perry, W. V.
20840	,,	Briggs, R.	20884	,,	Percival, A. L.
20843	,,	Cook, W.	20885	,,	Ridley, H.
20848	,,	Crabtree, F.	20887	,,	Smedley, A.
20850	,,	Evans, I.	20888	,,	Shaw, H.
20851	,,	Flynn, H.	20889	,,	Sewell, T.
20852	,,	Fielding, T.	20890	,,	Tracey, L.
20853	,,	Fairbrother, W.	20891	,,	Thomas, D.
20854	,,	Gardner, F.	21086	,,	Tabor, F.
20855	,,	Hamer, J.	20892	,,	Unsworth, R.
20856	,,	Hulmes, A.	20893	,,	Williams, E. M.
20857	,,	Hulmes, F.	20895	,,	Wilson, P. E.
20858	,,	Hallam, J.	20897	,,	Whittall, H.
20859	,,	Holt, W. P. B.	20899	,,	Wittmund, C.
20860	,,	Isherwood, C.	21155	,,	Morrell, W.
20861	,,	Jones, P.	21389	,,	Wild, W.
20863	,,	Jackson, R.	20845	,,	Cobb, A.
20864	,,	Johnson, D.	20847	,,	Cooke, L. H.
20865	,,	Leigh, W. R.	21381	,,	Hutton, T.
20867	,,	Logan, A.			

* For portrait, see Officers' Group, p. 305. † For portrait, see Sergeants' Group, p. 307.

22nd (Service) Battalion Manchester Regiment.

"D" COMPANY.

Officer Commanding Company - Capt. F. J. EARLES.*
Second in Command - - 2nd Lieut. W. J. COWAN.
Company Sergeant Major - - CUNNINGHAM, J.†
Company Quartermaster Sergeant - WILCOX, H.†

PLATOON NO. XV.

Platoon Commander - - - Lieut. W. E. GOMERSALL.
Platoon Sergeant - - HANNAH, W. G.

Roll No.	Rank and Name.		Roll No.	Rank and Name.	
17662	R.S.M.	HUGHES, J.	20908	Private	CLARKE, R.
21266	Sergeant	LEWTAS, T.	20947	,,	ORMEROD, J. T.
20919	L.-Sergt.	GRINDROD, J.	21149	,,	HARPER, A.
20927	Corporal	HOLLAND, F.	21120	,,	KINDER, J. T.
20929	L.-Corpl.	HEYWOOD, W.	20952	,,	SALISBURY, F.
20950	,,	SMITH, D.	20909	,,	CUMMINS, R. C.
20945	,,	MOON, J. A.	20904	,,	CLARK, D.
20907	,,	COPELAND, P. W.	20930	,,	HOYLE, H.
20902	,,	BENSON, G. J.	20912	,,	DEWHIRST, G.
20965	,,	WILLIAMS, W.	20946	,,	OWEN, E.
20422	Private	FREEMAN, R.	20951	,,	SMITHSON, W.
20749	,,	JACKSON, W.	20906	,,	CRYNE, T.
20910	,,	CRETNEY, W. G.	20915	,,	FIRTH, W.
20932	,,	JONES, R.	20955	,,	SHAW, H.
20938	,,	LAMBERT, W. R.	21270	,,	MEADOWCROFT, A.
20943	,,	MARSLAND, J. T.	21260	,,	JOHNSON, H. H.
20948	,,	ROBINSHAW, T.	21138	,,	PAVEY, F.
20953	,,	STANSFIELD, U.	21008	,,	MANTON, W.
20956	,,	TRAUNTER, R.	20905	,,	CLARKE, G.
20960	,,	WILLIS, C.	20959	,,	WAINWRIGHT, F.
20961	,,	WILLIAMS, S.	20916	,,	GIBSON, J.
20967	,,	YOUD, H.	20918	,,	GALLEY, A.
20935	,,	KAY, H.	20939	,,	LEECH, W.
20964	,,	WRIGHT, W.	20940	,,	LITCHFIELD, G.
20900	,,	BUNTING, S. H.	20962	,,	WALLER, F.
20903	,,	CHALLONER, W.	20920	,,	GANDY, T. M.
20963	,,	WILKINSON, T.	20901	,,	BRITTON, H.
20937	,,	LANDLESS, J. B.	20941	,,	LORD, E.
20922	,,	GOULD, A.	20957	,,	THRELFALL, F.
20914	,,	FEEHAN, J.	20924	,,	HEATHCOTE, A.
20934	,,	JARVIS, W.	20933	,,	JONES, W.
20928	,,	HALLIWELL, J.	20936	,,	KEAN, T.
20931	,,	HAMPSON, T.	21356	,,	TWINNING, W.
21236	,,	CARTMELL, D.			

* For portrait, see Officers' Group, p. 305.   † For portrait, see Sergeants' Group, p. 307.

22nd (Service) Battalion Manchester Regiment,

"D" COMPANY.

Officer Commanding Company	Capt. F. J. EARLES.
Second in Command	2nd Lieut. W. J. COWAN.
Company Sergeant Major	CUNNINGHAM, J.†
Company Quartermaster Sergeant	WILCOX, H.†

PLATOON NO. XVI.

Platoon Commander	2nd Lieut. J. L. M. MORTON.
Platoon Sergeant	LANCASTER, H.

Roll No.	Rank and Name.		Roll No.	Rank and Name.	
21039	Sergeant	DYSON, J. P.	20995	Private	HENNESSEY, E.
8234	,,	BISHOP, S. G.	21374	,,	JONES, E.
21005	L.-Sergt.	MACHIN, W.	20999	,,	JOHNSON, T. F.
21042	Corporal	KEWLEY, F.	21000	,,	JEFFREY, F. C.
21025	,,	SCHOFIELD, J.	20997	,,	JONES, A.
21026	L.-Corpl.	TUNSTALL, H.	21002	,,	LOMAS, R.
21036	,,	BULLOCK.	21267	,,	LISTER, H.
21027	,,	TAYLOR, S.	21003	,,	MARTIN, J.
21365	Private	ARDEN, A.	21006	,,	MCKEE, H.
20968	,,	BOOTH, C. L.	21007	,,	MELDON, S.
20971	,,	BARLOW, J. J.	21004	,,	MILLINGTON, C.
20970	,,	BUTTER, T.	21033	,,	MURPHY, H.
21225	,,	BLEASDALE, S. M.	21009	,,	OATES, J. H.
21235	,,	BURKHILL, J.	21007	,,	O'BRIEN, W.
21224	,,	BECKETT, J.	21013	,,	PHILIPS, W.
20975	,,	BAKER, W.	21014	,,	PENNY, C. H.
21035	,,	BURKE, M.	21012	,,	POLL, C.
20969	,,	BENT, W.	21011	,,	PARKES, H.
20973	,,	BOLTON, W. J.	21015	,,	RATHMILL, W.
20979	,,	CARTER, J.	21017	,,	ROYLE, J.
20978	,,	CRAWLEY, W. E.	21024	,,	SMITH, T.
20976	,,	CONOLLY, G.	21019	,,	SELLARS, J.
20980	,,	DALY, C.	21021	,,	SMITH, R. H.
20984	,,	DUNSTAN, H.	21018	,,	SCOTT, H.
20983	,,	DODD, W.	21020	,,	SHERRINGTON, T.
20985	,,	DAGLEY, C. W.	21028	,,	TAYLOR, J. J.
20986	,,	EVANSON, E.	21020	,,	WATSON, J.
20987	,,	FREETH, T.	21030	,,	WALKEY, S.
21254	,,	GLYNN, J. H.	21324	,,	WADDINGTON, J.
20988	,,	GRAY, R.	21032	,,	WILLIAMS, P.
20991	,,	HAWARTH, A.	21367	,,	WALLER, L.
20993	,,	HUGHES, J.	21332	,,	EVANS, A.
20994	,,	HANSON, H. B.	21330	,,	DAVIES, W. D.
20989	,,	HARTHILL, A.			

† For portrait, see Sergeants' Group, p. 307.

The following were not present when the Platoon Photograph was taken:—

21001	Sergeant	KNOX, T.	20992	Private	HARRISON, R.

22nd (Service) Battalion Manchester Regiment.

"E" COMPANY.

Officer Commanding Company - Capt. T. Etchells.
Second in Command - - Capt. C. M. Lloyd.*
Company Sergeant Major - Wagstaff, G.
Company Quartermaster Sergeant Yates, S.

PLATOON NO. XVII.

Platoon Commander - - 2nd Lieut. H. Grimwood.
Platoon Sergeant - - Tipper, A.

Roll No.	Rank and Name.		Roll No.	Rank and Name.	
21261	Sergeant	Jones, J.	20028	Private	Halliwell, W.
20446	,,	Leavey, G. R.	20497	,,	Hulse, E.
20069	Corporal	Ainsworth, H.	21344	,,	Jones, H.
21281	L.-Corpl.	Prior, J.	21363	,,	Jones, J.
21062	,,	Platts, J.	20510	,,	Lamb, T.
21089	,,	Skelton, H.	21364	,,	McCormick, J.
20101	Private	Levy, L.	21347	,,	Newton, C.
20954	,,	Steeley, J.	21350	,,	Osborne, A.
21178	,,	Edwards, E.	21059	,,	Pritchard, T.
21075	,,	Fletcher, E.	20390	,,	Pennell, W.
20027	,,	Hayes, J.	20532	,,	Turner, J.
20866	,,	Law, D.	21209	,,	Westwood, J.
21293	,,	Stretton.	21207	,,	Warburton, S.
21408	,,	Capper, T.	20268	,,	Wilson, E.
20982	,,	Delaney, W.	21387	,,	Barlow, G.
20003	,,	Asprey, J.	21399	,,	Carroll, W.
20472	,,	Anderton, G.	20420	,,	Emberton, T.
20604	,,	Burgess, A.	20437	,,	Harlow, P.
20782	,,	Cooke, E.	20038	,,	Jones, J.
20148	,,	Cunningham, E.	20452	,,	Mulvey, C.
21098	,,	Dixie, W.	21136	,,	Schofield, A.
20419	,,	Darke, V.	21396	,,	Jay, J.
20745	,,	Eaton, G. R.	21180	,,	Harper, J.
20085	,,	Grant, G.	21189	,,	Winston, T.
20361	,,	Hurley, T.			

* For portrait, see Depot Officers' Group, p. 401

The following were not present when the Platoon Photograph was taken:—

20773	Private	Bradley, J.	21406	Private	Boyle.
20972	,,	Burns, T.	20509	,,	Laurence, F.
20008	,,	Cunliffe.	20396	,,	Stonehouse.
20494	,,	Gunshon, E.	20489	,,	Dywer.
21341	,,	Hunt.	21253	,,	Gordon.
20874	,,	Mason.	20571	,,	Heaton, P.

22nd (Service) Battalion Manchester Regiment.

"E" COMPANY.

Officer Commanding Company - Capt. T. Etchells.*
Second in Command - - Capt. C. M. Lloyd.
Company Sergeant Major - - Wagstaff, G.
Company Quartermaster Sergeant - Yates, S.

PLATOON NO. XVIII.

Platoon Commander - - - 2nd Lieut. T. H. Barnard.
Platoon Sergeant - - Burrell, R. F.

Roll No.	Rank and Name.		Roll No.	Rank and Name.	
20876	L.-Sergt.	Midgley, E.	20789	Private	Husbands, G.
20199	Corporal	Dicken, T. W.	21080	,,	Gandy, E.
20156	,,	Hatch, W.	21160	,,	Pedder, M.
20596	L.-Corpl.	Southern, L.	21162	,,	Potter, W.
21122	,,	Follows, H.	20423	,,	Featherstone, S.
20505	Private	Knape, F.	21362	,,	Walker, A.
20349	,,	Davies, W.	21285	,,	Rooney, M.
20377	,,	Massey, W.	20521	,,	Price, W.
20373	,,	Lennon, W.	21112	,,	Riley, G.
21093	,,	Hulme, W.	21154	,,	Millington, S.
21303	,,	Andrews, E.	20398	,,	Threlfall, S.
20290	,,	Gibbon, E.	20727	,,	Segal, M.
21388	,,	Roberts, J.	21331	,,	Edwards, J.
20287	,,	Francis, A.	20539	,,	Willis.
20275	,,	Beresford, C.	21127	,,	Mitchell, H.
21159	,,	Peach, J.	20165	,,	Johnson, H.
21022	,,	Singleton, R.	21157	,,	Ostell, H.
21130	,,	Taylor, H.	21326	,,	Whiteley, W.
21016	,,	Roe, W.	20395	,,	Shaw, C.
21359	,,	Watts, D. W.	21161	,,	Salt, W.
21353	,,	Scowcroft, T.	21220	,,	Spencer, J.
21323	,,	Swindells, J.	21214	,,	Blomley, T.
20656	,,	Ruscoe.	21058	,,	Bayley, W.

* For portrait, see Depot Officers' Group, p. 401.

The following were not present when the Platoon Photograph was taken:—

20020	Sergeant	Elsworth, H.	20786	Private	Garland, W.
20383	Corporal	Edwards, T.	20794	,,	Jaycock, T.
20416	,,	Cotterill, J.	21145	,,	Farrington, E.
20208	L.-Corpl.	Blissett, A. A.	21144	,,	Felton, W.
20391	Private	Ryder, F.	21301	,,	Winward, H.
21111	,,	Melville, W.	21156	,,	Nuttall, T.

22nd (Service) Battalion Manchester Regiment.

"E" COMPANY.

Officer Commanding Company - Capt. T. Etchells.*
Second in Command - - - Capt. C. M. Lloyd.*
Company Sergeant Major - - Wagstaff, G.
Company Quartermaster Sergeant - Yates, S.

PLATOON NO. XIX.

Platoon Commander - - 2nd Lieut. A. O. Dowling.
Platoon Sergeant - - Alcock, F.

Roll No.	Rank and Name.		Roll No.	Rank and Name.	
20178	Sergeant	Pogson, W.	21436	Private	Booth, J.
21213	Corporal	West, A.	20370	,,	Kelly, J.
20925	,,	Howarth, E.	20846	,,	Cunningham, M.
20679	L.-Corpl.	Bolton, F.	21226	,,	Bolton, T.
21182	,,	Mullard, F.	20716	,,	Perry, W.
20083	Private	Foster, M.	20506	,,	Knowles, W.
20052	,,	Slater, S.	20380	,,	Middleton, W.
21133	,,	Armstrong, L.	20894	,,	Wild, W. H.
21176	,,	Bennitt, G.	20363	,,	Heaton, G.
21339	,,	Hamilton, I.	21276	,,	O'Gara, P.
20084	,,	Farnworth, A.	20643	,,	Jones, C.
21123	,,	Shawcross, J.	21152	,,	Martin, H.
21177	,,	Daly, P. J.	21342	,,	Jarvis, A.
20011	,,	Clarke, H.	21204	,,	Oakley, E.
21102	,,	Martin, H.	20722	,,	Sheridan, M.
20039	,,	Kenyon, W.	21349	,,	Napper, W. T.
20457	,,	Pilkington, J.	21292	,,	Storey, H.
20136	,,	Baker, J.	20340	,,	Booth, R. L.
21248	,,	Feeney, J. P.	21139	,,	Booth, C.
20123	,,	McGuire, J.	21227	,,	Booth, G.
21242	,,	Darlington, F.	21315	,,	Hepburn, R.

* For portrait, see Depot Officers' Group, p. 401.

The following were not present when the Platoon Photograph was taken:—

21054	Sergeant	Noon, E.	21249	Private	Frankland, N. H.
20944	Corporal	Moss, W.	20717	,,	Riley, D.
21166	L.-Corpl.	Wright, H. A.	21237	,,	Cartwright, H.
21089	,,	Hulme, W.	20445	,,	Kelly, C.
20309	,,	Kersley, R.	21388	,,	Graham, C. H.
21407	Private	Napier, G. D.	21151	,,	Harney, D.
20395	,,	Shanley, R.	20476	,,	Barlow, R.
20982	,,	Delaney, J.	20045	,,	Purcell, C.
20768	,,	Blackburn, J.	21117	,,	Lock, J. H.

22nd (Service) Battalion Manchester Regiment.

"E" COMPANY.

Officer Commanding Company   Capt. T. Etchells.*
Second in Command - - Capt. C. M. Lloyd.*
Company Sergeant Major - - Wagstaff, G.
Company Quartermaster Sergeant - Yates, S.

PLATOON NO. XX.

Platoon Commander   2nd Lieut. A. Walsh.
Platoon Sergeant - Jones, A.

Roll No.	Rank	and Name.	Roll No.	Rank	and Name.
25526	Sergeant	Strange, G. H.	21414	Private	Pickering, S.
21005	Corporal	Machin, W. A.	21413	,,	Maddox, P.
21171	L.-Corpl.	Lowe, S.	21415	,,	Richardson, H.
20193	,,	Davies, G.	21416	,,	Roberts, A.
20580	,,	Kirton, J. W.	21417	,,	Wilkinson, J.
20021	,,	Harper, L.	21418	,,	Byrne, J.
20538	,,	Woodcock, W. H.	21453	,,	Cartwright, E.
21194	Private	Oates, A.	21419	,,	Counsell, J.
21409	,,	Shallice, F. R.	21420	,,	Cook, F.
21439	,,	Capper, C. F.	21421	,,	Doherty, W.
21440	,,	Dickens, C.	21423	,,	Mitchell, A.
21441	,,	Eckersley, J. H.	21424	,,	Moores, W.
21450	,,	Bradley, F.	21425	,,	Sharpe, J. M.
21451	,,	Bagnall, E.	21426	,,	Waugh, J. W.
21452	,,	Chadwick, P.	21427	,,	Campbell, J.
21454	,,	Davies, R. E.	21428	,,	Cauldwell, E.
21455	,,	Dean, J. H.	21429	,,	Crabtree, A.
21456	,,	Drake, T. W.	21430	,,	Dunn, J.
21457	,,	Edwards, J.	21431	,,	Hughes, L.
21458	,,	Fox, H.	21432	,,	Openshaw, J.
21459	,,	Harrison, A. *killed July 1st 1916 age 32*	21433	,,	Heap, E. P.
21461	,,	Kelly, E.	21434	,,	Smith, J.
21462	,,	Moran, T.	21437	,,	Helme, F.
21463	,,	Redstone, J. W.	21438	,,	Higgins, G.
21464	,,	Sigsworth, E.	21439	,,	Bentley, J. H.
21466	,,	Quinn, T.	21442	,,	Fairhurst, W.
21467	,,	Whittaker, W. H.	21443	,,	Featherstone, S.
21410	,,	Andrews, C.	21444	,,	Jubb, T. H.
21411	,,	Hall, J.	21445	,,	Rodgers, J.
21412	,,	Heathcote, H.	20765	,,	Wood, F. S.

* For portrait, see Depot Officers' Group, p. 401.

The following were not present when the Platoon Photograph was taken:—

20289	Private	Gibbons.	21446	Private	Roper.
21465	,,	Stubbs, T.			

23rd (Service) Battalion

Officers' Roll.

Lieut.-Col.	HILL, Sir HENRY B., Bart.	2nd Lieut.	NOBLE, B.
Major	VAUGHAN, W. C.	,,	ROWLAND, F. E.
Capt. & Adjt.	ASHWORTH, J. H.	,,	HAMER, R. B.
Captain	GRIMSHAW, C.	,,	CAPSTICK, A. E.
,,	BATE, F. J.	,,	WARD, W. F.
,,	BETTELEY, C. E. R.	,,	WATSON, F.
,,	FYFE, C.	,,	FOULKES, J. S.
,,	COOPER, A. W.	,,	LENDON, H. C. G.
,,	HEATH, W. E.	,,	WATSON, J.
Lieutenant	GARNER, F. ST. J. W.	,,	KEELEY, A. W.
,,	GOSLING, F. W.	,,	HEARD, J. L.
,,	SIMPSON, G. E.	,,	FITZGERALD, L. D.
,,	HALL, T. B.	,,	SIMPSON, A.
,,	ROTHBAND, J. E.	,,	ALLEN, F. B.
,,	DIXON, T. H.	,,	DOUGLAS, P.
,,	GUILLET, J. C.	,,	BROWN, W. C. S.
,,	GIBBONS, W. P.	,,	SOMERVILLE, H.
,,	WHITE, J. H. B.	,,	WILSON, J.
		Lieut. & Q.M.	WILLIAMS, J. E.

The following were not present when the Photograph was taken:—

Lieutenant	TURRELL, J. W.	2nd Lieut.	JONES, R. H.
2nd Lieut.	ROBERTS, L. W.	,,	LEWIS, M. G.
,,	WOOD, J.	,,	HORLEY, E. L. R.
,,	MORLEY, A. S.		

23rd (Service) Battalion Manchester Regiment.

Non-Commissioned Officers' (Sergeants) Roll.

Warrant Officer.
22926 R.S.M. Dunn, J. E.

21767 R.Q.M.S. Higham, A.
21561 R.O.R.S. Whittaker, P. C.

Roll No.	Rank	and Name.	Roll No.	Rank	and Name.
21766	C.S.M.	Major, W.	22045	Sergeant	Danson, J.
23015	,,	Gorin, W.	22215	,,	Seddon, G.
22572	,,	Collins, E. G.	22245	,,	Cox, W.
22927	,,	Beamish, H.	22148	,,	Pugh, R.
21521	,,	Fisher, S.	22506	,,	Buchanan, A.
21768	C.Q.M.S.	Barrow, J. F.	22461	,,	Goldman, S.
21529	,,	Hunt, J.	22568	,,	Hughes, G.
21540	,,	Mather, S.	22545	,,	Sweatenham, J.
22337	,,	McManus, J. E.	22423	,,	Taylor, E.
22620	,,	Given, E. H.	22413	,,	Ramsden, S. E.
21509	Sergeant	Clare, J.	22314	,,	Fozzard, G.
21523	,,	Green, W. B.	22536	,,	McHardy, J. R.
21528	,,	Hopson, H.	22470	,,	Harris, J.
21604	,,	Lee, H. H.	22563	,,	Young, A.
21740	,,	Megson, C. F.	22628	,,	Baker, D.
21758	,,	Wolstenholme, W.	22615	,,	O'Neill, E.
21628	,,	Wray, S.	22575	,,	Lewis, W. C.
21738	,,	Megson, W.	22962	,,	Platt, J.
21544	,,	Needham, F.	22822	,,	Hobbs, H.
21560	,,	Taylor, T. H.	22847	,,	Woodcock, J.
22671	,,	Varley, B.	22034	,,	Flavell, T.
21962	,,	Tingle, A.	22745	,,	Hare, A.
21863	,,	James, W.	22756	Act. Sgt.	Hopper, F.
22023	,,	Sheridan, J. A.	22029	,,	Wallworth, R. H.
21883	,,	Royle, H.	22644	,,	Crowther, L.
22116	,,	Darby, J. H.	22655	,,	Farraghan, T.
22265	,,	Lister, W.	21880	,,	Pilling, A.
21862	,,	Jones, J.	21793	,,	Eastwood, J.
22134	,,	Keen, A.	21868	,,	Morris, J. T.
22076	,,	Lawson, W.	21818	,,	Prestwood, J.

Also on the Photograph: Lieut.-Col. Sir Henry Blyth Hill, Bart., and Capt. and Adjt. John Henry Ashworth.

The following were not present when the Photograph was taken:—

21612	Sergeant	Poyser, A.	22747	Sergeant	Hooper, W.
22406	,,	Mellor, E.	21951	Act. Sgt.	Ryan, J.
22595	,,	Renshaw, J.			

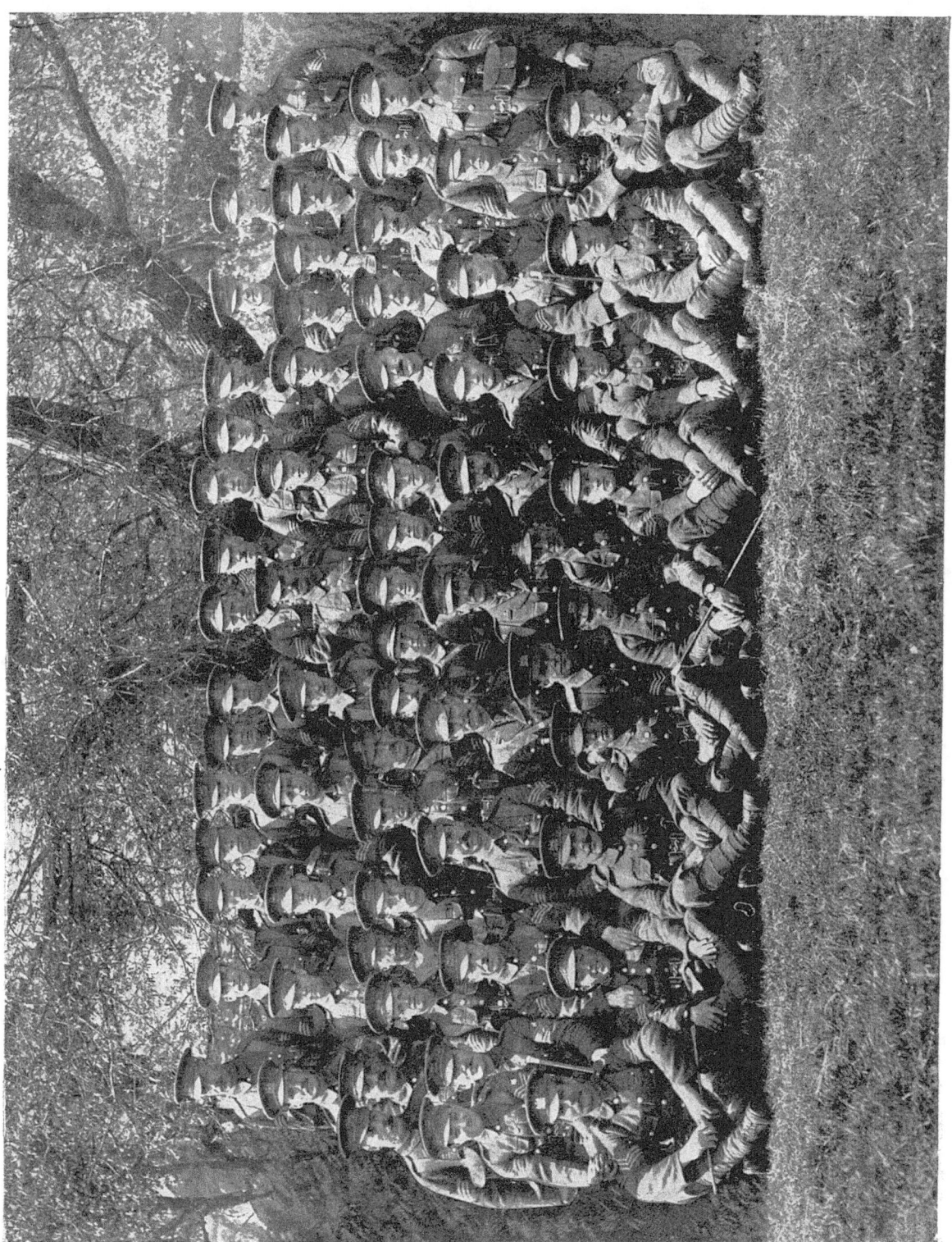

23rd (Service) Battalion Manchester Regiment.

Bugle Band.

Roll No.	Rank and Name.	Roll No.	Rank and Name.
22644	Sergeant CROWTHER, L.	21536	Drummer LORD, J.
22592	L.-Corpl. GARDNER, W.	21605	,, LAMB, D.
22602	Drummer ADAMS, J.	21867	,, MELLOR, N.
22171	,, BAKER, H.	21545	,, NEWBOULD, J.
22873	,, CLOUGH, H.	22146	,, OWEN, D.
22869	,, COSTELLO, T.	22861	,, PEARSON, J.
21645	,, DIGGENS, J.	22863	,, ROBERTS, A. E.
22054	,, DIXON, W. H.	22086	,, ROBINSON, A.
22247	,, FITTON, J. R.	21958	,, SHACKLETON, G.
22893	,, GRIMES, J.	21823	,, STEWART, G.
22769	,, GIFFORD, J. W.	22028	,, WALKER, S.
21662	,, HEAPS, J.	21834	,, WHARTON, W.
21660	,, HARWOOD, F.	21565	,, WHELAN, H.
22661	,, JAMESON, J.	22430	,, WEBSTER, A.
22330	,, KELLY, W.	21826	,, TAYLOR, R.
21602	,, KNOWLES, S.		

The following were not present when the Photograph was taken :—

22017 Drummer ROGERS.   22030 Drummer WILKINSON.

23rd (Service) Battalion Manchester Regiment.

"A" COMPANY.

Officer Commanding Company - Capt. Cleveland Fyfe.*
Second in Command - - - Lieut. F. St. J. W. Garner.*
Company Sergeant Major - - Major, Wm.
Company Quartermaster Sergeant - Barrow, J. F.†

PLATOON NO. I.

Platoon Commander - - - Lieut. F. St. J. W. Garner.*
Platoon Sergeant - - - - Hopson, Hy.

Roll No.	Rank and Name.		Roll No.	Rank and Name.	
21560	Sergeant	Taylor, T. H.	21535	Private	Lambert, R.
21544	,,	Needham, Fred.	21533	,,	Lambert, J.
21561	,,	Whittaker, P. C.	21537	,,	Lambert, Wm.
21532	Corporal	Leech, Percy.	21536	,,	Lord, T.
21562	L.-Corpl.	Webster, C. H.	21534	,,	Loughray, J.
21581	,,	Dolan, A.	21538	,,	Mills, W.
21501	Private	Ainsworth, F.	21543	,,	Millar, G.
21502	,,	Brookes, G.	21541	,,	Moore, T.
21507	,,	Brown, A.	21542	,,	Moran, D.
21505	,,	Brown, Lewis.	21539	,,	Molloy, J. H.
21504	,,	Birch, Wm.	21545	,,	Newbold, J.
21508	,,	Blake, J.	21552	,,	Rennie, R.
21513	,,	Carr, T. J.	21554	,,	Reid, D. C.
21510	,,	Clarke, G.	21551	,,	Ruler, J. W.
21511	,,	Carson, C.	21548	,,	Prince, A.
21512	,,	Clampitt, C. V.	21547	,,	Powell, F.
22598	,,	Crossley, P.	21553	,,	Roberts, J. E.
21516	,,	Davies, W. T.	21556	,,	Stanley, G.
21514	,,	Davies, J.	22593	,,	Salthouse, W.
21519	,,	Ferns, H.	21555	,,	Sloane, E.
21520	,,	Finn, P.	21559	,,	Seacy, J.
21522	,,	Farrand, B.	21557	,,	Senior, Amos.
21524	,,	Grange, W. H.	21558	,,	Vanden, F.
22597	,,	Herbert, F.	21566	,,	Watts, H.
21526	,,	Hassell, C.	21564	,,	Wilkinson, P.
21530	,,	Jones, G.	21563	,,	Wilson, H.
21531	,,	Knowles, A.	21565	,,	Whelan, H. T.

* For portrait, see Officers' Group, p. 353.   † For portrait, see Sergeants' Group, p. 355.

The following were not present when the Platoon Photograph was taken :—

| 21506 | Private | Butcher, J. E. | 21525 | Private | Hudson, F. |
| 21503 | ,, | Blackburn, E. | 21518 | ,, | Fish, R. |

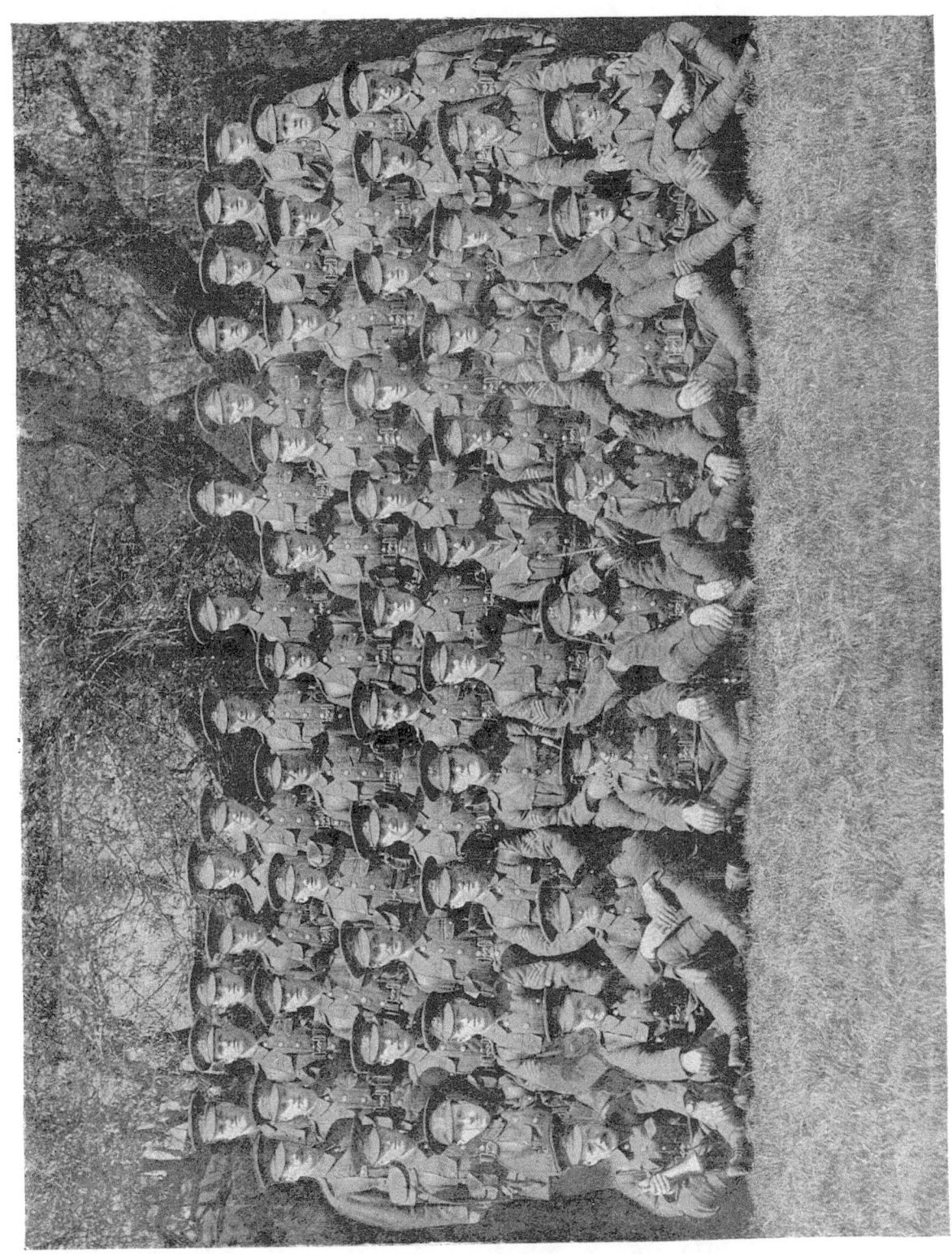

23rd (Service) Battalion Manchester Regiment,

"A" COMPANY.

Officer Commanding Company	Capt. CLEVELAND FYFE.*
Second in Command	Lieut. F. St. J. W. GARNER.*
Company Sergeant Major	MAJOR, WM.†
Company Quartermaster Sergeant	BARROW, J. F.

PLATOON NO. II.

Platoon Commander	2nd Lieut. H. C. G. LENDON.
Platoon Sergeant	MEGSON, WM.

Roll No.	Rank and Name.		Roll No.	Rank and Name.	
21624	Corporal	SCHOFIELD, L.	21597	Private	HILTON, J.
21578	,,	CREED, L.	21595	,,	HALDEN, J.
21619	L.-Corpl.	RANGELEY, C.	21601	,,	KING, A.
21582	,,	EDWARDS, A.	21602	,,	KNOWLES, S.
21567	Private	AYLWARD, C.	21607	,,	LAYCOCK, J.
21568	,,	BRADBURY, S.	21603	,,	LOWRY, A.
21569	,,	BELL, H.	21609	,,	MIDDLETON, G.
21570	,,	BENNETT, M.	21605	,,	LAMB, D.
21572	,,	BUCKLEY, W.	21611	,,	McCARTHY, J.
21573	,,	BROOME, J.	21613	,,	PRESCOTT, T.
21574	,,	COCKRANE, R.	21615	,,	PICKERING, E.
21575	,,	CRAWSHAW, S.	21616	,,	PENNINGTON, H.
21580	,,	CUNNINGHAM, A.	21618	,,	ROWLANDS, H.
21584	,,	FANNING, F.	22599	,,	ROYLE, J. H.
21583	,,	FLATLEY, J. D.	21617	,,	RUSSELL, J.
21585	,,	FORSTER, G.	21620	,,	STAHLER, A.
21587	,,	GREENHALGH, W. B.	21623	,,	SHEPHERD, J.
22601	,,	GREENLEES, W.	21621	,,	STOWE, E.
21586	,,	GREEN, J.	21622	,,	SMITH, R.
22600	,,	GARDNER, J.	21688	,,	SIMONS, A.
21591	,,	HATTON, S.	21625	,,	TAYLOR, J. W.
21594	,,	HOUGH, E.	21626	,,	TOWNLEY, W.
21592	,,	HAMILTON, B.	21632	,,	WALSH, M.
21599	,,	HOWARD, F.	21630	,,	WROE, W.
21600	,,	HANCOCK, G.	21631	,,	WHITE, W.
21598	,,	HUDSON, H.			

* For portrait, see Officers' Group, p. 353. † For portrait, see Sergeants' Group, p. 355.

The following were not present when the Platoon Photograph was taken:—

Roll No.	Rank	Name	Roll No.	Rank	Name
21612	Sergeant	POYSER, A.	21593	Private	HOGG, R.
21653	Private	FOWLER, H.	22657	,,	LANE, W.
21588	,,	GRIMES, J.	21627	,,	TAYLOR, F.
21589	,,	GUEST, J. J.	21629	,,	WROE, F.
21596	,,	HILL, A.	21633	,,	ZAMITEAS, F.

23rd (Service) Battalion Manchester Regiment.

"A" COMPANY.

Officer Commanding Company -	Capt. Cleveland Fyfe.*
Second in Command - -	Lieut. F. St. J. W. Garner.*
Company Sergeant Major -	Major, Wm.†
Company Quartermaster Sergeant -	Barrow, J. F.†

PLATOON NO. III.

Platoon Commander -	2nd Lieut. R. B. Hamer.
Platoon Sergeant - -	Green, W. B.

Roll No.	Rank and Name.		Roll No.	Rank and Name.	
21604	Sergeant	Lee, H. H.	21669	Private	Lewis, F. T.
21628	,,	Wray, T.	21670	,,	Lee, J. S.
21637	Corporal	Bowers, J.	21672	,,	Martin, A.
21679	,,	Percival, F.	21671	,,	Mansell, J. G.
21634	Private	Biggar, E.	21674	,,	McCrann, J.
21641	,,	Byers, S.	21667	,,	Kelly, J. J.
21636	,,	Bulger, H.	21675	,,	Ormrod, J. W.
21571	,,	Baxter, W.	21678	,,	Pontefract, R.
21638	,,	Bristow, H.	21677	,,	Parkinson, J.
21640	,,	Bagnall, Jas.	21683	,,	Reid, R. B.
21639	,,	Barker, H. C.	21681	,,	Royles, R.
21642	,,	Cain, T.	21682	,,	Riley, J.
21644	,,	Clare, E.	22604	,,	Reed, W. E.
21643	,,	Clarke, J. W.	21684	,,	Speed, W.
21645	,,	Diggens, R. B.	21687	,,	Shaw, R.
21649	,,	Ellis, Lewis.	21690	,,	Smethurst, T. W.
21651	,,	Ellis, Evan.	21691	,,	Smith, F.
21654	,,	Fernley, R.	21685	,,	Stirrup, S.
21652	,,	Forkin, J.	21692	,,	Talbot, E.
21657	,,	Grundy, C.	21696	,,	Timperley, A.
21590	,,	Gregg, E.	21694	,,	Taylor, W. O.
21658	,,	Gilluley, Wm.	21686	,,	Stretch, J.
21664	,,	Hammersley, J.	21693	,,	Turner, J.
21663	,,	Harrison, R.	21695	,,	Toal, C.
21660	,,	Harwood, F.	22603	,,	Henry, G. T.
21662	,,	Heaps, J.	21698	,,	Williams, J.
21666	,,	Jones, E.	21697	,,	Whittaker, J.
21668	,,	Lynam, L.	21699	,,	Washington, J.

* For portrait, see Officers' Group, p. 353. † For portrait, see Sergeants' Group, p. 355.

The following were not present when the Platoon Photograph was taken:—

Roll No.	Rank	Name	Roll No.	Rank	Name
21680	L.-Corpl.	Prescott, A.	21656	Private	Garland, M.
21646	Private	Davidson, A. P.	21661	,,	Hockenhull, T.
21649	,,	Ellis, L.	21673	,,	McDunnough, J.
21648	,,	Exton, J.			

23rd (Service) Battalion Manchester Regiment.

"A" COMPANY.

Officer Commanding Company - Capt. CLEVELAND FYFE.*
Second in Command - - - Lieut. F. St. J. W. GARNER.*
Company Sergeant Major - - MAJOR, WM.†
Company Quartermaster Sergeant - BARROW, J. F.†

PLATOON NO. IV.

Platoon Commander - - - Lieut. J. C. GUILLET.
Platoon Sergeant - - - WOLSTENHOLME, W. H.

Roll No.	Rank and Name.		Roll No.	Rank and Name.	
21740	Sergeant	MEGSON, C. F.	22654	Private	HUGHES, E.
21751	Corporal	SPRIGGS, W. D.	21736	,,	LAPPIN, W. J.
21727	L.-Corpl.	GRANNELL, M.	21735	,,	LOVETT, G.
21728	,,	GERAGHTY, W.	21737	,,	MILWARD, C.
21700	Private	ALDCROFT, A.	21741	,,	NIXON, A.
21701	,,	ATHERTON, S. W.	21743	,,	PARTINGTON, J. H.
21704	,,	BURNS, J.	21744	,,	PARNELL, R. E.
21702	,,	BROBBIN, G.	21747	,,	ROBERTS, T.
21706	,,	BUTLER, W.	21746	,,	RIGBY, W. J.
21703	,,	BROWN, J. E.	21748	,,	SEERS, E.
21710	,,	BAGGALEY, F.	21749	,,	SEERS, H.
21708	,,	BURDETT, G.	21753	,,	TAPLIN, A.
21713	,,	COOPER, R.	21759	,,	WHITE, J.
21711	,,	COTTON, G. W.	21757	,,	WHITBY, J.
21716	,,	CHARLSON, R.	21761	,,	WILSON, J. H.
21714	,,	CHORLTON, H.	21756	,,	WOOD, J.
21715	,,	CHORLTON, A. E.	21762	,,	WHITE, J.
21721	,,	DYSON, A.	21761	,,	WILSON, J. H.
21723	,,	EARITH, A. W.	21763	,,	WILLIAMS, J.
21726	,,	FIELDEN, S.	21764	,,	WHITE, T.
21725	,,	FIDLER, J.	21760	,,	WALKER, G.
21732	,,	HOLGATE, T.	22667	,,	HULME, H.
21734	,,	SHEA, C.	21765	,,	YATES, T.
21733	,,	HOWARTH, A.	21731	,,	GAVAGHAN, M.

* For portrait, see Officers' Group, p. 353. † For portrait, see Sergeants' Group, p. 355.

The following were not present when the Platoon Photograph was taken:—

21739	Corporal	MATTHEWS, A.	21722	Private	EBERT, F.
21724	L.-Corpl.	FLEMING, W.	21729	,,	GORDON, W. G.
21709	Private	BACKHOUSE, J.	21745	,,	ROBERTS, E. W.
21712	,,	CROOK, R. A.	21752	,,	SMITH, N.
21718	,,	DAVIES, D.	21755	,,	WILSHAW, W.
21720	,,	DEVONSHIRE, T.			

23rd (Service) Battalion Manchester Regiment.

"B" COMPANY.

Officer Commanding Company	Capt. F. J. Bate.*
Second in Command	Lieut. J. W. Turrell.*
Company Sergeant Major	Gorin, W.
Company Quartermaster Sergeant	Hunt, J.†

PLATOON NO. V.

Platoon Commander	Lieut. J. E. Rothband.
Platoon Sergeant	Varley, B.

Roll No.	Rank and Name.		Roll No.	Rank and Name.	
22644	Sergeant	Crowther, L.	21806	Private	Johnson, J.
21793	,,	Eastwood, J.	21828	,,	Worrall, J.
21818	,,	Prestwood, J.	21811	,,	Laithwaite, P.
21886	Corporal	Riley, R.	21775	,,	Bates, W. T.
21822	,,	Rowland, L.	21781	,,	Curran, C.
21813	L.-Corpl.	Mellor, J.	21773	,,	Beaver, E.
21778	,,	Bennell, H.	21833	,,	Wade, A.
21830	,,	Watson, J.	21774	,,	Bird, T.
21772	Private	Boardman, W.	21827	,,	Taylor, W.
21807	,,	Johnson, R.	21783	,,	Cusick, G. A.
21816	,,	Ogden, H.	21809	,,	Kelly, Joseph.
21787	,,	Dodd, F.	21782	,,	Cole, M.
21804	,,	Hall, S.	21808	,,	Kerwin, Wm.
21821	,,	Robinson, J.	21831	,,	Whyatt, H.
21780	,,	Cahill, A.	21795	,,	Floyd, H.
21810	,,	Kirkpatrick, J.	22295	,,	Warrender, B.
21786	,,	Collier, J. H.	21800	,,	Hatton, T.
21779	,,	Curley, M.	21895	,,	Thompson, J. W.
21975	,,	Cheetham, J.	21824	,,	Simons, C.
21794	,,	Firth, J.	21829	,,	Walker, G.
21820	,,	Slater, T.	21805	,,	Harvey, J.
21776	,,	Butterworth, J. H.	21801	,,	Hunter, D.
21771	,,	Aughton, R.	22625	,,	Nixon, J.
21791	,,	Dossantos, Wm.	21826	,,	Taylor, R.
21777	,,	Bowles, S.	21834	,,	Wharton, W.
21788	,,	Davies, H.	21823	,,	Stewart, G.
21785	,,	Cropper, J.	22610	,,	Kelly, John.
21789	,,	Donnelly, Wm.	21769	,,	Alban, S.
21803	,,	Haslam, W.	21817	,,	Poole, W. H.
21790	,,	Dainty, W.			

* For portrait, see Officers' Group, p. 353. † For portrait, see Sergeants' Group, p. 355.

The following were not present when the Platoon Photograph was taken:—

Roll No.	Rank	Name	Roll No.	Rank	Name
22756	Sergeant	Hopper, F.	21814	Private	McDonough, E.
21819	Private	Quinn, A.	21792	,,	Duffy, J.
21815	,,	Mitchell, W.	21797	,,	Gallahger, J.

23rd (Service) Battalion Manchester Regiment.

"B" COMPANY.

Officer Commanding Company	Capt. F. J. BATE.*
Second in Command	Lieut. J. W. TURRELL.
Company Sergeant Major	GORIN, W.†
Company Quartermaster Sergeant	HUNT, J.†

PLATOON NO. VI.

Platoon Commander	Lieut. G. E. SIMPSON.
Platoon Sergeant	JAMES, WM.

Roll No.	Rank and Name.	Roll No.	Rank and Name.
21883	Sergeant ROYLE, H.	21887	Private RILEY, W.
21880	„ PILLING, A.	21884	„ RODGERS, R.
21868	„ MORRIS, J.	21835	„ AMBROSE, J.
21840	Corporal BROWN, R. G.	21877	„ NUTTALL, J.
21859	„ HULSTON, W. E.	21858	„ HELINGOE, J.
21902	L.-Corpl. BROOME, H.	21845	„ CRANE, J.
21961	„ TOOHEY, B.	21839	„ BUTTERWORTH, H. S.
21890	Private SALISBURY, T.	21854	„ GARVEY, W.
21847	„ CUMMINGS, WM.	21893	„ TUCKEY, W.
21900	„ WAYWELL, E.	22609	„ LOCKETT, F.
21876	„ NEWTON, T.	21875	„ MAFFIA, C.
21849	„ DOYLE, L.	21897	„ WATSON, L.
21853	„ GREENHOW, A.	21891	„ TAYLOR, F.
21873	„ MAHONEY, J. T.	21894	„ TRIVETT, N.
21864	„ KELLY, T.	21837	„ BRADSHAW, C.
21836	„ BALL, T.	21885	„ RUSSELL, W.
21888	„ SMITH, J. F.	21856	„ HARROP, G. W.
21865	„ KITCHEN, L.	21879	„ PORTER, H.
21851	„ GRACE, J.	21882	„ GIDLEY, P. O.
21857	„ HARVEY, A. J.	21860	„ HELLIWELL, J.
21892	„ TUCKEY, E.	21881	„ ROGERS, E.
21895	„ THOMPSON, J. W.	21867	„ MELLOR, N.
21842	„ BREWER, A. W.	22613	„ DONOVAN, J. A.
21898	„ WILDE, W.	21866	„ MARTIN, J. T.
21843	„ BURKE, T.	21841	„ BROWN, J. H.
21846	„ COOPER, J.		

* For portrait, see Officers' Group, p. 353. † For portrait, see Sergeants' Group, p. 355.

The following were not present when the Platoon Photograph was taken:—

21889	Private	STEELE, S. F.	21899	Private	WILCOCKS, J.

23rd (Service) Battalion Manchester Regiment.

"B" COMPANY.

Officer Commanding Company - Capt. F. J. Bate.*
Second in Command - - Lieut. J. W. Turrell.
Company Sergeant Major - - Gorin, W.†
Company Quartermaster Sergeant - Hunt, J.†

PLATOON NO. VII.

Platoon Commander - - - 2nd Lieut. L. D. Fitzgerald.
Platoon Sergeant - - - Tingle, A.

Roll No.	Rank and Name.		Roll No.	Rank and Name.	
21951	Sergeant	Ryan, J.	21937	Private	Moss, J. R.
22655	,,	Faraghan, T.	22622	,,	Dyson, J.
22745	,,	Hare, A.	22616	,,	Johnson, E.
21929	Corporal	Higgins, M. J.	21903	,,	Barry, W.
21928	L.-Corpl.	Hughes, E.	21954	,,	Rogers, H.
21941	,,	Millington, R.	21908	,,	Conley, G. H.
21911	Private	Darlow, C.	21939	,,	Mitchell, A. L.
21924	,,	Gandy, F.	21959	,,	Tindall, M.
21933	,,	Kelly, W.	21952	,,	Reeve, G.
22629	,,	Parsonage, R.	21932	,,	Kershaw, G.
22614	,,	Clarke, F.	21953	,,	Robinson, G.
21946	,,	Nugent, L.	21917	,,	Dean, W.
22618	,,	Swallow, A.	21965	,,	Wolstenholme, W.
21907	,,	Cassell, A.	21920	,,	Flevill, C. H.
21923	,,	Forrest, J.	21957	,,	Sands, R.
21915	,,	Day, J. T.	21945	,,	Noon, J. W.
21949	,,	Oliver, T.	21926	,,	Haigh, J.
21944	,,	Mahoney, J.	21950	,,	Phillips, J.
21919	,,	Elliott, J. E.	21960	,,	Keelan, P.
21921	,,	Freer, G.	21905	,,	Brocklebank, Wm.
21931	,,	Kirkley, D.	21904	,,	Beswick, T. H.
21901	,,	Anderson, J.	21927	,,	Hollingworth, H.
21916	,,	Dakin, W. F.	21958	,,	Shackleton, G. E.
21935	,,	Lawson, S.	21925	,,	Green, J. S.
21918	,,	Donovan, W.	21906	,,	Barker, W.
21934	,,	King, O.	21955	,,	Simpson, H.
21938	,,	Mathews, J.	21948	,,	O'Brien, J.

* For portrait, see Officers' Group, p. 353.   † For portrait, see Sergeants' Group, p. 355.

The following were not present when the Platoon Photograph was taken:—

21956	Corporal	Sykes, J. A.	21964	Private	Wellings, A.
21930	Private	Hart, J.	21966	,,	Williamson, S.
21908	,,	Conley, G. H.	21936	,,	Lever, J.
21909	,,	Cramb, S.	21943	,,	Mayer, A.
21913	,,	Dixon, W.			

23rd (Service) Battalion Manchester Regiment:

"B" COMPANY.

Officer Commanding Company	Capt. F. J. Bate.*
Second in Command	Lieut. J. W. Turrell.
Company Sergeant Major	Gorin, W.†
Company Quartermaster Sergeant	Hunt, J.

PLATOON NO. VIII.

Platoon Commander	2nd Lieut. B. Noble.
Platoon Sergeant	Sheridan, J. A.

Roll No.	Rank and Name.		Roll No.	Rank and Name.	
22896	Sergeant	Royle, E.	21996	Private	Holt, A.
22029	,,	Wallworth, R. H.	21993	,,	Hutchinson, F. W.
21855	Corporal	Gill, W. H.	21999	,,	Ireland, B.
22005	,,	Mills, V. K.	21972	,,	Connolly, James.
21848	L.-Corpl.	Dodd, C.	22008	,,	Mason, W.
21977	,,	Chadwick, E.	22021	,,	Sheridan, M.
22010	Private	Parton, A.	21979	,,	Davies, A.
21971	,,	Connolly, John.	21974	,,	Clarke, S.
22004	,,	Murray, T.	21990	,,	Grundy, J.
22605	,,	Hayes, A.	22001	,,	Lewis, R. T.
21994	,,	Hagan, E.	22009	,,	Melia, G.
22032	,,	Walker, W.	21987	,,	Gillibrand, A.
21991	,,	Gregson, J.	21981	,,	Doyle, J.
22002	,,	Leith, G.	22611	,,	Axon, T.
21992	,,	Harvey, C. F.	22007	,,	Maggs, C.
21997	,,	Holl, R. S.	22027	,,	Ward, J. R.
22014	,,	Radcliffe, G.	22022	,,	Shawcross, J.
22026	,,	West, G. W.	22017	,,	Rogers, T.
22658	,,	Bullock, J. E.	21985	,,	Gill, G.
21978	,,	Dawson, H.	21850	,,	Farrin, L.
21986	,,	Gill, T.	22006	,,	Moore, W.
22024	,,	Thompson, T.	21983	,,	Forrest, J.
22015	,,	Ryan, W.	22897	,,	Landing, S. M.
21973	,,	Clarke, F.	22028	,,	Walker, S.
21968	,,	Burke, J. T.	22033	,,	Walker, J.
22000	,,	Kay, R.	21988	,,	Greenhalgh, A.
21984	,,	Files, R.	22617	,,	Beaumont, J. S.
22016	,,	Redikin, J.	22803	,,	Noton, I. J.
22031	,,	Whittaker, R.	21976	,,	Chadwick, M.

* For portrait, see Officers' Group, p. 353.   † For portrait, see Sergeants' Group, p. 355.

The following were not present when the Platoon Photograph was taken,

21982	Private	Foden, W. H.	21935	Private	Lawson, S.
22608	,,	Herrick, R.			

23rd (Service) Battalion Manchester Regiment.

"C" COMPANY.

Officer Commanding Company - Capt. C. GRIMSHAW.
Second in Command - - - Capt. A. W. COOPER.
Company Sergeant Major - - COLLINS, C. G.
Company Quartermaster Sergeant - MATHER, S.†

PLATOON NO. IX.

Platoon Commander - 2nd Lieut. A. W. KEELEY.
Platoon Sergeant - DARBY, J. H.

Roll No.	Rank and Name.		Roll No.	Rank and Name.	
22245	Sergeant	COX, W.	22039	Private	BENNETT, G.
22184	Corporal	DOYLE, P.	22093	,,	WILSON, C.
22278	,,	McHUGH, T.	22064	,,	HARRISON, S.
22149	L.-Corpl.	PLEASANT, W.	22085	,,	RILEY, M.
22172	,,	BULLOCK, S.	22051	,,	CARR, H.
22237	,,	BOWDEN, G.	22078	,,	McDONOUGH, F.
22040	Private	CLYNES, A.	22047	,,	CLARKE, A.
22062	,,	GREENFIELD, W.	22037	,,	BROTHERDALE, J.
22083	,,	POTTS, J. H.	22100	,,	WILKINSON, J.
22081	,,	NUTTALL, H.	22094	,,	WORRALL, S.
22087	,,	SPELLMAN, J.	22099	,,	WARDLE, A.
22038	,,	BURNETT, H.	22056	,,	DOBSON, F.
22088	,,	SCRAGG, R.	22077	,,	MANTON, J.
22071	,,	JONES, G.	22095	,,	WOODWARD, G.
22070	,,	JOWETT, C.	22045	,,	CONNOLLY, A.
22074	,,	KENNEDY, G.	22079	,,	MASSEY, A.
22052	,,	CLAXTON, J.	22092	,,	THOMPSON, W.
22861	,,	PEARSON, J.	22048	,,	CARTLEDGE, G.
22080	,,	PICKERING, A.	22061	,,	FAIRHURST, J.
22086	,,	ROBINSON, H.	22054	,,	DIXON, W.
22044	,,	CAMPBELL, J.	22073	,,	KAY, R. H.
22068	,,	JONES, D.	22075	,,	LOCKLEY, F.
22097	,,	WRIGHT, J.	22059	,,	ECKERSLEY, C. F.
22057	,,	DAVIES, G.	22096	,,	WARD, J.
22050	,,	CARTWRIGHT, W. O.	22069	,,	JENSON, C.
22058	,,	DREW, E.	22043	,,	COX, W.
22036	,,	BROADHURST, T.			

† For portrait, see Sergeants' Group, p. 355.

The following were not present when the Platoon Photograph was taken:—

22042	Private	COLLIER, R.	22066	Private	HART, P.
22049	,,	CRAWFORD, A.	22091	,,	TAYLOR, J.
28504	,,	LASCELLES, F.	22084	,,	PAXTON, T.
22983	,,	CARPENTER, F.	22063	,,	HANSON, E.
22089	,,	SUGRUE, C.	22060	,,	FLYNN, J.
22046	,,	CHAPMAN, E.			

23rd (Service) Battalion Manchester Regiment.

"C" COMPANY.

Officer Commanding Company	Capt. C. Grimshaw.*
Second in Command	Capt. A. W. Cooper.*
Company Sergeant Major	Collins, C. G.†
Company Quartermaster Sergeant	Mather, S.†

PLATOON NO. X.

Platoon Commander - 2nd Lieut. A. Simpson.
Platoon Sergeant - Seddon, G.

Roll No.	Rank and Name.		Roll No.	Rank and Name.	
22055	Sergeant	Danson, J.	22162	Private	Weston, W. H.
22076	,,	Lawson, W.	22145	,,	O'Brien, P.
22072	Corporal	Keighley, J.	22153	,,	Riley, W.
22098	,,	Whittaker, F.	22152	,,	Robinson, G.
22041	,,	Croft, S.	22123	,,	Harris, C. W.
22271	,,	Lunn, H.	22166	,,	Williams, S.
22270	L.-Corpl.	Langton, R.	22141	,,	McAlice, T.
22147	Private	Percival, J.	22161	,,	Taylor, R.
22151	,,	Roxby, F.	22121	,,	Gregory, C.
22122	,,	Hulme, F.	22113	,,	Coney, A.
22103	,,	Bullock, W.	22160	,,	Turner, T.
22139	,,	Mallinson, A.	22154	,,	Rothwell, T.
22136	,,	Lee, C.	22144	,,	O'Conner, J.
22115	,,	Conner, J.	22155	,,	Smith, J.
22132	,,	Henderson, T.	22156	,,	Sheridan, J.
22146	,,	Owen, J. D.	22163	,,	Ward, J.
22137	,,	Lilley, J.	22131	,,	Hannigan, T.
22573	,,	Matthews, S. J.	22135	,,	Kirwin, J.
22574	,,	Lord, E. J.	22112	,,	Condron, M.
22114	,,	Colman, R.	22108	,,	Bailey, W.
22863	,,	Roberts, A. E.	22133	,,	Jackson, E.
22157	,,	Shaw, W.	22150	,,	Phillips, J.
22159	,,	Slack, F.	22127	,,	Howarth, J.
22124	,,	Halstead, H.	22142	,,	Mills, H.
22111	,,	Clarke, H.	22130	,,	Hulton, E.
22105	,,	Blagg, J.	22119	,,	Entwistle, E.
22165	,,	Woodcock, N.	22128	,,	Hardman, J.
22107	,,	Barker, H.	22129	,,	Hardman, E. W.
22143	,,	Norbury, J.	22109	,,	Brierley, A.
22578	,,	Gillan, T.			

* For portrait, see Officers' Group, p. 353.   † For portrait, see Sergeants' Group, p. 355.

The following were not present when the Platoon Photograph was taken,

22125	Private	Hilton, J.	22577	Private	Barratt, J. T.
22106	,,	Blagg, A.	22140	,,	Miller, J.
22117	,,	Dinsdale, H.	22138	,,	Lees, B.

23rd (Service) Battalion Manchester Regiment.
"C" COMPANY.

Officer Commanding Company	Capt. C. Grimshaw.*
Second in Command	Capt. A. W. Cooper.*
Company Sergeant Major	Collins, C. G.†
Company Quartermaster Sergeant	Mather, S.†

PLATOON NO. XI.

Platoon Commander	Lieut. T. H. Dixon.
Platoon Sergeant	Lister, W.

Roll No.	Rank and Name.	Roll No.	Rank and Name.
22134	Sergeant Keen, A.	22222	Private Wall, G. F.
22148	,, Pugh, R.	22582	,, Walsh, P.
22118	Corporal Dodd, I. J.	22583	,, Cooney, H.
22082	L.-Corpl. Patchett, F.	22206	,, Pritchard, J.
22171	Private Baker, H.	22201	,, McGee, E.
22174	,, Bradley, J.	22220	,, Taylor, W.
22179	,, Cunningham, M.	22180	,, Carr, A.
22189	,, Hilton, H.	22199	,, May, E.
22195	,, Lynch, A.	22228	,, Willis, J.
22198	,, Milward, J.	22218	,, Tapp, J.
22211	,, Plevin, J.	22230	,, Waldron, W.
22203	,, Pritchard, S.	22231	,, Watkinson, J.
22212	,, Reynolds, J.	22191	,, Hall, R.
22580	,, Riley, J.	22192	,, Hughes, W.
22579	,, Tomlinson, A.	22229	,, Walker, A. S.
22224	,, Wych, Jos.	22842	,, Cooney, W.
22233	,, Wood, J.	22227	,, Wild, G.
22168	,, Ashton, T.	22197	,, Lees, H.
22178	,, Carter, W.	22173	,, Bannister, J.
22183	,, Dawson, A.	22226	,, Withers, J.
22185	,, Dalglish, W.	22177	,, Breheny, T.
22188	,, Hampson, S.	22207	,, Pope, G.
22193	,, Kay, B.	22181	,, Chapman, R.
22196	,, Lee, T.	22194	,, Keenan, E.
22204	,, Pickburn, C.	22221	,, Vakey, D.
22208	,, Parton, E.	22209	,, Prendergast, A.
22225	,, Woodward, L.	22584	,, Howarth, F.
22581	,, Jones, N.		

* For portrait, see Officers' Group, p. 353.　　† For portrait, see Sergeants' Group, p. 355.

The following were not present when the Platoon Photograph was taken:—

Roll No.	Rank and Name.	Roll No.	Rank and Name.
22170	L.-Corpl. Booth, T.	22219	Private Taylor, J.
22232	Private Wych, Jno.	22217	,, Scholes, A.
22869	,, Costello, T.	22213	,, Reeves, J.
22169	,, Allen, J.	22176	,, Bell, T.
22210	,, Preston, G.	22190	,, Holt, W.

23rd (Service) Battalion Manchester Regiment.

"C" COMPANY.

Officer Commanding Company -	Capt. C. Grimshaw.
Second in Command - -	Capt. A. W. Cooper.*
Company Sergeant Major - -	Collins, C. G.†
Company Quartermaster Sergeant -	Mather, S.

PLATOON NO. XII.

Platoon Commander - - -	2nd Lieut. J. Watson.
Platoon Sergeant - - -	Tuite, J.

Roll No.	Rank and Name.		Roll No.	Rank and Name.	
21862	Sergeant	Jones, J.	22254	Private	Hoyle, G.
22202	Corporal	McDermott, J.	22285	,,	Ravenscroft, T. H.
22294	L.-Corpl.	Thomason, H.	22238	,,	Brown, F.
22110	,,	Bailey, T.	22283	,,	Pearl, R.
22187	,,	Fowler, J. W.	22585	,,	Bennett, A. E.
22067	,,	Holland, F. S.	22262	,,	Homer, F.
22234	Private	Briddock, J.	22277	,,	Matthews, W.
22235	,,	Bird, W.	22260	,,	Hartley, W.
22236	,,	Bentley, H.	22296	,,	Wigg, F.
22288	,,	Sherrett, W.	22297	,,	Walton, R.
22280	,,	Nolan, C.	22276	,,	Mahon, J.
22286	,,	Reid, A. E.	22246	,,	Davies, E.
22298	,,	Wilcock, G.	22268	,,	Leech, H.
22242	,,	Bailey, P.	22255	,,	Holmes, J.
22287	,,	Robinson, A.	22256	,,	Hampson, C.
22292	,,	Sillitoe, W.	22269	,,	Lucas, R.
22273	,,	Lomas, G.	22250	,,	Fozzard, C.
22291	,,	Street, W. H.	22240	,,	Brown, S.
22241	,,	Barker, G.	22243	,,	Bambroffe, C.
22247	,,	Fitton, J. R.	22259	,,	Hargreaves, F.
22253	,,	Hacker, C. S.	22258	,,	Hayes, J.
22251	,,	Goulding, J.	22257	,,	Halson, E.
22267	,,	Lingard, J.	22263	,,	Johnson, H. D.
22281	,,	Noel, E.	22275	,,	Murray, F.
22293	,,	Torrens, G.	22290	,,	Simpson, N.
22248	,,	Fisher, M.	22299	,,	Young, W.

* For portrait, see Officers' Group, p. 353.   † For portrait, see Sergeants' Group, p. 355.

The following were not present when the Platoon Photograph was taken :—

Roll No.	Rank	Name	Roll No.	Rank	Name
22872	Sergeant	Baker, E.	22274	Private	Malackey, A.
22266	Private	Lockett, J. H.	22264	,,	Kellett, A.
22244	,,	Colburn, W.	22282	,,	Nibblet, H.
22284	,,	Read, R.	22289	,,	Summers, T.
22272	,,	Lomas, J. W.	22252	,,	Greenwood, J.

23rd (Service) Battalion Manchester Regiment.

"D" COMPANY.

Officer Commanding Company — Major W. C. Vaughan.
Second in Command - - - Lieut. F. W. Gosling.
Company Sergeant Major - - Beamish, H.
Company Quartermaster Sergeant - McManus, J. E.

PLATOON NO. XIII.

Platoon Commander - - - Lieut. J. H. B. White.
Platoon Sergeant - - - Sweatenham, J.

Roll No.	Rank and Name.		Roll No.	Rank and Name.	
22314	Sergeant	Fozzard, G.	22323	Private	Irving, T.
22354	Corporal	Slater, J.	22324	,,	Jones.
22336	,,	McFarland, G.	22326	,,	Jeffries, R. T.
22365	,,	Young, C.	22329	,,	Hearney, A.
22360	L.-Corpl.	Warden, E.	22328	,,	Kearns, R.
22301	Private	Atherton, J.	22331	,,	Lee, J.
22640	,,	Anderson, P.	22333	,,	Luckman, D.
22306	,,	Barrett, E.	22334	,,	Lawlor, T.
22307	,,	Barrett, P.	22632	,,	McLouglin, A.
22308	,,	Burke, C.	22335	,,	Moores, H.
22303	,,	Barker, S.	22340	,,	Newton, L.
22305	,,	Bonnar, R.	22339	,,	Noble, J.
22643	,,	Berrisford, J.	22344	,,	Penkethman, J.
22304	,,	Brown, B.	22346	,,	Parks, R.
22302	,,	Butterworth, J.	22345	,,	Porter, F.
22311	,,	Cooper, A.	22348	,,	Rodgers, C.
22309	,,	Carpenter, J.	22349	,,	Roberts, D.
22636	,,	Cartledge, S.	22351	,,	Roberts, E.
22300	,,	Cullen, F.	22633	,,	Rogers, J.
22310	,,	Croft, J. R.	22355	,,	Steele, J.
22646	,,	Conroy, W.	22357	,,	Stephens, R. B.
22312	,,	Danks, A.	22359	,,	Simpson, W. A.
22315	,,	Gill, J.	22352	,,	Seddon, A.
22316	,,	Garner, E.	22353	,,	Seddon, C.
22322	,,	Horridge, W.	22363	,,	Woodall, E.
22320	,,	Hassel, J. E.	22361	,,	Whitehead, T.
22321	,,	Hall, A.	22364	,,	Welch, J. J.
22317	,,	Heywood, A.	22634	,,	Wilkinson, L.
22319	,,	Hesford, T.	22661	,,	Jameson, J.
22325	,,	Johnson, E.	22330	,,	Kelly, W.

The following were not present when the Platoon Photograph was taken:—

| 22536 | Sergeant | McHardy, J. R. | 22359 | Private | Simpson, W. A. |
| 22639 | Private | Nixon. | 22362 | ,, | Westby. |

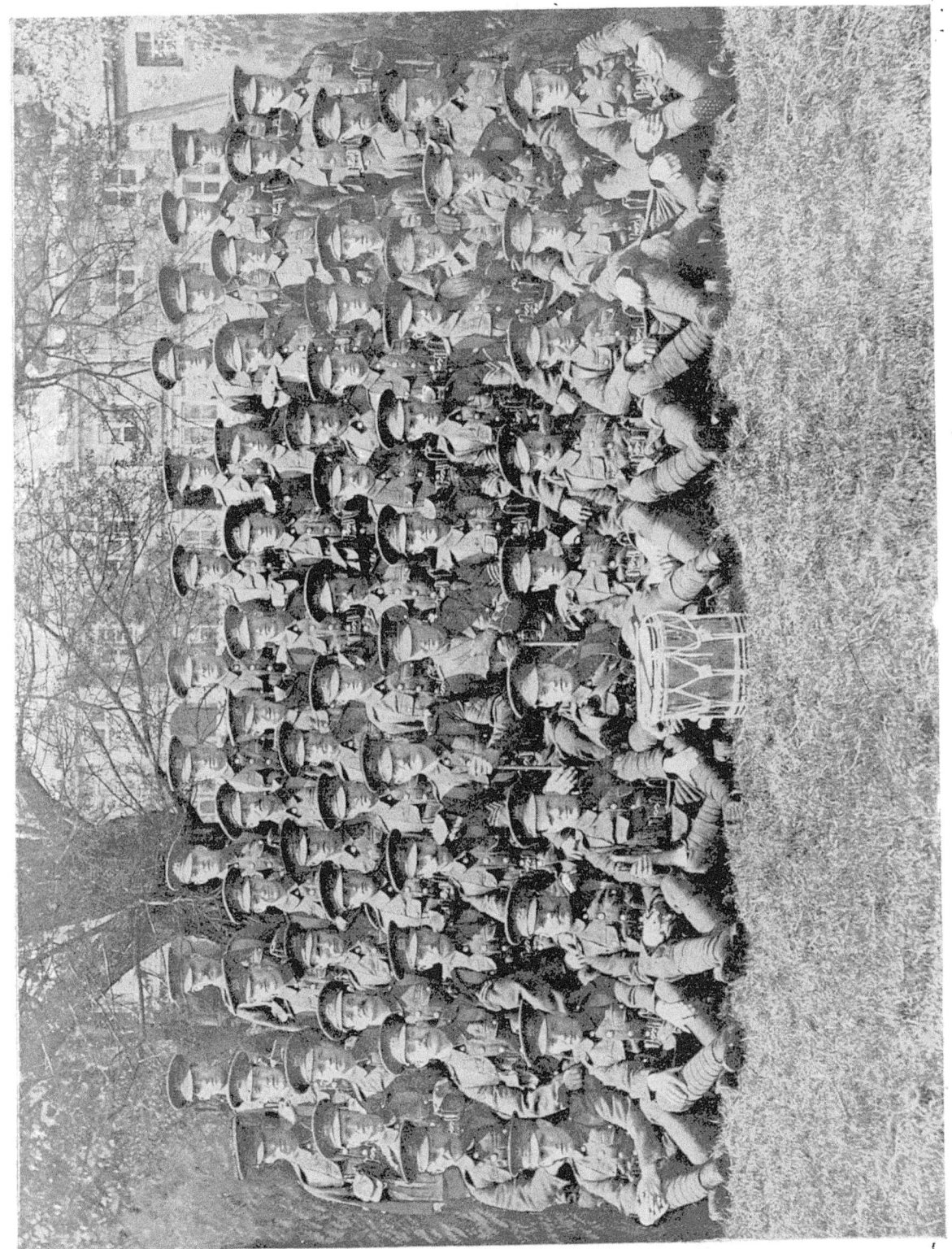

23rd (Service) Battalion Manchester Regiment.

"D" COMPANY.

Officer Commanding Company	Major W. C. VAUGHAN.
Second in Command	Lieut. F. W. GOSLING.
Company Sergeant Major	BEAMISH, H.
Company Quartermaster Sergeant	McMANUS, J. E.

PLATOON NO. XIV.

Platoon Commander	2nd. Lieut. F. E. ROWLAND.
Platoon Sergeant	TAYLOR, E.

Roll No.	Rank and Name.		Roll No	Rank and Name.	
22413	Sergeant	RAMSDEN, S. E.	22397	Private	JOHNSTONE, F.
22406	,,	MELLOR, E.	22399	,,	KILKENNY, E.
22421	Corporal	STREET, A.	22401	,,	LOMAS, O.
22395	,,	HARRISON, A.	22402	,,	LEVER, J.
22434	L.-Corpl.	PHILLIPS, J.	22649	,,	LEECH, C.
22592	,,	GARDNER, W.	22405	,,	McCULLOCH, D.
22367	Private	ASHTON, H.	22404	,,	McGEE, T.
22376	,,	BRADLEY, J.	22408	,,	McCOATES, D.
22374	,,	BYRNE, P.	22642	,,	MORGAN, E.
22375	,,	BROMLEY, B.	22407	,,	MIDDLETON, W
22371	,,	BUSHBY, F.	22409	,,	OLLERHEAD, G.
22372	,,	BARLOW, J. W.	22411	,,	PATON, W.
22650	,,	BRAMHALL.	22412	,,	POLLITT, J. W.
22638	,,	BUCKLEY, H.	22414	,,	PETTIGREW, J.
22373	,,	BROOME, T.	22699	,,	PEARSON, W. E.
22378	,,	CRABTREE, W.	22410	,,	PEARSON, A.
22382	,,	CLARKE, J.	22415	,,	ROBINSON, J.
22384	,,	COLWELL, H.	22416	,,	SMITH, J.
22381	,,	CAMPBELL, W.	22419	,,	SCHOLES, J.
22379	,,	CRABTREE, T. J.	22417	,,	SKIDMORE, F. J.
22386	,,	DAVIES, J.	22420	,,	TURNER, H.
22647	,,	DICKINSON, T.	22424	,,	WINTERBOTTOM, G.
22387	,,	DAVIES, W.	22422	,,	WHISTON, J.
22648	,,	EGAN, L.	22428	,,	WALSH, B.
22651	,,	FORTH, P.	22432	,,	WILLACEY, R.
22382	,,	GREAVES, J.	22433	,,	WALSH, H.
22391	,,	GILLOTT, J. H.	22410	,,	WAINWRIGHT, G. F.
22638	,,	HEALEY, D.	22431	,,	WRIGLEY, H.
22396	,,	HUTCHINGS, J.	22430	,,	WEBSTER, A.
22637	,,	HORTON, A.	22836	,,	RODD, T. H. J.
22398	,,	KENYON, A.			

The following were not present when the Platoon Photograph was taken:—

22385	Private	CROSS.	22394	Private	HOWARD.
22383	,,	CALVERT.	22429	,,	WILLIAMS.

23rd (Service) Battalion Manchester Regiment.

"D" COMPANY.

Officer Commanding Company - Major W. C. Vaughan.
Second in Command - - - Lieut. F. W. Gosling.
Company Sergeant Major - - Beamish, H.
Company Quartermaster Sergeant - McManus, J. E.

PLATOON NO. XV.

Platoon Commander - - 2nd Lieut. P. Douglas.
Platoon Sergeant - - - - Goldman, S.

Roll No.	Rank and Name.		Roll No.	Rank and Name.	
22470	Sergeant	Harris, J.	22468	Private	Holt, H.
22451	Corporal	McGinty, T.	22475	,,	Lowry, W.
22437	,,	Allam, G.	22558	,,	Lowe, A.
22465	L.-Corpl.	Hill, J.	22447	,,	Mallinson, T.
22454	,,	Dewhirst, T.	22479	,,	McNeil, T.
22436	Private	Acton, G.	22481	,,	Moran, J.
22439	,,	Ashworth, E.	22478	,,	Murphy, J.
22440	,,	Ashworth, L.	22471	,,	Platt, P.
22447	,,	Banks, J.	22492	,,	Sanders, H.
22448	,,	Blood, C.	22486	,,	Summers, F.
22444	,,	Berrisford, J.	22490	,,	Shenton, J.
22445	,,	Boddy, A.	22488	,,	Swindells, H.
22443	,,	Barrett, E.	22489	,,	Swain, F.
22442	,,	Basford, J.	22485	,,	Stephens, W. E.
22446	,,	Booth, A.	22491	,,	Shaw, J.
22450	,,	Cohen, F.	22487	,,	Sullivan, J.
22452	,,	Cuff, H.	22494	,,	Thomas, P.
22449	,,	Cummings, R. A.	22493	,,	Thompson, G.
22458	,,	Fielding, G.	22495	,,	Thornley, H.
22460	,,	Hannery, F.	22496	,,	Taylor, T.
22457	,,	Flaherty, W.	22634	,,	Theobold, J.
22455	,,	Fearnley, F.	22497	,,	Verity.
22463	,,	Gavin, N. J.	22499	,,	Wales, G.
22462	,,	Green, W. H.	22500	,,	Wych, B.
22467	,,	Hadwin, G.	22501	,,	Wade, F. J.
22464	,,	Hoole, J.	22502	,,	Worsley, H.
22472	,,	Johnson, W.	22662	,,	Adams, J.
22473	,,	Leadbeater, J.			

The following were not present when the Platoon Photograph was taken :—

| 22476 | Corporal | Langton, R. | 22455 | Private | Fletcher. |
| 22474 | Private | Langley. | | | |

23rd (Service) Battalion Manchester Regiment.

"D" COMPANY.

Officer Commanding Company - Major W. C. Vaughan.
Second in Command - - - Lieut. F. W. Gosling.
Company Sergeant Major - - Beamish, H.
Company Quartermaster Sergeant - McManus, J. E.

PLATOON NO. XVI.

Platoon Commander - - - Lieut. F. W. Gosling.
Platoon Sergeant - - - - Buchanan, A.

Roll No.	Rank and Name.		Roll No.	Rank and Name.	
22568	Sergeant	Hughes, G.	22565	Private	Knight, A.
22563	,,	Young, A.	22533	,,	Levy, M.
21509	,,	Clare, E.	22537	,,	Martin, T.
22547	Corporal	Robinson, J.	22438	,,	Manning, J.
22530	,,	Jennings, D.	22538	,,	Neal, F.
22562	L.-Corpl.	Wilcox, J.	22539	,,	Neal, H.
22506	Private	Astley, W.	22546	,,	Postill, P. C.
22511	,,	Baines, J.	22540	,,	Penlington, T. J.
22508	,,	Barlow, J. W.	22541	,,	Parr, H.
22510	,,	Barr, J.	22566	,,	Ryan, D.
22509	,,	Berry, A. F.	22555	,,	Renshaw, G. R.
22513	,,	Cochrane, S.	22552	,,	Rhodes, F.
22515	,,	Cruise, R.	22548	,,	Ralphs, G.
22366	,,	Conway, J. T.	22525	,,	Stott, T.
22512	,,	Crew, D. C.	22530	,,	Smethurst, J.
22569	,,	Devall, L.	22331	,,	See, A.
22516	,,	Dodd, L.	22549	,,	Smith, J.
22519	,,	Gavin, P.	22435	,,	Shepherd, E.
22518	,,	Griffiths, J.	22553	,,	Taylor, D.
22567	,,	Graham, J.	22551	,,	Taylor, R.
22527	,,	Hamil, E.	22560	,,	Warhurst, A.
22522	,,	Heany, A.	22556	,,	Wilson, R. L.
22523	,,	Holroyd, J. W.	22557	,,	Wilson, W.
22318	,,	Humphries, T. E.	22559	,,	Wilson, A.
22526	,,	Hemingway, S.	22558	,,	Watkinson, J.
22521	,,	Hirst, A.	22529	,,	Fitton, J. R.
22528	,,	Johnson, W.	22442	,,	Fletcher, F.
22531	,,	Kirkham, S.	22769	,,	Gifford.

The following were not present when the Platoon Photograph was taken:—

22507	Private	Backhouse.	22517	Private	Deakin, T.
22524	,,	Barton.	22534	,,	Hobson.

23rd (Service) Battalion Manchester Regiment.

"E" COMPANY.

Officer Commanding Company - Capt. C. E. R. Betteley.*
Second in Command - - - Lieut. F. St. J. W. Garner.*
Company Sergeant Major - Fisher, S.
Company Quartermaster Sergeant - Given, E. H.

PLATOON NO. XVII.

Platoon Commander - - - Lieut. A. E. Capstick.
Platoon Sergeant - - - Baker, D.

Roll No.	Rank and Name.		Roll No.	Rank and Name.	
22847	Sergeant	Woodcock.	22692	,,	Whitehead.
22743	Corporal	Baker, A. A.	22695	,,	Leeds.
22631	,,	Barron, J.	22665	,,	Smith.
22716	L.-Corpl.	Henderson, O.	22627	,,	Hall.
22664	,,	Gill, J. A.	22680	,,	Clapton.
22665	Private	Smith, A.	22663	,,	Barton.
22590	,,	Law, W.	22624	,,	Beddows.
22694	,,	Hardyman, B. J.	22729	,,	Pimlott.
22672	,,	Cain, J. J.	22858	,,	Keelan.
22682	,,	Hancock, A.	22901	,,	Davis.
22814	,,	Kay, T.	22702	,,	Axon.
22850	,,	McEneany.	22703	,,	Evans.
22662	,,	Fogg.	22849	,,	Rowlands.
22669	,,	Wood.	22678	,,	Blacklock.
22691	,,	Mathews.	22802	,,	Parker.
22656	,,	Batty.	22857	,,	Allmark.
22653	,,	Healey.	22674	,,	Ardern.
22848	,,	Shaw.	22660	,,	Fitton.
22659	,,	Keelan.	22864	,,	Devine.

* For portrait, see Officers' Group, p. 353.

23rd (Service) Battalion Manchester Regiment.

"E" COMPANY.

Officer Commanding Company	Capt. C. E. R. BETTELEY.*
Second in Command	Lieut. F. St. J. W. GARNER.*
Company Sergeant Major	FISHER, S.†
Company Quartermaster Sergeant	GIVEN, E. H.†

PLATOON NO. XVIII.

Platoon Commander	Lieut. J. S. FOULKES.
Platoon Sergeant	HOOPER, W.

Roll No.	Rank and Name.		Roll No.	Rank and Name.	
22626	Corporal	NEVILLE, J.	22753	Private	LINDSAY, W.
22666	,,	TURTON, W.	22719	,,	RYAN, T.
22681	L.-Corpl.	PRICE, J.	22720	,,	MOORES, H.
22724	Private	DAWES, A. M.	22735	,,	FOY, J.
22734	,,	BURKE, J.	22731	,,	MCLOUGHLIN, T.
22723	,,	SHEELAN, R.	22736	,,	MATHER, S.
22711	,,	KELTY, J.	22741	,,	FINN, J.
22742	,,	MULVEY, W.	22733	,,	EDMUNDSON, J. R.
22739	,,	HIBBERT, J. W.	22764	,,	PIMLOTT, J.
22771	,,	CONNOR, D.	22730	,,	SAXON, J. W.
22726	,,	ALLEN, W. H.	22744	,,	HACKNEY, H.
22770	,,	ROBINSON, W.	22728	,,	WHEELDON, J. W.
22749	,,	MULDOON, W.	22760	,,	CUMMINS, T.
22762	,,	DUNSCOMBE, H.	22718	,,	BLANTON, F.
22712	,,	VICKERS, C.	22755	,,	OSBORNE, J.
22768	,,	JONES, A. F.	22752	,,	PEERS, G.
22772	,,	ALDRIDGE, R.	22717	,,	BETHELL, A.
22652	,,	GORMAN, G. H.	22715	,,	SOUTHGATE, J.
22890	,,	LEONARD, J.	22766	,,	FRANKLAND, E.
22761	,,	BOWRING, A.	22721	,,	HEATHCOTE, A.
22765	,,	MULLIGAN, W.	22763	,,	SUNMAN, H.
22738	,,	LEE, E.	22979	,,	GORMAN.
22710	,,	TIPPETTS, W.			

* For portrait, see Officers' Group, p. 353.   † For portrait, see Sergeants' Group, p. 355.

23rd (Service) Battalion Manchester Regiment.

"E" COMPANY.

Officer Commanding Company	Capt. C. E. R. BETTELEY.*
Second in Command	Lieut. F. ST. J. W. GARNER.*
Company Sergeant Major	FISHER, S.†
Company Quartermaster Sergeant	GIVEN, E. H.†

PLATOON NO. XIX.

Platoon Commander	Lieut. F. B. ALLEN.
Platoon Sergeant	RENSHAW, J.

Roll No.	Rank and Name.		Roll No.	Rank and Name.	
22798	Corporal	LEWCOCK, R.	22794	Private	WHITBY, W.
22898	,,	KENNY, C.	22790	,,	DICKENSON, J.
22893	Private	GRIMES, J.	22788	,,	BYATT, A. L. S.
22935	,,	WILSON, R.	22777	,,	HADFIELD, J. A.
22841	,,	RUSHTON, J.	22800	,,	FOSTER, C. J.
22820	,,	CROWTHER, F.	22873	,,	CLOUGH, H.
22823	,,	COLLIER, J. B.	22818	,,	THOMAS, D.
22779	,,	RYAN, T.	22780	,,	WHITE, F.
22809	,,	HANLEY, WM.	22819	,,	PARRY, R. E.
22807	,,	WHEATER, J. H.	22053	,,	DOYLE, J.
22799	,,	MCLAY, A.	22789	,,	WATERHOUSE, S.
22808	,,	HUTTON, F.	22791	,,	DYSON, A.
22812	,,	SMITH, R.	22914	,,	QUIGLEY, W.
22883	,,	MULDOON, J.	22782	,,	WALSH, J.
22852	,,	BUCKLEY, M.	22781	,,	ROBINSON, F.
22801	,,	WILLIAMS, F. J.	22822	,,	ROSCOE, L.
22838	,,	POLE, R. G.	22641	,,	BOWERS, P.
22840	,,	EDWARDS, E.	22920	,,	WHITTINGHAM, R.
22811	,,	NALLY, J.	22829	,,	MASSEY, J.
22810	,,	JONES, T.	22832	,,	DOLAN, A.
22786	,,	FARRINGTON, N. F.	22948	,,	MCCULLOCH, P.
22813	,,	GOMERSALL, A.	22834	,,	BULL, D.
22776	,,	ASHWORTH, J.	22816	,,	SWIFT, S.
22792	,,	AGOMBAR, P.			

* For portrait, see Officers' Group, p. 353.   † For portrait, see Sergeants' Group, p. 355.

23rd (Service) Battalion Manchester Regiment.

"E" COMPANY.

Officer Commanding Company	Capt. C. E. R. Betteley.*
Second in Command	Lieut. F. St. J. W. Garner.*
Company Sergeant Major	Fisher, S.†
Company Quartermaster Sergeant	Given, E. H.†

PLATOON NO. XX.

Platoon Commander	Lieut. F. St. J. W. Garner.
Platoon Sergeant	Lewis, W.

Roll No.	Rank and Name.		Roll No.	Rank and Name.	
22822	Sergeant	Hobbs, H. V.	22901	Private	Davis, W.
22612	Corporal	Bridgehouse.	22882	,,	Butterfield, F.
22594	,,	Montgomery, H.	22922	,,	Pennington, G.
22746	L.-Corpl.	Nicholson, J.	22850	,,	Jones, N.
22849	Private	Rowlands, M.	22748	,,	Whiting, F.
22889	,,	Skeath, W. R.	22907	,,	Wolstencroft, S.
22931	,,	Lyons, B.	22918	,,	Barnes, H.
22928	,,	Pilling, J.	22868	,,	Schofield, C.
22881	,,	Hurst, E.	22859	,,	Rowlands, R.
22865	,,	Todd, J. W.	22939	,,	Travis, W.
22855	,,	Marshall, P.	22910	,,	Brownhill, H.
22117	,,	Dinsdale, H.	22879	,,	Heaton, M.
22895	,,	Marsh, W.	22591	,,	Causey, W. B.
22894	,,	Green, J.	22857	,,	Allmark, J.
22892	,,	Garner, E.	22976	,,	Adshead, H.
22877	,,	Leech, J. F.	22908	,,	Bardsley, F.
22870	,,	Tuley, E.	22880	,,	Horne, H.
22871	,,	Moss, E.	22888	,,	Cundiff, R.
22868	,,	Walker, A.	22854	,,	Childs, T.
22917	,,	Elwell, W.	22903	,,	Heeney, W.
22855	,,	Marshall, P.	22886	,,	Thornton, E.
22866	,,	Walker, W.	22858	,,	Keenan, J. H.
22949	,,	Hurst, W.	22947	,,	Higham, H.
22905	,,	Davis, W.			

* For portrait, see Officers' Group, p. 353.

† For portrait, see Sergeants' Group, p. 355.

91st Infantry Brigade Depôt Officers and Supernumerary Officers.

Colonel B. R. HAWES, C.B.
2nd Lieut. and Adj. J. F. LEWIS.

20th (Service) Battalion Depôt Company.

Captain	SAYCE, G. B.	2nd Lieut.	PERCY, G. B.
,,	HARRIS, T. A.	,,	CRAIG, J.
Lieut.	HARTLEY, R. L.	,,	WOOLLAM, G. L.
,,	DENTON-THOMPSON, B.	,,	LEVENSTEIN, G. E.
2nd Lieut.	HALDANE, C. K.	,,	OUTRAM, E.
,,	LOMAS, H.	,,	CLAYTON, J. L.
,,	KEMP, T.	,,	BLENCH, A. C.
,,	JENNISON, N. L.*	,,	THOMPSON, J.

21st (Service) Battalion Depôt Company.

Captain	MARSDEN, W. M.	2nd Lieut.	YEANDLE, G. G.
2nd Lieut.	PEASE, W. H.*	,,	CAULCOTT, J. E.*
,,	HARRIS, G. H.*	,,	DENNISON, G.
,,	CRUICKSHANK, G. G. L.	,,	COATMAN, G.
,,	MULHOLLAND, W.*	,,	PURVIS, W. B.
,,	BENTLEY, H.	,,	MILLER, J. H.*

22nd (Service) Battalion Depôt Company.

Captain	ETCHELLS, T.	2nd Lieut.	BARNARD, T. H.
,,	LLOYD, C. M.	,,	MORTON, J. L. M.*
Lieut.	COE, W. O.*	,,	STEAD, R.*
2nd Lieut.	PARR, E. H. T.	,,	WHEATLEY, T. L.
,,	COTTON, H. S.*	,,	ROYLE, H. W.
,,	WALSH, A.	,,	STREET, E. A.
,,	GRIMWOOD, H.	,,	BEARD.*
,,	FAULKNER, H. L.	,,	COWAN, W. J.*
,,	DOWLING, A. O.		

* Not present when the Photograph was taken.

RECRUITS

ROLL OF HONOUR

OF THE

Manchester Corporation

List of Employees who have joined the Colours.

City Architect's Department.

ANDREW, F. W.	GAUL, M.	PEARSON, R.
ARNOLD, E. D.	JAMES, H.	GRIMSHAW, C. E.
GAUL, E. P.	MITCHELL, W. H.	

City Art Gallery.

CORNTHWAITE, W. E. - 1/2nd East Lancs. R.F.A.
RICHARDS, W. - - - 17th S.Bt. Manchester Rgt.
HALLEY, J. C. - - - 3/8th Bt. Lanc. Fus. (T.F.)

Heaton Park Branch Gallery.

POWELL, F. - - - - Army Reservist, R.A.M.C.

Queen's Park Branch Gallery.

TAIT, F. W. - - - - 9th Bt. Royal Scots H.
BOWDEN, J. - - - - 18th S.Bt. Manchester Rgt.

Baths Department.

BEAVER, A. E.	HUMPHREYS, G.	MUSGROVE, S.
BEIRNE, P.	JACOB, A. E.	PATE, L. A.
BISHOP, A.	KAY, W.	PENDER, A.
BLAGBROUGH, W. J.	LOWTH, C.	PRINCE, C. H.
BROWN, J.	MAHER, A.	PRINCE, T.
CARTER, J.	MAHER, T.	PUGH, J.
CHARLESWORTH, S.	McKEIVER, L.	ROWORTH, L.
CORDT, J. P.	MARLAND, J.	ROYLE, H.
CORDT, T. H.	MAYCOCK, C.	SMITH, J. W.
COTTON, G.	MORRISSEY, D.	SMITH, G.
CURRELL, N.	(Died in hospital, the	STEARNE, T.
DAVIES, T. H.	result of wounds).	WILLIAMS, R. H.
DICKENSON, H.	MOWATT, S. B.	WRENSHALL, F.
FRANCIS, W.		

MANCHESTER CORPORATION
ROLL OF HONOUR.—continued.
Cleansing Department.

ALLEN, W.	BARNETT, C.	DUFFY, M.	GARNER, G.
AIDE, F.	BRADLEY, R.	DICKENSON, W.	GREGORY, F.
ATKINSON, A.	BAILEY, J. A.	DILLON, J.	GALLAGHER, J. J.
ADSHEAD, A.	BROADHURST, V.	DRINKWATER, W. J.	GILBERT, G.
ALDRED, H.	BARLOW, F.	DYER, T.	GOULDEN, A.
ATHERTON, J.	BAKER, J. H.	DIXON, J.	GRIMSHAW, W. E.
ANNISON, A.	BRUEN, J.	DOYLE, A.	GARSIDE, T.
ACTON, W.	COTTIER, J.	DAVENPORT, G. E.	GOODWIN, T.
ACTON, J.	CUMMINGS, J.	DEMPSEY, J.	GRIBBIN, J. H.
ACTON, T.	CRYNE, M.	DILLON, E.	GALLAGHER, J.
AYRTON, E.	COX, J. E.	DITCHFIELD, T.	GREGSON, A. E.
ARSTALL, J.	CHADWICK, W.	EDGE, H.	GREAVES, G.
ALEXANDER, T.	CORLETT, W.	ENGLAND, J. S.	GREAVES, S.
ALLEN, F.	CONNELL, E.	EDEN, W. H.	GREENWOOD, G.
ANDERSON, P.	CLOUGH, S.	EDWARDS, J.	GRAY, T.
ASHTON, R. W.	CATLIN, J.	ELLIOTT, H.	HINES, J. T.
AIKENHEAD, J.	CURTIS, J.	EVANS, G.	HAGAN, J.
ARCHER, J. A.	CLARKE, P.	EBOURNE, W.	HARRISON, J.
ATKINSON, J.	CRISP, T.	EVISON, M.	HILL, T.
ATKINSON, J.	CURTIN, J.	ELGER, S.	HESKETH, W.
BORN, F. C.	CRAWLEY, D.	ELLIS, S.	HORNSEY, E.
BIRD, W. F.	COSTELLO, J.	FROGGETT, A.	HALLSWORTH, E.
BLACKWOOD, W.	CARMICHAEL, W.	FLANAGAN, M.	HIGTON, A.
BOUSTEAD, R.	CARNEY, L.	FLYNN, P.	HAYES, C.
BAILEY, J. H.	CROMPTON, A.	FODEN, J.	HARDING, J. H.
BOND, J. A.	CASEY, P.	FORD, C.	HAMPSON, C.
BROPHY, T.	CALLIGAN, J.	FAIRHURST, J. W.	HILTON, G.
BUTLER, E. R.	CONNOR, D.	FOLEY, J.	HORAN, P.
BENNETT, H.	CLARKE, M.	FLANAGAN, J.	HARRIS, M. J.
BOLTON, J.	CRAWFORD, H.	FITZSIMMONS, A.	HOLLAND, W.
BREWER, P.	CARDY, T. B.	FARRELL, R.	HEMPSTOCK, N.
BLETCHER, J. T.	CONNOR, B.	FAIRHURST, F.	HENDERSON, J.
BARTLEY, G.	CARTLEDGE, E.	FLETCHER, T. M.	HULME, W. H.
BURROWS, J. W.	CLARKE, J.	FERNIE, J.	HULMES, F.
BARNES, W.	COSTELLO, P.	FRITH, A.	HULMES, J.
BRUNTON, G. F.	CAMPBELL, P.	FOX, W.	HUDSON, F.
BLACKHURST, F. W.	CLUNIE, A.	FAIRHURST, J.	HOLLAND, W. H.
BRADY, J.	COX, M.	FAHY, P.	HOYLE, W.
BOOTH, S.	CUNNINGHAM, J. E.	FRYLEY, M.	HELME, A.
BOHEN, M.	CLARKE, J. H.	FAZACKERLEY, Z.	HUNTINGTON, T.
BROWN, R.	COLEMAN, J.	FIELDEN, J. E.	HOLLAND, W.
BREWER, W.	CARTER, T.	FRITH, E.	HOLE, S.
BREWER, R.	CARPENTER, W. H.	FLINT, H.	HARDMAN, R.
BENNETT, F.	CURAN, H.	FAULKNER, A.	HOWARTH, M.
BURKE, J. T.	DAVIES, E.	FISHWICK, T. H.	HINDLEY, E.
BROWN, G.	DAVIES, W.	GOSS, T. J.	HOWLETT, J.
BAILEY, P.	DAVIES, H.	GILBERT, S.	HICKS, H.
BULLEN, G.	DAWSON, M.	GALLAGHER, J. H.	HOLCROFT, S.
BRADBURY, W. H.	DEGNAN, H.	GRIMSHAW, J. E.	HOGG, W.
BECKETT, J. A.	DOBSON, J.	GALVIN, S.	HARRIS, G.
BECK, J. H.	DOYLE, E.	GOULDEN, A.	HALL, A.
BAGGOLEY, R. E.	D'EATH, J. H.	GREENUP, J. W.	HALES, R. O.
BIGLAND, E.	DUNN, L.	GREGORY, T.	HILL, R.
BOLLINGTON, G.	DUFFY, T.	GORMLEY, T. B.	HADCOCK, J. J.

MANCHESTER CORPORATION
ROLL OF HONOUR.—continued.

Cleansing Department.

HALLIHAN, J. W.	LEAHY, W.	MIDDLETON, T.	RENSHAW, W.
HARRISON, W.	LEESON, W.	McMULLIN, A.	RICHARDSON, J.
HEATH, T. A.	LEIGH, H.	NUTTALL, W. A.	ROWLEY, J.
HOLT, E.	LEES, J. C.	NALLY, J.	ROWLINSON, W. C.
HARRISON, E.	LINEKER, G.	NELSON, G.	ROWEN, B.
HANVEY, D.	LYNCH, M.	NIXON, J.	RUTLEDGE, W.
HODGSON, A.	LEITH, G.	NASH, W.	RUTHERFORD, J.
HAMILTON, J.	LOFTUS, T.	NEVIN, J. E.	RAWLINGS, T.
HILL, J. W.	LEECH, P.	NORMAN, J. B.	SHARPLES, G.
HULME, W. H.	LONGSHAW, G.	NEWMAN, W.	SIMPSON, J.
HOYLE, J. A.	LEGGE, R.	NIXON, J.	SULLIVAN, J. W.
HEALEY, M. E.	LOWE, A.	NELSON, J.	SKARRATT, G.
HUGHES, J. N.	LONGDEN, M.	O'NEILL, J.	SMITH, H.
HOUGH, J. R.	LEWIS, E.	OLDHAM, T.	SMITH, T.
HARRISON, W.	LEACH, F.	O'DONNELL, C. E. A.	STARKEY, A.
HULME, W. H.	LOCKETT, F.	OLIVER, H.	SHAW, W.
HOGAN, J. J.	MAHER, T.	O'NEILL, E.	STONIER, J. E.
HIGHAM, T.	MAKIN, E.	O'BRIEN, T.	SHEEN, J. W.
HALL, J.	MORRIS, T.	OLDHAM, C.	SPAWTON, W.
HUTCHINSON, H.	MEALING, J.	ORMROD, H.	SMITH, D.
HAYES, T.	MOORES, W.	OWEN, G.	SEDDON, J.
IVISON, W.	METCALF, J. G.	OGDEN, J. A.	SUMMERS, D.
JEPSON, E.	McKENZIE, E.	O'GARA, J. P.	SOWERY, W.
JACKSON, P.	MOXON, J.	PARKER, W. J.	SMITH, J. J.
JONES, J. W.	MILLINGTON, J.	PILGINGTON, A. E.	SHIELDS, T.
JOHNSON, R.	MORRISEY, T.	PARKINSON, O.	SHEPHERD, A.
JOHNSON, T.	MORT, T.	PRIESTLEY, T. H.	STEWART, J.
JONES, E.	MARSH, T.	POWELL, H.	SHUTTLEWORTH, G.
JOYCE, T.	MELLOR, W. A.	PRIESTLEY, J.	SWEETMAN, J.
JONES, W.	MAHER, J.	PEACOCK, W. H.	SIMPSON, G.
JONES, R.	MURPHY, D.	PEARSON, W.	SLOANE, J.
JACKSON, J.	MANNION, J.	PICKERING, G. F.	SMALLSHAW, J T.
JARDINE, D.	MORRIS, J.	PINKNEY, C.	SEWARD, J. T.
JACKSON, W.	MADIGAN, J.	PARKINSON, W. J.	SCATTERGOOD, A. A.
JOHNSON, J. W.	MELIA, A.	POULTON, E.	SHAW, H. W.
JACKSON, A.	MOORFIELD, J. W.	PENKETHMAN, H.	SEDDON, T.
KEEGAN, D.	MOLLOY, J.	PLOVER, G.	TOOTILL, F.
KIRBOY, M.	MORRIS, A.	PLATT, H.	THORNEYCROFT, D.
KENNY, J.	McLOUGHLIN, W.	QUINN, J.	THOMAS, C.
KING, J.	MAYBURY, H.	QUINN, B. E.	THOMPSON, J.
KIDD, J. W.	MORGAN, G. H.	QUINN, J.	TOMLINSON, E.
KELLY, T. O.	MITCHELL, G. H.	RATCLIFFE, J.	THOMPSON, W. H.
KNIGHT, J. T.	MORAN, J.	RATCLIFFE, R.	TAYLOR, W.
KILLEEN, J.	McKALE, C.	ROBINSON, W. O.	TRACEY, T.
KNOWLES, J.	McGUIRE, J. P.	ROWBOTTOM, J. T.	TUSSLER, J.
KIMBER, J. C.	MASSEY, F.	ROWBOTHAM, S. H.	TURLEY, A.
KIRWIN, W.	MALONEY, T.	RICHARDSON, G.	THOMPSON, W.
KELLY, D.	McCORMICK, W.	RYAN, J.	TAYLOR, T.
KELLY, T.	MOORES, T.	ROBINSON, R. E.	TODMAN, J. J.
LANG, M.	MACBETH, A. E.	ROGERS, E.	TRAFFORD, J.
LEMONS, G.	MAHER, M.	ROGERS, W. H.	TAYLOR, A.
LEACH, J. A.	MADDEN, J.	ROGERSON, H. E.	THOMASSON, S.
LITHERLAND, J.	MANSON, H.	RIGBY, E.	TAGGART, H.
LEE, G.	McKENZIE, J.	ROURKE, J. E.	TAYLOR, A.

MANCHESTER CORPORATION
ROLL OF HONOUR.—continued.

Cleansing Department.

THOMPSON, T.
TOMKINS, W.
TOMLINSON, H.
VALENTINE, I.
VALENTINE, R.
WINTERBOTTOM, G.
WALKER, W.
WALL, J.
WATERFALL, T. J.
WHITEHEAD, J.
WILLAN, T.
WINKLE, W. A.

WILLIAMS, J. T.
WARD, J.
WALKER, S.
WILLIAMS, C. E.
WHITTAKER, I.
WISEMAN, J.
WILLIAMS, A.
WELSH, W.
WAKEFIELD, J.
WARREN, A.
WOOD, B.
WATSON, F.

WITHERS, J.
WARD, W.
WELSH, J.
WHITE, M.
WITHINGTON, F.
WARD, H.
WARD, J.
WARD, B.
WILSON, W.
WOOD, W. T.
WEBB, W.
WOOLHAM, W.

WAINWRIGHT, C.
WILSON, W. H.
WOOLRICH, E.
WOOLRICH, T. W.
WILLIAMS, W.
WILKINSON, W.
WARD, H.
WEBSTER, T. H.
WHITEHURST, J.
WRIGHT, R.
WILLIAMS, E.
WOODHOUSE, R.

Electricity Department.

ADDERLEY, W. E.
ANDERSON, J.
ANDERSON, S.
ANDERSON, W.
ARMSTRONG, W.
ARMITAGE, T.
ARCHER, F.
ARTUS, J.
BAILEY, H. S.
BAILEY, J.
BAILEY, N.
BAILEY, W. H.
BALDWIN, A.
BANKS, P.
BARBER, E.
BARNETT, J.
BARRATT, S. W.
BARRIE, L.
BARON, C. E.
BENNETT, S. A.
BELSHAW, N. E.
BELL, W.
BESWICK, H.
BETTRIDGE, E.
BEVAN, R. T.
BINNS, W.
BOTTRILL, J. T.
BOWDE, H.
BOWKER, J.
BROMLEY, J.
BRADE, J. R.
BROWN, S.
BREWER, E.
BRYANS, J.
BURGESS, O.
BROWN, I.
BRIDGFORD, H. H.
BLEMINGS, G.
BLOCKLEY, A.
BLOW, H.

BUDSWORTH, T.
  (Killed)
BUTCHER, C. A.
BUTLER, W.
CADMAN, T.
CAINE, N.
*CAVEY, H.
CAWTHORNE, A.
CHAPMAN, W.
CHEETHAM, J.
CHESTER, J. H.
CHANT, T. G.
CLARKE, A.
CLARKE, L.
CLEARY, W.
COLE, A.
COLLINS, J.
CONNOR, T.
COOKE, J. T.
COOKE, W. C.
COOPER, J.
COVERLEY, A.
CLARK, G. W.
CLARKE, J. E.
CROOK, F. G.
CROZIER, I.
CROSFIELD, H. B.
CURLEY, T.
CURRIE, J. R. W.
CUSICK, J.
DALY, T. J.
DANBY, G.
DAVIES, R.
DAVENPORT, J.
DAVIES, E.
DAWSON, J.
DICKINSON, P.
DILLON, P.
DOCKER, G. L.
DONIGAN, W.

DONOHUE, J.
DONAGHUE, F.
DONOHOE, A.
DUCKWORTH, J.
EARLAM, H.
EDWARDS, W. C.
  (Killed)
*EDWARDS, G.
EDWARDS, B.
EDWARDS, J. E.
EDWARDS, H. J.
EVANS, T.
ELKES, C. W.
ELLISON, A.
EMMETT, C. W.
ENGLISH, F.
ENTWISTLE, C.
ENTWISTLE, J.
FAGAN, J. H.
FAUX, T.
FEARNLEY, J. (Killed)
FEENEY, R.
FILDES, H.
FLEMING, F.
FOX, F.
FOX, G.
FOWLER, W. H.
FORSTER, J. B.
FRYER, A.
GARVIN, J.
GAMBLE, F. (Killed)
GATES, E.
GARSIDE, R. O.
GEE, J.
GIBSON, H.
*GILLIVER, H.
GILES, W.
GILLIVER, A.
GOUGH, P.
*GORDON, T.

GRAHAM, J.
GRUNDY, L.
GREEN, T. F.
GUNN, D.
HARPER, G.
HARDY, C.
HARRISON, R.
HALL, J.
HAMBLETON, P.
HAPGOOD, A.
HARLING, F. (Killed)
HASSALL, J. (Killed)
HARKNESS, F. (Killed)
HAWORTH, J. W.
HADFIELD, C.
HARTLEY, H.
HAYNES, T. H.
HEWITT, E. T.
HENEKE, P. D.
HEATON, W.
*HILL, J.
HINCE, T.
HINDS, J.
HIRST, H.
HOCKENHULL, H.
HOLDSHIP, G. E.
HORROCKS, A.
HOUGHTON, R. N.
HOWELL, J. (Killed)
HORNSBY, W. E.
HOWARD, P.
HUGHES, D. J.
HUGHES, J. E.
HUNT, J.
HURRELL, J. W.
HULME, H.
IRVINE, A.
IRVING, T. B.
IVISON, W.
JACKSON, H.

* Returned to civil life.

MANCHESTER CORPORATION
ROLL OF HONOUR.—continued.

Electricity Department.

- JONES, J. W.
- JONES, L. H.
- JONES, C. G.
- JORDAN, W.
- JONES, J.
- JONES, J. A.
- JONES, M.
- KEARNEY, W.
- KENNEDY, J.
- KELLY, J.
- KILROY, H.
- KNIGHT, J. A.
- KNOTT, F.
- KREUTZAHLER, G. F.
- LALLY, J.
- LAMB, J.
- LANE, F. G.
- LAWLESS, J.
- *LALLY, J.
- LANGSHAW, L. A.
- LEVER, T.
- LEES, J.
- LEARY, T. E.
- LEES, J. J.
- LIVESLEY, W.
- LOXLEY, E. (Killed)
- LUDLOW, H.
- LUNN, J.
- LYNCH, J.
- *MANNING, S.
- MASSEY, W. H.
- MACKAY, G.
- MACLENNAN, J. F.
- MACLEAN, L. C.
- MEREDITH, F.
- MILLER, A.
- MILLER, F.
- MILLS, J.
- MOFFATT, D. T.
- MOORE, R.
- MORRIS, E.
- MORRIS, J.
- MOULD, D.
- MOLINEAUX, R.
- MULLINS, E.
- MULLEADY, J.
- MURDOCK, A.
- *MURDOCK, J.
- MURPHY, J.
- McCARTHY, J.
- McCLENAHAN, R.
- McDERMOTT, C.
- McEVELLEY, H.
- McERLANE, M.
- McVEIGH, C. A.
- McLEISH, J.
- NEWTON, J. E.
- NEWTON T. (Killed)
- NIGHTINGALE, H. (Killed)
- NOBLE, S. E.
- NOLAN, J.
- NOLAN, R.
- NUGENT, C.
- OGDEN, A. E.
- OGDEN, G.
- OGDEN, P. G.
- OGDEN, T.
- O'NEILL, J.
- ONG. W. H. (Killed)
- PAINE, C.
- PARRY, J.
- PACEY, H.
- PALMER, F.
- PARROTT, C.
- PARKER, T.
- PATTON, W. P.
- PARKER, A.
- PERRIS, P. D.
- PEAK, A.
- PERCY, E.
- PENDLEBURY, H.
- PENDLEBURY, J.
- PEDUZZI, J.
- PIKE, H.
- PINDER, G. A.
- PRICE, J.
- PROBERT, H.
- QUINN, J.
- RALPHSON, R.
- RAMSBOTTOM, G. H.
- RAWLINSON, R.
- REID, J.
- *REILLY, B.
- REDFERN, T.
- REEVES, H. J.
- RILEY, T.
- ROBERTS, A. (Killed)
- ROBERTS, E.
- ROBERTS, D. A.
- ROBINSON, E.
- ROBINSON, H.
- ROBINSON, J.
- ROBERTSON, J. F.
- ROBSON, W. H.
- ROWE, V.
- ROWSON, W.
- *RYAN, J. J.
- SAMPLE, H.
- SEMAINE, J.
- SCHILLING, F.
- SCHOLES, H.
- SHEARER, A.
- SHEARER, W.
- SHENTON, J. W.
- SHARPE, C. H.
- *SLATTERY, M.
- SIMPSON, A.
- SIMPSON, Jr., A.
- SINCLAIR, J.
- SPENCER, J.
- STAFFORD, P.
- STEPHENS, J. (Killed)
- STOKES, W. G.
- STREET, W. H.
- STREETS, F.
- STUTTARD, W.
- SULLIVAN, T.
- SURRIDGE, T. (Killed)
- SUTTON, T. A.
- SWAIN, F.
- SWIFT, H.
- SYKES, A. C.
- TAYLOR, H.
- TAYLOR, J. H.
- *TAYLOR, J. A.
- TAYLOR, T. A.
- THOMPSON, F.
- *THOMPSON, M.
- THOMPSON, S. L.
- THOMSON, W.
- THORNHILL, R. (Killed)
- TIERNAN, W. J.
- TIMPERLEY, T.
- TINSLEY, A. W.
- TODD, D. W.
- TOFT, A. E.
- TOLAN, J. R.
- TOLAN, S.
- TOMKINSON, A.
- TOMMINS, W.
- TRIMBLE, W.
- TRANTER, W.
- TRIMBLE, J.
- TRELFA, J. W.
- TYREMAN, T.
- UPTON, C.
- VLIES, H. A.
- WALDRON, A.
- WALMSLEY, C.
- WALSH, J.
- WALL, J. W.
- WALKER, F. H.
- *WALKER, W. E.
- WALKER, J.
- WATSON, G. H.
- WARD, J.
- WELSH, J.
- WESTERMAN, H.
- WESTHEAD, J. B.
- WHITEHEAD, E. G.
- WHATMOUGH, J. W.
- WHARTON, F. L.
- WHITTAKER, H.
- WHITFIELD, G. W. S.
- WILLIS, W.
- WILSON, W. J.
- WILKINSON, J. N.
- WITHERS, J.
- WOOD, J.
- WOOD, W.
- WORTHINGTON, W.
- WRAY, A. E.
- WRIGHT, A.
- YATES, W.
- YOUNG, H.
- YOUNG, A. E.

Fire Brigade.

- BERWICK, G.
- BLACKWELL, G.
- BRAYSHAW, W.
- BRICE, H.
- BROWN, J. A.
- COUTTS, W. J.
- DOBBIN, J.
- DONNELLY, W.
- EGAN, L.
- GLENCY, H.
- JONES, W.
- KELLY, F.
- LEE, G. J.
- McGRATH, J.
- McLACHLAN, J.
- McNEILL, J.
- PEARSON, A. J.
- RENNIE, J. W.
- ROBINSON, W.
- SCHOFIELD, M.
- SCOTT, A.
- SIMPSON, L.
- TART, G.
- TAYLOR, A.
- WEBB, L.
- WRIGHT, J.
- YOULTON, F. T.

* Returned to civil life.

MANCHESTER CORPORATION
ROLL OF HONOUR.—continued.

Gas Department.
Clerical Staff—Town Hall.

ARRANDALE, S. R.
ATKINSON, H. C.
BALDWIN, F.
BALLARD, H.
BEAUPRE, H.
BELL, C. A.
BILLINGTON, H.
BRADBURY, A. H.
BUTTERWORTH, A.
BYRON, J. H.
CADMAN, H.
CUBBIN, R.
DAVIS, T. F.
DEWHURST, S. F.
ELLISON, C. H.
FOWLER, H. J.
FROELICH, C. A.
GATLEY, J. B.
HATTON, M.
HUNT, W. H.
JARMAN, J. T.
JOHNSON, P.
JONES, E.
LANCASHIRE, J.
MALCOLM, R.
ORMROD, S. M.
PARTINGTON, T. B.
RATCLIFFE, H. E.
REEVE, A.
RILEY, J. E.
ROBINSON, J. A.
ROBINSON, W.
SKIDMORE, S. E.
SPENCER, J. E.
SYKES, A.
STEPHENS, G. W.
TERRY, R. G.
WALKER, W.
WOOD, J. H.
WARBURTON, W. B.
WEBSTER, J.
WITHERS, A.
WOOD, F. D.

Ordinary Meter Department.

ANDREW, R. T.
BROWN, F. W.
BROWN, J.
BURGON, T.
BURKE, R. J.
CORBETT, W.
COWAN, J. A.
DUDLEY, W. H.
DUNSTON, F. J.
HEATHCOTE, W. E.
JOHNSTON, F. E.
JONES, T.
JONES, A.
LEES, F.
LLOYD, A.
MACBETH, L. A.
MASSEY, J.
MATHER, A.
MITCHELL, A.
MOLLOY, J.
RICHARDSON, A.
ROBERTS, W. P.
SANDFORD, G.
SAUNDERS, W. E.
SMITH, J. W.
SMITH, J. W.
SHAW, A. H.
WATERS, A. S.
WALLACE, T.
WEST, F. W.
WORTHINGTON, J.

Automatic Meter Department.

BARROW, J.
CARTER, S.
CRITCHLOW, A.
CUMMINGS, A.
DALE, C.
DICKENSON, E.
DUTSON, F. E.
FOX, R.
GARDNER, J. K.
HARRISON, T. H.
HARRISON, W. T.
HARROP, J. G.
HODGES, J. W.
HOOLEY, F.
HOULDSWORTH, T.
HUMPHREYS, R.
JEPSON, J. H.
KIRKLAND, S. A.
LEACH, H. A.
LECKENBY, E.
LOWE, V. J.
MILLER, G.
ORMEROD, S. J.
PEARSON, J. R.
PLANT, H.
RAWLINSON, W. R.
ROWLINSON, W. H.
STUBBS, F.

Meter Department (Stores).

BAKE, E. E.
BEARDMORE, P.
CALVERT, L.
DARKINSON, W. D.
DEANE, W.
DEVLIN, T.
FLETCHER, R.
JONES, C.
PAUL, R. W.
POWELL, R.
SMITH, W.
WATMOUGH, W.

Stoves Department.

AMOS, J.
ARNOTT, J.
ASHTON, J. T.
ATKINSON, A.
BAGULEY, J.
BAILEY, J.
BAMBER, R.
BEAL, S. J.
BELSHAW, W.
BENNETT, J.
BERESFORD, C.
BIRCH, G.
BOLLAND, H.
BOTTOMLEY, F.
BOTTOMLEY, J.
BRADBURY, J.
BRENNAN, T.
BROOKS, W.
BROWN, F.
CALLIGAN, W.
COLEMAN, A.
CONNOR, J.
COOPER, J. H.
COSTA, W.
CRANK, J.
CROFT, T.
CROFT, J.
DEAN, H.
DENSON, A.
DICKSON, R.
EDWARDS, E.
EDWARDS, T.
FIELDEN, T.
FOGG, E.
FOLEY, J.
GIBBON, W. E.
GIBBON, P.
GIBSON, G. R.
GILSON, A.
GRIFFITHS, E.
HALL, J. A.
HARRISON, F.
HART, O.
HATTON, S.
HENSHALL, J.
HILL, T. E.
HOLMES, J. W.
HOOLEY, C.
HOPKINS, O.
IDLE, T. H.
JACKSON, G.
JOHNSON, B.
JOHNSON, C. E.
JOHNSON, C. H.
KELLY, J. J.
KIRKLAND, H.
LAMB, H.
MARTIN, J.
MARTIN, J.
McCORMACK, H.
MELLON, J.
MILLAR, A.
MISKELLY, S.
MOORES, J.
NIGHTINGALE, R.
PARKINSON, A.
RADFORD, N.
RAVENSCROFT, F.
ROBINSON, B.
SCOTT, J.
SLATER, F.
SMITH, J.
SPENCER, R.
STANSFIELD, W.
TAWS, A.
TAYLOR, G.
TERRY, C.
TURNER, A.
WALMSLEY, J.
WEBSTER, J.
WHITWAM, B.
WILKINSON, G.
WILLIAMS, T.
WOOD, E.
WOODALL, F.

MANCHESTER CORPORATION
ROLL OF HONOUR.—continued.

Gas Department.

Private Lighting Department.

GULLAND, W. D.
BETTS, W. B.
DONNELLY, H. H.
HATTON, H.
HOWARD, W.
MACPHERSON, J. A.
ROWLINSON, J. H.

Gaythorn Station.

ALLATT, H.
BARTLETT, E. L. R.
BATTY, H.
BOULTON, T.
BROTHERTON, J.
CATCHASIDES, J.
COTGRAVE, G. H.
CULLENAN, A.
DEVINE, J.
DOHERTY, T.
DONLAN, P.
DUFFY, M.
DYER, T.
FELIX, J.
GARNER, J.
GRANTHAM, J.
HAMILTON, R. J.
HARE, T.
HASTINGS, T.
HEAP, T.
HOLLINS, W.
HYNES, D.
JONES, S.
KING, T.
KNIGHT, B.
LAWLESS, P.
MAHER, J.
MARTIN, J.
McDONOUGH, J.
McGOWAN, J.
MEADOWS, T.
MORRISSEY, E.
MURRAY, J. J.
NEAL, M.
NEY, J.
NUNNS, R.
PICKER, C. H.
PLATT, G. L.
RILEY, W.
ROWE, R. H.
SEARSON, E.
SHANDLEY, M.
THORNBURY, R. J.
WHELAN, J.
WILKINSON, J.
WILLIAMS, W.
WILSON, G.
WILSON, W.
WINSTON, A.

Rochdale Road Station.

ANNESLEY, J.
BROOKES, T.
BURY, H.
CASSIDY, J.
CASSIDY, M.
COWLEY, J.
DAVIES, J.
DONOHUE, T.
DOYLE, G.
DUFFY, S.
FERGUSON, J.
GALLOWAY, J. R.
GARRITY, T.
HEAFIELD, W.
HEWITT, C.
HUGHES, E.
JOHNSTON, F.
KEATES, G.
KING, A.
LEIGH, H.
McGRATH, J.
McMAHON, T.
MEEHAM, T.
MITCHELL, J.
MORAN, P.
MULREADY, J.
OLLERENSHAW, J.
PAINE, H.
PAUL, J.
POVER, F.
POWNALL, R.
TURNER, W.
WALKER, J.
WARHURST, W.
WILSON, C.
WRIGHT, J.

Bradford Road Station.

ALMOND, A.
ASHTON, W. E.
ASPINALL, W.
ASPINALL, W., Junr.
BARTON, C. H.
BECKETT, J., Junr.
BEDDOWS, J.
BELL, R.
BOWMAN, W.
BOWMAN, J. W.
BRADLEY, W. H.
BRADLEY, T.
BRADSHAW, C.
BROADY, J.
BROOKES, J.
BROOM, W.
BROUGH, R.
BROUGH, T.
BROUGH, J.
BURGESS, J.
BURGESS, J.
BURNS, J.
CADMAN, H.
CAINE, J.
CALDECOTT, F. W.
CAPPER, J.
CARROLL, W.
CHADWICK, E.
CHALLONER, P.
CODE, J. H.
CLOUGH, J.
COSTELLO, T.
CRONSHAW, J.
CROWE, E.
CROWE, W.
DAVIES, E. A.
DEVANEY, J.
DOYLE, M.
DUFFY, E.
DUFFY, L.
DUNN, W. E.
DUTTON, T.
ENTWISTLE, W. T.
EZARD, H.
FAY, T.
FENTON, J.
FITZGERALD, J.
FORD, J.
FORSYTH, J.
FRIER, F.
GIBBONS, P.
GLYNN, M.
GOLDBURG, F.
HART, M.
HATFIELD, C. F.
HILLS, D.
HOOPER, W.
HOPWOOD, J.
HOWLEY, P.
HULME, J.
HULME, S.
JOHNSON, J.
JONES, J.
KEANE, J.
KELLY, T.
KENNY, T.
LEATHER, J.
LENIHAN, E.
LITTLEWOOD, H.
LITTLEWOOD, H., Jnr
LOMAS, S. J.
LORD, S. G.
LOGAN, T.
LYNCH, C.
MAGUIRE, W.
McGREGOR, J.
McHUGH, J. W.
McKERNON, C.
McLOUGHLIN, J.
MERRILL, H.
MOFFITT, W.
MORAN, T.
MORGAN, M.
MORTON, C.
MURPHY, J.
MURRAY, C.
OLDLAND, G.
OWEN, A. E.
OWEN, E.
OWEN, R.
OWENS, J.
OWENS, J. E.
PARKER, A.
PEACH, A.
PETERS, H.
PINNER, J.
REEVES, J., Junr.
REGAN, M.
ROBERTS, E.
ROUGHSEDGE, J.
SAXON, J.
SCHOLES, A.
SCOTT, J.
SEDDON, R., Junr.

MANCHESTER CORPORATION
ROLL OF HONOUR.—continued.

Gas Department.

SHAW, E.
SHAWCROSS, W. A.
SHENTON, W.
SHEPHARD, E. E.
SLACK, H.
SOUTHALL, H. H.
SPENCER, T.
SPRUCE, D.
STANHOPE, J. H.
STAPLETON, J.
STAPLETON, T.
STOTT, C.
STRINGER, K.
TAYLOR, J. T.
THICKETT, S.
THOMASSON, H.
THORNHILL, W., Junr.
TULLY, J.
WALSH, J. T.
WALTON, J.
WARD, A.
WARDLE, P.
WATSON, S.
WHELAN, P.
WILLIAMS, J.
WILLIAMSON, F.
WITHINGTON, J. J.
WOOD, J.

Droylsden Station.

BANKS, A.
STANFIELD, J. W.

Street Mains and Lighting Department.

Mains.

BARBER, W.
BARNETT, W.
BIRTLES, W.
BLACK, G.
BLYTH, W.
BORTOFT, J.
BOSWELL, J.
BURNS, J.
BURNS, J.
CARPENTER, C. A.
CREEGAN, J.
CROWTHER, A.
COOTE, H. P.
DANIELS, H.
FITCHETT, A.
GRIFFIN, W.
GRIFFITHS, D.
HARTLEY, A.
HEMMINGWAY, J.
HOLT, W.
HOWE, T.
HUNT, J. E.
JONES, E.
JONES, R. W.
JOHNSON, T.
KELLY, T.
KERFOOT, T.
KITCHEN, T.
LEGGITT, A.
LYNCH, J.
MIDDLE, H.
MIDDLETON, W. T.
MILLETT, A.
MORAN, P.
MORRIS, H. T.
MULDOON, T. J.
OLIVER, J.
POWER, L.
RILEY, J., Senr.
RILEY, J., Junr.
ROBERTS, W.
ROBERTS, W. S.
SMITH, J.
SMITHIES, J.
STALEY, T. H.
STEELES, A. W.
STEELES, H.
SULLIVAN, M.
VARLEY, A.
WALTON, H.
WHITTAKER, T.
WILDE, P.
WINNINGTON, C.
WOOD, J.
WREN, W.

Lighting.

ALLCOCK, T.
ARROWSMITH, T.
ARROWSMITH, J. W.
ATKINSON, T.
BARLOW, H.
BEAHAM, W.
BENSON, J.
BIBBY, B.
BIBBY, J.
BOSTOCK, W.
BRIDDON, A.
BROOKES, T. A.
BROWN, JAS.
BROWN, JNO.
BURNS, J.
BURNSIDE, A.
BURROWS, T.
BUSTARD, W. E.
BUXTON, A.
CARLTON, J.
CARROLL, G.
CARTWRIGHT, F.
CHALLIS, G.
CHORLTON, J. W.
CLAYTON, E.
CLEGG, F.
COFFEY, R.
CONNOR, J.
CREACAL, J. H.
CURETON, C. F.
DAWSON, A.
DILLON, J.
DOWNING, T.
ELLIS, J.
FLEMING, C.
FODEN, C.
FOLEY, J.
FORD, J.
FOY, T.
FRANCIS, W. S.
FREEMAN, W.
FROST, W.
FURY, J.
GATLEY, J.
GIBBONS, J.
GILMAN, J.
GOODIER, J.
HAGUE, P.
HALL, W.
HALL, R.
HANLEY, J.
HANNAH, A.
HARRIS, A.
HARVEY, J. A.
HAMNETT, A.
HEAP, S.
HIGHAM, R.
HINDLE, W.
HITCHEN, T.
HOARE, J.
HUGHES, J.
HUGHES, R.
JAMIESON, J.
JERVIS, J.
JONES, C.
JONES, F. N.
KENNEDY, J.
KENNY, H.
KING, A.
LEIGH, W.
LOWE, A.
LUCAS, J.
McCARTON, F.
McFARLAND, S.
McGHEE, W.
McHUGO, P.
McMAHON, J.
McSPIRIT, G. P.
MELLING, W.
MELLING, J. W.
MITCHELL, F.
MOOR, H.
MOLLOY, J.
MORLEY, R.
MORRIS, J.
NEARY, J.
O'BRIEN, J.
ORRELL, P.
PALMER, W.
PAUL, J.
POTTAGE, C.
PORTER, B.
PRITCHARD, H.
PRITCHARD, E. W.
REED, G. W.
REID, W. E.
RICHARDSON, P.
RIX, J. W.
ROBERTS, J.
ROBINSON, H.
ROBINSON, H.
ROWE, J.
RYDER, W.
SIDDORN, W. A.
SMALLWOOD, J.
SMITH, R.
SPARLING, W.
STEELE, E.
STOTT, S.
STRINGER, A.
STRINGER, F. A.
TAYLOR, A. C.
TAYLOR, E. J.
THORBURN, E.
WADE, A. E.
WALTON, H.
WARD, F.
WARD, E.
WASHINGTON, T.
WHITELEGG, J.
WILDE, H.
WILLCOX, J.
WILLIAMS, R. H.
WILLIAMS, W.
WOLFENDEN, E.
WRENCH, G. E.

MANCHESTER CORPORATION

ROLL OF HONOUR.—continued.

Public Libraries.

Captain WILLIAM KELLY	7th Battalion Lancashire Fusiliers.
Captain Cyril E. SAUNDERS	7th Battalion Lancashire Fusiliers.
2nd Lieut. GEORGE W. P. SUTTON	8th Battalion Lancashire Fusiliers.
Colour Sergt. RICHARD G. DOWN	13th Battalion Lancashire Fusiliers.
Corporal THOMAS BOTT	3rd Manchester Regiment
Corporal ERNEST P. CLARKE	Royal Army Medical Corps.
Lance-Corporal JOHN DEARDEN	3rd Battalion Manchester Regiment.
Lance-Corporal JOHN GREEN	Highland Light Infantry. (Discharged through wounds).
Bombardier THOMAS M. FROST	15th Lancs. Batt. R.F.A., 2nd E. Lanc. Br.
Private THOMAS APPLEYARD	6th Battalion Manchester Regiment.
Private GEOFFREY R. AXON	Royal Army Medical Corps.
Private CHARLES H. BENNETT	6th Battalion Manchester Regiment (Discharged as medically unfit).
Private CHARLES A. BICKERTON	Royal Army Medical Corps.
Private WILLIAM BLEASE	27th Serv. Battalion Manchester Regiment.
Private ALBERT BROWN	2nd South Lancashire Regiment (Discharged as medically unfit).
Private JOHN A. CARTLEDGE	19th Serv. Battalion Manchester Regiment.
Private JAMES CROWTHER	6th Battalion Manchester Regiment.
Private JOSEPH FINN	16th Royal Welsh Fusiliers.
Private JAMES FLETCHER	6th Battalion Manchester Regiment.
Private HENRY B. HAMNETT	Royal Army Medical Corps.
Private HENRY HARRISON	Medical Unit, Royal Naval Division.
Private HARRY HILTON	7th Battalion Lancashire Fusiliers.
Private JOSEPH HOMPES	2nd Field Ambulance, R.A.M.C.
Private ARCHIBALD F. HUTT	Royal Field Artillery.
Private ALAN F. JONES	Royal Army Medical Corps.
Private EDMUND OGDEN	Royal Army Medical Corps.
Private JOHN F. RUSSELL	29th Battalion Royal Fusiliers.

Markets Department.

ATKINSON, F.	COYLE, J.	KILSHAW, H.	SANDHAM, T.
AVERY, S.	CROSFIELD, G. H.	LYDIAT, H.	STORER, W. H.
ANDREW, P. E.	CLEGG, A.	MOLLOY, J.	TONGE, S.
ALDCROFT, A.	DELANEY, R. J.	MILES, G. E.	WADE, T. W.
BEETON, H. W.	GLOVER, J. S.	PERCIVAL, J. J.	WILSON, W. F.
BOWDEN, F. (Killed)	JOHNSTONE, W. K.	REID, R.	WILKINSON, R.
CRAKE, J.	JONES, J.	SPRUELL, J.	WATTERSON, E. S.

Medical Officer of Health's Department.

BRIERCLIFFE, Dr. R. (Capt. R.A.M.C.).	CHALMERS, T.	HART, W.	PRICE, A.
BRITTLEBANK, J. W. (Capt. R.A.M.V.C).	COX, JOSEPH.	LORD, J. E.	YOUNG, Dr. W. A. (Lieut. R.A.M.C.).
	DRINKWATER, H.	MOORE, A.	
	EGERTON, DAVID.		

Tuberculosis Office.

DYER, W.	MOSS, A.
GILL, N. V.	THOMPSON, E.
GRIFFITHS, J. L.	REYNOLDS, M. F.
HOLLINGWORTH, W. F.	TINDALL, ALAN.

Baguley Sanatorium.

GARNER, T.

Abergele Sanatorium.

JONES, R.	CRAIG, Dr. C. McK. (Lieut. R.A.M.C.).

Monsall Hospital.

ARCHIBALD, P.	ISLES, W. B.
BARDSLEY, J.	MOSS, H. E.
BOLAN, W.	SMITH, E. F.
ELSE, J.	

MANCHESTER CORPORATION
ROLL OF HONOUR.—continued.
Parks and Cemeteries Department.

BAMFORD, S.
BANNISTER, G.
BARTON, T.
BIRCHALL, G.
BITHELL, J.
BLACKHURST, J.
BLACKSHAW, F.
BRADSHAW, H.
BROWNHILL, H.
BUCKLE, W.
CARTER, H.
COOKSON, H. W.
COWERDINE, J. O.
COXEY, G. N.
DAVENPORT, T.

DAVENPORT, T.
EVESON, J.
FENTON, J.
FIELD, T. H.
FOX, A. H.
GREAVES, J. H.
GREEN, W.
HADFIELD, J.
HARRIS, A. W.
HARRIS, G.
HARTLEY, J. W.
HOAR, A. D.
HODGES, H.
HUGHES, R.
KENYON, R.

LUCAS, J.
LLOYD, F.
MATHEWS, F. J.
MORGAN, R. T.
MORGAN, W.
NICHOLLS, D. D.
NIELD, J.
OLDHAM, W., Junr.
PRICE, H. (Killed).
RAMSEY, A.
RILEY, A.
ROBERTS, A.
ROYLE, L.
ROYLE, O.
ROYLE, S.

SANDERS, A. W.
SHARP, J. E.
STONIER, J.
TAYLOR, R.
TUNSTALL, T. J.
WALKER, R., Junr.
WARBURTON, J.
WEBB, F. A.
WILKINSON, E.
WILSON, H.
WITHNELL, T.
WALTON, J.
WOOD, T.
WOODRUFF, L.
YEOMANS, J. W.

Paving, Sewering and Highways Department.

ACKROYD, T.
AIREY, R.
ALLSOP, J. J.
ACKROYD, A.
ALLEN, H.
ALLEN, J.
ALLEN, J. E.
ALLSOP, G. F.
ALMOND, G.
ALMOND, W.
ARMSTON, F.
ARMSTRONG, W.
ARTHINGTON, H.
ATKINS, W.
BELL, W.
BERRY, H.
BERRY, J. A. (Dead).
BIRTLES, W. J.
BOOTH, D.
BROWN, J.
BURNS, J.
BARRATT, A. E. T. (Dead).
BOOT, J.
BOWERS, G. E. (Dead).
BRADLEY, R.
BROWN, W. B.
BERRY, F.
BAGLEY, J.
BAILEY, A. (Dead).
BAILEY, H.
BAKER, H.
BANCROFT, W.
BARBER, J.
BARLOW, G.
BAXENDALE, R.
BENNION, J.

BENSON, W.
BESWICK, A.
BIELBY, T.
BIRCH, L.
BLACK, E. C.
BOHANNON, L.
BONHAM, J.
BOYLE, T. O.
BRIERLEY, W.
BRIGGS, J.
BROADHURST, J. W.
BURGESS, F.
BURKE, T. (Dead).
BUTTERWORTH, T.
BUTTS, J.
BYRNE, T. H.
BLACKBURN, J.
BUTLER, J. H.
BROWN, P.
BAILEY, W.
BARLOW, J.
BEESLEY, W.
BRIERLEY, J.
CAUDWELL, G. F.
CHADWICK, J. L.
CHAPPELL, J. J.
COLLIER, A.
CRANE, R.
COPPOCK, W.
CAREY, J. J.
CONNOR, T.
COWGILL, T.
CROSS, W.
COX, T. D.
CAINE, J.
CARTER, H. L.
CARTER, J.

CARTER, J.
CARTWRIGHT, J. T.
CASSIDY, R. J. (Dead).
CHESWORTH, A.
CHESWORTH, T. H.
CHRISTIE, D.
CLARENCE, C. B.
CLARKE, A.
CLARKE, F.
CLAYTON, T.
CLAYTON, W.
CLEGG, J.
COBB, A.
COALING, W. G.
COMERFORD, T.
CONDUIT, G.
CONDY, H.
CONNOR, J. J.
CONNOR, M.
COOK, J.
COOK, T.
COOPER, J. J.
CORNTHWAITE, A.
CORRIE, F.
CORRIE, R. W. (Dead).
COX, G.
CRICK, C. A.
CROSBY, J. H.
CROSSLEY, S.
CORRIE, J. D.
CLARKE, E.
DAY, A. (Dead).
DUNNE, M.
DAVIES, T.
DIXON, A. G.
DALBY, J. S.
DALTON, J. H.

DAVIDSON, T. G.
DAVIES, C. H.
DAVIES, H.
DAVIES, J. E.
DAVIES, J.
DAW, J.
DAWSON, A.
DENTON, R.
DEWSNUP, N.
DILLON, J.
DOHERTY, J.
DOHERTY, M. E.
DOVER, R.
DOWNES, S.
DUDLEY, D.
DUNNE, J.
EDWARDS, E.
EASTWOOD, H.
EATON, H.
EATON, S. A.
EDWARDS, A.
EDWARDS, J.
EVANS, A.
EYES, J. C.
EDWARDS, G. R.
EGERTON, W.
EVANS, H. A.
FINCH, T. W.
FINLEY, H. W.
FLYNN, W.
FLAHERTY, E.
FORDHAM, A. J.
FORREST, W.
FROST, R.
FARRELL, J. E.
FERNLEY, G.
FIELDER, T. H.

MANCHESTER CORPORATION
ROLL OF HONOUR.—continued.

Paving, &c., Department.

- FLETCHER, J.
- FLETCHER, W.
- FORD, G. E.
- FORSTER, C.
- FORSTER, J.
- FOY, M.
- FISHER, W.
- GALLOWAY, J.
- GREGORY, E.
- GILFOYLE, A.
- GILL, R. E.
- GUEST, W.
- GALLOWAY, J.
- GARNER, F. St. J.
- GEE, J.
- GERRARD, S.
- GIBBONS, P.
- GIBSON, W. J.
- GILBERT, A.
- GLEESON, D.
- GLYNN, J.
- GOMERSALL, A.
- GRAHAM, W.
- GRAVEL, B.
- BRAVEL, R.
- GRAY, W.
- GREENHOUGH, P.
- GRIFFITHS, A.
- GRIFFITHS, H. A.
- GRIFFITHS, H. L.
- GRIMES, E.
- GRIMSHAW, J. H.
- GRIMSHAW, R. E.
- GOODWIN, T.
- GOODBEHERE, A.
- GRANT, C.
- HALLAS, J.
- HINCHLIFFE, W. (Dead).
- HUDSON, A. (Dead).
- HURST, H.
- HURST, J.
- HUSHION, M.
- HYDE, W. A.
- HALL, W.
- HARGREAVES, T.
- HOLT, E. T.
- HOPWOOD, G.
- HOWARTH, A.
- HORROCKS, J.
- HAIGH, R.
- HALL, G. E.
- HALL, P.
- HAMMOND, J.
- HANLON, G.
- HANSON, J.
- HARDY, J.
- HARVEY, J.
- HASLAM, J. W.
- HASLAM, S.
- HEATHCOTE, T. S.
- HEWITT, F.
- HEYWOOD, H.
- HIGGINSON, S.
- HILL, A.
- HILL, W.
- HINCHLIFFE, G. A.
- HOLDEN, J. F.
- HOLME, R. R.
- HOLMES, W.
- HOLT, C.
- HOLT, G.
- HOLT, J.
- HOOLIHAN, J. R.
- HUDSON, L.
- HULSE, H.
- HULSTON, A.
- HULSTON, J.
- HURLEY, A.
- HYDE, A.
- HAYERS, G. T.
- HALLIWELL, T.
- HALL, L.
- HARDIMAN, E.
- JACKSON, T.
- JONES, F. J.
- JACKSON, A.
- JACKSON, E.
- JACKSON, S.
- JENKINS, A.
- JEPSON, V.
- JOHNSON, C.
- JOHNSON, H.
- JOHNSON, T.
- JONES, A. S.
- JONES, D. C.
- JONES, E.
- JONES, E.
- JONES, W.
- JONES, W.
- JOYNT, E.
- JOYNT, H.
- JONES, J.
- JACKSON, W. T. N.
- JONES, R. W.
- KINSEY, C. A.
- KNOWLES, R.
- KEATING, J. W.
- KEELEY, J.
- KELSALL, T.
- KELTY, J.
- KERSHAW, T. M.
- KEVILL, W. J.
- KNIBBS, C.
- KNIGHT, W. J.
- LONGDIN, J.
- LEAH, G.
- LANE, W. H.
- LANGFORD, G.
- LANGFORD, J. A.
- LEAF, W.
- LEES, A.
- LEES, C. E.
- LEE, J. H.
- LENIHAN, M.
- LEWIS, G. A.
- LITTLER, J.
- LLOYD, G. A.
- LONGDIN, J.
- LOW, G. A.
- LYONS, A.
- LAMB, T.
- LAWLESS, G.
- LAWLESS, J.
- MYLCHREEST, W.
- MANNION, T.
- MANSFIELD, A.
- MOORE, J. A.
- MALONEY, E.
- MACHIN, C.
- MARSDEN, G. R.
- MASON, F. A.
- MELLOR, T.
- MOORE, G. E.
- MOORE, G. H.
- MORRIS, J.
- MORRISON, J.
- MORROW, J. J.
- MULLIN, M.
- MURPHY, H. W. S.
- MURPHY, L.
- McCARTHY, F. K.
- McCORMICK, J.
- McCULLOUGH, G. H. (Dead).
- McGUCKIN, C.
- McGUIGAN, P. J.
- McHUGH, P.
- McHALE, E.
- MORRIS, T.
- NEEDHAM, A.
- NAUGHTON, J.
- NEAL, H.
- NEIL, J.
- NORTH, H.
- O'CONNOR, J. T. (Won the D.C.M.).
- OAKES, S. T.
- O'BRIEN, J. W.
- O'CONNOR, T.
- OGDEN, J. J.
- O'NEILL, F.
- OWEN, D. J.
- PARRY, J.
- PHILLIPS, R.
- PALMER, F. L.
- PARKER, J.
- PARKER, R.
- PARKER, W. H.
- PARKES, S.
- PARRY, G.
- PATTERSON, J. S.
- PAYNE, A. P.
- PIMBLETT, T.
- PLATT, L. P.
- PRUNTY, P.
- PRATT, G.
- PRINCE, J.
- QUINN, J.
- RANFIELD, G.
- REDFERN, A.
- ROTHWELL, J. H.
- RAVENSCROFT, R.
- REYNOLDS, W.
- RILEY, A.
- ROBERTS, G.
- ROBINSON, H.
- ROYLE, R.
- ROSS, J. J.
- ROBERTS, R.
- ROGERS, S.
- SCOTT, A.
- SHARP, G.
- SINGLETON, T.
- SMITH, E. (Dead).
- STOREY, R.
- SHEEN, J.
- SMITH, S.
- SALISBURY, S. H.
- SAVAGE, H.
- SCAIFE, S.
- SCHOFIELD, C. H.
- SHAFTO, J.
- SHERRATT, W.
- SMEDLEY, J. W.
- SMITH, A.

MANCHESTER CORPORATION
ROLL OF HONOUR.—continued.

Paving, &c., Department.

SMITH, A. B.
SMITH, C.
SMITH, F.
SMITH, J. E.
SMITH, W.
SMITH, W. H.
SPRECKLEY, C. H.
STANWAY, J.
STANWORTH, J. R.
STATTER, H. E.
STONE, A. J.
SULLIVAN, J.
SUTCLIFFE, S.
STONALL, G. H.
SELLERS, J. W.
SNOWBALL, H. J.
TAYLOR, J.
THOMPSON, T.
TAYLOR, J. C.
TAYLOR, J. F.
TATTERSALL, A.
TAYLOR, A.
TAYLOR, E.
TAYLOR, W.
THEWLIS, D.
THORNTON, R. J.
TOWNSEND, T. A. (D'd)
TOWNSEND, W. H.
TRACEY, W.
TURNER, A.
TILSTON, S.
UTTLEY, J. A.
VERNON, W.
WAITE, J.
WALSH, W.
WRIGHT, J. H.
WILKINS, H. J.
WALKER, W.
WHITE, S.
WAITE, A.
WAITE, A.
WAITE, T.
WALKER, E.
WALKLETT, E. T.
WALMSLEY, E. W.
WALTON, R.
WARD, J.
WATERHOUSE, A. G.
WATKINS, J. T.
WATKINS, T. H.
WATMOUGH, A.
WATMOUGH, J. H.
WELCH, J.
WESTWOOD, J.
WHALLEY, L.
WHITE, T.
WHITTAKER, C. W.
WILLIAMS, A. E.
WILLOTT, J.
WILSON, G.
WILSON, N.
WINSON, J. W.
WINSTANLEY, J.
WOOD, G.
WOODBINE, J.
WORRALL, A.
WRIGHT, W. H.
WARD, A.

City Police.

ADAIR, ROBERT.
ALLCOCK, THOMAS.
ALLIBONE, JOHN W.
APPLEBY, SAMUEL.
APPLEYARD, JAMES.
ASHER, GEO. W.
ASHWORTH, ROBT. H.
ASTON, WILLIAM.
ASTBURY, WM. A.
ASTLEY, HERBERT.
BARBER, ROBERT.
BAXTER, W. H. J.
BARLOW, HERBERT.
BARKER, THOMAS.
BARSTOW, JOHN W.
BARDSLEY, THOS.
BARKER, ARTHUR.
BAGNALL, R.
BANNER, JESSE.
BAILEY, RICHARD.
BARRY, DENIS.
BEDDOWS, GEORGE.
BEECH, WM.
BELL, THOMAS.
BEDFORD, FRANK.
BENNETT, ALLEN.
BENNETT, ERNEST.
BENNETT, L.
BEES, FRANCIS G.
BERRY, WILSON.
BEAGLEY, JOHN.
BEARDSLEY, A.
BILLINGTON, H.
BIRDS, GEORGE.
BLACKMORE, F.
BLUFF, ISAAC.
BOSWELL, GEORGE.
BOSTON, JOHN.
BOULTON, JAMES R.
BOONE, ROBERT.
BOOTE, JOHN.
BOLTON, JOHN.
BOWEN, THOMAS P.
BRIDSON, ALFRED.
BRAHNEY, JAMES.
BRAILSFORD, JOHN.
BRAZNELL, JAMES.
BROWN, FRANK.
BROWN, ROBERT.
BROSTER, ALBERT.
BROOME, REGINALD.
BRIERLEY, JOHN.
BROMFIELD, S.
BROOKES, JOHN.
BRIERLEY, HENRY.
BRIERLEY, THOS. W.
BROOKS, JOHN CHAS.
BUCKLEY, RALPH.
BULLOCK, ALBERT.
BUNCE, THOMAS.
BURGESS, PETER.
BUTLER, HERBERT.
BYRNE, JOHN.
BYRNE, MICHAEL.
BYRNE, PATRICK.
BYRNE, WM.
BYWATER, GEORGE.
CAMPBELL, D. B. M.
CAPSTICK, HENRY.
CALOW, GEORGE F.
CARNES, W. B.
CADMAN, JESSE.
CARTER, JOHN S.
CAPPER, ARTHUR.
CAYGILL, GEORGE.
CAINE, THOS. HY.
CHIDLEY, A. (Died).
CHAPMAN, JAMES.
CHARD, HENRY.
CHEETHAM, W.
CHIDLEY, HAROLD.
CLARK, GEORGE.
CLARKE, JAMES.
CLARKE, THOMAS.
CLITHEROE, HENRY.
CLEMENTS, GEO. W.
COOPER, HERBERT.
COOPER, ERNEST.
CONDLIFFE, E.
CORCORAN, HERBT.
COX, MICHAEL.
COPLEY, WM. H.
CONROY, CYRIL H. D.
CODY, JOSEPH.
COOK, HERBERT.
COATES, WALTER E.
COVERDALE, T. H.
COWIN, JAMES.
COOKE, JAMES A.
COBHAM, GEORGE.
COTTAM, HARRY.
COOKSON, JOSEPH.
COOPER, JOHN.
CRANE, JOHN.
CRAVEN, WM.
CRABTREE, FRANK.
CRAGG, HAROLD.
CREWE, JOHN.
CREED, MICHAEL.
CROWE, STANLEY.
CRICHTON, N. D.
CROWTHER, EDW.
CROMPTON, ELLIS.
CROSSLEY, GEORGE.
CUTTS, JOHN.
DALE, MATTHEW.
DAVIES, FRANK.
DAVENPORT, F.
DAVIDSON, ALEXR.
DAVIES, RICHARD.
DAWSON, JOHN W.
DEAN JOHN (Killed).
DERBYSHIRE, R.
DICKENS, THOMAS.
DICKINSON, R. C.
DICKINSON, T. F. S.
DOWDING, F. J.
DOYLE, HENRY.
DOXEY, THOS. T.
DODDS, HENRY.
DONEVAN, ROBERT.
DONNELLY, H.
DORRICOTT, S.
DOWNS, R.
DRAYCOTT, THOS. H.
DUTTON, WM.
EARNSHAW, JOE.
EDWARDS, ERNEST.
EDWARDS, WALTER.
ELLWOOD, ROBERT.

MANCHESTER CORPORATION
ROLL OF HONOUR.—continued.

City Police.

ELLERSHAW, ROBT.
ELLERSHAW, T. W.
ELLISON, A.
ENTWISTLE, GEO. N.
EVANS, CHARLES.
EVANS, SAML. L.
FAWCETT, M. O.
FEARY, JOSEPH C.
FERRIDAY, ENOCH.
FINCH, RICHARD E.
FINCH, WM.
FINNEY, HERBERT.
FIELDEN, SAMUEL.
FISHER, JAMES.
FLEET, ALFRED.
FLEMING, ALEXR.
FLINDLE, PRYCE.
FORD, ERNEST.
FORDE, PATRICK A.
FOX, THOMAS.
FOX, WALTER.
FORSTER, RALPH.
FREEMAN, CHAS. W.
FREEMAN, WILLIAM.
FRYER, ARTHUR.
FRYER, HILARY.
FULLAM, CHARLES.
FURNIVAL, THOS.
GARDNER, FREDK.
GLADSTONE, THOS.
GEBBETT, FRED S.
GOLDEN, CHAS. W.
GILMOUR, WM.
GILRUTH, DURNO.
GOURLAY, A.
GILMAN, MATTHEW.
GASKELL, JOHN R.
GERRITY, JAS.
GARTSIDE, RUFUS.
GREGORY, FRANK.
GIBSON, WM.
GINNEVER, JOHN.
GOODWIN, GEORGE.
GLOVER, ARTHUR.
GREEN, LEONARD.
GORGE, ZACHARIAH.
GRUBB, HENRY.
GILL, WM.
GUTHRIE, HARRY.
GRIEVE, ANDREW.
GARNER, SAM.
GEE, JAMES.
GILBERT, WM. E.
GIBSON, JOHN.

GILLIBANKS, J. W.
GODDARD, DANIEL.
GOLDING, JAMES.
GRAHAM, PETER.
GREENHALGH, R.
GREENWOOD, E.
GREATOREX, WM.
GREENUP, JOHN.
GRIFFIN, THOMAS.
GRIMSHAW, PAUL.
HALL, JOHN.
HALLIWELL, WM.
HARGREAVES, J.
HAMILTON, GEO.
HALL, FRANK.
HARDMAN, ROBERT.
HASLAM, JOHN.
HARRIS, GEORGE.
HALL, ALAN.
HANCOX, ARNOLD.
HANDFORTH, WM.
HANNAH, J. J. (Killed).
HARRISON, W. F.
　　　　　(D.C.M.).
HARVEY, HARRY.
HARTLEY, M.
HANES, HERBERT.
HARTLEY, WM.
HARBURN, R.
HATTON, JOSEPH.
HACK, CHARLES.
HEWITT, GEORGE.
HESSION, JAMES.
HEY, ALBERT E.
HENRY, FRANCIS.
HELLAWELL, JESSE.
HESKETH, ROBT. H.
HEWITSON, JOSEPH.
HEWITT, FRANK.
HEYWOOD, FRED.
HICKINBOTHAM, J. R.
HIGGINS, EDWARD.
HILL, THOMAS.
HILL, WM. E.
HOBSON, JOHN T.
HODGSON, ALLAN.
HOWARTH, JOSEPH.
HOOD, ARTHUR.
HOLT, OSWALD.
HORGAN, A. H.
HOWE, G.
HOWSAM, ROBT. P.
HOLDEN, WM.
HOLLOWAY, W.

HOLMES, JOHN A.
HORTON, HERBERT.
HOUGHTON, H.
HUDDLESTON, F.
HUNT, HENRY A.
HUTTON, THOMAS E.
HYATT, WM. H.
IDLE, JOHN.
IRVING, GEORGE.
JEFFERAY, ROBERT.
JERVIS, ARCHIBALD.
JOHNSON, ARTHUR.
JOHNSON, FRANK.
JOHNSON, J. D.
JOHNSON, SAMUEL.
JOLLY, THOS.
JONES, HERBERT.
JONES, G. V.
JONES, JAMES E.
JONES, WM. M.
JONES, RALPH.
JONES, JOHN THOS.
JONES, ROBT. HY.
JONES, RALPH.
JOSEPHS, ALBERT.
KEEBLE, GORDAN.
KEELING, JOHN W.
KERR, WM.
KERR, FREDERICK.
KERSHAW, SAM.
KILCOURSE, JOHN.
KING, JAMES.
KNAGG, WM. Y.
LACEY, GEORGE.
LANGTHORNE, R.
LANGRILL, HENRY.
LAMBERT, JAMES.
LAWRIE, WM.
LEA, WALTER.
LEGG, GEORGE.
LEWIS, DAVID.
LIGHTON, WM. CHAS.
LITTLER, CHAS. WM.
LONGWORTH, A. J.
LUND, JAMES.
LOW, FRANCIS.
LLOYD, JOHN R.
LYNCH, JOHN.
MACLEOD, PETER.
MADDOCKS, THOS.
MANLEY, ALBERT.
MASKERY, THOS.
MANSELL, JOSEPH.
MARSHALL, JOSEPH.

MASON, ERNEST.
MARSHALL, FRANK.
MARSHALL, W.
MAYER, ALFRED.
MARSON, JOSHUA.
MASSEY, JAMES.
MAGOWAN, ALEXR.
MARTIN, GILBERT.
McCANN, WM.
McCARTHY, JOHN W.
McCLEAN, EDWARD.
MELLOR, HERBERT.
MELLOR, WM.
MELROSE, HAROLD.
METCALF, JAMES.
METCALF, THOS.
McDOWALL, CHAS.
McELROY, JAMES.
McFEELEY, EDW.
McMANUS, ALFRED.
MILLINGTON, D.
MIDDLETON, J. H.
MILLINGTON, GEO.
MITCHELL, R.
MOCHAN, FRANCIS.
MOFFATT, JOHN.
MOLYNEAUX, ALF.
　　　　(Killed).
MOLYNEUX, GEO.
MOONEY, JAMES.
MOONEY, PATRICK.
MOOR, JOHN.
MOORE, JONATHAN.
MOORE, THOS. G.
MOORE, R. (Killed).
MOORES, JAMES.
MORRIS, EDW. M.
MORGAN, HAROLD.
MURGATROYD, H.
MURRAY, JOSEPH.
MURRAY, WM.
NATHAN, WM. HY.
NEALE, WILSON.
NETHERWOOD, WM.
NEWTON, WALTER.
NICHOLSON, G. W.
NICHOLLS, JOHN HY.
NORMAN, C. E.
NOLAN, WM.
NUTTALL, JAMES A.
OAKDEN, DANIEL.
OGDEN, JARVIS N.
OLDALE, ALBERT.
O'REILLY, PATRICK.

MANCHESTER CORPORATION
ROLL OF HONOUR.—continued.

City Police.

O'REILLY, JOSH. F.
ORR, WM. J.
OWENS, THOS. W.
PASS, JOHN.
PARKER, WM. T.
PATTISON, R.
PATTINSON, JAMES.
PAYNTING, JOHN H.
PAYNE, WM.
PECK, ARTHUR WM.
PERRIN, HERBT. G.
PHOENIX, E.
PICKFORD, GEO. W.
PICKLES, ARTHUR.
PIGGOTT, THOMAS.
PLANT, JOSEPH.
PORTER, ERNEST.
POWELL, ERNEST.
PROUD, ARTHUR.
PUGH, EDWARD J.
PUGH, JOHN O.
RABBETT, THOMAS.
REDFEARN, HENRY.
REYNOLDS, JOHN.
RHODES, HAROLD.
RHODES, WM.
RIBCHESTER, JAS.
RICHARDSON, ROBT.
RIDGWAY, SAMUEL.
RIGBY, JAMES.
ROBB, WILLIAM.
ROBSON, JOHN WM.
ROBSON, WM.
ROBINSON, JOHN.
ROBINSON, P. G. E.
ROBERTS, WM. E.
ROGERS, TIMOTHY.
ROGERS, JOHN.
ROWE, JOHN JOSH.
ROWE, THOMAS E.
ROWLANDS, E.
ROYLANCE, JOHN.
RUSHTON, GEORGE.
RUSSELL, THOMAS.
RYAN, ERNEST.

SALSBURY, WALTER.
SALTER, THOMAS.
SANDERSON, E.
SAUNDERS, H. J.
SEVILLE, W. (Killed).
SCHOFIELD, JAMES.
SCHOFIELD, JAS. A.
SCHOFIELD, E.
SCOTT, HAROLD H.
SHARP, THOMAS.
SHARPLES, ERNEST
SHIRES, CHARLIE
SHARPE, EDWARD.
SHARD, FRANK.
SHELDON, WM.
SHIMMIN, A. M.
SHIRLEY, FRED.
SIDDLE, JAMES.
SIDWELL, HENRY.
SIMPSON, ARTHUR.
SKARRATT, JOHN.
SKELLY, CHAS.
SKERRATT, GEO. F.
SKETT, HERBERT.
SKILLING, R. (Killed).
SLADEN, JAMES.
SLOANE, WM.
SLEE, WM.
SLINGSBY, HARRY.
SMALLWOOD, JOHN.
SMEDLEY, GEORGE.
SMITH, ALLEN.
SMITH, C.
SMITH, JOHN.
SOHL, JOHN.
SPICER, WALTER G.
SPURR, FREDERICK.
STADEN, THOMAS.
STAGG, ERNEST G.
STANLEY, FRED.
STANTON, ALBERT.
STANAWAY, JAMES.
STARKEY, ALBERT E.
STARKIE, JOSEPH.
STEVENSON, W.

STREET, JOHN W.
STOCKTON, THOMAS.
STUART, THOMAS.
STUBBS, A. (Killed).
SUDLOW, WM.
SUMMERS, ALFRED.
SUMMERSBY, A.
SUMMERS, THOMAS.
SUTCLIFFE, A.
SUTTON, SAM.
SUTTON, JOSEPH.
SWIFT, WM.
SWINDELLS, H.
SYDDALL, JAMES.
SYKES, DAVID.
TAGGERT, DICK.
TAIT, JAMES A.
TAYLOR, ARTHUR.
TAYLOR, ERNEST.
TAYLOR, ERNEST A.
TAYLOR, GEORGE.
TAYLOR, ROBERT.
THICKENS, E.
THOMPSON, WM. W. (Killed).
THOMAS, GEORGE.
THOMAS, GEO. HY.
THOMPSON, JAMES.
THRELFALL, N.
TIPPING, EDWARD.
TITTERTON, GEO.
TOWNSON, HENRY.
TOWNSON, WM.
TRAVIS, GEORGE.
TREMLETT, HARRY.
TURNER, FRED. E.
TIMPERLEY, H.
TWINN, A. E.
VERNON, ARTHUR.
VERNON, EDWIN.
VOLANS, WM.
WADDINGTON, H.
WAGSTAFFE, GEO.
WAIN, GEORGE L.
WALKER, GEORGE E.

WALKER, ERNEST.
WALKER, ERNEST.
WALLACE, THOS.
WALLACE, JOSEPH.
WALMSLEY, WM.
WALMSLEY, WM. T.
WALSH, THOMAS.
WARR, WILLIAM.
WARREN, WM. F.
WATTS, WM. A.
WATERS, H. (D.C.M.).
WARNER, JOHN E.
WARBURTON, THOS.
WEBSTER, F.
WELSBY, JOHN E.
WHALLEY, JAS. WM.
WHATMOUGH, J.
WHEELER, CHAS. B.
WHEELDON, GEO.
WHITE, GEORGE C.
WHITELEY, JOHN W.
WHITFIELD, JOHN.
WHITTAKER, R.
WHITEHEAD, T. B.
WHITTLE, AMBROSE.
WILLIAMS, C. V.
WILLIAMS, JOHN G.
WILLIAMS, JOHN.
WILLIAMS, J. C.
WILLIAMSON, JAS.
WILLIS, ARTHUR.
WILSON, DAVID A.
WILSON, ERNEST A.
WILSON, JAMES.
WILSON, THOMAS.
WINDSOR, JOHN.
WOOD, JOHN A.
WOOD, JOSEPH.
WOODHEAD, J.
WORRALL, W.
WORSLEY, FRANK.
WRENCH, EDGAR.
WRIGHT, GEO. W.
WRIGHT, JOSEPH.

Rivers Department.

ADSHEAD, T.
ALLPORT, G.
AXON, R.
BENNETT, L. G.
BENNETT, R.
BRADLEY, T. W.
BROADY, G.

BROADY, J.
BARNES, J. W.
BARBER, J.
BLACKBURN, W.
BROOKS, N.
BURGESS, W. J.
CARTER, J.

CALDERBANK, A. E.
CHAMLEY, A.
CHAMLEY, J.
COLLINGE, J. E.
COLLYER, T. E.
COOKSON, F.
COUSINS, G.

CRONSHAW, J.
CUDDY, J.
DANIELS, J. H.
DAWSON, J.
DELANEY, J.
DERBYSHIRE, W.
DERVINN, J.

MANCHESTER CORPORATION
ROLL OF HONOUR.—continued.

Rivers Department.

DEVING, F.	JOYCE, T.	PEARSON, A.	TENCH, W.
DOHERTY, J.	KAY, J.	PERKS, C.	THACKER, G.
DRUMMOND, C.	KEAN, V.	POWER, J.	THORLEY, J.
FAREBROTHER, W.	KELLEY, H.	PRICE, J.	UPTON, W.
FIELD, G.	KETTLE, A.	RANKIN, W.	WADE, T.
FLANAGAN, T.	LIGHTFOOT, G.	RATCLIFFE, J. F.	WALKER, S.
FREEMANTLE, W. G.	LOWE, G.	RATCLIFFE, W.	WALTON, J.
FOGELL, C.	LUCAS, G.	RICHARDSON, B. S.	WALTON, A.
GARNER, H.	MAGSON, W.	ROBERTS, W.	WHITTAKER, J.
GIBSON, R. H.	MATTHEWS, J.	ROYLE, W.	WHITNALL, F.
GRIFFIN, M.	McCANN, J.	RUANE, J.	WILKINS, G.
HAMLETT, J.	McDERMOTT, P.	RUSH, P.	WILLIAMS, F. J
HIDES, G.	McGUINESS, H.	SCRUTON, R.	WILSON, R.
HIGGINS, C.	MOSS, P.	SHANNON, H.	WILSON, G. J.
HILL, F.	MULLARKY, J.	SHOTTON, S.	WOOD, E.
*HOLLINSWORTH, J.	MUNDY, R.	SINGELTON, C.	YOUD, F.
HOLLINSHEAD, P.	*NAUGHTON, J.	STABB, A.	WOODNETT, H.
HYNES, M.	NEWTON, A.	STEEPLES, E.	WYATT, F.
*JEFFREY, J.	NICHOLSON, F.	STILL, D.	YATES, H.
JOHNSON, S.	NOONE, E.	*STILL, W.	*YATES, W.
JONES, E.	ORPWOOD, G.	SUMNER, J. W.	YOUNG, A.
JONES, F.	PASS, T.	TAYLOR, H.	

Private P. Rush was killed in action on 20th October, 1914. Lieutenant W. G. Freemantle was killed in action in Gallipoli on 10th June, 1915.

Those marked thus (*) have since been rejected as unfit.

Sanitary Department.

ALLEN, W.	DUNMORE, F. T.	LAWSON, J.	POYSER, H.
ARNOLD, E. R.	FLYNN, F.	LEAR, C.	RISK, L. B.
BARLOW, F.	FORTH, H.	LENDON, H.	RONEY, A.
BEALES, S.	GRAVES, J. I.	LEE, G. R. (Killed)	SEED, A.
BEAUMONT, A. E.	HARPER, E.	MOORE, H.	SHEARMAN, E.
BULLOUGH, J. A.	HODGES, W.	McDOWELL, J.	SHIEL, E.
BURR, W. H. (Killed).	HOUGH, C.	McDOWELL, R. H.	VALENTINE, H.
CARTLAND, W. A.	JACKSON, H. M.	McQUIN, O.	WATERS, H.
CARTER, C. W.	KENDERDINE, C. A.	O'BRIEN, M. J.	WALTON, T. E.
DARBYSHIRE, J. A.	LANIGAN, J.	PAULSON, J.	WHITELEGG, J.
DARBYSHIRE, J.			

Stationery Department.

ALLMAN, W. A. - - - - Med. Unit., R. Naval Div.
*CHAPMAN, P. - - - - 7th Bt. Manchester Rgt.
DANIEL, B. - - - - D. of Lancaster's Yeom'y.
LINNEY, H. J. - - - - Army Service Corps.
THOMPSON, W. - - - - (City) Bt. Manchester Rgt.

* Discharged from the Army on August 10th, having lost his left leg in the Dardanelles, and is now at home. We expect he will resume his duties here when fit.

City Surveyor's Department.

ALLEN, R.	BROOK, F.	DAVIES, J. E.	GRANTHAM, W. H.
ASHTON, J.	BOOT, H. E.	DAVIES, R. H.	HART, G.
BIRCH, L.	BUTTON, F. E.	DORMAN, H. C.	HENDERSON, T. F.
BEAL, J. W.	CALVERT, C. P.	FARMER, C. H. C.	HOBSON, H. E.
BENTLEY, S.	COLLINS, C.	FLETCHER, W. D.	JACKSON, R. C.
BILLINGE, E.	CODLING, W. G.	FURNESS, D.	JEPSON, V.
BRIERLEY, H. C	CORDWELL, A.	GORDON, G. G.	JOHNSON, H.

MANCHESTER CORPORATION
ROLL OF HONOUR.—continued.

City Surveyor's Department.

KENT, C. G.	NEWTON, J. L.	SMITH, A.	WALMSLEY, E. W.
KNIGHT, W.	PLATT, L. P.	TAYLOR, C. N.	WILDE, E.
LISTER, R. W.	PRENTICE, H. J.	TATE, G. H.	WICKENDEN, E.
LAMOND, J.	ROWE, W. B.	THACKREY, T.	WILKINSON, H.
MIEDE, C. H. F.	REDFERN, J.	THOMSON, C. B.	YATES, J.
MOUNTAIN, F. W.	SAVAGE, R. B.	TILLEY, A.	YORSTON, J. H.
NEWTON, N.	SHAPLEY, A. E.	WALKER, G. D.	

Town Clerk's Department.

ADKIN, R.	COWAN, J. C.	HATTON, D.	PLANT, G.
BAKER, F.	COWX, W.	HAY, F. W.	REDFERN, C. H.
BANKS, A. H.	DEVONPORT, TOM.	HILL, R.	RICHARDS, H.
BARKER, J. W.	EATON, W.	HILL, S.	SEDDON, G. S.
BINKS, H. H.	FAIRWEATHER, T.	KNIGHT, F. A.	SHARPLES, T.
CALDWELL, H.	FINCHETT, S.	MOORES, H.	SHIRES, R.
CHAPMAN, B.	GENT, F. A.	OLLERENSHAW, J.	TAYLOR, H.
CHAPMAN, C. W.	HADDOCK, E. R.	PICKFORD, A. F. I.	WATSON, J. W.
COSTELLO, F.			

Tramways Department.

ABBERLEY, G.	ASTLE, S.	BASNETT, J.	BOLTON, F.
ABRAHAMS, J.	ATHERTON, W.	BASTIN, T. R.	BOND, H.
ACKROYD, J.	ATKIN, J.	BATES, W.	BOND, S. R.
ADAMS, F.	AUSTIN, H. C.	BATKIN, A.	BOOTH, G. E.
AFFLECK, J. H.	AYKROYD, A. S.	BATTY, S.	BOOTH, H.
AINSCOW, J. W.	BAGGOLEY, W. H.	BAXTER, G.	BOOTH, J. E.
AINSWORTH, D.	BAGULEY, C.	BAYLEY, J.	BOOTH, T.
ALLCOCK, G.	BAILEY, E.	BEARD, J.	BOOTH, W.
ALLENSON, G.	BAILEY, J. R.	BEAVER, J.	BOOTT, H. C.
ALLWOOD, J. W.	BAILEY, L.	BEBBINGTON, E.	BORKING, J.
ANDERTON, H.	BAILEY, R. W.	BEDDOW, R.	BOSTOCK, E.
ANDERTON, T.	BAILEY, W.	BEDDOWS, L.	BOTTING, R.
ANDERTON, W.	BAIN, J. W.	BEILBY, T. A.	BOUCHIER, G. C.
ANDREWS, F.	BAKER, A.	BELL, J.	BOULTON, J. H.
ANDREWS, J. G.	BAKER, G. H.	BELL, JAMES.	BOWDEN, J.
APPLEBY, G.	BANCROFT, L.	BELLIS, R.	BOWEN, G.
APPLEBY, J. H.	BANHAM, G.	BEMAN, H.	BOWKETT, F. R.
APPLEBY, H.	BANKS, J.	BENNETT, W.	BOWTELL, G.
APPLETON, T. H.	BANKS, T.	BENSON, W. H.	BOYLE, E.
ARNOLD, J. W.	BANN, S.	BENTLEY, J.	BOYLE, H.
ARROWSMITH, J.	BARDSLEY, W.	BETNEY, J. H.	BOYLIN, C. A.
ASCOTT, C. J.	BARKER, H.	BETTANY, H.	BRACEWELL, J.
ASHBURNER, T.	BARKER, W. H.	BIBBY, E.	BRADBURY, J. H.
ASHELBY, W.	BARLOW, A.	BICKERTON, J. H.	BRADLEY, J.
ASHTON, A. G.	BARLOW, JOHN.	BIDDLESTONE, W. H.	BRADSHAW, A.
ASHTON, E.	BARNES, J. R. H.	BIRCHALL, A.	BRADSHAW, J.
ASHTON, J.	BARNES, W.	BIRMINGHAM, J.	BRAND, H. G.
ASHTON, S.	BARRATT, J.	BIRTLES, H.	BRENNAN, J.
ASHWELL, L.	BARRATT, W.	BLACK, W.	BRENNAN, T.
ASHWORTH, L.	BARRETT, E.	BLAKELEY, W. H.	BRERETON, S. W.
ASPDEN, J.	BARRETT, H. S.	BLAKEMORE, T. A.	BRETSCHNEIDER, F. E.
ASPEY, H.	BARROW, W.	BLEASDALE, S.	
ASPINALL, J. S.	BARTH, A.	BLOOR, E.	BREWER, F.
ASPLAND, P.	BARTON, H.	BLUNDELL, W.	BREWETON, C. T.
ASTLE, J. H.	BARTON, T.	BOGG, F.	BRIGGS, W.

MANCHESTER CORPORATION
ROLL OF HONOUR.—continued.

Tramways Department.

BRIGGS, W. H.
BRIGHAM, T.
BROADHURST, T.
BROGDEN, N.
BROOKES, L.
BROOKS, S.
BROOKS, W.
BROOME, J. E.
BROTHERTON, J.
BROUGH, F.
BROWN, F.
BROWN, G. A.
BROWN, H.
BROWN, H. A.
BROWN, J.
BROWN, J.
BROWN, N.
BROWNHILL, T.
BRUCE, R.
BRUNT, H.
BUCHANAN, T.
BUCKLEY, A. J.
BUCKLEY, J. A.
BUCKLEY, J. T.
BUDGETT, H.
BUDSWORTH, T.
BULLOCK, G. H.
BUOTT, A.
BURGESS, B.
BURGESS, G.
BURGESS, J.
BURLEY, A.
BURNS, H.
BURNS, W.
BURTON, T. H.
BURY, C.
BUSS, H.
BUTLER, J. H.
BUTTERWORTH, J.
BUTTERWORTH, J. H.
BYRNE, A. E.
BYRNE, J.
BYRNE, P.
BYRNE, T.
BYRNE, T.
BYRNE, W.
CAIN, W.
CAINE, W.
CAREY, J. W.
CARLISLE, A.
CARLSON, N.
CARROLL, H.
CARTER, J.
CARTER, R.

CARTWRIGHT, A.
CARTWRIGHT, G.
CARTWRIGHT, T.
CASE, J.
CASEY, S.
CASH, J. E.
CASSIDY, J.
CASSIDY, T.
CAVENDER, S.
CHADWICK, A.
CHADWICK, G.
CHADWICK, R.
CHADWICK, W.
CHADWICK, W.
CHAMBERLAIN, J. E.
CHAMPION, A. L.
CHAPMAN, C.
CHAPMAN, E.
CHAPMAN, R.
CHAPMAN, S.
CHALONER, W.
CHEETHAM, S. C.
CHEETHAM, W.
CHESHIRE, J. W.
CHETWOOD, J. W.
CHRISTIE, J.
CHRYSTAL, J.
CLARKE, A.
CLARKE, J.
CLARKE, J. H.
CLARKSON, J.
CLAXTON, G.
CLEMINSON, J.
CLIFFE, G.
CLIFFE, H.
CLIFFE, J. E.
CLIFFE, W. R.
CLOUGH, H.
COATES, G. W.
COBURN, P. J.
COCHRANE, E.
COLDRON, C.
COLEMAN, A.
COLEMAN, W.
COLLINGE, S.
COLLINS, C. H.
COLLINS, J.
COLLINS, J. W.
COLLINS, J. A.
COLLINS, R.
CONNOLLY, J.
CONROY, H. J.
CONROY, JOHN.
CONRY, M. J.

COOPER, R.
COOPER, R. P.
COOPER, R. W.
CORCORAN, E.
COSTELLO, J.
COTTERALL, E.
COTTRELL, G.
COTTRILL, A.
COWARD, L. C.
COWBURN, R.
COXEY, C. E.
CRANE, J. W.
CRAVEN, C. W.
CRAWFORD, G.
CRIBBEN, H.
CRITCHLEY, A.
CROFT, F.
CROMPTON, A.
CROMPTON, G.
CROMPTON, J. E.
CROOKS, C.
CROPPER, J.
CRYAN, D.
CULLEN, P.
CUNLIFFE, H.
CUNNINGHAM, F.
CUNNINGHAM, F.
CURLEY, J. A.
DALE, A.
DALE, J.
DALEY, W.
DALTON, G.
DALY, J.
DANE, A.
DARBY, A. G.
DARBYSHIRE, W.
DAVENPORT, G. H.
DAVENPORT, G. T.
DAVIES, A.
DAVIES, A.
DAVIES, C.
DAVIES, C.
DAVIES, I.
DAVIES, J. E.
DAVIES, J. J.
DAVIES, J.
DAVIES, R.
DAVIES, W.
DAVINS, M. H.
DAVIS, R. F. W.
DAVISON, W.
DAWS, J. E. D.
DAWSON, C.
DAY, A.

DEAN, R.
DELANEY, W. H.
DERBYSHIRE, P.
DEVON, W.
DEWHURST, E.
DIAMOND, A.
DICKEN, H.
DICKENSON, J.
DICKENSON, J. G.
DIXON, F.
DODD, G. W.
DODD, W.
DODDS, J.
DOHERTY, J. W.
DONALDSON, W. D.
DOVE, W.
DOWNS, C.
DOWNS, G.
DOYLE, P.
DRINKWATER, W. A.
DUFFEY, H.
DUNKERLEY, W.
DUNN, F.
DURN, T.
DUTTON, A.
DWYER, A.
DYSON, A. L.
EADSFORTH, G.
EASTWOOD, H. H.
EATON, J.
ECCLES, F. C.
ECCLES, H.
EDWARDS, F.
EDWARDS, G.
EDWARDS, J.
EDWARDS, J. H.
EDWARDS, R.
EDWARDS, R.
EDWARDS, R.
EDWARDS, W.
EDWARDS, W.
EGAN, D.
ELLIOTT, A.
ELLISON, J.
ELLISON, W.
ELLISON, J. H.
EMMETT, A.
EMSON, J.
ENDERBY, C. W.
ERLAM, I.
EVANS, E. J.
EVANS, F. H.
EVANS, J. W.
EVANS, J. E.

MANCHESTER CORPORATION
ROLL OF HONOUR.—continued.

Tramways Department.

- EVANS, W. H.
- EYRE, A.
- EYRE, A.
- FAIRCLOUGH, T.
- FARRELL, G. H.
- FARRELL, J.
- FARRELL, P. J.
- FAUX, E.
- FEARNHEAD, T. A.
- FENDER, J.
- FERGUSON, A. G.
- FERGUSON, R. J.
- FESCO, J.
- FIFE, A.
- FINCH, J.
- FINCH, H. C.
- FINCH, T. G.
- FINDLOW, F.
- FINGLETON, E.
- FIRTH, J.
- FISHER, F. H.
- FISHER, G.
- FISHER, J.
- FISHER, S.
- FITTON, E.
- FITZGERALD, T.
- FITZPATRICK, T.
- FLATLEY, P.
- FLEET, F.
- FLETCHER, H.
- FLETCHER, J.
- FLETCHER, P.
- FLEVILL, C. H.
- FLITCROFT, H.
- FLYNN, W. J.
- FOGARTY, J.
- FOGG, J.
- FOOTITT, W.
- FORD, M.
- FORGHAM, G. E.
- FORSYTH, B.
- FOSTER, G.
- FOSTER, J. F.
- FOUCHARD, G.
- FOWLES, A.
- FOX, C. N.
- FOX, J.
- FOX, S.
- FOY, E.
- FRANCE, H.
- FRANKS, C. A.
- FRANKS, D.
- FRANKS, W. H.
- FREEMAN, J. L.
- FROGGART, W.
- FURNESS, F.
- FURNESS, J. A.
- FURPHY, H.
- GAGAN, W. A.
- GADD, C.
- GALLAGHER, R.
- GARDE, F.
- GARDNER, C.
- GARDNER, T.
- GARFIELD, A.
- GARLAND, F.
- GARNER, W. H.
- GARSIDE, H. R.
- GASKELL, A. E.
- GASKIN, A.
- GATLEY, W.
- GATWARD, A.
- GAUNT, W.
- GAYTER, E. H.
- GEE, J. B.
- GEE, W.
- GELSTHORPE, C.
- GESS, A. C.
- GIBSON, G.
- GILBERTSON, A.
- GILBERTSON, J.
- GILDEA, H.
- GILL, E.
- GILMORE, H.
- GLENNON, E.
- GLOVER, C. W.
- GOOCH, W.
- GOODWIN, T.
- GOODWIN, W.
- GORMAN, J.
- GORMLEY, C.
- GORNER, A.
- GOURLEY, A.
- GRADY, C.
- GRAHAM, F.
- GRAHAM, T.
- GRANTHAM, J.
- GRAY, C.
- GRAYSTOCK, J.
- GREATOREX, T.
- GREATOREX, J.
- GREEN, A. E.
- GREEN, H.
- GREEN, H. J.
- GREEN, J.
- GREEN, J.
- GREENFIELD, H.
- GREENHALGH, E.
- GREENWOOD, W.
- GREGORY, J.
- GREGORY, T.
- GREGSON, J. E.
- GROOM, J. R.
- HACKETT, S.
- HADFIELD, J. R.
- HALL, A.
- HALL, H.
- HALL, T.
- HALLWORTH, H.
- HALLWORTH, S.
- HAMILTON, J. J.
- HAMILTON, W. H.
- HAMMAN, F.
- HAMMERSLEY, A.
- HAMNETT, A.
- HAMNETT, J.
- HAMPSON, W.
- HAND, G.
- HAND, W.
- HANKINSON, F.
- HANSON, G.
- HARBRIDGE, G.
- HARDING, C.
- HARDSTAFF, A.
- HARDY, S.
- HARLEY, W.
- HARMSTONE, J. W. L.
- HARNEY, J.
- HARPER, G.
- HARRIS, H.
- HARRISON, J. E.
- HARRISON, T.
- HARRISON, T.
- HARROP, J. A.
- HARVEY, G. W.
- HARVEY, H.
- HARVEY, J. T.
- HASLEDENE, H.
- HATTON, A.
- HAWORTH, C. T.
- HAWORTH, W.
- HAWTHORNE, W.
- HAYCOCK, H.
- HAYES, E.
- HAYES, J. T.
- HAYMES, J. D.
- HAYNES, H.
- HAYWARD, J. R.
- HAYWARD, W. O.
- HEALD, J. E.
- HEALD, W.
- HEALEY, L.
- HERROD, A. E. B.
- HESELTINE, J. R. H.
- HESKETH, C. H.
- HESKETH, J. A.
- HEWITT, A.
- HEWITT, F.
- HEWITT, F.
- HEWITT, J.
- HEWITT, J.
- HEWITT, R.
- HIBBERT, E.
- HIBBERT, H.
- HIBBERT, J.
- HIGGINS, J.
- HIGGINS, N.
- HIGGINSON, C. T.
- HIGGINSON, J. A.
- HILL, C. A.
- HILL, M.
- HILLS, J. E.
- HINDLE, J.
- HINDLEY, J.
- HINTON, W.
- HIRD, E.
- HITCHEN, T.
- HOBBS, H. V.
- HOBSON, H.
- HOCKENHULL, W. R.
- HODCROFT, H.
- HODGKINS, H.
- HOLDING, F.
- HOLDING, F.
- HOLDING, G.
- HOLLAND, F.
- HOLLAND, J. E.
- HOLME, H. A.
- HOLMES, E.
- HOLMES, J.
- HOLT, C.
- HOLT, F.
- HOLT, J.
- HOOD, H.
- HOPE, A.
- HOPLEY, J. E.
- HORROCKS, J. H.
- HORROCKS, W. T.
- HORSFIELD, A.
- HORTON, W. A.
- HORTON, W. A.
- HOUGHTON, W.
- HOWARD, F.
- HOWARD, J. J.
- HOWARD, R. H.
- HOWARTH, H.
- HOWARTH, J.
- HOWARTH, J.
- HOWARTH, W.
- HOWELL, H.

MANCHESTER CORPORATION
ROLL OF HONOUR.—continued.

Tramways Department.

HOWELL, R.	JONES, A.	LANE, E.	LOWE, H.
HOWITT, A.	JONES, A.	LANE, J. A.	LOWIS, G.
HOWITT, H.	JONES, A.	LANG, J.	LOWNDS, C.
HUDSON, A. J.	JONES, C.	LAPPIN, T.	LUND, L. H.
HUDSON, J.	JONES, C.	LARGE, E.	LUND, T. W.
HUDSON, R.	JONES, C. W.	LAWRENCE, E.	LUNT, J. T.
HUDSON, W. A.	JONES, D.	LEACH, J. A.	LUSK, B.
HUFTON, W. E.	JONES, D. G.	LEAR, C. H.	LYON, A.
HUGHES, L. A.	JONES, G.	LEATHLEY, T. H.	LYONS, J.
HUGHES, H.	JONES, H.	LEDGER, H. J.	MACDONALD, J. G.
HUGHES, R.	JONES, J.	LEDGER, J. ST.	MACK, W.
HULME, A.	JONES, J. E.	LEE, A.	MACKESSY, W.
HULME, J.	JONES, S.	LEE, T.	MACKLIN, A.
HUNT, W.	JONES, S.	LEE, W.	MACLURE, A.
HUNTER, T. W.	JONES, W.	LEECH, F.	MADDICK, A.
HYNES, P.	JONES, W.	LEECH, W.	MADELEY, J. W.
ILES, N.	JONES, W. F.	LEEK, H.	MAGUIRE, E.
INGHAM, J. H.	JONES, W. H.	LEEK, J.	MAGUIRE, J.
INGHAM, R.	JORDAN, P.	LEES, F.	MAHER, P.
INGRAM, A. W.	KANOLTY, H.	LEES, F.	MAHER, W. J.
IRLAM, J.	KAY, F.	LEES, J. B.	MALE, F. W.
ISHERWOOD, J.	KEELER, T.	LEES, R.	MALLINSON, D. W.
JACK, J.	KEEANGHAN, P. A.	LEIGH, R.	MALLINSON, S.
JACKLIN, A.	KEITH, J. W.	LEIGH, R.	MALLINSON, T. W.
JACKLIN, P.	KELLY, E.	LEIGH, R.	MANFORD, C.
JACKLIN, R. G.	KELLY, J. F.	LEIGH, W.	MANN, E.
JACKSON, C. E.	KELLY, J. H.	LEONARD, H.	MANNING, F.
JACKSON, E. R.	KELSALL, A.	LEVER, F. T.	MANSELL, F.
JACKSON, T.	KELSEY, W.	LEVER, J. J.	MANTIGANI, C.
JACKSON, T.	KEMP, F.	LEWIS, G.	MARSH, R.
JACKSON, W. E.	KEMPSTER, A. E.	LEWIS, J. H.	MARSHALL, A. E.
JAMES, C.	KENNEDY, A.	LEWIS, W. H.	MARSLAND, W. H.
JAMIESON, J. H.	KENNEDY, A.	LIGHTFOOT, E.	MARTIN, J. R.
JAMIESON, J.	KENNEDY, F.	LILLEYMAN, R.	MASON, J. W.
JARMAN, F.	KENNY, P.	LINDSAY, J. A.	MASON, T.
JENKINS, J.	KENNY, W.	LITTLE, D.	MATTHEWS, B. T.
JENKINSON, D.	KENYON, B.	LIVESLEY, T.	MATTHEWS, H.
JENKINSON, R. A.	KERRIDGE, W. E.	LLEWELLYN, A.	MAUDSLEY, H. P.
JENKINSON, T. W.	KIDD, H.	LLEWELLYN, E.	MAURICE, A.
JOHNS, A. G.	KINSEY, J.	LLOYD, D.	MAWSON, F.
JOHNSON, A.	KIRK, R.	LLOYD, G. A.	MAWSON, H.
JOHNSON, A.	KIRKMAN, E.	LLOYD, J.	MAXWELL, C.
JOHNSON, E.	KIRKPATRICK, J.	LLOYD, L. S.	MAYFIELD, S. J.
JOHNSON, E.	KIRKWOOD, C. W.	LOCKE, A.	MAYO, F. W.
JOHNSON, H.	KIRTON, J. W. S.	LOCKETT, G.	MEAKIN, F.
JOHNSON, H.	KNAPE, J.	LOFTHOUSE, H.	MEAKIN, J.
JOHNSON, J. D.	KNEALE, S.	LOMAS, J.	MEE, H. B.
JOHNSON, S.	KNIGHT, T.	LOMAS, T. P.	MELBOURNE, F. N. C.
JOHNSON, W.	KNOTT, S.	LOMAX, A.	MELLOR, A.
JOHNSTON, B.	KNOWLES, E.	LONGSHAW, P. W.	MELLOR, J.
JOHNSTON, T.	LACEY, J. P.	LONGSHAW, R.	METCALFE, A.
JOHNSTON, T.	LAMB, J.	LORD, B. C.	METCALFE, G. W.
JOHNSTONE, F.	LANCASTER, J.	LORD, F. S.	METCALFE, W.
JOHNSTONE, H.	LANDING, H.	LOWE, C.	MILLS, F. C.

MANCHESTER CORPORATION
ROLL OF HONOUR.—continued.

Tramways Department.

MILLWARD, A.
MILNE, J.
MITCHELL, A.
MITCHELL, E.
MITCHELL, G. E.
MITCHELL, H.
MITCHELL, J.
MITCHELL, T.
MITCHELL, W.
MOFFATT, F.
MOONEY, T.
MOORE, A.
MOORE, E. G.
MOORE, J.
MOORE, J. C.
MOORE, W.
MOORE, W. R.
MOORES, G.
MORRIS, C.
MORRIS, E.
MORRIS, H.
MORRIS, R.
MORROD, H.
MORT, T.
MOSS, G. H.
MOSS, J. W.
MOSS, J.
MOUND, J. A.
MOUNTFORD, H. A.
MUIRHEAD, J.
MULHALL, M.
MULKERNS, P.
MURGATROYD, F.
MURPHY, J.
MURPHY, T.
MURRAY, A.
MURRAY, R. A.
MURRAY, T.
MURRAY, W.
MURTAGH, P.
MYERS, J.
MYLES, E.
MYOTT, J. E.
McCABE, F. W.
McCABE, J.
McCREAVEY, T.
McCLUSKEY, A.
McCOY, R.
McCULLOCK, H. B.
McCULLOGH, E.
McCURRIE, I.
McDERMOTT, J.
McDERMOTT, J.
McDONALD, W.
McDOWALL, D. R.
McELHATTON, J.
McELROY, W. H.
McGARRY, D.
McGARVA, J.
McGUIRE, T.
McGUINNESS, E.
McILWRAITH, C. B.
McINTYRE, C. T.
McKAY, J. R.
McLEAN, A. N.
McMAHON, T.
McMANUS, E.
McNAMARA, J. A.
McNAMARA, J. J.
McNULTY, E.
McQUADE, J.
McQUAY, J.
McQUAY, S.
NADEN, J.
NASH, F. A.
NAYLOR, J.
NAYLOR, T.
NELSON, A.
NELSON, O.
NESFIELD, J.
NESFIELD, J. E.
NEWELL, C. W.
NEWMAN, G. E.
NEWTON, A.
NEWTON, F.
NEWTON, P. G.
NEWTON, T.
NICHOLLS, W. H.
NICHOLS, S.
NICHOLS, W. H.
NICHOLSON, J.
NIXON, G. E.
NIXON, H.
NOONAN, J.
NORBURY, H. B.
NUTTALL, G.
OAKES, C. W.
OATES, H.
OATWAY, A.
O'BRIEN, F.
O'BRIEN, T.
O'CONNOR, C.
O'CONNOR, J. S.
O'CONNOR, M.
OGDEN, A.
OLDHAM, A.
OLDHAM, W. E.
OLEY, JOHN C.
OLLERENSHAW, R.
O'NEILL, J. H.
O'NEILL, J. J.
ORME, H.
ORMROD, J. R.
OSGOOD, J. E.
OWEN, C.
OWEN, F.
OWENS, R. T.
O'SHAUGHNESSY, J.
PAIN, R.
PALMER, F. H.
PALMER, J. H.
PALMER, R. L.
PANNELL, L.
PARFITT, G. F.
PARISH, J. H.
PARK, W. H.
PARKER, J.
PARKER, W.
PARKINSON, T.
PARKS, W. H.
PARKYN, E.
PARROTT, C. H.
PARSONS, W. H.
PARSONAGE, J. F.
PARTINGTON, T.
PATON, D.
PATRICK, A.
PAYNE, E.
PAYTON, H. H.
PAYTON, J.
PAYTON, P.
PEACH, A. E.
PEARSON, G.
PEARSON, S.
PEARSON, T.
PENLINGTON, F.
PENNELL, G. A.
PENNILL, G. A.
PENNY, J. H.
PENSON, J.
PEPPERDINE, P.
PERRIN, W.
PETIJEAN, E.
PHELAN, P. J.
PHILLINGHAM, H.
PHILLIPS, G.
PHILLIPS, G. P.
PHILLIPS, J. D.
PHILLIPS, J. Y. O.
PHILLIPS, T. H.
PHILLIPS, W.
PICKERING, A.
PICKERING, E.
PICKERING, E. H.
PILLING, T. H.
PINKERTON, W. M.
PITTS, J.
PLATTS, J. W.
POINTER, H.
POMFRET, G.
POOK, W. G.
POPE, C. F.
POPE, T.
PORTER, J. J.
POTTER, F.
POTTER, W.
POVALL, J.
POWER, E.
POWER, J.
POUNDER, W. H.
PRENDERGAST, W. F.
PRESTON, H.
PRICE, D. H.
PRIESTLY, R.
PRINCE, A.
PUGH, H.
PUGH, T.
PURCELL, J.
PURKISS, B. W.
PYATT, G. A.
PYATT, W. H.
PYCROFT, J.
PYE, F.
QUINN, E. P.
QUINN, R. H.
RAE, T.
RAMMELL, E. H.
RAMSAY, G.
RAMSBOTTOM, A.
RANDLE, E. G.
RANGE, A.
RASTALL, G.
RATCLIFFE, J.
RATCLIFFE, R.
RAWLINS, H.
RAWLINSON, G. W.
REDFERN, W. H.
REECE, W. H.
REID, J. W.
REILLY, T.
RELPH, J.
RELPH, W.
RENSHAW, H.
RENSHAW, W.
RICHARDSON, A.
RICHARDSON, S.
RICHMOND, A.
RICHMOND, S.
RIDLER, J.
RIGBY, J.

MANCHESTER CORPORATION
ROLL OF HONOUR.—continued.

Tramways Department.

RILEY, J.	SCOTT, J.	SNELSON, W.	TETLOW, J. M.
RILEY, W.	SCOTT, R.	SORAH, A. E.	THAW, J.
RINGER, H. R.	SCOWCROFT, J. H.	SOUTH, W. G.	THEWLIS, F.
RINGLAND, S.	SEARS, A. H.	SOUTHALL, A.	THOMAS, G.
RITSON, T. L.	SEDDON, W.	SPARLING, R.	THOMAS, H.
ROBERTS, A. F.	SEDDON, W.	SPEAKE, E.	THOMAS, H.
ROBERTS, B.	SELBY, J. A.	SPEIGHT, A.	THOMPSON, C.
ROBERTS, G.	SERVAN, A.	SPIERS, W. G. E.	THOMPSON, C.
ROBERTS, J. F.	SHARPE, J. M.	SPURR, A.	THOMPSON, E.
ROBERTS, J.	SHARPLES, L.	SQUIRE, J.	THOMPSON, H.
ROBERTS, J.	SHARPLEY, R.	SQUIRE, R.	THOMPSON, H. E.
ROBERTS, R.	SHATWELL, L.	SQUIRE, W. E.	THOMPSON, S. M.
ROBERTS, S. R.	SHAW, F.	SQUIRES, R.	THORLEY, F.
ROBINSON, J.	SHAW, J. E.	STAIT, T. A.	THORNLEY, R. A.
ROBINSON, J. O.	SHAW, W.	STANDRING, L.	THORP, J. W.
ROBINSON, J. H.	SHENTON, H.	STANSFIELD, H.	THORPE, H.
ROCHE, J.	SHEPHERD, G. H.	STANSFIELD, R.	THORPE, J. W.
RODDY, J.	SHONE, G.	STARKEY, W.	TILSON, A.
ROE, C. G. A.	SHORTT, S.	STEELE, F.	TILSTON, R.
ROLFE, H.	SIBBALD, W.	STEGGLES, V.	TIMPERLEY, G.
ROPER, J.	SIDDALL, B.	STENT, H.	TIMPERLEY, T.
ROSE, J.	SIDDALL, J.	STEPHENS, S.	TIMPERTON, E. W.
ROSS, H.	SIMMONS, J.	STEPHENSON, W.	TIPPING, A. E.
ROSS, H.	SIMMONS, W. L.	STEVENS, A. E.	TITLEY, T.
ROSTRON, G.	SIMPSON, J.	STEVENS, J. T.	TITTERTON, E.
ROUGHSEDGE, A.	SIMPSON, W. E.	STEVENSON, L. E.	TOD, C.
ROUNSEVELL, A.	SINGLETON, G.	STEWART, W.	TONROE, J.
ROWBOTHAM, T.	SINGLETON, H.	STOCKDALE, H.	TOON, J.
ROWBOTTOM, A.	SKELHORN, W. J.	STOCKTON, E.	TORKINGTON, F.
ROWBOTTOM, W.	SLACK, J. W.	STREET, C. E.	TORKINGTON, H.
ROWE, J.	SLAVIN, J.	STUBBS, C.	TOTTERDALE, N.
ROWLAND, J. E.	SMART, A.	STUBBS, C.	TRACEY, W.
ROWLAND, J. W.	SMETHURST, F.	STUBBS, L.	TRAFFORD, P.
ROYLE, H. T. C.	SMITH, A. E.	SULLIVAN, J.	TRAYNOR, A.
ROYLE, J. E.	SMITH, A. E.	SUMNER, H.	TRINICK, H.
RUSHBY, R.	SMITH, A.	SUMNER, J. W.	TURNER, H.
RUSHBY, W.	SMITH, A.	SUTCLIFFE, A.	TURNER, W. A.
RUTHERFORD, H.	SMITH, C. W.	SWAIN, J.	TURNER, W. B.
RUDD, C.	SMITH, E. E.	SWANWICK, J. J.	TURNER, W. E.
RYALL, R. P.	SMITH, E.	SWIFT, E.	TURPIE, R.
RYDER, H.	SMITH, F.	SWIFT, P. C.	TURPIE, W.
RYDER, N.	SMITH, H.	SYDDALL, A.	TYLER, A. W.
RYDER, W.	SMITH, H.	TANNER, E. A.	TYNAN, E.
ST. JOHN, W.	SMITH, H.	TARLTON, W.	TYNAN, J. H.
SALKELD, E.	SMITH, H.	TAYLOR, C.	TYSON, W.
SANDERSON, A.	SMITH, H. J.	TAYLOR, D.	UNWIN, H.
SANDERSON, G.	SMITH, J. F.	TAYLOR, F.	VANCE, J.
SANDIFORD, E.	SMITH, J. H.	TAYLOR, F.	VALENTINE, W.
SAVAGE, A.	SMITH, S.	TAYLOR, H. H.	VERNON, H.
SCHOFIELD, J. H.	SMITH, S.	TAYLOR, R.	VERNON, J. T.
SCHOLES, T.	SMITH, T. P.	TAYLOR, T. H.	VESEY, J.
SCHOLEY, H. H.	SMITH, W.	TAYLOR, W.	VESEY, P.
SCHOLLAR, A. J.	SMITH, W.	TAYLOR, W.	WADE, O.
SCOTT, H.	SMITH, W.	TEASDALE, A.	WADHAM, W. H.

MANCHESTER CORPORATION
ROLL OF HONOUR.—continued.

Tramways Department.

WAGSTER, W.
WAINHOUSE, F.
WAINWRIGHT, G. F.
WALBANK, W.
WALKER, A.
WALKER, J.
WALKER, R.
WALKER, W.
WALKER, W.
WALL, G. H.
WALL, L.
WALSH, H.
WALTER, P.
WALTERS, R. A.
WALTON, H.
WALTON, H.
WALTON, W. H.
WARD, J.
WARREN, T. E.
WARRINGTON, J.
WASHBOURNE, J. W.
WASHINGTON, W.
WATERS, R.
WATSON, P.
WATTERSON, A.
WAUGH, J. H.
WEBB, H.
WEBB, J. E.
WEBSTER, C.
WEBSTER, W.
WELCH, G.
WELLS, J.
WHALLEY, J.
WHARTON, A.
WHEELTON, S.
WHETTALL, W.
WHITE, J.
WHITE, R. W.
WHITEHEAD, G.
WHITEHEAD, J.
WHITEHOUSE, S.
WHITTAKER, G. H.
WHITTICK, J.
WHITTINGHAM, J.
WHITTLEWORTH, C. W.
WIDDOWS, R.
WILCOCK, F.
WILCOX, J. H.
WILD, E. M.
WILKINSON, W.
WILKS, C.
WILKS, H.
WILKS, J. W.
WILLANS, F.
WILLCOCK, T. J.
WILLIAMS, A.
WILLIAMS, B. H.
WILLIAMS, D.
WILLIAMS, F.
WILLIAMS, G. H.
WILLIAMS, J.
WILLIAMS, J.
WILLIAMS, J. H.
WILLIAMS, R.
WILLIAMS, S.
WILLIAMS, S. R.
WILLIAMS, T.
WILLIAMS, W. R.
WILLIAMSON, W.
WILLIAMS, W. R. O.
WILLIAMSON, A.
WILLIAMSON, J. N.
WILLIS, A.
WILMOTT, G.
WILMOTT, J.
WILSON, A.
WILSON, H. B.
WILSON, R.
WILSON, W. R.
WINSTANLEY, E.
WINTERBURN, H.
WITHINGTON, T.
WITHINGTON, W.
WOOD, A.
WOOD, J. A.
WOOD, P.
WOOD, R.
WOOD, T.
WOOD, W.
WOODCOCK, J. A.
WOODCOCK, J. W.
WOODFORD, P. C.
WOODHALL, G.
WOODHALL, J. T.
WOODHOUSE, R.
WOODMAN, S.
WOODING, F.
WOODWARD, J.
WOOTTON, T.
WORRALL, F.
WORSTENCROFT, J. V.
WORTHINGTON, J.
WORTHINGTON, J.
WORTHINGTON, T.
WORTHINGTON, W. R.
WORTHINGTON, W.
WRAY, W. L.
WRIGHT, A.
WROE, J. R.
WYETH, F.
YATES, A. H.

Tramways Department (Various).

ALLAN, W.
ALLCOCK, H.
ALLISON, A.
ALLEN, A.
ALLEN, J.
ANDERSON, J.
ANKERS, J.
ANKERS, W.
ANNFIELD, G.
ARUNDALE, R.
ASCOTT, C. J.
ASHCROFT, A. E.
ASHWORTH, T.
ASHWORTH, W. E.
ATKINSON, J.
AULT, J. W.
BAILEY, H.
BAILEY, W.
BAKER, E.
BAKER, R.
BAKER, W. R.
BALL, T.
BAMBER, W.
BANKS, E. J.
BANKS, J.
BANKS, J. T.
BARKER, J. H.
BARLOW, A.
BARLOW, J.
BARNES, G. A.
BARNETT, A.
BARRATT, J.
BARRETT, A. R.
BARRETT, W. A.
BARRON, J. H.
BARRY, F.
BARRY, T.
BASNETT, J.
BASNETT, W. F.
BATCHELOR, C.
BATEMAN, J. A.
BATER, C. E.
BATTY, J.
BEATTIE, R. R.
BEBBINGTON, A. E.
BEBBINGTON, S. H.
BEESLEY, J. E.
BELCHER, J. W.
YATES, H. W.
YATES, J.
YOUNG, J.
YOUNG, J. T.

BELL, A.
BELL, P. L.
BELL, S.
BENNETT, J. E.
BENNETT, R.
BENNETT, W. R.
BERRY, J. W.
BICKERS, J.
BINGHAM, A.
BISSELL, W. H.
BLACK, R.
BLACKBURN, T.
BLAKELEY, J.
BLANTON, H.
BLEZARD, I.
BOARDMAN, G.
BOARDMAN, T.
BOLAS, J.
BONNER, G. A.
BOOTH, A.
BOOTH, A.
BOOTH, A.
BOOTH, J.
BOOTH, J.
BOOTH, J.
BOOTH, R.
BOOTH, R.
BOOTH, T. C.
BOUCHER, J.
BOWERS, J. T.
BOWERS, T. S.
BOWKETT, F. R.
BOYLE, D.
BOYLE, F.
BRADFORD, R.
BRADSHAW, A.
BRADSHAW, J.
BRADSHAW, W.
BRADY, J. F.
BRAMHALL, J.
BRAMHALL, R. T.
BREW, C. P.
BREWER, R. F.
BRERETON, J.
BRIGHTY, J. H.
BRINDLEY, W.
BROAD, W.
BROADBENT, D.

MANCHESTER CORPORATION
ROLL OF HONOUR.—continued.

Tramways Department (Various).

BROADBENT, E.
BROGDEN, N.
BROOKES, N.
BROOKSHAW, J. B.
BROOME, G. E.
BROWN, A.
BRUCE, J. S.
BRUMAT, L.
BUBB, J.
BUCKLEY, J. T.
BUNTING, T.
BURGESS, H.
BURGESS, S.
BURKE, A.
BURKE, J. J.
BURNS, H.
BURTON, W.
BUTLER, B. J.
BUTLER, P.
BYATT, A. L. S.
BYRNE, J.
CABLE, W. E.
CADMAN, J.
CADMAN, J. A.
CALVERT, W.
CAMPBELL, W. E.
CARNEY, H.
CARRINGTON, T. F.
CARROLL, C.
CASEY, T.
CASSELL, F.
CAVANAGH, J.
CHAPMAN, J.
CHARNOCK, F.
CHEETHAM, J. H.
CHESTER, W.
CHICK, T. E.
CIRCUITT, C. A.
CLARIDGE, W. A.
CLARKE, A.
CLARKSON, J.
CLAYFORD, H.
CLIFTON, G. W.
CLOWES, S.
COLEMAN, J.
COLLIER, F.
COLLINS, R. H.
COLLINS, J.
COLUMBINE, C.
CONDON, D.
CONNAUGHTON, R.
CONNOR, J. J.
CONWAY, T.
COOKE, G. H.

COOPER, W.
CORBISHLEY, F. J.
CORBISHLEY, J. O.
CORDEN, C.
CORLETT, F. W.
CORNER, A.
CORNFORTH, J.
CORNTHWAITE, A.
COSTIN, J.
COTTRILL, W.
COWBURN, T.
CRAVEN, J.
CRAWFORD, C. L.
CRAWSHAW, S.
CROFT, F.
CROWTHER, J.
CUNLIFFE, J. H.
CUNLIFFE, R. G.
CUNNINGTON, J. J.
CURRAN, W. A.
CURRIE, J.
CURZON, G. N.
DALE, G. A.
DALTON, J.
DANIELS, J. H.
DAVIES, E.
DAVIES, T. H.
DAVIES, W.
DAWES, W. A.
DENNINGTON, J. H.
DENNIS, J.
DENT, F.
DICKENSON, J.
DINSDALE, J.
DIXON, H.
DOBSON, P.
DOBSON, T.
DODD, F.
DODD, T. A.
DOHERTY, J. F.
DONNELLY, R. J.
DOWLING, R.
DOYLE, C.
DRAPER, W.
DUDSON, W.
DUFFY, E.
DUTTON, J.
DUTTON, W.
EAKHURST, T. W.
EARDLEY, A.
ECKERSLEY, H. W.
EDGE, J. D.
EDGE, J. R.
EDGE, W. H.

EDWARDS, B.
EDWARDS, P.
EDWARDS, R.
EGAN, J.
EGAN, J.
ELLIS, E.
ELLIS, E. A.
ELLIS, J.
ELLIS, J. P.
ETCHELLS, A.
EVANS, G.
EVANS, W.
EXTON, W.
EYRES, C.
FARNWORTH, J.
FARR, W.
FARRELL, T.
FARRELL, W.
FARRINGTON, J.
FENNAH, W.
FERRIS, G.
FILDES, T.
FINLEY, W. H.
FIRTH, E. H.
FITZGERALD, T. J.
FLANAGAN, T.
FLEET, G.
FOLEY, M.
FORGHAM, J. W.
FORSYTH, D.
FORSYTH, F.
FORSYTH, J.
FOSTER, E.
FOTHERGILL, F.
FOULDING, F.
FOULKES, J. N.
FOX, J.
FRENCH, J.
FUDGE, J.
FURNISS, W.
FURNIVAL, E. H.
GANDY, G. A.
GANNON, J.
GARDNER, A.
GARDNER, W. H.
GARNETT, J.
GEE, W.
GEORGE, E. E.
GEORGE, F.
GIBSON, J. H.
GILL, I. I.
GILLARD, J.
GILLIGAN, J.
GITTINS, T. H.

GLANCY, O. J.
GLEADALL, E.
GLENNON, J. E.
GOODERIDGE, W. L.
GOODWIN, A.
GOODWIN, W.
GORDON, W. J.
GOSS, V.
GOUGH, S. H.
GRABHAM, T.
GRAHAM, J. T.
GRAHAM, T.
GRAYSTON, F.
GROOME, H.
GREATBANK, J. J.
GREATOREX, J.
GREEN, C.
GREEN, S.
GREEN, W.
GRIFFIN, M.
GROOMBRIDGE, W.
HALL, C.
HALL, H.
HALLIDAY, T. G.
HAMPSON, J.
HARDACRE, S.
HARDMAN, T.
HARRIS, H. J.
HARRIS, W.
HARRISON, A.
HARRISON, D.
HARRISON, T.
HARRISON, J.
HARROP, D.
HART, W. T.
HARWOOD, W. E.
HAWKSWORTH, G. J.
HAWORTH, C. T.
HAYES, H.
HEATHCOTE, T.
HEATLEY, R.
HEATON, A. R.
HEATON, S.
HENSHALL, A.
HERBERT, J.
HERBERT, J.
HERD, R.
HERON, S.
HESFORD, S.
HETHERINGTON, G. A.
HEWITT, R. H.
HIBBERT, W. H.
HIGGINBOTHAM, S. E.
HIGGINS, G.

MANCHESTER CORPORATION
ROLL OF HONOUR.—continued.

Tramways Department (Various).

HIGGINS, J.	JONES, J.	MACREATH, J.	McELROY, H.
HIGGINS, J. E.	JONES, R. D.	MAGUIRE, W.	McELROY, T.
HIGGINS, T.	JONES, R.	MAHER, W. J.	McGAW, A.
HIGSON, H. W.	JONES, S. E.	MAILE, C.	McGAW, A.
HILL, W.	JONES, T.	MALE, F.	McHUGH, M.
HILTON, V. R.	JOYCE, M.	MALIN, J. T.	McKEAN, A. J.
HINCHLIFFE, T.	JOYCE, J.	MALLEY, A. W.	McKENZIE, J.
HIPWORTH, W. E.	KAY, H.	MALONE, T.	McKINLEY, C.
HOARE, W.	KELLY, T.	MANDER, S. J.	McKNIGHT, T. H.
HOLLAND, C.	KELSALL, J.	MANGNALL, T.	McLAREN, J. H.
HOLLAND, E.	KEMP, J. W.	MANN, H.	McLEAN, J.
HOLME, G.	KENCH, F.	MARGERSON, T.	McMAHON, V. H. M.
HOLMES, W. H.	KENNEDY, H.	MARSH, W.	McMANUS, J. J.
HOLT, J.	KENYON, A. T.	MARTIN, G.	McNAMARA, J.
HOLYLAND, A. F. G.	KENYON, W.	MATTHEWS, E.	McNAMARA, T.
HOOPER, H.	KERRIGAN, M.	MATTINSON, H.	NAYLOR, R.
HOOPER, S.	KILLICK, G.	MATTISON, C. A.	NEEDHAM, J.
HOOPER, W. J.	KING, J.	MAY, S.	NEILLINGS, R.
HOPKIN, D. E.	KIRKLEY, F. H.	MAYELL, G.	NELSON, C. F.
HORNER, P.	KIRKMAN, J.	MELLOR, G.	NELSON, W.
HORROCKS, J.	KNIGHT, A.	MENZIES, A.	NEWBIGGIN, J. G.
HORROCKS, W. H.	LAMB, G.	MERRON, E.	NICHOLLS, W.
HOWARTH, D. A.	LAMB, J.	METCALFE, R.	NICHOLSON, H.
HUGHES, A. T.	LAMB, T. H.	MIDDLETON, F.	NICHOLSON, J.
HUGHES, E. J.	LAWSON, J. R.	MILES, C. H.	NUTTALL, R. H.
HUGHES, F. C.	LAWSON, H. R.	MILLAR, J. H.	OCKERBY, S.
HUGHES, H.	LEACH, J. E.	MILLER, J.	O'CONNELL, A.
HUGHES, T.	LEE, T.	MILNER, A.	O'CONNELL, T.
HULL, R. J.	LEES, F.	MILNER, G.	OGDEN, J.
HULME, P. J.	LEES, T.	MINTERN, S.	OGG, E.
HULSTON, J. M.	LEONARD, A. Y.	MITCHELL, J.	OLDFIELD, F.
HUMPHREYS, J. L.	LEONARD, J.	MOAN, D.	OLDHAM, J.
HUMPHREYS, W. H.	LEWIS, E. J.	MOLE, A.	OLDHAM, J. W.
HUNSTAN, J.	LEWIS, J.	MOLLOY, L.	OLDHAM, M.
HUNT, R.	LEWIS, J. W.	MOLONEY, G. H.	OLIVE, A.
HUTCHINSON, D.	LEWIS, T.	MONAGHAN, L.	O'NEILL, G.
HUTCHINSON, W. D.	LIGHTFOOT, E.	MONKS, J.	OPENSHAW, H.
HYNES, N.	LILLEY, E.	MONTAGUE, T.	OWEN, A.
HYNES, R.	LISCETT, W. B.	MOORE, W. (2).	OWEN, H. H.
JENKINS, J.	LISTER, G.	MORAN, J.	OWEN, W.
JEPSON, A.	LISTER, R.	MORGAN, W. H.	OWENS, E.
JEPSON, H.	LLOYD, E.	MORRELL, A.	PALMER, C.
JOHNSON, H.	LOCKLIN, J.	MORRIS, W. C. B.	PARKER, J. W.
JOHNSON, H.	LOFTHOUSE, W. F.	MORRISON, S.	PARKER, T.
JOHNSON, R. S.	LOMAS, JOHN.	MOSS, H.	PARKINSON, T.
JOHNSON, T.	LOMAX, W.	MUNRO, D. S.	PARTINGTON, H.
JOHNSON, W.	LONGDIN, S.	MUNTON, F.	PARTINGTON, S.
JOHNSON, W.	LORD, W.	MURPHY, H. M. J.	PATEFIELD, H.
JOHNSTONE, W. D.	LOVE, E. A.	MURPHY, J.	PATON, D.
JONES, B.	LUMSDEN, J. R.	MURRAY, W.	PAYTON, W.
JONES, E.	McCREAVEY, T.	McDARMAID, G.	PEARSON, J.
JONES, E.	MacALISTER, D.	McDERMOTT, W.	PEARSON, J.
JONES, J. O.	MACKAY, C. J.	McDONALD, J. W.	PEERS, S.
JONES, J.	MACKEN, W.	McDONALD, T.	PEGG, H.

MANCHESTER CORPORATION
ROLL OF HONOUR.—continued.

Tramways Department (Various).

PENDERGAST, W.	ROBINSON, A.	STAIT, H.	WALKER, A. S.
PENNY, W.	ROBINSON, J.	STATHAM, C. L.	WALKER, E.
PERKINS, G. E.	ROBINSON, J.	STATON, J. H.	WALKER, T.
PETFORD, G. R.	ROBSON, G. A.	STAVELEY, W. A.	WALKER, T.
PHILBIN, T.	ROGERS, J. W.	STEELE, J.	WALL, E.
PHILLIPS, J. D.	ROPER, J.	STEVENSON, H.	WALMSLEY, H.
PHILLIPS, J. W.	ROTHWELL, H.	STOCKTON, E. W.	WALSH, H.
PHILLIPS, W.	ROTHWELL, W.	STONEHEWER, A. H.	WALSH, J. H.
PICKERING, W.	ROWLAND, E.	STURLEY, W. J.	WALSH, M.
PICKFORD, S.	ROWLANDS, T.	STYLES, T.	WALTON, W.
PILKINGTON, H.	RUSHTON, C.	SULLIVAN, J.	WALTON, W.
PLAYFOOT, E. L.	RUTTER, J.	SUMMERSGILL, R. D.	WARBURTON, J.
POPPLEWELL, I.	RYAN, J.	SUTCLIFFE, C.	WARBURTON, T.
POPPLEWELL, S.	SALKELD, E.	SWAN, W.	WARBURTON, R. F.
PORTER, J. A.	SANDERSON, W.	SWINEY, J.	WARD, J.
PORTER, J. J.	SARGENT, A.	SWINSON, E. H.	WARD, M.
PORTER, W. R.	SAUNDERS, E.	SYKES, J.	WARD, M.
POTTS, J.	SAXON, H.	TALBOT, T. H.	WARD, T.
POWELL, C.	SCOTT, P.	TANSWELL, A. E.	WARDLEY, C.
POWELL, J.	SCHOFIELD, E.	TAYLOR, F.	WARE, F.
PRAILL, F.	SEDDON, E.	TAYLOR, F. T.	WARHURST, J.
PRICE, R. H.	SELVAGE, C. W.	TAYLOR, H.	WARING, T. H.
PRITCHARD, R.	SHARKEY, J.	TAYLOR, G. H.	WASHINGTON, E.
PRITCHARD, W. E.	SHAW, J. T.	TAYLOR, P. S.	WATERHOUSE, T.
PROCTOR, F.	SHAW, T. H.	TAYLOR, R. J.	WATSON, G.
PURSGLOVE, J. W.	SHAWCROSS, M.	TAYLOR, R.	WATSON, H.
QUINN, E. P.	SHELMERDINE, J.	TAYLOR, R. C.	WATSON, T.
RABY, J.	SHENTON, F. C.	TAYLOR, T.	WATTS, J.
RACE, J.	SHEPHERD, F.	THOMASON, E.	WEBB, H.
RADFORD, J. R.	SHERIDAN, P.	THOMPSON, J. A.	WEBB, H.
RANKIN, F.	SHROSBREE, H.	THOMPSON, R. S.	WEBSTER, T.
RAYNER, B. A.	SIDDALL, J. E.	THOMPSON, S.	WELCH, A.
REEVES, G.	SIDEBOTHAM, H.	THORLEY, A.	WEST, T.
REID, J.	SIDEBOTHAM, J. W.	THORNEYCROFT, T.	WESTON, H. T.
REILLY, P. T.	SIDEBOTTOM, A.	TICE, J. H.	WESTMACOTT, A.
REILLY, S. H.	SILLITOE, W.	TILSON, A.	WHARTON, W. G.
REILLY, W.	SIMPSON, C.	TINKER, F.	WHITE, H.
RELPH, W.	SIMPSON, J. E.	TIPPETTS, W.	WHITEHEAD, W.
REYNOLDS, J.	SIMPSON, T. E.	TIPPETTS, W. H.	WHITELEY, E.
REYNOLDS, P.	SKELHORN, H.	TOMLINSON, A. H.	WHITTAKER, A.
RHODES, A.	SLANEY, T.	TONGUE, E.	WHITTAKER, H.
RICHARDS, E. W.	SLICER, W. G.	TOWEY, G. A.	WILKINSON, A.
RICHARDSON, A.	SMITH, A.	TRY, E.	WILKINSON, F.
RICHARDSON, T.	SMITH, B. C.	TURNER, G.	WILKINSON, J. C.
RIDGWAY, J. G.	SMITH, J.	TURNER, H.	WILKINSON, J.
RIDYARD, J. W.	SMITH, J.	TYMAN, C. H.	WILLIAMS, A.
RIGBY, W.	SMITH, J.	UPTON, A.	WILLIAMS, C. R.
RIGNEY, J.	SMITH, J. H. C.	VALENTINE, E.	WILLAIMS, E.
RIGNEY, J.	SMITH, R.	VALENTINE, W.	WILLIAMS, H. V.
RILEY, J.	SMITH, R.	VESEY, P.	WILLIAMS, J.
RIMMER, W.	SMITH, W.	VOWERS, F.	WILLIAMS, J. H.
RIPPON, A.	SPENCER, E.	WAIN, R.	WILLIAMS, J.
ROBERTS, E. E.	SPURR, G. H.	WALKER, A.	WILLIAMSON, W.
ROBERTS, J.	STAHLER, J. A.	WALKER, A.	WILSON, R.

MANCHESTER CORPORATION

ROLL OF HONOUR.—continued.

Tramways Department (various).

WILSON, T.	WOODALL, T.	WORTH, R. A.	WRIGHT, C. J.
WINGRAVE, T.	WOODIWISS, A. E.	WORTHINGTON, A.	WRIGHT, S.
WOOD, J.	WOOLRIDGE, G.	WORTHINGTON, A.	WRIGHT, S.
WOOD, J. H.	WORSFOLD, W.	WORTHINGTON, J.	

Tramways (Miscellaneous).

BOARDMAN, J.	HERON, R.	NETTLETON, P.	SAUNDERS, G.
BOON, T.	HOLEBROOK, F.	O'HORA, T.	SIDEBOTHAM, J. T.
BOOTH, W.	HOWARTH, R.	REEVES, W.	SMITH, W.
BROMAGE, J.	INGLE, W.	RHODES, J. E.	SPENCER, C. H.
BUXTON, J. H.	JORDAN, G.	RIDGWAY, A.	SPROSON, W. J.
CHARNOCK, H.	KELLY, J. R.	RILEY, J. P.	TAYLOR, J. P.
CHORLEY, J. W.	KENNEDY, S.	ROBERTS, H.	TODKILL, H.
COATES, S.	LUDLOW, W.	ROBERTS, J.	WADE, I.
CRAGEN, A.	LORD, G. W.	ROBERTS, S. J. H.	WAKE, F.
EDWARDS, C.	METCALFE, R. L.	ROBERTS, T.	WHITWORTH, G. A.
FLOYD, A.	McCORMACK, J.	RODWELL, P. J.	WIGZELL, E.
GREGORY, W.	NALLY, A.	ROWDEN, G. E.	WILSON, R.

Treasurer's Department.

BAYLIS, H. W.	COBB, P.	MASON, W. E.	RICHARDSON, E. A.
BAXENDALE, A.	CARTLIDGE, V.	MORAN, E.	RIGBY, F.
BROOKES, H.	GARDNER, F.	MURGATROYD, G. C.	WARBURTON, H.
BOOTH, F. A.	GOODWIN, R. H.	SHAW, S.	WALKER, J.
BROWNRIDGE, F. W.	GREGORY, J.	SMITH, S.	WARWICK, H.
BRINDLE, A. E.	GRIFFITHS, J. A.	THATCHER, A.	WEBB, C. H.
BURTON, J. H.	LEA, A. E. (Discharged)	THOMPSON, H. W.	

Waterworks Department.

ANDREWS, J. E.	FISH, J.	LAW, D.	STROVER, G. W.
ASHTON, H.	FOOTE, F. A.	LAWRENCE, R.	SMITH, C. H.
BARBER, J. H.	FERGUSON, A. E.	LEIGH, R. A.	SMITH, W. G.
BALL, H. M.	GARLOCK, S.	LEWTHWAITE, H.	SCOTT, J. W.
BARROW, F.	GENDERS, W.	LONGWORTH, H.	SUTTON, F. W.
BALSHAW, E.	GILLETT, J. J.	MARSDEN, R.	TATTERSALL, J.
BATEY, J.	GRIMLEY, H.	MARSDEN, W. B.	THOMPSON, W.
BENN, T.	HALTON, J.	MILNER, F.	THOMAS, G.
BENTUM, T. W.	HARRISON, B.	MOORES, F.	THOMAS, J. E.
BELL, D. M.	HARRISON, W. A.	MULELLY, T. H.	THORBURN, G.
BEWLEY, J.	HARROP, F. J. A.	MURPHY, J.	TIMPERLEY, S.
BLOW, R.	HEAP, J. D. P.	McCULLOCH, E.	UNWIN, J.
BOOTH, P.	HENSHAW, W. H.	McCORMICK, S.	USHER, J.
BRERETON, E.	HILL, A.	McCRORY, J.	WAITE, F.
BROADY, Jr., G. H.	HORROCKS, E. H.	MUNRO, M. H.	WALKER, A. H.
BROADY, G. H.	HODGSON, W.	O'GARA, P.	WALKER, E. W.
BROWN, G. F.	HORNE, F.	PETTITT, E.	WARBURTON, A.
BUNTING, H.	JOHNSON, A. R.	POWELL, H. L.	WATERS, H. G.
CARLOS, H.	JONES, J.	POWELL, J.	WATSON, R.
COOKE, G. H.	JACKSON, J. W.	PREECE, E. J.	WILD, H.
CROSS, H. R.	JOHNS, E.	RIDINGS, J.	WILKINSON, H.
CROSSLAND, S.	JOHNSON, A.	ROBERTS, J. R.	WILKINSON, R. M.
CULBERT, W.	KEENAN, J.	SANDHAM, J.	WILLIAMS, H. G.
DANIELS, W. J.	KILNER, F. C.	SENIOR, W.	WILLIAMS, T. L.
DUDLEY, W. A.	KENNEDY, T.	SHAW, S. H.	WILLIAMSON, E.
DUTTON, J. C.	LASHMAR, G.	SHEPHERD, T.	WOOF, R.
EVANS, A.	LATER, J. O.	SPEAKMAN, W.	

Weights and Measures Department.

BRIEN, C. P. - - - -	Ryl. Naval Div. (Med. U.).	LOWDEN, C. - - - -	East Lancashire R.E.
DANBY, J. C. - - - -	9th Bt. Manchester Regt.	WALLACE, S. - - - -	20th Bt. Manchester Regt.
FIRTH, H. - - - -	7th Bt. Manchester Regt.		

ROLL OF HONOUR

Manchester Education Committee

Teachers serving with His Majesty's Forces:—

ALLAN, Capt. G. A.	7th Manchester Regiment.
ALLEN, ROBERT H.	18th Manchester Regiment.
ALLEN, WILFRID C.	Army Service Corps.
ALLISON, REGD. G.	A.S.C. (Mech. Transport).
ALLCOCK, FRANCIS	Royal Field Artillery.
ASHLEY, ERNEST	6th Manchester Regiment.
ATKINSON, HY. J.	18th Manchester Regiment.
BAGNALL, Lt. J. H.	7th Lancs. Fusiliers.
BALL, GEO. T.	Royal Army Medical Corps.
BARBER, CHARLES P.	16th Manchester Regiment.
BARDSLEY, JAS	Royal Army Medical Corps.
BATTERLEY, C. F. W.	Royal Garrison Artillery.
BEAL, CHAS. E.	Royal Flying Corps.
BEASTON, JOHN H.	Royal Army Medical Corps.
BEATTIE, FRANK	Royal Fusiliers
BEBBINGTON, B.	Royal Field Artillery.
BELL, 2nd-Lt. R.	7th Manchester Regiment.
BERRY, ARTHUR E.	16th Manchester Regiment.
BEVINGTON, H.	6th Manchester Regiment.
BOLTON, HARRY	8th Manchester Regiment.
BOODSON, DAVID	6th Manchester Regiment.
BOORMAN, SYDNEY	Royal Garrison Artillery.
BOWERS, ALFRED H.	18th Manchester Regiment.
BOWKETT, ERNEST C.	Royal Army Medical Corps.
BOWMAN, Lt. FRANK	Naval Instructor.
BRABIN, 2nd-Lt. H.	11th East Lancs.
BRADSHAW, HY. C.	19th Manchester Regiment.
BRADSHAW, 2nd-Lt. H.	Royal Garrison Artillery.
BRITTON, ALEC.	6th Manchester Regiment.
BROMLEY, 2nd-Lt. J. T.	3/7th Manchester Regim't.
BROOKES, F.	1/6th Manchester Regim't.
BROWN, WILLIAM S.	Royal Engineers.
BROWNJOHN, L. C.	Manchester Regiment.
BRYCE, JOHN M.	8th Royal Warwick Regt.
BUCKLAND, 2nd-Lt. A. E.	4th Royal Welsh Fusiliers.
BYRNE, JAMES F. (Died in hospital)	5th Irish Guards.
CANNAN, T. FRED	D. of Lancaster's Y'manry.
CHADWICK, GERALD	A.S.C. (Mech. Transport).
CHALLIS, VINCENT	Royal Army Medical Corps.
CHANDLER, F. E.	17th Manchester Regiment.
CHARLTON, JOHN	9th Royal Scots.
CHYNOWETH, A. S.	Royal Army Medical Corps.
CLAGUE, CLIFTON	8th Manchester Regiment.
CLARKE, 2nd-Lt. JOHN	14th Manchester Regiment.
CLARK, WILLIAM	14th Manchester Regiment.
COOKE, HERBERT S.	13th Ryl. Welsh Fusiliers.
COOKE, THOMAS	8th Manchester Regiment.
COOPER, WM.	Royal Garrison Artillery.
COTTERILL, ALBERT	16th Ryl. Welsh Fusiliers.
COWLEY, FRANK E.	Army Pay Corps.
CRESSWELL, FREDK.	18th Manchester Regiment.
CRETNEY, WM. G.	22nd Manchester Regiment.
CREWE, PHILIP (Killed in action)	6th Manchester Regiment.
CRICK, DOUGLAS W.	King's O. Ryl. Lancasters.
CROASDELL, A.	Royal Army Medical Corps.
CROFTS, WILLIAM	8th Manchester Regiment.
CROMPTON, WM. A.	7th Manchester Regiment.
CROSSLAND, L. W.	A.S.C. (Mech. Transport).
DANN, EDWARD J.	Royal Army Medical Corps.
DAWES, 2nd-Lt. C. E. (Killed in action)	1st Loyal N. Lancs. Regt.
DAWSON, 2nd-Lt. J.	8th Border Regiment.
DEIGHTON, H.	20th Royal Fusiliers.
DERBYSHIRE, JOHN	17th Manchester Regiment.
DIBB, Lt. H. W.	18th Lancashire Fusiliers.
DIBB, WILLIAM E.	Royal Army Medical Corps.
DICKIE, 2nd-Lt. A. C.	Manchester Univ. O.T.C.
DUDDLE, WILLIAM K.	6th Manchester Regiment.
DUROSE, RUPERT	8th Royal Warwick. Regt.

ROLL OF HONOUR—continued.

✱ ✱ ✱

Manchester Education Committee

Teachers serving with His Majesty's Forces :—

DYSON, JOHN	18th Manchester Regiment.
EGLIN, RICHARD	16th Ryl. Welsh Fusiliers.
ELLWOOD, A.	Royal Garrison Artillery.
EVANS, ERIC	Royal Engineers.
FEE, BERNARD W.	Royal Army Medical Corps.
FITTON, HARRY	Royal Army Medical Corps.
FOULDS, FRANK	A.S.C. (Motor Transport).
FREEMAN, PETER	Royal Garrison Artillery.
GAMBLE, Lt. C. W.	Royal Naval Air Service.
GEDDES, SAMUEL	Royal Army Medical Corps.
GRAVES, ALFRED	5th Hampshire Regiment.
GRIFFIN, LEOPOLD	6th Manchester Regiment.
HALLAS, JOSEPH	18th Manchester Regiment.
HALLWORTH, T.	Royal Field Artillery.
HANTON, 2nd-Lt. W. A.	Royal Engineers.
HARGREAVES, 2nd-Lt. CYRIL A.	6th Manchester Regiment.
HARPER, CHARLES	18th Manchester Regiment.
HAWORTH, CHARLES	3/2nd Royal Field Artill'y.
HAYES, FRANK	Royal Garrison Artillery.
HAYES, GEORGE W.	18th Manchester Regiment.
HETHERINGTON, W.	18th Manchester Regiment.
HILL, JOSEPH A.	6th Manchester Regiment.
HINDE, GEO. H.	Royal Fusiliers.
HOLDEN, 2nd-Lt. HENRY C. K.	8th Cheshire Regiment.
HOLLAND, 2nd-Lt. A.	King's O. Ryl. Lancasters.
HOPKINS, WM. G.	Royal Army Medical Corps.
HORSFALL, GILBERT	Army Service Corps.
HOYLE, Lt. BERTRAM	R.N.V.R.
HUNT, FRED	20th Manchester Regiment.
JAUNCEY, JAMES	Royal Army Medical Corps.
JONES, CHARLES F.	Royal Army Medical Corps.
JONES, FRANCIS	Royal Engineers.
JONES, JOHN	Royal Army Medical Corps.
JONES, JOSEPH	Royal Army Medical Corps.
JONES, WM. A.	
JOYCE, EDWARD	19th Manchester Regiment.
JOYNSON, WALTER	4th Manchester Regiment.
KEARNEY, 2nd-Lt. B.	3/5th Loyal North Lancs.
KELBRICK, T. V.	Royal Army Medical Corps.
KEMP, WILLIAM	Army Service Corps.
KITTO, THOMAS E.	Royal Engineers.
LANCASTER, R. W.	Army Service Corps.
LAPES, 2nd-Lt. J. E.	17th Lancashire Fusiliers.
LATHAM, WM.	18th Manchester Regiment.
LAWSON, 2nd-Lt. W. D.	Royal Scots.
LEES, Eng. Lt. S.	H.M.S. "Victory," Portsmouth.
LEIGH, FRED	18th Manchester Regiment.
LEIGH, ROBERT	6th Manchester Regiment.
LITTLER, JOHN H.	Royal Garrison Artillery.
LOFTHOUSE, F.	18th Manchester Regiment.
LOWTHER, CARL	12th Manchester Regiment.
McCANN, THOMAS	17th Manchester Regiment.
McINTYRE, CHAS. C.	20th Royal Fusiliers.
McINTYRE, DANIEL	18th Manchester Regiment.
McIVER, JOHN	Royal Army Medical Corps.
McNAMARA, JOHN	18th Manchester Regiment.
MARSDEN, HY. L.	20th Royal Fusiliers.
MARSDEN, JOHN W.	16th London Regiment.
MARSHALL, HY.	Manchester Regiment.
MARSLAND, WM. L.	Royal Engineers.
MASON, JAMES G.	18th Manchester Regiment.
MASON, JOHN A.	King's O. Ryl. Lancs. Rgt.
MASON, JOSEPH G.	A.S.C. (Motor Transport).
MASON, RICHARD	8th Yorkshire Regiment.
MAUDE, GEORGE W.	20th Royal Fusiliers.
MAYCOCK, WM.	8th Yorkshire Regiment.
MELEM, ERNEST	18th Manchester Regiment.
METCALFE, F. E.	7th Manchester Regiment.
MILLNER, GEO. H.	East Lancs. R. Engineers.
MOON, 2nd-Lt. HY. J.	10th King's O.R. Lancs. R.
MOORE, FREDK. G.	Royal Scots.
MOSES, 2nd-Lt. B.	12th Manchester Regiment.
MOWLE, H. W.	2nd Life Guards.
NEILSON, THOMAS	16th Ryl. Welsh Fusiliers.
NESBITT, GEORGE K.	Royal Army Medical Corps.
NUTTALL, JOS. W.	Royal Army Medical Corps.
OGDEN, 2nd-Lt. GRENVILLE W. E.	12th Lancs. Fusiliers.
ORMEROD, JAMES	18th Manchester Regiment.
OWEN, JOHN L.	1st C. of London Sanit'y C.
PARRY, EDWARD R.	Royal Scots.
PAYNE, JOHN	18th Manchester Regiment.
PEAKE, WM. E.	Royal Garrison Artillery.
PEARSON, JAMES T.	18th Manchester Regiment.
PHIBBS, ROBERT	Royal Army Medical Corps.
PICKUP, HERBERT	Royal Fusiliers.
PLATTS, ERIC	Royal Garrison Artillery.
QUINN, L. T.	Royal Army Medical Corps.
RAVENSCROFT, S.	16th Manchester Regiment.
REDFERN, ROBERT	Royal Army Medical Corps.
REDFERN, THOMAS	18th Manchester Regiment.
RENSHAW, CHAS. S.	6th Manchester Regiment.
RILEY, ALFRED	Royal Fusiliers.
ROBERTS, HAROLD	Royal Fusiliers.
ROBERTS, JAS. W.	Royal Army Medical Corps.

ROLL OF HONOUR—*continued.*

✱ ✱ ✱

Manchester Education Committee

Teachers serving with His Majesty's Forces :—

ROBERTS, MOSES	Royal Engineers.
ROBINSON, E. H.	Army Service Corps (M.T.).
ROLLINSON, FREDK.	Royal Engineers.
ROSCOE, ERNEST	Royal Engineers.
SCULLY, BERNARD F.	Royal Munster Fusiliers.
SHARP, PHILIP	18th Manchester Regiment.
SHATWELL, Lt. HUGH G.	9th Manchester Regiment.
SHAWCROSS, W.	6th Manchester Regiment.
SIMPSON, HERBERT	Royal Garrison Artillery.
SIMPSON, ROBERT	14th Manchester Regiment.
SINNATT, Capt. & Adj. FRANK S.	Manchester Univ. O.T.C.
SMITH, ALBERT E.	Royal Garrison Artillery.
SMITH, Lt. ALBERT G.	1st Lancashire Fusiliers.
SMITH, ERNEST	16th Manchester Regiment
SMITH, ROBERT F.	Royal Army Medical Corps.
SNAPE, HARRY	6th Manchester Regiment.
SOWERBUTTS, THOS.	Manchester Regiment.
SPEARS, STEPHEN	Royal Munster Fusiliers.
STAINER, 2nd-Lt. W. W.	3/4th Bt. R. Sussex Regt.
STANDEN, WM.	18th Manchester Regiment.
STANSFIELD, H.	Royal Army Medical Corps.
STOTT, JOHN E.	Royal Army Medical Corps.
STURLEY, THOS. R.	20th Royal Fusiliers.
STUTON, HARRY T.	Royal Army Medical Corps.
SUMMERSGILL, J.	Earl of Chester's Yeom'y.
TATTERSALL, 2nd-Lt. HAROLD N.	14th Manchester Regiment.
TAYLFORTH, WM. (Killed in action.)	6th Manchester Regiment.
TAYLOR, JOHN	Royal Welsh Fusiliers.
TAYLOR, RICHARD A.	22nd Manchester Regiment.
TAYLOR, WM. E.	8th Durham Light Inf't'y.
THOMAS, R. G.	Royal Army Medical Corps.
THORPE, R. O. V.	21st Royal Fusiliers.
THRUTCHLEY, J. G. R.	Royal Fusiliers.
TIMMS, W. JOS.	Royal Irish Fusiliers.
TODD, HOWARD C.	18th Manchester Regiment.
TRAVERS, GUSTAVE	18th Manchester Regiment.
TURNER, FREDK. H.	16th Manchester Regiment.
TURNER, JOSEPH	21st Manchester Regiment.
UNDERWOOD, P. A.	18th Manchester Regiment.
UPTON, JOSEPH S.	18th Manchester Regiment.
VALENTINE, C. K. (Killed in action.)	6th Manchester Regiment.
VERNON, NORMAN	King's Liverpool Regim't.
WALKER, SILVESTER	25th C. of London Cyc. R.
WASHINGTON, S. B.	A.S.C. (Mech. Transport).
WATSON, EDWIN	Army Service Corps.
WATSON, JOHN	King's Liverpool Regt.
WATSON, JOHN K.	Royal Garrison Artillery.
WHEALING, DANIEL	7th Manchester Regiment.
WHITTAKER, GEO.	6th Manchester Regiment.
WHITTAKER, T. W.	Royal Army Medical Corps.
WHITTINGHAM, S. H. B.	18th Manchester Regiment.
WIGGINS, RALPH	18th Manchester Regiment.
WILCOCK, H. A.	Royal Army Medical Corps.
WILCOCK, JOS. E.	Army Pay Corps.
WILLIAMS, F. J.	Royal Engineers.
WILLIAMS, R. H.	18th Manchester Regiment.
WILLOTT, HAROLD	20th Royal Fusiliers.
WILSON, GEO. T.	6th Manchester Regiment.
WILSON, 2nd-Lt. S. P.	10th South Lancs. Regt.
WOMACK, FRED W.	Royal Engineers.
WOOD, CLEMENT P.	King's Royal Rifles.
WOODS, GEORGE	21st Manchester Regiment.
WOODHOUSE, 2nd-Lt. MARCUS L.	13th Manchester Regiment.
WORSLEY, ALBERT	Royal Army Medical Corps.

The following Women Teachers have been granted leave of absence and are rendering full time service in Red Cross Hospitals :—

ALTMAN, FLORENCE.	BLOOR, LILIAN.	COX, GRACE E.	PARKER, MABEL.
ARMSTRONG, ALICE.	BOTHAM, M. A.	DYKES, MILLICENT.	SHEPHERD, AMY I.
*BAILEY, DOROTHY.	COX, AMELIA E.	INGRAM, GERTRUDE.	TINKER, NELLIE.

*Returned to school duty.

List of Employees (other than Teachers) serving with the Colours :—

ACTON, HARRY A.	8th Manchester Regiment.	AUSTIN, J. ALEX.	7th Manchester Regiment.
ALEXANDER, J. T.	Royal Army Medical Corps.	AYRES, ERNEST	Manchester Regiment.
ATKINSON, Lt. Dr. R. A. H.	Royal Army Medical Corps.	BAILEY, JAMES W.	Grenadier Guards.
		BAKER, ALBERT J.	South Lancs. Fusiliers.

ROLL OF HONOUR—continued.

* * *

Manchester Education Committee

List of Employees (other than Teachers) serving with the Colours:—

BALLANCE, JOHN	2nd Manchester Regiment.
BATES, JOHN H.	16th Manchester Regiment.
BRERETON, GEORGE	H.M.S. Terrible.
BROUGHTON, Lt. HY.	Royal Army Medical Corps.
BROUGHTON, JOHN	5th Manchester Regiment.
BREWER, ALFRED W.	23rd Manchester Regiment.
BROWN, GEORGE W.	Royal Horse Artillery.
BUCKLEY, M. J.	9th Manchester Regiment.
BROWN, JOHN T.	A.S.C. (Mech. Transport).
BUTTERWORTH, J. A.	6th Manchester Regiment.
CAMPBELL, WM.	7th Manchester Regiment.
CARRIER, WM. E.	H.M.S. "Kent."
CAULFIELD, JOSEPH	A.S.C. (Mech. Transport).
CLARKE, J. ERNEST	King's O. Scottish Bords.
CLIFFE, EDWARD S.	National Reserve.
CLOWES, SAMUEL	Royal Field Artillery.
COLLINS, JAMES	Royal Field Artillery.
COWSILL, JAS. H.	Royal Engineers.
COX, FREDERICK	Royal Marines.
CRAVEN, FRED	7th Manchester Regiment.
CRITCHLOW, G. H.	Royal Marines.
CRITCHLOW, JOHN	18th Manchester Regiment.
CRYNE, OWEN	King's Royal Rifles.
DAVIES, GEORGE	King's Shropshire Lt. Inf.
DAVIES, PETER	7th Lancashire Fusiliers.
DEAKIN, WALTER	East Lancs. R. Engineers.
DEAN, HARRY	7th Manchester Regiment.
DEARNALLEY, W.	Oxford and Bucks. Lt. Inf.
DEWHURST, T.	4th Manchester Regiment.
(Died of wounds.)	
EDWARDS, FRANK	7th Manchester Regiment.
ELLERY, FREDK. A.	6th Manchester Regiment.
ENNIS, JOHN	Royal Field Artillery.
FISHER, JOHN T.	Duke of Lancaster's Yeom.
FITZPATRICK, WM.	Royal Field Artillery.
FLEEK, JOHN	Royal Navy.
FORBES, JOHN	King's Royal Rifles.
FOSTER, FRANK A.	East Lancs. R. Engineers.
FOSTER, FREDK.	7th Manchester Regiment.
FOWLER, HENRY	23rd Manchester Regiment.
FREW, Lt. Dr. A. W.	Royal Army Medical Corps.
GARNER, WALTER F.	Royal Field Artillery.
GRAHAM, ROBT. C.	Royal Field Artillery.
GRANGE, WM. J.	7th Manchester Regiment.
(Killed in action.)	
GRIFFITHS, ALBERT	A.S.C. (Mech. Transport).
GRIFFITHS, JAMES H.	Royal Army Medical Corps.
GRIFFITHS, PERCY R.	A.S.C. (Mech. Transport).
GRIFFITHS, R. F.	6th Manchester Regiment.
HAIGH, JOHN H.	7th Manchester Regiment.
HALLWOOD, R.	18th Manchester Regiment.
HAMPSON, SAMUEL	Royal Engineers.
HAWLEY, GEO. A.	7th Manchester Regiment.
HEVICON, THOMAS	8th Lancashire Fusiliers.
(Died of dysentry.)	
HEYDON, JOSEPH	Loyal North. Lancs. Regt.
HILL, JAMES W.	Royal Garrison Artillery.
HITCHEN, EDWARD	King's Royal Rifles.
HOLLAND, JAMES	Royal Engineers.
HONEYBOURNE, Lt. Dr. WM.	Royal Army Medical Corps.
HUGHES, CECIL	20th Manchester Regiment.
HUGHES, FREDK.	8th Lancashire Fusiliers.
(Killed in action.)	
HULSE, Jnr., WM. H.	20th Royal Fusiliers.
JACKSON, WM.	8th Lancashire Fusiliers.
(Died of wounds.)	
JACKSON, CHAS. W.	Royal Army Medical Corps.
JOHNSON, ROLAND	Royal Army Medical Corps.
KELLETT, HARRY	7th Lancashire Fusiliers.
KENYON, CHAS. A.	Royal Navy.
KING, JOHN G.	National Reserve.
KIRBY, JOHN	Loyal North Lancs. Regt.
KIRTON, 2nd-Lt. G. G.	6th Cheshire Regiment.
KRUEGER, A. W.	Duke of Lancaster's Yeom.
LANGMEAD, G. H.	Royal Navy.
LEACH, Lt. Dr. A.	Royal Army Medical Corps.
LEARY, JOHN	Royal Field Artillery.
LEWIS, HAROLD	King's O. Ryl. Lancs. Rgt.
LYNCH, MICHAEL P.	Royal Horse Artillery.
McCORMACK, P.	A.S.C. (Mech. Transport).
MARSH, ALBERT	7th Manchester Regiment.
MATTHEWS, ROBERT	Royal Marines.
MILLNE, FREDK. A.	10th Lancashire Fusiliers.
MOSSMAN, HARRY	Royal Army Medical Corps.
NELSON, HORATIO	Royal Engineers.
NEWALL, WILLIAM	Cheshire Regiment.
NORTON, THOMAS	23rd Manchester Regiment.
PINNER, GEO. W.	4th Royal Scots.
PLATT, WILLIAM	King's O. Ryl. Lancs. Rgt.
POPPLEWELL, J. W.	7th Manchester Regiment.
POWELL, JAS. W.	7th Manchester Regiment.
PURDY, ERNEST H.	Naval Air Service.
REDDISH, WILLIAM	R.F.A., 2nd East Lancs.
REEVES, JOHN	Royal Engineers.
REYNOLDS, WM. A.	7th Oxon & Bucks Lt. Inf

ROLL OF HONOUR—continued.

* * *

Manchester Education Committee.

List of Employees (other than Teachers) serving with the Colours :—

ROBERTSHAW, R.	Royal Army Medical Corps.		TAYLOR, WM. H.	A.S.C. (Mech. Transport).
ROBINSON, ERNEST	King's Liverpool Regim't.		TEARE, JOHN A.	6th Manchester Regiment.
ROSCOE, SAMUEL	Royal Army Medical Corps.		THOMPSON, THOS. L.	6th Manchester Regiment.
ROTHWELL, T. W.	1st London Sanitary Corps.		THORPE, SAMUEL	King's O. Scottish Bords.
RUSSELL, JOHN W.	King's Own (R.L.).		TOMLINSON, Lt. J. H.	17th Manchester Regiment.
RYAN, PATRICK	20th Manchester Regiment.		TURNER, ARTHUR	Royal Army Medical Corps.
SAMMONS, JAS. D.	Royal Army Medical Corps.		WALTON, FRANK P.	Royal Army Medical Corps.
SELBY, HENRY	Rifle Brigade.		WARDEN, ROBERT	15th Lancashire Fusiliers.
SHORE, JOSEPH	South Lancashire Fusiliers.		WEBB, ARTHUR WM.	Lancers.
SIMPSON, ALEXR.	7th Manchester Regiment.		WHITE, F. H.	18th Manchester Regiment.
SLOAN, ROBERT	8th Lancashire Fusiliers.		WILLIAMS, T.	8th Lancashire Fusiliers.
SMITH, THOMAS	19th Manchester Regiment.		WILLMER, WILLIAM	Queen's Edinburgh Rifles.
SORO, WILLIAM	20th Royal Fusiliers.		WILSON, 2nd-Lt B.	12th Manchester Regiment.
STANFORD, JOS. A.	Royal Navy.		WINFIELD, EDWIN	20th Royal Fusiliers.
STAVELEY, FRANK	A.S.C. (Mech. Transport).		WHITE, THOS. H. J.	A.S.C. (Mech. Transport).
STRICKLAND, A.	Lancashire Fusiliers.		WOODHEAD, WM.	Royal Engineers.
SPARKES, ROBERT	Royal Marines.		WOOLFENDEN, F. W.	Royal Engineers, E.L.T.

The following members of the School Nursing Staff have been granted leave of absence and are now serving in Military and Red Cross Hospitals :—

ANDREW, MARION S.	DICKINSON, MARY E.	MARSDEN, LOIS.	SPROTT, MAUD H.
*BLOOR, LILIAN.	LEWIS, AGNES.	NODEN, NANCY.	

*Now returned to school duty.

ROLL OF HONOUR

The Manchester Grammar School

From School Staff

BROWN, M. W.
DANN, W. S.
FORSHAW, W. T.
FRY, C. E.
GRIFFITHS, D. H.
HAWCRIDGE, R. S.
LOB, H.
MAKIN, G.
MERRYWEATHER, C. W.
POTTS, C.
SADDLER, W.
WATERHOUSE, G.

Died (Pro Patria).

ALLEN, F.
BAILEY, G.
BARKER, W. R.
BAZLEY, W. N.
BICKERTON, N.
BINNS, C. F.
BURN, H.
BUTTERWORTH, EDWYN OFFER.
COOP, W.
CORY, BERNARD C.
DELEPINE, H. G. S.
DRESCHFELD, H. T.
EVANS, GEO.
EVANS, WM.
FOWKES, PERCY F.
HALL, S.
HAMER, FRANK.
HARRISON, FRANK
HELM, FRANK.
HEPBURN, A. J.
HICKSON, J. F.
HIGGINBOTTOM, J. B.
HOLDEN, A.
HOLDEN, G. A.
HOLDEN, N. V.
HOLME, Z.
HORRIDGE, R.
HOWARTH, N. D.
HUMPHREY, E. S.
JAGGER, W.
LODGE, G. A. B.
LOWERSON, H. B.
MOORHOUSE, R. C.
PILLING, STUART BOOTHE.
PORTER, T. C.
POWELL, ARTHUR E.
PRITCHARD, W. B.
ROBINSON, W. T.
ROBSON, J. M.
ROSE, H. J.
SCOTT, NORMAN S.
SPENCER, W. B. P.
STRINGER, GERALD M.
THEWLIS, HAROLD D.
TORKINGTON, RICHARD.
WALSH, E. A.
WIDDOWSON, A. J. H. R.
WOLF, PERCY.
WUNSCH, G. SANDYS.

Wounded.

ASHLEY, C. S.
BARNINGHAM, W.
BARRATT, H.
BEDSON, E. H.
BENTZ, F. COLIN.
BRAMWELL, T. R.
BREWIS, R. H.
BROADBENT, H. R.
BROADHURST, A. G. W.
BROCKLEHURST, E. W.
CLARK, G. N.
COLLIER, S.
GORDON, G.
HIGGINBOTTOM, E. E.
HIGHAM, C. E.
KAY, G. C.
LEACH, R. W.
LEEMING, J. A.
LINGS, H. C.
LOCKWOOD, G. S.
MAKINSON, H.
MAKINSON, J. R.
MANDLEY, H. C. F.
MAWSON, H. R.
MELLAND, F. B.
MOLESWORTH, W. N.
MOORHOUSE, A. E.
NORBURY, B.
OWEN, A. P.
ROBINSON, E.
SHELDON, R. M.
SPEAKMAN, HAROLD.
THOMPSON, J. W.
VOSE, J. H.
WALSH, FRANK.
WARING, J. L.
WHALLEY, C.
WILKINSON, ROY.
WILLCOCKS, W. H. E.
WILLIAMSON, C. H.
WILSON, A.

The Manchester Grammar School
ROLL OF HONOUR—Continued.

ABLE, A. W.
AINSCOW, H. W.
AINSWORTH, W. P.
AIREY, A. L.
ALBISTON, EDGAR.
ALCOCK, GEO.
ALDRED, A.
ALLEN, T. W.
ALLEN, V. M. B.
ALLTREE, E.
ANDERSON, F. McK.
ANDREW, G. P.
ANDREW, W.
APPLETON, A. H.
ARCHER, T. S.
ARMSTRONG, W.
ARMSTRONG, W. K.
ARNOLD, LESLIE.
ASHCROFT, K. H.
ASHLEY, C. S.
ASHLEY, W. S.
ASHTON, G.
ASHWORTH, R. S.
ASPINALL, IVOR.
ASPINAL, L.
ASTLE, H. C.
ATKIN, C. H.
ATKIN, S. E.
ATKINSON, C. S.
AUSTIN, F. E.
BACON, A. G.
BADDERLEY, REG.
BAGNALL, T.
BAILEY, A. J.
BAIRD, L. B.
BAIRD, S.
BALDWIN-WISEMAN, W. R.
BALL, A.
BALL, A. W.
BALL, C. H.
BALL, FRED.
BALMFORTH, A.
BALMFORTH, W.
BAKER, W. R.
BARBER, LEONARD H.
BARKER, C.
BARKER, GEOFFREY.
BARKER, J. H. J.
BARLOW, EDWIN.
BARNABY, W. R.
BARNES, E. G.
BARNES, J.
BARNES, W. T.
BARNETT, R. T.
BARNINGHAM, W.
BARRACLOUGH, J. A.
BARRATT, H.
BARRATT, R. F.
BARRETT, J. C.
BARRETT, W. H.
BARROW, E. I.
BATE, H.
BATE, N.

BATEMAN, G. A.
BATEMAN, R. W.
BATES, F.
BATT, C.
BATTERSBY, C. H.
BATTERSBY, D.
BAXTER, A. O.
BAXTER, C. H.
BEARD, F.
BEARN, F. A.
BEATTY, J.
BEATY, R.
BECKETT, F. P.
BEDALE, F. S.
BEDSON, E. H.
BEECH, J. L.
BEGGS, H.
BELL, H. S.
BENNETT, A. V.
BENNETT, H.
BENNETT, R. W.
BENTZ, F. C.
BENSON, H. T.
BENSON, W. J. P.
BERRY, T. A. S.
BERRY, W. J.
BESSO, M.
BESWICK, S.
BETTS, GEO.
BETTS, W.
BICKERTON, T. H.
BILLINGS, S.
BINNES, J.
BINNS, T. T.
BIRCHENALL, A. G.
BIRD, H. J. G.
BIRRELL, W.
BIRTILL, F. E.
BLACKLEDGE, R. D.
BLACKSTOCK, R.
BLAKELEY, A.
BLASON, C. H.
BLEAKLEY, A. D.
BLEAKLEY, E.
BLEARS, ERIC.
BLEARS, H. C.
BLINKHORN, F. B.
BLONDE, NEVILLE.
BLOOMER, G.
BLOOMER, W. C. K.
BLYTHE, PERCY A.
BOARDMAN, A. H.
BOARDMAN, GEORGE.
BONE, DENIS.
BOOTH, E.
BOOTH, HORACE.
BOOTH, S. B.
BOOTH, R.
BOOTH, W. O.
BOWES, J.
BOWES, ROY.
BOWDEN, T. H.
BOWMAN, C. H.
BOWMAN, F.

BOWSKILL, E.
BRABIN, E.
BRADBURY, G. S.
BRADLEY, R.
BRAMWELL, L. H.
BRAMWELL, T. R.
BRENTNALL, C. G.
BRENTNALL, E. S.
BREWERTON, R. H.
BREWIS, R. H.
BRIERLEY, E. E.
BRIERLEY, J. R.
BRIERLEY, W.
BRINE, H.
BRITCLIFFE, F.
BRITTON, A.
BROADBENT, C. J.
BROADBENT, HAROLD R.
BROADHURST, A. G. W.
BROADHURST, JOHN K.
BROADHURST, REX P.
BROCKLEHURST, E. W.
BROCKLEHURST, H. J.
BROOKE, S.
BROOME, J. C.
BROUGHTON, E. F.
BROWN, A. B.
BROWN, E. M.
BROWN, J.
BROWN, NORMAN.
BROWNING, W.
BROWNRIDGE, F. W.
BRYANT, F.
BUCKLE, J. F.
BUCKLEY, ALFRED.
BUCKLEY, C.
BUCKLEY, H. H.
BUCKLEY, J. C.
BURDITT, S. W.
BURMAN, A. P.
BURN, F. GREY.
BURN, HUGH
BURNS, C. F.
BURNS, G. C.
BURROWS, A. C.
BURROWS, H.
BURGESS, A.
BURGESS, H. R.
BUTLER, H.
BUTTERWORTH, H. L.
BUTTERFIELD, J. G.
CAIGER, F. G.
CALCUTT, C. P.
CALDWELL, N. J.
CALLISON, F. H.
CAMBELL, ARCH.
CAMBELL, C.
CAMPBELL, T. S.
CANNELL, F. E.
CAPSTICK, A. E.
CARMICHAEL, B. W.
CARMICHAEL, J. C.
CARSON, R. M.
CARVER, C.

CASSELL, M. C.
CAWE, C.
CHADWICK, GEORGE.
CHALLENOR, L. T.
CHAMBERS, LESTER C.
CHAMBLEY, R.
CHAPMAN, A.
CHAPMAN, C.
CHAPMAN, J.
CHATTERTON, W. O.
CHEETHAM, F. G.
CHEETHAM, G. R.
CHEETHAM, J. W.
CHISWELL, CLIFFORD H.
CHORLTON, A. F. T.
CLARK, A.
CLARK, G. N.
CLARK, H.
CLARKE, A.
CLARKE, L.
CLARKE, L. E.
CLARKE, S.
CLARKE, W. H.
CLARKE, W. M.
CLAYE, H. R.
CLAYTON, A. H.
CLAYTON, E.
CLAYTON, H. V.
CLEGG, A. M.
CLEGG, FRANK.
CLEGG, R.
CLEGG, S. J.
CLEMENT, L.
CLOUGH, E.
COACKLEY, J. R. V.
COBB, J. F.
COCKS, ROBT.
COHEN, D.
COHEN, S.
COLEBROOK, A. W.
COLEMAN, H. H.
COLLIER, E. D.
COLLIER, H. S.
COLLIER, S.
COLLYER, J. CLIEVELEY.
CONWAY, B. W.
COOKE, C. R.
COOMBER, H.
COOMBS, H. W.
COOMBS, J. R.
COOMBES, W. W.
COOP, H.
COOP, Rev. J. O.
COOPE, F. C.
COOPER, A. L.
COOPER, C. H.
COOPER, H.
COOPER, H. R.
CORE, D. E.
COWBURN, J. E.
COWEN, J.
COWEN, L. P. G.
COWIE, E. C.
COX, CLAUDE H.

The Manchester Grammar School
ROLL OF HONOUR—Continued.

COX, C. R.
CRASTON, F. M.
CRAVEN, E.
CRAWFORD, C.
CRAWSHAW, C. H.
CRAWSHAW, E.
CRAWSHAW, G.
CRAWSHAW, J. E.
CRESWELL, F. G.
CROKER, E.
CROOK, F. J. F.
CRONSHAW, A. E.
CROSLAND, J. C. H.
CROSSLAND, C. R.
CROSSLAND, N.
CROSSLEY, C.
CROSSLEY, H.
CROWE, F. G.
CRUMP, R. H.
CUERDEN, H. S.
CUNDALL, C. C.
CUNLIFFE, R. G.
DANZIGER, C. W. J.
DARLOW, J. J.
DAVENPORT, S. M.
DAVIES, E. A.
DAVIES-COLLEY, G. A.
DAVISON, N. H.
DEAN, H. R.
DEAN, W. H.
DEAN, W. P.
DEHN, H. G.
DEHN, R. M. R.
DEMEL, W. H.
DEMIERRE, H.
DESQUESNES, A.
DICKIE, H.
DIXEY, A. G. N.
DIXON, N. H.
DIXON, P.
DIXON, W. M.
DODSON, A.
DODSON, S. P.
DONALDSON, A.
DONALDSON, J.
DONNELLY, V.
DOOK, H.
DOOK, JOSEPH.
DOUGAL, D.
DOWNS, A.
DRAPER, J. E.
DUDDEN, A. C.
DUDDLE, W. K.
DUFFY, K.
DUGDALE, T. C.
DUGUID, L. N.
DUMVILLE, F.
EARLE, C. E.
EDGE, N. E.
EDWARDS, R. E.
EFFRON, G. H.
ELMORE, H.
ENGLAND, P. R.
ENTWISTLE, C. H.

ENTWISTLE, WM. C.
ENRIGHT, B.
EPSTEIN, B.
ERSKINE, J.
ESDAILE, G. A.
ESTILL, R. B.
ETCHELLS, HERBERT.
EVANS, ALFRED.
EVANS, HENRY.
EVANS, O. H.
EVANS, S. E.
EVERARD, R. W.
EVINGTON, C. B.
EWEN, GEORGE T.
FAIRLEY, W.
FARADAY, F. R.
FARRELL, C. F.
FARRELL, G. H.
FARROW, B.
FAULKNER, F.
FAULKNER, S.
FEARNHEAD, J. H.
FEENEY, F.
FENNEL, T. L.
FERNLEY, A. J. R.
FERNS, C. L.
FERNS, G. H.
FERGUSON, PHILIP.
FIDDES, R. S.
FINCKEN, V. S. T.
FISHER, K.
FITTON, R. A.
FLETCHER, F. S.
FLETCHER, HERMAN.
FLINN, N.
FORD A.
FOSTER, J. M.
FOSTER, REGINALD.
FOULDS, W. A.
FOULDS, W. G.
FOWKES, H. A.
FRANKENBERG, S.
FRANKENSTEIN, C.
FRANKLIN, C. L.
FRANKS, C. H.
FRESHWATER, A. J. C.
FROST, D.
FULLERTON, S. H.
FULTON, A.
FURNESS, A. F.
GADD, FREDK. G.
GANDY, F.
GANDY, L.
GARDNER, E. W. L.
GARNER, ARTHUR.
GARNER, LEO.
GARNER, W.
GATENBY, J.
GAYE, H. W.
GEORGE, A. H.
GEORGE, G. B.
GEORGE, P. M.
GEORGE, W. M.
GILES, A. E.

GLASS, L.
GLEDHILL, J. J.
GOLDSCHMIDT, C.
GOLDSELLER, L. D.
GOODE, R. E. D. P.
GOODMAN, G. D.
GOODWIN, H. L.
GOODWIN, H. S.
GOMERSALL, W. E.
GORDON, G.
GORDON, H.
GOUGH, J. S.
GOUGH, P. G.
GOWLAND, G. H.
GRAHAM, A.
GRAHAM, H.
GRAHAM, R. K.
GRANT, R. W.
GRAY, P.
GREEN, L.
GREENHALGH, F.
GREENWOOD, D. H.
GRESHAM, T. B.
GREY, E.
GRIBBIN, P. E.
GRIMSHAW, —.
GRIMSHAW, C.
GRIMSHAW, T.
GROVES, E.
GUISE, A. L.
HACKER, R. V.
HADFIELD, J. R.
HALL, B. C.
HALL, N.
HALL, W. COMPTON.
HALLATT, W. E.
HALLIDAY, G. A.
HAMLETT, W. A.
HAMER, H. B.
HAMER, S.
HAMPSON, EDGAR.
HANCOCK, J. A.
HANKINSON, R. H.
HANKINSON, W. C.
HARDY, L.
HARGREAVES, A. B.
HARDMAN, S. W.
HARREY, C. O.
HARRISON, E. Y.
HARRISON, F. E.
HARRISON, L. A.
HARRISON, P. A.
HARROP, R.
HARTSHORN, E. P.
HARTLEY, B. E.
HARTLEY, H.
HARVEY, G. M.
HASTINGS, J. L.
HAWKINS, G.
HAWKINS, P.
HAWKINS, W. P.
HAWORTH, E.
HAWORTH, G.
HAY, ATHOL J.

HAY, F.
HAY, T. P.
HAYDEN, J. S.
HAYHURST, W. L.
HEAD, JOHN.
HEADEACH, C. P.
HEALD, G. Y.
HEANEY, J.
HEAPE, E. A.
HEARN, J. R.
HEATHCOTE-HACKER, R.
HEBB, M. H. S.
HEIGHWAY, B. L.
HELSDON, W. G.
HENRIQUES, E. C. Q.
HENSHALL, C.
HEPWORTH, C. R.
HERTZ, G. B.
HERFORD, R. H.
HERFORD, S. W.
HESKETH, H. R.
HEWART, G. M.
HEWITT, B.
HEWITT, C.
HEYWOOD, G. BASIL.
HIBBERT, A.
HICKS, E. T.
HICKSON, C. G.
HIGGINBOTTOM, E. E.
HIGGINGBOTTOM, F.
HIGGINBOTTOM, G. L.
HIGHAM, C. E.
HIGHAM, H. W.
HIGSON, H. W.
HIGSON, R. H.
HIGSON, R. M.
HILL, R.
HILL, T. E.
HILL, W. W.
HINCHCLIFFE, G. N.
HIND, R. B.
HISLOP, J. A.
HITCHENS, J. H.
HODGSON-JONES, D. S.
HODGSON, F.
HOFFERT, W. H.
HOLDEN, A. H.
HOLDEN, E. AIRLIE.
HOLDEN, G. G.
HOLDEN, J. R.
HOLDEN, SIMEON.
HOLDEN, R. B.
HOLFORD, G. F.
HOLLAND, H. R.
HOLME, L.
HOLMES, C. L.
HOLMES, H.
HOLMES, H. W.
HOLMES, J.
HOLMES, N. B.
HOLMES, R. C.
HOLMES, Z.
HOLT, C.
HOLT, E.

The Manchester Grammar School
ROLL OF HONOUR—Continued.

HOLT, L.
HORTON, H.
HOTSON, S.
HOUGH, GEORGE.
HOUGHTON, J. R.
HOWARD, C. M.
HOWARD, D.
HOWARD, L. M.
HOWARTH, CHAS.
HOWARTH, D.
HOWARTH, F.
HOWARTH, GEO.
HOWARTH, G. D.
HOWARTH, T. E.
HOWE, H.
HUDDLESTON, L. F.
HUDSON, JAS.
HULME, EDWARD.
HULME, H.
HUNT, NORMAN.
HUNT, W. M.
HUNTER, F. R.
HUNTER, G. M.
HUNTER, J. K.
HYDE, EDWARD.
HYMAN, S. N.
INGHAM, J. S.
INNES, W. R.
IRELAND, A.
IVERS, C.
JACKSON, A. E.
JACKSON, F. D.
JACKSON, R. H.
JACKSON, W.
JACKLIN, A. H.
JARDINE, A. B.
JEFFERSON, J. C.
JENNISON, HUBERT.
JENNISON, R.
JEPSON, T. B.
JOHNSON, A. B.
JOHNSON, HAROLD F.
JOHNSON, H. H.
JOHNSON, J. M. O.
JOHNSON, T. G.
JOHNSTON, J. E.
JOHNSTON, W. H.
JOHNSTONE, J. S.
JONES, E. L.
JONES, F. W.
JONES, L. T.
JONES, R. E.
JONES, W. R.
KAY, E. C.
KAY, G. C.
KAY, H. D.
KAY, H. N.
KAY, M. A.
KAY, T. P.
KAY, W.
KEIGHLEY, P. L.
KELLY, A. J.
KELLY, N.
KEMPTON, J.

KERSHAW, P.
KERSHAW, S. S.
KING, J. H.
KIRK, ALLAN.
KIRKMAN, R. W.
KOCH, C. N. G.
KOHAN, C. M.
KNIGHT, P. C.
KNIGHT, W.
KNIVETON, C.
KNUDSON, O. J.
LAING, H.
LAING, W.
LAMB, A. F. T.
LAMB, E. H.
LAMB, S. H.
LANDLESS, C.
LANDLESS, G.
LANGTON, D. E.
LANGTON, R.
LASKI, NEVILLE.
LATIMER, F.
LAWSON, R. P.
LAWTON, R. A.
LEACH, G. B.
LEACH, R. W.
LEACH, W. R.
LEBELL, F. B.
LEECH, E. BOSDIN.
LEEMING, J. A.
LEEVES, A. H.
LEEVES, F. H.
LEIGH, H.
LEIGH, J. P.
LEIGHTON, G.
LEVI, A.
LEVY, R.
LIGHTFOOT, C. E.
LIGHTFOOT, H. B.
LILLIE, W. H.
LINDSELL, W. F.
LINGARD, W.
LINGS, H. C.
LISBONA, N.
LITCHFIELD, C.
LITTLEWOOD, F. W.
LLOYD JONES, P. A.
LOCKWOOD, E.
LOCKWOOD, G. S.
LODGE, K. A.
LODGE, R. N.
LONG, F. S.
LONGDIN, H. W.
LONSDALE, H.
LORD, E. B.
LORD, G. A.
LORDON, B. de.
LOVE, A. S.
LOVETT, G. C.
LOWE, G.
LOWE, W. H.
LUCAS, R.
LUCAS, W.
LYE, G.

MACARBORSKI, A.
MACDONALD, W. K.
MACKAY, R. H.
McBEATH, J. G.
McCABE, S. T.
McCLELLAND, H.
McGOWAN, A. G.
McGRATH, A.
McINTYRE, P. S.
McKILLOP, DOUGLAS.
McLEOD, K.
McMILLAN, H.
McMILLAN, S.
MacGREGOR, AMYAS.
MACKAY, A. M.
MACKENZIE, G. O.
MacLEOD, A. G.
MAKINSON, A. L.
MAKINSON, H.
MAKINSON, J. R.
MANDLEY, H. C. F.
MARKS, G. C.
MARLAND, HAROLD.
MARLAND, ROSCOE.
MARRS, F. W.
MARRS, R.
MARSH, A. J.
MARSHALL, C. B.
MARSHALL, J.
MARSDEN, R. W.
MARTIN, E. J.
MARTIN, H. R.
MARTIN, J. W.
MASON, F.
MASON, J. F.
MASSEY, H.
MASTERSON, E. C.
MATTHEWS, E.
MATTHEWS, F. J.
MAWSON, H. R.
MAXWELL, JAMES.
MAYCOCK, C. E.
MAYOH, S.
MEAD, A. de C.
MEAD, B. C.
MEADOWS, H.
MEAKIN, J. J.
MEALS, J. R.
MEGSON, A. E.
MELLAND, C. H.
MELLAND, F. B.
MELLOR, G. M.
METCALFE, H. R.
MICHAELIS, EDGAR.
MILBOURNE, L.
MILBOURNE, PHILIP.
MILLER, J. A.
MILNER, CYRIL W.
MILNES, F. W.
MITTON, H. M.
MOODIE, A.
MOORE, H.
MOORES, D.
MOORES, H. V.

MOORHOUSE, A. E.
MORING, F. H.
MORLAND, H.
MORRISON, J. R.
MORITZ, M.
MORTON, F.
MORTON, J.
MOSS, BEN.
MOSS, CHAS.
MOUET, W.
MOULD, G.
MUGGLETON, T. C.
MUMFORD, E. M.
MUMFORD, P. B.
MUIRHEAD, J. W.
MUTCH, C. H.
MYCOCK, E.
MYERS, J. WHEATLEY.
MYERS, W.
NABB, G. W.
NAYLOR, C.
NAYLOR, S.
NEAVE, E. M.
NELSON, L.
NEWELL, H. W.
NEWELL, L. E.
NEWELL, M. B.
NEWELL, R. L.
NEWNES, J.
NEWSOME, E.
NEWTON, C. E.
NICHOLS, A.
NICHOLS, H.
NICHOLSON, R. B.
NICKERSON, W. H. S.
NICKSON, J. F.
NICOLSON, M. A.
NIGHTINGALE, R. J.
NOALL, W. PAYNTER.
NORBURY, B.
NORCROSS, A.
NORRIS, E. B.
NORTHCOTE, T. V.
NORCLIFFE, A. C.
NOTON, H. H.
NUNN, E. C.
NUNWICK, A. C.
NUTCHEY, J. H.
NUTTALL, R.
O'CALLAGHAN, T.
O'GRADY, J. F.
O'MEARA, H.
O'SHEA, L. T.
OGDEN, J. S.
OGDEN, P. E.
OGLE, T. B.
OLDHAM, JNO.
OLDHAM, WILFRID.
OLIVER, J. M.
OLIVER, L. F.
OPPENHEIMER, F.
ORMEROD, F. C.
ORTON, D. C. L.
OSWIN, R. A.

The Manchester Grammar School
ROLL OF HONOUR—Continued.

OVEREND, F. L.
OWEN, A. P.
OWEN, W. H.
PALMER, B. H.
PALMER, R. W.
PARKER, W. H.
PARKINSON, J. N.
PATERSON, CLAUDE.
PATERSON, M. C.
PATERSON, M. W.
PATTEN, R. S.
PATTERSON, L. C.
PATTERSON, DOUGLAS.
PEACH, L. du G.
PEAKE, H. G.
PEARCE, R. N.
PEARSON, C. F.
PEARSON, S. O.
PELL-ILDERTON, PERCY.
PEMBERTON, E. V.
PEREZ, L.
PEWTRESS, A. W.
PICKERING, T. P.
PICKSTON, J.
PIGOTT, A. S.
PIKE, S. R.
PILCHER, A. J.
PILLING, E.
PILLING, F.
PINDER, G.
PINNINGTON, V.
PITT, B.
PLEVIN, W. H.
POGSON, J.
PORTER, ALEX.
PORTER, G. F.
PORTER, G. S.
PRESTWICH, E.
PRESTWICH, F. G.
PRESTWICH, H.
PRESTWICH, S.
PRICE, C. A.
PRICE, L. F. T.
PRINCE, G. F.
PRITCHARD, H. W.
PRITCHARD, S.
PROCTER, W.
PROUDFOOT, HAROLD.
PULMAN, C. W.
PURDY, E. C.
QUALYE, H. E.
QUINE, R. H.
QUINE, W. J. A.
QUINNEY, W. W.
RADCLIFFE, F.
RADCLIFFE, J.
RADCLIFFE, L.
RAINBOW, J.
RAMSBOTTOM, A.
RAMSKILL, J. K.
RANKIN, W. M.
RANKIN, S. W.
RATCLIFFE, ERNEST.
RAWLINSON, W. E.

REDFERN, A. R.
REEVE, A. J.
REEVE, P.
RENNARD, E. M.
REYNOLDS, A. V.
REYNOLDS, E. A. M.
REYNOLDS, H. J. B.
RHIND, E.
RHODES, BERTRAM.
RHODES, E.
RHODES, J. H.
RHODES, S.
RICHARDS, P. Q.
RICHARDSON, H. F.
RIDSDALE, W. K.
RIGHTON, J. R.
RIPPON, H. C.
RITCHIE, G. S.
RITSON, G.
ROBERTS, A.
ROBERTS, A. E.
ROBERTS, F. B.
ROBERTS, J. B.
ROBERTS, J. F.
ROBERTS, O. C.
ROBERTS, W.
ROBERTS, W. M.
ROBERTSON, ERIC.
ROBINSON, B. F.
ROBINSON, E. D.
ROBINSON, H. F.
ROBINSON, J. H.
ROBINSON, V. O.
ROBINSON, W.
ROFE, J. S.
ROGERSON, C. M.
ROGERSON, H.
ROSCOE, HAROLD.
ROSS, J. H.
ROTHBAND, B. H.
ROTHBAND, J. E.
ROTHWELL, S. B.
ROTHWELL, W. E.
ROWBOTHAM, J. C. S.
ROWBOTHAM, J. E.
ROWLINSON, J.
ROUNTREE, A. F.
ROYLE, R. H.
ROYLE, W. S.
RUSCOE, A. O.
RUSSELL, F. W.
RUSSELL, W. S.
SALMON, S.
SALOMON, S.
SAMUELS, L.
SAMUELS, S.
SAND, A.
SANDIFORD, C. R.
SANDIFORD, H. A.
SANKEY, S. H.
SAVAGE, R. H.
SAVILLE, A. C.
SAWER, E.
SAXON, C.

SCHOFIELD, J.
SCHOLFIELD, W. H. G.
SCHRODER, H.
SCIAMA, E. J.
SCOTT, F. G.
SCOTT, H. O.
SCOTT, J.
SCOTT, WM.
SCOTT-TAGGART, G.
SCHWEMMER, E. C.
SENIOR, J. W.
SEVER, JNO.
SEYMOUR, F.
SHAER, J.
SHAFFER, H.
SHALLCROSS, A.
SHANKS, E.
SHARP, H. H.
SHARP, W. D.
SHARRATT, H.
SHARRATT, R. W.
SHARRATT, W.
SHAW, A. H.
SHAW, N.
SHEARER, W. D.
SHEARER, W. M.
SHELDON, HAROLD.
SHELDON, R. M.
SHELDON, W. M. R.
SHEPHARD, F.
SHEPHARD, H. H.
SHERMAN, T. F.
SHREWSBURY, C. B.
SIMONS, GEO. DIGBY.
SIMPSON, D. C.
SINGLETON, F. C.
SINGLE, GEO.
SKINNER, A. L.
SKINNER, G. S.
SKINNER, J. M.
SLACK, GEO. WILFRED.
SLATER, F. C.
SLATER, J. H.
SLOMAN, A. J.
SMALLMAN, A. B.
SMITH, C. W.
SMITH, D. T.
SMITH, E. M.
SMITH, G. H.
SMITH, H. J.
SMITH, H. M.
SMITH, J. B.
SMITH, J. D.
SMITH, LEO.
SMITH, L. S.
SMITH, N. A.
SMITH, STANLEY.
SMITH, S. M.
SMITH, T. B.
SMITHARD, W. R. N.
SMYLIE, G. F.
SMYLIE, J. S.
SNAPE, A. E.
SPEAKMAN, H. C.

SPENCER, E.
SPILLER, P.
STANIFORTH, A.
STATHAM, A. J.
STATHAM, R. L.
START, S. P.
STEAD, G. H.
STEELE, L. E.
STEPHENS, A. M.
STEPHENSON, E. A.
STEPHENSON, C. G.
STEPHENSON, R. J.
STERN, HENRY S.
STEVENS, J. M.
STEWART, D.
STEWART, H. L. G.
STEWART, K. A.
STIEBEL, C. A.
STIEBEL, J. S.
STREET, F. G.
STOCK, R.
STOCKDALE, F.
STOCKS, A. V.
STODDARD, H.
STOKES, E.
STOKOE, H. N.
STOKOE, J. E.
STONE, G. K.
STONEHEWER, S.
STONEHOUSE, D.
STOTT, C.
STOTT, F.
STOTT, J. A.
STOTT, T. M.
STOTT, WALTER.
STRETCH, W. K.
STUART, F.
STUTTARD, M. E.
SUTCLIFFE, J. A.
SUTCLIFFE, NORMAN W.
SUTHERLAND, W. G.
SUTHERLAND, N.
SWAIN, W. G.
SWALE, ARTHUR T.
SWALE, F. E.
SWALE, J.
SWALE, W. M.
SWALES, W. A.
SWALLOW, L. J.
SWINDELLS, F. A.
SWINBURNE, A. T.
TABB, P.
TABERNER, T.
TALBOT, A. A.
TALBOT, A. E.
TANNER, H. P.
TATE, H. L.
TATTERSALL, NORMAN.
TATTERSALL, THOS.
TAYLOR, A. L.
TAYLOR, E. J. T.
TAYLOR, E. K.
TAYLOR, F. A.
TAYLOR, F. G.

The Manchester Grammar School
ROLL OF HONOUR—Continued.

TAYLOR, JAS.
TAYLOR, J. H.
TAYLOR, J. P.
TAYLOR, S. R.
TAYLOR, T. D.
TELFORD, E. D.
TEMPLAR, J. F. H.
TEMPEST, B.
THOM, S. D.
THOMSON, G. A.
THOMSON, H.
THOMPSON, A.
THOMPSON, C.
THOMPSON, F.
THOMPSON, F. R.
THOMPSON, G. M.
THOMPSON, H.
THOMPSON, H. L.
THOMPSON, J. W.
THOMPSON, W.
THORLEY, GORDON B.
THORNE, G. A. J.
THORNLEY, G. R.
THORP, C. E.
THORP, J.
THORP, L. T.
THORP, W. T.
THORPE, H.
TIMPERLEY, T. L.
TODD, C. GORDON.
TOMLINSON, F. K.
TOMLINSON, N.
TORDOFF, H. S.
TORRES, J. D.
TOWER, FRANK.
TRIPP, L. H.
TUNE, C. V.
TUNSTALL, G. S.
TURNBULL, J. A.
TURNER, A.
TURNER, A. N. T.
TURNER, C. G.
TURNER, E. J.
TURNER, H. E.
TURNER, NORMAN.
TURNER, S. A.

TURNER, W. B.
TWEEDALE, W. G.
TYSON, H. H.
USHER, H. YORKE.
VAUGHAN, A. N.
VERITY, R.
VOSE, J. H.
WADE, P. J.
WADSWORTH, G. W.
WAGSTAFF, J.
WALKER, C.
WALKER, F. J.
WALKER, J.
WALKER, J. T.
WALLACE, P. A.
WALMSLEY, C. A.
WALMSLEY, R.
WALMSLEY, S. H.
WALMSLEY, W. N.
WALSH, FRANK.
WALSH, J. N.
WALTER, E. R.
WALTON, C. H.
WALTON, H. W.
WALTON, R. W.
WALTON, W. L. P.
WARD, F. J.
WARD, G. F.
WARD, L.
WARD, R.
WARD, W.
WARD, W.
WARD-JONES, A. T.
WARDLE, R. A.
WAREHAM, G. S.
WARING, J. F.
WARING, J. L.
WATERHOUSE, HUGH.
WATSON, ARTHUR.
WATSON, C. JNO.
WATSON, J. M.
WATSON, W. BRADWELL.
WATTS, E.
WATTS, G. E.
WATTS, R.
WATTS, S.

WATTS, W. K.
WATTS, W. N.
WEAVER, J.
WEAVER, C. Y.
WEAVER, S. W.
WEBB, F. D.
WEBB, JOHN H.
WEBSTER, Dr. C. A.
WEBSTER, F.
WELLWOOD, T. G.
WELCH, L.
WELCH, O.
WEST, A.
WESTERBY, CAMPB. S.
WESTMACOTT, F. H.
WESTMACOTT, R.
WESTOBY, C. N.
WHALLEY, W. C.
WHEATLEY-JONES, F.
WHEATCROFT, F. W.
WHITAKER, FRANK.
WHITE, W.
WHITLEY, L. G. M.
WHITLEY, N. H. P.
WHITTAKER, D. G.
WHITWORTH, S.
WHITWORTH, T. S.
WIDDOWS, F. M.
WIGHTMAN, A. B.
WIGLEY, E.
WILCOX, E. H. W.
WILKS, S.
WILKIE, J.
WILKINSON, E.
WILKINSON, L.
WILKINSON, R.
WILKINSON, W. L. A.
WILLCOCKS, W. H. E.
WILLETT, A. J. C.
WILLIAM, C. à B.
WILLIAMS, A. S.
WILLIAMSON, A.
WILLIAMSON, C. H.
WILLIS, M. F.
WILSON, A.
WILSON, A. S.

WILSON, C. P.
WILSON, L. F.
WILSON, R. F.
WILSON, T.
WILSON, V. P.
WILSON, W.
WINTERBOTTOM, F. B.
WINTOUR, R.
WISEMAN, W. R.
WOLSTENHOLME, T. B.
WOLSTENHOLME, W. G.
WOMACK, JN. F. W.
WOOD, A. L.
WOOD, C. S.
WOOD, F. J.
WOOD, G. C.
WOOD, G. W.
WOOD, H.
WOOD, J. B.
WOOD, J. M.
WOOD, J. T.
WOOD, MORLEY.
WOOD, S.
WOOD, S. K.
WOODWARD, W.
WOOLLAM, S. E.
WORSLEY, D. R.
WORTHINGTON, J.
WRIGHT, C. H.
WRIGHT, E. M.
WRIGHT, F. H.
WRIGHT, V. C.
WRIGHT, W.
WUNSCH, A. S.
WUNSCH, THEODORE V.
WYKES, J. B.
WYLIE, D. S.
YARWOOD, W.
YATES, J. L.
YORETON, C. E.
YOUNG, A. B. FILSON.
YOUNG, J. E.
YOUNG, R. S.

ROLL OF HONOUR.

✱ ✱ ✱

Manchester Ship Canal

Alphabetical List of Employees who have Joined His Majesty's Forces.

✱ ✱ ✱

ADAMS, A.	ATKINSON, J.	BARNES, J. T.
ADAMS, W.	ATKINSON, J.	BARNETT, A.
ADAMSON, G.	ATLEY, W.	BARNETT, A. E.
ADSHEAD, A.	BACON, J. C.	BARNETT, F.
AINSWORTH, L.	BAGLEY, F.	BARNETT, J. D.
AINSWORTH, S.	BAGOT, J.	BARNETT, W.
ALDHOUSE, J. S.	BAILEY, A. E.	BARR, J.
ALDRIDGE, R.	BAILEY, B.	BARRATT, S.
ALLCOCK, G. W.	BAILEY, C.	BARRETT, C.
ALLCOCK, J.	BAILEY, G.	BARRETT, J.
ALLEN, J.	BAILEY, GEORGE.	BARRETT, T.
ALLEN, J. E.	*BAILEY, H.	BARROW, J.
ALMOND, D.	BAILEY, J. E.	BARRY, W.
AMBROSE, R.	BAILEY, R.	BARTER, F. E.
ANDERSON, T.	BAIN, J.	BARTON, W.
ANGELL, E.	BAINBRIDGE, H.	BASNETT, G.
ANKERS, R.	BAIN-WARDE, A. J.	BASNETT, H.
ANSELL, J.	BAKER, C.	BASNETT, S.
ANTHONY, R.	BAKER, C. W.	BATE, E.
APPLETON, W.	BAKER, JAMES.	BATE, J.
ARCH, H.	BAKER, JAMES.	BATE, R.
ARDREY, E.	BALE, H.	BATES, J.
ARIS, D.	BALL, H.	BATES, JAMES.
ARMISTEAD, J.	BARBER, H.	BATES, W. E.
ARMSTRONG, R. H.	BARBER, HENRY.	BATESON, T.
ARROWSMITH, J.	BARKER, G.	BAZLEY, J.
ASHCROFT, L.	BARLOW, A.	BEACH, J.
ASHLEY, J. T.	BARLOW, F.	BEALEY, F.
ASHWORTH, C. H.	BARLOW, G.	BEARD, J.
ASHWORTH, J. H.	BARLOW, H.	BEARDMORE, F.
ATHERTON, J.	BARLOW, S.	BEARDMORE, J.
ATHERTON, W.	BARNES, A.	BECKETT, T.
ATKINSON, G. M.	BARNES, C.	BEECH, A.

* Denotes killed.

NOVEMBER 24, 1915.

Manchester Ship Canal
ROLL OF HONOUR—continued.

BELL, J.	BOWLER, J.	BURKE, P.	CHADWICK, T.
BELL, J. H.	BOYERS, F.	BURKINSHAW, A.	CHARLESON, T.
BENBOW, E.	BOYERS, J.	BURNS, R.	CHARLESON, W.
BENNETT, C.	BOYLE, W.	BURNS, W.	CHARLESWORTH, N.
BENNETT, J.	BRACKENRIDGE, A. R.	BURROWS, F.	CHARLTON, T.
BENNETT, J. C.	BRADBURY, FRANK.	BURTON, J.	CHEETHAM, H.
BENSON, R. H.	BRADBURY, FRANK.	BURTON, W.	CHEETHAM, J. J.
BENT, J.	BRADBURY, FRED.	BUSHILL, G.	CHEETHAM, W.
BERISFORD, THOMAS.	BRADLEY, J.	BUTLER, W. G.	CHESHIRE, J.
BERISFORD, THOMAS.	BRADSHAW, A.	CAFFREY, R. E.	CLARE, C.
BERRY, E.	BRADSHAW, ARTHUR.	CAHILL, A.	CLARE, G.
BERRY, H.	BRADY, C. E.	CAHILL, D.	CLARE, S.
BESWICK, E.	BRADY, W.	CAHILL, P.	CLARKE, A. J.
BEVAN, J.	BRASSINGTON, T.	CALLAGHAN, J.	CLARKE, E.
BEVON, J. E.	BREEN, M.	CALVERT, B.	CLARKE, JOSEPH.
BIGNALL, I.	BRENNANN, W.	CAMPBELL, C. W.	CLARKE, J.
BILLINGTON, W.	BRERETON, G.	CAMPBELL, R. G.	CLARKE, JAMES.
BINFIELD, W. H.	BREWERTON, T.	CAULDWELL, J.	CLARKE, J.
BIRD, D.	BRIERLY, E.	CAPON, F. F.	CLARKE, N. V.
BIRD, W.	BRIERLY, W.	CARLON, J.	CLARKE, S.
BLACKHURST, E.	BRITT, R.	CARPENTER, J. E.	CLARKE, T. B.
BLAKE, A.	BROADHEAD, E.	CARRINGTON, E. D.	CLARKE, WALTER.
BLUCK, W.	BRODRICK, J.	CARROLL, P.	CLARKE, WILLIAM.
BLUNDELL, J. W.	BROOKS, J. H.	CARROLL, W.	CLARKSON, J. D.
BOARDMAN, C.	BROWN, A.	CARRUTHERS, G. H.	CLARKSON, R. W.
BOARDMAN, J. F.	BROWN, J.	CARSON, D.	CLARKSON, W. J.
BODEN, A.	BROWN, J. C.	CARTER, A.	CLIFTON, J. W.
BOLAND, J.	BROWN, J. E.	CARTER, F.	CLUCAS, J.
BOLD, R.	BROWN, J. J.	CARTER, R.	CLUCAS, N.
BOLLAND, C.	BROWN, J. S.	CARTER, T. W.	CLUTTON, H.
BOLTON, A. R.	BROWN, R. W.	*CAVANAGH, J.	CLUTTON, T.
BONNAR, R.	BROWN, SAMUEL.	CAWLEY, A.	COBURN, H.
BONNER, C.	BROWN, SAMUEL.	CAWLEY, T.	COCHRANE, A.
BOOTH, C.	BROWN, W.	CHADDERTON, A.	COCHRANE, D.
BOOTH, F.	BROWNE, A. D.	CHADWICK, J.	COFFEY, J. H.
BOOTH, J.	BRUCE, A.	CHADWICK, N.	COLCLOUGH, W.
BOOTH, JOSEPH	BRUCE, E.	CHADWICK, R.	COLEMAN, J.
BOOTH, J. W.	BRYAN, J.	CHADWICK, W.	COLES, J.
BORLE, L. A.	BRYCE, G.	CHADWICK, WILLIAM.	COLLIER, O. G.
BOSTOCK, R.	BULGER, T.	CHALLINDER, W.	COLLINGE, H. W.
BOSWELL, W. W.	BULL, J.	CHALLINOR, H.	COLLINGS, S. A.
BOWATER, W.	BURGESS, E.	CHAMBERLAIN, J.	COLLINGWOOD, A.
BOWE, J.	BURGESS, G.	CHAMBERS, C.	COLLINS, P.
BOWELL, C.	BURGESS, T.	CHANDLEY, B. J.	COLLINS, T. H.
BOWELL, J.	*BURGESS, W.	CHAPMAN, H.	COLLINSON, R.
BOWKER, F.	BURKE, J.	CHAPMAN, J.	COLLIS, E.

* Denotes killed.

Manchester Ship Canal
ROLL OF HONOUR—continued.

COLLIS, J. S.	CULSHAW, H.	DONLAN, P.	ELLIS, —
CONNELL, H.	CUNLIFFE, J.	DOOLAN, J.	ELLIS, C.
CONNOLLY, T.	CURRAN, F.	DOUGLAS, A.	ELLIS, J.
CONNOR, D.	CURRIE, W.	DOUGLAS, R.	ELLIS, J. A.
CONWAY, JOHN.	DAGGER, R.	DOWNES, S.	ELLIS, T.
CONWAY, JOHN.	DALE, J.	DOWNES, W.	ELLIS, W.
CONWAY, W.	DANKS, A.	DOWNIE, J.	ELLISON, J. E.
COOK, J.	DARSLEY C.	DOWNWARD, S.	ELSON, P.
COOK, F.	DARWELL, W.	DOYLE, J. R.	EMMS, A. W.
COOKE, G.	DAVENPORT, H.	DRAKE, F.	ENTWISTLE, C. V.
COOKE, H.	DAVIES, C.	DUFF, T.	ENTWISTLE, Wm.
COOKE, R.	DAVIES, C. W.	DUFFEY, T.	ETCHELLS, G.
COONEY, —	DAVIES, J.	DUFFICEY, S.	ETCHELLS, H.
COOPER, A.	DAVIES, J. W.	DUFFY, A.	EVANS, D.
COOPER, C.	DAVIES, W. A.	DUFFY, H.	EVANS, EDWIN.
COOPER, J.	DAVIES, W. H.	DUNBAVAND, E.	EVANS, ERNEST.
*CORCORAN, C.	DAWSON, THOMAS.	DUNCAN, A.	EVANS, ERNEST.
CORDERY, W. L.	DAWSON, THOMAS.	DUNCAN, J.	EVANS, H. W.
COSGROVE, T. P.	DEAN, A.	DUNN, J.	EVANS, J. M.
COSTER, G.	DEAN, J.	DUNN, J. J.	EVANS, T.
COUNSELL, W.	DEAN, P.	DUNN, RICHARD.	EVANS, W.
COWBURN, W.	DEEHAN, J.	DUNN, RICHARD.	EVANS, WILLIAM.
COX, E. L.	DELANEY, M.	DUNNING, G.	EVANS, WILLIAM.
COX, F.	DELVE, W.	DURKIN, J.	EVE, J.
COYNE, J.	†DERRY, W.	DURY, J. W.	FAHEY, M.
CRADDOCK, E.	DESFORGES, M.	DUTSON, W.	FAIRCLOUGH, R. W.
CRAIG, W.	DEWSNUP, FRANK.	DUTTON, T.	FARMER, A.
CRANE, A. W.	DEWSNUP, FRANK.	DWYER, P. A.	FARR, —
CRANFIELD, C.	DICKEN, C. E.	EARITH, A. W.	FARRAND, A.
CRANK, J.	DICKENSON, W.	EASDALE, R.	FARRELL, E.
CRAVEN, T.	DICKS, A.	EASTHORPE, A.	FARRELL H.
CRESSWELL, C.	DICKSON, F.	EASTON, F.	FARRELL, P. O.
*CRILLEY, H	DIDSBURY, G.	EASTUPP, E.	FARREN, F.
CRIMES, H.	DILLON, JAMES.	EDGE, D.	FARTHING, P.
CROFT, J.	DILLON, JAMES.	EDGE, F.	FAULKNER, B.
CROOK, D.	DIXON, H. V.	EDGE, H.	FAULKNER, G.
CROOKS, J.	DIXON, J.	EDWARDS, A.	FAULKNER S.
CROPPER, J.	DIXON, R.	EDWARDS, G.	FAWCETT, G. W.
CROSS, H.	DOBBS, F.	EDWARDS, J.	FEENEY, J.
CROSS, W.	DOBSON, T.	EDWARDS, L. E.	FEENEY, T.
CROSS, T. A.	DODD, W.	EDWARDS, T.	FENTON, S.
CROSSLEY, J.	DODD, W.H.	EDWARDS, W.	FEREDAY, T.
CROSSLEY, JOHN.	DODSON, M.	EGAN, T.	FERRIDAY, W.
CROSSMAN, J.	DOGGETT, F. J.	EGERTON, J. A.	FILKIN, J. W.
CROSTON, W.	DOIG, R.	ELGIN, C.	FILKIN, R.
CROWLEY, C.	DONE, R.	ELLINOR, J. C.	FINN, J. J.

* Denotes killed. † Denotes missing.

Manchester Ship Canal

ROLL OF HONOUR—continued.

FISHER, T.
FISHWICK, A.
FISHWICK, T.
FITTON, C.
FITZGERALD, D.
FLANNIGAN, J.
FLETCHER, F.
FLETCHER, J.
FLETCHER, R.
FLETCHER-EVANS, J. W.
FLINT, T.
FLITCROFT, J.
FLYNN, JOHN.
FLYNN, JOSEPH.
FOGG, W. E.
FORD, JAMES.
FORD, JOHN.
FORD, J. J.
FORD, THOMAS.
FORD, THOMAS.
FORDE, D.
FORWARD, W.
FOSTER, E. H.
FOSTER, J. M.
FOSTER, S.
FOULKES, J.
FOULKES, T.
FOXTON, H. D.
FOY, J.
FOY, T.
FRAZER, J. B.
FREER, P.
FREER, T.
FRIAR, G.
FROST, J.
FULLER, J. W.
GALLAGHER, J.
GARFORD, A.
GARFORD, F.
GARNER, T.
GARNER, W.
*GARRATT, J.
GATLEY, L. J.
GAUNT, C. H
GARVEY, J.

GEARY, G. J.
GERMAIN, J. T.
GIBBS, T. K.
GIBSON, H.
GIBSON, J. W.
GIBBINS, H.
GIBBONS, H.
GILL, M.
GILBERTS, J.
GILDEA, J.
GILDEA, J. F.
GILLASPY, H.
GINDER, A.
GINDER, ALBERT.
GLEAVE, J.
GLYN, J.
GLYNN, D.
GOODE, J. W.
GOODIER, S.
GOODIER, G.
GOODWIN, A.
GOODWIN, J. H.
GOODWIN, T. H.
GOONAN, M.
GORMAN, J.
GORTON, J.R.
GOUGH, W.
GOW, J.
GRADY, J. T.
GRAHAM, F.
GRAHAM, JOHN.
GRAHAM, JOHN.
GRAHAM, T.
GRANNELL, M.
GRAY, B.
GREAVES, —
GREEN, J. A.
GREEN, P.
GREEST, J. T.
GREENWOOD, W.
GREGSON, W.
GREGORY, C.
GREGORY, G.
GRESTY, J.
GREY, J.
GRINDROD, J.

GRIFFITHS, G. E.
GRIFFITHS, T.
GRIMSHAW, C. H.
GRINLEY, J.
GRINLEY, R.
GROGAN, M.
GROST, W.
GUIDER, J. W.
GUNN, G. W.
GUNN, J.
GUY, V.
GWYTHER, E.
HACKETT, T.
HAGUE, A.
HAGUE, J.
HAINSWORTH, H.
HALL, J.
HALL, P.
HALL, S.
HALL, T.
HALLIDAY, J. W.
HALLSWORTH, E.
HALLSWORTH, J. W
HAMER, A.
HAMER, J. R.
HAMILTON, G.
HAMMOND, J. E.
*HAMPSON, W.
HAMPSON, W. H.
HANCOCK, F.
HANDLEY, T.
HANLON, A.
HANNAN, D. J.
HANNAY, W.
HANSEN, —
HANSON, S.
HARCUP, F.
HARDMAN, J.
HARDMAN, JAMES.
HARDMAN, JOHN.
HARDY, R.
HARDY, G. R.
HARGREAVES, F.
HARLOCK, W.
HAROLD, J. E.
HAROLD, J. W.

HARPER, H.
HARPER, J.
HARPER, J. A.
HARRIS, J. E.
HARRIS, T.
HARRISON, F.
HARRISON, G. F.
HARRISON, J.
HARRISON, R. R.
HARRISON, W.
HART, W.
*HARVEY, G. H.
HASKELL, H. S.
HASLAM, H.
HATCLIFFE, W.
HAYDOCK, A.
HAYES, —
HAYES, H.
HAYES, J.
HAYES, JOHN.
HAYES, S.
HAYWARD, W.
HAYWARD, W. J.
HAZEL, G.
HEALEY, J. J.
HEALEY, R.
HEALEY, W.
HEANEY, B.
HEAP, H.
HEATHCOAT, D.
HEATHCOAT, W.
HEATON, JAMES.
HEATON, J.
HEDGECOCK, T.
HELPS, C.
HENDERSON, J.
HENSHALL, A. E.
HENSON, H.
HESK, R.
HEWITT, H.
HEWITT, J.
HEWITT, JAMES.
HEWITT, W. A.
HEYWOOD, W.
HEYWOOD, WILLIAM.
*HIBBERT, S. E.

* Denotes killed.

Manchester Ship Canal
ROLL OF HONOUR—continued.

HIBBERT, T.
HICK, J.
HIGGINS, C. E.
HIGNETT, G. H.
HIGSON, W.
HILL, E.
HINCHLIFFE, A.
HINDLE, W.
HIRST, W. W.
HOCTOR, J.
HODGSON, J.
HODGKINSON, F.
HODGKINSON, JOHN.
HODGKINSON, JOHN.
HODKINSON, G. R.
HOGAN, J.
HOGAN, T.
HOGG, J.
HOLBEN, J. H.
HOLDEN, J.
HOLLAND, A.
HOLLOWAY, A.
HOLLINGS, H.
HOLMES, JOHN.
HOLMES, JOHN.
HOLMES, T.
HOLT, J. P.
HOLT, T.
HOLT, T. W.
HOOLIGAN, M.
HOPE, A. E.
HOPLEY, C.
HOPLEY, J.
HOPWOOD, G.
HORSFIELD, T.
HORTON, G.
HOUGH, J.
*HOUGHTON, F.
HOUGHTON, S.
HOUGHTON, WALTER.
HOUGHTON, WM.
HOWARD, C. A.
HOWARD, W.
HOWARTH, C.
HOWARTH, E.
HOWARTH, F.
HOWARTH, G.
HOWARTH, J. R.
HOWARTH, W.
HOWE, J. T.
HOWLETT, H.
HOXWORTH, J.
HOXWORTH, R.
HOYLE, J. M.
HUBY, J. F.
HUDSON, A.
HUDSON, J.
HUGHES, A.
HUGHES, C.
HUGHES, CHARLES.
HUGHES, G.
HUGHES, H.
HUGHES, HUGH.
HUGHES, JAMES.
HUGHES, JOHN.
HUGHES, JOHN.
HUGHES, JOHN.
HUGHES, S.
HUGHES, T.
HUGHES, W.
HULME, J.
HULME, W. J.
HUMPHREYS, W.
HUMPHRIES, D.
HUNT, J. R.
HUNTER, R.
HURST, M.
HUSKIN, J.
HUTCHINSON, W.
HYDE, HARRY.
HYDE, HENRY.
HYDE, R.
HYDE, W.
ILLIDGE, J. H.
IRWIN, S.
JACKS, A.
JACKS, J.
JACKSON, H.
JACKSON, J.
JACKSON, J. J.
*JACKSON, J. T.
JACKSON, T.
JACKSON, THOMAS.
JACKSON, W.
JACKSON, WILLIAM.
JAMES, H.
JAMES, J.
JEFFERIES, W.
JEFFERS, P.
JEFFERSON, A.
JEFFREYS, W.
JEPSON, T.
JOHNSON, A.
JOHNSON, E.
JOHNSON, F.
JOHNSON, WILLIAM.
JOHNSON, W.
JOHNSON, W. E.
JOHNSON, W. M.
JOHNSTON, M.
JOHNSTONE, R.
JOHNSTONE-WALKER, J.
JOLLY, G. T.
JOLLY, W. H.
JONES, D. J.
JONES, D. W.
JONES, E. L.
JONES, FREDERICK.
JONES, FREDERICK.
JONES, G. V.
JONES, H.
JONES, JAMES.
JONES, JOHN.
JONES, JOHN.
JONES, JOSEPH.
JONES, J. F.
JONES, J. H.
JONES, J. R.
JONES, R.
JONES, R. R.
JONES, T.
JONES, W.
JONES, W.
JONES, WILLIAM.
JONES, W. H.
JONES, WM. HENRY.
JOYCE, W. H.
JOYNT, J. H.
JUDGE, P.
KEARNEY, R.
KEARON, P.
KEATING, M.
KEATING, V.
KEENAN, W.
KEILY, A. G.
KELLEY, E. J.
KELLY, E.
KELLY, J.
KELLY, P.
KELLY, T.
KELLY, T. J.
KENNEDY, J.
KENWRIGHT, B.
KENNY, R.
KETTLE, J.
KEYS, C.
KIGHT, D.
KILEY, P.
KING, J.
KING, T.
KINSEY, G.
KINSEY, J.
KORTENS, E.
KNOWLES, A.
KNOX, R.
LAING, J. W.
LALLY, J.
LALLY, W.
LAMB, J. W.
LAMBE, J.
LAMBE, W.
LAMBERT, J. H.
LANCASHIRE, J.
LANE, W.
LANGLEY, S.
LANGTREE, L.
LATHROPE, H.
LAWLEY, J.
LAWSON, D.
LEA, R.
LEAH, T.
LEATHERBARROW, T.
LEE, C.

* Denotes killed.

Manchester Ship Canal
ROLL OF HONOUR—continued.

*LEE, CHARLES.	McCAFFERTY, F. P.	MARSDEN, W.	MOORE, W.
LEE, H.	McCAFFERTY, P.	MARSH, T. A	MOORES, J. W.
LEE, J. W.	McCANN, J.	MARSH, J.	MORAN, JOHN.
LEE, W.	McCORMACK, —	MASON, H.	MORAN, JOHN.
LEECH, J.	McCORMICK, W. F.	MATHER, J. M.	†MORETON, B.
LEIGH, P.	McCREERY, J.	MATHEWS, E.	MORGAN, F.
LEMMON, M.	McCULLOUGH, G.	MATHEWS, J.	MORRIS, B. C.
LEONARD, J.	McCUNE, R.	MATHEWS, H.	MORRIS, E.
LEVER, G. W.	McDONALD, C.	MATTHEWS, F.	MORRIS, J.
LEWIS, G. L.	McDONALD, P.	MATTHEWS, F. J.	MORRIS, T.
LEWTAS, G.	McDONALD, J.	MATLEY, N. G.	MORRISEY, D.
LIGHTFOOT, E.	McDONNELL, J.	MATTRAVERS, —	MORROW, R. J.
LIGHTFOOT, J.	McDOUGALL, J.	MAUDESLEY, J.	MOSS, E.
LINCH, F. J.	McELROY, L.	MAXWELL, M.	MOSS, J. R.
LINES, J.	McENTEGART, J.	MAYCOCK, J.	MORTON, P.
LINES, S.	McEVOY, F.	MAYER, J.	MOSELEY, J.
LITTLE, H. J.	McGIVNEY, J.	MEADOWCROFT, J. E.	MOSSFORD, W.
LITTLE, T.	McGIVNEY, T.	MEARS, J. J.	MORTIMER, J. F.
LITTLER, J.	McGOVERN, J.	MEE, G. F.	MOUNTNAY, J.
LIVESEY, H. W.	McLEAN, W.	MEEHAN, B.	MUIR, R.
LIVISEY, J.	McLOUGHLIN, C. H.	MEEK, J.	MULLANE, J.
LLOYD, H.	McLOUGHLIN, G.	MELLOR, G.	MULLEN, M.
LLOYD, T.	McLEOD, J.	MELLOR, J.	MULLIGAN, D.
LLOYD, W.	McNEIL, J.	MELVIN, J.	MULLIN, S.
LOCKETTS, A.	McNAIR, G.	MERCER, J.	MULLINS, J.
LOCKLEY, G. E	McWILLIAMS, —	MERIDITH, W.	MULVEY, J. H.
LOCKLEY, J. B.	McWILLIAMS, J.	MERRIMAN, N.	MUNROE, W. A.
LONG, W.	McWILLIAMS, R.	MILES, H.	MURRAY, A.
LORD, D.	MADDOCKS, G.	MILEY, H.	MURRAY, T.
LOW, W. T.	MAHER, W.	MILLS, —	MURPHY, C. J.
LOWE, RALPH.	MAHON, P. A.	MILLER, J. W.	MURPHY, E.
LOWE, RICHARD.	MAIDENS, W. H.	MILLINGTON, J.	MURPHY, J.
*LUNN, J.	MALLINSON, J.	MILLINGTON, W.	MURPHY, JAMES.
LUNT, A.	MANLEY, C. S.	MITCHELL, A. P.	MURPHY, J. P.
LUXTON, T.	MANLEY, J. T.	MITCHELL, E.	MURPHY, H.
LYDIATE, J.	MANNING, D.	MITCHELL, F. W.	MURPHY, P.
LYDIATE, T.	MANNING, E.	MOCKRIDGE, G.	MURPHY, W.
LYDDLE, J. H.	MANNION, J.	MOCKRIDGE, W. R.	MURPHY, WILLIAM.
LYONS, E.	MANOCK, J.	MALLOY, H. E.	MUSGROVE, J. C.
LYONS, J.	MANSFIELD, J. A.	MONAHAN, W. H.	NAYLOR, E.
LYTHGOE, J. H.	MAGUIRE, A.	MONAGHAN, T.	NAYLOR, G.
MACDONALD, J.	MAGUIRE, M.	MONTAGUE, C.	*NAYLOR, J.
MACKAY, E.	MARTIN, H.	MOONEY, W.	NAYLOR, J. N.
MACKLENAHEN, W.	MARTIN, J.	MOORE, F.	NAYLOR, W. E.
McARDLE, J.	MARTIN, T.	MOORE, G.	NEILSON, E.
McAVORY, A. H.	MARTIN, W. F.	MOORE, J.	NELSON, A. F.

* Denotes killed.   † Denotes missing.

Manchester Ship Canal
ROLL OF HONOUR—continued.

NELSON, E.	PARKES, F.	POVEY, T.	RIDGWAY, J.
NEWNES, G.	PARKES, T. W.	POWELL, G.	RIDINGS, H.
NEWTON, A.	PARKINSON, E. G.	POWELL, I.	RIDINGS, J.
NEWTON, F.	PARKINSON, R.	POWER, J.	RIGBY, J.
NEWTON, H.	PARR, J.	POYNER, A.	RIGBY, JOHN.
NICHOLLS, S.	PARR, J. J.	PRACEY, H.	RIGG, W.
NICHOLLS, W.	PARROTT, J. D.	PRESCOTT, J.	RILEY, E.
NICHOLSON, J. C.	PARTINGTON, D.	PRESTON, F.	RILEY, W.
NIXON, C.	PATERSON, A.	PRESTON, W.	*RIMMER, W.
NOALL, W. F.	PATERSON, S.	PRICE, H.	RISTE, G.
NORBURY, C.	PATON, J.	PRICE, J.	ROBERTS, A. E.
NORBURY, G.	PAYNE, G.	PRICE, T.	ROBERTS, D.
NORMAN, J. E.	PEACOCK, G.	PRINGLE, R.	ROBERTS, F. M.
NORTH, G.	PEARSON, G.	PROBIN, W. R.	ROBERTS, J.
OAKLEY, J. M.	PEAURTE, J. E.	PURSLOW, W.	ROBERTS, JAMES.
O'BRIEN, —	PEDIGREW, T.	PYATT, J.	ROBERTS, JOHN.
O'BRIEN, J.	PEEL, J. E.	QUINN, W. G.	ROBERTS, J. H.
O'BRIEN, J. T.	PEERS, R.	RALPH, A.	ROBERTS, J. W.
ODDIE, J.	PENDLETON, C.	RAMMELL, J.	ROBERTS, T.
ODLING, —	PENTITH, H.	RAMSBOTTOM, R.	ROBERTS, THOMAS.
OGDEN, F.	PERCIVAL, W.	RANDALL, J.	ROBERTS, P.
OGDEN, JOHN.	PERCY, C.	RATCLIFFE, A. J.	ROBERTS, W.
OGDEN, JOHN.	PERRY, S.	RATCLIFFE, H.	ROBERTSON, F. C.
OGDEN, J. S.	PETERS, J.	RATCLIFFE, J.	ROBINSON, A.
O'HARE, P.	PETERS, R.	RATCLIFFE, W.	ROBINSON, ALFRED.
OLIVE, E.	PETERS, W. H.	RAVENSCROFT, F.	ROBINSON, C.
OLIVE, G.	PHELAN, W.	RAWSTHORNE, S.	ROBINSON, G. E.
OLIVE, T. W.	PHILLPOT, I.	RAWLINSON, T.	ROBINSON, G.
OLIVE, W.	PHŒNIX, L.	READ, T. J. E.	ROBINSON, GEORGE.
OLLERTON, H.	PICKERING, F.	REARDON, J. T.	ROBINSON, G., Jr.
O'LOUGHLIN, J. T.	PICKERING, H.	REASON, W.	ROBINSON, J.
O'MARA, J.	PICKSTOCK, G.	REDWOOD, L.	ROBINSON, J. W.
O'NIEL, J.	PILKINGTON, T.	REID, J.	ROBINSON, T.
ORME, J.	PIMLATT, W.	REILLY, M.	ROGERS, A.
*O'ROURKE, A.	PIXTON, A.	RENNIE, W.	ROGERS, B.
O'ROURKE, T.	PLANT, R.	RENSHAW, C. W.	ROGERS, H.
OVERTON, —	PLATT, E.	RHODES, W.	ROLES, C.
OWEN, C.	PLATT, H.	RICHARDSON, I. J.	ROOKE, H.
OWEN, H.	POLLITT, J.	RICHARDSON, T.	ROOKE, H.
OWEN, J. H.	POOLE, G.	RICHARDSON, W.	ROONEY, T.
OWEN, L.	POOLE, R.	RICHARDSON, W. L.	ROSAMUND, J. M.
PAGE, F.	POOLE, T. N.	RICHMOND, J.	ROSE, J. W.
PAGE, M. A.	PORTER, J.	RICHMOND, T.	*ROSE, S.
PALMER, G. H.	PORTER, T.	RIDDING, A.	ROSSALL, G.
PALMER, T.	POSTON, G.	RIDGEWAY, F.	ROTHWELL, J.
PARKER, H.	POTTS, J.	RIDGWAY, B. W.	ROUTLEDGE, —

* Denotes killed.

Manchester Ship Canal
ROLL OF HONOUR—continued.

ROWE, R.	SHAW, —	SOWTER, S.	SYNES, A.
ROWE-CASSIDY, J.	SHAW, F.	SPARKS, R.	TALLOW, W.
ROWLANDS, F.	SHAW, H.	SPENCER, F. R.	TANSLEY, W.
ROWLANDS, JOHN.	SHAW, J.	SPIERS, S.	TARRANT, A.
ROWLANDS, JOSEPH.	SHAW, R.	SPRECKLEY, G.	TAYLOR, A. M.
ROWLANDS, S.	SHAWCROSS, S.	STAFFORD, J.	TAYLOR, B.
ROYLE, R.	SHEARER, D.	STAFFORD, JAMES.	TAYLOR, C.
ROWLES, —	SHELLEY, C.	STANGER, A.	TAYLOR, G.
ROYSTON, A.	SHELTON, H.	STANLEY, E.	TAYLOR, J.
RUDMAN, F.	SHEPPARD, F.	STANNEY, J.	TAYLOR, JAMES.
RUSCOE, A.	SHERIDAN, R. J.	STATHAM, J. H.	TAYLOR, JOHN.
RUSSELL, W.	SHIELDS, A.	STEADMAN, A. I.	TAYLOR, R.
RUSTAGE, J.	SHINGLER, R.	STEELE, A.	TAYLOR, RICHARD.
RUSTAGE, W.	SHOREMAN, G.	STEELE, ARNOLD.	TAYLOR, T.
RUTTER, J. H.	SIDDELL, A.	STEELE, C.	TAYLOR, W.
RYAN, D.	SIDEBOTTOM, —	STEPHENS, F.	THEOBALD, S.
RYAN, J.	SIDWELL, R.	STERNBRIDGE, T.	*THOMAS, E.
RYAN, JOHN.	SIGHE, E.	STEWARD, T.	THOMASON, J.
RYAN, JOSEPH.	SIGHE, J.	STEWARD, W.	THOMPSON, A. H.
RYDER, F.	SIGHE, W.	STOCKTON, J.	THOMPSON, C.
RYDER, S.	SIMCOCK, L.	STORR, J. G	THOMPSON, JAMES.
SADDLER, A.	SIMMONDS, T.	STORR, T.	THOMPSON, JOHN.
SADDLER, J. W.	SIMPSON, THOS.	STOTT, J. D.	THOMPSON, W.
SALISBURY, W.	SKELTON, J.	STRAFFE, H.	THOMPSON, W. R.
SANDBACH, J.	SKERRITT, H.	STRATH, H.	THORNE, J.
SANGSTER, HAROLD.	SLADE, W.	*STRAW, J.	THORNTON, C.E
SANGSTER, JNO.	SLATER, N.	STREET, P.	THORNTON, R.
SAPPLE, W. J.	SMITH, A. T.	STRETCH, A.	THORNTON, W.
SAUNDERS, R.	SMITH, D.	STUBBS, S.	THORNHILL, E.
SAVAGE, G.	SMITH, D. H.	SULLIVAN, C.	THORNHILL, F.
SAXBY, L.	SMITH, HENRY.	SULLIVAN, DANIEL.	THORPE, ROBERT.
SCANLON, W.	SMITH, HERBERT.	SULLIVAN, DAVID.	THORPE, ROBERT.
SCHOFIELD, R.	SMITH, J.	SULLIVAN, F. J.	THREDGOLD, W.
SCHOLES, A.	SMITH, J. R.	SUMMERFIELD, A.	THRELFALL, A.
SCHOLTZE, E. C.	SMITH, SYDNEY.	SUMNER, F.	TIERNEY, J.
SCHON, D.	SMITH, S.	SUNDERLAND, W. H.	TIGHT, S. J.
SCOTT, J.	SMITH, SOLOMON.	SUTCLIFFE, F. W.	TINSLEY, H.
SCOTT, W. H.	SMITH, T.	SUTTON, W.	TIPPING, F.
SCRAGG, H.	SMITH, T. L. C.	SWALLOW, P.	TOBIN, J.
SCREETON, R.	SMITH, T.	SWANE, F.	TODD, T. A.
SECCHI, P.	SMITH, T. A.	SWATRIDGE, H.	TOMKINSON, H.
SEDDON, J.	SMITH, W.	SWEATMAN, P.	TOOLE, C.
SEDDON, N. R.	SMITH, W.	SWEETMAN, T.	TOOLE, J.
SETTLE, F.	SOUTHERN, L.	SWIFT, T.	TOWNSEND, T.
SHALLCROSS, A. C.	SOUTHERN, T.	SWINBURNE, S.	TRAVIS, A.
SHALLCROSS, T. B.	SOUTTER, W.	SWINDELLS, F.	TRAVERS, H. S.

* Denotes killed.

Manchester Ship Canal
ROLL OF HONOUR—continued.

TROTT, G.	WALSH, R.	WHIPDAY, J. W.	WILSON, E.
TROTT, H.	WALSH, THOMAS.	WHITBY, J.	WILSON, F.
TURNER, G.	WALSH, THOMAS.	WHITBY, W.	WILSON, H.
TURNER, H.	WALSH, W. B.	WHITE, C.	WILSON, JAMES.
TURNER, W.	WALTON, G.	WHITE, F. S.	WILSON, JOSEPH.
TWIGG, H.	WARBURTON, R.	WHITE, W. J.	WILSON, R.
TWISS, J.	WARBURTON, S.	WHITEHEAD, J. W.	*WILSON, WILLIAM.
TYRRELL, A.	WARD, J.	WHITEHEAD, W.	WILSON, WILLIAM.
UNSWORTH, J.	WARD, JOHN J.	WHITEHOUSE, I.	WILSON, WILLIAM.
VALENTINE, S.	WARD, JOSEPH J.	WHITELEGG, A.	WILSON, W. H.
VAN, A.	WARING, F.	WHITELEGG, H.	WILSON, W. W.
VARLEY, R.	WARNER, A.E.	WHITFIELD, J.	WITHALL, G. E.
VAUDREY, E.	WARREN, C.	WHITHAM, B.	WOOD, A.
VERNON, W. G.	WARREN, M.	WHITNEY, J.	WOOD, J.
*VINTON, G.	WARRINGTON, J.	WHITTAKER, E.	WOODS, T.
VOSE, C.	WATERWORTH, C.	WHITTINGTON, R.	WOODWARD, C.
VOSE, W. J.	WATKINS, A.	WHITTLE, T.	WOODWARD, J. W.
WADE, G.	WATSON, F.	WHITWORTH, J.	WOOLGAR, W.
WADSWORTH, J.	WATSON, W.	WHYTE, W. H.	WORRALL, W. R.
WAKEFIELD, C.	WEBB, C.	WILDE, J. H.	WORSWICK, L.
WAKEFIELD, L.	WEBB, R.	WILDING, R.	WORTHINGTON, J.
WALDRON, W.	WEBSTER, F.	WILKINSON, A.	WORTHINGTON, S.
WALKDEN, J. H.	WEBSTER, F. J.	WILKINSON, J. R.	WORTHINGTON, W.
WALKER, E. L.	WEBSTER, F. W.	WILKINSON, T.	WRIGHT, A.
WALKER, F.	WEIGHTMAN, A. E.	WILLIAMS, A.	WRIGLEY, S.
WALKER, H.	WELLINGS, A.	WILLIAMS, F.	WROOT, G. H.
WALKER, J. S.	WEST, G.	WILLIAMS, G. S.	YATES, A.
WALKER, J. T.	WESTHEAD, C.	WILLIAMS, H.	YATES, G. C. R.
WALL, A.	*WETHERALL, W. J.	WILLIAMS, H. J.	*YATES, G. H.
WALL, G.	WHAITES, J. H.	WILLIAMS, T.	YATES, JAMES.
WALL, J.	WHARTON, F.	WILLIAMSON, A.	YATES, JOHN.
WALL, J. W.	WHEATCROFT, S.	WILLIAMSON, J.	YATES, JOSEPH.
WALL, T.	WHEELER, W.	WILLIAMSON, J. W.	YATES, WALTER.
WALMSLEY, C.	WHEELDON, B.	WILSON, A.	YATES, WILLIAM.
WALSH, C.	WHEELDON, J.	WILSON, B.	YOUNG, G.
WALSH, J.	WHELAN, MICHAEL.	WILSON, C.	YOUNG, H.
WALSH, M.	WHELAN, MICHAEL.	WILSON, D.	

*Denotes killed.

Rolls of Honour

of some

Firms and Institutions

in

Manchester

Wherein are recorded the names of those who at the first call voluntarily placed their services at the disposal of their King and Country for the defence of Liberty and Civilisation.

ROLL OF HONOUR.

ADAMS & CO., LIMITED.
Chatham Mills, Manchester.

William Bradburn	Royal Engineers.
George F. Long	7th Batt. Manchester Territorials.
James McEvoy	Scottish Borderers.
Joseph McEvoy	4th Batt. King's Own Lancasters. (Killed in action).
Alfred Pikesley	Royal Army Medical Corps (Territorials).
William Wareham	19th Batt. Manchester Regiment.
Joseph L. Harper	H.M.S. "Powerful," Navy.

HILL, GODBERT AND CO.
62, Cannon Street, Manchester.

Charles Wilde	19th Batt. Manchester Regiment.

WASTE BLEACHERS LIMITED.
Holme Mill, Rawtenstall.

E. Woodworth	East Lancashire Regiment.
A. Heyworth	East Lancashire Regiment.
J. Dagg	East Lancashire Regiment.
B. Pooley	East Lancashire Regiment.
J. Healey	East Lancashire Regiment.
T. Rowan	Royal Irish Rifles.
A. Stevens	East Lancashire Regiment.
J. W. Tomlinson	East Lancashire Regiment.
F. Buck	Royal Field Artillery.
A. Fielding	Royal Field Artillery.
R. Rodgers	East Lancashire Regiment.
W. Manning	East Lancashire Regiment.
T. Cogan	East Lancashire Regiment.

ROLL OF HONOUR.

AFFLECK & BROWN LTD.
AND
BROWN BROS. LTD.

* * *

JACK BROWN.

R. ALDERSON.
A. APPLEYARD.
F. APPS.
RICHARD ARTHUR.
C. H. ASHTON.
J. A. BARBER.
F. BATES
    (since discharged, M.U.).
T. W. BATEY.
B. T. BLAKEMAN.
T. BOOTHROYD.
J. E. BOWEN,
H. L. BRADLEY.
HERBERT BRAY.
J. BREWER.
H. BROMPTON.
B. V. FORSTER BROWN.
R. A. BURN.
J. H. CANNELL.
A. CAYGILL.
W. J. CHAUNT.
J. CHIDLER.
R. D. CLARKE (died since joining).
F. L. CLARK.
G. E. CLUBB.
H. COOKE.
JOS. COOK.
P. A. COWAP.
R. F. COWLING.
J. J. CROSSLEY.
JOHN DAVIES.
D. DOUGLAS
    (since discharged, M.U.).
L. M. DYKE.
JAMES EASTWOOD.
J. EDDLESTON.
G. ELLIOT.
A. FRANKS.
J. A. FARRALLY.
R. FARRALLY.
W. FENLON.
J. T. GALLIMORE.
R. GILES.
J. H. GLEAVE.
J. C. GRANT.
A. GREENALL.
R. GREGORY.
R. R. GRIERSON.
J. A. HADDOW.
G. T. HARRISON.
R. HAIGH.
H. HALL.
S. HALL.
G. HALLAM.
W. B. HARRISON.

ROLL OF HONOUR
CONTINUED.

AFFLECK & BROWN LTD.
AND
BROWN BROS. LTD.

F. HENDERSON.
H. FRAZER HERBERT.
F. HEWIN.
J. HIND (killed in action).
W. HOPE.
W. HOUGHTON.
A. B. HUDDLESTON.
C. HULTON.
R. HUTCHINSON.
A. JOHNSON.
ALBERT JONES.
ARNOLD JONES.
G. JONES.
H. NEILSON JONES.
R. L. JONES.
R. JONES.
A. D. KNIGHTON.
T. LATHE.
ROBERT LATHE.
G. H. LAKING.
E. C. LITTLE.
FRANK LOWDE.
J. McCABE.
J. McCARDLE.
J. G. McGOW.
W. McLEAN.
F. MAFFEY.
JOHN MASSEY.
C. MELLOR.
H. A. MITCHELL.

G. H. MOORE.
THOMAS MOORES.
A. A. MORRIS.
J. H. MURFIN.
C. MURRAY
 (since discharged, M.U.).
H. MURRAY.
F. NASH.
W. NORTH.
A. NORTON.
T. O'CONNOR (killed in action).
J. O. PARKER.
JOHN PEAK.
WILLIAM PEAK.
R. PERT.
C. PRESTON.
A. PRIEST.
A. RAE.
C. RAYNOR.
R. H. RISDON.
F. ROBERTS.
R. E. ROBERTS.
JOHN ROBSON.
S. R. ROBSON.
TOM ROE.
J. B. ROEBUCK.
F. RONALD.
G. RUDDLE.

HARRY SANT.
W. M. SAUNDERS.
T. SEDGWICK.
E. SHELMERDINE.
A. D. SHERRATT.
H. SINGLETON.
HARRY SMALL.
E. D. SMITH.
J. B. SMITH.
O. SMITH.
G. SPRATT.
C. A. STARK.
W. SWAIN.
ARTHUR VARLEY.
R. VOSS.
JOHN WALKER.
J. K. WALTHEW.
F. S. WATLING.
A. E. WARD.
A. WATSON.
G. WEDDELL.
J. WILKINSON.
T. WILKINSON.
W. WITHINGTON.
J. WOOD.
F. WOOD.
G. ERNEST WRIGHT.
W. WALLAS.
E. YOUNG.

ROLL OF HONOUR.

Sir Elkanah Armitage & Sons Ltd.,
48, Mosley Street, Manchester.

* * *

Names of Employees who have Joined the Forces.

* * *

A. ALDCROFT.	P. DOYLE.	R. OVEREND.
T. ALDCROFT.	G. DYSON.	J. PAULDEN.
T. A. ALLSOPP.	R. EARDLEY.	P. POWELL.
W. ARDEN.	H. EASTHOPE.	A. ROACH.
J. ARMITT.	J. EVANS.	E. RODGERS.
C. ASHCROFT.	E. FALLOWS.	H. ROUSE.
J. ASTON.	W. FOULKES.	C. RUDINGS.
W. BARTON.	J. FRANCE.	G. SHAW.
J. BERTRAM.	J. GARNER.	L. SHAW.
E. BIRD.	W. GLEAVE.	W. SHAW.
T. BIRD.	B. GOODIER.	A. SIMCOX.
J. BOOTH.	W. HALLSWORTH.	G. SINDREY.
R. BORRICK.	R. HARDMAN.	S. SMITH.
A. E. BRADSHAW.	S. HISMAH.	W. SMITH.
R. BRIERLEY.	F. JACKSON.	C. STOREY.
T. BRODERICK.	H. JACKSON.	W. STOREY.
W. P. BURGESS.	J. JACKSON.	J. STOTT.
J. H. BURKE.	W. JACKSON.	N. STRINGFELLOW.
J. CARTER.	R. JOHNSON.	A. TAYLOR.
B. CARTER.	W. KENDRICK.	E. TOWERS.
T. CARTER, Junr.	G. K. LEE (Commission).	C. F. TURNER.
A. CASSON.	T. LEONARD.	T. TURNER.
W. CLARKE.	J. LOWE.	H. VAUGHAN.
F. CLIFFE.	P. LOWE.	W. WALFORD.
J. CONCANNON.	A. MAKIN.	J. L. WALKER.
W. CONWAY.	J. McCONVILLE.	C. WALSH.
H. COOPER.	J. McGUFFIN.	J. WINGFIELD.
C. CROSSLEY.	H. MOORES.	T. WILLIAMS.
P. CROSSLEY.	S. MOSS.	G. WILSON.
E. DANIELS.	J. MORRIS.	J. WOOD.
W. DOVE.	W. OBRIEN.	R. WOODWARD.
	R. OFFICER.	

ROLL OF HONOUR.

Sir W. G. Armstrong, Whitworth & Co. Ltd.
OPENSHAW.

BLETCHER, WM. H.
SCOTT, HEYWOOD.
LAWSON, E. LEONARD.
MASON, WILLIAM.
WRIGHT, ARTHUR.
WRIGHT, ROBT. WM.
PEARSON, JOS. A.
SWITZER, SIDNEY.
ROPITEAUX, MARK F.
McGREGOR, ALBERT E.
ALLOTT, GEORGE.
GARLICK, TOM.
FARRINGTON, CHAS.
MILLS, CHARLES.
RIDGWAY, GEORGE F.
RYDER, ERNEST.
LIGHTFOOT, SAMUEL.
BOOTH, FREDERICK.
WEAVER, ALFRED P.
SMITH, JOHN WM.
DELANEY, MATHEW.
CROSS, GEORGE WM.
ATKINS, DUNCAN W.
SIMPSON, HAROLD P.
WELCH, JOHN.
McCABE, THOMAS.
BARTON, JOHN THOS.
BRIDGE, ALBERT.
SYER, GEORGE.
HIGHAM, THOMAS.
HARGREAVES, G. H.
LOWE, JOHN.
LIDDIARD, JOS.
MURTAGH, PATRICK.
MORLEY, GEORGE.
TURNER, GEORGE.
CLARKE, ARTHUR E.
WAIN, SAMUEL, Jr.
EDMUNDSON, HARRY.
McKEW, REUBEN.
JONES, ERNEST.
BREW, LEWIS JOHN.
MAYO, JOHN HENRY.
HASLAM, JAMES.
GREEN, WALTER L.
NORMAN, EDWIN.
CASSIDY, JOHN.
SHUTTLEWORTH, J.
NUSSEY, WILLIAM.
HOWLE, HORACE.
ROBERTS, JAMES.
HUGHES, WALTER.
GREEN, FRANK.
HILL, FRED.
ATHERTON, PETER.
GOODMAN, DAVID.
EDGAR, JAMES F.
BERRY, DAVID.
SIMPSON, HERBERT.
JACKSON, JAMES.
EARLAM, HAROLD J.
THORNLEY, JOEL.
MOON, JOSEPH.
SMITH, CHARLES.
SHAW, CHARLES.
CLARKIN, ROBERT.
CHELMICK, CHARLES.
MALLALIEU, CHAS. A.
HEMPSTOCK, SAML. W.
GUILFOYLE, EDWARD.
DAVIES, ARTHUR.
PRICE, NELSON.
ATKINS, WILLIAM.
ROONEY, THOMAS.
BATES, FREDK. WM.
PRICE, PAUL.
COOK, ARTHUR.
WARDLE, EDWARD.
BERRY, FRANK JAS.
PASSMORE, THOMAS.
BARBER, PERCY.
LYNN, JOHN WALTER.
WILLIAMS, JOHN.
BARDSLEY, JOHN WM.
WILLIAMS, WILLIAM.
REYNOLDS, JAMES.
SMITH, TOM.
WYNNE, ROBERT.
WARD, FRANK.
ESTLES, GEORGE H.
CHAPMAN, JOS. E.
WARD, CHAS. HENRY.
SCHOFIELD, JAMES.
LEONARD, JOHN.
DAVIES, JAMES.
ASHCROFT, ARTHUR.
FIELDING, JAMES.
MULLOCK, ROBERT.
TAYLOR, ERNEST.
JACKSON, JOSEPH.
HUNT, ROBT. JAMES.
FOSBROOK, CHARLES.
HARRISON, FRANK.
SWITZER, WM. HENRY.
HARVEY, ALBERT.
TAYLOR, FRED CHAS.
HALEY, JOHN.
DANIELS, JOHN.
HULME, WILLIAM.
HOBSON, WM. HENRY.
McLEAN, ALEX. JOHN.
RUSHBY, CHARLES.
FEELEY, JOHN.
FITZPATRICK, JOHN.
CROMPTON, GEO. V.
PARKIN, SAMUEL.
BOWLES, WILLIAM E.
BELLIS, WILLIAM.
RILEY, WILLIAM.
DOOLEY, THOMAS.
DONOGHUE, EDWARD.
ANDERSON, THOMAS.
BLACKIE, SYDNEY.
FINLAY, THOMAS.
LEE, FRED.
McDOWELL, JAMES.
OWENCROFT, JAMES.
CLARKE, J. ANDREW.
TAYLOR, ALBERT.
PARKIN, WM.
DUTTON, THOMAS.
CAMPBELL, FREDK. J.
ROWLEY, BENJAMIN.
CLOUGH, JOHN.
READE, JOHN THOS.
BERESFORD, SAMUEL.
O'SHEA, JOHN M.
McCABE, JAMES.
RENNISON, GEORGE.
BENT, THOMAS.

ROLL OF HONOUR—Continued.

Sir. W. G. Armstrong, Whitworth & Co. Ltd.

JACKSON, JOHN THOS.
HURRELL, TOM.
BYROM, CHARLES.
COLEMAN, JOHN.
BRAIN, HARRY.
CHANDLER, HENRY.
GALE, GEORGE.
DOWDALL, GEORGE.
PERCIVAL, WM.
BARDEN, WALTER.
FENNA, WILLIAM.
WOOD, ROBERT.
GILLESPIE, WILLIAM.
BARNES, THOMAS.
LAND, JAS. HERBERT.
BILLINGTON, WM.
BACKHOUSE, FRED.
MOONAN, JOHN.
MASON, ROBERT.
SIMPSON, EDWARD.
STRINGER, JOSEPH.
JERVIS, WILFRED.
REED, JOSEPH.
FLETCHER, ALBERT S.
SHAW, HARRY B.
WEBSTER, WALTER.
CARTER, THOMAS E.
HARDACRE, RICHD. H.
HARGREAVES, J. H.
BRAMHALL, ISAAC.
BERESFORD, ROBT. S.
SNAPE, PETER JOHN.
McQUIRK, EDWARD.
HUME, ERNEST.
BURTON, FRED.
ROBINSON, WILLIAM.
LEES, ARNOLD.
WHITWORTH, HARRY.
DUTTON, GEORGE H.
HILTON, HAROLD.
IRLAM, WILFRED.
HILL, JOHN.
GREENHALGH, WM.
CODE, HAROLD.
HOGAN, JOSEPH.
TAYLOR, FRANK.
GARRATT, SAMUEL.
HARROP, WILLIAM.
HAMPSON, ROBERT.

KELLY, HENRY.
HEYWOOD, JOSEPH.
THOMPSON, WILLIAM.
BIGGAR, OSWALD.
COOPER, WILLIAM.
ANDREW, HAROLD S.
VICKERS, HAROLD.
MAYOR, ARTHUR.
WAIN, THOMAS.
WAIN, GEORGE.
ASHTON, ALBERT.
SMITH, JAMES.
ACKERMAN, ALBERT.
KEEFE, FRED.
WILSON, ALFRED.
SMITH, W.
WITHERS, G. F.
RILEY, JOHN.
DAVIES, EVAN H.
EDWARDS, H. THOS.
NEWBERRY, WILLIAM.
SCANLON, JAMES.
SNELSON, JAS. H.
GARRATT, JOSEPH.
MERIDITH, FRED.
BURGOYNE, JOHN.
DRINKWATER, FRED.
HAMER, SAMUEL.
MITCHELL, HARRY.
DALE, THOMAS.
McCABE, FRANCIS.
JOINSON, HARRY.
CAVANAGH, JOHN.
THOMASON, THOMAS.
HOOLE, JAMES WM.
MARSLAND, ERNEST.
GRIMSHAW, JOHN.
NOLAN, REUBEN.
ROBERTS, JOHN.
RICHARDSON, OLIVER.
McANDREW, JOHN.
EWINGTON, SIMON H.
FARINGTON, HARRY.
BALL, JOHN.
SAUNDERS, WM. H.
KNAGG, GEORGE.
BLEVINS, JOSEPH.
NICHOLSON, WM. GEO.
LODGE, HUGH THOS.

HORRIDGE, JOHN.
MITCHELL, ED. P.
SMITH, GEO. WM.
WILLIAMS, JAMES.
SHAW, NAT. RHODES.
ANDERSON, JAMES.
HEALEY, FAITHFUL.
KAVANAGH, FRANCIS.
DAGNALL, JOSEPH.
CLARKE, WM. HY.
ALLEN, JOHN WM.
LANGHAM, JOHN T.
ROSS, WM.
LUDGATE, JAS. WM.
McNALLY, THOMAS.
WINSKILL, JOHN.
TAYLOR, BEN.
MARRON, WM.
RICHARDSON, CHAS.
WILSON, HENRY.
HOLLINGWORTH, J.
LEWIS, JOHN.
RYDER, EDGAR.
HUMPHREYS, J. A. T.
ROONEY, ROBERT.
DAVIES, JOHN.
DUNN, ALBERT.
SNELSON, FRANK.
RIGBY, WM.
SMITH, JOHN.
MORRIS, WALTER.
LANGFORD, WM.
TRAVIS, THOMAS.
HOVINGTON, JAMES.
GETLIFFE, JOHN WM.
MASSEY, WM.
HOLMES, WM. F.
WHITELEY, CHARLES.
DAVIES, GEORGE.
DEAKIN, ALBERT.
ALLCOCK, JAMES.
THORPE, GEORGE.
BANNON, JOHN.
ASHCROFT, WM.
STATHAM, WM.
SANTI, JOHN.
SHAW, JOS.
CUMMINS, GEORGE.
ASTON, ALFRED.

PRINGLE, JOSEPH.
HENDER, JOHN HY.
NORMAN, GEORGE.
HARDMAN, GEO. WM.
KING, PATRICK.
BOOTH, WM.
COCKER, LEONARD.
FILDES, GEORGE.
GRIFFITHS, JOHN T.
BOYES, ALFRED.
WORSLEY, JAS. HY.
STRINGER, HUGH.
HAUGHTON, JOHN.
BINNS, THOMAS.
LESTER, THOMAS.
HARRISON, WM.
SWIRE, HARRY.
WALKER, GEORGE S.
FENTON, CHARLES.
MADDOCKS, HERBERT.
GREGSON, THOMAS.
BINNS, JAMES.
VAIL, GEORGE.
CORCORAN, JOHN.
JARMAN, ALBERT.
BLEMINGS, WM. THOS.
DENTON, JOHN.
SMITH, STEPHEN.
JAMES, WM.
ELLISON, THOMAS.
SEWELL, PERCY.
OGDEN, ALBERT.
HURCUM, FRANK.
BLEACKLEY, H.
LIVESEY, GEORGE.
WHARMBY, JAS. HY.
HAYES, JAMES.
BEAUMONT, WM.
PRICE, JAMES.
BARKER, HERBERT.
DAVENPORT, SIDNEY.
RYDER, JOHN HY.
HOLLAND, JAMES.
PLUNKETT, JOSEPH.
YOMANS, ED.
HEWITSON, ARTHUR A.
WOOD, WM.
PHILLIPS, CHARLES.
TURNER, EDWARD.

ROLL OF HONOUR—Continued.

Sir W. G. Armstrong, Whitworth & Co. Ltd.

SLINGER, JOS. HY.
CARS, ROBERT.
SHELDON, JOHN R.
ROBINSON, WM. HY.
HEWITT, WM. HY.
PEAKE, JOHN.
ROONEY, SAM.
MUTCH, DAVID.
DICKSON, WM.
WICKS, ALFRED.
ETHERINGTON, F.
BOARDMAN, FRED.
CARR, ALBERT.
SMITH, JOHN JOS.
HEAP, ERNEST.
ADAMS, ARTHUR.
SANTALL, ALBERT.
SMITH, PERCY.
OLDHAM, DAVID.
MOTTERSHEAD, WM.
BUNTING, JOHN ED.
FRYER, CHAS. THOS.
McGINN, WM. H.
DOLAN, PETER.
CRESSWELL, WM. L.
REDMAN, JOHN.
HULME, ROLAND.
FABBZ, JOHN ROBT.
BERISFORD, WM.
SMITH, THOMAS.
CALVERT, HENRY.
MASSEY, SAMUEL.
KILKENNY, EDWARD.
FAROGHER, JAMES.
McGRATH, JAMES.
JENKS, JACK.
WILKINSON, JOHN L.
McANDRY, THOS. A.
HANSON, THOMAS.
PIXTONE, JOHN.
JONES, WM. VICTOR.
WILSON, JOHN WM.
PHILIPS, MATTHEW.
CUMMINGS, ED. JOS.
LYNCH, JOHN JAMES.
LYNCH, JOSEPH A.
LASCELLES, E. M.
BROOKS, ALFRED.
DUCKETT, GEORGE.

BOYD, WM.
BRIDGEMAN, VICTOR.
WILSON, WM.
CHADWICK, JOHN R.
MARSDEN, NATHNL.
JONES, WALTER R.
HOLES, GEORGE.
McCORD, CHARLES.
DEAN, CHARLES.
MONTGOMERY, JOHN.
McMANUS, JOHN.
LITTLER, RALPH.
HOULTON, PETER.
GREENWOOD, GEORGE.
FLETCHER, THOMAS.
FLETCHER, HORACE.
DUGDALE, HORACE.
HULSTON, JOS. JAMES.
RENSHAW, FRANK.
CORNER, GEORGE.
WESLEY, ARTHUR.
CHADWICK, JOHN WM.
HARRISON, ROBT.
SMITH, JOSEPH.
STRINGER, PETER S.
FORREST, JAMES.
BROTHERTON, S.
ROGERS, THOMAS.
POUNTNEY, ANDREW.
SHAW, JOSEPH.
DEAN, FRANCIS.
ENGLAND, SAML.
HEATHCOTE, THOMAS.
POWELL, JOHN.
KNOTT, HARRY.
JOYNSON, GEORGE.
BLUNDELL, JAS.
STOREY, ARTHUR.
ATKINS, GEORGE.
GADSBY, FREDK. A.
WATKINSON, SAML.
ARMITAGE, FREDK.
McGUIRE, DANIEL.
JOHNSON, J. W.
FREESTONE, FRANK.
HANCOCK, CHARLES.
FOSTER, R. W.
PALMER, EDGAR M.
ADCROFT, CHARLES.

WILLINGHAM, GEO.
BOWERS, WM. M.
TEMPLE, JOS. WM.
BROTHERTON, THOS.
WITHERS, ALBERT E.
BOWMAN, JOHN.
DEAN, THOMAS.
HADFIELD, HAROLD.
MORRIS, ALFRED.
HEAP, WALTER.
DARBYSHIRE, G.
HENSHAW, GEO. H.
QUINN, JOHN.
WILKINSON, JAMES.
JONES, PERCY.
KINSELLA, PATRICK.
WORRALL, WM.
WALL, ALBERT.
SIMPKINS, WM. G.
ROBERTS, WALTER.
BETTRIDGE, ERNEST.
GREENWOOD, JOHN.
CARR, WM.
WALKER, HARRY.
LORD, JAMES.
MOULTON, JOHN.
ROBINSON, JAMES.
BEVINS, GEORGE.
MILNER, ERNEST.
McCARTHY, JOSEPH.
HARDING, THOMAS.
RIDGWAY, ALAN.
LEONARD, PAUL.
FOSTER, HARRY.
UNSWORTH, HENRY.
STEVENS, JAS. N. T.
SHAW, PERCY.
MITCHELL, THOMAS.
MAYO, JOSEPH.
PRICE, GEORGE C.
JACKSON, EDWIN.
AULTON, JAMES.
COOPER, THOS.
DAVIES, GEO. HY.
PIGGOTT, JAS. J.
HEALEY, EDWARD.
LAMBERT, THOMAS.
JONES, ALFRED.
SMITH, HENRY.

HEMLIN, THOMAS.
RAINSBURY, JOHN.
SCHOFIELD, L.
CUNLIFFE, JOSEPH.
PARKER, WM.
ELLIS, ARTHUR.
WILSON, FRANCIS.
DRINKALL, THOMAS.
DONOHUE, WM. P.
CREIGHTON, J.
CLARK, WM.
WETTON, GEORGE.
McILVENNY, JOSEPH.
CHAMBERLAIN, R. H.
CLEARY, JOHN.
DAVIES, JAMES.
GROVES, SAMUEL.
FRANCE, HERBERT.
HOSKINS, JAS. HY.
HARNEY, JAS. F.
WHITESIDE, LOUIS.
DELAHUNTY, RICHD.
WILLIAMS, ALFRED.
THOMPSON, JOHN.
WILLIAMSON, S. E.
MEADOWCROFT, WM.
BOARDMAN, JAMES H.
ROBERTS, WM.
MARTIN, A. WM.
WALKER, FRED.
BAGSHAW, ARTHUR W.
FAULKNER, WM.
WORMALD, ALBERT.
GIBSON, SAMUEL.
FITZMAURICE, E.
LIVESEY, PAUL.
DOWNS, CLARENCE.
McCLASKEY, WM. HY.
WALTON, JAMES.
EDWARDS, JAMES.
HAMER, THOS. A.
CAIN, THOMAS.
ROUTLEDGE, ALFRED.
FARRELL, FREDK. WM.
FARRELL, J. CHRIS.
GITTINGS, J. JAS.
NEWTON, SAMUEL.
PHILLIPS, JAMES.
OLIVER, JABEZ.

ROLL OF HONOUR—Continued.

Sir W. G. Armstrong, Whitworth & Co. Ltd.

BARNSLEY, ALFRED.
HOWELLS, JAMES.
WOODHEAD, JOHN WM.
WELLS, JOSEPH.
MILLIN, EDWARD S.
DONNER, JOS. WM.
WOLFENDEN, WM.
SLATER, FRANK HY.
ROBSON, WM. BROWN.
MAYERS, THOMAS.
FOULKES, ERNEST.
WRIGLEY, ARTHUR.
WRIGHT, JOHN A.
FARRELL, JOHN WM.
BAKER, EDWARD.
JONES, SYDNEY.
OGDEN, CHAS. THOS.
HEALEY, GEO. E.
BOOTH, WM.
McANDREW, JOHN.
MOORES, JAMES.
SMITH, ARTHUR.
SIMMONS, GEORGE H.
HUGHES, EDWARD.
NORTH, JAMES A.
YOUD, JOHN CHRIS.
HEWITSON, ALBERT.
MORAN, JOHN.
IVIN, CHAS. HENRY.
PENNINGTON, DAVID.
WOODROW, SAML. W.
CARROLL, THOS.
SMITH, GEORGE.
POVALL, GEORGE.
KIRKLEY, RALPH L.
JONES, JOHN.
RIDGWAY, OSWALD.
EURELL, CHRIS. JOHN.
CHADWICK, WM. HY.
FITZGERALD, JOHN.
ROURKE, THOMAS.
BURNS, DANIEL.
OAKDEN, HENRY.
PARKER, WILLIAM.
DUNN, WILLIAM.
BYRNE, MICHAEL.

KIRK, HENRY.
HAMER, SAMUEL.
ROE, JAMES.
GANSON, JOHN.
GANSON, CHARLES.
ROBINSON, JOSEPH.
TALBOT, JOHN.
GREENWOOD, JOHN.
POUNDER, WM. E.
SUTCLIFFE, ALBERT.
GANSON, JAMES.
GOOSTREY, JOS. WM.
MULVEY, CHARLES.
WOOD, JOHN.
SAUL, THOMAS.
JOHNSON, PAUL.
SHAW, ROBERT.
BARTON, JOS. E.
SOLLORY, JOHN.
McCABE, FREDK.
COFFEY, WM.
BAMFORD, ALFRED.
FIELDING, FREDK.
WOODSIDE, WM. S.
DOOLEY, JOHN.
HAWORTH, ALFRED.
DAXON, JAMES.
WHEELDON, THOS.
HOUGH, JAMES.
O'NEILL, THOS. CHAS.
RAMSDEN, HY.
CAWLEY, JOS.
NOTON, THOMAS G.
SLATER, JOS. FRANK.
LONGSDEN, JAMES.
MARTIN, MICH. JOS.
WOOLLEY, GEORGE.
CORK, ARTHUR.
BIRMINGHAM, JOHN.
WILLS, BENJ.
DALE, JAMES.
BARBER, JAMES.
WRIGHT, THOS.
HILL, JOHN HENRY.
CATTERALL, JOSEPH.
ROSE, JOHN WM.

MORGAN, ALEX.
DONLAN, JOHN.
BUXTON, ERNEST ED.
DAVIES, WM.
AULT, JOHN WM.
NICHOLSON, JAMES.
HEALEY, JOSEPH.
RUTTER, WILFRED.
RIDGWAY, WM.
ARNOLD, FREDK.
DELAHUNTY, W.
CHADWICK, JOHN.
GORSE, WM.
MILLER, FREDK.
SIMPKINS, WM. G.
WOODHEAD, ARTHUR.
JENKINS, JOSEPH.
WILLAN, JOHN.
OLIVER, JAMES.
TULEY, ERNEST.
CAFFREY, JOSEPH.
BURGESS, JOHN GEO.
SMITH, ALBERT E.
FARRICKER, JOSEPH.
FORD, FREDK.
JEFFRIES, PERCY H.
ORMROD, JAMES.
BUCKLEY, ALBERT.
TALBOT, JOHN HENRY.
SHAW, BERTRAM B.
DEAN, GEORGE.
ELLIOTT, GEORGE.
GALLOWAY, FREDK.
COSGROVE, GEORGE.
BRUID, R. WM.
WILSON, J. E.
HIGGS, MATTHEW.
BRAND, JAMES.
LLOYD, JOHN.
JACKSON, ALBERT E.
BEAMISH, JAMES.
BRITTLETON, W. HY.
CONROY, ALFRED.
MORRIS, HY.
DYKE, GEORGE W.

MORRIS, A. W.
BROWNHILL, W. L.
McQUIRE, THOMAS.
WHITEHURST, J. H.
TIMMIS, ERNEST.
WALES, JOHN CHAS.
O'NEILL, ALBERT V.
HARRISON, ERNEST.
HEATHCOTE, JOSEPH.
JONES, ALBERT.
BARBER, THOMAS.
HOGG, ANDREW.
MORRISON, JOHN.
BUNTING, JOE.
SAXON, W. HY.
WHITTLE, FRED WM.
BROWN, J. J.
BONNER, ALFRED.
DELAHUNTY, W.
GRIFFITHS, JAMES.
BIRTWISTLE, THOS.
BARRETT, J. W.
GRINDLEY, GEORGE.
FORD, SAMUEL.
DONE, FREDK.
GRAHAM, GEORGE.
QUALTERS, ELIAS.
SHERRATT, F.
TROUGHT, F.
MORRISON, H.
DUCKWORTH, ROBT.
FLETCHER, HORACE.
JONES, F. P.
LEWIS, FRED.
ASBRIDGE, J.
KEAVNEY, JOHN.
CUMMINS, WM.
BAMBER, FRANK.
WILKS, CHAS.
JOHNSON, WM.
WITHINGTON, FRED.
CHORLTON, A.
TROTTER, R.
ROBERTS, H.
WISE, P.

Private J. W. Lynn, 2nd Batt. Lancashire Fusiliers, was awarded the V.C., also the D.C.M. and the Cross of the Russian Order of St. George.

Roll of Honour.

ARNING & Co.,
MANCHESTER.

Members of our Staff who have joined His Majesty's Forces.

* * *

Lance-Corporal FRANK WARD,
   7th Batt. Lancashire Fusiliers.

Private A. DEAKIN,
   No. 17/8122. Signal Section. 17th Batt. Manchester Regiment. 90th Infantry Brigade. Headquarters, B.E.F., France.

Corporal T. McCORMACK,
   No. 8732. Quartermaster's Stores, 17th Batt. Manchester Regiment. 30th Division. B.E.F., France.

Private C. HIGGINSON,
   No. 24707. 11th Batt. Manchester Regiment. British Mediterranean Force.

Private T. RAMSDEN,
   Cheshire Field Artillery.

Roll of honour.

THE
Anglo-Syrian Trading Co.
LIMITED.

CONSTANTINE M. ELLIADI,
   2/6th Batt. Manchester Regt. (T.F.).
   Joined September, 1914.
   Now Sergeant Interpreter.

Private JESSE H. SIDDALL,
   19th Serv. Batt. Manchester Regt.
   Joined October, 1914.

Private ALFRED E. CHORLTON,
   2/3rd East Lancs. Field Ambulance,
   R.A.M.C. (T.F.).
   Joined September, 1915.

Private CLAUDE A. WHATHAM,
   6th Batt. Manchester Regt. (T.F.).
   Joined November, 1915.

European War, 1914.

Henry Bannerman & Sons Limited,
MANCHESTER.

Employees who, up to Dec., 1915, joined His Majesty's Forces.

AIREY, T.	FARRINGTON, J.	MORRISON, S.
ALLEN, J.	FIRTH, T.	MUSGRAVE, W.
ALMOND, A.	FISHER, A. E.	NORRIS, J.
ANDREW, R.	GANSON, W.	NUTTALL, A.
ASHTON, J.	GASKELL, F.	OLLERENSHAW, T.
ATHERTON, E.	GILLIBRAND, A.	OWEN, E.
AYLWARD, J.	GOSLING, F.	PARKER, C. T.
BARNETT, C.	GREEN, W.	PARKINSON, J. D.
BARNETT, G.	GRESTY, W.	PARRY, J. W.
BARROW, G.	GRIFFITHS, J. M.	PEACOCK, H.
BAXTER, J.	GRUNDY, J.	PERRIN, J. W.
BEAUMONT, H.	HAIGH, J.	PILLING, H.
BENNETT, T.	HALL, F.	POLLITT, W.
BIRKETT, H.	HALLATT, W.	POTTER, F.
BIRKETT, J.	HALLSWORTH, W.	POWERS, J.
BIRD, W. S.	HARPER, S. G. H.	QUICK, H.
BOOTH, G.	HARTLEY, E.	RADY, W.
BOTTOMS, J.	HAWORTH, R.	RAMAGE, W.
BOYD, S.	HEAVERS, W.	RATHBURN, V.
BROADHURST, R. P.	HEROD, A.	RHODES, G. W.
BROCKLEHURST S.	HIGGS, J.	RIDING, W.
BROWN, R.	HILL, W.	RODGERS, J.
BURNS, J.	HILLYARD, W.	ROTHWELL, J.
BURROWS, C.	HOLDEN, J.	SALT, H.
CAMERON, W.	HOLT, W.	SARSON, T.
CARLINE, W.	HOWARTH, R.	SAXON, J.
CLARKE, G. F.	HURST, F.	SCOTT, W.
CLARKSON, W.	INGHAM, J. G.	SHARPE, C.
CLAYTON, F.	JOHNSON, S. G.	SHAW, A.
CLAYTON, H.	KELLETT, J.	SHAWCROSS, L.
COOKE, T.	KERSHAW, E.	SLATER, A.
COPELAND, G.	KIDDY, J.	SNOW, W.
CRABTREE, H. H.	KINSEY, J.	STAFFORD, ERNEST.
CROOKE, A.	LANE, J.	STAFFORD, E.
DAVIES, F. J.	LAVIN, J.	STAFFORD, F.
DEAN, T.	LEE, J.	TATE, R.
DICKENSON, F.	LESLIE, J.	TAYLOR, J.
DODDS, T.	McKAY, J.	THOMAS, J.
DRUMMOND, J.	MEWHA, D.	WILCOX, J.
EASTWOOD, A.	MILWAIN, G.	WILCOX, L.
EXELBY, J.	MOORHOUSE, J.	WILLIAMSON, H.
FAIRBROTHER, C.	MORAN, S.	WOOD, A. C.
FARRELL, J. T.	MORRISON, F.	WOODALL, W.

ROLL OF HONOUR.

JAMES BARNES LTD.

PALACE SQUARE, MANCHESTER.

BARNES, WILLIAM,
Royal Flying Corps.

BREARLEY, FRED,
Seaforth Highlanders.

CALLAGHAN, JOHN,
9th Manchester Rifles (killed in action).

CAMERON, ALBERT,
1st Batt. Manchester City.

CORRIE, HARRY,
6th Manchester Territorials.

CRAWFORD, ARTHUR,
Royal Field Artillery.

GEORGE, DENIS,
3rd Batt. Manchester City.

HOSLER, JOHN,
Lancashire Fusiliers.

ROYLE, WILLIAM,
3rd Batt. Manchester City.

STABLEFORD, DONALD,
2nd Batt. Manchester City.

TAYLOR, LESLIE,
Royal Fusiliers, U.P.S. Batt.

WILKINSON, SIDNEY,
Border Regiment.

WITHERS, GEORGE,
Royal Field Artillery.

BARLOW & JONES, LTD.,
2, PORTLAND STREET, MANCHESTER.

AGNEW, T.
AINSCOW, E.
ALMOND, A.
ALMOND, J.
ANDERTON, T.
ASHTON, E.
ASPIN, H.
ASTLEY, F.
ATHERTON, R.
ATKINS, E.
BAGSHAW, G. H.
BAILEY, A. J.
BALL, J.
BALL, W. H.
BANN, N.
BARLOW, C.
BAYLISS, F.
BELL, F.
BELL, J. T.
BENYON, P.
BERESFORD, G.
BIGGS, P.
BINKS, S.
BIRCHALL, F.
BIRTLES, J.
BLACKBURN, E.
BOOTH, R.
BOOTH, W. J.
BOYD, G. A.
BOYERS, G.
BRADLEY, H.
BRIDGE, C. B.
BRINDLE, J.
BROOKES, W.
BROWN, H.
BROWN, F.
BROWN, J.
BROWN, L.
BROWN, W.
BRYAN, J. B.
BUTT, G. H.
BUTTNER, C. R.
CARR, W.
CARTER, C. F.

CARTER, E.
CARTER, F.
CAVANAGH, C.
CAVANAGH, H.
CHADWICK, R.
CHAPPELL, W.
CLARK, J.
CLEVELAND, J. E.
CRAWFORD, W.
CLOUGH, O.
COPSEY, H.
CROOK, C.
CROOK, J.
CROSTON, J.
CUNLIFFE, S.
DAVIES, H. O.
DAVIDSON, G.
DAY, F. J.
DEAN, G.
DENSON, J.
DIXON, R.
DODD, R.
DODDS, W.
DORNING, F.
DOWDALL, G. F.
DOWDING, C. S.
DOWNES, T.
DOYLE, B. M.
DUNN, S.
DUXBURY, J.
DYSON, H.
EAVES, H.
ENTWISTLE, J.
EVANS, H. KAY.
EVEREST, D.
FAIRHURST, A.
FARAGHER, E.
FEARNLEY, R.
FIELDING, E. J.
FLANAGAN, T.
FOREMAN, J.
FRANKLIN, S.
FRITH, W. H.
GADSBY, F.

GARDENER, A.
GIBBON, J. H.
GIBBONS, J.
GILLARD, W.
GODDARD, J. L.
GORTON, J.
GOTT, J.
GRADWELL, J.
GREENWOOD, J. W.
GRINDROD, W.
GRUNDY, G.
GUFFOGG, J.
HALL, F. McNEILL.
HALLSWORTH, J.
HAMER, J.
HAMER, S. R.
HAMPSON, W.
HAMS, F. J.
HANDLEY, W.
HARDY, F.
HARTLEY, H.
HATTON, W.
HAWES, P.
HOLROYD, H. L.
HELSBY, T.
HEWITT, T.
HEYES, H.
HIBBS, F. C.
HILES, L.
HILL, S.
HILLYARD, H. H.
HODGKINSON, L.
HOLLAND, J.
HOLLOWAY, F.
HOLT, L.
HOOLEY, A.
HOPE, J. H.
HORNBY, E.
HORROCKS, G.
HOWARD, A.
HOWIE, J. G.
HOYLE, J.
HUGHES, W. T.
HULME, A.

Barlow & Jones, Ltd.

ROLL OF HONOUR—Continued.

HULME, J.
HUNTER, N.
INCE, J.
IRELAND, J.
JACKSON, H.
JACKSON, J. S.
IRVINE, N.
JACKSON, W. T.
JEPSON, G. E.
JOHNSON, C.
JONES, A.
JONES, H. G.
KAY, J. E.
KEOWN, C.
KINDRED, J.
KIRKMAN, J. R.
KNOWLES, J. M.
LANE, R.
LANG, J. A.
LAWSON, A.
LAYCOCK, J.
LEE, W.
LEVER, R.
LOCKWOOD, A.
LOMAX, N.
LORRIMER, J. D.
LUCAS, F.
McCANNON, R.
McDERMOTT, J.
MALONEY, J.
MALONEY, P.
MANCKTELOW, W. H.
MARGINSON, H.
MARSHALL, A.
MATHER, E.
MATTHEWS, F.
MAYOH, A.
MEANLEY, H.
MELIA, W.
MILLER, H.
MILLS, H.
MOODY, A
MONKS, W.
MOORES, E.
MORRIS, N.
NEWTON, J.
NIGHTINGALE, L.
NIXON, G. B.
NORRIS, J.
NOWELL, W.
NUTTALL, P.
NUTTALL, J.

NUTTALL, S. W.
ORMROD, J.
PAILTHORPE, S. R.
PARKIN, T.
PARRY, D.
PEARCE, J.
PENNINGTON, J.
PENDLEBURY, F.
PHILLIPS, R. W.
PIPER, F.
POLLITT, M.
POTTER, F.
POTTER, H.
PRITCHARD, G.
RAMSBOTTOM, W.
RAMSDEN, F.
RICHARDSON, T. H.
RIDDEOUGH, F.
RIDINGS, A.
RIGBY, F.
ROBERTS, W.
ROBINSON, N.
ROBINSON, W. S.
ROSCOE, G.
ROTHWELL, J. W.
ROTHWELL, W.
ROYLE, J. C.
RYDER, J.
RYDEHEARD, W.
SARGINSON, H.
SCHOFIELD, J.
SCHOFIELD, T.
SCOWCROFT, J.
SEDDON, S.
SEDDON, W.
SHARPLES, J.
SHEARER, W. McD.
SHEPHERD, F.
SHURMER, F.
SIDES, W.
SIMPSON, H. J.
SINCLAIR, E.
SMITH, C.
SMITH, E.
SMITH, J.
SMITH, W. B.
SOUTHERN, W.
SPEIGHT, J.
STEPHENS, T.
SWIFT, S.
SWINGLEHURST, H. A.
TAYLOR, F.

TAYLOR, H.
TAYLOR, R.
TAYLOR, T.
THISTLETHWAITE H.
THOMAS, G. H. G.
THOMAS, W.
TIMPERLEY, A.
TONG, H.
TONGE, G.
TURNER, W. H.
TWIST, A.
UNWIN, W. H.
UNSWORTH, S.
VOSE, J.
WALKER, F.
WALKER, T. W.
WALL, D.
WALLACE, H.
WALMSLEY, J.
WALLWORK, A.
WALSH, T.
WATSON, A.
WEBB, J.
WEBSTER, H.
WEST, W.
WESTWOOD, A.
WHALLEY, H.
WHALLEY, P.
WHEELTON, J.
WHITEHEAD, W.
WHITELEGG, A.
WHITTLE, C.
WHITTON, W.
WILCOCK, R.
WIGGANS, A.
WILKINSON, A.
WILKINSON, C. L.
WILLIAMS, E. H.
WILLIAMS, H.
WILLIAMS, T.
WILSHAW, F. W.
WILSON, J. T.
WITHINGTON, H.
WOOD, H.
WOODBURN, L.
WORMALD, B.
WORTHINGTON, P. A.
WORTHINGTON, W.
WYCHERLEY, H.
YATES, S.
YATES, W. C.
YOUNG, R.

ROLL OF Beaty Bros (MCR) LTD HONOUR

MANCHESTER, OLDHAM, BOLTON, BLACKBURN, ROCHDALE, HANLEY, and BIRMINGHAM.

2nd Lieut. R. BEATY, 1st Garrison Batt. Manchester Regiment.

ANDERSON, H. S.,
  5th Bt. Loyal North Lancs. Regt.
BALLANTYNE, A.,
  4th East Lancashire Territorials.
BOYES, E.,
  Royal Field Artillery.
BELL, R.,
  11th Bt. King's O. R. Lancasters.
COTTAM, H.,
  15th Sv. Bt. Lancashire Fusiliers.
CARTER, J.,
  Royal Field Artillery.
CHADDERTON, J.,
  King's Own Royal Lancasters.
CARRUTHERS, J.,
  6th Manchester Regiment.
CARNALL, A.,
  Royal Field Artillery.
DEVENEY, J.,
  20th Sv. Bt. Manchester Regt.
DUNBAR, H.,
  6th Manchester Regiment (T.)
ENTWISTLE, J.,
  3rd Royal Scots.
FIRTH, W.,
  Royal Welsh Fusiliers.
GANDY, E.,
  22nd Sv. Bt. Manchester Regt.
GOLDSTRAW, A.,
  Royal Field Artillery.
GREENHALGH, E.,
  3rd Bt. East Lancs. R.F.A.
GRICE, A.,
  1st Manchesters.
GUNSHON, J.,
  King's Own Royal Lancasters.
HOLLAND, J.,
  Royal Engineers.
HOLLIDAY, W.,
  Royal Engineers.
HALL, H. E.,
  King's Liverpool.
HALL, R.,
  5th Loyal North Lancashires.
HEATON, W.,
  19th Lancashire Fusiliers.
HUGHES, S.,
  King's Liverpool Regiment.
KENNEDY, T.,
  Lancashire Fusiliers.
LEE, J.,
  3rd Manchester Regiment.
LAVER, B.,
  Royal Warwickshire Regiment.
LAW, J.,
  Loyal North Lancashire Regt.
McKENNING, C. M.,
  D. of Lancaster's Own Yeomanry.
McKIE, W.,
  10th Scottish Rifles.
ORMROD, J. R.,
  4th East Lancashire Territorials.
POWER, P.,
  Royal Engineers.
ROUSELL, W. S.,
  5th Bt. Loyal North Lancs. Regt.
SIMPSON, T.,
  Manchester Regiment.
SWANN, J.,
  Rifle Brigade.
SHANLEY, J.,
  King's Liverpool Regiment.
SMITH, J.,
  23rd Sv. Bt. Manchester Regt.
SIMMONS, W. B.,
  1st East Lancashire Regiment.
SALMON, P. H.,
  8th King's O. Royal Lancasters.
SMITH, A.,
  8th Manchester Regiment (T.).
TONGUE, H.,
  6th Manchester Regiment (T.)
WILSON, S.,
  7th Manchester Regiment (T.).

ROLL OF HONOUR.

Sir Jacob Behrens & Sons

MANCHESTER & BRADFORD.

"For King and Country."

Capt. HAROLD J. BEHRENS, 2/6th West Yorkshire Regiment.
Lieut. FRANK E. BEHRENS, 16th Manchester Regiment.
Lieut. EDGAR C. BEHRENS, Army Service Corps.
2nd Lieut. BRIAN FARROW, Lancashire Fusiliers.
Sergt. H. P. WARD, Royal Welsh Fusiliers.
L.-Sergt. DENIS GARBUTT, 1/6th West Yorkshire Regiment.
L.-Corpl. SIDNEY ATKIN, 22nd Manchester Regiment.
L.-Corpl. LEONARD PAERSCH, 2/7th Manchester Regiment.
Private W. ARMITAGE, Royal Army Medical Corps.
Private G. S. BOWDEN, 1/7th Manchester Regiment. (Died).
Private ALBAN CURTIS, 10th King's Own Ryl. Lancs. Regt.
Private STANLEY DUDSON, 16th Manchester Regiment.
Private J. W. GAUNT, 18th West Yorkshire Regiment.
Seaman J. H. GAZE, Royal Navy.
Private WALTER HITCHIN, 3/7th Manchester Regiment.
Private ARTHUR HOOLE, 3/6th Manchester Regiment.
Private H. HOLDSWORTH, Royal Army Medical Corps.
Private LEO LEATHLEY, 2/7th Manchester Regiment.
Private H. MIDDLEBROOK, 2/2nd West Riding R.F.A.
Private BERNARD MULLINS, 3/7th Manchester Regiment.
Private GEORGE OLIVER, Motor Transport Co.
Private JOHN PHILLIPS, 3/8th Manchester Regiment.
Private CHARLES SHARROCK, 2/7th Manchester Regiment.
Private ANDREW SLATER, 3/7th Manchester Regiment.
Private PERCY THRUSH, Queen's Own Yorkshire Dragoons.
Private HARRY TURNER, Queen's Own Yorkshire Dragoons.
Gunner H. W. WATSON, Royal Field Artillery.
Private ALFRED WHITEHEAD, 18th Manchester Regiment.
Private S. PATERSON, Royal Army Medical Corps.

ROLL OF HONOUR.

BEITH, STEVENSON & CO., LIMITED.
14, Bridge Street, Manchester.

✱ ✱ ✱

List of Names of Members of the Staff Serving with the Colours.

BRETT, Capt. H.C.	Duke of Cornwall's Light Infantry.
McNICOL, Capt. R. J.	8th Lancashire Fusiliers.
ANDERTON, 2nd-Lt. N. H.	Lancashire Fusiliers.
BURGESS, 2nd-Lt. C.	West Lanc. Terr. Brig. R.F.A.
FLANAGAN, 2nd-Lt. R. S.	4th Royal Inniskilling Fusiliers.
HAY, 2nd-Lt. E.	Cambridgeshire Regiment.
HUNT, 2nd-Lt. R. T.	4th East Lancashire Regiment.
OPENSHAW, 2nd-Lt. G. O.	5th East Lancashire Regiment.
HARVEY, Sergt. A.	7th Lancashire Fusiliers.
FREEBERNE, Cpl. S. L.	9th King's Royal Rifles.
JOHNSON, L.-Cpl. L. W.	6th Manchester Regiment.
OGDEN, L.-Corpl. G.	7th Lancashire Fusiliers.
ANDREW, Pte. F.	Royal Army Medical Corps.
BOWEN, Pte. J.	15th Lancashire Fusiliers.
BRACKENRIDGE, Pte. W.	Public Schools Batt. Royal Fusiliers.
BULLOCK, Pte. J.	6th Manchester Regiment.
BURGESS, Pte. J. S.	7th Manchester Regiment.
CARTER, Pte. T. H.	Army Service Corps.
COOLING, Pte. F. N.	Royal Army Medical Corps.
COX, Pte. H. C.	Public Schools Batt. Royal Fusiliers.
DARBYSHIRE, Trooper S.	"B" Squadron, Cheshire Yeomanry.
HUDSON, Pte. J. F.	14th King's (Liverpool) Regiment.
JONES, Pte. S. T. E.	17th King's (Liverpool) Regiment.
MONK, Pte. E.	6th Manchester Regiment.
MOORE, Driver F.	Motor Transport Section A.S.C.
PIGOT, Pte. L. V.	Royal Army Medical Corps.
RATCLIFFE, Pte. C. A.	7th Manchester Regiment.
RAVENSCROFT, Trooper F.	"B" Squadron Cheshire Yeomanry.
SMETHURST, Pte. W. K.	Public Schools Batt. Royal Fusiliers.
STEELE, Pte. E. D.	Public Schools Batt. Royal Fusiliers.
STOTT, Pte. J. A.	6th Manchester Regiment.
TALLENT, Gunner W.	2nd East Lancs. R.F.A.
TYRRELL, Pte. G.	8th Loyal North Lancashire Regiment.
WARD, Pte. N. E.	6th Manchester Regiment.
WISE, Pte. W. L.	Royal Army Medical Corps.
WOOLMER, Pte. S.	18th King's (Liverpool) Regiment.
YOUNG, Pte. L.	Motor Transport Section A.S.C.

ROLL OF HONOUR

Members and Employees of
Baerlein & Sons and Baerlein Bros
12 Blackfriars Street, Salford.

SONS OF PARTNERS.

Lieut. O. F. Baerlein	A.S.C.
2nd Lieut. A. A. Baerlein	68th Brigade R.F.A.

EMPLOYEES.

Harry Thomas	16th Lancashire Fusiliers.
Eric McKay	Lancashire Fusiliers.
W. Russell Jones	R.G.A.
Thomas Jackson	6th Border Regiment.
Sidney Herbert Pearson	8th Border Regiment.
E. Cheetham	Manchester Regiment.
Frank Hyde	8th Lancashire Fusiliers.
Walter Lewis	R.A.M.C.
Joseph Wade	H.M.S. "Tiger."
E. Bradshaw	16th Lancashire Fusiliers.
L. Cullerne	16th Service Batt. Manchester Regt.
Harold C. Gandy	H.M.S. "Roxburg."
C. W. Hopkinson	Royal Navy Medical Corps.
H. Hunt	16th Lancashire Fusiliers.
F. W. Webster	19th Rifle Brigade.
T. Wilkinson	7th Lancashire Fusiliers.
F. Leigh	6th Cheshires (T.F.).
A. Brooks	26th Manchesters.
J. Deasy	8th Manchesters (T.F., Ardwicks).

ROLL OF HONOUR.

BELSIZE MOTORS LTD.
Clayton, Manchester.

OFFICE.

CROWDER, S., *Royal Army Medical Corps.*
DUDLEY, Sergt. A., *Army Service Corps (M.T.).*
EARLE, A., *Army Service Corps.*
FLEMING, T., *Army Pay Corps.*
FOXLEY, J., *Army Service Corps.*
HALPIN, Corporal C., *Rifle Brigade.*
HAMBLIN, G., *6th Batt. Manch/r Regt. (T.F.).*
HARTY, W., *Royal Engineers.*
HAYNES, Bomb. E., *Cnty. Palatine Artillery.*
HIRST, E., *8th Batt. Manchester Regt. (T.F.).*
LYNCH, A., *8th Batt. Manchester Regt. (T.F.).*
MOLLARD, F., *4th Batt. Manchester Regt.*
SMITH, Sergt.-Major J. A., *W. Yorkshire Regt.*
TWISS, G., *Army Service Corps (M.T.).*
WHITNEY, R. J., *King's Liverpool Regt.*

WORKS.

ALDRED, R., *Rifle Brigade.*
ALLAN, W., *Army Service Corps.*
ASHTON, T., *9th Batt. Border Regt.*
ASHTON, F., *Royal Flying Corps.*
BARRACLOUGH, A., *Royal Engineers.*
BARTON, —, *6th Batt. Rifle Brigade.*
BAYBUT, H., *19th Batt. Manchester Regt.*
BAYLE, M., *8th Batt. Manchester Regt. (T.F.).*
BELLAMY, B., *Royal Naval Air Service.*
BENNETT, J., *Cheshire Regt.*
BICKERSTON, —, *7th Batt. Manchester Regt.*
BIANCHI, A., *Royal Engineers.*
BODEN, F., *8th Batt. Manchester Regt. (T.F.).*
BOOTH, J., *King's Own Lancaster Regt.*
BOULD, N., *Royal Scots.*
BOYLE, M., *7th Batt. Manchester Regiment.*
BRADDOCK, G., *8th Lancs. Fusiliers (Terr.).*
BRIGGS, J., *Royal Field Artillery.*
BRISCOE, D., *Royal Field Artillery.*
BUDD, C., *Army Service Corps (M.T.).*
BULLOCK, E., *13th Batt. Manchester Regt.*
BURNEY, W., *Army Service Corps (M.T.).*
BURNS, H., *Army Service Corps.*
CALDWELL, W., *8th Batt. H.S. Lancs. Fus.*
CHADWICK, H., *Army Service Corps (M.T.).*
CLANCEY, J., *Royal Engineers.*
COATES, W., *Army Vet. Corps.*
COUPE, —, *Army Service Corps.*
COPELAND, G., *Army Service Corps (M.T.).*
CROSBY, D., *Army Service Corps (M.T.).*
DANN, P. W., *Loyal North Lancashires.*
DAVIES, J., *Naval Reserve, H.M.S. "Canopus."*
DAWSON, T., *7th Batt. Manchester Regt.*
DEAN, C., *Royal Army Medical Corps.*
DEANS, J., *3rd Batt. Lancashire Fusiliers.*
DONBAVAND, J., *7th Batt. East Lancs. Regt.*
DORAN, —, *North Lancashire Regt.*
DUNN, H., *Royal Field Artillery.*
EARNSHAW, J., *Army Service Corps (M.T.).*
EDWARDS, A., *Army Service Corps.*
FEATHERSTONE, H., *8th Bt. Man. Rgt. (T.F.).*
FERUSON, V., *Army Service Corps.*
FITZSIMONS, R., *Rifle Brigade.*
FRASER, A. V., *Flying Corps, Furnborough.*
GARBUTT, —, *Army Service Corps.*
GILLARD, J., *8th Batt. Manchester Regt.*
GREAVES, A., *6th Batt. Cheshire Regt.*
GREEN, —, *Lancashire Fusiliers.*
GREEN, P., *Army Service Corps.*
GODDARD, Sergt. W., *11th Hussars (Res.).*

BELSIZE MOTORS LTD. Continued.

HADFIELD, S., *17th Batt. Manchester Regt.*
HASLAM, S., *6th Batt. Rifle Brigade.*
HEADING, J., *Army Service Corps (M.T.).*
HEBB, H. S., *2/8th Batt. Royal Fusiliers.*
HICKMAN, W., *Royal Garrison Artillery.*
HOLDING, P., *Royal Army Medical Corps.*
HORNBY, J., *Royal Engineers.*
HOUGH, H., *6th Batt. Manchester Regt.*
HOWARTH, E., *Royal Flying Corps.*
HURST, —, *Royal Marines.*
INGHAM, W., *Army Service Corps (M.T.).*
JACQUES, —, *9th Batt. Manch/r Regt. (T.F.).*
JOHNSON, C., *8th Batt. Manch/r Regt. (T.F.).*
JOHNSON, W., *Royal Field Artillery (Res.).*
JONES, J., Junr., *Army Service Corps.*
JONES, —, *7th Batt. Rifle Brigade.*
KELLY, —, *Manchester Regt. (Reservist).*
KNOWLES, —, *6th Batt. Manch/r Regt. (Terr.).*
KNOTT, D., *Army Service Corps (M.T.).*
LIVESY, Corpl. C., *Army Service Corps (M.T.).*
LONGWORTH, J., *Royal Field Artillery.*
MADELEY, A., *8th Batt. Manchester Regt.*
MANSFIELD, F., *8th Batt. Manchester Regt.*
McDOWELL, D., *King's Royal Rifles.*
McGREORY, J., *Royal Engineers.*
McMILLAN, D., *Royal Army Medical Corps.*
MOORES, H., *56th Infantry Brigade.*
MORTER, P., *Loyal North Lancashires.*
MORRIS, G., *Army Service Corps (M.T.).*
MOUNTFORD, H., *Royal Engineers.*
MULLANEY, Corp. J., *Army S. Corps (M.T.).*
NAIRN, H., *Royal Garrison Artillery (Res.).*
NEEDHAM, A., *Army Service Corps.*
OATES, J., *King's Royal Rifles.*
O'KELLY, D., *Royal Engineers.*
O'MARA, J., *3rd Batt. Lincolnshire Regt.*
O'NEIL, *Manchester Regt.*
PARKER, H., *2nd Batt. Manchester Regt.*
PARKER, H., *Lancashire Fusiliers.*
PARKIN, J., *6th Batt. Rifle Brigade.*

PEARSON, D., *King's Own Scottish Borderers.*
PEARSON, E., *Army Service Corps.*
PILLING, J., *Royal Engineers.*
PILKINGTON, T., *Army Service Corps.*
RAY, W., *Lancashire Fusiliers.*
REEVES, C., *Army Service Corps.*
RHODES, —, *Public Schools Batt.*
ROGERS, W., *Manchester Regt.*
ROPER, H., *Border Regt.*
ROWBOTTOM, J., *Army Service Corps.*
SCANLON, Sergt., *Rifle Brigade.*
SHARPLES, V., *8th (Irish) Batt. King's R.R.*
SHENTON, R., *8th Batt. K. O. Rl. Lanc. Regt.*
SHUTTLEWORTH, J., *7th Lancs. Fus. (T.F.).*
SLANEY, L.-Corp. J. S., *8th Batt. Man. Regt.*
STONE, J., *8th Batt. Manchester Regt.*
STOREY, H., *South Wales Borderers.*
THAW, W., *King's Own Scottish Borderers.*
TONGE, A., *Royal Engineers.*
VICKERS, —, *Manchester Regt.*
WALKENSHAW, A., *Royal Engineers.*
WALKER, D., *Public Schools Batt.*
WALLWORK, A., *Army Service Corps (M.T.).*
WARD, J., *Army Service Corps.*
WASHBOURNE, J., *Army Service Corps.*
WEBSTER, J., *King's Own Liverpool Regt.*
WHALLEY, L.-Corp. A., *8th Batt. Mancr. Regt.*
WHITING, A., *Army Service Corps (M.T.).*
WHITTAKER, A., *6th Batt. Manchester Regt.*
WILLIAMS, T., *Royal Engineers.*
WILLIAMS, J., *Scottish Borderers.*
WILLIAMS, J., *East Lancs. Artillery (R.F.A.).*
WILLIAMSON, B., *Army Service Corps.*
WILSON, E., *King's Own Lancaster Regt.*
WILSON, H., *King's Royal Rifles.*
WINSBOROUGH, Sergt. W., *R.A.M.C.*
WINTERS, C., *Army Service Corps.*
WITTINGHAM, G., *Border Regt.*
WOOD, N., *Rifle Brigade.*
YATES, L.-Corp. H., *Army S. Corps (M.T.).*

The following employés have left to join the Forces, but we have been unable to ascertain which Regiments they have enlisted in :—

BODDY, A.	JONES, —.	MEAKEN, J.	MURPHY, M.
HAMER, W.	KILCOYNE, —.	MOORES, —.	PERRY, J.
HITCHENS, H.	McCULLOCK, —.	MORSTON, P.	ROSE, E.
HOPKINSON, H.	McGRAY, —.	MOSELEY, —.	SMITH, —.

Roll of Honour.

* * *

Members and Employees of
S. D. BLES & SONS
54 Princess Street, Manchester

Serving with the Colours.

* * *

Partners and Sons of Partners.

Captain Arthur Bles	Royal Welsh Fusiliers.
2nd Lieutenant G. M. Bles	1st City Batt. Man. Regt.
2nd Lieutenant J. L. Bles	5th Cheshire Regiment.

Employees.

2nd Lieutenant E. Knott	1/6th Batt. Manchester Regiment.
Sergeant Bullmann	R.F.A.
Corporal E. Bamford	No. 2261, B. Co., 1/6th Batt. Man. Regt.
Corporal C. H. S. Moss	No. 2249, 1/6th Batt. Man. Regt.
Lance-Corporal V. Taylor	No. 17443, K.O. Royal Lancs.
Driver T. Barlow	No. 1159, 2/1st East Lancs. Div. A.S.C.
*Private H. Bebbington	No. 2253, B. Co., 1/6th Batt. Man. Regt.
†Private H. Chadwick	No. 3635, 8th Manchester Regt.
†Private M. Craddock	No. 17406, South Lancs. Regt.
*Private T. Eckersley	No. 2431, B. Co., 1/6th Batt. Man. Regt.
Private B. Halliday	No. 2402, B. Co., 1/6th Batt. Man. Regt.
Private D. Handley	No. 1190, Manchester R.F.A.
Private F. H. Jackson	No. 748, 8th Manchester Regt.
Driver W. G. Moult	No. 929, 1st Field Co., 3rd Lancs. R.E.
Private H. Pollard	No. 2353, 2nd South Lancs. Regt.
Private J. Rogerson	No. 2331, B. Co., 1/6th Batt. Man. Regt.
Rifleman R. Sumner	No. 2404, 9th Batt. Rifle Brigade.

*Killed in Action.   † Received Discharge Certificates.

The Bradford Dyers' Association Limited.

LANCASHIRE.

MANCHESTER OFFICE.

BOWLING, ALAN - - 20th S. Bt. Royal Fusiliers.
GALLOWAY, JOSEPH - 6th S. Bt. South Lancs.
SEXTON, WILLIAM - Naval Reserve.
WATERS, ARTHUR - 19th S. Bt. Manchester R.

ENGINEERING DEPARTMENT.

LOWE, THOMAS - - - Royal Fleet Reserve.
McCLUNEY, WM. - - 3rd Co., K. Bt. Man/r R.
REAVEY, WILLIAM - 3rd Bt. Manchester Regt.

THE ASHENHURST DYEING CO., LTD.

BANNISTER, F. O.
BAXTER, JOHN WM.
BARTLETT, GEORGE.
BRANDRICK, JOHN.
BRIERLEY, RD.
BROWN, WILLIAM.
CAVANAGH, JOSEPH.
CONDRON, JAMES.
CONDRON, JOSEPH.
COOPER, WM.
CRIGHTON, ARNOLD.
CUNNINGHAM, M.
CUNNINGHAM, P.
DUNN, NEWSOME.
GANT, HERBERT.
GANT, WILLIAM.
GILTRAP, ROBERT.
GLEADALL, FRANK.
HOBSON, RANDALL.
HUTCHINSON, W. G.
JONES, RD.
KAY, JONATHAN.
KELLETT, GEORGE.
KERSHAW, RD.
MORRIS, WALTER F.
OLIVER, JOSEPH.
PEOVER, HARRY.
PICKERING, FRED.
POLLITT, RD. A.
POPE, JOHN.
ROBERTS, A.
ROBERTS, JOHN B.
ROBINSON, JOHN.
ROUTLEDGE, H.
SALT, J.
TOMLINSON, P. L.
TOOTAL, ARTHUR.
TYSON, JAMES.
WAGSTAFFE, BENJ.
WRIGHT, WM. H.

MESSRS. J. and H. BLEACKLEY, LTD.

ASHWORTH, T. A.
BLAKELEY, HENRY.
CHAPMAN, SAMUEL.
COOPER, REG.
DAWSON, DAVID.
DAWSON, A.
DENNIS, JOS.
ECKERSALL, S.
FOSTER, FRED.
GREENHALGH, WM.
HANNAH, ROBT.
JACKSON, FREDK. A.
KIRKBRIDE, WM.
LEVER, ALFRED.
LLOYD, BEN.
LORD, EDWIN.
MALLINSON, TOM.
MALLINSON, CHAS.
MATHER, PERCY.
MEADOWS, WM.
PEARSON, HARRY.
PENSON, CHAS.
PLATT, J. W.
RACE, GEORGE.
ROTHWELL, J., Junr.
TAYLOR, WALLACE.
WILES, CHAS., Junr.
WILES, HENRY.
YATES, JAMES.

The Bradford Dyers' Association Ltd.
CONTINUED.

F. CAWLEY and CO., LTD.

ASHTON, FRANK.
ASHTON, WILLIAM.
BAGNALL, HARRY.
BAMFORD, F.
BEATSON, ARTHUR.
BENT, W.
BOOTH, T.
BOUGH, M.
BOULGER, J.
BOARDMAN, H.
BROWN, T. H.
BURKILL, G.
CARL, J.
CLUNEY, G.
CONWAY, J.
CORLESS, M.
CROASDALE, E.
DAVIES, A.
DAWSON, J.
DAWSON, JAMES.
DAWSON, JAMES.
DUNN, L. A.
EVANS, H.
EVANS, R.
GARNETT, F.
GARNETT, JOHN.
GIBLIN, J.
GREEN, J.
GRUNDY, F.
HADDOCK, JOHN.
HARRIS, C.
HEARNE, F. J.
HUGHES, T.
HUNT, FRANK.
HUTCHINSON, T.
JONES, J.
KINGHAM, J. E.
KYNASTON, J.
MARLAND, R.
McLOUGHLIN, A.
MEE, G.
MILLWARD, J.
NEWTON, T.
NICHOLS, W.
NORTH, F.
ORMROD, J.
PATTILLO, W.
POMFRET, V. L.
POTTER, WM.
QUIGLEY, J.
RENFREW, J.
RIGBY, J. W.
ROBINSON, T. B.
ROGERSON, J. E.
ROSTRON, W. H.
SALDARINI, C.
SALT, F.
SCHOFIELD, G.
SMITH, W. H.
SMITHIES, HARRY.
STORY, J. B.
TAYLOR, J. H.
THORNTON, JAMES.
TOFT, W.
WALL, F.
WALL, G. F.
WALKER, DOUGLAS.
WOLSTENHOLME, J.
YATES, SUDWORTH.

ADAM HAMILTON and SONS, LTD.

BARR, MICHAEL.
BENN, HARRY.
BOYLE, ED.
BROWN, WM.
BURKE, ED.
CHERRY, THOS.
CONNELL, JOHN.
COCHRANE, JAS.
CONNELL, ARCHIE.
COTTON, JOSEPH.
CRAIG, ROBERT.
CRAWFORD, WM.
CROMBIE, PAT.
CRUICKSHANKS, R.
DICKSON, JAMES.
DOUGLAS, JOHN.
DREGHORN, JAS.
DREGHORN, JOHN.
ESTLICK, GEO.
FAIRMAN, ED.
FORBES, ROBT.
FOSTER, PAT.
FORRESTER, H.
FULTON, H.
FULTON, WM.
GIBSON, WM.
HAMILTON, ROBT.
HAMILTON, WM.
HAMILTON, DAN.
HAMILTON, JOHN.
HELBURN, ROBT.
HOWATT, JAMES.
HUNTER, ARCH.
HUNTER, CONNEL.
HUNTER, DUGALD.
JOHNSTON, WM.
JACK, JAMES.
KANE, JAS.
KENNEDY, ARCH.
LAPSLEY, JAS.
LEONARD, FRANCIS.
LINDSAY, WM.
LOCHRIE, WM.
LOCHRIE, ED.
LEONARD, MICHAEL.
McAULAY, WM.
McDONALD, ED.
McDONALD, M.
McDONALD, JAS.
McLAREN, JOHN.
McMILLAN, PETER.
MAXWELL, S.
McGINN, JAMES.
McDONALD, NEILL.
McKENDRICK, JAS.
MEECHAN, SAM.
MEECHAN, JOS.
MURRAY, JOHN.
MUIRHEAD, JOHN.
MYLETT, HUGH.
NELLIS, JOHN.
PATON, WM.
PRICE, ED.
ROBINSON, FRANK.
RUSSELL, DUNCAN.
SCOBIE, STEWART.
SERVICE, ALEX.
SMITH, WM.
STEEL, JAS.
STEWART, JAMES.
STEWART, JAS.
STORRIE, DAVID.

The Bradford Dyers' Association Ltd.
CONTINUED.

ADAM HAMILTON and SONS, LTD.—Continued.

TONNER, GEORGE.
TRAYNER, JAMES.
WHITE, WM.
WHITE, HUGH.
WHITTON, EDWARD.
WILSON, JOHN.
YOUNG, ANDREW.

H. KERSHAW and SON, LTD.

ALLEN, ALBERT.
APLIN, CHAS. L.
BATTY, EDWARD.
BAKER, JAMES.
BALMFORTH, THOS.
BANKS, W.
BARLOW, EDGAR.
BODEN, F.
BRANDRICK, T.
BRISCOE, J. E.
BRUNDRETT, J.
CARR, R.
CAVANAGH, J. A.
CHARLTON, R.
COACKLEY, ASA.
COACKLEY, FRANK.
COLLIER, A.
COOKSON, JOSEPH.
COUSER, T.
DARLINGTON, F.
DAVIES, J. E.
DEAKIN, J. T.
DERBYSHIRE, J.
DUFFY, JOHN.
FULLER, JOHN.
GALLIER, J.
GARNER, C. F.
GASKELL, HAROLD.
GLOSSOP, ROBT.
GREEN, A.
GLEAVES, JOHN.
HAMER, JAS.
HAND, T.
HARWOOD, JAS. S.
HARWOOD, JOS. W.
HAWKINS, S.
HELLINGS, W.
HEYES, SAMUEL.
HOLDING, H.
HOLME, RICHARD.
HOLT, JAS.
HODGKINSON, A.
HODGSON, F.
HUDSON, ALLAN.
ILLSTON, C.
INGHAM, J. H.
KELLY, J.
LANSLEY, ALFRED.
LOCKETT, CHAS.
LOWE, JAMES.
MATHER, T.
McFARLANE, J.
McHUGH, T.
MOON, W.
MOON, JAS.
MORAN, R. F.
MORRIS, JAS. R.
MULVEY, SAMUEL.
NEILL, J.
ODDIE, JAMES.
OSBORNE, A. J.
PRYSE, J.
RENSHAW, J.
ROFF, H.
RUSSELL, GEORGE.
RUSSELL, J.
RUSSELL, T. P.
SHAW, ISAAC.
SIDDALL, CHAS.
SILCOCK, JAS.
SKELLERN, ERNEST.
SMITH, T.
SMITHSON, THOS.
STANSFIELD, J.
STEELE, J. T.
THOMAS, S.
TITLEY, S.
UNSWORTH, H. G.
WALLWORK, B.
WARE, T.
WHIPDAY, JOHN.
WILLIAMS, H.
WILLCOX, G.
WILLCOCK, J.
WILSON, SAMUEL.
WRIGLEY, LEO.
WIGLEY, A.

ROBERT PEEL and CO., LTD.

BAMBER, DAVID.
BATES, F.
BREARLEY, JAMES.
BROWNLOW, W. T.
BURDAKY, FRED.
CLACK, J. E.
COLLINS, J.
DOWNIE, J.
DOYLE, C.
EDGAR, W.
FARRELL, H.
FAULKNER, JAMES.
GILBERT, A. J.
GILLIBRAND, J. J.
GLEESON, J.
GORDON, WM.
GREEN, S.
HOWARD, H.
HOWELL, J.
HEAVISIDE, H.
HOPTON, T. W.
HUNT, ROBT.
KENDRICK, S.
KITE, NAT.
LOVATT, J.
MASSEY, HY.
MASTERS, E. H.
MATTHEWS, JOHN.
MEAKIN, J.
MOTTERSHEAD, R.
NICHOLL, GILBERT T.
NORMAN, J. J.
PEARCE, W.
RIDLEY, JOSEPH.
RYAN, JOHN.
SEVILLE, T.
SMITH, A.
STENNETT, W.
VESTY, WILLIAM.
WARD, C.

The Bradford Dyers' Association Ltd.
CONTINUED.

T. ROBINSON and CO., LTD.

ALTHAM, J. W.
BAILEY, T.
BALL, W.
BIRCHALL, J.
BOOTH, G.
BRIDGEHOUSE, J. H.
BROOKS, W.
BUTTERWORTH, J. H.
CRYNE, V.
CROMBLEHOLME, R.
DUCKWORTH, L. R.
DUCKWORTH, F.
EARNSHAW, F.
FOSTER, A.
GREENHALGH, H.
HALL, H. T.
HARRISON, T.
HARNMAN, J.
HIGGINS, R.
HIGHAM, W.
HOLT, F.
HORSFALL, F.
HOWARTH, H.
LABROW, W.
LOMAX, H.
McINNES, A.
McKAY, W.
MEALEY, P. O.
MILLS, F.
MOORE, J. W.
MULLIGAN, C.
NICHOLAS, G.
NUTTALL, R.
PEARSON, W. H.
PYECROFT, E.
RACE, A. E.
SHERIDAN, J.
SLATER, J. A.
SNAPE, R.
WALLBANK, J.
WARD, E.
WALSH, R.
WILDING, R.

THE STANDISH COMPANY, LTD.

ABBOTT, FRED.
ABBOTT, WILLIAM.
AINSCOUGH, J. W.
ALLEN, STANLEY.
ARROWSMITH, H.
ASHURST, JOHN.
ASPINALL, R.
BIBBY, ROBERT.
BIGGINS, PEARCE.
BROWN, EDWARD.
CHADWICK, J. R.
CHIPPENDALE, T.
COLEMAN, ALAN F.
COOPER, MILNER.
CROOK, HUGH.
CROOK, JOSEPH.
CULSHAW, JOHN.
CULSHAW, THOMAS.
CUSH, JAS. ALEX.
DAWSON, A.
DUCKWORTH, JAS.
EASTHAM, S.
FAIRHURST, A.
GOLDTHORP, L.
GOODWIN, J.
GRAY, HERBERT.
HART, RICHARD.
HART, THOMAS.
HADDON, SAMUEL.
HALL, F.
HAYDOCK, JOHN.
HARRISON, ROBT.
HILTON, JOHN.
HILTON, THOS.
HOCKING, FRED.
HOLMES, A. B.
HOPE, LEONARD.
HUNT, EDWARD A.
HUTCHINSON, JOHN.
JEFFREY, JAMES.
JACKSON, THOMAS.
KEIGHERY, THOS. P.
KNEALE, JAMES E.
KNOWLES, L.
LAWRENSON, JOS.
LEIGH, CHAS.
LIPPIETT, JOS.
LUCAS, WILLIAM.
MATTHEWS, J. J.
MAKINSON, WM.
McCARTNEY, ROBT.
MORLEY, JOHN B.
NORMINGTON, J.
PARKER, JOHN.
PEARSON, WM.
RAWSTERNE, JAS.
SHARP, HERBERT.
SKELLON, WM.
SMITH, JAMES.
SMITH, W. S.
SUTCLIFFE, JOSEPH.
SYNER, WALTER.
SYNER, WM. HENRY.
TAYLOR, JAMES.
TAYLOR, WALTER.
TRANTER, E. C.
WALSH, THOMAS.
WASS, TOM.
WARD, CHAS.
WARBURTON, H.
WEAVER, HENRY.
WESTHEAD, JOHN.
WHITTLE, RALPH.
WINSTANLEY, ROBT.
WOODHOUSE, JOS.
YATES, ERNEST.
YATES, JESSE.
YOUNG, SAMUEL.

The Bradford Dyers' Association Ltd.
CONTINUED.

YORKSHIRE.

THE BRADFORD DYERS' ASSOCIATION, LTD.
39, Well Street, Bradford.
Head Offices.

BENTLEY, J. E.	HODGKINS, HY.	STRINGER, H. G.
BROSCOMBE, I.	HURWORTH, HY.	STOTT, WALTER.
BINNS, HENRY I.	JOHNSON, VICTOR.	SCREETON, BERT.
BARRACLOUGH, F.	KAY, ARNOLD.	SIMPSON, HARRY.
BROADBENT, C. H.	KENYON, F. W.	SIMPSON, WM. GEO.
CALEB, WILLIE.	LISTER, PERCIVAL.	SHAW, L.
CULPAN, J.	LILLEY, H.	SMITH, WALT.
CLAPHAM, J. P.	LEIGHTON, GEO.	SIMPSON, F.
CHAMBERS, FRED P.	MARVELL, HERBT.	SPEAK, H.
EVANS, WM. GEO.	McPHERESON, W. G.	UNDERWOOD, H.
ELLIOTT, J.	MOORE, F.	WILD, JOS.
EDWARDS, IRVIN J.	MYERS, A. L.	WOOLLARD, G. F.
FOSTER, J.	MYERS, H. A. R.	WRIGHT, B. B.
FROOD, G. B.	NEALE, GEO.	WRIGHT, STANLEY.
GRIFFITH, F. R.	PARRINGTON, J. R.	WOOLLERTON, F.
GRIMSHAW, C. H.	PHILLIPS, A. E.	WISEMAN, WM.
GREENWOOD, H.	PEDLEY, EDGAR.	WILSON, EDGAR.
HEWITT, H.	PICKLES, WALTER.	
HOLMES, CHAS.	RIPLEY, EDGAR.	

Burrow Street, Manchester Road, Bradford.
Making-Up Department.

ATKINSON, H.	GILES, H. A.	NUTT, THOS.
CLARK, J.	HENDERSON, H. E.	TAYLOR, G.
COOK, H.	HEAD, V. G.	THOMAS, WM.
CRESSWELL, W. J.	MASON, P. R.	WALKER, A. C.
DUFTON, N.	MASON, ALB.	

Rosse Street, Thornton Road, Bradford.
Central Workshop.

BERRYMAN, JOHN W.	KAY, WILLIAM.	POYNTON, E. O.
CALVERT, W.	LODGE, THOS.	PRESTON, WM.
HARRINGTON, E. C.	MARSDEN, EDGAR.	RAMSDEN, F. G.

WILLIAM AYKROYD and SONS, LTD.
Oakwood Dyeworks, Bradford.

AYKROYD, Lt.-Col. H.E.	BOWER, THOS.	BLACKBURN, J. A.
BUTTERWORTH, A.	BARSON, WM.	BREWER, T. H.
BRIGGS, EDGAR.	BUTTERFIELD, ED.	BRADLEY, W. K.

The Bradford Dyers' Association Ltd.
CONTINUED.

WILLIAM AYKROYD and SONS, LTD.—Continued.

BURGESS, HY.
BROWN, ALBERT.
BEAUMONT, HARRY.
CRAVEN, SAM.
CATTON, FRED.
CRAVEN, T. W.
CLAYTON, HORACE.
DUCKETT, HY.
DEAN, FRED.
DELANEY, JAS.
DYKES, JAS.
EDWARDS, JAS.
FLETCHER, J.
FOSTER, FRED.
FISHER, HERBERT.
GAUNT, W.
GAUNT, H.
GIBBARD, L.
GILGAN, JAMES.
GOMMLICK, E. H. H.
ISITT, JAS.
JAGGER, WILLIAM.
KENNEDY, JOHN T.
LAYCOCK, WILLIE.
McAVAN, THOS.
McCANN, H. E.
MIDDLETON, M.
MORAN, F.
MURDOCK, JAS.
McAVAN, H.
OWEN, LEONARD.
PALLISER, JOHN.
PEARSON, THOS.
PINDER, ATKINSON.
PITTS, GEO.
PARKINSON, W.
PINDER, A.
ROBINSON, J. W.
ROWLEY, M.
RIX, ARTHUR.
RAWNSLEY, ED. L.
RAPER, MATTHEW.
SWAILES, HARRY.
SWAILES, E.
STEPHENSON, W. J.
SENIOR, NAYLOR.
TOMLINSON, S.
THOMPSON, C.
TANKARD, WILLIE.
THOMPSON, HORACE.
TETLEY, EDWIN.
THOMPSON, J. H.
TOMLINSON, FRED.
WHITAKER, W. H.
WALDRON, T. H.
WILKINSON, JOHN G.

GEORGE ARMITAGE, LIMITED.
West End Dyeworks, Halifax.

ARMITAGE, FRANK.
BALME, HARRY.
DENT, JAS.
FORT, JOS.
FLYNN, JAS.
FEATHER, ERNEST.
ILLINGWORTH, ALB.
KERR, JOHN A.
OSWIN, H.
VARLEY, HARRY.
WALKER, HAROLD.
YATES, EDWIN.

Thornton Road, Bradford.

ATKINSON, J.
ARMITAGE, H. G.
AUDE, J.
APPLEYARD, WM. B.
ARNOLD, WILLIAM.
BOYLE, W.
BEANLAND, WALT.
BARTLE, H. L.
BINKS, W.
BROWN, H. W.
BURGESS, J.
BARKER, CHAS.
BLAND, JOS.
CROSLAND, A.
COULTAN, J. T.
CHADWICK, H. R.
CATHERALL, FRED.
COCKETT, RICHARD.
DELANEY, R.
DIMBERLINE, W.
DODDS, JOS.
DYSON, JOHN.
FIELD, HARRY.
FIRTH, W. E.
GORMAN, JAS.
GREENHOUGH, A.
GORMAN, JOS. H.
HARLAND, A.
HARRISON, WM.
HALLIWELL, S.
HEWITT, ARTHUR.
HOWARD, E.
HILEY, SETH.
JOYNES, DAVID.
KENNINGHAM, ED.
KEATING, J.
KENNY, H.
KILBRIDE, V.
KNOWLES, JAS. WM.
KING, HUGH.
LONG, ARTHUR, E.
LEACH, WALTER.
LEIGH, ALBERT.
McDONALD, A.
McGOWAN, G.
MOORE, A.
MILLAR, G.
MURPHY, W.
MURPHY, E.
POTTER, WALTER.
PARKES, H.
SMITH, H. H.
SHAW, GEORGE.
STANLEY, SYDNEY.
THOMPSON, J.
TAYLOR, JOE.
VARLEY, H.
WARRENER, GEO.
WESTERMANN, WM.
WILKINSON, BENJ.
WILKINSON, J.
WOODHEAD, S.
WHITELY, J.
WALLACE, C.
YATES, JOHN WM.

The Bradford Dyers' Association Ltd.
CONTINUED.

AYKROYD and GRANDAGE, LTD.
Thornton Road, Bradford.

BARLOW, ALFRED.
BROGDEN, THOS.
BRAYSHAW, FRED.
BUTTERWORTH, P.
BEETHAM, JOS.
BENTLEY, GEORGE.
BERRY, OSCAR.
BRINKMAN, JOHN.
BURTON, ERNEST.
CRESSWELL, J. H.
COATES, JOHN.
CALVERT, L.
CULLEN, HAROLD.
CALVERT, THOS.
CUBLEY, F. S.
DELANEY, WM.
EMERY, CHARLES.
EDWARDS, THOS.
FLEMING, F. W. O.
FIELD, JAMES.
FIRTH, HANLEY.
FEATHER, ARNOLD.
FEARNSIDE, THOS.
FIELD, JOHN HY.
GALTRESS, FRANK.
GORMAN, THOS.
HOWARTH, JAMES.
HENDERSON, W.
HOLMES, HARRY.
HARDISTY, WM.
HICKS, SAM. ROBT.
HEELEY, ROBT.
JACKSON, HARRY.
KING, THOMAS.
KEMP, WILLIAM.
LONGBOTTOM, ALB.
LYMAN, WM.
MYERS, HARRY.
MITCHELL, E. T.
MARTIN, EDWARD.
MARSDEN, WM.
McGILL, WILLIAM.
MADDEN, WALTER.
MAHON, HARRY.
McINTYRE, JAS. ED.
NOBLE, FRED.
PRICE, CHAS.
POOLE, CHAS. H.
PICKERING, HERBT.
PATEFIELD, E.
PARKER, LEONARD.
PATEFIELD, L.
PATCHETT, B.
QUINN, JOS.
RILEY, HAROLD.
RALPH, JOSEPH.
ROBINSON, S.
RISDEN, HERBT.
SILSON, MAURICE.
SMITH, JOE.
SUTCLIFFE, ALB.
SUTCLIFFE, WM.
SWIRE, NORMAN.
STEPHENSON, F.
SIMPSON, PERCY.
TIPPING, JOHN.
THOMPSON, ED.
TOWERS, JOHN E.
WHITEFIELD, JOE.
WHEELHOUSE, W. H.
WALKER, HENRY.
WALKER, C. G.
WOOTTEN, ARTHUR.
WHITHAM, MILTON.
WARD, THOS. R.
WILLIAMSON, THOS.
WILLEY, FRANK.

CAWLEY'S (Cleckheaton), LIMITED.
Rawfolds Dyeworks, Cleckheaton.

BINNS, REUBEN.
BAILEY, WILLIAM.
BROADHEAD, J.
CROSBIE, S.
CLAY, GEORGE.
FISHER, WM. HY.
HOULDSWORTH, P.
KEIGHLEY, L.
KILBURN, S.
RICHARDSON, E.
THORPE, JOHN.

CRAVEN, PEARSON and CO., LTD.
Valley Dyeworks, Brighouse.

ASPINALL, J. C.
ALLEN, JOHN.
BARSTOW, E.
CHESHIRE, ARTHUR.
CHESHIRE, E.
FARRAR, J. E.
HOLT, ARTHUR.
HARGREAVES, JOS.
HIGSON, JOS.
JESSOP, HAROLD R.
KERSHAW, SAM.
KNAPTON, ED.
MARSDEN, F.
NETTLESHIP, ED.
PRATT, JAS. WM.
ROBINSON, JOS.
SHAW, J. W.
THOMPSON, JOHN.
WAINWRIGHT, P.
WHITELEY, C.
WOODS, H. F.
WHITELEY, L.
YOUNG, ERNEST.

The Bradford Dyers' Association Ltd.
CONTINUED.

"CRAVENETTE" COMPANY, LTD.
Ripley Road, Bowling, Bradford.

ALLISON, ANGUS.
BRAITHWAITE, B.
BARKER, ARCHIE.
GRAVES, CHAS.
GREENWOOD, WM.
GILL, HERBERT.
HUDSON, WALTER.
HETTHEN, FRED.
HUMBLE, JAMES.
MANN, WALTER.
NAYLOR, FRANCIS.
NORMAN, WILLIAM.
OTWAY, JOS.
RYAN, WILLIAM.
RAWLINGS, CHAS.
STEPHENSON, H.
SLATER, WM.
TETLEY, JOHN WM.
TEMPEST, WM.
WHITE, JOHN.

W. GRANDAGE and COMPANY, LTD.
Brownroyd Dyeworks, Bradford.

ATKINSON, FRANK.
BUCK, J. A.
BIRKBY, HARRY.
BARNETT, J. W.
BARRELL, ALBERT.
BOYLE, THOS.
BOWEN, WILFRED.
BENNETT, HENRY.
BLAMIRES, L.
BUSFIELD, G.
CLAPISON, JAMES.
CANNON, EDWARD.
COCKSON, JOHN.
CHAPMAN, S.
CRABTREE, L.
COLDWELL, W.
COWBURN, C.
COATES, G.
CERVI, A.
COATES, T.
COWGILL, H. P.
DONNELLY, T.
ELLWOOD, F.
EASTERBY, ALBERT.
EDWARDS, LEWIS.
FOX, HARRY.
FOX, T.
FIELDHOUSE, H.
FIELDHOUSE, JOS.
FOSTER, WM.
FARMER, CLIVE.
GALLAGHER, D.
GOODALL, WALTER.
GREW, L. L.
GRAYDON, R.
HIRST, T.
HITCHEN, ED.
HEBBLETHWAITE, J. H.
HINDLE, J. G.
HARRISON, GEO.
HILL, HERBERT.
HOBSON, G. W.
HILL, HARRY.
HARDY, RANDOLPH.
ILLINGWORTH, F.
JOHNSON, JOHN.
JOHNSON, G.
JONES, EDMUND.
JEFFERSON, P.
LEEMING, W. H.
LAVIN, THOS.
MOORE, WALTER.
MANNERS, WM. W.
MILNER, ALBERT.
MOUNSEY, A.
MARSHALL, W. H.
NOLSON, CHAS. HY.
NEWTON, ARTHUR.
PERKINS, RALPH.
PEERS, THOS.
PEDDER, JOSEPH.
ROE, A.
ROBINSON, H.
READ, THOS. R.
ROSE, ARTHUR.
SPELMAN, JAMES.
SMITH, HARRY.
SPENCER, W.
SMITH, THOS. H.
SCHOFIELD, L.
TOWNEND, J. A.
TORDOFF, WM.
THOMPSON, ERNEST.
VITTY, WALTER.
WOOD, EDGAR.
WATSON, THOS.
WALBANK, ARTHUR.
WHITHAM, HORACE.
WEBSTER, JAMES.
WATSON, H.
WADDINGTON, J.
WRIGHT, E.
WOOTTEN, J. W.
WHEELHOUSE, J.

GREENBOTTOM DYEING COMPANY, LTD.
Greenbottom Dyeworks, Guiseley, nr. Leeds.

BERRIMAN, GEO. W.
BIRKETT, H.
BRAYSHAW, EDWIN.
CROOK, J.
DOVE, J. C.
DOVE, C. E.
GREEP, F. T.
HUDSON, J. B.
HIRD, A.
KEIGHLEY, F. S.
KITCHEN, I.
KITCHEN, R.
LONG, J.
LIMMER, B.
RAWLING, J.
WATSON, H.
WOODHEAD, L.

The Bradford Dyers' Association Ltd.
CONTINUED.

GREETLAND DYEWORKS COMPANY, LTD.
Greetland Dyeworks, nr. Halifax.

- BETTERIDGE, C. E.
- BUTTERY, ARTHUR.
- BAKER, WM.
- BERRY, KENNETH.
- CORDINGLEY, A.
- DYSON, ALBERT.
- DYSON, HARRY.
- DYSON, ALBERT.
- DICKSON, CHAS. E.
- EASTWOOD, THOS. E.
- McCULLOCH, DAVID.
- McCULLOCK, WM.
- MITCHELL, F.
- MALONE, T.
- PORTEUS, S. W.
- SYKES, ERNEST.
- SMITH, WALTER E.
- SAUNDERS, B. A.
- TAYLOR, SIDNEY.
- TURNER, G. A.
- TURNER, BEN.
- TURNER, HENRY.
- THOMAS, F. C.
- WESTWOOD, GEO. T.
- WALTERS, HARRY.
- WEBSTER, LEWIS.

HALIFAX DYEING COMPANY, LTD.
Washer Lane Dyeworks, Halifax.

- BINNS, ABRAM.
- BARKER, NORMAN.
- BULL, FRED.
- BUCKLEY, A.
- CARTER, L.
- CALVERT, R.
- CROWTHER, E.
- DAWSON, FRANK.
- DUTCHMAN, A.
- EALHAM, L.
- FOX, FRIEND.
- HARDWICK, CHAS.
- HABERGAM, E.
- JONES, EDGAR.
- KNOWLES, WILLIE.
- MITCHELL, A.
- MARSHALL, E.
- MILNES, FRINDINS.
- NICHOLL, A. H.
- NICHOLL, HAROLD.
- PALFRAMAN, F.
- PEACOCK, FRANK.
- SIDDALL, NORMAN.
- SCOTFORD, G. H.
- WOODHEAD, J. E.

HUNSWORTH DYEING COMPANY, LTD.
Hunsworth Dyeworks, Cleckheaton.

- AIREY, JAS. W.
- ARMITAGE, T.
- BARKER, WILLIE.
- BARRACLOUGH, A.
- BASTOW, HARRY.
- BASTOW, FRED.
- BROOK, W. E.
- BOWLES, HENRY.
- BREARE, HAROLD.
- BROOKES, F. H.
- BARRACLOUGH, ALF.
- BENTLEY, H.
- BRADLEY, WM.
- BRADLEY, W. H.
- BASTOW, JOHN.
- BERRY, FRANK.
- BRIGGS, JOHN.
- CRAVEN, GEO. W.
- CLARKE, WM.
- CROSSLEY, CHAS. C.
- CLARK, RICHARD.
- CLOUGH, L.
- CRUMBIE, T.
- DOBSON, FRANK.
- DEAN, CHARLES.
- EASTWOOD, JAS.
- ELLIOTT, WM.
- EGAN, THOS.
- FENTON, ASA.
- GAUNT, EDWIN.
- GILL, ED.
- GILL, HENRY.
- HARGREAVES, THOS.
- HYDE, EUSTACE.
- HEWITT, EDWIN.
- HOLDROYD, PERCY.
- HODGSON, ALBERT.
- HARTLEY, PERCY.
- HILL, ERNEST.
- HEATON, HAROLD.
- HARGREAVES, F.
- HOLMES, CLARENCE.
- JEWITT, PERCY.
- KITSON, JOS. HY.
- KITCHINGMAN, W.
- KERSHAW, H. H.
- LAYCOCK, S.
- LITTLE, W. H. V.
- LEGGOTT, FRED.
- LAYCOCK, ALFRED.
- McKIM, WM.
- MURGATROYD, T.
- MASSEY, J. H.
- MITCHELL, JAS.
- McDONALD, ERNEST.
- NOLLER, JOS.
- PEACH, FRANK.
- PARKINSON, W.
- PRIESTLEY, R. H.
- SOOTHILL, ALBERT.
- SHEPLEY, ARTHUR.
- SMITH, WM. ED.
- SUGDEN, C. E.
- SMITH, W. E.
- SMITH, WM.
- SWAILES, NORMAN.
- SHEPLEY, FRED.
- SIMPSON, JOSEPH.
- STOTT, ELI.
- TRAYNOR, JAS. R.
- TETLEY, H. F.
- TAILFORD, N. M.
- WOODHEAD, J. J.
- WILKINSON, HERBT.
- WILKINSON, G.
- WATSON, FRED.
- WHITAKER, IRVINE.

The Bradford Dyers' Association Ltd.
CONTINUED.

SAMUEL KIRK and SONS, LTD.
Woodhouse Dyeworks, Leeds.

BARTLAM, T.	GARNETT, S.	STEVENS, A. E.
BERRY, J. W.	GERMAINE, H.	THOMAS, H.
BARNES, WM.	HOBSON, JAS.	THOMAS. H.
CALVERLEY, GEO.	HORSEY, EDWARD.	THACKWRAY, J. W.
COX, JOHN.	HARDY, J.	THACKWRAY, E.
CHILD, ALB.	LEE, SMITH.	THOMPSON, WM.
CLARK, SAMUEL.	LIGHT, B.	UMPLEBY, JOS. HY.
GERMAINE, E.	MURGATROYD, T.	WOOD, WM.
GREEN, PERCY.	MYERS, JOS.	WRIGHT, WM.
GREEN, W. P.	SUTCLIFFE, J. E.	

LINGFIELD DYEING COMPANY, LTD.
Lingfield Dyeworks, Bradford.

BRIGGS, JAS.	GARVEY, WM.	POWELL, JOSHUA.
BAIRSTOW, JOS.	GREEN, P.	PETTY, FRETWELL.
BOOTH, JOHN.	JAQUES, PERCY.	STANSFIELD, E.
COLLINS, EDWARD.	KING, JOHN.	SMITH, ALEX.
CROSS, JOE.	KETTLE, WM.	SPENCER, JOHN.
CRAVEN, GEORGE.	LOFTHOUSE, WALT.	SYKES, FRED.
COATES, W. N.	MILLER, HERBERT.	THOMPSON, M.
DRACUP, THOS.	MILLER, ARTHUR.	WRIGHT, BERT S.
FLYNN, JAS.	MACDERMOTT, C.	
FARRAR, ARTHUR.	NORTHROP, PERCY.	

NORCROFT DYEING COMPANY, LTD.
Norcroft Street, Thornton Road, Bradford.

ATKINSON, W.	HIRD, J. W.	PARKINSON, WM.
BENSON, ALFRED.	HODGSON, S.	PEDDER, J.
BOTTOMLEY, A.	HORNE, E.	PULLAN, S. J.
BATEMAN, CHARLIE.	KAYE, W. C.	SPENCE, B.
COGAN, FRANK.	KERSHAW, L.	TOMLINSON, GEO.
DELANEY, F.	LOVE, W. P.	TAYLOR, W.
GILL, GEORGE.	MANN, A.	TATE, J. E.
GILL, W. H.	MOULSON, FRANK.	TOPLEY, JOHN.
GIBSON, ROBT.	NEWTON, GEO. JAS.	
GREGSON, H.	NEWSOME, H.	

EDWARD RIPLEY and SON, LTD.
Bowling Dyeworks, Bradford.

ASHFORTH, RICH.	ACKROYD, F.	BRIGGS, F.
ARMITAGE, FRANK.	BIDGWOOD, DAVID.	BURRELL, FRED.
AUSTIN, ALB.	BAIRSTOW, T.	BRAND, JOHN WM.

The Bradford Dyers' Association Ltd.
CONTINUED.
EDWARD RIPLEY and SON, LTD.—*Continued.*

BELLFIELD, JAS.
BELL, ARNOLD.
BIRKBY, A.
BUTTERWORTH, WM.
BARRACLOUGH, E.
BENTLEY, H.
BROWN, GEORGE.
BARKER, WILLIE.
BANNISTER, WM.
BINDER, W. E.
BARRACLOUGH, F.
BELL, WILLIAM.
BARKER, WM.
BAXTER, FRANK.
BOTTOMLEY, F.
BROOKE, WM.
BRITON, ALF.
BRAY, HAROLD.
BRACEWELL, A.
BARRACLOUGH, HY.
BEAUMONT, THOS.
BATESON, ALFRED.
BEANLAND, JOE.
BARRETT, ALBERT.
BENN, WILLIE.
BURNS, JAMES.
BUTTERWORTH, W.
BRADLEY, HERBT.
CAMPBELL, ALB. E.
CUMMINGS, JOS.
CRAGG, JOSIAH.
CLAY, CECIL.
CHADWICK, GEO.
CHILD, CLARENCE.
CROSSLAND, N.
CROSSLAND, B.
CLOUGH, CHAS.
CREAR, ERNEST.
COLLINSON, M.
CALVERT, E. W.
COOPER, ROBERT.
DISBREY, G. W.
DRUMM, R. J.
DUTTON, J. E.
DRABBLE, L. H.
DELANEY, R.
DAWSON, J. H.
DEMAINE, SAM.
ELLIS, F.
ELSTUB, R.
ELLIS, HARRY.

ELLIS, GRAN.
FOSTER, ERNEST.
FENTON, E. J.
FOX, ARTHUR.
FOX, AMOS.
FORTUNE, NORMAN.
GRADWELL, ED.
GILLIAM, WM.
GREEN, HARRY.
GREED, ALB.
GREENWOOD, HEBT.
GREENWOOD, HY.
GALLAGHER, F.
HARTLEY, WILLIE.
HORSFALL, GEO.
HOPKINS, M.
HODGSON, W. E.
HARLING, W.
HEMINGWAY, J.
HAINSWORTH, M.
HACKETT, EDW.
HARDY, F.
HANDS, JAMES.
HOLMES, WM.
HEPTINSTALL, A. W.
HOLLOWAY, E.
HAYTON, ALB.
HOLROYD, BEN.
HORSFALL, THOS.
HOLROYD, SYDNEY.
HANNON, JAMES.
HODGSON, J. W.
HAIGH, CHAS.
HANSON, ARTHUR.
INGLETON, WALT.
IRVIN, PETER.
JOWETT, BEN.
JOHNSON, G. H.
JOY, GEORGE.
JACKSON, J.
JOWETT, H.
JESSON, ADOLPHUS.
KNOWLES, DAVID.
KERSHAW, C.
KAYE, JAMES.
KIRKWOOD, JOHN.
KENNY, FRANK.
KING, FRANCIS.
KENNEDY, J.
KAYE, HERBERT.
KIRKBRIGHT, WM.

LEWIS, EDWARD.
LIGHTOWLER, L.
LACEY, WALTER.
LEDDER, JOS.
LISTER, WADE.
LEEMING, DENIS.
LAWFORD, JOHN.
LARVIN, GEO. E.
McCREA, BENJ.
MITCHELL, E.
MACKENZIE, HERBT.
MANN, THOS.
MARVELL, JOHN.
METCALF, A.
MITCHELL, J. L.
McLEAN, D.
MITCHELL, HY.
MELTHAM, THOS. W.
MIDGLEY, ARTHUR.
MOULSON, JAMES.
MANN, JAS. ALF.
McLOUGHTIN, A.
MOORE, BERNARD.
MITCHELL, SMITH.
MALONEY, PETER.
MERRIN, HY.
McKENSIE, JAMES.
MORTON, GEO.
MALPRESS, R. F.
METCALF, URWIN.
NICHOLSON, P.
NELSON, WM.
OLDHAM, WM.
ODDY, ARTHUR.
PASHLEY, GEO. A.
PARKER, WM.
PORTER, LEONARD.
PORTER, F.
PAGE, TOM.
POLLARD, BERT.
PASHLEY, THOS.
PETTY, GEO. E.
POLLARD, ALB.
PEARSON, FRED.
PERKINS, JAS.
QUIRK, A.
QUEST, H.
REDDIOUGH, E.
RHODES, WM.
REDFEARN, THOS.
RHODES, CHARLES.

The Bradford Dyers' Association Ltd.
CONTINUED.

EDWARD RIPLEY and SON, LTD.—Continued.

RILEY, H.
SMITH, TOM.
STEAD, JOS.
SHEPHERD, JOE.
SMITH, ERNEST.
STEPHENSON, H.
SMITH, CHAS.
SOLOMON, HY.
SUGDEN, EDWIN.
SINGLETON, EDGAR.
STEELE, EDMUND.
SPEIGHT, HY.
SUTTON, GEO. A.
SMITH, HERBERT.
SWINDELLS, A.
SCULLEY, J. R.
STARR, ARTHUR.
SWAINE, H.
SYKES, A.
SMITH, THOS.
SHARP, HERBERT.
SCOTT, LEWIS.
SHAW, HERMANN.
SMITH, JOHN WM.
ROWNTREE, FRED.

RACE, BASIL.
RUSHWORTH, W.
SHOESMITH, FRED.
SURBUTS, ERNEST.
STEAD, H.
STOWELL, DAVID.
SUTTON, JOHN R.
SIMPSON, JOHN H.
SHARMAN, C.
STANSFIELD, A. J.
SMITH, GEORGE.
STEPHENSON, H.
SMITHIES, DAVID.
SCHOFIELD, A.
SMITH, ERNEST.
SADDINGTON, E.
TURNER, J. W.
THORNTON, F.
THIRKILL, RALPH.
TOWNEND, ERIC.
TAYLOR, E.
TEMPEST, FRED.
TURNER, HENRY.
TETLEY, W.
TAYLOR, H.

TIGHE, THOS.
TERRY, L.
THROP, THOS.
TRACEY, JOHN.
VICKERS, WM.
VERITY, HARRY.
WOODHOUSE, M.
WALLACE, J.
WHITTAKER, JAS. W.
WOOD, CYRIL.
WILSON, WM.
WILSON, CHAS. W.
WADDINGTON, F.
WARRENER, ENOS.
WEST, JOHN FRED.
WILKS, JAMES.
WATSON, FRED.
WILSON, BLAND.
WRIGHT, M. L.
WOOD, ROBERT.
WORSNOP, ALBERT.
WRIGHT, CHAS.
WOODHALL, JOS. H.
YEADON, HARRY.

JAMES and M. S. SHARP and COMPANY, LTD.
Low Moor.

APPLEYARD, GEO.
ALLATT, HARRY.
BARRACLOUGH, J. W.
BRIGGS, WILLIE.
BATEMAN, WALTER.
BROWN, ERNEST.
BINNS, ARTHUR.
BARTLE, HAROLD.
BARTLE, TOM.
BARTLE, ALBERT.
COOPER, RICH. B.
CROWTHER, FRED.
CRABTREE, IRVINE.
CROSSLAND, A.
ELLIS, JOS.
EMMETT, ERNEST.
FIRTH, ALBERT.
GRAVES, CHAS. HY.
GLEDHILL, C.

GLOVER, J. E.
HUDSON, EDWARD.
HOWARD, J. B.
HIRST, FRED.
HEPWORTH, FRANK.
HILL, FRED.
HARRISON, E.
HOWLETT, THOS. E.
HOLMES, HUBERT.
HIRST, HY.
HIRST, ALBERT.
LEE, CHARLES.
LONGBOTTOM, E.
LUPSON, MICHAEL.
MITCHELL, W.
McCREA, ED.
MANN, WALTER.
PRIESTLEY, HERBT.
PADGETT, FRED.

RIACH, JAMES.
RISHMAN, H. E.
SMITH, JOSEPH.
SMITH, ALBERT.
SMEDLEY, WALTER.
SMETHURST, F. W.
SHARP, H. E.
SCATCHARD, T.
UNWIN, JONAS.
WILLMAN, RICH.
WARD, DAN P.
WALKER, HERBT.
WALKER, ARTHUR.
WILKINSON, JOHN.
WRIGHT, BERNARD.
WILKINSON, J. T.
WOODHOUSE, F. J.
YATES, J. WM.

The Bradford Dyers' Association Ltd.
CONTINUED.

JAMES and M. S. SHARP and COMPANY, LTD.
Orchard Dyeworks, Heckmondwike.

AMOS, GEORGE.
AITKEN, A.
BATTLE, JAS.
BEAUMONT, JOE.
BARBER, FRED.
BROOKE, GEO. HY.
DENNISON, WALT.
DUFFIN, ARTHUR.
GOUGH, TOM.
HOFFLAND, JOHN J.
HIRST, CHARLES.
HAIGH, CLARK.
JACKSON, HAROLD.
LISTER, ARTHUR.
MALLIN, GEO.
MOSS, IRVIN.
PINDER, LEVI.
PARKER, J.
PORRITT, ARTHUR.
SCHOFIELD, E.
TOLAN, PATSY.
TAYLOR, WILLIE.
WALKER, ERNEST.

SHAW and COMPANY (Shipley), LTD.
Midland Dyeworks, Shipley.

AVEYARD, SAM.
BEECROFT, EDGAR.
BOURKE, EDMUND.
CRAIG, WM.
DOBSON, ED.
DICKERSON, W.
GREENWOOD, J.
HASTE, PERCY.
HOWARD, THOS.
HODGSON, JOS.
HUMBLE, W.
INGLE, J. A.
KENDALL, W.
KERSHAW, F.
LORD, HARRY.
MITCHELL, GEO.
MASON, WALT.
NORMINGTON, H.
PRESTON, WM. HY.
RICE, ERNEST.
RICE, WM. H.
ROBERTSHAW, J.
RAMSDEN, HAROLD.
SIMPSON, H.
SUNDERLAND, W.
SMITH, JOHN.
THORP, CLIFFORD.
THORPE, WM. HY.
TOPHAM, H.
WILKINSON, GEO.
WARD, RONALD.

JOHN SHAW and COMPANY, LTD.
Garnett Street, Bradford.

BEBB, NORMAN.
BENSON, EDGAR.
BROOK, J. W.
BROADBENT, W.
BROADBENT, J.
BRIGGS, W.
BLYTHE, JOHN H.
BROADBENT, B.
BEASLEY, JAS. A.
CLARKSON, H.
DARKIN, TOM.
FLETCHER, J.
FERDINAND, C.
GILL, T.
GILL, J.
HOLDSWORTH, W.
HALEY, JOHN.
HENSBY, EDGAR.
HAIGH, ERNEST.
HARRISON, J. W.
HENSBY, WM.
HELLIWELL, A.
LUMB, FRED.
LLOYD, JAS. J.
LLOYD, JOHN.
LLOYD, WM.
McHUGH, THOS.
METCALFE, D.
MILNES, B.
MASON, WM.
PETTY, WM. F.
PRATT, GORDON.
PYRAH, J.
RENARDSON, F.
RHODES, WM.
ROUSE, GEO. HY.
RHODES, HY.
SHOOTER, F.
TURNER, HY.
VERITY, WM.
WHITING, S.
WATSON, E.
WHITEHEAD, WM.
WILKS, HY.
WOOD, ARTHUR.

SAMUEL SMITH and COMPANY, LTD.
Horton Dyeworks, Bradford.

CARR, J. A.
EVANS, HARRY.
LODGE, BEDNA.
MACDONALD, WM.
METCALF, E.
SCHOFIELD, CHAS.

The Bradford Dyers' Association Ltd.
CONTINUED.

STOCKBRIDGE FINISHING COMPANY, LTD.
Bradford Road, Keighley,

ATTWELL, A.	FORTUNE, HARRY.	SAXTON, ARTHUR.
ATKINSON, BENJ.	FIELDING, HY.	TAYLOR, H.
ANDERTON, A.	GREENWOOD, FRED.	TEMPEST, A.
BILBROUGH, A.	HARDY, WM.	TERRY, H. C.
BRITTON, W.	JOHNSON, THOS.	TAYLOR, ALB.
BAIRSTOW, JOS.	KING, ARTHUR.	WILLOUGHBY, GEO.
BINGLEY, CHAS. S.	LARVIN, J.	WALMSLEY, A. G.
BELL, S.	POWELL, H.	WILKINSON, W.
COE, CHAS. W.	RENARDSON, J.	WATKINSON, J.
CRABTREE, LEWIS.	RAINFORD, T.	WILKINSON, R. O.
COATES, WILFRED.	SCOTT, DAVID C.	WHITAKER, H.
DAVY, HERBERT.	STOWELL, H.	WADE, NEWBY.
ELLISON, J.	SMITH, JOS.	

Horton Dyeworks, Bradford.

EASTWOOD, T.	OVEREND, ARTHUR.	STEELE, JOS.
HALEY, CHAS.	PARRISH, GEO.	WRIGHT, W. H.
LISTER, GEO.	QUIRK, CHRIS.	WOOLNER, JOS.
McEVOY, C.	ROYSTON, G.	WILSON, DAN.
OATES, HOR.	RIPLEY, EDGAR.	

THORNTON HANNAM and MARSHALL, LTD.
Brookfoot Dyeworks, Brighouse.

ASPINALL, J. L.	ERRATT, T.	HEPWORTH, T. A.
AKERS, A.	EXLEY, DYSON.	JOWETT, W.
AMBLER, FRED.	FITZJOHN, F. W.	JENNISON, H.
BAINES, J.	FOWLER, B.	KEAR, F.
BERRY, W.	FLETCHER, A.	LEAROYD, L.
BOOCOCK, A.	FORD, J.	LUNN, J. S.
BOOCOCK, H.	FAWCETT, W.	LEMM, ED.
BOOTH, A.	GIDLEY, W.	LEE, C. E.
BUTTERWORTH, A. L.	GIDLEY, H.	LENT, WALTER.
BATES, G. T.	GROVE, W.	LITTLEWOOD, G. H.
BINNS, F. H.	GOMERSAL, W. H.	LISTER, WADE.
BIRKBY, PARISH.	HARTLEY, L.	MARSDEN, A.
BLACK, N.	HORSFALL, J.	McFARLANE, W.
BRIGGS, H.	HIRST, W. H.	MITCHELL, S.
CROFT, J.	HIRST, J.	PATTERSON, J.
CROWTHER, C.	HELME, H.	PRYNN, A.
CROSSLEY, A.	HELME, T. W.	PAVIOUR, S.
COLLINS, A.	HEALEY, T.	RAVEN, C.
CLIFFE, K. A.	HILL, J.	ROPER, F.
DENTON, C. W.	HILL, W.	SAUNDERS, B.
EGAN, N.	HATTERSLEY, J. E.	SAUNDERS, J.
EGAN, C.	HARRIS, SAM.	SLATER, P.
ELLIS, F.	HULLAH, H.	SLANE, J.

The Bradford Dyers' Association Ltd.
CONTINUED.

THORNTON HANNAM and MARSHALL, LTD.—*Continued*.

SHARP, H.	SUGDEN, S. D.	WALKER, A.
STOTT, EDGAR.	THURLOW, G.	WOOD, H.
SHOOTER, WM.	THORNTON, H.	WOOD, I.
SPENCE, WALT.	THOMPSON, J. C.	WHITTLE, P. A.
SHAW, A.	THOMPSON, H. R.	WEBSTER, A.
SCHOFIELD, W.	THOMPSON, G.	WADDINGTON, T.
SETTLE, L.	WEBB, R.	WOGAN, J.
STEAD, J.	WHITELEY, V.	WARDINGLEY, A.
STRINGER, IRVINE.	WOOD, H.	YEADON, V.

WATER LANE DYEWORKS COMPANY, LTD.
Thornton Road, Bradford.

ALLSOPP, HARRY.	FIRTH, JOHN.	NAYLOR, JOSEPH.
BOLTON, GEORGE.	GOTT, ALBERT.	NAYLOR, FRED.
BRAYSHAW, H.	GRADWELL, WM. H.	NOLAN, GERALD.
BARKER, ARTHUR.	GLEDHILL, SAMUEL.	NICHOL, EDGAR.
BARNETT, WM.	GRANT, JACK.	OXLEY, HARRY.
BARBER, WALTER.	HARRISON, CHAS.	PICKLES, H.
CLIFFORD, E. R.	HILL, NORMAN.	POWELL, ERNEST.
CAHILL, WILLIE.	HOWLETT, WM.	RYAN, HARRY.
CARROLL, JAS. WM.	HANSON, BRINTON.	RAYNER, ARTHUR.
CRAVEN, RICHARD.	HOLLINGS, THOS.	ROBINSON, J.
COOPE, HAROLD	HODGES, S.	SHARMAN, ARTHUR.
COOPE, WILLIAM.	HOWARD, HERBT.	SAVILLE, JAMES.
CANNON, JAMES.	HAMMOND, GEO. S.	STEAD, H.
CHIPPENDALE, L.	HOLMES, EDGAR.	SWALES, ARTHUR.
CLARK, JOSEPH.	HODGSON, HERBT.	TURNER, ALBERT.
CRANSTON, ROBT.	HANSON, EVELYN.	TETLEY, ALBERT.
COLLETT, JOSEPH.	KEATING, DANIEL.	TETLEY, J. W.
DENNISON, M.	KING, GEORGE.	THORP, ARTHUR.
DEWHIRST, FRED.	KITCHINGMAN, A.	WALL, ALEXANDER.
ELLIS, HERBERT.	LEE, ALLAN.	WINTERBURN, ALF.
FOX, WILLIAM.	LUMLEY, ABM. R.	WILSHIRE, H. O.
FIELD, FRED.	LAMBERT, ROBERT.	WORSNOP, HY.
FISHWICK, G. A.	MITCHELL, ARTHUR.	WHEWELL, WM.

WHITAKER BROS. and COMPANY, DYERS, LTD.
Aire Vale Dyeworks, Newlay, nr. Leeds.

ALLISON, WM.	BLACKBURN, GEO. T.	BROADBENT, L.
ASKEY, F.	BARRETT, JAS. H.	BROGAN, J.
APPLEYARD, F.	BULMER, W.	BANNISTER, A. R.
AUSTWICK, C.	BOOTH, H.	BOWMAN, W.
AVERDIECK, G. G.	BLANCOUR, W. J.	BECKETT, J.
ALLANACK, E.	BAMFORD, ARTHUR.	BEAUMONT, H.
BRADLEY, WM.	BURKE, JAMES.	BRAITHWAITE, R.

The Bradford Dyers' Association Ltd.
CONTINUED.

WHITAKER BROS. and COMPANY, DYERS, LTD.—*Continued*.

BELLHOUSE, A.
BEST, G.
BIRCH, W.
CRAVEN, A.
CRAVEN, HAROLD.
CALVERT, T.
CREEK, T. W.
CLEMENTS, E.
CLAYTON, ASA.
COGGINS, ERNEST.
CLAYTON, TED.
COWGILL, THOS.
DICKINSON, H.
DUTHOIT, HY.
DARBY, C. L.
DOBSON, LEONARD.
DUTTON, T. H.
DENTON, A.
DRINKWATER, J.
DAVEY, J. T.
ELLIS, C.
ELLIOTT, ERNEST.
ECCLES, J. W.
EVERSON, JAS. A.
ETHERINGTON, J.
ERRINGTON, JOHN.
ETHERINGTON, H.
EASTWOOD, JAS. C.
FORREST, JOS.
FLETCHER, J. H.
FORD, JOSEPH.
GERMANY, GEO. K.
GAULTER, C.
GAULTER, N.
GAULTER, A.
GARDINER, V.
GATEHOUSE, FRED.
GAMBLES, WM.
HEY, J.
HUTCHINSON, J.
HOWLAND, C. H.
HOLMES, E.
HARGREAVES, J.
HAWKSWORTH, W.
HORNE, F. W.
HOLGATE, E. B.
HILL, H.
HAWKSWORTH, J.
HOWARD, F.
HALL, JOS. L.
HOUGH, J. J.

HILL, WILLIAM.
HOWARTH, J. J.
HAINSWORTH, J. H.
HARTLEY, WM.
HORNE, GEORGE.
HANDLEY, W.
HILL, J. B.
IVES, MARK.
JESSOP, SYDNEY.
JENKINSON, J.
JOHNSON, FRED.
KENDALL, W.
KEIGHLEY, L.
KENDALL, J. H.
KENNA, JOHN.
KENNA, J.
LAWSON, ARTHUR.
LAMBERT, GEORGE.
LUPTON, HENRY.
LAURIE, H.
LOCKWOOD, H.
LEAF, E.
LIDDAN, J. A.
LAWSON, THOS.
LAYTON, C.
MOODY, J. W.
MYERS, G.
McCULLA, T.
MITCHELL, L.
MIRFIELD, FRED.
MEGSON, FOSTER.
MINSKIP, CHAS.
MARSDEN, S.
MORLEY, GEORGE.
MURGATROYD, ED.
MERCHANT, J. H.
MARSDEN, J. D.
MYERS, CLEMENT.
MIDDLETON, WALT.
NORTH, HENRY.
NORTH, HAROLD.
NORMAN, H.
ODDY, ERNEST.
OLIVER, HENRY.
PANKHURST, L.
PARKER, A. W.
PRATT, WILF.
PATTERSON, A.
PRATT, TURNER.
REVELL, RICHARD.
ROO, R.

RAISTRICK, H.
RUTHERFORD, A.
RIPLEY, JAS. W.
RILEY, E.
SKIPPER, A. C.
STEAD, H.
SMITH, E.
SALMON, W.
SUTCLIFFE, L.
SCROGGINS, ROBT.
STANTON, WALTER.
STANDAGE, J.
SPLAIN, T.
SHEPHERD, W. R.
SILSON, J. W.
STRANG, J. W.
SUTCLIFFE, H.
SPLAIN, RICHARD.
SHORT, HERBERT.
SINGER, L. H.
SMITH, JOS. H.
SPLAIN, J.
THOMPSON, H.
TEALE, C.
TEALE, T.
TEALE, B.
TODD, A.
TOWERS, L.
TOTTIE, J. W.
THACKRAY, H. L.
TODD, ALEX.
TASKER, RICH. L.
TATE, WM. T.
THOMSON, J.
VINTER, E.
VINTER, H. A.
WESTERMAN, WM.
WESTERMAN, ALF.
WARD, ARTHUR.
WADE, C.
WAITE, ARTHUR.
WAKEFIELD, F. L.
WAKEFIELD, H.
WALKER, H.
WASP, WALTER.
WADKIN, W. L.
WILKINSON, F.
WAINWRIGHT, J.
YOUNG, W.
YOUNG, F.

ROLE OF HONOUR.

✱ ✱ ✱

Thomas Briggs (Manchester) Ltd.

List of Employees who have Joined the Colours.

Private P. Graham, 7th Batt. King's Own Scottish Borderers.
Private W. Taylor, 7th Batt. King's Own Scottish Borderers (Missing).
Private J. Quinn, 7th Batt. King's Own Scottish Borderers.
Private A. S. Cartledge, Army Service Corps.
Private J. Pollard, Army Service Corps (Pioneers).
Private V. Wilkinson, Army Service Corps (Pioneers).
Private G. McCartney, Army Service Corps (Pioneers).
Private W. Vipond, Army Service Corps (Pioneers).
Private T. Davies, Army Service Corps (Pioneers).
Lance-Corpl. C. Stocks, 12th Batt. King's Liverpool Regiment.
Private J. Briggs, 12th Batt. King's Liverpool Regiment.
Private J. Knott, 10th Batt. East Lancashires.
Private J. Murphy, 10th Batt. East Lancashires.
Private S. Smith, 8th Batt. Lancashire Fusiliers (T.F.) (Wounded).
Private W. Pike, 8th Batt. Lancashire Fusiliers (T.F.) (Wounded).
Private S. Charlesworth, 7th Batt. Lancashire Fusiliers (T.F.).
Private J. Gilmore, 2nd Service Batt. Lancashire Fusiliers.
Sergeant J. O'Mara, Lancashire Fusiliers (Killed).
Private T. Lucas, Lancashire Fusiliers.
Private J. Connor, 2nd Batt. Lancashire Fusiliers (Wounded).
Lance-Corpl. W. G. Earle, 1st Border Regiment.
Private A. Hamilton, 11th Batt. Manchester Regiment.
Private J. Roscoe, Army Service Corps.
Corpl. G. Bonter, 1st Batt. Dorset Regiment (Wounded).
Sergt. G. Bonter, 1st Garrison Devon Regiment.
Private J. Sherlock, Royal Army Medical Corps.
Private C. McCabe, Royal Field Artillery.
Private W. Ball, 2/4th South Lancashires.
Drummer W. Rutter, Royal Army Medical Corps (Invalided).
Private A. Mayoh, Royal Army Medical Corps.
Private T. A. Stansby, 20th Service Batt. Manchester Regiment.
Private A. Smith, 19th Service Batt. Manchester Regiment.
Corpl. S. Parkinson, 8th Batt. Duke of Wellington's Regiment.

ROLL OF HONOUR.

Wm. Briggs & Co. Ltd.

34 Cannon Street, Manchester.

Lt.-Col. C. M. ABERCROMBIE	16th Serv. Battalion Lancashire Fusiliers.
Lt. T. DOYLE	27th Battalion Northumberland Fusiliers.
2nd Lt. F. DURANDEAU	24th Serv. Battalion Manchester Regiment.
Corpl. J. JONES	Royal Army Medical Corps.
Pte. S. WORSLEY	Royal Army Medical Corps.
Pte. G. L. SHIELDS	9th Res. Batt. Royal Scots (Highlanders).
Pte. C. SMITH	11th Res. Battalion Black Watch.
Driver W. EDWARDS	2nd East Lancashire Royal Field Artillery.
Driver G. TAYLOR	2/2nd E. Lancashire Royal Field Artillery.
Pte. N. JONES	20th Serv. Batt. Royal Fus. (Pub. Sc. Batt.).
Pte. L. LEE	20th Serv. Batt. Royal Fus. (Pub. Sc. Batt.).
Pte. G. BUCKINGHAM	19th Serv. Batt. Royal Fus. (Pub. Sc. Batt.).
Pte. G. DOBSON	24th County of London Regt. (The Queens).
Pte. W. E. NICHOLL	8th Battalion Royal Fusiliers.
Driver H. MINORS	"B" Battery, Hon. Artillery Company.
Rifleman C. C. DONES	2nd Battalion Queen's Westminster Rifles.
Pte. F. E. MARLAND	24th Serv. Battalion Manchester Regiment.
Pte. J. H. GORDON	6th Battalion Lancashire Fusiliers.
Pte. S. JONES	1st Battalion East Lancashire Fusiliers.
Pte. F. E. TURNER	1/6th Battalion Manchester Regiment (T.).
Pte. S. HOLMES	7th Battalion Manchester Regiment (T.).
Pte. R. EVANS	7th Salford Battalion Lancashire Fusiliers.
Pte. F. L. JACKSON	8th Battalion Manchester Regiment.
Pte. F. SHELMERDINE	8th Battalion Manchester Regiment.
Pte. H. MOXON	Royal Naval Division (Medical Unit).
J. LLOYD BIRCH	Royal Navy (Writer).
Drummer KNIGHT	18th Serv. Batt. Manchester Regt. ("Pals").
Pte. H. WRIGLEY	18th Serv. Batt. Manchester Regt. ("Pals").
Pte. J. H. ANDREWS	18th Serv. Batt. Manchester Regt. ("Pals").
Pte. A. MILLWARD	18th Serv. Batt. Manchester Regt. ("Pals").
Pte. N. QUINN	18th Serv. Batt. Manchester Regt. ("Pals").
Pte. W. WINSBY	18th Serv. Batt. Manchester Regt. ("Pals").
Pte. J. HENNERLEY	18th Serv. Batt. Manchester Regt. ("Pals").
Pte. W. C. PAGE	18th Serv. Batt. Manchester Regt. ("Pals").
Pte. H. BARDSLEY	18th Serv. Batt. Manchester Regt. ("Pals").
Pte. H. POLLARD	19th Serv. Batt. Manchester Regt. ("Pals").
Pte. G. CASEWELL	19th Serv. Batt. Manchester Regt. ("Pals").

ROLL OF HONOUR.

The British Cotton and Wool Dyers' Association Limited.

HEAD OFFICE.

BARDSLEY, J. W.
CALDWELL, J. R.
CLEGG, S.
DERBYSHIRE, G.
FOULKES, Sgt. W.
FRANK, Lt. R. A.
GREENFIELD, A.
GWINNELL, L.
HASTINGS, Sgt. J. W.
HOLT, W.
HEWITT, J. G.
LEWIS, Lieut. M. P.
McCLINTON, Lt. E. E.
PRATT, Sgt. L.
ROBERTS, E.
SMETHURST, F. A.
TODD, Sgt.-Mjr. W.
TOPHAM, L.
WILSON, S.
WOOD, A.
WORSWICK, Cpl. L.

LANCASHIRE BRANCHES.

Burton and Slingsby, Ltd.

ADAMS, G.
BARRETT, E.
BARTLEY, J.
KAY, E.
KAY, T.
MATHER, F.
OLIVE, W.
POMFRET, T. H.

Cawdaw Dyeworks.

BARLOW, P.
BENNETT, H.
GARVEY, J.
JUDGE, H.
MACDONALD, H.
PICKERING, E.
ROTHWELL, S.

W. Eckersall and Co., Ltd.

BIRTWISTLE, H.
CHADWICK, E.
TURNER, S.

Jopson, Ashworth and Edmonds, Ltd.

BOOTH, S.
BUCKLEY, J.
CLARKSON, F.
GREENHALGH, D.
HALLWORTH, H.
LAMB, F.
MOTTERSHEAD, J. H.
SPEAKES, W.
SURRAGE, G.

Kearns, Allan and Co., Ltd.

BROOK, A.
CHEVIN, W. T.
DEWHURST, F.
FOOTE, F.
GAMMON, W. I.
GREENHALGH, L.
HAYWOOD, F. A.
HULME, W. G.
ISHERWOOD, P.
LUND, G.
SOURBUTTS, H.
STREET, D. H.
WHITCOMBE, R.

Kerr and Hoegger, Ltd.

BALLARD, J. R.
BARKER, H.
BARLOW, J.
BARNETT, J.
BEATTIE, S.
BLOOD, H.
BRENNAN, J.
BROWN, J.
BURKE, W.
BURROWS, E.
CHADWICK, E.
CRAWFORD, R.
ETTERY, T.
FARRINGTON, J.
FLANAGAN, P.
FLETCHER, J.
FORD, T.
GIBBON, A.
GILMAN, W.
GRICE, J.
HAIGH, G.
HALL, J.
HASLAM, H.
HASLAM, J. F.
HIGGINSON, J.
HOLT, M.
HOLT, S.
KERSHAW, F.
LANGFORD, W.
MARTIN, T.
MARTIN, W.
McCOMISH, J. J.
McGEE, J.
McGINTY, J.
McLEAN, J.
MENZIES, J. D.
MORLEY, J.
MORRIS, E.
MURPHY, F.
MURPHY, J.
NAYLOR, W.
NORBURY, J.
PALMER, J.
PARK, H.
PEACOCK, A., Senr.
PEACOCK, A.
PINDER, F.
ROBINSON, C. H.
ROWLANDS, E.
RYAN, M.
SCHOFIELD, F.
SMITH, R.
STEWART, C., Junr.
STRINGER, G.
TAYLOR, B.
TAYLOR, R.
THOMPSON, R.
WILLIAMS, J.
WOOD, A.
WRIGHT, G.

The British Cotton and Wool Dyers' Association Ltd.

ROLL OF HONOUR.—Continued.

Edward Lee, Ltd.

BRIERLEY, G. E.	JOHNSON, E.
CHADWICK, J. L.	LORD, J.
CHADWICK, T. E.	PERKINS, M.
DAWSON, J.	PINDER, T. F.
DICKINSON, J.	PRESTON, N.
DODD, F.	SCHOLEFIELD, E.
FIELDEN, D.	TROTTER, F.
HARDACRE, A.	WHITTAKER, W.
HARRISON, C.	

Mercer Co. (Manchester), Ltd.

HAZEL, W.   LOWE, W.

Robinson Bros. (Blackburn), Ltd.

CLIFFE, S.	KITCHER, W.
DICKENSON, G.	LAYCOCK, R.
KENYON, H.	ROBINSON, A.
KITCHER, G.	STOKES, H. B.

John Siddall, Ltd.

ARMSTRONG, G.	HOWARTH, G., Junr.
BRADLEY, A.	KAY, H.
BYRNES, JAS.	LATER, H.
BYRNES, JOHN.	LOMAX, J.
BYRNES, W.	LORD, J.
COOKE, J.	MELLOR, E.
EDWARDS, T.	PARKS, W.
ELLWOOD, E.	STANIFORTH, J.
HALL, H.	WARBURTON, J.
HARDMAN, J.	WILKINSON, K.
HAYES, O.	

S. Smethurst and Sons, Ltd.

ALSTON, J.	HOUGHTON, T.
ANSON, J.	HOWARTH, A.
BARLOW, W.	KAY, W.
BILSBERRY, E.	KERSHAW, W. P.
BIRTWISTLE, J.	LEE, W.
BOOTH, T.	LEVITT, C.
BROOKS, E.	LINTON, G.
BURNS, T. W.	LONGWORTH, W.
CARMAN, J.	MASON, T.
ECKERSALL, J.	MILLS, W.
GLEAVE, J.	MITCHELL, T. H.
GOLDSMITH, F.	MOGGERIDGE, J.
GREEN, J.	MONKS, W.
GRINDROD, A.	MOONEY, W. H.
HALL, F.	NEWBY, J.
HARKER, R. P.	NUTTALL, S.
HODGKINSON, F.	PARKS, W.

S. Smethurst & Sons, Ltd.—Continued.

PEERS, G.	TAYLOR, L.
PORTER, P.	TAYLOR, W.
RADCLIFFE, R.	TEALE, E.
REDFERN, J.	THOMPSON, B.
ROBINSON, J.	TURNER, R.
ROWLES, W.	WHITTAKER, RD.
SIMPSON, E.	WHITTAKER, ROBT.
SMITH, H.	WHITTAM, J.
SPEAKE, C.	WHITWORTH, F.
SPIVEY, A.	WOLSTENHOLME, T.
TAYLOR, F.	

YORKSHIRE BRANCHES.

Bradford Patent Dyeing Co., Ltd.

BURNETT, G.	WOLFE, H. H.
JENNINGS, B.	

John Buckle and Co., Ltd.

ALLINSON, G. W.	MITCHELL, L.
ALLINSON, T.	OVEREND, F.
EARLE, W.	PETCHER, R.
HARDY, J.	SUGDEN, R.
JOWETT, M.	TAYLOR, G.
LLANWARNE, G. L.	TERRY, C.

H. Fletcher and Co., Ltd.

AKROYD, J.	FORAN, G.
BRADLEY, W.	HALLIDAY, W.
BROWN, J.	HILEY, W.
BUCKLEY, J. H.	HOWARTH, F.
BURKE, J. T.	JONES, F.
BUTTERWORTH, H.	LONG, W. (D.C.M.)
CLARKSON, H.	O'BRIEN, J.
CONROY, T.	MAPLESON, C.
CRABTREE, C.	MORTIMER, W. E.
FLETCHER, G. M.	ROBINSON, H.

Fletcher Bros., Ltd.

ACKROYD, R.	CARTER, F.
AKED, T.	CLAYTON, J.
ARMITAGE, H.	CONWAY, F.
BENTLEY, S.	DUNN, W.
BISHOP, H.	EASTWOOD, W.
BOTTOMLEY, E.	FARNELL, F.
BROADBENT, H.	GOODALL, E.
BURROWS, J. W.	GREAVES, T.

The British Cotton and Wool Dyers' Association Ltd.

ROLL OF HONOUR—Continued.

Fletcher Bros., Ltd.—Continued.

HALLIDAY, H.	PEARSON, F.
HARRIS, W.	RALF, H.
HAWKINS, N.	REID, C.
HORSFALL, W.	RIGG, W.
JENKINSON, A.	SAVILLE, A.
KERSHAW, H.	SHAFE, J.
LANGHORN, G.	SHOOTER, S.
LAWSON, E.	SIDDAL, J.
LAXTON, W. A.	SIMPSON, C.
LUMB, A.	STEAD, L.
MAUDE, A.	TURNER, W.
MURRAY, H.	WILSON, H.
PARKER, E.	WINTERBOTTOM, W.

A. Goodall and Co., Ltd.

BAKER, G.	TAYLOR, G. A.
MAUDE, M.	WARWICK, W.
STRAFFORD, W. H.	

Grandages (Brighouse), Ltd.

MITCHELL, J. C.

Heppenstall Bros., Ltd.

BATES, E.	QUARMBY, D.
BENTLEY, J. A.	ROEBUCK, J. R.
DRIVER, H.	SOLLIS, J.
HARDCASTLE, W.	STRINGER, J.
JUBB, H.	SUNDERLAND, H.
MILLARD, H.	THOMPSON, R.
MOORHOUSE, B.	WADSWORTH, E.
NOBLE, F.	WINDLE, C.

Marshfield Dyeing Co., Ltd.

COONEY, W.	PEARSON, T.
CURREY, W.	POTTS, T.
HOWARD, H.	TOWNEND, E.
LEE, J. G.	WILKS, E.

Murgatroyd and Lister, Ltd.

FAWCETT, C. H.	PERKINS, J. A.
MALLINSON, H.	POLLARD, J.
MORRISON, T.	STIBBINS, J. R.
PARKIN, S.	

Hy. North and Sons, Ltd.

BANNISTER, J. W.	BETTS, A.
BANNISTER, W.	BLACKBURN, J.
BENNETT, E.	BLICK, T.

Hy. North & Sons, Ltd.—Continued.

CAWOOD, E.	HOLMES, T.
GILL, F.	ISHERWOOD, C.
GROSVENOR, R.	LEACH, E.
HAMMOND, H.	TARREN, A.
HARRISON, H.	WHEATER, T.
HOGAN, J.	WOOD, C.

Wm. North and Co., Ltd.

ANGEL, H.	JOY, H.
BAGULEY, H.	KEIGHLEY, J.
BATTYE, J. W.	KILBURN, W.
BENTLEY, T.	KNOWLES, F.
BOLTON, H.	KNOWLES, G.
BOOTHROYD, J.	LUND, R.
BOTTOMLEY, H.	McCUNLIFFE, J.
BOWEN, T.	McDONALD, J.
BRADO, W.	MERCER, W.
BREAR, J.	MILNES, N.
BROCKLEHURST, T.	MURGATROYD, W. M.
CHAMBERS, A.	O'NEILL, J.
CHAMBERS, E.	PARKINSON, W.
CLAUGHTON, H.	PENDLEBURY, R.
CLOUGH, F.	PETERS, E.
COLLINSON, J. E.	PICKARD, L.
CONLON, R.	PICKLES, W.
COOPER, R.	PIMM, H.
CRAVEN, W.	PROUT, E.
CULLING, T.	RICHARDS, W.
DILWORTH, A.	ROBERTSHAW, W.
EDMONDSON, W.	ROBINSON, H.
EMMOTT, S.	RUSHWORTH, C.
FERNSIDES, H.	SANDERSON, J. W.
FIRTH, A.	SMITH, J.
GALLAGHER, F.	TAYLOR, W.
GARNHAM, F.	THORNTON, T.
GREENWOOD, H. G.	TOWERS, J.
GREENWOOD, M.	TOWEY, P.
HARRISON, H.	VARLEY, E.
HEATON, J.	WARD, F.
HELLIWELL, H. M.	WATSON, W.
ILLINGWORTH, E.	WATMOUGH, F.
JACKMAN, I.	WILKINSON, E.

A. Peel Bros., Ltd.

AMBLER, S.	PEEL, L.
LINCOLN, S.	

I. Robson and Sons, Ltd.

MAY, F. D.	MOORE, C.

The British Cotton and Wool Dyers' Association Ltd.

ROLL OF HONOUR.—*Continued.*

SCOTCH BRANCHES.

Brownlee and Fyfe, Ltd.

MURRAY, P. C.　　　WELSH, R.

Cochrane, Smith and Co., Ltd.

ASHDOWN, H.　　　FORD, J.
BROWN, T.　　　　RATHIE, W.
DODDS, W.　　　　TAYLOR, G.

D. Macfarlane and Sons, Ltd.

BROWN, J.　　　　McCANN, J.
BROWN, S.　　　　McCAY, J.
CLOSE, J.　　　　McDONALD, C.
DEAN, W.　　　　 McGINNIGLE, A.
DONNELLY, JAS.　 McKAY, D.
DONNELLY, JOHN.　McKAY, J.
DOUGLAS, A.　　　McKAY, T.
DUNCAN, T.　　　 O'NEILL, A.
EAGLESOM, W.　　 O'NEIL, J.
FAULKNER, T.　　 PULLER, J.
HUGHES, B.　　　 SHAW, T.
INGLIS, J.　　　 SLATER, F.
LAWRIE, J.　　　 STEVEN, G.
LEES, J.　　　　 WARK, J.
LYONS, W.　　　　VICKERS, S.
MALCOLM, E.

J. and J. McCallum, Ltd.

ADAMS, R. J.　　　LINDSAY, J.
ALEXANDER, J.　　MALCOLM, W.
ALEXANDER, R.　　McCALLUM, J. K.
BARCLAY, J.　　　McCOLL, G.
BROWN, W.　　　　McGLYNN, W.
BURNS, R.　　　　McKENZIE, J.
CAIRNEY, J.　　　McLATCHIE, I.
CAMPBELL, J.　　 MILLER, J.
CHERRY, R.　　　 MITCHELL, J.
CUNNINGHAM, P.　 QUIN, P.
DONALD, J.　　　 REDDON, A.
FAULDS, R.　　　 REID, G.
GLANCY, F.　　　 REID, J.
GLEN, A.　　　　 REID, R.
GLEN, G.　　　　 ROBERTSON, A.
GORMAN, W.　　　 SMITH, W.
HAMILTON, J.　　 STORIE, D.
HUGHES, A.　　　 TIERNEY, J.
JEFFREY, A.　　　WALLACE, G.
LAMB, F.　　　　 YOUNG, J.

Wm. McConnell and Co., Ltd.

AITKEN, W.　　　 McCUDDEN, J.
ALEXANDER, R.　　McNINCH, J.
KEENAN, T.　　　 SHERIDAN, T.
McGAFFERY, J.　　SMITH, J.

Alex. Reid and Bro., Ltd.,

BOOTH, W.　　　　 LYLE, W.
BRAIN, G.　　　　 McCONNACHNIE, R.
BROWN, E.　　　　 McCONVILLE, F.
BYARS, J.　　　　 McFADYEN, W.
CUMMINGS, D.　　 MUIR, J.
CUNNINGHAM, P.　 O'NEIL, C.
CRAWFORD, R.　　 RITCHIE, T.
GERRAND, A.　　　SUMMERS, D.
HOLLAND, P., Junr.　THOMAS, E.
LOCHERIE, J.　　 YOUNG, D.

T. Simpson and Co., Ltd.

BALLANTYNE, J.　 MADDEN, A.
CAMPBELL, R.　　 McMILLAN, J.
DOUGLAS, J.　　　McNINCH, T.
FOY, J.　　　　　 RAMSAY, W.

J. Turnbull and Sons, Ltd.

AMOS, A.　　　　 JARDINE, W.
APPLEBY, W.　　　OLIVER, R.
BUTLER, J.　　　 ROBERTSON, G.
BUTLER, JAS.　　 RONALDSON, W.
CUNLIFFE, H.　　 STORRIE, R.
DECHAN, J.　　　 TAYLOR, D.
HAY, J.　　　　　 THOMSON, H.
HUTTON, F.　　　 WHILLANS, G.

Turnbulls, Ltd.

ANDERSON, G.　　 KELLY, J.
BEATTIE, J.　　　KYLE, J. H.
BOYD, C.　　　　 LAIDLAW, H.
BROWN, G.　　　　LUMSDEN, J.
COCHRANE, J.　　 MIDDLEMISS, R.
COLTMAN, J.　　　MILES, J.
DOUGLAS, A.　　　MILLAR, A.
DOUGLAS, G.　　　REID, C.
DRYDEN, T.　　　 SCOTT, T.
DUNCAN, A.　　　 SCOTT, W.
FEATHERSTONE, M.　STEWART, F.
FERGUSON, J.　　 SULLIVAN, F.
FERGUSON, R.　　 SWINTON, C.
GRAHAM, J.　　　 TAYLOR, A.
GOURLEY, F.　　　WILSON, A.
HALL, J.　　　　 WILSON, R.
HOGG, G.　　　　 WALDIE, T.
INGLIS, C.

ROLL OF HONOUR
OF
The British Reinforced Concrete Engineering Co. Ltd.
1. DICKINSON STREET, MANCHESTER.

✱ ✱ ✱

C. J. Allen.
J. M. Atlee. (Killed.)
S. Bumphrey.
G. Burnett.
S. L. Capes.
G. Clarke.
G. E. Dixon.
E. A. Dobbs.
W. Evans.
W. Ford.
T. A. Frost.
R. Grant.
George Gleave.
John Gleave.
E. Hawkins.
G. S. Heathcote.
S. Horsfield.
W. Hutchins.
G. Islay.
N. G. Isherwood. (Killed.)
A. H. Jones.
Arthur Kelly.

W. Lee.
C. F. Linton.
G. Matthews.
T. P. Miscampbell.
Hugh Owens.
W. Peate.
H. E. D. Pearce.
P. R. Pledger.
T. Pincutt.
G. F. Reeve.
Thomas Rusdale.
F. A. Sanders.
W. Smyth.
H. V. Stephenson.
F. Taylor.
John Tabbron.
J. Tuff.
A. B. Wallis.
J. Williams.
G. L. Wright.
John Woodward.

ROLL OF HONOUR.

Brookfield, Aitchison & Co.
LIMITED.
York Street, Manchester.

- J. Hart, "The Pals," 1st Manchester Battalion.
- F. W. Wiggins, "The Pals," 1st Manchester Battalion.
- A. Shaw, "The Pals," 2nd Manchester Battalion.
- E. Hawksworth, "The Pals," 2nd Manchester Battalion.
- F. Bunting, 2nd Manchester Battalion.
- H. A. Tant, 3rd Manchester Battalion.
- J. C. Wright, 3rd Manchester Battalion.
- E. W. Meadows, 4th Manchester Battalion.
- A. W. Higgs, Royal Fusiliers.
- E. P. James, Duke of Lancaster's Yeomanry.
- A. Blythe, Duke of Lancaster's Yeomanry.
- H. D. Woodhouse, Duke of Lancaster's Yeomanry.
- W. Wallace, Royal Field Artillery.
- F. Davis, "The Pals," 6th Manchester Battalion.
- A. Hooley, 2nd Salford Battalion.
- J. McCutcheon, H.M.S. Navy.
- D. J. Price, Public School Boys' Battalion.
- V. Birkby, 14th Manchester Regiment.
- S. Gordon, British Red Cross Society, Rouen, France.
- S. Wilson, Royal Army Medical Corps.
- W. Faulkner, "The Pals," 7th Manchester Battalion.
- S. Wilson, Royal Army Medical Corps.
- H. C. Brothers, Duke of Lancaster's Yeomanry.
- F. Wilson, 3/8th Manchesters.

ROLL OF HONOUR.

BROOME & FOSTER LTD.

17 and 19 Chorlton Street,
MANCHESTER.

Lieut. R. Harold Brewis	1/8th Lancashire Fusiliers (T.F.).
Q.M.-Sgt. H. St. John Stokoe	6th Manchesters (T.F.).
Harry Hunt	7th Manchesters (T.F.) (Killed).
A. Kennedy	R.A.M.C.
Thomas Fitzsimmons	14th King's Liverpool Regiment.
David Warren	20th Manchesters (Pals).
Victor Southcott	21st Manchesters (Pals).
L.-Corpl. Walter Vout	21st Manchesters (Pals).
L.-Corpl. Thomas Foley	Rifle Brigade.
J. A. Craig	R.F.A.
John Elliott	R.A.M.C.
Roger Milner	7th Manchester Regiment. (T.F.).
Thomas Halligan	15th King's Liverpool Regiment.
Joseph Henry Carter	Royal Garrison Artillery.
John Atkinson	R.F.A.
Herbert Bury	12th Manchester Regiment.

ROLL OF HONOUR.

The Broughton Copper Co. Ltd.

BROUGHTON WORKS.

DIRECTORS.

Major CRITCHLEY, E. A. | Captain SILTZER, F. J.

STAFF.

ASHTON, WILLIAM J.
BAMBER, GEORGE.
BENSON, JOHN S.
CAMPBELL, N. STUART.
CLARK, HAROLD.
FELLOWES, HARRY.
JACQUES, FRANK.
MILLWARD, BERTRAM.
NEWTON, JAMES B.
PRINCE, RICHARD WM.
STRACHAN, ALEX. G.
TOWER, PERCY KITSON.
WINDER, JOHN S.
YOUNG, P. RICARDO.

EMPLOYEES.

ABBOTT, CHARLES. (Wounded.)
ALDRIDGE, HENRY.
ALDRIDGE, JOHN.
ALLEN, ERNEST.
ALLEN, ROBERT. (Wounded.)
ARMSTRONG, WILLIAM. (Wounded.)
BACON, JOHN.
BARRETT, JAMES. (Wounded.)
BARRETT, THOMAS. (Accidentally Killed.)
BAUGHT, JOHN THOS.
BELCHER, JAMES.
BIRCH, FRANK.
BRADLEY, FREDERICK.
BREAKEY, PETER.
BRERETON, JOHN. (Killed in action.)
BRIDGE, THOMAS.
BRIGGS, ROBERT.
BUCKLEY, JOHN. (Gassed and Wounded.)
BUCKLEY, WALLACE. (Wounded.)
BURLEY, JAMES.
BYRNE, LAWRENCE.
BYRNES, GEORGE HY.
CAMPBELL, WILLIAM. (Wounded and prisoner.)
CARRUTHERS, WILLIAM.
CARTER, WARWICK.
CAWSON, JAMES.
CHURCHILL, TOM. (Wounded.)
CLANCY, DANIEL.
CLARE, JAMES THOMAS.
COLMAN, JOHN. (Gassed and Wounded.)
COONEY, JAMES.

COOPER, ALFRED. (Killed in action.)
CORLIS, JOSEPH.
COURT, GEORGE. (Wounded.)
CREIGHTON, JOHN.
CREIGHTON, THOMAS.
CUNNINGHAM, JAMES.
CUNNINGHAM, ROBERT. (Wounded.)
CUNNINGHAM, WM.
DAGNAN, JOHN HENRY.
DALEY, JOSEPH.
DARBY, CHARLES.
DAVIES, JOSEPH.
DAWSON, FRED.
DAWSON, WILLIAM M.
DAY, ROBERT.
DEAN, GEORGE.
DENGER, CHARLES W.
DERMODY, RICHARD.
DEVLIN, ROBERT.
DIBB, FRED.
DILLON, JOHN. (Died of Wounds.)
DONE, SAMUEL.
DOWD, WILLIAM.
DOYLE, THOMAS.
DUFFY, WILLIAM. (Wounded.)
EDMONDSON, WILLIAM.
EDWARDS, ROBERT.
EDWARDS, ARTHUR.
EDWARDS, CHARLES. (Wounded & Died on Service)
FARRELL, JOHN.
FARRINGTON, ROBERT.
FILDES, JOHN.
FINLAY, FRANCIS.
FLINN, EDWARD.
FOX, JOHN. (Wounded.)

GALVIN, HUGH.
GANNON, HERBERT.
GILMOUR, WILLIAM.
GIVERIN, JOSEPH. (Wounded.)
GLAVIN, JOHN. (Died of Wounds.)
GRAY, PATRICK.
GREEN, CHARLES W.
GREEN, JOHN.
HALL, JOHN. (Wounded.)
HAMILTON, RALPH.
HAMILTON, THOMAS.
HARDEN, GEORGE.
HARRINGTON, JAMES.
HARVEY, WILLIAM.
HART, GEORGE.
HEALEY, JOHN.
HERBERT, JOSEPH.
HEYWOOD, WALTER. (Wounded.)
HIGGINS, PAUL.
HOLLAND, JOHN.
HOLT, EDWIN.
HOOK, CHARLES.
HOPWOOD, ALFRED.
HUGHES, ALBERT.
HUGHES, CHARLES.
HULSE, JOHN T. (Wounded.)
HUTT, SAMUEL, Junr.
INGLIS, DANIEL. (Wounded.)
JENNINGS, WILLIAM. (Killed in Action.)
JONES, HAROLD.
KELLY, JOSEPH. (Killed in action.)
KELLY, THOMAS.
KENNEDY, ANDREW.
KILROY, JOSEPH.

ROLL OF HONOUR—continued.
The Broughton Copper Company Ltd.

KINGDOM, HARRY.
KINGSMORE, THOMAS.
KIRKHAM, JOHN T.
    (Wounded.)
KNOTT, ALFRED.
KNOTT, GEORGE.
    (Wounded and Prisoner.)
LANCASHIRE, HUBERT.
LAWLER, JOHN JOSEPH.
LESLIE, PATRICK.
LIVESEY, SAMUEL.
    (Wounded.)
LYONS, JOHN.
MADDEN, THOMAS.
McCREERY, WILLIAM.
McDERMOTT, EDWARD.
    (Prisoner.)
McDERMOTT, THOMAS.
McKAY, MICHAEL.
McKENNA, ALBERT.
McMAHON, THOMAS.
McMAHON, WILLIAM.
McMANUS, JOHN.
MAHER, JAMES.
    (Wounded.)
MANSELL, WILLIAM.
MASSEY, JOHN JOSEPH.
MATTHEWS, ERNEST.
MIDDLETON, GEORGE.
    (Died on service.)
MONKS, JAMES WM.
    (Wounded and Missing.)
MOONEY, CHRIS.
    (Killed in Action.)
MORGAN, JOHN.
MORRISON, JOHN W.
MOSS, JOHN HENRY.
NEWBROOK, ALBERT.
NORRIS, MAURICE.
NORRIS, MICHAEL.
NORRIS, PATRICK.
NURTNEY, THOMAS.
OGDEN, SAMUEL.
    (Wounded.)
O'NEILL, PATRICK.
    (Died on service.)
PATON, THOMAS.
PEELING, JAMES.
    (Wounded.)
PRENDERGAST, GEORGE
    (Wounded.)
PRESTON, FRANK.
PRICE, GEORGE.
    (Wounded.)
PRITCHARD, JOSEPH.
REYNOLDS, CHARLES.
    (Gassed and Prisoner.)
RHODES, HENRY.
    (Wounded.)
ROACH, GEORGE.
ROBERTS, JOHN.
    (Wounded.)
ROBERTS, JOSEPH.
ROBERTS, STEWART.
ROSE, JOHN.
ROWLANDS, WILLIAM.
RUSTIDGE, JOSEPH.
SALTER, EDWARD J.
SHAKESPEARE, ED.
SHERRY, JAMES.
    (Wounded.)
SHERRY, OWEN.
SHIELDS, JOHN.
    (Wounded.)
SHIELDS, THOMAS.
SINCLAIR, JOHN.
SKELLINGTON, JOHN.
SLATTERY, JAMES.
    (Wounded.)
SLOAN, JOHN.
SMITH, HARRY.
    (Killed in Action.)
SMITH, WILLIAM HY.
SOUTH, JAMES.
SOUTH, THOMAS.
SOUTHERN, JAMES.
STUBBS, ARTHUR.
STUBBS, FREDERICK G.
THORNTON, THOMAS.
    (Wounded.)
TOMS, ROBERT.
TRAYNOR, JOHN.
    (Wounded.)
TURNER, WALTER.
    (Wounded.)
TYNAN, ARTHUR JOHN.
TYRRELL, GEORGE.
TYRRELL, WALTER.
TYZACK, THOMAS.
    (Wounded.)
WADSWORTH, JOHN.
WALKER, JOHN.
WALKER, WILLIAM.
WALSH, FRANK.
WARREN, JOHN.
WARREN, PATRICK.
WATERS, HUGH.
WATERS, WILLIAM.
WHALLEY, JOHN HY.
WHALLEY, WILLIAM HY.
    (Wounded.)
WILLIAMS, JOHN.
WILLIAMS, JOHN JOS.
WILLIAMS, WILLIAM.
WOLFENDALE, CHAS.
WORTHINGTON, THOS.

DITTON WORKS.

FITZBROWN, GEOFFREY.

BLUNDELL, JOHN.
    (Missing.)
BYRNE, WILLIAM J.
    (Wounded.)
CAMPION, ROBERT HY.
CARNEY, THOMAS.
DITCHFIELD, WALLACE.
DOWNWARD, WILLIAM.
FALLON, JAMES.
HOUGHTON, ERNEST.
    (Wounded.)
HUNT, CHARLES.

STAFF.

CLAYTON, CHARLES.

EMPLOYEES.

LEATHER, RICHARD.
MASON, HERBERT.
MATHER, HAROLD.
MEADE, JOHN E.
MELIA, PATRICK.
MISKELLA, JOHN.
    (Wounded.)
MORGAN, ANDREW.
    (Wounded.)
MUSGRAVE, JOHN.
O'MALLEY, MARTIN.
PENNINGTON, JOSEPH.

HALFPENNY, JOHN.

PHYTHIAN, JOHN.
RILEY, WILLIAM.
SANDS, MATTHEW.
SMITH, W. H.
STEPHENS, ALCON.
    (Wounded.)
TAYLOR, DANIEL.
    (Killed in Action.)
WALTON, PETER.
    (Killed in action.)
WRIGHT, PETER.
    (Wounded.)

ROLL OF HONOUR.

Burgess, Ledward & Co.
LIMITED.
22 Dickinson Street, Manchester.

Lt.-Col. H. LEDWARD, V.D.	27th Reserve Batt. Manchester Regiment.
THOS ADSHEAD, L.Cpl.	7th Batt. King's Own Scottish Borderers.
LEONARD BEAVERS	Driver, East Lanc. Army Service Corps.
TOM BROWN, L.Cpl.	7th Batt. King's Own Scottish Borderers.
LEONARD CALDWELL	2nd Battalion Grenadier Guards.
FREDERICK DANSON	1/4th Batt. Ryl. Scots, Queen's Edin. Rifles.
SAMUEL HAMER	Temporarily with the Inn's of Court O.T.C.
J. F. HARDMAN	R.A.M.C. (T.F.), 2nd Western General Hpl.
F. L. HIRST	8th Battalion Manchester Regiment.
FRED HOSKINS, Dmr.	19th Service Batt. Manchester Regiment.
G. F. LEES	Army Service Corps.
HAROLD MATHER	2/4th Batt. Ryl. Scots, Queen's Edin. Rifles.
*FRANK MILLAR	7th Batt. King's Own Scottish Borderers.
RUD NEILSON	Royal Army Medical Corps.
ALFRED PARKYN	26th Battalion Manchester Regiment.
†HAROLD PARTINGTON	1/4th Batt. Ryl. Scots, Queen's Edin. Rifles.
J. D. PILKINGTON	3rd East Lancs. Royal Field Artillery.
JOSEPH SHAWCROSS	2/6th Battalion Manchester Regiment.
TOM SIMPSON	21st Service Batt. Manchester Regiment.
CHARLES SNAPE	1/6th Manchester Regiment (T.F.).
THOS. SUTCLIFFE, Cpl.	Army Service Corps, Trans. and Supply Col.
WM. SUTHERLAND	4th Res. Batt. Ryl. Scots, Queen's Edin. R.
H. WAREING	2/7th Battalion Manchester Regiment.
ALEX. WELLS	2/3rd East Lanc. Field Ambulance.

Weaving Department.

G. ARMITT	National Reserve.
H. BARHAM	Royal Army Medical Corps.
W. R. BERRY	Royal Field Artillery.
L. FARNWORTH	Royal Army Medical Corps.
S. GRUNDY	2nd Battalion Manchester Regiment.
O. HUGHES	5th Batt. Loyal North Lancashire Regiment.
J. HOWARD	Dublin Fusiliers.
W. HADCROFT	Royal Field Artillery.
P. HELM	Royal Garrison Artillery.
D. LONG	15th "S" Battalion Welsh Regiment.
H. MULLINEAUX	Royal Field Artillery.
M. MATHER	Army Ordnance Corps.
H. MORRIS	Royal Field Artillery.

*Killed in action. †Missing.

Burgess, Ledward & Co. Limited.
ROLL OF HONOUR—continued.

H. MORGAN	Army Ordnance Corps.
C. PRESTON	Army Service Corps.
C. POWELL	Royal Field Artillery.
A. ROWE	4th Battalion Manchester Regiment.
F. SMITH	East Lancashire Regiment.
H. SMETHURST	Army Ordnance Corps.
C. WORTHINGTON	6th Sussex Cycle Corps.

Dyehouse Department.

R. ASKEW	Royal Army Medical Corps.
T. ADAMS	Lancashire Fusiliers.
G. BOSTOCK	1/2nd N. Midland Brig. Ammunition Col.
J. BOOTH	Loyal North Lancashire Regiment.
E. BARNBY	Royal Army Medical Corps.
A. BOLTON	A.C.C.
T. A. COPE	King's Royal Rifles.
S. DARCY	National Reserve.
S. DARLINGTON	Royal Army Medical Corps.
J. FREY	Lancashire Fusiliers.
A. GRUNDY	6th Sussex Cycle Corps.
C. W. GREEN	3/6th Sussex Cycle Corps.
E. C. HODGINS, Lieut.	7th Battalion King's Liverpool Regiment.
F. HUDSON	3/6th Sussex Cycle Corps.
W. HOLDEN	Royal Field Artillery.
T. HOLMES	Royal Field Artillery.
W. E. JONES	Loyal North Lancashire Regiment.
J. JONES	Loyal North Lancashire Regiment.
T. D. JAMES	Lancashire Fusiliers.
R. JONES	Royal Field Artillery.
W. KNOWLES	Royal Army Medical Corps.
J. T. LIGHTBOWN	Ambulance Corps.
F. LYTHGOE	Royal Army Medical Corps.
R. LEACH	Loyal North Lancashire Regiment.
F. MATHER	King's Royal Rifles.
T. MOORES	Loyal North Lancashire Regiment.
J. MARSH	1st Sussex Cycle Corps.
H. MULLINEAUX	Royal Field Artillery.
W. MARLOR	Welsh Fusiliers.
I. McWILLIAMS	3/6th Sussex Cycle Corps.
A. McWILLIAMS	3/6th Sussex Cycle Corps.
T. E. OGDEN	Royal Field Artillery.
A. QUIGLEY	National Reserve.
A. RUSHTON	Loyal North Lancashire Regiment.
T. H. ROTHWELL	King's Royal Rifles.
R. RHODES	Royal Field Artillery.
J. STRINGFELLOW	Loyal North Lancashire Regiment.
W. SHAWCROSS	Lancashire Fusiliers.
W. A. TIBBS	6th Battalion Manchester Regiment.
F. TAITE	Royal Dublin Fusiliers.
W. VALENTINE	Loyal North Lancashire Regiment.
J. VICKERS	Loyal North Lancashire Regiment.
A. WOOLLARD	Loyal North Lancashire Regiment.
J. WILLIAMSON	Royal Army Medical Corps.
T. A. WILLIAMSON	3/6th Sussex Cycle Corps.
H. WALKER	Royal Field Artillery.
A. YOUNG	5th Battalion Manchester Regiment.

Roll of Honour.

Baxter, Woodhouse & Taylor
LIMITED
24 Mosley Street, Manchester.

Major F. J. TAYLOR,
　　7th Batt. Cheshire Regt.

Private J. F. COLLINGE,
　　Royal Army Medical Corps.

Private J. DAKIN,
　　25th Batt. Manchester Regt.

Private F. HARDY,
　　7th Batt. Manchester Regt.

Drummer A. HALLWORTH,
　　8th Batt. Manchester Regt.

Private W. LUXTON,
　　Royal Army Medical Corps.

Private J. C. PARKIN,
　　7th Batt. Royal Berk's Regt.

Drummer A. H. PERKINS,
　　8th Batt. Manchester Regt.

Private N. H. RAINS,
　　7th Batt. Manchester Regt.

Private A. WYETH,
　　Royal Army Medical Corps.

Roll of Honour.

Louis Behrens & Sons,
131, PORTLAND STREET,
MANCHESTER.

Roger G. Bird.
E. Holbrook.
A. Thomas.
F. Robinson.
H. E. Diggle.
H. F. Darbyshire.
W. Dixon.
R. Fielding.
F. Hills.
A. Abercrombie.
A. Jenkinson.
E. Valentine.
C. W. West.
E. Badcock.
A. Lauder.
H. Crompton.
C. Gardner.
T. Mullins.
W. Taylor.

ROLL OF HONOUR.
✱ ✱ ✱
S. & W. BERISFORD LIMITED,
20 and 22, Withy Grove,
Manchester.

2nd Lieut. FRANK BERISFORD,
　10th Durham Light Infantry.
　　Attached to
　　　11th King's Liverpool Regt., France.
Chief Petty Officer H. BATTERSBY,
　C/o Major Holmes,
　　R.N.D. Supply Depôt,
　　　M.E.F., Dardanelles.
Gunner J. E. HAMPSON, No. 1272,
　1/5th Battery, 42nd Division,
　　M.E.F., Dardanelles.
Sergt. H. G. RIDGARD, No. 10704,
　18th Service Batt., Manchester Regt.,
　　　B.E.F., France.
Private F. N. WOODWARD, No. 10735
　Signalling Section,
　　18th Service Batt., Manchester Regt.,
　　　B.E.F., France.
Private C. P. CUMPSTY, No. 10766,
　Signalling Section,
　　18th Service Batt., Manchester Regt.,
　　　B.E.F., France.
Drummer F. WILKINSON, No. 17530,
　20th Service Batt., Manchester Regt.,
　　　B.E.F., France.
Coy.-Q.M.-Sergt. H. THOMASON, No. 9038,
　35th Division Army Cyclists' Corps,
　　Lucknow Barracks, Tidworth.
Private W. WHITESIDE, No. 22132,
　1st Loyal North Lancashires,
　　Wounded in France, at present lying at
　　Balmer Lawn Hospital, Brockenhurst.
FRED BUDD,
　Royal Navy,
　　Appointed to Cruiser "Berwick."
Private A. ALDERSLEY, No. 43,
　66th Division, Casualty Clearing Station,
　R.A.M.C., East Lancs. Territorials,
　　　　　　　Imperial Service.
W. S. DUNNING,
　Y.M.C.A. Hut, France.
H. DUNNING,
　C/o Friends' Ambulance Unit,
　　17th Ambulance Train,
　　　　　　　France.

ROLL OF HONOUR.
✱ ✱ ✱
John Bolton & Co.,
7, Museum St., Manchester.

Lieutenant R. L. BOLTON,
　2/7th Batt. Manchester Regiment.

Lance-Corporal F. EMERSON,
　2nd Batt. Middlesex Regiment.

Private W. BUCHAN,
　7th Batt. Manchester Regiment.

*Private H. HARDING,
　Plymouth Div., Royal Marine L.I.

Private H. HOLLINGSWORTH,
　Army Veterinary Corps.

Private H. YOUNG,
　18th Batt. Manchester Regiment.

*Died of Enteric in the Dardanelles.

ROLL OF HONOUR.

C. H. Britton and Sons,

LLOYD'S HOUSE,
ALBERT SQUARE,
MANCHESTER.

L.-Corporal ALBERT BRITTON,
M.T.—Army Service Corps.

Sergt. CHAS. E. SMITH,
Army Veterinary Corps.

L.-Corporal ALFRED HUNT,
18th Service Batt. Manchester Regt.

Corporal FRANK PARTINGTON,
2/7th Batt. Manchester Regt. (T.F.).

Private FREDK. HODGKINSON,
18th Service Batt. Manchester Regt.

Gunner WALTER BLACK,
R.F.A., East Lancs. (T.F.)

FRANCIS PLUNKETT,
French Army

ALFRED BASTARD,
French Army.

Gunner ARNOLD SMITH,
R.F.A., East Lancs. (T.F.)

Corporal J. NASH JONES,
D. Batt. R.F.A., 55th Brig.

ROLL OF HONOUR.

Edward R. Buck & Sons

53, Dale Street,
MANCHESTER.

Sergeant J. N. BUCK,
Queen Victoria Rifles.

R. BUCK (Temporary Commission),
Royal Flying Corps.

Sergt.-Major G. J. INNES,
7th Lancashire Fusiliers.

Private D. GEE,
7th Lancashire Fusiliers.

Bombardier H. GOODBRAND,
Royal Field Artillery.

Private S. C. BAKER,
18th Manchester Regiment.

Private H. BILLINGTON,
Army Cycle Corps.

Private A. THORLEY,
Royal Scots Regiment.

Private A. LANGDON,
Royal Scots Regiment.

Private E. THOMAS,
Lancashire Fusiliers.

ROLL OF HONOUR.

Chorlton Brothers Limited,
49, 51 & 53, Piccadilly, Manchester.

BARLOW, H.   19th (Service) Batt. Manchester Regt.
BEESLEY, FRANK.   Royal Army Medical Corps.
BENNETT, S.   7th Batt. Lancashire Fusiliers.
BIRCHALL, HARRY.   17th (Service) Batt. Manchester Regt.
BURKE, STEPHEN.   17th (Service) Batt. Manchester Regt.
BURROWS, THOS.   Royal Army Medical Corps.
CAPSTICK, HUGH P.   14th (Service) Batt. Cheshire Regt.
CONNOLLY, W.   18th (Service) Batt. Manchester Regt.
COWDEN, ALAN.   7th (Territorial) Batt. Manchester Regt.
COYLE, A.   18th (Service) Batt. Manchester Regt.
DAVIDSON, G. H.   17th (Service) Batt. Manchester Regt.
DEWAN, THOMAS.   16th (Service) Batt. Manchester Regt.
DODGSON, REUBEN.   Royal Army Medical Corps.
GILBERT, J.   Royal Army Medical Corps.
GORNALL, ALFRED.   Royal Army Medical Corps.
HAYDEN, J.   Army Ordnance Corps.
HOPWOOD, FRED.   Army Ordnance Corps.
HUMPHREYS, J.   East Lancashire Regt.
JACKSON, ARTHUR.   Royal Navy.
JONES, W.   Royal Navy.
JONES, LEONARD BASIL.   Royal Army Medical Corps.
KAY, JOHN.   6th (Territorial) Batt. Manchester Regt.
LEWIS, W. T.   6th (Territorial) Batt. Manchester Regt.
LLOYD, PERCY.   7th South Lancashire Regt.
McLEOD, J.   Royal Field Artillery.
MAUGHAN, F.   4th Dragoon Guards.
MILLIARD, C.   7th (Territorial) Batt. Manchester Regt.
NEWTON, FRANK.   17th (Service) Batt. Manchester Regt.
NOBLE, GEORGE.   20th (Service) Batt. Manchester Regt.
PENDLEBURY, J.   6th (Territorial) Batt. Manchester Regt.
PENDLEBURY, R.   Royal Army Medical Corps.
PICKTHALL, HARRY.   17th (Service) Batt. Manchester Regt.
POTT, FRED.   6th (Terr.) Batt. Notts and Derby Regt. (Sherwood Foresters).
RABONE, ALFRED.   21st (Service) Batt. Manchester Regt.
RAVENSCROFT, JAMES.   20th (Service) Batt. Manchester Regt.
RIDDELL, ROBERT R.   19th (Service) Batt. Manchester Regt.
RILEY, W. L.   17th (Service) Batt. Manchester Regt.
ROSENBLOOM, JACOB.   6th (Territorial) Batt. Manchester Regt.
SOUTHERN, R.   Royal Army Medical Corps.
SPEARS, J.   19th (Service Batt. Manchester Regt.
SPENCER, ALBERT.   19th (Service) Batt. Manchester Regt.
TATTON, HAROLD.   17th (Service) Batt. Manchester Regt.
TYRRELL, G.   8th (Territorial) Batt. Manchester Regt.
WALKER, JOSEPH.   17th (Service) Batt. Manchester Regt.
WHITFIELD, JOHN W.   11th (Service) Batt. Border Regt.
WHITHAM, J.   21st (Service) Batt. Manchester Regt.
WILSON, JOE.   Duke of Lancaster's Yeomanry.
WILSON, N.   18th (Service) Batt. Manchester Regt.
WOOD, A. T. C.   6th (Territorial) Batt. Manchester Regt.
WOOD, H.   17th (Service) Batt. Manchester Regt.
YATES, A. L.   21st (Service) Batt. Royal Fusiliers.
YATES, LAWRENCE.   Duke of Lancaster's Own Yeomanry.

ROLL OF HONOUR.

✱ ✱ ✱

The Clayton Aniline Co.
LIMITED,
CLAYTON, MANCHESTER.

Private JOSEPH BERRESFORD	8th Battalion 23rd Manchester Regiment.
Private JOHN WILLIAM BERRY	1st Battalion 4th King's Own R. Lancasters (Prisoner of war).
Private FREDERICK BICKERTON	11th Battalion Lancashire Fusiliers.
Private FREDERICK CLAYFIELD	13th Battalion Manchester Regiment.
Private JAMES COLTAS	1st King's Liverpool Regiment.
Private EDWARD DOLAN	27th Battalion Manchester Regiment.
Private JOHN DONNELLY	3rd Battalion Manchester Regiment.
Private ALFRED CHAS. DOUGHTY	2nd Battalion Lancashire Fusiliers.
Private THOMAS DURKIN	2nd Connaught Rangers.
Private STANLEY ESILMAN	3/7th Battalion Manchester Regiment.
Lance-Corporal ALBERT FRASER	6th Battalion Manchester Regiment.
Private JAMES THOMAS GORDON	8th Battalion Manchester Regiment.
Private WILLIAM HY. GREAVE	3rd Battalion Manchester Regiment.
Lieut. EDWIN TURNER GRUNDEY	Royal Army Medical Corps.
Private JOHN HIGGINS	Coldstream Guards.
Private JOHN HOLMES	6th Battalion Manchester Regiment.
Private JAMES HOOPER	5th Battalion Manchester Regiment.
Private JOHN HOWSON	D Cy., 3rd Batt. The King's Liverpool Regt.
Private LEONARD JORDAN	Royal Army Medical Corps.
Private WILLIAM KERR	Royal Scotch.
Private WALTER LAWLESS	4th Battalion Lancashire Fusiliers. (Gassed; since died in hospital.)
Private JOHN LOMAS	9th Battalion East Lancashire Regiment.
Lance-Corporal MARSLAND	2/1st Army Service Corps.
Private JOHN McNICHOLLS	8th Battalion East Lancashire Regiment.
Private JOHN MORAN	Lancashire Fusiliers.
Private H. McCANDLISH	20th Battalion Royal Welsh Fusiliers.
Private PATRICK RATTIGAN	2nd Battalion West Riding Regiment.
Private BENJAMIN RAWCLIFFE	Royal Engineers.
Private JAMES RICHARDS	7th Battalion Lancashire Fusiliers.
Sergeant WILLIAM ROONEY	13th Battalion Manchester Regiment.
Private ERNEST SECREY	8th Battalion 2nd Rifle Brigade. (Prisoner of war).
Private FREDERICK SMITH	4th Battalion Manchester Regiment.
Sergeant FREDERICK SHUTLER	Manchester Regiment.
Private J. WALKER	6th Battalion Manchester Regiment.
Private JAMES WARD	Lancashire Fusiliers.
Private JAMES WELLS	Manchester Regiment.
Private THOMAS WILLIS	2nd Battalion Lancashire Fusiliers.
Private GEORGE WILLOTT	13th Battalion 4th King's Lancasters. (Prisoner of war).
Private JAMES WOOD	3rd Battalion King's Own Liverpool.
Private RUPERT WOOLLEY	1st Manchesters.

ROLL OF HONOUR.

I. J. & G. Cooper Limited,

DALE STREET, MANCHESTER.

Employees who have Joined His Majesty's Forces.

Manchester.

Name	Department	Regiment
ALDRED, T.	Silks	Manchester Batt. Kitchener's Army.
AINSWORTH, H.	Lace	Manchester Batt. Kitchener's Army.
AINSCOUGH, W.	Straws	4th Seaforth Highlanders.
ATTENBOROUGH, J. H.	Counting House	Royal Army Medical Corps.
BESWICK, A.	Millinery	Royal Army Medical Corps.
BOWKER, N. E.	Flowers	Manchester Batt. Kitchener's Army.
BELL, W.	Silks	Royal Scots Queen's Edinburgh Rifles.
BENT, J. A.	Neckwear	Manchester Batt. Kitchener's Army.
BUCKLEY, W. E.	Sales	Manchester Batt. Kitchener's Army.
BARROW, T.	Town-room	Manchester Batt. Kitchener's Army.
BEDNALL, A.	Order Office	10th Batt. Manchester Regiment.
BOARDMAN, J. H.	Gent's. Outfitting Dept.	Royal Army Medical Corps.
CAIN, J. L.	Blouse	6th Manchester Territorials.
CREWE, A.	Furs	Royal Army Medical Corps.
CONWAY, J.	Receiving Department	Manchester Batt. Kitchener's Army.
DAWSON, F.	Abstract Office	Naval Reserve (Medical Section).
DAWSON, R.	Fancy	Royal Field Artillery.
DANCE, J.	Lace	Manchester Batt. Kitchener's Army.
ELKIN, J.	Abstract Department	Royal Scots Queen's Edinburgh Rifles.
FITTIS, A.	Straws	Manchester Batt. Kitchener's Army.
FURLONG, F. P.	Straws	Manchester Batt. Kitchener's Army.
FRITH, J.	Mantle	Manchester Batt. Kitchener's Army.
FURNIFER, W.	Packing-room	Manchester Batt. Kitchener's Army.
GEE, A.	Neckwear	Manchester Batt. Kitchener's Army.
GILL, N.	Fancy	Manchester Batt. Kitchener's Army.
GODFREY, G. W.	Straws	Manchester Batt. Kitchener's Army.
GILLIGAN, W.	Lift	Manchester Batt. Kitchener's Army.
GOWER, J. B.	Counting House	Royal Fusiliers.
HALL, W.	Underclothing	Army Service Corps.
HEALEY, G. J.	Underclothing	Manchester Batt. Kitchener's Army.
HAWORTH, W.	Mantle	Manchester Batt. Kitchener's Army.
HARRISON, J. A.	Ribbons	Manchester Batt. Kitchener's Army.

ROLL OF HONOUR—Continued.

I. J. & G. COOPER LTD.

Manchester.

HOLT, J. W.	Straws	Manchester Batt. Kitchener's Army.
HEAPY, A.	Flowers	Royal Army Medical Corps.
HEYWOOD, J. H.	Abstract	Manchester Batt. Kitchener's Army.
INGHAM, W.	Millinery	Royal Fusiliers.
JACKSON, J. R.	Neckwear	6th Manchester Territorials.
JUPP, F.	Straws	Manchester Batt. Kitchener's Army.
JONES, W.	Mantle	Royal Field Artillery.
LEACH, H.	Abstract Office	6th Manchester Territorials.
LEACH, H. E.	Underclothing	6th Manchester Territorials.
LEE, J.	Millinery	6th Manchester Territorials.
LESTER, F.	Smallwares	Manchester Batt. Kitchener's Army.
LAWSON, J.	Packing-room	Manchester Batt. Kitchener's Army.
MADDOCKS, M.	Gent's. Outfitting	Manchester Batt. Kitchener's Army.
MACKERETH, F.	Gent's. Outfitting	Manchester Batt. Kitchener's Army.
MINTON, L.	Furs	Manchester Batt. Kitchener's Army.
MAGRATH, J.	Umbrellas	Manchester Batt. Kitchener's Army.
McHUGH, A.	Neckwear Dept.	7th Batt. Manchester Regiment.
NEWTON, J.	Straws	Manchester Batt. Kitchener's Army.
NICHOLSON, J.	Abstract Department	Royal Scots Queen's Edinburgh Rifles.
REYNOLDS, —	Mantle	Lancashire Fusiliers.
RAYNER, J. M.	Underclothing	Manchester Batt. Kitchener's Army.
RUSSON, A. H.	Packing-room	Royal Field Artillery.
ROYLE, WM. ALFRED	Underclothing	4th Batt. Seaforth Highlanders.
SMITH, T.	Packing-room	Royal Field Artillery.
SMITH, J. W.	Gent's. Outfitting	Manchester Batt. Kitchener's Army.
SMITH, JOHN	Underclothing	4th Batt. Seaforth Highlanders.
SHARP, H. H.	Fancy	Royal Army Medical Corps.
SEEL, W.	Manchester Dept.	Manchester Batt. Kitchener's Army.
TAYLOR, A.	Gent's. Outfitting	6th Manchester Territorials.
TYLDESLEY, A. J.	Straws	Manchester Batt. Kitchener's Army.
THOMPSON, R.	Mantle	Manchester Batt. Kitchener's Army.
TAYLOR, G. F.	Packing-room	Manchester Batt. Kitchener's Army.
WELCH, W. E.	Underclothing	6th Manchester Territorials.
WILLIS, J. M.	Mantle	Grenadier Guards.
WILSON, A.	Millinery	7th Manchester Fusiliers.
WOODHALL, F.	Straws	Manchester Batt. Kitchener's Army.
WILLCOCKS, L.	Ribbons	Manchester Batt. Kitchener's Army.
WESTWELL, A.	Forwarding Department	4th Batt. Seaforth Highlanders.

Liverpool Branch.

COLLINS, W. E.	—	Liverpool Batt. Kitchener's Army.
DUNN, H.	Traveller	Field Ambulance R.A.M.C. *In France*.
GOURLEY, R.	Furs, &c.	4th West Lancashire Artillery.
GAVIN, R.	Ribbons	1st Liverpool Scottish.
LOVELL, H.	Neckwear	Liverpool Batt. Kitchener's Army.
MILLS, C. O.	Ribbons	Birmingham Batt. Kitchener's Army.
MACDONALD, J.	Flowers	Liverpool Batt. Kitchener's Army.
NICHOLSON, G.	Ribbon and Silk	Liverpool Batt. Kitchener's Army.
PINFOLD, A.	Gent's. Outfitting, &c.	Liverpool Batt. Kitchener's Army.
SAVAGE, —		
WILSON, H.	Neckwear, &c.	Liverpool Batt. Kitchener's Army.
WALSH, H.	Porter	1st King's Liverpool.

ROLL OF HONOUR—Continued.

I. J. & G. COOPER LTD.

Leeds Branch.
DRIVER, W.	Packing-room	Royal Army Medical Corps.
FAWCETT, W. H. B.	Smallwares	Yorkshire Hussars.
FERGUSON	Fancy Linen	Royal Army Medical Corps.
HARDY, W.	Packing-room	17th West Yorkshire.
LAX, D. E.	Umbrellas	Yorkshire Hussars.
GILMOUR, D. M.	Silks	Royal Army Medical Corps.
MILBURN, H.	Mantle	Royal Army Medical Corps.
MORTIMER, A. O.	Flowers	Leeds Batt. Kitchener's Army.
ROSS, H.	Underclothing	Royal Army Medical Corps.
OTTER, J. R.	Millinery	Royal Army Medical Corps.
PARK, R. S.	Underclothing	Royal Army Medical Corps.
SPEIGHT, A.	Smallwares	Royal Army Medical Corps.

Birmingham Branch.
BOWER, A.	Fancy Linen	Royal Army Medical Corps.
BRADBURY, W. C.	Lace	Army Service Corps.
PRATT, H. S.	Flowers	Birmingham Batt. Kitchener's Army.
HOPKINS, H. G.	Furs	Birmingham Batt. Kitchener's Army.
RIDOUT, C.	Straws	Royal Army Medical Corps.
SUFFIELD, R. O.	Corset	Royal Army Medical Corps.
THOMPSON, A.	Packing-room	Worcestershire Regiment.
USHER, W.	Packing Room	Birmingham Batt. Kitchener's Army.

Newcastle-on-Tyne Br'ch.
BROUGH, T.	Packing-room	Northumberland Fusiliers.
BURNETT, J.	Fancy Linen	Northern Cyclists' Battalion.
CHARLESWORTH, T.	Neckwear	Northumberland Fusiliers.
CLARK, S.	Underclothing	Northumberland Fusiliers.
EMBLETON, J.	Corsets	Northumberland Fusiliers.
GILLENDER, J.	Underclothing	Northumberland Fusiliers.
GRAHAM, C.	Packing-room	Royal Army Medical Corps.
KITCHING, H.	Underclothing	Northumberland Fusiliers.
METCALF, —	Manchester Dept.	Royal Artillery.
MEY, W.	Underclothing	Northumberland Fusiliers.
PRITCHARD, R.	Straws	Northumerland Battalion R.F.A.
STUDDY, J.	Furs	Naval Brigade.
SMITH, R.	Packing-room	Northumberland Fusiliers.
TURNER, S.	Smallwares	Army Service Corps.
TEMPERLEY, E. F.	—	Royal Army Medical Corps.
WARD, C.	Lift Attendant	Northumberland Fusiliers.

Sheffield Branch.
ALLEN, C.	Office	Lancashire and Yorkshire Regt.
FORD, M.	Corsets	Sheffield Batt. Kitchener's Army.
WALKERDINE, L. A.	Packing-room	Royal Field Artillery.

Cardiff Branch.
FORSMAN, G.	Forwarding Department	Royal Field Artillery—Welsh Brigade.
PHELPS, W.	Laces, &c.	Royal Army Medical Corps.
SMITH, R. D.	Silks	7th Welsh Cycle Corps.
WARNER, P. H.	—	7th Welsh Cyclist Battalion.
WESTLAKE, P.	—	7th Welsh Cyclist Battalion.

ROLL OF HONOUR.

Co-operative Wholesale Society Limited

REGISTERED OFFICE:
1, BALLOON STREET, MANCHESTER.

List of Employees who have joined His Majesty's Forces.

ABBOTT, C.	ALLEN, H.	ARMSTRONG, J.
ABBOTT, J.	ALLEN, S. T.	ARMSTRONG, J. W.
ACKERLEY, G.	ALLEN, W.	ARMSTRONG, R.
ACKERLEY, G. (killed).	ALLEN, G. W.	ARMITAGE, H.
ACKERLEY, H.	ALLEN, A.	ARNOLD, F.
ACKERLEY, W.	ALLEN, G.	ARNOLD, F. W.
ACKERMAN, T. F.	ALLEN, H.	ARNOLD, W.
ACKROYD, J.	ALLAN, F.	ARNOTT, J.
ADAMS, A.	ALSTON, D. (killed).	ARSTALL, E.
ADAMS, B.	ALSTON, T.	ARSTALL, H.
ADAMS, E. H.	AMOS, P. A.	ASH, R.
ADAMS, J.	ANDERSON, W.	ASHBY, A. T.
ADAMS, W.	ANDERSON, W.	ASHCROFT, W. L.
ADSHEAD, S.	ANDERSON, R.	ASHER, G.
AGGIO, A.	ANDREWS, F. E.	ASHER, H.
AINLEY, S. W.	ANDREWS, W. T.	ASHFIELD, C. H.
AINSLEY, R. R.	ANDREWS, T.	ASHLEY, T. G. E.
AINSLIE, J.	ANKERS, S. B.	ASHLIN, W. R.
AINSWORTH, R.	APPLEBEE, G.	ASHMAN, J.
AISBITT, M.	APPLETON, J.	ASHTON, W.
AITKEN, A.	APPLEYARD, T.	ASHWORTH, A.
AKISTER, R.	ARCHER, H.	ASHWORTH, N.
ALBORN, H.	ARCHER, R.	ASKEW, T. W.
ALCOCK, E.	ARDERN, W.	ASPIN, R.
ALDERSON, A.	ARLOTT, A. E.	ATHERLEY, W.
ALLEN, J. B.	ARMSTRONG, C.	ATKINSON, G. V.
ALLDRED, C.	ARMSTRONG, E.	ATKINSON, G.
ALLISON, F.	ARMSTRONG, F. L. H.	ATKINSON, H.

Co-operative Wholesale Society Limited
ROLL OF HONOUR—Continued.

ATKINSON, J.
ATKINSON, W.
ATTRIBB, J.
AULK, E.
AUTY, A.
AVERY, R.
AYTO, A.
BAILEY, A.
BAILEY, A.
BAILEY, A. E.
BAILEY, H.
BAILEY, T.
BAILEY, T. H.
BAINBRIDGE, W. J.
BAKER, A. G.
BAKER, C.
BAKER, G.
BAKER, G. H.
BAKER, G. W.
BAKER, J.
BAKER, S.
BAKER, W.
BAKER, W.
BALKWILL, P. W.
BALL, H.
BALL, L. H.
BALMER, D.
BALMFORTH, H. B.
BANDY, G.
BANHAM, H.
BANKS, R.
BANNISTER, H.
BANNISTER, H. R.
BARBER, A.
BARBOUR, B.
BARBER, F.
BARBER, W.
BARDELL, A. C.
BARDSLEY, F.
BARDSLEY, N.
    (missing).
BARDSLEY, V. E.
BARE, A.
    (died of wounds).
BARFORD, H.
BARKER, A.
BARKER, H.
BARKER, J. (missing).
BARNARD, A. C.
BARNES, W.
BARNES, W. G.
BARNFIELD, P.
BARLOW, F.

BARLOW, S.
BARON, J.
BARRAS, H. V.
BARRATT, A. E.
BARRATT, C.
BARRATT, H.
BARRETT, A. F.
BARRETT, E.
BARRETT, E. A.
BARRETT, J. S.
BARRETT, L.
BARRON, A.
BARROW, P.
BARRS, H.
BARTLETT, S. G.
BARTLETT, W. H.
BARTON, F.
BARWELL, H.
BASKETTER, H.
BASKETTER, J.
BASS, A. (missing).
BASS, G. W.
BASS, R.
BASSETT, C.
BATE, F.
BATES, R.
BATES, W.
BATHGATE, W.
BATTERSBY, A. J.
BATTERSBY, J. A.
BATTLE, H.
BAUMBER, J. W.
BAWDEN, L.
BAWN, T. A.
BAYLEY, F.
BEADON, A. G.
BEAN, C.
BEANLAND, F.
BEARD, H.
BEARDSELL, B.
BEATTIE, J.
BEATTIE, S. J.
BECK, W.
BEDDERS, H.
BEE, W.
BEECH, G.
BEESLEY, A. E.
BELGIAN, W. (killed).
BELLINGHAM, R.
BELL, C. N.
BELL, E. (missing).
BELL, H. P.
BELL, J. W.

BELL, P.
BELL, P.
BELL, P.
BELL, R.
BELL, R. (killed).
BELL, W.
BELL, W.
BELLIS, L.
BELTON, C. E.
BENBOW, G. G.
BENFIELD, W.
BENFORD, H.
BENNETT, A.
BENNETT, C.
BENNETT, E. S.
BENNETT, G. H.
BENNETT, G.
BENNETT, H.
BENNETT, H.
BENNETT, H.
BENNETT, J. E.
BENNETT, S. C.
BENNETT, W. E.
BENSON, E. L.
BENTLEY, A.
BENTLEY, E.
BENTLEY, G. A.
BERBY, H.
BERESFORD, W.
BERRY, G. J.
BERSON, W. G.
BESSELL, W. H.
BESFORD, H.
BEST, A. W.
BESWICK, H.
BETHELL, A. W.
BETLEY, E.
BETTLEY, E.
BETTS, W.
BEVERIDGE, J.
BILLING, S. T.
BILLINGTON, H.
BILLS, A.
BINDLEY, H.
BINNS, F.
BINNS, H.
BINSTEAD, A. J.
BIRCH, W.
BIRCHALL, A.
BIRKETT, C. A.
BIRTWHISTLE, H.
BIRTWISTLE, W.
BISHOP, P. W.

BLACK, W.
BLACKEY, R.
BLACKLOCK, E.
BLACKMAN, H.
BLAINEY, E.
BLAKEMAN, C. J.
BLANCH, H.
BLAND, J.
BLAKEY, J. F.
BLENKIRON, J. J.
BLOCKLEY, P. J.
BLOGG, E.
BLORE, J. (killed).
BLORE, T.
BLUES, W.
BOARDMAN, E.
BOARDMAN, H.
BOARDMAN, J.
BOCKING, J. H.
BOLAM, G.
BOND, G. F.
BONNEY, C.
BONNEY, W.
BOOBYER, C.
BOON, C. C.
BOON, F. G.
BOOTHMAN, W.
BORE, W.
BORKIN, F.
BORLAND, D.
BORLAND, W.
BORROWS, W.
BOTT, F.
BOTTINSON, H. L.
BOTTOMLEY, J.
BOULD, L.
BOULTON, F. T.
BOUTLAND, J. G.
BOWE, T.
BOWEN, R.
BOWIE, W.
BOWKER, A.
BOWKER, R.
BOWLER, C.
BOYES, W.
BOYLE, J.
BOYLE, J. P.
BOYLE, T.
BOYSON, T.
BRABIN, C.
BRACK, G.
BRACEGIRDLE, A.
BRADFORD, F.

Co-operative Wholesale Society Limited
ROLL OF HONOUR—Continued.

BRADBURN, J. H.
BRADBURY, J.
BRADLEY, B.
BRADLEY, G. F.
BRADLEY, T.
BRADLEY, W.
BRADSHAW, A. S.
BRADSHAW, W.
BRAHAM, W.
BRAINES, C. F.
    (missing).
BRAMALL, J. T.
BRAMLEY, W. (killed).
BRANDON, W.
BRANNAN, F. G.
BRANSON, W.
BRAY, J. H.
BRAY, S.
BREEZE, G.
BRENDLEY, C.
BRENNAN, P.
BRENNEN, H.
BRERETON, R. F.
BRETT, G. E.
BREWIN, W.
BRICKELL, E.
BRICKILL, H.
BRIDDOCK, T.
    (died of wounds).
BRIDGEWATER, W.
BRIDLE, H. J.
BRIERLEY, S.
BRIGGS, E.
BRIGGS, G.
BRIGGS, J.
BRIGHT, W.
BRINDLE, V.
BRISCOE, E.
BRITTAIN, L. E.
BROADBENT, I.
BROADHURST, C.
BROADHURST, W.
BROBBINS, E.
BROCKHOUSE, G.
BRODERICK, R.
BRODRICK, B.
BROMLEY, S.
BROOKS, A.
BROOK, C.
BROOKS, E.
BROOKS, H.
BROOKS, W.
BROOKS, H.
BROOKS, H.
BROOKE, H. C.
BROOKS, L.
BROOKS, T.
BROOKSBANK, L.
BROTHERSTON, J.
BROTHERTON, G.
BROUGHTON, A.
BROUGHTON, S.
BROWN, A.
BROWN, A. E.
BROWN, C. H.
BROWN, E.
BROWN, E. S.
BROWN, F.
BROWN, H.
BROWN, H.
BROWN, J.
BROWN, J.
BROWN, J.
BROWN, J.
BROWN, J.
BROWN, J.
BROWN, N.
BROWN, R.
BROWN, R.
BROWN, W.
BROWN, W.
BROWN, W.
BROWN, W.
BROWN, W.
BROWN, W.
BROWN, W.
BROWN, W. J.
BROWNHILL, J. W.
BROXTON, W.
BRUCE, H.
BRUCE, H.
BRUMBY, J.
BRUTON, W. E.
BRYAN, T. W.
BRYANT, E.
BUCHANAN, A.
BUCHANAN, J.
BUCKLER, G. W.
BUCKLEY, A.
BUCKLEY, C.
BUCKLEY, G.
BUCKLEY, P.
BUCKMASTER, W. H.
BULCOCK, L.
BULLEN, G.
BULLOCK, T.
BULMER, J. W.
BUNDY, J.
BUNNEY, J.
BUNNEY, W. H.
BUNNING, C. H.
    (missing).
BURDEN, T.
BURDETT, A.
BURDETT, F.
BURDETT, J. T.
BURDITT, H.
BURGE, H.
BURGESS, E. W.
BURKE, J.
BURKE, M.
BURKETT, J.
BURN, J.
BURN, J. W.
BURNS, G. F.
BURNS, J.
BURNS, J. J.
BURNS, N.
BURROWS, A.
BURROWS, D.
BURROWS, H.
BURROWS, H.
BURT, J.
BURTON, A.
BURTON, F. B.
BURTON, H.
BURTON, T.
BUSH, H. V.
BUSHELL, C.
BUTCHER, R.
BUTLAND, M.
BUTLIN, E. R.
BUTLER, A.
BUTLER, H.
BUTTERFIELD, C. H.
BUTTERWORTH, A.
BUTTERWORTH, J.
BUTTERWORTH, J.
BYRNE, W.
CABLE, A. J.
CAFFERY, T.
CAGE, J. W.
CAIRNS, A.
CALLENDER, J.
CALVEZ, J.
CAMERON, R. M.
CANHAM, H.
CANN, W.
CANNE, H.
CANNING, D.
CANNON, J. E.
CAPPER, E.
CARR, F.
CARR, H.
CARR, T. H.
CARRICK, R.
CARRICK, R.
CARROLL, A.
CARROLL, H.
CARROLL, M.
CARRUTH, W.
CARTER, C. E.
CARTER, H.
CARTER, H.
CARTER, J.
CARTER, J.
CARTLEDGE, F.
    (missing).
CARTWRIGHT, H.
CARTWRIGHT, J.
CASEY, E.
CASSIDY, W.
CASSON, W. E.
CASSON, T.
CASWELL, S.
CATHART, S.
CATON, T.
CATTELL, A.
CATTERMALE, W. J.
CATTERALL, R.
CAVE, J.
CAVEN, W.
CAWSEY, W.
CHADWICK, A.
CHADWICK, C. E.
CHADWICK, J.
CHADWICK, W.
CHAPMAN, C. F.
CHARLTON, M.
CHAMBERLAIN, H.
CHAMBERLAIN, R.
CHAMBERS, F.
CHAMBERS, L.
CHAMBERS, P.
    (Drowned
      H.M.S. "Hogue.")
CHAMBERS, R.
CHAMBERS, R.
CHARMAN, W.
CHARNLEY, F.
CHANEY, M.
CHAWNER, J.

Co-operative Wholesale Society Limited
ROLL OF HONOUR—Continued.

CHILD, L.
CHITTY, J.
CHERRY, A.
CHEETHAM, H.
CHEETHAM, T. L.
CHRISTIAN, J.
CHURCH, G.
CHURCHARD, R. G.
CLARE, W.
CLARK, H.
CLARK, R.
CLARKE, A. (missing).
CLARKE, C.
CLARKE, E.
CLARKE, E. R.
CLARKE, E. W.
CLARKE, F.
CLARKE, F.
CLARKE, P.
CLARKE, R.
CLARKE, S.
CLARKE, S. G.
CLARKE, T.
CLARKE, W.
CLARKE, W.
CLARKE, W. A.
CLARKSON, R.
CLAY, D.
CLAYTON, E.
CLAYTON, W.
CLAYTON, W. T.
CLEGG, A.
CLEGG, P.
CLELAND, A.
CLEMENT, —.
CLIFTON, H.
CLINCH, S. J.
CLINTON, P.
CLOUGH, H.
CLOUGH, T.
CLOWES, J.
CLOWES, W.
CLUTTEN, J. T.
COADY, J.
COATES, L.
COATES, W.
COATSWORTH, W.
COBLEY, A.
COBURN, W.
COCKER, E.
CODLING, M.
COE, T.
COGHLAN, J.

COGLAN, J.
COKER, F. H.
COLCLOUGH, H.
COLCLOUGH, W.
COLE, J. E.
COLEMAN, C.
COLEMAN, E. J.
COLEMAN, H. B.
COLEMAN, J. J.
COLEMAN, J. W.
COLES, A. C.
COLINESE, L. P.
COLLIDGE, G.
COLLINS, H.
COLLINS, H. N.
COLLINS, J. G.
COLLINS, P.
COLLINS, W.
COLLINS, W.
COLLINSON, J. G.
COLTMAN, F. L.
COLTON, E.
CONBOYS, C.
CONNELL, J.
CONNELLY, J.
CONNOR, H.
CONWAY, T.
CONVILLE, J.
COOK, C.
    (died of wounds).
COOK, F. G.
COOK, W.
COOKE, C.
COOKE, F. W.
COOKE, G. W.
COOKE, W. B.
COOKSON, F.
COOPER, G.
COOPER, G.
COOPER, H. D.
COOPER, R.
COOPER, T.
COPPING, A.
COPSON, H.
COPSON, W.
CORDWELL, J.
CORFIELD, H.
CORNWELL, W.
COSTELLO, A.
COTTIER, J.
COUGHLAN, W.
COULBURN, G.
COULBOURN, M.

COULSON, A.
COULSON, J. W.
COUPE, A. F.
COWAN, W. H.
COWBORN, J.
COWELL, A. S.
COWELL, E.
COX, J.
COXON, W.
COXALL, E.
COYLE, JOHN (killed).
COYLE, J.
CRABB, D.
CRABBE, F. M.
CRABTREE, B.
CRABTREE, J. D.
CRABTREE, H. J.
CRABTREE, T.
CRADDOCK, C.
CRAIG, E.
CRAIG, J.
CRAIG, R.
CRAKE, F. W.
CRASHLEY, R.
CRATES, A.
CRAWSHAW, J. H.
CRAVEN, J. T.
CREE, A.
CREED, E.
CRICHTON, W. J.
CRIPWELL, W. H.
CROFT, W.
CROLLEY, J.
CROMER, H.
CROMWELL, E.
CROOKHALL, C. W. H.
CROOKHAM, W.
CROSS, G.
CROSS, J. F.
CROSSLEY, N.
CROSSLEY, W.
CROWTHER, H. M.
CRYER, H.
CUDDIHY, M.
CULLEN, H. J.
CULLIP, C.
CUNDALL, P.
CUNLIFFE, T.
CUNNINGHAM, M.
CUNNINGHAM, W.
CUQUEMELLE, G.
CURRY, J.
CURRY, R.

CURSON, R.
CURTIS, F. J.
CURTIS, G. A.
CURTON, H. G.
CUTHBERT, O.
CUTHBERT, W. J.
CUTHBERTSON, H.
CUTTERHAM, D.
    (killed).
DAKIN, R.
DALBY, W. E.
DALE, F. W.
DALE, H. E.
DALE, H. E.
DALE, M. (missing).
DALE, R.
DALE, R.
DALE, W. R.
DALEY, P.
DALGLIESH, J. P.
DANN, W.
DANIELS, E.
DANIELS, N.
DANIELS, W. H.
DARNTON, A.
DAVERAGE, W.
DAVEY, A.
DAVIDSON, C.
DAVIDSON, S. L.
DAVIES, A. D.
DAVIES, C. H.
DAVIES, C. I.
DAVIES, E.
DAVIES, H.
    (died of wounds).
DAVIES, J.
DAVIES, J. S.
DAVIES, J. W.
DAVIES, N.
DAVIES, R.
DAVIES, S.
DAVIES, T.
DAVIES, W.
DAVIES, W.
DAVIES, W. S.
DAVIS, J.
DAVIS, E. W.
DAVIS, P. T.
DAVIS, W. A.
DAVISON, A.
DAVISON, E.
DAVISON, G.
DAVISON, R.

Co-operative Wholesale Society Limited
ROLL OF HONOUR—Continued.

DAVISON, R.
DAVISON, R. W.
DAWES, A.
DAWES, W. A.
DAWSON, J.
DAWSON, J. S. G.
DAWKINS, C.
DAWSON, W.
DAY, A.
DAY, A. J.
DAY, G.
DAY, M.
DEADFIELD, J.
DEAN, H.
DEAN, J.
DEANE, A. B.
DEANE, A. T.
DEARDEN, G.
DEARNLEY, F.
DEARNLEY, H.
DENNETT, W.
DENNIS, J.
DENT, H.
DENTON, B.
DERRY, W.
DEVINE, J.
DEVONPORT, C.
DIAPER, F. J.
DICKENS, G.
DICKENS, J.
DICKENSON, J.
DICKENSON, T.
DICKER, G.
DICKINSON, T.
DICKSON, F.
DICKSON, G.
DICKSON, W.
DIGNAN, J. P.
DILLEY, F. (killed).
DISNEY, A.
DIX, G.
DIXON, G.
DIXON, H. S.
DIXON, H.
DIXON, J.
DOBBS, G. H.
DOCKERTY, W.
DODD, F.
DODDS, A.
DODDS, R.
DODDS, T.
DOHERTY, J. H.
DOLAN, T.

DONKIN, J.
DONLEY, H.
DONLON, J.
DONNELLY, A.
DONNELLY, J.
DONNISON, T.
DONOVAN, R.
DOOLEY, J.
DOODSON, E.
DORAN, T.
DORSETT, C.
DOSSETT, W. J.
DOUGHTY, A.
DOUGHTY, F.
DOUGLAS, W.
DOUGLASS, T.
DOWELL, F.
DOWNS, R.
DOWNS, H.
DOWNING, B.
DOWSON, T. W.
DOXEY, W.
DRAPER, B.
DRINKWATER, A. E.
DRIVER, S.
DRUMMOND, W.
DUCKITT, H.
DUFFY, J.
DUFFY, L.
DUKE, T. E.
DUNCAN, C. A.
DUNDAS, H.
DUNGAY, H. W.
DUNKIN, C. W.
DUNN, H. S.
DUNN, S.
DUNN, T.
DUNN, W.
DUNNE, R.
DUNNING, W. J.
DURHAM, J.
DURWARD, R.
DYCHE, R. A.
DYSON, F.
EADE, G. T.
EASON, W.
EAST, F. D.
ECKERSLEY, F.
EDDY, F.
EDEN, N.
EDMISTON, A.
EDMUNDS, A.
EDMUNDS, J. K.

EDMONDSON, B. G.
EDWARDS, C.
EDWARDS, F.
EDWARDS, G.
EDWARDS, H.
EDWARDS, H. G.
EDWARDS, J. E.
EDWARDS, T.
EDWARDS, W.
EGERTON, J.
EGAN, F.
EGLISH, W.
ELD, F.
ELLIOTT, A.
ELLIOTT, C. H.
ELLIOTT, G.
ELLIOTT, L.
ELLIOTT, W.
ELLIOTT, W. T.
ELLIS, A. H.
ELLIS, D. J.
ELLIS, G.
ELLIS, J.
ELLIS, J.
ELLIS, J. A.
ELLISON, G.
ELLISON, T.
ELLMORE, F.
ELSON, G. E.
EMERSON, C. N.
EMERY, H. W.
EMMOTT, F.
ENDERSBY, H. H.
ENGLISH, W. J.
ERRINGTON, H.
ESSEN, E. R.
EUSTACE, F.
EVESON, P.
EVANS, C.
EVANS, F.
EVANS, W. C.
EVANS, W. G.
EWART, L.
EXTON, H. C.
FAGAN, T.
FAGG, J. W.
FAIRBANK, F.
FALCUS, J.
FALCUS, R.
FALLAS, C.
FARCY, —.
FARISH, S.
FARLEY, J.

FARMER, H.
FARR, E.
FARRAR, W.
FARRELL, J. L.
FARROW, A.
FAULKNER, E.
FAULKNER, M.
FAULKNER, P.
FAWCETT, J. A.
FAWLEY, P.
FEATHER, H.
FEATHERSTONE, F.
FELL, J.
   (died of wounds).
FELLOWS, S.
FENDER, G. H.
FENDER, T.
FENTON, F.
FERGUSON, A.
FERGUSON, D. K.
FERGUSON, F.
FERNIE, J.
FIBBINS, J.
FIDDIS, J. S.
FIELD, G. G.
FIELDING, H. S.
FIFE, J.
FILDES, G. E. A.
FINDLAY, W.
FINDLEY, H. G.
FINCH, A.
FINN, J.
FIRTH, H.
FISHER, J.
FISHWICK, W.
FITTON, H.
FITTON, J.
FITTON, J. H.
FITTON, N.
FITTON, W. J.
FITZGERALD, H. P.
FITZPATRICK, J.
FLAVIN, T.
FLEMING, W. L.
FLETCHER, A.
FLETCHER, A.
FLETCHER, J.
FLETCHER, T. A.
FLINT, B.
FLOYD, G. F.
FOOT, J. A.
FORD, A. G.
FORD, G.

Co-operative Wholesale Society Limited
ROLL OF HONOUR—Continued.

FORD, J.
FORD, R.
FORD, W.
FORD, W. H. (killed).
FORREST, I.
FORREST, W.
FORSHAW, W. H. E.
FORSTER, A.
FORSTER, D.
FORSTER, J.
FORSTER, J.
FORSTER, J. D.
FORSTER, S. R.
FORSTER, W.
FOSTER, F.
FOSTER, P.
FOSTER, W.
FOURGEAND, F.
FOULKES, J.
FOULKES, J. R.
FOULKES, T. E.
FOX, A.
FOX, E.
FRANCIS, G.
FRANCIS, J. W.
FRANKLAND, J. E.
FRANKLIN, J. H.
FRANKLIN, T.
FREER, C.
FREER, O.
FREEMAN, A. H.
FREEMAN, E.
FREEMAN, G.
FRENCH, F.
FRETTINGHAM, A. C.
FREWIN, H.
FRIEND, A. O.
FRIMSTON, E.
FRIMSTON, H.
FRIMSTON, W.
FRITH, S.
FRYER, V.
FLYNN, J.
FUDGE, S.
FULLER, H.
FULLER, J.
FULTHORPE, R.
FURLONG, J. A.
GABRIEL, R.
GALE, W.
GALES, H.
GALLOWAY, J. C.
GAMBLIN, W. R.

GARAWAY, A.
GARAWAY, F.
GARDNER, J. J.
GARDNER, J. W. E.
GARDNER, W.
GARNER, F. V.
GARNER, G.
GARNER, H.
GARNER, J. H.
GARNER, W. A.
GARNETT, J.
GARRETT, F. J.
GARROD, L.
GARSIDE, E.
GARTSIDE, J. H.
GARVEY, H.
GARVEY, W.
GASCOIGNE, W.
GASKELL, J.
GASKELL, J. W.
GASTALL, H.
GATWARD, S.
GATENBY, H.
GATENBY, W.
GEARY, F.
GEARY, H. (missing).
GEARY, S. S.
GEATER, A. G.
GEE, E.
GEORGE, E.
GEORGE, F.
GEORGE, H.
GEORGE, J. L.
GENTLES, R.
GERDES, N. Y.
GERMAN, A.
GERRARD, P.
GETLIFFE, J. F.
GIBBS, W. J.
GIBBONS, H.
GIBBONS, W.
GIBSON, A. E.
GIBSON, E.
GIBSON, F.
GIBSON, H.
GIBSON, W.
GIFFORD, W.
GILBERT, H.
GILL, H.
GILL, N. (killed).
GILLAM, F.
GILLARD, A.
GILLARD, H.

GILLESPIE, E.
GILLETT, F.
GILLINDER, A. E.
GILLIVER, J.
GILMOUR, A.
GILROY, G. C.
GLADMAN, L.
GLYNN, J.
GOCKE, F. W.
GODDARD, C. E.
GODFREY, E. W.
GODFREY, V.
GOLDNEY, C.
GOLDSACK, C.
GOODALL, H. E.
GOODALL, L. Y.
GOODE, F.
GOODE, L.
GOODRUM, W.
GOODWIN, M.
GOODWIN, T.
GORING, J.
GORTON, A. E.
GORTON, A.
GORTON, W.
GOSNEY, W. E.
GOTHARD, J.
GOWER, W.
GRABHAM, H.
GRABHAM, H.
GRADY, M.
GRAHAM, R.
GRANT, A.
GRANT, C.
GRANT, G.
GRANT, R.
GRAY, A.
GRAY, I.
GRAY, J. H.
GRAY, W.
GRAY, W. G.
GREATOREX, A. L.
GREAVES, T.
GREEN, C.
GREEN, H.
GREEN, H.
GREEN, H. E.
GREEN, J.
GREEN, P.
GREEN, T. H.
GREENFIELD, H.
GREENHOUGH, W.
GREENHALGH, J. R.

GREENHALGH, T.
GREENING, J.
GREENHOW, I.
GREENHOUSE, A.
GREENWOOD, C.
GREENWOOD, J.
GREENWOOD, J.
GREGORY, G.
GREGORY, G. C.
GRICE, J.
GRIERSON, J. S.
GRIERSON, S.
GRIERSON, W. H.
GRIEVE, T.
GRIEVE, W.
GRIFFEE, C. P.
GRIFFEN, H. G.
GRIFFEN, J.
GRINDROD, R.
GRISDALE, H.
GROOM, M.
GROOME, R.
GROOMS, A. E.
GROVES, A.
GRUMMITT, J.
GRUNDY, A. (killed).
GUARD, P. B.
GUDGEON, F.
GUEST, N.
GUNN, G. H.
GURR, E.
GUTHRIE, D.
GUTTRIDGE, H.
HABRARD, H.
HACKER, H.
HACKER, C. S.
HADCOCK, W. L.
HADDOCK, W.
HAIG, F.
HAIGH, C. E.
HAIGH, G.
HAIGH, J.
HAIGH, N.
HAIGH, W.
HAINES, A.
HAINES, F.
HAINES, J. T.
HALL, A.
HALL, F.
HALL, G. E.
HALL, G. H.
HALL, H.
HALL, J.

Co-operative Wholesale Society Limited
ROLL OF HONOUR—Continued.

HALL, N.
HALL, P.
HALL, R.
HALL, T.
HALL, T. B.
HALL, W.
HALL, W.
HALL, W.
HALL, W. A.
HALL, W. W.
HALLAM, F.
HALLAM, T. C.
HALLAM, W.
HALLEY, P.
HALLIDAY, C.
HALLIER, W. J.
HALLIWELL, J.
HALLIWELL, S. S.
HALLIWELL, W. H.
HAM, C. W.
HAMBLIN, J.
HAMER, H.
    (prisoner of war).
HAMILTON, G.
HAMLETT, F.
HAMPSON, S.
HANDFORD, G. H.
HANGER, F.
HANLEY, J.
HANNING, W.
HANSON, F.
HANSON, L. E.
HAPPS, A. J.
HARA, R. A.
HARDCASTLE, H.
HARDING, T. R.
HARDING, J.
HARDING, P.
HARDY, E.
HARDY, J.
HARDY, J. A.
HARDS, J. E.
HARGRAVES, S.
HARGREAVES, H.
    (missing).
HARPER, F.
HARPER, J.
    (prisoner of war).
HARRINGTON, P. W.
HARRIS, E.
HARRIS, E. W.
HARRIS, F.
HARRIS, F. V.

HARRIS, R.
HARRISON, A. G.
HARRISON, E.
HARRISON, F.
HARRISON, G.
HARRISON, G. O.
HARRISON, H.
HARRISON, H.
HARRISON, J. H.
HARRISON, J. W.
HARRISON, P. L.
HARRISON, S.
HARRISON, T.
HARRISON, W.
HARRISON, W.
HARROP, G.
HARROP, J. E.
HART, W.
HARTLEY, G.
HARTLEY, H.
HARTLEY, S.
HARTSHORN, F.
HARWOOD, C. W.
HASWELL, A. H.
HATTERSLEY, J.
HATTON, H. C.
HAVEKIN, H.
HAWKINS, B. C.
HAWKINS, G. H.
HAWKES, W.
HAY, C. T. E.
HAY, G. H.
HAYES, E.
HAYES, J. H.
HAYES, T. W.
HAYMAN, W.
HAYNES, J.
HAYWARD, J. T.
HAZLEHURST, O.
HAZELL, A. H.
HAZELBY, L.
HEADLAM, J.
HEAL, H. W.
HEALD, W.
HEATH, E. S.
HEATH, T.
HEATH, W.
HEANAGAN, J. P.
HEANEY, B.
HEBRON, E.
HEIGHTON, T.
HELICON, F.
HELLOWELL, B.

HEMINGWAY, B.
HENDERSON, E.
HENDERSON, G.
HENDLEY, A.
HENDRY, T.
HENDRY, N.
HENDY, J. W.
HENSHALL, W.
HERBERT, C.
HERBERT, F.
HERBERT, P.
HERRERA, F.
HESFORD, W. A.
HESKETH, F.
HESKETH, H.
HESLOP, J. W.
HETHERINGTON, O. M.
HETHERINGTON, W.
HEWINS, A.
HEWITT, S.
HEWSON, E.
HEY, E.
HEYWOOD, A.
HEYWOOD, O.
HEYWORTH, G.
HIBBERT, W.
HICKEY, A.
HICKSON, C.
HIGBEE, C.
HIGGIN, O. C.
HIGGIN, R.
HIGGINBOTTOM, T.
HIGGINS, C.
HIGGINS, C.
HIGGINS, G.
HIGGINS, R.
HIGGINS, M.
HIGGINSON, J.
    (died of wounds).
HIGGINSON, J.
HIGGINSON, J.
HIGGINSON, S.
HIGGOTT, A.
HIGHAM, J. F.
HIGHAM, J. J.
HILL, C.
HILL, F.
HILL, H.
HILL, J.
HILL, W.
HILL, W.
HILLS, A.
HILLS, J.

HILTON, T.
HINGSTON, H.
HINDER, P.
HINDE, J.
HINES, J.
HINES, T.
HINDLEY, T.
HINTON, G.
HIRST, H.
HIRST, J. R.
HIRST, T. (killed).
HISTON, A. W.
HITCHEN, T.
HOBLEY, V. G.
HOCKEY, W.
HODGSON, J.
HODGKINS, R.
HODGSON, J. B.
HODSON, J. E.
HOGG, E.
HOGG, J.
HOLDEN, J.
HOLDEN, J. W.
HOLDSWORTH, H.
HOLE, F. G.
HOLEHOUSE, F.
HOLLAND, C. E.
HOLLAND, F. J.
HOLLIDAY, G. S.
HOLLINGWORTH, E.
HOLLIS, T. E.
HOLLIS, T. E.
HOLMAN, G. T.
HOLMES, H.
HOLMES, H.
HOLMES, H. G.
HOLMES, T. S.
HOLMES, T. U.
HOLMES, W. F.
HOLT, D. A.
HOLT, F.
HOLT, F.
HOLT, G.
HOLT, G.
HOLT, J.
HOLT, R. B.
HOLTBY, W.
HOLYOAK, E.
HOMER, R. H.
HONEYSELL, J.
HOOPER, W. H.
HOPE, H.
HOPE, H.

Co-operative Wholesale Society Limited
ROLL OF HONOUR—Continued.

HOPE, J.
HOPE, W.
HOPEWELL, A.
HOPKINSON, J.
HOPKINSON, R.
HOPPER, F.
HOPPER, H.
HORNBY, T.
HORSEY, R. T.
HORROCKS, F.
HORSFALL, C. J.
HORSFIELD, H.
HORTON, E.
HORTON, H.
HOWARD, D.
HOWARD, L.
HOWARD, W.
HOWARTH, A.
HOWARTH, E.
HOWARTH, F.
HOWARTH, W.
HOWDEN, B.
HOWES, A.
HOWKINS, J.
HOWKINS, J.
HOWLES, W. T.
HOYES, B.
HOYLE, J.
HUBBARD, A.
HUBBARD, B. J.
HUBBARD, C.
HUBBARD, F. E.
HUDSON, F.
HUDSON, G. H.
HUDSON, J. W.
HUGHES, A.
HUGHES, A.
HUGHES, C.
HUGHES, E. W.
HUGHES, F.
HUGHES, F. C.
HUGHES, H.
HUGHES, J.
HUGHES, W. T.
HULL, J.
HULME, C.
HULME, F.
HULME, J.
HULMES, H.
HULMES, J.
HULSE, W.
HUMBER, W.
HUMPHREY, G. A.

HUMPHREYS, W.
HUNN, J. E.
HUNT, A.
HUNT, A. E.
HUNTER, J. J.
HUNTER, T.
HURD, G. V.
HURLBUT, E.
HURLEY, E.
HURST F.
HUTCHINGS, G.
HUTCHINGS, J.
HUTCHINSON, H. J.
HUTCHINSON, I.
HUTCHINSON, T.
HUTCHINSON, W.
HYLAND, C.
HYDE, H. M. (killed).
IKIN, H.
INCH, F.
INGHAM, H.
INGHAM, L.
INKERSOLE, J.
INMAN, A.
IREDALE, H.
IRELAND, E.
IRELAND, W. A.
IRVING, R.
ISON, H.
IVESON, N.
JACKSON, A.
JACKSON, A.
JACKSON, A. W.
JACKSON, C.
JACKSON, G. W.
JACKSON, J. W. T. R.
JACKSON, P. H.
JACKSON, W.
JACOBSON, A. E.
JAMES, F.
JAMES, S.
JAMES, T.
JAMES, T. E.
JAMES, W. J.
JAMES, W. T.
JARVIS, J.
JARY, R. S.
JAY, P. W.
JEAVES, C.
JEAVONS, A.
JEFFERIES, C.
JEFFERS, M.
JEFFERY, O. E.

JEFFS, A. J.
JELLEY, J.
JENKINS, H.
JENKINS, J.
JENSEN, G.
JEPSON, H.
JEPSON, J.
JESSON, T.
JESSOP, F.
JOBE, N. W.
JOHNSON, A.
JOHNSON, C.
JOHNSON, C. M.
JOHNSON, E.
JOHNSON, E.
JOHNSON, E.
JOHNSON, F. E.
JOHNSON, G.
JOHNSON, H.
JOHNSTON, J.
JOHNSON, J. E.
JOHNSON, L.
JOHNSON, L. F.
JOHNSON, R. B.
JOHNSON, S.
JOHNSON, W.
JOHNSON, W.
JONES, A.
JONES, A.
JONES, C. L.
JONES, D.
JONES, D. R.
JONES, E.
JONES, H. A.
JONES, H. B.
JONES, H. M.
JONES, J.
JONES, J.
JONES, J.
JONES, J. (killed).
JONES, J. A.
JONES, J. S.
JONES, J. W.
JONES, L.
JONES, R.
JONES, R.
JONES, V. W.
JONES, W. B.
JONES, W. F.
JONES, W. H.
JORDAN, H.
JOSLIN, F.

JOWETT, J.
JOYCE, J.
JUSTHAM, J. F. R.
KAY, C.
KAY, H.
KAY, J.
KAY, L.
KAY, T. W.
KAY, W. H.
KAYE, T.
KEARNES, T.
KEAST, H.
KEEN, P.
KEEN, T. G.
KEETLEY, H.
KEILLER, R.
KELLIE, W.
KEELEY, M.
KELLY, C.
KELLY, D.
KELLY, G.
KELLY, W.
KELLY, W. E.
KEMP, A.
KELLETT, S.
KEMP, A.
KEMPSTER, J.
KENDALL, W. H.
KENNEDY, W.
KENNEY, E.
KENT, F.
KENT, F.
KENWORTHY, J. S.
KENWORTHY, R.
KERSHAW, F.
KERSHAW, J.
KERSHAW, J. H.
KERSHAW, J. H.
KETTLE, H. V.
KEYS, H.
KILBURN, E.
KILBOURNE, C. R.
KILMINSTER, A.
KIMPTON, J.
KINCH, A.
KING, A.
KING, H.
KING, J.
KING, J.
KING, T. C.
KING, W.
KING, H.
KINGHAM, W.

Co-operative Wholesale Society Limited
ROLL OF HONOUR—Continued.

KINGSTON, C.
KIRIVAN, L.
KIRKHAM, J. W.
KIRKLEY, C. A.
KIRKLEY, E.
KIRKMAN, A.
KIRKPATRICK, F.
KITCHINGMAN, G.
KNEESHAW, H.
KNIGHT, A.
KNIGHT, A. L.
KNIGHT, E.
KNIGHT, F.
KNIGHT, R.
KNIGHT, W.
KNOX, R.
KUBLER, A.
KYNASTON, A.
LABRON, P.
LACK, R.
LAIDLER, J.
LAFFERTY, J.
LAMBERT, A.
LAMBERT, F. J.
LANCUM, F. H.
LANCASHIRE, A. E.
LANCASTER, W.
LANGFORD, G.
LANGRIDGE, G.
LANGSTAFF, J. W.
LANGTON, A.
LANNING, E. C.
LAPTHORNE, T. H.
LARGE, P.
LARRADD, H. S.
LATHAM, J.
LATHAM, L.
LATTIMER, H.
LAVINGTON, E. R.
LAW, C.
LAWRENCE, W.
LAWRENCE, E.
LAWRENCE, E.
LAWSON, W.
LAWTON, R. A.
LEA, W.
LEABACH, F.
LEACH, F. (missing).
LEACH, J.
LEACH, M.
LEAH, A. E.
LEAH, H. S.
LEAH, W. R.

LEARY, D.
LEE, A.
LEE, H. O.
LEE, E. S.
LEECH, J.
LEECH, E.
LEECH, J. A.
LEES, T.
LEES, W.
LEES, M.
LEES, S.
LEEMING, T.
LEESON, J.
LEIGHTON, E.
LENNON, J. J.
LEONARD, F.
LESTER, W.
LETHORE, —.
LEVITT, C. E.
LEWIS, T.
LEWIS, W.
LEWIS, W.
LEWIS, E.
LEWITT, W.
LICHFIELD, W.
    (killed).
LIDGETT, C. G.
LIDGETT, C. G.
LIDINGTON, T.
LILFORD, H. E.
LINDLEY, G. R.
LINDLEY, H.
LINLEY, F.
LINNETT, R. L.
LINTOTT, A. L.
LISLE, J.
LISTER, J.
LITTLE, J.
LITTLE, W. E.
LITTLEWOOD, H. H.
LITTON, H.
LIVESEY, R. C.
LLEWELLYN, F.
    (killed).
LLEWELLYN, L.
LOBB, W.
LOCK, J.
LOCK, P. H.
LOCKER, F.
LOCKER, J.
LOCKETT, S.
LOCKEY, T.
LOCKTON, A.

LOCKWOOD, R.
LODGE, F.
LODGE, P.
LOFTUS, W.
LOMAS, A. T.
LOMAX, J. S.
LONDON, W.
LONG, F.
LONG, H.
    (died of wounds).
LONG, H. E.
LONGBOTTOM, H.
LONGDEN, E.
LONGHURST, A.
LONGLEY, L.
LONGWORTH, A.
LOOSELEY, S. H.
LORD, A. A.
LORD, E.
LORD, F.
LORD, G.
LORD, J.
LORD, T. H.
LORD, W.
LOUNT, J.
LOUNT, W.
LOVATT, G.
LOVE, A. H.
LOVE, B. (killed).
LOVELACE, J. (killed).
LOWE, W.
LOWE, T. W.
LOWES, A.
LOWRY, W. E.
LOYNES, W.
LOYND, J.
LUCK, F. (killed).
LUCKMAN, W. S.
LUKER, W.
LUMB, E. V.
LUMB, H.
LUMB, W. E.
LUMLEY, G. H.
LUMSDEN, G.
LUND, S.
LUND, T.
LUNDY, R.
LUNN, A.
LUNN, L.
LUNN, S.
LYALL, W.
LYNAN, L.
LYNASS, E. J.

LYONS, J.
LYONS, J.
MACFARLANE, T.
MACHIN, W. H.
MACKAY, J. A. C.
MACPHERSON, R.
MADDISON, W.
MADDISON, R.
MADDIX, J.
MAGUIRE, P.
MAHON, J.
MAHONE, D.
MAHONEY, G.
MAHONY, D. O.
MALABAR, D.
MALEY, M.
MALLINSON, A. E.
MALONEY, E.
MALTBY, T. W.
MANDALE, J. J.
MANN, W.
MANNERS, P.
MANNING, W. E.
MANSFIELD, A.
MAPSTONE, W. E.
MARDLE, H.
    (died of wounds).
MARGERISON, R.
MARKS, A.
MARKS, A.
MARLAND, H.
MARLOW, H.
MARLOW, H.
MARONEY, C. (killed).
MARR, C.
MARRION, L.
MARRION, W. M.
MARSDEN, L.
MARSH, S.
MARSH, T. H.
MARSHALL, A.
MARSHALL, A.
MARSHALL, C.
MARSHALL, F.
MARSHALL, T. V.
MARSTON, T. L.
MARTIN, A.
MARTIN, E.
MARTIN, J.
MARTIN, J.
MARTIN, P. L.
MARTIN, T. R.
MASON, F. R.

Co-operative Wholesale Society Limited
ROLL OF HONOUR—Continued.

MASON, O.
MASON, R. O.
MASON, T.
MASSON, A.
MASTERS, J.
MATHER, O. C.
MATHER, T.
MATHER, W.
MATHER, W.
MATHEWS, H. L.
MATHIESON, H.
MATHURIN, E.
MATTHEWS, G. T.
MATTHEWS, H.
MATTHEWS, W. J. B.
MATTOCKS, T.
MAUDE, J. W.
MAUNDERS, R. M.
MAYER, C. H.
MAYER, W.
MAYNARD, S.
MAYNE, G.
MacDONALD, R. R.
McAULEY, J.
McCALL, F. W.
McCANN, W.
McCARTHY, J.
McCARTHY, P.
McCARTHY, R.
McCLEVERTY, A.
McCLUSKEY, F.
McCORMACK, M.
   (killed).
McGLYNN, J.
McGLYNN, J.
McGLYNN, P.
McGOWAN, E.
McGUIRE, J.
McGUIRE, J. J.
McHAY, E.
McHALE, F.
McHALE, W.
McHENRY, J.
McHENRY, D.
McINERNEY, P. J.
McKAY, C.
McKENZIE, W.
McLAUCHLAN, P. S.
McLENNON, A.
McLOUGHLIN, F.
McMANUS, H.
McMULLEN, H.
McNALLY, M.

McRAE, C.
McROBERTS, G.
McWHIRTER, F.
McWILLIAMS, J. J.
MEAD, J. W.
MEAD, W. A.
MEADOWS, G. A.
MELLARD, G. A.
MELLOR, C.
MELLOR, E.
MELLOR, J.
MELVILLE, M. J.
MERRILL, A. W.
MERRYWEATHER,
   G. A.
MESSENGER, J. D.
MIDDLETON, A.
MIDDLETON, T. O.
MIDGLEY, J.
MIDGLEY, J. T.
MILBURN, J.
MILDENHALL, H.
MILES, W. J.
MILLER, A. D.
MILLETT, H.
MILLS, H.
MILLS, J. B.
MILN, R. B.
MILLIGAN, A. J.
MILLHOUSE, C.
MILLS, H.
MILLS, J.
MINARD, J.
MIRFIELD, E.
MITCHELL, H.
MITCHELL, J.
MITCHELL, J.
MITCHELL, J. F.
MITCHELL, L.
MIZON, C. P.
MOFFATT, F.
MOGG, C. T.
MONOGHAN, F.
MONOGHAN, T.
MONTGOMERY, J.
MOON, R. A.
MOONEY, J.
MOONEY, J. H.
MOORE, A. E.
MOORE, C.
MOORE, C. J.
MOORE, E.
MOORE, G.

MOORE, G.
MOORES, J.
MOORHOUSE, W. G.
MORGAN, A. J.
MORGAN, H.
MORGAN, G. H.
MORGAN, J. E.
MORRELL, A.
MORRELL, A. B.
MORRELL, H.
MORRIS, J.
MORRIS, J. A.
MORRIS, W.
MORRIS, W.
MORRISON, J.
MORRISY, J.
MORROW, G.
MORT, R.
MORTON, W.
MOSS, C. H.
MOSS, J.
MOSS, S.
MOTTERSHEAD, H.
MOUL, F. J. (missing).
MOULE, A.
MOULT, H.
MOUNSEY, G.
MOWBRAY, H.
MOWER, J.
MOYES, S. R.
MOYLAN, W.
MUDDIMET, J.
MULLOCK, H.
MULDOON, M. (killed).
MULLINS, —.
MUMBY, S. A.
MUNDEN, H. R.
MURPHY, J.
MURPHY, J.
MURPHY, J.
MURPHY, J. H.
   (killed).
MURR, C. R.
MURR, W.
MURRAY, J. A.
MURRAY, J.
MURTON, J.
MUSSON, E.
MYLCHREEST, J.
NAISH, H.
NARRAWAY, A.
NAPPIN, A.
NASH, M.

NAYLOR, R.
NAYLOR, R.
NEAL, B.
NEAL, P.
NEALE, W.
NEDEN, W.
NEEDHAM, S. E.
NEEP, S.
NELSON, C.
NELSON, G. W.
NELSON, T. (missing).
NENDICK, F.
NESBITT, A.
NEVILLE, J.
NEVILLE, M.
NEVILLE, T. W.
NEW, H.
NEWBOULD, T. H.
NEWGUIST, H. H.
NEWITT, T.
NEWMAN, F. W.
NEWMAN, G.
NEWMAN, W.
NEWNES, T. J.
NEWSOME, H.
NEWTON, A.
NEWTON, B.
NEWTON, G. W.
NEWTON, J. T.
NEWTON, S. G.
NEWTON, W.
NICHOL, T.
NICHOL, T. J.
NICHOLSON, G.
NICHOLSON, H.
NICHOLSON, T. W.
NIELD, F.
NIXON, H.
NOBLE, A.
NOBLES, W. H.
NOLAN, J.
NOLAN, N.
NORMINGTON, E.
NORRIS, W. H.
NORTON, W. A.
NUTTALL, H. L.
NUTTER, J.
OAKES, J.
OAKLEY, B.
OATES, A.
O'BRIEN, C.
O'BRIEN, D. (Killed).
O'BRIEN, W. E.

Co-operative Wholesale Society Limited
ROLL OF HONOUR—Continued.

O'CONNOR, A. E.	PARK, C.	PERCIVAL, W. J.	PRICE, J. T.
O'DONNELL, R.	PARK, J.	PERKINS, C.	PRICE, J. W.
ODLING, J. N.	PARKER, A. R.	PERKINS, H. A.	PRICE, O. S. D.
O'GARR, T.	PARKER, F.	PERKINS, W.	PRICE, P. (killed).
OGDEN, A.	PARKER, F.	PERRY, A. S.	PRINCE, K.
OGDEN, F.	PARKER, H.	PERRY, E.	PRINGLE, E.
OGDEN, G.	PARKER, H. V.	PERRY, E. H.	PRIME, G. W. J.
OGDEN, J. D.	PARKER, P. G.	PETERS, H.	PROCTOR, C. F.
OGDEN, J. E.	PARKER, R.	PHILIPSON, G.	PROCTOR, T. A.
OGDEN, S. B.	PARKER, R.	PHILLIPS, A.	PROFFITT, T.
OGDEN, T. G.	PARKER, W.	PHOENIX, W.	PROSSER, G. E.
OGDEN, T. H.	PARKES, C.	PICKARD, H.	PROSSER, J. W.
OLIVER, R.	PARKES, H.	PICKERING, E.	PROUDFOOT, A.
O'LEARY, D.	PARKES, I.	PICKERING, H.	PUGH, E.
O'LEARY, D.	PARKEY, G.	PICKERING, H. A.	PUGH, H.
OLDFIELD, W. L.	PARKIN, S.	PICKERING, J. A.	PUGH, H. H.
OLDHAM, H.	PARKINSON, F.	PICKERING, S.	PUGMORE, G. H.
OLDLAND, T. J.	PARKINSON, J.	PICKLES, W. H.	PULBROOK, F. W.
OLIVER, F.	PARKINSON, J. W.	PICKUP, A.	PURCH, J. T.
OLLERENSHAW, J.	PARR, N.	PICKUP, N.	PYE, W.
(killed).	PARROTT, W.	PIDGEON, J. T.	PYWELL, W. G.
O'MARA, R.	PARSONS, A.	PIERCE, J. W.	QUILLIAMS, R.
O'NEILL, C.	PARSONS, W.	PIERCE, V.	QUINN, P.
O'NEILL, J. L.	PARTRIDGE, E.	PILLING, H.	RAE, R. A.
O'NEILL, P.	PARTINGTON, H.	PINNINGTON, H.	RAILSTON, I.
O'NEILL, T.	PARTINGTON, R.	PIPE, W. J.	RAINES, G. A. E.
ORCHARD, P.	PATTERSON, H.	PIRRIE, J.	RALPHS, H. (missing).
ORMEROD, J.	PATTERSON, W.	PITTY, T. J.	RALPHS, W.
ORPHIN, T. W.	PATTISON, C. G.	PLANT, A.	RAMSAY, A.
OSBORNE, H.	PEACOCK, C. H.	PLANT, W.	RAMSBOTTOM, S.
OSCROFT, C.	PEARCE, O.	PLATTS, W.	RAMSDEN, E.
OTTLEY, L. S.	PEARSON, C. H.	PLESTER, G.	RAMSDEN, J.
OVEN, W.	PEARSON, E.	POLLARD, E. (killed).	RAMSDEN, W.
OVERFIELD, H.	PEARSON, H.	POLLARD, J.	RAMSDEN, W. T.
OWEN, F.	PEARSON, J.	POLLITT, G. S.	RAMSAY, J. E.
OWEN, J.	PEARSON, W.	POLLOCK, R.	RANDLE, A.
OWEN, J.	PEASGOOD, W. D.	POOLMAN, H. M.	RANDLE, F. O.
(Died of wounds).	PEAT, W.	(died of fever.)	RANDLE, G. W.
OWEN, R.	PECK, R. J.	POPPLETON, E.	RANSON, A. E.
OWEN, S.	PEDLEY, J. W.	PORTEOUS, J. M.	RATCLIFFE, E.
OVINGTON, H.	PEDUZZI, J.	PORTEOUS, M. H.	RATCLIFFE, J. A.
OXLEY, R.	PEEL, A.	POTTER, G.	RAWCLIFFE, W. D.
PAGE, H.	PEEL, J.	POTTER, H.	RAWLINSON, E.
PAGE, E.	PEMBERTON, H.	POTTS, L.	(died of wounds).
PAINTER, A.	PEMBERTON, W.	POTTS, F.	RAWNSLEY, J. G.
PAINTER, W. A.	PENKETHMAN, A.	POTTS, N.	RAY, T.
PALMER, A.	PENLINGTON, J.	POULTNEY, W. J.	RAY, W. E.
PALMER, A.	PENNINGTON, H.	POWELL, E.	RAYNOR, J.
PALMER, A. W.	PENNOCK, T.	POWLEY, A.	REANEY, F. M.
PALMER, E.	PENRITH, J.	POYNTON, C. W.	READ, W.
PALMER, H.	PERCIVAL, A. J.	PRESTON, R.	REDPATH, J.
PALMER, W.	PERCIVAL, J.	PRICE, A. E.	REDFERN, E.
PANTER, H.	PERCIVAL, P.	PRICE, H. W.	REDFERN, F.

Co-operative Wholesale Society Limited
ROLL OF HONOUR—Continued.

REDMAN, W.
REID, W. J.
REED, E. C.
REED, A. J.
REED, T.
REEVES, F.
REEVES, R.
REGAN, M.
RENNIE, W. T.
RENSONNET, J.
RENTON, H.
REYNOLDS, D.
RHODES, E.
RHODES, S.
RICCALTON, R.
RICE, E.
RICHARDS, J.
RICHARDS, W. V.
RICHARDSON, E.
RICHARDSON, F.
RICHARDSON, J.
RICHARDSON, R.
RICHES, C.
RICKARD, C.
RICKARD, G.
RIDDLE, D.
RIDGE, F. W.
RIGBY, T.
RILEY, T.
RILEY, W.
RIMMER, J. (killed).
RINGTOUL, W.
ROACH, E.
ROBBIE, A. (missing).
ROBERTS, A.
ROBERTS, B.
ROBERTS, C.
ROBERTS, C.
ROBERTS, C.
ROBERTS, D. A.
ROBERTS, F.
ROBERTS, F.
ROBERTS, J.
ROBERTS, J.
ROBERTS, J. F.
ROBERTS, N.
ROBERTS, R.
ROBERTS, R. D.
ROBERTS, S.
ROBERTS, T.
ROBINSON, C.
ROBINSON, G.
ROBINSON, L.

ROBINSON, O.
ROBINSON, T.
ROBINSON, R. C.
ROBINSON, R. C.
    (missing).
ROBINSON, T. R.
ROBINSON, W.
ROBSON, J.
ROBSON, J.
ROBSON, J.
ROBSON, L.
ROBINSON, F.
ROBINSON, S.
ROBINSON, C.
ROBINSON, A.
ROBINSON, E. W.
ROBINSON, H.
ROBINSON, J.
ROBSON, G.
ROCHE, R.
ROCHETTE, H.
RODGETT, J.
RODWELL, W.
ROE, R. C.
ROGERS, A. H.
ROGERS, H.
ROGERS, O.
ROGERS, W. G.
ROGERS, J. C.
ROGERSON, A.
ROGERSON, A.
ROLLS, A. J.
ROSCOE, E.
ROSCOE, F.
ROSE, S. G.
ROSE, L.
ROSS, J.
ROSS, T.
ROSS, W. B.
ROSTRON, J.
ROTHWELL, F.
ROUCHON, —.
ROUTH, G. W.
ROUTLEDGE, R.
ROUTLEY, R.
ROWAN, F.
ROWAN, G. (died).
ROWAN, J.
ROWBOTTOM, A.
ROWE, J.
ROWLAND, E.
ROWLANDS, F.
ROWLANDS, W.

ROWLEY, G.
ROWNTREE, B.
ROWSON, S.
ROYLE, E.
ROYLE, J.
ROYLE, J.
ROYLE, J.
ROYLE, J. A.
ROY, W.
RUDALL, F. L.
RUDDICK, J.
RUDGE, J. M.
RUFFLE, J. W.
RUGGLES, H.
RULE, G.
RULE, R.
RUSHTON, A.
RUSHTON, A.
RUSHTON, J.
RUSSELL, B. W.
RUTHERFORD, F.
RUTLEDGE, R.
RYAN, H.
RYAN, J.
RYAN, T.
RYDER, G. F.
RYDER, W.
RYDING, P.
RYDINGS, W. H.
RYLANCE, T.
RYLANCE, T.
SALISBURY, H.
SALT, F.
SALTER, W.
SANDERS, J. T.
SANDERSON, J.
SANDERSON, W.
SANSOM, W. H.
SANSOME, W.
SAUL, W. W.
SAUNDERS, J.
SAUNDERS, S.
    (missing).
SAVAGE, J. W.
SAWFORD, J.
SAWYER, J. W.
SAXBY, S.
SCARFE, L. (Killed).
SCATTERGOOD, H.
    (missing).
SCHOFIELD, H. R.
SCORER, J. R.
SCOTT, D.

SCOTT, F. W.
SCOTT, J.
SCOTT, L.
SCOTT, W.
SCOTT, W. R. (missing).
SCOTTON, W.
SEAGER, W.
SEAL, R. J.
SEATON, H.
SEATREE, J. A.
SEDDON, A. F.
SEGAL, M. M.
SEIG, S. T.
SELBIE, A. E.
SELWOOD, E.
SEVILLE, R.
SEVERN, C.
SEWELL, E.
SEWELL, W.
SEYMOUR, T.
SEYMOUR, W.
    (died of wounds).
SHORROCKS, A. H.
SHANN, A. P.
SHAW, A.
SHAW, C.
SHAW, G.
SHAW, H.
SHAW, H.
SHAW, R. C.
SHAW, R. W.
SHAW, W.
SHAW, W.
SHARMAN, A.
SHARMAN, J. T.
SHARP, F.
SHARP, J. W.
SHARPE, W.
SHARPE, B.
SHARPLES, F.
SHARPLES, R.
SHARWIN, R. H.
SHEA, G. (Killed).
SHEARD, W.
SHEARER, S.
SHEEN, W. J.
SHELMERDINE, A.
SHELMERDINE, J.
SHELMERDINE, W. B.
SHIELDS, W.
SHELDON, H.
SHEPHERD, A.

Co-operative Wholesale Society Limited
ROLL OF HONOUR—Continued.

SHEPHERD, A. E.	SMITH, F.	STACEY, F.	SUTHERLAND, J.
SHEPHERD, A. W.	SMITH, F.	STAFFORD, P.	SUTTON, A. E.
SHEPHARD, E.	SMITH, G.	STAFFORD, R.	SUTTON, G. (Killed).
SHEPHERD, S.	SMITH, G. E.	STALLARD, A.	SUTTON, G. W.
SHERBURN, A.	SMITH, H.	STALLARD, H.	SUTTON, H.
SHERIDAN, J.	SMITH, H.	STALEY, F.	SWADDLE, E.
SHIPMAN, J. H.	SMITH, H.	STANLEY, F.	SWADDLE, G.
SHOLL, O.	SMITH, H.	STANLEY, J.	SWAINE, H.
SHOREMAN, R.	SMITH, J.	STANLEY, T.	SWEENEY, D. (killed)
SHORROCKS, J.	SMITH, J.	STANCLIFFE, C.	SWEET, F.
SHORTLAND, A. J.	SMITH, J.	STANDRING, A.	SWEETING, J. A.
SIBLEY, A.	SMITH, J.	STANTON, G. C.	SWIFT, G. F.
SIDFORD, S.	SMITH, J. E.	START, W. H.	SWIFT, H.
SILLITOE, J.	SMITH, J. E.	STEELE, J. T.	SWIFT, J.
SILVERSIDE, J.	SMITH, J. G.	STEELE, W.	SWINDELLS, W.
SILVESTER, H.	SMITH, J. J.	STEVENS, J.	SWITZER, J. W.
SIMMONS, N.	SMITH, L.	STEVENS, W.	SYKES, G.
SIMMONS, W. R.	SMITH, M.	STENSON, S.	SYKES, J. H.
SIMPEY, P.	SMITH, P.	STEVENSON, F.	TABOR, W.
SIMPKINS, J.	SMITH, R.	STEVENSON, G.	TACEY, J. W.
SIMPSON, E.	SMITH, S.	STEPHENSON, J. H.	TAGG, E.
SINCLAIR, J. T.	SMITH, S.	STEVENSON, W. R.	TAGGART, G. F.
SINGLETON, A.	SMITH, S.	STEWARDSON, R.	TAIT, F.
SINGLETON, W. R.	SMITH, T.	STEWART, C.	TALLANT, J. W.
SIPPETT, R.	SMITH, W.	STEWART, E.	TANSWELL, R. E.
SKIDMORE, H. L.	SMITH, W.	STEWART, T.	TATE, R. G.
SKIDMORE, L.	SMITH, W.	STILES, B. E.	TATLER, G. A.
SKINNER, W.	SMITH, W. E.	STIRLING, W.	TATTERSALL, A.
SKEET, H.	SMITH, W. H.	STOBBART, R.	TATTERSALL, N.
SLADEN, T.	SMITHIES, H.	STOCKS, L.	TAYLOR, A.
SLANEY, W.	SMITHSON, N.	STODDART, A. E.	TAYLOR, A.
SLATER, L.	SMYTH, W.	STOKOE, B.	TAYLOR, A.
SLEET, A. E.	SNAPE, T.	STONIER, J. E.	TAYLOR, A.
SMALLRIDGE, T.	SNAPE, W.	STOREY, A.	TAYLOR, A. W.
SMALLEY, H.	SNOWDON, F.	STOREY, N.	TAYLOR, D.
SMART, A.	SOLOMAN, A. W.	STOTEN, H.	TAYLOR, E.
SMART, J.	SOMMERS, A.	STOTT, A.	TAYLOR, F.
SMEE, F. E.	SOMMERS, W. C.	STOTT, G. E.	TAYLOR, F.
SMETHURST, J. T.	SOUTH, A.	STOTT, J. W.	TAYLOR, F. W.
(died of wounds).	SOUTHERN, J.	STRANGE, J.	TAYLOR, H.
SMETHURST, S.	SPARK, J.	STRINGER, J. C.	TAYLOR, H.
SMILES, H.	SPARKES, T.	(died from fever).	TAYLOR, H.
SMITH, A.	SPEAKMAN, H.	STROUD, H.	TAYLOR, J.
SMITH, A.	SPEED, E.	STUBBS, O. B.	TAYLOR, J.
SMITH, A. H. A.	SPEED, W.	STURGEON, R. V.	TAYLOR, J.
SMITH, A. J.	SPENCE, T. H.	STURGESS, W.	TAYLOR, J.
SMITH, B.	SPENCER, F.	STURMAN, A.	TAYLOR, J. (Killed).
SMITH, C. G.	SPENCER, H.	STURROCK, R.	TAYLOR, J. B.
SMITH, D.	SPENCER, W. H.	SUGGETT, F.	TAYLOR, J. E.
SMITH, E.	SPIERS, W.	SUGGETT, I.	TAYLOR, J. J.
SMITH, E.	SPOONER, G. W. E.	SULLIVAN, D.	TAYLOR, P.
SMITH, E.	SPRINGTHORPE, E.	SUMNER, J. E.	TAYLOR, P.
SMITH, E. B.	STACEY, F.	SUSSUMS, T. A.	TAYLOR, R.

Co-operative Wholesale Society Limited
ROLL OF HONOUR—Continued.

TAYLOR, S. B.
TAYLOR, T.
TAYLOR, T.
TAYLOR, W.
TAYLOR, T.
TAYLOR, W.
TAYLOR, W.
TAYLOR, W. C.
    (Killed).
TEALE, R.
TEE, L. B.
TESTER, T.
TETHERINGTON, J.
TEVNAN, A.
THACKER, W.
THOMAS, D.
THOMAS, F.
THOMAS, J. H.
THOMAS, R.
THOMAS, W.
THOMAS, W. L.
THOMASON, T.
THOMPSON, A.
THOMPSON, A.
THOMPSON, A.
THOMPSON, A.
THOMPSON, A.
THOMPSON, D.
THOMPSON, E.
THOMPSON, G.
THOMPSON, G.
THOMPSON, J.
THOMPSON, J.
THOMPSON, J. D.
THOMPSON, J. R.
THOMPSON, W.
THOMPSON, W.
THOMPSON, W.
THOMPSON, W. A.
THORNLEY, G. H.
THORPE, C.
THORPE, A. W.
THORPE, J. W.
THORPE, W.
THREADKELL, H.
THRELFALL, L. H.
THRUSSEL, A.
THURGOOD, C. E.
    (missing).
TICKLE, F.
TIDDER, F.
TIFFEN, G. D.
TIFFEN, R. G.

TIMBERLAKE, A. R.
TINDAL, C.
TINDALL, J.
TILDESLEY, J.
TIPPER, G. W.
TIPPING, F.
TOBY, F.
TODD, J.
TOLLEY, B.
TOMLINSON, A.
TOMLINSON, T.
TOMLINSON, W.
TOOLE, A.
TOOTELL, W. D.
TOPPER, H. S.
TORRANCE, R.
TORRANCE, W.
TOSELAND, J.
TOUGH, C.
TOUILLETT, C.
    (Killed).
TOWERS, T.
TOWNSON, H.
TOWNSEND, C.
TOWNSEND, C.
TOWNSEND, H.
TOWLER, H.
TOWNSEND, S.
TRAVIS, F.
TREBLE, C.
TREBLE, W. T.
TREEBY, G.
TUCK, J.
TUCKER, G.
TUCKWELL, R.
TUCKWOOD, C.
TUGWELL, G.
TURNBULL, H.
TURNBILL, J.
TURNBULL, T. J.
TURNER, A. A.
TURNER, A. G.
TURNER, C. L.
TURNER, F.
    (died of wounds).
TURNER, F. J.
TURNER, J.
TURNER, L.
TURNER, S.
TUSTAIN, H.
TWEEDALE, W. L.
TYE, G.
TYNAN, J.

UNDERWOOD, J. B.
UNSWORTH, F.
UNSWORTH, F.
UNSWORTH, J. R.
URWIN, S.
USHER, J. W.
UTTLEY, J.
VALENTINE, W.
VALLINS, W. C.
VASEY, J.
VASEY, M.
VARTY, J. A.
VENN, A. H.
VERNALL, A. H.
VERNON, A.
VERNON, W.
VERNON, W. J.
VICKERS, H.
VICKERSTAFFE, E. B.
VINCE, A. D.
VINYCOMBE, W. L.
WADDINGTON, H. G.
WADDINGTON, S.
WADE, A.
WAGSTAFFE, T.
WAINWRIGHT, B.
WAILES, S.
WAISTELL, E.
WAISTELL, W.
WAITE, J. R.
WAKE, G.
WAKELING, C.
WAKELING, F.
WALE, H.
WALKER, D.
WALKER, D. J.
WALKER, F.
WALKER, H.
WALKER, H.
WALKER, J.
WALKER, N.
WALKER, N.
WALKER, W.
WALL, C.
WALLACE, A.
WALLER, W.
WALLIS, T.
WALLWORK, A.
WALLWORK, G.
WALMSLEY, H.
WALMSLEY, H. A.
WALSH, H.
WALSH, P.

WALSH, W.
WALTERS, L.
WALTON, A.
WALTON, C.
WALTON, F.
WALTON, H.
WALTON, T.
WALTON, T.
WANN, R.
WARBURTON, A.
WARBURTON, A.
WARBURTON, F.
WARBURTON, J.
WARBURTON, R. A.
WARBURTON, W.
WARD, A.
WARD, D. E.
WARD, E.
WARD, F. T.
WARD, V. S. J.
WARD, W. H.
WARD, W. J.
WARING, J. V.
WARMAN, H.
WARNER, W.
WARR, R.
WARREN, W. E.
WARREN, E. H.
WARREN, W. E.
WARRINGTON, E.
WARRINGTON, G. E.
WARSOP, A.
WARWICK, G.
WARWICK, J. H.
WATERS, J.
WATERWORTH, J.
WATKINS, A.
WATKINS, W.
WATSON, A.
WATSON, E.
WATSON, H. A.
WATSON, J.
WATSON, J. G.
WATSON, R.
WATSON, T. W.
WATTS, H.
WATTS, T.
WAUGH, T.
WEAVER, F.
WEBB, C. F.
WEBB, T.
WEBB, E.
WEBB, F.

Co-operative Wholesale Society Limited
ROLL OF HONOUR—Continued.

WEBBER, C.	WHITHAM, W.	WILSON, H.	WOODROW, F.
WEBDALE, P.	WHITTAKER, W.	WILSON, H. E.	WOODLAND, H. J.
WEBSTER, A.	WHITTER, J.	WILSON, H. P.	WOODWORTH, F. K.
WEBSTER, H. W.	WHITTLE, W.	WILSON, J.	WOOLISCROFT, W.
WEDGE, S.	WHITWELL, G.	WILSON, J.	WOOLLER, T.
WEEKLY, H.	WHITWORTH, G. H.	WILSON, L. M.	WOOLLERTON, G.
WELCH, A.	WHITWORTH, J. E.	WILSON, R.	WOOLSTENCROFT, T. W. L.
WELCH, H.	WICKEN, J.	WILSON, R. E.	
WELCH, W. H.	WICKS, G. R. A.	WILSON, S. F.	WOOLLAM, L.
WELSH, A.	WIGGINS, R.	WILSON, T.	WOOZENCROFT, H.
WELSH, A.	WILBERT, G.	WILSON, W.	WOODMAN, W. J.
WELSH, J.	WILCOX, F.	WILSON, W. J.	WORN, W. J. C.
WELSH, S. H.	WILDE, J. E.	WINKLE, A. E.	WORRALL, J.
WELLINGS, W.	WILDING, H.	WINN, J. B.	WORRALL, T.
WELLS, C. H.	WILKINS, H. W. P.	WINROW, H. P.	WORSLEY, G.
WESSON, C.	WILKINSON, A. E.	WINSTANLEY, E.	WOTHERSPOON, E. A.
WESLEY, A.	WILKINSON, H.	WINTERBOTTOM, A.	WOTHERSPOON, W.
WESTLAKE, H. L.	WILKS, J.	WINTERBOTTOM, J.	WRIGHT, D.
WEST, G.	WILLCOCK, R. B.	WITHINGTON, W. H.	WRIGHT, G.
WEST, G. A.	WILLIAMS, E.	WITHERS, E.	WRIGHT, H.
WEST, S.	WILLIAMS, G.	(died of wounds).	WRIGHT, H.
WEST, W.	WILLIAMS, H. (killed).	WOFFENDEN, H.	WRIGHT, J.
WESTON, A. C.	WILLIAMS, J.	WOLLEN, A.	WRIGHT, J. E.
WHALEN, T.	WILLIAMS, J. A.	WOLSTENHOLME, J. P.	WRIGHT, S.
WHELAN, J. A.	WILLIAMS, J. H.	WOMERSLEY, A.	WRIGHT, T.
WHEATON, T.	WILLIAMS, J. J.	WOOD, F.	WRIGHT, W.
WHEELDON, R.	WILLIAMS, T.	WOOD, F.	WRIGLEY, B.
WHITAKER, T.	WILLIAMS, T. G.	WOOD, H.	WRIGLEY, J.
WHITAKER, G.	WILLIAMS, W.	WOOD, H.	WYNDER, B.
WHITCOMBE, A.	WILLIAMSON, A.	WOOD, H. F.	YATES, F.
WHITEHEAD, J. C.	WILLIAMSON, C. H.	WOOD, T. E.	YATES, J.
WHITE, G. W.	WILLIAMSON, H.	WOODS, H.	YATES, J. H.
WHITE, A.	WILLIAMSON, H. S.	WOOD, H. C.	YEADON, A.
WHITE, C.	WILLIAMSON, J.	WOOD, J.	YEADON, J.
WHITE, C.	WILLIAMSON, W. A.	WOOD, J. A.	YORK, J. H.
WHITE, H.	WILLEY, J.	WOOD, L.	YOUNG, C.
WHITE, H. E	WILLIS, L.	WOOD, P.	YOUNG, C. J.
WHITE, T. B.	WILLS, A. G.	WOOD, T.	YOUNG, E.
WHITE, W. J.	WILLS, P. W.	WOOD, T.	YOUNG, J.
WHITE, W.	WILSON, A.	WOOD, T.	YOUNG, J.
WHITEHEAD, J. (killed).	WILSON, A.	WOOD, W.	YOUNG, G.
	WILSON, E.	WOOD, W.	YOUNGMAN, T.
WHITEHEAD, R.	WILSON, F. F.	WOODCOCK, J.	YOXALL, R.
WHITEHEAD, R.	WILSON, G.	WOODHOUSE, E.	

December 13th, 1915.   **Grand Total - - 2,975**

ROLL OF HONOUR.

CROSSLEY BROS., LTD.,
OPENSHAW, MANCHESTER.

Capt. E. CROSSLEY.
Lt. B. CROSSLEY.
    (Killed in action.)
Lt. B. C. CROSSLEY.
Lt. H. D. HAYWARD.
Lt. R. B. B. SMITH.
Lt. T. W. FAIRHURST.
2nd Lt. C. C. GREEN.
W. ADAMS.
E. ADAMS.
H. ALLEN.
C. ARDRON.
    (Wounded.)
W. ARMSTRONG.
A. ANDERSON.
H. BEDFORD.
W. BALL.
T. BROADBENT.
S. BLAND.
J. BARROW.
W. BOTHAM.
W. J. BELCHER.
J. W. BARKER.
C. BEAUCHAMP.
    (Killed in action.)
F. BRENTALL.
A. BROWNLOW.
A. BROWN.
J. BOUGHEY.
H. BLACKBURN.
C. BARDSLEY.
C. J. BECKETT.
A. H. BURROWS.
E. BEARPARK.
A. BURMAN.
E. BRERTON.
J. BARRETT.
J. BELL.
G. W. BRERETON.
F. BAYLISS.
S. BOUGHTON.
E. BANKS.
A. P. BLACK.
E. BARDSLEY.
F. BULLOCK.
E. BLACKBURN.
E. BONLAN.
J. CARTER.
J. CHATERS.
F. CHADWICK.

A. L. COLE.
H. COULTON.
    (Wounded.)
H. CRONSHAW.
    (Wounded.)
T. C. CARTER.
H. COLLINS.
J. CRAWLEY.
T. CONNOLLY.
    (Killed in action.)
W. H. CLEGG.
F. CLAYTON.
J. COTTIER.
J. CUNNINGHAM.
J. CASSIDY.
F. S. COLE.
J. COSGROVE.
G. F. COTTERILL.
J. CONNOR.
J. CUNLIFFE.
T. W. CARRELL.
J. CROMPTON.
A. CHAPPELL.
E. CAVANAGH.
H. CASHMORE.
G. DAVIES.
A. DAKEYNE.
A. DITCHFIELD.
W. L. DUGGAN.
N. H. DIXON.
S. DAVIES.
J. DAWLING.
E. DUCKWORTH.
J. DURWARD.
T. S. DRURY.
E. DONLAN.
S. EVERETT.
S. FENTON.
J. FARROW.
F. FORD.
F. FENNA.
H. FAWLEY.
T. B. FROGGART.
A. FANNON.
F. FIDLER.
W. FARRANT.
F. FINN.
G. FORSHAW.
O. FURNESS.
M. A. FURNESS.

A. GRIFFITHS.
R. GORDON.
J. GRATTON. (Missing.)
A. GILBERT.
W. GIBSON.
C. GREEN.
J. GRUNDY.
J. GARVIN.
P. GARSIDE.
A. W. HEGGS.
J. HILL.
J. HEAPS.
J. R. HAUGHTON.
    (Killed in action.)
J. HAMNETT.
W. HOLLAND.
J. HOGG.
P. HEALEY.
W. HEENAN.
J. HIGGS.
F. HINCHCLIFFE.
E. HALPIN.
E. HEYWOOD.
G. HOLLAND.
G. HULLEY.
A. HEATHCOTE.
F. HURST.
R. HALL.
F. HORNBY.
H. HERON.
R. HINDLAY.
T. HEYWOOD.
F. JOHNSON.
M. JOHNSON.
T. JENNINGS.
R. JONES.
H. JONES.
    (Killed in action.)
J. JEFFREY.
W. JONES.
J. JOYCE.
F. JAMES.
C. KENNY.
J. KENNEDY.
A. KIRVIN.
J. C. KEBBLE.
F. KELLY.
J. KIRKHAM.
R. KIRKHAM.
W. LATHAM.

ROLL OF HONOUR—Continued.

Crossley Bros., Ltd.,
OPENSHAW, MANCHESTER,

G. LEWIS.
D. LEWIS.
A. LEWIS.
H. LUCAS.
    (Died on service.)
F. LEE.
R. LEE.
W. LEE.
J. LEE.
W. LEE.
J. P. LEE.
R. W. LANDON.
J. LEISHMAN.
J. LOMAS.
N. LEACK. (Missing.)
H. MELLOR.
R. MAUDE.
G. F. MOORE.
J. McCLUSKY.
    (Killed in action.)
F. MULLEN.
J. MOSTYN.
C. MOWBRAY.
A. MONTGOMERY.
H. MASSEY.
J. MARSLAND.
C. MERCER.
J. MOULT.
F. W. MELTON.
G. MORRIS.
J. J. McKEOWN.
C. MITCHELL.
C. MORTON.
J. NEWTON.
R. NEILL.
R. NAYLOR.
J. OWEN.
F. OWEN.
T. O'CONNELL.
J. OLIVER.
W. O'NEILL.
J. OLIVER.
H. OLIVER.
E. OLIVER.
H. O'DONNELL.
T. O'CONNELL.
R. O'BRIEN.
E. OWEN.
J. F. PITTY.
F. PENNINGTON.
A. E. PHILIPS.

C. PYE.
W. F. PARSONSON.
H. PLATT.
O. POLLITT.
E. L. PARRY.
H. PERKINS.
T. PEETS.
J. PATON.
T. PASS.
    (Killed in action.)
W. PETERS.
N. RIDGE.
S. ROBERTS.
W. RIGGALL.
W. ROCHFORD.
E. ROSS.
W. ROGERS.
E. J. RAMSDEN.
A. RIDGEWAY.
G. ROSE.
J. ROBERTS.
R. RATHBONE.
J. REED.
A. REDMAN.
J. S. ROBERTS.
E. ROGERS.
A. RIDGARD.
W. H. ROBINSON.
A. ROUTLEDGE.
T. SMITH.
A. SHAW.
R. E. SUDDABY.
H. D. SCOTT.
W. SARGENT.
W. SHAW.
J. B. SMITH.
A. SCHOLFIELD.
J. STEVENSON.
T. SADLER.
R. SMITH.
A. F. SMITH.
F. STEEL.
W. SANDILANDS.
T. SYKES.
P. SMITH.
T. SPILLING.
A. SIMPKIN.
D. STIRLING.
A. SCRAGG.
H. STARR.
W. A. SMITH.

J. STERNDALE.
F. J. STOPFORD.
S. SHAW.
J. SHIEL.
G. N. STALEY.
J. SIMMONDS.
J. SLIMM.
J. TONLEY.
W. TIFFANY.
T. TAYLOR.
    (Wounded.)
T. TAYLOR.
R. THORLEY.
W. THOMAS.
J. H. THOMPSON.
E. TOWERS.
W. TOFT.
J. W. TERRY.
H. TURNER.
J. TETLOW.
    (Killed in action.)
T. THOMASSON.
J. TYLER.
J. TABNER.
H. THREADER.
    (Wounded.)
H. TAYLOR.
J. TOOHEY.
W. UNSWORTH.
J. URWIN.
R. WIGNALL.
R. WRIGHT.
F. WAGSTAFFE.
W. WHITTLE.
W. WALTON.
W. WEST.
R. WHITTINGHAM.
W. WRIGHT.
J. WALTON.
M. WHALEN.
A. WOLSTENHOLME.
F. WHITTAKER.
F. T. WARD.
W. WOLSTENHOLME.
J. WELFARE.
T. WEST.
E. WILLIAMS.
G. WAREHAM.
C. WOOD.
R. YOUNG.

ROLL OF HONOUR.

CROSSLEY MOTORS LTD.

* * *

Names of Men who have Joined His Majesty's Forces.

- A. WOOLNOUGH (Killed in action).
- L. ABELL.
- E. ABERCROMBIE.
- F. AKISTER.
- J. ALLEN.
- S. ALLEN.
- W. ALLEN.
- S. ANDREWS.
- H. ATKINS.
- R. BEARD.
- M. BEATTIE.
- J. BLAKELEY.
- J. BOULD.
- A. BRERETON.
- M. O'BRIEN.
- J. BOOTH.
- R. BROOKE.
- W. A. BROWN.
- T. BUCKLER.
- H. BUCKLEY.
- W. H. BYRNE.
- D. CAINE.
- S. COOK.
- T. CALL.
- T. CHADWICK.
- R. CHEETHAM.
- W. COLLET.
- T. CONLEY.
- R. COUZENS.
- F. COWAN.
- S. E. CROOKE.
- T. CROWLEY.
- H. CUMMING.
- T. DARBY
- E. DAVIES.
- T. DEAN.
- J. DERBYSHIRE.
- A. DINSDALE.
- A. DOYLE.
- A. FLEMMING.
- R. FORTUNE.
- J. FOSTER.
- A. GREGORY.
- R. M. HAMPSON.
- A. H. HARDMAN.
- C. HALL.
- F. HILL.
- A. HORTON.
- H. HEGGS.
- A. HOYLAND.
- J. JOHNSON.
- J. JOYCE.
- W. A. KERR.
- J. KEVINS.
- V. KNIGHT.
- J. LEES.
- W. LAWDER.
- E. LENNON.
- P. LITTON.
- H. LORD.
- W. M. LUCAS.
- E. MABON.
- J. McCALL.
- J. McEWEN.
- J. McLEOD.
- F. MOORE.
- E. MORGAN.
- E. MONTGOMERY.
- W. MYCOCK.
- F. MYERS.
- J. NORBURY.
- A. OWEN.
- J. PARKINSON.
- J. PILLINGER.
- R. PERRY.
- W. POTTS.
- J. POWER.
- A. RANDLE.
- H. REEVES.
- C. ROACH.
- F. ROBBINS.
- J. ROSCOE.
- E. SCHOLES.
- W. STABBS.
- I. SWINDELLS.
- F. SANDERSON.
- J. STEVENSON.
- J. SHAW.
- A. SWINGLEHURST.
- F. TAFT.
- A. TERRY.
- J. THATCHER.
- J. E. TURNER.
- F. UPTON.
- E. UTTING.
- F. WAITE.
- H. WALLACE.
- H. WALMSLEY.
- T. WATSON.
- C. WEBB.
- I. WESTERN.
- H. WHYTE.
- H. WIMBURY.
- A. WILLIAMS.

Roll of honour.

CLAUS & CO. LIMITED.

CLAUS, Lieut. F. H.
BIRKETT, E.
BOURKE, T.
BOWLER, E.
BURNEY, M.
ECKERSALL, E.
ENTWISTLE, S.
FENTON, E.
HAYHURST, F.
HONEYFORD, C.
HOPWOOD, S.
HOSKISSON, C.
HUGHES, A.
ISHERWOOD, L.
JACKSON, C.
KEAY, E.
LOGAN, A.
LORD, E. A.
McVETY, J.
REDFORD, J
REUBEN, H.
ROONEY, J.
RYDER, A.
SMITH, J.
STALEY, J
STARR, J. H.
WALSH, P.
WARD, D.

Members of the Staff of DONALD CURRIE & CO. who have joined H.M. Forces.

Manchester Office.

Staff Lt. G. P. DEWHIRST,
   Ass. Military Forw'g. Officer, A.S.C.
L.-Cpl. T. A. ELLISON,
   17th Bt. Manchester Regt. ("Pals").
Pte. J. WARDLE,
   19th Bt. Manchester Regt. ("Pals").
Pte. A. E. DAVENPORT,
   19th Bt. Manchester Regt. ("Pals").
Pte. H. F. MOE,
   19th Bt. Manchester Regt. ("Pals").
Pte. C. WATSON, Cheshire Regiment.
Pte. J. MAGUIRE, Royal Scots.

Liverpool Office.

Pte. E. C. GILMER, Army Pay Corps.
Pte. C. N. GULLAN,
   West Lancs. Territorial A.S.C.
Pte. T. JONES,
   2/4th W. Lancs. Howitzer Br. R.F.A.
Pte. A. GARVEN,
   87th Field Am., 29th Div., R.A.M.C.
Pte. D. J. HUGHES,
   87th Field Am., 29th Div., R.A.M.C.
Pte. J. TODD,
   87th Field Am., 29th Div., R.A.M.C.
Pte. J. HELSBY,
   West Lancs. Territorial A.S.C.
Pte. A. HELM,
   West Lancs. Territorial A.S.C.
Pte. G. R. JONES, R.A.M.C.
Pte. W. KERR, R.A.M.C.
Pte. B. HUGHES, Lancashire Hussars.
Pte. J. NEWSAM, Junr.,
   16th S. Bt. King's Lpl. R. ("Pals").
Pte. S. G. BLAND,
   Anti Air Craft Service.

Roll of Honour.

GEO. & R. DEWHURST, Ltd.
MANCHESTER.

AINSWORTH, J.	6th Bt. King's Own Rgt.
ALLEN, W.	King's O. R. Lancasters.
ALMOND, J.	East Lancs. Rgt.
ALSTEAD, R.	Loyal N. Lancs. Rgt.
ANDERTON, W.	2nd Devon Ammn. Column.
ARMSTRONG, R.	King's Own Lancs. Rgt.
ATHERTON, J.	King's Own Lancs. Rgt.
ATKINSON, P.	6th Bt. L. N. Lancs.
BAMBER, T.	2nd W. Lancs. Royal Field A.
BANNISTER, F. J.	1st Lancs. R. G. Artillery.
BARNES, F.	4th Bt. L. N. Lancs.
BARON, R.	No. 1 Army Service Corps.
BATESON, J. J.	1st West Lancs. B. Artillery.
BATTERSBY, J.	Loyal North Lancs.
BATTY, A.	Royal Army Medical Corps.
BAYLEY, E.	18th Sv. Bt. Manchester Rgt.
BEESLEY, F.	123rd Bt. Royal Field Arty.
BELL, J.	Army Ordnance Corps.
BELL, W.	Royal Garrison Artillery.
BENNETT, W.	Royal Army Medical Corps.
BENNISON, M.	8th Bt. L. N. Lancs. Rgt.
BILLINGTON, H.	Royal Field Artillery.
BILLINGTON, J.	Royal Field Artillery.
BIRCH, R.	Loyal North Lancs. Rgt.
BLACKBURN, H.	4th Birkenhead B. B.
BLAKENBERGER, O.	16th Sv. Bt. Manchester Rgt.
BOARDMAN, J.	Royal Field Artillery.
BOLT, W.	4th Bt. Royal Scots.
BOLTON, F.	12th King's Liverpool Rgt.
BOLTON, S.	Royal Engineers.
BOOTH, W.	16th Sv. Bt. Manchester Rgt.
BOYLE, A.	3rd King's Own Lancs. Rgt.
BRADLEY, J.	4th King's Own Lancs. Rgt.
BRADSHAW, A.	11th B. Royal Field Artillery.
BRADSHAW, H.	2nd W. Lancs. Royal Field A.
BRADSHAW, R.	2nd W. Lancs. Royal Field A.
BRENNAN, P.	16th Sv. Bt. Manchester Rgt.
BREWER, T.	11th W. Lancs. Ryl. Field A.
BROOME, E.	18th Sv. Bt. Manchester Rgt.
BUNTING, J., Junr.	Royal Field Artillery.
BURKE, T.	16th Sv. Bt. Manchester Rgt.
BURROWS, T.	16th Sv. Bt. Manchester Rgt.
CAIRNS, P.	3/12th B. Royal Field Arty.
CARTLIDGE, F.	7th Lancs. Fusiliers.
CANUCE, R.	2nd W. Lancs. Royal Field A.
CHARLESWORTH, R.	8th Manchester Rgt.
CHEETHAM, R.	Scots Guards.
CLARKSON, C. G.	7th Bt. L. N. Lancs. Rgt.
CLITHEROE, F.	2nd W. Lancs. Royal Field A.
COOPER, G.	Royal Engineers.
COTTAM, C.	11th W. Lancs. Ryl. Field A.
COTTAM, H.	B. Bt. Lancs. Fusiliers.
COTTAM, R. H.	Border Regt.
COTTERILL, W.	7th Manchester Rgt.
COULTHARD, S.	East Lancs. Regt.
COUNSELL, W.	1st W. Lancs. Royal Field A.
COUNSELL, W.	4th King's Own Lancs. Rgt.
COWAN, C.	7th Manchester Rgt.
COX, B.	4th Bt. L. N. Lancs. Rgt.
COX, J.	2nd W. Lancs. Royal Field A.
CRAWFORD, H.	16th Sv. Bt. Manchester Rgt.
CROOK, G.	11th B. Royal Field Arty.
CROOK, G.	11th W. Lancs. Ryl. Field A.
CROOK, L.	11th Bt. L. N. Lancs. Rgt.
CROOK, R.	6th Bt. King's R. R. C.
CROOK, T.	9th By. 2nd W. Lcs. R. F. A.
CROSS, A.	Loyal North Lancs.
DAGGERS, J.	Scottish Rifles.
DARWEN, H.	2nd W. Lancs. Royal Field A.
DELANEY, J.	L. Coy. Scots Guards.
DELANEY, J. R.	L. N. Lancs. 'C' Co.
DELANEY, JOHN	4th Bt. L. N. Lancs.

Geo. & R. Dewhurst, Ltd.
ROLL OF HONOUR—Continued.

DEWHURST, C.	Lancashire Hussars.		GLYNN, J.	Royal Engineers.
DEWHURST, G. C. L.	Rifle Brigade, 6th Division.		GORE, F.	Royal Army Medical Corps.
DEWHURST, G. P.	Cheshire Yeomanry.		GORE, J.	2nd W. Lancs. Royal Field A.
DEWHURST, R. C.	15th Bt. Rifle Brigade.		GORE, W.	2nd W. Lancs. Royal Field A.
DEWHURST, J.	Border Regt.		GORST, C.	2nd W. Lancs. Royal Field A.
DEWHURST, H.	Army Remount Department.		GOWAN, H.	16th Sv. Bt. Manchester Rgt.
DILLON, J.	16th Sv. Bt. Manchester Rgt.		GREEN, E.	21st Sv. Bt. Manchester Rgt.
DIXON, E.	Loyal North Lancs.		GREGORY, A.	East Lancs. Rgt.
DIXON, H.	2nd W. L. Royal Field Arty.		GREGSON, R.	2nd W. Lancs. Royal Field A
DOBSON, J.	12th Bt. King's Liverpool R.		GREGSON, T.	3rd Bt. Scots Guards.
DODSON, G. W.	18th Sv. Bt. Manchester Rgt.		GRIME, J.	Royal Marines.
DOLEMAN, A.	16th Sv. Bt. Manchester Rgt.		GRUNDY, E. R.	2nd W. Lancs. Royal Field A.
DOLEMAN, S.	16th Sv. Bt. Manchester Rgt.		HALE, J. H.	Royal Garrison Artillery.
DOOLAN, P.	7th Bt. L. N. Lancs. Rgt.		HALL, J.	Army Service Corps.
DOOMELEY, F.	2nd W. Lancs. Royal Field A.		HALLIDAY, F.	18th Sv. Bt. Manchester Rgt.
DOVER, W.	16th Sv. Bt. Manchester Rgt.		HALPIN, C.	2nd W. Lancs. Royal Field A.
DOWNHAM, H.	C. By. Royal Field Artillery.		HALPIN, J.	2nd W. Lancs. Royal Field A.
DOWNS, S.	7th Lancs. Fusiliers.		HALPIN, J.	11th By. Royal Field Arty.
EASTHAM, F.	11th Bt. Royal Field Arty.		HALPIN, W. H.	Royal Field Artillery.
EASTHAM, T.	B. Coy. L. N. Lancs. Rgt.		HALSHAW, J. T.	11th Lancs. Bt. Ryl. Field A.
EDMONDSON, C.	7th Bt. Royal Field Artillery.		HARDACRE, J.	3rd Bedford Rgt.
EDMONDSON, W.	46th Coy. Army Service C.		HARTLEY, J.	Loyal N. Lancs. Rgt.
EDWARDS, H.	L. N. Lancs. Rgt.		HATTON, J.	20th Sv. Bt. Manchester Rgt.
EVANS, W.	3rd Bt. Manchester Rgt.		HAWORTH, J.	Royal Field Artillery.
FAIRCLOUGH, F.	8th Lancs. Fusiliers.		HAYDOCK, N.	11th By. Royal Field Arty.
FARRELL, B.	4th Lancs. Fusiliers.		HENNISON, L.	2nd W. Lancs. Royal Field A.
FAZACKERLEY, T.	Loyal North Lancs. Rgt.		HEYES, I.	12th King's Liverpool Rgt.
FELL, T.	11th Bt. Royal Field Arty.		HILL, J.	11th W. Lancs. Ryl. Field A.
FERNHEAD, J. H.	Army Service Corps.		HOLLAND, F.	7th Bt. L. N. Lancs. Rgt.
FINCH, J.	E. Lancs. Royal Field Arty.		HOLMES, R.	Royal Army Medical Corps.
FINLOW, H.	22nd Sv. Bt. Manchester Rgt.		HOLMES, R.	8th Lancs. Fusiliers.
FRODSHAM, H.	King's Own Lancs. Rgt.		HOLT, H.	5th Cheshire Rgt.
FURNESS, S.	8th Division Army Service C.		HORROCKS, H.	2nd W. Lancs. Royal Field A.
FURNESS, W.	7th Bt. King's R. R.		HORROCKS, J.	2nd W. Lancs. Royal Field A.
GARDNER, H.	7th Bt. L. N. Lancs.		HOUGH, J.	8th Bt. L. N. Lancs. Rgt.
GARDNER, R.	Motor Transport.		HOUGHTON, J.	Coldstream Guards.
GARDNER, W. E.	5th King's R. R. C.		HOUGHTON, T. L.	Army Remount Department.
GARDNER, W. R. B.	Royal Engineers.		HOWELLS, A.	16th Sv. Bt. Manchester Rgt.
GARRATT, J.	Royal Engineers.		HUDSON, N.	Nat. Reserve, Lancaster.
GENT, J.	East Lancs. Rgt.		HULL, N.	Motor Transport.
GILL, T.	2nd W. Lancs. Royal Field A.		HULL, N., Junr.	Royal Engineers.
GILLETT, W.	King's Own Lancaster Rgt.		HUNTER, J.	2nd W. Lancs. Royal Field A.

Geo. & R. Dewhurst, Ltd.

ROLL OF HONOUR—Continued.

IDDON, J.	Birkenhead B. Bt.
IDDON, W.	Royal Engineers.
INGHAM, C.	Loyal N. Lancs. Rgt.
INGHAM, JOHN	2nd W. Lancs. Royal Field A.
INGHAM, J.	2nd W. Lancs. Royal Field A.
JACKSON, A.	Royal Army Medical Corps.
JACKSON, J.	8th Bt. L. N. Lancs. Rgt.
JACKSON, M.	3rd Royal Lancaster Rgt.
JACKSON, R.	Royal Garrison Artillery.
JONES, E.	22nd Sv. Bt. Manchester Rgt.
JONES, THOS. W.	A.S.C., 38th Welsh Division.
KAY, N.	E. Lancs. Royal Field Arty.
KELLY, C.	16th Sv. Bt. Manchester Rgt.
KILPATRICK, H.	16th Sv. Bt. Manchester Rgt.
KING, R. G.	Motor Transport A. S. C.
KIRKPATRICK, R.	16th Sv. Bt. Manchester Rgt.
KNOWLAND, G.	16th Sv. Bt. Manchester Rgt.
KNOWLES, H.	D. Coy. Border Rgt.
KNOWLES, H.	2nd W. Lancs. Royal Field A.
KNOWLES, J.	11th W. Lancs. Ryl. Field A.
LAMB, G.	18th Sv. Bt. Manchester Rgt.
LAMB, R.	7th Manchester Rgt.
LANE, W. G.	D. of Lancaster's Yeomanry.
LARKIN, F.	18th Sv. Bt. Manchester Rgt.
LAW, T.	6th Bt. King's R. R. C.
LEACH, G.	9th Bt. Royal Scots.
LEADBETTER, J. W.	9th Bt. Royal Scots.
LEEMING, W.	2nd W. Lancs. Royal Field A.
LIVESEY, J. T.	Scots Guards.
LONGTON, J.	2nd W. Lancs. Royal Field A.
LOVATT, T.	King's R. R. Corps.
LYTH, W.	7th Manchester Rgt.
McCANN, J. W.	11th Bt. Black Watch.
McCLEAR, J.	East Lancs. Rgt.
McDERMOTT, J.	2nd L. N. Lancs. Regt.
McMACKEN, J.	19th Sv. Bt. Manchester Rgt.
MACLAM, W.	117th By. Royal Field Arty.
MARGINSON, E.	Royal Army Medical Corps.
MARGISON, H.	11th W. Lancs. Ryl. Field A.
MARSDEN, R.	Army Service Corps.
MARSH, H.	27th By. Royal Field Arty.
MARSHALL, H.	4th Bt. L. N. Lancs. Rgt.
MARTLAND, L.	2nd W. Lancs. Royal Field A.
MARTIN, J.	1st W. Lancs. Royal Field A.
MARTIN, W.	2nd W. Lancs. Ryl. Field A.
MARTLAND, S.	8th By. Royal Field Artillery.
MAUDSLEY, T.	Royal Field Artillery.
MEEHAN, M.	Royal Engineers.
MELLING, A.	Royal Field Artillery.
MELLING, J.	Lord Derby's Battalion.
MELVILL, M. G. D.	6th Manchester Rgt.
MERCER, F.	Loyal North Lancs. Rgt.
MERCER, H.	11th By. Royal Field Arty.
MERCER, R.	8th King's Irish Rgt.
MILLER, J.	King's Own Lancs. Regt.
MOLYNEUX, W.	2nd W. Lancs. Royal Field A.
MORTON, J.	7th Bt. L. N. Lancs. Rgt.
MOSS, J.	2nd W. Lancs. Royal Field A.
NAYLOR, W.	16th Sv. Bt. Manchester Rgt.
NICKSON, T.	4th Bt. L. N. Lancs. Rgt.
NICKSON, T.	B. Bt. Lancs. Fusiliers.
NIGHTINGALE, J.	6th Bt. L. N. Lancs. Rgt.
NOBLETT, G.	2nd W. Lancs. Royal Field A.
NOBLETT, J.	10th L. N. Lancs. Rgt.
NORRIS, M.	2nd W. Lancs. Royal Field A.
NORTH, M.	5th King's R. Rifles.
OGDEN, G.	8th Lancs. Fusiliers.
PALIN, H.	16th Sv. Bt. Manchester Rgt.
PARKER, A.	2nd W. Lancs. Royal Field A.
PARKER, J.	King's Liverpool Rgt.
PARKER, N.	11th W. Lancs. Ryl. Field A.
PARKER, W.	2nd W. Lancs. Royal Field A.
PARKER, W.	Loyal North Lancs. Rgt.
PARKINSON, J.	2nd W. Lancs. Royal Field A.
PARKINSON, T.	Loyal North Lancs. Rgt.
PARKINSON, W.	8th King's Irish Rgt.
PEAK, J. F.	8th Manchester Rgt.
PEAK, W.	E. Lancs. Royal Field Arty.
PEARSON, J.	2nd W. Lancs. Royal Field A.
PENSWICK, A.	4th Loyal N. Lancs. Rgt.
PLUNKETT, G.	18th Sv. Bt. Manchester Rgt.
PORTER, G.	9th Bt. Lancs. Fusiliers.
PRATT, H. R.	E. Lancs. Royal Field Arty.
PRESTON, J. J.	2nd W. Lancs. Ryl. Field A.
READ, G.	1st Bt. East Lancs. Rgt.
REEVES, E.	Lancs. Fusiliers.
REDFERN, J.	16th Sv. Bt. Manchester Rgt.
RICHMOND, J.	Loyal North Lancs. Rgt.
RIDING, J.	2nd W. Lancs. Royal Field A.
RIDING, R.	2nd W. Lancs. Royal Field A.
RIDING, T.	Royal Army Medical Corps.
RIGBY, F.	1st W. Lancs. Royal Field A.
RILEY, T.	11th W. Lancs. Ryl. Field A.
ROBINSON, E.	19th Sv. Bt. Manchester Rgt.
ROBINSON, S. J.	Loyal North Lancs. Rgt.
ROBINSON, R.	Loyal North Lancs. Rgt.
ROE, E.	3rd Bt. L. N. Lancs. Rgt.
ROE, G.	16th Sv. Bt. Manchester Rgt.
ROONEY, W.	4th Bt. L. N. Lancs. Rgt.
ROSKELL, R.	2nd W. Lancs. Royal Field A.
ROWLANDS, H.	2nd E. Lancs. Brig. R.F.A.
RUSSELL, C. A.	16th Sv. Bt. Manchester Rgt.
RYDER, G.	18th Sv. Bt. Manchester Rgt.
RYDER, R.	6th Bt. Manchester Rgt.

Geo. & R. Dewhurst, Ltd.

ROLL OF HONOUR—Continued.

RYLANCE, J.	2nd W. Lancs. Royal Field A.
SAGE, G.	1st Birkenhead B. Bt.
SANDS, S.	7th Manchester Rgt.
SANDS, W. H.	19th Sv. Bt. Manchester Rgt.
SAUL, D.	2nd W. Lancs. Royal Field A.
SAUL, J.	2nd W. Lancs. Royal Field A.
SAUL, J.	11th W. Lancs. Ryl. Field A.
SAUL, J.	South Lancs. Rgt.
SCHOFIELD, J.	16th Sv. Bt. Manchester Rgt.
SCHOLES, H.	Royal Army Medical Corps.
SELKIRK, F.	7th Manchester Rgt.
SHARPLES, J.	Loyal North Lancs. Rgt.
SHARPLES, J.	1st W. Lancs. Ryl. Field A.
SHARPLES, P.	2nd W. Lancs. Royal Field A.
SHARPLES, T.	2nd Bt. Birkenhead B.
SHARPLES, W.	Scottish Rifles.
SHELMERDINE, B.	7th Lancs. Fusiliers.
SHELMERDINE, J. A.	22nd Manchester Rgt.
SHELMERDINE, P. A.	7th Lancs. Fusiliers.
SHENTON, T.	16th Sv. Bt. Manchester Rgt.
SHUTTLEWORTH, J.	7th Bt. Border Rgt.
SIBBERT, W.	9th L. N. Lancs. Rgt.
SLATER, W. H.	2nd Am. Col. Royal Field A.
SMALLEY, S.	2nd W. Lancs. Royal Field A.
SMITH, H.	8th Lancs. Fusiliers.
SMITH, J.	Army Service Corps.
SMITH, M.	6th Bt. King's R. R. Corps.
SNAPE, G. E.	11th By. Royal Field Arty.
SNAPE, R.	2nd W. Lancs. Royal Field A.
SNAPE, T.	11th By. Royal Field Arty.
SOUTHWORTH, J.	4th Bt. L. N. Lancs. Rgt.
STAFFORD, J.	4th Bt. L. N. Lancs. Rgt.
STEAD, J.	Loyal North Lancs. Rgt.
STEELE, L. E.	6th Manchester Rgt.
SULLIVAN, J.	10th Bt. L. N. Lancs. Rgt.
SUMNER, D.	Army Ordnance Corps.
SUMNER, F.	2nd W. Lancs. Royal Field A.
SUMNER, J.	2nd W. Lancs. Royal Field A.
SUMNER, J. (2nd)	2nd W. Lancs. Royal Field A.
SUMNER, R.	2nd W. Lancs. Royal Field A.
SWARBRICK, J.	4th Bt. Bantam Rgt.
SWINDLEHURST, A.	2nd W. Lancs. Royal Field A.
TAYLOR, F.	19th Sv. Bt. Manchester Rgt.
TAYLOR, H.	16th Sv. Bt. Manchester Rgt.
THOMPSON, J.	West Lancs. Royal Field A.
THOMPSON, W.	Royal Field Artillery.
TOMLINSON, A.	4th King's Own Rgt.
TOMLINSON, H.	3rd L. N. Lancs. Rgt.
TROLLOPE, S.	King's Own Lancs. Regt.
TURNER, J.	Loyal North Lancs.
TURNER, W.	Birkenhead B. Bt.
VOST, J.	7th Bt. East Lancs. Rgt.
WADGE, A.	3rd Bt. Scots Guards.
WAKEFIELD, G.	2nd W. Lancs. Royal Field A.
WAKEFIELD, J.	10th Bt. West Lancs. A.
WALSH, W.	6th Bt. King's R. R. Corps.
WARING, J.	B. Bt. Lancs. Fusiliers.
WASTLEY, J.	11th W. Lancs. Ryl. Field A.
WEATHERALL, R.	Loyal North Lancs. Rgt.
WEATHERALL, W.	Loyal North Lancs. Rgt.
WEBB, R.	11th By. Royal Field Arty.
WESTERN, J.	11th Bt. Lancs. Fusiliers.
WIGGINS, W.	12th King's Liverpool Rgt.
WILDING, G.	Loyal North Lancs. Rgt.
WILDMAN, R.	3rd King's Own Hussars.
WILSON, J.	4th Bt. L. N. Lancs. Rgt.
WOODBURN, R. M.	Scots Guards.
WOODCOCK, V.	2nd W. Lancs. Royal Field A.
WOODRUFF, J.	7th Bt. L. N. Lancs. Rgt.
WOODS, W.	9th Lancs. Bt. Ryl. Field A.
WOODS, L.	6th Bt. King's R. R. Corps.
WRIGHT, T.	South Lancs. Rgt.
WRIGLEY, N.	11th By. Royal Field Arty.
YATES, E.	11th By. Royal Field Arty.
YATES, G.	2nd W. Lancs. Royal Field A.
YATES, J.	11th Bt. L. N. Lancs. Rgt.
YATES, S.	Royal Army Medical Corps.

Duncan, Fox & Co. Manchester.
Members of the Staff who have joined the colours

 J. Allington
 F. D. Ashton
 W. E. Bennett
 A. J. Bridge
 A. Cross

 A. Davies
 S. Dickinson
 W. Evans
 W. Gibbons
 J. Gubbins

 W. Hamer
 N. Hunt
 C. Johnson
 A. Jones
 G. Lesk

 G. Macdonald
 A. E. Miller
 A. Taylor
 W. J. Thomas
 S. Wilson

GOD SAVE THE KING.

ROLL OF HONOUR.

Dugdale, Everton & Co.,

MANUFACTURERS AND MERCHANTS,

MANCHESTER.

F. Wilson	18th Batt. Manchester Regiment.
H. S. Devey	18th Batt. Manchester Regiment.
A. L. Gyves	18th Batt. Manchester Regiment.
T. Robertson	18th Batt. Manchester Regiment.
T. Cliffe	19th Batt. Manchester Regiment.
A. E. Taylor	19th Batt. Manchester Regiment.
J. Finnigan	3rd Batt. Manchester Regiment.
W. Barrow	2nd East Lancashire R.F.A.
N. B. Blackwell	2nd East Lancashire R.F.A.
G. Robertson	15th Battalion Royal Scots.
H. S. Henry	Army Service Corps.
Edgar Allen	6th Batt. Manchester Regiment (T.F.).
G. Dawson	17th Batt. King's Liverpool Regt.
Reg. Thom	30th Battalion Royal Fusiliers.
F. Whittaker	Duke of Lancaster's Own Yeomanry.
H. S. Gros	Officers' Training Corps.

Others have attested.

ROLL OF HONOUR.
✦ ✦ ✦
DEHN & CO.,
MANCHESTER.

2nd Lieut. HAROLD G. DEHN,
 3rd Batt. Wiltshire Regiment.
Private RICHARD DEHN,
 16th Batt. Middlesex Regiment.
Private C. ANDERTON,
 7th Batt. Manchester Regt. (T.).
Private T. ARCHER,
 17th Batt. Manchester Regt.
Private G. CARROLL,
 3/6th Batt. Manchester Regt. (T.).
Private R. COOPER,
 6th Batt. Man/r Regt. (killed). (T.).
Gunner T. CUNNANE,
 17th By. East Lancashire R.F.A.
Sergt. A. C. DAVIES,
 3/2nd By. East Lancashire R.F.A.
L.-Corpl. L. B. DAVIS,
 D. of Lancaster's Own Yeomanry.
Private S. EVERETT,
 6th Batt. Manchester Regt. (T.).
Sergt. J. GRISENTHWAITE,
 26th Batt. Manchester Regiment.
Private W. E. HORROCKS,
 7th Bt. Man/r Regt. (T.) (missing).
Private A. NICHOLLS.
 17th Batt. Manchester Regiment.
Private E. PARTT,
 6th Batt. Man/r Regt. (T.) (killed).
Piper R. ROUGH.
 6th Batt. Royal Scots.
Private E. THORNILEY.
 17th Batt. Manchester Regiment.

ROLL OF HONOUR.

Jas. L. Denman & Co. Ltd.
17, DEANSGATE,
MANCHESTER.

Staff Sergt. FRANK C. VINE,
 Altcar.

*Private WILLIAM ASHTON,
 6th Manchester Regiment (T.).

Private HARRY N. SNELSON,
 Duke of Lancaster's Yeomanry.

*Killed Dardanelles, 6th June, 1915.

Roll of Honour.

✶ ✶ ✶

ECKSTEIN HEAP & CO. LIMITED.

Employees who have Joined His Majesty's Forces.

D. V. Murphy	Cameronians (Scottish Rifles).
D. Flannery	Loyal North Lancashires (Killed).
F. Davies	8th Manchester Territorial Battalion.
J. Sanderson	7th Manchester Territorial Batt. (Missing).
B. Coxon	Royal Engineers, Manchester Territorials.
J. Allen	Cameronians (Scottish Rifles) (Killed).
A. Dowling	Royal Field Artillery.
T. Wallwork	Loyal North Lancashires.
J. Hampson	Royal Field Artillery.
H. Waters	South Wales Border Regiment.
J. Hall	7th Manchester Territorials.
F. Wilde	South Wales Border Regiment.
W. Naylor	South Lancashire Fusiliers.
B. Hardy	Royal Marine Light Infantry.
H. Carlton (Staff)	20th Serv. Batt. Manchester Regt. (Pals).
F. Cavanagh	14th Batt. Manchester Regiment.
A. Ball	
H. Young	Royal Army Medical Corps, Signal Service.
E. Lamb (Staff)	Royal Naval Division (Wireless).
F. Rylands (Staff)	18th Serv. Batt. Manchester Regt. (Pals).
A. Cadwallader	Lancashire Fusiliers.
A. Greer	King's Own Royal Lancashire Regiment.
J. Johnstone	19th Sv. Corps, Lancs. Fus., 3rd Salford Bt.
T. Evans	19th Sv. Corps, Lancs. Fus., 3rd Salford Bt.
E. Jones	Lancashire Fusiliers.
T. Carey	Lancashire Fusiliers.
F. Garnsworthy	Army Service Corps, Mechanical Transport.
E. Nixon	King's Own Royal Rifles.
N. Mason	Manchester Regiment (Pals).
T. H. Mitchell (Staff)	Royal Army Medical Corps.
H. Hornbrook (Staff)	6th Manchester Regiment (T.F.) (Killed).
H. Smith (Staff)	5th Manchester Regiment (T.F.) (Killed).
R. N. Harrison (Staff)	Royal Fusiliers, Public Schools Battalion.
G. A. Rowark	8th Battalion Lancashire Fusiliers.
J. Greenock (Staff)	Earl of Chester's Yeomanry.
W. Briggs (Staff)	8th Manchester Territorials.
A. Hallworth	Royal Scots.
H. Hardman	Lancashire Fusiliers.
J. Donnelly	2nd Manchester Regiment.
G. R. Hardstaff	Royal Engineers (Inland Transport Sect.).
T. Wunderly	
E. Evans	Royal Field Artillery.
S. Mathews (Chapel Walks)	16th Serv. Batt. Manchester Regt. (Pals).
D. H. Leah (Chapel Walks)	Army Service Corps (Mech. Transport).

ROLL OF HONOUR.

English Sewing Cotton Co. Limited

NATIONAL BUILDINGS, ST. MARY'S PARSONAGE,
——— MANCHESTER ———

HEAD OFFICE.

ALDRED, A. G.	DITCHFIELD, J. C.	MAKIN, A. W.	ROWBOTTOM, N.
ASH, C.	GODFREY, G. L.	MICKLEWRIGHT C.	ROGERS, J. H.
BERRY, T.	GREENHALGH, E.	MILLS, L.	SIDDALL, A. V.
BLEARS, H.	HALL, S. G.	MURPHY, D.	SHAKESHAFT, G. W.
CLARKE, C.	HARLING, J. T.	MUCKELT, H. C.	THORNHILL, W.
COOPER, C.	HOLTBY, W.	POTTS, C.	USHER, R. W. A.
DANIELS, F. T.	LILOF, G.	ROBERTS, A.	WALMSLEY, F. A.
DAVIES, H.			

STOCKPORT BRANCH.

BARRITT, P.	GRANT, T. E. B.	HALLWORTH, F.	SMITH, R. U.
BOOTH, T.	GRUNDY, G. F.	JONES, R. E.	VICKERS, G.
FOWLES, A. C.	HALLWORTH, H.	SANKEY, E.	

BELPER AND MILFORD BRANCHES.

BARFIELD, J.	FLINDERS, B.	LANDER, H.	SHAW, H.
BATTEN, J.	FOSTER, T.	LINTHWAITE, G. W.	SIMPSON, S.
BENNETT, S. A.	FREER, G.	McARTHUR, D.	SMITH, N. A.
BERESFORD, H.	HAGUE, A.	MEE, A.	STAMPER, E.
BOOTH, A.	HANDLEY, L.	MERRYWEATHER, R. H.	STEEPLES, J. W.
BOOT, E.	HALLAM, P. S.	MOODY, C. H.	STEVENSON, S.
BROWN, F.	HALLSWORTH T.	MOSELEY, P.	SWAIN, J.
CALOW, C. W.	HARESNAPE, A.	MELLOR, H., Jr.	TRUEMAN, E.
CHEETHAM, G., Jr.	HOBSON, H.	MELLOR, S.	TOPHAM, H.
CHEETHAM, H.	HOBSON, G.	McLEOD, J.	TOPHAM, J.
CHADWICK, A. N.	HURST, A.	NEEDHAM, W.	THROP, C.
CLAYSON, J. L. H.	HARLOW, F.	NIGHTINGALE, J.	WATSON, W.
COOPER, CHAS.	JANES, C.	OLDFIELD, H. H.	WIGLEY, A.
COOPER, F.	JENNISON, T.	PARKER, A. W.	WILLIAMS, L.
DAVENPORT, T.	JONES, H. M.	PARKER, A.	WINSON, WM., Jr.
DAY, W. H.	KIRKLAND, A.	PERRY, G.	WEBSTER, E.
DEANE, F.	LANDER, W.	PERCIVAL, H.	WEBSTER, A.
DEANE, H.	LAWRENCE, G. F.	REYNOLDS, W.	YEOMANS, S.
DEANE, W. H.	LANDER, F.	ROBINSON, V.	YEOMANS, H.
ELLIS, E.	LANDER, WM.	RYDE, L.	YOUNG, H.
FARRELL, J.	LANDER, A.	SANDERS, A.	

R. F. AND J. ALEXANDER AND CO., LTD., Neilston.

ADAMS, S.	CLARKIN, P.	LOVE, D.	SHEMWELL, T. E.
ALLISON, J.	COSH, W.	McARTHUR, R.	SINCLAIR, J.
AITCHISON, R.	CUMMOCK, H.	McLINTOCK, R.	SMELLIE, A.
ANDERSON, M.	DUNLOP, A.	McKENDRY, D.	THRELFALL, H.
BRIGGS, J.	GILLESPIE, J.	MUSHET, D.	TOMLINSON, R.
BRIGGS, V. B.	GORDON, J.	MATTHEWS, H.	WALKER, R.
BROWN, J.	GORDON, W.	McLELLAN, A.	WALKER, A.
BUCHANAN, A.	GORDON, WM.	O'NEILL, W.	WHYTE, A.
BRANNON, F.	HARESNAPE, C.	PATON, A.	WOOD, J.
CALDWELL, S.	HAY, J.	RANKIN, J.	WILSON, J.
CAMERON, P.	KEAN, D.		

English Sewing Cotton Co. Limited
ROLL OF HONOUR—Continued.

SIR RICHARD ARKWRIGHT AND CO., LTD., Matlock Bath.

ALLEN, J.	BROUGH, A.	GREGORY, J.	PARKS, C.
BATTERLEY, G. H.	BROUGH, W.	GREGORY, J. H.	PEARSON, S.
BIDDULPH, A.	DOXEY, G.	GROWCOTT, S.	PEARSON, W.
BODEN, F.	DOXEY, L. A.	HALL, A.	ROBINSON, G.
BOTHAM, J.	ELLIOTT, W.	HODGKINSON, G.	SAINT, N.
BRITLAND, H.	ELLIOTT, D.	KIRK, L.	STATHAM, H.
BROOKES, C.	ELSE, W.	MARSH, H.	SWIFT, J.
BROOKS, L.	FEARN, H.	MARSH, J.	WRIGHT, P.
BROWN, A.	GOULD, G.	OLDHAM, F.	WILBRAHAM, L.

JOHN DEWHURST AND SONS, LTD., Skipton.

ADAMS, H.	CLARKE, ALFRED.	LAMBERT, A.	RODGERS, P.
ANSLOW, H.	CLARKE, ARTHUR.	LAMBERT, H.	RUSSELL, J. W.
ARMITAGE, A.	CLARK, H.	LEE, R.	SCHOFIELD, W.
ATKINSON, H.	CHILD, C. V.	LEE, J. W.	SHERWOOD, F.
AUSTIN, F.	DEACON, G.	MASTERS, J. T.	SLAVEN, F.
BIRCH, H.	DAWSON, J.	MAUDSLEY, H.	SMITH, E. B.
BARLOW, A. E.	ELLIOTT, F.	METCALFE, A.	SMITH, J.
BARRETT, G. H	ERMEN, G. H.	McDERMOTT, O.	STEEL, R. H.
BARRETT, W.	FIELD, P.	MILES, C.	THOMPSON, W.
BEARD, F. W.	FRIEND, E.	MOORE, R.	THOMPSON, E.
BELL, H.	FLETCHER, B.	MOORBY, R.	TUER, W.
BELL, W. W.	GEMMELL, C.	MOORHOUSE, T.	TURNER, J. W.
BROWN, J. J.	GRAHAM, J.	MYERS, J. C.	TURNBULL, A.
BRYAN, F. W.	GRAY, W.	METCALFE, J. T.	THWAITES, C.
BURROWS, L. V.	HALL, J.	NUTTER, A.	UPTON, J.
BURTON, F. K.	HALLAM, J. W.	PASS, C.	VARLEY, J. W.
BAILEY, W. H.	HARTLEY, A.	PARKINSON, E.	WALLWORK, W.
BATES, C.	HESLOP, W.	PATCHETT, S.	WALTON, C. H.
CALVERT, H.	HORNER, G. H.	PEACOCK, J. L.	WALKER, I.
CARTER, A.	HAZLEWOOD, G.	PRESTON, F.	WALKER, W. H.
CARTLEDGE, C.	HOWARTH, J.	PATCHETT, E.	WALKER, H.
CASON, J. T.	INGHAM, H.	PEARSON, C. S.	WEAR, A.
CHAPMAN, JAMES	IRELAND, A.	QUINN, D.	WETHERELL, J. H.
CHAPMAN, JOHN.	KING, F.	RAMPLING, W. G.	WHITTAKER, C.
CHAPMAN, F.	KING, W. A.	READSHAW, T. L.	WILKINSON, D.
CHAMPION, E.	KING, R. E.	REYNOLDS, W.	WATSON, A.
CHEW, J. S.	KNIPE, J. W.	ROBINSON, E.	

ERMEN AND ROBY, LTD., Pendlebury.

ASHTON, E.	BLEARS, R.	HALLIDAY, R.	MILLAR, J.
BESWICK, W.	PARKER, R.		

ERMEN AND ROBY, LTD., Patricroft.

DANIELS, J.	JONES, J. A.	HESSIAN, J.	SMITH, J. H.
DAVIS, A.	RILEY, J.	MANN, J.	YATES, G. E.
HEWITT, G.	GORVETT, JOHN J.	POLLITT, ERIC.	

J. AND E. WATERS AND CO., LTD., Manchester.

HAWKINS, H.	WAKEFIELD, G.	RYDE, F.	LAWLESS, W.
BERRY, A.	OWEN, A.	THRELFALL, A.	WALTON, W.

J. AND E. WATERS AND CO., LTD., Longtown.

BATEY, T. W.	ROBINSON, J.	FOSTER, JOHN JAS.

ROLL OF HONOUR.

The English Velvet & Cord Dyers' Association, Limited.

The Names of those who in the time of need came forward in the service of their King and Country, and in defence of the liberties of Europe, 1914-1915.

HEAD OFFICES.

BROOKS, ARTHUR, Lieut.
CARTER, JOSEPH, Sergeant.
DALE, RICHARD.

FRANCIS, ALFRED E.
KENNY, J. E.
SHEASBY, LEONARD.

TURLEY, WILLIAM
WILLS, NORMAN T.

J. & J. M. WORRALL, LTD.

ALCOCK, BENJAMIN.
APPLETON, JOHN, Sr.
APPLETON, JOHN, Jr.
ASHWORTH, JOHN.
ASHTONHURST, J. W.
ASPREY, JOSEPH.
AIMSON, JOHN.
BANNER, W.
BERRY, GEO.
BLUNDELL, G. W.
BATES, JOHN.
BARKER, GEORGE W.
BAXTER, THOMAS.
BURNS, ALBERT.
BURNS, JAMES.
BROOKS, GEORGE.
BREWER, FRANK.
BREWER, GEORGE.
BYRNE, ARTHUR.
BEAUMONT, WILLIAM.
BUTLER, JAMES.
BRAMHALL, JNO.
BETTS, ALBERT.
BETHELL, THOMAS.
BAYBUT, GEORGE.
BISHOP, CHARLES.
BEAVER, ERNEST.
BRUEN, CHARLES.
CROFT, JOHN.
CARRUTHERS, ALEC.
CASSIDY, ED.
CROSS, ALFRED.

CHADWICK, JNO.
CARTWRIGHT, JNO.
CORCORAN, THOMAS.
CERES, HENRY.
CALLIGAN, THOMAS.
CHINN, GEORGE.
CALDWELL, GEORGE R.
CONNOR, JOHN.
CHATTON, FREDERICK.
COWPE, EDWARD.
CHADWICK, GEORGE.
CHAPMAN, ED.
CRIMBLEHOLME, S.
CAVANAGH, HERBERT.
CARTER, ARTHUR.
CURRAN, THOMAS
CROWTHER, JNO. J.
COYLE, JNO. T.
DYSON, GEORGE.
DENNELL, JOHN.
DEVINE, SAMUEL.
DALE, JNO. E.
DAVIES, RICHARD.
DESSENT, T. W. G.
DODD, EDWARD.
DENNIS, ERNEST.
DITCHBURN, CHARLES.
DOOLEY, PATRICK.
DOOLEY, JAMES T.
DOWLER, JAMES.
DOLAN, ARTHUR.
DAVIES, CYRIL.

DRAPER, JOS.
DUNN, R.
EYLES, SAMUEL.
ELLIS, JOSEPH.
EDWARDS, WILLIAM.
EMSLEY, WILLIAM.
ELLIS, HENRY.
EVANS, WALTER.
EDWARDS, ARTHUR.
FARNWORTH, ALFRED
FISHER, THOMAS.
FERNLEY, THOMAS.
FRANCIS, JAMES A.
GLYNN, MATTHEW.
GALLAGHER, JNO.
GREGG, EDWARD.
GLEAVES, ROBERT.
GLYNN, JOHN.
GRIBBEN, RICHARD.
GARNER, CHARLES.
GLYNN, WILLIAM.
GOODWIN, F
GOULD, W.
GRAHAM, JOSEPH J.
GREAVES, ERNEST.
GALLIMORE, GEORGE A.
HENDERSON, JOHN.
HARDMAN, ROBERT.
HOPCROFT, GEORGE.
HUGHES, W.
HUDSON, JOSEPH.
HAMNETT, JOHN.

The English Velvet & Cord Dyers' Association, Limited.

J. & J. M. WORRALL, LTD.—continued.

- HOBBS, WALTER.
- HOGGARTH, RICHARD.
- HEALD, JOHN.
- HOMAN, JOHN.
- HATCHER, GEORGE W.
- HOUGH, WILLIAM.
- HUMPHREYS, WILLIAM.
- HIGGINBOTTOM, H.
- HEALD, EDWARD W.
- HARDY, JAMES.
- HUDSON, JOHN.
- HODGKINSON, SIDNEY.
- HOPTON, ROBERT.
- IRLAM, ABRAHAM.
- JONES, GEORGE S.
- JONES, EDWARD.
- JENNINGS, JOSEPH.
- JONES, GRIFFITH.
- JOHNSON, JOHN.
- JULIAN, E.
- JENKINS, FREDERICK.
- JENSEN, CHRIS.
- JEMMETT, FREDERICK.
- JENNINGS, FREDERICK.
- JAMIESON, JOHN.
- KEATING, DOMINIC.
- KELSHAW, JAMES.
- LANE, G.
- LEE, ANDREW.
- LYNSKY, THOMAS.
- LANE, GEORGE H.
- LANE, FREDERICK.
- LEWIS, HERBERT.
- LARRAD, THOMAS.
- LOGAN, PATRICK.
- LEE, WILLIAM.
- LITTLER, ALFRED.
- MALONE, M.
- MASON, THOMAS.
- McDONALD, THOMAS.
- McKEEVER, JAMES.
- MEREDITH, THOMAS.
- MAJOR, ALFRED.
- McMORROW, M.
- MALAM, WILLIAM.
- MEREDITH, HERBERT.
- McKAY, JOSEPH.
- MERCER, HENRY.
- MATHER, HENRY.
- MATTHEWS, WILLIAM.
- MURPHY, ARTHUR.
- MALONE, JAMES.
- MILLS, JAMES.
- MASSEY, ALBERT.
- McCARTY, T.
- McCLURE, WILLIAM.
- McDERRA, P.
- McGREGOR, F.
- MAXWELL, JOSEPH.
- MITCHELL, ALBERT.
- MARRIOTT, JOSEPH.
- MEREDITH, ERNEST.
- MITCHELL, JAMES.
- NORTON, CHARLES.
- NORMAN, JOHN.
- NELSON, JOHN.
- NELSON, JOSEPH.
- NEWTON, ERNEST.
- NIXON, THOMAS H.
- OGDEN, JOSEPH.
- OSBORNE, A.
- OSBORNE, ARTHUR K.
- OSBORNE, HENRY.
- POLLITT, DAN.
- PILLING, WILLIAM.
- PRANGS, CHARLES.
- PAGE, JNO. C.
- PETERS, FREDERICK.
- PERCIVAL, JAMES.
- PETERS, WALTER.
- PRITCHARD, SIDNEY.
- PLATT, W.
- PARTINGTON, STANLEY.
- PAGE, JOSEPH.
- PLANT, HENRY.
- PRICE, THOMAS.
- ROBERTS, JAMES.
- ROBERTSON, WILLIAM.
- RICE, JAMES.
- ROGERS, CHARLES.
- ROWLES, ARTHUR.
- RYAN, JAMES.
- ROUTLEDGE, GEORGE.
- RYDER, HENRY.
- ROWBOTTOM, MATTHEW.
- RUSSELL, SANDY.
- RAVENSCROFT, JAMES.
- RICHARDS, WILLIAM.
- RATCLIFFE, F.
- REDFERN, WILLIAM.
- ROWBOTTOM, THOMAS.
- RODELEY, ALBERT.
- SAVAGE, ROBERT.
- SILCOCK, WILLIAM.
- SMITH, FREDERICK W.
- SHONE, JOHN.
- SMITH, ROBERT H.
- SHELDON, JAMES.
- SIMPSON, J. A.
- SWINDLES, J. W.
- SWEENEY, THOMAS.
- SUGRUE, CHARLES.
- SEDDON, H. S.
- SINGLETON, ROBERT.
- SIMMONS, H. S.
- STEVENSON, S.
- TAYLOR, WALTER.
- TYSON, WILLIAM.
- TUDOR, WILLIAM.
- TIMMS, JOSEPH.
- TIMMS, THOMAS A.
- TONGE, THOMAS.
- TINSLEY, JOHN.
- TERRILL, THOMAS.
- TAYLOR, ROBERT.
- TAYLOR, ROBERT.
- TARRANT, DAVID.
- TURNER, W.
- VARLEY, BENJAMIN R.
- WALTON, WILLIAM H.
- WALTERS, JAMES.
- WALLWORK, JAMES.
- WATSON, JOHN.
- WILLETTS, EDWARD.
- WOOD, WILLIAM.
- WORRALL, JNO.
- WALMSLEY, DAVID W.
- WALKER, ROBERT.
- WILLETTS, SAMUEL.
- WATERS, HENRY.
- WHITTALL, ROBERT.
- WEST, GEORGE.
- WILLIAMSON, JOHN.
- WELSH, JOHN.
- WALTER, J. W.
- WARREN, HAROLD.
- WORTHINGTON, J. H.
- WRIGHT, HAROLD.

SAMUEL ASHTON & CO. LTD.

- ADAMS, WILLIAM EDWARD.
- ANTROBUS, BENJAMIN.
- ASHTON, THOMAS.
- BIRTWISTLE, ARTHUR.
- BIRTWISTLE, ERNEST.
- BOWLES, SAMUEL.
- BOYLAM, WILLIAM.
- BRADBURY, JAMES.
- BRADLEY, HARRY.
- BRIDGE, HARRY.
- BROE, LEONARD.
- BUSHELL, LAWRENCE.
- CAIN, JOHN.
- CHILD, ARTHUR.
- CLOUGH, WILLIAM.
- COPE, RICHARD LAWTON.
- CONWAY, FRED.
- COPPLE, ERNEST.
- COOPER, FRANK.
- COPPLE, GEORGE E.
- COX, ARTHUR.
- DAVIES, HARRY.
- DEWHIRST, SAMUEL.
- DYSON, JOHN.
- EDDOWS, JOHN THOMAS.
- FLANNIGAN, JOHN.
- GLEAVE, HERBERT.
- HALL, GEORGE W.
- HALLIWELL, HARRY.
- HARDY, ALFRED.
- HARDY, FRED.
- HILL, BENJAMIN.
- HOOLEY, ALBERT.
- HOWELLS, THOMAS.
- JANION, JAMES HENRY.
- JONES, EDWIN.
- KELLY, JOSEPH.
- KITE, GEORGE.
- LAYTON, THOMAS.
- LEE, WILLIAM.
- LOGAN, DANIEL.
- LYNCH, JOHN.
- MATHER, ALFRED LEVI.
- MATHER, CHARLES.
- MATHER, LEVI.
- MAYCOX, ALFRED.
- McCORMICK, JOHN.
- MORAN, WALTER JOHN.
- MORRIS, JOSEPH.
- NAYLOR, JOHN.
- NEALE, JAS. ALEXANDER.
- PARKER, GEORGE.
- POTTS, RALPH.
- REECE, WILLIAM.
- ROBERTS, EDWARD.
- ROSCOE, FRANK.
- SCOTT, GEORGE.
- SEDDON, JAMES.
- SHAW, ARTHUR.
- SILLITOE, JAMES.
- SLATER, CLEMENT.
- SLAUGHTER, ARTHUR.
- SMITH, HAROLD.
- STAKE, RICHARD.
- STOKES, GEORGE.
- SUMNER, THOMAS.
- THROUP, HENRY.
- TURNER, ROBERT.
- VICKERS, JAMES.
- WILLIAMS, WALTER.
- WILKES, JOSEPH.
- WOOD, JOHN WILLIAM.

The English Velvet & Cord Dyers' Association, Limited.

THE LITTLEBOROUGH DYEING CO. LTD.

ADAMS, S.	CROSSLEY, O.	HOLT, A	ROBINSON, J.
ARMITAGE, A.	CROSSLEY, H.	HIBBERT, G.	ROYCE, A. E.
ANDERSON, W.	CROSSLEY, A.	HUTTON, J.	RHODES, J. T.
AUSTIN, J.	CROSSLEY, A.	HAIGH, A.	SCHOFIELD, S.
ASPINALL, H.	CRYER, J.	JACKSON, H.	SCOTT, J.
ANDERTON, J.	CRYER, F.	JONES, G. W.	SCOTT, J. W.
BAMFORD, C. A.	CARTWRIGHT, F.	KERSHAW, E.	STRAWSON, E.
BLACK, J.	DAY, W.	LONGLEY, F.	STOTT, E.
BUCKLEY, R.	DIXON, J.	McKENZIE, T.	TAYLOR, R.
BRIERLEY, N.	DUGGAN, D.	MATHIESON, J.	TETLOW, J.
BERNARD, F.	DAY, G.	MEADOWCROFT, R.	TEW, T.
BUCKLEY, R.	DEVINE, T.	MARTIN, J.	THOMPSON, J.
BENTLEY, H.	EGGLES, S.	MORRIS, E.	WARD, S.
BEMMINGTON, E.	EVES, J.	MARSH, W.	WALSH, J.
CARMAN, H. B.	FIELDEN, J.	MILLS, A.	WALSH, P.
CALVERT, T.	GRIFFEN, T.	NIGHTINGALE, C.	WALSH, T.
CONNOLLEY, J.	GRIBBEN, J.	PERKS, T.	WALKER, H.
COUNSELL, E.	GREENBANK, A.	PRIOR, H. W.	WHITWORTH, C.
CROSSLEY, C.	HOLMES, H.	PILLING, J.	

DRIVER, GOODIER & CO., LTD.

BAKER, A.	DAY, F.	HANDS, JNO.	MYLES, G.
BEVAN, P.	DARCY, J.	HANDS, JAMES.	SHEPLEY, E.
BIRCHALL, J.	DAVITT, H.	HARROP, JAMES.	SHUTTLEWORTH, D.
BESWICK, G.	DIXON, P. A.	HINDLEY, E.	WALTON, J.
BOLTON, WILFRED.	DOXEY, W.	JONES, S.	WALTON, W.
BRIDGE, J.	ELLISON, P.	LEVER, W.	WEST, G.
BURGESS, H.	ETCHELLS, A.	LINDLEY, J.	WILLIAMSON, W.
CARSON, H.	ETCHELLS, J.	MACLAREN, C.	WILSON, E.
CLAYTON, A.	FAGIN, W.	MAYO, J.	WHITEHEAD, E.
CLEWES, J.	GARVEY, L.	MELLOR, F.	
COLLINSON, J.	HALL, R.	MULLEN, JESSE.	

JOSEPH CLARE, LTD.

ANKERS, J. W.	EVANS, W.	INGHAM, R.	RUSHTON, H.
ANDREWS, F.	FULLER, T.	JONES, A.	RIGBY, R.
BARNES, J.	GROGAN, C.	KENWORTHY, R.	SOUTHWORTH, W.
BELL, W. H.	GREENHALGH, J.	LORD, D. E.	TAYLOR, E.
BELL, S.	HOLLOWAY, J.	LEYLAND, G.	WALKER, JOSEPH.
BETLEY, R.	HARDY, E.	LEE, F.	WALKER, JOHN.
COOKSON, E.	HILL, R.	MARSHALL, H.	WILLIAMS, A.
COOKSON, C.	HOWARD, W.	PALMER, T.	WILLIAMS, W.
DEWHURST, R.	HUSBAND, V.	POWELL, W. H.	

JOHN BROWN & CO. LTD.

BUCKLEY, JOSEPH.	HEPWORTH, FRED.	LOCKWOOD, HARRY.	STARKEY, ELLIOTT.
DENTON, CHARLES.	KAYE, JOE.	MORTON, RAWSON.	SKEEN, DENNIS.
DICKENSON, GEORGE EDW.	KENNERDALE, TOM.	RADCLIFFE, JOSEPH.	WATERTON, JOSEPH ALF.

CRIMSWORTH WATER DYEING CO. LTD.

ASHWORTH, T. R.	WADSWORTH, W.	WILDE, F.	WILDE, J. W.

STUBBIN HOLME DYEING CO. LTD.

RAWSON, LESLIE.	SMITH, EDWARD.	UTTLEY, ARNOLD.	WILLIAMS, CYRIL.

JOHN WHITELEY, LTD.

KEARNEY, J.	TAYLOR, W. H.	TREWARTHA, P.	WELBURN, W.

VARLEY BROS., LTD.

CLARKE, EDWARD.	MITCHELL, THOMAS F.	MULLEY, SAMUEL A.

ROLL OF HONOUR.

The East Lancashire Mills Company Limited.

82, Princess Street,
—MANCHESTER.—

Lance-Corpl. T. CHADWICK,
  18th Batt. Manchester Regt.

Private G. ROBBINS,
  18th Batt. Manchester Regt.

Private H. BRETT,
  20th Batt. Manchester Regt.

Private R. SIMPSON,
  20th Batt. Manchester Regt.

Private J. KEENAN,
  23rd Batt. Manchester Regt.

Lance-Corpl. W. EATOCK,
  2/1st Cheshire Yeomanry.

Private H. MYATT,
  South Lancashire Regt.

ROLL OF HONOUR.

Eadie Bros. & Co.

LIMITED.

(Manchester Office only).

ALBERT WARD,
  17th Batt. Manchester Regiment, 4th Platoon, A. Coy.

Private GEORGE McGREGOR,
  S4/085654, A. Coy., Army Service Corps.

2nd Lieut. DONALD EADIE,
  7th Dragoon Guards.

2nd Lieut. NORMAN EADIE,
  3/9th Glasgow Highlanders.

2nd Lieut. PETER EADIE,
  Renfrewshire (Fortress) Roy. Engineers.

Also 40 men from the Paisley Works.

Roll of Honour.

Sir James Farmer & Sons, Ltd.

List of Men Serving with the Forces.

Capt. D. G. NORTON	1/7th Batt. Lancashire Fusiliers.
G. BERRY	1/7th Batt. Lancashire Fusiliers.
W. BULLEN	1/8th Batt. Lancashire Fusiliers.
W. CLARKSON	King's Royal Winchester Rifles.
R. COPELAND	1/8th Batt. Lancashire Fusiliers.
J. CRAIGIE	1/8th Batt. Lancashire Fusiliers.
T. GREYSTOCK	6th Royal Scots.
E. GROVES	Royal Engineers, 5th Siege Co.
R. HORSFALL	East Lancashire Engineers (T.F.).
T. HURST	7th Batt. Lancs. Fusiliers (Bantams).
E. JONES	Royal Army Medical Corps (T.F.).
J. LEE	East Lancashire Engineers.
J. LEE	East Lancashire Engineers (T.F.).
R. PERKINS	7th Batt. King's Own Scottish Borderers.
T. PORTLOCK	1/7th Batt. Lancashire Fusiliers.
E. ROBERTS	7th Batt. Lancs. Fusiliers (Bantams).
J. SHEERIN	1/8th Batt. Lancashire Fusiliers.
J. WALKER	1/8th Batt. Lancashire Fusiliers.
J. WONDERLEY	2nd East Lancs. Royal Horse Artillery.

Roll of Honour.

THE FINE COTTON SPINNERS'
AND
DOUBLERS' ASSOCIATION LTD.

✶ ✶ ✶

CENTRAL OFFICE STAFF.

✶ ✶ ✶

OLDFIELD, Capt. E. G. W.
DIXON, Lieut. E. M.
DIXON, Lieut. A. E. B.
ALCOCK, JOHN.
BAGNALL, VINCENT.
BANKS, JOSEPH.
BATTERSBY, A.
BENNETT, FRANK.
BERESFORD, Junr., W.
BURROWS, W.
CATLOW, JAMES R.
COONEY, J. D.
COWDELL, A.
EDMONDSON, C. A.
EDMONDSON, L. A.
FARRELLY, J.
GOMERSALL, W.
GOSLING, JAMES.
GRIMSHAW, STANLEY.
HARRISON, Junr., THOMAS.
HILTON, H. A.
HIRST, GERALD WM.
HOUCHIN, B.

KNAGGS, W. H.
LINGARD, H.
MEIKLE, JOHN.
MERCHANT, ALFRED.
OWENS, JAMES J.
OWENS, T. C.
PANTER, EDGAR.
PARKER, N.
PORTER, T. C.
PRICKETT, RODNEY.
PRITCHARD, ARTHUR.
RAMSBOTTOM, F.
REILLY, E.
ROBERTS, JOHN.
ROYLE, STANLEY.
SILCOCK, FRANK HOWARD.
SILCOCK, W. S.
STOCKTON, ERNEST.
TWELLS, E. J.
UTTING, R. A.
WAITE, A.
WILSON, ERNEST.
WILSON, JAMES H.

THE FINE COTTON SPINNERS
AND
DOUBLERS' ASSOCIATION LTD.

Roll of Honour—continued.

BAZLEY BROS., LTD.

LANGTRY, Lieut. R. R.	GRIFFITHS, W.	MOORES, T.
ACTON, F.	HACKETT, H.	MORLEY, J.
ADSHEAD, J.	HARRIS, T.	NESBITT, J.
ALBISTON, J.	HAYES, E.	PARKER, T.
BAILEY, R.	HEWITT, T.	REGAN, G.
BARTON, A.	HOGAN, H.	ROBERTS, J.
BOLLINGTON, H.	HOULDSWORTH, A.	SLATER, F.
BURNS, A.	HUSSEY, L.	STOKES, G.
BURNS, T.	HURST, H.	STOKES, J.
BYRNE, J.	JONES, C.	SPENCER, G.
BYROM, G.	JORDAN, JAMES.	TAYLOR, F.
CHEETHAM, A.	JORDAN, JAMES.	TAYLOR, G.
CHERRY, B.	KYNSTON, J. R.	TAYLOR, N.
CLAYTON, A.	LEACH, N.	THORLEY, M.
CROPPER, A.	LYNCH, J.	TILLISON, C.
DAVIES, T.	MARLEY, T.	TIGHE, W.
EDWARDS, E.	McALLISTER, T.	TIMPERLEY, T.
FITZPATRICK, C.	McCORMICK, H.	TUHEY, P.
GILLESPIE, C.	McGREVEY, H.	WILD, G.
GREENHALGH, A.	MILLER, W.	

JAMES and WAINWRIGHT BELLHOUSE, LTD.

SWINDELLS, Captain ALAN CAWLEY.	BARNES, R.	PILLING, J.
ABRAHAMS, W.	DEAN, O.	RICHARDSON, J.
ATKINSON, J.	DRONSFIELD, S.	TAYLOR, R.
BAINBRIDGE, E.	GREENHALGH, H.	TRANTER, J.
	HOPKINS, A.	ROSE, W.

C. E. BENNETT and CO., LTD.

ALTY, ALBERT.	HALL, W.	MORGAN, W.
ANDERSON, G.	HARRIS, J. E.	MURPHY, F.
BENNETT, R. W.	HARRISON, E.	NEWTON, W.
BENNISON, A.	HART V.	PARKIN, E.
BLOOMFIELD, W. H.	HICKS, C.	PARSLOW, A.
BROADFIELD, L.	HIGGINS, E.	PHILLIPS, J. L.
CARROLL, T.	HODKINSON, J. W.	REGAN, J.
CHADWICK, H.	HOLT, A.	SANDS, R.
CHADWICK, W.	JOHNSTON, F. J.	SCOTT, G. E.
CHAPPELL, J.	KEELAN, P.	SHAW, D.
COSTELLO, L.	KEMP, M.	SHELDON, A.
CROFT, A.	LEACH, E.	SHERRATT, E.
DICKINSON, T.	LYNCH, H. T.	SMITH, R.
ENGLAND, F.	McEOWN, J.	SUGDEN, J. H.
FISHWICK, W.	MASSEY, W.	WALL, R.
FLETCHER, J.	MILLINGTON, S.	WILKINSON, J.
GILL, J.	MOLLOY, D.	WRIGHT, W. C.
GRAHAM, PHILIP.	MORRIS, S.	WYCH, H. L.

THE FINE COTTON SPINNERS
AND
DOUBLERS' ASSOCIATION LTD.

Roll of Honour—continued.

THE BOLTON SPINNING and DOUBLING CO., LTD.

BROWNLOW, JOSEPH.	HILL, JOHN H.	WALKER, HENRY.

F. W. BOUTH and CO., LTD.

ALDRED, F. W.	HOLMES, J. W.	WOOD, A. R.
GALVIN, JAMES.	LYTHGOE, THOMAS C.	WOOD, PERCY.
HINDLEY, JOSEPH.	PILLING, JOHN W.	WORRALL, GEORGE.
HINDLEY, SAMUEL.	SMITH, F. J.	YATES, OSMOND.

M. G. and A. BRADLEY, LTD.

THOMPSON, Captain H. B.	GILBERT, J. W.	HILL, F.
BARKER, CHARLES.	HALL, Lce.-Cpl. H.	LITTLEWOOD, Lce.-Cpl. H.
BODEN, J.	HALL, CHARLES.	MORRIS, S.

J. HENDERSON BROWN, LTD.

BARDSLEY, DANIEL.	HOLMES, JAMES.	McDERMOTT, JAMES.
CAMERON, JAMES.	JENNINGS, CHARLES.	MORAN, JOHN.
HEAP, WILLIAM.	MALONE, LAURENCE.	MORAN, JOHN HENRY.

BROWN and FALLOWS, LTD.

BOOTH, SIMEON.	FORSHAW, FRED.	OWEN, WILLIAM.
CARROLL, HARRY.	MARSH, ROBERT.	

JOHN CASH and SONS, LTD.

SAVAGE, Junr., CHARLES.

HECTOR CHRISTIE, LTD.

ABRA, GEORGE.	HERRINGTON, EDGAR.	ROBINSON, JOHN.
CARDUS, JOHN THOMAS.	HILTON, JOHN WILLIAM.	WHAITES, J. W.
FRANKLAND, THOMAS LORD.	REILLY, HENRY.	WOOFF, ROBERT.
HAYES, FRANK.	ROBINSON, ALFRED.	

GORSEY BANK DOUBLING CO., LTD.

ALLCOCK, WILLIAM.	HIGHAM, JOSEPH.	McCANN, ALBERT.
ARDEN, JAMES EDWARD.	HOPWOOD, JAMES.	PERKINS, JOHN.
ARRANDALE, JOSEPH.	JACKSON, GEORGE.	POTTS, ARTHUR.
BOOTH, RICHARD.	JONES, JOHN.	PRESCOTT, WILLIAM.
CUNNINGHAM, JOHN.	LEA, HERBERT.	RAYMENT, ALFRED.
EYRES, CHARLES WALTER.	LOFTUS, WILLIAM.	STUBBS, JAMES.
GRATRIX, JOHN.	MARSLAND, CHARLES.	WILSON, GEORGE.
HARRISON, WILLIAM.	MARSLAND, FRED.	

THE FINE COTTON SPINNERS AND DOUBLERS' ASSOCIATION LTD.

Roll of Honour—continued.

W. HOLLAND and SONS, LTD.

NATION, Capt. WILFRED C.
WARD, Lieut. G. S.
BLEARS, 2nd Lt. THOMAS E.
APLIN, CLIFTON.
BAGSHAW, WILLIAM.
BIRCH, THORNTON.
BROWN, WM.
CHIDGEY, JAMES.
CLOUGH, ROBERT.
COATS, W.
COOPER, ALFRED.
CROOK, J.
DICKINSON, PIERCEY.
DODD, ALFRED.
DODD, GEORGE.
EVANS, GEORGE BEVAN.
FAWCETT, JOHN.
FLANAGAN, ALFRED.
FRAZER, ALEXANDER.
GREENHALGH, JAMES.
GREGORY, WALTER.
GRIMSDITCH, JOHN HENRY.
HALL, SAMUEL.
HEADON, HARRY.
HEWITSON, THOMAS.
HOLLIS, ARTHUR.
HOLT, JAMES.
JONES, JOSHUA.
MAGUIRE, PATRICK.
MARKHAM, THOMAS.
McHENRY, ALBERT.
MULLEN, CHARLES.
OWEN, CHARLES.
PALMER, HERBERT.
PRICE, THOMAS.
QUINN, T.
RATCLIFFE, ARTHUR.
ROBINSON, WILLIAM.
ROWBOTTOM, GEORGE.
RUTHERFORD, JAMES.
RYAN, J. W.
SHARP, EDWARD.
SLATTERY, PERCY.
SMITH, W.
TAYLOR, A.
TRACEY, THOMAS.
TYLER, W.
WARD, ERNEST.
WEARDEN, THOMAS.
WHITWORTH, HARRY.
WRIGHT, CLARENCE CECIL.

THOMAS HOULDSWORTH and CO., LTD.

WRIGHT, 2nd Lieut. MARCUS T.
ARSTALL, GEORGE.
BANCROFT, ERIC.
BERRISFORD, THOMAS.
COLLINS, ERNEST.
CRAIG, SYDNEY.
CROSSLEY, WILLIAM.
DYSON, JOSEPH.
ECKERSLEY, WILLIAM.
GOODIER, ERNEST.
GOULD, FRANK.
GRADWELL, ALBERT.
GRIMSHAW, LEN.
HEMMINGWAY, THOMAS.
HILLIER, THOMAS.
HINDLEY, ROBERT.
HOLEHOUSE, WALTER.
HULLEY, WILLIAM.
KNOTT, ROBERT.
LONGDEN, ALBERT.
LOMAX, HENRY.
MAGEE, SIDNEY.
MacNEALL, ALOYSIUS.
MONKS, ARTHUR.
MONKS, DAVID.
MONKS, HENRY.
MOSS, JOSEPH.
STEVENSON, JACK.
TRAVIS, ALBERT.
UNSWORTH, BERNARD.
WILD, JOSEPH.

THE JACKSON STREET SPINNING CO., LTD.

ASTLEY, HENRY.
BATEMAN, G. BROOK.
BURT, W.
CONNOLY, A.
EVERY, JOHN.
FANNON, M.
FINN, W.
FLANAGAN, DENIS.
FRAIL, HENRY.
GOWRIE, T.
HALL, J.
HARWOOD, ROBERT.
HERRIOTT, NATHANIEL.
HORROCKS, EDWARD.
HULME, A.
ISHERWOOD, F.
LENEHAN, T. H.
LINDSAY, JAMES.
MASKREY, ERNEST.
MASKREY, JOHN.
McCABE, JAMES.
MULLEY, W.
RABY, WILLIAM.
RICHARDSON, JOSEPH.
RIDGARD, W.
ROTHWELL, R.
TOMLINSON, T.
WOOD, REGINALD M.

THE FINE COTTON SPINNERS
AND
DOUBLERS' ASSOCIATION LTD.

Roll of Honour—continued.

JOHN KNOTT and SONS, LTD.

ANDREW, HARRY.
BAIRSTOW, ARTHUR.
BAMFORD, ARTHUR.
BARRETT, FRED.
BENNETT, ALBERT.
BURROWS, JAMES.
CAINE, SYDNEY.
DAWSON, FRED.
DRINKWATER, WILLIAM.
JACKSON, GEORGE.
JONES, HARRY.
KINDER, HERBERT.
LEE, MATTHEW.
LIVESEY, ALBERT.
McDONALD, WILLIAM.
OGDEN, SAMUEL.
PENNY, THOMAS.
ROTHWELL, MILES.
SCHOFIELD, JOHN.
SQUIRES, FRED.
THORNLEY, ARTHUR.
TRAYERS, THOMAS.
WALKER, WILLIAM.
WHITEHEAD, JAMES.

H. W. LEE and CO., LTD.

BAILEY, HARRY.
BRAMWELL, THOMAS R. A.
BYRNE, JAMES.
DEWITT, PHILIP.
DUDLEY, WILLIAM.
EYRES, CHARLES WM.
JAMES, ALFRED.
JONES, EDGAR.
LIVSAY, ALFRED.
MURRAY, FRANK.
ROYLANCE, CHARLES.
STANLEY, CHARLES W.
TATTERSALL, LAWRENCE.
WHITEHEAD, THOMAS.
YEOMANS, GEORGE.

LEE SPINNING CO., LTD.

BEECH, CHARLES.
BLAKELEY, SAMUEL.
BOSTOCK, THOMAS.
GIDMAN, WILLIAM.
GOODMAN, JOSEPH.
HIGGINBOTHAM, CHARLES.
KNOWLES, JOHN.
LEE, JOSEPH.
McGOVERN, JAMES.
McGUINNESS, JAMES.
MORAN, STEPHEN.
O'BRIEN, JOHN.
OTTLEY, WILLIAM.
POWELL, WILLIAM.
PRESCOTT, FRED.
TIPLADY, J.
WILSON, JOB.
WYCHE, CORNELIUS.

McCONNEL and CO., LTD.
Ancoats.

ALLCOCK, GEORGE.
ANDREW, ERNEST.
ARMSTRONG, WILLIAM.
BAILEY, JOSEPH.
BAILIFF, WILLIAM.
BATES, JOSEPH.
BEARD, JOHN.
BEARD, JOSEPH.
BEARD, WALTER.
BECKETT, GEORGE.
BOWDEN, R. S.
BRADLEY, ERNEST.
BRANGHAM, DUDLEY.
BRICKELL, WILLIAM.
BRICKMAN, WILLIAM.
BRIDDON, JAMES.
BURGESS, ARTHUR.
BURNS, J.
CHADWICK, JOHN.
CHESNEY, JOS.
CLARE, DAVID.
COLLIER, JESSE.
COOKE, CHARLES.
DAVENPORT, RODGER.
DENNY, HENRY.
ENTWISTLE, JOHN RALPH.
EVANS, GEORGE.
FISHWICK, GEORGE.
FITZPATRICK, GEORGE.
FOY, THOMAS.
GAFFIN, WILLIAM.
GILL, HARTLEY.
GILLETT, THOMAS.
GREENWOOD, HARRY.
HADFIELD, FRED.
HANNIGAN, THOMAS.
HARDY, HARRY.
HARRISON, JAMES.
HASLAM, JOHN.
HASLAM, WILFRED.
HENNEGAN, WILLIAM.
HENTHORNE, JOSEPH.
HESSEY, NORMAN.
HIGGINS, ARTHUR.
HILL, JOSEPH.
HINCKLEY, WILLIAM.
HODGES, JAMES HUTTON.
HOLT, THOMAS.
ISAIAH, THOMAS.
KEELING, HARRY.
LANE, FRED.
LEADBETTER, JOHN.
LLEWELLYN, ERNEST.
LOMAX, ROBERT TAYLOR.
MACK, WM.
MALONE, EDWARD.
MARSH, HUBERT.

THE FINE COTTON SPINNERS
AND
DOUBLERS' ASSOCIATION LTD.

Roll of Honour—continued.

McCONNEL and CO., LTD.

MARSHALL, JOSEPH.
MATTHEWS, JAMES.
MATTHEWS, JOSEPH.
McCANN, JAMES HENRY.
McDONALD, SAMUEL.
McMAHON, JAMES.
MEREDITH, MAURICE.
MOON, FRED.
MOORE, ARTHUR.
MOORE, EDWARD.
MOORE, JOHN.
MOSS, ELLIS.
MULLIN, JAMES.
MURPHY, J. A.
NORCROSS, FRANK.
PAGE, JAMES HENRY.
PILLING, FRED.
POWNER, CHRISTOPHER.

PRICE, WILLIAM.
RIDDLE, T. R.
RILEY, WILLIAM.
ROBERTS, ARTHUR.
ROWLES, NED.
SCOWCROFT, ARTHUR.
SAXON, ALBERT.
SEATON, THOMAS.
SHARPLES, WILFRED.
SHERIFF, FRED'K. FRENCH.
SMITH, ARTHUR.
SMITH, EDWARD.
SMITH, WILLIAM.
SPENCER, ALEC.
SWEENEY, JOHN.
SWINDELLS, JOHN.
TAYLOR, GEORGE.
TAYLOR, JOHN RICHARD.

TUNNICLIFFE, ALBERT.
TURNER, ANDREW.
TURNER, ROBERT.
TURNER, THOMAS.
VENABLES, HARRY.
WALLACE, HAROLD.
WALLWORTH, HAROLD.
WARBURTON, JOHN HENRY.
WARD, TOM.
WATTS, WILLIAM HENRY.
WHITTAKER, H. W.
WHITTAKER, WM. ALBERT.
WHITTINGHAM, JOHN.
WILKS, FRED.
WILSON, MATTHEW.
WOOD, WILLIAM.
WOODWARD, JOHN ALBERT.
WORSWICK, JOHN.

Lumb Mills.

ANDREW, GEORGE.
BAGULEY, JOHN.
BAKER, GILBERT.
BARNES, FREDERICK.
BAILEY, EDWARD.
BAILEY, HARRY.
BELL, ERNEST RICHARD.
BELL, ROBERT.
BENNETT, JOHN.
BIBBY, EDMUND.
BIRKENSHAW, FRED.
CAMPBELL, JOHN WILLIAM.
CARLING, THOS.
CARROLL, JAMES.
CLEGG, ALFRED VINCENT.
COOKE, HARRY.
CUMMINS, ROBERT CHARLES.
DANIELS, JOHN.
DAVIES, GEORGE.
DOOLAN, JAMES ANDREW.
DOYLE, HENRY.
DOLAN, WILLIAM.
ECKERSLEY, JOHN WILLIAM.
ELLIS, GEORGE.
EVANS, CHARLES.
FLETCHER, RICHARD.
FORREST, THOMAS.

FOSTER, JOHN.
GOULD, ALBERT.
GREGORY, JOHN.
HALL, JOHN.
HANCOCK, LEONARD.
HANSON, GEORGE EDWARD.
HARDMAN, WALTER.
HARRIS, JOHN WILLIAM.
HAZEL, W. H.
HELME, JAMES.
HIBBERT, J. W.
HINDLE, PETER HOPKINSON.
HOLROYD, HARRY.
HOPKINSON, HAROLD.
HOWARD, FRANK.
JACK, LAWRENCE EDWARD.
JOBSON, ROBERT.
JONES, EDWARD.
LANGTON, AARON.
LANGTON, JOHN.
LAMB, GEORGE HENRY.
LANE, WALTER.
LEWIS, ALBERT.
LUMLEY, WILLIAM.
MARLAND, JAMES.
MARLAND, WILLIAM.

MILLS, PERCY.
OAKES, LEONARD.
PRIDHAM, JESS.
PUTTOCK, SYDNEY.
REEVES, CHARLES.
ROBERTS, JOHN THOMAS.
SAXON, T.
SHAW, HENRY.
SHEPLEY, JOHN WILLIAM.
SLATER, CHARLES.
SMITH, SAMUEL.
SMITH, WILLIAM.
SOUTHWORTH, STEPHEN.
SULLIVAN, JOHN.
SUMMERSGILL, JONATHAN.
TINKER, GEORGE.
TOWNLEY, THOMAS.
TRAVIS, HARRY.
VALENTINE, LARA.
WALL, RICHARD.
WATSON, LAWRENCE.
WILLEY, GEORGE.
WILSON, J.
WINWARD, THOMAS.
WORRAL, ALFRED ERNEST.
WRIGHT, HENRY ARTHUR.

THE FINE COTTON SPINNERS
AND
DOUBLERS' ASSOCIATION LTD

Roll of Honour—continued.

THE MANCHESTER REELING and WINDING CO., LTD.
Manchester.

ASHTON, JAMES.
BROWN, WILLIAM.
FUGE, ALFRED HENRY.
JENKINSON, JAMES.
PARKER, JAMES.
WILD, ROBERT.

JAMES MARSDEN and SONS, LTD.

CARROLL, Lieut.-Colonel.
MARSDEN, Lieut. H. R.
AINSWORTH, HARRY.
AINSWORTH, JOSEPH.
ASHTON, THOMAS.
ASPEN, ALBERT.
BARLOW, BENJAMIN.
BENTLEY, WM.
BERRY, JAMES.
BERRY, C. H.
BRABBING, DAVID.
BRABBING, JOSEPH.
BRAZIER, EDWARD.
BRIDGE, J. H.
BROUGHTON, J. H.
CHADWICK, JESSE.
CHADWICK, J.
CHADWICK, JOHN.
CHADWICK, JOSEPH.
CLARKE, ARTHUR.
CLARKE, FRED.
COLLIER, ROBERT.
COLLISON, W. K.
CROMPTON, G. W.
CROSSLEY, WILLIAM.
DAGNALL, OSWALD.
DANDY, WALTER.
DAVIES, EDWARD.
DEWHURST WILLIAM.
DICKINSON, JAMES.
DORNING, FRANK.
DOUGLAS, THOS.
DUNN, THOMAS.
EGLIN, THOMAS.
FURNIVAL, JOHN.
GOWAN, PETER.
GREENHALGH, JOHN.
GREENHALGH, RICHARD.
GREENHALGH, ROBERT.
HAMER, JAMES.
HARDY, JOS.
HASLAM, ALBERT.
HEALEY, JOSEPH.
HENNEFOR, DANIEL.
HENNEFER, WM.
HERIOT, DAVID.
HIBBERT, WM.
HIGGINS, B.
HODGES, E. A.
HODKINSON, PETER.
HOLLAND, HANDEL.
HOLMES, GEORGE.
HOLMES, HERBERT.
HOLMES, THOS.
HUGHES, THOMAS.
HUTCHINSON, G. T.
JONES, J. C.
JONES, JOHN E.
JONES, SAMUEL.
JOULE, WILLIAM.
KAY, ROBERT.
KELLY, JOHN.
KIPPAX, THOMAS.
LEATHER, JOSEPH.
LIVESEY, WILLIAM.
LONGWORTH, DAVID.
MAHR, THOS.
MARSH, T. H.
MARSH, W. E.
MARSHALL, E.
MARSHALL, J. R.
MATTHEWS, STEPHEN.
MATTHEWS, WALTER.
McARDLE, F.
McGRATH, F.
McGRATH, J.
McMILLAN, W.
McNICHOLAS, F.
MERCER, THOS.
MERCER, V.
MONKS, WILLIAM.
MORRIS, GEORGE.
MORT, A. R.
MOTTLER, ERNEST.
NAYLON, RICHARD.
NAYLOR, GEORGE A.
NEWSOME, JAMES.
NORRIS, H. S.
NORRIS, J.
NORTON, T. H.
PARKINSON, FRED.
PARTINGTON, H.
PEMBERTON, HAROLD.
PEMBERTON, JOHN.
PITFIELD, J. T.
PLATT, BRIDGMAN.
POLLITT, ALFRED.
RHODES, THOS.
RICHARD, W. J.
ROBINSON, EDWIN.
ROLLINSON, ROBERT.
ROSEVERE, HENRY.
SANDERS, THOMAS.
SEDDON, WILLIAM.
SHUTTLEWORTH, JAMES.
SHUTTLEWORTH, SAMUEL.
SHUTTLEWORTH, THOMAS (A).
SMEDLEY, J. S.
SOFIELD, SAMUEL.
SOUTHERN, GEO. T.
SPEIGHT, JAS. B.
THORNLEY, Junr., THOMAS.
TINDSLEY, DANIEL.
TINDSLEY, H.
TYRER, WALTER.
VICKERS, A. E.
WALKER, FRED.
WALSH, ROBERT.
WALLWORK, ROBERT.
WALWORTH, ALBERT.
WARWICK, COLIN.
WHALLEY, JOHN (A).
WHITTLE, EDWARD.
WHITTLE, JOSEPH.
WILKINS, NORMAN.
WILKINSON, JOS.
WILLETT, THOMAS.
WILLETT, WILLIAM.
WILLIAMS, A.
WILLIAMS, JOHN.
WILLIAMS, THOMAS.
WILLIAMS, WM.
WILLIAMSON, STANLEY.
WOODCOCK, HARRY.
WYRE, PATRICK.
YATES, ERNEST.

THE FINE COTTON SPINNERS
AND
DOUBLERS' ASSOCIATION LTD.

Roll of Honour—continued.

ROBERT MARSLAND and CO., LTD.

BEST, C.
BRADLEY, H.
BRATT, W.
BRINDLEY, J.
BROADBENT, G.
BROWN, D.
CAMPFIELD, J.
CARLINE, W.
CLARK, R.
CONOVAN, J.
DUCKWORTH, J.
DUNNE, G. A.
FROBISHER, J.
GILL, A.
GILL, E.
GOODWIN, FRED.
GREGORY, A.
HAVAKIN, T.
HENDERSON, J.
HICKLIN, JOHN.
HICKLIN, JOSEPH.
HIGGINBOTTOM, JOSEPH.
HIND, J.
HOWE, T.
HULME, G.
KEMP, JOSEPH.
KIERNAN, E.
LANNON, J.
LAVERTY, W.
LEESON, G.
LESTER, F.
LINGARD, F.
LUCAS, R.
MacKAY, S.
MADDEN, D.
McCANN, N.
OLDHAM, S.
PARKER, A.
PLANT, H.
POTTS, F.
RICHARDSON, E.
ROBINSON, J.
ROSS, J.
SEDDON, H.
SHAW, F.
WATTS, J.
WHITTAKER, G.
WHITTAKER, W.
WILKINSON, J.
WILSON, C.
WILSON, S.

SAMUEL MOORHOUSE, LTD.

Brinksway Bank Mill.

BENT, ALFRED.
BRADBURN, ROBERT.
BRITNOR, HAROLD.
CORAM, ERNEST.
CROSTHWAITE, JOHN.
HEAVYSIDE, ERNEST.
HEAVYSIDE, GEORGE.
HOLDEN, THOMAS.
ORR, DAVID.
RALPHS, HARRY.
SALT, WILLIAM.
TURNER, JAMES.

Wear Mill.

BARLOW, S.
BENT, S.
BOWEN, J.
BROWN, G.
CARSON, T.
COLLIER, R.
CORAM, W.
CROSSLEY, J.
FLANAGAN, J.
HADFIELD, J.
HATTON, W.
HEAVYSIDE, J.
HIBBERT, W.
HIND, J.
HOLLAND, S.
HOWSON, W.
JACQUES, J.
JEPSON, W.
JONES, J.
LEE, A.
LEE, J.
MADDEN, E.
MANFREDI, L.
McCOY, F.
MEAKIN, W.
MOORES, W.
PEARSON, H.
PEARSON, J.
PYOTT, F.
RANDALL, R.
RAWLINSON, A.
ROWLANDS, W.
TETLOW, H.
TRACEY, F.
WILLIAMSON, F.
WILLIAMSON, T.
WOODFINDERS, J.
WORSLEY, H.
YATES, J. T.

A. and G. MURRAY, LTD.

ALEXANDER, SAMUEL.
BETHELL, ALFRED.
BETHELL, ARTHUR.
BROWNLOW, WILLIAM HY.
CAVANAGH, THOMAS.
CLARKE, JOHN T.
COOPER, ARTHUR.
DREWERY, JIM.
ELTON, WALTER.
FITZGERALD, THOMAS.
GREGSON, JOSEPH J.
GRIMSHAW, JOHN W.
HALL, JOHN.
HARRISON, ROBERT.
HEATH, HARRY.

THE FINE COTTON SPINNERS
AND
DOUBLERS' ASSOCIATION LTD.

Roll of Honour—continued.

A. and G. MURRAY, LTD.—Continued.

HIGGINS, JOHN.
HILLIER, WILLIAM.
JACKSON, HAROLD.
JOHNSTON, JOHN.
KIRKMAN, WILLIAM.
MARTIN, THOMAS.
MAUDE, SHEPHERD.
McCANN, JOSEPH.
McCREERY, ERNEST.
OLDHAM, WILLIAM.
PEDDER, MATTHIAS.
PILLING, JAMES.
RIGBY, WALTER N.
SANDERSON, JAMES.
STRINGER, HARRY.
STRINGER, MATTHEW.
TAYLOR, JOHN.
WILDES, JOHN.

A. and G. MURRAY, LTD.
Newcastle, Staffs.

BROWNSWORD, GEORGE.
ELLIS, GEORGE.
HITCHIN, THOMAS.
HOLLINS, NORMAN.
SIMMS, ALFRED.
SMITH, GEORGE.

THE MUSGRAVE SPINNING CO., LTD.

SANDFORD, Lieut. E. C.
AITKEN, T.
ANDERSON, WILLIAM.
ARCHBOULD, ARTHUR.
ASHCROFT, T.
ASHWORTH, CALEB.
BANKS, W.
BARNES, JAMES.
BARNES, THOMAS.
BARNES, WIDMER.
BARTON, JOSEPH.
BEARDSWORTH, ALBERT
BEARDSWORTH, ARTHUR.
BENNISON, ARTHUR M.
BENTLEY, HERMON.
BENTLEY, JOHN.
BINKS, FREDERICK.
BIRCHALL, GEORGE.
BLINKHORN, ERNEST.
BLUNDELL, JOHN.
BOND, JOHN.
BOOTE, CHARLES HERBERT.
BOWMAN, JOSEPH.
BRINDLE, HARRY.
BROOKS, HAROLD F.
BROUGHTON, JAMES.
BROWN, HARRY.
BROWN, THOMAS.
BURNS, C. A.
BURTON, JOHN.
CALVERT, JOSEPH.
CARDWELL, ALBERT.
CARDWELL, JOHN.
CAROL, JOSEPH.
CARSON, JAMES.
CARSON, WILLIAM.
CHADBOND, NORMAN.
CHADWICK, ALBERT.
CHRISTIE, WILLIAM.
CLARK, HAROLD.
CLARKE, WILLIAM.
CLEGG, ROBERT.
COLE, WILLIAM.
COOP, THOMAS.
COOP, WALTER.
COOPER, CHARLES.
COOPER, FRED.
COTTAM, FRED.
COTTAM, HERBERT.
COTTON, WALTER.
COVELL, A.
CROSSLEY, FRED.
CUPITT, GEORGE.
CUPITT, WILLIAM.
DAVIES, F.
DAVENPORT, WALTER.
DAWSON, STANLEY.
DRAPER, ELLIS.
DUXBURY, LEWIS.
DUXBURY, W.
ELLIS, HUGH.
FALLOWS, JOHN.
FARGHER, T.
FARNWORTH, JAMES.
FARNWORTH, JOSEPH.
FARRINGTON, FRED.
FAULKNER, WALTER.
FIELDING, HARRY.
FRANCE, FRANK.
FRODSHAM, HAROLD.
GALLAGHER, JOHN.
GLADSTONE, SIDNEY.
GREEN, JOSEPH.
GREENHALGH, THOMAS B.
GREENHALGH, THOMAS.
GREGORY, ABRAM.
GRIME, ALEXANDER.
GRIME, HENRY.
GRIME, WILLIAM.
GRUNDY, ERNEST.
GRUNDY, WILLIAM.
HALL, CHARLES.
HALL, ROBERT.
HALLIDAY, ROBERT.
HAMER, JAMES.
HAMER, JOHN.
HAMER, THOMAS.
HAMPSON, FRED.
HARDMAN, T.
HARDMAN, WILLIAM.
HARRISON, THOS.
HART, ROBERT.
HART, THOS.
HART, WALTER.
HARTLEY, HAROLD NORMAN.
HASLAM, ARTHUR.
HAYDOCK, T.
HAZELHURST, JAMES.
HENLEY, HAROLD.
HEYES, JAMES.
HIGGINSON, JAMES.
HILL, JOSEPH.

The Fine Cotton Spinners and Doublers' Association Ltd.

Roll of Honour—continued.

THE MUSGRAVE SPINNING CO., LTD.—Continued.

- HILTON, EDWARD.
- HILTON, FRANK.
- HILTON, JAMES.
- HILTON, TOM.
- HODSON, ARTHUR.
- HOLLAND, HAROLD.
- HOLLIS, THOMAS.
- HORROCKS, ALFRED.
- HOWARTH, ALFRED.
- HOWARTH, GEORGE.
- HULME, NORMAN.
- HUMPHRIES, ALBERT.
- HUMPHRIES, HAROLD.
- ILIFF, HENRY.
- JACKSON, THOMAS.
- JONES, ALFRED.
- JOULES, HERBERT.
- KAY, FRED.
- KEATING, THOMAS.
- KEIR, FRED.
- KEIR, GEORGE.
- KENNY, WILLIAM.
- KERSHAW, JOSEPH.
- LAWTON, ARTHUR.
- LAWTON, RANDOLPH.
- LEACH, FREDERICK.
- LEACH, WILLIAM.
- LEATHER, ARTHUR.
- LEDWARDS, CHARLES.
- LEVY, J.
- LEWIS, THOMAS.
- LEWTAS, DAVID.
- LEWTAS, JOHN.
- LEWTAS, THOMAS.
- LILES, NORMAN.
- LYNN, ALBERT.
- LYNN, JOSEPH.
- McCAULEY, JAMES.
- McCONNEL, ANDREW.
- McCONNEL, JOHN.
- McHENRY, ALBERT.
- McINTYRE, ANDREW.
- MANN, LEONARD.
- MARKLAND, THOMAS.
- MARSDEN, ERNEST.
- MARSH, THOMAS.
- MASON, JAMES.
- MATHER, CHARLES.
- MATHER, HENRY.
- MEAKINS, WILLIAM.
- MORRIS, JOHN.
- MORRIS, WILLIAM.
- MORRIS, WM. G.
- NELSON, W.
- NUTTALL, JOHN.
- O'CONNOR, JOHN.
- OWEN, JAMES.
- OWEN, BEN.
- PAINTER, JOHN.
- PARKER, FRANK.
- PARKER, WALTER.
- PARKINSON, JOSEPH.
- PARTINGTON, ALLAN.
- PARTINGTON, FRED.
- PARTINGTON, J.
- PARTINGTON, THOMAS.
- PEARCE, JOHN.
- PEARCE, WALTER.
- PENDLEBURY, W.
- PETERS, HARRY.
- PIERPONT, HARRY.
- PIKE, GEORGE.
- PILLING, JOHN.
- PILLING, WILLIAM.
- POOLE, PERCY.
- POWELL, E.
- PRICE, WILLIAM.
- RALPHS, HERBERT.
- ROBERTS, ROBERT.
- ROBINSON, HARRY.
- ROEBUCK, JOHN.
- ROTHWELL, JOHN.
- RUSSELL, HERBERT.
- SALE, JOHN.
- SCOWCROFT, HARRY.
- SETTLE, ROBERT.
- SHARMAN, B.
- SHARPLES, H.
- SHUTTLEWORTH, FRANK.
- SIDDALL, JESSE.
- SMITH, ALFRED WILLIAM.
- STANDWORTH, FRANK.
- STOCKS, LAWRENCE.
- SYKES, ROBERT.
- TAYLOR, ALBERT.
- TAYLOR, ARCHIE.
- TAYLOR, FRED.
- TAYLOR, GEORGE.
- TAYLOR, JOHN.
- THOMASSON, JOHN MILLS.
- THOMPSON, NORMAN.
- THORNBER, JOHN.
- THORNLEY, ALFRED.
- THORNLEY, THOMAS.
- THWAITES, THOMAS.
- TOWELL, WILLIAM.
- TOWN, EDWIN.
- TURNER, JAMES R.
- TURNER, H.
- TURNER, THOMAS.
- TURTINGTON, EDWARD.
- UNSWORTH, J.
- WAIN, JAMES.
- WAIN, WILLIAM.
- WALES, PHILIP H.
- WALES, THOMAS.
- WALKER, A.
- WALKER, RICHARD.
- WALKER, JOHN.
- WALSH, JOHN.
- WALTERS, STANLEY.
- WARBURTON, NORMAN.
- WARDLEY, EDWARD.
- WEATHERALL, SAMUEL.
- WEBBER, JOHN.
- WESTHEAD, GEORGE.
- WHITTAKER, HENRY.
- WHITTAKER, JOHN.
- WHITTLE, THOS.
- WILDING, J. W.
- WILSON, WILLIAM.
- WOOD, NORMAN.
- WOOD, THOMAS.
- WOOD, WILLIAM.
- WOODCOCK, HAROLD.
- WORTHINGTON, W.
- YATES, FRED.
- YATES, ERNEST.
- YATES, JOSEPH.

THE FINE COTTON SPINNERS AND DOUBLERS' ASSOCIATION LTD.

Roll of Honour—continued.

THOMAS OLIVER and SONS (Bollington), LTD.

KNIGHT, Lieut. JOHN NORMAN.
ARNOLD, EDWIN.
ARNOLD, JOHN JAMES.
ARNOLD, WILFRED.
BANN, WILLIAM.
BAMFORD, ARTHUR.
BAMFORD, PERCY.
BIRCH, WILLIAM.
BRISTOW, WALTER.
BROADHEAD, ALBERT.
BROOKES, J.
BROOM, FRED.
BUNTING, PERCY H.
BUXTON, HARRY.
CARTWRIGHT, JOSEPH.
CLARKE, HAROLD.
COE, ALFRED.
FIELDSTEAD, JAMES.
FIELDSTEAD, JOHN.
FORD, ELLIS.
FOSTER, WILLIAM.
GIBBON, HAROLD.
HOLDCROFT, A.
HOLMES, JAMES.
HOLMES, WALTER.
ISHERWOOD, WILLIAM.
JACKSON, CHARLES.
LOWNDES, WILLIAM.
MAYERS, H.
MELLOR, T.
MILLWARD, JAMES.
MOTTERSHEAD, J.
NEEDHAM, F. E.
NEEDHAM, FRANK.
POYNTON, GEORGE.
POYNTON, WILLIAM.
PRESS, BENJAMIN.
PRESS, JOSEPH.
SNAPE, ALFRED.
SNAPE, HERBERT.
SNAPE, WILLIAM.
STANESBY, HARRY.
TAYLOR, JAMES.
TOMLINSON, BENJAMIN.
TOMLINSON, GEORGE.
USHER, JACK.
WALKER HILL, W.
WRIGHT, ARTHUR.
YOXALL, MOSES.

THOMAS OLIVER and SONS (Bollington), LTD.
Bamford.

ANDREW, C.
BENNETT, C.
DANIEL, J.
EYRE, J.
FINLAY, B.
FINLAY, W.
FARRELLY, J. J.
HALL, R.
HALLAM, THOMAS.
HARTLE, H.
ROSS, C.
UNWIN, R.
WRAGG, W.

ORMROD, HARDCASTLE and CO., LTD.

ALLEN, T.
BARNES, W.
BERRY, W.
BLEASE, G.
BROMILEY, R.
BROUGHTON, J.
BROUGHTON, W.
CHADWICK, J. W.
CHEETHAM, F.
CLARKE, A.
COSTELLO, T.
COUGHLIN, W.
CUNNINGHAM, J.
EASTWOOD, W.
EWINS, H.
FLETCHER, R.
FLITCROFT, T.
GARNER, R.
GARSTANG, A.
GAYLEY, T.
GREENHALGH, F.
GREENHALGH, T.
HAMER, F.
HARDMAN, A.
HASLAM, J.
HAYNES, G.
HEYES, H.
HILL, R.
HOUGH, J.
KELLY, J.
KNOWLES, R.
KNOWLES, W.
MATHER, W.
MILLINER, A.
MORRIS, T.
NABB, T.
NEWSHAM, J.
PASQUILL, E.
PASQUILL, R.
REARDEN, J.
SEDDON, H.
SELBY, W.
SHAW, J.
SLATER, S.
SMITH, J.
SMITH, W.
SUNTER, G.
TAYLOR, G.
THORNTON, W.
TURTINGTON, F.
WALLER, J. J.
WHITTLE, W.

THE FINE COTTON SPINNERS
AND
DOUBLERS' ASSOCIATION LTD.

Roll of Honour—continued.

ISAAC PEARSON, LTD.

GREENHALGH, Lieut. MAURICE L.
ATKINSON, WILLIAM.
BARDSLEY, HENRY.
BARLOW, JOSIAH.
BOOTHBY, RICHARD.
BOUCKLEY, E.
BOWERS, GEORGE V.
BRIDGE, GEORGE.
BURGESS, WALTER.
CANTWELL, JOHN W.
CHOLERTON, HENRY.
CONLON, DAVID.
COOKE, HARRY M.
COOPER, SAMUEL.
COOPER, WALTER.
FOX, GEORGE J.
HALES, JAMES.
HALFPENNY, H.
HARRISON, A.
KAY, JOHN.
KIMBER, LEGH.
LINES, JAMES.
MATHER, GEORGE.
McGOWAN, THOMAS.
MURPHY, JOHN.
NEWMAN, WALTER.
NORMANSELL, ALBERT.
OLLERENSHAW, GEORGE.
PALFREYMAN, HORATIO.
PEARSON, CHARLES.
PEARSON, GEORGE.
PEARSON, JAMES.
PERKINS, WILLIAM.
PICKFORD, J.
POLLITT, GEORGE.
RODGERS, WALTER.
SEEL, JOSEPH.
SHENTON, VICTOR.
SOUTHGATE, DAVID.
SUTCLIFFE, ROBERT V.
TOOLE, J. E.
TURNER, ROBERT.
WADSWORTH, FRANK.
WALSH, PATRICK.
WATTS, JOSEPH.
WHITTAKER, JOSEPH.
WILD, SAMUEL.
WILKINS, JAMES.
WOODHALL, JOHN.
WORSNUP, FRED.
YARWOOD, JAMES.

JOSEPH PEARSON and CO., LTD.

BROWN, GEORGE.
HAMMOND, HARRY.
MURDEN, THOMAS.

E. PEAT, SON and CO., LTD.

BEETON, FRED.
COMERY, ERNEST.
GILL, JESSE.
HURST, ABRAM.
NUTT, WILLIAM.
PICKERILL, WM.
SAVAGE, SAMUEL.
SMITH, JOHN H.
TOMLINSON, MARK.
WESTON, A. J.

THE REDDISH SPINNING CO., LTD.

BROCKLEHURST, Colonel R. W. D. PHILLIPS.
ADAM-STUART, 2nd Lieut. W.
ASTLEY, THOMAS.
ASTLEY, WILLIAM.
COCKSHOUT, HERBERT V.
COY, REGINALD.
CROFTS, EDWARD.
CUNNINGHAM, ALEC H.
DAVENPORT, ISHMAEL.
DAVIES, ARTHUR WM.
DITCHFIELD, SAMUEL.
ELWELL, JAMES.
FARRINGTON, WM.
GILL, FRANK.
GOOCH, ALBERT.
GOODIER, HAROLD.
GRIMSHAW, ARTHUR.
HALLIWELL, J.
HAMER, ALBERT.
HARRISON, JOS.
HAUGHTON, GEORGE.
HILL, HARRY.
HOLT, RALPH.
JONES, ROBERT.
KAY, THOMAS.
LITTLER, ALFRED.
LIVINGSTONE, EDWARD.
MATHER, SAMUEL.
MATKIN, ISAAC E.
MAYALL, SAMUEL.
MAYERS, CHAS. H.
MAYERS, HUBERT.
MAYNARD, ERNEST.
PLACE, JOS.
SUMNER, HARRY.
THORNTON, ALBERT.
WAGSTAFF, JAMES.
WAINWRIGHT, JOSEPH.
WALKER, GEORGE.
WILD, WILFRED.
WYNNE, JAMES ROBERT

THE FINE COTTON SPINNERS
AND
DOUBLERS' ASSOCIATION LTD.

Roll of Honour—continued.

THOMAS RIVETT, LTD.

RIVETT, Lieut.-Col. FRED.
BARNES, H.
BARRATT, J.
BOWDEN, ROBERT.
COLEMAN, W.
DEAN, G.
DEAN, J. W.
DIVINE, J.
DUDLEY, J.
FINDELL, E.
FROST, S.
   (Killed in France.)
GARNER, H.
GLEESON, J. H.
   (Killed in France.)
HARRIS, J.
HARRISON, F.
HODKINSON, A.
HULLEY, F.
HULLEY, J.
HUMPHRIES, J.
PENNY, ALBERT.
PRESTON, H.
REEVES, ELIJAH.
RIDGWAY, A.
ROWLINSON, H.
SHAW, R.
SHAW, THOS.
SLACK, J.
STANDRING, T.
THOMPSON, H.
TICKLE, H.
WHITEHEAD, G.
WRIGHT, F.

SHAW, JARDINE and CO., LTD.

ANDREW, A.
BOOTH, A.
BOOTH, S.
BOWDON, H.
BROOKS, W.
CHARLSWORTH, G.
CRESWELL, G.
DUNN, H.
FIELD, W. H.
FLETCHER, S.
GEORGE, F.
GRANTHAM, R.
HALL, W.
HELSBY, R.
HENDERSON, J. H.
HOPEWELL, T.
HOPWOOD, S.
HOTHERSALL, G.
HOTHERSALL, W.
HOUGHTON, A.
JACKSON, R.
JARVIS, A.
McKENNA, J.
MEADOWCROFT, A.
ORMEROD, F.
PALMER, F.
REDMAN, C.
RICHARDSON, G. H.
ROURKE, A.
SHARPLES, W.
TURNER, S. R.
WARD, A.
WARD, G.
WARD, G. H.
WEIR, J.

GEORGE SWINDELLS and SON, LTD.

SWINDELLS, Lieut.-Col. G. H.
DEBENHAM, Capt. A. M. G.
COBBOLD, Flight-Lieut. E. F. W.
ADAMS, EDWIN.
ARNOLD, MATTHEW JAMES.
ASHLEY, THOMAS.
BARTON, SAMUEL.
BASKERVILLE, JAMES.
BEARD, WILLIAM.
BELFIELD, ROBERT.
BETTLEY, JOSEPH A.
BEVAN, ARTHUR.
BRADDOCK, CHARLES.
BRADDOCK, WALTER.
BRADLEY, JOSEPH.
BROCKLEHURST, EDMUND.
BROOME, WILLIAM.
BROWN, JOSEPH.
BUCKLEY, JOSEPH.
BUCKLEY, WILLIAM.
CAPPER, ERNEST.
CASEY, BERNARD.
CASEY, ROBERT.
CASEY, THOMAS.
CAVENEY, THOMAS.
CLARKE, JOHN W.
CLARKE, JOSEPH.
CLAYTON, ARTHUR.
CLAYTON, DANIEL.
CLAYTON, EDWARD.
COLLIER, WILFRED.
CROMPTON, CHARLES H.
CUNNINGHAM, STEPHEN.
DANIELS, ALLEN.
DERBYSHIRE, ALBERT.
DODD, JOHN.

THE FINE COTTON SPINNERS
AND
DOUBLERS' ASSOCIATION LTD

Roll of Honour—continued.

GEORGE SWINDELLS and SON, LTD.—Continued.

DOWNES, THOMAS.
DRABBLE, JOHN.
DRABBLE, VAN MARTIN.
EGERTON, JOSEPH.
FEW, FRANK.
FLINT, GEORGE.
GALGANI, ALBERT.
GASKELL, ALFRED.
GAY, ROBERT.
GOODWIN, GEORGE.
GOODWIN, HARRY.
GOODWIN, JOHN.
GOSLING, GEORGE.
GREEN, SYDNEY.
HARDING, ALBERT.
HARDING, WILLIAM.
HARROP, JOHN W.
HARROP, PERCY.
HAWLEY, GEORGE.
HAWLEY, HARRY.
HAYMAN, JAMES.
HAYMAN, WILLIAM.
HINDLEY, GEORGE A.
HOLEHOUSE, WALTER.
HOLT, CHARLES.
HOPPER, FRANK.
HUGHES, JOHN.
HUGHES, RICHARD.
HUGHES, SAMUEL.
HUNT, SAMUEL.
HUNT, SIMON.
INGLEY, JOHN.
JACKSON, ALBERT.
JACKSON, HARRY.
JACKSON, THOMAS.
JEPSON, JAMES.
JONES, WILLIAM.
KING, JAMES.
KIRK, ISAAC.
LATHAM, JOHN.
LEIGH, ALFRED.
LEIGH, ARTHUR.
LINDOP, BERNARD.
LOMAS, CHARLES.
LOMAS, HARRY G.
MATTIMORE, LEO.
MAYERS, ARTHUR.
MORGAN, JOHN.
MORTON, WILLIAM.
NEEDHAM, WILLIAM HENRY.
NOLAN, BERNARD.
NOLAN, EDWARD.
NOLAN, GEORGE.
NOLAN, LEONARD.
NOLAN, THOMAS.
NOLAN, WILLIAM.
OLDFIELD, GEORGE.
PAGE, CHARLES.
PERKIN, JAMES.
POTTS, WILLIAM.
RILEY, EDWARD.
SHATWELL, HARRY.
SHATWELL, HARRY.
SHATWELL, JOSEPH.
SHATWELL, NATHANIEL.
SHUFFLEBOTHAM, WILLIAM.
SKIRVIN, SIDNEY.
SLATER, JOSIAH.
SNAPE, HAROLD.
STRINGER, ALLEN.
STRINGER, HARRY.
SUTTON, OSWALD.
SWINTON, ROBERT.
TAYLOR, ALBERT.
TAYLOR, HAROLD.
TAYLOR, JOHN W.
TAYLOR, JOSEPH.
THOMPSON, HAROLD.
THORLEY, BENJAMIN.
THORLEY, JAMES.
TINSLEY, WILLIAM.
TURNER, CHARLES H.
WALTON, HERBERT.
WARREN, JOSEPH.
WHISTON, DANIEL.
WILLIAMSON, JOHN.
WRIGHT, JAMES.
WRIGHT, Junr., JOHN N.
WRIGHT, STEPHEN.
WRIGHT, WILLIAM.

THOMAS TAYLOR and SONS, LTD.

ALLSOP, ALFRED.
ASHCROFT, JAMES.
ATKINSON, SAMUEL.
BAILEY, FREDERICK.
BOGLE, JAMES.
BOYLE, JOHN.
COATES, WILLIAM.
COGGINS, RICHARD.
COWARD, WALTER.
CRITCHLEY, JOSEPH.
DURKIN, THOMAS.
EDMUNDSON, GEORGE.
FOGG, JOSEPH.
GIDMAN, MILES.
GREGORY, JOHN.
HAMER, GEORGE.
HAYNES, HENRY.
HILL, JOSEPH.
HINCHCLIFFE, F.
HOOTON, ARTHUR.
HOUGH, THOMAS.
KAY, NATHAN.
LUBY, JAMES.
LUNNEY, PETER.
MARKLAND, HAROLD.
MAXWELL, STANLEY.
MOSCROP, SAMUEL.
PASQUILL, WILLIAM.
PICKVANCE, RICHARD.
RUSHTON, NORMAN.
SCHOFIELD, ALFRED.
SCROGG, RICHARD.
THOMPSON, GEO.
TONGE, HERBERT.
UNSWORTH, PERCY.
WHITTAKER, ROBERT.

THE FINE COTTON SPINNERS
AND
DOUBLERS' ASSOCIATION LTD.

Roll of Honour—continued.

J. L. THACKERAY and SON, LTD.

FINCH, GEORGE.	MAY, JOHN HENRY.	WARD, WILLIAM.
GILL, WALTER.	PEARSON, E.	WHYATT, J.
HART, ALFRED.	RUSSELL, ERNEST.	WIGGIN, ARTHUR.
HOWE, FRANK.	SMITH, G.	WOODWARD, WILLIAM.
MANTLE, GEORGE.	STRAW, W.	WRIGHT, T. E.

JOHN TOWLE and CO., LTD.

BARBER, THOMAS.   KINGHAM, JOHN.

J. TOWLSON and CO., LTD.

CLARKE, CUTHBERT.	GREAVES, ALBERT.	TANSLEY, HERBERT.
CLARKE, THOMAS.		

THE TUTBURY MILL CO., LTD.

PEARSON, HENRY.   WHITEHOUSE, WILLIAM.   WOOD, GEORGE.

J. and G. WALTHEW, LTD.

ARMSTRONG, EDWARD.	GIBSON, JOSEPH.	OWEN, A.
BAILEY, WILLIAM.	HADLEY, ARTHUR.	PLATT, HAROLD.
BENT, GEORGE FREDERICK.	HOBSON, JOSEPH.	RIDGWAY, JOHN.
BENTHAM, ARTHUR.	HOPWOOD, HAROLD.	ROBERTS, DANIEL.
BRADSHAW, RICHARD.	HOWARTH, W. H.	SHAWCROSS, SAMUEL.
BURTON, WILLIAM L.	LEIGHTON, J.	STANTON, JOHN.
BUTTERWORTH, SAMUEL.	LOFTUS, MARTIN.	THORLEY, FRANK.
CALVERT, J. S.	LONGSON, GEORGE VICTOR.	TOMKINSON, WALTER.
CHORLTON, ELLIS.	MOLYNEAUX, FRED.	WILLIAMS, JOHN.
CLARKE, SAMUEL.	MURPHY, H.	WILSON, HERBERT.
DEAN, A.	OGDEN, GEORGE.	WOOLEY, ROBERT.
EAGLAND, DANIEL.	OLDHAM, J. W.	WRIGHT, WILLIAM.
GEE, FRED.	ORR, HARRY.	

WOLFENDEN and SON, LTD.
Columbia Mill.

ATKINSON, WILLIAM.	HOGARTH, JOHN.	SPEDDING, STANLEY.
BARLOW, EDWARD.	HULME, WILLIAM.	TAYLOR, ALBERT.
CHARNLEY, FRED.	IRELAND, JAMES.	TAYLOR, JOSEPH.
CHEETHAM, ARNOLD.	KAY, NORMAN.	TOPP, BENJAMIN R.
CROOK, WILFRED.	NUTTON, CHARLES.	TOPP, JAMES.
DUNN, BENJAMIN.	POLLITT, HENRY.	TOPP, JOHN WILLIAM.
EVANS, JOHN.	READ, ARTHUR H.	YATES, H. F.
HARTLEY, ALBERT.	SEDDON, GEORGE JAMES.	YATES, JOHN G.
HARVEY, DAVID.		

THE FINE COTTON SPINNERS
AND
DOUBLERS' ASSOCIATION LTD.

Roll of Honour—continued.

WOLFENDEN and SON, LTD.—Continued.

Marsh Fold Mill.

BAINES, JOHN.
BAXENDALE, ALBERT.
DENNING, HARRY.
HIGSON, LEWIS.
HILL, JOHN R.
JONES, EDMUND.
LAITHWAITE, GEORGE S.
LANGSHAW, JAMES.
LOWE, JAMES.
MAKIN, JOHN.
MARKLAND, H. R.
MOLYNEAUX, ALFRED.
OLIVE, LEONARD.
ROYLANCE, HERBERT.
TAYLOR, ARTHUR.
TUDOR, GEORGE P.
WEBSTER, HENRY J.
WOODS, JAMES.

Asia Mill.

ASTLEY, H.
ATHERTON, HARRY A.
BALDWIN, HAROLD.
BARRATT, W. H.
BLACKLEDGE, JAMES.
BRIGGS, FRANK.
BROADHURST, ROBERT.
BURNS, ROBERT.
CHARNLEY, CHARLES G.
COLLIER, JAMES F.
DEARDEN, H.
GRIMSHAW, ELI.
HADFIELD, WILLIAM.
HIGSON, WRIGHT.
HILL, ALAN H.
HODKINSON, JOHN.
LAWSON, JOHN.
LOWE, PETER.
MANUELL, STANLEY.
MORRIS, FRANK.
NOON, JOHN.
O'HARA, PATRICK.
OWEN, THOMAS.
RIGBY, JOHN.
ROLLINSON, R. B.
SELBY, GEORGE.
SETTLE, JOHN.
TOMLINSON, A. E.
WEALL, F. B.

THE WOODEAVES CO., LTD.

ABBOTT, THOMAS.
BUNNEY, R.
FIGGINS, W.
STOTT, J.
WEATHERALL, JAMES.

CALEB WRIGHT and CO., LTD.

ALKER, FRANK.
BAXTER, HAROLD.
BAXTER, WILLIAM.
BENTHAM, FRANK.
BOARDMAN, JOSEPH.
CALLAND, STANLEY.
CRIPPEN, HARRY.
DAVENPORT, JOHN WM.
DAVISON, FRED.
EVANS, JOHN.
GARSTANG, JOHN.
GREEN, JOSEPH.
HEYWOOD, EDWIN.
HILL, EDWIN.
HILTON, FRANK.
HOLLIDAY, WILLIAM.
HUGHES, ROBERT.
JONES, GEORGE.
LEE, PETER.
LEIGH, WALTER.
LYON, HERBERT.
OWEN, JAMES.
PEMBERTON, JAMES.
ROACH, JOSEPH.
RODGERS, JOHN.
ROWLANDS, DAVID.
ROWTREE, SIDNEY.
SOUTHERN, HARRY.
STONES, JAMES POLLIT.
TAYLOR, THOMAS.
TYLDESLEY, WILLIAM.
VALENTINE, WILLIAM.
WALSH, WILLIAM.
WARBURTON, PERCY.
WOODS, JOSEPH.

ROLL OF HONOUR.

Bradford Collieries.
MANCHESTER.

ADAMS, T.
ABRAM, R., junr.
ADSHEAD, J.
ACKERS, J.
ALLCOCK, J.
ALLEN, H.
ARNOLD, C.
ASHCROFT, T.
ASHTON, D.
ASTON, J.
ASTON, R.
ASTON, D.
ATHERTON, S.
ATKINSON, T.
BACCHUS, G.
BAGGALEY, A.
BAGNALL, A.
BAILEY, H.
BAMBER, E.
BARBER, R.
BARNES, T. E.
BARNETT, G.
BARROW, L.
BARROW, J.
BARROW, J.
BATES, A.
BATTERSBY, H.
BEAUMONT, J.
BEE, W.
BELL, W.
BELSHAW, J.
BENNETT, E.
BENNETT, W.
BENNISON, S.
BENT, W.
BERRY, J.
BERRY, R.
BICKERDYKE, J.

BESWICK, C.
BLACKWOOD, W.
BLACK, A.
BLAIR, R.
BOARDMAN, B.
BOARDMAN, E.
BOARDMAN, M.
BOARDMAN, R.
BOON, E.
BOWDEN, T.
BOWERING, J.
BOWLER, F.
BOWKER, T.
BOWKER, S.
BOWKER, W.
BRADFORD, E.
BRADLEY, J.
BRADLEY, W.
BRASSINGTON, S.
BRAY, H.
BRIGGS, H.
BRISTOWE, F.
BROADHEAD, W.
BROADHURST, J.
BROADHURST, J.
BROADHURST, W.
BROODER, J.
BROOKS, F.
BROOKS, A.
BROWN, E.
BROWN, F.
BROWN, J.
BROWN, W.
BRYAN, J.
BRYAN, W.
BRYCE, W.
BUCKLEY, C.
BUCKLEY, J.

BUCKLEY, J.
BUCKLEY, E.
BURKE, T.
BURGESS, G.
BURNS, A.
BURGESS, A.
BURGESS, P.
BURGESS, S.
BURNS, J.
BOWKER, W.
BURNS, A.
BURKE, W.
BOSSOM, B.
BUTCHERS, C.
CAIN, J.
CAIN, T.
CAMPBELL, W.
CAREY, W.
CARNEGIE, C.
CARTLEDGE, H.
CARTER, C.
CAREY, S.
CHADWICK, E.
CHADDERTON, H.
CHAPPLE, J.
CHANDLER, B.
CHARNOCK, L.
CHORLEY, H.
CLARKE, F.
CLARKE, J.
CLINTON, A.
CLINTON, J.
COLCLOUGH, D.
COLEMAN, J.
COLEMAN, W.
COLLINSON, J.
CONCAH, A.
CONCAH, E.

BRADFORD COLLIERIES.

ROLL OF HONOUR—Continued.

CONCAH, M.	FISH, R.	HAMPSON, J.
COOK, R.	FORTH, HY.	HAMPSON, J. W.
COOMBES, W.	FOSTER, J.	HAMPSON, J.
COOPER, J.	FOX, E.	HANDS, S.
COOPER, W.	FOX, F.	HANLEY, W.
CORRIGAN, P.	FRANKLIN, A.	HANVEY, W.
COSTIGAN, R.	FLEET, E.	HARDING, H.
COTTRILL, W.	FLINT, W.	HARGREAVES, F.
COVERLEY, A.	FROST, A.	HARGREAVES, W.
CRIPPS, F.	FURNESS, T.	(deceased).
CROMPTON, E.	GALLAGHER, J.	HARPER, A.
CROSSLEY, J.	GALLAGHER, W.	HARRIS, J.
CUFTER, T.	GALLEY, J.	HARPER, S.
CURRIE, P.	GALLEY, J.	HARRISON, F.
CURRAN, C.	GALLIMORE, J.	HARRISON, J.
CURLEY, T.	GARNER, E.	HART, W.
DAKIN, W.	GARNER, E.	HARVEY, E.
DALE, F.	GARNETT, G.	HAYNES, W.
DANIELS, W.	GARNETT, J. H.	HEALD, W.
DAVIES, E.	GARSIDE, E.	HEALEY, J.
DAVIES, J.	GEE, J.	HEALEY, J.
DAVIES, J. H.	GILCHRIST, J.	HEANEY, WM.
DAVIES, T.	GILES, E.	HEANEY, J.
DAWSON, J.	GILL, R.	HEANEY, WALT.
DEAN, W.	GLENNON, A.	HEATON, E.
DEARNLEY, J.	GRANEY, G.	HERD, B.
DENHAM, A.	GOODWIN, W.	HEWITSON, E.
DODD, H.	GOODWIN, S.	HEYWOOD, T.
DODD, J.	GOODWIN, J.	HEYWOOD, W.
DOHERTY, M.	GOODWIN, J.	HIGHAM, S.
DOHERTY, M. J.	GOUGH, J.	HILLIKER, A.
DOODY, J.	GRAHAM, T.	HINCHCLIFFE, E.
DOUGLAS, J.	GREATBANKS, A.	HINDLEY, W.
DOWNING, C.	GREEN, A.	HITE, H.
DOYLE, W.	GREENHALGH, R.	HODSON, H.
DUNN, E.	GREGORY, L.	HODSON, W.
DUNN, W.	GREEN, R.	HOLDEN, A.
DYSON, T.	GRIMSHAW, W.	HOLT, S.
EASTHAM, E.	GRUNDY, A.	HOOLEY, A.
EDGE, S.	GRUNDY, F.	HOPKINS, J.
EDWARDS, J.	GRUNDY, N.	HOPKINSON, W.
EDWARDS, P.	HADLEY, C.	HORAN, J.
EDWARDS, R.	HALL, E.	HOUGH, H.
EDWARDS, T.	HALL, E.	HOUGHTON, J.
EDWARDS, J.	HALL, GEO.	HOWARTH, J.
ELLIS, B.	HALL, J.	HOYLAND, E.
ETCHELLS, S.	HALL, T.	HUFTON, G.
FEENEY, P.	HALL, W.	HOWARTH, J.
FERNLEY, W.	HALL, W.	HUGHES, E.
FIGG, R.	HALLOWS, A.	HUGHES, P.
FISHER, I.	HALLOWS, J.	HUGHES, T.
FISH, H.	HAMILTON, T.	HUGHES, W.

BRADFORD COLLIERIES.

ROLL OF HONOUR—Continued.

HUNT, A.
HUNTER, G.
HULMES, E.
IBBOTSON, JAS.
INGHAM, F.
IRVIN, R.
JACKSON, G.
JAGGAR, J.
JEPSON, J.
JOHNSON, J.
JOHNSON, T.
JOHNSON, W.
JOLLIFFE, F.
JONES, ALFRED.
JONES, ARTHUR.
JONES, D.
JONES, F.
JONES, F.
JONES, F.
JONES, F.
JONES, H.
JONES, H.
JONES, L. R.
JONES, O.
JONES, R.
JONES, R.
JONES, R. W.
JONES, T.
JONES, T.
KANE, R.
KEELAND, A.
KEELING, W.
KELLY, S.
KELLY, J.
KELLY, M.
KENNEDY, D.
KENNEDY, P.
KENDRICK, A.
KENYON, J.
KENYON, J. W.
KENYON, S.
KENYON, C.
KING, P.
KINSEY, W.
KIRKHAM, H.
KITCHEN, O.
LANGLANDS, A.
LANGLEY, J.
LEAH, H.
LEAH, J. W.
LEE, B.
LEE, E.

LEE, F.
LEE, G.
LEE, J.
LEECH, G.
LEONARD, A.
LEONARD, J.
LEVER, J.
LEWIS, W. E.
LINGARD, H.
LINES, W. H.
LINDLEY, J.
LINNEY, T.
LISTER, N.
LITTLEWOOD, R.
LIVESEY, F.
LOWE, J.
LLOYD, A.
LLOYD, W. H.
LOMAS, W.
LUDDON, J.
LYONS, R.
MACK, C.
MACKEY, R.
MALCOLM, J.
MANEY, E.
MANNING, J.
MANSFIELD, H.
MARSHALL, I.
MARSHALL, W.
MARSLAND, J., Senr.
MARSLAND, J., Junr.
MARKHAM, J.
MARTIN, J.
MAWDESLEY, H.
MAYBURY, A.
MAYER, J.
MAYLETT, G.
McBRIDE, J.
McCARTHY, A.
McCULLOCH, J.
McDOWELL, G.
McGAHAN, J.
McGOVERN, J.
McGRATH, H.
McQUIGGAN, W.
McLOUGHLIN, J.
McMANUS, B.
McNICHOLLS, J.
MEADOWS, G.
MEE, J.
MELLOR, S.
MILLIGAN, D.

MILLIGAN, I.
MILLIN, H.
MILLS, J.
MISKIMMON, S.
MOIR, J.
MOORES, E.
MOORES, J.
MORAN, E.
MORAN, P.
MORGAN, E.
MORRIS, J.
MOSS, W.
MOXON, J.
MULLIGAN, T.
MURPHY, T.
MURPHY, J.
MURTAGH, C.
NEILD, T.
NELSON, A.
NIGHTINGALE, T.
NOBLE, G.
NOBLETT, G. W.
OAKES, J.
O'BRIEN, F.
O'BRIEN, G.
O'BRIEN, J.
O'BRIEN, W.
O'DONNELL, R.
O'DONNELL, T.
O'NEIL, J.
O'SHEA, J.
OLIVER, J.
OWEN, C.
OWEN, HUGH.
OWEN, HY.
OWEN, M.
OWEN, T.
OUSBY, G.
PARKINSON, F.
PARKINSON, W.
PARDOE, A.
PARKES, J.
PEERS, R.
PEMBERTON, G.
PENNINGTON, G.
PENNINGTON, R.
PHILLIPS, J.
PHILLIPS, T.
PIDDINGTON, A.
PLATT, T.
POLLITT, T.
POOLE, W.

BRADFORD COLLIERIES.
ROLL OF HONOUR—Continued.

POTTS, D.
POTTS, T.
POULTON. E.
POWER, A.
POWER, W.
PRICE, J.
PRITCHARD, E.
PRITCHARD, W.
RAINFORD, J.
RAINFORD, P.
RAYNOR, W.
REDFORD, H.
REED, H.
RICHARDS, E.
RICHARDS, R.
RIDGWAY, J.
RIDGWAY, J.
RIMINGTON, GEO.
ROBERTS, J.
ROBERTS, T.
ROBERTS, W.
ROBERTSON, W.
ROBINSON, P.
ROONEY, T.
ROSCOE, R.
ROSS, J.
ROSTRON, I.
ROSTRON, W.
ROWDEN, W.
ROWLEY, C.
RYAN, G.
SALISBURY, T.
SAYERS, G.
SCANLON, T.
SCANLON, T.
SCHOFIELD, H.
SELLARS, J.
SENIOR, G.
SHEARD, C.
SHUTTLEWORTH, A.
SKADE, H.
SLACK, E.
SLACK, W.
SPENCER, J.
SPROSTON, F.
SMITH, A.
SMITH, H.
SMITH, J.
SMITH, J.
SMITH, J.
SMYTH, J.

SMITH, S.
SMITH, T.
SMITH, W.
SMITH, W.
SOUTHWARD, G.
SPARROW, E.
STAFFORD, T.
STANLEY, H.
STANSFIELD, T.
STEPHENSON, J.
STEPHENSON, L.
STOPFORD, JAS.
STOPFORD, JOS.
STOPFORD, J.
STRANGE, J.
SWALES, W.
SWANN, R.
SWATKINS, G.
SWINDELLS, J.
SWINDELLS, W.
SUNDERLAND, I.
TABNER, W.
TALBOT, S.
TALBOT, W.
TAYLOR, A.
TAYLOR, H.
TAYLOR, W.
THICKETT, J.
THORPE, T.
THOMAS, T.
THOMAS, C.
THOMPSON, B.
THOMPSON, W.
THOMAS, F.
THORLEY, H.
THORNTON, J.
TIPTON, A.
TIPTON, J.
TODD, W.
TOMLINSON, H.
TOMLINSON, M.
TOWNLEY, E.
TRACEY, J.
TRAVIS, G.
TURNER, C.
TURNER, C.
TURNER, J.
TYLER, G.
VAHEY, T.
VALENTINE, E.
VARLEY, R.

VAUGHAN, G.
VERNON, J.
WALKER, J.
WALKER, S.
WALKER, T.
WALSH, H.
WALSH, J.
WALSH, .
WALL, F.
WALL, T.
WARD, A.
WARD, H.
WEBB, W.
WEIGHTMAN, J.
WELBY, J.
WELSBY, J.
WETTON, J.
WHALLEY, R.
WHITE, S.
WHITEHEAD, J.
WHITEHEAD, T.
WHITELEY, B.
WHITTAKER, C.
WHITTHAM, T.
WILKINSON, R.
WILLIAMS, JOS.
WILLIAMS, JOHN.
WILLIAMS, W.
WILSON, F.
WILSON, H.
WILSON, J.
WILSON, J.
WILSON, J. B.
WINSTANLEY, I.
WINSTANLEY, WALT.
WINSTANLEY, W.
WINTERBOTTOM, H.
WINWARD, C.
WINWARD, J.
WOOD, F.
WOOD, M.
WOOD, T.
WOOLHOUSE, F.
WREN, J.
YARNALL, E.
YARWOOD, C.
YATES, W.
YUMBLETT, A.
YUMBLETT, F.

ROLL OF HONOUR.

FINNIGANS LIMITED,

DEANSGATE, MANCHESTER.

List of men serving with the Forces.

ACTON, Private F. (Wounded).	8th Batt. Man. Regt.
ARKINSTALL, Corpl. N.	Seaforth Highlanders.
ATKINSON, Driver J. W.	Army Service Corps.
BARRON, Sergeant A. (Killed).	8th Lancashire Fusiliers.
BARRON, L.-Corpl. J.	8th Lancashire Fusiliers.
BRENNAN, Driver TOM	Army Service Corps.
BRIDGE, L.-Cpl. FRANK	17th Batt. Man. Regt.
BRUNYEE, Private TOM	1st Grenadier Guards.
CAPPER, Co.Q.M.Sergt. J.	Royal Field Artillery.
CATLING, Corpl. H. T.	Westminster Dragoons (T.F.).
CLARKE, Pte. EDGAR	6th King's Liverpool Regt.
CLARK, Bugler C.	11th East Surrey Regt.
CLARKSON, Private H.	7th Batt. Man. Regt.
CUFF, Sapper E.	Royal Engineers.
CUNNINGHAM, Sergt. D.	16th Batt. Man. Regt.
DALE, Private GEORGE	Royal Naval Division.
DAWSON, Pte. HAROLD	17th Batt. Man. Regt.
DOYLE, Pte. BERNARD	7th Batt. Man. Regt.
EARNSHAW, Driv. W. E.	Royal Field Artillery.
EDMONDSON, Private W.	12th Batt. Cheshire Regt.
EYRE, Sergt. E. (D.C.M.)	R.A.M.C.
FARRAND, Private A.	9th Batt. Cheshire Regt.
FINN, Co.Q.M.Sergt. W.	1/8th Lancs. Fusiliers.
FINNIGAN, L.-Corpl. JOS.	16th Batt. Man. Regt.
FINNIGAN, Pte. CHAS. J.	12th Batt. R. W. Fus.
GILLINGHAM, Co.Q.M.S. A.	9th Batt. Cheshire Regt.
GOODWIN, Sergt. A.	South African Transport.
HAMILTON, Private R. (Killed).	8th Lancashire Fusiliers.
HARRISON, Corpl. A.	Army Veterinary Corps.
HAWKES, Driver N.	Army Service Corps.
HIGGINSON, Private J.	16th Batt. Man. Regt.
HIRSCHFIELD, Driver S.	Royal Field Artillery.
HITCHCOCK, Sadler J.	Army Service Corps.
HORNBLOW, Private J.	National Reserve.
HORNBLOW, jun., Driver Sadler J.	East Lancs. A.S.C.
JENNINGS, Private A.	9th Batt. Cheshire Regt.
JOHNSON, Private W.	6th Batt. Man. Regt.
JONES, Sergt. E.	20th Batt. Man. Regt.
LITTLE, Private FRED	25th Batt. Man. Regt.
LLOYD, Pte. HERBERT	5th King's Liverpool Rgt.
MASSEY, Pte. DUNHAM	7th Batt. Man. Regt.
McDONNELL, Private F.	6th King's Liverpool Rgt.
McHALE, Private J.	9th East Lancs. Regt.
MOSS, Private HENRY	17th Batt. Man. Regt.
PEARSON, Private WM.	16th Batt. Man. Regt.
PEERS, Private ARTHUR	16th Batt. Man. Regt.
PIERCE, Corpl. J.	1/2nd Field Ambulance R.A.M.C. (E.I.).
PIERCE, Pte. ARTHUR	R.A.M.C.
REBBITT, Private S.	6th Batt. Man. Regt.
ROBERTS, Gunner J.	Royal Field Artillery.
SCHUBROOK, Private S.	Mechanical Transport.
SHERWIN, Private W.	17th Batt. Man. Regt.
SHIPWRIGHT, Sergt. A.	National Reserve.
SMITH, Private A.	King's Own.
SMITH, Sadler STANLEY	Army Service Corps
SMITH, Sapper G.	212th Field Co. R.E.
SMITH, Sapper P.	Signalling Section R.E.
STEWART, Private J.	3rd Royal Fusiliers.
TROTT, Sergt. A.	Army Service Corps.
TAYLOR, Pte. THOMAS	10th Batt. Man. Regt.
WHEELDON, Driver S.	Army Service Corps.
WHITEHEAD, Private W.	17th Batt. Man. Regt.
WOODS, Private J.	Mechanical Transport.

ROLL OF HONOUR.

I. FRANKENBURG & SONS LTD.

Greengate Works, Salford, Manchester.

FRANKENBURG, SYDNEY (Director)	Sub-Lieut.	8th Manchester Regiment.
ABRAHAMS, B.	Garment Maker	Manchester Regiment.
AVITZ, ABRAHAM	Garment Maker	Field Artillery.
ATHERTON, JOHN	Mechanic's	Lancashire Fusiliers.
BRIERLEY, ALBERT	Rubber Shoes	Lancashire Fusiliers.
BAYLISS, BERTRAM	Office	12th Essex Regiment.
BROWNE, THOMAS	Leather	Scottish Rifles.
BAILEY, JOSEPH	Leather	13th Manchester Regiment.
BERNSTEIN, MORRIS	Garment Maker	King's Own.
BENTLEY, HENRY	Cable	8th Batt. South Lancashire Regiment.
BOWKER, EDWARD	Rubber	R.A.M.C.
BOTTOMLEY, SAMUEL	Showerproof	8th Lancashire Fusiliers.
BRINDLEY, FRED	Mechanic's	Manchester Scottish.
BURTON, JOHN NEWTON	Gent's Cutting	King's Own Scottish Borderers.
BURTON, GEORGE	Rubber Shoes	Manchester Regiment.
BURNS, EDWARD	Warehouse	Manchester Scottish.
BIRCH, FRED	Warehouse	Border Regiment.
BURNS, DAVID	Rubber Shoes	East Lancashire Fusiliers.
BRUCE, C.	Garment Maker	Royal Scots.
BATTEY, J. W.	Rubber	Manchester Regiment.
BOCK, BERNHARD	Warehouse	R.A.M.C.
BARNETT, LEWIS	Garment Maker	Lancashire Fusiliers.
BOARDMAN, ERNEST	Rubber Shoes	Manchester Regiment.
BROWN, JAMES	Cable	22nd Batt. Lancashire Fusiliers.
CHAPMAN, JAMES	Office	7th Batt. Lancashire Fusiliers.
COOPER, HARRY	Garment Maker	East Lancashire Regiment.
COHEN, PHILIP	Leather	Manchester Regiment.
COBLEY, JAMES	Leather	Loyal North Lancashire Regiment.
CLYNE, SOLOMON	Garment Maker	R.M.L.I.
CLARK, GEORGE	Cable	Manchester Regiment.
COHEN, ABRAHAM	Raincoats	Manchester Regiment.
CAREY, EDWARD (Killed)	Rubber	7th Batt. Lancashire Fusiliers.
CHADWICK, J.	Packing Room	7th Batt. Lancashire Fusiliers.
CARR, GEORGE	Rubber	7th Batt. Lancashire Fusiliers.
CARR, ALFRED	Rubber	7th Batt. Lancashire Fusiliers.
CURRIE, FRANK	Cutting Room	R.F.A.
CARR, FRED	Cable Dept.	Lancashire Fusiliers.
CARTIN, JOHN	Finishing Room	Royal Engineers.

ROLL OF HONOUR — I. Frankenburg & Sons Ltd.
Greengate Works, Salford, Manchester

Name	Department	Regiment
CUMMINGS, JAMES	Rubber	South Lancashire Regiment.
CLOUGH, JOHN	Leather	
CLASSIC, ELI	Raincoats	6th Manchester (Territorials).
DEWE, JOSEPH	Garment Maker	East Lancashire Fusiliers.
DARBYSHIRE, JOHN	Cable	Scottish Borderers.
DARBYSHIRE, HARRY	Leather	Manchester Regiment.
DAVIES, FRED	Rubber	
DIXON, HARRY	Cable	Scottish Borderers.
DEWE, THOMAS	Cable	7th Lancashire Fusiliers.
DUFFY, M.	Rubber Shoes	21st Batt. Manchester Regiment.
DONALDSON, R.	Rubber	R.A.M.C.
DEVINE, JOHN	Electrician	Lancashire Fusiliers.
DOWNES, H. L.	Cable	Liverpool.
DUFFY, CHARLES	Rubber Shoes	Lancashire Fusiliers.
EDWARDS, GEORGE	Leather	19th Batt. Manchester Regiment.
ECKERSALL, HARRY	Cable	Gordon Highlanders.
FINEBURG, HENRY	Garment Maker	Liverpool Regiment.
FARLEY, JAMES	Leather	Manchester Regiment.
FULLEN, HARRY (Killed)	Leather	Manchester Regiment.
FULLEN, ARTHUR	Rubber	King's Royal.
FROST, GEORGE	Gent's Cutting	King's Own.
FURBANK, ERNEST HARRY	Warehouse	R.F.A.
GOLDBERG, ALTER	Garment Maker	King's Own.
GOODMAN, FRANK	Mechanic's	Lancashire Fusiliers.
GALLAGHER, ANDREW	Mechanic's	Lancashire Fusiliers.
GALLAGHER, JOHN	Mechanic's	Rifle Brigade.
GLEEK, MYER	Raincoats	R.F.A.
GOWLIN, THOMAS	Ladies' Cutting	Liverpool Regiment.
GILBERT, H.	Garment Maker	Flying Corps.
GILL, W.	Leather	Manchester Regiment.
GUINN, C.	Cable	8th Lancashire Fusiliers.
HUSBORNE, G. W.	Electrician	Navy.
HULME, JOSEPH	Electrician	Manchester Regiment.
HOLT, ARTHUR EDWARD	Garment Maker	20th Batt. Manchester Regiment.
HIME, PERCY	London Office	H.A.C.
HOWLEY, ARTHUR (Killed)	Rubber	Lancashire Fusiliers.
HUNTER, CLARENCE	Gent's Cutting	Lancashire Fusiliers.
HALBUTZAL, WILLIAM	Gent's Cutting	Manchester Regiment.
HEWISON, FRANK	Warehouse	Border Regiment.
HOLT, ROBERT	Typist	Border Regiment.
HUMM, WALTER	Cloth	Argylle and Sutherland Highlanders.
HARES, JOSEPH ROBERT	Cloth	Shropshire Regiment.
HARES, VINCENT COLIN	Office	Shropshire Regiment.
HALL, G. (Died)	Cable	Manchester Regiment.
HEDLEY, ARTHUR	Rubber Shoes	Lancashire Fusiliers.
HORSEFIELD, WM. A.	Office	Royal Fusiliers.
HIGSON, JOHN	Garment Maker	R.H.A.
HOLT, ARTHUR	Garment Maker	Manchester Regiment.
HOLMES, PHILIP HENRY	Leather	19th Batt. Manchester Regiment.
HARRISON, WM. EWART	London	H.A.C.
HODGINS, WILL	Cutters'	7th Lancashire Fusiliers.
HANNAN, R.	Cable	Seaforth Highlanders.
HOWARTH, JOHN	Warehouse	Argylle and Sutherland Highlanders.
ISAACS, SAMUEL	Garment Maker	Liverpool Regiment.
JACOBSON, ABE	Garment Maker	King's Own.
JORDAN, JOHN	Cable	Scottish Borderers.
JORDAN, JOHN	Ladies' Cutting	6th Manchester Regiment.
JONES, ERNEST	Rubber	Rifle Brigade.

ROLL OF HONOUR - I. Frankenburg & Sons Ltd.
Greengate Works, Salford, Manchester

Name	Department	Regiment
JORDAN, JOHN MATTHEW	Rubber Shoes	Army Service Corps.
KILGOUR, ROBERT	Garment Maker	Rifle Brigade.
KILROY, JAMES (Killed)	Mechanic's	Lancashire Fusiliers.
LINDY, PHILIP	Garment Maker	King's Own.
LISTER, FRED	Commissionaire	1st Royal Dragoons.
LOWE, GEORGE	Rubber	Lancashire Fusiliers.
LORD, FREDERICK	Rubber Shoes	East Lancashire Royal Engineers.
LAVERTY, A.	A. Dept.	Lancashire Fusiliers.
LEYLAND, A.	Rubber	R.A.M.C.
LANE, HENRY	Leather	
MILLINSON, JOHN	Mechanic's	Lancashire Fusiliers.
MITCHELL, ROBERT	Leather	Lancashire Fusiliers.
McMELLOR, A.	Finishing Room	Rifle Brigade.
MALLON, WM. FRANCIS	Cable	Lancashire Fusiliers.
McGOWAN, PETER	Cable	
McNEIL, RICHARD	Rubber	Lancashire Fusiliers.
McMAHON, WILLIAM	Mechanic	King's Own.
MASON, WILLIAM (Killed)	Rubber	8th Lancashire Fusiliers.
MASON, JAMES	Rubber	8th Lancashire Fusiliers.
McGRATH, WILLIAM	A. Dept.	8th Lancashire Fusiliers.
MANLEY, FRED	Ladies' Cutting	Lancashire Fusiliers.
MIDWOOD, HERBERT	Cable	Royal Scots.
MARKS, LEO	Garment Maker	Cheshire Regiment.
McCORMACK, JAMES	Cutting Room	Royal Field Artillery.
MORRIS, FRANK	Rubber Shoes	Lancashire Fusiliers.
McGANN, D.	Finishers	Manchester Regiment.
MASSEY, G.	Cutters'	7th Lancashire Fusiliers.
MINOR, G.	Cutters'	7th Manchester (Territorials).
NEALON, CHRISTOPHER	Cable	Manchester Regiment.
ODENRODE, ERNEST	Cable	Lancashire Fusiliers.
OWEN, JACK	Leather	19th Batt. Manchester Regiment.
PALMER, GEORGE	Cloth	Argylle and Sutherland Highlanders.
PRINCE, JOHN	Leather	Lancashire Fusiliers.
PARTINGTON, GEORGE	Leather	Cheshire Regiment.
PRATT, FRANK	Rubber	R.A.M.C.
PADEN, PETER	A. Dept.	Lancashire Fusiliers.
POTTS, JAMES	Cable	22nd Batt. Lancashire Fusiliers.
PRINCE, J.	Cable	8th Lancashire Fusiliers.
RAFTRY, JOHN ROBERT	Gent's Cutting	South Lancashire Regiment.
ROBERTS, EDWARD	Garment Maker	Lancashire Fusiliers.
RIX, SYDNEY	Cable	Lancashire Fusiliers.
RICHARDSON, HAROLD V.	Cable	R.A.M.C.
ROBERTS, FRANCIS	Rubber	Cameron Highlanders.
RANFIELD, T.	Cable	Border Regiment.
RIX, THOMAS	Cable	Scottish Borderers.
RYAN, THOMAS	Rubber	Lancashire Fusiliers.
SILVERMAN, ISAAC	Garment Maker	Liverpool Regiment.
SHAW, THOMAS (Killed)	Warehouse	Border Regiment.
SALMON, CHARLES	Rubber	Argylle and Sutherland Highlanders.
SIMPSON, STANLEY	Cutters'	Lancashire Fusiliers.
THOMASON, ROBERT	Garment Maker	Rifle Brigade.
TITTERINGTON, JOSEPH	Watchman	Border Regiment.
TOMMONS, ALFRED	Cable	Scottish Borderers.
WARD, JAMES	Leather	Duke of Cornwall's Light Infantry.
WILSON, REGINALD V.	Cable	Lancashire Fusiliers.
WILSON, LAURENCE	Rubber	Scottish Borderers.
WILLIAMS, J. (Killed)	Showerproof	King's Royal Rifles.
WADCOCK, JOSEPH	Ladies' Cutting	Lancashire Fusiliers.
WATKINS, JOSEPH	Ladies' Cutting	Liverpool Regiment.
WILSON, THOMAS	Rubber	Royal Field Artillery.
WHITING, JOSEPH	Garment Maker	King's Own Liverpool Regiment
WHITTLE, THOMAS	Leather	R.A.M.C.
WARREN, THOMAS	Leather	Lancashire Fusiliers.

P. FRANKENSTEIN & SONS, LTD.
MANCHESTER.

List of Employees now Serving with the Colours.

Lce.-Corpl. CYRIL J. FRANKENSTEIN	Army Service Corp (Motor Transport).
Private W. COWAP	8th Battalion Manchester Regiment.
Private STEPHEN ROBERTS	10th Batt. South Lancashire Regiment.
Private E. BUCKLEY	7th Battalion Manchester Regiment.
Private H. DUNBAR	East Lancashire Regiment.
Private FRED COX	East Lancashire Field Ambulance.
Private GEORGE HART	East Lancashire Field Ambulance.
Private LOUIS BLACK	
Driver GEORGE BECKETT	East Lancashire R.F.A.
Private GEORGE BRAMHALL	6th Battalion Manchester Regiment.
Private J. TASSAKER	2nd Gars. Cheshire Regiment.
Private W. H. JONES	8th Batt. King's Own Royal Lancasters.
Private J. E. ROBERTS	8th Battalion Manchester Regiment.
Private ALFRED GILLASPY	7th Lancashire Fusiliers.
Private W. H. SMYTHE	4th King's Liverpool Regiment.
Private G. HARPER	
Private FRANK DAVIES	7th Gordon Highlanders.
Private WM. COOK	East Lancashire Field Ambulance.
Lce.-Corpl. C. A. CLAYBOROUGH	Army Cycle Corps.
Private F. GYVES	Manchester Regiment.
Private E. HEBDEN	King's Liverpool Regiment.
Private JOHN McMELLON	King's Own Scottish Borderers.
Private H. TYNAS	68th W.D.C.C.
Lce.-Corpl. SAMUEL MORGAN	3rd King's Liverpool Regiment.
Lce.-Corpl. H. MILLER	8th King's Own Royal Lancasters.
Private ROBERT SMITH	16th Lancashire Fusiliers.
Private JOHN TONGE	Manchester Regiment.
Private T. RATCLIFFE	Manchester Regiment.
Privatae A. THOMPSON	Manchester Regiment.
Private RICHARD SMITH	Manchester Regiment.
Private H. BROOKS	South Lancashire Regiment.
Private A. DAVIES	Gordon Highlanders.
Private R. BROWN	
Private J. HAYES	
Private L. LEVY	
Private W. LIMB	Welsh Regiment.
Private E. HUGHES	
Private W. YOUNG	
Private J. MOSTON	
Private H. PIVAWSKI	
Private J. SHIELDS	
Private F. WIGG	Manchester Regiment.
Private H. WOODS	
Private A. TINGLE	Manchester Regiment.

ROLL OF HONOUR.

Finlay, Campbell and Co.
LIMITED.

2nd Lieut. F. D. Mills,
 1st Batt. Cheshire Regiment.

2nd Lieut. R. H. Martin,
 3/7th Batt. Cheshire Regiment.

Sergeant G. Bamford,
 17th Sv. Batt. Manchester Regt.

Corporal H. Peart,
 21st Sv. Batt. Manchester Regt.

Private C. J. Anderson,
 15th Batt. Royal Scots.

Private E. Clutton,
 17th Sv. Batt. Manchester Regt.

Private J. Hamilton,
 King's Own Lancasters.

Private G. F. James,
 21st Sv. Batt. Manchester Regt.

Private W. Macintosh,
 17th Sv. Batt. Manchester Regt.

Private J. Shelmerdine,
 R.M.L.I.

ROLL OF HONOUR.

FORBES & CO.,
57, DICKINSON STREET, MANCHESTER.

Lieut. Albert Forbes,
 8th Manchester Regt

Sergt. J. Beardshall,
 8th Border Regiment.

Private E. A. Walsh,
 6th Manchester Regt.

Private F. Kenderdine,
 6th Manchester Regt.

Private A. Taylor,
 8th Manchester Regt.

Private A. McBride,
 17th Serv. Manchester Regt.

Private W. Scarr,
 6th King's Own R. Lancs Regiment.

ROLL OF HONOUR.

Felber, Jucker & Co.
LIMITED.

MANCHESTER.

BRITISH ARMY.

J. P. Andrews.
Wm. Foster.
W. Grisenthwaite.
R. A. Lowe.
Wilfred Gardner.
Frank Smith.
Oscar Fischer.
Saml. Jackson.

FRENCH ARMY.

Jean Heysch.
Jules Weinbrenner.

ITALIAN ARMY.

Mario Ronchi.
Ugo Pernetta.
A. Cavaciocchi.

ROLL OF HONOUR

G. Gottschalck & Co.
86, Major St., MANCHESTER.

Major N. G. FRANK,
 1/6th Manchesters.
J. CHANTLER,
 1/7th Manchesters (killed).
E. BROCKLEHURST,
 1/7th Manchesters.
C. PROST,
 A/67th Brigade R.F.A.
A. GRANT,
 Royal Field Artillery.
F. DUNN,
 Royal Field Artillery.
H. WALLWORK,
 Royal Garrison Artillery.
A. BARRATT,
 Royal Army Medical Corps.
J. TURNER,
 Royal Army Medical Corps.
J. JEFFS,
 Lancashire Fusiliers.
T. WOOD,
 10th Batt. Seaforth H'drs.
H. REYNOLDS,
 26th Manchesters.
T. DANIELS,
 23rd Manchesters.
A. BEETSON,
 H.M.S. "Black Prince."

ROLL OF HONOUR.

MESSRS. G. W. GOODWIN & SON
"IVY" SOAP WORKS, MANCHESTER.

* * *

*ATHERTON, T.	6th Batt. Royal Rifles.	*MULLEN, J.	South Lancashires.
BIRD, WALTER	Driver, East Lanc. Royal Engineers.	NICHOLLS, S.	Gunner, R.F.A.
*BLAIR, J.	"F" Coy. 6th Batt. Royal Rifles.	PARKINSON, W.	7th Manchesters.
		PRINCE, W. S.	Territorials.
BOARDMAN, R. A.	7th Manchesters.	RIDER, H. C.	Kings' Own Regt., Royal Lancaster Dragoons.
BURGESS, ALBERT	1st Salford Battalion.		
CHAMBERLAIN, D.	Royal Garrison Artillery. (Believe now transferred to King's O. Lancasters.)	ROBINSON, W.	Cycle Corps, London.
		RODGERS, Sig. A.	Royal Field Artillery, Territorials
COX, ARTHUR	Royal Marines.		
DALY, JOSEPH	Royal Field Artillery, Manchester Territorials.	SAMUELS, W.	8th Lancs., Salford Batt.
		*SHELMERDINE, J.	8th Lancashire Fusiliers.
DAVY, AUGUSTINE	8th Lancashire Fusiliers.	SKIMMINGS, JAS. W.	R.A.M.C., Manchester.
DISKIN, JOHN P.	Bantams, 4th Batt.	SMITH, J. C.	3rd Lancashire Fusiliers.
EXLEY, JAMES	Lancashire Fusiliers.	SNOWDEN, G.	Royal Army Medical Corps, 3rd East Lanc. Field Ambulance.
GILLAM, H. (Reservist).	Stationed at Internment Camps.		
LANGLEY, JOHN	6th Manchesters.	STONES, WILLIAM	King's Own.
LONG, JOHN	19th Batt. Lanc. Fusiliers	TYRER, WILLIAM	Salford Battalion.
MOORE, PETER (Reservist).	South Lancashires (since transferred to 53rd Welsh Regt.)	WALTON, A.	Lancashire Fusiliers, 10th Batt. No. 3 Coy.
		WILKINSON, A.	9th Batt. South Lanc. Regt.

* T. Atherton: killed in France, June 1915.   J. Shelmerdine: wounded in Dardanelles, June, 1915.
J. Mullen: killed in France, 1915.   J. Blair: wounded in France, May, 1915.

ROLL OF HONOUR.

RICHARD GOODAIR LIMITED,

8, Mosley Street, MANCHESTER.

* * *

AINLEY, F.	GRIFFITHS, W. A.	OLDFIELD, W.
BARLOW, M. G.	GRUNDY, S.	OWEN, W. E.
BAY, J. W.	HACKNEY, J.	OXLEY, G.
BOWLING, J.	HALL, P.	PICKERING, A.
BOOTH, W.	HARRISON, A.	ROBERTS, H.
BROWN, F.	HARRISON, L.	SHIERS, A.
CARTLEDGE, J.	HARTLEY, R. S.	SLATER, F.
CLARK, J.	HARGRAVES, J. A.	TOWNROW, W.
COOKE, W. H.	HORROCKS, T.	TUCKER, H.
DARBYSHIRE, R. A.	HOWSEN, E.	WATERHOUSE, A.
EDGE, F. G.	HYNCH, W.	WATKINS, H.
EUSTON, H.	KINDER, H. A.	WILD, H.
FELTON, H.	LAMBERT, J.	WILLIAMSON, A.
FOSTER, F.	LINDSAY, F.	WRIGHT, W.
GARDNER, F. W.	MELLOR, W.	
GREEN, G.	NEALE, C. A.	

Springfield Mills, Preston.

ATHERTON, T.	GREENWOOD, R.	PARKINSON, J.
BATTLE, J.	GREENWOOD, J.	PILKINGTON, A.
BERRY, T.	HIGGINSON, W.	PRINCE, J.
BILLINGTON, R.	HINDLE, A.	RAWCLIFFE, R
BLACKBURN, E.	HOWARTH, S.	SEED, F.
BLACKLEY, J.	HOLDEN, A.	SMITH, A.
CRANGLE, J.	HOYLE, H.	SPENCER, R.
CROSS, J.	HOYLE, T.	THOMPSON, H.
CROSSLEY, W.	JACKSON, J.	TURNER, T.
DAWSON, J.	KELLETT, T.	WAINMAN, A.
DUNN, W.	LEYLAND, T.	WALMSLEY, R.
FITZSIMMONS, W.	MILLER, C.	

ROLL OF HONOUR.

* * *

Goldschmidt, Hahlo & Co.
MANCHESTER.

* * *

Lieut.-Colonel SIDNEY G. GOLDSCHMIDT, R.F.A.,
Late Second in Command 20th Battalion Manchester Regiment.

2nd Lieut. ARTHUR TENNANT HARDY,
20th Battalion Manchester Regiment.

2nd Lieut. JOHN H. LOMAS,
4th Battalion The King's Liverpool Regiment.

2nd Lieut. ERNEST A. DAVIES,
10th Battalion Bedfordshire Regiment.

C.Q.M.-Sergt. T. WALTON,
14th Battalion The King's Liverpool Regiment.

Corporal JOHN CURRIE,
Army Pay Corps, Mediterranean Expeditionary Force.

Bombardier JOHN ALBERT ROSE,
2nd East Lancs. R.F.A., Mediterranean Expd. Force.

Private F. H. E. STANDISH,
28th Battalion Royal Fusiliers, U.P.S.

ROLL OF HONOUR.

H. T. GADDUM & CO.,
57, Brown Street,
MANCHESTER.

Sergt. P. S. McINTYRE,
1/6 Batt. Manch. Regt.

Sec. Lieut. A. A. McKAY,
1/7 Cheshire Regiment.

Private R. C. HOLMES,
R.A.M.C.

Corpl. T. H. ROBERTS,
16th Batt. Manch. Regt.

L.-Corpl. H. SCANLON,
1/7 Cheshire Regiment.

Sec. Lieut. N. EDGE,
2/7 Batt. Manchester Regt.

Private W. SMITH,
11th Batt. Manch. Regt.

ROLL OF HONOUR.

GREG BROS. & CO.,
MANCHESTER.

Colonel F. R. McCONNEL,
Com. 25th Batt. Manchester Regt.
Captain HUGH S. GREG,
16th Service Batt. Manchester Regt.
2nd-Lt. ANDREW M. MONCRIEFF,
Royal Garrison Artillery.
Sergeant CHARLES W. BARKER,
16th Service Batt. Manchester Regt.
Sergeant LEONARD C. COWARD,
25th Batt. Manchester Regiment.
Private P. T. ROE,
16th Service Batt. Manchester Regt.
Private G. W. HARRISON,
21st Service Batt. Manchester Regt.
Private ALFRED WATERHOUSE,
1st Batt. Manchester Regiment.
Private FRANK RENNIE,
21st Service Batt. Royal Fusiliers.
Bombardier STANLEY HOTSON,
Royal Field Artillery.
Gunner A. A. WRIGG,
Royal Field Artillery.
Gunner SAMUEL TASKER,
Royal Garrison Artillery.
Corporal E. P. TAYLOR,
Royal Army Medical Corps.
Private F. S. KOTT,
Royal Army Medical Corps.
Private E. H. E. LUEDER,
Royal Army Medical Corps.

ROLL OF HONOUR.

Hall, Higham & Co.,
6-14, DALE STREET, MANCHESTER.

Employees who have joined His Majesty's Forces.

Private G. B. ADSHEAD	Medical Unit, R.N.D.
Private B. BARKER	1st Battalion West Yorkshire Regiment.
Private F. BOND	Royal Army Medical Corps.
Private G. L. CARR	16th Battalion Manchester Regiment.
Driver A. B. CARRICK	Royal Garrison Artillery.
Sergeant H. K. COATES	17th Battalion Manchester Regiment.
Private J. COWIN	29th Battalion Royal Fusiliers.
Sec. Lieutenant R. CRESSY	20th Battalion Lancashire Fusiliers.
Private E. DAY	1st Battalion Border Regiment.
Private J. G. DOWNS	25th Reserve Battalion Manchester Regiment.
Driver A. DUMVILLE	17th Lancashire Battery, Royal Field Artillery.
Private F. W. DYDE	45th Provisional Battalion.
Private V. ELLOR	30th Division Cyclist Corps.
Private E. GIESENBERG	7th Battalion Manchester Regiment (Killed).
Trooper H. GREGORY	Duke of Lancaster's Own Yeomanry.
Private H. HIGGINS	7th Battalion Manchester Regiment.
Private H. HOLDEN	16th Battalion Manchester Regiment.
Sergeant T. F. HUGHES	Army Service Corps (Mechanical Transport).
Private P. JENKINSON	3rd Scottish Provisional Battalion.
Private G. KEATES	6th Battalion Manchester Regiment.
Private E. W. LANGLEY	6th Battalion Manchester Regiment.
Corporal W. LEE	14th Battalion Manchester Regiment.
Corporal W. LEAH	8th Battalion Manchester Regiment.
Private H. MELLALIEU	16th Battalion Manchester Regiment.
Sec. Lieutenant C. H. MOFFATT	5th Battalion Lancashire Fusiliers.
Driver J. P. NUNN	2nd East Lancashire Royal Field Artillery.
Private C. PARSONS	30th Reserve Battalion Royal Fusiliers.
Private G. PATRICK	90th Brigade Grenade Company.
Private A. POWELL	21st Battalion Royal Fusiliers.
Private H. RIGBY	16th Battalion Manchester Regiment.
Private J. ROBERTS	29th Battalion Royal Fusiliers.
Private G. ROBERTS	6th Battalion Manchester Regiment (Killed).
Lance-Corporal R. STODDARD	16th Battalion Manchester Regiment.
Gunner J. TURNER	2nd East Lancashire Royal Field Artillery.
Private G. A. WALTON	Royal Army Medical Corps.
Stretcher Bearer J. A. WESTERMAN	21st Battalion Royal Fusiliers.
Bandsman A. WHELAN	8th Battalion Manchester Regiment.
Lieutenant J. G. WHITEHEAD	19th Battalion Lancashire Fusiliers.
Private G. WHITEHEAD	17th Battalion Manchester Regiment.
Private P. J. WICKS	8th Battalion Lancashire Fusiliers.
Private L. E. WOODARD	16th Battalion Manchester Regiment.
Private S. WOODHEAD	18th Batt. King's Liverpool Regiment.
Mr. H. BRADDOCK	Army Y.M.C.A.
Mr. J. C. SCOTT	Army Y.M.C.A.

ROLL OF HONOUR.

HALL & PICKLES,

64, Port Street, MANCHESTER.

No. 8417.—C. BERRISFORD, 17th S. Batt. Manchester Regt.
„ 40180.—JOSEPH BRENTNALL, 80th Battery, R.F.A. (killed in action).
„ 5799.—ALBERT CARO, 2nd East Lancs. Regiment.
„ 6861.—H. DUNN, 16th S. Batt. Manchester Regiment.
„ 10640.—FRANK FARRELL, 18th S. Batt. Manchester Regt.
„ 41301.—F. HOWARD, Royal Engineers.
„ 8205.—W. KENYON, 17th S. Batt. Manchester Regiment.
„ 6896.—GEORGE A. KIRKHAM, 16th S. Batt. Manch. Regt.
„ 8217.—ARTHUR LLOYD, 17th S. Batt. Manchester Regt.
„ 6400.—CHARLES MATTARS, 2nd East Lancs. Regiment.
„ 8785.—WALTER OVENS, 17th S. Batt. Manchester Regt.
„ 6939.—F. J. TOLE, 16th S. Batt. Manchester Regiment.
„ 2766.—A. WARD, 7th Batt. Manchester Regiment (T.F.).
„ 8329.—E. H. WHITE, 17th S. Batt. Manchester Regiment.
„ 5012.—W. H. WILSON, Royal Army Medical Corps.
„ 8963.—JAMES WINTERBURN, 17th S. Batt. Manch. Regt

Roll of Honour.

Hardman & Holden, Ltd.

***

- P. McCARTHY.
- W. H. COVELL.
- J. TRACEY.
- J. WARD.
- W. JACKSON.
- J. VINTER.
- P. COWEN.
- J. H. MATHER.
- J. ROBSON.
- F. FINN.
- R. ROBERTS
- J. BOULGER.
- W. COLLINS.
- W. BURKE.
- H. COMER.
- E. McCLURE.
- J. MOORE.
- W. KNIGHT.
- C. ORMROD.
- T. CUSHION.
- J. BRODERICK.
- J. WEATHERALL.
- J. NEALD.
- A. CONWAY.
- JOS. MOORES.
- T. DUFFY.
- R. FORD.
- J. STEWARD.
- M. McGREAVY.
- H. FREAKES.
- J. LOCKEY.
- W. BATES.
- P. DUFFY.
- A. SMITH.
- J. HUGHES.
- W. GWYTHER.
- W. WHITTINGHAM.
- A. MORRIS.
- H. SMITH.
- C. McLOUGHLIN.
- G. SUTTON.
- T. ATHERLEY.
- J. STRONG.
- B. JUBBS.
- T. KELLY.
- W. ILLINGWORTH.
- J. MURRAY.
- J. MELINA.
- W. HOLLAND.
- W. JOHNSON.
- A. ACTON.
- F. TIMMS.
- F. BADLAN.
- R. HUGHES.
- F. SIMCOCK.
- J. THOMAS.
- J. SALMON.
- C. WARHURST.
- T. DALTON.
- E. RADCLIFFE.

ROLL OF HONOUR.

Richard Haworth & Co. Ltd.

35 Dale Street, Manchester.

Warehouse.

Private Frank C. Haworth, Fife and Forfar Yeomanry.
Lance-Corporal Gordon M. Haworth, 73rd Field Royal Engineers.
Sergeant C. Adams, Royal Field Artillery.
Private F. Aickmann, Royal Army Medical Corps.
Private John Andrews, 1st Manchester Warehouse Battalion.
Sergeant R. Armstrong, Salford Fusiliers.
Private F. Barton, 2nd Manchester Warehouse Battalion.
Private S. Beddow, Royal Garrison Artillery.
2nd Lieutenant H. A. Bedford, King's Own R. Lancasters, 10th Serv. Batt.
L.-Corpl. J. R. Berry, 3rd Manchester Warehouse Battalion.
Private A. Brooks, 3rd Manchester Warehouse Battalion.
Private T. Burns, 2nd Manchester Warehouse Battalion.
Private B. Caiger, 1st Manchester Warehouse Battalion.
Private J. Chapman, 1st Manchester Warehouse Battalion.
Private R. W. Chapman, 2nd Manchester Warehouse Battalion.
Lance-Corporal C. Chorlton, 3rd Manchester Warehouse Battalion.
Private A. Cowburn, 4th Manchester Warehouse Battalion.
Private H. Dean, 1st Manchester Warehouse Battalion.
Private R. Dickinson, Royal Flying Corps.
Private G. H. Dixon, Lonsdale Battalion.
Private A. Drummond, 1st Manchester Warehouse Battalion.
Private C. H. Edis, Duke of Lancaster's Yeomanry.
Private F. Evans, 3rd Manchester Warehouse Battalion.
J. Farnworth, Royal Navy.
Sergeant J. W. Farrow, 2nd Manchester Warehouse Battalion.
Private J. S. Fletcher, Army Service Corps.
Private J. Fudge, Border Regiment.
Private W. E. Gamble, Royal Army Medical Corps.

Richard Haworth & Co. Ltd.

ROLL OF HONOUR—continued.

Sergeant H. Grice, Lancashire Fusiliers.
Private A. T. Haddon, Officers Training Corps.
Private J. Hadfield, 6th Manchester Territorial Battalion.
Lance-Corporal R. Lockwood, 3rd Manchester Warehouse Battalion.
Private S. Moffatt, 1st Manchester Warehouse Battalion.
Corporal E. C. Morris, Cycle Despatch Rider.
Private F. G. Newland, 32nd Battalion Royal Fusiliers.
Private B. Norbury, 2nd Manchester Warehouse Battalion.
Corporal F. G. Nuttall, 3rd Manchester Warehouse Battalion.
Corporal H. Paice, Lancashire Fusiliers.
Private W. A. Powell, 6th Manchester Territorial Battalion.
2nd Lieutenant S. Ryley, Northumberland Fusiliers.
L.-Corporal C. Schaeffer, 1st Manchester Warehouse Battalion.
Corporal P. S. Senior, 3rd Manchester Warehouse Battalion.
L.-Corpl. W. Sharp, 18th Lancashire Fusiliers.
Private P. Smith, Manchester Battalion.
Private H. Stuffins, 1st Manchester Warehouse Battalion.
Lance-Corporal J. W. Thomas, 6th Manchester Territorial Battalion.
Private A. Taylor, City of London Yeomanry.
Private E. Uttley, Royal Army Medical Corps.
Private L. Walker, Royal Scots.
Lance-Corpal E. A. Warburton, 2nd Manchester Warehouse Battalion.
Private F. Wild, East Lancashire Royal Field Artillery.
L.-Corporal P. J. Willison, 2nd Manchester Warehouse Battalion.

From the Mills, Salford.

R. E. Ashcroft, 19th Battalion Lancashire Fusiliers.
Corporal H. Austin, Royal Army Medical Corps.
Sergeant A. Boyle, 1/5th Battalion Manchester Regiment.
T. Brooks, 3rd Battalion Manchester Regiment.
T. Bradbury, 3rd Battalion Lancashire Fusiliers.
A. Braithwaite, 2nd Company, 7th Battalion Lancashire Fusiliers.
J. Bird, 12th Battalion Lancashire Fusiliers.
J. Barry, 19th Service, 3rd Salford Battalion Lancashire Fusiliers.
G. Chamberlain, H. Coy., 3rd Battalion King's Own Scottish Borderers.
W. Crosbie, 2/7th Battalion Lancashire Fusiliers.
F. Cuthbert, B. Company, Royal Scots.

Richard Haworth & Co. Ltd.

ROLL OF HONOUR—continued.

J. Carr, 7th Battalion Lancashire Fusiliers.
Robert Cowell, 3rd Battalion King's Own Royal Lancasters.
T. Davies, 18th Battalion Lancashire Fusiliers.
M. Davidson, 21st Reserve Battalion Lancashire Fusiliers.
C. Foster, 3rd Battalion Lancashire Fusiliers.
H. Fowler, 18th Service Battalion Manchester Regiment.
J. Flatley, 23rd Battalion Manchester Regiment.
Corporal B. Grace, 1st Battalion Lancashire Fusiliers.
C. Garner, 7th Battalion Lancashire Fusiliers.
— Howarth, D. Battalion Royal Marines.
C. Howard, South Lancashire Regiment.
E. Hurst, 11th Battalion Lancashire Fusiliers.
T. H. Hart, 3rd Battalion Lancashire Fusiliers.
J. Harrison, 8th Battalion Lancashire Fusiliers.
J. Hulmes, Signaller, 16th Battalion Lancashire Fusiliers.
A. Hodge, 6th Battalion Royal Scots.
W. Lawson, 3rd Border Regiment.
J. Lyman, 2nd East Lancashire Regiment.
John Mooney, 2nd Battalion King's Own Royal Lancasters.
J. Moffatt, 3rd Border Regiment.
H. McKee, 1st Battalion King's Royal Rifles.
F. Millington, 1st Salford Battalion Lancashire Fusiliers.
A. Orford, King's Royal Rifles.
Edgar Parry, Royal Field Artillery.
Leonard Parry, 7th Battalion Lancashire Fusiliers.
O. Ryan, 8th Battalion Lancashire Fusiliers.
W. Robinson, 15th Service Battalion Lancashire Fusiliers.
Joseph Rothwell, 2nd East Lancashire R.A.
Joshua Rothwell, 3rd Company, Border Regiment.
H. Rostron, 2nd Lancashire Fusiliers.
H. Roberts, 6th Battalion Royal Scots.
C. Stones, 8th Battalion Lancashire Fusiliers.
H. Spencer, 1/8th Battalion Lancashire Fusiliers.
T. Swarbrick, 8th Battalion Lancashire Fusiliers.
Charles Stephens, 3rd Battalion Lancashire Fusiliers.
H. Sharpe, 12th Battalion Lancashire Fusiliers.
H. Tyson, 1/7th Battalion Lancashire Fusiliers.
J. Wilkinson, 2nd East Lancashire Regiment.
— Worsley, 8th Battalion Lancashire Fusiliers.
A. Wood, 1/7th Battalion Lancashire Fusiliers.
G. Warner, 11th Battalion Manchester Regiment.
H. Whitby, 18th Service Battalion Manchester Regiment.
A. Wood, C. Company, S.B.M.R.
Thomas Oliver, 8th Battalion Lancashire Fusiliers.

ROLL OF HONOUR.

Members of the Directorate and Staff of

M. Hertz & Co. Ltd.

Who have Volunteered and been accepted for Foreign Service.

Director.
Major GERALD B. HERTZ — 7th Batt. Manchester Regiment (T.).

London Office.
Major M. C. V. HERTZ — 2nd Bat. City of London Royal Fus. (T.)

Staff, Manchester Office.

J. BLEASDALE	Duke of Lancaster's Own Imp. Yeo.
W. BOWLER	3rd Batt. City of Manchester Regt.
W. BURTON	5th Batt. Manchester Regiment.
H. BUSBY	9th Royal Scots.
J. L. DAY	3rd Batt. City of Manchester Regt.
W. DERBYSHIRE	2nd Batt. City of Manchester Regt.
E. FARTHING	3rd Batt. City of Manchester Regt.
A. FEATHERSTONE	6th Batt. Manchester Regiment (T.).
D. FISHER	3rd Batt. City of Manchester Regiment.
J. HART	3rd Batt. City of Manchester Regiment.
A. HOBSON	6th Batt. Manchester Regiment (T.).
HARTLEY JACKSON	6th Batt. Manchester Regiment (T.).
H. JOHNSON	King's Own Scottish Borderers.
B. JOHNSON	Old Public Schools and Univ. Corps.
E. JONES	Royal Field Artillery.
J. H. KELLY	8th Batt. Manchester Regiment (T.).
F. L. LIVSEY	3rd Batt. City of Manchester Regiment.
P. MAGINNESS	East Lancs. Royal Engineers (T.).
*H. MORRIS	3rd Batt. City of Manchester Regt.
T. NELSON	Duke of Lancaster's Own Imp. Yeo.
R. SAUNDERS	8th Batt. Manchester Regt. (T.).
W. SCHOFIELD	Duke of Lancaster's Own Imp. Yeo.
J. SHAW	Royal Garrison Artillery.
W. H. SPENCELEY	3rd Batt. City of Manchester Regt.
J. TOMLINSON	3rd Batt. City of Manchester Regt.
H. TRUELOVE	Cheshire Yeomanry.
S. J. VALLENDER	2nd Lancs. Brigade Royal Field Art.
F. WILSON	3rd Batt. City of Manchester Regt.

* Killed in Flanders, 1916.

ROLL OF HONOUR.

HEYN FRANC & CO.,

4, Chepstow Street, MANCHESTER,
and
Eastern House, Harris Street, BRADFORD.

✱ ✱ ✱

List of Employees Serving with H.M. Forces.

ALDOUS, HAROLD, 16th Service Batt. Manchester Regt.
BEDFORD, F., 3/7th Batt. Manchester Regt. (Terr. F.).
BEECROFT, Sergt-Major J. H., National Reserve.
BERRY, Corpl. FRED, 16th Service Batt. Manchester Regt.
BOULTON, JAMES, National Reserve.
BRISTER, J. C., 16th Service Batt. Manchester Regt.
BUTLER, H., 3rd West Yorkshire Regt.
CORLEY, E., 16th Service Batt. Manchester Regt.
COATES, A. T., Royal Army Medical Corps.
CUMMINGS, C., 22nd Service Batt. Manchester Regt.
DUGGAN, Lce.-Corpl. JOHN, 4th Batt. Royal Scots Queen's Edin. R.
ETCHELLS, A., 8th Batt. Manchester Regt. (Terr. F.).
FOX, Lieut. ROBERT O., West Lancs. Garrison Artillery.
GATES, E. O., Royal Engineers, 32nd Signal Coy.
HIGSON, EDWARD, 16th Service Batt. Manchester Regt.
HIRST, JOSEPH, 16th Batt. West Yorkshire Regt.
HOLLAND, Sergt. GORDON, 10th Batt. King's Own. Yorkshire L.I.
HUDSON, Q.M.Sgt. HERBERT, 10th Batt. King's Own. Yorks. L.I.
HUGHES, Sergt. SYDNEY A., 17th Service Batt. Manchester Regt.
HORROCKS, ERNEST, 4th Batt. Royal Scots Queen's Edin. R.
KERR, JAMES, 4th Batt. Royal Scots Queen's Edin. R.
MOSS, Captain CECIL H., East Lancashire Royal Field Artillery.
MORAN, W., Seaforth Highlanders.
MUTCH, WILFRED, 4th Batt. Royal Scots Queen's Edin. R.
PINKERTON, NORMAN, 16th Service Batt. Manchester Regt.
RAILTON, Lce.-Corpl. DOUGLAS, 27th Res. Batt. Manchester Regt.
SANDFORD, GEORGE, 6th Batt. Manchester Regt. (Terr. F.).
SCOTT, ALBERT E., 22nd Res. Batt. Manchester Regt.
SIMPSON, Lieut. ALLEN, 23rd Service Batt. Manchester Regt.
TAYLOR, SYDNEY, 16th Service Batt. Manchester Regt.
UNTER, J., 8th Batt. Manchester Regt. (Terr. F.).
WALTON, A., 16th Service Batt. Manchester Regt.
WOOD, GEORGE H., 4th Batt. Royal Scots Queen's Edin. R.

ROLL OF HONOUR

***

The Hollins Mill Co. Ltd.

5, PORTLAND STREET, MANCHESTER.

Capt. GUY A. CARVER, A.D.C., Royal Field Artillery, Ches. Brigade.
Capt. OSWALD A. CARVER, East Lanc. Royal Engineers.
Lt. DOUGLAS FREARS LORD, Royal Field Artillery, Ches. Brigade.
Lt. REX HOLLINS LORD, Royal Field Artillery, Ches. Brigade.
2nd Lt. FRANK HOWARTH, 10th Batt. Manchester Regt.
2nd Lt. LEONARD KELLY, R.F.A., 1st East Lanc. Brigade.
2nd Lt. REGINALD KELLY, 9th Batt. Manchester Regt.
2nd Lt. JACK LEE, 6th Batt. Cheshire Regiment.
2nd Lt. REGINALD LETTON PERCIVAL, 2nd/8th Manchester Regt.
Col. Sergt. JOHN McQUINN, Munster Fusiliers.
Sergt. REGINALD ADSHEAD, 20th Batt. Manchester Regt.
Sergt. ARTHUR DENNEY, 16th Batt. Manchester Regt.
Sergt. J. MOLD, 12th King's Liverpool Regt.
Sergt. JAMES C. PEARSON, 19th Batt. Manch. Regt.
Corp. CHAS ARMITAGE, 7th Batt. Lanc. Fus. (T.F.).
Corp. FRED COPPARD, 5th Royal West Kents.
Corp. WILLIAM COXON, 16th Batt. Manchester Regt.
Corp. ALFRED FLETCHER, 19th Batt. Manch. Regt.
Corp. HARRY L. WAINE, 2nd/6th Batt. Manch. Regt.
L.-Corp. WALTER CORNER, 4th Batt. Seaforth H., T.F.
L.-Corp. THOMAS SHERLOCK, 7th Batt. Lanc. Fusiliers.
L.-Corp. FRANK SHERWOOD, R.A.M.C.
L.-Corp. GEORGE WILLIAMS, 18th Batt. Manch. Regt.
Pte. THOMAS HENRY BENNETT, 19th Batt. Manchester Regt.
Trooper HARRY BERRISFORD, Duke of Lancaster's Own Yeomanry.
Pte. AMOS BIRCHALL, 16th Batt. Manchester Regt.
Pte. FREDERICK BLEACKLEY, 17th Batt. Manchester Regt.
Pte. JAMES BOWKER, 17th Batt. Manchester Regt.
Driver M. H. BROWN, Army Service Corps, M.T.
Pte. HARRY CAWLEY, 16th Batt. Manchester Regt.
Pte. SAMUEL CROWTHER, 16th Batt. Manch. Regt.
Pte. JAMES DANIELS, 16th Batt. Manchester Regt.
Pte. EDWARD DUNKERLEY, 9th Batt. Royal Scots.
Pte. GEORGE EDMOND ESTILL, R.A.M.C. (T.F.).
Pte. DONALD M. FORBES, 6th Batt. Manchester Regt. (T.F.).
Pte. EDWARD FRITH, 17th Batt. Manchester Regt.
Pte. FRED GIBBONS, 3rd Batt. South Lanc. Regt.

ROLL OF HONOUR.
CONTINUED.

The Hollins Mill Co. Ltd.

Pte. HAROLD GILL, 6th Batt. Manchester Regt. (T.F.).
Pte. WILLIAM LEONARD GREENHOUGH, 4th Batt. Seaforth H. (T.F.).
Pte. WM. GURLING, — Batt. Manchester Regt.
Pte. JAMES HARRINGTON, 18th Batt. Manch. Regt.
Pte. ARTHUR HEYWOOD, 19th Batt. Manchester Regt.
Pte. WALTER HIBBERT, — Batt. Manchester Regt.
Pte. JOHN HIGSON, Public Schools Battalion.
Pte. STANLEY HILTON, 19th Batt. Manchester Regt.
Pte. THOMAS HOBBS, 7th Manchester Batt. East Lanc. Territorials.
Pte. JOSEPH HOLT, 19th Batt. Manchester Regt.
Pte. WM. HUNT, 7th Batt. East Lanc. Regt.
Pte. HERBERT INGOE, 18th Batt. Manchester Regt.
Pte. ALBERT JONES, 18th Batt. Manchester Regt.
Pte. SAMUEL KENDRICK, 7th Batt. East Lanc. Fusiliers (T.F.).
Pte. JOHN KIRELLY, 18th Batt. Manchester Regt.
Pte. ERNEST KIRKHAM, R.A.M.C.
Pte. PETER LLOYD, 3rd/2nd Lowland Field Ambulance, R.A.M.C.
Pte. EDWARD LOVATT, — Batt. Manchester Regt.
Driver STANLEY McDONALD, R.A.M.C., East Lanc Div. (T.F.).
Pte. ALFRED McGRATH, — Batt. Manchester Regt.
Pte. ALFRED MUMFORD, 15th Batt. Manchester Regt.
Pte. GEORGE PEARSON, 16th Batt. Manchester Regt.
Pte. RALPH PHILLIPS, 19th Batt. Manchester Regt.
Pte. GEORGE PRICE, 19th Batt. Manchester Regt.
Trooper ALBERT RAINES, Earl of Chester's Yeomanry.
Pte. ERNEST READ, 16th Batt. Manchester Regt.
Pte. FRED RICHARDSON, 16th Batt. Manch. Regt.
Pte. ERNEST RIGG, Argyle and Sutherland Highlanders.
Pte. FRANK ROE, 2nd Batt. Manchester Regt.
Pte. ALFRED ARMITAGE SLOMAN, R.A.M.C. (T.F.).
Pte. JAMES SMITH, 11th Batt. King's Own Royal.
Pte. JOHN STOCKS, 17th Batt. Manchester Regt.
Pte. FRED SUMMERFIELD, A.S.C., M.T. (T.F.).
Pte. JOHN THOMPSON, — Batt. Manchester Regt.
Pte. JAMES TITTLEY, — Batt. Manchester Regt.
Pte. STEWART L. WATSON, R.A.M.C. (T.F.).
Pte. CYRIL WHITNALL, Argyle and Sutherland Highlanders.
Pte. FRANK WILLIAMSON, 19th Batt. Manch. Regt.
Pte. LEONARD WOODALL, 18th Batt. Manch. Regt.
Pte. THOS. WATSON, 7th Batt. Manchester Regt.
Pte. ALEX. MacPHEE, Royal Army Medical Corps.

ROLL OF HONOUR

Holmes, Terry & Co. Ltd.,
MANCHESTER.

Members of the Staff now Serving in the Army.
Manchester City Battalions.

Pte. R. EVANS,
 27th Bt. Manchester Regt.
 (Single).

Sgt. L. McWILLIAMS, 6522,
 16th Bt. Manchester Regt.
 (Married).

Pte. W. BARNES, 6460,
 16th Bt. Manchester Regt.
 (Single).

Pte. A. MORAN, 11890,
 19th Bt. Manchester Regt.
 (Married).

Pte. RD. FURNESS, 11809,
 19th Bt. Manchester Regt.
 (Single).

Coy. Sgt.-Maj. CLARKE,
 16th Bt. Manchester Regt.
 (Married).

Pte. WILF HACKETT,
 16th Bt. Manchester Regt.
 (Married).

Pte. C. S. BERLIN, 17/8405,
 17th Bt. Manchester Regt.
 (Single).

Pte. H. BAMFORD, 8399,
 17th Bt. Manchester Regt.
 (Single).

Pte. N. FORTUNE, 7445,
 25th Bt. Manchester Regt.
 (Single).

Cpl. S. HARE,
 17th Bt. Manchester Regt.
 (Single).

Pte. A. NEWTON, 8255,
 17th Bt. Manchester Regt.
 (Single).

Pte. A. W. ANDREWS, 11731,
 19th Bt. Manchester Regt.
 (Single).

L.-Cpl. J. SHERLOCK, 8876,
 17th Bt. Manchester Regt.
 (Single).

Pte. J. MOORE,
 16th Bt. Manchester Regt.
 (Single).

Pte. C. SCHOLEY, 8875,
 17th Bt. Manchester Regt.
 (Single).

Sgt. G. DEANE, 6485,
 16th Bt. Manchester Regt.
 (Single).

Pte. E. FARRINGTON,
 25th (R.) Bt. Manchester R.
 (Single).

Pte. H. KELLEY, 17400,
 20th Bt. Manchester Regt.
 (Single).

Pte. S. ARMSTRONG, 8366,
 17th Bt. Manchester Regt.
 (Single).

Pte. W. R. CAMPBELL, 6473,
 16th Bt. Manchester Regt.
 (Single).

Pte. A. GOSLING,
 16th Bt. Manchester Regt.
 (Single).

Various Regiments.

Pte. C. WARD, 1660,
 7th Bt. Manchester Regt.
 (Single).

Pte. H. HASTINGS, 3835,
 3/7th Bt. Sherwood For.
 (Single).

Pte. F. BARBER,
 Royal Garrison Artillery.
 (Single).

Pte. G. W. WARD, 2854,
 9th Bt. Royal Scots H.
 (Single).

ROLL OF HONOUR—continued.

Holmes, Terry and Co. Limited.

Pte. J. SEREVITCH, 19956,
  3rd Bt. South Lancs. Regt.
  (Single).
Pte. F. C. PALMER, 2101,
  1/7th Bt. Manchester Regt.
  (Single).
Pte. J. H. LIVESEY, 34352,
  1st Bt. Welsh Regt.
  (Single).
Pte. J. ASTLE, S/10885,
  11th Bt. Gordon Highl'rs.
  (Single).
Pte. K. CAMERON, 3406,
  3/8th Bt. Arg. & Suth. H.
  (Single).
Pte. R. WILSON, 3610,
  9th Div. Cycle Coy., King's
  Own Scottish Borderers.
  (Married).
Pte. D. J. ROBERTS, 23612,
  16th Bt. Royal Welsh Fus.
  (Single).
Pte. V. SAVAGE, 18235,
  9th Bt. South Lancs. Regt.
  (Single).
Pte. S. SIDEBOTTOM, 1751,
  1/7th Bt. Lancs. Fusiliers.
  (Single).
Cpl. E. LASCELLES, 1445,
  1/7th Bt. Manchester Regt.
  (Single).
Pte. G. STEPHENS, 3483,
  3/8th Bt. Arg. & Suth. H.
  (Single).
L.-Cpl. J. H. HUDSON,
  3rd Bt. Manchester Regt.
  (Married).
Lt. J. W. BROUGHTON,
  2nd Gar. Bt. Northumb. Fus.
  (Single).

Pte. H. WHEELER, 789,
  R.A.M.C. Field Ambulance.
  (Single).
Cpl. S. BILLINGTON, 3698,
  3/7th Bt. Lancs. Fusiliers.
  (Married).
Pte. T. J. HILLBORNE,
  11th Bt. Welsh Regt.
  (Single).
Pte. H. LEVER, 438,
  1st Bt. Lancs. Fusiliers.
  (Married).
  Killed in Dardanelles.
Pte. W. LOWE, 2068,
  7th Bt. Manchester Regt.
  (Single).
Pte. T. C. JONES, 6359,
  Loyal North Lancs.
  (Single).
Pte. H. RUSSELL,
  Royal Army Medical Corps.
  (Single).
Pte. A. ROUGHSEDGE, 3888,
  3/7th Bt. Manchester Regt.
  (Single).
Pte. J. ELLIS, 788,
  R.A.M.C. Field Ambulance.
  (Single).
Pte. J. BAXTER, 1520,
  1/6th Bt. Manchester Regt.
  (Single).
Pte. B. ROACH,
  Royal Army Medical Corps.
  (Single).
Pte. ROBT. SMITH, 4332,
  8th Bt. Manchester Regt.
  (Single).

Pte. H. TIMMINS,
  6th Bt. Manchester Regt.
  (Single).
Gnr. H. F. TERRY,
  B. By, Hon. Artillery Coy.
  (Single).
Pte. J. HARNEY, 1483,
  1/6th Bt. Manchester Regt.
  (Single).
Pte. J. BERGIN,
  Winchester Rifle Brigade.
  (Married).
Cpl. D. COOKE,
  Lancashire Fusiliers.
  (Single).
  Killed in Dardanelles.
Pte. LUCAS,
  Army Service Corps.
  (Single).
Pte. R. CARDWELL,
  Motor Transport.
  (Married).
Pte. J. KARS,
  Royal Field Artillery.
  (Married).
Pte. J. HARDCASTLE, 26583,
  King's Liverpool Regt.
  (Single).
Pte. JONES,
  King's O. Liverpool Regt.
  (Single).
Lt. J. H. COOKE.
  9th Bt. Manchester Regt.
  (Single).
Pte. W. BATE,
  Motor Transport, A.S.C.
Pte. J. ROBERTS,
  Motor Transport, A.S.C.

List of members of above staff who have also offered their services but have been rejected for various reasons.

J. SPOONCER (Single).	W. HAMMERSLEY (Married).	S. BROWN (Single).
H. WALSH (Single).	F. GORTON (Married).	E. C. BROTHERTON (Married).
W. BENNETT (Single).	A. WHITE (Single).	J. HASSALL (Single).
L. FOSTER (Single).	H. SHERRATT (Married).	A. FINN (Single).
J. VAUGHAN (Single).	R. SHERSTONE (Married).	W. ROSSON (Single).
F. FODEN (Single).	J. STEINLOFT (Married).	

Sixty-five of our members have been attested and placed in their group under Lord Derby's scheme.

ROLL OF HONOUR.

***

HOGG & MITCHELL

BIRCHIN LANE, CHURCH STREET,
MANCHESTER.

Employees serving with His Majesty's Forces.

Pte. J. ATKINSON	13th Bt. King's Liverpool Regt.
Sergt. W. ADAMS	5th Scottish Rifles.
Pte. JOHN BOYD	2nd Bt. Royal Irish Rifles.

Wounded in action at Loos; since died in London.

Cpl. WILLIAM BELL	10th Bt. R. Inniskilling Fusiliers.
Pte. A. BROWN	10th Bt. R. Inniskilling Fusiliers.
Pte. ROBT. J. BIRNEY	3rd Bt. R. Inniskilling Fusiliers.
Pte. D. CURRAN	8th Bt. R. Inniskilling Fusiliers.
Pte. JOHN CRAIG	Royal Army Medical Corps.
Pte. DAVID CLARKE	12th Bt. R. Inniskilling Fusiliers.
Pte. R. H. ENGLAND	4th Manchester City Regiment.
Pte. F. EVANS	4th Manchester City Regiment.
Driver A. GILCHRIST	A.S.C., 6th Liverpool Rifles.
Pte. JOHN HYDE	8th Manchester Regiment (T.F.).
L.-Cpl. P. LOCKETT	6th Manchester Regiment (T.F.).
Cpl. R. M'CARTER	10th Bt. R. Inniskilling Fusiliers.
Pte. S. J. MERVYN	North Irish Horse Regiment.
Pte. ARTHUR MEARS	24th County of London F.S.R.

Killed in action.

Pte. J. McMILLAN	9th Highland Light Infantry.
Sergt. W. E. SMITH	8th Manchester Regiment (T.F.).
Pte. W. E. TAYLOR	2/6th City of London Rifles.
Pte. C. TAYLOR	7th Manchester City Regiment.
Pte. JOHN USSHER	12th Bt. R. Inniskilling Fusiliers.
Pte. WOODHEAD	Hon. Artillery Co. (Infantry Sect.).
Pte. H. BRAITH-WAITE	29th Batt. Royal Fusiliers.
Pte. D. TORRENS	12th Bt. R. Inniskilling Fusiliers.
Pte. F. W. PEARCE	Royal West Surreys.

List of Employees serving with the Colours.

Horrockses, Crewdson & Co.,
LIMITED,
107, Piccadilly, MANCHESTER.

Acheson, S. W.	Eardley, C.	Marsden, J.
Ashworth, A.	Fenton, J.	Massey, H.
Bamford, W.	Farrington, G. W.	Leatherbarrow, J. S.
Buckley, H.	Findlow, H.	Norwood, G.
Blount, H.	Foden, H.	Pollard, G. A.
Bruce, G. H.	Gallagher, T.	Rigg, J.
Broadmeadow, S.	Gribbin, P. E.	Riley, J.
Burke, E.	Heaton, J.	Robinson, F.
Burgess, H.	Hiorns, A.	Sheehan, B.
Bradshaw, W. H.	Howard, F. L.	Sparrow, J.
Cross, F.	Hughes, J.	Stringer, A.
Cookson, A. E.	Hulme, J.	Sullivan, J.
Cooper, D. C.	Johnson, A.	Turner, L. R.
Capstick, R.	Jones, C. O.	Tweddle, C.
Cooke, J. H.	Kitching, L. A.	Walker, H.
Crompton, P.	Knowles, A.	Wainwright, J. L.
Dunlop, W.	Leadbeater, G. V.	Warburton, J. W.
Evers, H. M.	Longworth, W.	Woodcock, W.

Of the above G. Norwood and J. L. Wainwright have received Commissions. There are also 652 enlistments from our mills, of whom two have received Commissions.

Dec., 1915.

ROLL OF HONOUR.

Joshua Hoyle & Sons Ltd.,
50, Piccadilly, MANCHESTER.

Directors and Sons of Directors.

Lieut.-Col. J. C. HOYLE, T.D., D.L.	5th Battalion East Lancashire Regt. (T.).
Lieutenant E. B. HOYLE, R.N.	H.M.S. "Azalea."
Lieutenant J. B. HOYLE	7th Battalion South Lancashire Regiment.
Lieutenant G. M. HOYLE	3rd Batt. Sherwood For. (killed in action).
2nd Lieutenant H. K. HOYLE	5th Batt. Lancs. Fus. (T.) (killed in action).
Corporal A. L. HOYLE	Nagpur Volunteer Mounted Rifles.

Employees.

J. L. HEARD, Lieutenant	23rd Battalion Manchester Regiment.
H. W. BRITTON, 2nd Lieutenant	3/5th M/r Regt. (T.).
W. C. LEES, 2nd Lieutenant	The Cameronians.
JOHN DARBYSHIRE	3rd King's Own Scottish Borderers.
J. McKEAN	Hampshire Regiment.
A. SOUTHERN	1st Battalion Loyal North Lancs. Regiment.
A. MAITLAND	Royal Naval Sick Berth Reserve.
J. PICKLES, Sergeant	5th Batt. Man/r Regt. (T.) (killed in action).
A. CLARKE	16th Battalion Manchester Regiment.
J. F. SHORROCKS	13th Battalion Rifle Brigade.
F. BROWN	2nd East Lancs. Brigade R.F.A. (T.).
H. FARRINGTON	7th Battalion Lancashire Fusiliers (T.).
J. BAND	18th Battalion Manchester Regiment.
T. DUTTON	18th Battalion Manchester Regiment.
A. PENNY	18th Battalion Manchester Regiment.
R. F. WHITEHEAD	18th Battalion Manchester Regiment.
E. POWNALL	18th Battalion Manchester Regiment.
A. DUCKWORTH	H.M.S. "Cæsar."
L. KIRBY	3rd Battalion King's Liverpool Regiment.
E. SUMMERS	8th Battalion Manchester Regiment (T.).
F. ROWE	Royal Army Medical Corps.
F. QUINN	8th Battalion Manchester Regiment (T.).
JOHN RICHARDSON	6th Battalion Manchester Regiment (T.).
G. B. COOPER	Victoria University O.T.C.
L. GREENWOOD	Cyclists' Corps.
JAMES CAIN	6th Battalion Manchester Regiment (T.).
J. G. STRADE	Royal Army Medical Corps.
J. W. BROOKES	Royal Army Medical Corps.
E. S. HOWARTH	13th Battalion Lancashire Fusiliers.
A. PYM	6th Battalion Manchester Regiment (T.).

ROLL OF HONOUR.

The Household Stores Association LIMITED.

Grocery and Provisions—
George Jones.
Henry Stott.
Hugh Taylor.
Alexander Poole.
John Butcher.
John H. Roby.
Richard Scholes.
John Latham.
William Morley.
Frank W. Cassidy.
Albert Booth.
J. Clegg (Williams).

Counting House—
Rich. L. Hardisty.
Geo. A. M. Bennett.
Bernard Halpern.
Wm. Hallatt, Jr.
Hugh Allen.
James H. Milne.
George Crighton.

Delivery Department—
Harry J. Walsh.
Joseph Welsh.
J. W. Millichap.
Alfred Bacchus.

Wine Department—
John Hendrick.
William Glynn.
Charles Anthony.

Tailoring Department—
A. Glazebrook.

Drug Department—
Ralph Bates.
H. Blomeley.

Men's Hosiery Dept.—
Alfred Kerr.

A record of their service and our pride in them.
THE STAFF AND MANAGEMENT.

THE HOUSEHOLD STORES ASSOCIATION LIMITED
KING STREET WEST, DEANSGATE, MANCHESTER

ROLL OF HONOUR.

Sydney Hudson Limited

18, Chepstow Street, Manchester.

1st Lieut. W. G. Higgins	A.S.C.
Sergeant T. Griffiths	26th Manchester Regiment.
Coporal Clifford Barrett	A.S.C. (T.F.).
Private Peter Carroll	Lancashire Fusiliers.
Private Jas. Cooke	Royal Scots (Discharged, too young).
Private John Dale	R.F.A.
Private H. Fitzwilliam	R.A.M.C. (T.F.).
Private Chas. Hart	16th Manchester Regiment.
Private Thos. Bramwell	18th Manchester Regiment.
Private Geo. Norbury	27th Manchester Regiment.
Private Sidney Price	Marines.
Private H. Patchett	R.A.M.C. (T.F.).
Private Geo. Simcock	R.A.M.C. (T.F.).
Private Wm. Stevenson	South Lancashire Regiment.
Private Richard Venables	R.F.A.
Private H. L. Seddon	A.S.C.
*Private E. J. Maddocks	8th Manchesters (T.F.).
Private D. Macfie	R.A.M.C.
Private Wm. Renwick	7th Manchesters (T.F.).
Private E. Billington	8th Manchesters (T.F.).
Private Geo. Pepper	R.A.M.C. (T.F.).

* Discharged, too young.

ROLL OF HONOUR.

Employees of
James F. Hutton & Company Ltd.
14 LLOYD STREET, MANCHESTER
Serving with the Colours.

†Staff Sergt. E. W. AKHURST	No. 382, Corps of the School of Musketry.
Private H. BLAKE	No. 3092, D Co., 2/6th Batt. Man. Regt.
Private W. BRACEWELL	No. P.S. 4552, C Co., 20th Batt. Royal Fs.
2nd Lieut. H. J. BROCKLEHURST	3/5th Batt. Hants. Regiment.
Private L. BRYON	No. 3849, A Co., 3/6th Batt. Man. Regt.
†Private A. CONDUIT	No. 10099, 18th Ser. Batt. Man. Regt.
Private A. DAVIES	No. 10105, No. 2 Co., 18th Ser. Batt. Man. Regt.
Corporal G. ELDING	Duke of Lancaster's Yeomanry.
Staff Sergt. S. FEARNHEAD	Army Service Corps.
*Private F. W. FISHER	No. S251, B Co., Plymouth Batt. Royal Marine Light Infantry.
†Sergeant A. O. HITCHEN	2nd City Batt. Manchester Regiment.
2nd Lieut. H. H. JACKSON	3/6th Batt. Man. Regt. (originally No. 2425, 1/6th Batt. Man. Regt., wounded at Gallipoli).
Corporal H. E. MORRIS	No. 142553, Royal Engineers.
Private J. S. SELBIE	No. 2432, 1/6th Batt. Man. Regiment (wounded at Gallipoli), now attached to 3/6th Batt. Man. Regt.
Corporal C. SOUTHERN	No. 2048, C Co., 1/8th Batt. Man. Regt.
Private H. TRUEMAN	No. 10221, No. 2 Co., 18th Batt. Man. Regt.
3rd Writer A. G. WEARING	H.M.S. "Ganges."

* Killed in Action.   † Received Discharge Certificate.

ROLL OF HONOUR.

✱✱✱

John Hall Ltd.,

11 Mosley Street, Manchester.

FRED BROOKS,
    19th Battalion Manchester Regiment.

HAROLD BLANKLEY,
    3/2nd Field Ambulance, R.A.M.C.

EPHRAIM GREENHALGH,
    Army Service Corps.

JOHN HOWARTH,
    17th Battalion Manchester Regiment.

WILLIAM HORNBY,
    22nd Battalion Manchester Regiment.

HARRY LEEMING,
    Royal Garrison Artillery.

JOHN MOORE,
    3rd Hussars.

CHRISTOPHER YOUNG,
    3/7th Lancashire Fusiliers.

Roll of Honour.

Hiltermann Brothers,

56, WHITWORTH STREET,
MANCHESTER.

Private W. W. BOX,
    Royal Army Medical Corps.

Gunner A. CHADDERTON,
    E. Lancs. Royal Field Artillery.

Private H. GARNER,
    7th Batt. Manchester Regiment.

Corporal E. HALL,
    16th Batt. Lancashire Fusiliers.

Grenadier A. E. HALLIDAY,
    13th Batt. King's Liverpool Regt.

Gunner W. HUNT,
    E. Lancs. Royal Field Artillery.

Private A. J. KNUDSEN,
    20th Batt. Royal Fusiliers.

Private H. McMILLAN,
    20th Batt. Royal Fusiliers.

Sec. Lieut. L. E. NEWELL,
    3rd Batt. Lancashire Fusiliers.

Private J. RICHARDSON,
    Royal Army Medical Corps.

Driver J. ROBERTS,
    E. Lancs. Royal Field Artillery.

Private F. THOMPSON,
    19th Batt. Royal Fusiliers.

Driver W. J. TURNER,
    Army Service Corps.

ROLL OF HONOUR.

HOUGH, HOSEASON & CO.

2, Bridge Street,
MANCHESTER.

Works:
HOLLAND STREET, PENDLETON.

Lieut. W. A. AMERY,
    Royal Army Medical Corps.

Lieut. H. G. ST. JOHN,
    14th Ser. Batt. Manch. Regt.

Sergeant R. BREAM,
    Loyal North Lancs. Regt.

Corporal C. F. JEBB,
    Royal Engineers.

*Private W. H. DINGLE,
    1/7 Batt. Manch. Regt. (T.).

*Private W. ABRAMS,
    Lancs. Fusiliers.

Private S. STANWAY,
    K.O. Liverpool Regt.

Private R. JONES,
    Army Service Corps.

Private A. DOBSON,
    Army Service Corps.

Private J. H. PORTER,
    Royal Army Medical Corps.

Private T. MCLOUGHLIN,
    Royal Army Medical Corps.
    * Killed.

ROLL OF HONOUR.

* * *

ALFRED HULME,
LIMITED,

Timber Importers and Merchants.

WITHINGTON STREET, . . .
    . . . . PENDLETON.

* * *

L.-Cpl. THOMAS ROWLES,
    Carter; Royal Irish Fusiliers. Killed Aug. 6th at Dardanelles.

L.-Cpl. ALFRED MORGAN,
    Foreman; Loyal North Lancs.

Pte. RICHARD HUGHES,
    Backer up to Circular Saw Bench; Lancs. Fusiliers.

Pte. HARRY SMITH,
    Clerk, R.A.M.C.

ROLL OF HONOUR.

✱ ✱ ✱

Irwell & Eastern Rubber Company
LIMITED.
ORDSALL LANE, SALFORD, MANCHESTER.

EUROPEAN WAR.

Names of Employees who have joined the Army or Navy.

COLSELL, Capt. R. F. J.	HAGUE, T.	PUGH, J.
TINTO, Lieut. W. A.	HASLAM, W.	PLUMB, E.
SWAIN, Lieut. T. L.	HUDDART, J.	POWER, H.
ARNOLD, P. W.	HOLDING, C.	PARRY, T.
AVERST, P.	HANDFORD, F.	TOWERS, F. R.
ALDOUS, W.	HARTLEY, T.	PEAT, J.
AULD, W.	HOY, J.	RODGERS, E.
BEARDALL, J.	HARDY, J.	RENSHAW, H.
BOND, J.	HESFORD, D.	REDMOND, J.
BINGHAM, C.	HILSON, J.	RIDGWAY, C.
BAINES, J.	JONES, W.	RENSHAW, J.
BERISFORD, S.	JONES, A.	RAMSDEN, T.
BURTON, A.	JONES, J.	SHAW, J.
BRIGHT, A.	JORDAN, A.	SHAW, W.
BOLLAND, A.	KERSHAW, E. (Killed).	(Prisoner of war).
BUNN, C.	KIRBY, E.	SIMPSON, E.
BARDSLEY, J.	KELLY, C.	SEE, A.
BURKE, E.	KEANE, J.	SOUTHERN, R.
CRAMPTON, A.	KELLY, F.	SLATER, J.
CROWLEY, W. (Killed)	KELLY, J.	SCHOFIELD, S.
CROWLEY, D.	LEE, S.	SCHOFIELD, H.
CLARKE, R.	LEWIS, A.	SPEDDY, J.
CARTER, T.	LEYLAND, J.	SEDDON, W.
CASH, S.	LATCHFORD, J.	SEALE, A.
CARNAJIA, J.	LANG, J.	STRICKLAND, H.
CLARKE, W.	LASCELLES, F.	THOMPSON, E.
CRAWFORD, F.	KINGSELLER, G.	TAYLOR, F.
CLARE, L.	MATHER, E.	TAYLER, G.
CONNOLLY, E.	McCANN, D.	TURNER, A.
CHAPMAN, C.	MULLEN, J.	TIMMIS, W.
CORRANCE, J.	MOORES, J.	USHER, G.
DUMPHY, E.	MILLS, J.	WILSON, W.
DAWSON, A.	MARSDEN, W.	WOOD, J. (Killed).
DENNEL, R.	McCRAE, G.	WOOD, J.
DAY, S.	MOSELEY, A.	WALSH, J.
DODD, H.	MURTAGH, P.	WHITELEY, W. H.
DONEGAN, J.	MURPHY, G.	WILLIAMS, C.
EMMERSON, T.	McMURDO, A.	WINSTANLEY, H.
EDWARDS, J.	McMURDO, B.	WARD, J. H.
ECCLES, H.	NOBLETT, J.	WILLIAMS, T.
FOLEY, J.	NESBITT, T.	WILLIAMS, J.
GOWTHORP, E.	OLDFIELD, R.	WISEMAN, J.
(Killed).	PAUL, H. C.	WOODBURN, J.
GOODWIN, J.	PETERS, A. (Killed).	WALKER, J. W.
GRIMES, W.	PERCIVAL, **W.**	

ROLL OF HONOUR.

Richard Johnson & Nephew, Ltd.,
Bradford Iron Works, Manchester.

* * *

JOHNSON, Col. H. A. - - 17th Manchester Regiment.
JOHNSON, Maj. ERNEST. Duke of L. Own Yeomanry.
PERSSE, Lieut. D. S. - - 30th Lancers, Ambala Cavalry Brig., Indian Exp. Force.
BADDELEY, 2nd-Lieut. PERCY, 8th Royal Warwickshire Regt.

ABBOTT, W. H.	2nd East Lancs.	CHARLTON, A.	
ACKERLEY, W.	Manchester Regt.	CARROLL, A.	
ADAMS, F.		CLAXTON, J.	Manchester Regt.
AIRD, W.		CHEETHAM, W.	
ALLEN, H.	1st Bt. K. O. Royal L. Regt.	CHESTERS, W.	6th Royal Lancs.
ALTON, B.	21st Manchester Regt.	CHINAR, E.	
ANDREWS, F.		CLINTON, A.	
ARMSTRONG, J.		CONNOR, F.	
ASHWORTH, R.	3rd Grenadier Guards.	CONNOR, M. J.	Liverpool Regt.
ASPIN, J.	2nd Manchester.	CONNOR, P.	8th Lancs.
BAILEY, A.	17th Manchester Regt.	COLFER, P.	Welsh Guards.
BAILEY, H.		COOKE, S.	4th Manchester.
BARNSLEY, M.		CORBETT, E.	
BARROW, P.		CHORLTON, J.	1/8th Lancs. Fusiliers.
BRADLEY, B.		CORNTHWAITE, W.	King's R. Liverpool Regt.
BRADY, J.	13th Manchester.	CROSSLEY, A.	Duke of Lancs. Yeomanry.
BECK, F.	East Lancs.	CUNCARR, W.	
BELL, J.	12th Manchester.	DAVIES, C.	
BEST, R.	Manchester.	DEPLEDGE, H.	
BETTISON, A.	D. of Lancs. O. Yeomanry.	DODD, J.	Manchester.
BIGLEY, W. H.	Royal Scots.	DOLMAN, J.	Manchester.
BRIDGE, J.	Lancs. Fusiliers.	DOUGLAS, J.	20th Manchester Regt.
BOWLER, M.	Royal Field Artillery.	DUCKWORTH, J.	Manchester Regt.
BOULGER, M.	Rifle Brigade.	DUNKERLEY, G.	Royal Field Artillery.
BROCKLEHURST, J.	Royal Field Artillery.	EDWARDS, H.	Scottish Borderers.
BURNS, J.		EDWARDS, J. T.	Royal Army Medical Corps.
CARPENTER, E.		EDWARDS, W. H.	6th Border.
CARR, G.	6th Bedford Regt.	ELLIS, G.	8th Manchester.
CARTER, E.		FAIRBROTHER, W.	
CHADWICK, F.	Loyal North Lancs.	FAIRCLOUGH, J. E.	King's Liverpool Regt.
CHADWICK, T. W.	Loyal North Lancs.	FAULKNER, T.	South Lancs.
CHARLOTTE, J.	Border Regt.	FRATER, T.	Manchester Regt.
CLARKE, F.		FEASEY, S.	2/8th Manchester Regt.
CLARKE, J.	Liverpool Regt.	FERGUSON, D.	8th Manchester Regt.

Richard Johnson & Nephew, Ltd.,
BRADFORD IRON WORKS, MANCHESTER.

***

ROLL OF HONOUR—Continued.

FOX, G.	South Lancs.
FRANKLIN, F. E.	5th Royal Warwick. Regt.
FURBER, J. T.	Rifle Brigade.
FURNIFER, J.	21st Manchester Regt.
GARDNER, S. C.	Lancs. Fusiliers.
GREAVES, H.	
GREEN, J.	5th Royal Field Artillery.
GILBERT, G.	Manchester Regt.
GILMORE, W.	3rd K. O. Royal Lancs.
GILL, H.	Lancs. Fusiliers.
GILL, J. P.	Seaforth Highlanders.
GILLIBRAND, R.	
GILSON, R.	8th Manchester.
GILDER, T.	
GRIFFITHS, W.	South Lancs. Regt.
GULLAND, T.	South Lancs. Regt.
HALL, C.	22nd Manchester Regt.
HALL, J.	Northumberland Fusiliers.
HAMILTON, H.	7th Royal Lancs.
HAMLETT, A.	East Lancs.
HARRISON, C.	Manchester Regt.
HARRISON, E.	
HASLAM, S.	
HAYHURST, N.	3rd Lancs. Fusiliers.
HEYWOOD, C.	9th South Lancs.
HIBBERT, C.	
HIGHAM, J.	Lancs. Fusiliers.
HIGHAM, W.	3rd Lancs. Fusiliers.
HILL, E.	19th Div. Cyclist Co.
HILL, T.	
HOATH, M.	
HOBSON, F.	6th Bt. 4th King's Own
HOLDEN, M.	2nd Connaught Rangers.
HOWARTH, J.	Manchester Regt.
HUDDERS, A.	
HULME, S.	
HULSE, D.	8th East Lancs.
HULSE, W.	8th Manchester.
HUNT, F.	
HUTTON, C.	8th Manchester.
JACKSON, J.	3rd Bt. Lancs. Regt.
JAMES, C.	4th Manchester.
JONES, E.	16th Manchester Regt.
JONES, E.	3rd King's Liverpool.
JONES, E.	1st Rifle Brigade.
JONES, J.	170th Brig. Royal Field A.
JOYCE, H.	East Lancs.
KELLY, Sgt.-Maj. A.	8th Manchester.
KELLY, E.	
KELLY, J.	2nd Manchester.
KENNEDY, J.	Manchester Regt.
KENNEDY, J. J.	
KENYON, J.	3rd Lancs. Fusiliers.
LANGLEY, G.	8th Manchester.
LAW, D.	
LITTLE, C.	1st Manchester Regt.
LOGAN, A.	22nd Manchester Regt.
LYONS, T.	R.L.R.
LORENZELLI, E.	King's Shrop. Light Inf.
LOUTH, T.	
LYNCH, L.	3rd Lancs. Fusiliers.
MADDEN, J.	South Staffs.
MAIRS, W. A.	A.S.C. East Lancs. Div.
McCRAITH, J.	
McNALLY, J.	
MANNING, H.	
MARTIN, H.	8th Bt. Manchester.
McCARTNEY, G.	8th Manchester.
McCARTNEY, R.	8th Manchester.
MAYBURY, A.	8th King's Own R.L. Regt.
MEACHIN, W.	18th Manchester Regt.
MERRIMAN, P.	
MIDDLETON, T.	Manchester.
MILLIGAN, J.	Manchester Regt.
MILLS, H.	
MINCHIM, W.	9th Lancs. Fusiliers.
MITCHELL, A.	Royal Lancs.
MOONEY, J.	Royal Field Artillery.
MOORE, H.	3rd King's Liverpool
MORTIMER, W.	
MULLIN, J.	4th Manchester.
MURRAY, T.	
MURRAY, J.	Royal Scots.
NEILD, A.	Manchester.
NEUMANN, ERNEST	4th Bt. Royal Fusiliers (T.)
OATWAY, H.	
OLDHAM, C. F.	8th Liverpool Rifles.
O'NEILL, F.	1/3rd Brig. East Lancs.
OVEREND, W.	Manchester.
PARR, T.	18th Batt. King's R. Rifles.
PEEOVER, A.	3rd Liverpool Rifles.
PRICE, H.	8th Manchester.
POLLITT, W.	
POYSER, C.	22nd Sv. Bt. Manchester R.
RANDALL, F. H.	London Rifle Brigade.
RATHBONE, J.	Royal Field Artillery.
READ, T.	18th Lancs. Fusiliers.
RICHARDSON, T.	1st Manchester Regt.
RICHARDSON, H.	
ROBERTS, S.	

Richard Johnson & Nephew, Ltd.,

BRADFORD IRON WORKS, MANCHESTER.

✶ ✶ ✶

ROLL OF HONOUR—Continued.

ROBINSON, G.	Royal Munster Fusiliers.
ROBINSON, W.	
ROBSON, H.	R.F.A. Res., 45th Brigade.
ROEBUCK, A.	
ROPER, T.	4th Royal Scots.
ROWDEN, W.	
SANDIFORD, J.	
STANSFIELD, E.	
STANSFIELD, W.	89th Field Co., R. E.
SLATER, R.	3rd Manchester, 8th Division.
SHAW, —.	South Lancs.
STREET, A.	8th King's Own R.L. Regt.
SYKES, W. H.	2nd Manchester Regt.
SIDEBOTTOM, W.	
SHERIDAN, W.	
SPIERS, J.	Rifle Brigade.
SPILSBURY, D.	
SMITH, T.	12th Lancs. Fusiliers.
SMITH, J.	11th Sv. Bt. Manchester Rgt.
STOPFORD, J.	7th Lancs. Regiment.
SOUTHWELL, E.	9th South Lancs.
SULLIVAN, J.	King's Royal Rifles.
SIM, Corpl. J. W.	Royal Engineers.
TAYLOR, A.	1st Rifle Brigade.
TAYLOR, J.	8th Manchester.
THOMASSON, W.	8th Manchester.
THOMPSON, W.	
TOWNLEY, J.	Duke of L. Own Yeomanry.
TOOLE, J.	
TUMULTY, L.	Manchester Regt.
VOLLNER, A.	North Lancs. Regt.
WALKER, G.	Royal Irish Fusiliers.
WALKER, H.	
WALKER, S.	South Lancs.
WALSH, J.	23rd Manchester.
WARDLE, A.	3rd Lancs.
WARDLE, W.	8th Lancs.
WATERWORTH, J.	202nd Co. Royal Engineers.
WATKINS, A. J.	
WATKINS, W.	20th Manchester Regt.
WATSON, J.	23rd Manchester Regt.
WRIGHT, J.	16th Bt. Liverpool Rifles.
WILKINS, C.	
WILLIAMSON, W. J.	
WILKS, W.	1st Border Regt.
WILSON, A.	
WILSON, C.	8th Manchester.
WINTERBOTTOM, J.	K Bt. Liverpool.
WHITEHEAD, J.	3rd Lancs. Fusiliers.
WOOD, J.	
WOOD, L.	
YEOMANS, W.	

Men Enlisted from our Ambergate Works:

ALLEN, W.	5th Notts and Derby T.F.
AMIABLE, J.	Royal Field Artillery.
BERESFORD, S.	6th Notts and Derby T.F.
BOTHAM, J.	6th Notts and Derby T.F.
BOWLER, G.	5th Notts and Derby T.F.
CLAMP, W.	5th Notts and Derby T.F.
CLARKE, J.	5th Notts and Derby T.F.
COOKE, D.	5th Notts and Derby T.F.
FAULKNER, J.	Yorkshire Light Infantry.
FEW, A.	5th Notts and Derby T.F.
GARLICK, S.	Grenadier Guards.
HALLSWORTH, E.	5th Notts and Derby T.F.
HALLSWORTH, H.	5th Notts and Derby T.F.
HIRST, G.	5th Notts and Derby T.F.
HITCHCOCK, T.	5th Notts and Derby T.F.
HITCHCOCK, F.	5th Notts and Derby T.F.
HOLLOWAY, A.	5th Notts and Derby T.F.
JOHNSON, J.	Derbyshire Yeomanry.
MASON, A.	Royal Field Artillery.
MELBOURNE, G. B.	5th Notts and Derby T.F.
MELBOURNE, R.	Royal Field Artillery.
MOXON, R.	6th Notts and Derby T.F.
MURPHY, C.	5th Notts and Derby T.F.
OLDFIELD, W.	Grenadier Guards.
PERRY, W.	5th Notts and Derby T.F.
RICHARDSON, W.	5th Notts and Derby T.F.
SELBY, W.	Army Service Corps.
SMITH, A.	5th Notts and Derby T.F.
SMITH, B.	5th Notts and Derby T.F.
SMITH, H.	6th Notts and Derby T.F.
SPENCER, J. J.	6th Notts and Derby T.F.
TAYLOR, B.	Grenadier Guards.
TOPHAM, W.	5th Notts and Derby T.F.
WAIN, T.	Royal Field Artillery.
WAIN, C.	Royal Field Artillery.
WEAVING, A.	5th Notts and Derby T.F.
WHAWELL, J.	Royal Field Artillery.
WHITTAKER, W.	5th Notts and Derby T.F.
WILLIAMS, A.	Royal Field Artillery.
WILSON, F.	5th Notts and Derby T.F.

he foregoing list is not complete owing to many of our men having enlisted without notifying us.

ROLL OF HONOUR.

Rd. Johnson, Clapham & Morris Ltd.

MANCHESTER & LIVERPOOL OFFICES
AND
NEWTON HEATH WORKS.

Capt. W. MORTON JOHNSON (Chairman of the firm)	16th Manchester Regiment.
2nd Lieut. RONALD JOHNSON	Royal Field Artillery, 103rd Brigade.
Capt. E. CROMPTON	16th Lancashire Fusiliers.
Lieut. E. GARNETT	3rd (attached 4th) King's (Liverpool) Regiment.
2nd Lieut. W. H. DEMEL	2/9th Manchester Regiment.
2nd Lieut. A. L. PAVEY	8th Wilts. Regiment.
2nd Lieut. J. K. BROADHURST	2/7th Lancashire Fusiliers

Priv. J. ACKRILL	8th Manchester Regiment.	Priv. P. BOYD	King's Liverpool Regiment.
— A. L. AIREY	Public Schools Batt. Royal Fus.	Priv. T. BRADBURY	R.F.A.
Priv. F. ANDERSON	27th Res. Batt. Man. Regt.	Priv. S. COHEN	16th Manchester Regiment.
Priv. W. ANDERSON	Army Service Corps.	Priv. F. COWMAN	17th Manchester Regiment.
Priv. P. Ausby	Lancashire Fusiliers.	Priv. W. COOK	22nd Manchester Regiment.
Priv. J. BATES	Yorkshire Light Infantry.	Priv. E. CAMPBELL	Sherwood Foresters
Priv. W. H. BOOTH	20th Manchester Regiment.	Priv. S. G. CUNLIFFE	6th Manchester Regt. (T.F.).
Trooper R. L. BOURNE	Cheshire Imperial Yeomanry.	Priv. E. COWAN	Manchester Regiment.
Priv. T. BOLTON	22nd Manchester Regiment.	Priv. H. COLLINGE	6th Lancashire Fusiliers.
Seaman W. BUCKLEY	Royal Navy.	Priv. T. COLE	Manchester Regiment.
Priv. H. BILLINGTON	21st Manchester Regiment.	Corpl. B. CARR	2nd City Batt. King's L'pool.
Priv. T. BROWN	12th King's Liverpool Regt.	Priv. P. COLLIER	9th King's L'pool Regt. (T.F.).
Priv. A. BERRY	11th Lancashire Fusiliers.	Priv. P. CROSS	Army Ordnance Corps.
Priv. G. BEECH	2/6th Batt. Manchester Regt	Priv. J. Cain	3rd Manchester Regiment.
Priv. W. BAKES	Royal Army Medical Corps.	Priv. T. CLAYTON	5th Manchester Regiment.
Priv. J. BARTLE	8th Manchester Regiment.	Priv. A. DUNKERLEY	Welsh Fusiliers.
Priv. O. BOARDMAN	8th Manchester Regiment.	Priv. G. DEWHURST	Bolton Regiment.
Priv. A. BOOTH	4th Manchester Regiment.	Priv. L. FEAY	16th Manchester Regiment.
Priv. J. BUCKLEY	King's Own Liverpool Regt.	Driver G. FRAMPTON	A.S.C. (Motor Transport).
Priv. W. BETHELL	7th Manchester Regiment.	Priv. J. FORD	Manchester Regiment.
Priv. T. BURKE	Royal Inniskilling Fusiliers.	Priv. C. FOY	Scottish Borderers.
Gunner A. BILLINGE	4th Howitzer Brigade West Lancashire Artillery (T.F.).	Priv. E. FIRSTBROOK	Royal Engineers.
		Sergt. J. FIRSTBROOK	Scotch Fusiliers.

ROLL OF HONOUR—continued.

Rd. Johnson, Clapham & Morris Ltd.

Priv. F. GATE	19th Manchester Regiment.
Priv. G. GOODBRAND	17th Manchester Regiment.
Priv. J. GLYNN	Lancashire Fusiliers.
Priv. C. GREGORY	9th Lancashire Fusiliers.
Priv. E. E. GREGORY	13th Manchester Regiment.
Priv. W. GRAINY	8th King's Liverpool Regiment.
Priv. T. GILPIN	2nd East Lancashire Regiment.
Priv. R. GLENNON	8th Manchester Regiment.
Priv. H. GREGORY	7th Manchester Regiment.
Priv. J. HOLMES	17th Manchester Regiment.
Priv. W. HIRST	East Lancashire Regiment.
Priv. J. HOYLE	16th Manchester Regiment.
Q.M.-Sergt. J. HEAP	King's Own Royal Lancs. Regt.
Priv. F. HORTON	Manchester Regiment.
Gunner H. HOLMES	Royal Field Artillery.
Priv. J. HAYES	22nd Manchester Regiment.
Priv. T. HARDMAN	Grenadier Guards.
Priv. W. HUGHES	3rd Manchester Regiment.
Trooper T. HOLT	Duke of Lancaster's Yeomanry.
Gunner E. HEALEY	Royal Field Artillery.
Priv. P. HEALEY	4th Manchester Regiment.
Priv. F. HINTON	4th City Batt. King's L'pool R.
Priv. R. HARTLEY	
Priv. J. IKIN	7th Manchester Regiment.
Seaman W. JACQUES	Royal Navy.
Priv. W. JACKSON	8th King's L'pool Regt. (T.F.).
Priv. J. KELLY	22nd Manchester Regiment.
L.-Corpl. R. KENYON	17th Manchester Regiment.
Priv. T. KAY	Royal Army Medical Corps.
Priv. D. KING	18th Lancashire Fusiliers.
Priv. H. KIRBY	7th Manchester Regiment.
Driver C. LEECH	1st East Lancs. Royal Eng.
Priv. W. LAMBERT	Manchester Regt. (Natl. Res.).
Driver T. LLOYD	A.S.C. (Motor Transport).
Priv. W. LOUDON	R.F.A.
L.-Corpl. R. MOTTRAM	R.A.M.C. (T.F.).
L.-Corpl. N. McILWREITH	8th Manchester Regt. (T.F.).
Sapper E. L. MALONE	Royal Engineers.
Priv. T. MATTHEWS	Manchester Regiment.
Priv. M. MORRISON	7th Manchester Regiment.
Priv. J. MOORHOUSE	Lancashire Fusiliers.
Priv. P. MANWARING	King's Own Royal Lancasters.
Gunner J. MARLEY	Royal Field Artillery.
Priv. W. MORGAN	Shropshire Light Infantry.
Gunner H. MURCH	Royal Field Artillery.
Priv. S. MALLINSON	27th Res. Batt Man. Regt.
Priv. T. MORRIS	6th King's L'pool Regt. (T.F.).
Priv. L. NUTTALL	1/7th Gordon Highlanders
Priv. B. NIGHTINGALE	2/7th Gordon High. (T.F.).
Driver W. S. NAPIER	Mechanical Transports.
Priv. C. NICHOLLS	22nd Manchester Regiment.
Priv. W. NORTON	17th Manchester Regiment.
Gunner F. OWEN	Royal Field Artillery.
Priv. P. OUSBY	Lancashire Fusiliers.
Priv. H. PARKINSON	5th Royal Fusiliers.
Priv. A. PERRIN	Lancashire Fusiliers.
Priv. W. PEAKE	8th King's Liverpool Regt.
Priv. H. PRIOR	Manchester Regiment.
Priv. J. PRIOR	6th Manchester Regiment.
Priv. W. POTTER	10th Scottish Batt. King's Liverpools (T.F.).
Priv. A. PEMBERTON	9th Batt. King's L'pool (T.F.).
Priv. W. PLATT	Coldstream Guards.
Priv. A. RICHARDS	4th Manchester Regiment.
Priv. J. RILEY	Welsh Fusiliers.
Gunner R. ROTHWELL	1st W. Lancs. R.G.A. (T.F.).
Driver W. SHAW	13th Div. Royal Field Artillery.
Priv. C. SOOTHERAN	16th Manchester Regiment
Priv. J. SMITH	8th King's Liverpool.
Priv. W. SCHOFIELD	South Lancashire Regiment.
Priv. C. STEWARD	2nd Argyll and Sutherland Highlanders.
Priv. S. STURGESS	7th Manchester Regt. (T.F.).
Priv. E. SMITH	Royal Army Medical Corps.
Priv. F. SHAW	Border Regiment.
Priv. A. V. STERRY	6th King's L'pool Regt. (T.F.).
Priv. H. THORNTON	Royal Scots (T.F.).
Priv. F. TAYLOR	1st Manchester Regt. (killed).
Gunner J. THOMPSON	Royal Field Artillery.
Priv. L. TRACEY	22nd Manchester Regiment.
Priv. J. TAYLOR	6th Manchester Regiment.
Co.-Sergt.-Maj. F. VENESS	2/8th Manchester Regiment.
Priv. T. VARLEY	Royal Irish Fusiliers.
Priv. J. WHITTINGHAM	21st Manchester Regiment.
Gunner H. WALKDEN	Royal Field Artillery.
Sergt. W. WORRALL	10th Manchester Regiment.
Priv. A. WILKINS	10th South Lancashire Regt.
Priv. R. WILSON	28th Royal Fusiliers.
Priv. C. WEBB	Manchester Regiment.
Priv. J. WHITTLE	Scottish Horse.
Priv. F. YARWOOD	17th Manchester Regiment.
Corpl. J. YOUDE	3rd City Batt. King's L'pool.
Gunner S. YOUNGMAN	R.G.A.

ROLL OF HONOUR

Jabez Johnson, Hodgkinson & Pearson,
LIMITED.
105 & 107, Portland Street, Manchester.

Major E. A. J. JOHNSON-FERGUSON - Dumfriesshire Squadron, Lanarkshire Yeomanry

Manchester Warehouse.

Pte. F. BENDALL	19th Service Batt. Royal Welsh Fusiliers.
Pte. J. BLACK	Salford Battalion Lancashire Fusiliers.
Pte. H. BRUNT	National Reserve, East Lancashire Division.
Pte. G. DAVIES	19th Service Batt. Manchester Regiment.
Pte. G. DEE	Army Cyclist Corps.
Pte. T. DENNY	2/4th Battalion Royal Scots Regiment.
Pte. A. EDWARDS	23rd Service Batt. Manchester Regiment.
Pte. W. JACKSON	Salford Battalion Lancashire Fusiliers.
Pte. D. J. JOHNSTON	6th Batt. Manchester Regiment (Territorial).
Sergt. J. LYTH	7th Batt. Manchester Regiment (Territorial).
Pte. T. LYTH	7th Batt. Manchester Regiment (Territorial).
Pte. H. MOTTRAM	8th Batt. Manchester Regiment (Territorial).
Pte. R. PETERS	8th Battalion Lancashire Fusiliers.
Pte. H. SCATTERGOOD	R.A.M.C. (T.), East Lancs. Division.
Corpl. H. S. SHIRRES	6th Batt. Manchester Regiment (Territorial).
Pte. F. SPEED	20th Service Batt. Manchester Regiment.
Pte. B. THORPE	National Reserve, East Lancashire Division.
Corpl. J. WILD	Salford Battalion Lancashire Fusiliers.
Sergt. R. WILFORD	18th Service Batt. Manchester Regiment.
Pte. A. WOOD	7th Batt. Manchester Regiment (Territorial).
Pte. G. YOUNG	St. John's Am. Brig., H.M.S. Prince George.
Gur. C. KIRKHAM	2/2nd East Lancs. Royal Field Artillery.

Victoria Mills, Bolton.

Pte. E. GOODRAM, R.F.A.
Sapper T. ROBINSON, W. Lanc. Div. R.E.
Pte. A. OPENSHAW, R.A.M.C.
Pte. E. A. CRITCHLEY, R.A.M.C.
Pte. J. A. KNOWLES, L.N.L. Regt.
Pte. H. COOKE, L.N.L. Regt.
Pte. R. CLARKSON, 3rd Border Regt.
Pte. J. NICHOLSON, L.N.L. Regt.
Rifleman H. RENSHAW, 16th Bt. King's R.R.

Driver J. PARTINGTON, 3rd E. Lanc. Div. R.F.A.
Pte. J. A. SUMNER, R.N.D.M.U.
Pte. C. MORRIS, R.A.M.C.
Pte. E. SMALLEY, R.A.M.C.
Pte. H. McCANN, 2/5 L.N.L. Regt.
Pte. H. BRANDWOOD, 3rd E. Lanc. R.F.A.
Pte. L. G. HEYES, R.N.D.M.U.
Pte. J. WOOD, Liverpool Scottish.

ROLL OF HONOUR
CONTINUED.

Jabez Johnson, Hodgkinson & Pearson,
LIMITED.

105 & 107, Portland Street, Manchester.

Moor Mills, Bolton.

Driver H. BOOTLE, 3rd E. Lanc. R.F.A.
Pte. T. HOOTON, R.A.M.C.
Driver T. WORTHINGTON, 3rd E. Lanc. R.F.A.
Pte. W. HIGGINS, R.A.M.C.
Pte. H. BIRCH, 2/5th L.N.L. Regt.
Pte. J. HUDSON, 1/5th L.N.L. Regt.
Corpl. F. SKILLEN, 8th L.N.L. Regt.
L.-Sergt. P. HARTLEY, 8th L.N.L. Regt.
Pte. W. OWEN, 1/5th L.N.L. Regt.
Pte. A. O. WHITTLE, 1/5th L.N.L. Regt.
Pte. C. A. NEWMAN, 8th L.N.L. Regt.
Pte. T. H. LYON, 1st L.N.L. Regt.
Gunner G. BINKS, 9th Batt. R.G.A.
Pte. J. W. BROOKS, 2/5th L.N.L. Regt.
Pte. JAS. BOOTH, 2/5th L.N.L. Regt.
Pte. JOS. BOOTH, 2/5th L.N.L. Regt.
Pte. J. J. ECCLES, 2/5th L.N.L. Regt.
Pte. J. BARON, R.A.M.C.
Pte. R. HAWORTH, 3rd L.N.L. Regt.
Pte. J. SCHOFIELD, 2/6th R. Sussex Regt.
Gunner V. MEADE, 3rd E. Lanc. R.F.A.
Gunner A. S. HORROCKS, 3rd E. Lanc. R.F.A.
Pte. H. NUTTALL, 3rd Batt. R. Welsh Fus.
Pte. J. SHEPHERD, 11th L.N.L. Regt.
L.-Corpl. J. MANN, 18th Batt. Lancs. Fus.

Pte. J. HOLDEN, R.A.M.C.
Pte. T. COPPERTHWAITE, 6th Border Regt.
Pte. W. STEEL, Coldstream Guards.
Pte. E. CAIN, 2/5th L.N.L. Regt.
Pte. A. J. MAYOH, R.A.M.C.
Driver H. HEYES, 148th Brig. R.F.A.
Driver F. MAKIN, Royal Marines.
Pte. C. PRICE, 5th L.N.L. Regt.
Pte. W. GREENHALGH, 5th L.N.L. Regt.
Pte. A. BUTTERWORTH, 5th L.N.L. Regt.
Pte. R. JAMES, 5th L.N.L. Regt.
Pte. F. HODGINS, Liverpool Royal Scots.
Pte. W. GANDY, Liverpool Royal Scots.
Pte. F. HARDIE, 20th Batt. Manchester Regt.
Pte. T. DUFFY, Loyal S. Lancs.
Pte. H. LONSDALE, 5th L.N.L. Regt.
Pte. J. CAULFIELD, 4/5 L.N.L. Regt.
Pte. QUIGLEY, 4/5 L.N.L. Regt.
Pte. G. GRANT, 4/5 L.N.L. Regt.
Pte. J. UNSWORTH, 11th Batt. L.N.L. Regt.
Pte. G. KEANE, R.A.M.C.
Pte. W. LEACH, R.A.M.C.
Pte. W. HOWARTH, D.L.O.Y.
Pte. G. APPLEYARD, R.F.A., 3rd E. Lancs
Pte. P. HARTLEY, Jnr., L.N.L. Regt.
Pte. G. CHAPMAN, A.S.C.

Ainsworth Mill, near Bolton.

Pte. A. LOMAX, K.O. Regt.
Pte. W. HEYWOOD, 5th L.N.L. Regt.
Pte. W. BAILEY, E. Lancs. Regt.
Pte. J. T. ATHERTON, R.A.M.C.
Pte. W. MORRIS, E.L. Regt. R.F.A.
Pte. R. WILSON, S. Wales Borderers.
Pte. J. LORD, Lancs. Fusiliers.
Pte. W. B. SIMPSON, Lancs. Fusiliers.
Pte. H. BROOKS, Border Regt.
Pte. F. LOMAX, 15th Welsh Regt.
Pte. J. BOOTH, E. Lancs. R.F.A.
Pte. N. HASLAM, E. Lancs. R.F.A.

Pte. F. LINGARD, E. Lancs. R.F.A.
Pte. F. WOOD, Lancs. Fusiliers.
Pte. W. SENNEY, Lancs. Fusiliers.
Pte. W. PILLING, Lancs. Fusiliers.
Pte. H. FISHER, L.N.L. Regt.
Pte. W. BARLOW, R.A.M.C.
Pte. J. BARLOW, R.A.M.C.
Pte. C. RAINES, D.L.O.Y.
Pte. E. RAINES, D.L.O.Y.
Pte. J. SETTLE, L.N.L. Regt.
Pte. W. GREEN, L.N.L. Regt.
Pte. J. HARDMAN, L.N.L. Regt.

ROLL OF HONOUR.

JONES BROTHERS LIMITED.

The following have already joined His Majesty's Forces in defence of King and Country.

DIRECTORS.

W. PIERS JONES, Capt. D.L. Yeomanry.

C. SHEPHERD CROSS, Capt. D.L. Yeomanry, attached to Indian Cavalry, British Expeditionary Force.

HARRISON M. BLAIR, Capt. 3rd. Batt. Welsh Fusiliers.

York Street Warehouse.

- R. BROMLEY, R.A.M.C.
- S. MULLIN, Sergt.-Major, A.S.C.
- L. L. BOARDMAN, 2nd Lieut., 6th M.T.
- R. WHITEHEAD, 12th Manchester.
- W. W. DODD, 6th M.T. (missing).
- A. HAYES, Sergt., 6th M.T. (killed).
- G. HILLMER, Sergt., Royal Warwick.
- A. BARTLETT, R.A.M.C.
- A. CORDWELL, 6th M.T.
- J. WILCOX, R.A.M.C.
- J. MILLWARD, 8th Cheshire.
- H. HUMPHREYS, Sergt., R.A.M.C.
- W. KAY, 6th M.T.
- M. GOUGH, 6th M.T.
- S. PRIEST, Sergt.-Major, R.A.M.C.
- F. WHITEHEAD, Sergt., R.A.M.C.
- R. TAYLOR, 6th M.T.
- L. MUNNINGS, 6th M.T.
- A. STANLEY, 6th M.T.
- H. REDING, M.B.
- A. STEWARD, Corp., M.B.
- T. ROOD, M.B.
- A. SYLVESTER, Sergt., M.B.
- W. LEE, M.B.
- H. BROWN, M.B.
- A. DEARDEN, Royal Navy.
- J. GIBBON, E.L.R.
- F. BOURNE, M.B.
- J. LITT, L.-Corp., M.B.
- H. CORDWELL, U.P.S.
- A. PROUDFOOT, U.P.S.
- E. HANNAY, L.-Corp., M.B.
- H. V. LARSEN, U.P.S.
- G. J. MASON, 7th M.T.
- J. V. PORTEOUS, King's Own Royal Lancs.
- F. D. ROWAN, Royal Edinburgh Rifles.
- A. N. SMITH, M.B.
- E. SHACKLOCK, Royal Navy.
- F. HYDE, 6th M.T.
- S. LEE, 6th M.T.

Booth Street, Salford.

- W. WILD, L.-Corp., 6th M.T.
- C. CASTLEDINE, M.B.

Bedford New Mills, Leigh, Lancs.

- E. LAWLESS, L.-Corp., South Lancs.
- E. MADDOCK, R.A.M.C.
- E. MOLYNEAUX, 10th Hussars.
- H. LYON, A.S.C.
- F. McGUIRE, A.S.C.
- T. MANLEY, A.S.C.
- P. T. LAURIE, 17th Batt. Bob's Own L.F.
- C. WHITTAKER, R.F.A.
- T. PEMBERTON, 17th Batt. Bob's Own L.F.
- J. JONES, R.F.A.
- J. HARDMAN, R.F.A.
- N. MAGILTON, Royal Navy.
- F. HILTON, L.-Corp., A.S.C.
- F. MURRAY, R.A.M.C.
- T. DUNN, A.S.C.
- C. CROMPTON, 5th Manchester.
- A. WORTHINGTON, R.F.A.
- A. FRANCE, R.A.M.C.

Belfast Branch.

- E. SMITH, Royal Fusiliers.
- J. McCULLOUGH, Sgt.-Maj., R. Irish Rifles.
- R. GREENLEE, Royal Irish Rifles.
- N. KIRKWOOD, Royal Irish Rifles.
- P. CLARKIN, Royal Irish Fusiliers.
- W. ANDERSON, A.S.C.
- GEORGE PETTY, A.S.C.
- ROBERT PEIRIN, Royal Irish Rifles.
- THOMAS WARREN, Royal Irish Rifles.

Roll of Honour.

W. W. Jones, Dooly & Co.

MANCHESTER & SALFORD.

FRANK NEEDHAM,
    6th Batt. Manchester Territorials.

ALLAN R. DAUNCEY,
    30th Reserve Batt. Royal Fusiliers.

GEO. W. DAUNCEY,
    18th Batt. Manchester Regiment.

CHAS. M. SYDER,
    3rd City Batt. King's Liverpool Regiment.

GEO. CHURCH,
    King's Own Scottish Borderers.

JAMES S. PEACH,
    11th Batt. Manchester Regiment.

JAMES FILDES,
    Army Service Corps.

GEO. FOSTER,
    11th Batt. Manchester Regiment.

JOHN MAGUIRE,
    Scottish Rifles.

FRANK E. ATTWOOD,
    2/1st S.W. Mounted Brigade.

JOHN NOLAN,
    Connaught Rangers.

H. ANDREW,
    Royal Naval Div. Medical Corp.

ROLL OF HONOUR.

KESSLER & CO. LTD.,

33, Dale Street, Manchester.

Captain EDGAR KESSLER,
6th Batt. The Manchester Regt. (T.F.)
(Killed).

*

Lieutenant C. E. KESSLER,
2nd Brigade East Lancs. R.F.A. (T.F.).

*

W. BALDWIN,
6th Batt. The Manchester Regt. (T.F.).

*

F. CHORLTON,
20th Batt. The Manchester Regiment.

*

T. A. ELLIS.
21st Batt. The Manchester Regiment.

*

A. KENNY,
Royal Garrison Artillery.

*

E. CLARKE,
Royal Navy.

ROLL OF HONOUR.

Kendal, Milne & Co.

A Roll of the Staff who Volunteered and were Accepted for Active Service.

* * *

ALLEN, S.
ASHWORTH, A.
AUSTIN, T. W. E.
BATTERSBY, R., Lieut.
BACON, J. L., Lieut.
BARLEY, J.
BARLOW, S. G., Lieut.
BAXENDALE, A.
BEAHAN, A.
BENNETT, H.
BLAYLOCK, G.
BOWLES, T.
BRIERLEY, C.
BROWN, F.
BURGESS, F.
BUTLER, F.
BULLOCK, R.
CARTER, W. J.
CONWAY, T.
COATES, F.
COOMBES, H.
COOPER, J.
COWGILL, J.
CRAGG, H. C.
DANIELS, A.
DICKINSON, S. J.
DORAN, H. A.
DUNN, J.
ECCLES, H.
EGAN, G.
EVANS, W. A. S.
FALLOWS, G.
FITTERS, S. H.
FRANKLAND, H.

GOULDING, W.
GRAHAM, A.
GRAINGER, M.
GREENHALGH, W.
GRIFFITHS, M.
HADDOW, J. L.
HANSON, E.
HARRISON, W. H.
HELSBY, E.
HERRING, A. G.
HETHERINGTON, T.
HEYWOOD, T.
HIBBERT, F.
HODGSON, O.
HIND, H. S.
HOLLAND, T.
HOOPER, S. B.
HOPWOOD, H.
JENKINS, T.
JOY, W.
KAY, J.
KENNEDY, D.
KIRK, A.
LANGTON, J. E.
LEE, R.
LLOYD, E.
MACKAY, J.
MARTELL, J.
MATTHEWS, H.
MANNING, A.
McMASTERS, J.
McMEEL, G.
MEDCALF, W.
McWILLIAM, W. J.

MILLER, F.
PEERS, T. E.
PICKLES, R.
RIGBY, A.
RALSTON, A.
ROUGHTON, A.
SHIELDS, A.
SMITH, G.
SMITH, S.
SMITHERS, G.
STOCKS, M.
SUTCLIFFE, J.
SUTTON, C. W.
SYMON, W.
TAYLOR, M.
THOMAS, A. E.
THOMAS, O.
THOMAS, R. A., Major.
TUDGE, A.
TWIGG, S. A.
TWIGG, F.
WALKER, C.
WALKER, G.
WALKER, A.
WARD, E.
WATSON, A., Lieut.
WEBB, R.
WHITE, C.
WHITELEGG, S.
WILLIAMS, L.
WOOD, H.
WORTHEN, A.

ROLL OF HONOUR.

LANGWORTHY BROS. & CO.
LIMITED.

ACKERLEY, J.	HAMBLETT, J.	ROBERTS, J.
APPLEBY, J.	HAMBLETT, T.	ROBERTS, W.
BONNY, A. H.	HIRST, I.	ROPER, E.
BREHENY, C.	HORNER, W.	STOCKLEY, A.
BELL, W.	JACKSON, A. E.	SPEED, G.
BARROW, A.	LOWCOCK, C.	SYLVESTER, H.
BIRD, G.	LOWCOCK, D. R.	SHAW, J.
BUTLER, W.	LIVESAY, J.	SWINDELLS, T.
BLEARS, H. C.	LOCKETT, J.	SHIELDS, A.
BURT-SMITH, B.	LYONS, E.	SHEPPERD, T.
CARROLL, M.	LAW, W.	SATCHELL, J.
CROWE, J.	LOGAN, J.	TOMKINS, W.
DEVANEY, G.	McBRIDE, J.	TOMKINS, J.
DOLAN, J.	McMANUS, N.	WILSON, T.
EDGE, J.	MOLLOY, W.	WARD, W.
FRAZER, J. L.	OATES, J.	WHITTAKER, J.
FERGUSON, —.	OATES, W.	WHITTAKER, W.
GOODWIN, J. J.	PARRY, W.	WILSON, A.
HOWELL, H.	PEERS, R.	WORSLEY, H.
HUNT, W.	ROWLANDS, F.	VESTY, H.
HUNT, J.	RUSHTON, W.	PINNINGTON, R.

Roll of Honour.

The Lancashire & Yorkshire Bank
LIMITED.
MANCHESTER.

H. ASHTON	Head Office.	T. E. BRITTAIN	-	Altrincham.
F. G. BEDFORD	,,	S. L. HALL	-	,,
W. E. BLACKWELL	,,	R. G. SMITH	-	,,
E. M. BLACOW	,,	C. L. CLARK	-	Blackburn.
E. H. BROWN	,,	N. J. FOULDS	-	,,
J. B. R. ELLISON (2nd Lieut.)	,,	H. BARNES (Killed)	-	Blackpool.
F. HAY (2nd Lieut.)	,,	J. W. BOOTH	-	,,
F. S. HELME (2nd Lt.)	,,	J. P. HEATON	-	,,
W. F. HIGSON	,,	S. T. BLANE	-	South Shore.
H. N. KAY (2nd Lieut.)	,,	A. SHEPHERD (Killed)		,,
H. C. LEAVER (2nd Lieut.)	,,	G. C. SAGAR	-	Bolton.
F. A. MAWDSLEY (2nd Lieut.)	,,	R. BALSHAW	-	Broadheath.
		H. WILKINSON	-	Burnley.
T. WEETMAN (S.-Maj.)	,,	R. WHITAKER	-	,,
A. WESTALL (2nd Lt.)	,,	R. SIMPSON	-	St. James Street.
N. WILSON (L.-Corpl.)	,,	E. ALCOCK (Wounded)		Bury.
W. S. JOHNSON	,,	F. HOWARTH	-	,,
T. R. BANKS (Sergt.)	,,	F. JACKSON	-	,,
W. W. ARNOLD (2nd Lieut.)	,,	R. SMITH	-	,,
C. G. BENNETT	,,	L. TAYLOR	-	,,
J. H. MARSDEN	,,	B. HALSTEAD	-	,,
D. PADFIELD	,,	E. A. COLLINS	-	,,
A. BEARDWELL	,,	R. P. PEACOCK	-	Buxton.
R. BRADBURY	,,	T. A. TEARE (Missing)		Cadishead.
A. C. BARLOW	,,	B. H. MILLS	-	Cheetham.
C. D. HAYWOOD	Accrington.	W. S. RUSSELL	-	,,
		L. M. NAYLOR	-	Chorlton.
		L. HEATON	-	Cleckheaton.

The Lancashire & Yorkshire Bank
LIMITED
ROLL OF HONOUR—*Continued.*

R. LLOYD	-	Darwen.
C. W. HULME	-	Deansgate.
G. F. HOLGATE	-	,,
E. BARLOW	-	Exchange.
D. COOMER (2nd Lt.)	-	,,
G. A. ELLAM	-	Dewsbury.
L. FISHER (Wounded)	-	,,
C. HIRST	-	,,
D. W. S. WATTS (2nd Lieut.)	-	,,
F. WILSON	-	,,
J. E. D. BARTHELEMY		Douglas.
L. W. CANNAN	-	,,
H. G. SCHOFIELD	-	,,
L. H. TRIPP	-	Hale.
H. S. LUMB (2nd Lt.)	-	Halifax.
C. E. ADKINSON (Wounded)	-	Heaton Chapel.
F. H. ASTLE (2nd Lt.)		,,
C. G. POSTLES	-	,,
W. O. DAVIES	-	Huddersfield.
T. S. G. MOXON	-	,,
J. A. PARKIN	-	,,
F. SAYLES (Killed)	-	,,
G. WALTON	-	,,
W. THORP (Died of Wounds)	-	,,
C. SYKES	-	,,
H. E. BROUGHTON	-	Hyde.
J. B. SMITH (2nd Lt.)	-	Levenshulme.
R. B. BEDFORD	-	Leeds.
J. T. WEST	-	,,
F. H. CLUBB	-	Liverpool, Castle St.
N. B. FOGG	-	,, ,,
A. TONGUE	-	,, ,,
E. WATERS (Liftman)	-	,, ,,
H. TAYLOR	-	,, ,,
S. A. G. FROST	-	Liverp'l, South John St
R. HARKNESS (2nd Lieut.)	-	,, ,,
R. G. ROGERS (2nd Lt.)		,, ,,
J. E. P. WILDE	-	,, ,,
S. H. BINGHAM (2nd Lieut.)	-	Mercantile.
G. GREENUP	-	,,
E. T. COLLINGE	-	Miles Platting.
E. FALLA	-	,,
H. FOSTER	-	,,
J. E. JONES	-	,,
F. J. SMETHURST	-	,,
G. H. STEELS	-	Mirfield.
S. B. HADFIELD	-	New Mills.
H. WARD	-	Nelson.
J. HEYWOOD (Killed)	-	Oldham.
K. McLEOD (2nd Lt.)	-	Oldham Street.
G. ALCOCK	-	,,
R. W. BUCKLEY (Missing)	-	Pendleton.
M. H. HUDSON	-	,,
C. H. BOWMAN	-	Portland Street.
W. L. A. WILKINSON		,,
J. D. GREEN (Killed)	-	,,
P. FAZACKERLEY		Preston.
J. H. HEALD	-	,,
W. A. D. EASTHAM	-	,,
F. J. MARSDEN (2nd Lieut.)	-	Queen's Park.
J. A. CORKILL	-	Ramsey.
N. NUTTALL	-	Rawtenstall.
H. H. WARBURTON	-	,,
E. C. ASPINALL	-	Shudehill.
J. A. TOMLINSON (2nd Lt., D. of Wounds)	-	,,
C. GRIFFITHS	-	Southport.
G. H. GRIMSHAW	-	,,
S. D. HARRISON	-	Southport, Eastbank St.
P. W. JACKSON	-	,,
J. A. CLAYTON	-	Stockport.
T. P. WILKINSON	-	,,
A. F. WALLACE	-	Swinton.
G. R. SNOWDEN	-	Todmorden.
W. S. ROYLE	-	Urmston.
J. T. PICTON (Major)	-	Warrington.
A. BOOTH	-	Waterfoot.
L. G. W. PILLING	-	,,
G. BARKER	-	West Didsbury.
A. T. FRANKISH	-	,,
S. A. BUXTON	-	Whitefield.
J. RANDLE	-	Widnes.
F. THOMPSON	-	Withy Grove.

ROLL OF HONOUR.
Levinstein Limited,
Aniline Colour Manufacturers, Blackley, Manchester.

ON ACTIVE SERVICE.
Offices and Dyehouse.

2nd Lieut. G. E. LEVINSTEIN, 20th Service Batt., Manchester Regt.
Captain E. R. BLANE, 2nd Batt. Manch. Regt.
Corporal H. GREEN, 19th Service Batt., King's Liverpool Regt.
H. NEWTON, 16th Service Battalion, Manchester Regiment.
L.-Corpl. H. LEATER, 16th Service Battalion, Manchester Regiment.
E. CASS, Public Schools Battalion, Royal Fusiliers.
H. HAMMOND, R.A.M.C.
L. TOMLINS, 6th Battalion Manchester Regiment.
L.-Corpl. ALBERT HALL, 6th Battalion Lancashire Fusiliers.
ERNEST WILKINSON, R.A.M.C.
SAMUEL HADFIELD, R.A.M.C.
RONALD CROZIER, Royal Naval Division.
H. H. STOCKS, Royal Engineers, Chemical Corps.
HECTOR McI. CROZIER, Black Watch.
J. C. CHAPMAN, 27th Service Battalion, Manchester Regiment.
F. HINDSHAW, Army Service Corps, T. & S. C.
P. LEESE, 6th Battalion Loyal North Lancashire Regiment.
A. BOYES, 6th Battalion Loyal North Lancashire Regiment.
JAMES RAYNOR, Black Watch.
J. PINKERTON, Royal Naval Division.
J. FLANAGAN, Royal Army Medical Corps.
R. McCARDELL, 2nd "Pals" Battalion Lancashire Fusiliers.

Workmen on Active Service.

S. MURPHY.	W. QUINN.	T. EDWARDS.	J. NUTTALL.
H. SMITHIES.	J. GALLAGHER.	S. BURGESS.	F. MOONEY.
R. CAMPBELL.	S. RADCLIFFE.	T. HEALD.	J. QUINN.
F. WHITTAKER.	G. MATTHEWS.	W. BAZENDALE.	J. WEEDALL.
A. JENKINS.	J. FLETCHER.	J. RATCHFORD.	G. BANKS.
F. HEALD.	T. MURPHY.	A. SALT.	J. OGDEN.
P. GREENHALGH.	T. BRIGGS.	R. HARTLEY.	T. JONES.
T. YOUNG.	R. HUGHES.	T. SMITH.	S. BATES.
R. PERCY.	A. SEDDON.	C. FARROW.	S. HEYWOOD.
J. BUCKWRIGHT.	J. GALLAGHER.	J. SPRAGGS.	J. GRADEY.
F. MURPHY.	J. BUCKLEY.	W. DUCKWORTH	F. PICKUP.

ROLL OF HONOUR.

George Lenthall & Sons,
3, Dale Street, Manchester.

Sub. Lt. CHAS. B. LENTHALL,
  Royal Naval Volunteer Res.
Private J. S. EVANS,
  3rd S. Batt. Manchester Regt.
Private S. W. CASSON,
  16th S. Batt. Manchester Regt.
Private J. WILCOX,
  17th S. Batt. Manchester Regt.
Private W. CROWE,
  18th S. Batt. Manchester Regt.
Private H. HARPER,
  18th S. Batt. Manchester Regt.
Private T. S. CAINE,
  20th S. Batt. Manchester Regt.
Private A. HUMPHREYS,
  20th S. Batt. Manchester Regt.
Private W. MAJILTON,
  Royal Army Medical Corps.
Private G. KIRKMAN,
  Royal Army Medical Corps.
Private A. LEWIS,
  Royal Army Medical Corps.
Private H. FIDLER,
  7th Batt. Manchester Regt.
Trooper J. W. GRANT,
  A. Squad., E.C.L. Yeomanry.
Trooper D. LAVIN,
  King's Own.
Private M. GROSSIER,
  French Army.
Private J. O. STRUTT,
  Royal Army Medical Corps.
Private D. PRIESTLEY,
  Royal Army Medical Corps.
Private R. S. TURNER,
  3/5th King's Own R.L.
Private W. HUDDART,
  Regular Army.

John T. Lewis & Sons
LIMITED.

List of Employees who have enlisted in the Army :—

BOOTHROYD, R. H., L.-Cpl. Signaller, 17299,
  20th (S.) Batt. Manchester Regt.

BAILEY, T. A., Pte.,
  22nd (S.) Batt. Manchester Regt.

BARCLAY, ALEXANDER, Pte.,
  Edinburgh Batt. Royal Scots.

BOLTON, PERCY, Pte.,
  2/6th Batt. Manchester Regt.

COURTIS, WILLIAM, Pte.,
  11th Batt. Lancashire Fusiliers.

HOLLAND, W. E., L.-Cpl., 2698,
  2/9th Batt. Royal Scots (H.).

PENNEY, HENRY, Pte.,
  19th (S.) Batt. Manchester Regt.

PEARCE, STANLEY, Pte., 12428,
  19th (S.) Batt. Manchester Regt.

ROYDS, EGBERT T., Pte., 10202,
  18th (S.) Batt. Manchester Regt.

WARBURTON, ARTHUR, Pte., 7381,
  16th (S.) Batt. Manchester Regt.

ROLL OF HONOUR.

J. Liotard & Sestier

4, Chepstow Street,
MANCHESTER.

Pte. THOMAS ATHERTON,
    6th Manchester Territorials.

Pte. VICTOR BERRY,
    Royal Scots (M/r Scottish).

Pte. FRED. BROWNE,
    4th Seaforth H. (Terr.).

Corpl. J. E. COTGRAVE,
    21st Bt. Manchester Regt.

Pte. JOHN FOSTER,
    16th Bt. Manchester Regt.

2nd Lt. DONALD MARSHALL,
    2/7th Bt. Lancashire Fus.

Pte. F. STEELE,
    13th S. Bt. Manchester Regt.

Pte. L. WELBY,
    Royal Marines.

Pte. J. WARDLE,
    Army Service Corps.

ROLL OF HONOUR.

Julius Liepmann & Co.'s Succrs.

Bridgewater House, Whitworth St.,
MANCHESTER.

Sergt.-Major JAMES GALE,
    17th Batt. Manchester Regiment
    (Formerly Dr.-Sgt. Leinster Regt.).

Driver FRANK CROCKER,
    R.F.A. (East Lancs. Division).

Pte. THOMAS CUNLIFFE,
    King's Royal Rifles.

Pte. SIDNEY GREEN,
    2nd Batt. Manchester Regiment.

Lce.-Corpl. HERBERT DEWHURST,
    16th Batt. Manchester Regiment.

Pte. JOHN W. FOULKES,
    7th Batt. Manchester Regiment.

Pte. FRANK CORRY,
    7th Batt. Manchester Regiment.

Pte. A. LAWRENCE EDWARDS,
    1/6th Royal Scots. (Since discharged as physically unfit.)

JOSEPH WATSON,
    Refused as physically unfit.

JOHN BROUGHTON,
    Refused as physically unfit.

WILLIAM JONES,
    Refused as physically unfit.

ROLL OF HONOUR

✶

J. O. Latham & Co.

Sussex Street and Cobden Street,

Lower Broughton.
MANCHESTER

✶

Harry Bower,
    12th Batt. Manchester Regt.

Tom Bower,
    15th Batt. Lancs. Fusiliers.

Charles Wells,
    8th Batt. Manchester Regt.

John Mason,
    7th Batt. Lancs. Fusiliers.

Wm. Farrell,
    4th Batt. Lancs. Fusiliers.

Sam Kirkman,
    Border Regiment.

Wm. Bolton,
    6th Batt. Manchester Regt (T.).

W. F. Wilson,
    6th Batt. Manchester Regt (T.).

John Massey,
    Not known.

R. J. LEA, LTD.

"CHAIRMAN" FACTORY, Manchester.

Lieut. D. N. Allen,
    Lanc. Fusiliers.
Lieut. L. Dale,
    E. Lancs. F.A.
Pte. A. Holden, King's Own.
 ,, J. Hughes, R.A.M.C.
 ,, H. Jenkinson,
    Manchester Regiment.
 ,, L. Lee, Lanc. Fusiliers.
 ,, A. Oaksworth,
    Manchester Regiment.
 ,, W. Pownall,
    Manchester Regiment.
 ,, T. Rathbone,
    Manchester Regiment.
Sergt. H. E. Sherlock,
    Military Mounted Police.
Pte. E. Smithies,
    Loyal East Lancs.
Pte. C. Wilson,
    Manchester Regiment.
Sergt. T. White,
    Manchester Regiment
W. Crewdson, R.N.
Pte. W. Jones,
    Argyll & Sutherland H.
 ,, T. Yates,
    Manchester Regiment.
 ,, A. Swan,
    Manchester Regiment.
 ,, W. Smith, Royal Fusiliers.
 ,, F. Moss, R.F.A.
 ,, A. Casey, R.I.F.
 ,, J. H. Dakin, R.N.
Pte. H. Jackson,
    Lanc. Fusiliers.
 ,, S. Walsh, R.A.M.C.
 ,, A. Irlam, Lanc. Fusiliers.
 ,, J. Bell, Lanc. Fusiliers.

Roll of Honour.

Lowthian, Drake & Co.,
MANCHESTER.

2nd Lieut. E. F. DRAKE,
  14th Bt. Cheshire Regiment.
2nd Lieut. M. T. DRAKE,
  1/2nd East Lancs. Brig. R.F.A.
2nd Lieut. T. ALLEN,
  Cheshire Regiment.
RICHARD BOARDMAN,
  17th Bt. Manchester Regt. ("Pals").
Corporal S. BROWN,
  2/6th Bt. Manchester Regiment.
F. HOBSON,
  17th Bt. Manchester Regt. ("Pals").
B. HOPEWELL,
  33rd Divisional Cyclist Corps.
Corporal H. LOWE,
  17th Bt. Manchester Regt. ("Pals").
H. LANGSTON,
  1/6th Bt. Manchester Regiment.
F. NEWLOVE,
  17th Bt. Manchester Regt. ("Pals").
H. ROGERS,
  17th Bt. Manchester Regt. ("Pals").
G. McPHERSON,
  2/9th Bt. Royal Scots.
H. JONES,
  3/6th Bt. Manchester Regiment.
E. ACTON,
  3/6th Bt. Manchester Regiment.
T. PRATT,
  2/2nd East Lancashire R.F.A.
J. PERCIVAL,
  3/6th Bt. Manchester Regiment.
H. JORDAN,
  2/6th Bt. Manchester Regiment.
J. H. PIMLOTT,
  2/8th Bt Nat. Res., Manchester R.
J. BARNES,
  3rd Bt. Cheshire Regiment.
E. T. MILLS,
  2/25th London Co. Cyclist Corps.

ROLL OF HONOUR.

SAM LUKE,
2, Chepstow Street & 32, Oxford Street
MANCHESTER.

Private JOHN BROWN,
  13th Manchesters.

* * *

2nd Lieut. HAROLD COLLIER,
  7th Manchesters.

* * *

Private ERNEST HANSON,
  6th Manchesters.

* * *

Private GEORGE H. SMETHURST,
  6th Manchesters.

ROLL OF HONOUR.

Mabbott & Co. Limited.

Phœnix Iron Works, Poland Street, MANCHESTER.

Pte. W. W. E. BARNSLEY	Royal Army Medical Corps.
Sapper C. BENNETT	Royal Engineers.
Pte. BORRELL	Manchester ("Pals") Battalion.
Sergt. T. E. CARTER	C. Company, King's Own Royal Lancaster Regiment.
Pte. CHORLEY	Worcestershire Regiment.
Pte. A. DEAN	King's Liverpool Regiment.
Bombardier D. GIBBONS	2/3rd London Brigade, R.F.A.
Pte. J. P. LITTLER	1st Cheshire Regiment.
Corpl. T. A. MABBOTT	8th Manchester Regiment.
Pte. NEWTON	Worcestershire Regiment.
Pte. W. VERITY	4th Seaforth Highlanders.
Sergt. L. VICKERS	22nd Service Batt. Manch. Regt.
Corpl. J. R. WOODS	C. Coy., 1st Cheshire Regiment.
Sergt. H. WOOLLEY	B. Company, 1/7th Batt. Lancashire Fusiliers, E. Lancs. Division.
Trooper W. WOOLLEY	No. 4 Troop, B. Squadron, 6th Dragoon Guards.

Chas. Macintosh & Co. Ltd.

EMPLOYEES' ROLL OF HONOUR.

ALLCOCK, SAMUEL.
AUSTIN, EDWARD.
AITKEN, WALTER.
ABRAHAMS, FRANK T.
ANDREWS, HENRY H.
ANDREWS, ERNEST.
ATKINSON, ED. H. W.
AUSTIN, WILLIAM.
AUSTIN, GEORGE WM.
ARMSTRONG, WILLIAM.
AUSTIN, GREGORY.
*BAKER, JAMES.
*BARDSLEY, P.
BEAUMONT, JOHN H.
BEAUMONT, WILLIAM.
BARLOW, THOMAS W.
BERRY, TOM.
*BELL, ARTHUR.
BURROWS, THOMAS.
BENT, JOHN.
BELL, JAMES.
BEAUMONT, D. W.
*BARKER, H.
BARNSLEY, SIDNEY.
    (Died of wounds).
BRINDLE, WILLIAM.
BARROW, HERBERT J.
BAINBRIDGE, ALFRED.
BROADFIELD, H. A.
BROCKWELL, T. J.
BROOME, ARTHUR.
BURGESS, Sergt. S. J.
BARCROFT, F.
BELL, WM. McGOWAN.
BERRY, R. H.
BRACEGIRDLE, H.
BEWLEY, HERBERT.
BARBER, STANLEY E.
BORKIN, J.
BOLWELL, HERBERT.
BOOTH, SAMUEL.
BLAIN, ARTHUR.
BROWN, J.
BROWN, ALEX.

†BARNES, THOMAS.
BURNS, JOHN.
BURNS, WILLIAM.
BELL, E.
BLOW, W.
BROSTER, ALBERT.
BURY, H.
CARTER, JOHN.
CHADWICK, WILLIAM.
CHOMELEY, RAYMD. A. C.
CLARKE, ALBERT E.
CHALLINOR, B. P.
CARNEY, ANDREW.
CONNELL, GEO.
CONNELL, T.
COLLINS, ALBERT.
COOK, BASIL E.
COOKE, JOHN.
CONWAY, GEORGE E.
CONWAY, THOS. R.
COOPER, WALTER.
COWIE, A.
CARTWRIGHT, J.
CARDON, OMER (of Liège).
CULLERTON, JEREMIAH.
CATLIN, JOSEPH.
CROSSLEY, Sergt. WM.
CORCORAN, JAMES.
COLEMAN, WILLIAM.
COLEMAN, PETER.
CURTIS, THOMAS A.
CAVANAGH, ALBERT.
CLIFFORD, MICHAEL.
COMERFORD, EDWARD.
CRANE, THOMAS.
CATTON, J. H.
COPPICK, WILLIAM.
CREWE, GEORGE.
COPE, J.
CHAPMAN, JOHN.
*CRUISE, F.
CHEADLE, F.
COCHRANE, J.
CHADWICK, WILLIAM.

CALLAGHAN, C.
COMRIE, ALEX.
CAMPBELL, J.
CHARLESWORTH, ROBT.
CHRISTIAN, F. W.
COWLEY, E.
CAINE, JOHN.
COPE, JOHN P.
CUMMINS, G.
*COMERFORD, JOHN.
DANIELS, GEORGE.
DWYER, Sergt. JOHN.
DAGGER, ROBERT.
*DILLON, T.
DALEY, JAMES.
DOBSON, Sergt. ALF. C.
DAVIES, THOMAS H.
DALE, T.
DAY, H. G.
DELANEY, JOHN.
DAVIES, EDWARD.
DAVIES, JOSEPH.
*DAVIES, ROBERT.
DUFFEY, J.
DUFFEY, WM. HENRY.
DUTTON, THOMAS G.
DYEHOUSE, WILLIAM.
DUTTON, JAMES.
DYEHOUSE, CHARLES.
DOLAN, THOMAS.
EARDLEY, JAMES.
ECCLESTON, JAMES.
EVANS, CHARLES.
*EDWARDS, L.
EDLESTONE, WALTER.
ELLIS, J.
ELLERSHAW, JOHN.
FARRELL, CYRIL.
FARRELL, E. T.
FOLEY, M.
FEATHERSTONE, CHAS.
FEATHERSTONE, JOS.
FEATHERSTONE, A.
FEATHERSTONE, MATT.

*Killed in Action.   † Drowned in Royal Edward.

Chas. Macintosh & Co. Ltd.

ROLL OF HONOUR—Continued.

FRANCIS, M. W.
*FISHER, THOMAS G.
FISHER, THOMAS.
FISHER, GEORGE A.
FINNERTY, JOSEPH.
FINCH, ARTHUR.
FILBROOK, JOSEPH.
FOLEY, GEO.
FOLEY, HENRY J.
FOY, WILLIAM.
FLANNERY, JAMES.
FITZPATRICK, WILLIAM.
FINNEY, JAMES.
FRANKLIN, JOHN.
FOX, THOMAS.
FOX, WILLIAM.
GRAHAM, T.
GILGRYST, WILLIAM B.
GREEN, THOMAS.
GARDNER, JOHN W.
*GLANCEY, J.
GLANCEY, F.
GREEN, ARTHUR.
GORTON, JOHN.
GORTON, BENJAMIN.
GOODWAY, W. R.
GREGORY, FRANK.
*GRIFFITHS, E.
GRIFFITHS, DAVID J.
GRIFFITHS, J. W.
GRIMLEY, JOHN.
GILLARD, J. A.
GEE, W. R.
GEE, RICHARD.
GOODWIN, T.
GIBSON, WILLIAM.
GRACE, B.
GRANT, JOHN.
GROSJEAN, JEAN M.
(of Liège).
HEVICON, WILLIAM.
HABISREUTER, ALBERT.
HYDE, FRED.
HYDE, W.
HERNON, Sergt. THOS.
HULSE, JOSEPH.
HORNBY, JOHN.
HEWITT, JAMES.
HUGHES, ROBERT.
HEYWOOD, ALFRED.
HUGHES, JAMES.
HARRISON, T. H.
HARRISON, W.
HEYWOOD, W.
HALLIWELL, JAMES.
HIGGIN, GEORGE A.
HARRIS, A.
HUNT, D.
HEATH, ARTHUR.
HAGAN, JOHN.
HOWSAM, G.

HULBERT, CHARLES A.
HULME, ELIAS SHAW.
HOPTON, H.
HOLT, E.
HILTON, W.
HACKETT, G.
HOLLES, JAMES.
HOOKWAY, J. W.
HURST, EDWARD.
HOLBROW, GERALD.
HILL, ARTHUR.
HARLING, WILLIAM C.
HEYWOOD, ARTHUR.
HAMPSON, FRED.
HULKS, J.
HANSON, THOMAS.
HARDING, DAVID.
HADDON, H.
HARRISON, ALBERT.
HAMPSON, CHARLES.
HAMPSON, W.
HEARNE, F.
HALL, JOHN.
HARROP, WILLIAM.
HARDING, SAMUEL.
HEYWOOD, THOMAS.
HULME, JOHN.
HENNESSEY, T.
HIGGINS, CHAS.
IGO, JOSEPH.
JONES, Qtr.-Master J. R.
JONES, HENRY.
JONES, HARRY.
JONES, JOSEPH.
JONES, THOMAS C.
JONES, WALTER N.
JONES, E.
JONES, EDGAR W.
JONES, E.
JONES, ERNEST.
JONES, JAMES.
JONES, WILLIAM.
JOHNSON, WALTER.
JACKSON, JAMES.
JACKSON, HENRY.
JACKSON, FRANCIS.
JACKSON, FRED.
JORDAN, ARTHUR.
JENKINS, JOSEPH.
JOHNSON, HAROLD.
JOHNS, A.
KENYON, HARRY.
KITCHIN, ALFRED.
KING, GEORGE.
KIDGER, JOHN W.
KNIGHT, WILLIAM S.
KEOGH, EDWARD.
KENNEDY, GEORGE.
KENNEDY, JAMES.
KENNEDY, WILLIAM.
KIRK, RICHARD.

*KENYON, H.
KERSHAW, ALFRED E.
KENNA, J.
KENNERLEY, JAMES.
KNIGHT, HERBERT.
KELLY, R.
KELLY, PATRICK.
KNIGHT, JAMES.
LEWIS, ANTHONY.
LEIGH, HARRY.
LILLIE, LOUIS.
LILLIE, A.
LITTLE, ROBERT J.
LYON, THOMAS.
LANDLESS, JOHN A.
LLOYD, H. J.
LUCAS, JOHN W.
LOFTS, ALFRED.
LOVETT, JOHN.
LINNEY, JOHN.
LEACH, JOHN M.
LOCKE, CECIL S.
LONGMIRE, WM. H.
LOWRY, MORRIS.
LOGAN, DANIEL.
LARRARD, J. W.
LEWIS, HARRY.
LISTER, THOMAS.
LITTLE, LOUIS.
MILLINGTON, ALBERT.
MILLINGTON, JOHN.
MULLINS, THOMAS.
MACK, WILLIAM.
MAGUIRE, E. ALFRED.
MARRS, JAMES.
MUSGRAVE, ALFRED.
McNEILL, MARTIN.
MILLS, GEORGE.
MILLS, ARTHUR.
MILLS, JOHN H.
MASON, CHARLES.
MORETON, CHARLES.
MORTON, GEORGE.
MYCOCK, WILLIAM.
MELLES, WILLIAM.
McCABE, THOMAS.
MOORE, ARTHUR.
McNEIL, JAMES.
MATHIE, JOHN.
MATHIE, ROBERT.
MORAN, EDWARD.
MUIRHEAD, E.
MURDOCK, THOMAS.
MONTON, HAROLD.
MENZIES, WILLIAM.
MOUNTAIN, E.
MADDOCKS, H.
McGLYN, J.
McELROY, J.
McSTAY, EDWARD.
MANNION, M.

*Killed in Action.

Chas. Macintosh & Co. Ltd.

ROLL OF HONOUR—Continued.

MULLIN, (Senior) CORNLS.
MORRIS, WILLIAM.
MAY, JAMES.
MORLEY, JOSEPH.
McRAE, JOHN E.
MEE, JAMES.
MARKHAM, ERNEST.
MULVEY, JOHN HENRY.
MATTISON, J.
McDONOUGH, EDWIN.
MILLINGTON, JOHN.
NICHOLSON, J. W.
NEWALL, HARRY.
NEWBERRY, J. A.
NIELD, DAVID.
NORRIS, A. G.
NELSON, JOHN.
NASH, ALBERT E.
NASH, GEORGE.
ODDIE, ALFRED.
OWEN, F.
OATES, THOMAS.
OATES, JOSEPH.
OSBORNE, ALBERT E.
OLDFIELD, WM.
O'NEILL, JACK.
O'NEIL, MARTIN.
PAYNE, E. J.
PETHICK, MAX.
POWELL, E.
POWELL, JOSEPH.
PHILLIPS, JOSEPH.
*PAUL, JOHN.
POOLE, W.
POOLE, WILLIAM.
POLLITT, C.
POWER, JAMES.
PORTER, JOHN.
POKE, JOHN.
PRICE, CHAS. E.
PROUDLOVE, CHARLES.
PICKLES, L.
PIM, CHRISTOPHER.
PIM, JOSEPH.
PRESTON, J.
POMFRET, G.
PATERSON, P.
RAYWOOD, OSWALD.
REID, J. G.
REED, GEORGE.
ROBINSON, H.
ROGERS, G. E.
ROBERTSON, WILLIAM.
RUAN, AUSTIN.
RILEY, EDWARD.
RONEY, THOMAS.
RICHARDS, AMOS.
RICHARDS, ARTHUR.
RAE, ROBERT.
RENSHAW, GEORGE.
RIGBY, THOMAS.
ROBERTS, W. P.

ROBERTS, THOS. (D.S.M.).
RATTCLIFFE, J.
REED, T.
RICHARDSON, A.
RIGBY, THOMAS.
RHODES, HARRY.
RIDGWAY, J.
ROSS, F.
ROCK, JAS. EDWARD.
SYKES, G. J.
SYKES, WILLIAM.
SILLCOCK, JOHN.
SAVAGE, THOMAS W.
SELLARS, J. J.
SLATER, ARTHUR.
SNAITH, H.
SNAITH, J. J.
STONEHEWER, GEORGE.
STOTT, J.
STOTT, R.
SHERGOLD, WILLIAM.
STEPHENS, WILLIAM.
SHELMERDINE, THOMAS.
SHARPE, HAROLD.
SPENCER, JOHN.
SAUNDERS, CHARLES.
STANIFORTH, JOHN.
SMITH, ARTHUR.
SMITH, G.
SMITH, J. P. G.
SMITH, JAMES.
SMITH, HUGH.
SMITH, JOHN HENRY.
SMITH, WILFRED.
STEPHENS, HENRY.
SHELTON, JOHN.
SHARKEY, ROGER.
STRETTON, THOMAS.
*STANTON, WM. (D.C.M.)
SUTTON, W.
SWARBRICK, F.
SILLS, H.
*SHANLEY, PATRICK.
SAXON, GEORGE.
SHANLEY, MICHAEL.
SHAW, E.
SLATER, NOEL ARTHUR.
SNAITH, J. J.
SANDS, JOSEPH A.
SMITH, HERBERT.
SHEERAN, EDWARD J.
SHELMERDINE, CHAS.
SWALLOW, FRANK.
SWINDELLS, W. A.
SHERLOCK, J. H.
SHAW, ARTHUR.
*SCHOFIELD, W.
SOUTHERN, A. H.
SLATER, ARTHUR.
*SHANDLEY, PATRICK.
TOMMIS, REGINALD.
THORPE, JOSEPH.

TOOLE, W. J.
*TYRELL, WALTER.
TWISS, W.
*TAYLOR, S.
TAYLOR, WM. THOMAS.
THERIANOUS, D. G.
TOWNSEND, JAMES.
TRUEMAN, BERNARD.
TRIMBLE, WILLIAM.
TRAINER, THOMAS.
THOMPSON, WILLIAM.
THORNE, G. A. J.
TANSEY, JOHN.
TANNER, EDWIN.
TRACE, G. W.
TROW, THOMAS.
VARDEN, P.
WILLIAMS, FREDERICK.
WILLIAMS, JOHN H.
WILLIAMS, J.
WILLIAMS, MAURICE.
WILLIAMS, T.
WALLIS, GEORGE A.
WILLIAMS, ERNEST R.
WILLIAMS, FREDERICK.
WEBSTER, A.
WAYNE, CHARLES A.
WARNER, GEORGE.
WHITE, JOHN.
WILSON, C. H.
WELSH, JOHN.
WALL, JOHN.
WARD, W.
WRIGHT, GEORGE.
WHITTAKER, ALBERT.
WILD, WRIGHT.
WALTON, FRANK.
WALKER, JOHN.
WESTON, JOSEPH.
WOODHOUSE, ROBERT.
WORSWICK, PERCY.
WILLINGS, ROBERT.
WRAY, R.
WARBURTON, JOSHUA.
WITHERS, J.
WEAVER, W.
WALKER, JAMES.
*WALKER, E. J.
WATERS, PERCY.
WINDLE, FRED.
WILLIAMSON, W.
WILLIAMSON, W.
WYATT, W.
WATSON, J.
WATSON, G.
WAITE, L.
WOOD, J.
WESTON, W. H.
WRIGHT, WILLIAM.
WILCOCK, GEO.
WOODRUFFE, F.
YARWOOD, E.

*Killed in Action.

ROLL OF HONOUR.

T. SEYMOUR MEAD & CO. LTD.

Manchester, Southport, Lytham, and Waterloo.

Captain A. SEYMOUR MEAD.
2nd Lieutenant BERNARD F. DRAPER.

APPLETON, J.
ASHBURY, F.
ALLCOCK, F. C.
ATHERTON, H.
ANDERSON, W. H.
ARTHUR, G.
ADAMS, A.
APPLEBY, R.
APPLEYARD, R.
ALCOCK, A.
ANSLOW, T.
ATHERTON, T.
BOWLING, H.
BRADBURY, J. A.
BARNES, T.
BOYNTON, E.
BISHOP, F.
BRAITHWAITE, G.
BRAITHWAITE, A.
BROWN, A.
BROOKS, A.
BROWN, S.
BARROW, E.
BARKER, W.
BURROUGHS, C.
BURTON, R.
BOND, W.
BANCROFT, A.
BRERETON, C. W.
BLUNDELL, F.
BREWER, E. W.
BOYER, H.
BROWN, R. T.
BOARDMAN, A.
BOWN, H. F.
BATTERSBY, P.
BUCKLER, A. G.
BUNT, T.
BOOTHROYD, J.

BEESLEY, C. C.
BURNS, L.
BURY, C. F.
BROWN, R.
BUCHANN, H.
BEST, J. J.
CRIGGALL, B.
CUMMINGS, P.
CHESWORTH, J.
CONNELL, J.
CHICK, A. J.
CROFT, B.
COX, A.
CORBISHLEY, L.
COOPER, A. A.
CRANE, W.
CLARKE, S. E.
CLAY, W. F.
COPELAND, H.
CAYGILL, R.
CROSBY, W. G.
COGAN, W.
CONNAR, J. A.
COOKSON, E.
CADEL, E.
CONNELL, F.
COLLINGWOOD, D.
CHINNERY, P.
CLANCY, Y.
COLGAN, W. H.
CARTER, T.
CARMEN, H.
CATTLE, W.
CRITCHLOW, J. C.
CARTER, R. A.
COPE, J. S.
DONOGHUE, F.
DAVIES, C.
DERRIG, A. S.

DIXON, J. A.
DRIFFIELD, E.
DAVIDSON, I.
DAVIES, R. B.
DYE, H.
DICKENSON, A.
DAVIES, H.
DURSTON, A. B.
DERRICK, O. W.
DOBSON, W. C.
DARRELL, A.
DAVIES, T.
EARNSHAW, J.
ELLIS, P.
EDWARDS, T.
EYES, R.
EDWARDS, E.
EVANS, W. P.
FOWLES, J.
FARIS, W.
FIELD, E. A.
FREEMAN, A.
FORD, J. E.
FALLOWS, D.
FARROW, J. R.
FIRTH, E. A.
FOXTON, C.
FORREST, A.
FENT, E.
FAIRWEATHER, F.
FERNIHOUGH, R. W.
FRANCIS, L.
FULLER, F.
FAIRHOLME, P.
FLETCHER, R. E.
FERGUSSON, J. E.
FLETCHER, F.
GREEN, A. G.
GIBSON, B.

GREENHALGH, S.
GILES, G.
GRINDROD, J.
GAINES, J. A.
GREEN, C. B.
GREEN, F. M.
GOSPEL, J. F.
GILL, A.
GODFREY, P. J.
HODSON, A.
HANNAH, J.
HONOUR, R. W.
HARSFALL, L.
HARRISON, C. W.
HELMS, C. W.
HANKIN, W.
HUGHES, R. W.
HUNTINGTON, R. T.
HILYER, C. F.
HORNER, E.
HAIGH, W.
HARKER, W.
HODGSON, P. N.
HICKEY, F.
HUGHES, R. D.
HUTCHINSON, A.
HAMMOND, C.
HARDICKER, G.
HALLIDAY, J.
HAYWARD, J.
HEWSON, J. E.
HOWARD, W.
HUDSON, G.
HARVEY, H.
HONOUR, L. L.
HARTLEY, J. O.
HOWARTH, H.
HUGHES, A.
HARDMAN, J. A.

T. SEYMOUR MEAD & CO. LTD.
ROLL OF HONOUR—continued.

HANSON, A.
HAWKYARD, A.
HART, G. E.
HIGGINBOTHAM, S. E.
HOWARD, R. W.
HAWTHORNE, G.
HAWKINS, C. H.
HIRST, T.
HOYLE, R.
IVISON, G. A.
ILLSLEY, W.
JOHNSON, H.
JONES, H.
JONES, L.
JONES, J. H.
JAMES, A. J.
JONES, A.
JOHNSON, M.
JOHNSON, H.
JONES, J. F.
JONES, T.
JERMYN, H.
JACKSON, F.
JONES, E.
JONES, J. T.
JOHNSON, F. W.
JACKSON, J. T.
KAYE, G.
KENDRICK, W.
KIRKPATRICK, J.
KINLEY, W. S.
KINGSTON, F.
KEELEY, A. A.
LOGAN, D. S.
LEES, G. R.
LANE, C. W.
LOFTHOUSE, J.
LOCKE, H.
LANE, W. H.
LINDSAY, S.
LOFTHOUSE, A.
LEADBEATER, L.
LEEMING, J.
LASKEY, R. J.
MORGAN, A. H.
MARSHALL, R.
MILLS, J.
MOORE, H. G.
MITCHELL, J.
MOSLEY, J. F.
MORTON, F. H.
MORAY, W.

McCLURE, W.
MICHAEL, G.
MONK, J.
MORGAN, W. P.
MUGAN, J.
MORRIS, T.
MOORE, G. A.
MILLWARD, W. G.
MADDEN, W.
MOORES, F.
MORRIS, A. W.
MARRIS, R. S.
MIDDLETON, T. W.
McCOY, W.
MELLOR, L.
NICHOL, D. J.
NOBLE, B.
NEWHAM, J. W.
NEATE, F.
NATTRESS, J.
OAKES, R. A.
OLDFIELD, J. H.
OWEN, R.
OWEN, W.
PROCTOR, R. W.
PEACOCK, M. G.
PEART, H.
PRINCE, A.
PARKER, F.
PROCTOR, J. B.
POTTER, G. E.
POMPHREY, H.
PARRY, J.
PITTS, S. L.
PRICE, T.
PARR, J.
PAGE, F.
PRICE, W.
PIMBLET, H.
PARSONS, C.
RAPIER, A. E.
ROBERTS, R. W.
ROBINSON, E. H.
RISELEY, T.
RYAN, E.
ROWE, T. H.
ROBINSON, J.
REESE, G.
ROWTON, J.
RUSSELL, H.
RISELEY, A.
ROSIER, M.
RAINE, W.

RICHARDS, W.
RAMSDEN, N. W.
RAWLINSON, W. T.
ROUTLEDGE, J. I.
ROBINSON, T.
ROBINSON, C.
RADCLIFFE, A.
RAINE, G. O.
RENSHAW, G.
ROBSON, J. W.
REDHEAD, F.
RAYNOR, G.
ROBERTS, E.
RATHBONE, A.
RAYNOR, J. B.
ROBERTS, J. W.
READ, J.
ROGERS, J. M.
RENSHAW, W.
ROBERTS, E.
RYDER, G.
RIGBY, J.
ROBERTS, C.
SMITHSON, M.
SIGSWORTH, H.
SMETHURST, W.
STAINTON, S.
SPURN, H. S.
SOUTHAM, H.
SELLARS, E. H.
SMITH, E. P.
SQUIRE, B. H.
STOBBS, W. E.
SHELMERDINE, J.
SHILLING, A.
SMITH, R.
STRICKLAND, F.
SKELLY, R. C.
SMEDLEY, W. A.
SIMPSON, J. B.
SWANN, C.
SPAKES, C.
SKELTON, R. F.
SHAW, M.
STANLEY, M.
STRONG, R. E.
STOWERS, G. F.
STEPHENS, W. P.
SCOTT, J.
SHEPHERD, R.
STOPFORTH, J.
SELLER, G. A.
SCHOFIELD, W.

THOMPSON, W. H.
TIPPIT, A.
TUNNICLIFFE, J.
TASKER, C. A.
THOMPSON, G. T.
TAYLOR, T.
TRAINGMAR, C.
TARPEY, J.
TRAVIS, A. C.
TABOR, A. G.
TAYLOR, T.
TUSTIN, R.
TAYLOR, J.
THACKRAY, J. W.
UTTING, C. A.
WHITESIDE, A. E.
WHARTON, T.
WRIGLEY, J.
WILDING, L.
WILLIAMS, T. J.
WILLIAMS, A.
WILKINSON, A.
WHITWORTH, P.
WORSDELL, A.
WARD, E. G.
WILLIAMS, E.
WILSON, E.
WAYMAN, W.
WHITEHOUSE, A.
WILLIAMS, R.
WILKINSON, L. E.
WILLIAMS, E. S.
WETTENHALL, W.
WOODHOUSE, D.
WILLIAMS, W.
WARRILOW, E.
WILKINSON, R.
WOODS, W.
WALL, A.
WALMSLEY, J.
WILLIAMS, W. T.
WALLEY, J. S.
WILLIAMS, H.
WILLIAMSON, E.
WINT, J. E.
WOODS, C. W.
WRIGHT, W.
WILKIN, H.
WALLEY, J. S.
YATES, W.
YOUNG, J.

MIDDLETON, JONES & CO. LTD.

ROLE OF HONOUR.

✶ ✶ ✶

David Midgley & Sons, Ltd.,

MANCHESTER.

✶ ✶ ✶

Employees who have joined the Forces.

L.-Corpl. C. H. OGDEN, 17th Service Batt. Manchester Regt.
Private J. OLDHAM, 17th Service Batt. Manchester Regt.
    ,, A. HOLT, 17th Service Batt. Manchester Regt.
    ,, J. LAW, 17th Service Batt. Manchester Regt.
    ,, H. DAVIES, 17th Service Batt. Manchester Regt.
    ,, P. HOWSON, 17th Service Batt. Manchester Regt.
    ,, R. SCHOFIELD, 17th Service Batt. Manchester Regt.
    ,, H. NEWTON, 17th Service Batt. Manchester Regt.
    ,, J. MULLIN, 18th Service Batt. Manchester Regt.
    ,, F. BELLIS, 21st Service Batt. Manchester Regt.
    ,, H. ISGROVE, 1/6th Batt. Manchester Regt. (T.F.).
    ,, W. THORNLEY, 1/6th Batt. Manchester Regt. (T.F.).
    ,, A. JOHNSON, 3/6th Batt. Manchester Regt. (T.F.).
    ,, R. FRANKLIN, 20th Service Battalion Royal Fusiliers.
    ,, E. MELLOR, 20th Service Battalion Royal Fusiliers.
    ,, J. H. RAMSKILL, 21st Service Batt. Royal Fusiliers.
    ,, F. HIBBERT, 19th Service Battalion Lancs. Fusiliers.
    ,, J. RENNIE, 15th Service Battalion Royal Scots.
    ,, W. E. COCKBAIN, Duke of Lancaster's Yeomanry.
Trooper P. PENDLEBURY, 5th Dragoon Guards.

Roll of Honour.

JAMES MOORHOUSE & SON LTD.,
10, CHARLOTTE STREET, MANCHESTER.

List of Employees Serving with the Colours.

Arthur Moorhouse	21st Batt. Royal Fusiliers (U.P.S.).
Richard Chaloner	2/2nd E. Lancashire Royal Field Artillery.
John R. N. Riley	3/5th Batt. Duke of Wellington's (West Riding Regiment).
Leslie Tapp	2/2nd E. Lancashire Royal Field Artillery.
William Jennison	King's Royal Rifles.
John Sumner	South Wales Borderers.
James Cornall	Duke of Wellington's W. Riding Regt.
Walter Riddiough	Duke of Wellington's W. Riding Regt.
James Smith	Lancashire Fusiliers.
Jerry Plumbley	Duke of Wellington's W. Riding Regt.
Harry Stott	28th Batt. East Lancashire Regiment.
James Thwaites	28th Batt. East Lancashire Regiment.
George Harwood	Duke of Wellington's W. Riding Regt. (Stretcher Bearer).
William Eccleston	Royal Army Medical Corps.
Carr Whipp	S.B.R. (Navy).
William Eastwood	S.B.R. (Navy).
Fred Exley	Army Service Corps.
Robinson Windle	Army Service Corps.

ROLL OF HONOUR.

Morreau, Spiegelberg & Co.

121 Princess Street, Manchester.

Men Serving with the Colours.

Lieut. T. Shorrocks	20th Service Batt. (Public Schools).
Lieut. C. Jordan	Royal Field Artillery.
Co.-Q.M.S. T. Wilkinson	8th Manchesters (T.F.).
Corporal C. E. Macdonald	3rd Rifle Brigade.
Corporal J. A. Best	Duke of Lancaster's Yeomanry.
L.-Corporal G. Hawkins	17th Service Battalion (Pals).
Drummer H. Midwinter	17th Service Battalion (Pals).
Private W. Arnfield	6th Manchesters (T.F.).
Private W. Barnett	6th Manchesters (T.F.).
Private S. Belcher	20th Service Batt. (Public Schools).
Private G. Carrol	6th Manchesters (T.F.).
Private A. Corner	R.A.M.C.
Private W. Cox	21st Service Battalion (Pals).
Private W. Craig	7th East Lancashires.
Private W. A. Dormer	2nd Manchester Regiment.
Private W. Hambleton	6th Manchesters (T.F.) (Missing).
Private C. Jackson	Duke of Lancaster's Yeomanry.
Private C. Kerr	17th Service Battalion (Pals).
Private J. Lyons	2nd Manchester Regiment.
Private F. Mayall	11th Lancashire Fusiliers.
Private A. Moore	7th East Lancashires.
Private H. Moritz	20th Service Batt. (Public Schools).
Private F. Pearson	Loyal North Lancs.
Private B. Penketh	18th Service Battalion (Pals).
Private A. Probert	6th Manchesters (T.F.).
Private S. Reynolds	20th Service Batt. (Public Schools).
Private F. G. Robinson	17th Service Battalion (Pals).
Private H. Shaw	11th Lancashire Fusiliers (Killed).
Private G. W. Smith	17th Service Battalion (Pals).
Private H. Southern	Loyal North Lancs.
Private T. Stephens	20th Service Batt. (Public Schools).
Private W. Taylor	8th Manchesters (Wounded).
Private E. Vickers	18th Service Battalion (Pals).
Private C. R. Webb	8th South Lancashires.

ROLL OF HONOUR.

Morris & Jones Limited,

8 and 10, Long Millgate, MANCHESTER.

Sapper J. W. SMITH	2nd Co., Royal Engineers.
Private CHAS. THOMPSON	2nd Batt. Duke of Wellington West Riding Regiment.
Private COLIN MACDONALD	H.M.S. "Mersey." (Killed.)
Gunner JOHN DAVIES	17th Battery, East Lancs. R.F.A.
Driver JOHN OWEN	16th Battery, East Lancs. R.F.A.
L.-Corpl. R. HYDE	"Pals," 16th Ser. Batt. Manchester Regt.
Sergeant S. IRWIN	C Coy., 2/8th Batt. Lancs. Fusiliers.
L.-Corpl. T. VICKERS	C Coy., 20th Ser. Batt. Royal Fusiliers.
Signaller HARRY BELL	Royal Engineers.
Private JOHN GRIFFITH	Royal Welsh Fusiliers.
Private J. KIRKHAM	16th Section, Army Veterinary Corps.
Private WM. KNOWLES	20th Batt. Lancashire Fusiliers.
Private W. H. ROUTLEDGE	3rd Batt. Manchester Regiment.
Driver H. FRENCH	No. 4 Coy., A.S.C. Motor Company.
Sergeant J. BUTTERWORTH	136 Depot, Unit of Supply, 54th Division.
Wireless Operator A. WILLIAMS	Royal Flying Corps.
Private CHAS. H. DAVIES	A.S.C. Supply Depot.
Private W. V. EVANS	68th Company Machine Gun Corps.
Private R. R. WILLIAMS	48th Company Army Ordnance Corps.
Trooper P. H. ROBERTS	Denbighshire Yeomanry.
Private PHILIP MORRIS	Medical Unit, R.N.D.

ROLL OF HONOUR.

David Moseley & Sons Limited,
Chapelfield Works, Ardwick, MANCHESTER.

*   *

List of our Employees who are serving their country.

Lieut. O. G. MOSELEY, Cheshire Yeomanry.
Lieut. R. MOSELEY, Royal Naval Volunteer Reserve.
2nd-Lieut. L. G. PETERS, Honourable Artillery Corps.

J. ANDREWS.	H. BENSON.	J. H. CLARKE.
W. H. ABBOTT.	H. BROADHURST.	F. CHARLTON (killed).
H. ADAMS.	P. L. BAINES.	T. COATES.
C. ANDREWS.	W. BROADLEY.	A. CARTLEDGE.
A. ABBOTT.	W. BRADLEY.	A. CLAYTON.
J. ARSTALL.	J. BROOKBANK.	A. CASH.
S. ACTON.	G. BROOKS.	F. CAVANAGH.
W. BEECH.	G. BELL.	J. CLARKE.
L. BAILEY.	A. BARLOW.	J. CLANCY.
A. BLACKBURN.	S. BROWN.	W. CUMBERBIRCH.
M. BLACK.	G. BARKER.	A. CLEARY.
F. BREWSTER.	J. BRENNAN.	A. CRAVEN.
J. BENTLEY.	T. BREASTON.	J. H. CROWLEY.
J. BARTON.	— BOOTH.	W. CONDON.
H. BROADHURST.	T. BRAMALL.	F. CHEETHAM.
J. BROWNSELL.	F. BURROWS.	C. CLARK.
T. BLACKBURN.	H. BALL.	T. W. CAIN.
H. BREAKEY (killed in action).	F. BOLTON.	D. CARTER.
	C. BARNES.	A. COOMBER.
F. C. BOULTON.	A. CARMICHAEL.	C. CHRISTANSEN.
F. BROOKES.	W. CLARKE.	W. DOBSON.
G. BRADBURY.	F. CLARKE.	F. G. DEAN.
W. BRADDOCK.	L. CARTER.	W. DERBYSHIRE.
E. W. BRIERTON.	A. CANNON.	W. DIXON.
E. BURTON.	R. J. COLE.	F. DAIN.
J. BARNES.	N. CHADDERTON.	F. DUNNE.
J. BOWDEN.	J. CASSIN.	T. DONOHOE.
W. BELL.	H. COOK.	J. DOUGLE.
W. BENT.	G. CHESTERS.	S. DAWSON.
H. BUTTRESS.	W. T. CAIN.	M. DOHERTY.
W. BAILEY.	J. COLLINS.	T. W. DIX.
J. BROPHY.	J. CREAMER.	W. DAVIES.
W. BURNS.		

ROLL OF HONOUR—continued.

David Moseley & Sons Limited.

A. DICKINS.
H. DENTON.
J. W. DUDLEY.
S. DENTON.
T. DAVIES.
C. EAST
    (killed in action).
T. EVANS
    (killed in action).
T. ELLIOTT.
G. EDWARDS.
A. EDINSBURY.
W. EZARD.
T. EDWARDS.
A. B. EVANS.
A. EVANS.
W. H. EDGE.
N. FINDLATER.
H. FARNWORTH.
E. FARNLEY.
C. FOSTER.
W. C. FROST.
A. FERGUSON.
W. FAIRBANK.
W. FAHY.
G. FLETCHER.
G. FLINT.
A. FROST.
J. FLYNN.
J. FARRELL.
W. FROST.
A. FRAMPTON.
W. FORSTER.
T. FROST.
T. GESS.
J. GARDNER.
T. GODWIN.
E. GRANT.
E. GIFFORD.
W. GRIFFITHS.
F. GREEN.
— GILL.
— GREENWOOD.
J. W. HILL.
J. HODSON.
W. HOLT.
W. HOWARD.
W. HENSHALL.
L. HAMMOND.
A. HOUGH.

J. W. HARDMAN.
W. HEYWOOD.
E. HILTON.
J. HADFIELD.
A. HARRISON.
W. HODSON.
W. H. HOWARD.
W. HUGHES.
C. J. HARRIS.
W. HIND.
E. HULMES.
W. HODSON.
W. HARRIS.
G. HASE.
W. HADFIELD.
J. W. HAMPSON.
T. HENDERSON.
E. HURST.
F. HENSON.
E. A. HAYMAN.
G. J. HADDON.
P. HORAN.
S. J. INGRAM.
A. J. JACKSON.
T. JACKSON.
R. JONES.
S. JONES.
E. KNIGHT.
J. KNIGHT.
E. KENNEDY.
J. KEEGAN.
F. KEEBLE.
T. KEEBLE.
W. KEENAN.
T. KEERAN.
T. KEELAN.
G. KING.
A. KIRBY.
A. KELLY.
P. KENNEY.
E. KINGSTON.
J. KEENAN.
J. KEENE.
W. KENNEDY.
W. D. M. LLOYD.
J. LEIPER.
H. LAWRENCE.
T. LOFTUS.
W. LEE.
J. E. LAWSON.

P. J. LYONS.
J. H. LUKE.
T. E. LATHWOOD.
F. LEE.
W. LOWRY.
J. W. LUBY.
H. LLOYD
W. LAWLER.
J. LOMAX.
W. LAWLER.
H. LEE.
F. LATHWOOD.
J. LEYLAND.
H. LEAH.
B. LEVER.
G. LEE.
J. MURPHY
    (killed in action).
W. MURRAY.
P. MATTHEWS.
P. MONKS.
W. H. MORGAN.
W. MILNER.
J. McDERMOTT.
W. MOTT.
F. MYERS.
D. MADDOCK.
J. MARSLAND.
L. MASON.
C. MORGAN.
J. MATHER.
J. MASON.
R. MORRISON.
H. MAHONEY.
T. MASON.
A. MELIA.
J. MURPHY.
J. MARTIN.
H. MILLS.
A. MITCHELL.
E. MITCHELSON.
C. MAHON.
A. MEADOWCROFT.
W. H. MORAN.
J. MOORE.
T. MURRAY.
J. MOODY.
P. McANDREW.
A. McKEE.
G. E. MARTIN.

ROLL OF HONOUR—continued.
David Moseley & Sons Limited.

C. NICKEAS.
J. NICKEAS.
W. NEILD.
W. NEWSOME.
A. NORBURY.
H. J. NAYLOR.
J. NALLY.
J. W. NEWTON.
E. NAPIER.
E. NAYLOR.
J. O'BRIEN.
W. OGDEN.
J. O'DONNELL.
P. O'CONNOR.
J. O'HARA.
H. ORME.
P. O'ROURKE.
J. ORME.
R. PICKSTONE.
G. PEARSON.
H. PEARSON.
T. PARKER.
A. PARSONAGE.
R. PHILLIPS.
F. PHELAN.
A. PILKINGTON.
H. PARSONS.
F. PEARSON.
A. PICKSTONE.
A. PEPPER.
— PICKBURN.
R. PRITCHARD.
— POWNEY.
C. PARSONS.
A. PANDALFO.
R. ROSSBOTTOM.
J. ROYLE.
J. ROONEY.
A. ROE.
C. E. ROBINSON.
M. ROBERTS.
T. RYAN.
J. ROBINSON.
J. RYAN.
J. REYNOLDS.
H. REDFERN.
J. H. ROBINSON.
J. ROGERSON.
T. ROBERTS.
A. ROBINSON.

C. RICHARDSON.
J. REID.
T. RODGERS.
R. RICHARDSON.
H. RUSSELL.
J. ROBINSON.
H. ROBINSON.
W. ROBERTS.
T. L. SCOTT.
A. SAUNDERS.
F. STANLEY.
J. STANTON.
S. SCOTT
   (killed in action).
W. SHERIDAN.
W. SUTTON.
J. SALE.
J. SCANLAN.
J. SCANLAN.
F. SMITH.
C. SMITH.
A. SCHOFIELD.
H. SCHOFIELD.
R. STUBBS.
C. STENNING.
J. SMETHURST.
J. J. SHAW.
A. STARK.
D. SPILSBURY.
J. STOPFORD.
F. SMITH.
H. SHAW.
F. SALTER.
B. W. SMITH.
J. H. SWIFT.
A. STOUT.
W. SCOTT.
H. SHEARER.
J. SELLARS.
T. SUTTON.
W. SUTTON.
A. J. SMITH.
T. SMITH.
F. STONE.
J. TURNER.
L. TULK
   (killed in action).
H. THOMPSON
   (killed in action).

J. THOMPSON.
J. TOMLINSON.
F. G. THORNHILL.
E. TOMMINS.
F. TOLTON.
J. THOMAS.
T. TOLLITT.
J. TOWEY.
E. TAYLOR.
T. THOMPSON.
J. THAKE.
J. TWYNHAM.
J. TAYLOR.
E. VAUGHAN.
E. WALKER.
A. WATMOUGH (killed)
A. WOODWARD.
P. WILLETT.
J. H. WALKER.
J. WALKER.
R. WRIGHT.
J. WRIGHT.
C. WOOD.
D. WHALLEY.
E. WOOLVIN.
— WARD.
P. WRIGHT.
W. WATTS.
M. WALSH.
J. WOLFENDALE.
C. WALKER.
H. WEBB.
D. WARING.
J. WHITTAKER.
W. WHITTAKER.
J. WHITTAKER.
C. E. WOOD.
J. T. R. WARD.
H. WOODWARD.
J. WOOTTON.
J. WAINWRIGHT.
A. J. WATSON.
C. J. WALKER.
T. WALKER.
S. WILKINSON.
J. WILLIAMS.
A. YATES.
W. H. YARDLEY.

Roll of Honour.

Manchester Liners
LIMITED.

ARMY.

HOWARD B. STOKER.
  Lieut. 13 Coy. Canadian A.S.C.
TOM HAYDOCK.
  Duke of Lancaster's Own Yeomanry.
JOSEPH TAYLOR.
  Duke of Lancaster's Own Yeomanry.
FRANK CLEGG.
  6th Manchester Regiment (T.F.).
FRANK WAINWRIGHT.
  Public School Batt. (Royal Fusiliers).
WILFRED YOUNG.
  Royal Scots.
EDMUND KERSHAW.
  4th Manchester Regiment.
G. W. NEELY.
  Denbighshire Hussars.
SIGNALLER PICKFORD.
  18th Hussars.
REGINALD HANNANT, R.A.M.C.
CYRIL J. RICHARDSON.
  Royal Fusiliers.
JOHN C. GUILDFORD.
  8th Manchester Regiment.
PETER CLEARY.
E. BYRNE.
— CROOKSEY.   } Irish Regiments.
A. DORAN.

NAVY.

GEO. GARNER.
  (Submarine Engineer).
E. W. E. CORDINGLEY.
B. W. DAVY.
W. H. WILKINSON.
R. H. CROUCHER.   } Ratings unknown
T. F. BALKWILL.
A. JOHNSTON.
J. UNWIN.

ARCHIBALD JACKMAN.
  Navy Wireless.
M. ALLEN.
  Lost in H.M.S. "Goliath."
A. E. MILNE.
  Lost in H.M.S. "Otranto."

Roll of Honour.

Mason, Scheidler & Co.
LIMITED.
MANCHESTER.

Private T. ANDREW,
  20th Batt. Royal Fusiliers.
Private J. COTTAM,
  7th Batt. Manchester Regiment.
Private R. COCKSON,
  Royal Army Medical Corps.
Gunner G. C. ELLIOTT,
  Royal Field Artillery (E. Lancs).
Private G. H. GWINNELL,
  20th Batt. Royal Fusiliers.
Coy. Q.M.S. W. HYDE,
  8th Batt. Lancashire Fusiliers.
Corporal W. JEPSON,
  7th Batt. Manchester Regiment.
    (Killed).
Private G. KEECH,
  9th Batt. Royal Scots.
Driver D. LOWE,
  R.G.A. (East Cheshire).
Private F. LEE,
  8th Batt. Rifle Brigade.
Private F. MASON,
  6th Batt. Manchester Regiment.
Private T. OWEN,
  5th Batt. Cheshire Regiment.
Sergeant H. POWELL,
  8th Batt. Lancashire Fusiliers.
Private D. ROSS,
  Earl of Chester's Yeomanry.
Private H. SHEARD,
  6th Batt. Manchester Regiment.

Roll of Honour.

Arthur McDougall Ltd.

City Flour Mills, Radium Street,
MANCHESTER.

Directorate—
  GEORGE McDOUGALL
  (Lieutenant).

Office—
  WILLIAM CULSHAW.
  JAMES KENNEDY.

Mill—
  THOMAS ASPINALL.
  JOSEPH EGAN.
  WILLIAM CONNOR.
  CHARLES QUARTON.
  ALFRED ROYLE.
  FRED HAND.
  HENRY MULLHOLLAND.
  STEPHEN FITZPATRICK.
  ALFRED BURGESS.

Packing Dept.—
  FRED FLETCHER.
  JOHN BALL.
  GEORGE BRIGHT.
  GEORGE BIRCHALL.
  J. QUARTON.
  ALBERT ELLIS.
  WILLIAM DUNSTAN.
  JAMES TUCKER.
  SAMUEL BENNETT.

Roll of Honour.

Merttens & Co. Ltd.,

76, NEWTON STREET,
MANCHESTER.

T. A. ADDISON,
  Royal Fusiliers.

T. A. BANNISTER,
  R.A.M.C.

G. L. COCKRELL,
  Royal Welsh Fusiliers.

F. FLINN,
  King's Own Royal Lancasters.

T. H. GEORGE,

S. HARRISON,
  R.F.A.

A. S. HARVEY,
  R.F.A.

F. HENDERSON,
  Manchester Territorials.

E. KAY,
  20th Batt. Royal Fusiliers.

J. MATHER,
  R.A.M.C.

J. A. MOORE,
  Royal Fusiliers.

A. O'ROURKE,
  R.A.M.C.

G. SUTCLIFFE,
  1/6th Manchester Territorials.

ROLL OF HONOUR.

N. P. Nathan's Sons

Sergeant J. COWSILL	Royal Army Medical Corps.
L.-Corpl. A. EVERALL	8th Manchester Territorials.
Private A. HARDY	Royal Army Medical Corps.
Private H. MAUDE	Royal Army Medical Corps.
Corporal W. PULFORD	8th Manchester Territorials.
Captain F. W. ROYLE	19th Battalion Manchester Regiment.
Private W. RICHARDSON	16th Battalion Manchester Regiment.
Private S. SIBLEY	Royal Marines.
Private W. WILLIAMS	Royal Army Medical Corps.
Corporal W. L. ORANGE	7th Lancashire Fusiliers.
Private HAROLD BOOTH	6th Royal Scots.
L.-Corpl. J. W. LEAH	7th Lancashire Fusiliers.
Private C. CALVERT	Lancashire Fusiliers.
Private S. DICKENSON	6th Royal Scots.
Private J. O'DONNELL	6th Royal Scots.
Private C. CALLAGHAN	6th Royal Scots.
Private F. LEA	6th Royal Scots.
Sergeant H. SCHOFIELD	Royal Army Medical Corps.
Private R. HOPWOOD	19th Battalion Manchester Regiment.
L.-Corpl. E. HODGES	Royal Army Medical Corps.
Private W. LOWE	Royal Field Artillery.
Private H. CARTER	Royal Army Medical Corps.
Private A. ISLIP	16th Battalion Manchester Regiment.

ROLL OF HONOUR.

The "Oak Tree" Hosiery Company Ltd.,

Formerly THOMAS GRIMSHAW & SONS Limited,

25 and 27, Dale Street, MANCHESTER.

2nd Lieut. T. GRIMSHAW (Director), 2nd—6th Battalion Sherwood Foresters.
" J. McGRATH, Duke of Lancaster's Own I.Y.
Sergeant W. BAILEY, Border Regiment.
Private F. MARSLAND, Manchester Regiment.
" H. DANIELS, R.A.M.C.
" MITCHELL, Manchester Regiment.
" A. YATES, R.A.M.C.
" J. SUTTON, Scottish Borderers.
" LINDSEY, Manchester Regiment.
" F. ERRINGTON, R.A.M.C.
" G. BROOKES, Manchester Regiment.
" R. MARSDEN, 8th Manchester Regiment (T.F.).
" V. CLAMPITT, Manchester Regiment.
" C. STANLEY, 8th Manchester Regiment (T.F.).
" G. BROWN, King's Own Liverpool Regiment.
" S. PAGE, Manchester Regiment.
" S. WATKINS, Manchester Regiment.
" H. HOWELLS, Manchester Regiment.
" L. HOWES, King's Own Liverpool Regiment.
Gunner F. HUXLEY, Royal Field Artillery Territorial Force.
Private L. SMITH, 6th Manchester Regiment (T.F.).
Gunner A. HARDMAN, Royal Field Artillery.
" J. H. SUTTON, Royal Field Artillery (T.F.).
Private S. WOLFENDEN, Manchester Regiment.
" W. G. WRATH, R.A.M.C.
" W. CHADWICK, R.A.M.C.
Driver E. WILKINSON, Royal Engineers.
" V. SHAW, Royal Field Artillery (T.F.).
" F. GRENVILLE, Army Service Corps.

ROLL OF HONOUR.

※ ※ ※

Wm. O'Hanlon & Co. Ltd.,

49—51, DALE STREET, MANCHESTER.

Employees serving with His Majesty's Forces.

Captain K. T. BLAMEY	8th Lancashire Fusiliers.
Lieut. E. O'HANLON	15th Ser. Batt. Lancs. Fusiliers.
W. CONDLIFFE	6th Manchester Regiment.
T. L. CROSSLEY	6th Manchester Regiment.
W. GERRARD	6th Manchester Regiment.
G. GRIFFITH	6th Manchester Regiment.
F. W. HAMPSON	2nd King's Dragoon Guards.
H. HARRISON	8th Manchester Regiment.
W. HASTINGS	19th Lancashire Fusiliers.
S. HEMINGWAY	23rd Manchester Regiment.
R. HILL	Royal Engineers.
E. JACOBS	7th Manchester Regiment.
J. JONES	Royal Engineers.
H. JONES	8th Manchester Regiment.
F. KITSON	6th Manchester Regiment.
H. MILNER	20th Manchester Regiment.
T. PALMER	6th Manchester Regiment.
C. POTTER	Army Ser. Corps (East Lancs.).
T. RALPHS	16th Manchester Regiment.
H. RAWLINSON	6th Manchester Regiment.
A. REDFERN	3rd Welsh Regiment.
H. S. SELBY	2nd East Lancs. R.F.A.
W. THOMPSON	6th Manchester Regiment.
G. H. WILCOCK	20th Manchester Regiment.

Roll of Honour.

Geo. Owen & Co.

15 Bloom Street, Manchester.

Captain D. BERRY,
  18th Batt. Manchester Regt.
Sergeant W. J. WALLIS,
  30th Divisional Cyclists' Corps.
L.-Corpl. A. MARSDEN,
  12th Batt. Manchester Regt.
Private JOHN CORRIS,
  7th Batt. Manchester Regt.
Private THOMAS CORRIS,
  2nd Batt. South Lancashire Regt.
Private ARTHUR CHAMBERS,
  19th Batt. Manchester Regt.
Private ALBERT CHAMBERS,
  4th Batt. King's Liverpool Regt.
Private FRED COYNE,
  14th Batt. Cheshire Regt.
Private WILLIAM DAVIS,
  19th Batt. Manchester Regt.
Private EDMUND McCUTCHEON,
  4th Batt. Seaforth Highlanders.
Private HAROLD OGDEN,
  15th Batt. Royal Scots.
Private THOMAS PARKER,
  7th Batt. East Lancashire Regt.
Private JOSEPH SHONE,
  19th Batt. Manchester Regt.
Private WILLIAM STUBBS,
  17th Batt. Royal Scots.
Private JOHN VIPOND,
  14th Batt. King's Liverpool Regt.
Private ARTHUR WILLIAMS,
  19th Batt. Manchester Regt.
Private A. D. WILLIAMSON,
  6th Batt. Manchester Regt.
Signaller SYDNEY STRAFFORD,
  H.M.S. "Magnificent."

ROLL OF HONOUR.

Oxendale & Co.,

MANCHESTER.

1st/6th Manchester Regiment.
  Pte. STANLEY TRUEMAN.
    (Killed in action, June 4th, 1915.)
17th Manchester Regiment.
  Pte. A. JACKSON.
  Pte. A. PRITCHETT.
  Pte. H. WHITE.
19th Manchester Regiment.
  Pte. W. P. ATKINSON.
  Pte. W. E. J. HALL.
  Pte. G. KENNEDY.
  Pte. J. LOCKWOOD.
  Pte. G. E. PATTINSON.
26th Manchester Regiment.
  Pte. R. J. TAYLOR.
3rd/6th Manchester Regiment.
  Pte. G. HULTON.
2nd/8th Manchester Regiment.
  Pte. F. TURNER.
The Rifle Brigade.
    (19th Western Battalion.)
  L.-Corpl. E. ECKERSALL.
15th Royal Scots Regiment.
  Signaller H. NAYLOR.
3rd/6th Cheshire Regiment.
  Signaller J. M. KNOWLES.
21st Royal Fusiliers.
  Pte. R. CUNNINGHAM.
Manchester Regiment (Depot).
  Pte. H. VARLEY.
Royal Army Medical Corps.
  Driver T. WILSON.
  Pte. A. EDMONDSON.
  Pte. H. OPIE.
Military Dock Police (France).
  Corpl. E. ROGERS.
Royal Flying Corps.
  Pte. P. BARRON.
Royal Marine Light Infantry.
  Pte. W. CLAYTON.

ROLL OF HONOUR.

George Peak & Co. Ltd.
Portland Street, Manchester.

AINLEY, W. E.
BARLOW, P.
BARTON, H.
BATES, C.
BELLAMY, H. S.
BEVERLEY, E.
BOOTH, F.
BOWLES, F.
BRIDGE, R.
BULMER, W.
BUXTON, A.
CAMPBELL, A. G.
CHAPMAN, R. W.
CLARKE, E.
CLEVELAND, W. H.
COCKS, B. C.
CRONSHAW, H.
EVANS, H.
FAUX, W.
FEAY, W. L.
FITZSIMMONS, A.
FOWLER, F.
HALL, J. E.
HALLETT, E.
HARCOURT, G.
HART, F. B.
HAWKER, F.
HAYES, J.
HEARN, S.
HENDERSON, W. L.
HIND, W. C.
HOLBROOK, T.
HOLLAND, J.
HOWARTH, E.
HOWARTH, F.
INGHAM, H.
JACKSON, W.
JENKINS, E.
JOHNSON, B.
KENDALL, J. M.
KERFOOT, W.
KILDING, A.
LAWRENSON, J.
MARTIN, F.
McCORMACK, J.
MORRIS, W.
MOTTERSHEAD, H.
OLDHAM, W.
ORTON, S.
PARK, W.
POLLARD, W.
RICHARDS, J. L.
SANDERSON, F.
SHEARSTON, J. A.
SMITH, S. D.
SUTTON, W.
TAYLOR, J.
THOMPSON, A.
THOMSON, W.
THORPE, S.
THREADGOLD, A.
TRAVIS, P.
WAINMAN, B.
WALDRON, B.
WALLWORK, T.
WARBURTON, P.
WATSON, A.
WHITTAKER, T.
WIGHTMORE, W.
WILLIAMS, E.
WOODS, R. J.

ROLL OF HONOUR.

Peel, Watson & Co. Limited,
6, Parker Street, MANCHESTER.

R. O. ASHTON	16th Service Batt. Manchester Regt.
F. ANTROBUS	6th Cheshire Regt. (T.).
J. AIKEN	17th Service Batt. Manchester Regt.
F. G. ALLSOPP	17th Service Batt. Manchester Regt.
W. E. BOTTOMLEY	Royal Army Medical Corps.
C. BUTLER	17th Service Batt. Manchester Regt.
F. BOOKER	7th Manchester Regt. (T.).
H. BOWER	2/53rd Welsh Division Cycling Corps.
E. BURGOYNE	21st Service Batt. Manchester Regt.
C. BAKER	4th Reserve Batt. Royal Scots.
H. BURTON	3/5th Batt. Manchester Regt. (T.).
A. CLOUGH	21st Batt. Ryl. Fus., Pub. Schools Brigade.
E. CRYER	Royal Garrison Artillery.
H. DAVIES	8th Batt. Lancashire Fusiliers (T.).
J. GLOVER	8th Batt. Manchester Regt. (T.).
B. GALLAGHER	8th Batt. Manchester Regt. (T.).
W. GILL	27th Service Batt. Manchester Regt.
E. HILL	8th Batt. King's (Liverpool) Irish Regt.
H. HUDSON	17th Service Batt. Manchester Regt.
G. H. HULME	4th Batt. Lancashire Fusiliers (T.).
J. HERBERT	21st Serv. Batt. Manchester Regt.
F. JOHNSON	6th Manchester Regt. (T.).
J. H. JONES	17th Service Batt. Manchester Regt.
R. LEVER	16th Service Batt. Manchester Regt.
G. G. LOUGHLAND	3rd Batt. Royal Fus., Public Schools Brig.
D. McCOURTS	23rd Service Batt. Manchester Regt.
H. E. MAY	Duke of Cornwall's Light Infantry.
J. McNALLY	19th Service Batt. Manchester Regt.
W. J. MERRICK	Royal Engineers.
W. MARTINDALE	9th Manchester Regt. (T.).
A. MYERS	7th Batt. Lancashire Fusiliers.
T. OLIVER	6th Batt. Royal Scots.
J. PALMER	Royal Naval Division.
B. PERKINS	R.A.M.C.
N. POLE	16th Service Batt. Lancashire Fusiliers (T.)
G. A. PITT	Royal Navy.
A. C. POULTON	London Rifle Brigade.
H. W. ROYLE	22nd Service Batt. Manchester Regt.
C. RUSHFORTH	Royal Garrison Artillery.
H. SOUTH	16th Service Batt. Manchester Regt.
T. C. SCHOLES	6th Reserve Batt. Manchester Regt.
A. E. TOWNSEND	7th Batt. Rifle Brigade.
J. TIGHE	17th Service Batt. Manchester Regt.
C. TAYLOR	20th Service Batt. Manchester Regt.
W. TAYLOR	7th Reserve Batt. Manchester Regt.
G. WALMSLEY	Army Service Corps.
A. V. WILKINSON	6th Batt. Manchester Regt. (T.).
F. WHATMOUGH	17th Service Batt. Manchester Regt.
V. L. WATTS	County of London Regt. (T.).
W. WILLS	3/6th Batt. Manchester Regt. (T.).

STAFF OF J. & N. Philips & Co.,
35 CHURCH STREET, MANCHESTER,
Who voluntarily offered their services in the great war.

* * *

ACKRILL, F.	BARTON, W. C.	CADMAN, W. H.
ADSHEAD, G.	BAUMER, F.	CAMPBELL, H. S.
AIREY, J. O.	BAXTER, J. H.	CAMPBELL, J. E.
ALBAN, L.	BEAN, W.	CARR, A. W.
ALCRUM, J.	BENNETT, F.	CARROTTE, F. C.
ALDCROFT, E.	BERRETT, T. G.	CARTWRIGHT, F.
ANDERSON, R. C.	BERTENSHAW, R. W.	CHAMBERS, L.
ANDERSON, W.	BESWICK, S.	CHAMP, W.
ANDREW, P.	BEVAN, H.	CHARLES, E. R.
ANDREWS, F.	BLAKE, L. O.	CHATTERTON, A.
ANNABLE, R.	BLEMARD, R.	CHECK, L. E.
ASHMAN, C.	BLOMILEY, J.	CHERRY, J. H.
ASHTON, V.	BLOOR, W.	CLAMP, G. W.
ASTLES, H.	BOARDMAN, W.	CLARE, J.
ASTON, L.	BOOTHMAN, A.	CLAYTON, H.
AUKLAND, W	BOWKER, S.	CLEGG, G. R.
BACON, A. B.	BOYD, F. P.	CLEGG, H.
BAILEY, F. C.	BRADBURY, B.	COATES, A. S.
BAKER, W. W.	BREWER, A. B.	COATES, J. W.
BALLARD, W.	BRINDLEY, J.	COCHRANE, A. G.
BARBER, C.	BROOKS, W. H.	CONNELL, D.
BARBER, A. J.	BROWN, F.	COOPER, A. R.
BARBER, A. L.	BRYANT, H.	CORBETT, W. A.
BARLOW, H.	BRYDEN, G. A.	COTTON, W.
BARNES, T. E.	BRYDEN, G.	COUZENS, H.
BARRETT, H.	BUCK, H.	COWSILL, A.
BARRY, E. H.	BULLOCK, A.	CROMPTON, F.
BARTHOLOMEW, J. E.	BURRELL, R. N.	CROMPTON, J. B.
BARTON, H.	BURROWS, H. J.	CRUTCHLEY, T.

STAFF OF
J. & N. Philips & Co.,
35 CHURCH STREET, MANCHESTER,
Who voluntarily offered their services in the great war.

Continued.

- COXON, J. H.
- DANN, W.
- DEACOCK, W. V.
- DART, F. T.
- DAVIS, A.
- DAVIES, H.
- DAVIES, T. K.
- DAVISON, F. H.
- DEAN, F. H.
- DEARN, P. L.
- DEAVILLE, A.
- DODGE, W. R.
- DOWNING, G. C.
- DUFFIN, G. H.
- DUNKLEY, F.
- EATON, C. W.
- EDGAR, J. L.
- EDGE, H.
- ELLOR, W.
- ENTWISTLE, E. C.
- ENTWISTLE, F.
- EVANS, P. C.
- FARRINGTON, C. M.
- FIELD, C. A.
- FLEMING, A.
- FLINT, W. E.
- FORD, A.
- FOSTER, J.
- FRASER, L.
- FROOD, C. T.
- FURNESS, T.
- GARTELL, H.
- GEARLE, E. B.
- GEE, W.
- GERMAN, G.
- GIBSON, R. D.
- GOODIER, A.
- GOODY, R.
- GOUGH, W. L.
- GOWING, S. A.
- GRAHAM, W.
- GREEN, E.
- GREENHALL, E.
- GRESTY, A.
- GRIFFITHS, W. H.
- GRIMSHAW, R. H.
- HALL, V.
- HAMNETT, E.
- HARDMAN, E.
- HARRIS, F.
- HARROP, E. A.
- HARROP, G.
- HART, L. F.
- HEATON, H. V.
- HERBERT, W.
- HERRING, W.
- HEYWOOD, S. H.
- HICKS, A.
- HILL, R.
- HILTON, C. H.
- HILTON, F.
- HINES, C. A.
- HODKINSON, R. F.
- HOGG, H. A.
- HOLLIDAY, W.
- HOLME, A. W.
- HOLMES, A. E.
- HORSEY, A. W.
- HOUGHTON, A.
- HUGHES, J. F.
- HULME, W.
- HUTTON, W.
- ISHERWOOD, W.
- JACKSON, H.
- JAMES, H.
- JENKINS, S.
- JENKINS, W.
- JENKINSON, J.
- JOHNSON, C. S.
- JOHNSON, J.
- JONES, J. E.
- KAYE, C.
- KELAWALA, J. M.
- KEMPLE, T.
- KERNAN, C.
- KERSHAW, G. A.
- KING, B. J. W.

STAFF OF
J. & N. Philips & Co.,
35 CHURCH STREET, MANCHESTER,
Who voluntarily offered their services in the great war.

Continued.

KING, G.
KNIGHT, D.
LANCASTER, D. G.
LANGLEY, E.
LEES, H. V.
LESTER, S. M.
LITTLE, W. G.
LITTLER, F. O.
LOCKWOOD, T. W.
LOMAX, G.
LOWE, D. C.
LUSCOMBE, L. A.
MAJOR, J.
MAJOR, L.
MARSHALL, W.
MASON, A.
MATHER, L.
MATTHEWS, F. J.
MAYER, H.
McCANN, J. H.
McGEE, J.
McGUIRE, W. D.
McLOUGHLIN, J.
McMASTER, A.
McPLAIL, L. B.
MEARS, W. P.
MENDES, N.
MILLS, A.
MILLS, E.

MINIATI, A.
MOFFET, E. H.
MOONEY, G.
MORRELL, F.
MORRIS, T.
MOSS, W.
MOUNTER, W.
NEILAN, J.
NEWMAN, S. N.
NOTTON, G. W.
NUTTALL, C.
NUTTALL, F.
NUTTALL, S. W.
OLDFIELD, J.
ORMSON, W.
OWEN, S.
OWEN, W. STANLEY.
PARKE, J.
PARKES, J. M.
PARKER, W.
PARSONS, H.
PARTINGTON, T. C.
PATON, R. L.
PAYNE, A.
PAYNE, J. A.
PAYNE, J. J.
PEARCE, H.
PEARSON, J. W. L.
PHETHEAN, T.

PHILIPS, H. B.
PHILIPS, H. N.
PICKSTONE, E.
PIGGOTT, F.
POLLITT, F.
POLLITT, H.
POWELL, R. M.
PRESTWICH, H. S.
RAMSDEN, H. W.
RATHBONE, T.
REDFEARN, J. W.
REDFORD, E.
REED, A. E.
REES, A. F.
RIDYARD, W.
RIGBY, T.
RILEY, H.
RIMMER, F. A.
ROBERTS, E. W.
ROGERS, G.
ROGERS, H.
ROSKELL, A. W.
ROSSITER, F.
ROYLE, T. R.
RYAN, J. P.
RYDER, H.
SENIOR, W. A.
SHARPE, C.
SHEPPHERD, W. A.

STAFF OF
J. & N. Philips & Co.,
35 CHURCH STREET, MANCHESTER,
Who voluntarily offered their services in the great war.

Continued.

SHELDON, G.	THOMPSON, W. L.	WHITTAKER, S.
SHELLY, C. R.	THORPE, E.	WHITWORTH, W. E.
SIMPSON, G. E.	THORNTON, W.	WILBY, G. H.
SLINGER, J. D.	TITTERINGTON, J.	WILLIAMS, G.
SMITH, A.	TOZER, G.	WILLIAMS, J. V.
SMITH, E.	TUCKER, D. W.	WILLIAMS, S.
SMITH, L.	TURNER, L.	WILLIAMS, S. R.
SMITH, W. D.	TURNER, S.	WILLIAMSON, H.
SNAPE, J.	TURTON, H.	WILLIAMSON, J.
SPRATT, H. J.	TYAS, G.	WILLOUGHBY, A.
STATHAM, A. J.	TYSON, T.	WILSON, W.
STINTON, W. J.	VERITY, G. H.	WILSON, W.
STOCKWELL, A.	WAIGHT, E. F.	WINDSOR, A.
STOCKWELL, S.	WARD, S. A.	WOOD, A.
TABBRON, A.	WARREN, C. W.	WOOD, H. R.
TAYLOR, E.	WATKINS, S. G.	WOODBURN, G.
TAYLOR, J. H.	WELCH, T. E.	WOODROFFE, F.
TAYLOR, W.	WELFORD, E. C.	WOODWARD, H.
THOMAS, F.	WELLS, F.	WOODWARD, W. A.
THOMAS, R. G.	WHATLEY, J.	WOOLLAM, S. E.
THOMSON, W.	WHITEHEAD, E.	WOLSTENCROFT, D.
THOMPSON, C.	WHITEHURST, E. M.	WREFORD, W. H.
THOMPSON, N.	WHITELEY, J. A.	WYATT, H.
THOMPSON, W.	WHITTAKER, H.	YATES, T.

ROLL OF HONOUR.

EMPLOYEES OF

W. & H. POWNALL LTD.

Daisy Bank Works, Stockport Road, Manchester,

WHO HAVE JOINED HIS MAJESTY'S FORCES.

C. H. ASHTON	2nd Battalion Manchester Regiment.
P. WALLACE	National Res., Con. Rangers, 5th Battery.
G. BARDSLEY	Army Service Corps.
F. BARKER	1/6th Batt. Manchester Regt.
D. WILLIAMS	25th Reserve Batt. Manchester Regt.
J. WORTHINGTON	1/8th Batt. Manchester Regt.
J. PINDER	25th Reserve Batt. Manchester Regt.
W. JACKSON	17th Service Batt. Manchester Regt.
J. ROURKE	18th Service Batt. Manchester Regt.
E. DAVIES	19th Service Batt. Manchester Regt.
W. McNEILL	9th Battalion, K.O.S.B.
A. WALKER	Royal Marines, Light Infantry.
A. WHITELEY	3/8th Batt. Manchester Regt., 2nd Lieut.
R. GARDE	8th Battalion Manchester Regiment.

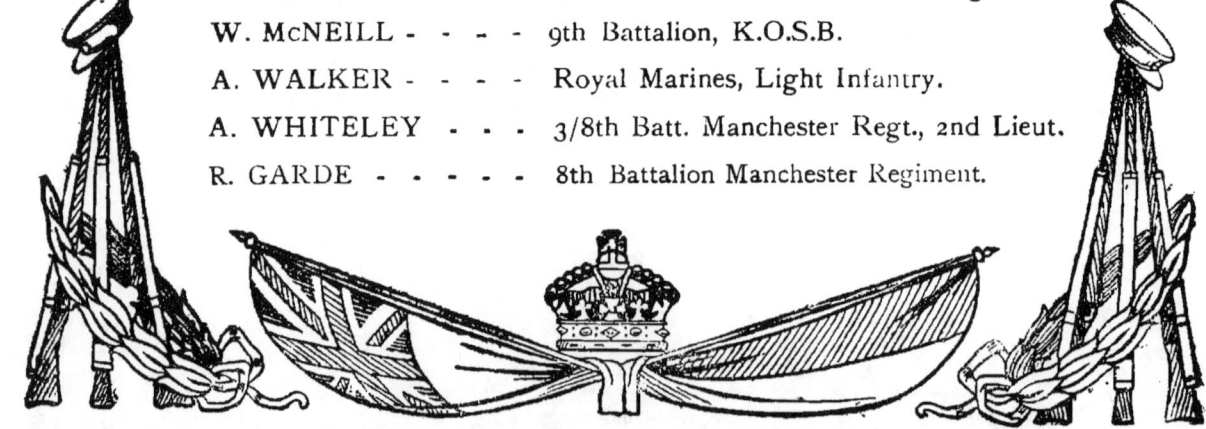

ROLL OF HONOUR.

The Premier Waterproof & Rubber Company Ltd.

DANTZIC STREET, MANCHESTER.

Men Serving with the Colours.

- Pte. J. ALLEN.
- Pte. J. ARMITAGE.
- Pte. W. ARMITT.
- Pte. R. BARKER.
- Pte. W. BARTHOLOMEW.
- Pte. T. BATH.
- Pte. A. BEARD.
- Pte. H. BEARD.
- Pte. T. BEDDOWS.
- Bomb. J. BOYLON.
- Pte. J. BOYD.
- Pte. G. BROWN.
- Pte. T. BRYAN.
- Pte. D. BURKE.
- Pte. B. BURKSON.
- Pte. C. BILLINGTON.
- Pte. J. W. BROMLEY.
- Pte. A. CARDEN.
- Pte. W. CARDEN.
- Pte. W. CARNEY.
- Pte. J. T. CARNEY.
- Pte. A. CARNEY.
- Pte. H. CARNEY.
- Pte. H. CHADWICK.
- Pte. A. COLLINGE.
- Pte. W. COLLIER.
- Pte. H. CONSTERDINE.
- Pte. J. CORRIGAN.
- Pte. J. COULBOURNE.
- Pte. R. COURTNEY.
- Pte. J. CROSSLEY.
- Pte. J. DEVANNY.
- Pte. E. DILLON.
- Pte. J. DODD.
- Pte. J. DONOGHUE.
- Sergt. J. V. EDGAR.
- Pte. P. FARRELL.
- Pte. S. FERRIS.
- Pte. J. FORAN.
- Pte. M. FORD.
- Pte. A. FORSHAW.
- Pte. J. FORSHAW.
- Pte. C. FREEDMAN.
- Pte. A. GANDY.
- Pte. W. GARDNER.
- Pte. F. GARSIDE.
- Pte. A. GRIFFIN.
- Pte. A. GRIMES.
- Pte. P. GRAHAM.
- Pte. M. F. GARTLEY.
- Pte. C. HARRIS.
- Corpl. W. HALL.
- Pte. R. HARGREAVES.
- Pte. D. HEALEY.
- Pte. E. HEALEY.
- Pte. B. HILLIDGE.
- Pte. J. HODSON.
- Pte. G. HOLDEN.
- Pte. W. HOLDEN.
- Pte. F. HOYLE.
- Pte. J. HOYLE.
- Pte. T. HUGHES.
- Pte. J. HUSHION.
- Pte. J. JACOBS.
- Pte. S. JAMES.
- Pte. J. JONES.
- Pte. J. P. KEELAN.
- Pte. P. KEELAN.
- Pte. J. KEELAN.
- Pte. W. LATIMER.
- Sergt.-Maj. LEAFF.
- Pte. T. LEES.
- Pte. J. LEIGH.
- Pte. H. LOWNSBACH.
- Pte. W. LOWE.
- Pte. F. LYST.
- Col.-Sergt. J. MALONEY.
- Pte. J. MACINTYRE.
- Pte. C. MELLES.
- Pte. J. McKINNELL.
- Pte. E. MOORE.
- Pte. A. ORANGE.
- Pte. T. PACE.
- Pte. G. PADDON.
- Pte. J. PARTINGTON.
- Pte. G. PEARCE.
- Pte. E. QUINN.
- Pte. G. RENSHAW.
- Pte. J. RILEY.
- Pte. W. ROACH.
- Pte. W. ROBERTS.
- Sergt. M. RATHMILL.
- Pte. A. E. RYDER.
- Lieut. W. A. SALT.
- Pte. O. SEEREY.
- Pte. A. SCHOFIELD.
- Sergt. J. SHERIDAN.
- Pte. F. SOUTHWORTH.
- Pte. H. SPELLMAN.
- Pte. F. SPELMAN.
- Pte. A. SILVERT.
- Pte. G. TAYLOR.
- Pte. J. TAYLOR.
- Pte. E. THEOBALD.
- Pte. E. VAUGHAN.
- Pte. F. WAINWRIGHT.
- Pte. J. T. WELSH.
- Pte. R. WOOD.
- Pte. R. WOLSTENCROFT.
- Pte. P. WORRALL.
- Pte. J. C. WAUDE.

ROLL OF HONOUR

Members of

Messrs. Ralli Brothers'
MANCHESTER STAFF
Who Joined His Majesty's Forces.

ARCHIBALD, W. J.	GANNON, H.	MOORE, C. A.
ASPINWALL, R. A.	GLEAVE, G.	NEWSHAM, C.
ASHWORTH, J. W.	GLEAVE, J.	NEWTON, J.
BROWN, A.	GLEAVE, T.	NEEDHAM, W.
BROWN, E.	GREELY, J. D.	O'CONNOR, T.
BRETT, T.	GREEN, H.	OGDEN, E.
BEBBINGTON, J.	HEIGHWAY, B. L.	OWEN, J. S.
BRASSINGTON, H.	HILL, W. W.	O'NEILL, P.
BAKER, S.	HOWARTH, A.	PARKS, C.
BARKER, J.	HENDERSON, T.	PRITCHARD, J.
BLAKE, H.	HAYHURST, T.	PLATTS, J
BUCKLEY, J. C.	HAMERTON, W.	RYAN, W.
CLARKE, G.	HAIGH, A.	RATCLIFFE, E.
CUMPSTY, S.	HACKETT, F.	REID, M.
CASSELS, J.	HUNTER, A.	ROBINSON, A. C.
COLLINS, F.	HAYHURST, W.	SAUNDERS, A.
COSADINOS, G. C.	HURST, J. W.	SHELDON, J.
CHALLENDER, T.	IONIDES, T. A.	SIMS, E. E.
CADMAN, C.	INGHAM, J.	SHELTON, A.
CLUNIE, A.	INGHAM, A. E.	SLATER, J.
COX, F. R.	JACKSON, R.	SLATER, J. T.
DRIVER, F.	JONES, E.	SHORROCK, F.
DIGGLE, H.	JONES, E. F.	THORP, N. H.
DENTITH, A. W.	JORDAN, M.	THOMPSON, W.
DENTITH, A.	KEDDY, J.	THOMPSON, H.
DILLON, S. B.	KIRKHAM, J.	TOMLINSON, W.
DUNN, E.	KING, E.	THOMPSON, F.
ELLISON, T.	KNOWLES, J.	WILLIAMS, H. H.
ELLIS, W. R.	LAMB, H.	WILLIAMS, J. W.
FAWCETT, T.	LAWLESS, T.	WILLEY, L. H.
EDWARDS, J.	LODGE, G.	WRIGHT, W. D.
EDWARDS, J. R.	MAGUIRE, S.	WHITEHEAD, A.
FOX, G. W.	MORRIS, T.	WITHERS, T.
FARRELL, W.	McMAHON, M.	WILLIAMSON, H.
FARRELL, A.	MOONEY, M.	WOLLASTON, K. R.
FOSTER, C.	MASSEY, J.	WHITTON, W.
FARRELL, G.	MOORE, J.	WOOD, E. H.
GREENWOOD, W. A.	McKNIGHT, E.	WOODWARD, W. J.
GRIFFIN, S.	MAGUIRE, A.	YATES, R., Junr.
GALVIN, T.	MILLWARD, G.	

ROLL OF HONOUR.

REISS BROTHERS,
MANCHESTER.
* * *

REISS, ALEC, Major, 12th Batt. Cheshire Regt.
REISS, ARTHUR, 2nd Lt., 17th Cheshires.
REISS, WILLOUGHBY, Capt., 2/6th Manch. Regt. (died of wounds, Gallipoli).

HANBURY-WILLIAMS, J., 2nd-Lt., 10th Hussars.
SICHEL, OLIVER W., Lt., 2/5th Warwickshire Regt.
MORRIS, W. R., 2nd Lt., 7th East Lancashires
    (killed in action, France).
ATHERTON, L., Manchester Regt. (Ashton)
    (killed in action).
BAMBER, A., R.A.M.C.
BARRATT, J., Lancashire Fusiliers.
BASTABLE, A., 21st Service Batt., Manchester Regt.
BAXTER, W., 23rd Service Batt. Manchester Regt.
BEAVER, J., Rifleman, King's Royal Rifles.
BLEARS, F., 19th Service Batt. Manchester Regt.
BOOTH, H., R.A.M.C.
BOOTH, S., 18th Service Batt. Manchester Regt.
BRADSHAW, J., 9th Royal Scots.
BROOKS, A., King's Own.
BROWN, W. K., 6th Batt. Manchester Regt.
BURROWS, R., R.A.M.C.
CLARKE, M., 6th Batt. Manchester Regt.
DARLINGTON, F., Cpl., Lancashire Fusiliers.
DAVIES, F., Lancashire Fusiliers.
DINSDALE, W., R.A.M.C.
ELLICOCK, W., Royal Engineers.
FANNING, L., 23rd Service Batt. Manchester Regt.
FRANCIS, J., Coy. Sgt.-Maj., 6th Batt. Manch. Regt.
HANRAHAN, J., 21st Service Batt. Manchester Regt
HARDY, W., Royal Navy.
HOUCHIN, H., R.A.M.C.
HOUGHTON, E., 21st Service Batt. Manchester Regt.
HUGHES, C., Lancashire Fusiliers.
INGRAM, J. A., 6th Batt. Manchester Regt.
JOHNSTONE, H., R.A.M.C.
JOHNSTONE, J. H., R.A.M.C.
JONES, W. H., Lancashire Fusiliers.
KNOX, A., King's Own.
LAMBERT, C., King's Own.
LLEWELLYN, H., 19th Service Batt. Manchester Regt.
McLEAN, R., 6th Batt. Manchester Regt.
MAITLAND, T., R.A.M.C.
MELLOR, J., 19th Service Batt. Manchester Regt.
MORRIS, E., King's Own.
OWEN, F., 18th Service Batt. Manchester Regt.
PEARSON, L., 6th Batt. Manchester Regt.
PICKERING, J., King's Royal Rifles (killed in action).
PIGGOTT, H., 6th Batt. Manchester Regt.
PLANT, A., R.A.M.C.
PROCTOR, C., King's Royal Rifles.
RAMSBOTTOM, E., 9th Royal Scots.
REDFERN, H., Cpl., Lancashire Fusiliers.
RICHARDS, E., 6th Batt. Manchester Regt.
ROBINSON, C., 8th Batt. Manchester Regt.
    (killed in action).
ROSS, J., 12th Batt. Manchester Regt. (Ashton).
ROYAL, A., 18th Service Batt. Manchester Regt.
SHARPLES, J. E., Lancashire Fusiliers.
SHAW, A., 7th Batt. Manchester Regt.
SWIFT, J., R.A.M.C.
TAYLOR, B., Earl of Chester's Yeomanry.
TATLOCK, J., L.-Cpl., 18th Service Batt. Manch. Regt.
THORNTON, W., East Lancashires.
TOMLINSON, F., Sig.-Sgt., 18th Sv. Bt. Manch. Regt.
WALSH, T., Border Regt.
WOOD, C., 21st Service Batt. Manchester Regt.
WOOD, G., Lancashire Fusiliers.
WOOD, S. W., 21st Service Batt. Manchester Regt.
WOODHEAD, J., 18th Service Batt. Manchester Regt.
WYATT, S., 7th Batt. Rifle Brigade.

REJECTED.—W. Hewson, T. Herbert, J. Jones, T. Robinson, A. Shallaker, W. H. Whittaker, W. Wilkes, S. Windram, T. Wilkinson, H. Housley, A. Harrop, H. Kershaw, S. Rogerson, A. Whitehill, T. Barnes, W. Poole, W. Pickering.

ROLL OF HONOUR.

F. REDDAWAY & CO. LTD.

PENDLETON, MANCHESTER.

ASHMAN, B.	3rd East Lancashires.
BROWN, F.	Nav. Res. H.M.S. 'Jupiter.'
BEAHAN, J.	7th Manchesters.
BATES, J.	King's O. Scot. Borderers.
BOUGHEY, W. H.	6th Batt. Border Regiment.
BERRY, A.	7th Lancashire Fusiliers.
BROADLEY, H.	King's Royal Liverpool.
BARWICK, J.	8th Batt. Manchester.
BERTRAM, H.	Royal Garrison Artillery.
BROWN, W.	7th Middlesex.
BROWN, E.	Royal Field Artillery.
CARTER, J.	1st Lancashire Fusiliers.
COLLINS, E.	2nd Batt. Yorkshire Regt.
CLARK, J.	7th Lancashire Fusiliers.
CLARE, M.	2nd Manchester Regiment.
CAREY, T.	King's Royal Rifles.
CLARK, W.	8th Lancashire Fusiliers.
CAREY, J.	8th Lancashire Fusiliers.
CLIFFORD, T.	11th Batt. Middlesex Regt.
CHAPMAN, E. F. G.	5th City Batt. Manchester.
CARROLL, J. O.	Loyal North Lancashires.
COLCLOUGH, J.	2nd Salford Battalion.
CROSSLEY, C.	Royal Irish Rifles.
CARTER, T.	8th Lancashire Fusiliers.
DUNBAR, J.	King's Shropshire Lt. Inf.
DOLAN, W.	Loyal North Lancashire.
DRAGE, H.	Royal Garrison Artillery.
ELLISON, R.	Army Service Corps.
EDWARDS, C.	8th Batt. King's R. Rifles.
ECCLES, W.	15th Serv. Batt. Lancs. Fus.
ELLISON, A. G.	6th Res. Batt. Lancs. Fus.
ELLWOOD, G.	2nd Batt. Middlesex Regt.
ELPHINSTONE, G.	7th Batt. Lancs. Fus. (T.).
FITZSIMMONS, H.	Lancashire Fusiliers.
FLANAGAN, W.	King's Royal Rifles.
FELSTEAD, F.	11th Batt. Middlesex Regt.
FEARNS, A.	8th Lancashire Fusiliers.
FLETCHER, G.	25th Res. Bt. Manchester R.
FOSTER, J. W.	2nd Bt. D. of Well'gt'ns R.
GARBUTT, E.	King's Royal Rifles.
GARBUTT, JAMES	7th Lancs. Fusiliers.
GODLEY, R.	Royal Irish Fusiliers.
GARSIDE, W.	Royal Army Medical Corps.
GARLAND, J.	7th Lancashire Fusiliers.
HIMSWORTH, J.	8th Lancashire Fusiliers.
HAMER, W.	7th Lancashire Fusiliers.
HOWARTH, E.	7th Lancashire Fusiliers.
HARRISON, J.	Spec. Res. 4th Lancs. Fus.
HOUGHTON, J.	4th Lancashire Fusiliers.
HASTINGS, P.	King's Royal Lancasters.
HANCOCK, W. A.	King's Royal Rifles.
HENSHAW, W.	2nd Salford Bt. Lancs. Fus.
HORSEY, E. H.	Royal Naval Division.
HOY, F. C.	159th Battery, R.F.A.
HARRISON, A.	8th Lancashire Fusiliers.
HORRIGAN, J. W.	Royal Garrison Artillery.
HOWSON, E.	1st Batt. E. Lancs. Regt.
HOWARTH, S.	Royal Field Artillery.
IVERS, CHARLES	Motor Transport Service.

F. REDDAWAY & CO. LTD.

ROLL OF HONOUR—continued.

JAMES, J.	- - - -	King's O. Scot. Borderers.
JENNINGS, J. H.	-	King's Royal Rifles.
JONES, H.	- - - -	King's Royal Rifles.
JONES, A.	- - - -	2nd 7th Batt. Lancs. Fus.
KENDRICK, R.	- - -	2nd Manchester.
KINDER, J. W.	- -	Lancashire Fusiliers.
KENYON, G. H.	- -	2nd Salford Bt., E. Lncs. R.
KIRKWOOD, A.	- -	Lancashire Fusiliers.
LEVAY, T.	- - - -	Army Service Corps.
LECKY, J.	- - - -	8th Lancashire Fusiliers.
LEE, J.	- - - - -	8th City Regt. (Bob's Own).
LADLER, E. G.	- -	20th Cnty. of London Regt.
LANE, W.	- - - -	Royal Garrison Artillery.
McCORMICK, W.	-	6th Batt. Manchester Regt.
McCORMICK, J.	- -	Scottish Borderers.
MARSON, S. B.	- -	Royal Horse Artillery.
McALICE, T.	- - -	27th Res. Batt. Lancs. Fus.
McELROY, JOHN	-	7th Lancashire Fusiliers.
McCAWLEY, J.	- -	7th Lancashire Fusiliers.
MURPHY, G. C.	- -	Wireless Operator, Navy.
MULHOLLAND, F.		7th Batt. Lancs. Fusiliers.
MARSHALL, G.	- -	Royal Field Artillery.
MITCHELL, T.	- -	Royal Garrison Artillery.
NORTON, J.	- - -	5th Manchester.
NASH, W.	- - - -	Royal Field Artillery.
O'NEILL, W.	- - -	7th Royal North Lancs.
PORTEOUS, G. D.		2nd Batt. London Rifle Br.
PAGE, W.	- - - -	Royal Naval Division.
PEIRCE, F.	- - -	27th Res. Bt. Manchester R.
PURCHASE, A.	- -	Royal Fusiliers.
REDDAWAY, H.	- -	Royal Fusiliers.
ROBBINS, W.	- - -	South Staffordshire.
ROSE, V.	- - - -	5th Batt. Middlesex Regt.
REDHEAD, T.	- - -	South Lancashires.
SHERRINGTON, J.	-	6th Manchesters.
SPENCE, S.	- - - -	4th City Batt. Manchester.
SKERMAN, CYRIL	-	10th Batt. Royal Fusiliers.
STOTT, W. H.	- - -	4th Hussars.
SMITH, R.	- - - -	Royal Irish Fusiliers.
STANDRING, FRED	-	Lancashire Fusiliers.
SIMPSON, F.	- - - -	1st Batt. Essex Regt.
SYKES, J.	- - - -	
TILDSLEY, D.	- - -	11th Batt. Rifle Brigade.
THORNTON, J.	- -	5th Manchesters.
THOMPSON, R. E.	-	13th Batt. Rifle Brigade.
TAYLOR, G. H.	- -	3rd Batt. King's O. Regt.
THORNTON, JAMES		1st Sv. Batt. Lancs. Fus.
TAYLOR, J.	- - - -	Royal Army Medical Corps.
VESTY, T.	- - - -	13th Batt. Lancs. Fusiliers.
WARING, A.	- - -	8th Batt. East Lancs. Fus.
WEBSTER, J.	- - -	Scots Guards.
WALTERS, A.	- - -	6th Batt. Manchesters.
WATERHOUSE, G.	-	4th Lancashire Fusiliers.
WISHART, W.	- - -	Royal Field Artillery.
WOOLLEY, W.	- -	12th Batt. Manchester Regt.
WAGSTAFFE, J. H.	-	13th Batt. Manchester Regt.
WALMSLEY, E.	- -	Royal Army Medical Corps.
WARD, H.	- - - -	7th Manchester Regt.
WARD, A. V.	- - -	Royal Fusiliers.
WISE, W. A.	- - -	Black Watch.
WILLIAMS, J.	- - -	Royal Field Artillery.

ROLL OF HONOUR.

The Refuge Assurance Co. Ltd.

Chief Office: Oxford Street, Manchester.

* * *

Adshead, J.	22nd	Cryer, G. F.	17th
Aitchison, R. B.	22nd	Davies, F.	16th
Ashmore, G.	16th	Davis, F. W.	16th
Ashton, C. E.	16th	Dawson, E. J.	21st
Atkinson, H. M.	22nd	Dowling, W.	16th
Baines, W. V.	22nd	Eglen, A.	19th
Ball, W.	18th	Ellis, E. A.	17th
Bingham, J. A.	16th	Forrest, A.	16th
Bower, A.	17th	Glessall, W. A.	23rd
Bowker, J.	19th	Gordon, P. N.	19th
Brierley, T.	17th	Gowen, R. E.	20th
Broadhurst, J	19th	Greaves, W.	16th
Brookes, Squire	16th	Green, R.	21st
Broome, T.	22nd	Hatton, G.	16th
Burgess, H.	16th	Hawxby, H.	16th
Burke, J.	16th	Hibbert, G. F.	16th
Burrows, R.	16th	Hirst, A.	19th
Caldwell, W.	16th	Hodgson, J.	16th
Campbell, J.	22nd	Hoyle, H.	22nd
Carroll, W.	22nd	Hulme, A.	16th
Cass, J.	20th	Ibbotson, A.	19th
Clayton, W.	16th	Jacobs, J. E.	20th
Colwell, J.	20th	Jones, Edgar	16th
Cosgrove, J. A.	16th	Kean, F. W.	20th
Cowap, J.	16th	Kelsall, E.	18th
Cowell, E.	17th	Kershaw, L.	22nd

ROLL OF HONOUR.
CONTINUED

The Refuge Assurance Co. Ltd.

Chief Office: Oxford Street, Manchester.

Kett, L.	18th	Scott, J.	16th
Kinsey, F.	16th	Slater, G.	21st
Lawson, L.	20th	Smith, H.	16th
Lock, A.	22nd	Smith, H. F.	16th
Lockwood, F.	16th	Snape, H.	21st
Lucy, T. G.	18th	Starkie, H.	17th
Marks, M.	21st	Stenson, J. W.	16th
Matthews, H. G.	16th	Stephenson, J. S.	22nd
Mollard, A. E.	21st	Stevenson, K.	16th
Moss, G. N.	16th	Strong, J.	16th
Murch, A.	18th	Stuttard, C. A.	16th
Murphy, D.	16th	Toft, H. D.	16th
Newton, L.	20th	Turner, W.	16th
Nuttall, J.	22nd	Upton, T.	16th
Orrell, H.	20th	Walkden, T.	18th
Owen, S.	20th	Walker, N.	17th
Pearce, W.	19th	Warburton, T.	20th
Pearson, A.	23rd	Warren, J. F.	16th
Penn, J.	16th	Watson, H.	21st
Platford, H. W.	17th	Webster, F.	16th
Pogson, W.	22nd	White, P.	18th
Ridgway, G. J.	21st	Wickman, W. E.	16th
Roberts, A.	20th	Wilkinson, M. C.	16th
Robinson, W. H.	17th	Windsor, S.	16th
Royle, L.	18th	Woodhead, E. J.	20th
Royle, R.	21st	Worthington, F. L.	17th
Rule, F. R.	17th	Yarwood, T.	16th

Enlistments from Chief Office 241.
Total enlistments from the Company's Staff 1,128.

November 30th, 1915.

ROLL OF HONOUR.

GEORGE ROBINSON & CO.

(109 Princess Street, MANCHESTER)

2-Lt. F. E. ASHWORTH	3/5th Cheshire Regt.	2-Lt. N. ARMSTRONG	3/5th Cheshire Regt.
Capt. W. G. HAYWOOD	19th Batt. Lancs. Fusiliers.	Pte. J. HIGGINS	D. of Lancaster's Yeomanry.
Capt. B. E. LANGFORD	12th Batt. East Surrey Regt.	Pte. C. JACKSON	8th Batt. Manchester Regt.
2-Lt. W. F. SIDEBOTHAM	3/9th Batt. Manchester Regt.	Pte. S. KENYON	1st Batt. King's Liv'p'l Regt.
Col-Sergt. D. FOWLER	Leicester Regiment.	Pte. J. W. KENYON	20th Batt. Manchester Regt.
Q.M. Sergt. P. H. JONES	17th Batt. Manchester Regt.	Pte. P. KERSHAW	6th Batt. Manchester Regt.
Sergt. I. BARTON	7th Batt. Manchester Regt.	Pte. A. KNOTT	8th Batt. Manchester Regt.
Sergt. A. HAMMERTON	Royal Army Medical Corps.	Pte. S. LABREY	17th Batt. Manchester Regt.
Sergt. S. MARCHINGTON	8th Batt. Lancs. Fusiliers.	Pte. J. LLOYD	7th Batt. Lancs. Fusiliers.
Sergt. W. H. RIDINGS	20th Batt. Manchester Regt.	Pte. W. C. OLIVER	Royal Army Medical Corps.
Corpl. W. A. BERRY	6th Batt. Manchester Regt.	Pte. T. S. O'GRADY	Royal Army Medical Corps.
Corpl. J. GEATER	7th Batt. Manchester Regt.	Pte. W. H. REDFERN	8th Batt. Lancs. Fusiliers.
L.-Corpl. G. CATTO	8th Batt. Black Watch.	Pte. G. H. SEDGLEY	17th Batt. Manchester Regt.
L.-Corpl. H. CATTRALL	16th Batt. Manchester Regt.	Pte. L. T. SMITH	6th Batt. Manchester Regt.
L.-Corpl. H. PLANT	6th Batt. Manchester Regt.	Pte. W. J. STACEY	6th Batt. Manchester Regt.
L.-C. G. SHELMERDINE	4th Batt. Manchester Regt.	Pte. A. R. TETLOW	20th Batt. Royal Fusiliers.
L.-Corpl. J. SMITH	7th Batt. L. N. Lancs. Regt.	Pte. W. TODD	8th Batt. Lancs. Fusiliers.
Gnr. T. HEALD	Royal Field Artillery.	Pte. H. TOPHAM	21st Batt. Royal Fusiliers.
Pte. R. L. BRYANT	17th Batt. Manchester Regt.	Pte. H. WHITEHEAD	6th Batt. Manchester Regt.
Pte. C. CLAYTON	6th Batt. Manchester Regt.	Pte. H. A. WHITTENBURY	16th Batt. Man. Regt.
Pte. C. CRITCHLOW	17th Batt. Manchester Regt.	Pte. H. WILKS	9th Batt. Royal Scots.
Pte. J. EMERSON	17th Batt. Manchester Regt.	Pte. A. WILSON	30th Batt. Royal Fusiliers.
Pte. J. GILBODY	8th Batt. Manchester Regt.	Pte. C. R. WILSON	Royal Army Medical Corps.
Pte. C. HARRISON	2nd Batt. Cheshire Regt.	Pte. W. L. WRAY	17th Batt. Manchester Regt.
Pte. A. HAZLEY	17th Batt. Manchester Regt.	Bugler G. CARTER	18th Batt. Manchester Regt.

ROLL OF HONOUR
OF
GEORGE ROBINSON & CO.

ROLL OF HONOUR.

J. F. and H. Roberts Limited,
Portland Street, MANCHESTER.

* * *

ARDRON, F.	HASTINGS, J. L.	WILLAN, G.
BANKS, J.	HAYES, E.	WILLIAMS, E.
BERRY, B.	HEYWOOD, H.	WOODS, R.
BENSON, J. W.	HIGGINBOTHAM, A.	WOODWARD, E. L.
BRIGGS, F.	JOHNSTON, J. R.	WOOLLEY, J.
BRITTAIN, H.	LARMOUR, W. T.	WRIGHT, A.
CHARLTON, A.	LEAHY, G.	YATES, J.
CLIFFE, R.	LEWIS, H.	
CORBETT, H.	LOWE, R. H.	
COLLINSON, H.	MASSEY, G.	
COUCHER, E. J.	MASTYN, J.	*REJECTED.*
CREACAL, E.	MORELLO, J.	AUSTIN, H. M.
CRISPIN, F.	MUNCASTER, A. B.	BARTON, E.
CROSSLAND, C.	OWENS, J. P.	BOOTHWAY, J. F.
DALE, C. R.	PARSONAGE, G.	GREENWOOD, R.
DEAN, F.	POTT, T.	HODGSON, A.
DERWENT, R.	REDFORD, G.	MACKENZIE, E.
DOBSON, F. C.	SHAW, C.	MERRICK, A. E.
FERGUSON, S.	SIMPSON, D. C.	FRANCE, M.
FLINDLE, H.	THOMSON, W.	RUCKER, J.
GREEN, E.	THORPE, F.	SANDERSON, F.
GREENHALGH, R.	TOYN, E.	SINGLETON, J.
HADFIELD, L.	WEBB, M.	TAYLOR, D.
HALL, C.	WELCH, J. J.	TURNER, A.
HALLIWELL, S.	WILSON, W.	WADE, A. C.
HARRISON, H.	WILDE, W.	WILKINSON, J.

ROLL OF HONOUR.

Rose, Hewitt and Co.,
10, MINSHULL ST., MANCHESTER.

WAREHOUSE, MANCHESTER.

JAMES COLBRIDGE	National Reserve.
F. BROADHURST	1st Lancashire Fusiliers.
JOHN GANNON	Manchester Pals (7th Battalion).
FRANK GENT	R.A.M.C.
JOHN HOLT	Earl of Chester's Yeomanry.
TOM MITCHELL	Manchester Pals (8th Battalion).
ROBERT MYERS	7th Battalion Manchester Regt.
F. PURVIS	A.S.C.
B. SUTTON	R.F.A.
J. WEBSTER	9th East Lancashire Regiment.

MILL, SKIPTON.

JOHN ASHWORTH	3rd West Riding.
ALLAN HALL	1st/6th Duke of Wellington.
LESLIE BERRY	1st/6th Duke of Wellington.
WALTER HOLMES	1st/6th Duke of Wellington.
ERNEST WHITAM	1st/6th Duke of Wellington.
FRED THOMPSON	3rd West Riding.
WILLIAM MAYOR	Kitchener's Army.
ROBT. WHITTAKER	3rd/4th H.B. R.F.A.
RICHARD HUMPHREY	2nd/6th West Riding.
ALFRED MARONEY	Coldstream Guards.
HARRY LEET	Royal Naval Reserve.
ARTHUR GOUGH	1st/6th West Riding.

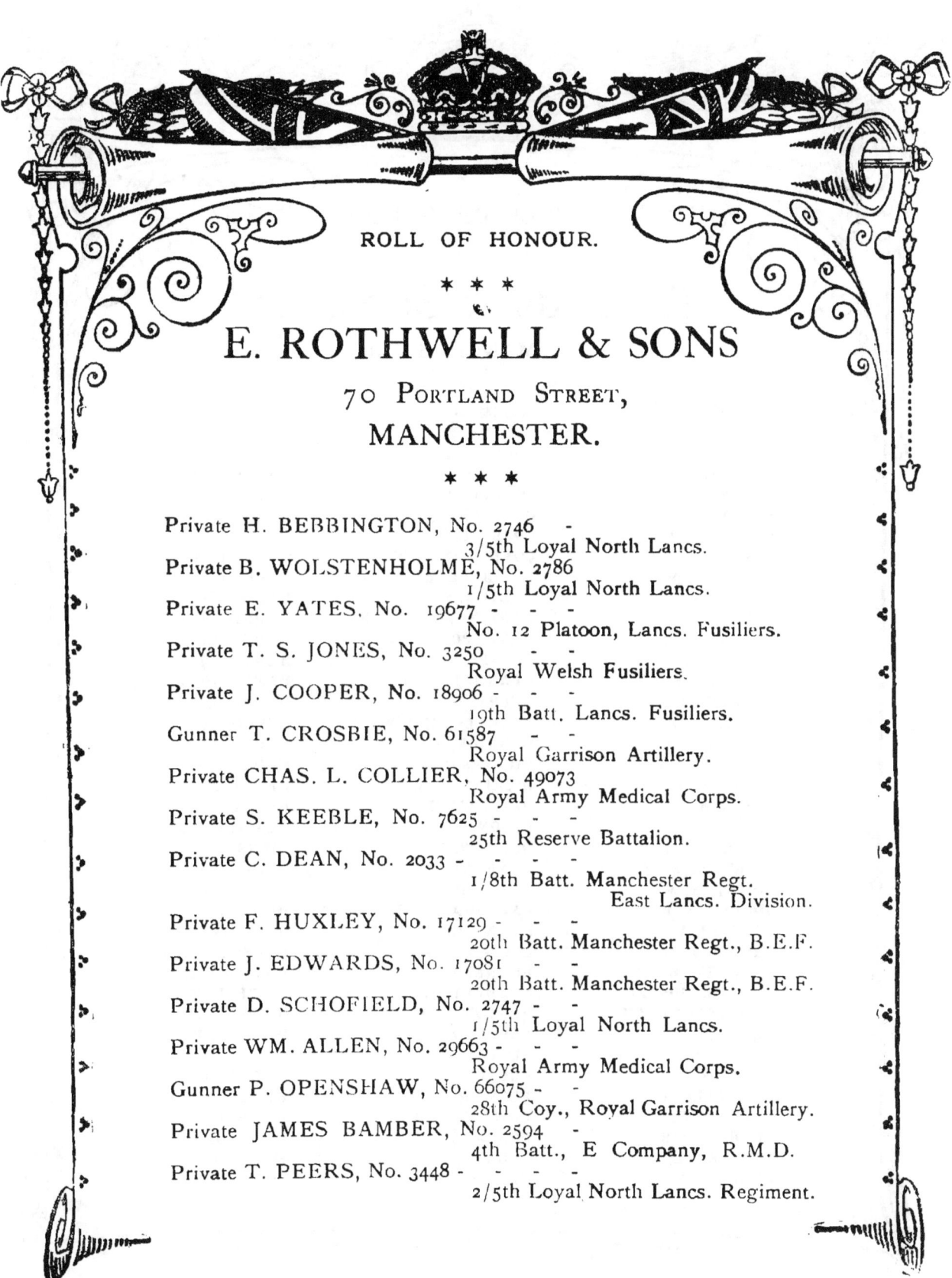

ROLL OF HONOUR.

* * *

E. ROTHWELL & SONS

70 Portland Street,
MANCHESTER.

* * *

Private H. BEBBINGTON, No. 2746 -
    3/5th Loyal North Lancs.
Private B. WOLSTENHOLME, No. 2786
    1/5th Loyal North Lancs.
Private E. YATES, No. 19677 - - -
    No. 12 Platoon, Lancs. Fusiliers.
Private T. S. JONES, No. 3250
    Royal Welsh Fusiliers.
Private J. COOPER, No. 18906 - - -
    19th Batt. Lancs. Fusiliers.
Gunner T. CROSBIE, No. 61587 - -
    Royal Garrison Artillery.
Private CHAS. L. COLLIER, No. 49073
    Royal Army Medical Corps.
Private S. KEEBLE, No. 7625 - - -
    25th Reserve Battalion.
Private C. DEAN, No. 2033 - - - -
    1/8th Batt. Manchester Regt.
        East Lancs. Division.
Private F. HUXLEY, No. 17129 - - -
    20th Batt. Manchester Regt., B.E.F.
Private J. EDWARDS, No. 17081 - -
    20th Batt. Manchester Regt., B.E.F.
Private D. SCHOFIELD, No. 2747 - -
    1/5th Loyal North Lancs.
Private WM. ALLEN, No. 29663 - - -
    Royal Army Medical Corps.
Gunner P. OPENSHAW, No. 66075 - -
    28th Coy., Royal Garrison Artillery.
Private JAMES BAMBER, No. 2594 -
    4th Batt., E Company, R.M.D.
Private T. PEERS, No. 3448 - - - -
    2/5th Loyal North Lancs. Regiment.

ROLL OF HONOUR.

Rylands & Sons, Ltd.,
MANCHESTER.

New High Street.

- ALDRED, J.
- AMBLER, J.
- ANDREWS, T.
- ATHERTON, H.
- AVERY, H.
- ATKINSON, J.
- ARMSTRONG, R. H.
- BAILEY, J. W.
- BAILEY, W.
- BLAKELEY, G. J.
- BARDSLEY, H.
- BARKER, J.
- BARLOW, W.
- BEATSON, J. E.
- BECKETT, H.
- BECKWITH, H.
- BELLERBY, W. E.
- BELSHAW, R.
- BESWICK, C.
- BETTS, A.
- BRIDGE, W. J.
- BRIERLEY, A.
- BRIERLEY, W.
- BRODIE, J. W.
- BOWKER, A.
- BROWN, J. W.
- BUCKLEY, H.
- BURGESS, JOSEPH.
- BURGESS, JOSIAH.
- BRYAN, C.
- CALDWELL, A.
- CALE, W.
- CAMPBELL, J.
- CLARKE, J. J.
- CLARKE, R. B.
- CATTERALL, B.
- CHALLINOR, S.
- COLEMAN, S.
- COATES, T.
- COLLINS, E.
- COLLINS, H.
- COOPER, J. H.
- COPPOCK, A.
- CROSS, T. F.
- COVENTRY, J. W.
- CUNLIFFE, E.
- DALTON, S.
- DARLING, E.
- DAVENPORT, T. J.
- DAVIES, J. G.
- DEARNALEY, A.
- DELPH, T.
- DENNELL, GEO. H.
- DERRICK, A.
- DICKINSON, F. E.
- DICKINSON, W.
- DRINKWATER, H.
- DIXON, A.
- DOLMAN, J.
- DONEGAN, P.
- DOWD, H.
- EARNSHAW, C. F.
- EVANS, G.
- ELLIS, J. A.
- EBURN, F.
- FRADLEY, H.
- FENTON, H. M.
- FERGUSON, F. D.
- FINAN, G.
- FROST, G.
- FLOWER, E.
- FOWLER, J. A.
- FOX, A.
- FLUX, L. T.
- GARNER, W.
- GREENHOUGH, P.
- GIBBONS, W.
- GRIFFIN, W.
- GODSALL, E.
- GOLLINGS, C. F.
- GRESTY, T.
- GRIMSHAW, J.
- GRUNDY, A.
- HALL, A.
- HARDMAN, J.
- HARRISON, A.
- HARRISON, A. E.
- HARVEY, H.
- HAYWOOD, T.
- HEALD, E.
- HELLIWELL, H. G.
- HERBERT, H.
- HEWSON, G. H.
- HEWITSON, F.
- HEY, W.
- HEYWOOD, J.
- HICKS, A.
- HIGGS, C. C.
- HILL, H. A.
- HILTON, J.
- HORSFALL, J.
- HOUSLEY, C. A.
- HOWARD, T. H.
- HOWELL, T.
- HOWELL, H.
- HUGHES, H.
- HUGHES, T.
- HULME, D.
- HUNTINGDON, W
- HYDE, J.
- INGHAM, A.
- INNES, J.
- JACKSON, F. S.

ROLL OF HONOUR—continued.

Rylands & Sons, Ltd.

New High Street.

JELLY, F.
JENNINGS, G.
JOHNSON, A.
JOHNSON, F.
JOHNSON, H.
JONES, B.
JONES, H.
JONES, G.
JONES, T.
KEATINGE, H.
KELLY, J. H.
KENYON, E.
KETTLE, A.
LAMB, J.
LEECH, S.
LENNOX, H.
LEWIS, J.
LEYLAND, F.
LINDSAY, J.
LIPP, J. A.
LONGWORTH, F.
LLOYD, J. G.
MARSDEN, E.
MASSEY, C. W.
MASSEY, C.
MASSEY, E.
MAXWELL, T. D.
MITCHELL, T.
MORT, W.
MYERS, G. W.
NICHOLSON, G.
O'BRIEN, T.
O'CONNOR, C.
OPENSHAW, H.
OWEN, J.
OWEN, J. S.
PLANT, C.
PRATT, N.
PEARSON, J. E.
PEEL, H.
PRESSLER, G. H.
PILOT, R.
PODMORE, A. B.
POINTER, H. B. D.
PYMM, E.
RAMSDEN, J. W.
RATCHFORD, E. A.

RIDDELL, H.
RIDDICK, W.
RHODES, A.
RIGBY, S.
ROBERTS, C. H.
ROBINSON, H.
ROSE, A.
ROSE, J.
ROSS, W.
ROUSHAM, F.
SADLER, D. W.
SAUNDERS, W.
STANWAY, R. H.
SHAW, G.
SHELMERDINE, E. S.
SHENTON, J. A.
SHEPLEY, G. W.
SMETHURST, J.
SWIFT, G. V.
SMITH, H. V.
SMITH, HERBERT.
SMITH, HENRY.
SMITH, LEONARD.
SOUTHERN, T.
SUMMERS, H.
SUTTON, H.
TAYLOR, S. W.
TIERNEY, G.
TIGHE, A.
TOLLETT, H.
THOMAS, J. R.
THOMAS, P. S.
THOMAS, W.
TOMKINSON, E. A.
TOMLINSON, H. H.
THOMPSON, G. A.
THOMPSON, W. A.
THOMPSTONE, F.
TYRRELL, W.
WARBURTON, A.
WARBURTON, E.
WARBURTON, E.
WARHURST, A.
WARING, S.
WARRINGTON, B.
WRAY, E.
WIGGINS, C. A.
WRIGHT, H. A.
WILD, A.

WILD, G.
WILKINSON, ALFRED.
WILKINSON, ARTHUR.
WILKINSON, J.
WILLIAMS, G. W.
WILLIAMSON, W. R.
WILMOTT, J.
WILSON, A.
WILSON, JOHN.
WILSON, JOSEPH.
WHITTAKER, E.
WHITE, E.
WHITE, J.
WOOD, T.
WOOD, J.
WOODHOUSE, G.
WOOLFENDEN, R. M.
WOODCOCK, W. H.
YOUNG, A.

Longford Works.

ATHERTON, J.
BATEMAN, W.
BOUCH, R.
BURGESS, S.
DANIELS, A.
DOWLING, H.
EVANS, T. E.
ELLIS, H.
FRANCIS, W.
FOLLOWS, T.
GARDNER, H.
GOLTON, J.
GOOCH, A.
GUILDFORD, W.
HALL, H. G.
HODSON, F.
HYNES, J.
INGHAM, L.
JACKSON, T.
JONES, A.
KELLY, W.
KILCOYNE, J.
LANGSHAW, W.
NELSON, O.
RICHARDSON, C.
RIDINGS, W.

ROLL OF HONOUR—continued.

Rylands & Sons, Ltd.

Longford Works.
- SHELMERDINE, A.
- WHITTLE, T.
- YOUNG, A.

Liverpool.
- ALLEN, F.
- ANDREWS, W. J.
- CARR, E.
- CORSON, D.
- DAVIDSON, T. R.
- EDWARDS, T.
- FELL, J.
- FORBES, G. E.
- FOX, G.
- GRAVES, L.
- JONES, C.
- JONES, S.
- JONES, W. E.
- KINDER, J. E.
- LLOYD, T. D.
- MANSON, R. A.
- MUSKER, A.
- MURRAY, J.
- PARKER, H.
- PERRY, T.
- RICHARDSON, H. K.
- ROBINSON, R. G.
- SPENCER, R.
- WELSBY, G.
- WILLIAMS, W. H.
- WHITTLE, T.

Dacca Twist Co.
- CAIN, P. R.
- FRENCH, E.
- GOUGH, C.
- KELLY, W.
- KIRKHAM, S.
- McCONNELL, W.
- OWEN, J.
- SIDEBOTHAM, R. J.
- TIMPERLEY, C.
- THOMAS, D.

100, Portland Street.
- BANCROFT, J.
- BOLLAND, H.
- GLEAVE, E.
- JONES, C.
- McCULLOCH, M.
- OWEN, J.
- SMETHURST, R.
- SCHOFIELD, J. F.

Heapey.
- ABBOTT, W.
- AINSWORTH, J.
- ALLISON, A.
- BAILEY, W. H.
- BALDWIN, G. W.
- BAYBUTT, R.
- BLACKHURST, T.
- BRANAGAN, P.
- BRADLEY, E.
- BILLINGTON, S.
- BRINDLE, J.
- BROMILEY, J.
- BOWLING, W.
- BURNS, J.
- CLARKSON, A.
- CARR, J.
- CHRISTIE, H.
- COLLINSON, E.
- COMPTON, T.
- CORKLIN, T.
- CULLEN, J.
- COULTHARD, W.
- DICKINSON, F.
- ELLISON, J. W.
- ENTWISTLE, T.
- FARNWORTH, A.
- FARNWORTH, F.
- FARNWORTH, R.
- FLEVILL, F.
- FINCH, T.
- FOWLER, G.
- FOWLER, H.
- FOWLER, R.
- FOX, J.
- FOY, J.
- GASKELL, J.
- GERAGHTY, J.
- GRIFFITHS, T.
- HALLATT, G.
- HART, G.
- HOOLTON, G.
- JENKINS, E.
- JOLLY, R.
- JORDAN, P.
- JOYCE, M. J.
- LEIGHTON, R.
- LISTER, A.
- MARSDEN, J.
- McDONALD, W.
- McMINN, W.
- MOORE, J.
- MURTHA, J. J.
- NIGHTINGALE, H.
- PARKER, G.
- PRESSLER, W.
- PILKINGTON, G.
- POOLE, T.
- RAMSBOTTOM, G.
- REDSHAW, J.
- RIDINGS, J.
- ROUGHLEY, J.
- SAULT, H.
- STRAIN, R. W.
- SHARPLES, J.
- SMITH, HY.
- SCOTT, G.
- SPEAK, E.
- STOCK, J.
- TRAFFORD, J.
- TAYLOR, F.
- TROUGHT, J.
- TURNER, J.
- URQUHART, C.
- WESTHEAD, W.

ROLL OF HONOUR—continued

Rylands & Sons, Ltd.

Chorley.
ADAMS, J. H.
BLACKLEDGE, R.
BLACKLEDGE, W.
BALDWIN, H.
BONEDING, G.
BUTLER, J.
CATTERALL, J.
COLEMAN, M.
COLLINSON, J.
COMMONS, J.
DARBYSHIRE, G.
DEAVES, G. F.
DOHERTY, M.
DUXBURY, G.
FAIRCLOUGH, R.
GASKELL, W.
GERMAN, G. H.
GRIMSHAW, J.
GRUNDY, P.
HALL, T.
HARGREAVES, W.
HOLDEN, W.
JOYCE, W.
LEAVER, F.
LLOYD, J.
McCANN, A.
McNALLY, F.
MARSDEN, T.
MITCHELL, C.
MITCHELL, J.
MURRAY, J.
MYERSCOUGH, T. H.
MYERSCOUGH, T. A.
NIGHTINGALE, H.
NIGHTINGALE, S.
RILEY, F.
ROBINSON, J.
SMALLEY, J. R.
SHELDON, S. T. R.
SMITH, R.
SMITH, T. P.
TAYLOR, J.
WALSH, J. A.
WALSH, R.
WIGGANS, J.
WILSON, T. S.

Gorton.
ASQUITH, D.
BRADLEY, R. K.
BARLOW, S.
BARRETT, H.
BROWN, F.
BURGESS, W.
CHICKEN, J.
COONEY, W.
CROPPER, J.
FRANCES, D. J.
GREAVES, J.
HATTON, A.
HOWARD, H.
IRELAND, R.
JONES, E.
KEMPSTER, A.
LEWIS, J.
MARTIN, P.
MAWDSLEY, J.
MONTGOMERY, E.
MORRIS, J.
MORRISEY, E.
PHILLIPS, J.
ROBERTS, J.
ROWLANDS, L.
SHARPE, M.
SHAWCROSS, W.
SHEPLEY, J.
THELWELL, T. H.
TOPPING, P.
UFF, A. J.
WAKLER, J.
WILKINSON, A.

Gorton Waddings.
DARLINGTON, I.
DIXON, H.
JOHNSON, A.
MASSEY, W.
SELLERS, H.
SCHOFIELD, W.
WILKINSON, JOSEPH.
WILKINSON, JAMES.

Wigan.
APPLETON, T.
GREENALGH, J.
GILL, J.
KINSEY, H.
LEATHER, J.
LEATHERBARROW, J.
LORD, F.
SCOTT, W.
TABBERNER, J.
TOWNSEND, R.
WINNAIRD, J.
WORTHINGTON, J.

Swinton.
BERRY, T.
DELLHIDE, E.
GOODALL, E.
MARSH, G.
WILKINSON, H.

New High Street Warehouse	225
Longford Works	29
Liverpool Warehouse	26
Dacca Twist Co.	10
100, Portland Street	8
Heapey Works	74
Chorley Works	46
Gorton Mill	33
Gorton Wadding Works	8
Wigan Mill	12
Swinton Mill	5
	479
Including London Warehouse	225
Total	704

Scottish Widows' Fund & Life Assurance Society.

Directors and Officials on Naval or Military Service.

ON NAVAL SERVICE.

Royal Navy.
Stoker Thomas Chudley - - - Bristol.

Royal Marine Light Infantry.
Corpl. H. J. Page - - - - London.

Royal Naval Volunteer Reserve.
Sub-Lt. J. C. Murdoch - - - Glasgow.
Petty Officer R. H. Quick - - Bristol.
(Interned in Holland)

ON MILITARY SERVICE.

Staff.
Personal Staff.—Lieut. (temp.) J. A. B. Urquhart, N. Mid (Staff.) R.G.A., Bristol.

Cavalry, Special Reserve, and Yeomanry.

1st Life Guards.
Lt. The Marquis of Tweeddale   Extray. Director.

11th (Prince Albert's Own) Hussars.
Lce-Corpl. C. E. W. Speller - - Birmingham.
(Died in Aldershot Hospital).

South Irish Horse.
Trooper A. B. Thomson - - - Dublin.

Lothians and Border Horse.
Lieut.-Col. Lord George Scott - - Director.
Lieut. The Marquis of Linlithgow Vice-President.
Sq. Qr.-Mr. Sgt. R. S. Caverhill - Head Office.
Lce.-Cpl. Robert Logan - - - ,,
Trooper J. A. Mann - - - - ,,
Trooper J. G. Simpson - - - ,,

Scottish Horse.—Trooper Matthew Harvie, Head Office.

Artillery.
1st Lowland Brigade Royal Field Artillery.—2nd-Lieut. Thomas Fairley, Head Office.
4th West Riding (Howitzer) Brigade.—Gunner H. R. Hornby, Leeds.
Lowland (City of Edinburgh) Royal Garrison Artillery.—Sergt.-Major Adam Currie, Head Office.

Infantry.

The Royal Scots (Lothian Regiment).
Capt. F. W. Robertson - - - Head Office.
Lieut. W. S. Ferrier - - - ,,
,, A. M. Ballingall - - - ,,
2nd-Lt. F. B. Saunders - - - ,,
,, F. W. Paulin - - - ,,
,, R. Armstrong - - - ,,
,, R. F. W. Henderson - - ,,
Lce-Sgt. W. W. Meikle - - - ,,
Lce.-Cpl. S Burrows - - - ,,

The Royal Scots (Lothian Regiment)—continued.
Lce-Cpl. M. Wilson - - - Birmingham.
Private M. S. Barclay - - - Head Office.
,, W. Campbell - - - ,,
,, J. Deuchars - - - ,,
,, H. J. Herd - - - ,,
,, C. S. F. Mackenzie - - ,,
,, W. C. Reid - - - ,,
,, H. F. Tait - - - ,,

(Continued on next page).

ROLL HONOUR—continued.

The Scottish Widows' Fund & Life Assurance Society.

Infantry—continued.

The Northumberland Fusiliers.
Private R. H. Penney - - - - Newcastle.
" J. Duckworth, Jr. - - - - "

The Royal Warwickshire Regiment.
Major A. D. Fleming - - - Head Office.
Lce-Cpl. F. Clarke - - - - Birmingham.

The Royal Fusiliers (City of London Regiment).
Private A. Evans - - - - - Leeds.

The King's (Liverpool Regiment).
Private J. S. Kitchen - - - - Liverpool.
" L. N. Winder - - - - "

The Prince of Wales's Own (West Yorkshire Regiment).
Lce.-Cpl. J. T. C. Margetts - - - Leeds.

The Cheshire Regiment.
Lieut. J. A. L. Barnes - - - Manchester.
Private J. A. Tait - - - - Liverpool.

The Worcestershire Regiment.
Sergt. P. Russell - - - - Birmingham.

The Black Watch (Royal Highlanders).
Capt. F. W. L. May - - - Manchester.
Private C. M. Martin - - - - Belfast.
" Harry Young - - - - "

The Queen's Own (Royal West Kent Regiment).
2nd-Lt. R. Wade - - - - - London.

The King's Own (Yorkshire Light Infantry).
2nd-Lt. I. L. Harison - - London (West End).

The Duke of Edinburgh's (Wiltshire Regiment).
2nd-Lt. C. G. C. Fisher-Brown - - London.

The Manchester Regiment.
Private L. Burne - - - - Manchester.
" A. H. Fry - ⎱ Killed in - "
" R. B. Hind - ⎰ Gallipoli - "

The Highland Light Infantry.
Lce.-Cpl. C. J. Bruce - - - - Glasgow.
Private William Parker - - - "

The Gordon Highlanders.
2nd-Lt. E. G. Mackean - - - Head Office.

The Queen's Own Cameron Highlanders.
Lt.-Col. D. W. Cameron of Lochiel Extr. Director.
2nd-Lt. N. D. Macfadyen - - - London.
Private W. Lawrie - - - Head Office.
" E. M. Morison - - - - "

The Royal Irish Rifles.
Rifleman C. Hind - - - - Belfast.

The Royal Dublin Fusiliers.
Private A. H. Murray - - - - Dublin.

The Rifle Brigade (The Prince Consort's Own).
2nd-Lt. E. V. Townshend - - - Liverpool.

The London Regiment.
Rifleman H. E. Armitage (Qn. Vict.'s Rifles), County of London Battalion - London.
Private R. W. Lee (London Scottish), County of London Battalion - - - Do. (West End).
Private L. F. Rees (The Queen's), County of London Battalion - - - Do.
Corpl. Edward Allen (Artists' Rifles), County of London Battalion - - - Do.
Lce-Cpl. H. V. S. Hawes (Artists' Rifles), County of London Battalion - Do.

The Hertfordshire Regiment.
2nd-Lt. David F. Cowie - - - - - - - - - - - Do. (West End).

The Army Service Corps.
Private H. V. Baker - - - - - - - - Dublin.

The Royal Army Medical Corps.
Private Ernest B. Philpot - - - London. Private S. C. Tully (57th Field Ambulance) Dublin.

MANCHESTER OFFICE:—21, ALBERT SQUARE.
HEAD OFFICE :—9, ST. ANDREW SQUARE, EDINBURGH.

30th MARCH, 1915.

ROLL OF HONOUR.

* * *

SCHILL BROTHERS, LIMITED.

* * *

Private W. R. ASHWORTH	6th Battalion Manchester Regiment (Terr.).
Private J. F. BLEAKLEY	18th Battalion Royal Fusiliers.
2nd Lieutenant GEO. C. BUTTERLY	1/5th Battalion King's Liverpools.
Sergt.-Major T. J. BUTTERWORTH	6th Service Battalion Loyal North Lancs.
Private W. BARDSLEY	18th Service Battalion Manchester Regiment.
Private N. A. BROCKLEHURST	12th Rifle Brigade (Lost his left arm).
Private B. DALE	19th Service Battalion Manchester Regiment.
Private W. ENDSOR	7th Gordon Highlanders.
2nd Lieutenant J. FIDDES	Public Schools Battalion.
2nd Lieutenant R. E. FLINN	5th Battalion Manchester Regiment (Terr.).
Private S. GREEN	1/8th Manchesters (Terr.).
Private J. GRAY	Driver, Motor Transport, Army Service Corps.
Private R. E. LEMMON	2nd E. Lancashire Brig., Royal Field Artillery.
Sergeant H. LOCKE	2/7th Manchesters (T.). (Back hurt by mine explosion).
Private A. MacDONALD	12th Rifle Brigade.
Lieutenant E. GUY MELLAND	8th Battalion Cheshire Regt., attached to 1st Battalion West Yorkshire Regt. (Killed).
Sub-Lieutenant B. T. R. MELLAND	Royal Marines, Anson Battalion (Killed).
Lance-Corporal B. MILNE	A Company, 7th Battalion Loyal North Lancs.
Private S. MOORE	2nd East Lancs. R.F.A. (Terr.) (A.C.).
Sergeant A. MILLS	20th Serv. Batt. Manchester Regt. (5th City).
Lieutenant E. W. PARROTT	12th Batt. Manchester Regiment (Wounded).
2nd Lieutenant E. M. SCHILL	21st Battalion Lancashire Fusiliers.
Private J. SELBY	9th Serv. Batt. King's Own Royal Lancasters.
Private T. SHAW	2/7th Manchesters (T.) (Died from wounds).
Private L. SMITH	B. Company, 11th Batt. Lancashire Fusiliers.
Private J. H. TETLOW	National Reserve.
Private J. TETLOW	7th Gordon Highlanders.
2nd Lieutenant H. THORNLEY	14th Reserve Battalion Manchester Regiment.
Private H. TOWLE	7th Gordon Highlanders.
Private H. WHITEHEAD	Royal Army Medical Corps.
Private E. WRAY	19th Service Battalion Manchester Regiment.

REJECTED.—GEO. CHEETHAM, A. B. EVERETT, GEO. HALL, STANLEY HOLT, N. V. HUDDLESTON, A. SCHOLES.

ROLL OF HONOUR.

SIMON-CARVES, LTD.
20 Mount Street, Manchester.

O. B. BELL (2nd Lieut.)	Royal Engineers.
C. F. BOWHILL (2nd Lieut.)	Royal Engineers.
C. T. BOWLING	Royal Fusiliers.
F. CUMMINS	Royal Fusiliers.
H. FULLWOOD	Royal Engineers.
P. GREGORY	French Artillery.
H. W. HAGGIS	Manchester Regiment.
T. HALTON	Loyal North Lancs.
W. HINKS	Field Engineers (Naval Division). (Killed in action—Dardanelles.)
P. LONGWORTH	Royal Flying Corps.
E. MARSDEN	Royal Fusiliers.
J. E. PARR	South Lancs. Regiment.
S. RHODES (Captain)	5th York and Lancaster Regiment.
L. SEED	Manchester Regiment.
J. B. THOMPSON (2nd-Lieut.)	Manchester Regiment.
A. WALLACE	Argyll and Sutherland Highlanders.

Roll of Honour.

Robert Scott & Co.

16, Nicholas Street,
MANCHESTER.

Capt. Thomas Entwisle (Partner)

*

Albert McPhail.

*

Robert Hopkins.

*

Alan Young.

*

Hubert L. Jones.

*

Donald Chambers.

*

Lindsay Earl.

*

William Schofield.

*

W. G. Ramsden.

*

William Keeling.

Roll of Honour.

Simon, Son & Co.,

32, Oxford Street,
MANCHESTER.

Sergeant Joyce,
    Warwickshire Regiment.
Driver F. Thompson,
    East Lancs. Field Artillery.
Private Mark McEwen,
    7th Lancashire Fusiliers.
Private E. Moir Brown,
    6th Batt. Manchester Regt.
    (Killed Gallipoli, June 6).
Gunner Robert Sharp,
    Royal Garrison Artillery.
Private Harry Brittain,
    16th Service Batt. Man. Regt.
Private James McCaig,
    17th Service Batt. Man. Regt.
Private Arthur Tawn,
    18th Service Batt. Man. Regt.
Private William Naylor,
    18th Service Batt. Man. Regt.
Private Joseph Edmondson,
    1st Batt. Manchester Regt.
Corporal E. Butterworth,
    6th Batt. Manchester Regt.
Private Robert McDonald,
    Argyll and Sutherland
                    Highlanders.
Gunner Robert McCulloch,
    Royal Garrison Artillery.

ROLL OF HONOUR.

HENRY SIMON Ltd.

20 Mount Street, Manchester.

Captain H. SIMON	R.F.A., 15th Lancs. By., 2nd E. Lancs. Br.
Captain F. MARSHALL	24th Serv. Battalion Manchester Regiment.
Lieutenant F. C. PALMER	7th Battalion Manchester Regiment.
2nd Lieutenant B. W. BENNETT	R.F.A., D/89 Brigade, 19th Division.
2nd Lieutenant F. R. JOLLEY	R.F.A., 73rd Brigade.
2nd Lieutenant J. R. BIRCH	Royal Engineers, Sussex R.G.A.
2nd Lieutenant G. A. HUXLEY	Royal Engineers.
Quartermaster Sergeant J. WOOKEY	19th Serv. Battalion Manchester Regiment.
Sergeant W. HOWE	9th Reserve Regiment Cavalry.
Sergeant S. B. BOWES	D. of Lancaster's Yeomanry, C Squadron.
Sergeant F. KARGE	R.A.M.C., 2nd West. Gen. Hosp., Man/r.
Sergeant F. W. BOWER	20th Serv. Battalion Royal Fusiliers.
Corporal J. V. TAYLOR	20th Serv. Battalion Royal Fusiliers.
Corporal J. W. TRUEBLOOD	2/6th Batt. Manchester Regiment (T.F.).
Lance-Corporal J. CARTLAND	2/6th Batt. Manchester Regiment (T.F.).
Lance-Corporal J. DOYLE,	18th Serv. Battalion Manchester Regiment.
Lance-Corporal L. K. CAMERON	7th Cameron Highlanders.
Lance-Corporal B. DAVIES	21st Serv. Battalion Manchester Regiment.
Lance-Corporal H. HAGGER	Seaforth Highlanders, 191st Infantry Brig.
Lance-Corporal R. WOODALL	16th Serv. Coy., Army Ordnance Corps.
Private GEO. BREW	1/6th Battalion Manchester Regt. (T.F.).
Trooper C. HOWARD	Duke of Lancaster's Own Yeomanry.
Private E. W. K. FOOTE	19th Serv. Battalion Royal Fusiliers.
Private H. R. HUGHES	20th Serv. Battalion Royal Fusiliers.
Private T. W. KELLY	20th Serv. Battalion Royal Fusiliers.
Private F. W. HARDACRE	1/4th Battalion Royal Scots.
Private J. CASTELL	20th Serv. Battalion Royal Fusiliers.
Private B. HEWITT	20th Serv. Battalion Royal Fusiliers.
Private F. G. BLAKE	2/6th Battalion Manchester Regt. (T.F.).
Private O. WELCH,	21st Serv. Battalion Royal Fusiliers.
Private H. KARGE	R.A.M.C., 2nd West. Gen. Hosp., Man/r.
Driver S. ASPINALL	2nd East Lancashire Brigade, R.F.A.
Gunner W. BUTTERWORTH	R.G.A., 37th Siege Battery, 32nd Brigade.
Private A. COULTHURST	3/6th Manchester Regiment.
Sapper G. W. STOCKWELL	Royal Engineers (T.).

ROLL OF HONOUR

✶ ✶ ✶

EMPLOYEES OF

Simpson & Godlee Ltd.,

Who Responded to their Country's Call.

Warehouses.

G. W. BAGULEY.	W. HEYES.	A. MONTGOMERY.
T. SPEED.	J. BONYNGE.	C. KELLETT.
F. MOTTRAM.	J. WATKIN.	A. WOOD.
T. LEEMING.	W. T. ROBINSON.	J. F. WILLOTT.
D. E. GORTON.	J. MELLOR.	J. W. MOSS.
G. BERRY.	S. JORDAN.	H. KNOWLSON.
F. N. R. WARREN.	J. CUMMINGS.	P. GODLEE.
J. RANDLES.	E. JONES.	W. C. BATES.
F. McDERMOTT.	G. HERBERT.	J. WARD.
T. JAQUES.	G. KIRKLEY.	E. C. POYSER.
R. CROOK.	F. GARSIDE.	W. MARSH.
W. H. WROE.	H. BARRINGTON.	E. JACKSON.
E. C. ROYLE.	W. WAINE.	C. CONNOLLY.
A. HARRISON.	G. POTTS.	W. E. WOOD.
C. DYER.	H. LUCAS.	H. ROSS.
G. BAINES.	A. JACKSON.	J. MORRISSEY.
W. SPENCER.	H. BROWN.	J. J. LILLAS.
W. PARRY.	J. WOOD.	F. PHILLIPS.
J. H. LEES.	W. ROBINSON.	F. STREET.
R. LEE.	L. SEDDON.	W. K. BURN.
E. FLANAGAN.	E. BRADSHAW.	H. MORTON.

ROLL OF HONOUR
CONTINUED.

EMPLOYEES OF
Simpson & Godlee Ltd.,
Who Responded to their Country's Call.

* * *

Deans Mill.

W. BROOKES.	J. FANNING.	J. WIGGANS.
W. H. PARTON.	G. HARRIS.	H. LEACH.
B. WINKWORTH.	R. JONES.	G. L. MAYBURY.
H. WOODFIN.	J. HURST.	C. WHITEHEAD.
H. HAYES.	H. H. JONES.	

Know Mill Printing Company.
PORTLAND STREET.

S. CHEETHAM.	P. HOLLINSHEAD.	T. C. JACKSON.
H. ABBOTT.		

Entwistle.

R. BALDWIN.	JOS. WALMSLEY.	P. SMITH.
R. BARLOW.	E. COOPER.	L. SEDDON.
E. BARTON.	J. MALKIN.	T. WILSON.
J. A. CURLE.	E. HOWARTH.	K. TAYLOR.
W. BRIGGS.	S. HOLDEN.	G. BRIGGS.
H. BRINDLE.	H. KILBURN.	J. RAMSBOTTOM.
E. GRIME.	H. LEIGH.	T. REDMAN.
T. DUCKWORTH, Jr.	J. G. MAINWARING.	E. TRIM.
J. ENTWISTLE.	R. HOWARTH.	J. WALMSLEY.
W. J. SHARPLES.	E. EMBRA.	G. WARREN.
T. KNOWLES.	J. REYNOLDS.	H. TAYLOR.
F. CRAWLEY.	H. HAYWARD.	S. LOMAS.
T. EMBRA.	R. RAMSBOTTOM.	F. TURNER.
J. HACKETT.	S. MATHER.	J. J. MATHER.
S. HAYWARD.	W. MATHER.	S. WARRINGTON.
W. HANKIN.	A. RABY.	
T. YATES.	D. REYNOLDS.	

Bevis Green.

T. E. ACTON.	F. BROWN.	R. READ.
F. STANLEY.	F. STUART.	L. MORT.
T. READ.	S. JAMES.	J. W. WINTERBURN.
D. H. SIMPSON.	A. HOWARTH.	
J. EARNSHAW.	J. WALKER.	

ROLL OF HONOUR.

Sivewright, Bacon & Company

Lieutenant A. H. BACON	7th Batt. Manchester Regiment (killed in action in Gallipoli, 7th Aug., 1915).
Lieut. W. J. SIVEWRIGHT	7th Batt. Manchester Regiment.
2nd Lieutenant E. S. BACON	17th Battery 2/3rd Brigade, East Lancs. Royal Field Artillery.
Sergeant G. M. SHEPPARD	10th Batt. East Yorkshire Regiment.
Lance-Corporal W. H. KEY	Machine Gun Section, 6th Batt. King's Liverpool Regiment.
Private A. JAMESON	45th Prov. Batt. Manchester Regiment.
Private G. BARKLAM	19th Batt. Manchester Regiment.
Private W. FLETCHER	25th Batt. Manchester Regiment.
Rifleman R. E. WILLIMOTT	6th Batt. King's Liverpool Regiment.
Private FITZPATRICK	8th (Irish) Batt. King's Liverpool Regt.
Private P. McKENNA	5th Batt. King's Liverpool Regiment.
Private E. O. CLEGG	Machine Gun Section, 10th Batt. East Yorkshire Regiment.

The following also offered his services, but was not accepted:—
F. SIVEWRIGHT.

ROLL OF HONOUR.

Henry & Leigh Slater Ltd.

HARTER STREET, MANCHESTER.

Pte. A. ARDERN, 7th Cheshire Regiment (T.F.).
Pte. F. AUSTIN, 7th Cheshire Regiment (T.F.).
Pte. W. BAGULEY, 7th Cheshire Regiment (Killed in action)
Pte. J. BALL, 3rd Lancashire Fusiliers.
W. BARBER.
W. BROADHEAD.
Driver R. H. CALCRAFT, Cheshire R.F.A.
Pte. F. COPE, 7th Cheshire Regiment (T.F.).
Pte. F. DRABBLE, 8th Cheshire Regiment (T.F.).
J DRABBLE.
W. DRABBLE.
W. DUFFIELD.
A. GASKELL.
Sergt. G. GASKELL, 7th Cheshire Regiment.
Pte. H. GASKELL, 7th Cheshire Regiment.
Pte. H. GIBSON, 10th Cheshire Regiment (T.F.).
W. GOODWIN.
Sergt. J. W. HART, 21st Service Batt. Manchester Regiment.
Pte. H. HART, 1st Cheshire Regiment.
Pte. J. HEALD, 2nd Cheshire Regiment (T.F.).
Pte. H. HOLMES, 16th Lancashire Fusiliers.
Pte. N. HOWARD, 7th Cheshire Regiment (T.F.).
Pte. F. C. JOHNSON, 18th Service Batt. Manchester Regiment.
G. LOMAS.
Pte. H. MAYERS, 2nd Cheshire Regiment (T.F.).
H. MAYERS.
Sergt. W. McGUIRE, 20th Service Batt. Manchester Regiment.
Pte. P. OBBARD, 18th Service Batt. Manchester Regiment.
Sapper P. PARROTT, 41st Signalling Corps R.E.
Pte. J. T. POTTS, 7th Cheshire Regiment (T.F.).
Pte. J. PIMLOTT, 12th Cheshire Regiment (T.F.).
V. STEWART.
Pte F. TINSLEY, 7th Cheshire Regiment (T.F.).
Pte. W. TRAFFORD, 7th Cheshire Regiment (T.F.).
Pte. G. WOOD, 7th Cheshire Regiment (T.F.).
Pte. A. K. WOOD, 18th Service Batt. Manchester Regiment.
Pte. R. WRIGHT, 3rd Lancashire Fusiliers.

ROLL OF HONOUR.

✱ ✱ ✱

J. T. Smith & J. E. Jones, Ltd.

✱ ✱ ✱

      2nd Lieut. L. NELSON, 18th (Ser.) Batt. Manchester Regt. ("Pals")
632 Co. Sergt.-Major T. HEAP, 8th Manchester Regiment (T.F.).
491 Co. Sergt.-Major H. TANNER, 8th Manchester Regiment (T.F.).
11983 Sergeant L. BUTLER, 19th (Ser.) Batt. Manchester Regt. ("Pals").
11883 Sergt. B. MCGRATH, 19th (Ser.) Batt. Manchester Regt. ("Pals").
1523 L.-Corporal B. GLAISTER, 7th Manchester Regiment (T.F.).
1417 Bombardier F. POPPLETON, East Lancashire Royal Field Artillery.
2855 J. BRADLEY, 8th Manchester Regiment (T.F.).
11758 J. BRITTEN, 19th (Ser.) Batt. Manchester Regiment (Pals").
      E. BROCKLESBY, British Red Cross.
11778 W. COTTON, 19th (Ser.) Batt. Manchester Regiment ("Pals").
404 G. CRAWFORD, East Lancashire Royal Engineers.
11787 W. DAWSON, 19th (Ser.) Batt. Manchester Regiment ("Pals").
2481 E. DICKIN, 6th Scottish Provincial Battalion.
      F. EDWARDS, not appointed yet.
11825 W. HALL, 19th (Ser.) Batt. Manchester Regiment ("Pals").
11842 H. HOLLAND, 19th (Ser.) Batt. Manchester Regiment ("Pals").
11849 A. HORTON, 19th (Ser.) Batt. Manchester Regiment ("Pals").
1120 J. HOWARD, East Lancashire Royal Engineers.
11865 E. JONES, 19th (Ser.) Batt. Manchester Regiment ("Pals").
11872 J. LAMBERT, 19th (Ser.) Batt. Manchester Regiment ("Pals").
11882 E. MAGEE, 19th (Ser.) Batt. Manchester Regiment ("Pals").
2857 W. MANNING, 8th Manchester Regiment (T.F.).
5290 T. MAWDSLEY, 20th (Ser.) Batt. Royal Fusiliers.
10511 A. E. NUTTALL, 15th (Ser.) Batt. Lancashire Fusiliers.
11915 H. PUGH, 19th (Ser.) Batt. Manchester Regiment ("Pals").
11918 L. ROBINSON, 19th (Ser.) Batt. Manchester Regiment ("Pals").
11933 F. SMITH, 19th (Ser.) Batt. Manchester Regiment ("Pals").
11948 W. WARDEN, 19th (Ser.) Batt. Manchester Regiment ("Pals").
11951 H. WATTS, 19th (Ser.) Batt. Manchester Regiment ("Pals").
11953 R. WEST, 19th (Ser.) Batt. Manchester Regiment ("Pals").
11945 O. WALKER, 19th (Ser.) Batt. Manchester Regiment ("Pals").

J. T. SMITH & J. E. JONES LTD.

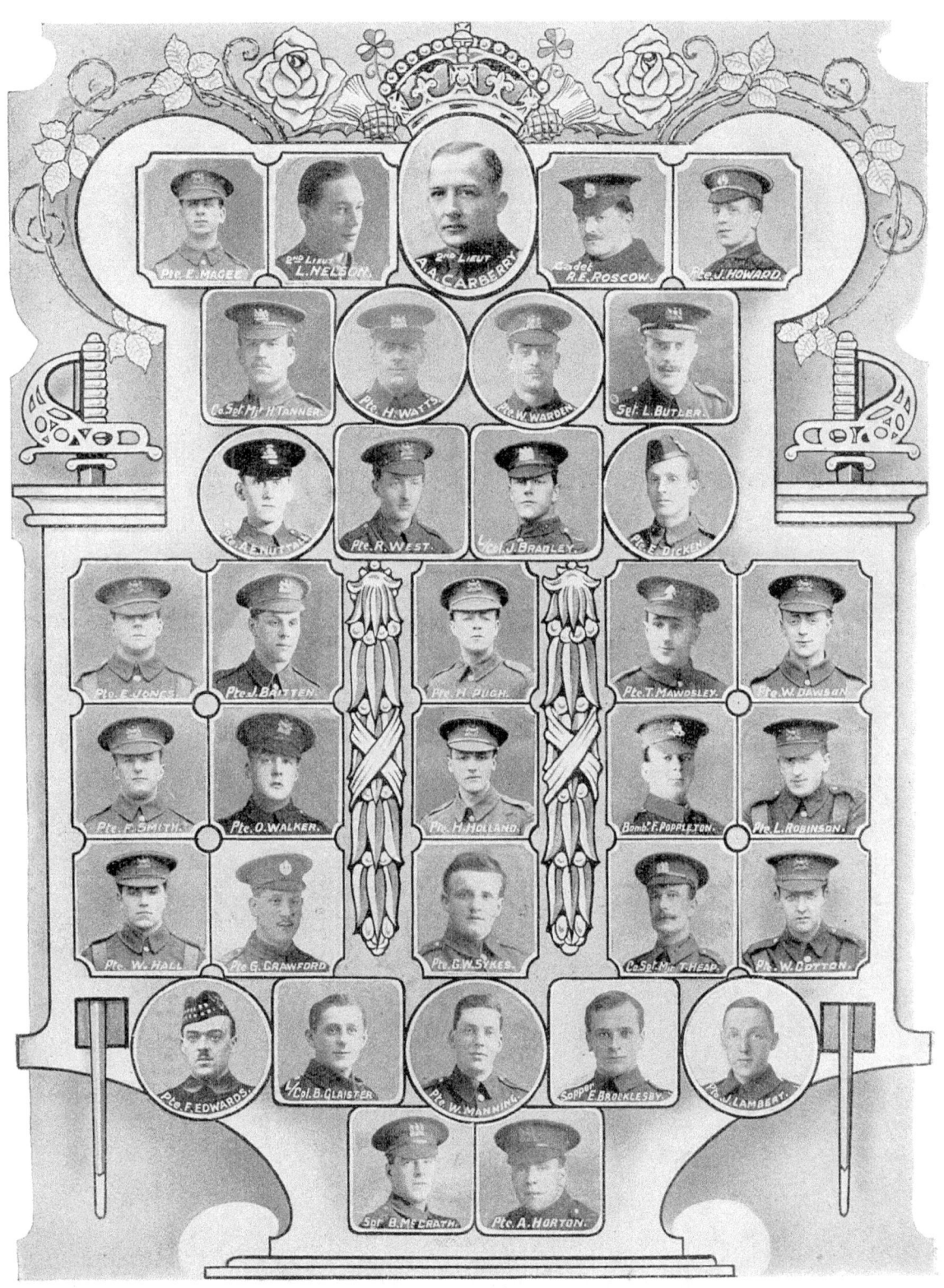

ROLL OF HONOUR

✱ ✱ ✱

SMITH & COVENTRY LIMITED

Gresley Iron Works, Salford,
MANCHESTER.

✱ ✱ ✱

Names of men who have joined His Majesty's forces since the outbreak of the war.

J. ASKEW.	W. FOSTER.	J. MOLLOY.
D. BURKE.	N. FOGG.	W. MARSDEN.
W. BURKE.	J. GRINDROD.	G. F. MELLOR.
O. BENNION.	J. GORST.	J. McCONVILLE.
H. BRITLAND.	J. GREENHOUGH.	C. MOORES.
F. BERRY.	E. HAYHURST.	A. MARSHALL.
S. BANNER.	W. HIGGINS.	W. MASON.
E. BRIDGE.	S. HAYDOCK.	H. NODEN.
H. BLACKBURN.	F. HARRISON.	J. NODEN.
R. BARRON.	H. HOWARD.	E. A. PIMLOTT.
S. BROUGHTON.	S. HUMPHERYS.	W. RIDINGS.
A. BEDGOOD.	J. HAWTHORN.	R. ROBERTS.
A. COWIE.	J. H. JONES.	W. RICHARDSON.
T. CHAMBERS.	R. JONES.	E. ROBINSON.
J. CUNLISS.	S. JACKSON.	J. ROYLE.
W. G. COOK.	J. KENYON.	T. SHANAHAN.
H. CLARENCE.	J. KNIGHT, Senr.	H. STOKES.
S. COOKE.	J. KNIGHT, Junr.	J. STEWART.
J. CAIN.	F. LAVERTY.	W. SALT.
H. CAVANAGH.	J. LONGWORTH	A. TAYLOR.
W. COOKSON.	A. LOMAS.	J. UNSWORTH.
G. J. CUBITT.	E. LAMB.	S. WHITTAL.
W. A. DRAPER.	R. LOWE.	J. WOODWARD.
F. DUCKWORTH.	A. LAKE.	A. WOODWARD.
J. DODD.	T. LEACH.	R. WOODMAN
T. DWYER.	T. LLOYD.	H. WILCOCK.

ROLL OF HONOUR

JOSHUA SMITH (1908) LIMITED,

6, Oxford Street, St. Peter's Square,
MANCHESTER.

Lieut. JOSHUA H. SMITH	6th Lancashire Fusiliers. (Killed in action, Dardanelles.)
2nd Lieut. H. C. SMITH	Royal Flying Corps.
2nd Lieut. H. M. SMITH	2nd Batt. Scottish Rifles.
2nd Lt. RONALD SMITH	King's Liverpool Rifles.
Pte. HAROLD CROWTHER	6th Lancashire Fusiliers. (Killed in action, Dardanelles.)
L.-Cpl. SYDNEY COOKE	6th Lancashire Fusiliers. (Killed in action, Dardanelles.)
Pte. WALTER FARRAR	6th Lancashire Fusiliers. (Killed in action, Dardanelles.)
Pte. HARRY BARON	6th Lancashire Fusiliers.
Pte. HUBERT HOWARTH	6th Lancashire Fusiliers.
Pte. JOHN HEYS	6th Lancashire Fusiliers.
Pte. WM. SNAPE	6th Lancashire Fusiliers.
Pte. TOM STAINWORTH	6th Lancashire Fusiliers.
Pte. SYD. WHITEHEAD	6th Lancashire Fusiliers.
Pte. HAROLD COOPER	2nd East Lancs. (Killed in action, France.)
2nd Lt. ARTHUR H. MILES	Lancashire Fusiliers.
Pte. GREENWOOD CROWTHER	Lancashire Fusiliers.
Pte. CHAS. CROWTHER	Lancashire Fusiliers.
Pte. WALT. GREENWOOD	Lancashire Fusiliers.
Pte. RD. E. GREENWOOD	Lancashire Fusiliers.
Pte. WILB. GREENWOOD	Lancashire Fusiliers.
Pte. THOS. W. HARDY	Lancashire Fusiliers.
Pte. JOHN MACINTYRE	Lancashire Fusiliers.
Pte. JOSEPH MILLS	Lancashire Fusiliers.
Pte. HY. N. MARSHALL	Lancashire Fusiliers.
Pte. LD. N. MARSHALL	Lancashire Fusiliers.
Pte. ERNEST RAYNOR	Lancashire Fusiliers.
Pte. HARRY TREGAY	Lancashire Fusiliers.
Pte. HARRY STOTT	Lancashire Fusiliers.
Pte. HENRY SOWERBY	Loyal North Lancs.
Pte. JOSIAH TREGELLIS	6th East Lancs.
Pte. B. GODDARD	7th Lancs. Fusiliers.
Pte. F. GRIFFIN	12th Lancs. Fusiliers.
Bandsman WALTER HOWARTH	7th Manchesters.
Pte. T. ANDERSON	6th Manchesters.
Pte. F. FAULKNER	6th Manchesters.
Pte. F. W. WOOD	6th Manchesters.
Pte. L. STINTON	King's Shropshire L. Infan.
Pte. W. BAGLEY	20th Service Manchesters.
L.-Corpl. F. BUCKLAND	20th Service Manchesters.
Pte. B. CAUFIELD	20th Service Manchesters.
Pte. F. HOCKADAY	20th Service Manchesters.
L.-Corpl. P. THOMAS	4th King's Liverpool.
Pte. WILLIAM REDMOND	Devons.
Pte. JOSEPH SHAW	Suffolks
Pte. MILTON CRABTREE	Army Service Corps.
Pte. JOHN W. LEDGARD	Army Service Corps.
Pte. PERCY DEAN	R.A.M.C.
Pte. BERN. SOUTHWELL	R.A.M.C.
SYDNEY BLACKBURN	H.M.S. "Impregnable."
B. SPEARS	Naval Air Service.

DERBY GROUPS.

Pte. JOHN H. ORMEROD	Royal Field Artillery.
Pte. HUBERT DAWSON	West Riding (Duke of Well.)
Pte. HARRY GRAHAM	West Riding (Duke of Well.)
Pte. JOHN HEYS	West Riding (Duke of Well.)
Pte. ABRAHAM SMITH	West Riding (Duke of Well.)
Pte. GEORGE P. LEE	14th Service Manchesters.

Roll of Honour.

*

J. Smedley & Co. Ltd.

18, LONDON ROAD,
MANCHESTER.

Captain Harry Smedley,
1/7th Batt. Manchester Territorials.

Sergeant Gilson,
1/7th Batt. Manchester Territorials.

Albert Towle,
East Lancs. Royal Engineers (T.).

Charles Scott,
20th Service Batt. Manchester Pals.

James Bird,
3rd Batt. Lancashire Fusiliers.

Robert Jones,
1/20th Batt. Welsh Fusiliers.

Roll of Honour.

Robert Spencer & Nephews

LIMITED,

1, Church Street, Manchester.

Corporal T. NEEDHAM,
  18th Service Batt. Manchester Regt.

Private C. P. BEAGLEY,
  18th Service Batt. Manchester Regt.

Private W. MAGRATH,
  18th Service Batt. Manchester Regt.

Private H. KIRK,
  19th Service Batt. Manchester Regt.

Sergeant F. W. RITCHIE,
  East Lancs. R.A.M.C. (T.F.).

Private V. L. HADFIELD,
  1/6th Batt. Manchester Regt. (T.F.).

Private H. BROADBENT,
  1/8th Batt. Manchester Regt. (T.F.).

Bombardier J. A. HOUGHTON,
  Royal Field Artillery (T.F.).

Trooper R. P. JONES,
  Montgomeryshire Yeomanry.

Private L. ADDERLEY,
  Edinburgh Rifles.

Private C. ELLIOTT,
  Rifle Brigade.

Roll of Honour.

Southern Cotton Oil Co.
OF GREAT BRITAIN LTD.
Trafford Park, Manchester.

BAKER, A. A.	Married	23rd Manchester Regiment.
BAKER, W. H.	Single	7th Battalion Manchester Regiment.
BARLOW, H.	Married	1st Manchester Regiment.
BARNETT, W.	Married	Royal Scots.
BATTY, J.	Single	Royal Garrison Artillery.
BAXENDALE, C. E.	Married	3rd Battalion Lancashire Fusiliers.
BLAND, H. W.	Single	7th Battalion Manchester Regiment
BROOKING, E.	Single	2nd West Lancs. Field Amb. R.A.M.C.
BROUGH, G.	Married	2nd Battalion South Lancs. Regiment.
CATCHPOLE, S.	Single	Royal Navy.
CARROLL, T.	Married	K.O.S.B.
CHADWICK, J.	Single	7th Manchester Regiment.
CHORLTON, G.	Married	Salford Bantam Battalion.
CHRISTY, E.	Married	Loyal North Lancashires.
CLARK, J. C.	Single	20th County of London Regiment.
COATES, F.	Married	Driver, Motor Transport, A.S.C.
CONST, W.	Single	6th Battalion Manchester Regiment.
CORNES, H.	Single	19th Battalion Manchester Regiment.
COURT, G.	Single	Driver, Motor Transport, A.S.C.
CRAIG, W.	Single	19th Battalion Manchester Regiment.
CROKER, A.	Single	18th Battalion Manchester Regiment.
CROWHURST, G.	Married	8th Lancashire Fusiliers.
DOUGHTY, H.	Married	Royal Engineers.
EDWARDS, A.	Single	R.N.R.
FRASER, J.	Single	South Lancashire Regiment.
GILMAN, A.	Single	Lancashire Fusiliers.
GREEN, A.	Married	Royal Engineers.
HAWKINS, L.	Single	7th Battalion Manchester Regiment.
HIGGINSON, J.	Married	6th Manchester Regiment.
HOLDEN, W.	Single	Royal Field Artillery.
HUGHES, R. A.	Married	South Lancashire Regiment.

Roll of Honour.

Southern Cotton Oil Co.
OF GREAT BRITAIN LTD.
Trafford Park, Manchester.

CONTINUED.

HUNT, J. H.	Single	6th County of London Regiment.
KELLY, W.	Single	Gunner Royal Field Artillery.
KING, S. P.	Married	Queen's Own Yorkshire Dragoons.
LANGE, T.	Single	2nd Manchester Regiment.
LINCOLN, E.	Single	13th County of London Regiment.
McKEAN, W.	Single	10th South Lancashire Regiment.
MILLARD, E. G.	Single	London Irish.
MILLS, S.	Single	6th Manchester Regiment.
MONTAGUE, F.	Married	Royal Field Artillery.
MUIR, R.	Single	17th Highland Light Infantry.
NORRIS, W.	Single	7th Manchester Regiment.
PYBUS, H.	Single	Cheshire Regiment.
ROBERTS, A.	Single	18th Battalion Manchester Regiment.
ROBERTSON, J.	Single	3rd Battalion Lancashire Fusiliers.
ROLLINSON, R.	Married	1st Battalion Lancashire Fusiliers.
RUSHTON, G.	Single	18th Battalion Lancashire Fusiliers.
RYDER, R.	Married	Royal Engineers.
SCHOFIELD, J.	Married	15th Battalion Lancashire Fusiliers
SMITH, W.	Single	18th Battalion Lancashire Regiment.
STREET, H.	Single	7th Lancashire Fusiliers.
STUBBS, J.	Single	South Lancashire Regiment.
THOMPSON, R.	Married	5th Manchester Regiment.
TREVELYAN, J. H.	Single	18th Battalion Manchester Regiment.
TREVITT, E.	Single	Driver, Motor Transport, A.S.C.
TYLEE, G. T.	Married	Driver, Motor Transport, A.S.C.
WAINE, T.	Married	R.A.M.C.
WALLER, F.	Married	Lancashire Fusiliers.
WATSON, A.	Married	3rd Manchester Regiment.
WEILDING, J. H.	Married	Royal Field Artillery.
WINSTANLEY, S.	Married	2nd Lancashire Fusiliers.
WORRALL, H.	Married	8th Lancashire Fusiliers.
WORTHINGTON, R.	Married	National Reserve.
YATES, S.	Single	6th Manchester Regiment.

ROLL OF HONOUR.

Sparrow Hardwick and Co.

The following Employees of the firm served their King and Country in the Great European War, 1914.

OFFICERS.

SPARROW, Lt. W. G. K.	E. of Chester's Yeomanry.
NIDD, Lt. H. H.	7th (T.) Bt. Manchester R.
SMITH, Lt. O.	9th East Lancashire Regt.
WALSH, Lt. L. E.	Army Service Corps.

NON-COMMISSIONED OFFICERS AND MEN.

ROBINSON, S.-Maj. A.	9th Bt. Lancs. Fusiliers
WOODVILLE, Cpl. T. W.	6th (T.) Bt. Manchester R.
ALLCOCK, T.	6th (T.) Bt. Manchester R.
CORBISHLEY, R. P.	6th (T) Bt. Manchester R.
ECCLES, A. D.	6th (T.) Bt. Manchester R.
HIGHAM	6th (T.) Bt. Manchester R.
LEES, J. E.	6th (T.) Bt. Manchester R.
MARTINEZ	6th (T.) Bt. Manchester R.
RODGERS, W. P.	6th (T.) Bt. Manchester R.
SHELDON, R.	6th (T.) Bt. Manchester R.
WORSWICK, W.	6th (T.) Bt. Manchester R.
WILLIAMS, F.	6th (T.) Bt. Manchester R.
THORNLEY, T.	6th (T.) Bt. Manchester R.
TOMLINSON, J. H.	Royal Army Medical Corps.
BRADLEY, Cpl. J.	16th (S.) Bt. Manchester R.
INGHAM, L.-Cpl.	16th (S.) Bt. Manchester R.
MARSLAND, L.-Cpl. H. K.	16th (S.) Bt. Manchester R.
EDWARDS, J.	16th (S.) Bt. Manchester R.

ROLL OF HONOUR
CONTINUED.

* * *

Sparrow, Hardwick and Co.

GOODSON, F.	16th (S.) Bt. Manchester R.
GOSLING, H.	16th (S.) Bt. Manchester R.
HALSALL, S. A.	16th (S.) Bt. Manchester R.
HENDERSON, F.	16th (S.) Bt. Manchester R.
MESSENHEIMER, H. G.	16th (S.) Bt. Manchester R.
MONKS, A.	16th (S.) Bt. Manchester R.
PIKE, S. R.	16th (S.) Bt. Manchester R.
POINTON, T.	16th (S.) Bt. Manchester R.
SPINKS, H. E.	16th (S.) Bt. Manchester R.
SINCLAIR, J.	16th (S.) Bt. Manchester R.
SHEARD, G. S.	16th (S.) Bt. Manchester R.
TAYLOR, P. C.	16th (S.) Bt. Manchester R.
WILSON, R.	16th (S.) Bt. Manchester R.
WARRINGTON, S.	16th (S.) Bt. Manchester R.
BAKER, P.	17th (S.) Bt. Manchester R.
CLARK, E.	17th (S.) Bt. Manchester R.
EARLAM, E.	17th (S.) Bt. Manchester R.
IRLAM, D.	16th (S.) Bt. Manchester R.
ORR, W.	17th (S.) Bt. Manchester R.
STRINGER, W.	17th (S.) Bt. Manchester R.
SMITH, W.	17th (S.) Bt. Manchester R.
WILLIAMS, R.	17th (S.) Bt. Manchester R.
RIGBY, R.	18th (S.) Bt. Manchester R.
PILKINGTON, A.	19th (S.) Bt. Manchester R.
RACE, A. J.	19th (S.) Bt. Manchester R.
MURPHY, S.	20th (S.) Bt. Manchester R.
DUCKWORTH, B.	Old Boys' Epsom, Attached 18th R.F.
DAWSON, J. F.	Loyal North Lancashires.
DYER, B.	Loyal North Lancashires.
DONALDSON, T.	Manchester Scottish.
FILLINGHAM, W. F.	Manchester Scottish.
MUIR, A.	Manchester Scottish.
FOWELL, F. A.	5th Dragoon Guards.
IRVING, W.	Royal Scots.
KERFOOT, J.	5th Bt. Loyal N. Lancs.
NIXON, T.	5th Royal Scots.
HILDITCH, A.	9th Royal Scots.
NORBURY, A.	8th (T.) Bt. Manchester R.
OLIVER, A. E.	7th E. Lancs. R.F.A. (T.).
PEARSON, A.	King's Royal Rifles.
STEWART, G. A.	Queen's Edinburgh Rifles.
WEBSTER, J.	Scottish Borderers.
KENNEDY, A.	4th King's Liverpool Regt.
ROONEY, W.	D. of Lancaster's Yeom'ry.
HEPPLE, I.	D. of Lancaster's Yeom'ry.
KIDD, J.	Royal Warwicks.
BROUGHTON, J. M.	E. of Chester's Yeomanry.
HANNING, Cpl. W.	7th (T.) Bt. Manchester R.
BARLOW, D.	A.S.C. (Transport Section).
HASTINGS, G.	2nd Bt. Lancs. Fusiliers.
WARD, W. J.	H.M.S. "Powerful."
FOTHERGILL, F. A.	New Zealand Contingent.
BOYLE, J. P.	Royal Army Medical Corps.
ROYLE, A. J.	Royal Army Medical Corps.
ALLEN, C.	6th Manchesters.
EVANS, R.	Royal Welsh Fusiliers.
JAFFREY, C.	Sports Battalion.
MORTON, W. J.	Royal Army Medical Corps.
MANN, F.	17th Royal Scots.
ROBERTS, D.	Royal Welsh Fusiliers.
SIMCOCK, H.	Royal Army Medical Corps.
WRIGHT, A.	8th Manchesters.
WAINWRIGHT, J.	Royal Army Medical Corps.
PRITCHARD, A.	Royal Naval Marines.

The following offered their services but were unable to pass:—
McILROY.   TAYLOR, G.   TENCH, J.

ROLL OF HONOUR.

Names of Employees of
Peter Spence & Sons Ltd.
on Active Service.

APPLEYARD, J. M.
ALDERSON, E.
ALLAN, W.
ASHLEY, R.
BURY, E.
BINKS, F. R.
BAMBER, G.
BARKER, J. S.
BRANDON, J.
BROWN, J.
BRIDGE, W. H.
BOWIE, J. W.
BOWLER, H.
BISSETT, W.
BUDD, J.
BURKITT, C.
BURKITT, M.
CLEGG, J.
CODD, A.
CHAPMAN, W.
CARR, W. H.
CARR, J.
CARR, C.
CHANDLER, J.
CHAPMAN, W.
CODD, J.
CORFIELD, R.
COULTISH, W.
CRACKLES, E.
CRAIG, L.
DAWSON, A. H.
DICKS, T.
EYRE, H.
FITZGERALD, G.
GLEAVES, W. E.
GRASBY, J.
GREIG, W.

GOODWIN, J.
GWYTHER, J.
GRANTHAM, H.
HAINES, A.
HEDLEY, A.
HUNT, A.
HOBSON, W.
HOLLIDAY, H.
HOWARTH, F.
ISHERWOOD, H.
IRELAND, F.
ISLES, T.
JOHNSON, W.
JOYNSON, D. A.
JONES, J.
KIRBY, H.
KYNMAN, H.
LEAKE, C. C.
LESTER, G.
LOCKWOOD, J.
LEE, J.
LANE, H.
LEECH, R.
McCABE, J.
McVEETY, W. H.
McGARRY, N.
McALISTER, M.
McGARRY, W.
MOORE, H.
MOORE, R.
NEEDHAM, H.
NOON, G.
OUNSLEY, —.
PARKER, G.
PORTER, E.
PHILLIPSON, L.
POLLEY, R. W.
PHILLIPS, R.

PHILLIPS, J.
RAWLINGS, W.
RICHARDSON, G. H.
RHODES, G.
ROBERTS, —.
REECE, J.
RYAN, R.
READ, A.
SHAW, J.
SHERIFF, B.
SHIPLEY, A.
SPANTON, R.
SUTCLIFFE, E.
SCHOFIELD, J. J.
SHANNON, E.
SHERRY, J.
SIDEBOTTOM, A.
SMITH, G. A.
SILCOCK, W.
SMITH, G.
SMITH, J.
THOMPSON, T.
THOMPSON, B.
VANSON, J.
VICKERS, G.
VICKERS, H.
WILSON, J.
WARD, J. W.
WHITTAKER, S.
WHELDRAKE, A.
WELCH, C.
WELSH, J.
WATSON, T.
WOOD, H.
WOODWARD, J. M.
WHITE, T.
WALL, W.

ROLL OF HONOUR.

Members and Employees of

STADELBAUER & CO.,

50, BLOOM STREET, MANCHESTER,

Serving with the Colours.

Partner.

Sec. Lieut. ERIC PRESTWICH	25th Res. Batt. Manchester Regiment.

Employees.

Sec. Lieut. EDGAR MICHAELIS	3/8th Batt. Manchester Regiment.
Sec. Lieut. ARTHUR COLLING	3/10th Batt. Manchester Regiment.
Quar. Serg. E. J. V. WOOD	No. 24166, 57th Brigade R.F.A.
Corporal A. E. BRADBURY	No. 2918, 2/7th Manchester Regiment.
Bombd. CHARLES PERCY CHAPMAN	No. 4876, Manchester R.F.A.
Gunner RONALD LEASK	No. 24251, 27th Batt. Res. R.F.A.
Gunner JOHN PLANT	No. 24139, 26th Batt. Res. R.F.A.
Sergt. WILLIAM DAWSON	No. 24171, 57th How. Brigade R.F.A.
Rifleman ARTHUR GRESTY	No. 1265, 8th Rifle Brigade.
Private FRED FORSYTH	No. 8547 1st Gar. Batt. Manchester Rgt.
Private L. C. T. CLAPHAM	No. 2021, 1/6th Batt. Manchester Regt.
Lce. Corpl. FRED HEDGES	No. 1534, 1/6th Batt. Manchester Regt.
Lce. Corpl. SAM ENTWISTLE	No. 916, 1/6th Batt. Manchester Regt.
Sapper JOHN TOOLE	No. 770, 3/1st Batt. East Lancs. R.E.
Private JOSEPH CORLEY	No. 17857, 15th Royal Scots.
Private HERBERT LEIGH	No. 18644 21st Batt. Manchester Regt.
Bugler W. J. LEES	No. 395, 19th Western Batt. Rifle Brigade.
Driver ERNEST OLLERENSHAW	R.H.A.
Private H. BELFIELD FLOWERS	No. 75585, 143rd Field Ambul. R.A.M.C.
Private STANLEY BAILEY	3/8th Batt. Manchester Regiment.
Gunner J. W. PEAKE	No. 57481, Royal Garrison Artillery.
Private W. H. DODD	No. S 4085, M.U. Royal Naval Division.
Private JOHN A. DAVIDSON	No. 4721, 2/7th Batt. Manchester Regt.
Private EDWARD DEAN	No. 4604, 2/6th Batt. Manchester Regt.
Sapper J. R. WILLIAMS	66th East Lancs. Royal Engineers.
Sapper WILLIAM NUTTALL	No. 4821, 2/7th Batt. Manchester Regt.

ROLL OF HONOUR.

Hugh Stevenson & Sons Limited,

Cardboard Box Manufacturers,

Victoria Mills, Pollard Street, Manchester.

Employees who have joined His Majesty's Forces (prior to Lord Derby's Scheme)

Captain Frank Berridge	Dorset. Regt. and Royal Flying Corps
Captain F. A. W. Brown	Royal Engineers.
Sec. Lieut. M. Joynson	South Wales Borderers.
Sec. Lieut. Robert Johnson	21st (Res.) Batt. Lancs. Fusiliers.
Regt. Qr. Sergt. J. Maguire	19th Batt. Manchester Regiment.
G. Scott	E. Lancashire Regiment.
J. Moore	Kitchener's Army.
J. Ashworth	Loyal North Lancashire Regiment.
J. Horrocks	King's Own Royal Lancasters.
J. Dewan	Connaught Rangers.
T. Hopkins	19th Batt. Manchester Regiment.
F. Lister	57th Howitzer Brigade, R.F.A.
John Buxton	Royal Scots.
F. Rockliffe	21st Batt. Manchester Regiment.
Lance-Corporal A. Garton	21st Batt. Manchester Regiment.
H. Bashall	21st Batt. Manchester Regiment.
G. Redford	9th Batt. East Lancashire Regiment.
W. Williams	King's Royal Rifles.
T. Edwards	Scottish Borderers.
Sergeant R. Robinson	18th Batt. Manchester Regiment.
R. Power	Loyal North Lancashire Regiment.
R. Partridge	3rd Batt. Manchester Regiment.
S. Gough	Lancashire Fusiliers.
J. Beck	Kitchener's Army.
R. Dawson	Royal Field Artillery.
J. Lingard	Lancashire Fusiliers.
E. Eardsley	East Lancashire Regiment.
W. Proudman	Salford Batt. Lancashire Fusiliers.
W. Wright	Royal Navy.
W. Dodd	9th Batt. East Lancashire Regiment.
J. Billington	Scottish Borderers.
J. Hough	Lancashire Fusiliers.
W. Bell	Irish Fusiliers.
H. Mitchell	19th Batt. Manchester Regiment.
J. Gee	22nd Batt. Manchester Regiment.
W. Whitehead	Kitchener's Army.
Sergeant W. Young	Lancashire Fusiliers.
W. Clifford Royle	Royal Field Artillery.
A. Smith	Kitchener's Army.
P. Killorin	Lancashire Fusiliers.
R. Cullen	Lancashire Fusiliers.
R. Crossland	7th Batt. Manchester Regiment.
S. Sesar	7th Batt. Manchester Regiment.
R. Power	East Lancashires.
C. Baxendale	King's Own Royal Lancasters.
J. Whalley	Royal Engineers.
J. Platts	8th Batt. Manchester Regiment.
J. Routledge	2nd Batt. Manchester Regiment.
T. Tynan	8th Batt. Manchester Regiment.
W. Ferns	Royal Army Medical Corps.

ROLL OF HONOUR — Continued. Hugh Stevenson and Sons Limited.

E. Day	27th Batt. Manchester Regiment.
J. Davenport	Royal Army Medical Corps.
Lance-Corporal Thos. Reader	Wiltshire Regiment.
Lance-Corporal W. McIntosh	Wiltshire Regiment.
A. Budd	Wiltshire Regiment.
J. Trigg	Wiltshire Regiment.
W. Pledger	Wiltshire Regiment.
A. Calver	Wiltshire Regiment.
A. Clark	East Surrey Regiment.
J. Andrews	East Surrey Regiment.
J. Baldwin	East Surrey Regiment.
C. Weller	East Surrey Regiment.
G. Thompson	Dragoon Guards (Queen's Bays).
Sergeant D. Clark	8th Buffs.
E. H. Cartwright	Royal Engineers.
Sergeant E. Foden	Army Ordnance Corps.
J. McAllan	21st Middlesex Regiment.
E. Iles	21st Middlesex Regiment.
T. Bramley	21st Middlesex Regiment.
A. Abbott	21st Middlesex Regiment.
W. Stewart	National Reserve.
T. Westbrook	Mechanical Transport (A.S.C.).
C. Taylor	Mechanical Transport (A.S.C.).
J. Phillips	Mechanical Transport (A.S.C.).
W. Doer	Mechanical Transport (A.S.C.).
H. G. Holmes	Mechanical Transport (A.S.C.).
Quartermaster Sergt. J. Parr	23rd County of London Regiment.
J. Frost	23rd County of London Regiment.
A. Stenning	Royal Army Medical Corps.
W. Pescud	Royal Army Medical Corps.
F. W. Thorn	County of London Yeomanry.
W. Goodman	5th East Surrey Regiment.
J. Acres	13th East Surrey Regiment.
H. Poole	13th East Surrey Regiment.
A. Taylor	13th East Surrey Regiment.
A. Riggs	13th East Surrey Regiment.
W. Winton	Royal Field Artillery.
A. Sippett	Royal Field Artillery.
F. Haworth	Royal Field Artillery.
E. S. Strong	Royal Field Artillery.
T. Harwood	Queen's R.W. Surrey Regiment.
H. J. Battershaw	Army Pay Corps.
H. Good	Queen's Westminsters.
H. W. Smith	Royal Navy.
E. Chapman	Royal Marines.
W. Newman	Royal Marines.
R. Menzies	Black Watch.
A. Henderson	Royal Scots.
Sergeant H. Falconer	Royal Garrison Artillery.
C. Forrester	Royal Field Artillery.
A. Wallace	Royal Army Medical Corps.
H. Stanway	Royal Garrison Artillery.
G. Leggatt	Highland Light Infantry.
J. Menzies	Royal Scots.
D. Drummond	Royal Garrison Artillery.
J. Wight	Royal Garrison Artillery.
B. Dutton	2nd City Batt. Royal Warwicks.

ROLL OF HONOUR.

Stewart, Thomson & Co., Limited,
17, TODD STREET, MANCHESTER.

Pte. P. N. APPLEBY	17th Sv. Bt. Manchester Rgt.
L.-Corpl. A. BARRATT	17th Sv. Bt. Manchester Rgt.
Bugler F. BARROW	R.A.M.C. (T.)
	(Killed at Dardanelles.)
Pte. T. BATES	16th Sv. Bt. Manchester Rgt.
Pte. P. BATES	Lancs. Fus. (Salf'd Pals' Bt.).
Pte. E. BOWLES	16th Sv. Bt. Manchester Rgt.
Pte. F. BOWLES	16th Sv. Bt. Manchester Rgt.
Pte. T. BRYANT	8th Bt. King's Liverpool Rgt.
Sergt. R. CLIFFE	16th Sv. Bt. Manchester Rgt.
Pte. W. COCHRANE	8th Bt. Manchester Rgt. (T.).
Corpl. C. COLLINS	6th Bt. Manchester Rgt. (T.).
Pte. J. COLLINS	7th Bt. Lancs. Fus. (T.).
Corpl. H. CRETNEY	8th Bt. Manchester Rgt. (T.).
Pte. L. J. DAVIES	16th Sv. Bt. Manchester Rgt.
Pte. C. DEAVILLE	15th Lancs. Fus.
	(Salford Pals' Bt.).
Corpl. E. DICKINSON	3rd Bt. Scottish Rifles.
Pte. C. DINWOODIE	18th Sv. Bt. Manchester Rgt.
Pte. D. H. DUNBAR	16th Sv. Bt. Manchester Rgt.
Pte. T. EDWARDS	11th Bt. King's Own Royal Lancs. Rgt.
Pte. J. GIBBONS	16th Sv. Bt. Manchester Rgt.
Pte. A. GARNETT	20th Sv. Bt. Manchester Rgt.
Pte. W. GORWOOD	10th Bt. South Lancs Rgt.
Pte. C. GILES	7th Bt. Manchester Rgt.
	(National Reserve).
L.-Corpl. W. HARRIS	2nd Bt. Cameron Highl'ders.
	(Missing).
Pte. H. HEATON	17th Sv. Bt. Manchester Rgt.
Pte. J. HINDLE	King's O. Scottish Borderers.
Pte. A. HOLDEN	8th Bt. Manchester Rgt. (T.).
Pte. H. HOPKINSON	6th Bt. Manchester Rgt. (T.).
Pte. S. HOWARD	16th Sv. Bt. Manchester Rgt.
Pte. A. IMRIE	R.A.M.C.
C. Q.-Sgt. W. R. IREDALE	A.S.C.
Pte. C. KELLY	17th Sv. Bt. Manchester R
Pte. B. LEWIS	Royal Naval Division, Medical Unit
Pte. H. LONSDALE	King's O. Scottish Bordere
Pte. H. LOUGHLAND	6th Bt. Manchester Rgt. (T.).
Pte. H. McFARLANE	16th Sv. Bt. Manchester Rgt.
Pte. R. A. MITCHELL	16th Sv. Bt. Manchester Rgt.
Pte. T. MITCHELL	20th Sv. Bt. Lancs. Fus.
Pte. A. MILLWARD	16th Sv. Bt. Manchester Rgt.
Pte. R. O'BRIEN	7th Bt. East Lancs. Rgt.
Driver G. E. ROURKE	R.F.A.
Trooper H. PARDOE	Duke of Lancaster's Own Yeoman
Pte. H. PERCIVAL	8th Bt. Lancashire Fusilier
Pte. W. RAVENSCROFT	7th Bt. Manchester Rgt. (T.).
Q.-Sgt. W. H. RENSHAW	R.F.A. (T.).
Pte. R. ROWLEY	6th Bt. Manchester Rgt. (T.).
Pte. R. ROBINSON	A.S.C.
2nd-Lieut. R. H. SMITH	1st City Bt. King's Own Liverpool Rgt.
2nd-Lieut. B. W. SIMS	11th Bt. East Lancs. Rgt.
Pte. U. SPENCER	17th Sv. Bt. Manchester Rgt.
Pte. G. E. STAFFORD	3rd Bt. Manchester Rgt.
Pte. G. TROWBRIDGE	7th Bt. Manchester Rgt. (T.).
Pte. A. TROW	6th Bt. Manchester Rgt. (T.).
C.S.M. W. N. WADDICOR	18th Sv. Bt. Manchester Rgt.
Pte. W. WILKINSON	17th Sv. Bt. Manchester Rgt.

ROLL OF HONOUR.
✱✱✱
STOTT & SMITH LTD.
4, MINSHULL ST., MANCHESTER,
AND
EMPIRE MILLS, CONGLETON.

Lieut.-Colonel Herbert Stott.
Sergt.-Major Harman.
Private Jas. Parsonage.
Private H. Hargreaves.
Sergeant F. Kershaw.
Private J. Berry.
Private J. Atkin.
Sergeant Makin.
Lce.-Sergeant A. Knowles.
Bombardier G. Hough.
Private T. Shepley.
Corporal E. Millar.
Private F. Leah.
Private A. Rushton.
Private E. Hart.
Private J. Crosby.
Private A. Daley.
Corporal Harold Smith.
Gunner W. Crowther.
Captain G. O'Mackenzie.
Private J. H. Macdonald.
Private A. Knight.
Corporal E. Wallwork.
Private G. Taylor.
Private F. N. Hassall.
Private F. Hughes.
Private W. Webb.
Private H. J. Wood.
Private F. Furness.
Corporal W. Glew.
Private E. Bradley.
Private Eric Spratt.
Private James Bennett.
Private E. E. Newton.
Private E. Calverley.
Private L. Lorant.
Private H. Williams.
Private J. M. Keymer.
Private R. C. Harrison.
Private J. H. Coates.
Private T. L. Lewis.

EMPIRE MILLS.

Sergt.-Major Gallimore.
Corporal W. Jackson.
Private J. Kendall.
Corporal C. Gibson.
Private H. Burgess.
Private W. Foster.
Private F. Bailey.
Private G. Hood.
Drummer W. Stubbs.
Bandsman W. Knight.
Private F. Turnock.
Private W. Sherratt.
Private W. Williamson.
Private T. Johnson.
Private J. Duckworth.
Private A. Green.
Private H. Williams.
Private E. Lear.
Private G. Sherratt.
Private J. Knight.
Private W. Swindells.
Private S. Joynson.

A further 18 men offered for enlistment but were not accepted.

ROLL OF HONOUR.

JOSEPH STUBBS LTD.,
MANCHESTER.

List of Names of our men who are serving in H.M. Forces.

STUBBS, W. LYON.

ASHCROFT, J.
ALLEN, J.
BANKS, M.
BOLTON, H. G.
BERISFORD, A.
BOWMAN, J.
BELL, J.
BARRACLOUGH, E. L.
BROWN, A.
CARROLL, T.
CROSSLEY, J.
CHARLESWORTH, A.
CORCORAN, J.
CLAYTON, ED.
CONNELL, ALF. T.
CASSIN, WM. J.
DEARDEN, B.
DILLON, J.
DAWSON, T.
DAWSON, J.
DONALDSON, F.
EGERTON, H.
EGERTON, JAMES.
ERASMUS, A.
EGAN, H.
ENTWISTLE, C.
ELLIOTT, HENRY.
EMMERSON, JOHN J.
FAIRCLOUGH, H.
FARROW, W. H.
FISHER, JOHN.
FLETCHER, JAMES.
FISHER, WM.
GORDON, F.
GORMLEY, J.
HASSALL, T. A.
HADSKISS, W.
HALLOWS, F.
HARDMAN, W.
HOLMES, J.
HOLLINGWORTH, A.
HOPWOOD, R. T.
HEALEY, J.
HURST, R. E.
HURST, HAROLD.
HACKNEY, A.
HAWTHORN-
　　　THWAITE, F.
JAMIESON, J.
JONES, JOHN.
KEATES, C.
KENNAH, T.
KERR, R.
KAY, J.
LANCASTER, J. W.
LANGRON, M.
LOMAS, WM.
LOMAS, JOHN.
LITTLE, JOHN T.
LETCHFORD, J. H.
McGRATH, J.
McGRATH, B.
McCLUSKIE, C.
MOORE, J. T.
MAGUIRE, J.
MARSDEN, J.
MARR, C. A.
MacGUINESS, T.
McIVER, G.
McMANUS, J.
MORAN, WM.
MATTHEWS, ALBERT.
NOBLE, W. H.
NUTTALL, A.
PALMER, ERIC.
PRIOR, H. J.
PILSTON, W.
PARKINSON, E.
PEARSON, J.
PEARSON, W.
PRESTON, S.
ROONEY, C.
ROBINS, J.
RYDER, A.
ROBERTS, T.
SAULL, R.
SMITH, A.
STUBBS, W.
STAFFORD, F.
SMITH, W.
STEVENS, J.
SCULLY, J.
SIDDERLEY, D.
SALT, J.
SILCOCK, D.
THORNHILL, J. R.
TINKER, E.
TULEY, J.
THOMPSON, A.
TRAVIS, J. P.
THOMAS, L.
WORTHINGTON, G.
WRIGHT, W.
WRIGHT, A.
WALLEY, R.
WILCOX, E.
WHITE, JOS.
WALTON, T.
YATES, C.
WEAVER, H.

ROLL OF HONOUR.

* * *

Henry Tetlow & Sons,
VARLEY STREET, OLDHAM ROAD, MANCHESTER.

Employees who have joined His Majesty's Forces.

Lieut. HENRY TETLOW	22nd Battalion K.L.R.
Pte. K. B. TETLOW	O.T.C., Inns of Court.
Bandsman N. McANULTY	C. Coy., 3/8 Manchester Regt.
Pte. E. BARNSHAW	Royal Field Artillery.
Pte. E. BILLINGTON	Welsh Fusiliers.
Pte. F. BOND	Rifle Brigade.
Pte. J. BOND	Lancashire Fusiliers.
Pte. J. CASEY	South Lancashire Regiment.
Pte. W. CASHION	Royal Field Artillery.
Corpl. M. CAVANAGH	Rifle Brigade.
Pte. J. CONLEY	3/7 Manchester Regiment.
Pte. J. CRITCHLEY	Lancashire Fusiliers.
Pte. G. DUNNING	1st Batt., C. Coy., K.L.R.
Pte. J. P. FEELEY	Welsh Fusiliers.
Pte. G. HARRINGTON	Border Regiment.
Pte. J. LONGSHAW	8th Manchester Regiment.
Pte. J. McCARTHY	6/7 Lancashire Fusiliers.
Pte. J. McDONALD	2nd Manchester Regiment.
Pte. J. McCORMICK	8th Manchester Regiment.
Pte. H. OWEN	19th Batt. Manchester Regt.
Pte. W. PARKINSON	6th Batt. Manchester Regt.
Pte. F. POPPLEWELL	21st Batt. Manch. Regt. ("Pals").
Ord. Seaman C. RILEY	Royal Navy.
Pte. G. SAUNDERS	Lancashire Fusiliers.
Pte. A. SACHEL	King's Own Regiment.
Pte. A. SLACK	King's Royal Rifles.
Pte. G. WALKER	Manchester Bantams' Regiment.
Pte. J. WALKER	14th Manchester Regiment.
L.-Corpl. J. W. WILKINSON	A.S.C., Mechanical Transport.

ROLL OF HONOUR.

TOOTAL BROADHURST LEE COMPANY LTD.

List of Employees who have joined the Colours.

Private A. Aldcroft, 23rd Batt. Manchester Regiment.
Mr. D. Allen, Young Men's Christian Association.
Private W. F. Armstrong, 16th Batt. Manchester Regiment.
Private R. J. Baddeley, 20th Batt. Royal Fusiliers.
Private K. C. Bailey, 1/6th Batt. Manchester Regiment.
Private J. Baird, 3/6th Batt. Manchester Regiment.
Private W. A. Ball, 45th Provisional Battalion.
Private J. Barnes, 8th Batt. Manchester Regiment.
Private F. Barrett, 6th Batt. Manchester Regiment.
Driver A. Baskerville, Signal Service Company, R.E., East Lancs.
Private I. Bates, 16th Batt. Manchester Regiment.
Private L. Battlemuch (Nottingham), "A" Sub-Section, Notts. R.H.A.
Private A. Bayes, 20th Batt. Manchester Regiment.
Private A. Beal, 5th Batt. Manchester Regiment.
Private W. Beasley, 17th Batt. Manchester Regiment.
Private C. P. Beaver, 16th Batt. Manchester Regiment.
Private A. N. Bennett, 16th Batt. Manchester Regiment.
Driver E. Berriman, 2/1st Batt. Army Service Corps, East Lancs. Div.
Trooper O. Berry, Duke of Lancaster's Own Yeomanry.
Private N. Bickerton, 6th Batt. Manchester Regiment.
                                          (Died of Wounds, June 14th, 1915.)
Sergeant G. Birch, 2/6th Batt. Manchester Regiment.
Driver G. H. Blakey, 12th Reserve Battery, Royal Field Artillery.
Sergeant C. Bolton, 17th Batt. Manchester Regiment.
Private W. Bowers, 6th Batt. Manchester Regiment.
Corporal F. R. Bradley, 16th Batt. Manchester Regiment.
Rifleman H. Brett (London Branch), 11th Batt. King's Royal Rifles.
Private J. Brett (London Branch), 9th Batt. Worcester Regiment.
                                        (Died of Wounds, October 12th, 1915.)
Private J. Briggs, 16th Batt. Manchester Regiment.
Sergeant G. Broadbent, 16th Batt. Manchester Regiment.
Lieutenant A. F. B. Broadhurst, 1st Batt. Highland Light Infantry.
Private A. Broughton, 16th Batt. Manchester Regiment.

ROLL OF HONOUR—Continued.

TOOTAL BROADHURST LEE COMPANY LIMITED.

Drummer J. BROWN, 16th Batt. Manchester Regiment.
Lieutenant J. P. BRUCE, 16th Batt. Manchester Regiment.
Private A. J. BUCKLEY, 16th Batt. Manchester Regiment.
Private T. A. BUTLER, 17th Batt. Manchester Regiment.
Qr.Mr.-Sergeant H. BURTON, 121st Company Army Service Corps.
Private T. A. CALVERT, 18th Batt. Manchester Regiment.
Corporal A. B. CAMPBELL, Army Service Corps, East Lancs. T.S.C.
Mr. C. CARTER, Ammunitions.
Private B. W. CARMICHAEL, 6th Batt. Manchester Regiment.
Private H. W. CASTLE, Royal Naval Division, Medical Unit.
Private C. CHAMBERS, 6th Batt. Manchester Regiment.
Private J. H. CHAPMAN, 17th Batt. Manchester Regiment.
Sapper C. B. CHAPMAN (Nottingham), 17th Divisional Signal Co.
Private J. W. CHEETHAM, 1/6th Batt. Manchester Regiment.
Private R. CLARKE (Ten Acres Mill), Lancashire Fusiliers.
Private C. W. CLIFTON (London), 2/15th London Regt., Civil Ser. Rifles.
Captain S. F. COLLIER, 3/6th Batt. Manchester Regiment.
Lieut. S. COLLIER, 6th Batt. Manchester Regiment.
Private J. C. COLLINGE, Royal Army Medical Corps, East Lancs. Division.
Private W. COLLINSON, 3/7th Batt. Manchester Regiment.
2nd Lieut. R. N. COMPTON-SMITH, 6th Batt. Manchester Regiment.
(Died of Wounds, 29th May, 1915.)
Private A. COOK, 13th Batt. Royal Scots.
2nd Lieut. A. J. B. CORADINE, 6th Batt. Somerset Light Infantry.
Private H. CORKER, 2/6th Batt. Manchester Regiment.
Private W. CRAIG, 17th Batt. Manchester Regiment.
Lieutenant F. CROSSLEY, 6th Batt. Manchester Regiment.
Private A. W. DAVIS, 17th Batt. Manchester Regiment.
Sapper W. H. DITCHFIELD, Royal Engineers, East Lancashire Signal Coy.
Private H. J. DOYLE, Officers' Training Corps.
Driver R. DUNN, Royal Field Artillery.
Private G. EDMUNDS, 16th Batt. Manchester Regiment.
Private R. ELLIS, 17th Batt. Manchester Regiment.
Private G. B. ELLIOTT, 3rd Batt. Manchester Regiment.
Private G. ELSWORTH, 48th Coy. Army Ordnance Corps.
Private J. F. ENGLISH, Army Service Corps (Transport Section).
Private W. ETCHELLS, 3/7th Batt. Cheshire Regiment.
Private E. R. EVANS, 25th Batt. Manchester Regiment.
Private T. EVANS, 16th Batt. Manchester Regiment.
Private D. FERGUSON, 2/6th Batt. Manchester Regiment.
(Died of Fever, October 13th, 1915.)
Private T. FESMER, 7th Batt. Lancashire Fusiliers.
Private J. FITZPATRICK, 17th Batt. Manchester Regiment.
(Killed in action, February 29th, 1916.)
Driver C. V. FLETCHER, Cumberland Artillery, 2nd Battery.
Sergeant W. N. FLETCHER, 26th Reserve Batt. Manchester Regiment.
Sergeant E. FOALE, 17th Batt. Manchester Regiment.
Private C. FOGG, 2/6th Batt. Manchester Regiment.
Private W. FOX (Leeds), Army Ordnance Corps.
Private W. GAFFNEY, 16th Batt. Manchester Regiment.

ROLL OF HONOUR—Continued.

TOOTAL BROADHURST LEE COMPANY LIMITED.

Private H. GIBB, 18th Batt. Manchester Regiment.
Private A. GITTINS, 13th Batt. Royal Welsh Fusiliers.
Private W. B. GOODWIN, 6th Batt. Lancashire Fusiliers.
Private G. GORDON, 17th Batt. Manchester Regiment.
Sergeant D. J. GORDON (Glasgow), 5th Scottish Rifles.
Lieut. C. B. GORTON, 12th Batt. Cheshire Regiment.
Private W. J. GOTHARD, 20th Batt. Manchester Regiment.
Private J. GRAHAM, 7th Batt. Lancashire Fusiliers.
Bombardier R. A. GRENVILLE, 10th Division Artillery.
Private A. J. GRUMMITT, Royal Army Medical Corps.
Private W. HAND, 8th Batt. Manchester Regiment.
Corporal C. HARRISON, 16th Batt. Lancashire Fusiliers.
Private J. W. HARRISON, 16th Batt. Manchester Regiment.
Private F. HAYES, Royal Army Medical Corps.
Mr. W. HERK, Royal Army Medical Corps.
Private J. HERON, 20th Batt. Manchester Regiment.
Sapper C. HEWITT (Ten Acres Mill), Royal Engineers.
Lance-Corporal W. HIGSON, 8th Batt. Manchester Regiment.
Private J. HILL (Ten Acres Mill), 27th Batt. Manchester Regiment.
Lance-Corporal T. HORFORD, 16th Batt. Manchester Regiment.
Private F. HOWCROFT, 6th Batt. Manchester Regiment.
Gunner A. G. HOYLAND, Royal Garrison Artillery.
Private T. HUGHES, 16th Batt. Manchester Regiment.
Lance-Corporal G. HULL, 16th Batt. Manchester Regiment.
Lance-Corporal T. HULME, 7th Batt. Manchester Regiment.
2nd Lieut. L. B. HUMPHREYS, 17th Batt. Manchester Regiment.
Corporal J. IBBOTSON (Ten Acres Mill), 113th Brigade R.F.A.
Private F. JACKSON, 16th Batt. Manchester Regiment.
Private W. J. JAMIESON, 17th Batt. Manchester Regiment.
L.-Corpl. H. C. JEBSON, 1/6th Batt. Manchester Regiment.
Private F. JEFFERSON, 3/1st West Division Cycling Corps.
Private B. JOHNSON, Royal Army Medical Corps, East Lancs. Division.
Qr.Mr.-Sergeant C. R. JOHNSON, 17th Batt. Manchester Regiment.
Private M. JONES, 16th Batt. Manchester Regiment.
Private F. KEARSLEY, 25th Batt. Manchester Regiment.
Private T. J. KEECH, 16th Batt. Manchester Regiment.
Private E. D. KNAGGS, 17th Batt. Manchester Regiment.
Lance-Corporal G. KNOWLES, Royal Army Medical Corps.
Lance-Corporal J. LANCASHIRE, 17th Batt. Manchester Regiment.
Private A. L. LEAVER, 23rd Batt. Welsh (Cycling) Division.
Brig.-General Noel LEE, Com. Manchester Infan. Brig. at the Dardanelles.
(Died of Wounds, June 23rd, 1915.)
Private F. LEIGHTON, British Red Cross Society.
Private T. LESLIE, 6th Batt. Manchester Regiment.
Private T. LINDSAY, 2/4th Batt. Royal Scots.
Private W. LINDSAY, 6th Batt. Manchester Regiment.
Acting Corporal A. LOUGHEED (London), 8th Batt. Wiltshire Regt.
Private F. LOPEZ, 9th Batt. Royal Scots Highlanders.
Gunner E. LOWE, 3/2nd East Lancs. Brigade Royal Field Artillery.
Captain T. A. LOWE (Belfast), 2nd Batt. Royal Irish Regiment.

ROLL OF HONOUR—Continued.

TOOTAL BROADHURST LEE
—— COMPANY LIMITED. ——

Lance-Corporal G. LYNE, 17th Batt. Manchester Regiment.
Captain BRUCE MACPHERSON, 8th Batt. Lancashire Fusiliers.
Private J. F. MAHER, 16th Batt. Manchester Regiment.
Private L. C. MALKIN, Liverpool Scottish Regiment.
2nd Lieutenant B. MANNING (London), 1a Reserve Brigade R.F.A.
Private G. MARRIOTT, 16th Batt. Manchester Regiment.
Private E. MARSDEN, 30th Res. Batt. Royal Fusiliers.
Private J. MAYORS, 16th Batt. Manchester Regiment.
Private A. MCADAM, 8th Batt. Manchester Regiment.
Private W. T. MCEWEN, 17th Batt. Manchester Regiment.
Private J. MCKEOWN (Ten Acres Mill), 26th Reserve Batt. Manch. Regt.
Driver A. MCPHERSON, Army Service Corps, Lancashire Fusiliers.
Private J. MCTIGHE, 2/4th South Lancashire Regiment.
Private J. MELLOR, 8th Batt. Manchester Regiment.
Sergeant S. MERRY, 3/7th Batt. Manchester Regiment.
Bombardier W. MOORE, Royal Field Artillery.
Private F. MORLEY, 17th Batt. Manchester Regiment.
Private J. MURRAY, 16th Batt. Manchester Regiment.
Private W. NAYLOR, 16th Batt. Royal Welsh Fusiliers.
Lance-Corporal W. NEWALL, 7th Batt. Manchester Regiment.
Private R. E. NEWTON, 6th Batt. Manchester Regiment.
Private J. H. NIXON, 17th Batt. Manchester Regiment.
Private W. NORTHEND, 18th Batt. Manchester Regiment.
Sergeant J. O'HARA, 17th Batt. Manchester Regiment
Private A. M. ORMEROD, 6th Batt. Manchester Regiment.
2nd Lieutenant A. W. OSBORNE, East Lancs. Brigade R.F.A.
Lieutenant E. N. OUGHTRED, 6th Batt. Manchester Regiment.
Private W. A. PART, 21st Reserve Batt. Manchester Regiment.
Private T. PASQUILL (Ten Acres Mill), Royal Army Medical Corps.
L.-Sergeant H. PEARSON (Ten Acres Mill), 1st Garrison Batt. Man. Regt.
2nd Lieut. H. A. PEARSON, Accrington and Burnley Howitzer Brig., R.F.A.
Private S. PEARSON, 17th Batt. Manchester Regiment.
Private J. PENNY, Royal Army Medical Corps.
Private W. PENNY, 17th Batt. Manchester Regiment.
Private A. PETERS, 16th Batt. Manchester Regiment.
Private J. PLANT, 16th Batt. Manchester Regiment.
Private R. POWELL, Royal Fusiliers.
Private W. N. PROPHET, 1/6th Batt. Manchester Regiment.
Private J. RADFIRTH, 7th Batt. Cheshire Regiment.
Private J. W. RAMSEY, Royal Army Medical Corps.
Corporal J. E. RAYNER, 16th Batt. Manchester Regiment.
Private J. REYNOLDS, 26th Batt. Manchester Regiment.
Lance-Corporal A. R. RICKARD, 2/7th Batt. Manchester Regiment.
Private T. RIDING, 17th Batt. Manchester Regiment.
Private A. RIMMER, 17th Batt. Manchester Regiment.
Private T. ROBERTS, 23rd Batt. Manchester Regiment.
Private T. W. ROBINSON, 16th Batt. Manchester Regiment.
Private F. ROTHWELL, 6th Batt. Manchester Regiment.
Private R. E. SAWER, 3/5th Batt. Manchester Regiment.
Corporal J. E. SCOTT, 15th Batt. Royal Scots.

ROLL OF HONOUR—Continued.

TOOTAL BROADHURST LEE COMPANY LIMITED.

Private H. Scott, 16th Batt. Manchester Regiment.
Private W. C. Scott, 2/7th Batt. Manchester Regiment.
Private F. Seal (Ten Acres Mill), 25th Batt. Manchester Regiment.
Private J. S. Seed, 2/8th Batt. (Cyclists) Essex Regiment.
Private E. H. Shaw, 1/6th Batt. Manchester Regiment.
Private A. Shepherd, 1st Batt. Field Ambulance, Royal Army Medical C.
Private E. H. Sherwood, 6th Batt. Manchester Regiment.
Private J. A. Siepen, 16th Batt. Manchester Regiment.
Private W. B. Simpson, 20th Batt. Royal Fusiliers.
Private J. Singleton, 17th Batt. Manchester Regiment.
Private W. Skelton, 3/6th Batt. Manchester Regiment.
Private L. Slater, 3/8th Batt. Manchester Regiment.
Captain A. W. Smith, 6th Batt. Cheshire Regiment.
Gunner F. L. Smith, 16th Battery, Royal Field Artillery, 2nd East Lancs.
Private L. Smith (Notts. Branch), Royal Horse Artillery.
Trooper J. N. Smith, 2nd Batt. Earl of Chester's Yeomanry.
Private H. Smith (Ten Acres Mill, Newton Heath), Royal Irish Fusiliers.
2nd Lieut. H. C. Speakman, 8th Batt. Lancashire Fusiliers.
Gunner A. Staley, Royal Field Artillery.
Signaller C. Stansfield, Royal Engineers, East Lancashire Division.
Captain A. Storey, Army Service Corps.
Private W. Swindell, 17th Batt. Manchester Regiment.
Gunner W. Tasker, Royal Garrison Artillery.
2nd Lieutenant A. B. Taylor, 6th Batt. Manchester Regiment.
Private G. E. Taylor, 2/6th Batt. Manchester Regiment.
Sergeant T. F. Taylor, 2/6th Batt. Manchester Regiment.
Lance-Corporal E. Thomas, 10th Batt. King's Own Royal Lancasters.
Driver M. Thorneycroft (Ten Acres Mill), Royal Garrison Artillery.
Private F. Thorp, 2/7th Batt. Manchester Regiment.
Captain J. E. Townsend, 22nd Batt. Manchester Regiment.
2nd Lieut. I. C. Trench, 4th Batt. Wiltshire Regiment.
Driver J. Turner, 1st Batt. Royal Field Artillery.
Private C. Tyson, 7th Batt. Manchester Regiment.
Private A. Walker, 16th Batt. Manchester Regiment.
Private H. Walker, 17th Batt. Manchester Regiment.
Private B. Wade (Ten Acres Mill), 21st Batt. Manchester Regt.
Private W N. Ward, 16th Batt. Manchester Regiment.
Private H. Waring (Ten Acres Mill), 1st Cheshire Garrison.
Acting Lieut.-Col. R. D. Waterhouse, 8th Batt. Lancashire Fusiliers.
Gunner O. A. Welch, 2nd Batt. East Lancashire Brigade, R.F.A.
Private T. Whaling, 17th Batt. Manchester Regiment.
Private W. Whelan, 17th Batt. Manchester Regiment.
Private C. Whitley, 16th Batt. Manchester Regiment.
Lance-Corporal I. Wild (Ten Acres Mill), 25th Batt. Manchester Regt.
Private C. Wilkinson, 21st Batt. Manchester Regiment.
Bugler J. Wilson, 8th Batt. Manchester Regiment.
Trooper W. Wilson (Glasgow Branch), Queen's Own Royal Glasgow Yeo.
Private B. Wood, 8th Batt. Manchester Regiment.
Trooper A. E. Worthington (Ten Acres Mill), Cheshire Yeomanry.
Private A. Wright, Royal Army Medical Corps.

ROLL OF HONOUR—Continued.

TOOTAL BROADHURST LEE
—— COMPANY LIMITED. ——

Private T. W. Wright, 8th Batt. Lancashire Fusiliers.
Driver C. Wynn, 1st Field Coy. East Lancashire Royal Engineers.
Private A. C. Yates, 6th Batt. Manchester Regiment.
(Died of Wounds, July 8th, 1915.)
Private W. C. Yates, 6th Batt. Manchester Regiment.

Employees who have joined the Colours from our Bolton Mill.

Private A. Anderson, 2nd Garrison Batt. Royal Welsh Fusiliers.
Private C. Anderson, Royal Army Medical Corps.
Lance-Corporal G. Aspinall, 4/5th Batt. Loyal North Lancashires.
Driver C. Bailey, 1/3rd East Lancs. Royal Field Artillery.
Armourer H. Banks, H.M.S. "Erin."
Private W. Banks, 4/5th Batt. Loyal North Lancashires.
Drummer A. E. Barlow, 3/5th Batt. Loyal North Lancashires.
Gunner H. Barlow, Royal Garrison Artillery.
Private R. Barnes, 4/5th Batt. Loyal North Lancashires.
Gunner T. Barnes, 171st Brigade, Royal Field Artillery.
Sapper T. H. Boardman, Royal Engineers.
Corporal C. Booth, 5th Reserve Batt. Coldstream Guards.
Private J. H. Brooks, Loyal North Lancashires.
Sergeant H. Clark, Royal Garrison Artillery.
Sergeant W. A. Cliff, Loyal North Lancashires.
Private R. Clough, Shropshire Light Infantry.
Driver E. Cooke, 2/3rd East Lancs. Brigade Royal Field Artillery.
Driver H. Daniels, 32nd D.A.C.
Private W. Davies, Loyal North Lancashires.
Private H. Donaldson, Royal Scots.
Private R. Durning, Loyal North Lancashires.
Bombardier D. Edmondson, 3rd East Lancs. Royal Field Artillery.
Drummer J. A. Ellwood, 10th Batt. Loyal North Lancashires.
Bombardier S. Flinders, 116th Brig. Ammunition Column, R.F.A.
Private J. Fletcher, 3/5th Batt. Loyal North Lancashires.
Private J. France, 3/5th Batt. Loyal North Lancashires.
Private A. Frodsham, Shropshire Light Infantry.
Private J. W. Gillard, 1st 12th Pioneers.
Lance-Corporal J. Grace, Loyal North Lancashires.
Lance-Corporal J. Greenhalgh, Loyal North Lancashire Regiment.
Lance-Corporal A. H. Greenhalgh, 2nd Batt. Royal Scots.
Lance-Corporal T. A. Gregory, 2nd/3rd Lancs. Field Ambulance.
Private A. Hailwood, Loyal North Lancashires.
Drummer H. Hamilton, 3/5th Batt. Loyal North Lancashires.
Signaller W. Hamilton, 3rd Batt. South Wales Borderers.
C.P.O. R. Haslam, Naval Sick Berth Reserve.
Sergeant W. Hardman, Loyal North Lancashire Regiment.
Private J. Healey, Loyal North Lancashires.
Driver F. Holden, 170th Brigade Royal Field Artillery.
Lance-Corporal A. Holt, 3/5th Batt. Loyal North Lancashire Regiment.

ROLL OF HONOUR—Continued.

TOOTAL BROADHURST LEE
—— COMPANY LIMITED. ——

Private W. Hough, 42nd Provisional Batt.
Private H. Howarth, Loyal North Lancashires.
1st Air Mechanic J. Howcroft, Royal Flying Corps.
Private A. Hunt, Loyal North Lancashires.
Private E. Hurst, Loyal North Lancashires.
Private R. S. Hulme, Royal Army Medical Corps.
Sergeant T. Hyam, 10th Batt. Lancashire Fusiliers.
Private W. Lane, Loyal North Lancashires.
Private J. Jepson, 4/5th Batt. Loyal North Lancashires.
Drummer A. Kitchen, 3/5th Batt. Loyal North Lancashires.
Private A. Lewis, 8th Service Batt. R.O.R. Lancs.
Driver A. Lord, Royal Field Artillery.
Private P. Lowe, 4/5th Batt. Loyal North Lancashires.
Attendant W. Lythgoe, Naval Sick Berth Reserve.
Corporal E. Maguire, Loyal North Lancashires.
Driver C. Manley, 1/3rd East Lancs. Army Service Corps.
Lance-Corporal J. Marsden, Royal Army Medical Corps.
Private W. McCall, Army Service Corps.
Lance-Corporal H. Monks, Loyal North Lancashires.
Driver T. Olive, Royal Field Artillery.
Private E. Ormesher, King's Own Royal Lancasters.
Private J. Partington, 6th Batt. Manchester Regiment.
Private C. Povey, Naval Sick Berth Reserve.
Private F. Pye, Loyal North Lancashires.
Private F. Rae, Royal Army Medical Corps.
Driver J. Reason, 1/3rd East Lancs. Army Service Corps.
Bombardier E. Reynolds, Royal Field Artillery.
Private H. Richards, Royal Army Medical Corps.
Private H. Riley, Naval Sick Berth Reserve.
Bugler J. Seed, Royal Army Medical Corps.
Corporal T. Shaw, Royal Field Artillery.
Gunner C. H. Simmons, Royal Field Artillery.
Private A. S. Simpson, Royal Army Medical Corps.
Private N. Smith, Loyal North Lancashires.
Signaller S. Smith, 15th Batt. Welsh Regiment.
Private J. Snape, Naval Sick Berth Reserve.
Private J. Stevens, 4/5th Batt. Loyal North Lancashires.
Private E. A. Taylor, 42nd Provisional Batt.
Private H. Turner, Welsh Regiment.
Private F. C. Wallis, 5th Batt. Loyal North Lancashire Regiment.
Sapper J. Walmsley, West Lancs. Division, Royal Engineers.
Sergeant W. Wells, East Lancashire Regiment.
Driver W. Wharton, 171st Brigade, Royal Field Artillery.
Private H. W. Whitehead, 2/5th Batt. Loyal North Lancashire Regt.
Corporal J. Wilcox, 23rd Batt. Manchester Regiment.
Private N. Wilkinson, 19th Batt. Manchester Regiment.
Private T. Wood, 3/4th Batt. Loyal North Lancashires.
Gunner J. Wright, Royal Field Artillery.
Trooper W. Young, Yeomanry.

ROLL OF HONOUR.

Tennants (Lancashire) Ltd.

1 Booth Street, Manchester.

A. EARL.	HUGH DAVIES.
JOS. COOKE.	H. HINSLEY.
GEO. DAVIE.	H. TAYLOR.
A. GRIFFITHS.	H. HOLME.
A. ROONEY.	B. MORTON.
J. CARMICHAEL.	CHARLES COOMBS.
J. GOODWIN.	A. HINDLE.
J. W. SMITH.	M. WHALEN.
J. OWEN.	J. BAGNALL.
J. FALKNER.	J. KIRKLAND.
J. LYON.	T. DICKSON.
W. WARTON.	FRED. A. HART.
J. SUTTON.	W. MOORE.
J. DAWSON.	J. MUBRYAN.
T. GREENOUGH.	J. COONEY.
J. BELL.	J. F. KEELAN.
J. COOK.	S. JACKSON.
L. D. BEVINS.	A. THOMAS.
F. FIGHT.	J. HAMNETT.
T. KEELING.	J. TULEY.
A. MAWSON.	J. H. PENDLEBURY.
J. HARDMAN.	J. DAWSON.
JOS. THOMPSON.	J. H. HALLETT.
J. LOLLY.	E. WESTWOOD.
B. BEASLEY.	

Roll of Honour.

Bertram Thomas,

WORSLEY STREET, HULME.

A. J. BAILEY.
F. BLACK.
T. BLAND.
W. BURKE.
C. COX.
H. CRITCH.
A. DONEVAN.
G. GREGORY.
W. HAMPSON.
C. HILL.
T. HULME.
H. JONES.
K. A. LODGE.
B. MONKS.
E. MOORE.
W. MOORE.
A. E. RAWSON.
G. SMETHURST.
D. G. THOMSON.
D. TREVOR.
W. TRUEMAN.
W. WHITE.
E. WHITLEY.

ROLL OF HONOUR.

The Union Bank of Manchester Ltd.

Members of the Staff serving with His Majestys Forces during the War.

Director: COLONEL (Temp. BRIGADIER-GENERAL) The Rt. Hon. LORD ROCHDALE, 6th Batt. Lancashire Fusiliers (Terr.).

†Arnold, Lieut. P. F.	8th Batt. Lancashire Fusiliers (T.F.).
Bardsley, Lieut. G. S.	10th Batt. East Lancashire Regiment (T.F.).
Barritt, Coy. Q.M. Sergt. N.	2/6th Batt. Manchester Regiment (T.F.).
Battye, Corporal S. L.	East Lancashire Royal Engineers.
*Binns, Private C. F.	6th Batt. Manchester Regiment (T.F.).
Blomeley, Private G. C.	20th (Ser.) Batt. Royal Fusiliers (U.P.S.).
Boardman, Private H.	21st (Ser.) Batt. Royal Fusiliers (U.P.S.).
Bolsover, Corporal J. H.	3/6th Batt. Manchester Regiment (T.F.).
Booth, Driver H.	2/2nd East Lancashire R.F.A.
Booth, Lance-Corporal H. L.	2/5th Batt. Cheshire Regiment (T.F.).
Bowers, Private H.	20th (Ser.) Batt. Royal Fusiliers (U.P.S.).
Bridge, Bombardier A.	3/1st East Lancashire R.F.A.
Burgess, Private C.	19th (Ser.) Batt. Manchester Regiment.
Burman, Private J.	20th (Ser.) Batt. Royal Fusiliers (U.P.S.).
Cannell, Private W. R.	3rd Batt. Sherwood Foresters.
Chambers, Private R.	Royal Army Medical Corps.
Charlesworth, Private A. P.	A.S.C. (Mechanical Transport).
†Chesters, Corporal S. W.	7th Batt. Cheshire Regiment (T.F.).
Coop, Private G. H.	26th (Ser.) Batt. Royal Fusiliers.
Coop, Lieut. R.	2/4th West Lancashire R.F.A.
Cross, Private C. S.	6th Batt. Cheshire Regt. (T.F.) (Attached A.S.C.)
Dalton, Corporal P. F.	17th (Ser.) Batt. King's Liverpool Regiment.
Darwell, Lance-Corporal T. W.	3/5th Batt. Manchester Regiment (T.F.).
Davies, Private R. B.	O.T.C. (Manchester University).
Dixon, Private H. L.	Royal Army Medical Corps.
Donnelly, Private J. V.	5th Batt. Manchester Regiment (T.F.).
Driscoll, Driver W.	2/2nd East Lancashire R.F.A.

* Killed in Action.   † Wounded.

ROLL OF HONOUR.
Continued.

The Union Bank of Manchester Ltd.

†EDWARDS, Captain D. G.	5th Batt. East Lancashire Regiment (T.F.).
EMERY, Corporal L. C.	3/6th Batt. Cheshire Regiment (T.F.).
EVANS, Private J. R.	6th Batt. Royal Scots (T.F.).
FALLON, Jean	(Vol.) Belgian Heavy Artillery.
FISH, Sub. Lieut. S. H.	Royal Naval Volunteers.
FITTON, Private N.	21st (Ser.) Batt. Royal Fusiliers (U.P.S.).
FINCH, Private J.	10th (Scottish) King's Liverpool Regiment.
GANDY, Private T. M.	22nd (Ser.) Batt. Manchester Regiment.
GARFITT, Private C. E.	20th (Ser.) Batt. Royal Fusiliers (U.P.S.).
GEORGE, Lance-Corporal L. S.	Duke of Lancaster's Yeomanry (T.F.).
GREENWOOD, Lieut. A.	3/6th Batt. Lancashire Fusiliers (T.F.).
GRIMES, Private W. R.	26th (Ser.) Batt. Royal Fusiliers.
GUY, Private H. N.	29th (Res.) Batt. Royal Fusiliers (U.P.S.).
*HAHN, Lance-Corporal W. F.	2/6th Batt. Manchester Regiment (T.F.).
HALL, Private R. H.	29th (Res.) Batt. Royal Fusiliers (U.P.S.).
HALLIWELL, Private G.	29th (Res.) Batt. Royal Fusiliers (U.P.S.).
HARPER, Lance-Corporal E. N.	21st (Ser.) Batt. Manchester Regiment.
HEAP, Private J. A.	2/9th Batt. Royal Scots.
HEATON, Private M.	19th (Ser.) Batt. Manchester Regiment.
†HEATON, Private T. M.	5th Batt. Loyal North Lancashires (T.F.).
HESKETH, Sec. Lieut. H. A.	170th Brigade Royal Field Artillery.
HIGGINSON, Private J. B.	Royal Army Medical Corps.
*HOLME, Private Z.	6th Batt. Manchester Regiment (T.F.).
HORSFALL, Lance-Corporal J.	9th (Ser.) Batt. East Lancashire Regiment.
†HOWARTH, Private W.	14th (Ser.) Batt. Middlesex Regiment.
JEPSON, Sec. Lieut. S.	4th Batt. North Staffs. Regt. (Attached 1st.)
LANG, Sergt. C. H.	2/6th Batt. Cheshire Regiment (T.F.).
LARSEN, Sec. Lieut. L. W.	3rd (Res.) Batt. South Lancashire Regiment.
LAWLER, Bugler W.	Royal Army Medical Corps.
LAWTON, Gunner A. M.	1/2nd East Lancashire R.F.A.
LIVESLEY, Sergeant W. A.	Royal Army Medical Corps.
McCLUNG, Lance-Corporal G.	5th (Royal Irish) Lancers.
McROBIE, Private H. D.	17th (Ser.) Batt. King's Liverpool Regiment.
MADELEY, Private B.	19th (Ser.) Batt. King's Liverpool Regiment.
MAKINSON, Sec. Lieut. A. L.	3/5th Batt. Manchester Regiment (T.F.).
MARSDEN, Sub-Lieut. W. D.	Royal Navy. (Asst.-Paymaster.)
MARSHALL, Private C. H.	26th (Ser.) Batt. Royal Fusiliers.
MEADOWCROFT, 2nd Air Mechanic C.	Royal Flying Corps (Wireless Section).
MILES, Corporal W. J.	17th (Ser.) Batt. King's Liverpool Regiment.
MORETON, Sec. Lieut. H.	3/7th Batt. Cheshire Regiment (T.F.).
MORRIS, Sub-Lieut. J. W.	Royal Navy (Asst. Paymaster).
MORTON, Corporal H.	Cheshire Brigade R.F.A. (T.F.).

ROLL OF HONOUR.
Continued.

The Union Bank of Manchester Ltd.

Ney, Sec. Lieut. G.	24th (Ser.) Batt. Manchester Regiment.
Nuttall, Trooper J.	2nd Line Westmoreland & Cumberl'd Y. (T.F.).
Nuttall, Private S. L.	5th Batt. Lancs. Fusiliers (T.F.).
*Oakes, Private J.	5th Batt. Loyal North Lancs. (T.F.).
Parsons, Sub-Lieut. R. L.	Royal Navy (Asst. Paymaster).
Philips, Private N. S.	2nd Batt. King's Liverpool Regiment.
Preston, Sergeant E. C.	West Lancashire Division A.S.C. (T.F.).
‡Riley, Private H.	Royal Army Medical Corps.
Robinson, Private T.	20th (Ser.) Batt. Royal Fusiliers (U.P.S.)
Robinson, Sec. Lieut. W. H.	17th (Ser.) Batt. Lancs. Fusiliers.
Roe, Private H.	26th (Ser.) Batt. Royal Fusiliers.
Rostron, Sec. Lieut. H.	13th (Ser.) Batt. West Yorkshire Regt.
Royley, Lance-Corporal H.	5th Batt. Loyal North Lancs. (T.F.).
Rounding, Private T. A.	21st (Ser.) Batt. Royal Fusiliers (U.P.S.).
Scantlebury, Private G. B.	26th (Ser.) Batt. Royal Fusiliers.
Schofield, Private E.	20th (Ser.) Batt. Royal Fusiliers (U.P.S.).
Shaw, Private A.	1/7th Batt. Manchester Regiment (T.F.).
†Shaw, Major A. Ll. B.	8th Batt. Lancashire Fusiliers (T.F.).
Smith, Private J.	20th (Ser.) Batt. Royal Fusiliers (U.P.S.).
Sneddon, Private R.	17th (Ser.) Batt. King's Liverpool Regiment.
Sparke, Private D. A.	17th (Ser.) Batt. King's Liverpool Regiment.
Spiers, Private J.	2/5th Batt. East Lancashire Regiment (T.F.).
Steeple, Private J.	21st (Ser.) Batt. Royal Fusiliers (U.P.S.).
Striffler, Sergeant A. R.	2/6th Lancashire Fusiliers (T.F.).
Stubbs, Private E.	Royal Army Medical Corps.
Thomas, Private F.	17th (Ser.) Batt. King's Liverpool Regiment.
Tyldesley, Private S.	5th Batt. Loyal North Lancashires (T.F.).
Uren, Private A. S.	O.T.C. (Inns of Court).
Wainwright, Private O.	26th (Ser.) Batt. Royal Fusiliers.
Walsh, Sec. Lieut. H. G. V.	9th (Res.) Batt. East Yorkshire Regt.
Ward, Private R. W.	20th (Ser.) Batt. Royal Fusiliers (U.P.S.).
Watson, Sec. Lieut. F.	3rd (Ser.) Batt. Connaught Rangers.
Watson, Private J. P.	5th Batt. Loyal North Lancashires (T.F.).
Webster, Private V. A.	2/8th Batt. Manchester Regiment (T.F.).
Whitehead, Private A. W.	2/6th Batt. Manchester Regiment (T.F.).
Whitehead, Sec. Lieut. F. B.	Army Pay Corps.
Whyte, Private J.	17th (Ser.) Batt. King's Liverpool Regiment.
Willett, Private R.	O.T.C. (Inns of Court).
Wrigley, Private C.	26th (Ser.) Batt. Royal Fusiliers.
Yates, Rifleman F. S.	17th (Ser.) Batt. King's Liverpool Regiment.

* Killed in Action.   † Wounded.   ‡ Died.

ROLL OF HONOUR.

List of Employees of the

United Yeast Co. Ltd., Manchester

Who are at present serving with His Majesty's forces.

Aerts, H. J. E.	Gladstone, S.	Pearce, W. J.
Atkins, J.	Gradwell, J.	Penny, A. C.
Avery, G.	Gradwell, V.	Percy, G.
Ayard, C.	Guy, J. R.	Portwaine, G.
Baggaley, W.	Golledge, B.	Powell, W. J.
Belcher, J. G.	Greenwood, H.	Parsons, T.
Bentley, F.	Hancocks, F. S.	Powell, W.
Bookham, G.	Hardaker, J. S.	Palmer, J. T.
Bright, W.	Henwood, R.	Payne, B.
Bishop, H.	Hines, G. J.	Redfarn, F.
Bowell, J.	Holmes, H.	Ridley, L. J.
Briggs, W.	Honey, F.	Rout, F.
Bury, W. H.	Hutchinson, H.	Rowell, A. E.
Carr, W.	Hall, A. O.	Reid, A. J.
Christy, D.	Henderson, H.	Robson, E.
Court, W.	Hansford, W.	Reynolds, E.
Crew, F. W.	Harris, B.	Salisbury, E.
Curtis, L.	Hancock, F.	Salisbury, W.
Crowther, F.	Jowett, A.	Shufflebotham, J.
Crapper, B.	Kirtley, J. W. S.	Smith, D.
Clarke, E.	Kendrick, A.	Sparrow, T.
Coldwell, R.	Lester, C. W.	Stephens, H.
Cole, A. E.	Lester, T. S.	Street, E. S.
Cheetham, W.	Lewis, G.	Shore, F.
Carr, B.	Light, H. J.	Scanes, H. J.
Chadwick, E.	Marshall, G.	Saunders, T.
Denham, A. J.	May, T.	Southeran, W.
Duncliffe, P.	Methley, A.	Taylor, H.
Dunk, C.	Mulberry, G.	Taylor, W.
Elliott, E.	Marshall, J.	Tomlinson, R.
Evans, N. R.	Marshall, F. W.	Talman, P.
Easton, W.	Marriott, W.	Tooms, W.
Exton, H. V.	Metcalfe, S.	Thatcher, W. P.
Flett, H.	Milner, O.	Wallace, M. P.
Fletcher, J.	Newman, R.	Waters, C. H.
Ford, J. H.	Nicholson, A. F.	Watkins, F. C.
Fortune, J.	Newsome, H.	Watson, J. H.
Farrer, F.	Old, S.	Williams, F.
Fisher, W.	Orton, —.	Wills, T. B.
Fairbrother, J.	Packam, C. M.	Wright, H.
Gotley, G. S.	Parker, S. J.	Young, R.
Galley, A. W.	Parkinson, P.	

ROLL OF HONOUR.

S. & J. Watts & Co.,
MANCHESTER.

✱ ✱ ✱

WATTS, H., Major.
WATTS, H. L., 2nd Lt.

ARNFIELD, T.
ARNOLD, S. W.
ASHTON, J. W.
ADAMSON, JAS.
ASHTON, J.
ANDREW, A.
ANGEL, W.
ANSTEE, E. H.
ATTWOOD, A. J.
AUSTIN, —.
BACKHOUSE, A. R.
BARNSLEY, F.
BATEMAN, W.
BECKITT, JAS.
BIRKETT, A. S.
BARNES, B.
BRIDGE, J.
BROWN, W.
BURGESS, C. V.
BENTLEY, A. C.
BULLOCK, W.
BENNETT, P.
BIRCH, F. J.
BERRESFORD, W. D.
BLACK, A.
BOYD, H. T.
BUNBURY, C.
BUTTERWORTH, D.
BOOTH, A.
BROOKE, A.
BURNETT, H.
BARRON, F.
BUERDSELL, E.
BURGESS, S.
BARKER, I.
BRITLAND, J. W.

BAMFORTH, J. G.
BROWN, W. J.
BURNS, —.
BRUCE, W. A.
BARDSLEY, W.
BROWN, H.
BENNION, A.
BRANT, A.
BAGSHAW, A.
BLACKBURN, E.
BEAVAN, J.
BECKETT, W.
BAXTER, H.
CATON, G. L.
COCHRANE, W.
COULTHARD, P.
COLLINGE, F.
CLEGG, J.
COOKE, A.
CLEMENTS, A.
CORBETT, F.
CRAIG, H.
COLLIER, F.
CARTER, E.
CAVANAGH, W.
CHADWICK, A.
CARLINE, —.
CURRAN, T.
COPE, C. W.
COBBETT, W. O., 2nd Lt.
CONNOR, H.
CRAWSHAW, J.
CALLISON, F.
COOPE, F. W.
CLAYTON, W. L.
CARSWELL, I. H.
CIRCUIT, F. J.
DAY, F. G.
DAVIES, E. R. I.

DEWAR, H.
DUCKWORTH, G.
DAWSON, T.
DAVENPORT, J.
DAVIES, C. E.
DANIELS, G. H.
DAVENPORT, —.
EDGE, F.
EDGE, GEO.
EATON, M.
ELLSE, J.
ENGLISH, J. H.
FENNELL, P., 2nd Lt.
FLETCHER, J.
FRANCIS, H.
FISHER, J.
FOULKES, H.
FORSYTH, J.
FAWKES, E. G.
FORREST, J. G.
FIZZELLE, T.
FOSTER, —.
FARNWORTH, W. H.
FOLEY, C.
FOLEY, N.
FITCHETT, —.
GILLIATT, H.
GERRARD, T.
GASKELL, A.
GORNER, F.
GREER, H.
GALWAY, F.
GATE, K. C.
GEORGE, J.
GREEN, F.
GRIMSHAW, F.
GAFFNEY, S.
GREEN, D.
GLEDHILL, J. E.

S. & J. WATTS & CO.

ROLL OF HONOUR—Continued.

GARNER, T.
GALSTON, E.
GRIFFIN, J.
GIBSON, J.
GRANGE, R.
HEARD, R. L.
HOWELL, A.
HOPE, A.
HARE, C. R.
HART, H.
HIBBITTS, H.
HOWMAN, A.
HODGE, H. B.
HUGHES, W. F.
HEATON, C.
HAWLEY, J. P.
HILL, F. W.
HILL, T.
HENSHAW, E.
HALLAS, JOS.
HARTLEY, R. L., Lt.
HIPKINS, H.
HARRISON, P.
HANDFORD, F.
HAMNETT, BOB.
HOWARD, H.
HULL, F. V.
HALLIWELL, F.
HORSTELL, H.
HURNELL, W. H.
HENDERSON, W.
HAULDREN, J. A.
HAY, J.
HARDMAN, —.
HOWARD, W.
HENLEY, —.
HAMNETT, —.
HUNT, H.
IRLAM, W.
IRELAND, S.
IRLAM, J.
JAMES, J.
JOHNSTONE, A.
JOHNSTON, F. S.
JONES, R. W.
JONES, C. H.
JAMES, —.
KNOWLES, R. H.

KNOX, F.
KIRKLEY, B.
LAWSON, J. N.
LEIGH, H.
LAMBERT, JOS.
LEATHER, A.
LOCKWOOD, C. D., 2nd-Lt.
LIGGETT, H.
LEVINGS, S.
LATHAM, H.
LOMAX, H.
LANCASHIRE, A.
LEE, J.
MATHER, T.
MOLLOY, V.
MILLER, S. R.
MINAY, J. H.
MARTIN, H.
McCABE, W.
MACAULAY, W.
MAWSON, R. H.
McDONALD, F.
MULHEARNE, J.
MEADEN, P.
McNALLY, S.
MATHER, T.
NORMINGTON, F.
NUGENT, J.
NUTTALL, O.
NADEN, F.
NOLAN, J. F.
NEWMAN, A.
OUSEY, F.
OWEN, P.
OWEN, W. G.
OGDEN, F. E.
OWEN, H.
PERRY, J.
PALMER, F. S.
PEERS, J. A.
PLEWS, F.
PARSONS, G. M.
PAYTON, G.
PEDDER, S. H.
QUIRK, S.
ROYLE, W.

ROWLAND, H.
REDHEAD, T. J.
RIDGARD, R.
ROBINSON, K.
ROBINSON, H.
ROBERTS, V.
ROYLE, G.
ROWE, A. E.
RINGHAM, H. T.
ROBERTS, J. D.
ROBERTSHAW, A.
ROWLINSON, E.
RILEY, F. C.
ROBERTS, F.
RAYNES, E.
RICHARDSON, W. T.
ROBINSON, H.
RUFUS, E.
RUSSELL, W.
RUSSELL, J. P.
ROBERTS, C. E.
SCOTT, T. S.
SHAW, A.
SIMPSON, J. F.
SHAW, P.
SHERRING, F.
SMITH, W.
STREAT, B. R.
STARKIE, W.
SMITH, F. R.
SLACK, J.
SADLER, J.
SHORE, J.
STREET, A.
SMITHER, M. C.
STONE, J. E.
SCHOFIELD, A.
SWINDELLS, P.
SMITH, J. H.
SMITH, G. H.
SKINNER, J.
STAFFORD, S.
SMETHURST, C. W.
SHEPHERD, F.
SCHOFIELD, A.
SCARBORO, H.
TAYLOR, G.

TAYLOR, J.
THOMAS, N.
TOVELL, C.
TAYLOR, A.
THOMPSON, S.
THOMSON, J. N.
TAYLOR, S.
TWYNHAM, W.
THORNLEY, —.
UNSWORTH, T.
VAUGHAN, W.
WILLS, E.
WHILES, T.
WEATE, H.
WILSON, J.
WILSON, L.
WILLIAMS, H.
WYNN, W.
WARD, R.
WOOD, J.
WALSH, A.
WHITTAKER, J.
WARWICK, H.
WOMBY, T.
WATSON, T.
WARDLE, W.
WALKER, L.
WAREHAM, W. G.
WOOD, J. B.
WILSON, J. F.
WILD, T. T.
WHITE, R.
WALTERS, WM.
WALKER, W.
WYLDE, C. C.
WILSON, L.
WATSON, F.
WALL, H.
WORRALL, F.
WISWALL, H.
WAINWRIGHT, G. H.
WILLIAMS, A.
WRIGHT, —.
WALKER, J.
WAGSTAFFE, A.
WILD, T.
YOUNG, A.

ROLL OF HONOUR.

Walker & Homfrays Limited
AND
Manchester Brewery Company, Limited.

J. ASHMAN.	J. FOWLER.	W. OWEN.
J. W. ASHTON.	T. FOX.	J. PALMER.
S. BACON.	T. GARNETT.	J. PARKES.
H. BARNETT.	A. GATENBY.	A. PETTITT.
H. BEAUMONT.	T. GOODS.	J. PHIPPS.
G. H. BELFIELD.	J. HALLIDAY.	R. PILLING.
R. BELFIELD.	T. HALLSWORTH.	H. PRINDLE.
C. BELL.	W. HARDMAN.	H. PATCH.
E. BELL.	W. A. HARVEY.	J. POTTS.
R. BEWLEY.	W. HAUSMAN.	G. REDFORD.
B. BISHOP.	J. HAYLE.	H. RICHARDSON.
W. BORRELL.	R. HEARD.	J. SHAWCROSS.
J. BOWERS.	W. HICKSON.	F. SNOWDEN.
J. BRADBURY.	C. E. HOLDEN.	H. SPENCER.
P. F. BRANCHFLOWER.	J. JACKSON.	V. STERLING.
E. BRODERICK.	C. JAMES.	A. TEANBY.
C. BROOKS.	J. JOHNSON.	W. TALLIS.
C. J. BRYAN.	F. W. JONES.	H. TAYLOR.
T. BARNETT.	G. JONES.	S. E. TAYLOR.
T. BUTLER.	M. J. RILEY.	T. THOMAS.
F. BUNNELL.	W. LAWLER.	C. TONGE.
A. CHADWICK.	T. LEIGH.	L. TRIGG.
C. CLAYTON.	W. LEYLAND.	R. VALENTINE.
S. CHRISP.	G. LIGHTFOOT.	J. WALKER.
T. W. COLLINS.	J. H. LYONS.	J. WARD.
S. COOK.	J. MARSH.	ALFD. WATKINS, Jnr.
J. GORMAN.	W. MARSHALL.	ALBERT WATKINS.
J. COWSILL.	A. MAXWELL.	C. WILCOCK.
J. CROMPTON	H. MAXWELL.	A. WHITEHEAD.
JAS. DAVIES.	T. McKEE.	E. C. WILLIAMS.
JNO. DAVIES.	J. W. MEADOWCROFT.	G. WILLIAMS.
E. DUFFIELD.	F. MEADOWCROFT.	H. WILLIAMS.
E. F. ECKERSLEY.	W. MOLLOY.	R. WILSON.
J. ELLISON.	A. MOREWOOD.	R. WINN.
S. ELLISON.	J. MOREWOOD.	R. C. WOODCOCK.
M. EVISON.	C. E. MULRAINE.	H. WRIGHT.
C. FIRTH.	J. MURREY.	C. WALSHE.
F. FIRTH.	J. NUTTALL.	H. YATES.
T. FRENCH.	W. OGDEN.	W. YOUNG.

ROLL OF HONOUR.

Herbert Watson & Co.

108, DEANSGATE, MANCHESTER.

J. L. Wood.

W. G. Browning.

J. L. E. Wright.

G. Holt.

H. L. M. Dodson.

G. Cracknell.

L. Beasley.

ROLL OF HONOUR.

Welsh, Warburton & Co.

16 Aytoun Street, Manchester.

Captain J. S. GEMMELL, 20th Service Batt. Manch. Regt.

L.-Corpl. E. BOWDLER, 15161, B Coy., 7th Batt. K.O.S.B.

Sergt. A. R. FRANKS, 086957, A Company, A.S.C.

Gunner F. R. GIBBON, 25031, D Batt., 59th Brigade, R.F.A.

Driver G. H. SWAINE, 1185, 15th Lancs. Battery, R.F.A.

Pte. H. URWIN, 12006, B Batt., 3rd Border Regiment.

Pte. R. FROST, 8553, 17th Batt. Manch. Regt. B Company.

Pte. J. BRIERLEY, Army Service Corps.

Pte. F. SKERRITT, 7th Manchester Regiment.

Pte. T. WILCOCK, Ryl. Naval Div., Med. Unit.

ROLL OF HONOUR
OF
EDWARD WOOD & CO., LTD.
OCEAN IRON WORKS, MANCHESTER.

The Names of those who in time of need came forward in the service of their King and Country and in the Defence of the Liberties of Europe in the Great War which began in August, 1914.

ELWELL, Capt. E. M. - Lancashire Fusiliers.
DENTON, Lt. H. B. - Royal Engineers.
GRIBBELL, Lt. L. T. - 3rd Devons.
LEWIS, Lt. N. A. - Royal Fusiliers.
McKENZIE, Lt. J. - Seaforth Highlanders.
McCALLUM, Lt. W. A. Royal Engineers.
ABLE, A. W. - Manchester Regiment.
ALCOCK, J. - Manchester Regiment.
ALDEN, W. -
ALLEN, W. -
ARTHUR, J. - Royal Scots.
ASTON, J. - Royal Engineers.
BAILEY, W. - Royal Scots.
BAKER, E. - Lancashire Fusiliers.
BALL, J. H. - Manchester Regiment.
BANNISTER, A. - Manchester Regiment.
BASSON, J. -
BEBBINGTON, C. - Royal Engineers.
BENTLEY, H. - Field Telegraph Service.
BERRY, J. - Manchester Regiment.
BOYLE, W. - Royal Army Medical Corps.
BRASSINGTON, J. -
BRIGGS, J. - Manchester Regiment.
BROCKLEHURST, V. - 5th E. of Chester's Infantry.
BROWN, F. - Manchester Regiment.
BUCKLEY, W. -
BURKE, W. - Royal Engineers.
BURNS, G. -
BUTTERFIELD, J. - Manchester Regiment.
BUTTERWORTH, J. - Royal Navy.
CHAPMAN, C. R. - Royal Marine Light Inf'y.
CLARKE, J. - Lancashire Fusiliers.
COE, R. -
COLES, G. S. - Manchester Regiment.
COLLIER, S. - Cheshire Regiment.
CONNOR, G. -
CONNOR, J. O. -
CONNOR, T. -
COTTON, W. - Lancashire Fusiliers.
CROMBLEHOLME, F., Sen. Manchester Regiment.
CUMMOCK, G. - Royal Field Artillery.
CUNNINGHAM, J., Jr. Loyal N. Lancashire Regt.
CUNNINGHAM, JAS. - Lancashire Fusiliers.
CUTTING, E. - Royal Navy Reserve.
DAVIES, C. F. - Duke of Lancaster's Yeo.
DAVIES, D. -
DAVIES, S. - Lancashire Fusiliers.
DAY, G. -
DEMAINE, W. - Manchester Regiment.
DIXON, A. - Manchester Regiment.
DIXON, H. - Manchester Regiment.
DODDS, W. - Manchester Regiment.
DOHERTY, C. -
DUFFY, T. -
DUGGAN, P. -
DYE, H. (Killed) - Manchester Regiment.
EDWARDS, J. W. - Manchester Regiment.
EGAN, T. -
ELLISON, E. -
FALLON, M. - Royal Army Medical Corps.
FALLOWS, E. -
FARNELL, F. B. - Royal Fusiliers.
FERNS, M. - Manchester Regiment.
FIELDING, H. - Royal Naval Vol. Reserve.
FITZPATRICK, D. - Lancashire Fusiliers.
FLEMING, T. -
FLITCROFT, J. - Lancashire Fusiliers.
FORSYTH, D. G. - Border Regiment.
FOY, J. - King's O. R. Lancs. Regt.
GANDY, J. -
GANNON, J. -
GILLIGAN, P. - Manchester Regiment.
GLOSSOP, B. (Killed) - Lancashire Fusiliers.
GREENOUGH, W. - Manchester Regiment.
GREGORY, G. - E. Lancs. Royal Engineers.
HALL, G. - King's O. Liverpool Regt.
HALLIDAY, J. - Manchester Regiment.
HALLOWS, J. -
HALLSWORTH, R. - Lancashire Fusiliers.
HANDS, W. - King's Royal Rifles.
HARPHAM, C. - Manchester Regiment.
HARRISON, H. -
HARRISON, H. O. F. - Royal Engineers.
HAZZLEWOOD, N. - Motor Transport.
HEMMINGS, A. - Lancashire Fusiliers.
HENNESLEY, W. -
HESLOP, F. - Lancashire Fusiliers.
HILL, J. -
HOLLWOOD, J. -
HOLT, J. - Lancashire Fusiliers.
HORN, WALTER - King's O. R. Lancs. Regt.
HORN, G. - Lancashire Fusiliers.
HORN, R. - King's O. R. Lancs. Regt.

ROLL OF HONOUR—continued.

EDWARD WOOD & CO. LTD.

ISHERWOOD, T.	Royal Navy.
JACKSON, H.	
JACOBS, J.	17th Sig. Co. R. Engineers.
JOHNSON, A.	
JOHNSON, T.	Manchester Regiment.
JONES, G.	
JURGENS, P.	
KAY, A.	Lancashire Fusiliers.
KELLEY, J.	
KIRBY, A.	King's O. R. Lancs. Regt.
KNOTT, R.	East Lancashire Fusiliers.
LAMBOURN, E.	Manchester Regiment.
LEATHERBARROW, A.	
LEMMON, J.	King's O. R. Lancs. Regt.
LETT, S.	Lancashire Fusiliers.
LIGHTFOOT, T.	
LISTER, T.	
LLOYD, A.	
LOVETT, J.	
LUFKIN, F.	Loyal North Lancs. Regt.
MACK, L.	
MACK, W.	
MADDOX, A.	Lancashire Fusiliers.
MARGETSON, E.	
MARSDEN, J.	11th Hussars.
MARSLAND, H.	Manchester Regiment.
MATHER, E.	
MARTIN, S.	Lancashire Fusiliers.
McGUIRE, J. B. (Killed)	Royal Marine Light Inf'y.
McLAREN, J.	
McNAMEE, J.	Lancashire Fusiliers.
McNULTY, T.	Royal Scots.
MITCHELL, G.	Lancashire Fusiliers.
MONKS, T.	
MURPHY, E.	Royal Fusiliers.
MURPHY, W.	City of Edinb'gh R. Scots.
NETTLE, L. (Killed)	Lancashire Fusiliers.
NIGHTINGALE, J.	Lancashire Fusiliers.
NOON, J.	Manchester Regiment.
NUGENT, J.	Lancashire Fusiliers.
OAKLEY, J.	Royal Field Artillery.
O'BRIEN, I.	
O'CONNOR, J.	Army Service Corps.
OULTON, T.	Lancashire Fusiliers.
PACKHAM, G.	King's Liverpool Regt.
PATON, J.	Lancashire Fusiliers.
PATTEN, H.	Lancashire Fusiliers.
PATTEN, W.	Lancashire Fusiliers.
PENKETHMAN, T. (Killed)	Lancashire Fusiliers.
PHILLIPS, T.	
PITT, S. R.	Royal Garrison Artillery.
POTTER, H.	
PRICE, J.	
PROCTOR, D.	
RAYNOR, E.	
REGAN, J.	Lancashire Fusiliers.
RICHARDSON, R.	Lancashire Fusiliers.
ROBERTS, S.	Lancashire Fusiliers.
ROBINSON, G.	Army Service Corps.
ROBINSON, R.	Royal Navy.
ROGERS, H.	Scottish Borderers.
ROGERSON, J.	
ROLLISON, A.	
ROSEBERRY, S.	20th Hussars.
ROWLANDS, J.	Lancashire Fusiliers.
RUDDY, P.	R. Scots Edinburgh Rifles.
RUSHTON, S.	Royal Field Artillery.
SHARKLEY, J.	
SHENLEY, E.	
SHERIDAN, T.	Royal Irish Fusiliers.
SIMMS, M. J.	
SIMPSON, H.	Manchester Regiment.
SKERRETT, E.	Royal Engineers.
SLATER, J. R.	E. Lancs. Royal Field Art.
SMITH, STANLEY	Manchester Regiment.
SMITH, T. (Killed)	Lancashire Fusiliers.
SPEAKMAN, C.	
SPARKES, J.	Loyal North Lancs. Regt.
SWIFT, J.	Royal Engineers.
SWINDELLS, J.	Lancashire Fusiliers.
TAYLOR, C. H. (Killed)	Manchester Regiment.
TAYLOR, J.	
THORNHILL, A.	Manchester Regiment.
THORNTON, G.	
THORNLEY, W.	
TINSLEY, D.	
TOOLAN, J.	Royal Field Artillery.
TOOLE, J.	
TREACY, F.	Royal Field Artillery.
WALKER, C.	
WALSH, H.	Manchester Regiment.
WALSHE, H.	King's Liverpool Regt.
WALSHE, J.	
WARD, W. R.	Royal Engineers.
WELLINGS, D.	Manchester Regiment.
WHITELING, C. E.	Loyal North Lancs. Regt.
WILD, F. C.	Royal Fusiliers.
WILDING, J.	City of Edinb'gh R. Scots.
WILLIAMSON, R.	Royal Field Artillery.
WILLIAMS, W. (Killed)	King's Liverpool Regt.
WILLIS, J.	
WILLOUGHBY, S.	Lancashire Fusiliers.
WILSON, E. R.	Royal Engineers.
WILSON, J.	Royal Munster Fusiliers.
WORSLEY, H.	Manchester Regiment.
WRIGHT, A. E.	Royal Marine Light Inf'y.
WRIGHT, S.	Motor Transport.
YOUNG, J.	Royal Engineers.

ROLL OF HONOUR.

James Woolley, Sons & Co. Ltd.

Employees Serving in the Great European War.

Lieut. STANLEY WATSON, Cheshire Regt.
Pte. F. ABRAMS, Cheshire Regt.
Pte. T. ALDERSHAW, Loyal North Lancs.
Pte. E. ASPINALL, A.S.C.
A.B. G. ASPRAY (Naval Reserve).
Pte. J. ATKINS, Loyal North Lancs.
Pte. J. C. BARBER, R.A.M.C.
Staff-Sgt. T. F. BARROW, A.S.C.
Pte. WILFRID BARROW, K.O.R.L.
Pte. A. BAXENDALE, Montgomery Yeomanry.
Pte. F. BEARD, R.A.M.C.
Cpl. A. J. BLOMERLEY, A.S.C.
Pte. W. O. BRENNAN, Lancs. Fusiliers.
Pte. V. BROSTER, A.V.C.
Pte. G. W. CARTER, Lancs. Fusiliers.
Cpl. FRANK CLAGUE, Lancs. Fusiliers.
Pte. C. COLLINS, Manchester Regt.
Pte. J. R. COOPER, 3rd Border Regt.
Pte. H. CUNLIFFE, R.A.M.C.
Pte. W. DAINE, 7th Manchester Regt.
L.-Cpl. ALFRED DEAN, Lancs. Fusiliers.
Pte. RICHARD DENTITH, Lancs. Fusiliers.
A.B. H. G. DINGLE (Naval Reserve).
Pte. T. DOVE, Royal Scots.
Pte. C. W. EASTWOOD, R.A.M.C.
Pte. H. EDGE, R.F.A.
Pte. S. EDWARDS, Manchester Regt.
Cpl. J. FARTHING, Lancs. Fusiliers.
Sgt. JOHN FROST, Lancs. Fusiliers.
Sgt. WM. HANCOCK, Lancs. Fusiliers.
Pte. FRED HARRISON, Lancs. Fusiliers.
O.S. JACK HAYWARD, Royal Naval Div.
Pte. G. HENSHALL, Lancs. Fusiliers.
Pte. A. HILL, R.F.A.
Pte. ALFRED HILTON, Lancs. Fusiliers.
Pte. C. HOBBS, Manchester Regt.
GEORGE HOLT, Royal Navy.

ROLL OF HONOUR—continued.

James Woolley, Sons & Co. Ltd.

Pte. J. INGHAM, R.A.M.C.
Pte. A. R. JOHNSON, King's Royal Rifles.
L.-Sgt. ARTHUR KIRBY, Manchester Regt.
Pte. W. KNOWLES, Navy.
Pte E. KYTE, King's Liverpool Regt.
Pte. JOHN A. LADD, Manchester Regt.
Sgt. W. L. LAURIE, Royal Scots.
Pte. T. H. LEWIS, K.O.S.B.
Pte. H. LONGFIELD, Lancs. Fusiliers.
Pte. H. MACDONALD, 7th Manchester Regt.
Pte. R. MATHER, Loyal North Lancs.
Pte. J. H. L. MILLWARD, Manchester Regt.
Pte. F. MOORE, King's Liverpool Regt.
Pte. P. MUIR, Royal Engineers Oversea.
Pte. J. O'CONNOR, A.S.C.
Pte. W. OLDFIELD, Ryl. Light Naval Marines.
Pte. LESLIE PARKER, Lancs. Fusiliers.
Pte. J. PEACOCK, East Lancs. Regt.
Pte. J. W. PEOVER, Manchester Regt.
Pte. H. PIMLOTT, 8th Manchester Transport.
Pte. ARTHUR ROBINSON, Lancs. Fusiliers.
L.-Cpl. H. E. ROBINSON, Seaforth Highlanders.
Pte. WM. ROYLE, Lancs. Fusiliers.
Sgt. F. G. SMITH, Lancs. Fusiliers.
Pte. H. SPRUCE, Manchester Regt.
Pte. R. TALBOT, King's Liverpool Regt.
Pte. G. THOMPSON, 7th Manchester Regt.
Pte. JAMES TIMMIS, Lancs. Fusiliers.
Cpl. T. TUDOR, R.A.M.C.
Pte. A. TURNER, R.A.M.C.
Pte. J. TURTON, A.V.C.
Pte. JOHN WARD, National Reserve.
Pte. G. WILLIAMSON, Seaforth Highlanders.
L.-Cpl. W. WILLIS, K.O.S.B.
Sgt. H. WOODBOURNE, Border Regt.
Pte. A. WORTHINGTON, S. Lancs. Regt.
Pte. J. WORTHINGTON, Cheshire Regt.

ROLL OF HONOUR.

WILSON BOTHAMLEY & SON,

58, 60, 62, High Street,
Manchester.

Private J. Beswick, No. 8065,
 C. Co., 17th Bt. Manchester Regt.
Private J. Coates, No. 8103,
 Sig. Sect., 17th Bt. Manchester Regt.
Private S. Cooke, No. 3587,
 4 Pl., A. Co., 3/6th Manchester Regt.
Private G. Cuffwright, No. 8108,
 C. Co., 17th Bt. Manchester Regt.
Private A. R. Edwards, No. 8133,
 C. Co., 17th Bt. Manchester Regt.
Sergeant H. Fitch, No. 11544,
 Ord. Room, 19th Bt. Manchester R.
Lance Corporal D. O'Brien,
 B. Co., 5 Plat., 11th Welsh Regt.
Private S. Parkin, No. 8266,
 17th Batt. Manchester Regiment.
Private G. Pollitt, No. 6921,
 C. Co., 16th Bt. Manchester Regt.
Private A. Rogers, No. 28819,
 Royal Army Medical Corps.
Private W. Kelsey, No. 6895,
 (Trans.), 16th Bt. Manchester Regt.

The following also offered their services but were not accepted:—

H. Ashton.   V. Humphreys.
R. Bullough. R. Meek.
A. Greaves.

Wilson, Latham & Co.

have serving with His Majesty's Forces

J. R. Abercrombie,
 Indian Reserve of Officers.

I. M. Orr,
 Indian Reserve of Officers.

R. Chaworth-Musters,
 Lieutenant, King's Royal Rifles.

E. O. Holmes,
 Middlesex Regiment.

W. Raynor,
 Royal Scots.

W. Grainger,
 Manchester Regiment.

T. Hateley,
 Manchester Regiment.

L. Moores,
 Manchester Regiment.

S. Bone,
 Manchester Regiment.

A. J. Cann,
 Manchester Regiment

F. Oldham,
 Seaforth Highlanders.

Roll of Honour.

Woodhouse, Hambly & Coy.

105 & 107, Princess Street,
Manchester.

WOODHOUSE, FRANK (Captain),
    1/9th Manchester Regiment.
HAMBLY, J. LYTTLETON (Captain),
    6th Manchester Regiment.
MOORHOUSE, B. (Sergeant).
    20th Royal Fusiliers.
GALLAGHER, J. (Sergeant),
    Drill Instructor, National Reserve.
VEVERS, G. (Corporal),
    Cheshire Yeomanry.
WALLWORK, FRANK,
    1/6th Manchester Regiment.
BONNER, E.,
    16th Service Batt. Manchester Regt.
HOWARTH, N. D.,
    1/6th Manchester Regiment.
HAWORTH, G. R.,
    2/9th Royal Highlanders.
BRAITHWAITE, J.,
    1/7th Manchester Regiment.
PRINCE, A.,
    3/6th Manchester Regiment.
WHALEY, W.,
    Royal Engineers.
WALLWORK, FRED,
    3/6th Manchester Regt.
BROOMHEAD, W. B.,
    26th Reserve Batt. Manchester Regt.
ORSON, J.,
    Royal Navy, H.M.S. "Powerful."
FAULKNER, A.,
    Royal Field Artillery.

ROLL OF HONOUR.

Alfred Young & Co. Ltd.

INDIA HOUSE,
75, WHITWORTH STREET,
MANCHESTER.

Quartermaster Sergt. JOHN KAY,
    5th Loyal North Lancs. (T.) Regt.

Sergeant ARTHUR D. HALLOWS,
    7th King's O. Royal Lancs. Regt.

Private STANLEY COOKE,
    6th Bt. Manchester Regiment (T.)

Private JACK COOKE,
    6th Bt. Manchester Regiment (T.).

Private SAM B. JAMES,
    6th Bt. Manchester Regiment (T.).

Private W. PHILLIPS,
    6th Bt. Manchester Regiment (T.).

Private HAROLD WHIMPENNEY,
    26th Bt. Manchester Regt. (Pals).

Private W. KELSALL,
    8th Bt. Manchester Regiment.

ROLL OF HONOUR.

H. White Wilson & Co.
(A Branch of LARRINAGA & CO. LTD.)
MANCHESTER.

Private J. DANIEL,
18th Service Battalion Manchester Regiment.

*

Private J. DANIEL,
18th Service Battalion Manchester Regiment.

*

Private W. GIBBON,
1/6th Royal Scots.

*

Private A. GIBBON,
2/8th Batt. Argyle and Sutherland Highlanders.

ROLL OF HONOUR.

* * *

J. D. Williams & Co.
53, Dale Street, MANCHESTER.

* * *

Sergt. AIRLEY, A. W.,
    18th Manchesters.
Private CALDERBANK, B. V.,
    6th Manchesters (died in hospital).
Private FISHER, G. J.,
    20th Manchesters.
L.-Corpl. HONEYMAN, F.,
    18th Manchesters.
Private HUGHES, W.,
    Lancashire Fusiliers.
Private KING, J.,
    8th Ardwicks.
Private JONES, C.,
    21st Manchesters.
Private LOCK, F.,
    Signaller attached to 18th M/sc.
Private MAHER, J.,
    8th Ardwicks.
L.-Corpl. MAKIN, A.,
    18th Manchesters.
Private MATSON, V.,
    Royal Army Medical Corps.
Private PEAKE, F. E.,
    20th Manchesters.
Private SHEARMAN, S. E.,
    Signaller attached to 18th M/sc.
Private STEIN, J.,
    Naval Division.
Private TAYLOR, G.,
    Naval Division.
Private WILLMOTT, A.,
    8th Ardwicks.
Private WITTER, W.,
    Army Service Corps.

Supplementary List

ROLL OF HONOUR.

ARMITAGE & RIGBY LTD.,
MANCHESTER.

Directors of the Company.

Capt. Philip M. Armitage	Cheshire Brigade, R.F.A. (T.F.).
Capt. Ralph Armitage	Cheshire Brigade, R.F.A. (T.F.).
Capt. Kenneth Rigby	Duke of Lancaster's Yeomanry.
1st Lieut. Noel Armitage	Scottish Horse.

Warehouse Staff, 95 Portland Street, Manchester.

Lance-Corpl. C. Spring	97 A. Section, 2nd Field Ambulance, East Lancs. Division R.A.M.C. (T.F.).
Private H. Hayes	30th Battalion Royal Fusiliers.
Private J. Openshaw	7th Manchester Regt., B. Coy.
Private J. S. McCrohan	B. Coy. 1/7th Gordon Highlanders, 2nd Highland Infantry Brigade.
Private H. White	13 Platoon, D. Coy., 19th Service Battalion Royal Fusiliers.
Corpl. A. Hemmingway	3rd Coy. 5th Cheshire Regiment.
Private A. Amatt	C. Coy. 19th Manchesters, 90th Brigade, 30th Division.
Private John Allen	D. Coy. 18th Service Battalion Manch. Regt.
Gunner W. McNally	R.F.A., 2nd Cheshire Brigade.
Private J. Farnell	2/4th Seaforth Highlanders, B. Coy., No. 2. Platoon.
Private T. S. Campbell	16th Service Batt. Manchester Regiment.
Private William Bate	A. Coy., 87th Brigade, 1st Battalion K.O.S.B., 29th Division.
Private J. Langan	No. 4 Platoon, 22nd Div. Cyclist Company.
Private J. Snelson	Royal Engineers.
Able-bodied Seaman J. W. Tomkinson	Naval Brigade.
Brigade Sergt.-Major E. Sidgreaves	10th Siege Battery.
Private J. Flavell	D. Coy., 21st Batt., Manch. Regt., 91st Brigade, 30th Division.
Private Leslie Uttley	3/7th Manchester Regt.
Private Augustine Hughes	No. 2 Coy. Royal Fusiliers.
Private Herbert Bromfield	3/7th Manchester Regt.
Private John E. Taylor	F. Coy. 25th Reserve Batt. Manchester Regt.
Private James Moston	3rd Cheshire Regiment.
Private Joseph Black	26th Manchesters.

Roll of Honour—continued.

ARMITAGE & RIGBY LTD.
Cockhedge and Rodney Mills, Warrington.

Private Harry Holt	A. Coy. 4th Batt. South Lancs. Regt., 7th Brigade, 3rd Division.
Private John Holt	Grenadiers Coy., 4th Batt. South Lancs. Regt.
Rifleman C. H. Scruton	C. Coy. 4th Rifle Brigade.
Private W. H. Jenkinson	4th South Lancs. Regt.
Corporal Wm. Bailey	
Bugler P. M. Wright	1/4th Batt. South Lancs., C. Coy.
Rifleman Thomas Hayes	2nd Batt. Rifle Brigade.
James Roylance	H.M.S. "Juno."
Private Walter Brookes	2/4th South Lancs. Regt.
Private George Brown	A.S.C., 8th Field Bakery.
Rifleman Robert Hill	A. Coy., 2nd Batt. Rifle Brigade.
Drummer Harold Ashton	2/4th South Lancs. Regt.
Lance-Corpl. Frank Haslam	
Private Ernest Jones	Lancs. Hussars.
Driver Frank Rostron	4th South Lancs. Regt.
Driver Richard Rostron	19th New Heavy Battery, R.G.A., 21st Bgde.
Rifleman Thomas Sudell	8th Batt. Rifle Brigade, C. Coy.
Rifleman James H. Kay	B. Coy. 13th Batt. King's Royal Rifles.
Rifleman James Firth	10th Batt. Royal Welsh Fusiliers, C. Coy.
Lance-Corpl. Fredk. Brierley	C. Coy. 10th Batt. Royal Welsh Fusiliers.
Private John Hughes	
Lance-Corpl. Fred Smith	D. Coy. 2nd R.M. Fusiliers.
Gunner Edward Riley	A. Sub. A. Battery, 151 Brigade R.F.A.
Private William Wilcock	C. Coy. 2/4th South Lancs. Regt.
Private Henry Skelhorne	A. Coy. 2/4th South Lancs. Regt.
Private Peter Peers	A. Coy. 3/4th South Lancs. Regt.
Private Ernest A. Wallington	B. Coy. 18th Batt. Royal Fusiliers.
Private Philip Johnstone	7th Batt. South Lancs., 56th Brigade, 19th Div.
Driver James Sudell	A.S.A. Battery, 151st Brigade R.F.A., 30th Division.
Private Joseph Stacey	A. Coy. 3rd Batt. South Lancs.
Private Joshua Gregory	R.N. Barracks.
Private Samuel Hassall	A. Coy. 3/4th South Lancs. Regt.
Private James Wakefield	A. Coy. 3/4th South Lancs. Regt.
Private Ernest Davies	F. Coy. Royal Marines.
Private Harold Higginbottom	A. Coy. 3/4th South Lancs. Regt.
Private John Thomas Harrison	3/4th South Lancs. Regt.
Private Joseph Potter	10th Batt. South Lancs. Regt.
Private Joseph Preston Jones	12th Batt. South Lancs. Regt.
Private Thomas Litherland	
Sergeant W. Litherland	A. Coy. 2/4th South Lancs. Regt.
Private W. Critchley	C. Coy. 2/4th South Lancs. Regt., 49th Provisional Batt.
Private W. Holmes	4th South Lancs.
Private Thomas Donbavand	Royal Engineers.
Private T. Littlefair	A. Coy. 7th Brigade, 3rd Division Machine Gun Section 4th South Lancs. Regt.
Lance-Corpl. H. Skelland	1/1st Lancs. Hussars, C. Squadron.
Signaller C. Darbyshire	3rd Batt. 10th Coy. Royal Welsh Fusiliers.

Roll of Honour.

E. Ascoli and Son,
Asia House, Princess Street,
MANCHESTER.

Lieut. Walter S. Ascoli,
  Machine Gun Training Centre.
2nd-Lieut. George H. D. Ascoli,
  2nd Reserve Cavalry Regiment.
Arthur Anderson,
  2nd East Lancashire R.F.A.
Charles Barlow,
  Army Service Corps.
George Bowers,
  Territorial Reserve.
Bernard Capes,
  6th Bt. South Lanc. Regiment.
William Fairhurst,
  22nd Bt. Manchester Regiment.
Joseph F. Hampson,
  Duke of Lancaster's Yeomanry.
Frank Harrington,
  7th Bt. Manchester Regiment.
William Kelsall,
  6th Bt. Manchester Regiment.
Herbert Mills,
  7th Bt. Manchester Regiment.
2nd-Lieut. Charles Williams,
  9th Bt. South Lanc. Regiment.
John Carter,
  6th Bt. Manchester Regiment.

ROLL OF HONOUR.

Ashton & Co. (Estd. 1787) Ltd.
45, Chorlton Street, Manchester.

*Private R. Brindle,
  2nd Lancashire Fusiliers.
Sergeant W. Bennett,
  6th Cheshire Regiment.
Private C. Benville,
  17th Manchester Regiment ("Pals").
Private D. Brown,
  5th Royal Scots Q.E.R.
Private R. Cundiff,
  Divisional Cyclist Corps.
Sergeant H. Elsworth,
  22nd Manchester Regiment ("Pals").
Private E. Faragher,
  20th Manchester Regiment ("Pals").
Private T. Hirst,
  7th Welsh Regiment.
Private H. A. Hill,
  Duke of Lancaster's Own Yeomanry.
Private H. Macdonald,
  19th Manchester Regiment ("Pals").
Private S. Mardy,
  26th Manchester Regiment.
Private J. Perfect,
  8th Lancashire Fusiliers.
Private S. Turner,
  20th Manchester Regiment ("Pals").
Private H. White,
  7th Manchester Regiment (T.F.).
L.-Corpl. F. Woollerton,
  6th Manchester Regiment (T.F.).

  * Killed in action in Flanders.

Roll of Honour.

Barber & Colman, Limited,

10, Charlotte Street,
MANCHESTER.

Lieut. JOHN RUSSEL MAKINSON,
    8th Batt. Manchester Regiment
       (Wounded in Dardanelles).

2nd Lieut. FREDERICK G. GADD,
    10th Batt. Royal Lancasters.

Sergt. GEORGE WILLIAM HOLT,
    18th Batt. Manchester Regt.

L.-Corpl. SYDNEY T. HOVELL,
    9th Batt. Royal Scots.

Private LAMBERT BERRY,
    20th Batt. Manchester Regiment.

Sapper H. BOARDMAN,
    Royal Engineers, East Lancs.

Private ALBERT BRANDRETH,
    19th Batt. Manchester Regiment.

Private WILFRED CURTIS,
    4th Batt. Manchester Regiment.

Private JOSEPH MOORES,
    8th Batt. King's Liverpool Regt.

Private J. PEARSON,
    Royal Irish Fusiliers.

Sapper THOMAS VEAR,
    Royal Engineers, East Lancs.
       (Wounded in Dardanelles).

ROLL OF HONOUR.

James Barber & Co. Ltd.

6, Fairfield Street,
—MANCHESTER—

LEONARD H. BARBER.

JOSEPH ADSHEAD.

W. H. WHITE.

JAMES GIBBS.

THOMAS WOOD.

GEORGE I. SAUNDERS.

FRED. ARTHUR CAPSTICK.

JOHN McSPIRIT.

RICHARD STOTT.

ROLL OF HONOUR.

S. L. Behrens (Manchester) Limited.

16 Oxford Street, Manchester.

2nd Lieut. C. W. Lamb	3/1st East Lancashire R.F.A.
Sergt.-Major C. H. Martin	44th Field Ambulance.
S.Q.M. Sergt. J. Reilly	11th Service Coy., Army Ord. Corps.
Sergt.-Major C. Bonehill	No. 4 Royal Army Medical Corps.
S.Q.M. Sergt. H. Dawson	3rd Earl of Chester's Yeomanry.
Sergt.-Major Leeming	Royal Field Artillery.
Corporal F. Evans	2/5th Provisional Battalion.
L.-Corpl. S. Austin	6th Battalion Manchester Regiment.
Private B. H. Buckland	20th Battalion Royal Fusiliers.
Private H. S. Hargreaves	2/7th Battalion Manchester Regiment.
Private C. Smallshaw	2/6th Battalion Manchester Regiment.
Private W. Keating	2/6th Battalion Manchester Regiment.
Private W. Newman	6th Provisional Batt. Royal Scots.
Private T. Hampson	6th Provisional Batt. Royal Scots.
Private W. Broady	18th Service Batt. Manchester Regt.
Private A. Fletcher	2/8th Battalion Manchester Regiment.
Private J. Gawkrodger	11th Batt. Loyal North Lancs. Regt.
Sapper R. Toole	Royal Engineers.
Private G. Millett	12th Batt. King's Liverpool Regt.
Private A. S. Wright	King's Liverpool Regiment.
Driver W. McKinnell	Motor Transport A.S.C.
Driver J. W. Carlile	Army Service Corps.
Private G. Walker	Duke of Lancaster's Yeomanry.
Private R. Radcliffe	2/7th Battalion Manchester Regiment.
Gunner T. Kelly	1/2nd E.L. R.F.A. Ammunition Col.
Private F. Wheeldon	9th Battalion Rifle Brigade.
Private D. Heaton	Welsh Border Mounted Brigade.
Private W. Mills	16th Service Batt. Manchester Regt.
Private C. H. Kerr	2/6th Battalion Manchester Regiment.
Private S. B. Sweetman	2/6th Battalion Manchester Regiment.
Private R. Mason	20th Service Batt. Royal Fusiliers.
Private H. G. Metcalfe	6th Batt. Manchester Regiment. (Killed in action 7th Aug.)
Private H. V. Heywood	Royal Marines, Light Infantry.
Private G. Allen	25th Batt. Manchester Regiment.
Private G. McCubbin	2/7th Battalion Manchester Regiment.
Private J. E. Holford	25th Reserve Batt. Manchester Regt.

ROLL OF HONOUR.

List of Men who have Joined His Majesty's Forces from

John & William Bellhouse, Ltd.

City Road.

Pte. H. TYREMAN	- -	1/8th Manchester Regiment.
Pte. E. SCOTCHFORD	-	1/7th Lancashire Fusiliers.
Pte. CARTER	- - - -	L.N.L.
Pte. BARLOW	- - - -	1/7th Lancashire Fusiliers.
Pte. BECKETT	- - - -	2/7th Manchester Regiment.
L.-Corpl. EDWARDS	- -	3rd East Surrey Regiment.
Pte. S. ALDRED	- - -	8th K.O.R.L.
Pte. J. JOHNSON	- - -	K.L.R.
Pte. SMITH	- - - - -	Royal Scots.
Pte. W. JOHNSTONE	-	R.F.A.
Pte. E. McCORMICK	- -	Border Regiment.
Pte. W. McCORMICK	-	12th Manchester Regiment.
Pte. F. KERSHAW	- -	8th K.O.R.L.
Pte. PHILIPS	- - - -	2nd Salford Pals.
Bombardier J. WRIGHT	-	R.F.A.
Pte. BRINDLEY	- - -	K.L.R.
Pte. KENNY	- - - -	R.A.M.C.
Pte. HARPER	- - -	K.O.R.L.
Pte. MARTIN	- - - -	K.O.R.L.
Pte. ATHERTON	- - -	24th Royal Fusiliers.
Pte. R. ALDRED	- - -	A.S.C.
Pte. CHILDS	- - - -	East Lancashires.

Miles Platting.

DAWSON, WILLIAM E.	Royal Naval Air Service.
JONES, ERNEST	King's Own Royal Lancaster Rgt.
SPARROW, ALFRED	A.S.C.
DAVIDSON, JAMES	Shropshire Light Infantry.
FEARNS, FRANK	15th Royal Scots.
SUDLOW, ALFRED E.	A.S.C.
MANGNALL, CHARLES	15th Royal Scots.
GREEN, JOSEPH	7th Manchesters.
McGHIE, ALEXANDER	
CHAPPELL, PERCY	15th Royal Scots.
McVET, WILLIAM	
McCLELLAN, WILLIAM	Army Police.
AINSWORTH, THOMAS	R.F.A.
KEYS, JAMES	
TOBIN, JOHN	
McNALLY, THOMAS	Lancashire Fusiliers.
MORRIS, JOHN	
CLARK, GEORGE	
DELLAFIELD, JOHN	
COYNE, PETER	Army Police.
JONES, EDGAR	
TAYLOR, HENRY	South Lancashire Regiment.
HARTLEY, WILLIAM	Motor Transport Section.
BAMFORD, ROBERT	
BISHOP, HENRY	
HILTON, W.	
FOX, W. C.	
CHAPMAN, JOHN	
RUDMAN, ARTHUR	
TAYLOR, THOMAS	8th Manchester Regiment.
BAILEY, ARTHUR	Royal Scots.
NOBLE, ALBERT	69th Welsh Regiment.
RUSE, JOHN	R.M.L.I.
McDONOUGH, JOSEPH	O.S.

Roll of Honour.

Beatty, Altgeldt and Co.,

2, Brazil Street, Sackville Street,

List of our Employees serving with the Colours.

2nd Lieut. W. B. DIERDEN,
 2nd Gloucester Regiment,
  81st Brigade, 27th Division.

Private RALPH BOLT, No. 8408,
 "B" Company, 17th Battalion,
  Manchester Regt., 30th Division.

Private SIDNEY HIND, No. 2579,
 Royal Scots Reserve.

Private FRANK BRADLEY, No. 2701,
 "B" Coy., 2/4 Seaforth High'rs.

Private ERIC HALL, No. 517,
 3/1st Welsh Div. Cyclist Corps.

Trooper HERBERT TAYLOR, No. 3955,
 Duke of Lancaster's Own Yeo'nry.

Roll of Honour.

C. Binks Ltd.

Church Street,
ECCLES, MANCHESTER.

MONRO, H. J. G., Corpl.,
 Army Service Corps (M.T.).
M'CAW, T.,
 Army Service Corps (M.T.).
DALTON, ARTH.,
 Hussars.
WORTHINGTON, JAS.,
 Lancs. Fusiliers (Wounded).
CHEETHAM, ARNOLD,
 Lancs. Fusiliers.
ROSEWAREN, T. R.,
 Lancs. Fusiliers.
DALEY, WM.,
 Army Service Corps.
REDFERN, EDWIN,
 Lancs. Fusiliers.
BOOTHMAN, CLARENCE,
 Duke of Wellington's Own.
ROBY, JACK,
 Lancs. Fusiliers (Wounded).
VALENTINE, FRED,
 Lancs. Fusiliers (Wounded).
AITKEN, DAVID,
 Gordon Highlanders.
MONRO, KENNETH,
 Despatch Rider.

ROLL OF HONOUR.

Blakeley and Beving, Limited,

MANCHESTER.

Lieut. E. P. HARTSHORN, D.C.M.

T. ANDERSON.	F. HINSON.
J. BLAIR.	F. HOUGH.
P. BRISLAND.	J. KERSHAW.
B. BROWN.	G. W. MASON.
G. BROWNLOW.	W. G. MOORHOUSE
E. CLARKE.	W. SHORT.
J. COGGER.	A. TREANOR.
A. ELLISON.	H. G. WALLER.
T. GIDLEY.	J. S. WHITELEGG.

ROLL OF HONOUR.

Blyton, Astley & Co.
MANCHESTER.

Capt. C. H. WILLIAMSON,
  1/7th Manchesters.
HUGH WATERS,
  7th Manchesters.
E. HOOLEY,
  8th Lancashire Fusiliers.
I. HARDING,
  R.A.M.C.
L. CAREY,
  East Lancashires.
WM. FISH,
  8th King's Own.
ALBERT ROBINSON,
  8th Manchesters (Terr.).
A. STAPPLETON,
  1st Liverpool Regiment.
A. POLLARD,
  Border Regiment.
W. LINDSEY,
  King's Own.
R. CROOK,
  Lancs. Fusiliers (Terr.).
W. SIBLEY,
  8th Manchesters.
P. COTT,
  Lancs. Fusiliers (Terr.).
A. GOODWIN,
  Lancs. Fusiliers (Terr.).
L. COTT,
  Lancs. Fusiliers (Terr.).
J. PHILLIPS,
  8th Batt. Lancs. Fusiliers.
E. SHAEBOTTAM,
  King's Own Lancasters.
A. BARLOW,
  Manchesters.
J. HOGG, Manchesters.

Roll of honour.

Herbert B. Bowen
33, CHORLTON STREET, MANCHESTER.

Trooper E. BRICE BOWEN,
  Warwickshire Yeomanry.

L.-Corpl. B. OLDFIELD,
  3rd East Lancs. Transport,
  R.A.M.C. Territorial Force.

Pte. A. BADDELEY, No. 272,
  3rd Batt. East Lancs. Territorial Force.

Pte. T. BENNETT,
  Military Headquarters, Gibraltar.

Pte. S. TOWNLEY,
  17th Batt. Manchester Regt.
  Machine Gun Section.

Pte. H. GREEN, No. 8587,
  C Co., 17th Batt. Manchester Regt.

Pte. J. STEAD,
  6th Manchester Territorial Force.

Pte. A. VIPOND, No. 8924,
  17th Batt. Manchester Regt.

Pte. R. PRIEST, No. 103303,
  R.A.M.C.,
  Royal Free Military Hospital, London.

Pte. S. MURPHY, No. 4599,
  3rd/7th Batt. Manchester Regt.

Pte. J. FALLON, No. 5027,
  3rd/7th Batt. Manchester Regt.

Pte. J. STREET, No. 8887,
  C Co., 25th Manchester Regt.

Second Lieut. L. GANDY,
  14th Div. 11th Manchester Regt.
  (Attached to.)

ROLL OF HONOUR.

✱ ✱ ✱

H. O. Brandt & Co.,
63, Granby Row,
Sackville Street, Manchester.

Private R. V. Cash,
 Black Watch.

Corporal John Edward Coutts,
 2nd East Lanc. Field Ambulance.

Private Alexander Dick,
 15th Serv. Batt. Lancs. Fusiliers.

Private Charles Garner,
 16th Serv. Batt. Manchester Regt.

Private Henry Lionel Griffiths,
 2nd East Lanc. Field Ambulance.

Private John Johnson,
 15th Serv. Batt. Lancs. Fusiliers.

Private James Kennedy,
 18th Serv. Batt. Manchester Regt.

Private Clifford Warburton,
 6th Manchester Regt. (T.F.).

Private Frank Watson,
 16th Serv. Batt. Manchester Regt.

Private Charles Albert Wilson,
 2nd East Lanc. Field Ambulance.

ROLL OF HONOUR.

Thomas Brayshay & Sons,
LIMITED,
10, Dantzic Street, Manchester.

Private Jas. Berry,
 26th Batt. Manch. Regt.

✱

Private Reg. Hopkins,
 No. 2 Co., Grenadier Guards.

✱

Private Oswald King,
 19th Ser. Batt. Man. Regt.

✱

Private Chas. Raeper,
 B. Co., 2nd K.O.S.B.

Roll of Honour.

Fredk. Brine & Co.,

Worsley Street, Chester Road,
MANCHESTER.

- Brine, H.
- Buckley, J.
- Bond, F.
- Brittain, R.
- Barrey, D.
- Ambrose, J.
- Campbell, P.
- Cawley, H.
- Delany, J.
- Evans, A.
- Foster, R.
- Healey, F.
- Malone, P.
- McBride, F.
- Miles, G.
- Simon, R.
- Jones, T.
- Slattery, M.
- Timperley, W.
- Vernon, D.

Roll of Honour.

Brisbane, Jones & Co. Limited

10, Aytoun Street,
Manchester.

Sergt. THOMAS HIBBERT,
8th Batt. Manchester Regt.

*

Pte. JOHN SMITH,
R.A.M.C., East Lancs. Division.

*

Pte. JOHN HOLLAND,
3rd Manchester Regiment.

*

Pte. PHILIP BERRISFORD,
2/6th Batt. Sherwood Foresters.

ROLL OF HONOUR.

Brown & Forth
10 Dolefield, Bridge Street,
MANCHESTER

Sergt. RUSSELL BROWN,
29th Royal Fusiliers.

★

Sec. Lieut. ERIC FORTH,
2/2nd East Lancashire R.F.A.

★

CHARLES FORTH,
Manchester University O.T.C.

★

Sapper PERCY HALL,
E.L.R. Engineers.

★

Driver FRED. JEVONS,
A.S.C. M.T.

ROLL OF HONOUR

A. BURGON & CO. LTD.
Card and Paper Box Manufacturers,
75, 79 & 104, Sackville Street,
Manchester.

List of Employees who have Joined the Army since War was Declared.

ROWLAND ATKINSON,
  Manchester Pals Battalion.
GEORGE BEAUMONT,
  South Lancashire Regiment.
JOHN R. BROWNSELL,
  8th Manchester Regiment.
JOHN CAUDWELL,
  Royal Welsh Fusiliers.
LAUNCELOT P. CLAYTON,
  Royal Field Artillery.
PERCY COOKSON,
  Royal Field Artillery.
NORMAN DABBE,
  6th Batt. Manchester Regiment.
ROBERT DAWSON,
  Lancashire Fusiliers.
GEORGE DEPLEDGE,
  Royal Field Artillery.
PHILIP K. HALL,
  East Lancashire Territorials A.S.C.
THOMAS HARRISON,
  Royal Army Medical Corps.
LEONARD HEATH,
  Royal Garrison Artillery.
JOSEPH KENNEDY,
  Royal Irish Fusiliers.
ARNOLD LUCAS,
  6th Batt. Manchester Regiment.
RICHARD O'NEILL,
  Manchester Pals Battalion.
RICHARD TWIGG,
  Bury Fusiliers.
ARTHUR WOOD,
  Royal Field Artillery.

ROLL OF HONOUR

ISAAC BURY LTD.,

ADELPHI DYEING AND FINISHING WORKS,

SALFORD

Men serving with the Colours.

T. ARMSTRONG.	WILLIAM MORRIS.
J. BAXTER.	G. MARSDEN.
FRED BATES.	T. McENEANY.
W. BAXTER.	W. McMULLAN.
C. BAXTER.	W. PURSGLOVE.
J. BERRY.	JOHN ROGERSON.
WM. COSTELLO.	J. H. ROGERSON.
T. CUNNINGHAM.	J. ROGERSON.
PHILIP DONOHUE.	F. A. SLEGG.
H. GORTON.	T. H. SMITH.
ARTHUR HEALD.	HAROLD SYKES.
JAS. HORFORD.	GEORGE TYLDESLEY.
C. HALL.	J. TAPP.
G. HUSBAND.	W. TOWNSEND.
T. HAYDEN.	THOMAS WILD.
STANLEY JACKSON.	THOMAS WARBURTON.
JAS. KELLY.	W. WILLIAMSON.
RICHARD KIRK.	B. WALKER.
JOHN LOWE.	R. WALKER.
EDWARD MAY.	THOMAS YATES.
THOMAS MORRIS.	HORATIO YALE.

Roll of Honour.

Emmanuel Casdagli & Sons

32 Oxford Street,
MANCHESTER.

CARL POTTS,
17th Batt. Manchester Regiment.

HARRY BROWN,
17th Batt. Manchester Regiment.

ALFRED GARNER,
17th Batt. Manchester Regiment.

ROLL OF HONOUR.

William Champness & Sons

Rusholme, Road, Manchester.

Corpl. MARK SMITH,
    6th Batt. Manchester Regiment.
                  (Killed in action.)

Pte. WM. CHAMPNESS,
    Army Service Corps.

Pte. JAMES C. STEWART,
    Royal Army Medical Corps.

Regt. Q.M. Sergt. JOHN ORME,
    11th Royal Welsh Fusiliers.

Lce. Corpl. GEORGE WATSON,
    13th Manchester Regiment.

Pte. CHAS. PETRIE,
    21st Manchester Regiment.

Pte. PERCY FORD,
    1/7th Manchester Regiment.

Pte. WM. PARRY,
    4th Batt. Manchester Regiment.

Pte. FRANK STREET,
    9th Batt. South Lancs. Regiment.

Pte. ROBERT MCCONVILLE,
    21st Batt. Lancs. Fusiliers.

Pte. WALTER WITHINGTON,
    1/7th Man. Regt., Machine Gun Sect.

The Churchill Machine Tool Co. Ltd.

LIST OF MEN ON ACTIVE SERVICE.

Corporal Harrison, E.	East Lancs. Royal Engineers (Signaller).
Linney, P.	Army Service Corps (M.T.).
Willoughby, W.	6th Manchesters.
Lloyd, F.	7th Manchesters.
Douglas, W.	Seaforth Highlanders.
Hunter, W.	Lancashire Fusiliers (Killed in Action).
Sergt. Satterthwaite, H.	Royal Ordnance Corps.
Foster, A.	
Gilder, H.	
Ancell, E.	East Lancs. Royal Engineers.
Jennings, J.	
Rowbottom, A.	
Connor, J.	7th Lancashire Fusiliers.
Lomax, F.	East Lancs. Royal Engineers.
Ramage, F.	
Daly, M.	Killed in Action.
Rooney, A.	11th Manchester Regiment.
Grundy, J.	
Sheldon, T.	Royal Ordnance.
Merrill, L.	
Satterthwaite, F.	Royal Navy.
Wood, J. T.	6th Royal Lancaster King's Own.
Renshaw, T.	Killed in Action.
Gough, S.	Killed in Action.
Burrows, J.	
Foster, R.	
Whittaker, E.	1st Lancashire Fusiliers.
Campbell, G.	
Hossack, S.	3rd Batt. Liverpool Regiment.
Simpkins, T.	
Lance-Cpl. Willers, F.	8th Royal Lancaster Regiment.
Grummitt, W. C.	
Bent, H.	
Skidmore, E.	
Western, H.	East Lancs. Royal Engineers.
Barker, J. W.	3rd Lancashire Fusiliers.
Sergt. O'Neill, T.	3rd Lancashire Fusiliers.
Lance-Cpl. Robinson, J. A.	Royal Engineers
Carr, T.	
Parker, L.	16th Lancashire Fusiliers.
Watts, W.	
Sergt. Ellison, W.	Ordnance Corps.
Sergt. Roberts, J.	7th Lancashire Fusiliers.
Hall, T.	Army Service Corps (M.T.).
Thompson, J.	10th South Lancs.

Roll of Honour.

Coates, Wilson & Co.
(Late COATES, HODGKINSON & CO.)

38, Bloom Street,
MANCHESTER.

Sec. Lieut. R. HODGKINSON,
　North Staffs. Regt.

Sec. Lieut. M. WOOD,
　14th Manchesters.

Drummer A. W. COWAN (killed),
　1st/6th Manchester Regt. (T.F.).

Pte. L. BRIERLEY,
　11th King's Liverpool Regt.

Pte. L. DEAN,
　6th Cheshire Regt. (T.F.).

Pte. L. P. TRUELOCK,
　30th Batt. Royal Fusiliers.

Lce. Corpl. J. J. DAVISON,
　King's Shropshire L.I. (9th Batt.).

Roll of Honour.

Harold Daniels & Co.

11, Whitworth Street,
—MANCHESTER—

PERCY HOWARD.

ARTHUR PUGH.

GEORGE MORRISON.

DAVID ROWLANDS.

VICTOR J. WAGSTER.

EDWIN B. TILLEARD.

JOHN F. COPLEY.

FRANK S. BRADLEY.

Roll of Honour.

F. A. DEAN.
75, WHITWORTH STREET, MANCHESTER.

Sec. Lieut. FREDK. FOSTER,
  8th Batt. Manchester Regiment.

Sergt. CHARLES HERBERT CARTWRIGHT,
  9th Batt. Royal Scots.

Private HERBERT COLIN SAMES,
  6th Batt. Manchester Regiment.

Private PERCY LINCOLN KEIGHLEY,
  20th Batt. Royal Fusiliers.

Private JAMES NOEL FIELDING,
  R.A.M.C.

Private RICHARD JONES,
  27th (R.) Batt. Manchester Regt.

Private CHARLES BEHAN,
  7th Batt. Lancashire Fusiliers.

Roll of Honour.

C. C. Dunkerley & Co.
LIMITED.

JAMES BARRETT,
  1st Batt. Rifle Brigade.

JOHN MATHIE FOSTER,
  6th Batt. Man. Regt. (T.F.).

ALBERT GILL,
  3rd Batt. South Lancs. Regt.

FREDERICK GOULDEN,
  2nd Batt. East Lancs. Fusiliers.

HARRY NANSON HARRIS,
  Pals Batt. Manchester Regt.

JAMES KERR,
  9th Bt. King's Own Lanc. Rgt.
  (Prisoner in Bulgaria.)

ARTHUR KNOTT,
  Lancashire Fusiliers (T.F.).

THOMAS LEACH,
  14th Batt. Manchester Regt.

ARCHIBALD ROUTLEDGE,
  8th Batt. Man. Regt. (T.F.).
  (Reported Missing in Gallipoli.)

JOHN STRINGER,
  7th Batt. Lancashire Fusiliers.

WILLIAM STRINGER,
  13th Batt. Manchester Regt.

J. FRENCH,
  Lancashire Fusiliers.

ROLL OF HONOUR.

A. K. Dyson & Co. Ltd.

88-90 George Street,
Manchester.

H. Simpson,
　18th Field Ambulance, R.A.M.C.

A. Berry,
　Royal Army Medical Corps.

J. Murphy, D.C.M.,
　6th Manchester Regiment.

J. A. Ellison,
　8th Batt. Lancashire Fusiliers.

J. W. Barton,
　6th Manchester Regiment.

G. Nicholson,
　Royal Army Medical Corps.

G. Wilson,
　Army Service Corps.

C. H. Luke,
　4th Seaforth Highlanders.

H. H. Midwinter,
　2nd East Lancs. R.F.A.

A. Lambert,
　5th Cheshire Regiment.

W. B. Bardsley,
　7th Manchester Regiment.

Roll of Honour.

Edwards, Cunliffe & Co. Ltd.

16, Byrom Street,
MANCHESTER.

Captain Harold H. Cunliffe,
　25th Manchester Regiment.

Captain William R. Cunliffe,
　1st East Lancs. R.F.A.

Lieutenant Neville Bull,
　Army Service Corps.

Sergt. Arthur Pye,
　21st Royal Field Artillery.

Corpl. William Burton,
　1st East Lancs. R.A.M.C.

L. Corpl. Joseph Murphy,
　18th Manchester Regiment.

Private John W. Hulley,
　6th Manchester Regiment (T.F.).

Private Walter Welch,
　King's Liverpool Regiment.

Private William Hill,
　Royal Welsh Fusiliers.

Private William Heaford,
　3rd Manchester Regiment.

Private Michael Reilley,
　13th Lancashire Fusiliers.

Private Albert Hall,
　15th Lancashire Fusiliers.

Private George Henry Smith,
　8th Lancashire Fusiliers.

ROLL OF HONOUR.

Ehrenbach Brumm & Co.

BRADFORD,
MANCHESTER.

- J. Beall.
- F. Hazeldine.
- N. Henderson.
- J. H. Hodgson.
- F. Jackson.
- J. Lea.
- F. Maskew.
- E. Pickering.
- E. Pickstone.
- W. Price.
- S. Shaw.
- H. Shoesmith.
- E. Smith.
- P. Thompson.
- J. Turton.
- G. Walker.
- W. Wakefield.
- S. Wass.
- L. Waterworth.
- E. Wolstenholme.

Roll of Honour.

Elson & Neill

45 Faulkner Street,
—Manchester—

Seaman THOS. BURKE,
    4 Mess H.M.S. "Brisk."

Corpl. GILBERT CLARIDGE, 1452,
    G. Co. 6th Manchester (T.F.), B.M.E.F.,
        42nd East Lancs. Division.

Corpl. FRED EVANS, 8536,
    C. Co. 17th Manchester ("Pals").

Pte. NORMAN GREENWOOD, 8591,
    D. Co. 17th Manchester ("Pals"), B.E.F.

Pte. SYDNEY HANDFORD, 4347,
    C. Co. 3/6th Manchester (T.F.),
        42nd East Lancs. Division.

Pte. JOHN HYDE, 4840,
    D. Co. 3/8th Manchester (T.F.).

Drummer ERNEST LESSER, 1320,
    A. Co. 1/7th Manchester (T.F.), B.M.E.F.,
        42nd East Lancs. Division.

Driver JOSEPH McCARTHY, 096769,
    Co. 570, Motor Transport Sec., A.S.C., E.A.E.F.

Pte. SAM MYERS,
    A. Co. Royal Marines, Depôt, Deal.

Lance-Corpl. BEN NEWTON, 6661,
    B. Co. 16th Manchester Ser. Batt. ("Pals"), B.E.F

Lance-Corpl. GEORGE E. TURNER, 18741,
    A. Co. 21st Manchester Ser. Batt. ("Pals"), B.E.F.

Pte. ELLIS WARRENDER, 24618,
    B. Co. 3rd Manchester ("Regulars"), B.M.E.F.

ROLL OF HONOUR

Etchells, Congdon & Muir,
Limited.
MANCHESTER.

Capt. H. J. Rose,
 1/8th Batt. Man. Regt. (T.F.).
 (Killed in action at Achi Baba,
 June 4th, 1915).

Sergt. R. L. Stevenson,
 1/6th Batt. Man. Regt. (T.F.).

Corpl. S. R. Topping,
 Duke of Lancaster's Yeomanry.

Pte. C. Uttley,
 1/6th Batt. Man. Regt. (T.F.).
 (Killed in action in Gallipoli.)

Pte. J. Pennington,
 Loyal North Lancashire Regt.

Pte. A. J. Bramhall,
 2nd King's Rifles.

Pte. P. Humphries.

Pte. E. W. Parkin.

Pte. J. Dignan.

Pte. Harold Loynd.

Roll of Honour.

FLETCHER, ARTHUR & Co.

Steam Ship Owners & Brokers,

207, Deansgate,

MANCHESTER.

Serving in France.

Corporal CHARLES HOLTUM,
 21st Service Batt. Manchester Regt.

Private SYDNEY OWEN,
 16th Ser. Batt. Lancashire Fusiliers.

Attested.

FRED WALLWORK.

ARTHUR FAULKNER.

CHARLES GRADWELL.

FRANK CLARK.

ROLL OF HONOUR.

Fothergill & Harvey Ltd.
MANCHESTER.

Reservists called to the Colours at the outbreak of the War.

TRACEY, PETER — King's Royal Rifles. (Time expired 9/10/14; Discharged 9/10/15; Re-enlisted Nov., 1915.)
MILLICAN, RICHARD — Royal Garrison Artillery.

Territorials called to the Colours at the outbreak of the war.

CRASTON, NOEL — 6th Manchesters.

Men who enlisted prior to the Derby Scheme.

ASHWORTH, NORMAN — Salford Fusiliers.
ROYCE, ARTHUR — 19th Batt. Manchester Regiment.
KEIGHLEY, ROBERT — Loyal North Lancs.
HUGHES, WILLIAM — Welsh Fusiliers.
McGUIRE, WILLIAM — Royal Engineers.
BISHOP, ARTHUR — Royal Field Artillery.
MILLAR, WILLIAM — R.A.M.C.
JONES, LEONARD — King's Own Lancasters.
STEELE, ARTHUR — Noncombatants' Corp. (Sent out by the Society of Friends to the Front.)

Men who have enlisted under the Derby Scheme and who have now gone.

SHAW, CYRIL — Shropshire Light Infantry.
DYSON, EDWARD — Lancashire Fusiliers.

Men who have attested under the Derby Scheme but who have not yet been called up.

Sandys, Francis G. C.   Lord, Thomas.   Richards, George.
Moores, Richard.   Wragge, Walter.

N.B.—The above List, together with those rejected, comprises the whole of our staff eligible for the Army according to the age limit.

ROLL OF HONOUR.

***

GATLEY, VICKERS & CO.

***

ARCHER, S.	GILLETT, T.	McBRIDE, S.
ASHWORTH, J.	GLYNN, A.	McFARLANE, T.
ATHERTON, C.	GOODWIN, W.	NEWTON, S.
BEDDOWS, A.	GRUNDY, T.	NICHOLAS, A.
BERRY, J.	HALLWOOD, D.	NOLAN, C.
BESSELL, A.	HARRISON, H.	NORRISS, T.
BEVAN, G.	HAYES, A.	O'BRIAN, J.
BELLESTY, W.	HEYWOOD, H.	PARKER, G.
BOTTOMLEY, J.	HICKSON, C.	PRITCHARD, J.
BRAITHWAITE, H.	HINDLEY, T.	RAMSBOTTOM, W.
BRENNAN, H.	HINDLEY, W.	RAYNOR, G.
BUCKLEY, R.	HOLT, A.	RATIGAN, J.
BURNS, W.	HOLT, S.	REDMOND, M.
CARROLL, S.	HOLT, W.	REVILL, F.
CAREY, T.	HOPWOOD, E.	RIGBY, A.
CLARKE, A.	HOPWOOD, W.	ROEBUCK, C.
CLARKE, E.	HOUGH, G.	ROGERSON, H.
CLYNES, F.	HUMPHREYS, S.	ROUND, G.
COLE, M.	JAMES, A.	ROWLES, J.
COLLIER, J.	JAMES, A.	RUSHTON, S.
COLLIER, W.	JACKSON, P.	SANDERSON, S.
CONLAN, L.	JEFFERSON, J.	SANDIFORD, A.
COOKE, F.	JOHNSON, C.	SEAL, H.
COURTNEY, J.	JONES, J.	SESSNON, W.
CUMMINDS, J.	JONES, S.	SHAWCROSS, E.
DENHAM, J.	KELLY, J.	STEELE, R.
DENHAM, W.	KINDER, E.	TOMNEY, A.
DILLON, J.	KINLEY, A.	TURNER, C.
DOHERTY, J.	KNIGHT, J.	WALKER, D.
DONE, M.	KNIGHT, W.	WALLACE, J. W.
DONEGAN, P.	LEE, W.	WARD, F.
DUFFY, T.	LEVIS, J.	WALSH, J.
EDWARDS, E.	LIVESEY, S.	WEDDLE, E.
ELLISS, H.	LOMAS, A.	WIDDESON, G.
FALLOWS, H.	LYONS, J.	WHITEHEAD, R.
FALLS, T.	MASSEY, E.	WILLCOCK, R.
FARRELL, R.	MEAKIN, B.	WISEMAN, T.
FARROW, W.	MOLYNEAUX, W.	WOLSTENHOLME, J.
FERNLEY, A.	MONKS, T.	YATES, A.
FOSTER, J.	MORRISS, E.	YATES, E.
FOSTER, W.	MORTON, B.	YATES, J.
GERRARD, J.		

ROLL OF HONOUR.

Groves & Whitnall Ltd.

Lieut.-Col. J. E. G. GROVES, T.D.　　Lieut. W. PEER GROVES, R.N.A.S.

Captain W. VERNON.

- ALLMARK, S.
- ALLMAN, A.
- ASHWORTH, G.
- ASHCROFT, A.
- BURGESS, J.
- BUNTING, G.
- BLACKFORD, H.
- BRADBURY, W.
- BENEDICT, A.
- BAILEY, J.
- BROOKS, S.
- BURNS, J.
- BROWN, J.
- BRINDLEY, A.
- BROWN, F.
- BIRCH, H.
- BIRKBY, W.
- CONWAY, R.
- CUTTING, E.
- COOK, A.
- CLARKE, F.
- CLARKE, C.
- CLARE, H.
- CRONSHAW, H.
- CARROLL, P.
- CHAPMAN, W.
- CHAPMAN, J.
- COOPER, J.
- CHANTLER, A. J.
- CHAPMAN, W.
- DAINES, H.
- DINNEN, R.
- DAVIES, S.
- DAWSON, C.
- DAVENPORT, W.
- DAGNALL, T. N.
- DELANY, C. M.
- EVANS, H.
- FOY, A.
- FULLER, —.
- GREEN, D.
- GRIFFITHS, F.
- GILLINGHAM, J.
- GREEN, W. H.
- GILL, S.
- GOUGH, H.
- GOULBOURNE, J.
- GAHAN, J.
- HAYES, F.
- HUGHES, S.
- HOLDEN, J.
- HOWARD, P.
- HARDMAN, J. W.
- HODGE, A.
- HULL, O.
- HITCHEN, J.
- JONES, I.
- JACKSON, A.
- JONES, H.
- JONES, I.
- JONES, J.
- JELLY, H.
- KELLY, W.
- KELLY, E.
- KAY, A.
- LLOYD, T.
- LANCASTER, J.
- LANG, P.
- MARTIN, E.
- MILLINGTON, J.
- MACDONALD, T.
- McALPINE, J.
- MURPHY, J.
- MOLLARD, E.
- MILLS, C.
- McKIE, T.
- MONKS, A.
- MORRISON, R.
- NELSON, E.
- OATES, T.
- OGDEN, K.
- PEARSON, J.
- PEARSON, E.
- PERCIVAL, E.
- ROACH, J.
- ROACH, A.
- REASON, J.
- ROWLINGS, F.
- ROBINSON, J. P.
- STEPHENSON, E.
- SUTTON, J.
- STANLEY, A.
- SHAW, J.
- SPROSTON, F.
- SYKES, H.
- SYKES, D.
- SKELTON, R.
- SHAW, H.
- STAINTON, F.
- SPENCER, R.
- SEDDON, T.
- SKEVENEY, F.
- SOUTHERN, R.
- SANGER, C.
- SMITH, J. D.
- TARR, S.
- THOMPSON, J.
- TILLEY, H.
- TATE, G.
- TOWERS, S. V.
- TOMKINSON, F.
- URMSON, C.
- VALENTINE, W.
- WOOLEY, A.
- WATSON, A.
- WRIGHT, S.
- WHARTON, W.
- WHELAN, J
- WEBSTER, S.
- WALSH, T.
- WILLIAMS, W.
- WILLIAMS, G. S.
- WINKLEY, H.
- WALKER, W.

Roll of Honour.

Haugk, von Zabern & Co.

24, Sackville Street,
Manchester.

HAROLD PICKERING.
Lancashire Fusiliers.
(Killed in Action at Gallipoli.)

WILLIAM EVANS.
17th Serv. Batt. Manchester Regt.

GEORGE S. GARBUTT.
17th Serv. Batt. Manchester Regt.

GEOFFREY LEATHER.
17th Serv. Batt. Manchester Regt.

JONATHAN H. BRADSHAW.
R.A.M.C., East Lancashire.

JOHN YATES.
3rd Manchester Regt.

REGINALD RUSSELL.
Royal Scots.

FREDERICK WOOD.
26th Batt. Manchester Regt.

FREDERICK MINSHULL.
Lancashire Fusiliers.

Roll of Honour.

S. Hinrichsen & Co.

24 Sackville Street,
Manchester.

CHAS. J. ARON.

FRED A. ARON.

WM. BURLEY.

RICHARD E. CLARKE.

JOSEPH COOPS.

JAS. E. COWLEY.

A. J. C. FRESHWATER.

DONALD F. HAY.

F. HEARDMAN.

ERNEST HEWITT.

FRED JOHNSON.

ROBT. H. JONES.

THOS. MILLICHAP.

A. E. POTTS.

JAS. RILEY.

WM. RAYSON.

ED. SHERRATT.

ROLL OF HONOUR

Heynssen, Martienssen & Co.,
MANCHESTER.

List of men who have joined up:

Private W. BATTEY	20th Ser. Batt. Manchester Regt.
Trooper W. J. BRINDLE	3rd Cheshire Yeomanry.
Bombardier J. CALDWELL	2nd East Lancs. Royal Field Artillery.
Gunner F. COOPER	2nd East Lancs. Royal Field Artillery.
Private A. COLLINGE	6th Batt. Manch. Regt. (T.F.), Killed.
Private J. CONEY	Royal Army Medical Corps.
Private A. DAVIES	6th Batt. Manchester Regt. (T.F.).
Private E. DARBYSHIRE	Royal Army Medical Corps.
Private G. DOBSON	Prince of Wales Own W. Riding Rgt.
Private H. FRASER	6th Batt. Manchester Regt. (T.F.).
Lance-Corpl. A. GIDLEY	9th King's Shropshire Light Infantry.
Private J. HUDSON	6th Batt. Manchester Regt. (T.F.).
L.-Corpl. H. JOHNSON (killed)	21st Ser. Batt. Manchester Regt.
Corporal T. JONES	6th Batt. Manchester Regt. (T.F.).
Private H. KAY	16th Ser. Batt. Manchester Regt.
Private WALTER KAY	21st Batt. Royal Fusiliers.
Private W. O'NEILL	7th Batt. Manchester Regt. (T.F.).
Private G. PALIN	6th Batt. Manchester Regt. (T.F.).
Private H. PARKER	18th Ser. Batt. Manchester Regt.
Private A. PETTY	Royal Army Med. Corps, Transport.
Private H. PIMLOTT	10th Batt. King's Royal Rifles.
Driver H. ROWLANDS	2nd East Lancs. Royal Field Artillery.
Private W. O. SMITH	6th Batt. Manchester Regt. (T.F.).
Driver S. TAFT	2nd East Lancs. Royal Field Artillery.
Sergeant T. WALKER	16th Ser. Batt. Manchester Regt.
Private F. WILLIAMS	8th Argyle & Sutherland Highlanders.
Bandmn. A. WORTHINGTON	28th Batt. Royal Fusiliers.

ROLL OF HONOUR.

List of Employees of

Thos. G. Hill & Co. Ltd.,
MANCHESTER,

Who have enlisted, and now serving with the colours.

*

Sec. Lieut. J. P. CARRINGTON	Royal Welsh Fusiliers.
Corpl. H. CARR	6th Lancashire Fusiliers.
Corpl. J. H. HITCHENS	5th Cheshires.
Corpl. A. SLATFORD	13th Manchesters.
L. Corpl. H. HOWCROFT	5th Cheshires.
Private J. R. WALLACE	R.A.M.C.
Private H. WILKINSON	Pals, 20th Manchesters.
Private E. P. ROBERTS	Pals, 18th Manchesters.
Private M. ROGERS	Pals, 20th Manchesters.
Private J. BAILEY	Pals, 20th Manchesters.
Private F. HYDE	Pals, 20th Manchesters.
Private A. WALKER	Pals, 20th Manchesters.
Private E. M. WILLIAMS	Pals, 22nd Manchesters.
Private A. READ	Pals, 21st Manchesters.
Private V. J. WEST	Royal Fusiliers.
Private G. NIXON	Lancashire Fusiliers.
Private F. PARKINSON	R.A.M.C.
Private A. HAND	27th Manchesters.
Corpl. G. CARROLL	R.E., Motor Cyclist Section.
Trooper H. HOULDSWORTH	Cheshire Yeomanry.
Private P. ELDING	9th K.S.L.I.
Private R. SHAW	16th Lancashire Fusiliers.
Private A. POWELL	Royal Marine Artillery.
Cadet J. MORRISON	Victoria University O.T.C.
Cadet H. BLACKSTOCK	Victoria University O.T.C.
3rd Writer H. INNERDALE	H.M.S. "Victory," Royal Navy.
Private J. KERSHAW	25th Manchesters (Reserve).

Roll of Honour.

KAY and LEE Ltd.

17, High Street, Manchester
AND
Perseverance Mills, Allum Street.

BOOTH, G. H.	DIXON, H.
BRIDGE, G.	GANNON, P.
BROTHERTON, J.	†GODWIN, J.
BROUGHTON, H.	§LEE, W. H.
BURKE, M.	LEES, A.
*CLIMO, J.	MASKELL, T.
DAVIES, W.	RUSCOE, C.
DAY, ALBERT	STANWAY, J.
DAY, ARTHUR	WARD, E. O.

* Killed in action in the Dardanelles, June 4th, 1915.
† Killed in action in France, October 13th, 1915.
§ Killed in action in Gallipoli, December 25th, 1915.

ROLL OF HONOUR.

I. KRIEGSFELD,

BRIDGEWATER RUBBER WORKS,

GREENGATE, SALFORD.

J. ANDERSON.	Z. MAYBLOOM.
ARTHUR BARRATT.	R. POVEY.
W. BESWICK.	A. THORP.
A. COOKE.	W. TOOLE.
P. CLAYTON.	F. THOMPSON.
E. DAVIS.	A. WOOLLEY.
H. FOSTER.	C. WILD.
P. GLENNON.	H. WILCOCK.
W. GRISDALE.	A. LUKE.
M. MORTIMER, Senr.	M. LYNCH.
M. MORTIMER, Junr.	J. HANWAY.

Roll of Honour.

Members of Kidsons, Taylor & Co.'s
Staff who are serving with His Majesty's Forces.

Private C. H. C. CHOWN,
London Rifle Brigade.

Private H. COCKER,
9th Bt. King's Shropshire Light Infantry.

Sapper W. N. DIAPER,
Royal Engineers, East Lancs.

Private J. GRINDROD,
19 S.B.M.R.

Private M. HART,
R.A.M.C.

Lieutenant A. G. HEWATT,
East Surrey Regiment.

2nd Lieut. E. L. JONES,
Loyal North Lancs.

Private W. V. PERRY,
22 S.B.M.R.

Driver S. POOLE,
3/1 Essex Battery R.F.A.

Private GEO. SCHOFIELD,
19 S.B.M.R.

Private HARRY TWEEDALE,
Royal Marine Submarine Miners.

Private P. WELLS,
6th Manchesters (T.F.).

ROLL OF HONOUR.

George Leek & Sons, LIMITED.
Hope Street Foundry, Salford, Manchester.

H. LEEK,
Lancashire Fusiliers.

G. WHARFE,
Lancashire Fusiliers.

E. BAIRD,
Lancashire Fusiliers.

H. SMALLMAN,
Lancashire Fusiliers.

W. BREHENY,
Lancashire Fusiliers.

F. LANGHORNE,
Border Regiment.

R. JONES,
South Wales Borderers.

W. EDMUNDS,
King's Own Royal Rifles.

R. MORRIS,
Royal Army Medical Corps.

J. McMAHON,
Royal Irish Rifles.

S. OLDHAM,
Royal Irish Rifles.

G. GRIFFITHS,
Manchester Regiment.

D. ALLCOCK,
Royal Field Artillery.

T. WARD,
Royal Engineers.

J. WALLWORK.
W. BEATTIE.
J. H. EAVES.
P. TRAYNOR.
J. BARLOW.
J. J. NORRIS.

Roll of Honour

J. & E. LICHTENSTEIN LIMITED,

Gordon Street Works, Broughton,

MANCHESTER.

M. BLACK.

N. BRAMWORTH.

F. DOBSON.

H. FINKLESTEIN.

J. FISH.

J. GERSHON.

L. HARRIS.

H. HEATON.

H. LEVI.

J. LEWIS.

S. PAYMAN.

L. ROSE.

G. SHEARER.

A. SMITH.

H. VAUGHAN.

B. WEILOW.

B. WILKS.

ROLL OF HONOUR.

✱ ✱ ✱

Thos. Livesey & Son

Cotton Manufacturers,
Bridge Mill, Pendleton

A. JACK,
　1st Leinster Regiment.

J. POOLE,
　Royal Field Artillery.

J. SCOTSON,
　2/5th Lancashire Fusiliers.

W. LAMBERT,
　23rd Serv. Batt. Manchester Regiment.

T. HOWARTH,
　16th Serv. Batt. Lancashire Fusiliers.

J. BRIERLEY.
　3/7th Lancashire Fusiliers (T.).

E. DOOLEY,
　19th Serv. Batt. Lancashire Fusiliers.

D. DITCHFIELD,
　19th Serv. Batt. Lancashire Fusiliers.

H. AINSWORTH,
　2/7th Lancashire Fusiliers (T.).

T. BROE,
　3/7th Lancashire Fusiliers (T.).

W. RUSSELL,
　3/1st East Lancs. R. Engineers (T.).

Roll of Honour.

HENRY MARCHINGTON,

68, Mosley Street,
Manchester.

2nd Lieut. DOUGLAS ADAMS,
14th Royal Fusiliers.

Corpl. GEORGE MITCHELL,
2nd Manchester Regiment.

L.-Corpl. WILLIAM DALY,
Royal Irish Fusiliers.

L.-Corpl. ARCHER SEARLE HOYE,
" B " Co., 16th Manchester Regt.

L.-Corpl. WILLIAM LOMAS,
" B " Co., 16th Manchester Regt.

Private BERTRAM COX,
King's Own Royal Lancashire Regt.
(Killed in Battle of the Aisne.)

Driver WALTER GIBBS,
East Lancashire R.F. Territorials, 42nd Division.

ROLL OF HONOUR.

* * *

B. Muratti, Sons & Co.,
LIMITED,

Whitworth Street, Manchester.

T. MADDOX.

E. PROCOPIDES.

G. HODGINS.*

J. WEATE.

G. JACKSON.

J. LEAVY.

F. OUSEY.

F. SUTTON.

A. HODGES (R.A.M.C.—Home).

Sergt. HOWARD.

* Killed in action.

ROLL OF HONOUR.

NASMYTH, WILSON & CO. LTD.

Locomotive and Hydraulic Engineers,

BRIDGEWATER FOUNDRY, PATRICROFT,

MANCHESTER.

H. J. Alger.	A. Clarke.	W. Fearneough.
C. Appleton.	W. Clarke.	H. Ferns.
S. T. Arnott.	T. Clayton.	T. Freeman.
H. Ashton.	J. Clements.	W. Fryatt.
C. Aulie.	J. Clutterbuck.	W. Golding.
C. J. Bamford.	J. J. Coffey.	Thomas Grayson.
A. Band.	W. Cooper.	T. W. Green.
A. Brannagan.	J. Cowan.	J. W. Griffiths.
T. J. Bell.	E. L. Cowley.	T. Griffiths.
A. Bennett.	G. H. Crane.	J. Hawkins.
W. J. Bennett.	J. Croft.	G. Hatton.
J. Blackwell.	E. Dale.	J. Henshaw.
Leigh Blears.	B. Darby.	J. Hamer.
J. Bossons.	F. Davies.	F. Holding.
A. Bowker.	G. A. Dentith.	A. Haden.
W. Bowker.	W. Drinkle.	B. Harrison.
H. Bradwell.	*T. Duffy.	H. Hampson.
S. Britch.	E. Dunn.	S. Hamilton.
H. Bronson.	*E. Dyson.	A. Hardie.
F. G. Brooksbank.	J. S. Edmundson.	H. Harding.
A. E. Brown.	H. Edwards.	J. Hesford.
J. Brown.	H. W. Eggington.	W. Hesketh.
H. Burbridge.	E. Eggleston.	G. Horner.
F. Burgess.	S. Ellis.	E. Houghton.
W. Burrows.	C. M. L. Everett.	C. Howard.
J. Burns.	T. Fallows.	T. Jameson.
A. Clare.	Jos. Farrell.	

* Killed or died on active service.

ROLL OF HONOUR—Continued.

NASMYTH, WILSON & CO. LTD.

James Johnson.
J. H. Johnson.
H. Jones.
Jno. Jones.
W. Kelly.
C. Kennils.
W. J. Kirwin.
W. Knight.
E. E. Lawson.
F. Leeson.
W. Leish.
P. Long.
J. McCormick.
H. McNiell.
D. Madden.
H. Marsh.
W. H. Martin.
E. Massey.
E. Meadows.
A. H. Moore.
S. Morris.
J. Morrison.
*W. T. Murphy.
T. Murtagh.
P. T. Nicholls.
T. Nicholls.
G. Nuttall.
H. Oakes.
J. C. Oldfield.
C. Orr.

J. Patten.
J. Pennington.
F. Percival.
L. Perry.
F. Pilling.
A. Pinnington.
J. Platt.
J. Pollitt.
T. Priest.
J. Radford.
H. Rangeley.
W. H. Ratcliffe.
H. Rawlinson.
J. W. Rigby.
J. Riley.
Jno. Ritchie.
A. Rogers.
T. Roberts.
J. Robinson.
R. Royle.
A. Royle.
T. W. Russell.
H. D. Shawcross.
R. Schofield.
J. E. Scott.
T. Scott.
W. Seddon.
J. Sharples.
J. Sheldon.
J. Sidebotham.

F. Simpson.
J. Simpson.
J. Skeech.
J. Sloane.
J. H. Smith.
W. H. Stanley.
T. Stanton.
B. Stockey.
J. Stockey.
*C. Stell.
S. Streets.
W. Stott.
Chas Taylor.
J. Tonge.
J. Tillbrook.
A. H. Timperley.
P. Turner.
A. E. Twigg.
Edward Twigg.
F. Unsworth.
F. Unsworth.
J. Valentine.
J. Walton.
P. Ward.
G. Westbrook.
H. Wharmby.
A. Whitehead.
W. Williamson.
*E. Wilson.
E. Yates.

* Killed or died on active service.

ROLL OF HONOUR.

James E. Ogden & Sons Ltd.

New Bridge Street,
MANCHESTER.

Corporal FRANK SCOTT,
  New Zealand Contingent

Corporal TOM R. DALE,
  1/6th Manchester Regt. (T.F.).

Private ROBERT PRESTON,
  1/7th Manchester Regt. (T.F.).

Private WILLIAM GRIMSHAW,
  18th Serv. Batt. Manchester Regt.

Lce.-Corp. EDWARD LIDBETTER,
  19th Serv. Batt. Manchester Regt.

Private FRED EASTWOOD,
  2/8th Batt. Manchester Regt.

Private JOHN KAY,
  2/6th Lancashire Fusiliers.

Private ARTHUR BAILEY,
  Royal Scots.

Private B. BELLINI,
  Royal Garrison Artillery.

Roll of Honour.

G. B. Ollivant & Co. Ltd.

3, Albert Street,
MANCHESTER

Private H. DIMELOW, 6486,
  D. Co., 16th Ser. Batt.
    Manchester Regt.

Drummer A. GRIFFITHS, 6991,
  D. Co., 16th Ser. Batt.
    Manchester Regt.

Lance-Corpl. W. MIEN, 6527,
  5th Pl. B. Co., 16th Ser. Batt.
    Manchester Regt.

Private J. MacMAHON, 6521,
  B. Co., 16th Ser. Batt.
    Manchester Regt.

Private J. McKENZIE, 634,
  R.A.M.C.

Lance-Corpl. C. NIXON, 17/8773,
  B. Co., 17th Ser. Batt.
    Manchester Regt.

Private F. POTTER, 6554,
  Signal Section, 90th Brigade
    (Headquarters).

Private H. T. RATCLIFFE, 7485,
  B. Co., 5th Pl., 19th Batt.
    Royal Fusiliers.

Private J. SMITH, 6557,
  B. Co., 16th Ser. Batt.
    Manchester Regt.

Private E. V. VLIES, 9457,
  B. Co. 8th Pl., 17th Ser. Batt.
    Manchester Regt.

Driver H. F. VOSE, 159838,
  Base Horse Transport Depot,
    Army Service Corps.

Roll of Honour.

✶

Paterson, Zochonis & Co.,
LIMITED,
42 Whitworth Street, Manchester.

✶

Corporal Frank Entwisle,
  Manchester Regiment (T.F.)
Private Edward Grimshaw,
  Manchester Regiment (T.F.)
Private Arthur Whitnall,
  Manchester Regiment (Pals).
Private Fred. Whittaker,
  Manchester Regiment (Pals).
Private Frank Holt,
  Manchester Regiment (Pals).
Private G. W. Careswell,
  Manchester Regiment (Pals).
Private Arthur Windle,
  Manchester Regiment (Pals).
Gunner Harold Nickson,
  Territorials R.F.A.
Private James Chrystal,
  East Lancashire Regiment.
Private William Wilson,
  Royal Engineers.
Private R. C. R. Robinson,
  E. of C. Yeomanry.
Private James Goodwin,
  Legion of Frontiersmen.
Private Leonard Hayes,
  Sportsman's Battalion (Royal Fusiliers).
Private Thomas Spencer,
  Royal Army Medical Corps.

Roll of Honour.

Paulsen, Kóedt & Co.
2 Fairfield Street,
Manchester

Pte. F. R. Hodgson,
  19th Royal Fusiliers
    (Public School Batt.).

✶

Pte. Joseph Wallworth,
  9th King's Shropshire Light Infantry.

✶

Pte. Austin Armitage,
  Royal Marine Artillery.

✶

Pte. W. H. Wilks,
  9th Royal Scots.

ROLL OF HONOUR.

ROYCE LIMITED,
TRAFFORD PARK, MANCHESTER.

Employees who have Enlisted.

ANDREW, J. J.	7th Batt. East Lancs. "C" Company.
BAILEY, J. H.	1st Cheshire Yeomanry.
BINNS, N. H.	King's Own Royal Lanc.
BISHOP, T. W.	1st Field Co. East Lancs. Royal Engineers.
BRIDGE, C. K.	King's Own Royal Lanc.
BRIDGES, J.	Loyal North Lancs.
BROOMHEAD, J.	No. 2 Coy. A.S.C.
BROWN, J.	8th Manchesters.
BROWNE, H. P.	Royal Scots.
BURGESS, S.	7th Batt. East Lancs.
COTTAM, F. A.	13th Batt. "D" Coy. Lancashire Fusiliers.
COWELL, J.	Royal Engineers.
CHARNLEY, W.	Royal Flying Corps.
DAVIES, W. H.	19th Batt. "C" Co. Royal Welsh Fusiliers.
DOHERTY, H.	Royal Scottish Fusiliers.
DOOLAN, J.	Manchesters.
DOYLE, T. J.	National Res. E. Lancs. Division.
FERGUSON, W.	R.A.M.C.
FISHER, H.	"B" Co. Lancs. Fusiliers.
FOSTER, G.	6th Batt. Inniskillen Fus.
FOXCROFT, W.	18th Hussars.
GILSON, W.	Duke of Lancaster's Own Yeomanry.
HARTLEY, F.	1st Field Coy. E. Lancs. Royal Engineers.
HOME, J.	Pendleton Batt. Lancs. Fusiliers.
HORNER, W. R.	2/7th Manchester Regt.
JACKSON, T.	East Lancs. Royal En'rs.
JONES, A. E.	10th Batt. South Lancs.
KERSHAW, W. H.	Royal Irish.
LAPPIN, W. J.	8th Manchesters.
LORD, J.	5th Cheshires.
MASON, T.	6th Cheshires.
MATHER, A. B.	12th Service Batt. King's Liverpool.
MATHER, J.	Royal Irish Rifles.
McDONALD, J.	Loyal North Lancs.
McKNIGHT, J.	8th Manchesters.
McMILLAN, A.	8th Lancashire Fusiliers, Transport Dept.
MELLOR, H.	1st Batt. Royal Scottish Fusiliers.
MILLHOUSE, A. P.	East Lancs. Royal En'rs.
MORGAN, J.	Welsh Fusiliers.
MORRIS, W.	Royal Navy.
ORAM, H.	15th Service Batt. Lancs. Fusiliers.
PILKINGTON, G.	Royal Navy.
RILEY, T. W.	Royal Naval Reserve.
RYAN, R.	7th Batt. "C" Coy. Rifle Brigade.
SCHOFIELD, C.	Royal Field Artillery.
SHAW, T. H.	Lancs. Fusiliers.
SIMMS, R.	Lanc. Fusiliers, Bantams.
SLATER, R. A.	Army Service Corps.
TURNER, A.	3rd Batt. Lancs. Fusiliers.
WAGSTER, S.	Duke of Lancaster's Own Yeomanry.
WARREN, F.	5th Cheshires.
WIGHT, J.	6th Cheshires.
WILLIAMS, R. S.	Royal Flying Corps.
WOOLLEY, A.	9th Batt. Lancs. Fusiliers.
WORSLEY, W. S.	East Lancs. Royal Engs.

ROLL OF HONOUR.

Redpath, Brown & Co. Limited.

Edinburgh Staff.

Gnr. BLYTH J.	- - - -	Royal Field Artillery.
Driv. BROWNLEE W.	-	Royal Field Artillery.
Pte. CAMERON G.	- - -	9th Batt. Royal Scots.
Sgt. GRAY J.	- - - -	5th Batt. Royal Scots.
Cpl. KINNEAR W.	- - -	Black Watch.
Pte. McDOUGAL A.	- -	Black Watch.
L. Cpl. McMILLAN R.	-	5th Batt. Royal Scots.
Pte. MILNE A.	- - - -	Lochiel's Cameron Hghlrs.
Pte. PORTEOUS J.	- - -	6th Batt. Royal Scots.
Pte. RITCHIE, G.	- - -	Royal Army Medical Corps.
Sec. Lt. SIMPSON J. C.	-	4th Batt. Royal Scots.
Sec. Lt. WALLACE A.	-	8th Batt. Royal Scots.

Edinburgh Works.

Pte. ALLAN W.	- - - -	16th Ser. Batt. Royal Scots.
Pte. ANGUS D. R.	- - -	7th Batt. Royal Scots.
Pte. ANGUS J.	- - - -	16th Batt. Royal Scots.
Pte. BAIN P.	- - - -	1st Batt. Royal Scots.
Gnr. BARCLAY D.	- - -	Royal Garrison Artillery.
A.B. BARRON H.	- - -	R.F.R. H.M.S. "Majestic."
Pte. BLACKIE T.	- - -	Arg. & Suth. Highlanders.
Pte. BOW J.	- - - -	16th Ser. Batt. Royal Scots.
Pte. BRIEN E.	- - - -	9th Batt. Royal Scots.
Pte. BRIEN W.	- - - -	Gordon Highlanders
Pte. BROCK R.	- - - -	16th Batt. Royal Scots.
Pte. CAIRNS C.	- - -	7th Batt. Royal Scots.
Instructor CAMPBELL K.-		13th Ser. Batt. Royal Scots.
Pte. CAVANAGH M.	- -	9th Batt. Gordon Highlrs.
Pte. COATS J.	- - - -	9th Batt. Royal Scots.
Drmr. CONNOLY R.	- -	9th Batt. Royal Scots.
SAP. COSSINS A.	- - -	Royal Engineers.
Pte. CUMMING S.	- - -	Lovat's Scouts.
Bglr. CUMMING T.	- -	7th Batt. Royal Scots.
Pte. DALGLEISH J.	- - -	3rd Royal Naval Division.
Pte. DALRYMPLE J.	- -	Black Watch.
Pte. DAVIDSON C.	- -	Scottish Horse.
Pte. DEMPSTER G.	- - -	16th Batt. Royal Scots.
Pte. EASTERN J.	- - -	Royal Field Artillery.
Pte. FAIRLEY E.	- - -	16th Ser. Batt. Royal Scots.
Pte. FERGUSON C.	- - -	4th Royal Scots.
Pte. FERGUSON J.	- - -	Gordon Highlanders.
Pte. FERGUSON M.	- -	7th Batt. Royal Scots.
Pte. FRASER C.	- - - -	Highland Light Infantry.
Pte. FRASER HOMER	-	7th Batt. Royal Scots.
Pte. FRASER HUGH	- -	Gordon Highlanders.
Pte. DALE J.	- - - -	13th Hussars.
Pte. GALLAGHER J.	- -	Highland Light Infantry
Pte. GILBERTSON E.	- -	7th Batt. Royal Scots.
Pte. GILBERSTON H.	- -	5th Dragoon Guards.
Pte. GILBERTSON J.	-	7th Batt. Royal Scots.
Pte. GRAHAM J.	- - -	16th Batt. Royal Scots.
Pte. GRAHAM R.	- - -	Royal Army Medical Corps.
Pte. GRANT J.	- - - -	16th Ser. Batt. Royal Scots.
Pte. GULLAND F.	- - -	Royal Garrison Artillery.

ROLL OF HONOUR—continued.

REDPATH, BROWN & CO. LIMITED.

Edinburgh Works—continued.

Pte. HANLEY D.	Black Watch.
Pte. HARDIE T.	K.O. Scottish Borderers.
Pte. HENDERSON R.	Gordon Highlanders.
Pte. HENDRIE J.	7th Batt. Royal Scots.
Gnr. HORSLEY R.	Royal Garrison Artillery.
Gnr. INGLIS J.	Royal Fleet Res. Chatham.
Band. KEENAN W.	9th Batt. Royal Scots.
Pte. KELLY J.	16th Ser. Batt. Royal Scots.
Pte. KIRK J.	7th Batt. Royal Scots.
Pte. LAING P.	16th Ser. Batt. Royal Scots.
Pte. LATIMER A.	7th Batt. Royal Scots.
Pte. LATTOE J.	9th Batt. Royal Scots.
Gnr. LEGGAT A.	Royal Field Artillery.
Pte. LIDDELL G.	7th Batt. Royal Scots.
Pte. McCOLL T.	15th Ser. Batt. Royal Scots.
Stkr. McCOMBE J.	R.F.R. H.M.S. "Cyclops."
Pte. McKAY D.	Royal Naval Reserve.
L.-Cpl. McKAY G.	7th Batt. Royal Scots.
Pte. McKAY H.	7th Batt. Royal Scots.
Pte. McKAY, W.	4th Batt. Royal Scots.
Pte. McKINNEY S.	Edin. Batt. Royal Scots.
Gnr. McLEAN J.	Royal Garrison Artillery.
Pte. McQUEENIE T.	Gen. Service Special Res
Pte. MAIN R. Gnr.	16th Ser. Batt. Royal Scots.
L.-Cpl. MENNAMEN W.	7th Batt. Royal Scots.
Pte. MILLAR G.	16th Batt. Royal Scots.
Gnr. MOODIE A.	Royal Garrison Artillery.
Drmr. MOODIE J.	7th Batt. Royal Scots.
Pte. MONAGHAN J.	7th Batt. Royal Scots.
L.-Cpl. MORLEY T.	6th Batt. Royal Scots.
Pte. MORTON C.	2nd Seaforth Highlanders.
Pte. MORTON D.	16th Ser. Batt. Royal Scots.
Pte. MOYES W.	Scottish Horse.
Pte. NEIL C.	3rd Batt. A. & S. Hghlrs.
Pte. NICOL A.	7th Batt. Royal Scots.
Pte. O'BRIEN J.	7th Batt. Royal Scots.
Pte. O'NEILL J.	K.O. Scottish Borderers.
Pte. O. REILLY J.	Royal Dublin Fusiliers.
Pte. PERRILA D.	6th Batt. Royal Scots.
Pte. PRIEST H.	6th Batt. Royal Scots.
Driv. PRIOR G.	Lowland Div. Trans. Col.
Pte. REID A.	Gordon Highlanders.
Bglr. REID R.	6th Batt. Royal Scots.
Pte. RODGERS J.	Royal Field Artillery.
Pte. ROLLO J.	Second Life Guards.
Pte. ROSS W.	Lowland Div. Heavy Batty.
Pte. RUTHERFORD A.	7th Batt. Royal Scots.
Pte. RUTHERFORD R.	7th Batt. Royal Scots.
Pte. RUTHERFORD W.	7th Batt. Royal Scots.
Pte. SCOTLAND H.	16th Ser. Batt. Royal Scots.
Pte. SHAND W.	4th Batt. Royal Scots.
Pte. SIMPKINS C.	4th Batt. Royal Scots.
Pte. SMITH A.	16th Batt. Royal Scots.
Pte. SMITH J.	Arg. & Suth. Highlanders.
Pte. TAIT H.	7th Batt. Royal Scots.
Sap. THOMSON ADAM	Royal Engineers.
Driv. THOMSON ARTH.	Lowland Div. Trans. Col.
Corpl. TODD C.	2nd Batt. Royal Scots.
Pte. WEIR G.	Lowland Div. Heavy Batty.
Pte. WEIR W.	Lowland Div. Heavy Batty.
Pte. WEST W. T.	7th Batt. Royal Scots.
Gnr. WILSON D.	Royal Garrison Artillery.
Pte. WISHART J.	7th Batt. Royal Scots.
Pte. WYBURN P.	Royal Field Artillery.
Sgt. YOUNG G.	7th Batt. Royal Scots.

Glasgow Staff.

Sgt. JOHNSTON T.	6th Batt. Cameron Hghlrs.
Pte. LAW F. E.	5th Batt. Cameron Hghlrs.
Pte. LIDDELL R.	Queen's Own Cameron H.
Pet. Off. TEMPLEMAN D.	R.N. Volunteer Reserve.

Glasgow Works.

Pte. BELL J.	10th Batt. Seaforth Hghlrs.
Pte. BEATON D.	8th Batt. Roy. Scots Fus.
Pte. BROWN J.	9th Batt. Scottish Rifles.
Pte. CRAWLEY T.	8th Batt. Seaforth Hghlrs.
Pte. CORBETT J.	9th Batt. Scottish Rifles.
Pte. CORBETT JOHN	4th Batt. A. & S. Hghlrs.

ROLL OF HONOUR—continued.

REDPATH, BROWN & CO. LIMITED.

Glasgow Works—continued.

A.B. FERRIS J.	- - - -	H.M.S. "Prince George."
Sa. GILLAN W.	- - - -	72nd Coy. Royal Engineers.
Pte. GOW A.	- - - -	5th Batt. High. Light Inf.
Pte. HARKNESS J.	- - - -	64th Coy. Royal Engineers.
Band. JEFFERSON A.	- - - -	9th Bt. H.L.I. (Glas. Hdrs.).
Pte. MACDONALD J.	- - - -	3rd Seaforth Highlanders.
Pte. McCALLUM J.	- - - -	9th Batt. Seaforth Hghlrs.
Pte. McINROY J.	- - - -	7th Serv. Batt. R.S. Fus.
Pte. McATEER M.	- - - -	5th Batt. High. Light Inf.
Pte. McGRORY F.	- - - -	Royal Field Artillery.
Pte. MILLS J.	- - - -	Army Service Corps.
Pte. NIXON J.	- - - -	1st Glas. Batt. H.L.I.
Pte. RYAN T.	- - - -	Army Ordnance Corps.
Pte. STAFFORD T.	- - - -	1st Glas. Batt. H.L.I.
Pte. SPEIRS J.	- - - -	7th Batt. Roy. Scots Fus.
Pte. SMALL L.	- - - -	19th Batt. R.F.A.
Pte. SUTHERLAND J.	- - - -	Royal Field Artillery.

East Greenwich Staff.

Pte. BARRATT A.	- - - -	Royal West Kent Regt.
Cpl. BURNSIDE W.	- - - -	Seaforth Highlanders.
Pte. COLLINS A. F.	- - - -	Royal Engineers.
Pte. CRICKETT M. E.	- - - -	Royal Field Artillery.
Sap. DIXSON F.	- - - -	Royal Engineers.
Pte. GOWLETT	- - - -	3rd Dragoons.
Pte. HENDRY J. M.	- - - -	London Scottish.
Pte. SARGEANT L.	- - - -	3rd Dragoons.
Pte. WHIDDINGTON F. P.		R.N. Div. Engineers Unit.
Pte. YOUNG E. L.	- - - -	Royal Naval Division.
Pte. CLARK H.	- - - -	Army Service Corps.

East Greenwich Works.

Pte. ALLWRIGHT E.	- - - -	Royal Garrison Artillery.
Pte. ARNOTT J.	- - - -	Royal Fort Artillery.
Sap. BEAGLE S.	- - - -	Royal Engineers.
Sap. BILBY H.	- - - -	Royal Engineers.
Pte. BORELAND D.	- - - -	Gordon Highlanders.
Sap. BOYENS S.	- - - -	Royal Engineers.
Sap. BROOKER H.	- - - -	Royal Engineers.
Sap. BROOM E.	- - - -	Royal Engineers.
Pte. BROWN C.	- - - -	Army Service Corps.
Cpl. BURGESS G.	- - - -	Royal Fort Artillery.
Pte. CLARKE H. J.	- - - -	12th Lancers.
Pte. COLLEY J.	- - - -	Army Service Corps.
Pte. COLLINS M.	- - - -	Northamptonshire Regt.
Pte. DOWNES A.	- - - -	Royal West Kent Regt.
W.O. DOWNES J. L.	- - - -	W.E. H.M.S. "Revenge."
Stkr. EARLE W. C.	- - - -	Chatham Barracks.
Sap. ELLESTON E.	- - - -	Royal Engineers.
Pte. FROOMS H.	- - - -	Army Ordnance Corps.
Pte. FULLER J.	- - - -	Grenadier Guards.
Pte. GIBBS A. H.	- - - -	20th Co. of London Regt.
Cpl. GREGORY C. L.	- - - -	Army Service Corps.
Pte. HENDERSON A.	- - - -	Royal Garrison Artillery.
Pte. HENNING F.	- - - -	Royal West Kent Regt.
Pte. JOHNSTON J.	- - - -	Royal Garrison Artillery.
Pte. KEBBLE E.	- - - -	Royal Fort Artillery.
Pte. KEMP F.	- - - -	Royal Garrison Artillery.
Sap. KILLICK A.	- - - -	Royal Engineers.
Pte. KING C.	- - - -	Army Service Corps.
Sap. McCORMICK J.	- - - -	Royal Engineers.
Pte. McDONALD H.	- - - -	Royal Fort Artillery.
Stkr. McDONALD J. J.	- - - -	H.M.S. "Juno."
Pte. McEWEN J.	- - - -	Gordon Highlanders.
Pte. MILLER A.	- - - -	Middlesex Regiment.
Stkr. MURPHY W.	- - - -	H.M.S. "Edgar."
Pte. PEARCE W.	- - - -	Royal West Kent Regt.
Pte. POWELL J.	- - - -	Gordon Highlanders
Pte. QUILTER C.	- - - -	Royal Horse Artillery.
Pte. RAE D.	- - - -	Gordon Highlanders.
Sap. RAMSAY W.	- - - -	Royal Engineers.
Sap. RICHARDS R.	- - - -	Royal Engineers.
Pte. ROBERTS J.	- - - -	Middlesex Regiment.
Sap. ROBINSON G.	- - - -	Royal Engineers.
Pte. ROSIER P.	- - - -	Royal Field Artillery.
Pte. SCALES C.	- - - -	20th City of London Regt.

ROLL OF HONOUR—continued.

REDPATH, BROWN & CO. LIMITED.

East Greenwich Works—continued.

Sap. SCALES F.	- - -	Royal Engineers.
Pte. SCANLON C. A.	- -	Royal Field Artillery.
Sap. SCOGING G.	- - -	Royal Engineers.
Pte. SMITH H.	- - - -	Royal Field Artillery.
Pte. STANLEY C.	- - -	20th City of London Regt.
Pte. STARKEY A.	- - -	Royal Field Artillery.
Sgt. STEMP W.	- - - -	Royal Army Medical Corps.
Pte. STEWART J.	- - -	Gordon Highlanders.
Pte. TURNER W. T.	- - -	South Wales Borderers.
Sgt. WADE A.	- - - - -	Army Service Corps.
Pte. WALTERS S.	- - -	Royal Garrison Artillery.
Pte. WARBOYS T.	- - -	Royal Field Artillery.
Pte. WESTROPE G.	- -	Royal Field Artillery.
Sap. WATSON W.	- - -	Royal Engineers.

Manchester Staff.

Pte. ARNOLD C.	- - - -	Royal Garrison Artillery.
Sec. Lt. COWAN J. A.	- -	Queen's Roy. West Surreys.
Pte. CHRISTIAN M. R.	- -	20th Batt. Manchester Regt.
Pte. CLARKE J. A.	- - -	6th Batt. Manchester Regt.
Pte. DOWNS C J.	- - -	6th Manchester Regt.
Pte. DUNT R. W.	- - -	5th Manchester Regt.
Pte. FEACHNIE A.	- - -	19th Batt. Manchester Regt.
Cpl. GENESE R.	- - - -	6th Batt. Manchester Regt.
Pte. HOLLAND E.	- - -	6th Manchester Regt.
Pte. HUTCHINSON W.	-	Staffordshire Yeomanry.
Pte. JOHNSTONE T.	- -	6th Batt. Manchester Regt. (Wounded).
Pte. KAY H.	- - - - -	Warwickshire Yeomanry.
Pte. LOGAN A.	- - -	Royal Garrison Artillery.
Pte. MARTIN A.	- - -	Lancashire Fusiliers.
Pte. MURRAY N.	- - -	6th Manchester Regt.
Sap. NOBBS S.	- - - -	Royal Engineers.
Sgt. NOBLETT A.	- - -	East Lancashire Regt.
Pte. NORBURY E.	- - -	6th Manchester Regt.
Pte. PARKINSON J. A.	- -	Earl of Chester's Yeomanry.
Pte. ROBERTSHAW C.	- -	6th Manchester Regt.
Sgt. WORTON H.	- - -	7th Batt. Lancs. Fusiliers. (Wounded).

Manchester Works.

Pte. BATTY H.	- - - -	8th Lancashire Fusiliers. (Wounded).
Pte. BECK S.	- - - - -	Shropshire Light Infantry.
Pte. BOLTON J.	- - - -	Cheshire Regt. (Wounded).
Pte. BURGESS D.	- - -	Manchester Regiment.
Pte. COATES A. H.	- - -	Lancashire Fusiliers.
Pte. COOPER J.	- - - -	9th Rifle Brigade (Killed).
Driv. DRINKWATER A.	-	Royal Field Artillery. (Wounded).
Pte. FELLOWS S.	- - -	Royal Garrison Artillery. (Wounded).
Pte. HILTON L.	- - - -	8th Lancashire Fusiliers.
Pte. HOMER D.	- - - -	3rd Bt. Loyal North Lancs.
Pte. HUGHES J.	- - -	Lancashire Fusiliers.
Pte. HUGHES W.	- - -	9th Rifle Brigade.
Pte. JENNINGS G.	- - -	8th Lancashire Fusiliers.
Driv. JOHNSTON C.	- -	Royal Field Artillery.
Pte. LONGWORTHY H.	-	Rifle Brigade.
Pte. McCLENNON J.	- -	8th Lancashire Fusiliers.
Pte. NORBURY J. W.	-	1st Liverpool Regt. (Wounded).
Pte. PARKER F.	- - - -	11th Manchester Regt.
Pte. PRESTON F.	- - -	10th Bt. Loyal North Lancs. (Wounded).
Pte. PRICE W.	- - - -	East Lancashire Regt.
Pte. QUANN J.	- - - -	Manchester Regiment.
Pte. RANDALL R.	- - -	Loyal North Lancs.
Pte. SADLER T.	- - - -	11th Lancs. Fusiliers.
Pte. SPARKES J.	- - -	Manchester Regiment.
Pte. STEWART J.	- - -	A.S.C., Motor Transport.
Pte. TAYLOR F. C.	- - -	29th Brigade R.F.A.
Pte. TAYLOR W.	- - -	3rd Lancs. Fusiliers. (Wounded).
Pte. THOMPSON R.	- -	Lancashire Fusiliers.
Pte. YATES J.	- - - - -	7th Lancs. Fusiliers. (Killed).

ROLL OF HONOUR

RITCHIE & EASON,

26 Dickinson Street, Manchester.

Lieut. E. A. EASON	Cheshire Yeomanry.
Lieut. R. HASHIM, D.C.M.	Joined 6th Manchesters, since received Commission in the 2/7 Cheshires.
Private J. WOODROFFE	1/7th Lancashire Fusiliers.
Private E. H. DAWBER	A.S.C. (Transport Supply Column).
Private R. E. BRUNTON	16th Batt. Manchester Regt. (Pals).
Private J. HUGHES	16th Batt. Manchester Regt. (Pals).
Sergeant F. WIMBURY	18th Batt. Manchester Regt. (Pals).
Private J. MARTIN	6th Manchester Regt. (T.F.).
Private C. WHITTLE	Royal Scots.
Private F. MILLER	Royal Scots.
Private L. HART	Army Service Corps.
Private E. GERRARD	Mechanical Transport.
Private F. SPEDDING	Royal Field Artillery.
Private W. BEVERLEY	Royal Army Medical Corps.
Private E. HODGSON	Argyle and Sutherland.
Private E. HUGHES	Army Service Corps.
Lance-Corpl. H. HENSHALL	Middlesex Regiment.
Private C. WILSON	7th Manchester Regiment.
Private J. BROMAGE	Regiment not known.

ROLL OF HONOUR

Renshaw & Barrow

52, Princess Street,
—MANCHESTER—

List of Employees who have enlisted.

2nd Lieut. GERALD W. S. FRANKLIN,
7th Batt. Manchester Regiment.

Bombardier V. ASHTON,
30th Siege Battery, Royal Gar. Artillery.

Private JOHN PARSONAGE,
7th Batt. Manchester Regiment.

Private A. KEATES,
Machine Gun Section,
20th Manchester Regiment.

Private W. MACKAY,
21st Batt. Manchester Regiment.

Private JOSEPH JUDGE,
8th Batt. Lancashire Fusiliers.

Private JOHN M. BEE,
9th Batt. Manchester Regiment.

Private S. POOLE,
4th Batt. Royal Scots,
Queen's Edin. Rifles.

Private REG. S. HOPKINS,
6th Batt. Manchester Regiment.

ROLL OF HONOUR.

G. Roskill and Co.,

20, CHEPSTOW STREET.

2nd Lieut. W. G. ROSKILL.
Lieut. E. D. MATHER.
Private JOHN BAGULEY.
Private ALFRED R. CRAVEN.
Private F. DAVIES.
Private H. HAWTHORN.
Private SIDNEY JONES.
Private REGINALD G. LAWTON.
Private WILFRID RUSSELL.
Sergeant EDWARD THOMAS.
Private ALBERT WILLIAMS.
Private JOHN HARRY BEBBINGTON.
Private WILLIAM HENRY BUCKLEY.
Private EDGAR CAWTHRAW.
Private CLIFFORD CHISWELL.
Corporal CLIFFORD DAWSON.
Private GILBERT VINT PARKINSON.
Private J. RICHARDSON (Wounded).
Private WILLIAM ASHWORTH.
Private ARTHUR HAYWARD.
Private THOMAS MELIA (Killed).
Corporal R. M. S. BRUCE.
Corporal J. CARMICHAEL.
Private ARTHUR CALVERT.
Signaller ERIC CAWTHRAW.
Private JOSEPH CULLENANE.
Rifleman JAMES FILDES (Wounded).
Private — GILLAND.
Private JOSEPH GATELEY.
Private THOMAS PROPHET (Wounded).
Gunner THOMAS PARKER.
Private JAMES EDWARD RENSHAW.
Private CHARLES REES.
Private SYLVESTER SIMPKINS.
Driver ARTHUR SHAW.
Private C. SHAW.
Private CLIFFORD SHARPLES.
Gunner OLIVER WHITE.
Private DONALD GORDON WHITTAKER.
Private — WHITTLE.
Driver THOMAS WALSH.
Gunner WILLIAM WALKER.

ROLL OF HONOUR

G. I. Sidebottom & Co.,

12, CHORLTON STREET, MANCHESTER.

Thomas Hibberd	8th Lancashire Fusiliers (T.F.).
Corporal Ernest Makin	25th (Res.) Manchester Regt. (Pals).
William E. L. Shields	Royal Field Artillery.
R.Q.M.S. Franklin W. Horsley	101st Canadians.
Frank Kirk	4th Batt. (Res.) Royal Scots.
J. W. Gifford	23rd Manchesters (Pals).
Germain Dieltiens	Belgian Army.
Frank Crossley	Canadians (Cycle Corps).
F. Stanley Carden	Sea Scouts.
William C. Fay	Royal Field Artillery.

Roll of Honour.

C. E. Samuels & Co.,
MANCHESTER.

Captain Kenneth Waterhouse,
2/5th Lanc. Fusiliers (T.F.).

*

L.-Corpl. J. E. Entwistle,
25th Serv. Batt. Man. Regt.

*

Private H. Shaw,
1/6th Manchester Regt. (T.F.).

*

Private W. Warhurst,
2/6th Manchester Regt. (T.F.)

*

Private S. Andrew (4385),
30th Royal Fusiliers.

Roll of Honour.

Paul Susmann & Co.
MANCHESTER.

Lieut. F. Grey Burn,
7th Batt. Manchester Regt. (T.F.).

Sergt. Ernest Sorton,
6th Batt. Manchester Regt. (T.F.).
(Killed in action in the Dardanelles, June 5th, 1915.)

Private Frank Brierley,
6th Batt. Manchester Regt. (T.F.).

Private George Thomas Owen,
16th Service Batt. Manchester Regt.

Private Ernest Tattersall,
16th Service Batt. Manchester Regt.

Private Harry Billsborough,
16th Service Batt. Manchester Regt.

Private Harry George Hermon,
17th Service Batt. Manchester Regt.

Private Frederick Cowley,
18th Service Batt. Manchester Regt.

Private Frank Green,
18th Service Batt. Manchester Regt.

Private Richard Griffiths,
19th Service Batt. Manchester Regt.

Roll of Honour.

Sutcliffe and Bingham,
Limited,

"KKOVAH" WORKS,

Manchester.

2nd Lieut. HAROLD SUTCLIFFE,
  East Lancs. Royal Engineers.
Sergeant W. SCOTT,
  2nd Cavalry, A.S.C.
Corporal J. SHAWCROSS,
  1st/5th Man. Transport Sect.
Private W. PLUMMER,
  16th Service Batt. Man. Regt.
Private E. JONES,
  19th Service Batt. Man. Regt.
Private T. WARBURTON,
  Royal Army Medical Corps.
Private R. LLOYD,
  Royal Army Medical Corps.
Private W. NEWMAN,
  3rd/8th Manchester Regt.
Private E. SHARPLES,
  3rd/8th Manchester Regt.
Private J. HAMLETT,
  Royal Marines.
Private J. BACON,
  Army Service Corps.
Private A. KIRKWOOD,
  Royal Army Medical Corps.
Private W. E. COYSH,
  London Scottish Regiment.

Roll of Honour.

W. Sutcliffe & Son

Egerton Street, Hulme,
MANCHESTER.

Office.

E. G. GOUGH,
2/6th Territorials, Manchester Regt.
W. A. HULME,
4th Manchester Regiment.
M. A. JOHNSTONE,
R.A.M.C.
A. E. WRIGHT,
Earl of Chester's Yeomanry.

Mill.

J. ADDISON,
2/7th Territorials Manchester Regt.
A. CALLAGHAN.
J. GRAINGER.
H. HOLT,
6th Border Regiment.
P. HANCOCK,
Shropshire Light Infantry.
T. HATTON,
8th Manchester Regiment.
C. LINETON.
E. J. LOWE, R.A.M.C.
W. MILNER.
H. OWEN, Rifle Brigade.
W. RACKSTRAW,
5th Cheshire Territorials.
P. REGAN.

ROLL OF HONOUR.

✱ ✱ ✱

THRELFALL'S BREWERY COMPANY
LIMITED.
- MANCHESTER -

✱ ✱ ✱

ANDERSON, T. - - - Lancashire Fusiliers.	RAVENSCROFT, H. V. 18th Bt. Manchester Regt.
ASPINALL, S. - - - - Lancashire Fusiliers.	WORSWICK, C. - - - 15th Lancashire Fusiliers.
BORDERS, J., D.C.M. - King's Liverpool Regt.	JOHNSON, G. - - - - 15th Lancashire Fusiliers.
CHAPMAN, H. - - - 7th Lancashire Fusiliers.	FROST, C. - - - - - 16th Lancashire Fusiliers.
COLEMAN, T. - - - - 10th Hampshires.	HILLARY, W. - - - - 13th Lancashire Fusiliers.
HARRISON, H. - - - 8th Lancashire Fusiliers.	GRUNDY, H. - - - - 16th Lancashire Fusiliers.
KINGHAM, W. - - - 8th Manchester Regt.	HADFIELD, M. - - - Army Service Corps.
LANGLEY, W. - - - - 10th Hampshires.	SHAW, J. - - - - - - 15th Lancashire Fusiliers.
PARRY, T. - - - - - 7th Lancashire Fusiliers.	HOLLINGSWORTH, W. 8th Lancashire Fusiliers.
PHELAN, J. - - - - - 8th Lancashire Fusiliers.	SKEVY, W. - - - - - 8th Lancashire Fusiliers.
PROBERT, D. - - - - Lancashire Fusiliers.	LEATHER, F. - - - - 16th Lancashire Fusiliers.
PERKINS, J. - - - - Royal Engineers.	BADHAM, W. - - - - Royal Field Artillery.
TAGGART, J. - - - - 10th Hampshires.	PAUL, W. - - - - - 16th Lancashire Fusiliers.
THOMPSON, A. - - - 1st Lancashire Fusiliers.	DEANE, R. - - - - - 8th Lancashire Fusiliers.
TOMKINSON, J. - - - 1st Lancashire Fusiliers.	EVANS, H. - - - - - 11th Hampshires.
WALKER, H. - - - - 10th Hampshires.	TERILL, E. - - - - - Lancashire Fusiliers.
WANSKILL, W. H. - - Cameronian Highlanders.	GLYNN, J. - - - - - National Reserve.
WIBBERLEY, J. - - - 7th Lancashire Fusiliers.	SWINDELLS, J. - - - National Reserve.
WHITWORTH, C. - - 8th Lancashire Fusiliers.	BOHANNA, A. - - - - Royal Fusiliers.
WORSLEY, R. - - - - 7th Lancashire Fusiliers.	TITLEY, A. - - - - - 20th Lancashire Fusiliers.
WISEMAN, W. - - - - 14th King's Liverp'l Regt.	CORDY, E. - - - - - Royal Army Medical Corps.
LYONS, G. - - - - - 15th King's Liverp'l Regt.	CHAPMAN, J. - - - - 8th Lancashire Fusiliers.
ROYLE, R. - - - - - 15th King's Liverp'l Regt.	MASON, T. - - - - - 6th Manchesters.
BOTHWELL, J. - - - Lancashire Fusiliers.	GOODFELLOW, R. - - Army Service Corps.
BROTHERTON, J. - - Lancashire Fusiliers.	HORSEFIELD, H. - - Lancashire Fusiliers.
RIGBY, J. - - - - - - 12th Lancashire Fusiliers.	BINNS, G. W. - - - - Royal Army Medical Corps.
POMFRET, J. - - - - Lancashire Fusiliers.	EVANS, A. - - - - - Lancashire Fusiliers.
CHAPMAN, A. - - - - 15th Lancashire Fusiliers.	POLLITT, J. S. - - - 10th Seaforth Highlanders.
CHAPMAN, ISAAC - - 1st Hampshires.	TOMSON, H. P. - - - Motor Ambulance.

ROLL OF HONOUR.

THRUTCHLEY & CO.,
LIMITED
22, St., Mary's Gate, MANCHESTER.

Mr. A. BERTENSHAW,
"B" Coy., 20th Manchester Regt.
Mr. C. BROWN,
"B" Coy., 10th Seaforth Highlanders.
Mr. J. BETHELL,
2 Coy., 22nd Div. Train., A.S.C.
Mr. E. BOND,
"A" Coy., 6th Seaforth Highlanders.
Mr. W. BULLOCK,
2/3 Field Company, W.L.D.R.E.
Mr. F. DEEKS,
4th Battalion Seaforth Highlanders.
(Killed in action Neuve Chappelle, May, 1915.)
Mr. H. HILLER,
3rd Earl Chester's Yeomaury.
Mr. D. W. JENKINS,
C.I. Section, 1st Lincs. R.N. Div.
Mr. J. P. LEATHER,
"A" Coy., 16th Manchester Regt.
Mr. F. LEE,
"C" Coy., 20th Manchester Regt.
Mr. H. OATES,
"A" Company, 3/6th Cheshire Regt.
Mr. E. A. OVENDEN,
"A" Coy., 1/1st Kent Cyclists' Batt.
Mr. G. RICHARDSON,
R.A.M.C.
Mr. A. WINCHESTER,
Army Service Corps.
Mr. R. WATERMAN,
2/16 County of London "D" Coy.
Mr. F. BODDY,
Lancashire Fusiliers.

Roll of Honour.

W. H. Tutton & Co., Ltd.,
Lancaster Avenue, Fennel Street, MANCHESTER.

Sergt. JAMES BLAIR,
351A Battery, R.F.A.
Private ARTHUR BRATT,
18th (S.) Bt. Manchester Regt.
Private HAROLD ELTON,
18th (S.) Bt. Manchester Regt.
Private JOSEPH BOTTOMLEY,
19th (S.) Bt. Manchester Regt.
Private LESLIE SHEASBY,
12th Bt. King's O. Lanc. Regt.
Private WM. ARMSTRONG,
15th Bt. Lancashire Fusiliers.
Driver DAVID GYLES,
Divisional Team of the A.S.C.
Private HAROLD GRIFFITHS,
6th Bt. Manchester Regt.
(Killed at the Dardanelles.)
Private ED. MOULTON,
Grenadier Guards (Sig. Sect.).
Private THOS. LEE,
R.F.A. (Mounted Section).
Private GILBERT WESTWELL,
Royal Flying Corps.
Lieut. FRANK MERRIT,
Serving on H.M.S. 'Partridge' at sea. (Formerly in the firm's employ.)

Roll of Honour.

HENRY TURNBULL & CO.
THOMAS STREET, MANCHESTER.

Private P. Turnbull	Liverpool Scottish.
Corporal J. R. Bullivant	Royal Army Medical Corps.
Private J. Archer	18th Batt. Manchester Regiment.
Private W. Wood	18th Batt. Manchester Regiment.
Private J. Lloyd	18th Batt. Manchester Regiment.
Private R. Rogerson	18th Batt. Manchester Regiment.
Private C. Oswald	18th Batt. Manchester Regiment.
Gunner F. Gregory	Lancashire and Cheshire R.G.A.
Private B. Howarth	Lancashire Fusiliers.
Private F. Evans	R.M.L.I. Decoy.
Trumpeter H. Gregory	Lancashire and Cheshire R.G.A.
Private E. Coghlan	13th Batt. Royal Welsh Fusiliers.
Private J. H. Bradshaw	Army Service Corps.
Private F. Simpson	19th Batt. Manchester Regiment.
Sergeant L. Crowther	23rd Batt. Manchester Regiment.
Private J. Johnson	1st Batt. Manchester Regiment.
Private J. Denby	South Lancashires.
Private G. Levy	Flying Corps.
Sapper M. H. Barrans	East Lancashire Royal Engineers.
Private G. Davies	6th Batt. Manchester Regiment.
Private R. Moyse	25th Lancashire Fusiliers.
Signaller R. Gorton	Lancashire Fusiliers.

Roll of Honour.

UNION MILLS CO.

8-10 Brazennose Street, Manchester.

OFFICE.

ARTHUR A. NAHUM.	A.S.C. (M.T.)
P. HILL	East Lancashire R.A.M.C.
A. WATSON	Duke of Lancaster's Own.
L. STUBBS	30th Division Cyclists' Company.
F. STARBUCK	Royal Marine Light Infantry.
H. WOOD	7th Batt. Manchester Regiment.
J. FISHWICK	Mechanical Transport Section A.S.C.

HOLMFIELD MILL.

F. WALSH	Royal Field Artillery.
G. A. RUSSELL	4th West Yorks.
S. BROADBENT	Royal Army Medical Corps.
F. WALSH	4th West Yorks.
F. BURKE	Highland Light Infantry.
H. NUTTALL	Cameron Highlanders.
G. WALSH	4th West Riding Regiment.
W. KERSHAW	4th West Riding Regiment.

OLDHAM MILL.

A. LAW	Royal Army Medical Corps.
J. CALLINAN	14th Cheshires.
T. WHITEHEAD	10th Manchester Regiment.
J. ANCHOR	10th Manchester Regiment.
J. L. FROBISHER	9th Manchester Regiment.
HAROLD COCKER	10th Manchester Regiment.

SOWERBY BRIDGE MILL.

J. GREENWOOD	4th West Riding Regiment.

Roll of Honour.

Thomas Vickers & Sons
LIMITED.
Miles Platting, Manchester.

Ernest Holt, Private, 8th Lancs. Fusiliers.
John Bowyer, Private, 20th Manchester Regt.
James Schofield, Private, 1st Loyal North Lancs. Regt (Killed).
William McGee, Private, Royal Scots Fus. (Killed).
John Murphy, Private, Royal Scots Fusiliers.
John Mills, Private, Lancs. Fusiliers.
James Dunn, Private, K.O.L. Lancasters.
Thomas Mort, Private, 12th Manch. Regt.
George Goodwin, Driver, R.G.A.
John Lanagan, Private, 1st Batt. King's Garr. Regt.
Jeremiah Cunliffe, Private, 20th Man. Regt.
James Kemp,   T
Joseph Steventon, Private, 24th Man. Regt.
William Irving, Gunner, R.F.A.
George Hill, Private, South Lancs. Regt.
George Garland, Private, Rifle Brigade.
Joseph Conway, Private, 1/7th Manch. Regt.
Henry Allen, Private, 1/7th Manch. Regt.
Anthony Walsh, Private, East Lancs. Regt.
John Waugh, Private, Manchester Regt.
William Morris, Bombadier, R.G.A.

ROLL OF HONOUR.

G. & G. WHITEHEAD,
LIMITED.

FARRELL STREET, ELTON STREET,
LOWER BROUGHTON,
Manchester.

James Allen.
Roland Blackburn, Junr.
James Catherall.
Henry Derbyshire.
Robert Groves.
Joseph Hamilton.
William Kay.
Francis Kelly.
James Moran.
William Moran.
James Pilling.
William Rawlinson.
Samuel Smallshaw.
Robert Taylor.

ROLL OF HONOUR.

THE Wall-paper Manufacturers LIMITED.

LIGHTBOWN ASPINALL BRANCH.

ANDERSON, A.	FISH, H.	LANGDEN, J.	SPELLMAN, JOS.
BLACKBURN, J.	FOSTER, F.	LAMB, A.	SMITH, H.
BRADSHAW, J.	GOULDIN, H.	MAGILL, H.	SMITH, C.
BUCKLEY, JAS.	HURST, F.	MESSER, J.	SMITH, A.
BOOTH, W.	HACKWELL, W.	MORAN, J.	TURNER, R.
BUSH, G. W.	HOUGHTON, J.	MINSHULL, J.	TOOLE, C.
BARLOW, H.	HOWARTH, W. H.	MINSHULL, L.	WATSON, W.
BRENNAN, T.	HILL, F.	MOORE, F. D.	WHEELER, H.
BODEN, J.	HOWSON, G.	MOYNIHAN, T.	WARBURTON, W.
COOKE, T.	HAWARD, C.	OGDEN, S.	WADE, D.
COOKE, F.	HORTON, H.	PARKINSON, A.	WEAVER, E.
CHADWICK, J. E.	HALL, C.	PENNY, J.	WELCH, A.
CHADWICK, T.	JONES, J.	PETERS, E.	WILLIAMS, C.
CARTER, W.	KNAPE, O.	RIGBY, R.	WILSON, L.
CAHILL, T.	KIELEY, J.	STONEHEWER, J.	WARBURTON, J.
DAWBER. J. V. S.	KELLY, J.	STEWART, A.	WHITE, J. A.
DUCKWORTH, H.	KENNEDY, H.	SEAMAN, F.	WHITTAKER, G. R.
DUTTON, W.	LAW, R.	SPELLMAN, JOHN.	

WALKER CARVER BRANCH.

ASHLEY, J.	HANNON, F.	MACKIE, J.	SHARPE, F.
BAKER, G.	HIGSON, T.	MARTIN, C.	STAHAM, T.
BARRETT, F.	HAMILTON, W.	McKENNA, H.	SIDLOW, A.
BECKETT, J.	HORNBY, B.	McFARLANE, W.	SUTCLIFFE, H.
BYRNE, F.	HINDE, G. A.	McCAWLEY, A.	THOMPSON, J.
BOWDEN, H.	HORTON, W.	MAYO, L.	WORSLEY, W.
BLAKEMORE, H.	INGLESENT, J.	MORAN, J.	WALSH, A.
BRIGGS, W.	JONES, S.	McKAY, C.	WALSH, T.
BURNS, T.	JONES, B.	PARKINSON, N.	WALKER, W.
BINGHAM, A.	KITE, G.	PIKE, T.	WILD, G.
CROSSLEY, J.	KNOWLES, T.	REYNOLDS, F.	WOOD, J.
GROOME, T.	LEONARD, H.	ROGERS, J.	WOODFORD, W.
GRAHAM, J.	LEWIS, G.		

ROLL OF HONOUR

James Wheeldon & Sons, Ltd.

Regent Road Saw Mills, Glasshouse Street, ——SALFORD——

Abbott, Harry.
Atkins, William.
Axon, Robert.
Benson, Benjamin.
Blackham, John.
Bostock, Arthur.
Carpenter, William.
Cooper, James.
Edge, John.
Eyres, George.
Eyres, William.
Ferguson, Joseph.
Fitzsimmons, Robert.
Foulkes, Robert C.
Griffiths, James.
Hand, John.

Healer, George.
Healey, Joseph.
Hickford, Alfred.
Hickford, Thomas.
Hoey, Frederick.
Howard, John.
Huby, James.
Jackson, James.
Joule, Frederick.
Lindley, James.
Lomax, George.
McKearney, Ernest.
Mockridge, George.
Molloy, Joseph.
Morgan, George.
Morgan, Frederick W.

Newton, Albert.
Nugent, James.
Perkins, Charles.
Pritchard, Stephen.
Shenton, Joseph.
Turbine, Arthur.
Wallwork, James.
Wallwork, William.
Wheeldon, Robert.
Whitehead, William.
Whittaker, John.
Whittaker, Samuel.
Wood, Thomas.
Worthington, Kay Walter.
Wright, William.

ROLL OF HONOUR.

Whitworth & Mitchell Ltd.,
97, Portland Street,
MANCHESTER.

Pte. F. Bowes, 19th Batt. Manchester Regt.
Pte. W. Jones,
    2/7th Batt. Manchester Regt.
Sergt.-Major C. R. Clare,
    R.A.M.C., East Lancs.
Pte. E. Rose, 3/8th Batt. Manchester Regt.
Sergt. J. Knott, 1/8th Lancashire Fusiliers.
Sergt. J. H. Bowler, 7th Batt. Rifle Brigade.
Bombardier W. H. Jacques,
    2nd East Lancs. R.F.A.
Lance-Corpl. T. P. Foy,
    2904 Rifle Brigade (Killed in action).
Pte. F. Tonge, 3/6th Batt. Manchester Regt.
Pte. J. Hartley, 22nd Batt. Manchester Regt.
Pte. J. H. Holland,
    1/7th Bt. Man. Rgt. (Killed in action).
Pte. G. W. Brown,
    3/6th Batt. Manchester Regt.
Pte. C. Bradley,
    3/6th Batt. Manchester Regt.
Bandsman J. Hopkins,
    8th Batt. Manchester Regt.
        (Invalided out of Army).
Lance-Corpl. E. Marsden,
    12th Lancashire Fusiliers.
        (Invalided out of Army).
Pte. R. Horrox, 25th Batt. Manchester Regt.
        (Invalided out of Army).
Pte. J. L. Graham, 2/4th K.S.L.I.
Pte. G. Kerwin, 21st Lancs. Fus. R.A.M.C.
Pte. E. Wells, K.S.L.I.
Pte. A. Wilkinson,
    6th Batt. Manchester Regt.

ROLL OF HONOUR.

John H. Widdowson,
Engineer,
Britannia Works, New Park Road,
Ordsall Lane, Salford, Manchester.

Lieut. E. Percy Widdowson,
    3rd Batt. South Lancashire Regt.
2nd Lieut. Harold R. Widdowson,
    2nd Batt. South Lancashire Regt.
Sergt. J. Crowley Smethurst,
    8th Lancashire Fusiliers (Terr.).
Private W. Nash,
    8th Lancashire Fusiliers (Terr.).
Private S. Cryer,
    8th Lancashire Fusiliers (Terr.).
Private J. Farmer,
    7th Lancashire Fusiliers (Terr.).
Private J. Schofield,
    7th Lancashire Fusiliers (Terr.).
Private F. McCallum,
    7th Lancashire Fusiliers (Terr.).
Private Allan Doyle,
    2nd Lancashire Fusiliers.
Private A. Bolton, 3rd Welsh Regiment.
Private F. Hartley,
    19th Serv. Batt. Lanc. Fusiliers.
Private W. Widdows,
    19th Serv. Batt. Lanc. Fusiliers.
Private W. Darbyshire,
    18th Serv. Batt. Manchester Regt.
Private J. Davies,
    23rd Serv. Batt. Manchester Regt.
Private T. Hannigan,
    23rd Serv. Batt. Manchester Regt.
Private A. Hewitt,
    6th South Lancashire Regiment.
Private J. Powell,
    6th South Lancashire Regiment.
Private B. Doyle,
    2/8th Argyle and Sutherland H.

Roll of Honour.

Wilson, Knowles & Co.

48, George Street,
MANCHESTER.

Private JOHN B. BEVERLEY,
  7th Lancashire Fusiliers (Missing).

Sergt. HAROLD BROADBENT,
  1/4 Royal Scots, Q.E.R.

L.-Corpl. FRANK CLIFFE,
  1/4 Royal Scots, Q.E.R.

Private SAMUEL FORTH,
  1/4 Royal Scots Q.E.R. (Killed).

L.-Corpl. GEORGE ROBINSON,
  4th Royal Scots, Q.E.R.

Private THOMAS DOW,
  9th Black Watch.

Private GEORGE F. PHILLIPS,
  24th Royal Fusiliers.

Private ARTHUR WITHINGTON,
  8th T. Manchester Regiment.

GEORGE ASPINALL (Rejected).

Roll of Honour.

F. Phillips & Company

96, Deansgate,
MANCHESTER.

List of Employees who have enlisted.

Capt. FREDERICK PHILLIPS,
  Attached Royal Dublin Fusiliers.

Pte. FRED HOLDEN,
  21st Royal Fusiliers.

Sergt. FRED ROBINSON,
  Machine Gun Sec., 7th Rifle Brigade.

L.-Corpl. JOHN THOMPSON,
  19th Motor Ambulance Corps, A.S.C.

L.-Corpl. A. V. HOUGH,
  14th Cheshire Regiment.

Pte. ROSS GARLICK,
  Inns of Court O.T.C.

Corpl. A. H. MURPHY,
  32nd Field Ambulance, R.A.M.C.

Pte. KENNETH HINDE,
  61st Field Ambulance, R.A.M.C.

ROLL OF HONOUR.

ROBERT BARCLAY & CO.

35, Whitworth Street West,

MANCHESTER

BAGNALL, T.
BARLOW, F.
BILLINGTON, N.
BOWCOCK, E.
BROADBENT, J. (2nd Lt.)
DALBY, D. H.
DENHAM, R.
DODDS, J. (Killed).
DONOUGHUE, M.
GLENDINNING, W. D.
GREENUP, J.
HADFIELD, J. H.
HALLIWELL, J. H.
HENDRY, W. L.
HEWITT, C.
HOWARD, T. V.
HODGKINSON, F.
JONES, C.
KELLY, J.
KELLY, A.
KENDALL, S.
LINNEY, W. H.
LOVELACE, H.

MASSEY, E.
MITCHELL, WM.
MORAN, B.
MURPHY, A.
McWILLIAMS, J. H., Jr.
NATHANIEL, T. P. (Killed).
OAKES, J.
OLIVER, H. C. C. (2nd Lt.)
PAGE, H.
PARKINSON, F.
PLATT, F. L. (2nd Lt.)
ROGERS, J. R.
RYLE, T.
STOTT, F. C. (Lieutenant).
STRUTHERS, S.
THOMAS, D. H.
TONGE, E. S.
WALTON, E.
WARD, C. D.
WILKINSON, W. D.
WOOLLERTON, H.
WHITTAKER, A.

ROLL OF HONOUR.

Manchester Evening News
3 Cross Street, Manchester.

- J. Arden.
- W. Baxter.
- J. Boardman.
- E. Booth.
- J. Borkin.
- A. S. Brabin.
- W. Brown.
- H. Buckley.
- J. Burns.
- A. Cade.
- F. Carter.
- W. Choyce.
- T. Code.
- P. Connor.
- E. Cureton.
- W. Davenport.
- J. Denholm.
- H. W. Doughty.
- A. Dowling.
- N. Dowling.
- H. Edwards.
- H. Evans.
- W. Firth.
- S. Foulkes.
- W. Garner (Killed).
- A. Georgeson.
- S. Gregory.
- W. Griffin.
- T. Hammond.
- J. Handley.
- A. Hargreaves.
- W. Henshaw.
- F. Henthorn.
- T. Hewitt.
- J. Hobson.
- J. Holbrook.
- G. Holehouse.
- R. Horrocks.
- A. Hough.
- J. Hunstan.
- W. Hunt.
- F. Hutchinson.
- R. Hyde.
- A. Jenkinson.
- E. Jones.
- T. Jones.
- W. Leigh.
- W. McGeary.
- M. McKie.
- E. Mason.
- E. May.
- A. S. Mellor.
- J. Mitchell.
- A. Mobey.
- H. Moores.
- W. Morris.
- W. Mosdale.
- J. Murphy.
- J. Murray.
- A. Myers.
- J. R. Parkyn (Killed).
- C. Partington.
- W. Plant.
- J. Portlock.
- F. Preece.
- J. Quarmby.
- A. B. Roberts.
- W. Roberts.
- H. Rogerson.
- T. Sharp.
- F. W. H. Singfield.
- E. Smith.
- J. Smith.
- J. Smith.
- F. Smyth.
- A. Spooner.
- B. Stiles.
- A. Taylor.
- A. Tomkinson.
- J. Thompson.
- A. Travis.
- J. Walsh.
- W. Walsh.
- J. Watson.
- T. Wielding.
- H. Wilde.
- B. Wilkinson.
- W. Williams.
- R. Willoughby.
- J. Wilson.

Employees of
WILLIAM GRAHAM & CO.
48 Sackville Street, Manchester, and 3 Lees Street, Ancoats.

ARCHER, F.
   Died of wounds—Mesopotamia.
ALLEN, L.
   Slightly wounded—Gallipoli.
ADSHEAD, A.
ANDREWS, J.
BOOLE, S.
BELSHAW, G. R.
BARNETT, M.
BAGGOLEY, A.
   Died of wounds—France.
BARKER, T.
BALDWIN, F.
BURKE, W.
BERRIMAN, P.
BRITTAN, J.
BRIERLEY, J.
   Accidently killed—England.
COLEBECK, H.
CONSTABLE, G. R.
COTTRELL, G. H.
   Killed in action—Dardanelles.
COOPER, A.
CROOK, J.
CARROLL, J.
CLARK, H.
DUNKERLEY, H.
DANIELS, J.
   Slightly wounded—Gallipoli
DEAKIN, J.
   Wounded—France
DERBYSHIRE, A.
DARBYSHIRE, G.
DERBYSHIRE, J. R.
DORNING, E.
DUFFY, W. H.
DONOHUE, J.

EDWARDS, P. H.
ELLIOTT, W. H.
FAWCETT, H.
FERNLEY, G.
FITZGERALD, F.
   Severely wounded—Gallipoli.
FOSTER, W.
FORGO, T.
FROGGATT, G.
GREENWOOD, E.
GREENWOOD, H.
GAITSKELL, R.
   Killed—France
GIBBON, F.
GOODALE, A.
GREEN, F.
GRIFFITH, W. T.
   Killed in action—Gallipoli.
HADLAND, R.
HOPE, A. S.
HALL, P.
   Severely wounded—France.
HARRISON, G.
HARRISON, J. W.
HARRISON, T.
HARWOOD, J.
HEALD, J.
HOOD, A.
HOOD, W.
HUSSEY, W.
HUTCHINSON, A.
IRELAND, B. T.
JAMES, A.
JONES, A.
JONES, D. O.
JONES, G. T.

JONES, R.
JONES, J. T.
KELLY, E. J.
KINGSTON, J.
LAMBERT, H.
LANE, A.
LAWSON, W.
LILLEY, S.
*LLOYD, J.
MONTGOMERY, A. G.
MATTINSON, T.
MINSHULL, A. T.
MULLINIEUX, S.
MARKLAND, L. H.
MATTISON, A.
MORAN, J.
MORRIS, J.
   Wounded by Zeppelin—England.
NEEDHAM, L.
ORANGE, A. E.
OLIVER, A.
OWEN, A.
OWEN, J.
OWEN, J. W.
PORTER, R.
PERCIVAL, J. H.
PARRY, A. H.
*PALFREYMAN, A.
PARKINGTON, J.
PAYTON, J.
POLLITT, W.
PHILIPPS, C.
PLANT, F.
PROCTER, S.
   Killed in action—France.
QUINN, W.

ROBINSON, J. H.
RAW, T.
RAW, W.
REDFERN, E.
REID, W.
ROBINSON, T.
ROTHE, A. J.
SCOTT, F. G.
SHAW, W.
   Twice wounded—Dardanelles.
   Missing since 7/8/15.
SWAN, J.
SHAW, J. M.
SHARP, P.
SALT, G.
   Killed—France.
SEEL, J. (Junior).
SIBBETT, F.
SIMMS, A.
SKELHORN, J.
   Severely wounded—Gallipoli.
SWEENEY, J.
TAYLOR, A.
*TAYLOR, J.
TAYLOR, R.
TEE, A. W.
*TWEMLOW, C. R.
WHITE, A.
WALLACE, G. D.
WATSON, C.
WARRINER, J.
WHITEHEAD, J.
WHEELDON, J.
WILCOCK, R
WILKINSON, F.
WINSTANLEY, H.
*WOTHERSPOON, J.

*Invalided out.

ROLL OF HONOUR.

WRIGHT & GREEN LTD.

7, 9 and 11, DANTZIC STREET, MANCHESTER.

Pte. W. SNAPE	6th Manchesters.		Driver W BROWN	A.S.C.
(Killed in Gallipoli.)			Pte. J. GREENHALGH	12th Manchesters.
Pte. E. MILES	23rd Royal Fusiliers.		(Killed in France.)	
Pte. T. E. BRETHERTON	R.A.M.C.		Pte. S. INGLEFIELD	Roy. Welsh Fusiliers.
Trooper R. FARMER	D.L.O. Yeomanry.		Pte. A. BAILEY	King's Royal Rifles.
Pte. H. GOLDSBOROUGH	17th Manchesters.		Pte. M. CARKEET	14th Manchesters.
Pte. S. HILL	Cyclists' Corps.		Pte. C. PALMER	Royal Navy.
L.-Corpl. E. C. KELSALL	17th Manchesters.		Pte. W. JOHNSON	Lancs. Fusiliers.
(Died of Wounds.)			Pte. W. BARKER	Roy. Welsh Fusiliers.
Corpl. E. EDGAR	Lancs. Fusiliers.		Pte. M. HAMILTON	14th Manchesters.
Pte. G. S. CRAMPTON	18th Manchesters.		Pte. G. PARKIN	
Pte. A. HANDFORD	7th Manchesters.		Pte. J. E. HEWITT	Roy. Welsh Fusiliers.
J. F. KNOWLES	Telegraphist, R.N.		Pte. J. S. THORPE	Royal Scots Guards.
Pte. J. C. COWDEN	23rd Royal Fusiliers.		Pte. J. DONNOLLY	14th Manchesters.
Pte. H. PAYTON	7th Manchesters.		Corpl. F. BROOMER	K. O. Royal Lancs.
Pte. J. CULLEY	4th Manchesters.		Pte. C. HACKETT	46th Provisional Bat.
Pte. P. SLINN	18th Manchesters.		Pte. A. WALKER	Royal Marines.
Pte. J. HORSFIELD	11th Manchesters.		Pte. W. LEATHERBARROW	R.A.M.C.
Pte. J. WARD	21st Manchesters.		WALTER HOYLES	Royal Navy.
Pte. H. TAYLOR	27th Manchesters.		Pte. JOS. NEWTON	14th Manchesters.
Pte. J. PENKETHMAN	21st Manchesters.		Pte. JAS. HY. TURNER	14th Manchesters.
Pte. A. DAVENPORT	12th Manchesters.		Pte. REG. WORDSWORTH	Royal Gar. Artillery.
Pte. W. DUNN	Lancs. Fusiliers.		Pte. A. RIDINGS	Royal Gar. Artillery.
Pte. J. L. INGLEFIELD	Motor Transport.		Pte. FRED. AINSWORTH	

Roll of Honour.

E. H. Hollings & Sons
22 Lever Street, Manchester.

Employees Enlisted.

R. Barratt, R.A.M.C.
C. E. T. Billing, 19th Manchesters.
W. Corrigan, R.F.A.
J. Cunliffe, 20th Manchesters.
J. W. Haughton, 8th Manchesters.
R. G. Henderson, Med. Unit Nav. Div.
W. Johnston, Royal Engineers.
W. Lowe, 19th Manchesters.
H. Manton, 19th Manchesters.
J. Rostron, 2/4th South Lancs.
Lt. and Q.M. White, G. P., Man. Rgt.
A. Williams, Med. Unit Nav. Div.
O. Whittaker, 6th Manchesters.
D. Merron, 27th Manchesters.
F. McEwen, 2nd/7th Lanc. Fusiliers.
J. P. Davies, 21st Lanc. Fusiliers.

Employees Rejected.

A. W. Brown.
L. B. Crough.
W. E. Fletcher.
A. Poole.
J. B. Taylor.
J. A. Wilbraham.

ROLL OF HONOUR.

Manchester Steam Users' Association.

*

W. H. RAVEN,
    Lieut. and Q'master Army Service Corps, Mech. Transport Dept.
H. FOYSTER,
    Royal Artillery.
R. SWEENEY,
    Royal Engineers.
JOHN BENTLEY,
    Royal Engineers. (Died during training.)
DAVID CORMACK,
    Royal Scots.
RUSSELL TAYLOR,
    Machine Gun Section, B. Co., 13th Batt. Middlesex Regt. (Killed in action.)
E. BRAME,
    Army Service Corps (Driver).
W. H. FERRAND,
    Army Service Corps (Clerk).
A. ARDERN,
    Royal Army Medical Corps.
FRANK WARDLE,
    Royal Field Artillery.
A. H. SIMS,
    Royal Flying Corps.
C. R. TALBOT,
    Royal Navy.
W. H. CHADWICK,
    2nd/5th Liverpool Regt. (The King's).
FRED HARTLEY,
    Army Service Corps, Mech. Transport.

ROLL OF HONOUR.

H. N. MORRIS & CO. LTD.

Gorton Brook Chemical Works,
MANCHESTER.

MEN SERVING.

ERNEST WINDSOR	Egypt (Regiment not known).
HERBERT WHITEHEAD	23rd Serv. Batt. Manchester Rgt.
HAROLD BELL	1st Border Regiment.
JOHN HENRY VICKERS	7th Manchesters, Territorials.
ROBERT WARD	1st Border Regiment.
JAMES POWER	1st Royal Lancashires.
— GRATTON	Regiment unknown. (Killed.)
J. MacFARLANE	1/6th Manchester Regiment.
G. DORLING	Royal Scots.
E. MAKIN	Loyal North Lancashires.
R. KELSHAW	12th King's.

Roll of Honour.

A. Prestwich & Co. Ltd.

13. Major Street, Manchester.

WAREHOUSE.

Pte. Reginald Prestwich	Duke of Lancaster's Own Yeomanry. (Signaller)
Pte. Percy M. Hibbert	Manchester Regt.
Pte. Ernest Wheawell	Lancashire Fusiliers. (Signaller)
Pte. Albert Scarr	Manchester Pals.
Pte. Joseph Bennett	Royal Fusiliers.
Pte. H. Grimshaw	Duke of Lancaster's Own Yeomanry.
Pte. Stanley E. Harper	— — — — — — — — —
Pte. Thomas Wilson	— — — — — — — — —

SALFORD MILL, TODMORDEN.

Corpl. B. Beaumont	Mechanical Transport Section.
Pte. F. Eastwood	Mechanical Transport Section.
Pte. E. Pickles	Lancashire Fusiliers.
Pte. W. Hargreaves	Lancashire Fusiliers.
Pte. F. Parker	Lancashire Fusiliers.
Pte. F. Pickles (Killed)	Lancashire Fusiliers.
Pte. F. Spencer	R.A.M.C.
Pte. W. Barker	R.A.M.C.
Pte. W. Toothill	Duke of Wellington's Regt.
Pte. W. Marshall	Duke of Wellington's Regt.

Roll of Honour.

PUGH, DAVIES & CO. LIMITED
29 Dale Street, MANCHESTER.

V. C. STAFFORD-BADGER (Lieutenant)	11th Batt. Man. Regt.
O. FAIRBANK (Sergt.)	16th S. Bt. M/c Rgt. B.E.F.
C. T. BOTTRILL (Corpl.)	16th S. Bt. M/c Rgt. B.E.F.
S. CROMPTON	16th S. Bt. M/c Rgt. B.E.F.
W. ELLIS THOMAS	16th S. Bt. M/c Rgt. B.E.F.
A. E. SHAW	16th S. Bt. M/c Rgt. B.E.F.
B. SWAIN (Lce.-Corpl.)	18th S. Bt. M/c Rgt. B.E.F.
T. A. PUGH	19th Ser. Bt. Manchester Rgt. (B.E.F.) France.
R. CONNOLLY	22nd S. Bt. M/c Rgt. B.E.F.
T. J. OWEN (2nd Lieut.)	Royal Welsh Fusiliers.
R. BOUD	Royal Welsh Fusiliers.
F. CLARK	6th Man. Terr. Regt.
C. A. CROSS (Killed in Gallipoli.)	6th Man. Terr. Regt. (Egypt).
V. C. H. ROBERTS (Sgt.)	6th Man. Terr. Regt.
B. STUBBS	6th Man. Terr. Regt.
C. W. BAILEY	7th Man. Terr. Regt.
H. E. WILD (Lce.-Corpl.)	7th Man. Terr. Regt.
J. COONEY	7th Man. Terr. Regt.
W. H. LEES	East Lanc. Field Amb. (Egypt).
C. BROOME	East Lanc. Field Amb.
F. E. WILLIAMS	East Lanc. Field Amb. (Egypt).
W. C. BATES	East Lanc. Field Amb. (Egypt).
W. MILLER	R.A.M.C. (B.E.F.).
A. F. WILLIAMS (L.-Cpl.)	R.A.M.C.
C. WALLWORK	A.S.C. Motor Transport.
J. BIRCH (Corpl.)	A.S.C. Motor Tr. (B.E.F.)
H. M. HUGHES	A.S.C. Motor Tr. (B.E.F.)
E. DOBSON	7th Res. Bt. Man. Regt.
J. DICKENSON	26th Res. Bt. Man. Regt.
J. W. CONNOR (L.-Cpl.)	3rd Res. Bt. Lanc. Fus.
V. P. HIND	4th Res. Bt. Royal Scots.
G. WESTWELL	Royal Flying Corps in France.
A. O. SMITH (Bomb'dier)	Royal Field Artillery.
E. ROBERTS (2nd Cpl.)	Royal Marine Submarine Miners.
G. HODGSON	Royal Engineers.
P. JONES	Royal Naval Air Service.
H. M. CROWTHER	30th Royal Fusiliers, Sportsmen's Batt.
J. ROBERTS	30th Royal Fusiliers, Sportsmen's Batt.
W. DAVIES (Bugler)	13th King's Liverpool Regt. (B.E.F.).
B. SMITH (Killed in France.)	16th Bt. Northumberland Fusiliers.
W. H. JONES	2/2nd London Field Amb.

ROLL OF HONOUR.

Ph. Ziegler & Co.,

2, BOMBAY STREET,
MANCHESTER.

Mr. P. H. Ziegler, partner,
  19th Batt. Royal Fusiliers.

C. F. Mather,
  R.A.M.C.T. East Lancs.

R. Jackson,
  Attached 1st City of London F.A.,
  R.A.M.C., Staff.

J. Morris,
  20th Serv. Batt. Manchester Regt.

R. Preece,
  20th Serv. Batt. Manchester Regt.

G. H. Sproston,
  20th Serv. Batt. Manchester Regt.

A. Wilkinson,
  20th Serv. Batt. Manchester Regt.

ROLL OF HONOUR.

SHERRATT & HUGHES,

34, Cross Street
and
1, Hulme Street, Deansgate,
MANCHESTER.

Baldwin, F. W., Manchester Rgt.
Bayes, N., Garrison Artillery.
Cheetham, G., 10th Seaforth Highlanders.
Denham, F., Border Regt.
Emerson, E. W., 6th Bt. Man. Rgt. (T.F.).
Fish, R., Lancashire Fusiliers.
Grant, E., Royal Navy.
Lee, P., 24th (Ser.) Batt. Manc. Regt.
  (Died from Wounds).
Nixon, J. W., R.F.A. (T.F.).
Read, J. N., 21st Royal Fusiliers.
Roberts, E., 8th Batt. Man. Rgt. (T.F.).
Rosenthal, V., 1st Batt. Kent Cyclists.
Scott, A. D., 18th Batt. Manchester Rgt.
  (Killed in action.)
Smithies, W., King's Liverpool Regt.
Stevens, A., Royal Navy.
Taylor, J., Royal Fusiliers.
Trite, George R., 22nd Royal Fusiliers.

At Duty's Call.

The following employees of

The SHREWSBURY & CHALLINER TYRE Co. Ltd., Manchester,

served with HIS MAJESTY'S FORCES during the GREAT WAR.

STAFF.

Priv. W. BAKER	Royal Fusiliers.
Priv. F. DAVIES	5th Roy. Welsh Fusiliers.
Priv. G. R. DEXTER	Royal Flying Corps.
Priv. W. GIBSON	Royal Fusiliers.
Priv. J. HEAP	Manchester Regiment.
Priv. G. HOARE	A.S.C., M.T.
Corpl. R. HUNT	10th Batt. Rifle Brigade.
Priv. R. JACKSON	Seaforth Highlanders.
Priv. H. G. MANN	A.S.C., M.T.
Sergt. R. MASKELL	Manchester Regiment.
Priv. H. PHILIP	A.S.C., M.T.
Trooper W. A. PLANT	15th Hussars.
Priv. H. RICHARDSON	6th Manchesters.
Priv. F. YATES	7th Manchesters.

WORKS.

Priv. A. BATES	8th Batt. Manchester Rgt.
Priv. F. BELMAN	Royal Navy.
Priv. W. BEVINGTON	The Manchester Regt.
Priv. H. BIANCHI	King's Own.
Priv. H. BOWDON	Rifle Brigade.
Priv. E. BROOKS	Royal Welsh Fusiliers.
Priv. H. BUCKNALL	11th Hussars.
Priv. A. CATTON	8th Batt. Manchester Rgt.
Priv. M. CALLAGHAN	East Lancs. Regt.
L.-Corpl. W. CARSON	Border Regiment.
Ser. Major R. CHEETHAM	King's O. Lancaster Rgt.
Priv. F. CLARKE	Army Service Corps.
Priv. S. COLLINS	Royal Field Artillery.
Priv. F. COLE	Royal Field Artillery.
Priv. R. COOKE	Army Service Corps.
Priv. T. COOLE	South Lancs. Regt.
Priv. M. COLLINS	Dublin Fusiliers.
Priv. J. COADY	Dublin Fusiliers.
Priv. M. CRABB	14th Hussars.
Priv. W. DANIELS	8th Batt. Manchester Rgt.
Priv. W. ECKFORD	Royal Welsh Fusiliers.
Priv. W. H. ELLIOT	Rifle Brigade.
Priv. A. EVERALL	7th Batt. Manchester Rgt.
Priv. T. EVERALL	The Manchester Regt.
Priv. F. FARROW	Border Regiment.
Priv. J. W. FIELDING	7th Batt. Manchester Rgt.
Priv. W. FISK	R.A.M.C.
Priv. W. GORING	8th Batt. Manchester Rgt.
Bugler L. HARRINGTON	7th Batt. Manchester Rgt.
Priv. J. HUGHES	8th Batt. Manchester Rgt.
Priv. T. JONES	Rifle Brigade.
Priv. J. JONES	The Royal Scots.
Priv. W. JONES	The Royal Scots.
Priv. A. KAY	Royal Field Artillery.
Priv. J. LANG	8th Batt. Manchester Rgt.
Sergt. W. LANG	The Manchester Regt.
Priv. C. MOODY	Royal Garrison Artillery.
Priv. C. MOORES	8th Batt. Manchester Rgt.
Priv. D. PETRIE	Royal Engineers.
Priv. R. PETRIE	Royal Garrison Artillery.
Priv. H. PRIOR	Royal Engineers.
Priv. H. ROBERTS	Royal Welsh Fusiliers.
Priv. T. S. ROBINSON	South Lancs. Regt.
Priv. J. RUSSELL	Dragoon Guards.
Priv. J. SMALL	Royal Marines.
Priv. W. SMITH	8th Batt. Manchester Rgt.
Priv. W. STRONG	Royal Field Artillery.
Priv. J. TRIGG	Royal Field Artillery.
Priv. L. WEBB	The Royal Fusiliers.
Priv. N. WHITTLES	Royal Engineers.
Priv. H. WILD	8th Batt. Manchester Rgt.
Priv. R. WILSON	Royal Engineers.
Priv. H. WITHERS	8th Batt. Manchester Rgt.
Priv. H. WOODWARD	Royal Flying Corps.

ROLL OF HONOUR.

Schmidt's Superheating Co. (1910) Ltd.

Offices:
Locomotive Dept., 28, VICTORIA STREET, WESTMINSTER, S.W.
Marine Dept., BILLITER BUILDINGS, BILLITER STREET, LONDON, E.C.

Works: TRAFFORD PARK, MANCHESTER.

LONDON OFFICES.

Lieut.-Colonel H. A. STENNING	25th Battalion County of London.
Captain H. GODSAL	Hampshire Carbineers Yeomanry.
Captain H. A. BOWSER	Royal Field Artillery.
Lieutenant R. GUEST	Railway Transport.
Lieutenant G. DICKSON	Royal West Kents.
Lieutenant R. S. YORK	Royal Garrison Artillery.
Sergeant P. COOPER	East Yorkshire Regiment (Killed in Action).
Lance-Corporal R. H. BURNETT	London Scottish.
Private J. J. HEALEY	Royal Naval Air Service.

TRAFFORD PARK WORKS.

Sergt.-Major T. TURNER	21st City of Manchester.
Private S. CLARKSON	17th City of Manchester.
Private J. A. TAYLOR	6th Manchester Regiment (T.F.).
Private D. SHARPE	7th Manchester Regiment (T.F.).
Private H. SUMMERS	7th Manchester Regiment (T.F.).
Corporal J. H. WILDING	Lancashire Fusiliers.
Private J. P. CUMMINGS	Lancashire Fusiliers.
Private D. KELLY	Lancashire Fusiliers.
Private W. KELLY	Lancashire Fusiliers.
Private A. HACKNEY	Lancashire Fusiliers.
Private H. HUDSON	Lancashire Fusiliers.
Private J. H. LUMLEY	Lancashire Fusiliers.
Lance-Corporal F. PHILLIPS	Lancashire Fusiliers.
Private F. McCANN	Loyal North Lancs.
Trooper W. LEWIS	18th Hussars.
Private F. DELANEY	King's Own Royal Lancasters.
Private T. HARRISON	King's Own Royal Lancasters.
Private G. THORNLEY	King's Own Royal Lancasters.
Sapper H. ATKISS	Royal Engineers.
Sapper B. BOYES	Royal Engineers.
Sapper E. A. HULSE	Royal Engineers.
C.P.O. S. TATTERSALL	Royal Naval Air Service.
Private I. NEVILL	Royal Naval Division.
Driver E. BAKER	Royal Field Artillery.
Private F. DOWSON	Army Service Corps.
Driver J. E. McBLUNT	Army Service Corps.
Private W. A. SINGLETON	Army Service Corps.
Private R. DOBSON	10th Seaforth Highlanders.
Private R. HOLDEN	2/7 Cheshire Regiment.

ROLL OF HONOUR.

JOHN MILNER LTD.

Tetlow Street, Manchester.

Driver ROBERT BIRCH	- -	Army Service Corps.
Private WM. CARTNER	- -	8th Manchester Regiment.
Driver ALBERT GOODWIN	- -	Royal Field Artillery.
Driver WM. GREENWOOD	- -	Royal Field Artillery.
Driver PETER KELLY	- -	Army Service Corps.
Driver JOHN MACHIN	- -	Royal Field Artillery.
Private ALFRED MILNER	- -	R.A.M.C.
Private FRANK NICHOL	- -	R.A.M.C.

Attested.

Chapman, Elijah.	Milner, Richard H.
Chapman, Thos.	Nichol, Joseph.
Hartley, Thos.	Nuttall, Edward.
Machin, Abraham.	Scott, John.
Mathieu, Samuel.	Turner, Joseph.

ROLL OF HONOUR.

Lawton & Stevenson, Ltd.

12 Bradshaw Street, Shudehill
AND
2 & 4 Amber Street
MANCHESTER.

GUNNER WILLIAM KEADY, 1008,
1/15 Lancs. Battery, Royal Field Artillery.

ALFRED N. HULME,
6th Manchesters.

GILBERT FLEMING,
5th Batt. Rifle Brigade, Machine Gun Section.

SYLVESTER OLDFIELD, 34580,
17th Battalion Manchester Regiment.

CLARENCE FAULKNER, 5935,
2/4 East Yorkshire Regiment,

SIDNEY BARTON, 5956,
Mess 4, H.M.S. "Powerful."

Roll of Honour.

Spurrier, Glazebrook & Co., LIMITED.

8, Market Place,
MANCHESTER.

CAPTAIN GERALD DUGDALE,
Royal Flying Corps.

STAFF-SERGEANT WILLIAM POWELL,
R.A.M.C., East Lancs.

COY.-SERGEANT-MAJOR WM. JOHNSON,
South Staffs.

PRIVATE ERNEST NUTTALL,
A.S.C. Motor Transport.

PRIVATE CLARENCE BARBER,
13th Manchester Regiment.

B. J. WAYGOOD,
Royal Navy, Signalling Section.

ROLL OF HONOUR.

E. Hulton & Co. Limited
MANCHESTER.

Engraving Dept.
HARDLEY, W. G.
RHODES, F.
HAYWARD, W. S.
SMITH, H.
CALLAN E.
HINSON, V
BULLEN, W.
BUTLER, F.
ROBERTS, F.
NORMAN, H.
EVANS, W.
BARNES, A. J.

Photographic Dept.
CHADWICK, F.
SKINNER, F. S.
GRUNDY, G. V.
MARSDEN, R.

Editorial Dept.
RUDD, P.
KIRK, J. T.
STOWELL, —
BALL, A.
READING, R.
STOREY, F. A.
ARKINSTALL, R. A.
EDWARDS, R.
RAFFERTY, D. L.
ROBERTS, E.
WOODBRIDGE, J. A.
CARLEY, L.
TURNER, F. P.
HARRISON, C. E.
WITHERS, J.
CAMPBELL, A.
LYNCH, P.
McGARRIE, —
VICKERSTAFF, —
COONEY, S. J.
HOOLAHAN, J. A.
FIFE, F. A. (Liverpool)
FYFE, G.   ,,
SHEPHERD, —   ,,
COOPER, —   ,,
LAVIN, —   ,,
BARLOW, H. (Bolton).
HANDLEY, B. W.

Cashiers Dept.
BATTLE, E. R.
CAMPBELL, C.
WEIGHTMAN, W. J.

Mechanics.
COOKSON, E.
JOHNSON, A.
WOOD, J.
SMALLEY, J. V.

Advertisement Dept.
ASHE, S.
BODDY, J.
BROWN, F. A.
BUCKLER, A. J.
COWAN, W. J.
DAVIES, S.
DUNKERLEY, C. G.
HALL, G.
HEATON, T. E.
HOLT, E. C.
JACKSON, R.
LAWTON, S. J.
NEWMAN, W.
NUTTALL, H. V.
PRICE, A. J.
ROBINSON, E. C.
SCHOFIELD, E.
SMITH, W.
TERRELL, G. A.
VINCENT, J.
WOODS, S.

Electricians.
THOMPSON, J.
THOMPSON, G. R.
WEBB, C.
WALLACE, N.

Painter.
PIKE, C.

Joiners.
BRIGGS, F.
McMASTER, A.

Labourers.
GARVIN, A.
TAVO, C.
DILLON, J.
ILLINGWORTH, F.
SUTCLIFFE, C.
FINLOW, F.
SIMMONS, A.
WELLS, McCULLOUCH
  T.
BURTON, J.
CAMPBELL, T.

Accountants.
TAYLOR, J.
SWANN, H.
SWINDELLS, H.
PRIESTLEY, T.
SCHOLES, H.
BATTERSBY, W.
GOODWIN, C. W.
NADIN, S.
HEYWOOD, C. V.
EGAN, N.

ROLL OF HONOUR—Continued.

E. Hulton & Co. Limited

Liftmen.
GARVIN, H.
NORMAN, F.

Cleaners.
LINDSAY, H.
ROBINSON, J.
RICHMOND, H.
BELL, W.
PERRY, A.
McVETY, J.
BRIERLEY, W.
GEE, F.
KINSEY, H.

Branch Office Assistants.
JENNINGS, J.
RILEY, J.
WALTON, J. E.
RANDLES, J.
ROTHWELL, J.
BLACKWELL, T.
VICKERS, C.
PHILLIPS, H.
SEDDON, C.
MORTON, A.
KELTY, C.
REA, C.
PROCTOR, R.
MULTOCK, A.
HAMER, W.
LANCELOTT, J.
VICKERS, W.
STOCKTON, H.
BRAMHILL, A.
BENTLEY, E.
PICKLES, E.

Lino. Dept.
ASHLEY, E.
DAWSON, J.
ELDRED, —
GILDER, D.
SKINNER, D.
GOUGH, L.
PARKYN, W. E.
PRITCHARD, W.
RYAN, A.
SIMPSON, J.
TOWNLEY, H.
COGHLAN, E.
MILLER, G.
SHARP, F.
VICKERS, E.
HARPER, T.
THOMAS, L.
GERRARD, A.
COWLISHAW, T.
HOWELL, T. V.
ROSS, J. M.
COOPER, J. R.
MORLING, A. G.
CAWTHORNE, J. W.
ROYLE, H.
COTTIER, W. F.
BARNETT, N.
BURT, A. G.
FAIRWEATHER, P. G.
SHORROCKS, H.
CLARE, E.
MANSELL, A. F.
LATHAM, G.
BROOKMIRE, A.
BAILEY, J.
M'HARDY, P.
ATHERTON, S.

Newsagents' Accounts.
BROWN, C.
CONROY, B.
CRAWFORD, W. H.
FORRESTER, J.
HALL, J.
KENYON, G.
LEES, B.
PERCIVAL, G. R.
TUNNAH, W.
WILLIAMS, V.

General Printing Dept.
CASSERLEY, P.
BANNISTER, T.
BASKETTER, B. P.
ELLIS, G. T.
FRIPP, A.
GILLETT, J. C.
GREGORY, J. A.
HACKETT, M. F.
JONES, J. H.
LAYLAND, A.
MASHEDER, R. W.
NEWMAN, A. G.
OGDEN, T.
SIMM, A.
SPENCER, H. B.
TAYLOR, T.
WILLIAMS, H. H.
WOLSTENCROFT, H.
ATKINSON, H. C.
BARNETT, R.
BURKE, J.
COGHLAN, F. A.
McALLISTER, P.
QUINN, J.
SCANLON, A.
WILLIAMS F.
GREEN, T.
EVANS, G.
BOARDMAN, A.
GOULDING, J.
THOMPSON, A.
SMITH, H.
JONES, S.
SHERWIN, J.
BASSNETT, T.
NUTTALL, E.
DOWEY, J.
CLARKE, J.
EATON, J.
SIMISTER, R.
ROEBUCK, H.
SINCLAIR, F.
POLE, H.
BOOTH, J.
WILLIAMS, W.
SEWTER, L.
PRIEST, R.
COSGROVE, H.
SHUTTLEWORTH, A.

Publishing Dept.
SKELHORN, T.
GOLDSBORO, W. E.
LARGE, E.
ANDREWS, H.
WESTWOOD, E.
FOX, J.
RIDLEY, H.
BODDY, F.
BARRATT, P.
COLTON, M.
KNOTT, A. K.
SHAW, R.
FEARN, H.
SLACK, G. W.
NAYLOR, F.
BRADLEY, G.
SALE, J.
MARSDEN, W.
WHITTAKER, A.
DICKINSON, J.
BOOTH, E.
WALKER, J.
BURKEY, R.
WHITTAKER, W.
HENSHAW, A.
WATKISS, R.
COLLETT, L.
MILLS, J. H.
JOHNSTONE, R.
ROYLE, J. J.
HEATHCOTE, R. H.
DOLAN, J.
MANION, J. E.
BAILEY, W.
WOOD, J. H. R.
KEELING, G.
KILBURN, G.
SENIOR, A.
MYCOCK, A.
BRITTAIN, L. A.
RENNIE, J.
MORRISAY, A.
REA, G.
TOFT, L.
DOLBY, R.
SCOTT, J. H.
HATCH, A.

ROLL OF HONOUR—Continued.

E. Hulton & Co. Limited

Stereo Dept.

EYRE, J.
LEAHY, D.
HOLMES, E.
LOMAS, —
TASKER, A.
DICKSON, G.
MITCHELL, R.
WOODHOUSE, J.
LITTLEWOOD, H.
PICKTER, —
PICKERING, —
DILLON, —
HULME, F.
AITKEN, W.
PRIESTLEY, H.
WARD, A.
WHITTLE, H.
ROACH, J.
TAYLOR, H.
McKAY, R.
JAMIESON, R.
FELLOWS, C.
SYKES, A.
ELLIS, G.
KENDALL, R.
DALY, J.

Machine Dept.

ATKINSON, J.
BLACKBURN, C.
CORRIGAN, J.
KELLY, P.
MILLWARD, C.
ORRY, T.
CONNATTY, A.
JENKINS, J.
ENTWISTLE, J.
GREEN, G.
FORD, T.
ROSS, F.
WHITTLE, T.
WELSH, W.
COLE, C.
EVANS, T.
MILLAR, S.
TALLON, G.
BUCKLEY, J.
ROBERTS, J.
HALL, C.
GOLDIE, A.
LEWIS, A.
PARKER, G.
BLACKIE, T.
COSGROVE, J.
DEAVILLE, E.
LYNCH, J.
MORTON, T.
PURCELL, F.
PAGE, —
COSGROVE, C.
EDMONDSON, E.
HICKEY, E.
HOWARD, C.
JENKINS, E.
ROBINSON, R.
WILSON, T.
DONLEY, J.
EAGLES, J.
FLOOD, H.
HOWLEY, W.
MORTON, G.
MAYCOCK, E.
DICKENSON, J.
WILSON, W.
COWLEY, G.
OWEN, J.
LEWIS, H.
BUTT, J.
CURRAN, W.
DIXON, T.
MAYCOCK, W.
MOUND, W.
PEARSON, H.
REDDY, J.
EDWARDS, H.
FITZPATRICK, T.
FLANAGAN, J.
HUDSON, F.
RENSHAW, E.
WORRALL, F.
DOBSON, —
CLELLAND, F.
TAYLOR,
LEAVY, J.

Machine Dept.

GRAHAM, W.
HALL, W.
ALLISON, E.
ALLISON, H.
AVERY, A.
ABBOTT, W.
BURNS, R.
BUXTON, G.
BAILEY, H.
BRADBURN, G.
BROAD, L.
BOYD, C.
CURRAN, F.
CURRIE, W.
COLLINS, J.
COOPER, W. H.
COOPER, R.
CARROLL, T.
DAWSON, S.
DAVIES, C.
DOWNIE, J.
DIXON, J.
DUFFY, J.
EDWARDS, J.
FLATLEY, J.
FLYNN, D. R.
FIELDSEND, J.
GILLOTT, W. H.
GOODWIN, W.
GOODRIDGE, H.
HARRIS, J.
HOWITT, J.
HANNAN, H.
BUTLER, S.
JOSS, W.
HYDE, H.
DOOLEY, T.
GIBBS, J.
WARREN, —
KANE, J.
KIRKHAM, R.
LEIGHTON, J.
LANGTON, R.
LEATHLEY, H.
MILLS, J.
NAYLOR, T.
PITCHFORKE, A.
QUIRK, F.
ROYLE, A.
SHAW, H.
SYKES, H.
SANDERSON, A. E.
TANSLEY, P.
THORNTON, W.
TOMLINSON, T.
TOWNLEY, G.
VAUGHAN, H.
WARDLE, W. H.
WILLIAMS, F.
YARDLEY, W.
YATES, G.
BARDSLEY, W.
CRISP, C.
LOMAS, —
LEWIS, —

Carters.

SUTTON, J.
RIDYARD, H.
WOOD, W.
WOOD, T.
STEWART, W.
HORSFALL, J.
COYLE, J.
MELLOR, N.
MOODY, —
JOLLY, —
WOOD, C.
TARRY, C.
TARRY, T.
BUTLER, F.
ROMANS, H.
MOORE, P.
McCARTHY, P.
TOMLIN, C.
RAYMOND, A.
BEESLEY, E.
MOLINEUX, J.
KEDIE, A.
TYRIE, W.
LEEMING, E.
HARRISON, R.
BERRELL, A.

ROLL OF HONOUR

de JERSEY & CO.,

Manchester and Liverpool.

Serving.

Captain JERSEY DE KNOOP	6th Cavalry Brigade.
W. BELLIS	D.L.O. Yeomanry.
G. BOEUFVE	French Army.
J. CHAMBERS	South Lancashire Regiment.
G. H. CROWTHER	184th Siege Battery, R.G.A.
W. J. DAVIES	10th King's Liverpool Regiment.
R. W. FALKINER	18th Service Battalion K.L.R.
I. GRACE	43rd Provisional Battalion (T.F.).
C. W. HORSLEY	R.A., Section G.H.Q.
L. LEWIS	London Welsh.
A. ROSE	18th Service Battalion K.L.R.
F. RYLE	10th King's Liverpool Regiment.
G. WILLIAMS	1st West Lancashire R.A.M.C.

Attested.

W. JOHNSON.	R. D. SACHS.
G. DUNN.	T. WESTWOOD.
D. HINDLE.	

Rejected.

J. H. CLEGG.*
J. W. FIELDEN.*
J. H. ROBINSON.*

* Medically unfit.

ROLL OF HONOUR.

List of Men from
A. V. ROE & CO. LIMITED
Who have Joined H.M. Forces.

Name.	Rank.	Regiment.
ADKIN, J.	2nd A.M.	Royal Naval Air Service.
ALDCROFT, P.	2nd A.M.	Royal Flying Corps.
ALLEN, ALBERT	Private	Royal Engineers.
ARMSON, FRED	Private	Royal Garrison Artillery.
AUSTIN, FRANK	Private	Black Watch.
BANCROFT, ALFRED	2nd A.M.	Royal Flying Corps.
BELL, HARRY, L.	2nd A.M.	Royal Flying Corps.
BENTLEY, SIDNEY	2nd A.M.	Royal Flying Corps.
BETTLES, SAMUEL	2nd A.M.	Royal Flying Corps.
BOWYER, ALFRED	Private	Army Service Corps (M.T.)
BURNETT, H. C.	2nd A.M.	Royal Flying Corps.
CHAPMAN, JAMES	2nd A.M.	Royal Flying Corps.
COLLIER, HERBERT	Petty Officer	Motor Boat Section, R.N.A.S.
DURTNALL, HAROLD	2nd A.M.	Royal Flying Corps.
EARLE, WILLIAM HY.	A.B.	Royal Navy.
ECCLES, S.	2nd A.M.	Royal Flying Corps.
FARRINGTON, WALTER	Sergeant	King's Royal Rifles.
FOOT, J.	2nd A.M.	Royal Flying Corps.
FRIER, J.	Private	Argyle & Sutherland Highlanders.
GREENWOOD, HENRY	1st A.M.	Royal Naval Air Service.
HAMPSON, ABRAHAM	1st A.M.	Royal Naval Air Service.
HANNA, WILLIAM	1st A.M.	Royal Naval Air Service.
HOLMES, FRED J. V.	1st A.M.	Royal Naval Air Service.
HOLT, JAMES	Private	8th Batt. Manchester Regiment.
HORTON, WILLIAM	Private	Royal Field Artillery.
HOULDSWORTH, WILLIAM	2nd A.M.	Royal Flying Corps.
HOWARD, —	2nd A.M.	Royal Flying Corps.
JENNISON, —	2nd Lieut.	
KELLY, —	Private	10th Batt. Manchester Regt.
KENT, MARK	2nd A.M.	Royal Flying Corps.
LAND, WILLIAM HY.	2nd A.M.	Royal Flying Corps.
LUCAS, CLIFFORD	1st A.M.	Royal Naval Air Service.
MARTINDALE, WILLIAM	Staff Sergeant	Army Ordnance (Artificer).
MATHEWS, —	2nd A.M.	Royal Flying Corps.
MOORE, W.	Private	Royal Engineers.
NORWOOD, HUGH	Private	Grenadier Guards.
OAKES, WILLIAM	Petty Officer	Motor Boat Section, R.N.A.S.
PARRY, HENRY	2nd A.M.	Royal Naval Air Service.
PENDLEBURY, JAMES	2nd A.M.	Royal Flying Corps.
PEMBERTON, SAMUEL W.	Private	Grenadier Guards.
RAWSTHORNE, A.	Private	Royal Field Artillery.
RHEAN, ALLEN	2nd A.M.	Royal Flying Corps.
ROBERTS, CHARLES	2nd A.M.	Royal Flying Corps.
SCHOFIELD, RALPH	Private	9th Batt. Manchester Regt.
SKIDMORE, GEORGE	2nd A.M.	Royal Flying Corps.
SMITH, F.	2nd A.M.	Royal Flying Corps.
SMITH, G.	2nd A.M.	Royal Flying Corps.
SMYLIE (D.S.O.), GILBERT F.	Flight Sub.-Lieut.	Royal Naval Air Service.
STEVENSON G.	Private	Royal Engineers.
STRINGER, JAMES	2nd A.M.	Royal Flying Corps.
SWAN, I.	Private	Royal Field Artillery.
TAYLOR, FRANK	Private	9th Batt. Manchester Regt.
TAYLOR, SIDNEY	E. R. Artificer	Royal Navy.
TAYLOR, WILLIAM	A.B.	Royal Navy.
WALTON, FRANK S.	Private	Royal Engineers.
WAINWRIGHT, EDWARD	Private	Royal Field Artillery.
WORSLEY, FREDERICK	2nd A.M.	Royal Flying Corps.

ROLL OF HONOUR.

R. JOHNSON & SONS, LTD.

52 The Crescent,
—SALFORD—

H. F. JOHNSON	Royal Garrison Artillery.
JAMES JOHNSON	5th Manchesters.
FRED SLOAN	16th Lancashire Fusiliers.
FRED BEVINS	16th Lancashire Fusiliers.
EDWARD PARKINSON	19th Lancashire Fusiliers.
WILLIAM JACKSON	South Lancashire Regiment.
JOE COOK	19th Lancashire Fusiliers.
LEONARD PLATTEN	19th Lancashire Fusiliers.
ALFRED BROOKS	Royal Flying Corps.
ARTHUR CRYER	7th Lancashire Fusiliers.
ARTHUR JOHNSON	Royal Field Artillery.
JAMES GREGORY	Royal Welsh Fusiliers.
ARTHUR OPENSHAW	7th Lancashire Fusiliers.
JOHN WEBB	Royal Navy.
L. BERRY	Loyal North Lancashire Regiment.
EDWARD PARKER	Lancashire Fusiliers.
WILLIAM CAMPBELL	Lancashire Fusiliers.
A. W. HAWORTH	Seaforth Highlanders.
W. MANNING	Lancashire Fusiliers.
GEORGE LIVESEY	3/7th Lancashire Fusiliers.
CYRIL PALMER	Royal Navy.
HAROLD JOHNSON	18th Lancashire Fusiliers.
CHAS. JACKSON	South Lancashire Regiment.

ROLL OF HONOUR.

GEO. H. WALKER & SON,

3, Chepstow Street, MANCHESTER.

SERVING WITH THE FORCES.

WILLIAM BOOTH	3/6th Manchesters.
STANLEY DAVENPORT	2/7th Chesters.
FRED DAVIES	Cyclists, 8th Manchesters.
CHARLES DEWSBURY	Royal Field Artillery.
GEO. HANNAY	6th Manchesters.
H. HONAN	Royal Welsh Fusiliers.
H. B. RAINES	Royal Field Artillery.
E. WHITTLES	6th West Yorks (Wounded).
E. KREUTZ	R.F.A., 59th Brigade, 11th Division.
H. SHOESSMITH	1st Gar. Battery, Yorks. Regt. In India.
P. HARE	R.F.A., 1st West Riding Batt. (R.A.M.C.)
W. LEECHMAN	Royal Navy, H.M.S. "Comas."
A. THORNTON	3/6th West Yorks.
F. HOLDSWORTH	3/6th West Yorks.
T. ARMSTRONG	3/6th West Yorks.
S. FIELD	Not known
H. POLLARD	R.F.A., 53rd Brigade, 9th Division.
A. RICH	20th West Yorks.

Roll of Honour.

Black & Green Ltd.
MANCHESTER.

Pte. SEDDON,
    Loyal North Lancashires.
Pte. LEATHER,
    Manchesters.
Pte. YATES,
    Manchesters.
Pte. DANIELS,
    Manchesters.
Sgt. TANNER,
    Motor Transport, A.S.C.
Pte. ROBERTS,
    Army Service Corps.
Pte. ROBSON,
    Lancashire Fusiliers.
Pte. SHARPLES,
    Manchesters.
Pte. WINDER,
    Motor Transport, A.S.C.
Pte. JONES,
    Royal Field Artillery.
Pte. SLEE,
    Royal Garrison Artillery.
Pte. FLEMING,
    Army Service Corps.
Sgt. BROOKSBANK,
    Sherwood Foresters.
Sgt. BARTON,
    Army Veterinary Corps.
Pte. ROSCOE,
    Royal Field Artillery.
Cpl. WILSON,
    Army Service Corps.
Pte. CRASTON,
    Army Service Corps.
Pte. PYCROFT,
    London Rifles.
Pte. FRYER,
    East Yorks.
Pte. LONGFELLOW,
    Army Veterinary Corps.
Pte. LANE,
    King's Liverpools.

Roll of Honour.

John Ditchfield

54, & 56, Dantzic Street,
15, & 17, Mayes Street,
SHUDEHILL,
MANCHESTER.

CUTHBERT KELLETT.
R.A.M.C.

WALTER KAY,
R.F.A.

KENNETH LISTER,
Royal Scots.

SYDNEY ROYLE,
R.N.V.R.

LESLIE RYMAN,
A.S.C., Motor Transport.

E. RIMMER,
Lancashire Fusiliers.

JOHN SMITH,
A.S.C.

JOHN CROOK.
Shropshire L. I.

ROLL OF HONOUR.

MATHER & PLATT LTD.
MANCHESTER.

Royal Navy.
Lieut. S. H. HALL, Naval Ordnance, Electrical Sect.
Pte. E. H. WEBB, H.M. Hosp. Ship "Garth Castle."
Pte. F. W. WINDYBANK (498), R.M.L.I., Plym. Batt.
Pte. H. BATTLE (33440), Roy. Nav. Div., "Benbow" Bt.
Pte. D. ELLIS, Royal Marines.
Seaman J. W. WOODWARD, H.M.S. "Brilliant."
A.B. Seaman A. WIGNALL, (Z. 332 C.), 2nd Royal Naval Div., "Collinwood" Batt.
Stoker T. PLIMMER, H.M.S. "Aurora."
Stoker G. HUMPAGE, H.M.S. "Canopus."
Wire. Op. H. TOLLEY (8531), H.M.S. "Impregnable."
Appentrice H. EMERY, Royal Nav. Barr., Portsmouth.
Seaman C. E. SAVAGE, H.M.S. "Tiger."
5th Eng. T. HOWARTH, Troopship "City of Dunkirk."
1st Cl. Boy A. BARNES (J. 34599), H.M.S. "Minataur."
Pte. T. HAWKRIDGE, R.N.V.R. "Mersey" Dv., 2nd Co.
Boy B. ROBEY, H.M.S. "Powerful," Devonport.
Boy J. HUGHES, H.M.S. "Powerful," Devonport.
Boy Telegraphist J. ASHTON, H.M.S. "Iron Duke"
Seaman A. TUNSTALL, H.M.S. "Powerful."

Royal Naval Air Service.
2nd Lt. F. H. HAYWARD, Nav. Air Ser., Arm. Car Sec.
2nd Lt. W. BUCKLEY, Royal Naval Air Service.
Petty Officer R. MASON, Nav. Air Ser., Arm. Car Brig.
1st Mech. R. MORRISON, Royal Naval Flying Corps.

Cavalry.
Corpl. A. CARTER, 20th Brig. Military Mounted Police.
L.-Corpl. A. G. HODGSON, City of London Yeomanry.
Trooper T. R. ROBINSON (5117), 4th Dragoon Guards.
Trooper C. BRADY (22024), 4th Dragoon Guards.
Trooper D. CLARE (22804), 4th Hussars.
Trooper F. CONNORY, 17th Lancers.
Trooper C. GALE, 7th Cavalry Reserve.
Trooper A. M. SMITH, D.L.O. Yeomanry.
Trooper S. Garcia, D.L.O. Yeomanry.
Trooper R. OAKLEY, Worcester Yeomanry.
Trooper T. E. GUNSON, Norfolk Yeomanry.

Royal Garrison Artillery.
Lieut. A. C. HARDY, Harwich.
2nd Lieut. H. B. EDWARDS, 129th Heavy Battery.
2nd Lieut S. SMITH, 19th Heavy Battery.
Gunner W. LESTER (49326), Plymouth.
Artificer S. R. A. STERLING, 120th Battery.
Gunner J. HEBB (278), 133rd Heavy Batty.
Gunner H. JOHNSON (7210), Fort Rowner, Gosport.

Army Ordnance Corps.
Staff-Sergt. H. McPHEE (88526), 89th Brigade R.F.A.
Sgt. J. W. DUNLOP, 157th Heavy Batt. R.G.A., Deptf'd.

Machine Gun Corps.
Pte. W. YORKE.

Royal Field Artillery.
Lieut. L. G. WORMALD, 132nd Battery.
Lieut. O. G. SHERWELL, 364th Battery. Mil. Cross.
2nd Lieut. C. E. SKINNER.
L.-Corpl. S. BATESON, 351st Battery.
Signaller E. HURST (86409), 212th Battery.
Driver H. HARRISON (24074), 25th Battery.
Driver W. LATHROPE (27897), 27th Brigade Am. Col.
Driver A. GIBSON, "D" Battery, 103rd Brigade.
Gunner T. PRINCE (24274), 59th Brigade Am. Column.
Gunner E. R. BRISCOE (37584), 305th Battery.
Gunner P. RUSH, 1st London.
Driver J. BYROM (47670), 4th Battery, 79th Brigade.
Gunner J. RILEY.
Gunner J. W. WARREN (97163), 176th Battery.
Gunner J. BEATHAM (4889), 179th Battery.
Gunner J. R. DYSON (25020), 11th Battery.
Bbr. W. A. BOWMAN (69886), 52nd Bat., 6th C. Res. Br.
Driver T. NODEN (70442), 20th Division Am. Column.
Driver R. W. WEEDS (98893), 23rd Battery.
Gunr. A. D. EMSLEY (1744), Motor Cycle Mac. Gun Sec.
Gunner F. JARVIS.
Gunr. G. BARRATT (117532), 9th Depot Batt., Preston.
Gunner J. DERBYSHIRE, 72nd Brigade Am. Column.

Mather and Platt Ltd.

ROLL OF HONOUR—continued.

County Palatine R.F.A.
Sergt. T. WOODS (18361), 170th Brigade, "B" Battery
Bombr. W. COOP (9435), 4th Brigade.
Gunner W. H. SCHOFIELD (9849), "K" Batt.
Gunner J. C. BROWNHILL (10878), 169th Brigade.
Gunner P. J. HAYES (16082), 169th Bridage, "D" Batt.
Driver H. OSBALDESTON (34525), 181st Brigade.

East Lancashire R.F.A.
Sergt. W. LANE (122), 2nd Am. Column.
Driver G. WILKINSON (1254), 2nd Battery.
Gunner J. HOLLINGWORTH, 2nd Battery.
Gunner E. STRANGE (20226), 2/3rd Battery.
Gunner G. HOWELL (1742), 2/3rd Battery.
Gunner G. CONWAY (732), 1/4th Battery.
Gunner W. BAILEY (1251), 1/5th Battery.
Gunner J. JONES (1181), 17th Battery.
Bombr. G. H. SMITH, 16th Battery.
Gunner F. H. CRAWSHAW, 17th Battery.
Gunner B. BESWICK (1857), 2/2nd Battery.
Gunner T. SIMMONDS (2922), 2/2nd Battery.

West Riding R.F.A.
Corpl. C. J. BRENTNALL (791), 3rd Battery.

Nottingham R.H.A.
2nd Lieut. E. J. H. LONERGAN.

Indian Army.
Lieut. A. MACBETH, Head-Quarters Staff.

Royal Flying Corps.
Lieut. C. H. WHITTINGTON. Head-Quarters Staff.
2nd Lieut. C. DRABBLE.
2nd Lieut. P. S. BUTTERWORTH, 14th Res. Aero Squadron.
Corpl. J. KIRBY, Hounslow.
2nd Mechanic F. DAVENPORT (3377), 3rd Res. Aero Squadron.
2nd Mechanic C. DALEY (4456), 3rd Res. Aero Squad.
2nd Mechanic E ORMONDROYD (4390), 2nd Res. Aero Squadron.
2nd Mechanic C. F. ABBOTT, Kite Balloon Section.

Glamorgan Fortress.
2nd Lieut. A. R. PERTWEE, 3rd Co. El.
Sapper T. DAVIES, 4th Co. El.

Royal Anglesey Engineers.
Sapper J. F. MADELEY (7334).

County Palatine Royal Engineers.
Driver J. M. FOX (83044), 201st Coy.
Sapper E. BEDDOES (99731), 200th Coy.

Royal Engineers.
Major R. THOMAS, Dep. A. Director Canal Transport.
Lieut. F. W. CLARK, 231st Field Co., 40th Division.
2nd Lieut. V. J. HOOK.
Cpl. E. D. FINLAYSON (42989), 16th Sig. Co., Mot. Cyc.
Corpl. G. M. ROWLANDS (75163), Despatch Rider,
L.-Cpl. R. MATHER (45454), 19th Sig. Co., 56th Brig.
L.-Corpl. J. ROBINSON (42993), 83rd Field Co.
L.-Corpl. A. SLACK (142646), No. 2 Wireless Squad.
Driver J. KENNEDY (45963), 10th Signal Co.
Sapper G. WOOD, 19th Signal Co., 56th Brigade.
Pioneer H. OWEN (44581), 21st Signal Co.
Driver L. FRY, 29th Signal Co.
Sapper W. STUART (45456), Reserve, Haines Park.
Sapper C. GRANT (31554), Reserve.
Sapper W. MOFFATT, 62nd Field Co.
Sapper R. COOPER (40245), 69th Field Co.
Sapper H. BUTTERWORTH (44835), 84th Field Co.
Driver W. SHERRATT (51901), 104th Field Co.
Sapper W. DONNELLY (31555).
Sapper W. HANSON (105765), Railway Troops Co.
Sapper R. S. PALMER (35059).
Sapper F. PAXTON (9005).
Sapper W. EARLEY (35154), 143rd Army Troop Co.
Sapper P. HEALEY (16869).
  Signal Depot.
Sapper H. A. HANDS (97635), 167th Fortress Co.
Sapper R. HARTLEY (28625), 20th Fortress Co., 3rd Army Corps.

Lancashire Fortress Royal Engineers.
Sapper R. A. BALDWIN (667), No. 2 Coy.

Army Service Corps.
Sgt. J. JONES (22370, Motor Tran., 1st Cav. Supply Col.
Lieut. E. P. F. EDWARDS, 2nd Army Headq. Office.
Driver H. MORRIS, Motor Transport.
Driver A. POWNALL (O. 8335), Motor Tran., 80th Co.
Driver C. S. HORSBURGH (6133), Motor Transport, 2nd Cavalry Supply Col.
Driver A. TAYLOR, Motor Transport.
Pte. R. STARKEY (734), Motor Transport.
Pte. W. TRAVIS (T. 1826), 15th Divisional Train.
Pte. S. CRAWSHAW (O. 54753), Mechanical Transport.
Pte. J. CLARKE, 187th Co., 25th Division.
Pte. G. DICKINSON (O. 53936), Mechanical Transport.
Pte. E. WRIGHT (O. 54778), Mech. Tran., 29th Div.
Pte. A. WILLIAMS (O. 53952), Mechanical Transport.
Pte. H. ROYLE (O. 53816), 175th Co., 12th Supply Col.
Driver H. REDFEARN, Motor Transport.
Pte. F. BATESON, Mechanical Transport.
Pte. B. LLOYD (17112), 4th Co., Labour Section.

Mather and Platt Ltd.

ROLL OF HONOUR -- continued.

East Lancashire Royal Engineers.
Captain L. E. MATHER, 2/1st Field Co.
Captain R. F. SUTCLIFFE, 6th Prov. Field Co.
Lieut. O. H. TAUNTON, 1/1st Field Co. Mil. Cross.
Lieut. D. E. GOUGH, 1/1st Field Co.
Lieut. R. L. GRACEY, 1/2nd Field Co.
2nd Lieut. A. ROBERTS, Signal Co.
Corpl. G. WALKER (1393), 2/1st Field Co.
Corpl. B. WHITTY (733), 1/1st Field Co.
L.-Corpl. F. HUTCHINSON (782), 1/2nd Field Co.
L.-Corpl. H. SWIFT (901), 1/2nd Field Co.
Sapper L. WARD, 1/1st Field Co.
Driver E. WOOD, 1/1st Field Co.
Sapper J. CATTERALL (823), 1/1st Field Co.
Sapper R. COULTHURST, 1/1st Field Co.
Sapper W. DUNNING, 1/1st Field Co.
Sapper G. H. WALKER (1039), 1/1st Field Co.
Sapper A. HUGHES (1011), 1/1st Field Co.
Sapper W. G. ECCLES, 2/1st Field Co.
Sapper R. BARRITT (1082), 2/2nd Field Co.
Sapper F. J. DYKES, 2/ Field Co.
Sapper J. H. PARKIN (1406), Signal Co.
Sapper T. CULLY.
Sapper S. T. HOWE (1048), 1/2nd Field Co.
Sapper J. A. PRICE (2823).
Sapper M. K. GODLEY (3265), 2/3rd Field Co.
Sapper J. R. SWARBRICK (3266), 2/3rd Field Co.
Sapper E. NEWALL (3394) 2/3rd Field Co.

Royal Army Medical Corps.
Sergt.-Major A. RIDYARD, 17th Co., Congleton Hosp.
Corpl. J. THOMPSON, Rouen Stationary Hospital.
L.-Corpl. J. FIELDING (11101), 39th Field Ambulance.
Pte. F. HEEDY (18096), 17th Rail Head Sanitary Squad.
Pte. F. DANIELS (37711), 35th Feild Amb., 11th Div.
Pte. A. HORSFIELD, 30th Field Ambulance.
Pte. H. BROMLEY, 7th Sec., "H" Co.
Pte. W. HIGGINSON (1912), No. 6 Amb. Train, France.
Pte. R. JAMES (380), 1st Field Ambulance.
Bugler J. REID (152), 2nd Western Hosp., Manchester.
Pte. H. DUTTON (150), 2nd Western Hosp., Manchester.
Pt. W. NOBLE (126), 2nd Field Ambulance.
Pte. O. & SMITH (637), 3/2nd Field Ambulance
Pte. J. W. NEWTON (635), 3/2nd Field Ambulance.
Driver C. THOMPSON, 1st Sec. Motor Amb., Dijon.
Pte. T. HEAPHEY (612), Lily Lane Hosp., Manchester.
Pte. E. RUSHTON (68487), Twedledown Camp, Farnham
Pte. P. ALLEN (75670), 17th Field Amb., 6th Division.
Pte. H. DRYSDALE (62254), Litchfield Military Hosp.
Pte. D. BEATTIE (38), 66th E.L. Division.
Pte. S. WILLIAMSON (625), Whitworth St. Hospital.

South Midland Royal Engineers.
Sapper A. G. TUTTON, 2/1st Field Co., 28th Div.
Sap. E. W. HOLLWAY (1775), 2/1st Field Co., 28th Div.
Sapper C. COOK (2750), 2/2nd Field Co., 28th Div.

Manchester Regiment.
Major F. BRYANT, 20th Batt. Military Cross.
Captain R. C. MATHER, 19th Batt.
Lieut. H. N. McLELLAN, 2nd Batt.
Lieut. H. H. CRAWSHAW, 18th Batt.
2nd Lieut. S. JARVIS, 13th Batt.
2nd Lieut. B. TEMPEST, 13th Batt.
2nd Lieut. H. V. BARKER, 15th Batt.
2nd Lieut. C. W. K. HOOK, 16th Batt.
Q.M.Sergt. J. JOYCE (1504), 7th Batt.
Sergt. C. WHITTAKER, 8th Batt.
Sergt. J. HOLMES, 16th Batt.
Sergt. L. D. BOYD (2083), 6th Batt.
Sergt. G. H. WOOD, 6th Batt.
Sergt. J. BAINBRIDGE (2536), 7th Batt.
Corpl. H. CROFTS, 8th Batt.
Corpl. G. MATHER, 8th Batt.
Corpl. D. L. JONES (13186), 12th Batt.
Corpl. J. E. LORD (13612), 14th Batt
Corpl. J. H. SEARS, 16th Batt.
Corpl. S. WINTERBOTTOM (20469), 22nd Batt.
Corpl. J. COCHRANE (9836), 2nd Batt.
Corpl. H. ARUNDALE (4001), 3rd Batt.
L.-Corpl. W. PEACOCK (48), 7th Batt.
L.-Corpl. E. H. S. HALL (2737), 8th Batt.
L.-Corpl. T. SHAUGNESSY, 8th Batt.
L.-Corpl. W. F. JACKSON (31364), 25th Batt.
L.-Corpl. A. TOMMINS, 1st Batt.
Pte. W. GRAVES, 1st Batt.
Pte. J. A. CASSON (2231), 1st Batt.
Pte. J. BENSON, 2nd Batt.
Pte. F. MORRIS, 2nd Batt.
Pte. C. HORTON (24596), 3rd Batt.
Pte. G. QUINLESS (7748), 3rd Batt.
Pte. J. BESWICK, 3rd Batt.
Pte. W. GAVIN (1710), 3rd Batt.
Pte. J. HAMER, 3rd Batt.
Pte. E. WHITE (1551), 3rd Batt.
Pte. W. DERBYSHIRE (16823), 3rd Batt.
Pte. J. McGARY (6904), 3rd Batt.
Pte. G. ATHERTON (2877), 3rd Batt.
Pte. C. WALKER (16776), 3rd Batt.
Pte. W. JOWETT (40405), 3rd Batt.
Pte. T. R. BROWN (23010), 3rd Batt.
Pte. D. HANNAN (1108), 4th Batt.
Pte. J. MYCOCK, 4th Batt.
Pte. H. WHITEHEAD, 4th Batt.

Mather and Platt Ltd.

ROLL OF HONOUR—continued.

Manchester Regiment—continued.

- Pte. H. B. SMITH (2814), 4th Batt.
- Pte. J. WILLIAMSON, 4th Batt.
- Pte. D. KILCOURSE, 4th Batt.
- Pte. A. STRAFFORD (2575), 4th Batt.
- Pte. A. TONGS (16958), 4th Batt.
- Pte. J. WHITE (5240), 4th Batt.
- Pte. R. BRIERLEY (16381), 4th Batt.
- Pte. F. McDONOUGH (2331), 4th Batt.
- Pte. H. HEWITSON (24334), 4th Batt.
- Pte. J. R. NEWALL (37894), 4th Batt.
- Pte. A. BOALER, 6th Batt.
- Pte. H. TURNBULL (1386), 6th Batt.
- Pte. C. P. WILD (2463), 6th Batt.
- Pte. E. M. WHITE, 6th Batt.
- Pte. W. HOLT, 6th Batt.
- Pte. A. TWEATS, 6th Batt.
- Pte. W. HILTON (1291), 6th Batt.
- Pte. J. STANYARD (4122), 6th Batt.
- Pte. A. SHAW (4107), 6th Batt.
- Pte. W. CLARKE (1306), 7th Batt.
- Pte. J. PEACOCK, 7th Batt.
- Pte. N. WILKINSON, 7th Batt.
- Pte. H. GRIFFIN, 7th Batt.
- Pte. R. BOWERS, 7th Batt.
- Pte. G. TEALEY, 7th Batt.
- Pte. J. STOCKS, 7th Batt.
- Pte. J. R. HALL, 7th Batt.
- Pte. F. SALMON (1629), 7th Batt.
- Pte. T. UNSWORTH (3836), 7th Batt.
- Pte. H. DETHERIDGE, 7th Batt.
- Pte. R. MORRIS, 7th Batt.
- Pte. A. ROGERS, 7th Batt.
- Pte. T. RAWSON (3835), 7th Batt.
- Pte. J. H. BAILEY (3637), 7th Batt.
- Pte. W. E. RAWLINSON, 7th Batt.
- Pte. W. RILEY, 7th Batt.
- Pte. H. BOYD (5291), 7th Batt.
- Pte. H. WHITTAKER (2481), 7th Batt.
- Pte. J. HOWARTH (4073), 7th Batt.
- Pte. R. ARMSTRONG (4709), 7th Batt.
- Pte. A. V. ROBINSON (5390), 7th Batt.
- Pte. T. BURKE, 8th Batt.
- Pte. C. SHAW, 8th Batt.
- Pte. P. O'BRIEN (1932), 8th Batt.
- Pte. T. KEIG, 8th Batt.
- Pte. S. INGHAM, 8th Batt.
- Pte. C. E. JONES, 8th Batt.
- Pte. — WILLIAMS, 8th Batt.
- Pte. J. BOAHAN (830), 8th Batt.
- Pte. W. GAUNT (2286), 8th Batt.
- Pte. L. GARDNER (2779), 8th Batt.

Manchester Regiment—continued.

- Pte. E. D. HOWELLS (2762), 8th Batt.
- Pte. E. D. HALL, 8th Batt.
- Pte. J. C. CROSS, 8th Batt.
- Pte. E. WAREHAM, 8th Batt.
- Pte. F. WALSH, 8th Batt.
- Pte. W. ISHERWOOD, 8th Batt.
- Pte. G. WARBURTON, 8th Batt.
- Pte. G. A. ABBOTT, 8th Batt.
- Pte. A. HANCOX (2427), 8th Batt.
- Pte. A. MORRAN, 8th Batt.
- Pte. E. SNOWDON, 8th Batt.
- Pte. J. W. STONE (1927), 8th Batt.
- Pte. W. HOLT, 8th Batt.
- Pte. H. BRADWELL, 8th Batt.
- Pte. W. TAYLOR, 8th Batt.
- Pte. J. C. BECKWITH (2189), 8th Batt.
- Pte. G. WARBURTON, 8th Batt.
- Pte. J. AUBREY (3560), 8th Batt.
- Pte. J. E. HUGHES, 8th Batt.
- Pte. R. WHARTON (3159), 8th Batt.
- Pte. W. JAMES (9885), 8th Batt.
- Pte. J. H. WELBOURNE (9888), 8th Batt.
- Pte. H. ASHTON, 8th Batt.
- Pte. H. A. BARRATT (5385), 8th Batt.
- Pte. J. IRVING, 9th Batt.
- Pte. E. WOOD (2884), 9th Batt.
- Pte. J. MARTIN, 9th Batt.
- Pte. S. LESTER (1987), 10th Batt.
- Pte. B. SUTTON (4540), 10th Batt.
- Pte. W. HARRISON (5259), 10th Batt.
- Pte. F. ALLEN (9635), 11th Batt.
- Pte. E. ALDRED (3169), 11th Batt.
- Pte. J. HAMILTON (27924), 11th Batt.
- Pte. R. SMITH (4905), 12th Batt.
- Pte. W. JORDAN (4770), 12th Batt.
- Pte. G. HUDSON (5286), 12th Batt.
- Pte. R. SCOTSON (4771), 12th Batt.
- Pte. W. HARDING (5262), 12th Batt.
- Pte. H. KELLY (5193), 12th Batt.
- Pte. E. VALENTINE, 12th Batt.
- Pte. E. HOUGHTON (5951), 12th Batt.
- Pte. J. WRIGHT (3897), 12th Batt.
- Pte. W. TAYLOR (553), 12th Batt.
- Pte. W. COOPER, 13th Batt.
- Pte. H. McMAHON (7893), 13th Batt.
- Pte. J. O'HARA (13591), 14th Batt.
- Pte. W. SYKES (24475), 14th Batt.
- Pte. H. ROSS, 14th Batt.
- Pte. H. ROYLE, 14th Batt.
- Pte. H. SWEETMAN (1217), 16th Batt.
- Pte. H. HILTON (27037), 16th Batt.

Mather and Platt Ltd.

ROLL OF HONOUR—continued.

Manchester Regiment—continued.

Pte. G. C. CHASE (7646), 16th Batt.
Pte. H. FEARNS, 17th Batt.
Pte. A. ADAMS, 17th Batt.
Pte. T. REEVES, 18th Batt.
Pte. T. BAILEY, 18th Batt.
Pte. C. MOLDEN, 18th Batt.
Pte. W. H. HEWITT, 18th Batt.
Pte. C. GARLICK, 18th Batt.
Pte. C. MORGAN, 18th Batt.
Pte. G. A. PERKINS, 18th Batt.
Pte. W. WEBB, 18th Batt.
Pte. A. SPACKMAN, 18th Batt.
Pte. T. SNELSON, 18th Batt.
Pte. G. R. BOULTON (9808), 18th Batt.
Bugler A. RAMSDEN, 18th Batt.
Pte. C. R. WILLCOCKS, 19th Batt.
Pte. T. PARKER, 19th Batt.
Pte. A. REID (12442), 19th Batt.
Pte. E. SAVAGE, 19th Batt.
Bugler G. GORMAN, 19th Batt.
Pte. J. SIMPSON, 19th Batt.
Pte. W. CONNOLLY, 20th Batt.
Pte. H. SCOBLE, 21st Batt.
Pte. F. LINDON, 21st Batt.
Pte. A. SIMMONDS, 21st Batt.
Pte. A. FLINT, 21st Batt.
Pte. W. MATTHEWS, 21st Batt.
Pte. G. GOSNELL (7501), 21st Batt.
Pte. F. THRELFALL (20957), 22nd Batt.
Pte. G. HORROCKS (20294), 22nd Batt.
Pte. W. F. BINNS (20205), 22nd Batt.
Pte. J. McHARDY, 23rd Batt.
Pte. F. DOBSON, 23rd Batt.
Pte. J. DANSON, 23rd Batt.
Pte. S. RICHARDSON, 23rd Batt.
Pte. E. BRADLEY, 24th Batt. (Oldham).
Pte. J. CAVEY (15417), 24th Batt. (Oldham).
Pte. S. J. SMITH (15111), 24th Batt. (Oldham).
Pte. A. BESWICK (25500), 26th Batt.
Pte. R. RALPHS (29380), 26th Batt.

East Lancashire Regiment.

Corpl. R. A. LIVESEY, 9th Batt.
Corpl. T. BROWN (14524), 9th Batt.
L.-Corpl. I. UPTON (14325), 9th Batt.
Pte. J. HORRIDGE (7050), 3rd Batt.
Pte. J. HARTLEY, 3rd Batt.
Pte. T. PARRY (18397), 3rd Batt.
Pte. W. MATTHEWS (17078), 6th Batt.
Pte. J. GRIMSHAW (14099), 7th Batt.
Pte. T. W. KELLY (14259), 7th Batt.
Pte. H. JUDD (13051), 8th Batt.

East Lancashire Regiment—continued.

Pte. T. BUTTERWORTH, 8th Batt.
Pte. S. LORD, 8th Batt.
Pte. R. C. WOODHOUSE, 9th Batt.
Pte. H. MERRICK (14121), 9th Batt.
Pte. A. DUNN (14604), 9th Batt.
Pte. T. KINGSMORE, 9th Batt.
Pte. R. LEES (14231), 9th Batt.
Pte. JAS. DAWSON (14285), 9th Batt.
Pte. A. HARDING, 9th Batt.
Pte. G. ANDERTON (14320), 9th Batt.
Pte. H. H. SHAW (14271), 9th Batt.
Pte. A. FROST (14730), 9th Batt.
Pte. P. BROWN (14123), 9th Batt.
Pte. F. BERRY (14336), 9th Batt.
Pte. W. HEATON (14338), 9th Batt.
Pte. F. SMITH (14036), 9th Batt.
Pte. C. W. LONG (14039), 9th Batt.
Pte. J. CLARKSON (14543), 9th Batt.
Pte. T. DAVIES (14007), 9th Batt.
Pte. V. ALLATT (14622), 9th Batt.
Pte. C. A. MORGAN (14109), 9th Batt.
Pte. J. A. BOWERS (19642), 9th Batt.
Pte. S. HEYWOOD (14319), 9th Batt.
Pte. J. ORCHARD (14279), 9th Batt.
Pte. C. H. GOODLIFFE (14117), 9th Batt.
Pte. W. LAWSON (14280), 9th Batt.
Pte. H. TOWNEND, 9th Batt.
Pte. D. SUTCLIFFE (14341), 9th Batt.
Pte. J. CONNOR (13724), 9th Batt.
Pte. R. LUCAS, 9th Batt.
Pte. W. FRASER (14118), 9th Batt.
Pte. J. HARTLEY, 9th Batt.
Pte. H. SLATER, 9th Batt.
Pte. E. WILLIAMS (14323), 9th Batt.
Pte. M. BOOTH, 9th Batt.
Pte. A. MORGAN (14100), 9th Batt.
Pte. H. TOMLINSON (14051), 9th Batt.
Pte. J. EXELBY (14298), 9th Batt.
Pte. A. GRIFFITHS (14125), 9th Batt.
Pte. J. MACK (14003), 9th Batt.
Pte. E. BLAKER (14621), 9th Batt.
Pte. G. STIRRUP (13839), 9th Batt.
Pte. B. CASEY (14024), 9th Batt.
Pte. W. HACKIN (14226), 9th Batt.
Pte. M. G. WATSON (14221), 9th Batt.
Pte. J. BENTHAM, 9th Batt.
Pte. C. H. MATTHEWS, 9th Batt.
Pte. J. DAWSON (14399), 9th Batt.
Pte. A. MOORE (14004), 9th Batt.
Pte. E. PHAIR, 9th Batt.
Pte. S. HOBSON, 9th Batt.

Mather and Platt Ltd.

ROLL OF HONOUR—continued.

Lancashire Fusiliers.

Captain W. CARTWRIGHT, 7th Batt.
Captain F. H. WILLIAMSON (Adj.), 7th Batt.
Staff-Sergt. A. SPONG (2413), 8th Batt.
Co.Q.M.Sergt. T. ELLY, 8th Batt.
Co.Q.M.Sergt. H. BARBER (2411), 8th Batt.
Q.M.Sergt. J. HALSALL, 7th Batt.
Sergt. J. McLAUGHLIN (6780), 11th Batt.
Sergt. A. COATES (1829), 8th Batt.
Sergt. A. SCRIVEN (1295), 8th Batt.
Corpl. J. H. CONWAY, 2nd Batt.
Corpl. G. E. HODGSON (3194), 7th Batt.
Corpl. A. THOMAS (2098), 8th Batt.
Corpl. C. LEMON (4096), 8th Batt.
Corpl. F. BIRMINGHAM (6978), 11th Batt.
L.-Corpl. J. WHITTLE (5356), 4th Batt.
L.-Corpl. E. DAVEY, 7th Batt.
L.-Corpl. J. WARD (1632), 7th Batt.
L.-Corpl. G. GULLY (4146), 8th Batt.
L.-Corpl. H. C. WILLIAMS, 12th Batt.
L.-Corpl. C. H. BIRD, 12th Batt.
Drummer J. MOSS (2329), 8th Batt.
Pte. W. HIRD (711), 2nd Batt.
Pte. H. BARRATT, 2nd Batt.
Pte. J. GARTSIDE (9397), 2nd Batt.
Pte. J. TAYLOR (3852), 2nd Batt.
Pte. N. BRADY, 3rd Batt.
Pte. J. JOHNSON, 3rd Batt.
Pte. J. FARRELL (4558), 3rd Batt.
Pte. R. THOMAS, 3rd Batt.
Pte. J. GALLAGHER, 3rd Batt.
Pte. W. TAYLOR (4933), 4th Batt.
Pte. A. LORD (3804), 4th Batt.
Pte. E. SMITH (9063), 6th Batt.
Pte. J. ASHLEY, 7th Batt.
Pte. J. MULLIGAN (1476), 7th Batt.
Pte. W. ASHLEY, 7th Batt.
Pte. A. SCHOFIELD, 7th Batt.
Pte. J. H. JOHNSON (1442), 7th Batt.
Pte. G. PALMER (2379), 7th Batt.
Pte. J. W. HUGHES (1800), 7th Batt.
Pte. R. GRAHAM, 7th Batt.
Pte. F. UPTON, 7th Batt.
Pte. J. SOUTH, 7th Batt.
Pte. V. HEALEY, 8th Batt.
Pte. E. SIDEBOTHAM (2410), 8th Batt.
Pte. H. PALMER, 8th Batt.
Pte. A. SMETHURST, 8th Batt.
Pte. E. E. SHEPHERD, 8th Batt.
Pte. D. BENSON (116), 8th Batt.
Pte. W. R. MARSHALL, 8th Batt.
Pte. F. BUTTERFIELD, 8th Batt.

Lancashire Fusiliers—continued.

Pte. T. THORNHILL (2387), 8th Batt.
Pte. H. WELSH (1950), 8th Batt.
Pte. J. T. BOYES (8237), 8th Batt.
Pte. J. FLETCHER, 8th Batt.
Pte. A. D. LEVER (1398), 8th Batt.
Pte. R. CREWDSON, 8th Batt.
Pte. T. CARLISLE, 8th Batt.
Pte. P. GENT (2991), 8th Batt.
Pte. T. DAVIES, 8th Batt.
Pte. S. RADFORD, 8th Batt.
Pte. H. PEARSON (3314), 8th Batt. ...
Pte. J. E. KILROY, 8th Batt.
Pte. F. HORAN (3506), 9th Batt.
Pte. H. FORRESTER (7920), 9th Batt.
Pte. E. W. KINGTON, 9th Batt.
Pte. E. P. SMITH (3218), 9th Batt.
Pte. A. TOOLE (4265), 10th Batt.
Pte. J. WILSON, 11th Batt.
Pte. J. DAVISON, 11th Batt.
Pte. E. GRANT, 11th Batt.
Pte. W. WATERMAN (7056), 11th Batt.
Pte. W. A. RUSHTON (7305), 11th Batt.
Pte. S. ANDERTON, 11th Batt.
Pte. E. SMITH, 11th Batt.
Pte. T. ROBERTSON (7053), 11th Batt.
Pte. W. H. JONES (8399), 11th Batt.
Pte. G. BAND, 12th Batt.
Pte. J. NORRIS (724), 12th Batt.
Pte. T. BIRCHALL (13243), 13th Batt.
Pte. J. WILLIAMS, 15th Batt.
Pte. G. LEEMING (10096), 15th Batt.
Pte. J. W. WHITE, 15th Batt.
Pte. W. D. MARRS (13024), 15th Batt.
Pte. G. A. CROSBY (15829), 17th Batt.
Pte. A. BEARDOW, 19th Batt.
Pte. J. COOPER (33556), 21st Batt.
Pte. S. BLACKWELL (35044), 21st Batt.
Pte. G. WOOD (34443), 22nd Batt.

South Lancashire Regiment.

Sergt. J. W. BLACKWELL (14101), 9th Batt.
Pte. S. ROBERTS (2530), 3rd Batt.
Pte. W. BLAKELEY (18805), 3rd Batt.
Pte. A. MARK, 4th Batt.
Pte. H. DAVIES, 4th Batt.
Pte. H. SWAIN (K. 335), 9th Batt.
Pte. E. WILLIAMS (14040), 9th Batt.
Pte. T. W. BLACKWELL, 9th Batt.
Pte. L. COATES (18056), 10th Batt.

North Staffordshires.

Pte. J. C. NEWTON (7955), 3rd Batt.
Pte. W. ROBINSON (2125), 6th Batt.

Mather and Platt Ltd.

ROLL OF HONOUR—continued.

Black Watch.
2nd Lieut. W. J. DUFFY, 10th Batt.
Pte. W. STANLEY (S. 11472), 11th Batt.

Cameron Highlanders.
Pte. W. RAWLINGS, 3rd Batt.

Scottish Rifles.
Rfn. W. HUGHES (6481), 1st Cameronians.
Rfn. P. BARNES (14489), 11th Cameronians

Highland Light Infantry.
Corpl. H. A. SIMMS, 9th Batt.
Corpl. J. ANDREWS (16195), 17th Batt.

Seaforth Highlanders.
L.-Corpl. T. BURKE, 4th Batt.
Pte. A. REEDER (10208), 3rd Batt.
Pte. W. SANT, 4th Batt.
Pte. R. CASHELL (3797), 4th Batt.
Pte. E. LEES (2687), 4th Batt.

Argyll and Sutherland Highlanders.
2nd Lieut. W. PATE, 7th Batt.
Pte. D. H. SHEEHAN, 8th Batt. (Argyll).
Pte. J. R. BUTLER (3273), 8th Batt. (Argyll).
Pte. S. TYERS (3002), 8th Batt. (Argyll).

Royal Scots (Lothians).
Corpl. E. SAXON (8626), 2nd Batt. Lothians.
Corpl. J. B. McCORMACK, 9th Batt. Highlanders.
Pte. W. GREENHALGH (2529), 4th Batt. Q.E. Rifles.
Pte. T. LOCKYER (2577), 4th Batt. Q.E. Rifles.
Pte. A. McCORMACK, 4th Batt. Q.E. Rifles.
Pte. A. SMITH (2932), 4th Batt. Q.E. Rifles.
Pte. S. McDONALD (2955), 6th Batt. Lothians.
Pte. J. JONES (17409), 9th Batt. Highlanders.
Pte. W. FAULKNER (17624), 15th Bt. Edinburgh.
Jte. JSH. JACKSON (17406), 15th Bt. Edinburgh.
Pte. J. M. CAIN (18199), 15th Batt. Edinburgh.
Pte. P. CHAPPELL (29464), 18th Batt. Reserve.

King's Own Scottish Borderers.
Corpl. J. EBREY (12468), 6th Batt.
Pte. S. KING (20131), 3rd Batt.
Pte. A. SCOTT (13541), 3rd Batt.
Pte. J. LEISHMAN (11880), 6th Batt.
Pte. F. DAWSON, 6th Batt.

County of London Regiment.
Pte. T. BUSH (231), 10th Batt.
Rfn. E. MARSHALL, 11th Batt.
Pte. B. G. G. ANDERSON, 14th Batt. (Scottish).
Pte. T. H. BOULTON (4395), 19th Batt.
Rfn. E. C. BARKER, 21st Batt.
Rfn. R. C. NASH, 23rd Batt.
Pte. W. N. LITTLE, 25th Batt.

Royal Sussex Regiment.
Pte. E. D. HARRIS (35977), 3rd Batt.

Royal Berkshire Regiment.
Lieut. R. W. POULTON PALMER, 4th Bt. (Reading).

South Staffordshires.
Pte. M. EDWARDS (12137), 4th Batt.

Essex Regiment.
Pte. E. CAPON, 3rd Batt.

East Surrey Regiment.
Pte. J. COOK (7192), 1st Batt.
Pte. H. PAXTON, 1st Batt.

Middlesex Regiment.
L.-Corpl. W. DYERS, 6th Batt.
Pte. H. BOND (3851), 6th Batt.

The Suffolk Regiment.
L.-Corpl. G. F. CAPON, 10th Batt.
Pte. A. SWINDELLS (20865), 3rd Batt.

Royal Welsh Fusiliers.
Sergt. H. BEARD, 17th Batt.
Sergt. H. KAY (25162), 17th Batt.
Pte. F. GOSTELLO (8276), 1st Batt.
Pte. W. V. BEESTON, 14th Batt. (Public School).
Pte. T. RACKETT, 14th Batt (Public School).

South Wales Borderers.
Pte. A. MOORES (14963), 7th Batt.
Pte. R. ORMROD (45925), Defence Corps.

The Welsh Regiment.
Pte. W. ROYLE, 3rd Batt.
Pte. W. TWOHY, 3rd Batt.
Pte. A. WORSLEY, 3rd Batt.

King's Shropshire Light Infantry.
Pte. E. MORRIS, 1st Batt.
Pte. E. F. O'GARR (19904), 9th Batt.

The Buffs (East Kent Regiment).
2nd Lieut. L. ANDERSON, 8th Batt. Military Cross.

Yorkshire Regiment.
Pte. W. BESWICK, 2nd Batt.

King's Own Yorkshire Light Infantry.
Pte. A. E. COPLEY (2145), 2nd Batt.

West Riding Regiment.
Lieut. F. D. CHADWICK, 2nd Batt.
Pte. E. OLDHAM (1955), 7th Batt.

West Yorkshire Regiment.
Pte. G. P. ALVEY (1105), 6th Batt.

East Yorkshire Regiment.
Pte. A. TIMPERLEY (6059), 4th Batt.

Leicester Regiment.
Pte. S. CLAY (12561), 2nd Batt.

Royal Warwickshire Regiment.
Pte. S. W. PLATT, 5th Batt.
Pte. A. G. TROWMAN, 5th Batt.
Pte. R. S. LITTLEWOOD, 6th Batt.

Hampshire Regiment.
Pte. S. D. CORPS (2651), 3rd Batt.

Mather and Platt Ltd.

ROLL OF HONOUR—continued.

Sherwood Foresters.
Pte. P. WHITE (25092), 15th Batt.

King's Liverpools.
Sergt. H. FLEWITT (20210), 12th Batt.
Pte. J. L. SMITH, 4th Batt.
Pte. W. H. DYER (26789), 4th Batt.
Pte. H. LOWE, 8th Batt.
Pte. H. WOOD, 8th Batt.
Pte. J. P. GILLIBRAND, 8th Batt.
Pte. C. BARLOW (19215), 8th Batt.
Pte. J. McCLELLAN (20363), 12th Batt.
Pte. P. J. KILLORAN (19184), 12th Batt.
Pte. H. WOOD, 12th Batt.
Pte. J. CHAPMAN, 12th Batt.
Pte. T. ROBERTS (19928), 12th Batt.
Pte. T. LIVESEY (20407), 12th Batt.
Pte. V. GRIFFITHS (20242), 14th Batt.
Pte. J. HUGHES (45196), 23rd Batt.
Bugler J. H. BRADSHAW (20015), 14th Batt.

Loyal North Lancashires.
Sergt. D. LANG (3314), 7th Batt.
Pte. J. O'CONNOR, 1st Batt.
Pte. J. C. JOHNSON (21328), 3rd Batt.
Pte. T. MATHER (3724), 3rd Batt.
Pte. C. HIGGINBOTTOM (4839), 5th Batt.
Pte. W. BATESON (15876), 7th Batt.
Pte. T. H. HILLIER, 8th Batt.
Pte. C. E. MATTHEWS, 9th Batt.
Pte. T. MUSCHAMP (21459), 11th Batt.

Royal Inniskilling Fusiliers.
Corpl. H. CLAYTON, 5th Batt.
Corpl. J. GODSALL (16650), 5th Batt.
L.-Corpl. G. WATTS (14784), 5th Batt.
Pte W. BALDWIN, 5th Batt.
Pte A. WHALLEY, 5th Batt.
Pte. R. J. PUGH, 5th Batt.
Pte. D. DICKSON, 5th Batt.
Pte. E. THOMAS, 6th Batt.
Pte. H. LYNCH, 6th Batt.
Pte. J. E. GRIFFITHS (16768).

Border Regiment.
Pte. J. HIGHAM (6157), 2nd Batt.
Pte. F. ALTOFT (20218), 3rd Batt
Pte. G. PHILLIPS (16814), 3rd Batt.
Pte. J. BLEASDALE (18187), 3rd Batt.
Pte. F. DAWSON (10874), 6th Batt.
Pte. J. HARDIE (19339), 6th Batt.
Pte. G. W. HARDY (18765), 10th Batt.

Royal Irish Fusiliers.
Pte. G. W. HILL, 6th Batt.
Pte. T. ROGERS, 6th Batt.
Pte. G. DUNSCOMBE, 6th Batt.

King's Own Royal Lancasters.
Sergt. W. MOULTON (5935), 1st Batt.
Sergt. T. HEYWOOD, 4th Batt.
Sergt. J. I'ANSON (14159), 9th Batt.
L.-Corpl. W. J. WHITLOCK (12414), 4th Batt.
Pte. W. SCOTT, 1st Batt.
Pte. P. MORAN (6859), 3rd Batt.
Pte. H. DAWSON (12054), 3rd Batt.
Pte. T. SEVILLE (13973), 4th Batt.
Pte. C. DAWSON, 4th Batt.
Pte. J. E. DAVIES, 4th Batt.
Pte. R. BOWKER, 4th Batt.
Pte. W. JONES, 4th Batt.
Pte. J. GREENWOOD, 4th Batt.
Pte. H. NICKSON (3103), 5th Batt.
Pte. C. GRAHAM (12199), 6th Batt.
Pte. W. HESLOP (12102), 6th Batt.
Pte. E. CAVEY, 7th Batt.
Pte. A. BRITTAIN (14431), 8th Batt.
Pte. A. INGHAM (14430), 8th Batt.
Pte. J. RYAN (15471), 8th Batt.
Pte. H. HAUGHTON (14154), 9th Batt.
Pte. J. McDONALD, 9th Batt.

Cheshire Regiment.
Corpl. M. CONROY, 3rd Batt.
L.-Corpl. E. CLAYTON (11872), 2nd Batt.
Pte. G. ALLABY (1578), 5th Batt.
Pte. J. HOLROYD (1492), 6th Batt.

Rifle Brigade.
Sergt. J. HARWOOD (1543), 9th Batt.
Corpl. J. GLASS, 2nd Batt.
Corpl. F. CROCKWELL (1540), 9th Batt.
Rfn. W. T. EVANS, 5th Batt.
Rfn. A. MORTON (13473), 5th Batt.
Rfn. G. FILDES, 7th Batt.
Rfn. A. HORN (1257), 8th Batt.
Rfn. T. FISH (3332), 9th Batt.

King's Royal Rifle Corps.
Captain R. G. TAYLOR, 17th Batt.
Rfn. W. DIXON, 1st Batt.
Rfn. W. SOUTHWOOD (8486), 5th Batt.
Rfn. H. TAYLOR (2246), 3rd Batt.
Rfn. D. INGLIS (4879), 6th Batt.

Royal Fusiliers.
2nd Lieut. O. THOMAS, 14th Batt.
Pte. H. HOWELL, 2nd Batt.
Pte. D. PATTERSON, 3rd Batt. (Public Schools).
Pte. H. J. IBBERSON, 19th Batt.
Pte. A. C. SCOTT (4251), 21st Batt.
Pte. J. CURRAN (13092), 25th Batt. (Frontiersman).

Worcestershire Regiment.
2nd Lieut. A. K. WHITE, 5th Batt.

MANCHESTER STOCK EXCHANGE.

LIST OF MEMBERS AND CLERKS

WHO HAVE JOINED THE ARMY SINCE OUTBREAK OF WAR.

Rank and Name.	Regiment.	Firm.
Lt.-Colonel D. ABERCROMBIE	5th Batt. Cheshire Regiment (T.)	David Abercrombie.
Private C. G. ARDERN	Royal Welsh Fusiliers	Dimmock Bros. & Cowtan.
Lieut. W. P. ASHWORTH	Light Motor Battery, 14th Brigade	W. R. Ashworth & Sons.
Lce.-Corpl. T. S. AUSTIN	16th Serv. Batt. Man. Regt. (Prisoner)	F. W. Staveacre & Co.
2nd Lieut. E. N. ASHE	3/8th Manchester Regiment (T.)	Fernyhough & Ashe.
Private J. APPLEBY	3/8th Man. Regt. (T.), Cyclist Corps	J. E. Winder & Son.
Staff-Sergt. HAROLD BAKER	7th Batt. Man. Rgt. (T.), now att. A.S.C.	Mewburn & Barker.
Gunner KENNETH BARKER	Howitzer Brigade, attach. to Headquarters	Mewburn & Barker.
NORMAN BARKER	Royal Naval Air Service	Mewburn & Barker.
Private R. BROOKES	16th Service Batt. Manchester Regiment	P. H. & F. C. Mosley.
Private C. BARNETT	K. O. Royal Lancasters (Killed)	P. H. & F. C. Mosley.
Lieut. P. E. BRIERLEY	7th Lancashire Fusiliers (T.) (Wounded)	J. H. Lancashire & Co.
Private A. BALLINGER	4th Cheshire Regiment (T.)	J. H. Lancashire & Co.
Private J. BELL	16th Serv. Batt. Man. Regt. (Wounded)	A. W. Walton & Co.
Private H. BLEASE	22nd Service Batt. Manchester Regiment	Lawson & Ormrod.
Bombardier T. BRIGGS	Royal Field Artillery	Goodwin & Ambery.
Capt. & Adjt. W. T. L. BECKER	7th York and Lancaster Regt. (Pioneer)	Becker & Carington.
Private H. BATLEY	16th Serv. Batt. Man. Regt. (Missing)	Becker & Carington.
Major T. J. BIDDULPH	7th Lancashire Fusiliers.	Dimmock Bros. & Cowtan.
Private W. BUXTON	Royal Naval Division (Medical Unit)	Dimmock Bros. & Cowtan.
Private W. BLORE	3/6th Manchester Regiment (T.)	E. H. Roylance.
Sergt. A. BROCKLEHURST	Royal Field Artillery	R. Whitehead & Co.
Private E. BURNS	Lancashire Fusiliers	Fernyhough & Ashe.
Private A. BUCKLEY	Motor Transport, A.S.C.	A. Buckley.
2nd Lieut. S. H. BRATBY	Army Service Corps	Coppock & Bratby.
Cadet ALEC BELL	Artists' Rifle O.T.C.	H. Cooke & Son.
Private W. BROWNHILL	(Public School) Royal Fusiliers	H. Cooke & Son.
Corporal A. BOYES	71 Co., Machine Gun Corp	C. W. Lambert.
Private S. BRITTAIN	Artists' Rifle O.T.C.	C. W. Lambert.
Private E. BROWN	25th Service Batt. Manchester Regiment	M. M. Speakman.
Private W. BURGESS	Rifle Brigade (Wounded & Discharged)	McEwen & Burgess.
Private C. G. COOPER	16th Serv. Batt. Man. Regt. (Prisoner)	W. A. Arnold & Sons.
Pioneer R. COSSINS	Signal Co., Royal Engineers	W. A. Arnold & Sons.
Lt. JOHN C. CLOSE-BROOKS	1st Life Guards (Missing, Oct. 1914)	Marsden, Close-Brooks & Robertson.
Private E. CONNOR	20th Serv. Batt. Man. Regt.	Marsden, Close-Brooks & Robertson.
Corporal L. H. COOKE	22nd Serv. Batt. Man. Regt. (Killed)	J. Siddall & Son.
Private R. L. COPPOCK	16th Serv. Batt. Man. Regt. (Wounded)	F. W. Staveacre & Co.
Private G. CUSICK	3/8th Man. Regt. (T.), Cyclist Corps	Charlton, Illingworth & Co.
Seaman T. CASH	Royal Navy	Halliday, Blakeway & Teasdale.
Private Arthur DAVIES	16th Serv. Batt. Man. Regt. (Discharged)	F. W. Staveacre & Co.
Private HERBERT DAVIES	Rifle Brigade	Becker & Carington.
Sergeant HORACE DAVIES	16th Batt. South Lancashire Regiment	Bell, White & Hardy.
Private J. H. DAVIES	3/6th Manchester Regiment	H. Cooke & Son.
Lieut. T. G. DOWSON	3rd Sherwood Foresters	T. Greg Dowson.
Lce.-Corpl. A. DRABBLE	16th Service Batt. Manchester Regiment	Robinson & Mothersill.
2nd Lieut. H. C. ELLIS	2/9th Manchester Regiment (T.)	Coppock, Stanley & Ellis.

MANCHESTER STOCK EXCHANGE.
CONTINUED.

Rank and Name.	Regiment.	Firm.
Private M. J. EARL	2/4th King's Shropshire Light Infantry	Mewburn & Barker.
2nd Lieut E. ENTWISLE	R.F.A., East Lancashire	E. Entwisle, Junr.
Corpl. H. W. FILDES	6th South Lancashire Regiment.	W. A. Arnold & Sons.
Lce.-Corpl. E. FLINT	Royal Army Medical Corps	D. Q. Henriques & Co.
Private H. C. FEARNELY	Lancashire Fusiliers	Coppock, Stanley & Ellis.
2nd Lieut. D. G. K. GARNETT	1/3rd East Lancashire Brigade, R.F.A.	D. G. K. Garnett.
Lieut. E. L. GOODWIN	13th Manchester Regiment	Goodwin & Ambery.
Lce.-Corpl. H. GUNTRIP	16th Serv. Batt. Man. Rgt. Machine Gun	Stock Exchange, Sec.'s Office.
Capt. C. H. GOODE	1st Garrison Batt. Manchester Regiment	Langston, Goode & Challinor.
Lce.-Corpl. R. GOTT	8th Manchester Regiment (T.)	F. F. Page & Co.
Private A. J. GUILFOYLE	Army Service Corps	F. W. Staveacre & Co.
Trooper J. H. HAMER	1st Lancashire Hussars	W. A. Arnold & Sons.
Gunner F. HALLAM	Royal Garrison Artillery	W. A. Arnold & Sons.
Private H. HUNT	Royal Engineers (Transport Section)	J. H. Lancashire & Co.
Major W. D. HEYWOOD	1/6th Batt. Lancashire Fusiliers	W. D. Heywood.
Drummer L. HOLDEN	21st Royal Welsh Fusiliers	Kerr & Lowe.
Sergt. R. HINCE	16th Service Batt. Manchester Regiment	Lawson & Ormrod.
Trooper H. V. HILLIER	Earl of Chester's Yeomanry	Oliver & Co.
Trooper H. HORNER	Duke of Lancaster's Yeomanry	A. & J. J. Arnold.
2nd Lieut. G. L. Q. HENRIQUES	16th Service Batt. Manchester Regiment	D. Q. Henriques & Co.
Capt. R. H. HASLAM	2/5th Cheshire Regiment	R. H. Haslam.
Private W. R. HOLT	20th Serv. Batt. Roy. Fus. (Discharged)	Langston, Goode & Challinor.
Private G. HOWSAM	Royal Field Artillery (T.)	F. W. Staveacre & Co.
Lce.-Corpl. J. HIBBERT	West Kents	R. Whitehead & Co.
Private S. HEAP	Army Pay Corps	Fielding & Hayes.
Lieut. D. B. HARDY	Army Service Corps.	Bell, White & Hardy.
Private E. HENRY	16th Serv. Batt. Man. Regt. (Killed)	Coppock & Bratby.
Private T. H. HARRINGTON	King's Shropshire Light Infantry	T. M. Davies.
Lieut. D. F. HUNTER	2nd Manchester Regiment	H. Cooke & Son.
Cadet J. HUNTER, Junr.	Inns of Court O.T.C.	H. Cooke & Son.
Private F. H. HALLIDAY	6th Manchester Regiment (Killed)	Halliday, Blakeway & Teasdale.
Private K. HAWORTH	25th Service Batt. Manchester Regiment	Fernyhough & Ashe.
Private J. HELM	Royal Engineers	T. M. Davies.
Sergt. G. A. IRLAM	16th Serv. Batt. Man. Regt. (Wounded)	W. A. Arnold & Sons.
Capt. S. F. JACKSON	6th Batt. Manchester Regt. (T.) (Killed)	S. F. Jackson.
Lce.-Corpl. H JACKSON	Royal Army Medical Corps	Marsland & Smethurst.
Private H. JONES	R.A.M.C., East Lancashire	Kerr & Lowe.
Private W. JACOBSEN	6th Batt Manchester Regiment (T.)	Dimmock Bros. & Cowtan.
2nd Lieut. A. JOHNSTON	Cameronians, Scottish Rifles	Charlton, Illingworth & Co.
Private J. JOYCE	Argyll and Sutherlandshire Highlanders	H. Cooke & Son.
Battery Sergt.-Major F. JONAS	R.F.A., East Lancashire	C. H. Stott & Son.
Bombardier B. JACQUES	R.F.A., East Lancashire	McEwen & Burgess.
Private J. JENKS	6th Batt. Manchester Regiment (T.)	F. W. Staveacre & Co.
Private J. D. KITCHIN	30th Batt. Royal Fusiliers	Coppock, Stanley & Ellis.
Sergt. E. LIVESEY	6th South Lancashire Regiment	W. A. Arnold & Sons.
Sapper J. LYONS	Royal Engineers	W. A. Arnold & Sons.
Private J. LYONS	Manchester Regiment	P. H. & F. C. Mosley.
2nd Lieut. C. P. LEESE	7th Batt. Lanc. Fusiliers (T.) (Retired)	C. P. Leese.
Lieut. H. G. LANGLEY	Cheshire Regiment	D. Q. Henriques & Co.
Corpl. F. G. MONNINGTON	16th Serv. Batt. Man. Regt. (Prisoner)	F. W. Staveacre & Co.
Capt. W. M. MARSDEN	26th Service Batt. Man. Regt.	Marsden, Close-Brooks & Robertso
Private T. MACHIN	8th Batt. South Lancs. Regt. (Wounded)	Bell, White & Hardy.
Private R. McHUGH	16th Serv. Batt. Man. Regt. (Wounded)	D. Q. Henriques & Co.

MANCHESTER STOCK EXCHANGE.
CONTINUED.

Rank and Name.	Regiment.	Firm.
Private R. MORTIMER	Rifle Brigade (Wounded)	Dimmock Bros. & Cowtan.
Private J. S. MOSS	3/4th Royal Scots	Lawson & Ormrod.
Private J. MAXWELL	10th Seaforth Highlanders	Dimmock Bros. & Cowtan.
Lieut. S. NAYLOR	9th Manchester Regt. (T.) (Wounded)	P. H. & F. C. Mosley.
Lieut. H. ORMROD	3/7th Lancashire Fusiliers	Lawson & Ormrod.
Private W. OVERTON	4th Royal Scots (Discharged)	Langston, Goode & Challinor.
Private W. PORTER	R.A.M.C., East Lancashire	J. H. Lancashire & Co.
Private A. D. PIXTON	Army Service Corps	A. W. Walton & Co.
Private T. PIMLOTT	Army Service Corps	Murray, Bythell & Co.
Lce.-Corpl. G. W. POTTS	Royal Engineers, East Lancashire	Stock Exchange, Sec.'s Office.
2nd Lieut. S. L. REDFERN	Loyal North Lancashires	J. Siddall & Son.
Lieut. J. W. A. RAMSDEN	Duke of Wellington's Own, West Riding	Coppock, Stanley & Ellis.
Private T. ROWLANDS	Royal Welsh Fusiliers	H. Cooke & Son.
Flight Lieut. J. C. RAILTON	Royal Naval Flying Corps	Railton, Sons & Leedham.
Corpl. G. C. ROBIN	18th Service Co., A.O.C.	O. Yates.
Private P. RHODES	2/6th Manchester Regiment (T.)	Lawson & Ormrod.
Private A. ROBINSON	King's Liverpool Regiment	Charlton, Illingworth & Co.
Private G. O. REMOND	Royal Garrison Artillery	D. Q. Henriques & Co.
Private F. SWALE	King's Shrop. Light In., attach. R.A.M.C.	J. Swale & Son.
Private J. R. SIDDALL	1/6th Manchester Regiment (T.)	J. Siddall & Son.
Private GUY STATHAM	Liverpool Scottish	Murray, Bythell & Co.
Coy.-Sergt.-Major J. SCOTT	Attached 9th Scottish Cadet Battalion	Railton, Sons & Leedham.
2nd Lieut. J. SEAL	6th Manchester Regiment (T.)	Coppock & Bratby.
2nd Lieut. R. J. STEPHENSON	6th Lancashire Fusiliers	Coppock & Bratby.
Lce.-Corpl. H. STANWAY	21st Service Batt. Manchester Regiment	O. Yates.
Private N. SIMMONS	8th Manchester Regiment (T.)	F. F. Page & Co.
Private. A. SHERWIN	Royal Army Medical Corps	Goodwin & Ambery.
Private C. B. SUTCLIFFE	Royal Garrison Artillery	Goodwin & Ambery.
Private W. SHELLEY	King's Shropshire Light Infantry	Becker & Carington.
Private T. SMITH	2/7th Cheshire Regiment	Kerr & Lowe.
Private A. SCHOFIELD	2/6th Manchester Regiment (T.)	J. H. Lancashire & Co.
Sergt. F. W. TAYLOR	Army Service Corps	J. Swale & Son.
2nd Lieut. G. E. TAYLOR	York and Lancaster Regiment	E. Entwisle, Junr.
Private E. TAYLOR	R.A.M.C., East Lancashire	Kerr & Lowe.
Private E. TOOTILL	16th Service Batt. Manchester Regiment	A. & J. J. Arnold.
Private F. H. TURNER	16th Service Batt. Manchester Regiment	Stock Exchange, Sec.'s Office.
Capt. M. TWEEDALE	7th King's Liverpool Regt. (Killed)	Coppock & Bratby.
Private G. TYSOE	16th Service Batt. Manchester Regiment.	Illingworth & Agnew.
Private H. VESEY	King's Liverpool Regiment	Illingworth & Agnew.
Private A. VERNON	2/6th Manchester Regiment	H. Cooke & Son.
Corpl. C. M. WILLIAMS	20th Serv. Batt. Man. Regt. (Killed).	Marsden, Close-Brooks & Roberts
Private T. WHITTAM	Army Service Corps	W. A. Arnold & Sons.
Lieut. F. B. WILD	Royal Army Medical Corps (T.)	J. H. Lancashire & Co.
Corpl. J. G. WOOD	Army Service Corps	W. R. Ashworth & Sons.
Private A. WOLFENDEN	Army Service Corps	Murray, Bythell & Co.
Private E. H. WARD	3rd Seaforth Highlanders	Railton, Sons & Leedham.
Private F. A. WILLS	Army Service Corps	Murray, Bythell & Co.
Private A. WALKER	Motor Section, Royal Flying Corps	W. R. Ashworth & Sons.
Sergt. L. WHITEHEAD	16th Serv. Batt. Man. Regt. (Killed)	Ogden, Whitehead & Smale.
Corpl. A. WILLIS	16th Service Batt. Manchester Regiment	D. Q. Henriques & Co.
Private A. WOOD	Royal Army Medical Corps	Dimmock Bros. & Cowtan.
Private T. L. WILSON	16th Service Batt. Manchester Regiment	A. & J. J. Arnold.
Bugler W. WROE	Royal Army Medical Corps	J. E. Winder & Son.

ROLL OF HONOUR.

H. D. POCHIN & CO. LTD.

WORSLEY STREET, SALFORD, MANCHESTER.

HEAD OFFICE.

A. Cowburn.	F. H. Grime.	S. Rowley.

WARRINGTON WORKS.

John Kelly.	George Turner.	Peter Bate.
William Keating.	James Traynor.	Thos. Muckley.
Thos. Keating.	Wm. Weigh.	Fred Banner.
Wm. Mills.	Joseph Riley (Navy).	Thomas Riley.
Wm. Sixsmith (Killed).	Joeph Tomkins.	James Whalley.
Samuel Hawkes.	Patrick Starkey.	Richard Urey.
Alfred Denny.	James Healey.	Frank Chambers.
Fredk. Massey.	Joseph Tyrell.	J. Cumberbirch.
James H. Atkinson.	Thos. Collins.	L. Lefort (serving in French Army).
James Turner.	Joshua Raymond.	

NEWCASTLE WORKS.

Jas. Usher (Missing).	Thos. Dunlop (Wounded and Prisoner).	Robt. Hewitt.
Wm. Helm.	Wm. Hopper (Killed).	Arthur Cottiss.
Thos. Hopper.	Steven McVay.	Elijah Sudworth.

GOTHERS CLAY MINE.

W. Bennetts, Jr.	Moses Kent.	W. Glanville.
S. Tabb.	J. Bullock.	Herbert Crowle.
L. Chapman.	C. Grigggs, Sr.	J. Caddy.
L. Trudgeon.	A. Pooley.	F. Runnalls.
G. Runnalls.	J. Burton.	M. Docking.
W. Allen.	G. Ball.	J. Colwill.
G. Hayden.	F. Liddicoat.	H. Roberts.
W. Geach.	J. Stocks.	G. Mably.
Reginald Tabb.	C. Polkinhorne.	T. Vincent.
J. Sloman.	A. Grigg.	C. Blamey.
J. Carpenter, Sr. (Killed).	T. Barnicoat.	J. Skinner.
W. Spry.	F. Vincent.	T. Martyn.
S. Selby.	J. Carpenter, Jr.	Alfred Best.
J. Stanton.	J. Bennetts.	H. James.
C. Griggs, Jr.	S. Roberts.	F. Brewer.
T. Tucker.	W. Hawke.	T. Stacey.
W. Solomon.	E. Stoneman.	L. Stoneman.
B. Kent.	C. Rowe.	W. Rowe.
Jas. Martyn.		

H. D. POCHIN AND CO. LTD.

Roll of Honour—Continued.

BRISTOL WORKS.

Harry Bridle.	Wm. Silman.	Wm. Tasker.
Albert Helps.	Joseph Browning.	

HALVIGGAN CLAY MINE.

C. Hocking.	A. Whitford.	H. Legg.
N. Whitford.	H. Lintern.	T. Hawkey.
F. Barrett.	W. Phillips.	J. Richards.
F. Hawkey.	H. Mellow.	P. Hore.
W. King.	J. Hall.	W. Trembath.
C. Cornelius.	H. Rickard.	W. Dean.
M. Clatworthy.	J. Bawden.	W. Hore.
H. Harper.		

LESWIDDEN CLAY MINE.

T. Bolitho.	W. Bolitho.	A. Guy.
A. King.	W. B. Searle.	H. Trevurrow.
J. Hall.	R. J. Hitchens.	J. Rogers.
E. Rowe.	A. Key.	F. Best.
T. Reynolds.	R. Warren.	R. Ellis.

PARK CLAY MINE.

J. Woodridge.	R. Hosking.	E. Olver.
S. Wilton.	T. Hooper.	E. Bufton.
J. Semple.	C. Avent.	R. Rogers.
J. Hosking.	Jas. Hooper, Sr.	W. Tamblin.
J. Mallett.	J. Doney.	L. Snell.
R. Angove.	A. Gerry.	John Meech.
W. Harris.	W. Northcott.	J. Hodge.
B. Netherton (Killed).	E. Rowe.	A. Yeo.
J. Clark.	W. Wilton, Jr.	J. Angove.
C. Hares.	C. Stanaway.	W. Stanaway.
E. Reed.	A. Arthur.	A. Mitchell.
J. Redler.	J. Vincent.	P. Hosking.
J. Cowling.	W. Hosking.	A. Langdon.
H. Holman.	W. Hares.	A. Holman.
E. Langdon.	W. Hill.	J. Whell.
Jas. Hooper, Jr.		

BALLESWIDDEN CLAY MINE.

H. Glasso.	E. Boynes.	W. Casley.
T. Strick.	W. Richards.	W. J. Chapell.
J. Strathen.	L. Matthews.	W. Hocking.
J. Williams.		

CLAY MINES STAFF.

T. Rowse.	L. G. Hooper.

ROLL OF HONOUR.

JOHN HEYWOOD LTD.,

121, Deansgate, Manchester.

DIRECTORS.

Major L. E. WALKER. | F. K. HEYWOOD.

DEANSGATE AND RIDGEFIELD STAFF.

Lieut. F. Nasmith.	T. Needham.	H. Mallett.
F. Holmes.	C. Chadwick.	N. Herold.
J. McMeel.	L. Thompson.	W. D. Campfield.
W. F. Fanning.	B. E. McBride.	A. E. Still.
W. Jones.	W. McNally.	R. B. Garrett.
A. McKay.	T. Hancock.	E. Perry.
A. Cave.	J. W. Healey.	H. B. Fielding.
F. Burke.	J. Kelly.	H. A. Marchant.
F. Nugent.	G. A. Murnaghan.	W. H. Wood.
F. Mawdsley.	W. Fox.	A. Wallace.
R. Horan.	H. Warburton.	E. Smith.
H. Story.	H. Wilson.	A. Greenway.
H. Goodwill.	J. Blackett.	A. E. Bickerstaffe.
G. H. Gordon.	A. Rylance.	E. Scanlon.
S. Foster.	E. Whyatt.	F. C. Sharp.
W. E. Sigsworth.	W. Thorpe.	G. Allen.
W. West.	A. Armstrong.	T. Smith.
H. Hadshern.	W. Holiday.	H. Smith.
G. Davies.	A. Tavernor.	I. Tregan.
H. B. Todd.	A. Scanlon.	H. Bamber.
T. Wright.	A. Brill.	— Swindlehurst.
R. Makinson.	A. Topping.	— Atkinson.
W. Tingey.	T. H. Mattinson.	— Adamson.
A. B. Penney.	W. K. Macgarvie.	— Cundiff.
D. Moore.	J. A. Barnes.	— Palmer.

EXCELSIOR WORKS AND ALBERT MILLS,

Hulme Hall Road, Manchester.

F. Shields.	A. Blackburn.	J. Saville.
J. Johnson.	H. Nuttall.	S. Harris.
B. Jarvis.	J. W. Dick.	A. Washington.
J. Ralston.	A. Sweeney.	F. Benskin.
W. Miller,	G. Lodge.	T. Battell.

ROLL OF HONOUR—continued.

JOHN HEYWOOD LTD.

Excelsior Works and Albert Mills—continued.

- C. H. ROWLANDS.
- H. FLETCHER.
- C. BOOTH.
- G. W. GOULD.
- S. WALSH.
- E. MEEK.
- G. HADFIELD.
- J. WILLIAMSON.
- H. MEYERS.
- H. LUNN.
- W. KINSHIN.
- A. POOLE.
- A. DOHERTY.
- W. OWENS.
- A. ASHES.
- H. WALKER.
- J. CHOLLERTON.
- S. ROSE.
- W. HETHERINGTON.
- H. EDGE.
- H. BALLINGALL.
- F. JACKSON.
- G. DUNN.
- F. BRADSHAW, JR.
- F. LLOYD.
- A. POLLITT.
- A. WHITTAKER.
- S. TWIGG.
- F. CONLON.
- A. HEWITT.
- H. MARSHALL.
- — ASKEW.
- — BARWICK.
- — MCLAREN.
- — RYDER.
- — PERRY.
- — POLLITT.
- — BRADSHAW.
- — MOORES.
- — DOWLING.

SCHOOL FURNITURE WORKS,
Weaste, Manchester.

- J. KEOHANE.
- C. BUTTERWORTH.
- J. D. PEMBERTON.
- J. ONG.
- T. ANDERSON.
- J. HOYLE.
- J. RIDGEWAY.
- A. GRIFFITHS.
- E. NORMAN.
- W. GEE.
- G. N. BROWN.
- W. HAWKIN.
- T. CONWAY.
- A. HOWARD.
- J. PEMBERTON.
- T. HART.
- R. NEWBURY.
- J. HARGREAVES.
- S. LATCHFORD.
- G. BROOME.
- A. BUTLER.
- J. SMEDLEY.
- P. THOMAS.
- — LAWTON.

CARTING DEPARTMENT.

- T. LEE.
- B. SUMMERS.
- A. RICHARDSON.
- R. NASH.
- R. SMETHURST.
- W. MCELROY.
- P. HERON.
- G. KERRY.
- A. JOHNSON.
- W. GRIMSHAW.
- J. LEE.
- T. FARRELL.
- J. BEACHAM.
- S. HAMETT.
- G. LAWSON.
- H. HERBERTS.
- P. NOBLE.
- W. RIGBY.
- S. YATES.
- E. MURRAY.

LONDON STAFF.

- W. B. MURPHY.
- A. GUEST.
- G. O. KING.
- P. DARE.
- A. HUNT.
- W. PATON.
- E. SHAW.
- A. W. MYERS.
- J. H. MASON.
- G. S. BLOOMFIELD.
- F. SHAW.
- S. PAGE.
- W. WALKER.
- W. J. SIBLEY.
- H. SPENCER.
- W. A. LOWE.
- A. GILL.

BLACKBURN STAFF.

- A. KENYON.
- C. WORDEN.
- J. RAKESTRAW.
- R. FOULKES.
- J. CROSSLEY.
- W. SMITH.
- E. NEWSHAM.

ROLL OF HONOUR.

HERBERT WHITWORTH LTD.
MANCHESTER.

Private W. BAILEY,
  7th Batt. Cheshire Regt.
Co.-Sergt.-Major F. J. BANNER,
  12th Royal Welsh Fusiliers.
Corpl. T. BANNER,
  Royal Engineers.
Private R. BARRETT,
  3/7th Batt. Manchester Regt.
Private E. BARTLEY,
  27th Batt. Manchester Regt.
Private E. CALVERT,
  13th Batt. Lancashire Fusiliers.
Driver A. COLMAN.
  2/2nd East Lanc. R.F.A.
Rifleman W. COLLINGE,
  19th R. Bt. King's Roy. Rifle Corps.
Sergt. H. COOPER,
  8th Batt. Rifle Brigade.
O.T. GEO. F. COOPER,
  R.N. Wireless Service.
Corpl. G. DAVIES,
  The Border Regt. (Wounded).
Private W. H. DAY,
  6th Batt. Man. Regt. (Wounded).
Rifleman A. F. DICKSON,
  7th Batt. Rifle Brigade (Wounded).
Private F. FINN,
  The Border Regiment (Wounded).
Private T. W. GREENHALGH,
  28th Batt. Royal Fusiliers.
Private E. GERDES,
  7th Bt. K.O. Roy. Lancaster Rgt.
       (Killed).
Corpl. S. GERMAN,
  6th Batt. South Lancashire Regt.
       (Wounded).
2nd Lieut. H. L. GIBSON,
  6th Batt. Manchester Regt.
Driver J. HOPPER,
  Royal Army Medical Corps.
Private E. HOPWOOD,
  9th Bt. King's Shrop. Light Inft.
Private E. A. HOYLE,
  7th Batt. Manchester Regt.

Trooper B. HURST,
  Essex Yeomanry (Killed).
Private E. W. KIRBY,
  6th Bt. K.O. Roy. Lancaster Regt.
Trooper J. L. OGDEN,
  Duke of Lancaster's Yeomanry.
Private C. OWENS,
  6th Cheshire Regiment.
Private A. C. PARKER,
  3rd Batt. Manchester Regt.
Private G. PILLING,
  Royal Army Medical Corps.
Private. J. C. PORTER,
  30th Res. Batt. Royal Fusiliers.
Private F. D. REDFERN,
  6th Bt. K.O. Roy. Lancaster Rgt.
       (Wounded).
Private B. RILEY,
  9th Batt. Royal Scots.
Private E. RILEY,
  9th Batt. Royal Scots.
Private S. RILEY,
  26th Batt. Manchester Regt.
Private W. ROGERS,
  2nd Batt. Loyal North Lancashires.
Co.-Sergt.-Major J. A. STEWART,
  20th Service Batt. (5th City)
       Manchester Regt.
Private F. TAYLOR,
  6th Bt. Manchester Regt. (Killed).
Corpl. W. TAYLOR,
  7th Batt. Rifle Brigade (Wounded).
Private A. H. TOBIN,
  8th Batt. Lancashire Fusiliers.
Private J. TOWNSEND,
  7th Batt. Rifle Brigade.
Sergt. H. WALKER,
  21st Service Batt (6th City)
       Manchester Regt.
Private WM. WHITTLE,
  3/6th Batt. Manchester Regt.
Private E. WOOD (Killed),
  30th Batt. Manchester Regt.

The Associated Newspapers Limited

("DAILY MAIL" & "WEEKLY DISPATCH"),
DEANSGATE, MANCHESTER.

List of Members of the Manchester Office who have joined H.M. Forces since August 4th, 1914.

Antwiss, E. J.	Harrison, R.	Quinn, M.
Arber, W.	Hart, H.	Rafferty, E.
Armstrong, J. E.	Hay, W. S.	Rand, G. C.
Barker, R.	Heath, H. D.	Renshaw, C.
Barlow, G.	Heathcote, L.	Roberts, H.
Barnfield, T.	Heathcote, R.	Rogerson, T.
Barratt, A.	Hodson, J.	Roots, F. W.
Basford, W.	Holmes, C.	Royle, E.
Burleigh, Bennet.	Howell, C. T.	Ruddock, J.
Butler, W.	Hyde, A. E.	Senior, C.
Byrne, J.	Isherwood, W.	Seymour, H.
Camille, J.	Jolley, E.	Sharman, F.
Campbell, J.	Jones, A. A.	Sharples, L.
Clough, G. H.	Jones, T.	Shaw, J. W.
Connor, J. R.	Kelly, T. J.	Sisson, J.
Corbett, G.	Laverack, F.	Smith, H.
Copeland, R.	Lomas, R.	South, P.
Croal, D. A.	Lowe, A. W.	Sykes, C.
Daly, J.	Martin, H.	Taylor, G.
Denton, F.	Marshall, W.	Thomas, G.
Downing, G. W.	Marsland J.	Thornhill, F.
Edge, J.	McCarty, T.	Tompkins, W.
Evans, L.	McLachlan, P.	Toole, W.
Fearn, J.	McPartlin, H.	Tucker, A.
Fildes, T.	Mellor, F.	Turner, O. B.
Flower, L.	Mills, T.	Walker, W.
Foster, E.	Mossey, D. J.	Walsh, J. V.
Foster, H.	Murray, C.	Webster, A. B.
Green, J.	Myrtle, W.	Wilson, L.
Gregg, H.	Newsham, R.	Wood, H.
Griffiths, J. A.	Norris, S. E.	Woodings, T. R.
Griffiths, T.	O'Brien, E.	Wright, T.
Hallard, D.	Peel, G. E.	Youell, R.
Hannaford, R. S.	Potter, H. W.	

ROLL OF HONOUR.

Fisher Renwick Manchester-London Steamers Limited

Directors.
Major G. A. RENWICK, Northumberland Fusiliers.
Lieut. G. F. FISHER, Westmorland and Cumberland Yeomanry.

Staff.
Capt. S. RENWICK Northern Cyclists.
Capt. G. RAE SIMS, Royal Irish Rifles.
Lieut. C. S. BOWMAN, Northumberland Fusiliers.
Sub-Lieut. H. W. PARSONS, R.N.R.

E. G. ASHLEY.	F. HORNSEY.	A. V. SNEEZUM.
H. G. BANISTER.	H. HOWE.	F. SQUIRE.
A. FAULKNER.	J. LAWS.	A. B. TAYLOR.
T. D. FENWICK.	A. G. MEREDITH.	P. W. TAYLOR.
P. J. FISHER.	F. PERCY.	H. WITHINGTON.
C. GARDNER.	W. SLAUGHTER.	S. WRIGGLESWORTH.

Wharf Staff—Manchester.

C. AKERS.	G. GRAHAM.	C. SIDWELL.
H. BAILEY.	R. HARGREAVES.	D. SMITH
W. BARNWELL.	H. HULME	J. SUTTON.
J. BOWELL.	G. HURST.	G. W. TAYLOR.
W. CAULFIELD.	E. JACKSON.	J. UNSWORTH.
C. A COULTER.	F. JACKSON.	F. WALKER.
R. DEARDEN.	A. MCCORMICK.	D. WILSON.
G. H. DODDS.	F. MUNDAY.	W. WILSON.
C. J. FERRIDGE.	G. NUNNES.	

Wharf Staff—London.

E. ARNOLD.	E. HALES (Killed in action).	J. R. PINNELL.
A. BARBER.		W. PULLEN.
B. BRAZIER.	F. HASSELL.	G. REGAN.
J. BROOKES.	H. HILL.	H. E. RINGROSE (Killed in action).
J. BROWN.	C. HUGHES.	
W. CARD (D.C.M.).	A. ILES.	R. RUFF.
S CHATTAWAY.	C. KING.	J. SAUNDERS, Junr.
H. COOKE.	L. LANG.	R. SAUNDERS, SENR.
D. COUGHLIN.	J. LODMORE.	T. SMITHERS.
J. COUGHLIN.	C. MARSH.	A. SOLLIEUX.
W. CRUTCH.	J. MASON.	A. THEOBALD.
J. CUNNINGHAM (Killed in action).	E. MATTHEWS.	G. THOMPSON.
	C. A. MCCARTHEY.	E. TOPPS.
W. CUNNINGHAM.	T. MILLHOUSE, Senr.	G. TUTTHILL.
J. DAVIDSON.	T. MILLHOUSE, Junr.	G. WEIDIG.
D. DAVIS.	M. MITCHERSON.	A. WHITMARSH.
F. DEARLOVE.	M. MORRIS.	A. WILLIAMS.
E. DOYLE.	G. OLIVER.	G. WILSON.
P. FINIAN.	A. OLLEY.	W. WILSON.
G. GLAZEBROOK.	G. PARNELL.	W. R. WOOD.
	F. PEACHY.	

ROLL OF HONOUR.

JAMES S. BLAIR & SON,
Great Ancoats Street, MANCHESTER.

From Manchester.

Lieut. JOHN BLAIR	17th Batt. Northumberland Fusiliers.
Private JAMES F. BLAIR	14th Cheshires.
L.-Corp. RICHARD DEWHURST	East Lanc. Royal Engineers (wounded).
Sergt. ALBERT N. STREAT	17th Batt. Manchester Regt. (wounded).
L.-Corp. FRANK A. JACKSON	17th Batt. Manchester Regt. (missing).
Corp. HAROLD TEE	6th East Yorkshire Regt.
Private ROBERT HEPWORTH	17th Batt. Manchester Regt.
Private ARTHUR MILLWARD	1st Batt. Border Regt. (wounded).
Private ALGERNON E. SMITH	R.A.M.C.
Gunner THOMAS WILSON	West Lanc. R.F.A.
Rifleman EDWARD MARTIN	King's Royal Rifles (killed),
L.-Corp. JOHN HAINES	16th Batt. Manchester Regt.
Private JOSEPH MARSDEN	1/8th Batt. Manchester Regt.
Private FRED BELL	25th Batt Manchester Regt.
Private THOMAS MOSS	King's Shropshire Light Infantry.
Private JOHN GIBBONS	1/7th Batt. Manchester Regt. (killed).
Private ARTHUR DIMELOW	14th Batt. Manchester Regt.
Private EDWARD GALLAGHER	1st Batt. Manchester Regt. (killed).
Private JOHN GALLAGHER	1/8th Batt. Manchester Regt.
Trooper JAMES JOHNSON	11th Hussars (gassed).
Private JOSEPH SIMPKINS	17th Batt. Manchester Regt.
L.-Corp. THOMAS CARTLEDGE	1/7th Batt. Manchester Regt.
Private GILBERT SPENCER	18th Batt. Manchester Regt.
Private WILLOUGHBY MILLS	17th Batt. Manchester Regt. (killed).
Private FRANK PARKER	3/4th Batt. Border Regt.
Private HARRY MAY	4/5th Batt. Lancashire Fusiliers.
Cyclist WILLIAM HYDE	Army Cyclist Corps.
Gunner EDWARD DAVIES	R. G. A.
A. M. GEORGE FENSOME	Royal Flying Corps.
Private ARTHUR YEOMANS	41st Provisional Battalion.
Gunner WILLIAN MARTIN	R. F. A.
Private THOMAS MCKENNA	1/8th Batt. Manchester Regt.
Bombardier JOHN W. DUCK	R. G. A.

From London.

Rifleman W. ACOURT	6th Batt. Rifle Brigade.
Sergeant R. J. DURWARD	Seaforth Highlanders.
Private W. PAYNE	Royal Fusiliers.
Private A. RADLEY	Middlesex Regiment.

ROLL OF HONOUR.

MYRTLE, BURT & CO.,

MANCHESTER.

List of Men with the Colours.

Sergt.-Major ROBT. BLACKSTOCK - 20th Batt. Royal Fusiliers.
　　　　　Killed in France.
Private WM. OWEN DIBMON, R.A.M.C.　Attached to 6th Manch'r Regt.
　　　　　Killed in Gallipoli.
Private WM. ERNEST COCKCROFT　　Royal Garrison Artillery.
Private WILFRED HANBURY - 26th Batt. Manchester Regiment.
Private THOS. PERCY HEPWORTH - 4th Batt. Cheshire Regiment.
Private JAMES JACKSON - - - 26th Batt. Manchester Regiment,
Sergeant FRANK LOFTHOUSE - 14th Batt. Royal Welsh Fusiliers.
Private FRANK MAHER - - - 10th Commercial Batt. Royal Dublin
　　　　　　　　　　　　　　　　　　　　Fusiliers.
L.-Corp. CHAS. H. RATCLIFFE - 20th Batt. Royal Fusiliers.
2nd Lieut. W. S. SCOTT - - - Royal Flying Corps.
Private PETER TURNER - - - 2nd Batt. Monmouthshire Regiment.
Private THOMAS H. WINDSOR - 26th Batt. Manchester Regiment.
Ord. Seaman ARTHUR WILDING - Wireless Section, Royal Navy.
Lieut. SYDNEY CROSSLEY* - - 16th Batt. Lancashire Fusiliers.

From Java to Enlist.

Private E. MARSHALL STEVENS - Royal Engineers.

*Retired. Ill-health.

ROLL OF HONOUR

OF THE MANCHESTER STAFF OF

Messrs. E. D. SASSOON & CO.,

INDIA HOUSE, 73, WHITWORTH STREET.

Joined the Army—on Active Service.

- H, K. ANDREWS.
- H. AYKROYD.
- A. BATES.
- A. BERRY.
- S. BODEN.
- E. BROWNHILL.
- W. S. BRUCE.
- J. CLARKE.
- A. H. CLAYTON.
- S. CLIFFE.
- A. M. CUNINGHAM.
- N. DANIELS.
- T. FLETCHER.
- W. HAMILTON.
- E. HORRIDGE.
- L. IDDISON.
- J. F. A. JAMES.
- T. R. JONES.
- C. JOHNSON.
- G. KENT.
- A. LEE.
- J. W. LITTLE.
- T. OLDHAM.
- T. PARRY.
- V. RAINES.
- E. RYDER.
- F. L. SEWELL.
- J. SHEASBY.
- F. SHEPPARD.
- F. SMITH.
- F. W. SUMNER.
- J. SUTTON.
- A. E. TAYLOR.
- O. WILD.
- T. J. WILSHAW.
- F. WOLFENDEN.
- J. H. WOOLFORD.
- C. YOUNG.

ROLL OF HONOUR.

Isaac Booth & Son,

58, 60, 62, 64, MULBERRY STREET,
HULME, MANCHESTER.

- E. Vernon Booth, 6th Manchesters. (Son of E. I. Booth).
- F. C. Griffiths, Royal Field Artillery.
- A. Litherland, Army Veterinary Corps.
- E. J. Harrison, R.A.M.C.
- F. Parker, R.A.M.C.
- W. Street, Rifle Brigade.
- J. Holmes, Highland Light Infantry.
- F. Henthorne, Cheshire Regiment.
- F. Battersby, 2nd Welsh Regiment.
- G. Richardson, 2nd Welsh Regiment.
- W. Pottage, 7th Manchesters.
- T. Jones, 7th Manchesters.
- S. Wrigley, 27th Manchesters (Pals).
- H. Smith, 27th Manchesters (Pals).
- J. Batchelor, 27th Manchesters (Pals).
- H. Sands, King's Liverpools.
- A. Dorman, King's Own Royal Lancasters.
- S. Williams, Royal Field Artillery.
- C. Roberts, 6th Manchesters.
- J. Shearson, Lancs. Fusiliers.
- E. Cresswell, King's Own Royal Lancasters.
- A. Ryder, 6th Manchesters.

Roll of Honour.

GRANDAGE & CO.,

India House,
Whitworth Street, Manchester.

- Private Charles Bentley, 16th Serv. Batt. Man. Regt. (Killed).
- Private Albert Tabron, 17th Serv. Batt. Man. Regt. (Killed).
- Private A. O. Jessop, 16th Serv. Batt. Manchester Regiment (Reported Missing).
- Private S. Tristram, 18th Serv. Batt. Manchester Regiment
- Private Charles Hannan, 25th Serv. Batt. Man. Rgt. (Discharged)
- Private George Bowler, Duke of Lancaster's Yeomanry.
- Private William Catton, Royal Garrison Artillery (Discharged).
- Capt. H. F. Hobbs, 10th Batt. Welsh Regiment.
- Lieut. C. Woodall, Royal Flying Corps.
- Lieut. E. Newman, Army Ordnance Corps.
- Private C. D. Mayhew, Royal Army Medical Corps.
- Ship Steward Asst. A. J. Clark, Royal Navy.

Roll of Honour.

Falk, Stadelmann & Co. Ltd.

Veritas House,
Rochdale Road
MANCHESTER.

BARNARD, H. E.,
 Manchester Regiment.
BOURNE, F. H.,
 Manchester Regiment.
BURL, E.,
 Manchester Regiment.
CADWALLADER, C. W.,
 Manchester Regiment.
CLARKE, A. H.,
 North Staffordshire Regiment.
HANCOCK, R.,
 Royal Engineers.
HAYES, W.,
 Royal Engineers.
LEECH, K.,
 Motor Transport.
MAGUIRE, H. H.,
 2nd East Lancashire Regiment.
McEVOY, G.,
 3rd Lancashire Fusiliers.
McEVOY, T. G.,
 Manchester Regiment.
MILLER, C. E.
 7th King's Own Royal Lancs.
SHACKLETON, G.,
 Manchester Regiment.
STANDING, A. J.,
 2nd East Lancashire Regiment.
SWARMAN, C.,
 King's Royal Rifles.
TAYLOR, F. J.
 Manchester Regiment.
TAYLOR, H.,
 Manchester Regiment.

Above from Manchester Branch only.

RICARDO MÖLLER,

Great Marlborough Street,

MANCHESTER.

JOHN THORNEYCROFT,
 6th Manchester Regiment.

ALBERT KAY,
 17th Manchester Regiment.

ELLIS HERBERT,
 17th Manchester Regiment.

ALBERT PARR,
 6th Manchester Regiment.

FRANK GREEN (Killed in Action),
 13th Royal Welsh Fusiliers.

JOHN DAVENPORT,
 King's Own Rifles.

WILLIAM CUMMINGS,
 Lancashire Fusiliers.

THOMAS HORRIDGE,
 7th Welsh Fusiliers.

STANLEY STEWART.

ROLL OF HONOUR.

Steinthal & Co.

53, WHITWORTH STREET,
MANCHESTER.

Captain N. H. Zimmern,
    8th Lancashire Fusiliers.

Sergt.-Major C. K. Cope,
    1/17th Lanc. Battery, R.F.A.

Sergeant R. Gourley,
    7th Manchester Regiment.

Sergeant R. Anderton,
    8th Lancashire Fusiliers.

Sergeant R. Bateman,
    12th Lancashire Fusiliers.

Sergeant A. Mottershead,
    22nd Manchester Regt. (Killed in action in France, 1st July 1916).

Signaller J. Habershon,
    19th Lancashire Fusiliers.

Trooper N. Stansfield,
    2nd Cheshire Yeomanry.

Driver C. R. Simister,
    89th Field Co., R.E.

Private E. Heenan,
    20th Manchester Regiment.

Private A. Tuck,
    South Lancashire Regiment.

Private J. Fleming,
    R.A.M.C.

ROLL OF HONOUR.

C. BENTON,

58 Peter Street, Manchester,
and Branches.

2nd Lieut. F. C. Benton,
    6th Manchesters.

Private A. Benton,
    4th Dragoon Guards.

Trooper C. Benton,
    Australians.

Corporal R. H. Benton,
    Motor Dispatch Rider, R.E.

D. T. Clark (Attested).

F. R. Walker,
    180th Siege Battery, L.G.A.

F. Hilton (Attested—Rejected)

Private E. F. Reynolds,
    1st Cam. T. Rifles.

ROLL OF HONOUR

OF

Smethurst & Holden Ltd.

Gunner H. BRADBURY,
79th Section A.A.S.

Sergeant J. BROCK,
1/1st Cheshires, 267th Brigade, R.F.A.

Private G. BOWMAN,
"D" Company, 1/7th Manchesters.

Trooper G. COOKE,
Duke of Lancaster's Own Yeomanry.

Private G. A. HOLDEN,
"D" Company, 1/6th Manchesters.

Private E. HOLDEN (Killed),
"A" Company, 20th Royal Fusiliers (3rd Public Schools).

Private G. H. HOWARTH,
"C" Company, 18th Service Battalion, Manchester Regiment.

Private T. HALPIN,
6th Manchesters.

Driver B. HAMMAN,
55th Company Machine Gun Corps.

Private P. JENYON,
B" Company, 1/7th Manchesters.

Signaller W. KERR,
3/5th Cheshires.

Sergeant S. G. MELLOR (Killed),
"D" Company, 18th Service Battalion, Manchester Regiment.

Private W. MEARE,
50th Company Machine Gun Corps.

Private A. ORR,
"A" Company, 14th Manchester Regiment.

Signalman J. O. SEDDON,
Royal Naval Division.

FRED TAYLOR & SONS,

Cotton Manufacturers and Merchants,

— 17, BLOOM STREET, MANCHESTER —

The following have joined H.M. Forces up to September 1, 1916.

Staff Captain ARTHUR TAYLOR, 90th Infantry Brigade.
Captain L. F. WILSON, 16th Battalion Manchester Regiment.
Lieut. R. L. JOHNSTON, 17th Battalion Manchester Regiment (Killed in action).
Lieut. C. D. SCHULZE, 13th Argyle and Sutherland Highlanders.
Sergeant G. A. RICHARDS, 6th Battalion Manchester Regiment (Killed in action).
Sergeant G. EYRES, 9th Battalion Manchester Regiment (Killed in action].
Sergeant F. RUSHOLME. 6th Battalion Manchester Regiment.

W. H. MUSSON, R.F.A.
F. COOPER, R.G.A.
J. MIDDLETON, 6th Batt. Manchester Regiment.
E. BROOKES, R.F.A.
A. CARRUTHERS, R.A.M.C.
A. FREEMAN, R.E.
L. PORTER, R.G.A.
W. HOPKINS, Manchester Regiment.
G. A. TURNER, 3rd Batt. Manchester Regiment.
F. CAUDWELL, 6th Batt. Manchester Regiment.
J. RAWSTHORNE, R.E.
H. SPENCER, 6th Batt. Manchester Regiment.
F. H. FOX, 13th Batt. Royal Welsh Fusiliers.
R. WALMSLEY, 7th Batt. Manchester Regiment.
H. SEDDON, 18th Batt. Manchester Regiment.

F. HOWARD, R.A.M.C.
C. BAILEY, 6th Batt. Manchester Regiment.
L. RILEY, R.G.A.
G. KAY, R.G.A.
G. R. CHEETHAM, 6th Batt. Manchester Regt.
F. BOX, R.F.A.
W. TULIP, Royal Welsh Fusiliers.
F. JOHNSON, Royal Flying Corps.
G. FERNELEY, R.G.A.
C. JOHNSON, 6th Batt. Manchester Regiment.
F. T. ROBINSON, R.E.
H. BROOKS, Earl of Chester's Yeomanry.
H. LOCKE, 3rd Batt. Manchester Regiment.
G. G. JOHNSTON, Hon. Artillery Company.

Pioneer Mills, Radcliffe.

ALBERT TURNER.
JONATHAN BERRY.
ALFRED A. MOUNTFORD.
GEORGE GUFFOG.
THOS DOBSON.
JOHN HALLIGAN.
RICHARD DIGGLE.
SQUIRE ASHWORTH.
JAMES E. HAIGH.
MILFORD BROOKS.
WILLIAM MILLS.
ALBERT E. BELL.
GEORGE BELL.
JOSEPH WILLIAMS.

JAMES HADFIELD.
JAMES PENDLEBURY.
HARRY SANDIFORD.
STANLEY GREENHALGH.
ELIJAH YORK.
DAVID HAIGH.
JOHN HALL.
ARNOLD DOBSON.
WILLIAM SLATER.
WILLIAM BROOKS.
JACK BOYLE.
RICHARD ALLEN.
JOHN SMITH.

NORMAN OLIVE.
JOSEPH TAYLOR.
JOHN TONG.
THOS. CLARK.
JOHN CHADWICK.
EDWARD STOCK.
H. WOLSTENHOLME.
JOHN HOLDEN.
ERNEST PILKINGTON.
HARRY WATERS.
JOHN PROFFIT.
PERCY FRANCIS.
HAROLD HARDMAN.

Prospect Mill Hindley.

Pte. VINCENT CAWLEY, 14th King's Royal Rifles.
Pte. JONATHAN CHEETHAM, Signaller Royal Naval Volunteer Reserve.
Pte. NORMAN WILLIAM DUCKWORTH, 2/9th Royal Scots.
Gunner GEORGE DOOTSON. 169 Brigade R.F.A.
Pte HARRY DEAN, 9th Loyal North Lancs. Regt.

Pte. ALBERT EDWARD POTTER, 7th Royal Enniskillen Fusiliers.
Pte. FRED WALMSLEY, 11/5th King's Own Royal Lancaster Regt.
Pte. ARTHUR WADSWORTH, 345 Co. Motor Transport, A.S.C.
Pte. HARRY WINSTANLEY, 12th R.W.F.

The Manchester Guardian

ROLL OF HONOUR.

MONTAGUE, C. E. \
SCOTT, E. T. } *Directors.*

ASHCROFT, J.
ARMSTRONG, H.
BRADY, K. R.
BRADY, H. W.
BURDETT, S.
BERRY, S.
BENSON, W.
BURROWS, S.
BARRETT, A.
BAKER, R.
BEEVERS, J. G.
BERGIN, J.
BARBER, W.
BEARD, S.
BRANNEY, J.
CARTER, J. W.
CLARK, H. F.
CALVERLEY, T.
COOKMAN, C. V.
CODE, T.
CAWARDINE W.
CUMMINGS, H. R.
CRAWFORD, J.
DAVIES, J.
DEAN, A. W.
EDWARDS, H.
FIRTH, J.
GLEAVE, P.
GILLIGAN, J.
GILMORE, J.

GRAVETT, H.
HORNER, F.
HUGHES, H. P.
HEDDLE, J.
HARGREAVES, H.
HODGERT, W.
HARGREAVES, A.
HOUGH, E.
HOUGH, A.
HOBBS, C.
HICKS, C.
IRWIN, W. L.
JACK, W.
KIPPAX, J.
KNIGHT, P.
KEELEY, W.
KENYON, T. W.
LOWE, F.
LAWLESS, J.
LEACH, R. W.
LETHAR, J. H.
LONG, F.
MITCHELL, H.
MURPHY, H.
MORGAN, J.
MORAN, T.
McDONALD, J.
MORRIS, A.
MORETON, V.
MOSSEY, J. E.

NICHOLS, H. D.
NORTHCOTE, A. N.
NEILL, E. S.
PILLING, J.
ROUSE, H.
RILEY, H. J.
RONAN, J.
ROEBUCK, A.
ROSS, S.
SCANLON, S.
SINGFIELD, F.
SAVAGE, R. H.
SMITH, A.
SHAW, T.
SPRING, R. H.
SARGOOD, T.
SUTTON, J.
SHERIDAN, J.
SHERIDAN, B.
SMITH, S.
SOMERVILLE, H.
TOOTILL, E.
TONER, F.
TOPPING, T.
VERE DE VERE, E.
WILSON, F. H.
WYRILL, H.
WELSBY, J.
WILLIAMSON, H. W.
YATES, J. W.

"THE DAILY NEWS" LTD.

(NORTHERN EDITION)
DALE STREET, MANCHESTER.

ADAMS, H.
ASHBROOK, J. W.
ASTON, H.
ATKINSON, E.
BAXTER, W.
BENTHAM, J. W.
BROADHURST, C.
CARROLL, S.
CARTER, F. R.
CLARK, W.
COOPER, A. G.
DOWNS, C.
EATON, J.
EDMUNDS, G.
EDMONDSON, T.
EDWARDS, C.
FALLON, F.
GAUNT, J. T.
GIBSON, W.
GLASS, J.
GORMAN, D. W.
*GRANTHAM, W.
GRAY, J.
GREAVES, G.
GREGORY, R.
HAGAN, C.

HAGAN, J.
HALL, J.
HARRISON, W.
†HEATHCOTE, A. V.
IVESON, J.
JACKSON, F.
JOHNSON, P.
JOHNSTON, J. H.
JONES, J. W.
JONES, R.
†KAY, D.
KILROY, D.
LANCASHIRE, J. R.
LEIGHTON, D.
LODGE, H.
*LONGWORTH, T.
MATTHEWS, J.
MITCHELL, G.
MITCHELL, W.
MOFFATT, L.
MOSS, F.
MOSS, T.
NAYLOR, W. W.
NEILD, A. J.
NOLAN, J.
OLIVER, J.

OLIVER, W.
PARKER, O.
PEARSON, J.
PERKIN, J. W.
PHELAN, T.
RENSHAW, J.
RICHARDSON, C.
*RIDSDALE, W. B.
ROOME, J.
SALMON, S.
SCOTT, H.
SMALLEY, J.
SMITHIES, R. J.
*TARPEY, W.
†TASKER, J.
TAYLOR, A.
THOMAS, E. A.
TULEY, T.
TULEY, W.
WARBURTON, W.
WHALING P.
WHITTALL, N.
WILKES, J. T.
WILKINSON, R.
WILSON, W.
WINTER, G. L.

* Commissioned Officers.   † Died on Service.

ROLL OF HONOUR.

Samuel Heginbottom & Sons Ltd.

Junction Mills, Ashton-under-Lyne.

HAROLD HIBBERT	Assistant Salesman	Welsh Fusiliers.
JOSEPH CHADDERTON	Weavers' Overlooker	9th Batt. Manchester Rgt. (T.)
JOHN HAMPSON	Jacquard Assistant	9th Batt. Manchester Rgt. (T.)
JAMES PLAYER	Jacquard Assistant	9th Batt. Manchester Rgt. (T.)
JOHN DODD	Jacquard Assistant	9th Batt. Manchester Rgt. (T.)
SAMUEL GILMORE	Jacquard Assistant	9th Batt. Manchester Rgt. (T.)
WILLIAM GRIMSHAW	Jacquard Assistant	Lancashire Fusiliers.
WILLIAM ROBERTS	Jacquard Assistant	Royal Garrison Artillery.
JOHN GASKELL	Cloth Looker	County Palatine Heavy Artil.
GEORGE MEAKIN	Slashers' Labourer	King's Own Royal Lancasters.
WILLIAM HIBBERT (Died, Dardanelles.)	Weavers' Overlooker	East Lancashire Regiment.
ARNOLD BOOTH (Killed, Dardanelles.)	Piecer	9th Batt. Manchester Rgt. (T.)
GEORGE BOOTH	Piecer	9th Batt. Manchester Rgt. (T.)
REUBEN TYSON	Piecer	9th Batt. Manchester Rgt. (T.)
THOMAS KERSHAW	Piecer	9th Batt. Manchester Rgt. (T.)
ALFRED HARROTT	Piecer	9th Batt. Manchester Rgt. (T.)
SYDNEY WILDE	Piecer	9th Batt. Manchester Rgt. (T.)
ARTHUR LILLEY	Lap Carrier	9th Batt. Manchester Rgt. (T.)
JOSEPH ANDREW	Lap Carrier	9th Batt. Manchester Rgt. (T.)
FRED CARR	Assistant Carder	1st Batt. Cheshire Yeomanry.
TOM MILLER	Piecer	Duke of Wellington's Regt.
REG. KERSHAW	Piecer	9th Batt. Manchester Rgt. (T.)
JOE HALLIWELL	Jacquard Assistant	3rd Batt. Cheshire Regiment.
JOE ALLEN	Cloth Folder	Royal Field Artillery.
ALFRED HIPWELL	Piecer	9th Batt. Manchester Rgt. (T.)
JAMES BRADLEY	Piecer	9th Batt. Manchester Rgt. (T.)
ERNEST TYSON	Piecer	Royal Army Medical Corps.
JOSEPH BROOME	Piecer	Loyal North Lancs.
ROBERT GRIFFITHS	Spinner	Kitchener's Army.
GEORGE SAXON	Spinner	Royal Army Medical Corps.
JOE WOOLEY	Cloth Folder	Welsh Fusiliers.
HARRICK YATES	Book-keeper	Royal Garrison Artillery.
JAMES SYKES	Cloth Looker	9th Batt. Manchester Rgt. (T.)
SAM TAYLOR	Joiner	E.L. Royal Engineers.
THOMAS WILLIAMS	Piecer	9th Batt. Manchester Rgt. (T.)
HARRY CARTER	Card Lacer	9th Batt. Manchester Rgt. (T.)

ROLL OF HONOUR.
H. Wallwork & Co. Ltd.
Roger Street, Red Bank, Manchester.

Captain HERBERT WALLWORK, 2/10th Manchester Regiment.
2nd Lieut. EDGAR WALLWORK, 1/10th Manchester Regiment.

A. ADDERLEY	Royal Garrison Artillery.
JOHN ALLEN	3rd Batt. Manchester Regiment.
R. ALLEN	1st Batt. Lancashire Fusiliers.
JAMES H. ANNING	6th Batt. K.O.S.B. Regt.
W. J. ARCHER	9th Batt. Lancashire Fusiliers.
W. ATKINS	10th Batt. Loyal North Lancs.
J. BOWMAN	6th Batt. East Lancashire Regt.
P. BRABAZON	2nd Royal Irish Regiment.
W. BRADBURY (Killed)	1st Manchester Regiment.
R. BROWN	Dorset Regiment.
JAMES BUCKLEY	Royal Engineers.
J. J. BURNS	Royal Field Artillery.
G. CARAHER	14/5th Bt. King's Liverpool Rgt.
J. CARROLL (Killed)	1st Lancashire Fusiliers.
T. CASE (Killed)	10th Batt. Loyal North Lancs.
S. CHESTERS (Killed)	99th Field Coy. Roy. Eng.
F. COLE	12th Bt. Royal Welsh Fusiliers.
T. COYNE	22nd Serv. Bt. Manchester Regt.
A. CRONAN	6th Batt. East Lancashire Regt.
R. DAVENPORT	9th Batt. East Lancashire Regt.
C. DAWSON	10th Batt. Lancashire Fusiliers.
T. DOLMAN	Motor Transport, A.S.C.
D. ELLINSWORTH	9th S. Batt. East Lancs. Regt.
J. ENGLISH	K.O. Royal Lancaster Regt.
W. J. FINCH	No. 1. Company R.G.A.
F. FOULKES	9th Batt. South Lancs. Regt.
JAMES FOX	2nd Batt. K.O.S.B. Regt.
T. FOY	No. 9 Squad. Royal Flying Corps.
J. GARRY	16th Batt. Lancashire Fusiliers.
J. GAVIN	10th Bt. Loyal North Lancs. Rgt.
D. GIBSON	9th Batt. East Lancashire Regt.
J. GREEN	9th Batt. East Lancashire Regt.
W. GREEN	Lancashire Fusiliers.
G. H. GRIMSHAW (Killed.)	Royal Engineers.
J. HILL	Royal Defence Corps.
R. HINDS	21st Serv. Batt. Manchester Rgt.
A. HOOPER (Killed)	8th King's Own Royal Lancasters.
A. HORNE	13th Batt. King's Liverpool Rgt.
R. HUDSON	Manchester Regiment.
J. HUSBAND	King's Own Scottish Borderers.
W. INGRAM	King's Own Scottish Borderers.
A. JONES	Royal Engineers.
G. JONES	16th Batt. Manchester Regt.
J. KELLY	13th Batt. Manchester Regt.
W. KERWIN	Manchester Regiment.
W. LENNARD	1st Batt. South Lancs. Regt.
JAMES LYNCH	2nd Manchester Regiment.
JOHN MANNION	1st Batt. Manchester Regiment.
G. MASSEY	10th Batt. South Lancs. Regt.
F. MATTHEWS	Royal Field Artillery.
W. MAXFIELD	Manchester Regiment.
J. McCRANN	1st Gar. Batt. Manchester Regt.
F. MITCHELL	12th Batt. Lancashire Fusiliers.
J. MORRIS	11th Batt. Lancashire Fusiliers.
J. MURRAY	Lancashire Fusiliers.
J. NAYLOR	11th Batt. Loyal North Lancs.
W. J. NEILD	Grenadier Guards.
J. NUTTALL	1/8th Batt. Manchester Regt.
J. A. ORMAN	11th Batt. Lancashire Fusiliers.
R. PICKLES	Leicester Regiment.
J. PILOT	13th Batt. Lancashire Fusiliers.
J. ROBERTS	13th Batt. Lancashire Fusiliers.
G. ROBINSON	Royal Field Artillery.
S. SHANLEY	1st Batt. Lancashire Fusiliers.
J. SHARPLES	2/7th Lancashire Fusiliers.
W. S. SMITH	21st Batt. Manchester Regt.
W. SYKES	98th Field Coy. Royal Eng.
G. H. THEWLIS	14th Batt. King's Liverpool Regt.
W. TIMES	18th Batt. Manchester Regt.
C. TOMLINSON	King's Own Scottish Borderers.
S. WALKER (Killed)	1st Batt. 7th Manchester Regt.
J. F. WALSH	10th Batt. Border Regiment.
T. WHELAN	Lancashire Fusiliers.
D. WHISTON	2/3rd Field Co. E.L. Royal Eng.
C. WHITE	13th Batt. King's Liverpool Rgt.
H. WINSTANLEY (Killed.)	6th Batt. South Lancashire Regt.
E. E. WOOD	12th Batt. King's Liverpool Rgt.
S. WOODHEAD (Killed)	11th Batt. Lancashire Fusiliers.
T. WORRALL	1st Air Mechanic R.F.C.
W. WRIGHT	4th Hussars.

ROLL OF HONOUR

* * *

J. H. AGNEW & BRO.

5, Mount Street, Manchester.

* * *

NAMES OF EMPLOYEES WHO HAVE JOINED HIS MAJESTY'S FORCES.

Capt. F. M. BLATHERWICK	6th Batt. Manchester Regiment.
Capt. W. E. LEAVER	2/9th Batt. Manchester Regiment.
Capt. J. S. FOX	2/5th Batt. Manchester Regiment.
2nd Lieut. P. A. WOODHOUSE	2/9th Batt. Manchester Regiment.
2nd Lieut. W. H. DEAN	East Lancashire Regiment.
2nd Lieut. E. E. TWEEDALE	Loyal North Lancashire Regiment.
Corpl. W. LONGWORTH	6th Batt. Manchester Regiment.
Lce.-Corpl. T. RENSHAW	King's Own Lancaster Regiment.
Lce.-Corpl. S. MULLINEAUX	Royal Field Artillery.
Private C. BOOTH	7th Batt. Pals.
Private R. WILKINSON	6th Batt. Manchester Regiment.
Private A. WARK	6th Batt. Manchester Regiment.
Private J. McNICHOLLS	Royal Army Medical Corps.
Private E. GUNSHUN	7th Batt. Pals.
Private R. SUMMERFIELD	Argyle and Sutherland Highlanders.
Private W. MOORES	6th Batt. Manchester Regiment.
Private F. ROGERS	4th Batt. Manchester Regiment.
Private W. WARK	1/6th Batt. Manchester Regiment.
Private F. S. BRADLEY	1/6th Batt. Manchester Regiment.
Private C. HOLLOWAY	Lancashire Fusiliers.
Private R. WADSWORTH	Lancashire Fusiliers.
Private L. TEFFT	6th Cheshire Regiment.
Private R. BUCKLAND	27th Batt. Royal Fusiliers.
Private J. BRIGGS	Royal Field Artillery.
Private H. H. PROFFITT	King's Liverpool Regiment.
Private JOS. WINDLE	Army Pay Corps.

ROLL OF HONOUR.

***

HENRY BOND & CO. LTD.

12, Tariff Street, Dale Street, Manchester, and
Milton Mills, and Thyme Street Works, Bolton.

JOHN BLEAKLEY	3rd Batt. Loyal North Lancashire Regiment.
WALTER BROWN	5th Batt. Loyal North Lancashire Regiment.
JOSEPH BENTLEY	Royal Army Medical Corps.
RICHARD COOKE	5th Batt. Loyal North Lancashire Regiment.
CHARLES COOP	3rd East Lancashire Brigade R.F.A.
ALBERT DERBYSHIRE	15th Batt. Welsh Regiment.
JOHN DORNAN	13th Batt. The Royal Scots.
JAMES FLETCHER	County Palatine R.F.A., 148th Brigade.
THOMAS F. GRUNDY	2nd Batt. Lancashire Fusiliers.
ALFRED HEATON	11th Batt. Manchester Regiment.
JAMES F. HUNT	3rd East Lancashire Brigade R.F.A.
JOHN KELLY	93rd Brigade R.F.A., National Reserve.
WALTER KIRKMAN	9th Batt. Loyal North Lancashire Regiment.
CLARENCE LOW	5th Batt. Loyal North Lancashire Regiment.
GEORGE PENNANCE	County Palatine R.F.A., 148th Brigade.
ROBERT SYDDALL	5th Batt. Loyal North Lancashire Regiment.
JOHN SYDDALL	County Palatine R.F.A., 148th Brigade.
GEORGE E. WILLIAMSON	16th Batt. King's Royal Rifle Corps.
THOMAS WILSON	18th Batt. Welsh Regiment.
JAMES H. RUSHTON	Royal Garrison Artillery.
THOMAS WARBURTON	Lancashire Fusiliers.
ANDREW MONKS	Army Cyclists Corps.
WILLIAM H. STRONG	Royal Garrison Artillery.
CHARLES NUTTALL	Lancashire Fusiliers.
JAMES HOLT	Pioneers' Battalion.
JAMES BANNISTER	Loyal North Lancashire Regiment.
SAMUEL HOLDEN	Loyal North Lancashire Regiment.
ALBERT BROOKS	Loyal North Lancashire Regiment.
HORACE E. HALL	O.T.C. Inns of Court.
JAMES HORSEFIELD	7th Batt. Manchester Regiment.

ROLL OF HONOUR.
T. TAYLOR LTD.
44, George Street, Manchester, and
. . Saville Mills, Bolton. . .

Capt. H. TAYLOR	King's Royal Rifle Corps.
C. AINSCOW	King's Royal Rifle Corps.
R. ASPINALL	King's Royal Rifle Corps.
Sgt. R. BERTWISTLE	Loyal North Lancs.
Sgt. R. SPENCER	Loyal North Lancs.
Sgt. R. BULLOUGH	Loyal North Lancs.
J. CLEMSON	Loyal North Lancs.
S. WOODALL	Loyal North Lancs.
J. BABER	Loyal North Lancs.
T. PETERS	Loyal North Lancs.
T. GUYNAN	Loyal North Lancs.
J. WARBURTON	Loyal North Lancs.
J. SEDDON	Loyal North Lancs.
F. LIDDELL	Loyal North Lancs.
C. AINSCOW	Loyal North Lancs.
D. HEYWOOD	Loyal North Lancs.
I. ENTWISTLE	Loyal North Lancs.
M. VALENTINE	Loyal North Lancs.
R. WALMSLEY	Loyal North Lancs.
T. WORSLEY	Loyal North Lancs.
W. GRUNDY	Loyal North Lancs.
P. BROWN	20th Hussars.
N. KAY	Royal Engineers.
Cpl. A. S. POLLITT	Royal Engineers.
L.-Cpl. J. HAMER	5th Manchester Regt.
R. PENNANCE	King's Own Lancasters.
J. JERSTICE	King's Own Lancs.
J. BOARDMAN	King's Own Lancasters.
J. PARKER	Welsh Regiment.
L.-Cpl. J. DEMAINE	Welsh Regiment.
W. SMITH	King's Royal Lancasters.
J. W. PROCTOR	8th King's Liverpools.
H. SENIOR	Royal Naval S.B.A.
A. CARDWELL	Royal Naval S.B.A.
Cpl. R. ASHWORTH	Royal Field Artillery.
J. DISLEY	Lancashire Fusiliers.
H. ADDISON	Army Service Corps.
S. BOWLING	Army Service Corps.
A. AUSTIN	Army Service Corps.
E. KNOWLES	Temporary Coastguard.
G. GOODMAN	Sherwood Foresters.
W. GREENHALGH	Royal M.L.I.
H. MOORES	Royal Garrison Artillery.
R. BINKS	Royal Garrison Artillery.
J. HOLLAND	Royal Garrison Artillery.
W. WOOD	East Lancs. R.F.A.
J. TATTERSALL	Loyal North Lancs.
H. SWINDLEY	Cycle Corps.
Cpl. R. CALLISTER	8th Manchesters.
J. WOOTON	2nd Manchesters.
L.-Cpl. T. LUCAS	Lancashire Fusiliers.
H. RYLANCE	Royal Field Artillery.
J. YATES	6th Manchesters.
J. LAWSON	Royal Sussex Cycle Corps
S. HENSON	2nd 4th Yorkshire Regt.

Attested : J. T. BRIDGE and A. SIMMONDS.

ROLL OF HONOUR.

JOHN BOOTH & CO. LTD.,
1, DICKINSON STREET, MANCHESTER.

MILLS—Walkden and Radcliffe.

NORMAN DAWES.	SAM. BARROWCLOUGH.
THOMAS RILEY.	HARRY HENSHALL.
CHARLES EDWARDS.	DUNCAN McPHERSON.
ERNEST BITHELL.	LEONARD GRIFFITHS.
JOHN McPHERSON.	SILAS GRUNDY.

ATTESTED LIST.

THOMAS ANDERSON.	H. HICKSON.
H. J. HAMPSON.	JOHN W. HOLT.
FREDERICK BARNES.	CHARLES PICKSTONE.
R. MULLINGER.	R. THORPE.
JOSEPH FLETCHER.	H. G. BOOTH.
FRANK NIXON.	PERCY LOWE.
THOMAS EVANS.	FRED WOLSTENHOLME.
W. R. TALLEY.	JOHN FLETCHER.
JAMES HOLDSWORTH.	

ROLL OF HONOUR
John Phethean & Company Limited,
30, GEORGE STREET, MANCHESTER.   MILLS: Moses Gate, Nr. Bolton.

Manchester Warehouse.

CHARLES PHETHEAN	Manchester Regiment.
HARRY BROOKES	Manchester Regiment.
ERNEST BARDSLEY	Manchester Regiment.
JOHN GREENHALGH	Royal Garrison Artillery.

No. 1 Mill.

JAMES SMITH	East Lancashire Regiment.
WILLIAM WALKER	Lancashire Fusiliers.
WILLIAM GREEN	Coldstream Guards.
JOSEPH WHITEHEAD	Royal Army Medical Corps.
WILLIAM MARSH	Royal Army Medical Corps.
JOSEPH BOHANNON	Royal Field Artillery.
JOHN WALCH	Royal Army Medical Corps.
JOSEPH BLAKELEY	Royal Army Medical Corps.
SYDNEY BLAKELEY	Royal Army Medical Corps.
HERBERT PROUDFOOT	Loyal North Lancashire Regiment.
GEORGE WILLIAM PROUDFOOT	Sick Berth Reserve.
FRANK EVANS	King's (Liverpool).
R. LYTHGOE	
JOSIAH BURGUM	Motor Machine Gun.
GEORGE COOPER	Loyal North Lancashire Regiment.
JOHN COLLISON	Cheshire Regiment.
ALBERT HOWCROFT	Loyal North Lancashire Regiment.
ALBERT WELSBY	Cheshire.

No. 2 Mill.

PETER HOWCROFT	Royal Field Artillery.
JOHN THOMAS MOBEY	D.C. Light Infantry.
RICHARD MASSEY	Loyal North Lancashire Regiment.
THOMAS ATHERTON	Loyal North Lancashire Regiment.
WALTER ROUTLEDGE	Royal Army Medical Corps.
JOHN OWEN	Loyal North Lancashire Regiment.
JAMES MEDCROFT	Yorkshire Light Infantry.
GEORGE HASTIE	King's Own Scottish Borderers.
HENRY HOWARTH	Loyal North Lancashire Regiment.
FRED HOPKINSON	Loyal North Lancashire Regiment.
EWART W. LUND	Loyal North Lancashire Regiment.
FRED GREENHALGH	15th Cheshires.
F. HIGGINBOTTOM	Loyal North Lancashire Regiment.
THOMAS HANLEY	Loyal North Lancashire Regiment.
H. OPENSHAW	Loyal North Lancashire Regiment.
JOHN EYLAND	Loyal North Lancashire Regiment.

New Mills, Derbyshire.

FRED WHARMBY	12th Sherwood Foresters.
MARK WHITTAKER	Royal Welsh Fusiliers.
—— BURNS	York and Lancaster Regiment.
J. S. GRIMSHAW	Royal Army Medical Corps.
ARNOLD HILL	21st Heavy Battery Ammunition Column.
HAROLD T. BARBER	3rd Sherwood Foresters.
J. W. RIDGEWAY	Sherwood Foresters.
WALTER BATES	Sherwood Foresters.

Linotype and Machinery Limited.

ROLL OF HONOUR
EUROPEAN WAR, 1914—16.

The Directors and Staff of Linotype and Machinery Limited place on record with pride the names of their Colleagues who are serving with the Allied Forces.

* The names starred indicate those who have given their lives for the cause.

Head Office, London.

AKERMAN, H. D.	R.A.M.C.	HEWLETT, A. M.	Civil Service Rifles.
BAKER, S. G. R.	12th Gloucesters.	HUNT, G. O.	A.S.C., Motor Transport.
BLAKER, T. J.	R.A.M.C.	JACKSON, C. E. H.	10th Middlesex.
BRIDGMAN, H A.	15th Batty. R.F.A. London.	JOBSON, L. A.	25th County of Lond. (Cycl.).
BUGLER, A. V.	R.N.V.R., H.M.S. Conqueror.	KING, J.	King's Royal Rifles.
BURDON, C. S.	15th Middlesex.	LEEGOOD, W. J.	24th County of London.
CADMAN, F. S.	3rd Sussex Yeomanry.	LIGHTFOOT, J.	R.N. (H.M.S. "Prince of Wales").
CAINE, C. V.	1st Northants.		
CAMP, W. S.	R.F.A., 2nd East Anglian.	MORGAN, W. C.	Royal Flying Corps.
CLEWES, W. F.	Army Service Corps.	PRITCHARD, H. H.	5th East Surrey.
CRABBE, T. H.	9th Middlesex.	PRYKE, W. P.	Roy. Flying Corps, Wire. Sec.
CRADDOCK, W.	R.A.M.C.	READER, J. W.	8th East Surrey.
EDWARDS, A.	R.A.M.C.	SHRUBSHALL, H.	6th Batt. Essex Regiment.
FENTUM, A. L.	10th County of London.	STRATTON, E. C.	Army Pay Dept.
GELLAN, R. A.	5th Royal Fusiliers.	WADESON, R. E.	Army Pay Dept.
GODFREY, E.	9th Lancers.	WEEKS, E. W.	Durham Light Infantry.
GOLDSMITH, C. E.	10th County of London.	WOOD, F. W.	A.S.C. (Motor Transport).
GOULD, J. H.	8th Northamptons.	WOODHAM, G.	6th Rifle Brigade.
GREEN, A.	17th County of London.	WRIGHT, L. S.	4th Suffolk Regiment.
GRIFFITHS, T.	Army Service Corps.		

London Depôt.

DUNN, W. S.	London Scottish.	LANDER, S. A.	Royal Field Artillery.
FIRMAN, A.	Royal Naval Division.	LAWLER, G.	A.S.C.
HARPER, E. J.	Army Ordnance Corps.	MITTON, H.	Royal Naval Division.
HUGHES, M. O.	Royal Field Artillery.	SIMMONDS, W. J.	Royal Engineers.
KINGSTON, H.	A.S.C.	TRODD, A. E.	Royal Field Artillery.

Broadheath Works.

ACTON, F. A.	1st Royal Scots.	BARKER, J.	East Lancs. Royal Engineers.
ALLEN, G.	Royal Inniskilling Fusiliers.	BARNETT, W.	11th Scottish Rifles.
ALLEN, R.	Army Service Corps.	BARTON, J.	11th South Lancashires.
ALSTON, C.	Royal Engineers.	BATTELL, C.	East Lancs. Royal Engineers.
ARNOLD, J.	8th Cheshires.	BEESLEY, C.	6th Manchesters.
ATKINSON, W. J.	5th Cheshires.	BEESLEY, W.	Army Service Corps.
BABBINGTON, W.	6th Connaught Rangers.	BEIGHTON, L.	A.S.C. (Motor Transport).

Linotype and Machinery Limited.

ROLL OF HONOUR—continued.

BROADHEATH WORKS—continued.

BENNETT, G. A.	Seaforth Highlanders.		EUDALE, F.	8th Cheshires.
BEECH, J. W.	R.G.A.		EUDALE, H.	5th Cheshires.
BESWICK, F.	5th Cheshires.		*EVENSON, G.	11th Scottish Rifles.
BEVAN, T.	2/1st East Lancs. R.E.		FERGUSON, F.	41st Battery, R.F.A.
BIGGS, A.			FIELDING, C.	78th Field Co. Royal Eng.
BLACKSHAW, F.	3rd Cheshires.		FLETCHER, J.	
BLEASE, J. H.	3rd Cheshires.		FLYNN, A.	
BOARDMAN, J.	9th R.E. (Signal Co.).		FORSTER, H.	5th Cheshires.
BOOKER F.	5th Cheshires.		FOTHERINGHAM, T.	8th Royal Scots Fusiliers.
BOWETT, A. E.	7th K.O. Royal Lancasters.		FOY, A.	5th Cheshires.
BRADE, J. F.	21st Lancers.		FOY, P.	Royal Engineers.
BRADLEY, C. H.	2nd East Lancs. R.E.		GALLIARD, W. G.	11th Scottish Rifles.
BROOKER, J. E.	8th King's Liverpool.		GAYTER, H.	5th Cheshires.
BROWN, W.	5th Cheshires.		*GIROD, MILTON.	Royal Flying Corps.
CALDERBANK, J.			GLEAVE, W.	Royal Field Artillery.
CANTWELL, P.	8th Cheshires.		GOLDSTRAW, E.	1st Cheshires.
CARR, J. W.	8th Cheshires.		GOUGH, A. T.	181st Co. A.S.C., Motor Tran.
CARSON, H. R.	5th Cheshires.		GRAHAM, F.	R.F.A.
CARVILL, T.	5th Cheshires.		*GREGORY, F. C.	1st Cheshires.
CHADWICK, T. J.	East Lanc. R.E., 1st Field Co.		GREGORY, J.	18th Welsh Regiment.
CHAMBERS, R.			GREGSON, G.	Royal Eng. (92nd Field Co.).
CLARKE, J. A.	22nd Manchesters.		GRETTON, B.	Army Ordnance Corps.
CLARKE, W.	5th Cheshires.		GRIFFITHS, H.	A.S.C. (Motor Transport).
COHN, S.	5th Cheshires.		GROARK, M.	3rd Cheshires.
COLE, C.	Royal Welsh Fusiliers.		HALL, W.	1st Manchesters.
COLLINS, J.	6th Manchesters.		HAMPSON, J.	
COOK, H.	3rd Cheshires.		*HANLEY, D.	8th Cheshires.
COOPER, F.	5th Cheshires.		HANLEY, J.	8th Cheshires.
COOPER, R.			HANLEY, J.	Royal Irish Rifles.
COOPER, J.			HANSON, T.	Cheshires.
COMAR, H.	R.F.A.		HARRINGTON, T. J.	83rd Army Service Corps.
CORRIGAN, J.	R.A.M.C.		HARRISON, C.	14th Manchesters.
CORRIN, H.			HARRISON, E.	5th Cheshires.
COTTINGHAM, E.	10th Cheshires.		HARRISON, G. F.	3rd Cheshires.
COWLISHAW, H.			HARRISON, R.	3rd Cheshires.
CUNNANE, J.	11th Cheshires.		HARROP, J. W.	R.F.A.
DEAN, J.			HARROP, J. H.	
*DEVONPORT, H.	5th Cheshires.		HARTLEY, G. C.	Army Service Corps.
DIXON, H.			HEALEY, J.	Royal Engineers.
DODD, H.	9th Cheshires.		HEARNE, J.	3rd Cheshires.
DOIG, E.			HENNERLEY, M.	8th Cheshires.
DOYLE, G.	Royal Engineers.		HIGGINS, T.	Royal Irish Rifles.
DRAKE, C.	5th Cheshires.		HIGGINS, W.	18th Lancs. Fusiliers.
EASTHAM, T.	5th Cheshires.		HIGGS, G. A. C.	6th Manchesters.
EATON, F.	10th Cheshires.		HOLMES, W.	
*EATON, G.	8th Cheshires.		HOLT, D. R.	18th Royal Fusiliers.
ENTWISTLE, F.	68th Welsh Div. (Cyclists).		HOPKINSON, R.	6th Roy. Inniskilling Fusiliers.
*ENTWISTLE, H.	5th Cheshires.		HORLOCH, A.	
EPPLESTON, W.	5th Cheshires.		HORSLEY, F. W.	5th Cheshires.
ESPIN, J. H.	6th Manchesters.		HOUGHTON, J. T.	Lancashire Fusiliers.

Linotype and Machinery Limited.

ROLL OF HONOUR—continued.

BROADHEATH WORKS—continued.

HOUGH, W.	19th Manchesters.	PEACOCK, J.	5th Cheshires.
HUFF, H.		PEARSON, H.	6th Cheshires.
HUGHES, A.	5th Cheshires.	PERKIN, D.	5th Cheshires.
HUXLEY, R.	8th South Lancashires.	PERKIN, F.	10th Cheshires.
INGLE, E.	17th Manchesters.	PINDER, E.	King's Royal Rifles.
JACKSON, H.	6th East Lancashires.	POOLE, A.	3rd Cheshires.
JACKSON, S.	5th Army Service Corps.	POOLE, E.	5th Cheshires.
JOHNSON, H.	20th Manchesters.	POWELL, J.	9th K.O. Yorks. L.I.
JONES, W.	3rd K.O. Royal Lancasters.	PRIGG, W. M.	10th Cheshires.
KELLY, E.	R.F.A.	PURCELL, H.	National Reserve (2nd Class).
KENYON, F.	Red Cross Ambulance.	RICKARDS, O.	7th Manchesters.
KERSHAW, A.	East Lanc. R.E. (2/1 Sig. Co.)	ROBINSON, F.	Royal Welsh Fusiliers.
KING, H.	8th King's Liverpools.	ROBINSON, G.	Royal Engineers.
KITCHEN, E.	5th Cheshires.	ROGERSON, W.	1st Cheshires.
KNOWLES, R.	Royal Eng. (92nd Field Co.).	RUBBATHAN, A. J.	7th Cheshires.
LAMB, H.	1st Cheshires.	SECKER, H.	7th South Lancashires.
LEE, A.	8th South Lancashires.	SHAW, A.	5th Cheshires.
LEES, J.	Royal Engineers.	SHERWOOD, F.	
LEONARD, A.	5th Cheshires.	SHORT, W.	6th Manchesters.
LEYLAND, W.	8th Manchesters.	SIMPSON, W.	
LITTLEWOOD, G.	3rd Lancashire Fusiliers.	SIMISTER, J.	6th Manchesters.
LOVESAY, F.	5th Cheshires.	SIMPER, H.	Royal Scots.
LUCAS, J. H.		SMITH, J. F.	R.A.M.C.
LYNCH, J.	20th Manchesters.	SMITH, H.	
MACDONALD, A.	3rd Cheshires.	SNOW, R.	
MACKENZIE, L. A.	E. Lanc. R.E. (2nd Field Co.)	SOUDEN, D.	2nd Scots Greys.
MACNAMARA, T.	3rd Cheshires.	SPARKES, H. G.	6th Manchesters.
McCARTIE, R. J.	Royal Engineers.	SPEAKMAN, F.	2nd Lancashire Fusiliers.
MARSH, C.		SPENCE, J. J.	19th Manchesters.
MASON, W.	Royal Scots Fusiliers.	SPENCER, G. A.	Naval Sick Berth.
MERRELL, C.	Gordon Highlanders.	STACEY, R. L. O.	8th Cheshires.
*MILLER, A.	10th Cheshires.	STOKES, F.	K.O. Scottish Borderers.
MILLER, T.		STRADLING, H.	3rd Cheshires.
MOORES, W.	Royal Welsh Fusiliers.	STREET, D.	5th Cheshires.
MORGAN, J.	R.A.M.C.	STREET, F.	
MORLEY, P.	5th Cheshires.	STUART, W.	7th Manchesters.
MORT, G.	6th R.A.M.C (Field Amb.).	THOMPSON, J.	2nd East Lancs. R.E.
MUGAN, A.	R.F.A.	TIERNEY, W.	5th Cheshires.
MURRAY, J.	K.O. Royal Lancasters.	TURNER, H.	5th Cheshires.
MYATT, R.	5th Cheshires.	WALKER, J.	R.F.A.
MYLES, P.	Royal Naval Stores.	WALLACE, F.	6th East Lancashires.
NEWTON, A.	3rd Cheshires.	WALTON, F.	Naval Sick Berth Reserve.
NOLAN, J.	Royal Field Artillery.	WARBURTON, H.	Royal Engineers.
NORRIS, T. C.	11th Scottish Rifles.	WARBURTON, J.	5th Cheshires.
NORTON, J.	Argyll & S. Highlanders.	WEBB, N.	Sherwood Foresters.
OKELL, S.	3rd Cheshires.	WEETMAN, J. H.	East Lancashire Regiment.
OLLIER, R.	Royal Engineers.	WILD, F. C.	R.F.A.
PARKINSON, A.	Lancashire Fusiliers.	WILKINSON, S.	5th Cheshires.
PARSONAGE, J.	R.F.A.	WILLIAMS, F.	A.S.C. (83rd Co. Motor Tran.)

Linotype and Machinery Limited.

ROLL OF HONOUR—continued.

BROADHEATH WORKS—continued.

WOLSTENHOLME, K.	East Lancs Royal Engineers.	WRIGHT, A.	5th Cheshires.
WOODHEAD, G.	Grenadier Guards.	WRIGHT, J.	
WORRALL, A. L.	A.S.C. (4th Co. Motor Tran.).	YARROW, A.	5th Dragoon Guards.
WORTHINGTON, G.	13th King's Royal Rifles.	YARWOOD, G.	3rd Cheshires.
WORTHINGTON, T.	5th Cheshires.	YEARSLEY, A.	Royal Irish Rifles.

Glasgow Depôt.

HUGHES, A.　　K.O. Scottish Borderers.

Barcelona Branch.

GIROD, PERCY.　　20th (P.S.) Royal Fusiliers.

Athens Branch.

SAINSOT, A.　　Corps d'Avation (Armée Française).　　VALLIN, J.　　(Armée Française).

Cairo Branch.

TIZORIN, E.　　282me Inf. (Armée Française).

Societe Linotype Française, Paris.

BERLAUD, M.	32me Inf. (Armée Française).	MERIOT, R.	8me Artillerie (A.F.).
CONTASSOT, A.	8me Artil. (Armée Française).	PERIN, G.	8me Génie (Armée Française).
DUCHEMIN, E.	(Armée Française).	PINET, M.	105me Territorial (A.F.).
DUPUY, H.	80me Inf. (Armée Française).	PIQUET, C.	1er Bat. Chass. Alpins (A.F.).
FERGANT, P.	28me Inf. (Armée Française).	RAYMOND, A.	Infirmier (Armée Française).
FLEURY, L.	89me Inf. (Armé Française).	RAYMOND, G.	356 Reserve de Ligne (A.F.).
GRAEBER, A.	2me Régiment Etranger, A.F.	RAYNAUD, G.	7me Groupe Artillerie (A.F.).
HAEN, G.	6me Artil. (Armée Française).	ROUX, E.	14me Génie (Armée Française)
*HIAM, G.	368me Inf., Armée Française.	SALBREUX, J.	1er Génie (Armée Française).
LANTIER, L.	(Armée Française).	SEILLAN, E.	86me Infanterie (A.F.).
MAISTRE, J.	144me Infanterie (A.F.).	VALLIERE, F. H. J.	300me Inanterie (A.F.).

Societa Linotype Italiana, Milan and Rome.

DELON, A.	22me Inf. (Armée Française).	TOCCHIO, C.	2nd Aviatori (Exercizio Italiano).
BORGIOLI, A.	4th Automobilisti (Exercizio Italiano.)	RENATO, U.	81st Fant. (Exercizio Italiano).

ROLL OF HONOUR.

J. Mandleberg & Company Ltd.

ALBION WORKS . .

Cobden Street, Pendleton.

Directors - { Colonel S. L. MANDLEBERG.
2nd Lieut. J. H. MANDLEBERG.
Captain P. L. ROTHBAND. }

ASPERY, STANLEY.	CONNELL, RICHARD.	*DUTTON, ARNOLD.
ALLEN, CHARLES.	CORCORAN, JAMES.	ECOB, H. L.
*AMOS, W.	CLEGG, THOMAS.	EMSLEY, ALFRED.
BERRY, ARTHUR.	COLLINS, JOHN.	ENGLESBERG, N.
BARNFIELD, HARRY.	CHATHAM, WALTER.	FISHER, HORACE.
BROUGHAM, STANLEY.	*CROMPTON, J.	*FILDES, JAMES.
BROGAN, JOHN.	*CRABTREE, C.	FLETCHER, WILLIAM.
BAILEY, WILLIAM.	*CRAWSHAW, J.	GREER, J. H.
BARKER, JOSEPH.	*CUNLIFFE, JOHN.	GORTON, F. L.
BOYD, THOMAS.	*CLARKE, JOHN.	GILMOUR, JACK.
BELLERBY, RICHARD.	DENTITH, ALFRED SAM.	GAUNT, WILLIAM.
*BELLIS, OSWALD.	DEVLIN, CHARLES.	GEE, RICHARD.
*BOOTH, J. H.	DICKINSON, HERBERT.	GREGG, WILLIAM.
*BERRY, W.	DUGGLEBY, DIGBY.	*GRATRIX, WILLIAM.
*BIRCHWOOD, ARTHUR.	DUNN, DANIEL.	HAND, GEORGE.
*BROWN, JOHN.	*DEAN, JAMES.	HUGHES, JOSEPH.
*BLEARS, CYRIL.	*DEAN, W.	HORSFALL, WILLIAM.
CALVERT, JOHN.	*DUTTON, J.	HUGHES, HARRY.
CLOWES, WILFRED.		

* Derby Men called up.

ROLL OF HONOUR—Continued.
J. Mandleberg & Company Ltd.

HORROCKS, DAVID.
HALLAM, JOHN ROBT.
HOBSON, THOMAS.
HORSFALL, GEORGE.
HEALD, PETER.
*HODDY, WILLIAM.
*HARRIS, J. H.
*HORRIGAN, THOMAS.
*HARDEN, JOSEPH.
ISHERWOOD, JAMES.
JACKSON, HARRY.
JONES, ALBERT.
JONES, ARTHUR.
*JONES, MARCUS.
*JONES, ALBERT.
*JONES, W. D.
KELLY, ANDREW.
*KERSHAW, JOHN.
*LEIGHTON, C.
LOMAX, ABRAHAM.
LOWTHIAN, JACK.
MAXWELL, ROBERT.
MOODY, TOM.
MARRIOTT, ROBERT W.
MANSON, JAMES.
MOFFATT, J. W.

*MERRY, GEORGE.
NASH, JOHN B.
NEWNHAM, HENRY J.
NICKSON, HARRY.
NIGHTINGALE, WM.
NOCK, H.
*NEWEY, A. E.
OGDEN, HARRY.
PRICE, JAMES.
PELLOWE, BEN.
PEARSON, JOHN.
PERKINS, SIDNEY.
*POTTS, J.
*PENNANCE, J.
ROBERTS, SAMUEL.
RUSHTON, PERCY.
RAYMOND, J. W.
*ROBINSON, PERCY.
*ROTHWELL, J.
STRONG, JOHN.
SEDDON, ALFRED JAS.
SCHOFIELD, THOMAS.
SMART, GEORGE.
SHORTEN, FRANK C.
SMITH, J.
SCOTT, F.

*SABEY, WILLIAM.
*SEDDON, FRED.
*SWANN, N.
THOMASSON, ROBERT.
TAYLOR, RICHARD H.
TAYLOR, JOHN.
TIMMS, JESSE.
*TOWNSON, W.
TAYLOR, HAROLD.
WILKINSON, JAMES.
WARD, JOSEPH.
WALKER, WM. HENRY.
WORSLEY, AARON.
WHITTAM, ARTHUR.
WADE, JOHN.
WIGGINS, ROBERT.
WHINFIELD, ERNEST.
WRAY, JOHN.
WILLIAMSON, J. E. C.
WILSON, G.
*WOOF, J.
*WOOD, B.
*WILCOX, H.
*WESTERN, A. R.
*WILLIAMSON, BEN.
*WILLIAMS, HERBERT.

* Derby Men called up.

Roll of Honour.

The Calico Printers' Association Ltd.

ST. JAMES'S BUILDINGS, OXFORD ST., MANCHESTER

MANCHESTER, GLASGOW AND LONDON OFFICES.

AINSWORTH, R.
AINSWORTH, R. W.
AINSWORTH, T. A.
ANDERSON, C.
ANDERTON, F.
ANDERTON, G.
ANDREW, A.
ARMSTRONG, J.
ARNFIELD, T.
ASPINALL, A.
ATTWOOD, E.
BARBER, G.
BARCLAY, J.
BARNES, H.
BATLEY, T.
BARRETT, J. S.
BEBBINGTON, N.
BELL, F. J.
BELL, T.
BENNETT, J.
BENNETT, T.
BENTLEY, H.
BERISFORD, W.
BILLINGE, J.
BIRCH, G.
BIRMINGHAM, A.
BLANCHARD, N.
BLUNDELL, G.
BOARDMAN, H.
BONNEY, H. F.
BOOTH, G.
BOWDEN, H. B.
BOWDEN, C.
BOWES, P.
BOWKER, F.
BOWKER, A.
BOZELLEC, Y.
BRADBURY, S.
BRANWOOD, W.
BRAY, S.
BROADMEADOW, W.
BROWN, J.
BROWN, J.
BROWN, L.
BROWN, T.
BROWN, W. H.

BROWN, R.
BROWNING, J.
BRUCKSHAW, G.
BRYSON, W. L.
BURGESS, J.
BURGESS, O.
BURNS, G.
BUTLER, W.
BYWATER, W. H.
CARLEY, F.
CASSIN, W. A.
CARVER, P. L.
CHADWICK, S. S.
CHAMP, H. V.
CHAPMAN, F.
CHRISTIE, R.
CLAY, G. W.
CLOUGH, H.
CLOUGH, L.
COFFEY, T.
COUPS, H.
COX, A. E.
CRAMPTON, H.
CREER, F.
CROMPTON, T.
CRONIN, C.
CROOK, J.
CROSBY, J. G.
CROUCH, N. S.
DALTON, A.
DARLINGTON, H. C
DARROCH, J.
DAVIES, F.
DAVIES, J.
DEMAINE, H.
DENHAM, S.
DERWENT, A. S.
DICK, H.
DICKINSON, F.
DIMOND, A.
DIXON, A.
DIXON, S.
DIXON, T. H.
DUNCAN, J. A.
DUNLOP, A. S.
DYSON, E.

DYSON, J.
EARWAKER, R. N.
EASTWOOD, J. E.
ENSTONE, A.
EVANS, H. R.
FESMER, W.
FIDLER, G. W.
FITZPATRICK, J.
FODEN, W. S.
FRANKLAND, L.
FLETCHER, H.
FRASER, J. B.
FOUCHARD, W.
FULCHER, J. M.
FYFE, A.
GARDNER, J.
GEE, J.
GENTLES, E.
GILKS, S.
GLOVER, C.
GOFF, W. A.
GOODALL, L.
GOLDTHORPE, F.
GORTON, J. P. P.
GRAY, C.
GREEN, J.
GREGORY, E.
GREGORY, J.
GREGSON, H.
GRICE, L. V.
GRINDLEY, H.
GOUGH, F.
HADFIELD, V.
HALL, F.
HALLAM, J.
HAMMOND, F.
HAMPTON, A.
HARDY, H.
HARDY, T.
HAILWOOD, G. A.
HARRISON, J.
HARRISON, W. E.
HARVEY, H.
HAWORTH, L.
HAYDOCK, T.
HEAP, J.

HELM F.
HEWITT, E. J.
HIBBERT, J.
HIGGINGS, J.
HIGHAM, G.
HILTON, O.
HIRST, H.
HITCHEN, L. F.
HOBSON, E.
HODGKINSON, J. N.
HODGKINSON, W. P.
HOLDEN, P. C.
HOLT, H. W.
HOLT, W. P.
HOPWOOD, H.
HOUGH, J.
HOWARD, J.
HOWDEN, S.
HOWE, T.
HOWELL, F.
HUBBARD, T. H.
HULL, J. B.
HURST, J. T.
ILIFFE, H.
IRVING, W.
JACKSON, A.
JACKSON, C. A.
JACKSON, H.
JACKSON, R.
JAMES, W. P.
JENKS, E. B.
JOHNSON, A. E.
JONES, E. T.
JONES, R. H.
KAY, J.
KIRK, I.
KELLEY, A.
KELLY, J.
KERSHAW, T. R.
KERSHAW, W.
KNIGHT, A.
LANDLESS, C.
LANG, F. S.
LATHAM, C.
LEE, G. B.
LEE, J. C.

ROLL OF HONOUR—continued.

THE CALICO PRINTERS' ASSOCIATION LTD.
Manchester, Glasgow and London Offices—continued.

LEES, A.
LEES, B. J.
LEES, E.
LEITCH, R.
LEWIS, R.
LIVESEY, G.
LOUGHMAN, J. H.
LOWE, J. W.
LUDLAM, A.
MACKAY, D.
McDOWELL, N.
McEVOY, W.
McEWAN, A.
McGINNIS, T.
McKELLEN, I.
McKENZIE, A.
McLEAN, H.
McMANUS, J.
McNALLY, W.
MALE, F.
MARKENDALE, J. H.
MARTIN, H.
MASSEY, F. N.
MATHIESON, W.
MAUDSLEY, H.
MAUGHAN, K.
MIDGLEY, A. W.
MILLIGAN, A.
MILLS, N. R.
MILNE, D. F.
MILNER, A.
MITCHELL, A.
MITCHELL, A.
MITTON, A.
MOLESWORTH, W. N.
MONKHOUSE, H.
MOSLEY, H.
MOTTRAM A.
MUNRO, J.
MURPHY, J.
NEALE, S. H.
NEEDHAM, E.
NEWTON, A.
NICHOLSON, W. F.

NORTON, F. E.
NUTTALL, A.
OATES, J. W.
ODELL, W.
O'DONOGHUE, T.
OGDEN, W.
OLDLAND, J.
OLIPHANT, J.
OSBORNE, C. F.
PARKINSON, J. R.
PARKINSON, W.
PARRY, J.
PARSONS, E.
PEARSON, G.
PETTIGREW, W.
PILKINGTON, A.
PILLING, S. B.
PORTER, N.
POULTER, A.
PRICE, H.
PHYTIAN, T.
QUINN, G.
RAINEY, T.
RAMSBOTTOM, S. W.
RATHBONE, F.
RATHBONE, J. A.
RAYNOR, J.
REBBITT H. R.
REEDER, W.
REEVES, W.
REYNOLDS, W. L.
RIDDELL, P.
RILEY, E. L.
ROBERTS, J. W.
ROBINSON, H.
RODGERS, W.
ROGERS, J.
ROGERS, W.
ROTHWELL, C.
ROWBOTHAM, J. E.
ROYLE, J.
REDFERN, L.
RICHENS, A.
RUCKER, H.

RUMNEY, R. B.
RUSSELL, A.
RUSSELL, H. McP.
RUSSELL, R. B.
RYAN, J.
SAGAR, J. A.
SANDIFORD, C. H.
SCANLON, J. W.
SCHOFIELD, W.
SEDDON, A.
SHELDON, F.
SHELMERDINE, F. L.
SHIEL, J.
SIBBLES, J.
SIMPSON, A.
SIMS, E. V.
SMITH, F.
SMITH, R.
SMITH, T.
SMITH, T.
SMITH, W. F.
SMYTH, W.
SOWERBUTTS, A.
SPEAKMAN, C.
STATHAM, J.
STEVENSON, A.
STEVENSON, D.
STEWART, A.
STEWART, I.
STIRLING, Miss.
STOTT, J.
STRATTON, R. D.
STUBBS, J.
SWINBURN, H.
TAYLOR, E. L.
TAYLOR, O. A.
TELFORD, W.
THOMAS, L.
THOMSON, J.
THORP, L.
TOMKINS, H. L.
TOWLER, J.
TOWNLEY, G.
TOWNLEY, J.

TOWNSEND, A.
TRAVIS, W.
TRUIN, H.
TRUSSELL, E. C.
TUCKER, J.
TUNNINGLEY, O.
TURNER, P. W.
UREN, P. D.
VALENTINE, A. G.
VINCENT, E.
WALKDEN, R.
WALKER, A.
WALKER, J. L.
WALKER, W. E.
WALTERS, A.
WARBURTON, A.
WATSON, W.
WAYGOOD, C. W.
WEBSTER, F. T.
WELFARE, W.
WESTRY, J.
WHATMOUGH, A.
WHATMOUGH, J.
WHITEHEAD, W.
WILCOCK, A.
WILKINSON, R.
WHITEHURST, F.
WHITLOCK, S.
WILKS, G.
WILLIAMS, E.
WILLIAMS, W.
WILLSHAW, E.
WILSON, E.
WILSON, L.
WISEMAN, A.
WOOD, C.
WOOD, E.
WOOD, R.
WOOD, F. L.
WOOD, H.
WORTHINGTON, C. S.
YELD, R. B.
YELD, R. N.

AGECROFT PRINT WORKS.

BATES, A.
BATES, R.
BELL, A.
BENNETT, G.
BESWICK, J.
CONNOR, V.
CROKER, F.
ELLIS, J.
GOULD, F.

HAMPSON, H. B.
HENSHALL, H.
HENSHALL, W. R.
HIGGINBOTTOM, R. P.
HOPWOOD, J.
IRELAND, A.
JENKINS, W. H.
JONES, G. J.

JONES, H.
JONES, J.
LEACH, F.
LEWIS, S.
MAGHILL, J.
MILLER, W.
PENNINGTON, J.
ROBERTS, T.

RUTTER, G.
SALT, E.
SMITH, J.
STOTT, R.
THOMAS, E.
TOMLINSON, J. W.
TOMLINSON, M.
TURNER, A.

ROLL OF HONOUR—continued.

THE CALICO PRINTERS' ASSOCIATION LTD.

ALBION MILL.

DONLAN, J.	DONLAN, J. T.	STEVENS, J.	WESTON, J. C.

ARROWSCROFT MILL.

DANIELS, G.	KEATINGS, J.	QUINLIN, J.	SMITH, T.
HOBSON, G.	MITCHELL, H.	REVELL, R.	STEELE, C.
HOWARD, E.	NINNIES, W.	SHIRT, P.	TIMPERLEY, J.

BINGSWOOD PRINT WORKS.

ASHMORE F.	DYER, W.	JODRELL, E.	PLATTS, H.
ASHMORE, H.	FENTON, W.	JOHNSON, A.	SHAW, H.
BAGSHAW, G. P.	FIDLER, A.	JOHNSON, C.	SHIRT, F.
BENNETT, W. T.	GODDARD, G.	LONGDEN, E.	SMITH, H.
BRADLEY, R.	GRAHAM, A.	MARSHALL, T. G.	THOMASSON, F. R.
BRAMWELL, A.	HIBBERT S.	MATHER, J. W.	TOWNSEND, G. W.
BRAMWELL, H.	HILL, F.	MELLOR, W.	WALKER, J.
BROADHURST, W.	HILL, G.	MELLOR, W. H.	WALKER, J.
BUCKLEY, A.	HILL, J.	MILLER, J.	WILD, T.
COLLIER, A.	HILL, T.	MOON, J. H.	WOOD, J.
COLLIER, W.	HOWARTH, J.	ORMROD, H.	WOOLLEY, P. T.
DARBY, T.	HUTCHINSON, F.	ORMROD, J. W.	WRIGHT, J. F.
DEPLEDGE, J.	HUTCHINSON, H.	PASCALL, A.	YATES, W.
DUCKWORTH, W.			

BIRCH VALE PRINT WORKS.

ADAMS, W.	FIELDING, G.	JACKSON, H.	ROBINSON, H.
ARCHER, F.	GALBRAITH, A.	KAY, J.	ROGERS, J.
BAGSHAW, A.	GARLICK, J.	LEVER, J. H.	ROGERS, J. H.
BARBER, A.	GARSIDE, J.	LIDDEARD, F.	ROWBOTTOM, T.
BARBER, J.	GASKELL, H.	LITTLEFORD, J.	SIMISTER, A.
BEARD, J.	GOODWIN, B.	LITTLEFORD, S.	SINGLETON, F.
BENNETT, A.	GREAVES, F.	LOMAS, L.	SMITH, F.
BENNETT, J.	GREAVES, W.	LOMAS, T.	SMITH, H.
BOWDEN, L.	GREENWOOD, W.	LOMAS, W.	SMITH, JNO.
BRADLEY, A.	GRESTY, A.	McMANUS, J.	SMITH, JOS.
BRADLEY, F.	HALL, E.	McNEE, G.	SMITH, JOS.
BRANSON, J.	HALL, J.	MASON, F. H.	SMITH, R.
BUCHANAN, R.	HALL, R.	MONKS, H.	SUDDERS, F.
BULLOCK, J.	HALSTEAD, J.	MOORCROFT, G.	SWIFT, G.
BURNS, J.	HAMPSON, J.	MOSELEY, J. H.	THORNLEY, J.
CHATTERTON, W.	HAMPSON, J. W.	MURFIN, J.	TOMLINSON, J. T.
CLARKE, A.	HANDFORD, J. U.	NADIN, J.	TURNER, R.
CLEGG, T.	HAWKER, F.	OAKES, F.	TYRER, T.
COFFEY, J.	HIGGINBOTTOM, W. H.	PHILIPS, W.	UNWIN, H.
COUPE, W.	HILL, G.	PLUMMER, J. A.	WALSH, A.
CRABTREE, E.	HILL, J. J.	POLLARD, F. H.	WALTON, G.
CRABTREE, F.	HOWARD, J.	PRICE, W.	WARDLE, W.
CRANKSHAW, E.	HOWARD, H.	RAMWELL, I.	WATERHOUSE, F.
DARBY, R.	HOWITT, G. W.	RANGELEY, A.	WATERHOUSE, W.
DOUGLAS, S.	HUGHES, J.	RATCLIFFE, J.	WILD, W.
DRAPER, F.	HYDE, A.	REDFERN, J.	WILSON, L.
ELY, J.	HYDE, H.	REDFERN, JABEZ.	WRIGHT, F.
EVANS, C.	HYDE, S.	REDFERN, T.	WYATT, S.
FINLAY, H.	HYDE, W.	RICHARDSON, F.	YATES, J. F.
FLINT, W.	IBBOTSON, F.	RICHARDSON, J.	YATES, R.

ROLL OF HONOUR—continued.

THE CALICO PRINTERS' ASSOCIATION LTD.

BIRKACRE PRINT WORKS.

ALLEN, T.	CROMPTON, A.	LEVER, J.	SHERRINGTON, J.
ARROWSMITH, S.	DARCY, J.	LIGHTBOWN, F.	SLATER, J.
BAKER, A. F.	DICKINSON, J.	LONGTON, R.	SLATER, W.
BARKER, W.	GENT, J.	OWENS, S.	SMALLEY, T.
BARKER, WM.	GILMAN, W. E.	RIMMER, J.	SPEAKMAN, J.
BERRY, J.	HARLING, J.	ROBERTS, P.	SUMNER, W.
BIBBY, T.	HART, R.	ROGERSON, J. W.	TAYLOR, R.
BLACKBURN, J.	HATCH, W.	ROGERSON, R.	UPTON, W.
BOLTON, H.	HODGKINSON, T. H.	ROSCOE, J.	WATMOUGH, R.
BOLTON, W.	HUNTER, J.	ROTHWELL, M.	WATMOUGH, T.
CALDERBANK, J.	JONES, W. S.	SCHOLES, W. A.	WIGNALL, H.
COWNSELL, W.	KINLOCH, C.	SEWELL, B. R.	WIGNALL, J.
CROASDALE, A.			

BRINSCALL PRINT WORKS.

ASHWORTH, J.	DOBSON, F.	MONK, W.	SUMNER, J.
BAIN, W.	HALL, T.	MOORE, F.	SUMNER, T.
BARGE, A.	HALLIWELL, F.	MOREY, R.	TAYLOR, D.
BAKER, A.	HALLIWELL, P.	PEARSON, F.	TAYLOR, L.
BARRY, J.	HOYLE, G. W.	PRESCOTT, E.	TAYLOR, R.
BRIERS, D.	IRONFIELD, W.	PRESSLER, F.	TINDALL, H.
BRINDLE, F.	JACKSON, E.	QUINN, T.	WALSH, A.
BRINDLE, J.	JOLLY, F.	REID, F.	WALSH, M.
BRINDLE, W.	KEIGHLEY, T.	RITCHIE, S.	WHITEHOUSE, J.
BROADHEAD, H.	KENNEDY, G.	SCHOLES, A.	WHITTLE, H.
CALDWELL, H.	McFARLANE, W.	SHACKLETON, E.	WHITTLE J.
COOKSON, J.	MILLER, E.	SHACKLETON, J.	WOODS, G. E.
DIXON, H.	MILLER, W.	SHAW, W.	WOODS, J.
DIXON, J.	MONK, J.	SMETHURST, R.	WYATT, A.

BROAD OAK PRINT WORKS.

ALDERSON, G.	CHADWICK, E.	DAKIN, E.	ENTWISTLE, H.
BAILEY, W.	CHADWICK, H.	DARCY, C.	EVANS, L.
BALDWIN, P.	CHADWICK, J.	DAVIS, H.	FELL, H.
BARLOW, F. H.	CHAPMAN, F.	DAWSON, R.	FINN, H.
BARROW, H.	CHAPMAN, H.	DEAN, A.	FLANNERY, J. W.
BARTON, F. T.	CHATBURN, R.	DEAN, H.	FORD, J.
BASSINDER, A.	CHRISTY, J.	DEAN, T.	GARTON, J.
BENT, T.	CLARKE, H.	DEMAIN, G. A.	GLOVER, J.
BLACKBURN, T.	CLAYTON, G.	DEWHURST, A.	GREASLEY, H.
BLACKLEDGE, T.	CLAYTON, W.	DEWHURST, A.	GREASLEY, W.
BRADSHAW, T.	CLINCH, W.	DEWHURST, H.	GREENWOOD, W.
BRADSHAW, W.	CLITHEROE, J. T.	DEWHURST, H.	GREGSON, H.
BRAYSFORD, H.	CLOUGH, J. A.	DEWHURST, H.	GRUNALL, A. E.
BRIGGS, W.	CLOUGH, K.	DEWHURST, W.	HALSTEAD, W.
BRIMLOW, J.	COLCLOUGH, L.	DICKINSON, H.	HARDMAN, G.
BROWN, R.	COOKE, W.	DOBIE, J.	HARGREAVES, A. E.
BULLOCK, H.	CORNWALL, T.	DOBIE, J. A.	HARGREAVES, I.
BURGESS, C.	CRABTREE, H.	DONOVAN, J.	HARTLEY, WILLIS.
BURY, A.	CRAWSHAW, D.	DRINKWATER, F.	HARTLEY, WILSON.
BURY, P.	CROSS, E.	DUCKWORTH, C.	HARTLEY, W. H.
BYWATER, E.	CROWDER, G.	DUERDIN, R. E.	HEAP, C.
BYWATER, F.	CROWDER, W. R.	EATOUGH, J. P.	HEAP, R.
CARTER, J.	CROWTHER, E.	ELLIS, C.	HEATON, J.
CAVENEY, J.	CUNLIFFE, H.	ELLSON, J.	HEATON, T.

ROLL OF HONOUR—continued.

THE CALICO PRINTERS' ASSOCIATION LTD.

Broad Oak Print Works—continued.

HEBSON, E.
HEBSON, R.
HEYS, A.
HEYS, G.
HICKIN, J.
HILL, A.
HILTON, S.
HINDLE, A.
HINDLE, J.
HODSON, J.
HURTLEY, W.
ILLINGWORTH, F.
ISHERWOOD, E.
JAMES, T.
JOHNSON, J. W.
JONES, A. S.
JONES, J. T.
JORDAN, A. W.
KENYON, N.
KENYON, W.
KERSHAW, J. H.
KILLOWAY, G.
KNOWLES, B.
LANTY, J. B.
LIGHTFOOT, A.
LINDSAY, F.
LOCKHART, G.
LONSDALE, R.
LUNT, A.
McCARTHY, C.
McKENNA, W.
McKILLOP, J.
McLARNON, D.
McMILLAN, W.
McMYLER, T.
McNAMARA, J.
MADEN, F.
MAKIN, T.
MASON, R.
METCALF, F. A.
MIDGHALL, W. J.
MITCHELL, J.
MOIZER, W.
MORRIS, W.
NADEN, A.
NEWLOVE, H.
NUTTALL, A.
NUTTALL, W.
O'BRIEN, J.
O'BRIEN, W.
ORMEROD, J.
ORRELL, B.
PALMER, G. F.
PARKINSON, J. A.
PARKINSON, J. W.
PEEL, J. R.
PEMBERTON, H.
PETTY, F. H.
PICKUP, H. A.
PICKUP, J. R.
PILKINGTON, T.
PILKINGTON, T. T.
POLLARD, J. R.
POPE, A.
POPE, A.
POPE, J.
PROUDLOVE, W.
PRICE, R.
PUTTICK, A.
RAWCLIFFE, E.
RIGBY, R. W.
RILEY, E. W.
RILEY, J.
ROBERTS, T.
ROGAN, J.
RONEY, J. A.
RUSHTON, W. F.
SCHOFIELD, J.
SHARP, J. H.
SHEDDON, D.
SHERBURNE, E.
SINCLAIR, F.
SLATER, A.
SLATER, H.
SLATER, J. W.
SLATTERY, A.
SLATTERY, P.
SMITH, E.
SMITH, H.
SMITH, R.
SOUTHWELL, W.
SOWERBUTTS, G. W.
SPENCER, W. E.
STEELE, G. C.
SWALLOW, W.
SYKES, D.
TASKER, N.
TATTERSALL, W.
TAYLOR, P.
TAYLOR, T.
TAYLOR, T.
TESTA, V. T.
THORNTON, E.
TOMLINSON, B.
VINGE, B.
WALLWORK, J.
WALMSLEY, F. A.
WALMSLEY, H.
WALSH, M.
WARD, A.
WARWICK, H.
WATTS, H.
WELLS, F.
WHATMOUGH, W.
WHEWELL, S.
WHISTON, W.
WHITTAKER, A.
WHITTAKER, WAL.
WHITTAKER, WM.
WHITTAKER, W.
WHITTAM, R. V.
WILD, B.
WILKINSON, H.
WILLCOCK, R.
WILLIAMS, H.
WILSON, D.
WILSON, H.
WISEMAN, J. R.
WOOD, A. V.
WOOD, H. E.
WOOD, W. C.
WORTHINGTON, G.
YATES, A.
YATES, W. E.

BUCKTON VALE PRINT WORKS.

ANCKERS, L.
ARMITAGE, T.
ASHTON, S.
BAILEY, H.
BARDSLEY, T.
BARKER, W.
BATTY, F.
BELL, E.
BENNETT, J.
BENNETT, J. H.
BENNETT, T.
BIRD, T.
BOALE, J.
BOLTON, J. E.
BOOTH, G. H.
BOOTH, H.
BOWYER, J.
BRETT, B.
BRIDGE, E.
BRIDGE, H.
BRIGGS, A.
BROOKE, J. H.
BROOKS, J.
BROOKS, W.
BROWN, E.
CHRISTOPHER, F.
CLARK, A. T.
CLEGG, T.
CLEGG, W.
CHASE, C.
COLE, R.
COLLISON, J.
COOPER, W.
CUNNINGHAM, W.
DARBY, J.
DARROUGH, T.
DAVIES, W.
DAVIS, R.
DAWSON, C. H.
DAWSON, J.
DAWSON, W.
DAY, H.
DAY, T.
DEARNALLEY, H.
DENNIS, G.
DERBY, H.
DODD, J.
DOODSON, G.
DOODSON, T.
DORSEY, P.
DOWNS, W.
DOYLE, W.
DUGDALE, A.
EASTWOOD, S.
EDMONDS, J.
EDWARDS, C.
EDWARDS, S.
FALLAS, B.
FARRINGTON, A.
FERNIHOUGH, F.
FIELDING, W.
FLETCHER, J.
GALT, P.
GILLOTT, A.
GILLOTT, F. E.
GOULDEN, H.
GRAHAM, F.
GRAHAM, I.
HADFIELD, J.
HADFIELD, J.
HAGUE, F.
HAGUE, H.
HALL, J. E.
HALLAS, T.
HALLSWORTH, G.
HANSHAW, W.

ROLL OF HONOUR—continued.

THE CALICO PRINTERS' ASSOCIATION LTD.

Buckton Vale Print Works—continued.

HARBEN, O.
HARDWICK, J. H.
HARDY, W.
HASLAM, E.
HASSELL, H.
HAWORTH, W.
HERON, H.
HILL, J.
HILTON, H.
HINCHCLIFFE, J.
HITCHMAN, F.
HITCHMAN, H.
HOGAN, J.
HOGAN, JOHN.
HOLLAND, B.
HOPKINS, A. W.
HOPWOOD, J.
HORAN, E.
HORROCKS, G. H.
HOSKIN, I.
HOUGH, F.
HOWARD, E.
HOWARD, H.
HOWARTH, J.
HOWARTH, J. T.
HOWARTH, S.
HOYLE, A.
HOYLE, S.
HYDE, A.
JACKSON, E.
JEPSON, N.
JOHNSON, W.
JONES, C.
JONES, J.
JONES, J. W.
JONES, S.

KAY, A. T.
KAYE, A.
KEELEY, A.
KEELEY, W.
KERR, W.
LEES, W.
LESLIE, J.
LLOYD, J. D.
LOCKWOOD, H.
McARTHUR, F.
McKENZIE, J.
McMANUS, J.
MALONEY, J.
MALONEY, W.
MANTON, F.
MARKLAND, J.
MARLAND, J.
MARLAND, J.
MELLETT, W.
MEEHAN, L.
MEREDITH, R.
METCALFE, H.
MIDDLETON, J.
MILHENCH, H.
MORRIS, S.
MOSS, R.
MUNDY, J.
MURPHY, J.
NAIGLE, D.
NASH, J. W.
O'BRIEN, J.
O'BRIEN, T.
ONIONS, W.
OUSEY, W.
PARKER, G.

PIERCE, T.
PIERCE, W.
PLANT, H.
PRESTON, T.
RADCLIFFE, H.
REYNOLDS, M.
RICHARDSON, J.
ROBINSON, F.
SCHOFIELD, H.
SHARPLES, F.
SHAW, A. D.
SHEPLEY, A.
SIDEBOTTOM, R.
SIDEBOTTOM, T.
SIMISTER, D.
SMETHURST, P.
SMITH, J.
SMITH, J.
SMITH, W.
STEGER, T.
STOCKLEY, T.
STOCKTON, J. W.
STRINGER, J.
STUBBS, F. W.
SWANN, H.
SYKES, H.
TAYLOR, J.
TAYLOR, W.
TEEVANS, A.
THOMAS, W.
THORPE, G.
THORPE, L.
TOLLIS, W. F.
TOWLE, J.
TOWLE, W.

TRAVIS, G.
TUCK, W.
TURNER, G.
TURNER, J.
UTTLEY, W.
WADE, J.
WAINWRIGHT, J. A.
WAINWRIGHT, W.
WAKEFIELD, H.
WAKEFIELD, J.
WALMSLEY, J.
WARING, T.
WELLS, J. W.
WHARTON, G.
WHELAN, J.
WHITTAKER, W.
WILLIAMS, E.
WILSON, F. C.
WILSON, G.
WILSON, J.
WILSON, J.
WINTERBOTTOM, F.
WINTERBOTTOM, J.
WINTERBOTTOM, P.
WOLFENDALE, W.
WOOD, H.
WOOD, J. T.
WOOD, O.
WOOD, W.
WOOD, W.
WOODHOUSE, J. J.
WRIGHT, G. H.
WRIGLEY, E. H.
WYKES, F.
YATES, H.

CENTRAL LABORATORY.

COOPER, C. H.
COSTOBADIE, H. C.

ELLIS, G. H.
HAMPSON, A. E.

HARDMAN, F.
LAYCOCK, C.

SMITH, L.

CHADKIRK PRINT WORKS.

ABBOTT, G. R.
ASHWORTH, J.
BAILEY, J.
BARBER, T.
BEECH, A.
BOOTH, J.
BRUCKSHAW, S.
BUXTON, G.
CLARKE, A.

CLAYTON, C.
CRICHTON, A.
EUSTACE, E.
EVANS, A.
FERNLEY, W.
GOSLING, R.
HANSON, E.
HUGHES, E.
HUGHES, J.

MALPAS, J. V.
MASON, S.
MOORES, J.
MOTTERSHEAD, F.
REDSHAW, F.
ROBERTS, S.
SCHOLES, F.
SCHOLES, J.
STAFFORD, H.

STENTON, J.
SWINDELLS, W.
TAYLOR, J.
TETLOW, W.
TREEWEEK, G. W.
WHITE, S.
WHITELEY, J.
WILLIAMS, W.
WINNETT, L.

COMPSTALL MILL.

BELFIELD, J. W.
BURROWS, J.
CLARKE, F.
HARTLEY, J.
HEGINBOTHAM, W.

HIBBS, N.
HIGGINS, T.
INGHAM, A.
MARKLAND, W.
MARSLAND, N.

MULLINEAUX, H.
RIDGWAY, C.
SHALLCROSS, G. S.
SIMPKINS, W.
WATERHOUSE, S.

WATERS, F.
WATERS, G.
WHALLEY, A.
WOOD, J.
YARWOOD, H.

ROLL OF HONOUR—continued.

THE CALICO PRINTERS' ASSOCIATION LTD.

CRAWFORD EASTON.

BIRRELL, A.
CHRISTIE, R.
DILLON, P.
KELLY, J.
LITTERICK, R. B.

DALMONACH PRINT WORKS.

BARR, A.
BARR, M.
BOYD, J.
BROADIE, A.
BROOKES, R.
CAMPBELL, P.
CHRISTIE, J.
CLARK, J.
CUNNINGHAM, W.
DENNETT, J.
DENNIE, F.
DUNN, P.
DUNWOODIE, D.
FORREST, J.
GETTY, J.
GRANT, P.
HUNTER, M.
HUNTER, W.
LOGAN, J.
LOY, M.
McALISTER, C.
McAULAY, A.
McBETH, C.
McCAFFRETY, T.
McCOLL, H.
McDERMID, J.
McDONALD, T.
McGARRY, J.
McGILL, J.
McLELLAN, J.
McRAE, W.
MALLOCH, JAS.
MALLOCH, JNO.
MALTMAN, R.
NEWTON, R.
REID, J.
SKELLY, R.
STEVENSON, A.
STRUTHERS, J.
STRUTHERS, W.
TANNICH, A.
TAYLOR, J.
WARK, R.
WARK, W.
WILSON, J.

DINTING VALE PRINT WORKS.

AINSWORTH, J. W.
ALCOCK, L.
ARTHERN, S.
BARDSLEY, E.
BARDSLEY, W.
BENNETT, J.
BENNETT, W.
BETHEL, G.
BLEASDALE, J.
BOND, A.
BOOTH, J.
BOOTH, T.
BRADBURY, E.
BRADBURY, J. R. T.
BRADBURY, W.
BRADSHAW, A.
BRADSHAW, F.
CAIRNIE, J.
CHADWICK, J.
CHESTER, H.
CLARKE, G.
COLLINS, J.
COLLIS, H.
CRANSHAW, F.
DALE, G.
DAVIES, T.
DAWSON, J.
DAWSON, J.
DEARNALEY, J.
DICKSON, G.
DOWNS, E.
DUCKWORTH, A.
DYSON, R.
ELLIOTT, G.
FENNELL, J. W.
FLETCHER, F.
GARLICK, A.
GARLICK, E.
GARLICK, J.
GARSIDE, F.
GRAY, J.
GREGORY, H.
GRIME, G.
GRIMSHAW, W.
HADFIELD, J.
HARDWICK, J.
HARRISON, J.
HEPPINSTALL, H.
HIBBERT, W.
HIGGINS, J.
HINCHCLIFFE, F.
HINCHCLIFFE, J.
HOOD, S.
HORNSBY, J.
HOYLAND, W.
ISAACS, A.
JACQUES, V.
KANE, J.
LACEY, S.
LALLY, J.
LEACH, W.
LOMAS, T. A.
LEIGHTON, W.
McARTHUR, D.
McNABB, D.
MARSDEN, H.
MILLS, T. H.
MOON, A.
MORRIS, O.
MORTON, R.
MOSS, J.
MOSS, W.
MOTTRAM, E.
MYERS, W.
NEWSHAM, D.
NIXON, E.
NUTTAL, J.
O'KEEFE, C.
OLDHAM, J.
OLLERNSHAW, J.
O'SHEA, J.
PALFREYMAN, W.
PALMER, J.
PARKIN, T. W.
PATTERSON, W.
PRICE, T.
RATCLIFFE, J.
RATCLIFFE, R.
RAWSON, J.
REVELL, C.
REVELL, J.
RIDGWAY, T.
ROBERTS, W.
SCARRATT, G.
SHEPPARD, S.
SHEPPARD, T.
SWANN, F.
SWINDELLS, A.
TEASDALE, JAS.
TEASDALE, JNO.
TITTERINGTON, J.
TOOLE, R.
TOOLE, J.
WALMESLEY, T.
WALMESLEY, H.
WALSH, J.
WALSH, M.
WALTON, J.
WARHURST, R.
WARHURST, W.
WINTERBOTTOM, J.
WOOD, J.
WOOD, T.
WOODACRE, H.
WRIGLEY, A.
WYCH, T.

EDMONDSON BROS.

BREARLEY, A.
CALVERT, T.
CASSIDY, G.
CHAPMAN, W.
COX, S.
CRANSHAW, J. T.
DAWSON, S.
DILLON, H. J.
DILLON, J. H.
DODSON, W. J.
FAULKNER, C.
GALLIMORE, G.
GAREHAM, D.
GEMMELL, D.
GOODFELLOW, J.
GREGORY, J.
JONES, H.
KELLY, T.
KENNEDY, J.
LEES, W.
McGREGOR, J.
NADEN, T.
OAKES, J.
QUARMBY, W.
SAUNDERS, W. H.
SEYMOUR, W.
VICKERS, T.

ROLL OF HONOUR—continued.

THE CALICO PRINTERS' ASSOCIATION LTD.

FERRYFIELD PRINT WORKS.

GALLOCHER, G.	McDERMID, D.	MILLS, E.	SPENCE, J.
GOLDIE, J.	MALARVIE, J.	MURRAY, P.	TURNBULL, J.
McBRIDE, J.	MELVIN, J.	REID, J.	WHITE, A.

FURNESS VALE PRINT WORKS.

ATTWOOD, B.	FORD, G.	MIDDLETON, J. P.	SHIRT, D.
BEARD, H.	GOULD, J. W.	MIDDLETON, N. G.	SHIRT, R.
BEARD, J. A.	GRAHAM, J. T.	NUTTALL, J.	SHIRT, S.
BOARDMAN, A.	HADFIELD, C. C.	O'CONNELL, M.	SWIFT, H.
CHEETHAM, L.	HALL, E.	OULTON, F.	TAYLOR, J.
COOK, A.	JENNINGS, W.	OULTON, T. E.	TAYLOR, R.
COOK, A.	JOHNSON, C. E.	ROUKE, A.	WALKER, T.
CRIBBE, A. W.	JORDAN, H.	SECOMBE, J.	WATSON, F.
DRINKWATER, G.	MAKIN, J. C.	SHARPLY, J.	WHARMBY, J. T.
DRINKWATER, D.			

GATESIDE PRINT WORKS.

ANDERSON, J.	CARSLOW, J.	POLLARD, Z.	SMILLIE, J.
BROOKS, W.	LESLIE, A.	PORTER, T.	WATSON, G.

KELVINHAUGH FACTORY.

HASTIE, A.

LENNOXMILL PRINT WORKS.

ANDERSON, J.	DUNWOODIE, J.	McCAHILL, D.	McKAY, G. G.
BARR, J.	GALT, A.	McCORMICK, J.	McKELLAR, D.
BLACKWOOD, A.	GRAHAM, A.	McDONALD, D.	McPHERSON, W.
BOLTON, J.	HUNTER, JAS.	McDONALD, J.	RAE, J.
BOLTON, R.	HUNTER, JNO.	McDONALD, R.	RODGER, J.
BRITTON, H.	KELLY, J.	McDONALD, W.	ROURKE, J.
CRAWFORD, R.	KELLY, P.	McFARLANE, R.	STEWART, R.
DICKSON, W.	KELLY, W.	McGRORTY, J.	WALKER, W.
DUFFIELD, J.	KINCAID, J.	McHOWAT, R.	WYLLIE, N.
DUNWOODIE, G.	McALLAN, J.	McIWEE, C.	

LEVENSHULME WORKS.

BENNETT, H.	EDEN, E.	HOLLAND, A.	MOSS, H.
BENNETT, J.	FARNWORTH, R. H.	HUMPHREYS, J.	MOSTYN, W.
BINNS, E.	FERGUSON, C.	IBBOTSON, R.	NEILD, J.
BOWER, W. J.	FORD, C.	KAY, E.	STEVENSON, A.
BURN, J. S.	FRANCIS, T.	KIRKMAN, F.	STORAH, P.
BUTTERWORTH, J.	GALVIN, T.	LEAH, A.	SUTTON, J.
CALCUTT, J. H.	HAINES, S.	MAHON, J.	WALKER, S.
COLLINS, S.	HAMPSON, J.	MASSEY, H.	WOOD, F.
CUMMINS, J.			

LILLYBURN PRINT WORKS.

DEMPSIE, P.	FLETT, D.	KELLY, J.	TURNBULL, A.
DOUGAN, J.	FLETT, M.	KINCAID, R.	

LOCHERFIELD PRINT WORKS.

BRODIE, J.	FORSYTH, W.	McINTOSH, C.	WELSH, T.
DOUGLAS, J.	LAVERTY, J.	McKEE, G.	

ROLL OF HONOUR—continued.

THE CALICO PRINTERS' ASSOCIATION LTD.

LOVE CLOUGH PRINT WORKS.

ALLEN, J.	GREEN, F.	MILLER, G.	TAYLOR, J.
ASPIN, E.	HALSALL, J. H.	MOLLOY, T.	TAYLOR, V. H.
BINNS, H.	HEYS, W.	NELSON, G. H.	TRICKETT, H.
BIRD, W. O.	HEYWORTH, H.	POLLARD, A.	TRICKETT, J.
BREAKWELL, R.	HEYWORTH, J.	POLLARD, T.	TRICKETT, J. E.
BRIDGE, H.	HITCHIN, J.	POUNDER, L. H.	WALSH, J.
BUFTON, W.	HARGREAVES, R.	PROCTOR, T.	WATSON, J.
CARR, E.	HAWKINS, A.	QUINN, G. E.	WESTALL, R.
COOKSON, G. T.	HINDLE, J.	READ, J. E.	WHALLEY, J. W.
CUNLIFFE, J. W.	JACKSON, J. W.	ROTHWELL, G.	WHITE, P.
DICKENSON, T.	LIVESEY, E.	RUSHTON, G.	WOOD, J.
DUST, F. T.	MARSDEN, W.	RUSHTON, G.	WRIGHT, J.
EASTWOOD, G.	MEDLOCK, F.	SEEDALE, W.	WRIGHT, P.
EASTWOOD, R.	METCALF, J. A.	SMITH, T.	WROE, A.

LOW MILL PRINT WORKS.

ALMOND, J.	HARTLEY, J.	MELLING, F.	SCHOFIELD, W.
ASTLEY, M.	HODGKINSON, J.	MOCKETT, A.	SMITH, J. H.
CARTER, H.	HODGSON, J.	MOON, J.	WEAVER, M.
CARTER, W.	HOPWOOD, H.	RIDING, W.	WILKINSON, T.
CHRISTIAN, J. L.	LANGTON, A.	ROBINSON, W.	WITHNELL, T.
CRAVEN, J.	LONGTON, R.	ROTHWELL, C.	WOOD, S.
FIELDING, I.	McCLELLAN, R.		

NEWTON BANK PRINT WORKS.

ADAMSON, J.	GOODWIN, F.	LEECH, J.	SPENCER, E.
BARKER, E.	GRACE, J.	LOWE, H.	SPENCER, F. A.
BRADDOCK, H.	GREEN, J.	MANN, W.	SPENCER, W.
BRELSFORD, E.	GREENHALGH, A.	OGDEN, H.	STAFFORD, G.
BRITTON, H.	GREGORY, S.	PARKER, W. A.	STAPLETON, C.
BRUCE, H.	HAMILTON, T.	POULTON, R.	SUTCLIFFE, J.
BRUNT, W.	HARRISON, G.	ROWBOTHAM, J.	TAYLOR, G.
CAPEL, G. H.	HILL, G.	SHEPLEY, J.	TAYLOR, J.
CAVENY, W.	HOLLINGWORTH, T.	SLATER, F.	TOLSON, J. E.
CLAYTON, L.	HOWARTH, H.	SLATER, H.	TRAVIS, J.
DAKIN, E.	JOHNSON, H.	SLATER, T.	WARBURTON, W.
DELANEY, J.	KELLY, J.	SLATER, W.	WILDGOOSE, J.
GARDINER, H.	KENDAL, J.	SMITH, C. W.	WRIGHT, W.
GARDINER, J.	LEAH, E.		

OAKENSHAW PRINT WORKS

ALDRED, D.	CALVERT, J.	LIGHTBOWN, F.	SCHOFIELD, J. P.
BALDWIN, J. W.	CASE, P.	LONG, C. H.	SKILLBECK, A. C.
BATTRICK, J. C.	DUCKWORTH, J. L.	McCANN, G.	TOWNLEY, C. E.
BERRY, F.	DUERDEN, A. W.	MUIR, A.	TOWNSEND, T.
BERRY, R.	ECCLES, A.	OLDHAM, J. E.	WALMSLEY, W. T.
BERRY, T. H.	FITCHETT, J. W.	PYE, R. A.	WESTWELL, J.
BIRTLES, T.	HINDLE, H.	ROBINSON, R.	WHELAN, D.
BLACKWELL, G. O.	HOWSON, A. H.	ROGERS, A. E.	WHELAN, L.
BLAIR, A.	LIGHTBOWN, C.	ROSE, I.	YATES, A.
CALVERT, R.			

PIN MILL RAISING DEPT.

CURTIN, C.	HOLLINWORTH, S.	WORSLEY, J. J.

ROLL OF HONOUR—continued.

THE CALICO PRINTERS' ASSOCIATION LTD.

POLAND STREET.

ASHLEY, G.
BAILEY, A.
BARTLEY, D.
BLYTHE, E.
BRIDGE, D. H.
BROSTER, W.
BROUGH, J.
CRUTCHLEY, F. J.
FAIRFOUL, A.
FARRER, J.
FITZGERALD, M.
GRIFFITHS, J. W.
HENNEGAN, J.
HIGGINS, J.
HOLMES, J.
HOPKINS, J.
HORAN, C.
JAMES, G.
JOHNSON, A.
JOHNSON, W. E.
KELLY, F. A.
KERRIGAN, W.
LAFFERTY, J.
LEWIS, J. W. G.
LORD, E.
LYNAM, J.
McCORMACK, J.
McDONALD, W.
McEWEN, W.
MAHER, N.
MAUNSEY, P.
MOORHEAD, J.
MURRAY, A.
OLDFIELD, L.
REED, J. A.
ROEBUCK, J. B.
ROGERS, J.
SLATER, S.
SMITH, P.
SOUTH, J. R.
STRONG, J. R.
SUTTON, J. E.
TEASDALE, G. E.
WHEATON, G.
WHITE, M.
WILLIAMS, D. I.
WILLIAMS, J.
WOOD, G.
WRAY, A.
WRIGHT, B.

PROCESS ENGRAVING.

KER, J.
McMURRAY, E.
PAUL, J.

REDDISH VALE PRINT WORKS.

BAILEY, A.
BAILEY, J.
BARDSLEY, J.
BEELEY, R.
BENT, J.
BERESFORD, H.
BOWLING, T.
BRITTAIN, A.
BUCKLEY, A. V.
CAMPBELL, F.
CAMPION, M.
CHAPMAN, J.
CLEGG, F.
CULVERWELL, A.
CUMMINGS, J.
DALZIEL, R.
DEAN, T.
EARLAM, J.
FARRELL, D.
FULLER, C.
HALL, J.
HARROP, J. A.
HENSHALL, J.
HIBBERT, H.
HOWARTH, S.
KELLY, JAS.
KELLY, JOS.
KELSALL, A.
LAMBERT, E.
LEE, J.
LEWIS, D.
MASON, J.
MELLOR, H.
NEIGHBOUR, T.
OGDEN, H.
OLDHAM, T.
PEARSON, S.
PLESTED, J.
POTTS, L.
READ, B.
ROWLEY, E.
ROWLEY, F.
SHORROCKS, J.
SNELGROVE, A.
SUMMERS, J.
SUMNER, A.
TANZIE, J.
WALKER, S.
WILD, G.
WOOD, A.
WOOD, W.

RHODES PRINT WORKS.

ALBESON, E.
AMOR, B.
AMOR, J.
BANCROFT, H.
BARRETT, N.
BASTOW, E.
BATES, F.
BEAMAN, P.
BEESE, W. H
BELL, A.
BESWICK, J.
BLACKSHAW, H.
BOARDMAN, C.
BOARDMAN, J.
BONNEY, C.
BOULTON, W. H.
BRIGGS, H.
BRIGGS, HAROLD.
BRIGGS, M.
BRINDLE, H.
BRIDEN, W.
BUCKLEY, T.
BULCOCK, J.
BURROWS, J.
BUTLER, A.
CAIN, P.
CALVERT, C.
CAMPBELL, J.
CARR, F.
CARTER, A.
CHADWICK, A.
CLARKE, F. C.
CLARKSON, H. G.
CONNOLLY, T.
COOGHAN, B.
CORCORAN, P.
COX, J.
CUMMINS, H.
DALEY, G.
DALEY, J.
DARKE, E. V.
DAVIES, W.
DAWSON, J.
DIXON, A.
DOOLAN, M.
DURR, J.
ECCLESTON, J.
FISHER, C.
FITTON, W.
FITTON, WM.
FOGG, B.
FORREST, J. R.
FOXALL, H.
FOXALL, W.
FOXCROFT, F. H.
GALLAGHER, J.
GARNER, F.
GORDON, F.
GORDON, J. J.
GRINDERICK, J.
HAGUE, J. F.
HALL, H.
HALL, R.
HALL, S.
HALLIWELL, T.
HANDS, J.
HANNAH, H.
HARDMAN, F.
HARDMAN, R.
HARTLEY, E.
HASLAM, F.
HASLAM, W.
HENSHALL, H. S.
HEYWOOD, A.
HEYWOOD, E.
HEYWOOD, J. H.
HILL, J.
HILTON, P.
HOPWOOD, F.
HORRIDGE, J.
HORROCKS, F.
HOSEY, H.
HOSEY, J.
HOSKER, H.

ROLL OF HONOUR—continued.

THE CALICO PRINTERS' ASSOCIATION LTD.

Rhodes Print Works—continued.

HOWARD, E.	McELROY, G.	RANDLES, M.	TAPSON, F.
HOWARD, F.	McGANNITY, A.	REVINGTON, A.	TAYLOR, A.
HOWARD, HY.	MATHER, W.	REVINGTON, G.	TAYLOR, D.
HOWARD, HY.	MATHER, W. E.	REVINGTON, J.	TAYLOR, W.
HOWARD, W.	MILLARD, J.	ROBERTS, W. E.	TEECE, J.
HOWARTH, J.	MILLS, F.	SANDIFORD, C.	TEECE, J.
HOWARTH, R.	MINGHAM, J.	SCHOFIELD, H.	TENCH, H.
HOWARTH, V.	MINGHAM, W.	SEVILLE, W.	THORNLEY, S.
HOYLE, H.	MITCHELL, A.	SHARPLES, T.	TIPPET, J. T.
HULSE, E.	MOORES, A.	SHAW, J.	TODKILL, G.
HULSE, J.	MORRIS, W. J.	SHEPLEY, H.	TODKILL, W.
HUNT, C.	NUTT, J. L.	SHEPLEY, W.	TURNER, H.
INGHAM, R.	OGDEN, R.	SHORROCKS, M.	TURNER, W.
JACKSON, E.	PAGE, H.	SHORROCKS, R.	WAIT, C.
JOHNSON, W.	PARKEY, A.	SMETHURST, A.	WALSH, J.
KEATE, R.	PARTINGTON, J.	SMETHURST, J.	WARBURTON, A.
KEEFE, JAS., Senr.	PARTINGTON, JAS.	SMETHURST, T.	WATERHOUSE, C.
KEEFE, J., Junr.	PARTINGTON, JOS.	SMITH, G.	WATSON, J.
KENYON, A.	PEARSON, WM.	SMITH, J.	WESTWELL, V.
KIRKMAN, G.	PEARSON, W.	SOUTHERN, J.	WHEELHOUSE, J.
KYMER, A.	HARDMAN, F.	STANSFIELD, V.	WHITEHURST, C.
LEE, E.	PHILLIPS, R.	STEAD, J.	WHITTAKER, R.
LEICESTER, H.	POWER, T.	STEADMAN, F.	WILLIAMS, A.
LEIGH, J. W.	PRESTWOOD, J.	STOTT, C.	WORRALL, J.
LEVER, J.	PRESTWOOD, J.	STOTT, J.	WRIGHT, H.
McCANN, J.	PRICE, J. W.	STRINGER, F.	WRIGHT, J. H.
McCONDACH, W.	PRIESTLEY, V.	STRINGER, R.	WRIGLEY, H.
McCONVILLE, J.	QUINCEY, F.	TAINSH, A.	WROE, W.

SOUTH ARTHURLIE PRINT WORKS.

AGNEW, J.	DOCHERTY, JOHN.	KERR, M.	McMILLAN, J.
AIRD, A.	ELLIOTT, F.	LAIRD, A.	MARTIN, W.
ANDERSON, J.	ELLIOTT, J.	LAIRD, W.	MAXWELL, C.
ANDERSON, M.	FLYNN, J.	LAWNS, J.	MILLAR, A.
ANDERSON, W.	FOSTER, J.	LECKIE, P.	MILLAR, J.
ARMSTRONG, T.	GALBRAITH, W.	LEONARD, J.	MUIR, R.
ARMSTRONG, W.	GALLOCHER, J.	LIGGAT, F.	MURRAY, J.
BOYD, J.	GALLOCHER, W.	LINDSAY, W.	O'DONNELL, W.
BUTTERS, D.	GEORGE, J.	McBRIAR, J.	O'NEIL, P.
CAIRNEY, W.	GILMOUR, T.	McCHESNEY, W.	PATTISON, W.
CAREY, T.	GOODWIN, A.	McCORMACK, J.	PINKERTON, G.
CARROLL, J.	GRANT, R.	McCREADY, D.	RITCHIE, J.
CARROLL, W.	HALDANE, R.	McCROSSAN, M.	RITCHIE, JAS.
CLABBURN, W.	HAMILTON, J.	McDADE, J.	ROBERTSON, T.
CLANNACHAN, R.	HANDLEY, J.	McDONALD, J.	ROSS, W.
CLARK, H.	HAWTHORN, J.	McDOUGALL, J.	SCOTT, A.
COLLINS, G.	HAY, J.	McDOUGALL, W.	SMITH, T.
CONWAY, W.	HILL, E.	McFARLANE, W.	TAIT, J.
COWAN, S.	HILLANS, J.	McGWIRE, D.	WALLACE, C.
COYNE, P.	IRVINE, J.	McINTYRE, —	WALLACE, J.
CURRANS, H.	JAMIESON, A.	McKECHNIE, T.	WILSON, D.
DOCHERTY, JAS.	KELLY, P.	McLEAN, A.	WILSON, W.
DOCHERTY, JAS.	KELLY, T.	McLINTOCK, A.	

ROLL OF HONOUR—continued.

THE CALICO PRINTERS' ASSOCIATION LTD.

SPRINGFIELD PRINT WORKS.

AIRLIE, J.
AUBREY, W.
BOWMAN, J.
BRYSON, A.
BURNS, M.
CALDERWOOD, A.
CANTLEY, A.
CHAPMAN, J.
CONNELLY, J.
CONNELLY, W.
CONNER, W.
CRAWFORD, D.
CRAWFORD, J.
CURRIE, A.
DEMPSEY, R.

DOCHERTY, J.
EARLEY, J.
FLATLEY, T.
GILLIGAN, J.
GRAHAM, J.
GRAHAM, W.
GRANT, H.
GREIG, J.
HAY, W.
HIGGINS, J.
HOLLIS, E.
JOHNSTON, C.
JOHNSTON, J.
KELLY, P.

KENNEDY, J.
KIRK, J.
LEGGAT, A.
LEIGHTON, H.
LIDDELL, R.
McARTHUR, K.
McARTHUR, T.
McCANN, W.
McCRANN, J.
McDERMAID, T.
McDERMAID, H.
McGARRIGLE, J.
McGUINNESS, J.
McILREE, R.

McKISSOCK, R.
McLEAN, A.
McLEAN, W.
McMENEMY, JAS.
McMENEMY, J.
MOFFAT, W.
MURDOCK, T.
NELLANY, R.
REILLY, J.
SPENCER, J.
WARREN, J.
WARREN, L.
WILSON, J.
WILSON, J.

STRINES PRINT WORKS.

ANTROBUS, G. W.
ARDERN, J.
BAGSHAW, A.
BARRATT, A.
BENNETT, L.
BOLD, H.
BOTTOMLEY, W.
BRADBURY, H.
COCKER, A.
COLLIE, A.
DAVIES, H.
DRAPER, W.
GARLEY, T.
GASKELL, J. R.
GRIFFIN, H.

HAMPSON, H.
HAMPSON, T.
HARDY, H.
HARRISON, J.
HAZLEHURST, J. T.
HIBBERT, G.
HIBBERT, J.
HOWE, A.
HOWE, J.
INGHAM, H.
INGHAM, W.
JACKSON, F.
JONES, W.
KIGHTLY, A.

LOMAS, J.
LOMAS, L.
MARSDEN, F.
MASKELL, H.
NADIN, F.
NADIN, G.
PARROTT, T.
PARSONS, J. F.
PEARSON, W.
PLATT, W.
RAMSEY, E.
REYNOLDS, J. W.
RHODES, C.
ROXBY, F.

RYAN, J.
SMITH, A.
SWINDELLS, M.
THORPE, E.
WHALLEY, T.
WHITAKER, H.
WHITEHEAD, A.
WILD, A.
WILD, J. W.
WOOD, H.
WOOD, R.
WOODWARD, A.
YOUD, HY.
YOUD, HERBERT.

THORNLIEBANK PRINT WORKS.

ARCHIBALD, J.
ANDERSON, JAS.
ANDERSON, JNO.
BEGGS, H.
BENNETT, J.
BERNEY, D.
BIGGINS, H.
BRADSHAW, J.
BRITTON, J.
BRITTON, W.
BROWN, W.
BURKE, T.
CALDER, D.
CAMERON, J.
CAMERON, J.
CAMERON, R.
CAMERON, W.
CARSLAW, H.
CAVES, D.
CLUGSTON, J.
CRAWFORD, JAS.

CRAWFORD, JNO.
CROMBIE, H.
CRONE, T.
DALGLISH, D.
DOWIE, D.
DUFF, R.
DUNLOP, W.
EAGLESHAN, M.
EASTCROFT, W.
EDGAR, J.
EDGAR, S.
ELDER, S.
EVANS, RICH.
EVANS, ROBT.
EVANS, W.
EWART, J.
FARRAR, E. K.
FRANCIS, S.
GALBRAITH, J.
GALLACHER, J.
GILLON, E.

GILLON, J.
GILMOUR, J.
GILMOUR, W.
GRAHAM, T.
HALLIDAY, H.
HAMILTON, J.
HAMILTON, J.
HANDVIDGE, H.
HART, AND.
HART, ARCHD.
HART, T.
HENRY, J.
HIMLIN, A.
HIMLIN, W.
HOLLIS, F.
HUGHES, T.
HUNTER, J.
JACKSON, W.
JOHNSTONE, D.
JOHNSTONE, W.
KELLY, J.

KERR, W.
KYLE, J.
LONGWELL, D.
LONGWELL, J.
LOVE, J.
LYONS, D.
McCAFFERTY, G.
McCANDLISH, C.
McCANDLISH, R.
McCONNELL, T.
McCOURT, P.
McCUTCHEAN, G.
McKELVIE, A.
McDONALD, J.
McDONALD, W.
McFETRIDGE, J.
McGARTH, T.
McGINLEY, J.
MACKIE, R.
McKINLEY, A.
McKINLEY, W.

ROLL OF HONOUR—continued.

THE CALICO PRINTERS' ASSOCIATION LTD.

Thornliebank Print Works—continued.

McLUGGAGE, T.	MURPHY, G.	RANKIN, JAS.	SURGENOR, J.
McMASTER, T.	MURRAY, H.	RANKIN, W.	TIMLIN, J.
McMURRAY, A.	MURRAY, J.	REID, W.	TELFORD, A.
McMURRAY, J.	MURRAY, W.	ROBSON, J.	TODD, JAS.
MAIR, S.	NICHOLSON, J.	SHIELDS, E.	TODD, JNO.
MEWHA, W.	PATERSON, L.	SHEARER, S.	TODD, JOS.
MILLER, J.	PETERS, T.	SLATER, W.	TONNER, P.
MILLER, S.	PICKETT, J.	SMITH, G.	WATSON, A.
MILLS, W.	PROW, C.	SNODGRASS, D.	WATSON, W.
MITCHELL, J.	QUIGLEY, J.	STEVENS, W.	WEIR, A.
MONAGHON, B.	RANKIN, A.	STOCKMAN, S.	WILLIAMS, S.
MONAGHON, P.	RANKIN, A., Jnr.	SURGENOR, A.	WILSON, W.
MUIRHEAD, G.	RANKIN, J.	SURGENOR, G.	YUILLE, W.

TOTTINGTON PRINT WORKS.

ASHWORTH, F.	FENTON, A.	KAY, R.	SHAW, J.
BAILEY, T.	FORSTER, H. V.	KAY, ROBT.	SHEPHERD, J.
BARTON, E.	FOX, C. J.	KENYON, H.	SNOWDEN, G.
BRADBURN, J. R.	GIFFARD, W.	LOMAX, S.	STANDING, F.
BEAUMONT, R.	GILBERT, J.	LONSDALE, T.	SUMPTER, A.
BRIGGS, V.	GOVIER, J.	McEWAN, W.	TAYLOR, H.
BRITTON, B.	HALL, R. H.	MANTLE, W.	TAYLOR, HY.
BROOKE, A. E.	HARDMAN, C.	MEAKES, A.	WADDINGTON, H.
BROOKE, J. H.	HARDMAN, T.	MELELEU, A.	WALKER, F.
BROOKE, H.	HARRISON, J.	MINSHULL, D. S.	WALKER, G.
BROOKE, W.	HEAP, T. P.	MULROONEY, F.	WARBURTON, D.
BROOKS, E.	HEAP, W. S.	NEWSHAM, J.	WARDLE, R.
BUTTERWORTH, S.	HEWITT, T.	NUTTALL, J.	WARRINGTON, J. G.
BUTTERWORTH, W. J.	HIBBERT, S.	NUTTALL, J. W.	WHEELER, H.
CHADWICK, J.	HIGGINS, W.	NUTTALL, S.	WHITTAM, G.
COARD, W.	HORROCKS, T.	NUTTALL, W.	WIKE, G. W.
COLLINSON, E.	HOWARTH, A. E.	O'CONNELL, J.	WIKE, R.
COOPER, R.	HOWARTH, E.	PRICE, H.	WILD, E.
CROMPTON, J.	HOWCROFT, E.	REID, W.	WILKINSON, C.
DALE, R.	HUDDLESTONE, A.	RIGBY, J. W.	WILLOUGHBY, S. R.
DAVIES, T.	HULTON, J.	ROBINSON, G.	YATES, J.
DOLPHIN, F.	IRVINE, J.	ROTHWELL, S.	YATES, W.
EARNSHAW, W.	KAY, E.	SHAW, H.	YESFORD, W.
EATOCK, J.			

WATERSIDE MILL.

AUSTEN, F.	GODDARD, J.	METCALFE, T.	ROWBOTTOM, S.
BEELEY, P.	GODDARD, S.	NEWTON, S.	SHEA, M. O.
BENNETT, E.	GOULD, R.	PAYNE, A.	SNAPE, T.
BURNS, J.	HADFIELD, E.	PLATT, G.	SWALLOW, W.
BUTCHER, S.	HARRISON, J.	PLATT, G.	WADSWORTH, A.
CARPENTER, E.	HARROP, E.	PLATT, W.	WILLIAMSON, M.
CATTERALL, N.	HOOLAN, J.	RIDGEWAY, W.	WILSON, J.
CHADWICK, G.	HOWARD, H.	RIGGE, F.	WILSON, R.
COFFEY, M.	LEAH, G.	ROBERTS, H.	WILSON, W.
CROOKS, J.	LEE, H.	ROBERTS, W.	WOODROW, W. T.
FISH, J.	MARSHALL, T.	ROBINSON, W.	WOODWARD, J.
GARLICK, W.	MARSTON, F.	ROWBOTTOM, E.	WOODWORTH, F.

ROLL OF HONOUR—continued.

THE CALICO PRINTERS' ASSOCIATION LTD.

WATFORD BRIDGE PRINT WORKS.

ARDERN, G.
BAGSHAW, L.
BAILEY, P.
BARTON, F.
BARTON, J.
BENNETT, J.
BENNETT, W.
BLAKE, A.
BROMILOW, G.
BULLOUGH, S.
BURGESS, E.
BURGESS, J.
BYRNE, J.
CAUKELL, W.
COVERLEY, C.
CRAVEN, W.
DEAN, J.
DEVLIN, C.
DOWNS, W.
EDWARDS, E.
FOX, E. B.
GALBRAITH, F.
GREEN, P.
GUEST, W.
HAMMOND, G.
HANNON, F.
HARROP, JAS.
HARROP, J. W.
HEATHCOTE, B.
HIBBERT, H.
HIGGINBOTTOM, J. J.
HILL, E.
HILL, G.
HILL, S.
HOOLEY, J. H.
HOWARD, W.
JOHNSON, E.
JONES, N.
LEACH, T.
LEE, S.
LOMAS, W.
LYNE, J.
MARSH, E.
MARSH, T.
MARSLAND, S.
PLATT, J.
REDFERN, W. J. B.
SCHOFIELD, H.
SHIRT, W.
SIDEBOTTOM, W.
SIMISTER, W.
SWANN, J.
SWEATMORE, H.
TALBOT, H.
TAYLOR, J.
WADSWORTH, S.
WAIN, A.
WALKER, J. W.
WARING, J. A.
WETHERLEY, F.
WHARMBY, S.
WORTHINGTON, P.
WRIGHT, A.

WELLINGTON MILLS.

ARNOLD, H.
ASHMORE, W.
BALLAM, J.
BARBER, S.
BARBER, W.
BARRETT, H.
BENNETT, G. H.
COCHRANE, F. A.
COLLIER, W.
DRINKWATER, G.
FINNERTY, T.
GEE, E.
HARROP, R.
HEELIS, J.
KEMP, E.
KINDER, W.
MITCHELL, P.
MUTTER, W.
NEWTON, G.
OGDEN, W.
RICHARDSON, P.
STANSFIELD, T.
STARKEY, G.
THWAITES, J. H.
TURNER, J.
VINEY, W. H.
WARNER, W.
WILD, R.
WILSON, R.
WRAGG, W.
WRAY, C.
WYATT, A.

WHALLEY ABBEY PRINT WORKS.

ABRAHAM, J.
ARNFIELD, D.
ASHCROFT, H.
ASHCROFT, J.
BALL, J.
BARTLETT, F.
BARTLETT, J.
BARTLETT, M.
BENTLEY, A.
BENTLEY, A.
BENTLEY, R. H.
BOARDMAN, F.
BOOTH, J. W.
BOWKER, J.
BRAYSHAW, H.
BRIDGE, H. H.
BRIDGE, J.
BRIGGS, D.
BURNETT, N.
BUSHY, A. V.
CALVERT, J. A.
CALVERT, W.
CARDEN, J.
CHATBURN, J.
COLLINSON, J. J.
COOK, H. R.
CORMICK, W.
CRAWFORD, D.
CROWTHER, B.
DEAN, R.
DENNETT, A.
DEVINE, D.
DEWHURST, H.
DOUGLAS, W.
DYER, J.
EVERTON, C.
FENTON, W. E.
FENWICK, J.
GOODMAN, S.
GORNALL, J. T.
GRIMSHAW, J.
HACKETT, W. A.
HALL, J.
HARGREAVES, JAS.
HARGREAVES, JNO.
HARGREAVES, W.
HARPER, E.
HARRISON, C.
HAYHURST, L.
HENVY, D.
HINDLE, S. J. S.
HOLT, J.
INCE, A.
INCE, E.
JONES, ALBERT.
JONES, AMOS.
JONES, P.
KIRBY, H.
KNOWLES, W.
LANCASTER, H.
LAWRENCE, A.
LOCKLEY, C.
LUPTON, J. F.
LYNE, F.
McHALE, J.
McLAREN, D.
MANLEY, G.
MANLEY, G.
MORTIMER, W.
MUMBY, J. W.
NELSON, V.
NUTTER, J.
NUTTER, T.
O'NEIL, J.
PATEFIELD, W.
PENNY, J.
PRICE, J.
PUNCHARD, E. W.
PYM, A.
RICHARDSON, J.
RIDSDALE, G.
ROBERTSON, P.
SCOTT, W.
SIBSON, E. B.
SIMPSON, T.
SLINGER, H.
SMITH, J.
SMITHIES, J.
SOUTHERN, E.
SOUTHWORTH, H.
SPEAK, H.
SWARBRICK, E.
TAYLOR, A. M.
THORNBER, A.
THORNBER, L.
WALKER, C.
WELSH, G.
WHALLEY, J.
WHIPP, J.
WHITTAM, J.
WHITTAM, J. W.
WILKINSON, A.
WILKINSON, J.
WRIGHT, W. F.
YATES, H.
YOUNG, W.

WOOD (HAYFIELD) PRINT WORKS.

BAXTER, J.
BENNETT, R.
BROCKLEHURST, W.
BURWELL, W. K.
ELLIOTT, J.
FURNESS, J.
GARSIDE, A.
HADFIELD, S.
HARRISON, W.
HIBBERT, P.
HILL, J.
HILL, W.
HUDSON, H.
HUGHES, A.
KING, H.
KIRTON, J. T.
MATE, J. W.
METCALFE, J.
PILKINGTON, G. E.
RANGELEY, S.
ROBINSON, U.
VERNON, R.
WALSH, J.
WILSON, O.

ROLL OF HONOUR—continued.

THE CALICO PRINTERS' ASSOCIATION LTD.
FRANCE: MALAUNAY WORKS AND PARIS OFFICE.

ALLAIN.	CHAUVET.	GENIN.	LEGRAND, P.	PETIT, EMILE.
ALLAIS, F.	CHERON.	GENTIL, A.	LELIÈVRE.	PETIT, PIERRE.
ALLEAUME.	CLAUDE.	GENTIL.	LELONG.	PETIT PAUL.
AMELIN.	COCAGNE.	GENTIL.	LELOUARD.	PETITON.
ANDRIEUX.	CONSEIL.	GIBON.	LEMORT.	PICARD.
ANQUETIL, MARCEL.	COQUEMENT, H.	GIBOURDEL.	LEROUX, H.	PIGAULT.
ANQUETIL, MAURICE.	COQUIN, G.	GILLES.	LETACQ.	PINAIRE.
BAPTISTE.	CORMON.	GILLET.	LEVEILLARD.	PINOEL.
BAPTISTE.	COUTURIER.	GOSSAY.	LIBERGE.	PLANQUAIS.
BAPTISTE, G.	DAVID.	GOUDEY, M.	LINOT, A.	POLLET.
BAPTISTE, M.	DAVID.	GRANCOURT.	LINOT, A.	POY.
BAUCHET.	DELAHAYE.	GRENIER, H.	LOISELIER.	PRÉVOST.
BAUDÈRE.	DELAUNAY, A.	GRISEL, O.	LUCAS.	QUEMIN.
BAZIN.	DELU.	GUÉVILLE.	MAINEULT.	QUESSYAC.
BÉCHERELLE.	DENIS, F.	HAMEL.	MALANDAIN.	RADENEZ.
BECK.	DENORMANDIE.	HENQUINQUANT.	MALLET.	RASSE.
BÉCUE, L.	DEPREAUX.	HAREL.	MALLET.	RICHARD.
BELLAMY, G.	DESCHAMPS, R.	HAZEL, E.	MANCHION.	RIVIÈRE.
BELLAMY.	DESHAYES.	HEBERT.	MARCADÉ.	ROUSSEL, R.
BENARD.	DEVAUX.	HENNETIER, A.	MARCOTTE.	ROUX, E.
BÉNARD.	DEVAUX, G.	HENNETIER.	MARETTE.	SAUNIER.
BENARD.	DEWER.	HENRY.	MARTIGNY.	SAUNIER.
BÉNARD.	DEYBER.	HERICHER.	MARTIGNY.	SCHMIDT, E.
BENNETOT.	DIEUL.	HERICHER, S.	MARTIN, H.	SEIDLER, E.
BETHON, J.	DIGARD.	HEYSSE.	MARTIN, F.	SEMARD.
BETHON.	DOUDEMENT.	HUCHON.	MARTIN.	SIMON.
BETHON, ALF.	DOUDET.	HUET.	MAUROUARD.	SIRE.
BIVA, LUCIEN.	DOUDET.	HUMBERT, B.	MEGEL.	SORET.
BLANCHARD.	DOUDET, G.	JACQUET.	MEGEL, J.	TASSERY, H.
BLANCHEMAIN, L.	DREYFUS.	JOUBERT, A.	MESSIÉ.	TERRIEN, A.
BONAMY.	DROUET.	KLUMPP.	MESSIÉ.	TERRIEN, ED.
BOREL.	DUBOC.	KLUMPP.	MESSIÉ.	THIEURY.
BOULARD.	DUBUC.	KOCK.	MEYER, G.	TIERCELIN.
BOULET, J.	DUFROY.	KOECHLIN.	MEYER, J.	TISSE.
BOURGEOIS, H.	DUPAIN.	LACAILLE.	MILLE, A.	TOSTAIN.
BOUTTE.	DUQUESNE.	LAINÉ.	MILLE, L.	TOUZÉ.
BOYER, J.	ENGRAND, C.	LAMOTTE.	MOLLARD.	TREVET.
BOYER.	ESCALAIS.	LAROCHE.	MONDET.	TREVET, C.
BRARD.	EVRARD.	LAYETT.	MORIGOT.	TROCHET.
BREDIF.	FERET, E.	LEBOUC.	MORIN.	TROPPÉE.
BRELLMANN.	FLAHAUT.	LEBRUN, J.	MOUQUET.	TROTTEL.
BUÉ.	FOITIER.	LEBRUN, E.	MULLET.	VANDRILLE.
BULAN.	FOLLIOT, E.	LECLERC.	NEVEU.	VAUSSIER.
BUQUET.	FONTAINE.	LECLERC.	NICOLLE, G.	VAUTIER.
CANVILLE.	FONTAINE.	LECOQ.	NOEL.	VIARD.
CARMENT, P.	FOULON.	LECOQ.	OLLIVIER.	VILLETTE.
CAUDRON, G.	FOURNIER.	LECOQ.	PAPLOREY.	VILLETTE.
CAUMONT.	FOURNIER, G.	LECOQ.	PAUL, A.	VILLIERS.
CAUMONT, H.	FOUSTREL.	LEFEBVRE.	PÉRUELLE, A.	VIRMONTIER.
CAUVIN.	GAMBÉ.	LEFEBVRE.	PETER.	VISTRES.
CAVELIER.	GAUDINIERE, H.	LEGROS.	PETIT.	WALTER.
	GENET, A.			

In addition to the above names there are 3,080 men who have attested.

DANIEL LEE AND CO., LTD.

CRAVEN, J. H.	KANE, P. J.	MILLAR, J.	SHAW, T. R.

APPENDIX.

Names of Men who have attested under the Group System.

Affleck and Brown, Ltd., and Brown Bros., Ltd.
(See p. 406 in Roll of Honour.)

AMBLER, F. R.
ALDERSLEY, J.
BRAY, R. A.
BAYSTON, A.
BENNETT, J. B.
BROWN, J.
BROWN, T. J.
BROWN, W.
BLEASBY, C.
BROOKS, J. A.
BATES, W. E.
COOKE, J. L.
CHADWICK, H.
CASBOLT, A. E.
COPPACK, W. J.
CARTER, G.
CURTIS, N.
DAVIES, W. O.
DODD, W. H.
DAWBER, H.
DEAN, W.
DEES, O.
EDWARDS, E. W.
EVANS, M.
EVANS, J.
FAWCETT, J. F.
FERGUSON, J.
FORD, W.
GRIFFITHS, R. T.
GARNETT, L. W.
GRIFFITHS, T. J.
GOSSON, P.
GOUGH, A.
GIBBON, S.
HARDY, A.
HARTLEY, C. J.
D. B.
HUGGINS, R. C.
HAWORTH, T.
HIGGINS, R.
HAINING, R.
HERBERT, J. T.
HILL, S.
HOWATSON, J.
HEALEY, F. R.
JACKSON, A. E.
JARDINE, A.
JONES, R. J.
JONES, D. J.
JONES, C.
JONES, W. E.
JONES, H.
JUDGE, T.
KENNEDY, T.
KINSELLA, J.
KING, W. B.
LIGHTFOOT, G.
LATHAM, W.
LAWSON, F. W.
LUND, S.
LIFE, G.
LUCKHAM, R. A.
LOCKE, H.
MUNDELL, S.
M'MILLAN, L.
MITCHELL, A.
NIELD, J.
NEWBY, A.
NORMANTON, C.
OSWELL, W.
O'REILLY, G.
POWELL, W. C.
PLANT, F.
PROCTOR, L.
POWELL, W. P.
PEARSE H. G.
PETERS, W.
ROUTLEDGE, J.
ROBINSON, J. W.
RUSHTON, G.
ROWLAND, F.
ROBERTS, A.
STYLES, W. F.
THOMAS, T. H.
TOMES, E. W.
THOMAS, J. I.
THOMAS, E. A.
THORBURN, W.
TAYLOR, C. F.
WATSON, J. B.
WHITFIELD, J. V.
WILLIAMS, G. E.
WILLIAMS, G. H.
WILLIAMS, J. R.
WILLIAMSON, G. H.
WILLIAMSON, H.
WRIGHT, J. W.
WELSBY, H.
WALKER, W. M.
WESTON, W.

Aitken, Campbell and Co., Ltd.
HUNTER, H.
*DOBSON, T.
*ROSCOE, T.
*ELLISON, H.
*COOKE, R.
*YARDLEY, H.
*CARSON, L.
*KERRIDGE, G.

The Anglo-Syrian Trading Co., Ltd.
(See p. 413 in Roll of Honour.)

HOULT, J. P.
MARSHALL, C. E.

Arning and Co.
(See p. 413 in Roll of Honour.)

APTED, F. W.
BAGOT, F.
BENNETT, G.
BOHANNA, A.
BRODIE, A. K.
BROWN, J. A.
DAVIES, S.
KIRKHAM, J.
RALPHS, C.
RISING, W.
REDMAN, J.
ROYLE, J.
URMSTON, J. F.

* Serving with the Colours.

Armitage and Rigby, Ltd.
(See p. 656 in Roll of Honour.)

Cockhedge and Rodney Mills, Warrington.
TAYLOR, H. E.
SAVORY, J. W.
HINDE, J.
HOLT, W.
BAILEY, W.
TICKLE, J.
MORRIS, J.
AINSWORTH, J.
DITCHFIELD, E. S.
NORTH, C.
BURLAND, W.
SEAGAR, J. W.
ANSON, T.
MAGUIRE, T.
TOFT, J.
PERCIVAL, J.
GARRATT, G. M.
MILLER, C.
AINSWORTH, J., Junr.
SAVORY, R.
BOLAND, W.
HEAP, H.
ALLCOCK, D.
HARDMAN, J.
SMITH, T.
FIRTH, S.
BATE, S.
WYKE, A.
LORD, E.
RILEY, S.
GILL, F.
SHARPLES, C.
SHAW, C.
EDWARDS, S.
WILLCOCK, S.
LOGAN, J.
GREGORY, W.
HAMMON, W.
HAYES, A.
JOHNSTONE, W.
JACKSON, J.
WORRALL, T.
WHITTAKER, J.
WRIGHT, G.
HOLBROOK, H.
SLOANE, J. R.
HIBBERT, B.
CANN, L.

Warehouse, 95, Portland Street.
ARMITAGE, G. W. (Managing Director)
BUCKLEY, J. E.
BRATLEY, C. E.
LUCAS, C.
HAMNETT, H.
EASTWOOD, W.
MASON, J.
PENDLEBURY, A.
MILLWARD, H.
HESKETH, T. B.
FENTON, H.
LILL, G.
LARNER, E.
NELSON, W.
APPLETON, H. J.
CAVILL, F. E.
RICHARDSON, S.
LONGSTAFF, J.
HEYWOOD, W.
McHUGH, E.
CHAPPELL, C.
FARNWORTH, W.
POTTS, J.
TURNER, F.
MEADOWCROFT, H.
BUZZA, J.
FARRELL, T.

E. Ascoli and Son.
(See p. 658 in Roll of Honour.)

HONEYBILL, W.
GILLET, W.
GUTTERIDGE, E. H.
KELLY, F.
RICHARDSON, J.
†ANDREWS, A.
†JORDAN, F.
†PODMORE, E.
†GUINANE, J.

Ashton and Co. (estd. 1787), Ltd.
(See p. 658 in Roll of Honour.)

ALLEN, A. S.
CONNOR, T.
OWEN, J.
*SMITH, T.
†HUGHES, S.
MALCOLM, J. M.
†CANNON, R.
†LUSTGARTEN, I.

Baerlein and Sons and Baerlein Bros.
(See p. 421 in Roll of Honour.)

BAERLEIN, H. A.
BAERLEIN, E. M.
BRIDGWOOD, C.
LAVERY, W.
MACKIN, W.
PRESTON, A.
LONGY, R.
HANNAH, E.
WRIGLEY, W.
TAYLOR, C.
WARD, H.
ARNOLD, S.
OLDHAM H.
BEVERLEY, J. R.
BECKETT, H. E. V.
JONES, A.
LEANG, J.
PARSONS, J. H.
BOOTH, L.
WHITELEY, J.
COTTRILL, J.
KIRKMAN, H.
CARTER, P.
POLLITT, E.

* Accepted for home service only.
† Rejected.

Henry Bannerman and Sons, Ltd.
(See p. 414 in Roll of Honour.)

†ALLEN, H.
ALLMARK, A. E.
†BANNERMAN, R. H. W.
BARLOW, C.
BATTERSBY, W.
BOOTH, J.
BRADLEY, J.
†BRADLEY, W.
BROCKBANK, J.
BROWN, J.
BUCKLEY, C. S.
†BUCKLEY, R.
BURGESS, J.
CARTER, W.
CHANDLER, G.
CHETHAM, H.
CLAYTON, F.
CLETHERO, G.
COCHRANE, S.
COOK, E.
COOKE, F. P.
COPSON, J.
COPSON, S.
CRAWSHAW, F.
CROSSLEY, J.
CUTTLE, H.
DAVIS, J.
†DAWSON, T.
DEASEY, W.
DEASEY, D.
DIXON, J. W.
DYSON, R.
EASTWOOD, D.
EDWARDS, J. T.
FAIRBROTHER, J. H.
FARRINGTON, J.
FAULKNER, J.
FEATHERSTONE, G.
†FINDLAY, H.
FITTON, H.
†GLEAVE, E.
GOODALL, D.
GREEN, H.
GREEN, J.
GREGORY, J.
GRUNDY, R.
HADFIELD, W.
HALTON, F.
HAYES, JAMES.
HAYES, JOHN.
HINCHCLIFFE, H.
†HINCHCLIFFE, W.
HUNT, C. W.
IVES, T.
JORDAN, J.
KEY, L.
KINGSTON, C.
LAWTON, A.
LLOYD, J.
LOWE, J.
MACARA, W. C.
MACKIE, W. L.
McCORMICK, T.
McKENNA, T.
†MEEKS, G.
†MELLOR, A.
†MELLOR, W.
MILLAR, W. G.
MOUNTEER, W.
NEEDHAM, J.
NIELD, J.
OATES, W.
ODDY, H. S.
PARR, J.
PREECE, H. J.
RIDINGS, F.
RIGGS, E.
ROGERS, T.
SANDERSON, F. D.
SIMPSON, JAS.
SIMPSON, JOHN.
SLEIGH, J. W.
SMITH, C. V.
SMITH, F. W.
SOUTHWORTH, G.
SWINDELL, J.
TEER, F. A.
THORPE, G.
†VALENTINE, S. H.
†WATSON, W.
WATTS, V.
†WELBERRY, J.
WEST, H.
WILLIAMSON, A.
†WOOD, C.
WOOD, F.
WORSLEY, C. L.
†WRIGHT, R. L.

Barber and Colman, Ltd.
(See p. 659 in Roll of Honour.)

COUSEN, F.
FARRELL, W.

James Barber and Co., Ltd.
(See p. 659 in Roll of Honour.)

ACASTER, E.
SUTTON, B.
KIDNEY, R.
WEBB, T.
STOCKDALE, P.
FORREST, G.
HULL, A.

Robert Barclay & Co.
(See p. 710 in Roll of Honour.)

CHOLLERTON, F. A.
FARRELL, F.
FORREST, J.
JONES, H.
KING, A.
LINNEY, S.
SMITH, A.
THORPE, A. W.
WARBURTON, C. K.
DONEVAN, W. E.
CROOK, H.
GOODWIN, I. D.

James Barnes, Ltd.
(See p. 415 in Roll of Honour.)

BARNES, T. B.
BUCKLEY, W. H.
DAVENPORT, J. B.
CHARNLEY, R.
STRINGER, A. J.
DODD, A.
CALDWELL, J.
CHAPPELL, R.
BAYLEY, G.
HALPERN, W.
COOPS, G.
DORE, J.
FERNIE, F.
LEWIS, W.

Beaty Bros. (M'ter), Ltd.
(See p. 418 in Roll of Honour.)

ASPINALL, E.
BROWNFIELD, C.
BROOKS, H.
BROOKES, C.
BARRON, W.
BAZLEY, T. W.
COTTERILL, G.
CLAPHAM, C.
CUNLIFFE, J.
COOPER, E.
CASEY, S.
DOWNS, J.
EASTHAM, W.
EVANS, R.
GALE, W.
GISBOURNE, G.
GUY, M.
GIBBS, S.
HOOLOHAN, J.
HUBBALL, C. S.
KENNEDY, S.
KENT, G. T.
LENTON, M.
LANE, R.
McGORLICK, F.
McDONNELL, J.
McCONNELL, A.
QUEENAN, M.
RAILTON, J. R.
ROSCOE, J.
ROBB, A.
SPALL, C. G.
SKIDMORE, T. W
SULLIVAN, T.
TATLER, W.
TARR, A.
THAELL, I. J.

Sir Jacob Behrens and Sons.
(See p. 419 in Roll of Honour.)

BRIERLEY, C. C.
WALKER, E.
YATES, L.
ALLEN, A.
LIGHTOWLER, M.
MELLOR, H.
KELLETT, J.
FAWCETT, A. E.
RAWSON, H.
GILDERDALE, J.
SLADEN, J.
MATHER, E.
ROBINSON, W. S.
NORTHWOOD, T. G. P.
WILSON, W. V.
CHUBB, A.
SKINNER, A. M.
LOCKING, A. P.
BLACKBURN, S.
DAWSON, W.
HUNTER, S.
BOWLER, H. B.
GLEAVE, H. B.
HODGSON, C. A.
CHADWICK, A.
THOMPSON, F.
†RHODES, W.
†BOOTH, F.
†RUDD, J. W.
†WRIGLEY, G. H.
†STEUART, W. W.
†BOVINGTON, E. W.
†ASHWORTH, W. H.

Barlow and Jones.
(See p. 416 in Roll of Honour.)

*BICKERTON, J. A.
*BUNTING, W.
*DAVENPORT, H.
*HOWARTH, D.
*KENNERLEY, F. R.
*MORT, H.
*NEEDHAM, S.
*OLDFIELD, E.
*ROWE, H.
*STEWART, A. R.
*STIRLING, W.
*WAITE, P.
*WOOD, J.
*PLIMMER, B. H.
ADCOCK, H. L.
ADDI, ——
ARDRON, J. E.
ASQUITH, W. C.
BARLOW, P. B.
BARLOW, T. D.
BARNETT, S.
BAXTER, T.
BEDFORD, J. E.
BENNETT, J. W.
BEVINS, T.
BICKERTON, A.
BIRD, H.
BLACKHAM, E.
BLETCHER, E.
BOWERS, H.
BRADBURY, G.
BRAMHALL, T.
BROAD, S. S.
BROMLEY, J.
BROOKES, H.
BRUCE, J. R.
BURROWS, N.
CARTER, E.
CARTWRIGHT, E.
CAVE, F. N.
CHAPMAN, H.
CHEETHAM, J. W.
CHORLTON, T.
CLARKE, H.
CLARK, W.
CLAYTON, A.
CLIFTON, H.
COOKE, C.
COOPER, P.
COSTIGAN, T.
COULDOCK, E.
COXHILL, W. H.
COXON, J.
CROMPTON, W. R.
DAWSON, F. F.
DAVIES, J.
DEBELLE, J.
DRURY, P.
FAIRCLOUGH, G. R.
FEARNEOUGH, F.
FEATHERSTON, F.
FERGUSON, J.
FIRTH, J. G.
FIRTH, W. J.
FOX, A.
FRANK, F.
GALE, G.
GANDY, D.
GERRARD, H.
GILBERT, R.
GILMOUR, T.
GRAHAM, W.
GREEN, W.
GREEN, W.
GREGSON, H.
GURNHILL, W.
HAGGER, C. W.
HAIGH, W.
HAMER, L.
HARGREAVES, W.
HARLAND, F.
HARTLEY, C.
HEALD, L. J.
HEAP, J. R.
HEGINBOTHAM, H. W.
HETHERINGTON, H.
HEWITT, S.
HEYWOOD, J. R.
HILL, T.
HOLLAND, J. D.
HOLLIDAY, R.
HOPE, C.
HOPPER, J.
HOWARD, H.
HUGHES, W. F.
IRLAM, L.
ISHERWOOD, V.
JACKSON, H. N.
JOHNSON, A.
JOHNSTONE, W.
JONES, I.
JONES, J.
JONES, W. A.
KELLETT, S.
KENYON, A.
KNOTT, C.
LANGSHAW, G.
LEES, H.
LEMON, J.
LINNEY, F.
LITHERLAND, E.
LOCKETT, J.
LOMAS, E.
LORD, A.
LOWNDES, D. B.
LUPTON, H. G.
McCARTHY, W.
METTAM, J.
MILBURN, J.
MITCHELL, W
MOORES, I.
MURPHY, A. V.
NEEDHAM, H.
OPENSHAW, E.
OWEN, H.
PARRY, G.
PAXTON, J. W.
PILKINGTON, P.
PINKERTON, W.
PLANT, A.
PLATTS, J.
POYSER, G. P.
PURKIS, W. T.
RAMSBOTHAM, J.
REDFORD, T. J.
RENSHAW, L. W.
REYNOLDS, F.
ROBINSON, G.
ROBINSON, W
ROBY, R. H.
ROGERSON, N. K.
ROSSITER, A. E.
RUTHERFORD, R.
RUTTER, R. T.
RUTTER, R. S.
SALMON, W. W.
SAYER, T.
SCHOLES, S.
SCRAGG, E.
SHAW, G.
SMITH, B.
SIMPSON, H.
SPEAKMAN, F.
STAMBOROUGH, H.
STREET, H.
TAYLOR, G. A. H
TAYLOR, H.
TARR, V. K.
THOMASSON, W
THOMPSON, J.
THOMSON, D.
TINDALE, J. H.
WALKER, A. B.
WALKER, J. H.
WALTON, J.
WARBURTON, A.
WELBERRY, W.
WESTALL, F. D.
WHEADON, R.
WHITWORTH, F.
WILKINSON, C.
WILSON, A.
WILSON, A. J.
WILSON, J. H.
WINN, W.
WOLSTENCROFT, J. H.
WOOD, H.
WOOD, P.
WOOD, R. A.
WOOLLEY, A. J.
YARWOOD, G.

Beatty, Altgeldt and Co.
(See p. 662 in Roll of Honour.)

HUTCHINSON, W. H.
BACON, R
†POWELL, G.
†STACEY, H.
†WINTERBOTTOM, F. S.

† Rejected.

Baxendale and Co., Ltd.
(See p. 418a in Roll of Honour)

†DARRAH, E. DARRAH, A. L. DARRAH, P.

AINSWORTH, H. L.
ALLEN, E.
ANDERSON, C.
APPLETON, W. E.
AYRES, S.
BAILEY, W. H.
BALL, T.
BALLINGER, F.
BAND, E.
BARTON, O.
BEECH, W.
BENNETT, I.
†BENTLEY, G.
BERRISFORH, H.
BICKERTON, W.
BIRCHALL, J.
BLACKETT, J.
BLAKELEY, H.
BLOMLEY, W.
†BOLTON, G.
BRADBURY, G.
BRADLEY, D.
BRADSHAW, S.
BREAKELL, W.
BRIGGS, H. N.
BRIGHOUSE, S.
BROOKS, J.
BRYDON, G.
BUTTERWORTH, R.
CAFFREY, C.
CAMPBELL, M.
CARROLL, A.
CAYTON, J.
CLARKE, B. P.
†CLARKE, J. B.
†CLARKE, J.
CLARKE, W.
COAKLEY, J.
COLLIE, H.
CONDRON, J.
CONNAUGHTON, P.
CONSTERDINE, F.
COOKE, R.
COOPER, J.
COUPE, S.
CRANNA, W.
†CRAVEN, C.
CROCKER, W.
†CROSSLEY, A.
DARRAH, H., Jnr.
DAY, W.
DELVES, H.
DENNIS, J. W.
†DICKENSON, W.
DOODSON, G.
DONOGHUE, J.
DUDLEY, W. J.
DUGDALE, C.
DWYER, A.
†EDWARDS, J.
EGAN, J.
ELLISON, A.
ELLISON, E.
EVANS, A.
FALLOWS, T.
FARMER, J. W.
†FARTHING, H.
FAULKNER, F.
†FEARNLEY, G.
FERRALL, W.
FIELDING, B.
FINLEY, J. W.
†FLETCHER, W.
†FOSTER, J. W.
FOSTER, P.
POWELL, G. F.
†GARNER, A. E.
GARDNER, P.
GIBBISON, P.
†GIBBONS, F.
†GIBSON, W.
GRAVES, J.
GREEN, D.
GREENHALGH, J.
GREGORY, L.
GOODWIN, H.
GORTON, J.
†GUY, G.
HALLSWORTH, S.
†HAMPSON, W.
†HAMMETT, S. H.
HANNON, R. J.
HARRISON, R.
HAY, J. T.
HEATON, G.
†HERON, T.
HILDITCH, W.
HILLS, J.
HODSON, E.
HODGSON, P.
HOLME, J.
HOLT, F.
HOLT, P.
HORSFIELD, F.
HORWOOD, T.
HOWARD, H.
HOWARTH, J.
JACKSON, H.
JACKSON, R.
JONES, J.
JONES, J. H.
JONES, T.
†KEATING, J.
KING, C.
LAMPTON, H.
LAWTON, A.
LEE, A.
†LICKERISH, J.
†LIPTROTT, W.
LLOYD, F.
†LOCKETT, A.
LOUNSBACH, J.
LOWE, J.
LUDLAM, T.
LYMER, F.
LYTH, F.
†MACCARTER, J. H.
McCORMICK, H.
McCRACKEN, W.
McCULLEY, E.
McGOVERN, A.
†McWATT, A.
MAIRS, S.
MARSH, G.
MASSEY, T. M.
MAYOR, T.
†MELROSE, W.
METCALF, W.
MILBURN, J.
MILLWARD, J.
MORGAN, E.
MORRIS, A. E.
MORRIS, B. H. B.
†MOTLER, J. H.
MOTTRAM, J. E.
NELSON, R.
†NESBITT, F.
NIELD, H.
†NOBLE, C.
NUTTALL, J.
OFFICER, T.
†O'BRIEN, W.
†O'GARR, J.
†OWEN, W.
PARKINSON, G.
†PARTRIDGE, R.
PEARSON, J.
PEARSON, T.
†PERCIVAL, W.
PERRINS, F.
POWER, J. W.
PRATT, H. R.
QUALTER, E.
†QUEALEY, J.
RANSFORD, C.
†RENNIE, A.
†RESBEC, G.
RIGGALL, F.
†ROUCHETTI, D.
ROWLANDS, A.
†RUTHERFORD, C.
†SALT, S.
SCOTT, F.
SCOTT, J.
SHARPLES, A. E.
SHAW, J.
SHAW, J. W.
SHAW, O.
SHELTON, E.
SHEPPERD, T.
SHERIDAN, L.
SHERLOCK, H.
SHIPPOBOTTOM, F.
†SIMKIN, W.
SIDEBOTHAM, J.
SLACK, E.
SLACK, J.
SLATER, W.
†SMETHURST, G.
SMITH, E. J.
†SMITH, W.
SNAPE, W.
STALEY, J.
STAPLETON, T.
STOKES, H.
†STONEHOUSE, H.
†STUBBS, J. C.
SUTCLIFFE, D.
SWEENEY, J.
†SWETTENHAM, A.
THEXTON, J.
THOMAS, E.
THOMAS, H.
THOMAS, S. H.
TINKER, R.
TIPLADY, G.
TROUSDALE, I.
†TURNER, F.
TURRELL, S.
†TYLDESLEY, F.
TYSALL, A.
WALKER, W.
WALKLATE, A.
WARD, G.
WARD, H. V.
†WARRINGTON, J.
WATSON, J. R.
WEBSTER, J.
†WEST, C. F.
WHARTON, J.
WHITE, A.
WHITE, G. W.
WILD, ART.
WILD, ALB.
WILD, J. W.
WILKINSON, ALB.
WILLIAMS, H.
WILLIAMS, T.
WILSON, A.
†WILSON, HAROLD.
WILSON, HARRY.
WILSON, J.
WOODS, F.
WORRALL, A.
†WORTHINGTON, ALF.
†WORTHINGTON, ART.
WRIGLEY, M.
WYNNE, H.
YATES, L.

John Bolton and Co.
(See p. 455 in Roll of Honour.)

BOLTON, J., Junr.
WIGLEY, A. S.
TAYLOR, G.
RODGERS, T.
HUTCHINSON, B. B.
ASHTONHURST, G.
HARRISON, W. H.

† Rejected.

Louis Behrens and Sons.
(See p. 454 in Roll of Honour.)

BIRD, G. G.
LONG, E.
BROWN, W.
COOPER, J.
MILBURN, A.
HESKETH, J.
HALL, P.
HEWITT, S.
HANDLEY, H.

S. L. Behrens (Manchester), Limited.
(See p. 660 in Roll of Honour.)

WARDLE, R.
GASKILL, S.
HOLFORD, J.
WRIGHT, F.
TAYLOR, S.
ALLEN, H.
SUNDERLAND, A.

J. and W. Bellhouse, Ltd.
(See p. 661 in Roll of Honour.)

(City Road.)

REYNOLDS, H.
EASTHOPE, J. H.
JACKSON, A. E.
LYON, J.
KENNEDY, C.
LYNCH, W. J.
FROST, T.
LEES, R.
WILLIAMSON, J.
BENNETT, W.
GAFFNEY, T.

(Miles Platting.)

CARR, J.
HILLMAN, W.
GREENLEES, C.
LYDAN, W. G.
OGLE, P. L.
SPARROW, J.
CRELLIN, G.
MEADOWCROFT, F.
TRANTER, R.
LILLEY, R.
GILBERT, E.
GORMAN, J.
YOUNG, F.
PILLING, R.

S. and W. Berisford, Ltd.
(See p. 455 in Roll of Honour.)

BERISFORD, S. R.
BERISFORD, H.
†HILTON, L.
BRIGGS, J.
JEPHSON, A.
†GORNALL, J. F.
CODDINGTON, H.
NEEDLE, H.
GILBERT, J. F.
RUTTER, J.
CHADWICK, J.
MOORES, J.
ASPINALL, J.
†STANLEY, R.
†MAWDSLEY, T.
†GRIFFITHS, S.
McBRIDE, H.
SIDDALL, J.
SMITH, H.
JACKSON, F.
MYERS, F.
NICHOLLS, W.
NIELD, H.
ISHERWOOD, J.
BROWN, J.
†PLATT, N.
†ANDERSON, F.
†BROWN, G.
CRANFIELD, J. F.

C. Binks, Ltd.
(See p. 662 in Roll of Honour.)

BINKS, C. L.
WARD, A. C.
TOWNSEND, S. R.
COTTOM, T.
STAITE, A. R.
ANDERTON, W.
FOSTER, A.
HERON, J. R.
NIELD, C.
LEWIS, J. W.
TOWNSON, F.
KING, D.

Blakeley and Beving, Limited.
(See p. 663 in Roll of Honour.)

BEVING, C. A.
ASHTON, A. E.
BROOME, A.
CARRINGTON, A.
DEARDEN, J.
DUFF, A.
ESHBORN, C.
FRANCIS, J.
GILL, A.
JONES, G.
JONES, W. H.
OLEY, A.
POWNAL, E.
ROUTLEDGE, J.
ROWLANDS, J.
SMITH, F. S.

S. D. Bles and Sons.
(See p. 424 in Roll of Honour.)

†ASHTON, T.
‡BANKS, I.
BAUM, F. P.
†BINKS, I.
†CRITCHLEY, S.
DOWSON, F.
ETTENFIELD, W.
HOMER, C.
‖HORBURY, E.
†HUNT, J.
*HURD, G.
†ISHERWOOD, W.
MACKIE, W.
McGILLIVRAY, J.
‖MORRIS, W. A.
NUTTALL, J. R.
PARRY, A.
TODD, W. H.

Isaac Bury Ltd.
(See p. 668 in Roll of Honour.)

ASPRAY, J.
ALLEN, J.
BIRD, J.
BARROW, J.
BARNES, T.
CROOK, J.
DEVENPORT, W.
HOOPER, A.
HARWOOD, W.
HANNAH, A.
HAMPSON, J.
KEEFE, A.
LEACH, T.
MOULDING, J. T.
MAGOWAN, G. H.
MORETON, G.
MARSDEN, H.
PRIOR, T.
OLDHAM, R. G.
PETERS, J.
POLLITT, F. T.
POWELL, A.
ROSE, T.
REDFORD, J. T.
STUBBS, J.
SLEGG, F.
TURNER, S.
TOMLINSON, H.
TURNER, J.
WALKER, G.
WRIGHT, E.
WOODHOUSE, R.
WHITE, J.

* Serving with the Colours. † Rejected.
‡ Accepted for Home Service.
‖ Temporarily medically unfit.

The Bradford Dyers' Association, Ltd.
(See p. 425 in Roll of Honour.)

Head Office.

AIREY, E. R.
BEACH. R. H.
STEAD, H. S.
MANN, H. W.
KENDALL, F.
SHAW, E. W.
BROOK, G.
BOOTH, J. H.
BLAMIRES, H.
WOOD, H.
CHAMBERS, L. B.
THORNTON, G. S.
FORSYTH, F. C.
EVANS, H. L.
HODGSON, A.
ROSE, C. J.
AKEROYD, F. P.
JOWETT, A.
SIDDONS, R. B.
MARTINDALE, H.
DUNNINGTON, J. E.
FOSTER, J. W.
FEATHER, T.
HUGHES, P. E.
SHAW, J. G.
HANSON, M. E.
EWING, J.
DUNN, H.
ROOLEY, A. J.
ELLIS, A.
GRAHAM, C.
BUTTERCASE, T. D.
FLEMING, S.
REID, F. A.
WELCH, W.
FLETCHER, J.
SMITH, H. B.
BOLGER, M. J.
TORDOFF, S.
BAXTER, E.
HASLAM, G. S.
LAW, W.
CARTER, C.
RIPLEY, A.
HARDIE, J. A.
EVANS, D.
RAPER, W.
JACKSON, H.
HARTLEY, W.
ROBERTS, A.
DEWHIRST, H. R.
DARNBOROUGH, L.

Making-up Department.

PHILLIPS, A.
MOORHOUSE, A.
GAUNT, J.
MAXFIELD, J.
BRAITHWAITE, J.
QUIGLEY, T.
SCHOFIELD, W.
SCHOFIELD, C. W.
MITCHELL, J.

Central Workshop.

SHACKLETON, F.
AYRE, E. H.
DIXON, G. F.
FIRTH, A.
THEAKSTON, J.
BROADLEY, W.
GLOVER, F.
BEDFORD, H.
HALEY, H.
MANN, G.
RUSHWORTH, T.
BAINES, F.
LLOYD, F.
WATERHOUSE, T.
AYRE, E. H.

Sub-Station.

RAISTRICH, H.
EMMOTT, C.
AMBLER, H.
ELLIS, A. P.
PENTY, P. W.
RHODES, F.
HIRD, J. H.
DYER, A.
BARRACLOUGH, H.
DAVIES, S.
MARGETTS, R.
WILSON, W.
HORNER, S. S.
BROAD, F.
ROMAINE, H.

George Armitage, Limited.

ABBOTT, E.
BENTLEY, J. W.
SAXTON, J. J.
KENNEDY, W.
HUDSON, M

PEDDAR, B.
LOCKWOOD, H.
BREWER, G.
MURGATROYD, H.
LAYCOCK, W.
TERRY, J.
THRESH, C. H.
GREEN, W.
BIRKENSHAW, H.
WALLACE, A.
WALKER, J.
FLEMING, P.
HOLLAS, A.
STURDY, T. A.
ATKINSON, J.
MOSS, A.
BLAKEY, G. A.
HILEY, M.
PEARSON, A. C.
MIDGLEY, I.
WILKINSON, E.
WOOLLER, B.
STANSFIELD, W.
MANN, J.
SCARBOROUGH, F. W.
NORTHERN, M.
NICHOLSON, V.
FARRELL, P.
WOODHEAD, A.
ELLERY, B.
TITHERINGTON, J. J.
CULLING, A.
LISTER, H.
ELLIS, C. H.
LOCKWOOD, H.
MURGATROYD, H.
PEDDAR, B.
BREWER, G.
ABBOTT, E.
TERRY, J.

AKROYD, W. E.
BARRACLOUGH, E.
STEAD, J.
WELLS, G.
RILEY, W.
OSWIN, A.
GREAVES, A. W.
HILEY, H.
HILTON, H.
OLDFIELD, E.
CROWTHER, W.
WILSON, A. E.
HALL, C.
WOODHEAD, G. E.
STOTT, H.
HIRST, T.
BARRACLOUGH, F.
SQUIRE, J. H.
NIXON, G. W.

William Aykroyd and Sons, Limited.

SCHULTEN, A. H.
HARTLEY, F.
PRICE, H. H.
HUDSON, W.
McDOWELL, E.
WILKINSON, L.
SMITH, W.
WHITLEY, H.
NEAL, J.
SUNDERLAND, E.
CHADWICK, J.
SKELLY, H.
RAYNER, H.
ATHERTON, A.
WHITLEY, W. H.
LONG, C. A.
BUCK, G.
DUFFEY, E.
HOLMES, W.
WHITEHEAD, J.
MITCHELL, G.
STERLING, J.
ROWNTREE, A.
STEPHENSON, N.
WIDDOP, C. F.
BROSCOMBE, J. W.
HAMILTON, A.
BLAMIRES, W.
DODSWORTH, A.
JOHNSON, L.
NELSON, C.
GOODALL, H.
HOLDEN, T.
PARKER, J. W.
SCOTT, J.
BATTY, H.
SAMPSON, J. T.
SMITH, J.
SIMPSON, A. C.
WADDINGTON, W.
INGHAM, S.
HOLDSWORTH, H.
WOODHEAD, W.
NUTTER, H. N.
ANDREWS, E.
RAMSDEN, W.
FAWCETT, T.
HODGSON, L.
MORRELL, A.
AMBLER, J.
GALLAGHER, H.
KNAPTON, G. F.
EASTWOOD, J.
MASKELL, J.
HEAP, A.
PEARSON, G. F.
PARKER, W. B.
CULL, J.
NICHOL, J.
CRESSWELL, W. F.
DAWSON, H.

The Bradford Dyers' Association, Ltd.—Con.

Ashenhurst Dyeing Company, Limited.

STRETTON, E.
YEWDALE, T. A.
TUPPEAR, P.
YEWDALE, E.
COOPER, W.
YEWDALE, J.
CARTER, T.
WILLIAMS, W. C.
LAMB, J.
BURNS, T.
ARCHER, J.
DUNN, B.
LEWIS, I.
BERRISFORD, H.
COTTRILL, A.
HANDLON, T.
KENYON, G.
SOTHERN, J. T.
SOTHERN, W. T.
CROSSFIELD, F.
ROYLE, J.
CONNOR, J. E.
NEWTON, H.
STANDING, T.
GRINDROD, H.

Aykroyd and Grandage, Limited.

McGEE, J. J.
WALTON, L.
HALEY, F.
TETLAW, J.
WALTON, L.
SPENCER, J.
BRAY, H.
DOLAN, P.
FLETCHER, G. E.
FLETCHER, G.
SILSON, B.
ASPINALL, W.
COCKER, L.
PENNY, J.
HUDSON, L.
ROBERTSHAW, J.
FOSTER, H.
BILBROUGH, W.
McGUINNESS, —
KAYE, W. H.
TORDOFF, S.
GALLAGHER, T.
DAY, J.
INGRAM, A. E.
CLAYTON, T. C.
AYKROYD, J.
JOHNSON, T.
BRIGGS, F.
JENNINGS, C.
BARRACLOUGH, A.
HATFIELD, J.
BLACKWELL, E. N.
HOLMES, A.
ORMONDROYD, J.
RIDDIOUGH, J.
HALEY, D.
RUSHWORTH, A.
DUCKWORTH, M.
PATCHETT, P.
POLLARD, S.
DOBSON, A. E.
WAINWRIGHT, D.
CALVERT, B.
PEEL, J. W.
CHIPPINDALE, W.
BURNS, W.
GOTT, E.
RICHARDSON, J. H.
BOWYER, J.
SINGLETON, C. H.
TURNER, F.
CLAPHAM, M. W.
DUGGAN, J.
JONES, J.
HOPKINSON, J.
SMITH, W.
PAMINGTON, A. E.
BENTLEY, J.
NEWMAN, F.
ROSS, H.
LONGLEY, F.
CRAVEN, E.
NOBLE, A.
ACKROYD, A.
PROCTOR, E.
THOMPSON, H.
DUNWELL, E.
BROADBENT, J.
SHEPHERD, S.
MARSHALL, E.
CHIPPINDALE, E.
FIRTH, J.
BIRKENSHAW, G. F.
EAST, W.
DYER, P.
PAUL, G. E.
ROBINSON, H.
ILLINGWORTH, C.
RILEY, F.
WHEELHOUSE, J.
SCAIFE, H. G.
MORGAN, F.
CAWTHRA, E.
BARR, E.
WHELAN, T.
STEPHENSON, J. T.
KERSHAW, W. H.
BRADBURN, W.
THROP, S.
BROADBENT, E. H.

William Bancroft and Sons, Limited.

FOSTER, A.

John and Henry Bleakley, Limited.

TAIT, L.
BARLOW, T.
PEATFIELD, F. B.
MATHER, H.
HEYWOOD, F.
WOODHOUSE, J.
RALLY, J. E.
CHAPMAN, J.
ASHWORTH, E.
MATHER, E.
HAMPSON, T.
WEBSTER, W.
BROOKS, J.
DONNELLY, H.
RAMSBOTTOM, J.
HARDMAN, J. H.
MATHER, W. H.
HOUGHTON, T.
BOOTH, G. H. D.
OWEN, E.
GILLIBRAND, W.
LORD, F.
DYSON, T.
MATHER, B.
DAWSON, F.
LEES, S.
LEWIS, H.
FLETCHER, A.
PEEL, C.
HEYWOOD, J.
GILLIBRAND, T. H.
HAYES, J. W.
SIMPSON, G.
BARKER, W.
HEYWOOD, F.
DICKINSON, E.
SHARP, J. J.
ASHWORTH, D.
BROOKS, N.

Cawley's (Cleckheaton), Limited.

ILLINGWORTH, F.
BROADBENT, J.
PERRINS, E.
RAMSDEN, H.
WALSH, T.
WAINWRIGHT, E.
CRAWSHAW, G.
ROSS, I.
WOOD, H.
THORPE, E.
HADDON, J.
WOOD, J. H.
WATSON, F.
LIGHTOWLER, W.
HIRST, J.
ORAM, W.
BROOME, J. K.
BRAITHWAITE, W.
NUTTER, W. A.
BARKER, W.
WADSWORTH, J.
SMITH, J.
CRAVEN, R.

Greetland Dyeworks Company, Limited.

TAYLOR, W.
BUNNISS, J.
TAYLOR, H.
HELLIWELL, C.
THOMAS, W. C.
GREEN, H.
HEYS, J. W.
BERRY, H.
RAYNOR, A. R.
SMITH, H.
WHITELEY, J. D.
THOMAS, G. C.
JOHNSON, T. H.
FARNELL, H.
HANSON, W. H.
WRIGGLESWORTH, H.
HOLMES, D.
LAMBERT, C. H.
WILKINSON, F. W.
AKROYD, A. N.
BARRETT, E.
ACKROYD, O.
PARR, E.
HORNER, H.
HODGSON, A.
FOX, G. A.
DYSON, F.
McCULLOCK, M.
HIGGINS, G. W.
MONAQUE, T.
HARE, T. P.
GORDON, J.
BARNETT, J. A. D.
HAMER, J. F.
WOOD, W.
BARRON, R.
TAYLOR, B.
SCOTT, J. W.
TURNER, J.
FIELDING, F.
SMITH, W. H.
DIXON, J.
KAYE, F.
SENIOR, W.

The Bradford Dyers' Association, Ltd.—Con.

F. Cawley and Company, Limited.

ROSTRON, R.
RIGBY, H.
COLLINGE, A. E.
COSGROVE, W.
BALL, W.
SHORE, H.
ELSON, A.
GRESTY, H. H
GORDON, C.
PICKFORD, H.
ADAMS, W. H.
HESKETH, W. H.
BUTTERWORTH, J.
GRESTY, W.
CRETNEY, E. F.
PERKINS, G.
COOK, J. E.
WHITELL, C. R.
HOWARTH, J.
ORMSON, T.
HESKETH, T.
WARREN, E.
WILSON, G.
FARNWORTH, P.
CROSSLEY, J.
TRESADERN, J.
KAY, J.
BERRY, T.
AINSWORTH, J.

Craven, Pearson and Company, Limited.

BARSTOW, R.
WATSON, T.
NETTLESHIP, E.
DRAKE, L.
RUDDY, W.
GRAYSON, C. T.
WALSH, J.
LEE, J.
ELLIS, S. M.
CLAY, L.
DRAKE, W.
SAUNDERS, K.
HAIGH, L. J.
TYAS, J. E.
HODGSON, H.
WILKINSON, T.
FAWCETT, R.
BROWN, W.
TURNER, A. E.
BAIRSTOW, J. C.
KAYE, N.
DRAKE, L.
WATSON, T. W.

"Cravenette" Company, Limited.

WINDSOR, A. E.
CRABTREE
ROBINSON, C.
GREENWOOD, F.
WAITE, J.
NICHOL, F.
SMITH, D.
PRIESTLEY, K.
SHARMAN, W.
PARRY, J.
BRAY, J. E
DUNWELL, J. S.
REDFEARN, F.
TAYLOR, J.
HESLING, J.
COCKROFT, H. F.
MURBY, B.
FIRTH, L.
STEPHENSON, E.
TURNER, H.
PICKARD, A.
RUSHWORTH, R.
MORRIS, W.
JACQUES, H.
SMITH, S.
BAINES, A.

William Grandage and Company, Limited.

IRVIN, J. M.
FEATHER, G. H.
ABBOT, S.
HOLMES, F.
SHEARER, H. N.
WIDDOP, P.
HADDOCK, H.
LANCASTER, W.
ROBINSON, H.
MORRISON, J. B.
WHITELEY, F.
LEACH, E. D.
BARTON, J.
ROBERTSHAW, H.
HARVEY, C.
KENDRICK, O.
COCKSHOT, F.
BULLOCK, W.
HARDY, T.
HARTLEY, G.
TURNER, F.
CUSACK, T. F.
BIRTWISTLE, J. F.
HELLIWELL, S.
HARRISON, B.
REVILL, F. R.
HOWARD, H.
BENTLEY, A.
NICHOLLS, H.
GODWARD, A.
STURGESS, C.
STOTT, A.
YEOMAN, F.
PARKER, A.
ARCHER, F.
BRAYSHAW, J. B.
BOOTH, F.
HARDAKER, H.
CLARK, S.
WILLIAMSON, S.
JENNINGS, W.
LIVSEY, E.
KERSHAW, W.
WILSON, J.
BLAND, C.
KAY, E.
BAXTER, W.
CARR, J.
FAIRS, A. H.
HOLDSWORTH, A.
LEATHLEY, R.
AIREY, T.
BLACKMORE, W.
SMITH, J.
BLACKBURN, W.
MAY, H.

Greenbottom Dyeing Company, Limited.

LAW, W.
YEADON, J.
RAWNSLEY, B. A.
STEPHENSON, C.
HART, J. C.
CLARKE, H.
SUNDERLAND, G.
FLETCHER, H.
CROWTHER, J. M.
HOLLINGS, G.
WORMALD, W.
BRIGGS, W.
ARMITAGE, H.
LUPTON, G.
HINCHCLIFFE, R. H.
ARMITAGE, J. W
STEEL, A.
WATSON, W.
YEADON, J. T.
ABBOTT, J. W.
MARSHALL, R.
ROSS, J. N.
BOULTON, G. A.
ROBSON, G.
CHIPPINDALE, A. O.
POPPLEWELL, W.
LAYCOCK, J. W.
LEE, G.

Halifax Dyeworks Company, Limited.

WIGGLESWORTH, F.
HEAP, M.
ROEBUCK, J.
GREENWOOD, A. J.
WOODHEAD, J. E.
FOX, N.
PITTS, H.
SCOTT, R.
STOTT, V.
ACKROYD, H.
BINNS, E.
HARVEY, S.
BROOK, C. E.
MALLINSON, J.
WARNER, D.
WHITE, H.
HOWARD, G. F.
WIDDOP, H.
FOX, C.
PATTINSON, C.
STOTT, J. W.
CLARKE, G. L.
NICHOLL, G. M.
HELPS, F.
WARNER, G.
BROOKE, A.
HALLSWORTH, H.
OATES, J.
DIXON, W.
MIDGLEY, E. A.
WARNER, C.
TAYLOR, E.
GEORGESON, F.
CLEGG, E.
HELLIWELL, J.
SMITH, F.
BOTTOMLEY, J. W.
HELLIWELL, R.
KAY, H.
LUMB, F.
HOYLE, A.
SENIOR, G.
HOYLE, R. J.
BROOKSBANK, E.
SIMPSON, S.
EASTWOOD, T. H.
HALEY, W.
HOLROYD, G.
BINNS, E.

The Bradford Dyers' Association, Ltd.—Con.

Adam Hamilton and Sons, Limited.

FERGUSON, A.
CONVERY, J.
DOCHARTY, J.
FISHER, A.
DICKSON, W.
BROWN, T. J.
DUNSMORE, D.
GILLESPIE, W.
BROWN, D.
SCOTT, H.
CARSE, W.
GARVIN, W.
McLACHLAN, J.
HENDERSON, D.
HANSON, F.
DEVENEY, J.
SMITH, W.
FOSTER, R. D.
STEVENSON, D.
CONNELL, W.
FERGUSON, H.
DUNLOP, R. A.
GIBSON, M.
HUNTER, W.
BLYTH, J.
PATERSON, J.

Hunsworth Dyeing Company, Limited.

RUSHTON, L.
BENTLEY, A.
WILSON, H.
THOMPSON, A.
GARBUTT, E. P.
GARSIDE, H.
POLLARD, F.
WESTERMAN, D.
CROWTHER, H.
ROBERTSHAW, S.
BENNETT, J.
GAULKROGER, W.
BILSBOROUGH, T.
SYKES, H.
CLOUGH, R.
BENN, J.
BASHFORTH, G. E.
HUTCHINSON, H.
SHAW, F.
WALSHAW, A.
BATEMAN, A.
HARRISON, S.
HANSON, F.
HOLDSWORTH, W.
RILEY, W.
BROADLEY, A.
HOLT, J.
MACHELL, H.
WOODHEAD, J. W.
NAYLOR, W. H.
KELSALL, E.
PICKLES, H.
McMORGAN, C.
GREEN, W. H.
BOTTOMLEY, W.
HIRST, E.
HOLMES, F.
COCKETT, A.
TAYLOR, W.
CARTER, F.
BOOTHAM, E.
COLBERT, J. R.
BECK, A.
DAWSON, J. W.
BROOK, J.
SHARP, W.
BELLFIELD, H.
GLENTON, T.
GREEN, R.
WADSWORTH, J. W.
HAIGH, T.
ACKROYD, W.
WRIGHT, T.
FLETCHER, E. C.

H. Kershaw and Son, Limited.

BAGNALL, A.
KNOTT, W. F.
ALPIN, C.
SIDDALL, J.
MOSTYN, A.
CARTRIDGE, A.
SHERRATT, H.
FISHER, G.
COATES, H.
LEE, P.
MILLARD, J.
STAFFORD, C.
WOOD, G.
McKEEVER, L.
BRADBURY, A.
STRETCH, J.
BATTERSBY, A.
BAILEY, E.
JONES, W.
HILTON, N.
SHEENE, T.
RILEY, W.
PRICE, W.
BALMFORTH, F.
HEYWOOD, F.
WRIGLEY, J. H.
WORTHINGTON, R.
MURPHY, G.
WALL, E.
GILL, F. F.
MULVEY, J.
LOMAS, E.
SELLARS, J.
LEE, T.
MILLER, F.
BUCKLEY, W.
SILVESTER, P.
JACKSON, C.
LLOYD, W. H.
JOHNS, J.
HARDWICK, A. G.
PARKINSON, H.
WROE, H.
SEDDON, W.
WAIN, W.

Samuel Kirk and Sons, Limited.

INGHAM, A.
HIGGINS, W.
MURRILL, A.
KROPFF, E.
LONSDALE, A.
JOHNSON, H. F.
MARSHALL, A.
HARDAKER, M.
WAITE, J.
BRITTON, P.
MARSHALL, J.
WILSON, W.
AUDSLEY, J.
WOODHEAD, C.
BANNISTER, W.
ROMAYNE, A.
ATKINSON, C. R.
HALTON, A.

Lingfield Dyeing Company, Limited.

STEPHENSON, W.
SLATER, H.
KAY, R.
GOLDTHORPE, A.
HACKEN, H.
MAWSON, H.
EDWARDS, H.
JACKMAN, J. T.
WORSNOP, O.
SHARP, H.
DAVY, G.
TUNNICLIFFE, F.
THACKRAY, F.
CARR, W.
CARTLEDGE, J.
THORNTON, A.
GALLOWAY, J.
PRIESTLEY, E.
WALKER, R.
MURGATROYD, H.
SIMPSON, A.

Norcroft Dyeing Company, Limited.

BIRKENSHAW, N.
MIDGLEY, T.
LEACH, H.
TRETT, A.
BENNETT, T.
YEWDALL, W.
KENDALL, G. W.
COOKE, W.
CHAMBERS, W.
COWBURN, R.
LEE, A.
WILKINSON, R.
BOOTH, J.
FLEMING, G.
INGHAM, E.
GOTT, H.
BATES, H.
GARLICK, J.
BEESLEY, W.
GRIFFIN, A.
SUTCLIFFE, A.
MACKRILL, J.
ROBERTSHAW, J. W.
RHODES, W. H.
RHODES, S.
SPURR, T.
BLAGBOROUGH, H.
NEWSOME, F.
SCHOFIELD, F.
SWIFT, E.
DODSON, J. B.
HOLDSWORTH, A. C.
DALBY, R.
FIRTH, R.
BARRETT, J. A.
HEATHCOTE, H. J.
PRATT, E.
TOPHAM, C.
DOBSON, H.
HEELEY, F.
HOLGATE, T.
HOWARD, E.
RAMSDEN, S.
HOYLE, F.
HARBISHER, W.
GILL, H.

The Bradford Dyers' Association, Ltd.—Con.

Robert Peel and Company, Limited.

THORNE, H.
NEALON, M.
BURDAKY, W. H., Junr.
HARRISON, W., Junr.
BROWN, F.
BELLERBY, C. H.
JEFFS, C. H.
CARROL, C.
THORPE, J. L.
BUTTERWORTH, J.
ROUTLEDGE, J.
CRITCHLEY, R.
TATTERSALL, E. S.
HALL, H.
BEECH, W. H.
HARDMAN, N.
WILLIAM, G. S.
HOLLAND, W.
KENDRICK, T.
SMITH, J.
GRINSHAW, G.
SMETHURST, P. L.
TAYLOR, E.
WORTHINGTON, F.
SWINDELLS, T.
GILLIBRAND, J.
COWLISHAW, D.
CROSS, J.
CROSSLEY, J.
RILEY, R.
MILLARD, N. S.
MURPHY, T.
COWLISHAW, W. E.
MILLIGAN, J.
LARGE, J.
BARTLETT, J.
ROBINSON, J.
BRIERLEY, J.
MYCOCK, G. D.
TISSINGTON, T.
BARTRAM, W.
ROYLE, J. K.

Edward Ripley and Son, Limited (West).

BENNETT, H.
HOLT, W.
CARR, A. E.
COULTER, N.
REED, E.
STEVENSON, F.
HUDSON, J.
WADDINGTON, F.
WINDER, H.
RUSHWORTH, J. W.
PRICE, C.
REYNOLDS, E.
BARKER, F.
GEE, F.
SEED, M.
WESTMAN, H.
WEATHERHILL, H.
PRICE, J.
BENNETT, H.
SMITH, A.
THRETWAY, C.
BIRKBY, A.
FENTON, N.
CORDINGLEY, W.
SHAW, H.
HOGG, J.
SMITH, T.
KIDD, R.
JENNINGS, S.
NELSON, G. W. (HOWARD.)
RAISTRICK, F.
TURNER, W.
WILKS, A.
HUDSON, L.
WRIGHT, D.
WORSMAN, T.
WILLCOCK, A.
SUGDEN, F.
BENTLEY, I.
COULTER, A.
PICKLES, F.
MYERS, W.
THORPE, H.
BENN, A.
CROWTHER, C.
WATSON, L.
HOGG, E.
BEEVERS, S.
HAILK, J.
BROWN, W. A.
QUAYLE, W.
SHARP, S.
HILLAM, H.
ROGERS, B.
CLAYTON, F.
SMITHIES, W.
TORDOFF, H.
BURNLEY, J. W.
MORTON, J. T.
HARRISON, H.
TAYLOR, L.
POPPLEWELL, J.
WOOD, J. W.
WILSON, H.
WILSON, A.
WALKER, A.
CLAYTON, E.
GREENWOOD, A.
PHELPS, A.
DENNISON, A. H.
SENIOR, J. A.
MALLINSON, A.
ELLISON, T.
JENNINGS, S.
SPURR, E. J.
WRAGG, T.
WRIGHT, C.
AUSTICK, H.
AMBLER, A.
WILKINSON, S.
FINCH, J.
WROE, T.
WOODCOCK, H.
WHITE, W.
ALFRED, H.
NEWBY, J.
LOCKWOOD, W.
BELLFIELD, F.
RYAN, T.
BROWN, J.
LEEMING, G.
BARKER, E.
NORTHIN, B.
LAMBERT, J.
ROLLINSON, A.
HAINSWORTH, S. W.
LEE, F.
KERWIN, W.
JACKSON, F.
HINDLE, J.

Edward Ripley and Son, Limited (East).

SMITH, S.
HILL, A.
HARRISON, J. M.
BOLTON, M.
HEATON, E.
SENIOR, H.
CONLEY, F.
RICHARDS, H.
COOPER, D.
WOODRUFF, W.
WORMALD, F.
JAGGER, F.
STEWART, D.
BATES, C.
LUPTON, J.
PEARSON, W.
HOWITSON, O.
BARRETT, J.
NORTHIN, V.
PRIESTLEY, W.
MONAGHAN, P.
SHARP, C.
FLATT, G.
MELVILLE, S.
HOLDSWORTH, J. H.
STOTT, A.
NAYLOR, F.
PARKIN, W.
HOPKINSON, G.
GREEN, E.
WRIGHT, H.
CHAPMAN, W.
GILL, S.
STONES, H.
HENEGAN, J.
HARRISON, F.
BELL, S. E.
HANSON, D.
THOMPSON, G. H.
SHARPE, J.
LUND, J.
LONGHORN, R.
BATEMAN, L.
SHEPHERD, A.
PRIESTLEY, H.
LEACH, H.
OLDFIELD, J. W.
HARTLEY, R.
ACKROYD, W.
BROADBENT, F.
HELM, L.
TAYLOR, F. H.
HEAVSIDES, F.
PETTY, H. F.
STANLEY, J.
BOTTOMLEY, T.
LANCASTER, F. S.
HOLMES, B.
THORLEY, G. A.
DOBBY, A.
MITCHELL, H. H.
MUFF, J. H.
PADGETT, W.
METCALF, T.
GIBSON, L.
BARKER, H.
PARKER, J.
KELLETT, W.
HUDSON, J. W.
HAINSWORTH, H.
SIMPSON, E.
INESON, C.
BEANLAND, J.
LODGE, J. A.
STOBATTS, H.
PEARSON, H.
HOLMES, H.
GIBSON, C.
DARBY, F.
CLARKSON, S.
BOOTH, G. W.
SHARP, S.
WINTERBURN, W.
SUGDEN, H.
PRATT, A.
MAUD, E.
WALLACE, T.
HOLROYD, S.
FLATHER, S.
HEPWORTH, J.
ANTCLIFFE, A.
INESON, T. H.
HARRISON, J.
SCOTT, T.
STOCKS, B. H.
TAYLOR, C.
CRABTREE, A.
MIDDLETON, H.
SUNDERLAND, F.
STANSFIELD, T.
DIXON, B.
PARKER, F.
BENNETT, E. E.
LIGHTOWLER, J. W.
BLYTHE, T.
WALTON, F.

The Bradford Dyers' Association, Ltd.—Con.

PARKER, J. R.
ARNETT, W.
ALDERSON, J.
BRIGGS, F.
BENNETT, W.
ODDY, J.
PERIGS, M.
RILEY, B.
CROSSLAND, H.
KIPLING, T.
ILLINGWORTH, B.
NICHOLS, F.
NICHOLS, F.
ANDREWS, J.
MARFLEET, F.
HAIGH, H.
OLIVER, E.
AMBLER, J.
LYONS, T.
BLAND, H.
FAWCETT, G.
WHITAKER, C.
FASHLEY, F. L.
COTTINGHAM, A. S.
FLESHER, H.
WOOD, H.
APPLEYARD, C.
COLBERT, A.
MORRELL, T. F.
LOBLEY, I. S. W.
DOBSWORTH, J.
BASSETT, R.
PENSHION, J.
SHAW, J. D.
CARR, J. W.
REDFEARN, F.
SIMPSON, A.
COE, F.
LUDLAM, E.
GILL, W.
WILKINSON, A.
WHONE, W.
BOYES, S.
RILEY, F.
ARMITAGE, H.
DARBY, J.
BARRETT, W.
STEVENSON, F.
WILSON, V.
YORKE, G. A.
SUTCLIFFE, H.
BARRETT, F.
STOW, T.
GORELL, R.
SHAW, G.
TOMLINSON, A.
GORMAN, M.
PRIESTLEY, S.
HILLAS, W.
TANE, J. W.
PARKER, A.
KING, L.
HALL, H.
NELSON, J. H.
HANSON, T.
MALLOW, J.
BROOKE, J.
BARKER, H.
CROWTHER, D. C.
NAYLOR, C. D.
WOODHEAD, F.
WILKINSON, S.
RADFORD, J. H.
BROOK, A. W.

T. Robinson and Company, Limited.

HORROCKS, J.
BUTTON, J.
CANDLER, J. H.
DUCKWORTH, J.
HODKINSON, F.
ROTHWELL, G. A.
KNOWLES, J.
FRENCH, T.
MASON, G.
HINDLE, R.
TAYLOR, H.
BARNES, F.
CLOUGH, W.
KAY, J.
KAY, A.
HAYHURST, J.
HASLAM, W.
DUNN, J.
CHATTWOOD, S.
DAVIS, L.
HOLDEN, W.
LOMAX, J.
HAWORTH, F.
MORRIS, M.
WILKINSON, H.
DENTON, R.
EWING, T. C.
EMMETT, J. L.
HOUSE, I.
BIRCH, S.
DUNN, J.
MORTON, F.
WALKER, H.
FAIRCLOUGH, J.
WILD, N.
CAMPBELL, J.
SNOWDEN, C.
ISHERWOOD, J.
AINSWORTH, R.
TAYLOR, A.
NUTTALL, H.
KENYON, F. L.
THOMAS, P.
EVANS, E.
BAILEY, J.
JOHNSON, H.
EWING, A.
NEWTON, J.
SMITH, W.
BUCKLEY, W.
STARKEY, W.
LEGGE, M. W.
BARLOW, H.
KENYON, F.
HOLDEN, J. K.
BEARD, P. W.
SAVIN, J. R.
ASPIN, J. W.
HUNT, E.

James and M. S. Sharpe and Company, Limited.

HOLLIS, G.
PROSSER, J. W.
BOOTH, W.
JONES, W.
HOOD, W.
EMMETT, N.
BOYES, F.
HODGSON, C.
BUTTERWORTH, J.
MARSH, A.
WILKINSON, J. W.
WATSON, L.
BARKER, F.
PARKINSON, H.
TERRY, L.
OWEN, S.
HOLMES, L.
KELLETT, H.
FARRER, G. W.
SMITH, H.
KING, J. H.
HOLDSWORTH, W.
ELLIS, W.
BROOK, L.
McVAN, G.
FIRTH, H.
BARBER, F.
JACKSON, B.
PEARSON, H.
TAYLOR, S.
KAYE, F.
WESTERMAN, A.
STEINTHORPE, J.
WORMALD, H.
BRAHEN, J.
PINFIELD, E.
SCOTT, A.
HOPPER, E.
BAXTER, H.
HARRISON, V.
TAYLOR, J.
BEST, F.
WHITE, R. Y.
SCHOFIELD, J. C.
HOYLE, J.
LIGHTOWLERS, F.
WOOD, F.
DALBY, H.
HARLOW, E.
REYNOLDS, H.
PRIESTLEY, G.
COLLINSON, R.
SHARP, H.
SPEIGHT, C. H.
BUTTERWORTH, J.
SHARP, M.
HORNER, A.
STEAD, W.
BELL, G. A.
WATSON, H.
SUTCLIFFE, L.
BROCKHAM, G. D.
JAGGER, A.
BAKES, A.
JAGGER, J. E.
INGHAM, H.
KERSHAW, H.
TOWNEND, H. G.
WOOD, E. C.
HOLT, C.
SENIOR, P.
STOCKS, G.
FLINT, J.
WILSON, J.
PORRITT, G. H.
THORNTON, W.
MICHELL, G. W.
WHITTINGHAM, J. W.
INGHAM, W.
HAIGH, G.
COLLINS, F.
SUCKSMITH, P.
FAWTHROP, L.
BARLOW, F.
PORTER, G.
HOLDSWORTH, J. T.
HOYLE, E.
ICKE, E.
AINSWORTH, N.
HOLROYD, E.
JEWITT, A.
BARRACLOUGH, J.
GREENOUGH, J.
PEARSON, W.
BROOMHEAD, F.
JACKSON, W.
LEE, F.
BENTLEY, F.
CHARNOCK, H.
LIGHTOWLERS, A.
JACKSON, J.
SHAW, C.
LOCKWOOD, F.
JEFF, H.
BARRACLOUGH, D. E.
ROBINSON, W.
HIRST, G.
ROBERTS, A.
BUCKLEY, H. L.
MALLIN, J. H.
SMITH, M.
INGHAM, D.
HILL, J.
AYKROYD, S. W.
PRESTON, S.
WHITEHEAD, J. W.
CLIFF, W. H.
STOTT, F.
TAYLOR, W. J.
FOX, A. E.

The Bradford Dyers' Association, Ltd.—Con.

Shaw and Company (Shipley), Limited.

CONSTANTINE, B.
DRAKE, J.
FORREST, J.
KITSON, W. H.
SMITH, A.
BRANNAN, H.
RHODES, E.
SMITH, L.
BROWN, H.
MITTON, A.
ROPER, H.
PERRIN, W.
KENDALL, F.
GORELL, W.
HILL, A.
BUTLIN, P.
STEPHENSON, W.
CLOW, W.
HATTON, J. H.
GRIEVE, W.
POWELL, W.
THOMPSON, F.
JUDSON, W. E.
PROCTOR, J.
TOWNEND, A.
SIMMS, J.
BAILEY, F.
WOOD, C.
ROSS, G.
FURNESS, H.
THOMAS, J. J.
DICKERSON, W.
KENDALL, H.
MULLANEY, R.
WAITE, A.
OVERING, H.
COOPER, F. W.
BANNISTER, F.
LIGHTOWLER, H.
WEST, G.
HOLROYD, C.
WALKER, F.
MITCHELL, F.
DYSON, W. T.

John Shaw and Company, Limited.

HARTLEY, A.
SILSON, E.
PORTER, P.
SENIOR, J.
SHAW, A.
GIBSON, W.
MORAN, W.
STEWARD, H.
BARRACLOUGH, R.
TRAINOR, A. F.
MASON, C. G.
HARRISON, J. T.
BENISTONE, J. A.
THORNTON, A.
HILL, W.
SIDES, A.
THOMPSON, H.
KELLETT, H.
JOWETT, H.
CARTER, J.
MARSDEN, E.
DICKINSON, F.
HORNER, A.
SHARP, J. W.
OLDROYD, E. H.
LIGHTOWLER, F.
ANDERSON, E.
BATESON, A.
ILLINGWORTH W.
CHAPMAN, J.
CARROL, J.
SUGDEN, C.
DICKINSON, W.
PHILLIP, W.

Samuel Smith and Company, Limited.

EMSLEY, J.
THOMPSON, F.
SOOTHILL, F.
ROBERTS, J.
MACAULAY, A.
PARKER, S.
KITSON, R.
WINNETT, A.

The Standish Company, Limited.

URMSTON, N.
WORSLEY, J.
NORRID, J. H.
NORRIS, S.
MOSS, J.
NORIS, E., Jun.
BIBBY, J. E.
ASHCROFT, T.
BIGGINS, J.
PARKER, J.
WHITE, C.
MASON, G. H.
DEAN, H. A.
TAYLOR, W.
WOODHOUSE, C. E.
NORRIS, E. H.
MAKINSON, S., Jnr.
MARTINDALE, W.
HOCKING, B.
HANSON, W.
MASON, W. H.
HAYES, F.
ECCLESTON, J.
ALKER, F.
MacGRATH, J.
PITTS, W.
BENTHAM, B.
YATES, F.
PRESTON, J.
ROSCOE, J.
ASHCROFT, R.
HITCHEN, W.
HOLLAND, V.
YATES, E.
RIGBY, W. H.
MURRAY, A.
CARRINGTON, G.
OLLERTON, W. J.
COMPTON, F.
GREGORY, G. T.
McCARTNEY, W. J.
BARTON, W.
ROPER, A.
MEAKIN, S.
DARBYSHIRE, E.
WHITE, H.
BROOKS, R.
BLACKBURN, J.
MULDOON, J.
ARLINE, J. McF.
HEAP, J.
WHITTAKER, A.
JONES, J. B.
DARBYSHIRE, W.
LAIRD, R.
DARBYSHIRE, W. H.
BALL, E.
SNAPE, W.
LEIGH, R.
MADDISON, G. W.
FISHER, J.
ARMER, W.
FORSTER, J.
SUTTON, H. B.
GREGORY, W.
LATHAM, R.
HUXLEY, J. H.
RAWLINSON, J.
HAZELDINE, W. H.
CROOK, A.
JEFFREY, J.
MAKINSON, J.
COWARD, S.
MAKINSON, S. R.
LOXHAM, J.
COUSINE, F.
SMITH, M.
BIBBY, J.
BOARDMAN, E.
COLE, W.
GOODWIN, J., Jnr.
RATCLIFFE, J.
MOLYNEAUX, J.
AUSTIN, W. E.
CHARNOCK, H.
HOCKING, H.
MULSE, J.
HAYES, T. J.
LIPTROT, J.
DICKINSON, T.
CARRINGON, T.
WHITE, A. E.
SCHOFIELD, W.
HOCKING, A. E.
LOWE, F. W.
SMITH, A.
WILSON, J. W.
MURRAY, A.
WHALLEY, J.
ARSTALL, W.
HEATON, I.
MAIDEN, G.
DOUTHWAITE, G.
KING, J.
GRIMSHAW, J.
SHARP, M.
KELLY, J.
CLARKE, W. H.
VALENTINE, J.
HALLIWELL, R.
MOSS, J. H.
ACTON, H. S.
BARTON, J. T.
FADDEN, P.
MAIDEN, F. O.
ROSTRON, J.
BOOTH, J.
ROPER, J.
SHARROCK, W. T.
BIBBY, E.
BURTON, R. M. W.
LAVIN, J.
WYATT, H.
MOORE, H.
CALDWELL, F.
MALYNEAUX, G.
SHERIFF, D.
OVERTON, T.
YAPP, A.
OLLERTON, W. H.
WHITTLE, T.
WESTHEAD, W.
BALL, J.
BALL, E.
McFARLIN, J.

Stockbridge Finishing Company, Limited.

PRIESTLEY, A. J.
JACKSON, J.
WILKINSON, H., Junr.
WOOD, H. J.
NAYLOR, S.
RAINFORD, H.
ORTON, A.
KNOWLES, A. H.
RAINFORD, A.
CONROY, H.
WINDER, A.
NAYLOR, H.
JACKSON, J.
GLEDHILL, D.
BATTYE, J. W.
BURGESS, A.
ACKROYD, J. W.

The Bradford Dyers' Association, Ltd.—Con.

Stockbridge Finishing Company, Limited.

EARNSHAW, W.
WILSON, H.
WINDLE, J.
MOORE, A.
BROOKE, H.
WILKINSON, S. A.
LAMBERT, A.
BECK, J.
CLARKE, P.
CLARKE, J. W.
MASON, T.
BELL, M.
DRIVER, G.
SYKES, E. R.
DRIVER, J. H.
CLARKE, J.
LEACH, T.
CLOUGH, H.
SEXTON, T.
JARMAN, A. E.
HAIGH, E.
BECK, J.
EVERETT, G.
TETLEY, P.
BLAKEY, H.
HEPWORTH, A.
CLARKE, W.
RUSHWORTH, H. H.
CUTTER, H.
SLATER, E.
FAKY, W.
DAWSON, H. W.
LIVERSEDGE, A.

Thornton, Hannam and Marshall, Limited.

PADGETT, E. M.
RAMSDEN, W.
MARSDEN, N.
DOBSON, E.
HEATH, J. H.
THORNTON, J.
BRIER, E.
KEAR, A. C.
DYSON, J. E.
BATES, H.
GREEN, E.
FIRTH, W.
BRIGGS, W.
SMITH, T.
MALTBY, H. C.
CLIFFE, H. E.
RUSHTON, S.
SLACK, N.
RUSHWORTH, I.
SUCKSMITH, W.
BINNS, S.
HOWE, W.
LONGBOTTOM, F.
BROWN, J. W.
STUART, C.
DEIGHTON, S.
FIRTH, A.
DOYLE, W.
WOOD, R. J.
BROOK, A.
MARSDEN, J.
FARRER, G.
RUSHWORTH, T.
FOSTER, P.
SKITMORE, J.
PARKER, W. M.
SHEPHERD, A.
KELLETT, I.
JAGGER, J. A.
MALTBY, P.
THORNTON, J.
BENSON, A.
WILKINSON, C.
BYROM, R. R.
SUGDEN, J. W.
HADFIELD, T.
HOUGH, G.
HADFIELD, B.
DEACON, W.
WHITELEY, E. N.
SIDDONS, W. S.
THOMPSON, J. E.
SCRIVEN, A.
SHAW, A.
RICHMOND, M.
FOX, Y. T.
SPENCER, W. K.
MONKMAN, H.
STOCKS, J.
DAWSON, C.
CLEGG, E.
SUTCLIFFE, H.
COCKROFT, S.
CLAY, A.
SUTCLIFFE, H.
KELLETT, C.
PRIESTLEY, L.
CROWTHER, J.
BARBER, H.
COCKROFT, F.
ATKINSON, F.
LEE, H.
GOODISON, S.
CLEGG, J.
WHITEHEAD, J.
STRINGER, T.
SLATER, E.
HAMER, F.
LUMB, D.
THOMAS, A.
BAYLIFFE, H.
DENHAM, W.
WILKINSON, A.
BROOK, H.
EAGLING, G.
HODGSON, C. W.
LIGHTOWLER, I.
LEIGHTON, J.
HADFIELD, A.
SCHOLEFIELD, F.
HANEY, F.
MARSDEN, A.
HOLDSWORTH, G. W.
HEMINGWAY, W.
WYMAN, W.
BARBER, H.
McBURNEY, R.
COLLINS, A.
MURGATROYD, E.
HARDAKER, D.
FELTHAM, H.
SWAINE, E.
NORTHEND, J.
LAVERS, E.
STUART, G.
BOTTOMLEY, T.

Water Lane Dyeworks Company, Limited.

MOORHOUSE, A. L.
SHARP, H.
LONGBOTTOM, S.
MAHONEY, W.
BREAKS, J., Junr.
PETTY, H.
HADCROFT, N.
BENTLEY, A.
McKEOWN, W.
ABBEY, W.
MEE, T.
WILMAN, C.
COOPE, H.
COSTIN, C.
HARRISON, A.
EMSLEY, A.
QUIRK, W.
BOLTON, E.
NEUMANN, W.
SMITH, W.
TOWNSLEY, T.
KING, T.
NORMINGTON, E.
ASQUITH, A.
KELLETT, H. B.
ROBINSON, L.
HOLMES, W. A.
PEDDER, G. H.
BROOK, J. M.
TURNER, F.
METCALFE, H.
DENNISON, T.
BENTLEY, J.
LONG, J. H.
DAWSON, W.
TORDOFF, H.
WADDINGTON, J. A.
KELLY, W.
GORMAN, P.
GILL, A.
BOYES, H.
HUDSON, E.
CLIFFORD, A.
SHAW, J.
SPAFFORD, A.
GLEDHILL, A.
HAMMOND, E.

Whitaker Bros. and Company, Dyers, Limited.

HUNTER, J.
ELSWORTH, A. W.
KEMP, F.
TATSON, E.
HAWKE, G.
WADKIN, J. B.
BARTON, T. H.
SMALES, C.
WEBSTER, C.
MITCHELL, H.
BARTON, A.
HALL, J.
HOLGATE, F.
COOK, R.
BROADBENT, J.
STANTON, O. T.
BATTYE, H.
WAINWRIGHT, W.
SHAW, A.
KITCHEN, J. B.
NORTON, W.
FENTON, J.
BOOTH, E.
BARKER, W.
CLAYTON, G.
WAINWRIGHT, E.
LONG, J. E.
KEIGHLEY, A.
DICKINSON, H.
HILL, A.
SWAILES, W.
DENTON, H.
ROPER, H.
ETHERINGTON, R.
EARNSHAW, J. W.
KITCHEN, H.
ROO, D.
SCROGGINS, S.
BAXTER, W.
ROSE, B.
HOYLE, A.
LIGHT, J.
MANNERS, P.
LORRIMER, J.
HUNTER, J. R.
SILSON, H.
MATTHEWS, E. L.
ROBERTSON, E. R.
POPPLEWELL, A.
RICHMOND, E.
HARRISON, J.
WALKER, F.
WOOD, J.
STOCKHILL, S.
DICKINSON, J. W.
KENDALL, R.
WHITAKER, T.

The Bradford Dyers' Association, Ltd.—Con.

WEBSTER, G.
ABBOTT, M.
MARSDEN, H.
WOOD, D.
GLEDHILL, P. S.
GREEN, H.
FENTON, H.
LEAF, G.
RHODES, G.
PILKINGTON, H. T.
DYSON, T.
PEEL, T.
DICKINSON, A.
McDOWALL, O.
MORRIS, J. C.
HOPKINSON, F.
WEBSTER, G. A.
HONIWELL, H.
WISE, W. L.
MASON, C. W.
APPLEYARD, H.
CROSSLEY, J. W.
KITSON, G. H.
PERIGO, T.
GAUNT, J.
STANDAGE, E.
MIRFIELD, F.
WHITTINGHAM, W.
TATE, R.
COOK, S.
WILFORD, J.
SHIRES, W.
WHITHAM, H.
SCROGGINS, F.
BRADSHAW, W.
MOSS, J. W.
GAUNT, M.
COWGILL, W.
LEES, T.

PETTY, L.
LONG, E.
AMBLER, H.
DENBIGH, J.
WALSH, A. B.
HUSTLER, F.
WATERHOUSE, H.
DICKINSON, J.
ASHFORTH, A.
COWGILL, H.
SCOTT, W.
ATKINSON, W.
SMITH, B.
WESTERMAN, A.
CRAWFORD, R. A.
HUSTLER, H.
FORREST, H.
LEE, H.
RHODES, M.
CHAPMAN, A.
BODEN, J. W.
MIRFIELD, R.
BRIGGS, L.
RAWNSLEY, B.
COOPER, W.
BUTLER, A.
JACKSON, F.
BINNS, J. H.
ATHA, E.
SMITH, J. W.
WATERHOUSE, F.
JACKSON, F.
GAINES, W.
EVERSON, A.
LONG, J.
WILSON, F.
BEST, W.
HALLAM, H.
TWEEDALE, G.
LEE, A.
WOOD, C. M.

OLIVER, J. W.
KIRK, A.
JACKSON, J. E.
RAISTRICK, W. A.
FIELDHOUSE, F.
FOSTER, H.
MIRFIELD, H.
BROOKSBANK, J. W.
O'NEILL, T.
KENDALL, E.
WORSNAM, A.
BEDFORD, J.
FOSTER, T.
HARLING, J. E.
LEE, T.
EVERSON, T.
WILSON, T.
WATERHOUSE, M. L.
KNAPTON, H.
FISHER, A. H.
JACKSON, A.
WEBB, W. H.
SOWDEN, L.
DOUGILL, W.
GARNER, H.
AVISON, W.
CLARK, L.
COWGILL, A.
RILEY, W. H.
RHODES, H.
LUNN, A.
DIBB, J. W.
HOLDSWORTH, N.
RAWNSLEY, G.
BLACKBURN, A.
WILSON, T. W.
BARRATT, W.

Manchester Offices.

CARTRIDGE, W. E.
EASTWOOD, E.
CLOUGH, R. W.
BLAND, J. W.

GARLICK, H.
MELLOR, F.
STAFFORD, A. B.
TOWNSEND, W.

WILKINSON, E. J.
HANCOCK, F.

The British Cotton and Wool Dyers' Association, Ltd.

(See p. 443 in Roll of Honour.)

Head Office Staff.

ALLEN, C. W.
COWAN, J. W.
CROMPTON, L.
ORR, G. M. E.
SLATER, S. A.
THORNLEY, F.
WILKINSON, F.

AUSTIN, J.
COCKER, A. H.
MURGATROYD, N. O.
ROGERSON, H.
SHAW, T.
WHITTAKER, A.

CLARKSON, F. G.
CRAVEN, A.
O'LEARY, C.
SILVERWOOD, F.
SMITH, J. E.
WHITEHEAD, A.

LANCASHIRE.

Burton and Slingsby, Ltd.

ORMEROD, R. A.
TIPPING, H.
CLARKSON, H.
JACKSON, W.
SIDDALL, C.
LEE, J.
DRINKWATER, E.
HARDMAN, E.
LOMAX, J.

SOUTHWORTH, J.
OLIVE, N.
WALKER, J.
RIMMER, S. R.
FRAY, E.
BLEAKLEY, D.
TAYLOR, E.
THORNLEY, T.
BURTON, F.

WOLSTENHOLME, J.
CRAVEN, L.
HOUGHTON, J. T.
PICKVANCE, J.
WALKER, J.
HASLAM, A.
CROOK, F.
TAYLOR, W.

Cawdaw Dyeworks.

PICKUP, J.
DAVENPORT, J.
BAGBY, T.
FENN, T.

PICKERING, W.
PARTINGTON, E.
BARBER, C.
JONES, E.

MASON, R.
HOLT, O.

The British Cotton and Wool Dyers' Association, Ltd.—Con.

W. Eckersall and Co., Ltd.

MAGNALL, W.
FRENCH, W.
JONES, C.

ROBERTS, O.
SHEPHERD, W.
CLOUGH, C.

THOMPSON, F.
FARROW, J.

Jopson, Ashworth and Edmonds, Ltd.

HILTON, H.
STARKEY, F. E.
REILLEY, J. B.
DAWSON, A.
MELLING, J.
SHEPHERD, F.
REID, P.
THORPE, J.
FITTON, W.
HALLIWELL, J.
PARTINGTON, W.

BARLOW, W.
HEYWORTH, G.
JACQUES, B.
BRADLEY, L.
WHATMOUGH, D.
FLITCROFT, A.
BRIERLEY, H.
WATERHOUSE, A.
COOPER, J.
ADEY, H.
CROWTHER, W.

OGDEN, W.
THOMAS, H.
SMITH, G.
WHITEHEAD, H.
HOWARTH, H.
FOGG, J.
ALBISTON, T.
LEE, J., jun.
YEARSLEY, S.

Kearns, Allan and Co., Ltd.

DAWSON, I.
HINDLE, A.
WHITELEY, H.
BERRY, H.
SANDERSON, D.
WHITTAKER, J. S.
ASPDEN, T.
WHITEHEAD, G.
RUSSELL, D.
FURNELL, J.

STREETS, J. R.
HARGREAVES, J.
SUNDERLAND, J.
WHITTAKER, J.
KNOWLES, H.
BAMBER, A.
WALMSLEY, J.
SPROUL, G.
LEWIS, W. J.
SMITH, W.

WHITTAKER, T.
JOHNSTONE, J.
SALLOWAY, H. E.
CONDRON, J.
CAVE, E. J.
EMMS, J.
HOLLAND, R.
ROTHWELL, J.

Kerr and Hoegger, Ltd.

HATTON, R.
TAYLOR, G. F.
TAYLOR, J.
KILPATRICK, H.
BUTCHER, J.
McGEE, W.
MASSEY, J.
McLEAN, J.
McGROGAN, J.
ANDERTON, W.
CHATTERTON, T.
TITTERINGTON, J.
HEYWOOD, W.

CLOUGH, I.
MITCHELL, A.
JONES, J.
ALLEN, J.
ROBERTS, W.
ILLINGWORTH, A.
FARRINGTON, E.
PATTERSON, J.
GLEDHILL, A.
WAREING, J.
CLIFF, J. W.
GREENHALGH, J. L.

BROWNBILL, W.
TAYLOR, J.
WRIGHT, J.
McGROGAN, J.
JACQUES, A.
RITCHIE, H.
SCHOFIELD, C.
SMITH, J.
MACHIN, P.
HINCHCLIFFE, H.
PRITCHARD, F.
KENNEDY, H.

Edward Lee, Ltd.

DONOGHUE, W.
DAVIES, G. W.
TAYLOR, R.
POLLARD, W.
ROBINSON, J. W.
RIDING, H.
McDADE, D.
BARROW, G.

BERRY, B.
CUNLIFFE, W.
STOTT, M.
POMROY, F.
HITCHEN, H. B.
ASPDEN, A.
STANWORTH, A.
LORD, H. F.

SULLIVAN, J.
DERBYSHIRE, J. W.
STANTON, P.
ASHWORTH, A.
HORNER, W.

The Mercer Co. (Manchester), Ltd.

WOOTON, F.

Robinson Bros. (Blackburn), Ltd.

MARSHALL, H. P.
SHARPLES, H.
HALEWOOD, G.
ROWE, A.
WILKINSON, T.
PEMBERTON, J.
READ, W.
COCKER, JOHN.
DEAN, A.
CRUICKSHANK, W.
JACKSON, C.
PEMBERTON, J.

ETHERINGTON, W.
WHITTAKER, A.
WHITTAKER, E.
ETHERINGTON, E.
THRELFALL, W.
WEBSTER, W.
READ, J.
COHEN, T.
BURGESS, W.
COCKER, JAS.
ELLISON, W.
STOCKDALE, T.

ASTLEY, J. R.
STARKIE, M.
TAYLOR, W.
WINWARD, S. H.
BRINDLE, T.
BRIGGS, A.
CRONSHAW, H.
STOCKDALE, J.
WILLIAMS, T.
HINDLE, T. A.
ETHERINGTON, A.

John Siddall, Ltd.

BARLOW, D.
BARLOW, J.
BARNETT, A.
BUCKLEY, T.
CHILD, T.
CARTER, W.
CROMPTON, J. W.
EASTWOOD, G.
ENTWISTLE, W.
HOLT, F.

JONES, E.
KELLY, E.
LATER, F.
MELLING, J.
MOSELEY, E.
MORLEY, C.
PILLING, E.
PILLING, J.
EDWARDS, J.
GRUNDY, R.

HARGREAVES, S.
HOLDEN, R.
HASLAM, E.
TURNER, E.
PENDLEBURY, F.
STANNIFORTH, H.
TAYLOR, S.
TAYLOR, H.
TRAVIS, J. R.
WILLIAMS, W.

The British Cotton and Wool Dyers' Association, Ltd.—Con.

S. Smethurst and Sons, Ltd.

NEWBY, W.
COOPE, J.
ROWLES, W.
NEWBY, G.
SMITH, J.
REED, W.
MORROW, R.
JACKSON, M.
DAVIES, W.
HASLAM, F. J.
MAY, P.
PARKS, H.
DEARDEN, W.
CHADWICK, J.
WILDING, J.
FLOOK, T.
HARDMAN, A.
TOOTILL, R.
ROBINSON, T.
ROWLES, W.
FLETCHER, H.
ECKERSALL, F.
SPENSER, W.
WILD, L.
HAMER, J.
SMITH, S.
HOLDSWORTH, H. V.
TAYLOR, J. W.
WHITTAKER, S.
HAND, E. M.
WHITTAKER, F.
PILKINGTON, J.
SMITH, E.
HAMPSON, N.
HARDMAN, J.
WOOD, A.
CROMPTON, H.
WHITTAKER, S.
THORPE, F.
ISHERWOOD, C.
HOWARTH, E.
BRIDGE, J.
OLDFIELD, B.
MARSDEN, F.
TURNER, W.
LONGWORTH, J.
AINSWORTH, H.
ENTWISTLE, J.
HAMER, H.
SANDERSON, A.
ELLIOTT, W.
YATES, J.
BRADBURY, T.
ORRELL, T.

YORKSHIRE

The Bradford Patent Dyeing Co., Ltd.

JOWETT, A.
HARRISON, J.
AUSTIN, J.
MILLICAN, —
FIRTH, —
PRIESTLEY, H.
TAYLOR, J.
AUSTIN, A.
THIRKILL, —

John Buckle and Co., Ltd.

CLIFFE, A.
SMITH, A.

Fletcher Bros., Ltd.

SANDERSON, W.
HACKETT, L.
REDMAN, L.
BROOKSBANK, C.
NETTLETON, P.
HEY, C. H.
HARRINGTON, D.
WALDRON, T.
MOSEY, G.
HOLROYD, F.
DORAN, T.
BURNS, J.
BOLTON, C.
SPENCER, C.
ATKINSON, C.
GREENWOOD, L.
PICKLES, J.
WADDINGTON, F.
TAYLOR, J. W.
CLEGG, W.
BIRTWHISTLE, C.
DOBSON, W.
TOMLINSON, R.
SMITH, J. H.
FAWCETT, W.
GOODRICH, W.
McDERMOT, T.
BEAUMONT, W.
SLATER, J.
ROBINSON, H.
CLARK, E.
KIRBY, J.
CROWTHER, H.
WATSON, C.
SMITH, C.
HARGREAVES, J.
WOODHOUSE, A.
ELLIOTT, J.
HOLTEN, J.
FLAHARTY, P.
PETTY, H.
HARGREAVES, J.
CRAWSHAW, H.
FLATHERS, H.
TORRIS, C.
MOSEY, F.
SWEENEY, B.
HIGHLEY, H.
WELLS, C.
VENTING, C.
ASPINALL, C.
ROBINS, H.
SULLIVAN, J.
ARMITAGE, S.
CASSON, E.
DICKS, L.

H. Fletcher and Co., Ltd.

ISLES, E.
CROOK, C. A.
MITCHELL, J.
DENTON, J.
HEATON, F.
OGDEN, C.
CULPAN, S.
FOSTER, S.
SORSBY, H.
JOWETT, W.
GREENWOOD, J. W.
WHITAKER, J.
NETTLETON, A.
CARLTON, F.
SUTCLIFFE, W.
TANKARD, A.
SPENCER, J. W.
FORAN, E.
TASKER, A.
BINNS, S.
MORLEY, C.
CLEARY, M.
NORTH, G.
HILEY, P.
SMITH, E.
MORGAN, J.
DEWHIRST, C.

A. Goodall and Co., Ltd.

WILKINSON, G. W.
WHITELEY, E.
LOWE, S.
WOOD, J.
LEE, E.
FRANKLAND, P.
FITZPATRICK, W.
CLAY, W.
HIGHLEY, A. E.
CARTER, T.
WOOD, R.
BROWN, H.
FRANKLAND, A.

Heppenstall Bros., Ltd.

POTTER, J. H.
CRUMPTON, E.
DITCHFIELD, E.
LAVENDER, E.
CROWTHER, W.
EXLEY, A.
SARGENT, R. C.
FIRTH, S.
HAWLEY, W. H.
BRIGGS, H. R.

The Marshfield Dyeing Co., Ltd.

CARROLL, A.
CROSSLEY, F.
PRIESTLEY, C.
LIGHTOWLER, E.
TAYLOR, H.
PLEWS, S.
LAWSON, V.
NUTTER, W.
METCALFE, W.
JACKSON, A.
LOWES, R. H.
HUDSON, J.

The British Cotton and Wool Dyers' Association, Ltd.—Con.

Murgatroyd and Lister, Ltd.

GREED, A.
GUNN, L. N.
CLANCEY, J. E.
FITZPATRICK, W.
BARRACLOUGH, H.
FOUNTAIN, B.
GREGSON, J. R.
METCALFE, F.
CHAMBERS, J.
MURGATROYD, L.

Wm. North and Co., Ltd.

BARTLE, J.
POLLARD, F.
CHAMBERS, S.
NICHOLSON, W. H.
INGHAM, E.
THOMPSON, C.
CHAMBERS, A. E.
GUY, W.
SUTCLIFFE, H.
HAMMOND, W.
LORD, A. H.
WIDDOP, H.
NEWSHOLME, R.
DALBY, —
GARNHAM, E.
WOODHEAD, H.
QUIRK, J. W.
REID, F.
COATES, E.
LAWRENCE, H.
SUTCLIFFE, L.
CROWTHER, J. W.
VARLEY, H.
LISTER, F.
ELLIS, S.
LAYTE, S.
HOLDSWORTH, F.
MOSSLEY, E.
ORMANDROYD, T.
SUGDEN, J. W.
CHAPMAN, W.
ROOT, E.

Abram Peel Bros., Ltd.

PEEL, S.
JEFFERSON, A.
METCALF, H.
HALL, J.
THOMPSON, R. E
MIRFIELD, I.

Adam Robinson and Son, Ltd.

CLAPHAM, H.
TASKER, C.
LEGGETT, J.
WOOD, S.

I. Robson and Sons, Ltd.

KAYE, W.
PEAL, T.
WOOD, A.
WHITTAKER, J.
PIPER, J.
HAMER, H.
SCOTT, J. W.
PEAL, A.
THOMAS, P.
WILKINSON, T.
DICKENS, J.

The Silsden Dyeing Co. (1915), Ltd.

PRESTON, P.
TURTON, A.
COOPER, E.
TOWNEND, H.
MORRELL, J.
DENISON, J.
BANCROFT, F.
BOGG, A.
TAYLOR, F.
BARKER, C. E. J.
DABLE, H.

SCOTLAND.

Cochrane, Smith and Co., Ltd.

INGLIS, J.

D. MacFarlane and Sons, Ltd.

McLAREN, W. P.
McLELLAND, D.
McCAFFERY, J.

J. and J. McCallum, Ltd.

BREE, H.
REID, J.
CORRIGAN, D.
PATERSON, G.
YOUNG, A.
ORR, J.
SHAW, J., Junr.
CONNELL, W.
BROWN, N.
McCALLUM, J.
MULLEN, E.
BROWN, T.
MOFFAT, G.
WALLACE, J.
YOUNGER, J.
WILSON, J.

Wm. McConnell and Co., Ltd.

SIMPSON, A.
PARK, G.
MURPHY, P
RODDEN, A.
McCARTHY, T.
BISLAND, T.
McGREGOR, A

Alex. Reid and Bro., Ltd.

MATHESON, A.

T. Simpson and Co., Ltd.

PEDLOW, R.
CREAMER, J.
PETTIGREW, A.
HERD, J.
REDDAN, A.
PEDLOW, J.
MURPHY J.

J. Turnbull and Sons, Ltd.

BELL, W.
RICHARDSON, G.
WILSON, J.

Turnbulls, Ltd.

STEWART, T. B.
TURNBULL, W. D.
ABBEY, J. G.
STORRIE, W.
BELL, R.
McLEAN, D.
LITTLE, W.
TURNBULL, W.
FORREST, A.
McGINLAY, T.

The Broughton Copper Co., Ltd.
(See p. 450 in Roll of Honour.)

Office Staff.

GRIFFITHS, W. L.
WINTERBOTTOM, J.
SMITH, W. D.
MALLIN, E. W.
JENKINS, S. G
DEAKIN, J.
INGRAM, J.
COOPER, F.
TROW, G. E.
STEWART, J. M.
COX, G. H.
WHITE, H.
ALBISTON, R.
BATTY, E.
GEE, F.
†NIGHTINGALE, G.
†ROBERTSON, D. A.
†ROSS, E. W.

Employees.

TAYLOR, W. H.
ASHLEY, R. F.
COOK, A.
APPLETON, C.
WRIGHT, H.
HAMILTON, J.
HILTON, J.
McBRIDE, J.
ISHERWOOD, D.
HOLDSTOCK, G.
FOSTER, E.
ROBERTS, J.
DEAVENPORT, S.
CORLIS, T.
HAGUE, W.
DURKIN, W.
HARRIS, T.
HILTON, W. E.
TAYLOR, D.
GREEN, P.
LANG, P.
SMITH, A.
CAMP, W.
QUARMBY, H.
THICKETT, W.
GENTRY, T.
COLLIER, W.
SMITH, A.
WHITBY, W. A.
FLINN, J.
TIGHE, M.
CLAYTON, F.
THORNLEY, T.
HEMSLEY, H.
FARRELL, T.
GARFORTH, H.
KNIPE, I.
MOULDING, G.
VALENTINE, W.
JOHNSON, A.
DICKENS, T.
ECKERSALL, J.
MATHER, W.
HARDY, J.
EVANS, G.
SLATER, T.
BECKETT, J.
PEMBERTON, J.
KERSHAW, W.
BURTON, G.
WHEALING, T.
ALDRIDGE, D.
BARNES, J.
SHAKESPEARE, L.
MILLER, W.
DUNN, W.
EVANS, S
KNIPE, J. W.
GREENHILL, A.
DEAN, A.
GALLIMORE, R.
WELSBY, B.
GARDINER, J
PENNINGTON, S.
FORSHAW, J.
WHITEHEAD, H.
BARLOW, H.
BOOTH, J. W.
KINDLEY, G.
MASON, J.
GRIFFIN, J.
BRADLEY, H.
ROBY, H.
BIRCHALL, E.
OATES, J. H.
WELLS, W.
TAYLOR, C.
CARROLL, P.
WHARMBY, W.
SMITH, J.
SMITH, C.
MANSELL, M.
DOYLE, J.
MULLANEY, J.
HARRISON, G.
SCOTT, C.
COUPE, R.
WAGSTAFF, H.
CORRIGAN, I.
WATERS, M.
BAIN, J.
BROWN, J.
BROOKES, G.
POTTS, J.
RUCKER, F.
TOOLE, T.
SINCLAIR, J.
CHADWICK, P.
WEEKS, C.
DERMODY, D.
GREGORY, A.
BOOTH, C.
MASSEY, C.
ETTEY, R.
WALSH, W.
HEALD, W.
BROOKES, G. H.
LOGAN, P.
MARSH, E.
WHITEHEAD, F.
DEAN, E.
HUNTER, S.
WILSON, J.
RAWSON, R.
WAIN, T.
TOOLE, C.
SULLIVAN, F.
HEYWOOD, E.
ALDRIDGE, T.
BUSH, D.
BLACK, J.
CONROY, J.
NORRIS, J.
GINDER, J.
RYDER, H.
MOSS, J.
SINCLAIR, W.
BRANDRETH, B.
BELCHER, J.
DOYLE, J.
KELLY, J.
FOSTER, J. E.
KNAPE, A.
CUNLIFFE, H.
WILLIAMS, E.
FOXCROFT, C.
MOULDING, W.
GRIFFITHS, W.
WILSON, G.
HORAN J.
OATES, J.
WALKER, T.
SAUNDERS, C.
TOMLINSON, E.
SMITH, E.
MATHER, A.
LAWLER, M.
PRESTON, J. W.
BATES, W.
INGHAM, F.
CAMP, F.
TAYLOR, W.
MORLEY, T.
GILLULEY, T.
JACKSON, C.
BALLARD, C.
BRADLEY, F.
LIVERSEDGE, G.
ROBINSON, F.
REEDY, T.
ROBERTS, W.
RYDER, W.
TYNAN, J.
BROOKES, S.
KILLON, J.
KNAPE, H.
NUTTALL, E.
HUGHES, H.
SPENCER, F.
ACTON, H.
STUBBS, C.
HAYES, W.
COFFEY, M.
JACKSON, H.
HOPKINSON, R.
PRICE, H.
CHADWICK, C.
McCARTHY, W.
LOUGHMAN, L.
ACKERLEY, W.
DONOHUE, J.
COLEMAN, T.
MOORES, J.
PARKINGTON, A.
O'DRISCOLL, P.
CASEY, F.
WARD, F.
VIPOND, M.
TAYLOR, W.
BERRY, W.
BURGESS, W.
OGDEN, E.
EVANS, J. W.
LANG, A.
DERMODY, J.
CALVERT, A.
LOGAN, S.
SWINDELLS, R.
DUTTON, A.
MILLS, J.
CRONIN, M.
SHIPLEY, H.
CUNLIFFE, W.
MASSEY, T.
CUNNINGHAM, J.
MILLER, W.
HASTIE, R.
SMITH, J.
NIGHTINGALE, S.
LEADBETTER, N.
IRELAND, I.
FITELSON, H.
ASPDEN, H.
CONWAY, J.
HARRIS, H.
MANLEY, C. I.
†SUTCLIFFE, A.
†ASTON, J.
†McDONALD, G.
†ROBINSON, J.
†MOSS, W. H.
†THORP, H.
†AULT, T.
†McCOLM, A.
†BAILEY, A.
†BROWN, J.
†HASTIE, J.
†CROWE, H.
†RHODES, D.
†HAYDOCK, J.
†BOOTH, R.
†MARTIN, J.
†TOMLINSON, J.
†PROCTOR, C. E.
†MULLANEY, T.
†COUPE, E.
†COCKER, F.
†ROGERS, G.
†WHITING, A.
†RECKLESS, J.

The Broughton Copper Co., Ltd.—Con.

MEHOMET, B.
ROEBUCK, C.
HAMILTON, H.
HARVEY, R.
BAKER, S.
BROOKE, C. E.
DAVIES, O.
RAMSBOTTOM, C.
BRIGGS, W.
MATHER, F.
HESTIE, R.
TALBOT, R.
ECKERSLEY, J.
CURZON, A.
GREAVES, H.
SCHOFIELD, E.
WEISBERG, C.
HARRIS, R.
SUTHERLAND, A.
MEACHIN, J. C.
MELLING, W.
JONES, B.
WADE, H.
McCURDY, C.
SHAW, H.
SOUTHWARD, J.
KAVANAGH, W.
SAVAGE, T.
LILLEY, J.
KENIVAN, W.
SOLMAN, C.
LANGDEN, G.
DALE, J.
MACCABE, J.
OLDHAM, A.
BAZLEY, E. S.
WHITTAKER, A.
PEARSON, J.
SCOTT, T.
ATHERLEY, W.
CARNELL, L.
MULLANEY, W.
HIGHAM, I.
POWELL, J.
FAIRCHILD, E.
WILSON, D.
HODGSON, A.
CRABSTICK, E.
†BESWICK, J.
†PLEACE, C.
†RYDER, A.
†EARNSHAW, F.
†WHITTAKER, H.
†WHITE, T.
†GRIBBON, W.
†DICKENSON, J.
†ORMONDY, H.
†BRADLEY, H.
†WATERS, H.
†GOODWIN, J.
†HIGHAM, W.
†RICE, J.
†CARR, J.
†CONNELL, J.
†WILLIAMS, J.
†NEALSON, R.
†ASTON, J.
†ELLIS, C.
†MANSFIELD, D.
†ECKERSLEY, H.
†OATES, J.
†OGDEN, J.

Ditton.

BEESLEY, E. T.
DUCKETT, S.
STEAD, R. H.
ROBERTS, A.
WILLIAMS, W.
BURNS, D.
RILEY, T.
TURTON, G.
DEVANEY, J.
SEFTON, T.
YOUNG, H.
GILL, W.
GREENWOOD, H.
MULLEN, M.
HOUGHTON, J.
HALE, W.
BROOME, A.
OWENS, J. W.
WHITLEY, H.
PROUD, E.
RADLEY, J.
HASTINGS, J.
SIMMONS, G.
KIRKHAM, W.
WILLIAMS, J.
BARTON, H.
HARDING, R.
BROMILEY, G.
DONOGHUE, J.
LEATHER, R.
GILBRIDE, D.
LOTT, W.
WOOLRICH, H.
GRACE, R.
MAGUIRE, F., Jr.
GRIFFITHS, T.
RIMMER, R.
MURRAY, H.
WATKIN, B.
CAMPBELL, M.
HIGGINS, T.
CARTER, T.
STEPHENS, H.
STEPHENS, M.
BARNES, W.
HOUGHTON, W.
PYE, W.
DALE, J.
STUBBS, T.
MASON, G.
KETTERICK, J.
HOUGHTON, J.
LEATHER, W.
McGARTY, P.
PRITCHARD, J.
WILLIAMS, W.
HENSLEY, T.
FLETCHER, W.
PRITCHARD, E.
LEACH, H.
MURPHY, W.

H. O. Brandt and Co.
(See p. 665 in Roll of Honour.)

HAMPSON, G. B.
ATCHESON, A. S.
BOWDEN, W.
FOSTER, J.
McNAB, W.
MARSHALL, W.
PEARSON, T.

Thomas Brayshay and Sons, Ltd.
(See p. 665 in Roll of Honour.)

BAXENDALE, W. T.
BLOOR, T. W.
HOLT, J. A.
MOORES, H.
PORT, J.

Wm. Briggs and Co., Ltd.
(See p. 442 in Roll of Honour.)

SHARPLEY, A.
HEATHCOTE, F. P.
KNIGHT, E. G.
BILLINGHAM, C. E.
WARD, W.
YATES, S. C.
YATES, L.
CADMAN, W. H.
BENNETT, P.
FIRTH, H. O.
BODDY, J.
THOMPSON, F. D.
BENTLEY, C. R.
CONRY, J. M.
BROWN, T.
TAYLOR, F. E.
CASEWELL, H.
ROGERSON, H.
FERRY, B.
DOMBAVAND, H
TUCKER, G.
YATES, A.
POLLITT, J.
TENCH, J.
CHADWICK, F.
HOBSON, R.
GWINNETH, A.
FODEN, T.
THOMPSON, J.
McLACHLAN, A.
O'CONNELL, J.
TAYLOR, J.
KIRKLAND, T.
GILL, H.
SHARPLES, L.
PUGH, W.
HAMILTON, J.

C. H. Britton and Sons.
(See p. 456 in Roll of Honour.)

BRITTON, H.
KINSELLA, H.
SKERRATT, J.
PRICE, T. W.

Brown and Forth.
(See p. 667 in Roll of Honour.)

BROWN, HORACE
EVANS, THOMAS

† Rejected.

The British Reinforced Concrete Engineering Co., Ltd.
(See p. 447 in Roll of Honour.)

BUTLER, J. F.
BUSBY, C.
BRADLEY, J.
*COOKE, R.
CROWTHER, F. S.
DIGBY, H.
DUFF, S.
FOSTER, P.
GRAY, L.
GRIFFITHS, J. B.
GLEAVE, A.
IMBER, R. J.
KERSHAW, J.
MacDONALD, J. A.
POTTS, S. J.
PRIESTLEY, C. F.
SIMPSON, T. G.
SHIPLEY, F.
SOUTHERN, J. H.
SUMMERGILL, J.
TURNER, F.
VINSON, A. J.
WEBSTER, H. R.
*WARWICK, B.
WHITTAKER, W.
WILSON, W.
YEARSLEY, H. A.

Broome and Foster, Ltd.
(See p. 449 in Roll of Honour.)

ANDREWS, H.
BRIERLEY, W.
BAILEY, H.
APLIN, W.
COOKE, H. W.
†FAIRHURST, C.
HANMER, A.
†INMAN, H.
†MOORE, T.
RAYNOR, R. W.
SCOTT, E.
†TAYLOR, G.
DARBYSHIRE, R. E.
†BARNES, S.
CLARK, J.
ELLISON, J.
RACKSTRAW, W.
REEVES, C.
SIMPSON, H.
†STOCKER, C.
SMITH, S.

Burgess, Ledward and Co., Ltd.
(See p. 452 in Roll of Honour.)

ASHCROFT, R.
BURGESS, S. H.
BELLIS, A.
BURROWS, H.
BEDFORD, H.
BARLOW, H.
CHORLTON, T.
CORY, E. B. F.
CROWTHER, F. M.
DRUMMOND, F. A.
GULLIFORD, R.
GREY, W. E.
HUGHES, H. H.
HURST, S.
HURST, N.
LAMBERT, J.
McDOWELL, W.
McGIVERN, W. B.
POTTS, I.
PYE, W. E.
PENNEY, W.
SHORE, W. H.
STOCKER, J.
WOODHOUSE, A.
ATKINSON, J. H.
BALL, M.
BALL, D.
BARHAM, J. S.
BARNABY, C.
BAXENDALE, W.
BENNETT, H.
BENNETT, J. E.
BERRY, J.
BERRY, H.
BERRY, G.
BINNS, A.
BLOWER, W. A.
BRADBURY, J.
BROOKES, A. B.
BROOKES, H.
BURGESS, G. E.
COOKE, H.
COOKE, J.
CHAPMAN, E.
CHAPMAN, H.
CROMPON, L.
CROMPTON, R. H.
CROOKE, W.
CROOKE, T.
CROSSLEY, H.
DAVIES, H.
DEAN, H.
DEARDEN, S.
DENNER, N.
DODGSON, H.
ECKERSLEY, W.
ECKERSLEY, A.
ELLAM, T.
ENTWISTLE, J.
EVANS, H.
FARNWORTH, J.
FLANNIGAN, J.
FOX, H.
GARWOOD, F.
GRIMSHAW, J.
GRIMSHAW, F.
GRUNDY, J.
GRUNDY, R.
HAYES, J.
HARDMAN, G.
HARDY, E.
HEYS, H.
HILTON, J. C.
HOLMES, J.
HOLLAND, J.
HOPE, A.
HURST, T., Junr.
JACQUES, J.
KILEY, T.
KING, J.
KINNISTON, A.
KNIGHT, A.
LAW, J. R.
LEATHER, H.
LIGHTFOOT, J.
LOWE, E.
LOWE, P. H.
LOXHAM, J.
MARSHALL, J.
MARSHALL, T.
MASON, J.
MATHER, J.
MAWDESLEY, T.
MILLS, J. H.
MORGAN, J.
MULLINEAUX, T.
NORBURY, J.
NORTH, F.
OLIVE, J.
PEAKE, S.
PEERS, S.
PENNINGTON, R. W.
REVELL, J.
RHODES, J.
RIGBY, A.
RILEY, J.
RODGERS, J.
ROTHWELL, J.
RUSHTON, W.
SHAW, J.
SHAW, J.
SPENCER, H.
STUBBS, H. L.
SCHOLEFIELD, F.
TAITE, E.
TATTON, G.
THOMPSON, A.
TIBBS, W.
TONGE, W.
TOZE, J.
WALKER, D.
WALKER, S.
WALKER, W.
WALKER, W. J.
WALSH, J.
WARDLE, J.
WATTS, W.
WEBB, G. R.
WILLIAMSON, C. J.
WILLIAMSON, F.
WILLIAMSON, H.
WILLIAMSON, H.
WILLIAMSON, J.
WINSTANLEY, A.
WORSLEY, W. T.
YATES, A.
YATES, E.

Brisbane, Jones and Co., Ltd.
(See p. 666 in Roll of Honour.)

BROWN, J.
FERNELEY, H.
PILKINGTON, A.

Edward R. Buck and Sons.
(See p. 456 in Roll of Honour.)

BUCK, R. R.
BUCK, E. S.
BUCK, W. M.
BUCK, F. M.
BROWN, T.
GODWIN, J. A.
LEE, G.
ABERCROMBIE, A.
ROBINSON, W.
WALSH, M.
RIDGEWAY, W.
WORSLEY, R.

A. Burgon and Co., Ltd.
(See p. 667 in Roll of Honour.)

KELLY, S.
BLASDALE, H. C.
LAMBERT, A.
OSBORNE, C.
HERSTELL, F.
NEWTON, W.
JONES, S.

* Serving with the colours. † Rejected.

Chorlton Bros., Ltd.
(See p. 457 in Roll of Honour.)

BADLEY, G.
BARONS, B. W.
BARTON, W.
BEARD, J. H.
BLAKEY, L. H.
BOOTHBY, S.
BORROWS, P.
BRADY, H.
BROWN, A. L. P.
CANNON, W. R.
CARROLL, L.
CHURCH, W.
COHEN, M.
CUNNINGHAM, A.
DAVIES, S.
DEMBORITCH, M.
ELMORE, A.
FORBES, G.
HEATON, T.
HOLMES, R.
HURST, F.
JACKSON, T.
LEAREY, J.
LEE, J.
LEWIS, M.
LINDSAY, A. H.
MAY, J.
MORLEY, E.
NAYLOR, P.
ORMSON, S. W.
PEARSON, F.
PROSSER, J.
READE, W.
ROBERTS, D.
ROSEBY, L.
SLATFORD, W. J.
SMETHURST, A.
SMITH, J.
SMITH, H.
SUTTILL, A.
THOMPSON, W.
TILLEY, F.
TRUE, W.
WHITWORTH, E.
WOODMAN, L.

The Churchill Machine Tool Co., Ltd.
(See p. 670 in Roll of Honour.)

ASBRIDGE, H. H.
JACKSON, W.
JONES, H.
ADAMS, H. G.
LOCKHART, J. M.
SPROSON, H.
LARKIN, W.
MORRIS, J.
†MURRAY, E.
HUNT, A.
SMART, A. P.
MACCONWELL, N.
JONES, A.
SIDEBOTHAM, S.
WATERS, A.
†WOOD, A.
PIKE, R.
BOWDEN, A.
HUDSON, G.
HOPE, T.
READ, W.
WOOD, H.
COLLINS, D. A.
LONGTHORPE, H.
†MOORES, F. H.
†HUDSON, T. H.
KINSEY, W.
ECKERSALL, G.
WILKINSON, H.
NEWMAN, F. C.
EDDEN, J.
LORD, R.
BARRACLOUGH, E.
ALLEN, J.
ATKINSON, A. C.
ASPINALL, J. E.
ALLEN, G. N.
BAGGLEY, E.
BARNES, D.
BINNS, M.
BARLOW, P.
BALL, T.
BARCLAY, H.
BERRY, L.
BARCLAY, J.
BROWN, A. W.
BATY, R.
BATES, J.
BATES, H.
BURCIN, F.
BIRCH, J.
BURKE, J.
BEETHAM, R.
CONNOR, J.
COOMBS, W.
CONNOR, W. W.
CORDWELL, R.
CARR, I.
CROOKELL, G. H.
CROMPTON, J. B.
CHADWICK, N.
DIXON, H.
DAVIES, E.
DAVIES, B.
DUNN, W.
DEAN, R.
DELANEY, J. B.
DAVENPORT, S.
DAVIES, T.
DEAN, T.
DRAKE, W.
DEAN, W.
EDMONDSON, H.
FORD, F.
FLETCHER, W.
FURMINGER, J.
FRANCE, R.
GARNER, J. W.
GRADY, J.
GLYNN, W.
GEORGE, F.
HEALEY, T.
HAMPSON, J.
HODSON, W.
HOSIE, J. A.
HICKSON, J.
HORRIDGE, T.
HOLDEN, W.
HUGHES, T. A.
HARSLEY, A.
HINDLE, W.
HATTERSLEY, J.
HOWARTH, T.
HAWORTH, J.
HAYES, H.
HORRIDGE, E. A.
JENNINGS, T.
JONES, A.
JONES, E.
JAMES, E.
JONES, W. G.
JACKS, W. H.
JENKINSON, A. P.
JOHNSON, A.
KEENAN, W.
KIRKHAM, S.
LANSLEY, T.
LARKIN, A.
LEWIS, T.
LANCASTER, J. L.
MAUNDER, F. E.
MATTHEWS, F.
McLEAN, R.
McKERNAN, H.
MYCOCK, T.
MARSH, S.
MORTON, C.
McLEAN, D.
McKENNA, J.
McALPINE, R.
MADDY, W.
MATTHEWS, J.
NORREY, E.
NEWTON, F.
OKELL, A.
O'CONNOR, E.
PROCTOR, A.
PILLING, F.
POYNTON, F.
PILLING, W. H.
PITTILLA, H.
PETERS, A.
ROBINSON, A.
RIDGWAY, V.
RIDGWAY, C. A.
REECE, J.
RUDDICK, W. H.
RICHARDS, H.
REDFORD, J. B.
SMITH, W.
SANDS, H. J. H.
STEPHENS, C.
STEWART, W.
SWINDELLS, J.
SUMNER, A.
STOKES, J.
STARKEY, H.
SMITH, S. A.
SENIOR, J.
SMITH, H.
SIMPSON, A.
STANSFIELD, W. H.
TAYLOR, J.
TUCKER, L.
THOMSON, H. A.
TICKLE, E. J.
THOMAS, F. W.
TYRER, E.
THOMPSON, W.
TAYLOR, H. H.
THOMPSON, E.
UNSWORTH, W.
VAUGHAN, W.
WYCH, J.
WRIGHT, R.
WILLIAMS, R.
WALKER, W. C.
WILKINSON, A.
WEBSTER, S. G.
WHEALING, S.
WALMSLEY, E.
WILSON, J.
WHITNEY, W.
WYCH, J.
WINWARD, A.
†PORTLOCK, J.

Claus and Co., Ltd.
(See p. 480 in Roll of Honour.)

ATACK, F. W.
ALCOCK, J. E.
BENNETT, J.
BOURKE, J.
BOWKER, J.
BRADLEY, G.
BULLOCK, J.
CLAUS, W. L.
CLOWES, J.
COLLIER, W.
COOPER, H.
CROPPER, J.
EARDLEY, J.
EMERSON, F. W.
FORNACHON, A.
GATH, F.
GOWER, J. B.
GRAHAM, R.
HAMLETT, G.
HOWARD, T.
ISHERWOOD, J.
JOHNSON, A.
McCURRIE, J.
McINTYRE, A.
MATTHEWS, T.
MORT, J.
MURRAY, W.
PLATT, J. H.
ROBINSON, A.
ROBINSON, H. S.
SIRRELL, J.
SLEAFORD, J.
TIMMS, E.
TRACEY, D.
VLIES, L. E.
WAKEFIELD, G. H.
WHITESIDE, K.
WILKINSON, T.
YATES, G.
YATES, W.
YEARSLEY, J.

Emmanuel Casdagli and Sons.
(See p. 669 in Roll of Honour.)

CASDAGLI, X.　　BATHO, J.　　MATHEWS, H.

William Champness and Sons.
(See p. 669 in Roll of Honour.)

HOOK, J. P.　　WOOD, W. H.　　ALDRIDGE, T.
JOHNSON, T.　　CHAMBERLAIN, H.　　MYERS, T. E.

Clayton Aniline Company, Ltd.
(See p. 458 in Roll of Honour.)

ALLCOCK, F.	GREENOUGH, J.	ROWLANDS, E
ARMSTRONG, C.	HIBBERT, H.	RYDER, J.
ARDEN, R.	HAWKINS. R.	ROBINSON, M. A.
ALLPASS, J. T.	HILL, C. W.	RUNCIMAN, J.
BRADBURY, R. H.	HANNS, H.	SWAN, H. H.
BLYTH, E.	HOUGHTON, R. W.	SHIRT, A.
BIRCH, W.	HORROCKS, G.	SANDBACH, J. H.
BEDDOWS, J.	HARRIS, F.	STANSFIELD, J.
BAILEY, J.	HIGGINBOTHAM, H.	SCULLY, J.
BANKS, R.	HOLE, W. C.	SNELL, W.
BRIDGE, A.	HENDERSON, J. R.	SMITH, A.
BARRETT, F. W.	HAWKESFORD, G.	SHERRATT, E
BRACEGIRDLE, R.	HIBBERT, J. W.	STRINGER, C.
BEALE, F.	HICKMAN, F.	SLOANE, J.
BLAKELEY, W. S.	HEATHCOTE, T.	SHIELDS, H.
BRACEGIRDLE, H. W.	HIGNETT, J. P.	TAYLOR, F.
BRADBURY, H.	HIGHAM, H.	TAYLOR, A.
BOTTOMLEY, E.	HAGUE, G. A.	TAYLOR, G. E.
BOLAND, T.	HUGHES, R.	TOOMEY, C. J.
BRUCE, —	HOSKING, W. A.	THOMPSON, S.
CARDWELL, D.	JOBEY, J.	VERITY, F.
COWIN, D.	JONES, S. V.	WELLS, E.
CASTLE, W. J.	JENNINGS, W.	WORLAND, F. J.
COTTRELL, J.	JACKSON, A. A.	WINGFIELD, B.
CALVERT, J. E.	JONES, A.	WALKER, T.
DONNETT, J.	JACKSON, S.	WOOD, J.
DAVIES, W. O.	KENNEDY, T.	WALKER, J. H.
DARLINGTON, H.	KING, A.	WHITHAM, W.
DAVIES, J.	KERFOOT, J.	WEBSTER, R.
DAWSON, T.	LEIGH, F.	WALMSLEY, F.
DERBYSHIRE, J.	LONG, T.	WOOD, C.
DAGLEY, W.	LOGAN, D.	WHARTON, J.
DREW, J.	LOMAS, J.	WINGFIELD, J.
DEMPSEY, R. E.	LEWIS, A. F.	WARRINGTON, F. C.
EVENSON, J.	LLOYD, J.	WALKER. A.
EVANS, T. W.	McNICHOLLS, J.	WHITWORTH, H.
EMERY, T.	MANN, S.	WOOD, S. S.
FOWLER, W.	MOTTERSHEAD, J.	WALKER, G.
FULLER, W.	MOORE, H. A.	WHITTINGSLOW, G.
FAIRCLOUGH, J. T.	MELLOR, A.	WALKER, F.
FULLER, E.	NUTTALL, A.	WILDE, C.
FOX, G.	PICKERING, H. R.	WADE, J.
FROGGATT, F.	PENDLEBURY, E.	WRIGHT, A.
FIELDING, P.	PRIESTNELL A.	WYLDE, J. T.
FOY, T. H.	PARRISH, J.	WARD, G.
GUTZMER, H. V.	PEARCEY, F.	WILD, C.
GRADWELL, R.	PARKER, F.	WILKINSON, J.
GARNER, C.	PEDLEY, J.	WAUGH, B.
GUINN, M. A.	PEAK, A. E.	WARD, F. J.
GLOISTER, H. F.	RILEY, J.	WOLSTENHOLME, A.
GOUGH, G.	RILEY, T.	
GUDGEON, W.	RYAN, A.	
GRIFFITHS, J. H.		

I. J. and G. Cooper, Ltd.
(See p. 459 in Roll of Honour.)

ARMYTAGE, F. J.	GADD, W.	MEGSON, W. J.
ARMITAGE, H.	HUFTON, F. G.	MYLECHREEST, W. E.
ANDERSON, J.	HARBORROW, W. E.	NORTON, E. H.
ACTON, A.	HARRISON, H.	POTTS, E.
BARLOW, A. E.	HARBRON, E.	POOLE, F. A.
BAILEY, J. E.	HOSEASON, G. B.	PRATT, C.
BLEAKLEY, W.	HENRY, J.	RAMSBOTTOM, A.
BEWLEY, W. T.	HILTON, W.	RITCHIE, T. R.
BAILEY, T.	HARDIE, R.	ROSEWARNE, W.
COVENTRY, W. A.	HYDE, J.	RILEY, J.
CONN, H.	HOLDEN, A. E.	RIDGEWAY, J.
CARTER, H. E.	HAYES, S.	SOUTHGATE, F.
CHEETHAM, G.	ISHERWOOD, T.	SMITH, C. W.
DEWHIRST, T.	JONES, E. E.	SIMPSON, L.
DIXON, J.	JONES, E.	SPEAR, H. W.
DIXON, T. A.	LOMAS, E.	STRINGFELLOW, B.
DUNN, J.	LAWSON, H. B.	SMETHURST, J. C.
EVANS, W. J.	LEE, T. A.	TAYLOR, H.
FARNWORTH, W.	LONGDEN, H.	THORNHILL, E.
FISHER, G.	McKEE, G. S.	WILKINSON, R.
FLETCHER, L. N.	McWILLIAMS, F.	
GREEN, A.		

Co-operative Wholesale Society, Ltd.
(See p. 462 in Roll of Honour.)

ALLEN, R. E.	ATKINSON, J.	BARRETT, J.
ASHWORTH, H. R.	ALDERSON, W.	BELL, H. J.
ATCHERLEY, F.	ATKIN, H.	BRIGGS, H.
ADSHEAD, G. A.	ADSHEAD, G. A.	BUTCHART, J.
ATKIN, H.	ARMITAGE, H.	BORROWDALE, J.
ARMITAGE, H.	ATKIN, H.	BLACKHALL, G.
ASHTON, E.	AINGE, H.	BLOOMFIELD, J.
ATKIN, H.	AUSTIN, W.	BURKETT, R.
ARNOLD, J.	ATKINS, J.	BERRY, J.
ANSON, A. J.	AIREY, A. E.	BURN, A.
AINSWORTH, F.	ALLEN, R.	BULLEN, G.
AISTON, T.	AYTO, E.	BROOKER, C. G.
ALEXANDER, R.	AINGES, J.	BAUER, E.
ARMSTRONG, J.	ALLEN, F.	BRADSHAW, W. L.
ANDERSON, J.	ARCHER, G.	BENNETT, F. J.
ATTRIDGE, R.	ATKINSON, T. W.	BARNETT, F.
ADKINS, G.	ARSTALL, W.	BIRD, D.
ALDOUS, H.	ASHTON, A.	BUTLER, A. E.
ALDOUS, H.	ALLEN, H.	BARRETT, W.
ANDERSON, G.	ARSTALL, C.	BREEN, J. P.
ADLAM, J. G.	ALLEN, C.	BOWLER, E.
ASHWIN, H.	ARSTALL, J.	BEARD, J.
ALDRIDGE, J.	ACKERLEY, H.	BARRETT, J.
ALDRIDGE, A. E.	ACKERLEY, T.	BUCKLAND, J. H.
ALLEN, F.	BOTTOMLEY, W.	BOVEY, H. E.
AYRES, C. W.	BATTY, G.	BAKER, G. W.
AYRES, H.	BROWNING, H.	BARNES, G. H.
ALLEN, A. M.	BENNETT, A. G.	BAKER, E.
ATKINSON, E.	BENT, F.	BAMBER, C. A
ASHTON, A.	BURN, E. J.	BUSSELL, —
ALLEN, C.	BRIGGS, J. A.	BURNELL. S.
ASHTON, A.	BRADBURY, F.	BEVAN, R. A.
ASHWORTH, E.	BRITTON, F.	BISHOP, R. H.
ALLISON, T. B.	BRICKLES, T.	BENNETT, H. E.
ANDREWS, H. T.	BARDSLEY, F.	BURGESS, F.
ABBEY, F.	BRADLEY, F.	BUSHIN, W.
ATKINSON, T.	BURTON, S.	BEAT, E. E.
ALLWOOD, P. S.	BATCHELOR, C	BRADBURN, E.
ARMSTRONG, E.	BENNISON, J.	BROUGH, —
ALDERSON, A. J.	BIRCHENOUGH, J. A.	BOOTH, —
ASKEW, W.	BRERETON, J.	BOOTH, —
ATKIN, H.	BAXTER, J.	BONE, E.
ARSTALL, J. H.	BOWDEN, F.	BENGER, C.
ALDRED, F.	BRADLEY, H.	BACON, J.
ARSTALL, T.	BROOKES, E.	BOND, H.
ASHTON, J.	BAILEY, A.	BINHAM, G.
ALVEY, J	BOFFEY, A.	BROOKES, F.
ALLEN, W.	BURKE, T.	BAILEY, H.
ALEXANDER, D.	BOWDEN, H.	BROWN, A.
ATHERTON, G.	BESWICK, J.	BRADSHAW, F
ACKLAND, W.	BRADDOCK, G.	BURGESS, R.
ALMOND, H.	BOARDMAN, R. M.	BURN, R.
ATHERTON, P.	BARLOW, W.	BRADSHAW, F.
AINSWORTH, H.	BATES, E.	BAMFORD, W.
ASHTON, W.	BURCHAM, C. H.	BLACKBURN, M.
ASHTON, H.	BOYES, W.	BENNETT, J.
AINSWORTH, J.	BOYES, W. H.	BENNETT, T.
AGGIS, W.	BRIERLEY, H. N	BIRD, A.
ATKINSON, R.	BATEMAN, J.	BAILEY, T.
ARCHER, A.	BUCKLEY, T.	BESWICK, J.
ARCHER, J.	BROOKS, P.	BEESTON, F. C
ALLEN, J.	BAILEY, R.	BATESON, W.
ANSELL, H.	BURGESS, C.	BATES, F.
ANDERSON, J. H.	BANNISTER, J.	BOHL, A.
ANDERSON, H.	BROOME, J.	BLUNDELL, W.
ANDERSON, A.	BENNISON, S.	BROMLEY, C.
ALBERY, T.	BOOTH, E.	BELL, E.
ANN, E.	BAKER, J.	BRADY, L.
ANDREW, W.	BOWKER, H.	BISHOP, W.
ALDRIDGE, C.	BOWE, J.	BARRATT, S.
AUDSLEY, A.	BLACK, W.	BOWERS, W.
ALLATT, P.	BAUGLEY, A.	BELL, G.
ATKINSON, S.	BATEMAN, J.	BLAND, E. T
ALLEN, W.	BARBER, W.	BROMLEY, S.
ANTHONY, J.	BROWN, J.	BENTLEY, J.
ATKINSON, E	BELLAMY, A. H.	BATTEN, J.
ATACK, G.	BELL, R.	BEARDMAN, S.
ALLEN, W.	BATEY, M.	BURKE, J.
ADAMS, W.	BEARD, A.	BLADES, W.
ANDERSON, F.	BACKLEY, J.	BARRY, J.
ALLEN, S.	BREWIS, J.	BROWN, F.
ATKINSON, E.	BELL, G.	BECK, J.
ALDRED, C.	BERRY, A.	BARNES, H.
ASHTON, T.	BLACKLOCK, J.	BOWES, H.
ARMITAGE, C.	BELL, F.	BUTLER, A. H.
ALLEN, J.	BOWE, T.	BURDETT, J.
AUSTIN, A.	BLACK, J.	BEDFORD, A. J.
ARMISTEAD, R	BATEY, E. J.	BARROW, J.
ASHER, E.	BARNES, T.	BIRTLES, A.
ASQUITH, F.	BULMAN, R.	BRADBURN, W.
ABBOTT, W. H.	BREWIS, J.	BRIERLEY, F.
AYRES, G.		BENSON, J. J.

Co-operative Wholesale Society, Ltd.—Con.

BLACKLEDGE, J.
BIRTLES, G.
BEAVER, W.
BARRINGTON, J. W.
BARLOW, T.
BROOKS, W.
BAXTER, G.
BANKS, C.
BROOKS, H.
BRANES, F.
BRADSHAW, T.
BANDY, T.
BESFORD, J. W.
BURKE, J.
BLACKBIRD, E.
BLAKEY, R.
BROWN, H. A.
BALL, W.
BAKER, J.
BODLEY, W.
BURWOOD, W.
BAILEY, C.
BAILEY, J.
BURNS, J.
BISPHAM, P.
BRADLEY, H.
BAMFORD, D.
BALL, W.
BEDDOWS, C.
BURKILL, G.
BOSTOCK, C.
BICKERDIKE, T.
BICKERDIKE, D.
BOWERS, J.
BLACKEY, R.
BELFIELD, T.
BROOME, J.
BOWDEN, J. E.
BAXTER, J. H.
BAGOT, W. W.
BAYLISS, S. A.
BRODRICK, R.
BROWN, A.
BATEY, F.
BROWN, W.
BOSTON, J.
BOSTON, W.
BLACKBURN, W.
BLENKINSOP, A.
BROWN, J.
BAKER, T.
BENNETT, H. E.
BULLOCK, N.
BREWER, G.
BATEMAN, T. H.
BROOKS, G. F.
BROOMHEAD, W.
BROMLEY, W.
BETTS, A.
BRIDGES, C. F.
BRIGHAM, J.
BAKER, A. H.
BACKHOUSE, A. W.
BEASANT, H.
BRACEY, A. C.
BRAGG, W. C.
BUCKLAND, G. E.
BUCK, E.
BEBBINGTON, H.
BARRETT, H. S.
BALE, H. H.
BRAMWELL, C. G.
BUCKLE, W.
BERRY, W.
BROOKS, W.
BEATON, A.
BREARS, T.
BEAUMONT, E.
BEDFORD, A. E.
BROOKE, S.
BARDON, R.
BRAWN, W.
BARNES, S.
BLACKWELL, H. G.
BRIDGEFORD, L.
BRAMPTON, G. A.
BALLARD, F. W.
BRIDGEFORD, E. W.
BRITTEN, R.
BRITTEN, N.
BAYES, C.

BETTS, E.
BECKETT, W.
BARKER, F.
BIRKETT, J. W.
BRAYSHAW, J. W.
BRITTON, J.
BRISTOWE, T.
BISHOP, J.
BAKER, E.
BOWMAN, W.
BAKER, W.
BROADHEAD, E.
BURROWS, F.
BEDDAMS, J.
BENNETT, F.
BLUNT, A.
BELL, T. C.
BRUCE, F.
BARCLAY E.
BARRATT, A.
BURNLEY, B. W.
BISHOP, A.
BESS, H.
BAKER, W.
BRIGHT, W.
BRINE, E.
BOWDEN, J.
BEATY, A.
BARNES, E.
BLOMELEY, H.
BAMFORD, J. S.
BARLOW, J. H.
BRUNT, F.
BARROW, C.
BOLTON, S.
BENNETT, M.
BUCKLEY, L.
BARKER, F.
BOWERS, J.
BREEZE, J.
BARRATT, A.
BROCKLEHURST, H.
BOWDEN, G.
BARLOW, A.
BROOKES, W.
BRINDLE, F.
BIFFEN, R.
BOOTH, H.
BARNES, G.
BOOTH, T.
BOYER, C.
BOYER, C. T.
BUTLER, S.
BLACKBURN, H.
BERRY, A.
BOYES, R.
BRIGHT, J.
BEST, J.
BUTTERFIELD, E.
BERRY, W.
BIRCH, W.
BUTTERWORTH, W. E.
BECKWITH, P.
BRIGGS, J. A.
BUTTERWORTH, F.
BARRATT, F.
BODECOAT, H.
BROWN, F.
BOWLER, E.
BAILEY, T.
BAILEY, J.
BURROWS, E.
BLOCK, P.
BARNES, W.
BROOKS, P.
BARRATT, W.
BATTYE, W.
BRUMBY, G. H.
BEAUMONT, W. H.
BOOTH, A. B.
BRADLEY, R. B.
BROWN, F.
BOTTOMLEY, W.
BENSON, P.
BUCKLEY, E.
BRITTON, F.
BRICKLES, T.
BOOTH, H.
BUTTERWORTH, J
BOTTELEY J.
BENT, F.

BURN, E. J.
BATTY, G.
BROWNING, H.
BIRD, T.
BENNETT, A. G.
BRADLEY, F.
BURTON, S.
BATCHELOR, C.
BLAKELEY, F.
BROADBENT, J.
BRERETON, J.
BAXTER, J.
BENNISON, J.
BIRCHENOUGH, J. A.
BOWDEN, F.
BRADLEY, H.
BROOKES, E.
BOARDMAN, R. M.
BURNHAM, T.
BENNETT, A.
BELLWOOD, F.
BUSBY, W.
BROWN, W.
BOWLES, A.
BURTON, C.
BROMLEY, F.
BUTLER, H.
BERRY, A.
BURDETT, W.
BROWN, E.
BECK, P.
BATTERSON, A.
BURTON, A. L.
BOUSER, J.
BRIAN, J.
BRANDRETH, A.
BISHOP, G.
BURDETT, H.
BOTTOM, T.
BETTS, H.
BALDWIN, J.
BUSWELL, W.
BROOKS, R.
BRUIN, E.
BRADSHAW, R.
BROOKS, H.
BRAISBY, H.
BRAUN, F.
BRADSHAW, W.
BROOKS, S.
BICKERTON, E.
BROOKS, C. E.
BURY, J.
BURTON, H.
BENTHAM, A.
BOND, J.
BARROW, F.
BANKS, J.
BRICKHILL, N.
BROOKS, G.
BROOKS, H.
BROOKS, W.
BROOKS, F.
CARTER, H.
COOPER, F. W.
COATES, C.
COLLIER, F.
CHADWICK, D.
COULDING, J. W.
CAPPER, J.
COOPER, F.
CLARKE, H.
CHADWICK, W.
CORDINGLEY, J.
CROSS, G.
CHAPMAN, T.
CORLESS, W.
CORRY, P.
CROSS, D. J.
CLAYTON, A.
COPPELL, A.
CLINTON, T. C.
CLINTON, M.
CRIBB, J.
CROSS, A.
COX, J.
CRAGG, W.
COURT, W. E.
CAFFREY, J.
CONLEY, H.
CHEETHAM, J.
CRAMP, T. H.

CRISP, S.
CHARLTON, G.
COLE, W. E.
CRAIG, J. H.
CAWTHORN, H. L.
COLE, W. G.
CLARK, T.
COXON R.
CLARK, P.
CLARK, R.
CLEGG, N.
CASH, P.
COLE, H.
CRAGGS, J.
CRAIG, A.
CROW, A.
COOK, W.
COULSON, F.
COLE, D.
CARR, J.
CORBETT, T.
CHALMERS, D.
CANNAWAY, E
COOPER, J.
COLLINGE, H. G.
CONNOR, H.
CUNNINGHAM, A
CROME, E. W.
CONNOR, F.
CLARK, H.
COLLINS, J.
CAMPION, W. H.
CLARK, E.
COLLETT, J.
COLE, S.
CHAPMAN, E. J.
COLE, M.
COCKBAINE J. K.
CLEPPIT, C. H.
CLEAK S.
COOMBS, A. F.
CHILDS, A.
CURTIS, G.
CAUSELEY, M.
CHILCOTT, H.
CARTER, C.
CHAPLIN, T.
COX, H. T.
COSH, A.
COLTON, S. M.
CHAMBERLAIN, R.
CLARKSON, J.
COOKSON, A. J.
CATHERALL, T. C.
CROMPTON, F.
CONOLLY, J. H.
CLARKE —
CONWAY, —
COWELL, —
CARDWELL, A.
CHAPLIN, F.
CLARK, T.
CROSBY, B.
CLARK, F.
CLARK, R.
CLARK, S.
CATLIN, A.
CARTER, T.
CREE, H.
COLLINS, A.
CATLIN, P.
COLLINS, A.
CHIPPERFIELD, C.
CHERRY, H.
CRINNION, F.
COOKE, H.
CHAPPELL, I.
CORRAN, H.
CRESSWELL, W.
COLE, H.
CLARK, W.
CONWAY, J.
CLEGG, J. V.
CUSS, W. G.
CAVANAGH, T.
CASH, J.
CARSON, A.
CHORLTON, E.
CULLEN, F.
CUFFWRIGHT, R.
COLE, R.
COLE, C.
COXEY, F.

Co-operative Wholesale Society, Ltd.—Con.

CHALLINOR, W.
COLEMAN, H.
CAMPBELL, J. W.
COLEMAN, J.
CAVERHILL, W.
COFFEY, F. W.
CROMPTON, H.
CANNON, J.
COLLIER, W.
COWARD, I. J.
CHADWICK, G.
CARR, T.
COLLINS, J.
CONNOR, J. H.
CAUSER, G.
CLARE, R.
CORNER, J.
CARTER, J. G.
CUTHBERTSON, G.
CLARKSON, W.
COCKRAM, R.
CARRUTHERS, N
CROOK, E.
CARROLL, W.
CRABTREE, S.
CHANDLER, W.
CONNOR, G.
COLLINGE, H.
COLLINGE, H.
COATES, J.
COLLINGE, A.
CROPPER, A.
CHEETHAM, H.
COYNE A.
COTTON, C.
CAILEY, J.
COOK, J.
CONNOLLY, P. J.
COOK, W.
CHARLTON, I.
CHARLTON, J.
CLARK, A.
CHAMBERS, E.
CREED, H.
CLARK, C.
CLARK, W.
CLARK T.
CAIN, C. J.
CORDEN, A. H
COUPE, L.
CLULOW, J.
COBBIN, G.
CROMPTON, R.
CHATTERTON, S.
CLARKE, F.
COOK, J.
CROCKER, C. J.
COLE, R. H.
CROSS, A.
CAPEIN, E.
CHISWELL, J.
CHANDLER, W. F. H.
CRONSHAW, R.
CRIPPS, W. A.
CAMERON, H.
CRABTREE, F.
CATER, J.
CARTER, J.
CAVE, H. M.
COLLINS, S. B.
COOPER, R.
CHARLESWORTH, F.
COUGHLAN, F.
CLAYTON, H.
CHADWICK, H.
CARRACK, J.
CARRACK, JOE.
COOPER, F. E.
COLEMAN, G. W.
CHILDS, A.
COLEMAN, J. J.
CUMBERPATCH, A. P.
CLEGG, T.
COLLISON, J.
CORK, A.
COLLEDGE, W.
COLBOURNE, I.
COLBOURNE, J.
CABLE, W.

CHARLTON, M. W.
CLARE, E.
CASELEY, J. J.
CLAYTON, R.
CORSER, F.
CARTWRIGHT, F.
COATES, W.
CHERRY J.
CLARKE, F.
CHARLESWORTH, J.
CHADWICK, J. H.
COOPER, F.
CHADWICK, H.
CAMPBELL, L.
CHAMPION, H.
COPLEY, N.
CLEGG A.
COLLINS, J.
CHINAR, J.
CHARLESWORTH, H.
CROWE, W.
CHADWICK, H.
CARTLEDGE, W. G
CHEERS, H.
CRICHTON, W.
CALVERT, E.
CHALLONER, F.
CAMPBELL, J.
CHORLTON, J.
COCHRANE, D. T.
CLEGG, N.
CRAWFORD, T.
CADMAN, H.
CORNES, J.
CHADWICK, A.
CRABTREE, A.
CARLTON, C.
CONALTY, B.
CROMACK, H.
CASHON, J.
CONNAUGHTON, J.
CALVERT, —
CUTTER, L.
CHESTERS, J.
CARVLIN, R. J
CRAIG, S. F.
COATES, T. B.
CARR, W. H.
COLSH, P.
COLEMAN, E
CLEGG, F.
COOK, E.
CORE, H.
CARRACHER, T
CLARK, A.
CROSBY, G.
CHADWICK W.
CHADWICK, D.
COULDING, J. W.
CAPPER, J.
CLARKE, H.
CORDINGLY, J.
CROSS, G.
COOPER, E.
CAW, C. W.
CLINTON, F. J.
CLAYTON, A.
COPPELL, A.
COLEY, J.
CAWTHORN, E.
CLARK, C.
COOPER, E.
COLTMAN, A. H. C
CLARKE, J.
COPSON, F.
CLARKE, L.
COPLEY, H.
CROXTALL, W.
CARTER, J.
COUSINS, J. R.
CLARKE, T.
COX, J. H.
CARTWRIGHT, W.
CORT, F.
CARTER, J.
COOKE, H.
CHAPLIN, J.
COLVER, A.
CHARLESWORTH, J.
CHAPLIN, A

Co-operative Wholesale Society, Ltd.—Con.

CRAMP, A.
CLARKE, J.
CROWSON, W.
CLEAVER, G.
CORDWELL, J.
CORDER, B.
CLARKE, H.
CARTER, W.
CAWLEY, W.
CLARKE, S.
CLARK, P.
CRIPPEN, W.
CAMPBELL, M.
DYSON, F.
DOUGLAS, W.
DRONSFIELD, F.
DOBSON, T.
DAWSON, J.
DOWN, A. H.
DOBSON, H.
DAVIES, S.
DAVIES, T. B.
DAVENPORT, W.
DUNN, H.
DYSON, F.
DERBYSHIRE, J.
DOWSON, C.
DOULANE, J.
DOBSON, T.
DUNCAN, E.
DUTHIE, W.
DODGSON, J.
DUNCAN, R.
DODDS, E.
DIXON, W.
DYER, J.
DALTON, F. J.
DOLLING, W. L.
DONOVAN, E. P.
DURRANT, W.
DURRANT, D.
DERHAM, A.
DREW, A. J.
DAWES, A. E.
DELL, W.
DAY, G.
DEE, F.
DARROCH, J.
DUEMAN, F.
DEUTRIS, H.
DORMAN, L.
DEAN, W. H.
DRYHURST, R.
DOOKER, J.
DAVIDSON, F.
DELVES, J.
DAWSON, W.
DICKENSON, F.
DEVLIN, J.
DUXBURY, J.
DAVIS, F.
DANCE, G.
DALTON, W.
DEAN, J.
DIMELOW, B.
DAVIES, A.
DEAN, S.
DULANTY, D.
DONOVAN, A.
DICKENSON, R.
DAWSON, A.
DAVIES, A.
DAVIES, H.
DAWSON, H.
DICK, J.
DUFFY, A.
DODSON, G. W.
DUCKWORTH, F.
DANIELS, E.
DUNBAR, J.
DAVISON, J.
DORMAN, F.
DIXON, E.
DIXON, F.
DAWNES, J. J.
DANBY, W. J.
DURDEN, G.
DAWSON, J.
DAVIS, D. R.
DOUGLAS, H.
DAVIES, I.
DUCKER, W. J.
DALTON, F. B.

DAVIES, T.
DRUGGITT, G.
DAVIS, W.
DOWNING, W.
DUFFET, F. J.
DAWSON, E.
DANIELS, A.
DEAN, F.
DOVE, C.
DENTON, A.
DODGSON, A.
DURHAM, W.
DEANE, G. J.
DESBOROUGH, A. E.
DRAGE, A.
DICKENS, L.
DAWSON, J.
DOUGILL, W.
DRIVER, W.
DAVIES, J.
DAWSON, L. H.
DICKSON, J.
DREWITT, J.
DAVIS, R. J.
DRAKE, C.
DEARNLEY, H.
DENWOOD, M.
DE LUCEY, T.
DAVIS, T.
DERBYSHIRE, J. W.
DICKENSON, R.
DALTON, J.
DAVIS, J.
DAVIES, A.
DENNETT, A.
DAY, J.
DRAKE, H.
DIXON, J.
DOLAN, J.
DEVITT, J.
DIRKEN, A.
DIAMOND, G. M.
DEARNLEY, A.
DAWES, E.
DAVIS, G.
DAWSON, L.
DENNIS, W.
DICKEN, F.
DRONSFIELD, F.
DOWN, A. H.
DAWSON, J.
DOBSON, H.
DYSON, F.
DOUGHTY, T.
DIXON, F.
DILLEY, W.
DAYMAN, E.
DAWKINS, E.
DORE, P.
DUMELOW, G.
DODSON, C.
DARNS, C.
DALBY, W.
DARNTON, S.
DYSON, W.
DALE, T. W.
DAWSON, J.
DALTON, M.
ELSAM, T.
EGERTON, A. E.
EVERETT, C. A.
ELLIS, A.
EVANSON, A.
EARNSHAW, R. H.
ECKERSALL, G. M.
ENGLAND, A.
ELLIS, J.
EDWARDS, A.
EDMONDSON, H. S.
ENGLAND, G. W.
EKINS, L. G.
EDEN, W.
EDMONDSON, F. K.
ERRINGTON, R.
ETHERINGTON, R.
ELLIOTT, W.
EDWARDS, D.
EGLIN, G.
ELLIOTT, H. C.
ELLMAN, W.
ESBESTER, P. J.

EVETT, F. W.
EDWARDS, J.
EASTMENT, C.
EDWARDS, J.
EVANS, H.
EVERITT, J.
EVANS, J.
ELLINGHAM, W.
EMMETT, J. T.
EVANS, A.
ELWOOD, J.
ELLIS, A. L.
ELAM, B.
EARDLEY, H.
EASTMENT, S.
ELLIOTT, J.
EAVES, J.
EMERY, J.
EDMONDSON, G.
EDMONDSON, T.
ELLIOTT, F.
EVANS, C.
ELLIOTT, T.
ERRINGTON, R.
EASTON, B. B.
EDWARDS, H.
EDMUNDS, J.
EDSER, H.
EDWARDS, G.
EDMONDS, H.
ELLIS, F.
EASTWOOD, G.
EMSLEY, W.
EXLEY, F.
EDDISON, W.
ELDRIDGE, F.
EMERY, E.
EVANS, W.
ECKERSALL, H.
EVERETT, E. H.
EDE, J.
EASTWOOD, W.
ECKERSALL, F.
EVANS, G.
ECKERSLEY, A.
EVES, G.
EWART, J.
EGERTON, A. E.
ELSAM, T.
ELLIS, A.
EAGAR, G.
EVENSON, A.
ECKERSALL, G. M.
ELLIOTT, A.
EDGERLEY, A.
EVANS, J.
ELLIOTT, C.
FOSTER, J.
FRANKLAND, W. A.
FISHER, T. E.
FEBER, L.
FOSTER, R. S.
FEARNLEY, T.
FLANAGAN, E.
FIELDEN, I.
FELL, A.
FARRAR, W.
FOX, F.
FLANAGAN, M.
FORREST, J.
FLOYD, T.
FROST, J.
FARRAR, F.
FOGGON, R. S.
FINLAY, J. M.
FISHER, P.
FRATER, —
FLETCHER, T.
FOSTER, R.
FOGGIN, W.
FRASER, G. W.
FENWICK, R.
FRENCH, W.
FINDLAY, A.
FALLA, C.
FRANKS, H.
FORSYTH, G.
FOLLOWS, J.
FISHER, A.
FOORD, H.
FORD, H.

Co-operative Wholesale Society, Ltd.—Con.

FEREDAY, S.
FOXLEY, C.
FLACK, E.
FITTON, —
FERGUSON, —
FOSTER, C.
FELLOWS, F.
FRANCIS, G.
FREEMAN, F.
FLETCHER, A.
FLETCHER, E.
FOULKES, F.
FAIRBROTHER, S.
FOLEY, S. H.
FORD, J.
FITZJOHN, R.
FOSTER, W.
FREEMAN, J. E.
FINDLEY, A.
FRASER, F.
FEATHERSTONE, T.
FOULKES, T.
FEIGHNEY, T.
FORSTER, J.
FERRIER, J. W.
FARRER, J.
FRANKLIN, H.
FLAVELL, H.
FINDLATER, A.
FOSTER, J.
FULTHORPE, R.
FLETCHER, J.
FARRELL, E.
FORD, E. W.
FLOCK, F. W.
FRANKLIN, F.
FENNELL, T.
FENNEY, F. W.
FORSYTH, T. D.
FUDGE, B.
FRANCIS, A. L.
FELTHAM, W. A.
FRY, H.
FIELDS, G. R.
FOWLER, H.
FLEMING, W.
FLITCHCROFT, W.
FIRTH, P.
FLANAGAN, J.
FIRTH, A.
FIRTH, B.
FIRTH, A.
FIRTH, H. S.
FOX, E. A.
FRISBY, W. J.
FELCE, P. W.
FRANCIS, W.
FLEETHAM, T.
FINCH, W.
FIELDHOUSE, T.
FARMAN, W.
FROGGATT, J. A.
FRESHNEY, C.
FRIDAY, L.
FOX, H.
FALSHAW, J.
FRIEDRICH, H.
FRANKLIN, G. D.
FURBY, R.
FOSTER, L.
FINLAY, A.
FISH, A.
FENTON, —
FOY, J.
FOLWELL, W.
FIRTH, G. H.
FISHER, P.
FISHER, T. E.
FRANKLAND, W. A.
FOSTER, J.
FEBER, L.
FOSTER, R. S.
FEARNLEY, T.
FREESTONE, J.
FREESTONE, J.
FOX, T. E.
FOSTER, T.
FARMER, A.
FRODSHAM, H.
FREER, W.
FOULKES, W.
FREESTONE, H.

FIELDING, S.
FARDON, H.
GUEST, W.
GRIFFITHS, W. H.
GRATTON, J.
GREENWOOD, H.
GODDARD, F. D.
GALL, J. A.
GARTSIDE, W.
GREENHALGH, E.
GARNETT, S.
GILL, L.
GREENWOOD, R.
GWINNELL, H. A.
GREENHALGH, A.
GOODERHAM, A.
GARSIDE, F.
GUEST, T. F.
GASS, R. L.
GILTRAP, H.
GLYNN, M.
GIBBONS, M.
GRIFFIN, E.
GARDINER, J.
GRYSTON, C.
GRIFFITHS, W.
GREY, A.
GREETHAM, J. J.
GREY, J. E.
GREAVES, J.
GILHESPIE, F.
GIBB, J.
GLEN, J.
GIBB, H.
GREY, T.
GAYNER, A. E.
GARTH, W. F.
GEACH, —
GOVETT, A.
GRANGER, R.
GOODALL, J.
GREENAWAY, W. E.
GIBBS, C. A.
GREEN, E. G.
GRIMES, P.
GOSS, R.
GITSHAM, A.
GEORGE, J.
GREEN, W. J.
GRIFFITHS, H.
GORE, W.
GREENWOOD, C. W.
GRAINGER, A. H.
GREAVES, —
GREEN, J.
GARRATT, W.
GEIRS, F.
GRUNDY, D.
GARSIDE, H.
GELL, W.
GEARY, W.
GERHOLD, J.
GANE, A.
GREGORY, P.
GILLISON, J. W.
GRAY, H.
GENT, H.
GOSS, H.
GREENER, J.
GARDNER, C.
GIBSON, W.
GIBBINS, H.
GODDARD, T.
GODDARD, E.
GREEN, W. H.
GODDARD, A.
GREY, A.
GOODWIN, C.
GIBBS, P.
GRIFFITHS, J.
GILLIGAN, E.
GORDON, D.
GRIFFITHS, J.
GODDARD, W.
GILMOUR, J.
GRIERSON, R.
GLAZE, A.
GREAVES, J.
GREGORY, J.
GARNER, W.
GREEN, F. J.
GIBSON, J.

GREENER, J.
GOULBOURN, J.
GILHOLM, N.
GREEN, W. E.
GREEN, A. H.
GARDNER, E.
GASKELL, J. A.
GALLOWAY, J.
GALLOWAY, A.
GREAVES, F.
GLOVER, C.
GARNETT, G. H.
GIBSON, J.
GOODALL, G.
GREEN, A.
GREENWOOD, N.
GAUTREY, A.
GREAVES, J. W.
GEORGE, E.
GEORGE, J.
GINNS, C.
GREEN, G.
GILBERT, A.
GILL, A.
GRAINGER, A.
GRIFFITHS, A.
GOULD, J.
GLAISTER, G.
GOUGH, T. M.
GILCHRIST, J.
GREAVES, T.
GARDNER, A.
GREENWOOD, A.
GEE, T.
GOODWIN, J.
GORDON, C.
GRIFFITHS, T.
GARBUTT, J.
GARFORD, F.
GILCHRIST, F.
GILMORE, J.
GILMORE, —
GREY, T.
GILMORE, H. E.
GARTSIDE, B.
GAMBLE, J.
GAMBLE, D.
GREEN, W.
GOWER, J.
GODLEY, F.
GOTHARD, C.
GLEDHILL, T.
GREENWOOD, H.
GARNETT, W.
GREAVES, H.
GOODIER, A.
GALL, J. A.
GARTSIDE, W.
GREENHALGH, E.
GODDARD, F. D.
GREENWOOD, H.
GREENWOOD, R.
GARNETT, S.
GILL, L.
GWINNELL, H. A.
GREGORY, H.
GREENHALGH, A.
GUEST, W.
GARSIDE, F.
GRAYSON, A.
GRANT, E. L.
GRANT, B. T.
GROOCOCK, A. W.
GREEN, W.
GLOVER, B.
GRANT, E.
GIBSON, J. H.
GAMBLE, T.
GOODYER, E.
GAMBLE, E.
GILLIVER, H.
GEARY, H.
GRIMES, T.
GRIFFITHS, L.
GORDON, R.
GREENWOOD, T.
GILLESPIE, H.
GELL, H.
HOLDEN, H.
HARTLEY, R. I.
HILL, T.
HIGGIN, E.
HAIGH, F. C.

Co-operative Wholesale Society, Ltd.—Con.

HALL, J.
HULME, F.
HARDMAN, E.
HARDMAN, A.
HIND, W.
HOLLAND, J.
HOLMES, A.
HOWARD, J.
HOWARTH, J. A.
HORSFIELD, G. A.
HILL, F.
HOPE, L.
HALLIDAY, J.
HODSON, F.
HARTLEY, H.
HOWARTH, J. H.
HARTLEY, A.
HADFIELD, A.
HOLLINS, F.
HARRISON, S.
HARDMAN, A.
HOLDEN, H.
HEAPS, J.
HARVEY, H.
HUTTON, A.
HAGGERSTONE, E. M.
HEDLEY, T. L.
HOLMES, H.
HAYES, A.
HOUGHTON, W.
HOLLAND, P.
HOLMES, L.
HARRISON, A.
HAYLOCK, A.
HOLLINS, WM.
HOBSON, A. J.
HYMERS, R.
HERON, G.
HODGSON, C.
HILL, W. T.
HOWAT, J.
HODGSON, T.
HALL, E. J.
HEADLAM, G.
HANCOCK, A.
HETHERINGTON, L.
HOWSON, T. W.
HERON, A. H.
HENDERSON, J.
HERON, M.
HUDDANT, J.
HARRISON, J.
HARDMAN, G.
HAWKINS, F.
HURT, J. A.
HARRIS, T.
HILL, G.
HETHERINGTON, J.
HANSELL, W.
HALSTEAD, A. W. P
HAYWARD, E.
HOWELL, D. H.
HEALES, J.
HARWOOD, J.
HASELER, P.
HEATHER, H. H.
HANCOCK, R. W.
HOARE, J.
HEATHCOTE, L.
HAMPTON, M.
HILTON, W.
HANCOCK, G.
HASTINGS, G. H.
HASLOP, R.
HARRIS, F.
HOOPER, F.
HOWLETT, A.
HOPPER, H.
HEELAS, G.
HUTTON, J.
HARRINGTON, S.
HOWARD, W. S.
HONE, J. R.
HALLIDAY, R. J.
HADDOCK, H.
HELLIER, H. H.
HARRIS, V.
HALLETT, L. G.
HOPKINS, W. E. C.
HORNE, J. E.

HAM, G.
HARRIS, P.
HAWKINS, H.
HOBBS, J.
HEADON, W.
HALLIWELL, A.
HAMILTON, R.
HARPHAM,—
HOLT,—
HOWARD,—
HEPBURN, A.
HARRIS, W.
HORWELL, S.
HUBAND, W.
HILLIS, B.
HILL, H.
HOAR, F.
HARDMAN, R.
HARRISON, T.
HEYWOOD, T.
HILTON, A.
HOPE, N.
HOYLAND, F.
HODSON, H.
HURT, W. H.
HUGUES, M.
HESELTINE, F.
HANDS, W.
HUGHES, T.
HUGHES, J.
HUDSON, H.
HIGGIN, A. H.
HAIGH, G. A.
HIGGINBOTTOM, T.
HINCHCLIFFE, B.
HEPBURN, A.
HOPKINSON, J.
HODSON, J.
HUMPHREY, A.
HUMPHRIES, W.
HARDING, R.
HARRIS, J.
HORSFIELD, W.
HOLMES, J.
HOULSTON, A. F.
HARVEY, G.
HIGGINS,—
HUTCHINSON, R.
HOPWOOD, J.
HAMMERSLEY, F.
HOWARTH, T.
HAMPSON, W.
HILL, D.
HEATON, R.
HODGKINSON, S. E.
HARROP, F.
HOWARTH, R.
HIGGINBOTHAM, F.
HOWARD, T.
HEATH, G.
HARRISON, A.
HANKINSON, J.
HOUGHTON, R.
HIGGINBOTTOM, S.
HOWARD, W. J.
HAMPSON, H.
HINDLEY, A.
HEAP, G.
HUGHES, D.
HEWIT, W.
HARPER, C.
HIGNETT, J.
HESFORD, D.
HOPE, J.
HARRIS, J.
HAMPSON, T.
HARRIS, R.
HOWELL, S.
HOWARTH, F.
HOLT, J.
HEYWOOD, R.
HOUGHTON, W.
HUTCHINSON, N.
HOWARTH, H.
HUTCHINSON, P.
HILTON, W.
HULME, H.
HALLIWELL, H.
HOWARTH, J.

HALL, J. P.
HOWARTH, A.
HEALEY, W.
HULME, A.
HARGREAVES, W.
HOLLAND, J.
HOLT, E. W.
HALL, H.
HOLT, W.
HUTCHINSON, J.
HEMMINGS, A.
HAYTON, G.
HALL, A. K.
HAWTHORNE, C.
HILLS, S.
HILLS, T.
HALL, G.
HOGGINS, W.
HUNTER, J.
HEDLEY, J.
HAY, J.
HEDWORTH, S.
HARRIS, C.
HAMLIN, W.
HARRIS, W.
HARRIS, J. W.
HAYNES, D.
HARRINGTON, E.
HERBERTSON, J. H.
HAMPSON, A.
HARRISON, W.
HAYHURST, W.
HEWITT, J.
HORROCKS, J.
HOWARTH, L.
HOLGATE, J. A.
HYDE, M.
HAINES, W. H.
HONEYBALL, J.
HEADFORD, T.
HALE, W. G.
HARDING, C.
HOBBS, F. R.
HAINES, J.
HALES, R.
HOLLOWAY, H.
HOLT, S.
HOLLINGWORTH, M. W.
HAMER, W.
HANSON, L.
HERON, J.
HOLMES, T.
HOWARTH, H.
HELLIWELL, F.
HAIGH, P.
HOWARD, W.
HUDSON, D.
HOLMES, S.
HOCKLEY, J.
HOLMES, R.
HOLMES, H.
HARDIMAN, J.
HAYES, G.
HALL, G.
HAYES, A.
HILLARD, J.
HUNTINGTON, J.
HARTLEY, T. W.
HIRST, A.
HEPWORTH, H.
HOPPER, I.
HINCHCLIFFE, H.
HALL, F. F.
HOLT, J.
HEPWORTH, C. H.
HILL, F.
HANSON, J. A.
HARTLEY, G. H.
HUTCHINSON, J.
HIBBERT, G. W.
HANKINS, W.
HEFFORD, J. C.
HARRIS, J.
HILLS, W.
HOUSEAGO, A.
HOLLINGS, J.
HARDMAN, C.
HUDSON, G.
HOLT, A.
HARTLEY, P. G.
HICKS, H.

Co-operative Wholesale Society, Ltd.—Con.

HEATHCOCK, J.
HAWTHORNE, E.
HARTSHORNE, G.
HARTLAND, J.
HENDERSON, W. T.
HAULT, W. E.
HEWISON, J.
HURLSTONE,—
HEYWOOD, H.
HINDLE, J.
HOLLAND, H.
HAWKSWORTH, S.
HAWKSWORTH, J. A.
HOLLAND, J.
HURT, E.
HILL, J.
HARRISON, A.
HARTLEY, A.
HORROCKS, T.
HAMEY, W.
HASLAM, W.
HALL, G.
HICKS, S.
HALL, J.
HARDMAN, T.
HIBBERT, A.
HANDLEY, J.
HOWARTH, H.
HOWARTH, F. E.
HUMPHREYS, F.
HARDCASTLE, J.
HOPWOOD, N.
HEGINBOTTOM, H.
HOPE, T.
HOLMES, S.
HANCOCK, G.
HEALEY, I.
HINDE, F. H.
HAIGH, E.
HASSALL, A.
HUGHES, W.
HURST, E.
HODSON, W.
HEMINGWAY, S.
HOEY, A. E.
HART, F. W.
HOLT, W.
HOLDEN, J.
HUMPHRIES, G
HORNE, R.
HARVEY, D.
HURT, J. A.
HARRIS, T.
HILL, G.
HOBBS, C.
HOWARD, A. H.
HAWKINS, J.
HYMERS, W. J.
HORN, J. J.
HANLON, R.
HARTLEY, J. J.
HODGSON, G. E.
HARGREAVES, J. A
HANCOCK, G. G.
HYDE, H.
HALL, H.
HARDY, G. A.
HEATHCOTE, W.
HICKLING, E.
HALL, H.
HARRISON, P.
HEPWORTH, S.
HIRST, J. A.
HOBSON, H.
HULLEY, S.
HEYS, H.
HILL, J. W.
HUMPHREYS, J. D.
HESSELGRAVE, E. W.
HOLMES, A.
HODKINSON, F. J.
HIGGINS, E.
HOPE, L.
HORSFIELD, G. A.
HODSON, F.
HILL, F.
HALLIDAY, J.
HOWARD, J.
HAIGH F. C.
HALL, J.
HIND, W.

HULME, F.
HARDMAN, E.
HARDMAN, A.
HOLLINS, F.
HARTLEY, A.
HOLDEN, H.
HOYLAND, F.
HODSON, H.
HADFIELD, A.
HEIGHTON, F.
HOUSEMAN, J.
HULETT, D. E.
HEAWOOD, G. H.
HUNT, H. E.
HADDON, C.
HELAM, W. R.
HEATH H.
HENSON, G. K.
HORTON, J. E.
HOLMES, J. H.
HALL, H.
HACKETT, H.
HEATH, W.
HURST, F.
HAINES, W.
HARRIS, W.
HUBBARD, J.
HASSEL, A.
HEARD, R.
HARRIS, B.
HALL, J.
HEARN, S.
HERBERT, A.
HUDSON, W.
HOGG, J. H.
HENSON, T.
HARRISON, A.
HAMPSON, J.
HESFORD, W.
HICKSON, F. O.
HAZELHURST, I.
HINDLEY, J. J.
HOWAT, W. B.
HICKSON, H.
HOLMES, E.
HAMER, T.
HALLIWELL, F.
HILTON, W. A.
HARRISON, W.
HAZELHURST, M.
HILL, A.
HOLT, A.
ISHERWOOD, P.
INCE, J. H.
ISHERWOOD, P.
IRWIN, R.
ISAACS, W.
IRONS, C.
IDLE, H.
IRONS, F.
INGRAM, W.
IRONS, P.
INESON, J.
INGHAM, G.
IRVING, M.
INMAN, R.
INGLE, A.
INGHAM, W.
IDLE, B.
INCE, J. H.
ISHERWOOD, P.
ILIFFE, E. W.
ILIFFE, G.
IRWIN. W.
ILLINGWORTH, T.
INTIN, J.
JONES, J. H.
JONES, H. S.
JAMES, J. J.
JACKSON, J.
JEWITT, W.
JOHNSON, J.
JONES, E. W.
JOHNSON, J.
JACKSON, R.
JUDGE, J.
JOHNSON, W. A.
JACKSON, A.
JACKSON, H.
JACKSON, A.
JACKSON, W.
JOLLEYS, P.
JOHNSON, W.

JONES, E. P.
JOHNSTONE, J.
JOHNSON, P.
JACKSON, A. T.
JOHNSTONE, J.
JOHNSON, T. H.
JOBLING, E.
JONES, H.
JOB, A.
JOSHUA, R. J.
JONES, S. T.
JONES, W.
JENKINS, E.
JAMES, W. F.
JACKSON, A.
JONES, J. P.
JONES, C.
JACKSON, H.
JEPSON, J.
JONES, W. A.
JACKSON, A.
JACKSON, C.
JOHNSON, E.
JACKSON, J.
JACKSON, J. F.
JORDAN, P.
JOHNSTON, R.
JACKSON, H.
JEFFREY, A.
JONES, T.
JOHNSON, S.
JONES, W.
JOHNSTON, J.
JONES, W.
JONES, W. D.
JOY, W.
JOHNSON, P.
JACKSON, G.
JARVIS, R. C.
JACKSON, H.
JEWETT,—
JONES, A.
JACKSON, J.
JONES, D.
JEFFREY, A.
JONES, J. A.
JOHNSON, T.
JOINSON, J.
JARRETT, A.
JEWISON, J. H.
JOWETT, R.
JACKSON, J.
JACKSON, J.
JOHNSON, H.
JARMAN, W.
JARMAN, A.
JARMAN, C.
JEWKES, E.
JOHNSON, J. W.
JOHNSON, A.
JOHNSON, J.
JARVIS, J.
JONES, G.
JACKSON, T.
JOHNSTONE, W
JONES, J. W.
JENKINSON, F.
JOHNSTON, F.
JESSOP, J. B.
JENYON, G.
JACKSON, J.
JONES, J. T.
JUMP, J.
JOHNSON, W.
JOHNSON, H.
JENNINGS,—
JONES, H.
JACKSON, G.
JORDAN, B.
JACKSON, S.
JAMES, J. J.
JAMES, A.
JACKSON, J.
JEWITT, W. J.
JOHNSON, J.
JOHNSON, J.
JONES, F.
JOHNSON, C.
JORDAN, R.
JACOBS, A. J.
JOHNSON, A.
JAMES, E. J.
JACKSON, W.

15

Co-operative Wholesale Society, Ltd.—Con.

JACKSON, J.
KNOWLES, W.
KITSON, A.
KEANE, J.
KIRKMAN, H. E.
KUHN, L.
KELLY, T. G.
KILBY, J.
KNOX, T. W.
KOCH, O.
KINGHORN, W.
KNOWLES, J.
KING, L.
KINGDOM, F. S.
KILLICK, A.
KNOWLES, S.
KELDWELL, J.
KNIGHT, A.
KIRKHAM, C.
KERR, F.
KILDAY, T.
KIRKBRIDE, A.
KING, J.
KILDAY, —
KENYON, J.
KEAVNEY, P.
KIRSOP, W.
KING, J.
KENYON, J.
KENYON, W.
KNIGHT, H.
KELLY, F.
KNOTT, R.
KEMP, R.
KNIGHT, A.
KENDALL, W.
KITCHINGMAN, H.
KITCHINGMAN, F.
KITCHINGMAN, J.
KEMP, W.
KITCHINGMAN, R.
KNOWLES, P.
KNOTT, J.
KING, C.
KEAY, H.
KENYON, A.
KENYON, J.
KIRKHAM, W. R.
KENYON, T.
KENT, J. W.
KENT, H.
KELLETT, A.
KERSHAW, O.
KIRBY, J. W.
KAY, J.
KELLY, J. W.
KNIGHT, H.
KILBURN, G. R.
KING, F. J.
KNOWLES, W.
KING, W.
KING, T.
KING, A.
KIDGER, F.
KIRBY, F.
KING, W.
KAY, R.
LEES, T.
LAIRD, P.
LUCE, S. P. J.
LOMAN, C. W.
LONG, G.
LANG, J. H.
LEIGH, J.
LEONARD, J.
LEECH, G.
LEAKE, H.
LYALL, J.
LUMSDEN, R. W.
LUMLEY, R.
LAWSON, —
LONGSTAFF, W.
LEE, E. L.
LEE, R.
LEWINS, T.
LONG, J.
LITTLE, W.
LOWES, T.
LAMB, T.
LOUGHBOROUGH, F.
LECTOMERE, C.
LOCKYER, W.

LONGSON, J.
LEONARD, J.
LETHBRIDGE, H.
LEWIS, —
LEWIS, G. H.
LEECE, A. S.
LOMAS, J.
LOWE, E.
LUNN, G.
LEECH, G.
LODGE, W.
LEE, J.
LEACH, J. R.
LAMBERT, T.
LEE, R.
LUNT, T.
LEE, W.
LEES, W.
LOWE, H.
LEVICK, A.
LEVER, T.
LORD, A. B.
LOWE, J.
LANGDON, L.
LOKES, T.
LATIMER, D.
LANGTON, A.
LOWE, T.
LEES, H.
LONERGAN, D. C.
LOCKETT, W.
LEE, A. E.
LANGLANDS, A.
LIVESEY, T.
LEE, A.
LICKLEY, J.
LEACH, R.
LEACH, J.
LOWE, W. W.
LEEMING, A.
LEACH, C.
LANDLESS, G. C.
LAWTON, J. E.
LUKE, G.
LANCASTER, T.
LIGHT, R.
LAMBERT, T.
LAMBERT, J.
LOWE, H.
LOFTS, J.
LAVIN, F.
LOMAS, G.
LOCK, J.
LEVER, W.
LOVELL, S.
LEES, P.
LAWTON, J.
LAZENBY, A.
LLOYD, G.
LEWIS, T.
LISTER, A.
LEE, J. W.
LAWTON, W.
LEE, H.
LONGBOTTOM, S.
LISTER, T.
LINDSAY, T.
LANGFORD, E.
LANGLEY, F.
LEE, F. J.
LOAK, G.
LEECH, W. H.
LINDSAY, J.
LEIGHTON, R.
LOCKLEY, J.
LEETH, T.
LEETH, J.
LLOYD, F. C.
LEYLAND, H.
LOCKWOOD, F.
LINDLEY, A.
LAMBERT, D.
LONGFIELD, W.
LORD, W.
LOCKETT, R.
LAST, A.
LEVAY, F.
LATHAM, J.
LONGSON, H.
LOCKWOOD, F.
LEE, H.
LAWRENCE, H.
LLOYD, A.

LUND, W.
LAMONT, A. C.
LEGGATT, A.
LAW, H.
LEE, R.
LUMB, F.
LEES, J.
LOVELOCK, H.
LEECH, J.
LEES, F.
LOMAX, C. W.
LUCE, S. P. J.
LEACH, A.
LONG, G.
LAW, H.
LISTER, E.
LOWE, J.
LOWE, A.
LORD, R. R.
LORD, E. J.
LOWNDES, J.
LOWNDES, E.
LONGBOTTOM, W.
LEEDER, J. A.
LEIGH, H.
MART, T. H.
MARKAM, H.
MORRIS, S.
MORLAND, W. J.
MILES, N. W.
McLENNON, J. E.
McGRATH, J.
MARSHALL, F.
McCORMACK, W.
MESSENGER, A. H. G.
MOORES, G.
MORTON, H.
McINTYRE, J.
MONKS, J.
MORAN, J.
McLOUGHLIN, T.
MAY, L.
McLOUGHLIN, H.
MYLREA, D.
MELVIN, H.
MATHER, G. H.
MARKS, E.
McKAIG, W.
MOORES, H.
McKINLEY, J.
McFARLANE, C.
McLELLAND, J.
MEYER, J.
MEALING, T.
MILNE, J.
McCULLOCH, J.
MOORE, J.
MACBEAN, J.
MURTON, J.
MURRAY, J.
McKINLEY, J.
MASSON, T. K.
MOFFATT, J.
MITCHELL, R. W.
McKAY, R.
MELLING, J.
MITCHELSON, C.
MILNE, G.
MOORE, J.
McGINNETY, F.
MEADES, M.
MARTIN, J.
MANIFORD, F.
MATHEWS, T. G.
MOYNIHAN, A.
MASSEY, H.
MENNELL, E. H.
MONKSFIELD, H.
MAGNUS, R.
MAYES, F.
MAY, —
MARKS, —
MILTON, N.
MOORBY, F.
MORTIMER, J.
MELVILLE, J.
MORRIS, D. T.
MINES, A. J.
MARTIN, H.
MORGAN, —
MORRIS, F.
MORGAN, G. O.

Co-operative Wholesale Society, Ltd.—Con.

MORRIS, W. J.
MORGAN, E. J.
MORGAN, G.
MARKS, W.
MARKS, P.
McCLURE, H. W.
MILNE, —
McARTHUR, J. D.
MOLE, E.
MASON, A.
MONK, R.
MARCHANT, G.
MORRIS, J.
McLINTOCK, H.
McNEIL, J.
MARSHALL, F.
MARDLE, E.
MAYLES, F.
MURPHY, E.
MOULSON, L.
MATHER, W.
MORGAN, J.
MORRIS, H.
MAWDSLEY, W.
MARTIN, W.
MAHER, F.
MUIRHEAD, D.
McNICHOLAS, P.
MORRIS, H.
McWATUS, J.
MITCHELL, H. I.
MARSHALL, M.
MILLS, R.
MAYBURY, B.
MOSS, H.
MULDOWNY, J.
McGEARY, P.
MILLS, W.
MOORE, J.
MILLER, W.
MILLS, W. S.
McHUGH, W.
MANTON, C.
MAWSON, G.
MALONE, W.
McCLEAN, B.
MARLEY, F.
MAWBY, W.
MERRALL, E.
MARTIN, A.
MOSLEY, H.
MATHEWSON, W.
MOORE, H.
MORRIS, T.
MARSHALL, T.
MEADE, G. H.
MILNE, S.
MORRISON, J.
McHUGH, A.
MALCOMSON, S.
MASON, M.
MARSHALL, W.
MAKIN, W.
MILLS, F.
MILLS, W.
McGURK, B.
McGHEE, J.
MAJOR, W.
MACHIN, E.
MARSHALL, W.
MULLINER, A.
MOXFIELD, J.
MEADOWCROFT, T. H.
MULLINOR, G.
McKENZIE, A.
McCALL, J.
MULLEN, J.
MILLS, J.
MORRELL, E.
MILLS, J.
MARCROFT, L.
MOSS, F.
MOSS, J.
MORRIS, J.
METCALFE, E.
M'CLEAN, J.
M'CLEAN, G.
MAIN, C.
McNEILL, R.
MILLER, W.
McHENRY, W.
MALLETT, P.

MASON, W.
MULVANEY, J.
McDOUGALL, J.
MORRIS, R.
MORRIS, A. W.
MAGGO, W. H.
MORRIS, A.
MERRYWEATHER, G.
McINNES, G.
MALLINSON, F.
MILLS, H.
MOSS, J. W.
MACARTNEY, A.
MIDDLETON, W.
MITCHELL, H.
MURGATROYD, R.
MIDDLETON, H.
MONKMAN, G.
MURRAY, J.
MYERS, R. J.
MILLS, E.
MORRIS, E. B.
MINNEY, E. B.
MARTIN, W.
MINNEY, F.
MILLWARD, P.
MILLER, J.
MIZON, H.
MEREDITH, W. E.
MILLER, A.
MANDERS, Z.
MEEK, J. A.
MASON, W.
MERRICK, —
MAXWELL, J.
MARSH, B.
MATHER, F.
MILLS, J.
MOORES, H.
MATHER, H.
MILLER, D.
MYLES, J.
McMEEL, C.
MARTINCROFT, A.
MOORE, E.
MACDONALD, G.
MATHER, J.
McEVOY, J.
McBURNEY, J.
MESSENGER, T.
McLEAN, A.
MYFORD, P.
MARTINDALE, W.
McMAHON, —
McCABE, C.
MICHAM, J.
MASTERMAN, G.
MITCHELL, F.
MAWSON, B.
McGREGOR, —
MANN, E.
McCONKEY, A.
MITCHELL, J.
MACKENZIE, G. B.
MILLER, C.
MELLOWS, T.
MELLOWS, L.
MORLEY, E.
MURDEN, S.
MAY, H.
MARLOW, C.
MILNES, C.
MIDWOOD, E.
MILNES, B.
MARSDEN, F.
MILLS, W.
MANIFIELD, G.
MORRIS, S.
MATHER, H.
McCORMACK, W. W.
MESSENGER, A. H. G.
MOORES, G.
MORTON, H.
McGRATH, J.
McLELLAN, J. E.
MILES, N. W.
MONKS, J.
MORAN, J.
McINTYRE, J.
MAY, L.

McLOUGHLIN, T.
MOORE, E.
MARKHAM, W.
MATLOCK, W.
MATHERS, A.
MERRICKS, L.
MILLER, T.
MARRIOTT, W.
MARTIN, G.
MARTIN, J.
MARBY, S.
MATHEWS, E.
MARTIN, H.
MARTIN, A.
MOORE, E.
MATHERS, H.
MASSEY, E.
MASSEY, J.
MASSEY, T.
McLINTOCK, W.
McKAY, R.
MORT, A.
MORT, J. T.
MORTON, R.
MERRICK, W.
MELLOR, H.
MORGAN, G. E.
MITCHELL, G.
McCULLOCH, H.
NELSON, H.
NELSON, J.
NELSON, F.
NOEL, A.
NIGHTINGALE, A.
NEWHALL, H.
NIBLETT, E.
NEWTON, H.
NICHOLLS, E.
NODDINGS, R. G.
NESBITT, J.
NICHOLSON, R.
NICHOLSON, A.
NOBLE, P.
NIHELL, E.
NEVILL, W. J.
NOBLE, A.
NEWBERRY, A. S. T.
NICHOLSON, —
NEWTON, A.
NOLAN, I.
NEVIN, J.
NICHOLSON, E.
NELSON, C.
NEDEN, A.
NOBLE, J.
NIELD, H.
NORMAN, F.
NAYLOR, T.
NUTTALL, W.
NEWTON, F. P.
NUTTALL, F.
NEWTON, A. W.
NATTRESS, G.
NEALING, J.
NIELD, J.
NICHOLSON, T.
NASH, A.
NORRISH, P.
NEWSOME, A.
NAYLOR, C.
NAYLOR, A.
NAYLOR, H.
NELMES, E. C.
NEALE, H.
NICKLIN, W.
NICKLIN, J.
NAYLOR, S.
NETTLESHIP, F.
NUTTALL, T.
NAYLOR, F.
NEWBY, W. H.
NICHOLSON, T. A.
NEAL, R. W.
NEAL, J.
NEWSOME, J. W.
NELSON, H.
NELSON, J.
NIGHTINGALE, A.
NOEL, A.
NEWCOMBE, W.
NOBLE, W.
NOBLE, A.

Co-operative Wholesale Society, Ltd.—Con.

NEAT, W.	POTTS, J. E.	PETTIFER, A.
NEWCOMBE, G.	POTTS, C.	POWELL, A.
NEAL, E.	PEELE, J.	PRICE, H.
NEALE, J.	PEARCE, C. H.	PRYER, W.
NICOLLS, W.	PASKELL, R.	PRYER, T.
OLDBURY, J.	PAGE, F.	PITTAM, W.
OVERALL, W. C.	PAGE, A.	PARROTT, C.
ORANGE, S. A.	PILLER, H.	PRINOLD, F.
OGDEN, G. H.	PHILLIPS, J.	PRICE, G.
OGDEN, J.	PLUME, J.	PICKIN, G.
OWEN, F. L.	PERCIVAL, H.	PRINCE, W.
OWEN, H.	POWELL, J.	PREECE, J.
OLIVER, J.	PALMER, C. E.	PILKINGTON, F.
OSWELL, E.	PERRYMAN, G. W.	PATERSON, H.
O'HARA, J.	PADFIELD, J.	PARR, A.
OAKLEY, T.	PAUL, P. C.	PLUMB, H.
ORRICK, W.	PADFIELD, G.	PILKINGTON, J.
ORFORD, G.	PARSONS, F.	PARKER, J. E.
OXLEY, J.	PARSONS, A.	POWELL, F.
OSBORNE, J.	PULLEY, F.	POOLE, E.
OWEN, W.	PETRIE, A. G.	PONTING, F.
OSWALD, T.	POLLITT, —	PLANT, L.
OAKES, A.	PARK, G.	PILKINGTON, J.
O'NEIL, A.	PIMLEY, A.	PRESTON, H.
OWEN, D.	PENDLEBURY, P. W.	POLLITT, S.
ORR, G.	PORTER, W. E.	PAUL, H.
OGDEN, B.	PAYNE, J.	POCHIN, J.
OGDEN, S.	PEARCE, W.	PHOENIX, H.
OXLEY, JNO.	PATES, A.	PARROTT, W.
OXLEY, JOS.	PATTINSON, R.	PHILLIPS, —
OGLE, H. C.	PEARSON, T. J.	PRITCHARD, R.
OLSEN, H.	PAGET, S.	PROCTOR, W.
O'NEILL, J.	PRITCHARD, D.	PERRY, H. R.
OAKLEY, B.	PRICE, J. A.	PHIPPS, W. H.
ORGAN, E. R.	PENDLEBURY, C.	PEPPER, W.
OATES, J. S.	PARKER, F.	PARKER, H.
OLDROYD, J. W.	PEARSON, T.	PICKERING, H.
OAKLEY, H. E.	PICKFORD, J.	PARTINGTON, A.
ORR, D.	PENNINGTON, A.	PATEFIELD, H.
O'NEILL, J.	PEMBERTON, R.	PICTON, H.
OPENSHAW, A.	PERRIN, J.	PICKUP, J. R.
O'SHAUGHNESSY, G.	PENNINGTON, A. W.	PIKE, W.
		PEDUZZI, J.
OLIVER, D.	PINNINGTON, F.	PECKET, A.
OLDFIELD, E.	PARKIN, W. J.	PARTINGTON, R.
OLDROYD, B.	PENGELLY, J.	PLUMB, J. J.
OWEN, E.	PERRY, W.	PILKINGTON, H.
OAKES, J. F. L.	PATTISON, W. S.	PUGH, R.
OVERALL, W. C.	PATTISON, J.	PEARSON, H.
ORANGE, S. A.	PRICE, S.	PARR, H.
OWEN, B.	PARKINSON, F.	PHILLIPS, G.
OCCLESTON, J.	PARKINSON, R. T.	PRESCOTT, J. W.
O'HARE, J.	PEDLEY, M. R.	PRESTON, A.
OWEN, J.	PENKETHMAN, F.	PRINCE, D.
OWEN, R.	PERRIN, J.	PAGET, S.
PENDLETON, W. H.	PERRIN, H.	PRINCE, D.
PRESTWICH, J. W.	PURDY, M.	PLUMB, W.
PARTINGTON, A.	PEMBERTON, R.	PYWELL, A.
PRINCE, D.	PLANT, W.	PUTT, W. J.
PARTINGTON, R.	PENDLEBURY, W.	PEARSON, F.
PLUMB, J. J.	PARKINSON, W.	PERCIVALL, A.
PICKET, A.	PACEY, P.	POTTERTON, C.
PIKE, W.	PURCELL, A. L.	PERKINS, J.
PILKINGTON, H.	PESTAL, H.	POWERS, W. C.
PUGH, R.	PEARCE, A.	PAGE, F.
PEARSON, H.	PEARSON, J.	PICKERING, H. E.
PARR, H.	PENMAN, O.	PARSONS, J.
PRESCOTT, J. W.	PRINGLE, J.	PHIPPS, E.
PHILLIPS, G.	PULLINGER, E. A.	PIKE, J.
PULLAN, J.	PHIPPS, C.	PAGE, H.
PRINCE, D.	POUILLEY, C.	PRINCE, E.
PRESTON, A.	PEARCE, O. J.	PRICE, F.
PURSGLOVE, A.	POOLE, C. W.	POLLARD, G.
PEARSON, H. B.	PIPER, W. B.	PORTEOUS, A.
PRINCE, D.	PETERS, A. H.	POSTLES, F.
PICKERING, A.	PEATTY, E.	PINNION, A.
PEARSON, R.	POWELL, R. J. H.	PRESCOTT, J.
POLLOCK, A.	POTTER, F.	PRIEST, J.
PATCHETT, J.	PRESTON, J. W.	PLANT, J.
PRICE, A.	POPPLEWELL, G.	PERKINS, H.
PHILLIPS, J.	PARKER, C.	PARR, A.
PILLING, H.	PRINCE, G. A.	QUIGLEY, J.
PALMER, H.	PHILBY, G. A.	QUARTLEY, B.
PARKHOUSE, W.	PAGE, B. V.	QUALTER, J.
PERRY, F.	PEGG, J. I.	QUALTERS, E.
PEACOCK, B.	PERCIVAL, S. R.	RYDINGS, E.
PIGG, W.	PERCIVAL, H.	ROBINSON, E. S.
PROUD, J. W.	PORT, J.	RIGG, J.
PURVIS, —	PRENTICE, E.	RICHARDS, S.
PURDY, J.	PROCTOR, C.	RATCLIFFE, S.
PATTISON, J. S.	PHILLIPS, C.	ROGERSON, R.
PALMER, H.	POOLE, T.	RIDING, W. S.
PENNETT, E.		RAW, J. W.

Co-operative Wholesale Society, Ltd.—Con.

RAY, J.	ROBSON, —	RAY, J.
REDFORD, H.	ROY, H.	REDFORD, H.
ROTHWELL, T.	RUSSELL, I.	ROYLE, J. R.
ROYLE, J. R.	RUTHERFORD, T.	RYDINGS, E.
ROBINSON, G. W.	RUTHERFORD, J.	REEVES, S.
ROSS, I.	REID, J.	RYAN, J.
RYAN, J.	ROSS, A.	ROSS, I.
REEVES, S.	RUSSELL, J.	RANDALL, C.
ROTHWELL, H.	ROSS, A.	ROGERS, W. E.
ROBINSON, G.	ROBSON, W.	ROBERTS, W. T.
RUSSELL, J.	ROBSON, T.	RUDKIN, H.
RIGBY, S.	ROSE, F.	RUDKIN, E.
ROYLE, A.	ROWE, W.	ROWE, G.
ROBSON, W.	ROLTON, B. O.	RIDDINGTON, H.
RICHARDSON, S.	ROBERTS, O.	ROGERS, J.
RAFFLE, G.	RODEN, A.	RICHARDSON, J.
ROBERTSON, F.	RAWLINS, E. R.	RENSHAW, A.
RICHARDSON, J. T.	RIDINGS, J. E.	RYAN, J.
ROBINSON, E. A.	ROSE, E. A.	ROGERSON, J. J.
ROBSON, L.	RENTON, H.	RIGBY, F.
REYNOLDS, C.	RIDGEWAY, J.	ROBERTS, E.
REID, J.	REDMAN, A.	RENSHAW, J. W.
ROSIE, D.	ROSSITER, W. G.	RATCLIFFE, J.
ROYSTON, J.	ROTHWELL, G.	SLACK, J. E.
REEMAN, R.	RAYNOR, A.	SIDEBOTHAM, J.
RENDLE, W. L.	ROBINSON, P.	STAFFORD, H. E.
REDSELL, W.	RATCLIFFE, E.	SIDDALL, J. W.
ROBERTSHAW, J. W.	ROBINSON, E.	SPENCER, J. R.
	ROBINSON, A.	STEWART, McL.
ROBERTS, B.	ROBINSON, I.	J. A.
RICHARDS, F.	ROTHERY, T. S.	SIDDALL, J. A.
RICHARDSON, F.	ROSENDALE, R.	SCORE, W. L.
ROWLES, R.	ROGERS, J. C.	SHERRATT, F.
ROSE, G.	ROBINSON, J.	SIDDALL, J.
ROBSON, W.	ROGERS, W. E.	STAFFORD, A.
RAY, R.	ROWTHORN, W. O.	SETON, D.
REES, T. A.	RICHARDSON, J. T.	SHAWCROSS, H.
REYNOLDS, D.	RADCLIFFE, T.	SHAW, E.
ROBINSON, W. E.	RHODES, J. W.	SHAW, H.
RUGEN, L.	ROE, J.	SIMMONS, J.
RAMSDEN, W.	RESTALL, W.	STONEHOUSE, W.
RICKETTS, H. J.	ROBINSON, J.	SCOTT, N.
RIMMER, F.	RUSSON, A.	STANSFIELD, H.
RANDALL, W.	RUSSON, H.	SHEPHERD, R.
ROGERSON, J.	ROUND, E. A.	SPRINGALL, W. T.
ROWBOTTOM, F.	RIDLEY, A. J.	SCAIFE, E. J.
ROYLE, H.	RUDIFERTH, A. E.	STRATH, J.
ROGERS, J.	ROBINSON, G.	SPENCER, J.
RICHMOND, H.	RODERICK, S.	SUTTON, H.
ROBERTS, W. H.	ROBERTS, T.	SMITH, G.
ROWBOTTOM, T. P.	ROBINSON, J.	STOPFORD, W.
ROBERTS, J.	ROSCOE, A. E.	SMITH, G.
ROSENBERG, H.	ROSCOE, A.	STOTT, W.
ROBINSON, W.	ROBERTS, H.	SHAUGNESSEY, T.
RADCLIFFE, L.	RIGBY, A.	STEELE, T.
ROBINSON, S.	REVETT, E.	SHEARD, G.
RICHARDSON, R.	RADCLIFFE, S.	STEEL, E.
RICKERS, C. H.	REDFERN, J.	SCOTT, J.
ROBERTS, H.	ROBINSON, H.	SLACK, J.
RICHARDSON, J.	ROBERTS, J.	SOAR, F.
RIDLEY, B.	ROYLE, J.	SCORER, T.
ROFFE, E.	ROBINSON, H.	STRICKSON, A.
ROBINSON, T.	RADCLIFFE, E.	SHERREN, G.
RICHARDSON, G.	REID, H.	STEWART, T.
ROXBURGH, A.	REDFORD, T.	SNOWDON, C. W.
ROYLE, W.	ROTHWELL, W.	SMITH, E.
RENSHAW, F.	ROBERTS, A.	SPOORS, W.
ROTHWELL, P.	ROYLE, C.	STOREY, H.
RYAN, W.	RUSSELL, F.	SMITH, J.
ROYLE, J.	RUSCOE, H.	SIMM, J.
ROYLE, E.	RAPER, F.	SHADWICK, R.
ROBERTS, L.	RICHARDSON, T.	SCOTT, W.
RUSHTON, B.	RAMSDEN, W.	STUBBS, H. P.
RICHARDSON, J.	REED, A. H.	SHEPHERD, J.
RIGBY, A.	RHODES, E.	SEDGEWICK, N.
ROBERTS, R.	ROBERTS, J.	SCOTT, A.
ROYLE, J.	RUSHWORTH, G.	SANDERSON, R.
ROBERTS, E.	RATLEDGE, A.	SCOTT, J. G.
ROYLE, J. T.	RIDLEY, R. O.	SCORER, G.
RUNCIMAN, J.	ROSE, A. R.	SMITH, J.
ROGERS, W. S.	ROBERTS, G.	STEPHENSON, J.
ROSE, —	ROWLES, T.	STEVENS, L.
RODEN, T.	RICHARDSON, H.	SILLS, L.
ROWLES, T.	RAMSBOTTOM, J.	SMITH, E. C.
ROOKE, A.	ROBERTS, H. T.	SELF, E.
RUSSELL, R.	ROBINSON, E. S.	SILLS, C.
RICHES, S.	RIGG, J.	SHUTER, H.
RHODES, B.	RATCLIFFE, S.	SHEPHERD, W.
RABY, J.	ROGERSON, C.	STOWE, C.
REED, G. R.	RIDINGS, W. S.	SILLIS, W.
RANDALL, G.	RAW, J. R.	SAUNDERS, W. J.
ROUSE, R.	ROYLE, R. N.	SMITH, J. E.
RICHARDS, S.	ROTHWELL, T.	

Co-operative Wholesale Society, Ltd.—Con.

SEAGRAM, A.
STONIER, A.
SOMERVILLE, J.
SCHRAM, M.
STOREY, F.
SERVIS, M.
SOWERBY, —
SHEPHARD, F.
SUSSEX, J.
SPACCATROSI, A. G.
SHORT. P. C.
SNOW, H. T.
SUMMERS, W. A.
SUMMERFIELD, A.
SEIG, T.
SIMPSON, A.
STARK, W.
SMITH, P.
SURRIDGE, G. A.
SHORES, S.
STARK, G.
SCHOFIELD, L.
SHORES, H.
SKEGGS, B.
SULLIVAN, J.
STAMBROOK, L.
STARLING, W.
SERVIS, J.
SHAW, J.
SCRUTTON, J.
SULLIVAN, J.
SMITH, W.
STAPLES, W.
SMITH, G.
SMART, S.
SELBY, R.
SCHOFIELD, J. R.
SCHOFIELD, C.
STOTT, R. D.
SHERBURN, R.
SCARTH, J. S.
SMITH, G.
SAUL, H.
SALMON, H.
SHAW, J.
STOTT, W.
SAMUEL, E. A.
SMITH, J. E.
SMITH, H.
SCHOLES, T.
SKEWES, J.
SUTCLIFFE, C.
SHAW, W.
SMITH, F.
STONELY, J.
SIMPSON, O.
SCOULER, P.
SMITH, P.
STODDART, T. H.
SOAR, G. H.
STAINES, J.
STURROCK, H.
STURROCK, J.
SMITH, R. H.
SAWYER, F.
STIRLING, W.
SHELMERDINE, R.
SCHOFIELD, J.
SCRAGG, G.
SIGSWORTH, W.
SHAWCROSS, P.
STONE, F.
SCOTT, R.
STOCKWELL, G.
SANSON, J.
SHAW, J.
SHARP, J.
SHAWCROSS, J.
SHAW, J.
SHAW, G.
SINBLETT, W.
SMITH, W. H.
SAUNDERS, A. G.
STANLEY, W.
SULLIVAN, J.
SMITH, W.
SMETHURST, J.
SHARP, W.
SHARP, L.
STONE, J. G.
SIBBLES, G. H.
SINKINSON, F.
SMITH, J.
SALMON, G.
STAMP, C. F.
SWALLOW, G.
SALMON, P.
SMITH, T.
SIMPSON, J.
SMITH, S.
STEVENSON, G.
SPENCE, R.
STILWELL, T.
STOKER, J.
SCOTT, J.
SLEIGH, G.
SOULSBY, W. T.
SKOYLES, A.
SIMPSON, C.
SHRIMPTON, F. C.
SHRIMPTON, E. B.
SMITH, F.
STOCK, G.
STEVENS, G.
STEELE, F. J.
SCHOFIELD, J. W.
SEABORNE, J. W.
SAVAGE, J.
SUTTON, J. E.
SANDERSON, H.
STRONG, R.
SHINGLER, W. H.
SAUNDERS, H.
SEABORNE, W. S.
SANSUM, G.
SERLE, E. J. G.
SMITH, G.
SMITH, A.
SAUNDERS, E. C.
SLATTERY, W.
STANLEY, J.
SIDDAL, R.
STEPHENSON, J. W.
SEVILLE, J.
STOWE, J.
SUGDEN, T.
SPIVEY, R.
STURGESS, H.
SMITH, C.
STOTT, J.
SWIFT, W.
STOCKS, H.
SMITH, E.
SMITHSON, J.
SMITH, H.
SANDS, G. H.
SMITH, I.
SENIOR, T.
SWIFT, A.
STOTT, A.
STOTT, E.
SUMMERSCALES, F.
SMITH, W.
SCATCHARD, B.
SHEARD, W.
SPENCE, B.
SUTTON, H.
SHARPE, J.
SMYTH, A.
SPENCER, C.
SMITH, S. E.
SNELLING, R. H.
SHARMAN, W. A.
SKINNER, H. E.
SUGARS, E. A.
SMITH, C.
SMITH, F. A.
SEAMARKS, W. E.
SWINGLER, E. E.
SAFFORD, G.
SPRING SMITH, J. A.
SINFIELD, W.
SMITH, C. W.
SHELDRICK, H.
SCHOFIELD, F.
SMITH, A.
SLATER, W.
SHACKLETON, H. R.
SLINN, A.
STIRLING, A.
SIDDALL, S.
SIMPSON, G.
SUMMERS, H.
SHINGLER, J.
SIMS, P.
SLOPER, F.
SMITH, G.
SWINDALE, W.
SHOVELTON, T.
SHINTON, H.
SHARROCKS, R.
SIDDALL, H.
SCHOFIELD, F.
SWINDELL, H.
SHORROCKS, J.
SHORES, E.
SHANNON, C.
STRINGER, S.
SHAW, F.
SHARPLEY, W.
SALTER, W.
SIPE, A.
SLATER, F.
SWINDELLS, C.
SHORROCKS, C.
SCHOLES, W.
SMITH, W.
SLATER, C.
SMITH, C.
SMITH, H.
SMITH, J.
SHARP, J.
SMITH, G.
SHOREMAN, T.
SIMS, A.
SADLER, H.
SMITH, —
STEVENS, L.
SMITH, E.
SWAN, J. T.
SMITH, T. A.
SUNDERLAND, L.
STOTT, J. T.
STUART, J.
SMITH, C.
SMITH, G. H.
SHEARD, H.
SEARS, H. A.
SYKES, G. W.
SMITH, J. A.
SMITH, W.
STOTT, W.
SWIFT, F.
SHAW, J.
SIDDALL, J. A.
STAFFORD, H. E.
SLACK, J. E.
SIDEBOTHAM, J.
SIDDALL, T.
SHERRATT, F. H.
SCORE, W. L.
STAFFORD, A.
SETON, D.
SHAWCROSS, H.
SCOTT, H.
STANSFIELD, H.
SCARRETT, W.
SCOTTON, C.
STEVENS, J. A.
STAFFORD, H.
STOCKER, J. A.
SNAPE, A.
STEELE, J. H.
SIMONS, P.
STANYON, T.
STANDLEY, F.
SMITH, T. F.
SHORT, H.
STEVENSON, C
SHARMAN, F.
SPENCE, T.
SPENCE, J.
SOUTHAM, W.
SMITH, F.
SIBSON, J.
SIBSON, A.
SIMPKINS, W.
SHARMAN, B.
SHAW, T.
SMALLEY, B.
SMITH, B.
STEWART, C.
SWINDLES, E.

Co-operative Wholesale Society, Ltd.—Con.

SHAW, J.
STOREY, J.
SHAWCROSS, T.
SWINDLES, J.
SAVERY, A.
SCHOLES, N.
TAYLOR, H.
TAYLOR, H. P.
THORPE, H.
THOMPSON, W.
TAYLOR, L. B.
TAYLOR, W. P.
TWEEDALE, H. A.
THOMAS, T. C.
TILDSLEY, A. E.
TOMKINS, F. W.
TONGE, I.
TURNER, P.
TURNER, C.
THORNLEY, W.
TURNER, F.
TAYLOR, S.
TAYLOR, G.
THOMAS, S.
TOOR, J.
TAYLOR, G.
TAYLOR, C.
TILSTON, F.
TOOBY, J.
THOMAS, D.
TAYLOR, E.
TAYLOR, W.
TITHERINGTON, A.
TROUT, H.
TILLEY, H. F.
THOMPSON, J. T.
TODD, S.
TURTON, S.
TAYLOR, J. G.
TULIP, J. C.
THOMPSON, S.
THORNTON, A.
TREWEEKS, T.
TIMMINS, A.
THORNER, T.
THOROGOOD, C.
TRAIN, A.
TAYLOR, A. G.
TIETGEN, H.
THOMPSON, E.
TYLER, W.
TOOMEY, J.
THOMASSON, F.
TINEY, J.
TALBOT, A.
TITMARSH, V.
TEMPLAR, J.
TUCKER, A. E.
TIPPETTS, T.
THOMAS, E.
TURNER, A.
TAYLOR, C.
THOMAS, J. A. G.
TEUCHER, F. B.
TYLER, H. W.
TOMPKINS, W.
TRIVETT, E.
TEENDALL, F.
TOOMEY, J.
TARRANT, G.
TREERS, C.
TREEN, C.
THOMPSON, W.
TUCKER, F.
TIPTON, C.
TURNER, H.
THEAKER, H.
TAYLOR, J.
THOMPSON, J.
TELFORD, T.
TODD, R.
TURNER, E.
TAYLOR, G.
THOMPSON, J. J.
THOMPSON, J.
TAYLOR, F.
TOFT, W.
TAYLOR, M.
TALLENTYRE, T.
TEMPEST, T.
TAYLOR, E.
THOMPSON, A.
TODD, J.
TEMPERLEY, A.
TAYLOR, H.
TAYLOR, H.
TAYLOR, T.
TEASDALE, E. G.
TAYLOR, S.
TAYLOR, H. P.
TASEY, J.
TOWNS, T.
TATTON, C.
TAYLOR, H.
TOWNS, A.
TAYLOR, R.
TRAVIS, F.
TAYLOR, T.
TOVEY, C. W. G.
TARRY, G.
TAYLOR, J. T.
TINSLEY, J. W.
TRAVIS, H.
THOMAS, J. A.
TURNER, J.
TERRY, S.
TATTERSFIELD, C.
TOWNEND, A.
THEWLIS, E. A.
TOWNEND, A.
TURNER, G.
THORNTON, L.
THEWLIS, J.
THORNE, F. R.
TODD, A.
TRAYNAR, R. T.
TRIGG, A.
TAYLOR, J.
TYNDALL, J.
TYSON, T.
THOMPSON, R.
THOMAS, W.
THOMAS, E.
THOMAS, A.
TONGE, A.
TIGHE, F.
TAYLOR, D.
TAYLOR, H.
THISTLETHWAITE, A.
TUTTIETT, S.
TAYLOR, S.
TRAVIS, J. W.
TAYLOR, H.
TRAVIS, H.
TOWNSON, L.
TANSEY, C.
THORLEY, S.
TEWSON, F.
THOMASON, J.
THORNEYCROFT, J.
THORNLEY, A.
TAYLOR, A.
TRENELL, H.
TAYLOR, T.
THOMPSON, G.
TATE, E.
TUFLE, S.
TRUSCOTT, G. A.
TUCKWOOD, E.
TAYLOR, A.
THORNTON, J.
TAYLOR, G.
THOMAS, T. C.
TAYLOR, L. B.
TAYLOR, W. P.
THOMPSON, W.
THORPE, H.
TILDSLEY, A. E.
TOMKINS, F. W.
TONGE, T.
TURNER, F.
TURNER, C.
THORNLEY, W.
TAYLOR, G. W.
TEBBUTT, G.
TESTER, P.
TOONE, A.
TOWNSEND, A.
TOSELAND, F.
TAYLOR, A.
TIBBLES, S.
TAYLOR, L.
TINSLEY, J.
TAYLOR, S.
TAYLOR, G.
TAYLOR, J.
THOMASON, J.
THIRSK, G.
TAYLOR, F.
TITMARSH, F.
TAYLOR, A.
URWIN, J. J.
UNDERHILL, J.
UNSWORTH, E.
UPTON, W.
UNSWORTH, G.
UNDERWOOD, T.
UNDERWOOD, N.
UTTLEY, T.
VARLEY, P.
VALENTINE, J. W.
VANN, W.
VERNON, R. J.
VINCENT, A.
VENUS, G.
VAUDRY, J.
VANHEE, G.
VARTY, G.
VARTY, J.
VARLEY, A.
VOYCE, P.
VARLEY, P.
VERNON, J. E.
VOSS, T.
VAUDREY, T.
WHITTLE, P.
WARBURTON, F.
WORTHINGTON, W. L.
WILLIAMS, J. A.
WOOD, W. M.
WILLIAMS, H. T.
WALKER, J. T.
WOLSTENCROFT, W.
WHITEHEAD, W. E.
WHITTAKER, A. V.
WHITE, H.
WILD, H.
WOOD, ALBERT.
WOOD, ALF.
WALKER, W.
WARD, J. D.
WOODS, J. T.
WILKINSON, C.
WRIGHT, W.
WILD, E.
WHIPP, W.
WELBURN, H.
WRAY, W. R.
WARBURTON, H.
WALKER, W.
WALSH, G.
WYNN, J.
WHITTAKER, J.
WARREN, G.
WALKER, R.
WAKEHAM, W.
WELCH, W.
WILLIAMS, J.
WRIGHT, R.
WALTON, W. R.
WEIGHTMAN, J. W.
WILSON, H.
WILKINSON, W.
WOOD, E.
WATKINS, A.
WALTON, J. A.
WHITE, J. A.
WADDELL, R.
WAUGH, W.
WELSH, J.
WISELY, G. A.
WILSON, J. H.
WORTHY, H.
WILSON, B. B.
WILSON, J. H.
WHALEY, W.
WHITE, N.
WILKINSON, W.
WILSON, W.
WHEATLEY, W. H.
WRAGG, A.

18

Co-operative Wholesale Society, Ltd.—Con.

WILSON, S.	WILKINSON, J. E.	WALLWORK, J.
WILSON, A.	WINKLE, J. A.	WARBURTON, J.
WILCOX, S.	WILSON, P.	WILLIAMS, S.
WILCOX, S.	WHITEHEAD, A.	WIGGINS, L.
WHITEHOUSE, J.	WAGSTAFF, S.	WHITTAKER, A.
WRETHAM, S.	WILSON, W.	WATERHOUSE, H.
WALPOLE, J.	WHITE, D.	WALLEY, T.
WHITE, H.	WILSON, T. H.	WRIGHT, C.
WARNE, —	WHIPPS, T.	WATKINS, A.
WILLIS, S.	WATKINS, H. D.	WAINWRIGHT, W.
WHETSTONE, G.	WRIGHT, F.	WOOOD, E. H.
WADE, E.	WALTER, J.	WINKLEY, W.
WOOD, S.	WRIGHT, A.	WHITE, E. C.
WYATT, W.	WALKER, R.	WALTON, F.
WINTER, A. B.	WATSON, J.	WATSON, J.
WHITEHEAD, E.	WOOD, A.	WILSON, E.
WALKER, A.	WATSON, G.	WILKINSON, I.
WATTS, F. J.	WHARRIER, N.	WILLIAMS, L.
WHITE, R. W.	WILSON, J.	WHITEHOUSE, F.
WILLIAMS, D. J.	WINFIELD, H.	WILKINSON, E. G.
WALLINGTON, H.	WOODWARD, E.	WILSON, J.
WHITCHURCH, G.	WILSON, W.	WRIGHT, M.
WILLIAMS, D. H.	WEISS, W. A.	WORTHY, A.
WINN, H.	WOOD, T.	WILKINSON, G.
WILLIAMS, I. J.	WHITELEY, L.	WOOD, J. C.
WEBLEY, N. H.	WEBB, A. E.	WOOLFENDEN, J. W.
WATERS, G.	WELSH, G. E.	
WILLIAMS, P. E.	WRIGHT, A.	WOODHEAD, J. T.
WHITE, H.	WHITING, A. E.	WILLCOX, L. J.
WATERFIELD, G.	WELSH, E.	WOOD, J.
WRIGHT, C. H.	WILD, J. W.	WARREN, W.
WOOD, E. L.	WOOD, W.	WOOD, W.
WINSTANLEY, H.	WILBRAHAM, S.	WOMERSLEY, W.
WHEELER, A. N.	WILKINSON, F.	WHITWORTH, F.
WARD, E.	HARDMAN, T.	WILSON, B.
WILLIAMS, E.	WEBSTER, H.	WARD, A.
WALLACE, E.	WRAY, R.	WOODWARD, J.
WESTBROOK, C.	WALKER, P.	WOODCOCK, F.
WARDELL, J.	WALKER, M.	WHITTLE, P.
WHITEHEAD, T.	WHITE, G.	WARNER, R. H.
WASH, S.	WOODCOCK, G. H.	WHITE, H.
WARBURTON, W. H.	WOOD, G. A.	WILD, H.
	WOODCOCK, P.	WOOD, ALBERT.
WILD, E.	WILSON, P.	WOOD, ALF.
WHITEHEAD, A. B.	WILSON, G.	WHITEHEAD, W. E.
WILD, W.	WAINWRIGHT, G.	
WARBURTON, H.	WHITLEY, J.	WHITTAKER, A. V.
WOOD, H.	WORMALD, A.	WORTHINGTON, W. L.
WOOLASS, T.	WOOD, E.	
WRIGLEY, J. G.	WYKES, A.	WOOD, W. M.
WOODCOCK, W.	WHITWORTH, H. D.	WOLSTENCROFT, W. A.
WEAVER, J.		
WALKER, G.	WRIGHT, N.	WILLIAMS, H. T.
WADDINGTON, S.	WATTS, F.	WALKER, J. J.
WOOLLEY, T.	WHITWORTH, A.	WARBURTON, F.
WILLETT, H.	WREN, J.	WILLIAMS, J. A.
WILLETT, A.	WRIGHT, H.	WALKER, W.
WALKER, R.	WOOTTEN, F.	WARD, J.
WALKER, T.	WHALLEY, E.	WILKINSON, C.
WHITE, F.	WALMSLEY, N.	WHITING, J. K.
WATTS, H.	WALKER, D.	WILLIAMS, T. H.
WILKINSON, H.	WALKER, C.	WELLS, C. G.
WARBURTON, B.	WHITEHEAD, T.	WELLS, J. H.
WATSON, O.	WHITEHEAD, W.	WHEATLEY, A. P.
WHITESIDE, E.	WATSON, J.	WILSON, G.
WOODWARD, F.	WOMACK, W.	WARD, T.
WITHERS, S.	WEBB, G.	WILSON, B.
WAITE, J. H.	WRIGHT, F.	WORTH, F.
WEATHERHEAD, J.	WILLS, F.	WELLS, A.
	WOOD, B.	WELLS, W.
WARNER, A. E.	WADE, J.	WELLS, A.
WILSON, W.	WALKER, W.	WHEATLEY, W.
WORSLEY, T.	WATSON, F.	WILCOCK, R.
WILSON, J. L.	WALTON, C.	WRIGHT, C.
WORSLEY, W.	WILLIAMSON, J.	WILDE, J.
WARBURTON, H.	WINTERBOTTOM, S.	WILLIAMS, F.
WENHAM, G.		WHITEFIELD, A.
WHITTAKER, E.	WILSON, L.	YATES, T.
WALTON, G.	WATERS, F.	YATES, N.
WHITTAKER, J.	WILSON, J.	YOUNG, A.
WHITTAKER, R.	WALKER, G. E.	YOUNG, F.
WHITELEGG, E.	WAIN, R. J.	YOUNG, O.
WADDELL, W.	WINTERBOTTOM, J. S.	YOUNG, T.
WESTLAKE, A.	WILLIAMS, A. T.	YOUNG, E. C.
WALLINGTON, H.	WILKINSON, A.	YARDLEY, J.
WYNN, G.	WOODS, F.	YOUNG, E.
WATTS, J.	WATSON, T.	YEARSLEY, W.
WILKINS, C.	WILSON, R.	YATES, J.
WILLIAMSON, E.	WILLIAMSON, J.	YATES, J.
WRIGHT, F.	WHITTAKER, J.	YOUNG, M.
WALL, T.	WORTHINGTON, T. J.	YATES, T.
WHITEHEAD, H.		YARE, W. H.
WOODHEAD, G.		

Co-operative Wholesale Society, Ltd.—Con.

YATES, J.	YATES, A. A.	YOUNG, S.
YATES, T.	YATES, C. T.	YATES, J.
YATES, N.	YORK, S.	YATES, F.

Crossley Motors, Ltd.

(See p. 479 in Roll of Honour.)

MABON, W.	GREGORY, W.	KELLY, J.
NEARY, A.	SNOWDEN, R.	KIRKHAM, R.
DARBY, F.	GRAYDON, R.	OSBORNE, J.
ALLEN, W.	BROWN, F.	ENTWISTLE, J.
ARMSTRONG, J.	BRERETON, W.	CAHILL, W.
BODEN, E.	GOODWIN, A.	CLARKE, W.
THOMPSON, F.	BAGNALL, H.	COLLINS, H.
STEPHENSON, H.	HOCKHEIMER, H.	ROPER, R.
BUTTERWORTH, S.	SMITH, R.	CONNOR, W.
INMAN, J.	BROWN, J.	HOYLE, A.
BARLOW, C.	TOMLINSON, H.	SMITH, F.
WOODHEAD, T.	FREEMAN, B.	BATES, J.
HUDSON, R.	ATHERTON, M.	CHESHIRE, A.
BRUNT, J.	HOOLEY, T.	GALLAGHER, T.
COOPER, J. W.	ASPINALL, J.	MILLINGHAM, E.
MOSS, J.	CRITCHLOW, E.	THAW, W.
SANDERSON, A.	GOODWIN, A.	DRANSFIELD, J.
HAMPSON, W.	WARBURTON, H.	RYAN, H.
ALLEN, J.	MULRYAN, P.	SIMPSON, W.
JONES, H.	DOUGLAS, T.	ELLAMS, A.
TOWNSEND, G.	BOYES, A.	DANIELS, E.
BROWNHILL, W.	WILKINSON, A.	SMITH, R.
LANE, W.	RUSSELL, W.	YEADON, W.
LOMAX, T.	VERNON, A.	BRIGGS, W.
BOORMAN, G.	CARTER, W.	REGAN, M.
MAUND, J.	TAYLOR, J.	CARTER, J.
GILL, F. J.	OWEN, A. E.	FAIRHURST, G.
HIDE, M.	CRABTREE, H.	READETT, W.
EDE, J.	REYNOLDS, J.	FISH, L.
HARRISON, A.	FRANKLAND, T.	MITCHELL, H.
AINSWORTH, T.	DIXON, H.	LUPTON, J.
NICKLIN, F.	MANUEL, A.	JONES, W.
DOWNS, F.	BENNETT, S.	SMITH, F.
MAUND, E.	HUNT, G.	TODD, D.
McELEAVEY, T.	WALMSLEY, W.	MARSH, R.
BATES, R.	MORREY, J.	BLAKEWAY, G. W.
BOWMAN, A.	KINSEY, T.	LAWTON, J.
MARTIN, C. F.	COOPER, F.	BIDDLE, A.
HOLCROFT, F.	EHLERS, J.	BOOTH, J.
MAYOH, J. D.	ORRELL, A.	SMITH, W. A.
JONES, J.	CALDWELL, J.	BROOKES, H.
MATHER, T.	HARDMAN, R.	POWELL, W.
SMALL, F.	WATSON, F.	FOX, W.
TAYLOR, T.	JONES, J. A.	TAYLOR, L.
WHITEHEAD, J. H.	HEATON, J.	THOMPSON, J.
INGLEBY, W.	MILLINGTON, C.	DUNBERVAND, F.
HISCOCK, C.	PEARCE, G.	WAY, G. E.
PAYNE, H.	ROBINSON, F.	WITHERS, A.
DUGDALE, S.	TAYLOR, F.	CONNOLLY, J.
CHAPPELLS, R.	CONNOR, C.	FAIRHOLM, W. C.
PALIN, C.	ANTROBUS, J.	EDWARDS, W.
PIKE, S.	MILLS, F.	TETLOW, P.
NEARY, A.	COOK, C.	CAIRNS, W.
CROSSLEY, G.	WILLIAMS, J.	BRADSHAW, W.
DAVIES, O. E.	WOOLFENDEN, F.	MERCER, W.
HOWARD, H.	CONNOLLY, R.	HARDING, G.
HIGGINSON, R.	GROVES, G.	THAW, R. M.
KEAN, T.	HARDMAN, S.	SIXSMITH, W.
DAVIES, C.	HARRISON, F.	BOULTON, A.
DAVIES, W.	PARKIN, F.	BACHE, H.
DAVIES, R.	ANTHONY, B.	GASKELL, W.
HILL, S.	HEWITT, A.	BARLOW, F.
LODGE, J.	SLOANE, F.	JONES, W.
BUCKLE, A.	BROWN, F.	TURNER, T.
JOHNSON, W.	DARLINGTON, W.	JACKSON, G.
KELLY, W.	MURGATROYD, F.	PRIESTNALL, J.
CHISNALL, J.	MABON, W.	JENKINSON, E.
HYDE, G.	BRIDDON, I.	MURDEN, M.
MASTERS, T.	SCHOLES, A.	KELLY, D.
HOWARD, W.	CHAPPELL, A.	ELLIS, J.
WARBURTON, F.	WILBURNE, H.	BAMFORD, J.
DONOGHUE, J.	RENNY, J.	AUSTIN, A.
WALKER, G.	MYLES, T. G.	COLLINGE, J. H.
FENTON, H.	BARNETT, R.	BARRETT, S. T.
GASKIN, L.	DYER, H.	WHITFIELD, D.
TWISS, W.	BURROWS, F.	JACKSON, H.
NEILL, J.	HEALEY, A.	MYCOCK, R.
FOSTER, S.	ROBINSON, J.	SINGER, G.
GRAHAM, W.	BEARD, J.	DRAKE, H.
GALGANI, E.	DIAMOND, F.	BALL, H.
HOPKINSON, F.	GLEDHILL, F.	RICHARDS, F.
HEAP, W.	GIFFORD, H.	HALL, F. E.
RUTTER, J.	HADFIELD, B.	BIANCHI, C.
HOULKER, J.	WALKER, T. G.	STAFFORD, C. E.

Crossley Motors, Ltd.—Con.

HARVEY, J.
ALDCROFT, W.
TETLOW, B.
WATT, E.
BURKE, E.
GRUNDY, L. H.
HIBBERT, J.
HOLLOWAY, E.
RAWSON, T.
TOWNSON, W.
KAY, H.
WARBURTON, J.
MOTTERSHEAD, T.
MIDDLETON, G.
ALDRED, J.
WOODCOCK, A.
BOWERS, W.
RILEY, W.
BUTTERWORTH, R
MORGAN, A.
GREENWOOD, L.
CASHEL, R.
MOORES, F.
HIGGINS, J.
SMITH, L.
McGARRY, E.
ELLIS, A.
LEES, W.
MOORES, J.
LOMAS, W.
HADFIELD, A.
PHILLIPS, J.
WRIGHT, J.
HALES, J.
CRUMPTON, W.
BUSBY, J.
BRERETON, E.
IVESON, R.
MAGUIRE, T.
BLACKBURN, J
COSTELLO, J.
HUCKLEBRIDGE, E.
WRIGHT, J.
COOK, E.
SWINTON, F.
SHAW, D.
TOOTHILL, F.
HENDLEY, J.
KING, J.
WALKER, E.
HAGUE, S.
KNOTT, J.
WOOD, T.
MINSHALL, H.
PENNY, W.
BULMER, F.
BOUGHEY, W.
ARMSTRONG, J.
JOWETT, W.
MILNER, W.
NEWSOME, J.
COUSINS, R.
MADDOCKS, T.
MAUGHAN, R.
JONES, J.
HOYLE, H.
HYDE, T.
THOMPSON, S.
CALDICOTT, F.
MARTIN, L.
DERBYSHIRE, W.
CLOWES, G.
CROOK, F.
BREEZE, E.
HANDS, J.
SIMPSON, J. S.
MOSDALE, F.
COOK, A.
RIDINGS, E.
JACKSON, J.
WATERHOUSE, J.
ROBERTS, W.
BRADLEY, F.
BELLE, J.
GRIMES, W.
FITZHUGH, H.
MOTH, E.
JACKSON, J. M.
TAYLOR, W. O.
LUCAS, F. W.
HOWELL, S.
BARNES, J. W.
JACKSON, L.
HANSON, W.
HOPKINSON, F.
BELL, L.
GITTINS, N.
SKITT, C.
SMYLIE, N.
HOWE, S.
MUSGROVE, T.
FORSYTH, J.
NEWSHAM, E.
WHITEHEAD, A.
JURY, A.
TATHAM, E.
MULLINS, N.
TOWEY, J.
SINCLAIR, W.
SCHOFIELD, L.
DOYLE, W.
WILLIAMS, T.
OGDEN, S.
VAIL, R.
BUCKLEY, J. E.
LOWE, E.
STUBBS, R. C.
FORD, A.
DIMELOW, J. V.
OGDEN, A.
LEESON, W.
ARMSTRONG, G.
HEMMINGS, L.
ASHBY, T.
CLIFTON, A.
HUBBLE, A. W.
SHUTTLEWORTH, H. E.
WAKEFIELD, E. B.
REID, L. B.

Donald Currie and Co.
(See p. 480 in Roll of Honour.)

COOPER, W. S.
LUMB, H. P.

Harold Daniels and Co.
(See p. 671 in Roll of Honour.)

BALL, H. M
ACTON, A
BURGESS W
ROBERTS, H. N.
ROSSALL, J
MARCHANT G. H.
GREENHALGH, W.

Decorators' Supply Co.

*PRICE, T.
*KNOWLES, S.
*KNOWLES, R.
*BIRTWISLE, C.
*BRUCE, A.
*HORRIDGE, J.
HEIGHWAY, G.
HEIGHWAY, A.
BEESLEY, J.
PHILLIPS, F. H.
MADDOCK, H.
NELSON, G.

Dehn and Co.
(See p. 486 in Roll of Honour.)

ROBERTS, T.
WHITTAKER, F.
SHAKESHAFT, N.
†PERKS, T.
†BENTLEY, F.
†SHAW, J. W.

Geo. and R. Dewhurst, Ltd.
(See p. 481 in Roll of Honour.)

SHERWIN, J.
LAWSON, E.
WIGGINS, M.
NORRIS, T.
MILLER, R.
GRASS, W.
CROOK, J.
FERNLEY, A.
SHORROCK, A.
RIDING, M.
HUNTER, P.
AIREY, E.
BURTON, J.
LAW, G.
MORGAN, J.
HARDACRE, J. T.
NAYLOR, E.
EASTHAM, J.
MOON, T.
BARON, J.
RICHMOND, J.
PARTINGTON, R.
PORTER, W. H.
DERHAM, R.
WIGGINS, J.
BATTY, J.
PARKINSON, D.
HEATON, J.
RIDING, J.
POULTON, H.

Geo. and R. Dewhirst, Ltd.—Con.

SUMNER, J.
THRELFALL, G.
COULTON, J.
COULTON, E.
BLUNDELL, R.
SWALES, J.
CALVERT, J
SLATER, F.
RIDING, J.
BAXENDALE, R.
BARNES, G.
STOPFORD, R.
BARNES, J.
WILDMAN, W.
HARRISON, J.
KAY, O
THOMPSON, J.
HIGGINS, L.
YATES, J.
YATES, H.
STAFFORD, W.
CARTER, J.
WATKINSON, H.
WALGHE, A.
TURNER, J.
APPLEBY, F
INCE, T.
SIMMS, W.
SAGE, I.
CORBETT, D.
SHARPLES, J
COLLINSON, W.
WHITTLE, H.
HEAPS, E.
HARGREAVES, J.
THORNLEY, G.
KERIN, W.
HEAPS, C.
GORE, J.
TOMLINSON, J.
CLARKE, C.
KING, W.
WALMSLEY, C.
BARON, J.
SIMMS, A.
BATTY, R. H.
COUPE, J.
CROOK, R.
ORRELL, R.
WOODCOCK, W.
LAW, A.
TOMLINSON, H.
WORDEN, F.
HARDACRE, H.
HARDACRE, W.
HUNT, G. E.
HUNT, H.
WOODRUFF, E.
BATESON, W.
COOPER, J.
NAYLOR, W.
MOLYNEAUX, J.
MARTIN, R.
MOEN, H.
CESTIGAN, M.
THORNLEY, W.
LAW, J. J.
CROOK, W.
LIVESEY, J.
COX, J.
THORNLEY, W.
TURNER, M.
NOBLETT, W.
REED, R.
WOODS, H.
COUNSELL, J.
BAILEY, W.
KITCHEN, W.
MARGISON, F.
BREWER, W.
WORDEN, J.
CROOK, W.
WOODS, T.
ARMSTRONG, J.
SLATER, J.
LAWSON, P.
PENNINGTON, J.
HOUGH, H.
HOWARTH, G.
MOORHOUSE, D.
GREGSON, S.
McILROY, A.
PENDLEBURY, W. H.
LERINE, S.
JONES, W.
NUTTALL, H.
SCHOLES, T.
HEYWOOD, G. T.
SHUFFLEBOTTOM, J.
DAWSON, E.
RILEY, W.
BLOOD, E.
LEE, W.
TENCH, T.
COLLINS, R.
SHERIDAN, I.
BROCK, T.
SLATER, G.
BERGIN, T.
FOWLER, C.
MARSH, J.
DOOSEY, W.
TAYLOR, F.
O'DONNELL, D.
ATKIN, W.
GLAISTER, J.
REDFERN, A.
REDFERN, J.
ROBERTS, D.
VOST, T.
NEWTON, A. E.
HASSALL, J.
POTTS, W.
KENNY, J.
BEEVERS, G.
LOCKYER, J.
HUNTER, W.
FOSTER, W.
FITTON, H.
DICKINS, J.
VASEY, F.
DALE, P.
URE, W.
BELL, W. G.
BENTLEY, J.
BOARDMAN, J.
BROWN, H. H.
COOKSON, G.
CRAWLEY, E. E.
DICKEN, S.
FARRELL, R.
HARGREAVES, W. G.
WALTERS, H.
TURNER, W.
DERHAM, L.
SPENCER, G.
FAWCETT, A.
FAWCETT, R
KAY, L.
MATTHEWS, D.
DARLINGTON, J.
RICHMOND, W.
ORME, S.
SAUL, J.
GRIME, J.
FOXEN, A.
BRADSHAW, W.
JACKSON, J.
BANKS, G.
SHORRECK, W.
GREGSON, T.
ROBINSON, J.
COATES, W.
WATERHOUSE, P.
HOUGHTON, R.
PARKINSON, T.
CLARKSON, H.
PARKINSON, E.
WATERHOUSE, J.
SNAPE, W.
COCKER, T.
COCKER, R.
BOLTON, J.
O'DONNELL, J. W.
DAGGERS, W.
PRESCOTT, C.
PARKER, J.
WHARTON, W.
WILCOCK, A.
PARKINSON, R.
INGHAM, P.
ROBERTS, F.
WARBRICK, J.
BARTON, J.
SCOTT, W.
WOODS, G.
LEONARD, J.
LAKIN, A.
ECCLES, R.
GORST, E.
WHITTLE, A.
BLACKBURN, J.
MERCER, J.
SHARPLES, J.
MERCER, W.
WOODS, J.
SHARPLES, H.
DIXON, E.
SUMNER, J.
LONGTON, J.
NICKSON, W.
RIDING, P.
BRADSHAW, J.
INGHAM, C.
HARRISON, H
BAMBER, W.
SIMPSON, W.
KETTLEWELL, E.
OLDFIELD, H.
DUXBURY, W.
DITCHFIELD, J.
DUXBURY, J.
ASHTON, J.
GRASS, W.
WOODCOCK, J.
CLARKSON, J.
PRESCOTT, H.
BENNETT, J.
SHARPLES, R.
WOODCOCK, W.
PRESTON, C.
SWARBRICK, W.
PRESCOTT, J.
TURNER, D.
MERCER, W.
BRINDLE, J.
WOODBURN, A.
HOUGHTON, R.
HOULDING, A. F.
ORME, S.
THOMAS, G.

F. A. Dean.
(See p. 672 in Roll of Honour).

LAMB, T. R.
HIGGINSON, S.
DEAN, J. W.
BAKER, W. T.
CLARK, J.
TODD, C. H.
BERRY, S.

Duncan, Fox and Co.
(See p. 484a in Roll of Honour.)

*BEECH, B. J.

* Serving with the Colours.   † Rejected.

C. C. Dunkerley and Co., Ltd.
(See p. 672 in Roll of Honour.)

DUNKERLEY, E.	SHARWIN, H.	MAHER, W. A.
DAVIDSON, A. L.	TITLEY, J.	ROBINSON, A.
STENHOUSE, G. A.	WHITING, J.	ROEBUCK, J.
SCOTT, J. H.	GRIMSHAW, R.	HEWITT, J.
HADFIELD, V.	COOPER, H.	

A. K. Dyson and Co., Ltd.
(See p. 673 in Roll of Honour.)

PENRICE, H.	ROBERTS, D.	GREEN, J.
MYERS, J. A.	MEE, C. F.	YOXALL, G. W.
MARSH, H. W.	CRITCHLOW, G. R.	JERVIS, L.
BEARD, W.	LUKE, A. H.	SANDS, A.
BRINDLE, H. W.	WORMALD, L.	

East Lancashire Mills Co., Ltd.
(See p. 493 in Roll of Honour.)

HEARON, W.	LOFTS, T. M.	MIDGLEY, G.
HOWARD, T.	MARGROVE, J. H.	URMSTON, R.

Eckstein, Heap and Co., Ltd.
(See p. 487 in Roll of Honour.)

BUTTERWORTH, J.	HOGG, J. M.	PANTER, E.
BRAMBLE, W.	HOPE, J.	PIMLOTT, H.
BURY, J.	HORNER, F.	POLLARD, T.
BODEN, J. W.	HOULDSWORTH, M.	RAMWELL, H.
CARTER, R.	HOWE, J.	ROBERTS, P.
COOKSON, J.	HULME, A.	SANDFORD, T. A.
CRITCH, L.	HULME, A. E.	SHANKLAND, J.
EMMETT, J.	JONES, E.	SMITH, J.
EVANS, W.	KENEALY, F.	SUNMAN, J.
ELLIOTT, S. H.	KIRBY, E.	SYKES, H.
FIELDING, J.	MILROY, W. J.	TAYLOR, F.
GOLIGHTLEY, G. A.	MOOTZ, H.	VALLELY, A.
GORDON, A.	MORRIS, F.	VICKERS, H.
HALL, P. B.	NESTOR, H.	WALKER, H.
HARROLD, E.	OWEN, W.	WALSH, C.
		WATERHOUSE, F.

Ehrenbach Brumm and Co.
(See p. 674 in Roll of Honour.)

ALDRED, H.	HOLMES, A.	†SCHOLEY, F.
ARMITSTEAD, W.	†HOLMES, W.	SCHOLEY, W.
BARRINGTON, J.	JACKSON, F.	*SHAW, S.
*BEALL, J.	†JAGGER, A.	*SHOESMITH, H.
BOWER, T.	JEFFERSON, J. R.	*SMITH, E.
†CROFT, W.	KING, A.	*THOMPSON, P.
†DEWHIRST, H.	*LEA, J.	*TURTON, J.
EVANS, C.	†LEE, A.	VERITY, H.
†GEE, F.	LODGE, R.	*WAKEFIELD, W.
HARWOOD, C. E. L.	MARSH, J.	WALKER, G.
*HAZELDINE, F.	*MASKEW, F.	*WASS, S.
*HENDERSON, N.	MAYHEW, F.	*WATERWORTH, L.
HODGSON, J.	*PICKSTONE, E.	WESTERMAN, A.
*HODGSON, J. H.	*PICKERING, E.	*WOLSTENHOLME, E.
HOLDSWORTH, J.	*PRICE, W.	

Elson and Neill.
(See p. 674 in Roll of Honour.)

JOHNSTON, E.	HIGHAM, H.	†BROPHY, F.
MELLOR, H. H.	KELSHAW, J. W.	†WILD, THOMAS.
HOLLAND, E. F.	FARRELL, J. W.	

English Sewing Cotton Co., Ltd.
(See p. 488 in Roll of Honour.)

R. F. and J. Alexander and Co., Ltd.

BARBER, T.	WILLIAMS, T.	EDGAR, J.
HIGGINS, J.	FISHER, J.	BARLOW, H.
HENDERSON, W.	FAULDS, C.	CHARLESWORTH, W.
WILLIAMS, R.	McARTHUR, A.	HARRISON, W.
McGEACHAN, J.	COSH, J.	DRIVER, D. E.
ROBINSON, A.	HUGHES, J.	WILLIAMS, R.
HANNIGAN, F.	BROWN, J.	DONNELLY, P.
STEWART, D.	KINCAID, A.	McFADEN, J.
MOSGROVE, J.	DANNFAULD, F.	McFADEN, W.

English Sewing Cotton Co., Ltd.—Con.

LAWS, A.	†KIRK, R.	†McFADEN, D.
McMILLAN, D.	†STEWART, R.	†ROBERTSON, R.
McFADEN, R.	†BALFOUR, A.	†YOUNG, R.
ARMSTRONG, H.	†ALLAN, W.	†RODGER, R.

English Sewing Cotton Co., Ltd., Stockport.

ROSE, J. W.	BOOTH, W.	†SANDBACH, W.
HOUGH, S.	LEE, C.	†DARBYSHIRE, J.
ARMITAGE, W., Jr.	MARRIOTT, W.	†WILLIAMSON, D.
WILD, R.	HAMBLETT, J.	†HOLT, R.
WYCHE, P.	ROSE, J.	†SANKEY, J.
PEARSON, H.	HUGHES, A.	†HACKING, A.
BROMAGE, A.	ARTHUR, J. S.	†PERCIVAL, W.
BIRDS, J.	†GARSIDE, W.	†PEARSON, C.

Sir Rd. Arkwright, Ltd.

BUNTING, E.	ALLSOP, J.	†SWIFT, J.
DOXEY, S.	BROWN, J. T.	†HODGKINSON, S.
BROWN, C.	SHAW, J.	†BUNTING, W.
DOXEY, N.	WRIGHT, W.	†MILLWARD, G.
TREECE, G.	WALTHALL, H.	†SEEDS, A.
DOXEY, J. F.	FROST, F.	†BUNTING, T.
ELSE, W.	MASSEY, A.	†GREGORY, E.
WOOD, G.	BROWNE, L.	†BRAILSFORD, J.
HALLOWS, S.	SPENCER, I.	†WILD, H.
STATHAM, J.	CARLINE, J.	†MASSEY, T.
HALL, T.	SWIFT, J.	†GREGORY, R.
DOXEY, H.	†ALLSOP, H.	†SWIFT, J.
STAFFORD, J. H.	†BATTERLEY, G.	†WILD, W.
OLIVER, J.	†BROWN, W.	†KAY, J.
FOWKES, F.	†MILLWARD, A.	†BODEN, A.

John Dewhurst and Sons, Ltd., Skipton.

DONALD, E.	ELLISON, W.	†HUDSON, A.
TEMPEST, W.	LAYCOCK, W.	†WADDINGTON, P.
SCOTT, W.	HULL, W.	†FLETCHER, A.
CLARKE, T.	HOLMES, E.	†BARRETT, A.
PRESTON, J. M.	FURNESS, S.	†SMITH, W.
CARR, E.	SIMPSON, W.	†MOORHOUSE, H.
DENT, J. W.	CROOK, J. H.	†WHITAKER, G.
PRESTON, W.	HORNER, C. M.	†HUDSON, J.
BRIGGS, F.	PATCHETT, R.	†HUDSON, T.
PENDLEBURY, F.	BERRISFORD, C.	†ATKINSON, T. W.
TAYLOR, G.	DIXON, W.	†PICKLES, D.
GELDART, H.	AYRTON, J.	†ROBERTSON, N. T.
HOLE, W. R.	MAXFIELD, J. H.	†COATES, L.
COWGILL, J. W.	FORELAND, J. T.	†RATCLIFFE, J. H.
ATKINSON, T.	NUTTER, J.	†BARRETT, C.
SCHOFIELD, A.	SEED, E.	†GARWOOD, A. G.
NUTTER, W.	†OLDFIELD, S.	†GREEN, J.
WHITTAKER, W.	†HANSON, A. P.	†BURNETT, W. R.
WHITTAKER, J.	†BARKER, W.	†HOLMES, J. H.
RAMPLING, E. J.	†GREY, A.	†BRAYSHAW, G. W.
REED, W.	†RAMPLING, A.	†HANHAM, B. H.
NEWALL, J.	†WEEKS, H. J.	†BELL, J.
CORE, C.	†WATSON, T.	†GARWOOD, A.
WHITTAKER, F.	†COATES, G.	†MOUNT, R.
WHITEOAK, J.	†PRESTON, E.	†BEARD, G. C.
PEARSON, J. H.	†THORNTON, H	

Ermen and Roby, Ltd., Patricroft.

SUTCLIFFE, T.	†FISHWICK, F.	†MULLIN, M.
HIGGINS, J.	†JACKSON, J.	†EVANS, F.
†HORNER, W.	†THOMPSON, W.	†SMITH, A.
†TAYLOR, J.	SNAPE, T.	†JACKSON, J.
†SMITH, H.	†BAYLEY, E.	†BLINKHORN, W.
†DEVINE, J. H.	†GRAYSON, A.	

Ermen and Roby, Ltd., Pendlebury.

FORD, J.	LODER, C.	†WHITEHEAD, E. M.
SHARPLES, T. W.	POYNTON, D. C.	†TAYLOR, W.
BOARDMAN, T. A.	NIGHTINGALE, D.	†WHELAN, P.
BLEARS, H.	RAFERTY, B.	

Belper and Milford.

SIDDONS, H.	JENNISON, T.	WILCOX, J.
CALOW, J.	HARRIS, T.	YOUNG, A.
SMITH, S.	BRIDGES, T.	ROBINSON, G.
HALL, W.	ASHMORE, E.	TAYLOR, H.
STONE, J. W.	BARR, G.	WOOLLEY, B.
WESTON, H.	LOMAS, J.	RICHARDSON, W.
BUTLER, W.	MAYES, J.	ROBERTSON, A.
STANHOPE, G.	ALLSOPP, E.	GAUNT, W.
HUNT, G., Jr.	ROLLINSON, G.	HALL, E.
BENNETT, B.	HOWARTH, F.	SMITH, H.
ROBERTS, G.	SANDERS, H.	ROBERTSON, G.
BENNETT, E.	WOODWARD, J.	WALDRON, B.

* Serving with the Colours. † Rejected.

English Sewing Cotton Co., Ltd.—Con.

GRACE, E.
LANCASTER, H.
OSBORNE, J.
YEOMANS, A.
HATTON, J.
STONE, T. W.
HOLBROOK, W.
HICKING, H.
WALKER, A.
LAND, J.
OLDERSHAW, G.
WHITE, F.
WEBSTER, W.
BECKWITH, W.
PERCIVAL, E.
CHILD, E.
GLEW, H.
FORD, W.
GODBER, H.
BOOTH, H.
HITCHCOCK, G.
TAYLOR, W.
BUTLER, H.
SELLORS, H.
SWINDELL, A.
HODSON, J.
†BRIGGS, W.
†FAULKNER, J. H.
†SHARDLOW, W.
†BODELL, A.
†STONE, C.
†OLDKNOW, F.
†JACKSON, A.
†VARNEY, S.
†STAINFORTH, W. H.
†DILLINGHAM, J.
†BRIDGES, E.
†YEOMANS, C.
†PEDEN, J.
†RYDE, G.
†STAINFORTH, W.
†STEVENSON, G.
†CHEETHAM, A.
†LANDER, A.
†STAPLES, T. W.
†BRIDGES, H.
†MORRELL, S.
†BARTRAM, J.
†GODDEN, S.
†HOWCROFT, P.
†BASHFORD, C.
†HODGKINSON, G.
†TAYLOR, R.
†HODGKINSON, H.
†DOXEY, A.
†TOPHAM, G.
†JOHNSON, C.
†HASLAM, B.
†BOSTOCK, J. F.

Waters, Manchester.

HAWKINS, S. B.
WATKISS, J.
JONES, G.
WILLIAMS, J.
BENNETT, A.
GRIFFITHS, A.
ARMSTRONG, M.
RICHBELL, F.
HETHERINGTON, A.
†McDONALD, N.
†BERRY, A.

Waters, Longtown.

BARNFATHER, J.
BARNFATHER, C.
GADDES, C.

Head Office.

BROOKES, R.
PARKER, B
EALES, W.
MORGAN, S.
STAFFORD, S.
WOOLRICH, W.
CRAWSHAW, G.
SCHOFIELD, W.
BARKER, G. E.
ASHWORTH, P.
HALFORD, J. C.
KERSHAW, C.
SWINDELLS, C.
MICKLEWRIGHT, F.
POOLE, R. J.
WALSH, F.
BURNSIDE, C.
GARDNER, G.
NICHOLSON, W.
HARRISON, J.
HESKETH, T.
SMITH, H.
†DEAN, S.
†TELFORD, J.
†HARRISON, E.
†CORKER, W.
†REDFERN, J. W
CAMERON, W.
†ELLISON, J.
†ELLERSHAW, J. H.
†WARBURTON, G.
†JONES, A. E.
†MARSHALL, E.
†PLANT, H.
†WOODS, R.
†BROTHERTON, C. H.

Sir James Farmer and Sons, Ltd.
(See p. 494 in Roll of Honour.)

NORTON, W. J.
ETCHELLS, W.
NEWBERY, E.
BARNES, J. H
CROSBY, E.
WOLSTENHOLME, W. B.
WELCH, C. A.
BRUCE, P. G.
NOWELL, H.
CROCKWELL, H.
NEWTON, J.
CHAPMAN, J.
HUCKLE, T. W.
ASHCROFT, T.
HOUGHTON, W.
GREENHALGH, C.
CATTERALL, G.
DOOTSON, L.
DALBY, H.
GRIFFITHS, T. H.
SHAFT, T.
FLETCHER, J. W.
RUSSELL, E.
BERRY, W.
GREENHALGH, S.
DAVIES, T.
ENNION, G.
FAIRCLOUGH, J.
SKELLERN, A. H.
WYNN, F.
ALLEN, W.
GROCOTT, G. H.
BRADSHAW, J.
GRIFFITHS, J.
RICE, W.
LAWRENCE, T.
NORMAN, H.
HOLMES, H.
HEWITT, H.

P. Frankenstein and Sons, Ltd.
(See p. 519 in Roll of Honour.)

FRANKENSTEIN, P. G.
ASHTON, C.
BAINES, J.
BRADY, E.
BRADY, J.
BRENNAN, T.
CARRIGAN, M.
CHAPMAN, F.
COHEN, A.
COLEMAN, M.
COLLINS, A.
COOK, H.
CORCORAN, H.
CRAWFORD, G.
DAVIES, W.
DEAN, G.
ECKERSLEY, S.
FIDLER, R. M.
FITZSIMMONS, P.
FOSTER, J.
FROST, H.
HALL, J.
HALL, J. A.
HARRIS, W.
HARTSHORN, C.
HILL, R.
HOOSEN, E.
HOPWOOD, T.
HOWARTH, A.
HOWLES, E.
HOWLES, T.
JOHNSTON, C.
JONES, F. H.
JONES, W.
KAY, H.
KAUFMANN, I.
KIRWIN, J. E.
LAW, F.
LAW, D.
LUCAS, J.
MAINWARING, G.
MASON, F.
MOORE, W.
MORGAN, G.
MURRAY, E.
NORRIS, W.
PEMBERTON, J.
RAMSEY, R.
ROBERTS, A.
ROGAN, W.
ROGERS, E.
SHIELDS, W.
SINGLETON, T.
SINGLETON, W.
SINGLETON, W.
TAYLOR, M.
TAYLOR, T.
WALMSLEY, T.
WHELAN, G.
WILD, J.
YARWOOD, J.

† Rejected.

The Fine Cotton Spinners' and Doublers' Association, Limited.
(See p. 495 in Roll of Honour.)

Central Office Staff.

BAILEY, W.
BAILEY, W., Junr.
BANKS, B. S.
BATES, J. H.
BATTERSBY, J.
BEECROFT, J. B.
BELL, R.
BENNETT, H.
BLAIR, H. M.
BOURNE, C. P.
BRIARS, J.
BULLIVANT, F.
CADMAN, S. J.
CLIFTON, H.
DODDS, A.
DRISCOLL, J.
DUXBURY, L.
EADIE, H. C.
FALLON, A.
GALLAGHER, C. F.
GAUNT, B.
GREEN, L. S.
GRIMSHAW, J. E.
HAGUE, H.
HOWELL, H.
HUNT, G. H.
JOHNSON, T.
KEMP, W.
LEYLAND, T. A.
LONGMIRE, F.
LOWE, H.
MASON, W. S.
MONAGHAN, J. C.
O'BRIEN, A.
PARTINGTON, S. G.
PICKFORD, F.
PORTER, H. S.
ROSTRON, G.
SCHOFIELD, F.
SMITH, A.
STARKEY, A. H.
STEVENSON, E.
STEVENSON, O.
STEWART, J. A.
STOCKTON, W.
WATKINS, C.
WILDING, T. W.
WILKES, H. Y.
WILKINSON, J.
WILLIAMSON, S.
WILSON, E. S.

Bazley Brothers, Ltd.

AITKEN, A.
ARMSTRONG, E.
BELL, W. R.
BOLLINGTON, E.
BURGESS, A.
CARRINGTON, A.
GARNER, W.
GRANGE, H.
HALL, F.
HARPER, E.
HARRINET, T.
HEALEY, W. E.
HEYWOOD, E.
HICKSON, J. M.
HOLES, J.
LINNEY, W.
McALLISTER, A.
MASON, H.
MORRIS, J.
PARKER, F.
PATRICK, J.
POUNDER, J.
SCOTT, J.
SHEPERLY, W.
SPEAT, W. T.
STANLEY, E.
TILLISON, H.
TOWLSON, H. J.
TRILLOW, T.
WHARMBY, S.
WILLIAM, E.
WILSON, H. R.
YATES, T.

James and W. Bellhouse, Ltd.

ALDRED, A.
ATHERTON, H.
COOK, J.
CROSSLEY, A.
DEAN, S.
DENTON, W. H.
DUNN, T. P.
GRIME, J. R
HODGSON, G.
HOLLAND, E.
JOHNSON, C. E.
KELSEY, F. M.
KEMP, R.
MARGINSON, H. H.
MARSDEN, J. T.
MAYO, J.
MAYO, T.
MELLING, T.
OAKES, G. J.
REYNOLDS, J. T.
ROBINSON, S.
ROWEN, P.
SHARPLES, J.
WRIGHT, J.

C. E. Bennett and Co., Ltd.

ARRANDALE, J.
BENNETT, F. R.
CANNING, A.
CORDINGLEY, T.
CUMMINGS, G.
HAMILTON, J.
HEMBOROUGH, J.
HOBSON, P.
HODGETTS, J.
HODSON, F. C.
HOLT, T.
KEMP, H.
McCARTHY, J.
McDONALD, J.
MASSIE, F.
MELLOR, J.
MILLS, H.
MINSHALL, H.
OAKES, H.
O'NEILL, J.
PARSLOW, E.
PEMBERTON, J.
PHILLIPS, H.
QUINN, A.
ROACH, J.
SELLERS, C. H.
SHEPHERD, G.
SHEPHERD, G. J.
SHERIDAN, P.
SILL, H.
WOOLMER, J.
WRIGHT, J.

F. W. Bouth and Co., Ltd.

ALDRED, J.
BREESE, H.
GARFIN, G. W.
HEYWOOD, W.
HIGGINSON, F.
JOHNSON, W. J.
KELLAR, J.
PASQUIT, J.
SANKEY, A.
SANKEY, A.
SANKEY, J.
SANKEY, P.
WARD, H.
YATES, F.

M. G. and A. Bradley, Ltd.

BICKERTON, E.
BUNTING, A.
DAVIS, J. L.
GIRLING, C.
HALL, J. T.
MYERS, F. H.
PLATT, H.
ROBINSON, E.
THOMPSON, G. H.

J. Henderson Brown, Ltd.

MARSDEN, E.
RICHMOND, T.
WAINWRIGHT, J.
WOOD, J.

Brown and Fallows, Limited.

COOK, A.
HOLT, G.
O'BRIAN, W.
SCOWCROFT, E.

John Cash and Sons, Limited.

BELL, H.
BURTON, J. F.
SAVAGE, B. M.
WOOD, G.
WRIGHT, J.

Hector Christie, Limited.

COX, R.
EASTER, T.
HALLAM, G. A.
HEELIS, J.
INGHAM, W.
LEAWORTHY, A.
MARSDEN, T.
MORTIMER, G.
POTTER, D.
PRATT, R.
RALPH, A.
WEST, R.
WHITMORE, W.
WILLIAMS, F.
WOOLERTON, H.

The Fine Cotton Spinners' and Doublers' Association, Limited.—Con.

Gorsey Bank Doubling Co., Limited.

BEELEY, W.
BIBBY, J.
BOHEN, T.
DOLAN, W.
GRIFFIN, J.
HULLEY, F.
HYDE, J.
ORR, H.
PLANT, J.
POLLITT, G.
RODGERS, J.
SMITH, W.

William Holland and Sons, Ltd.

ANDREWS, M.
BAKER, M.
BARNETT, E. W.
CALDWELL, A.
CARTLEDGE, J. H.
CLARKE, J. H.
COCHRANE, J.
COLLINSON, W.
CROMPTON, J.
CROOK, J.
DAVIES, H.
DAWSON, J. E.
ETCHELLS, W.
GARNER, J.
HALLSWORTH, J. W.
HEATON, H.
HILTON, J. P.
HINCKLEY, T. A.
HODKINSON, T.
HOLLYWOOD, A. E.
JEFFERSON, E.
JOHNSON, H.
LANCASHIRE, C. E.
LYONS, G. F.
MANSELL, J.
MATHER, E.
MELLING, R.
MORRIS, J.
MORTON, F.
MOSS, J.
NEWTON, S.
OWEN, T.
PARKINSON, B.
PARKINSON, W.
PARTINGTON, H.
QUIGLEY, D.
ROYLE, N.
SEWART, J.
SMITH, J.
STREET, W. E.
SUTTON, J.
SYKES, J. W.
WHITWORTH, J.
WILDE, J.
WILSON, D.
WOOD, J. N.
WOODS, J.
WRIGLEY, J.

Thomas Houldsworth and Co., Limited.

ADSHEAD, F.
BALL, T.
BROOKS, W.
COOKE, E.
COOPER, J.
CUTHBERT, S. W.
ECKERSLEY, J.
ECKERSLEY, J.
DARWEN, H.
DUNCAN, J. W.
HARRIS, C.
HARRIS, J.
HEATHCOTE, A.
HIGGINSON, D.
HIGGINSON, E.
HIGGINSON, J.
HOLEHOUSE, A.
JOHNSON, T.
KNOWLES, R.
LEVER, J.
LEVER, R.
MAYERS, R.
MELLOR, H. A.
NEWTON, J.
PARKINSON, C.
PICKFORD, J. T.
WATSON, R. H.
WATSON, W. H.
WILDING, A.

Jackson Street Spinning Co., Ltd.

BAXENDALE, W.
BAXENDALE, W.
BORSEY, W.
BRIDDON, L.
GLYNN, W.
HARDMAN, W.
HARGREAVES, J.
HASSALL, C.
HOLT, A. E.
LEE, J.
MARRISON, W.
MASKREY, C. H.
MASKREY, J.
MASKREY, W.
PIMLOTT, S.
PRYCE, E.
REYNOLDS, A.
RIGBY, W. R.
SCHOFIELD, H.
SIDDERLEY, R.
TATTERSALL, J.
WALMSLEY, L.
WALMSLEY, R.

John Knott and Sons, Limited.

BAILEY, W.
BROMLEY, W.
CROMPTON, P.
EDWARDS, T.
GEE, J. W.
HOPKINS, J. W.
KENWORTHY, J.
NEWTON, E.
OLDFIELD, F.
PERKINS, W.
ROBERTS, H.
ROTHWELL, A.
SAMPLE, T.
SMITH, J. W.
THORNLEY, A.
TURNER, W.
WALLACE, J.
WHITHAM, H.
WILDE, G.
WILSON, G. R.

H. W. Lee and Co., Ltd.

ARMITT, A.
BAIRD, T.
BENNETT, W.
BILSBORROW, A.
BLAIR, C. H. M.
CANNING, H.
CLIFTON, J. F.
ELEY, J. W.
FOSTER, W.
GEE, J.
HALL, J.
HARRIS, A.
LAWTON, T.
LOUGHLAN, P.
MURRAY, B.
SMITH, H.
WARDLE, W.
WINTER, D.
YATES, J.

Lee Spinning Company, Ltd.

BERESFORD, S.
BOWERS, W.
CONNER, J.
DEAKIN, E.
GREEN, S.
HARRISON, C.
HUDSON, C. E.
KIRKMAN, W.
LEIGHTON, A.
LOCKETT, H.
MASSEY, J.
WHITMORE, J.

McConnel and Co., Ltd.

(Ancoats Mills.)

ANDREWS, W. J.
BAGNALL, J.
BARTON, R. E.
BERRY, T. W.
BOWCOCK, E.
BRIDGE, R.
BRIMELOW, W.
BROADHURST, J.
BULLOUGH, W.
CATTERAL, W.
CHESTERS, J.
COLLIER, A.
CROOK, F.
DAVENPORT, R.
DOVER, W.
DRINKWATER, C.
DUGDALE, T.
ECCLES, E.
GORDON, L.
GOUGH, T.
GREGORY, G.
HARDMAN, S.
HARRISON, F.
HARRISON, F.
HARRISON, W.
HASLAM, W.
HEPWORTH, J.
HERRIOTT, H.
HINCKLEY, P.
HODGKINSON, J. A.
HOLDEN, J.
HOWARD, J. A.

HOWARTH, J.
ISHERWOOD, R.
KAY, J.
KAY, R.
KNOWLES, J.
LANE, J.
LEATHER, F.
LEE, W. H.
LEIGH, H.
LEVER, H.
LOMAX, J. W.
MARSDEN, H.
MELLOR, G.
NEWTON, J.
O'NEILL, J.
OSWELL, W. J.
OWEN, T.
PENDERGAST, S.
PENDLEBURY, A.
PERRY, W. A.
POWELL, E.
POWNER, G.
POWNER, J.
PYE, J.
QUAYLE, T.
RIDINGS, R.
RUSCOE, F. L.
SAXON, R.
SLACK, J.
STOTT, J.
TAYLOR, J.
TUNNICLIFFE, H.
TUNNICLIFFE, J.
TURNER, R.
UNSWORTH, J.
UNSWORTH, P.
WADSWORTH, W.
WHITTAKER, H. A.
WHITTLE, W.
WHITWORTH, C. W.
WORTHINGTON, J. H.
WRIGHT, A.

(Lumb Mills.)

AINSWORTH, W.
BANCROFT, R.
BROWN, F.
BRYAN, J.
FERNLEY, W.
FINNIGAN, J.
FLETCHER, R. G.
FLETCHER, W.
FOGG, J. J.
HEYWOOD, J.
HILL, H.
HOBSON, H.
HOLLAND, W.
HOOLEY, A.
HOWARTH, C.
JACKSON, C.
KENYON, J.
LAX, C.
McCLELLAND, E.
McKENNA, A.
MANN, W. H.
MASON, A.
MILLER, J.
MITCHELL, J. W.
MOYLE, A.
O'KEEFE, J.
RICHARDSON, A.
SLACK, J.
SOMNERS, J.
SPENCER, J.
STREET, H.
WELLS, W.
WILSON, W.
WOOD, H.

Manchester Reeling and Winding Co., Limited.

GREEN, J.
PEACH, A.
PICKUP, J. W.
THOMPSON, W.
WHITTINGHAM, W.

James Marsden and Sons, Ltd.

ASHTON, P.
ATHERTON, J.
BEDDOWS, A.
BERRY, J. H.
BRABBIN, J.
BRITTLES, A.
BROMLEY, J. H.
CADLE, W.
CAMPBELL, C.
CAWFIELD, G.
CHADWICK, E.
CLARKSON, J. T.
COCKER, A.
COLDERLEY, W.
COOPER, J.
CULLINAN, J.
DARBY, O.
DENTON, C.
DUGDILL, R.
ECCLES, J.
FEARNLEY, J.
FIELDING, A.
FIELDING, W.
GRAHAM, A.
GRIMSHAW, J.
HAMER, E.
HARDMAN, J.
HARTLEY, W.
HEAPS, J.
HIBBERT, H.
HIGGS, J.
HINCHCLIFFE, W.
HINDLEY, F.
HOLDEN, H.
HOLT, J.
HOWARTH, A.
HOWARTH, F.
HOWARTH, J.
HUGHES, J.
IREDALE, J.
JACKSON, W.
JONES, J.
KING, W.
LEACH, J.
LEYLAND, H.
LOFTHOUSE, J.
MOLLOY, P.
MONKS, J.
NORRIS, A.
NORRIS, T.
OAKES, A.
OAKES, J.
ORRELL, C.
OWEN, J.
PARTINGTON, J.
QUINN, W.
RISHTON, J.
ROBERTS, T.
ROBERTS, W.
ROBINSON, F.
ROBINSON, H.
ROTHWELL, J.
RUSHTON, D.
SCOWCROFT, A.
SELBY, J.
SHEFFIELD, J.
SHUTTLEWORTH, J. J.
SHUTTLEWORTH, T.
THOMPSON, R.
TYRER, H.
WHALLEY, J.
WILKINSON, S.
WILSON, G.
YATES, F.
YATES, T.
YATES, W.

Robert Marsland and Co., Ltd.

BAXENDALE, J.
BOWERS, W.
BROOKES, E.
BROWN, J. R.
BROWN, S. W.
CLAPHAM, W. W.
CLARE, D.
COOKSON, S.
CROOK, H.
CROOK, I.
DUNN, F.
DUNN, S.
EATON, W.
FLETCHER, A.
FOSTER, S.
FOWLER, J.
FREEBOROUGH, J.
GLENNON, J.
GOODWIN, J. M.
GREGSON, F.
GRIFFITHS, E.
GRIFFITHS, J.
HALL, F. W.
HAMMOND, J.
HIGSON, J.
HILTON, T.
LIVESEY, W.
LYNCH, L.
MACK, D.
MACK, J. T.
MOLLOY, T.
MOORES, W. H.
OAKDEN, A.
O'NEILL, W.
OWEN, E.
OWEN, F.
PARKER, J. H.
RAMSDEN, J.
RILEY, A.
ROURKE, W.
SOUTHERN, J.
WITHINGTON, H.
WORTHINGTON, J.
YATES, A.

Samuel Moorhouse, Limited.

(Brinksway Bank Mill.)

ADSHEAD, F.
BIRTLES, H.
CHAPPELL, H.
CLARKE, D.
CLARKE, M. P.
CLAYTON, J. W.
CREWE, W. B.
GERRARD, F.
HARDACRE, W.
JACKSON, D.
JACKSON, S.
LEAH, G.
MORTON, J.
MORTON, T.
RALPHS, R. E.
ROY, G.
SOMERVILLE, H.
WHITEHEAD, R. J.

The Fine Cotton Spinners' and Doublers' Association, Limited.—Con.

(Wear Mills.)

ARTHERN, W.
BALDWIN, F.
BURKE, B.
CALDERBANK, J.
COPPOCK, H.
CRAIG, P.
DICKENSON, T.
EAGLAND, R.
FILDES, G.
FINLEY, F.
GOULDEN, J.
HARRISON, P.
HENSHALL, W.
HEYS, G.
HIGGINBOTHAM, F.
HODSON, A.
JACKSON, S.
JONES, F.
LANCASHIRE, E.
MARSHALL, F.
MORAN, P.
OLDHAM, W.
RAWLINSON, W.
RHODES, W.
ROBINSON, J.
ROONEY, J.
ROWLANDS, W.
SHAW, J.
SMIRTHWAITE, J.
SWINDELLS, T.
TOFT, J.
TYLDESLEY, A.
VERNON, A.
WHITEHEAD, J.
WINFIELD, H.
WYCHE, R.

A. and G. Murray, Limited.

ALLEN, T.
ATKINSON, W.
BESWICK, J.
BETHELL, F.
BETHELL, T.
COOKE, H.
CUPPELLO, B.
CUPPELLO, J. L.
DAVIES, A. E.
DAVIES, J. H.
DEAN, P.
DENTON, R.
DODD, W. H.
HODGKINSON, J.
HORNER, T.
KAY, J.
MACKEY, H.
MARLEY, J.
MAYO, H.
MAYO, J.
MAYO, L.
MAYO, W.
MEADEN, J.
MELLOR, J.
MELLOR, J. H.
MORRIN, J.
NORBURY, B.
PAGET, T.
STEELE, J.
SULLIVAN, S.
WADDINGTON, D.
WOODWARD, J.

Cross Heath Mill.

BLOOR, A.
BUTTERS, G.
COTTON, W.
DALEY, B.
EARDLEY, L.
ELKS, E.
FARAM, F.
FORRESTER, A.
JOYNSON, H.
MASON, J.
RATHBONE, S.
TEW, A.
VARE, J.
WHEATLEY, P.
WILD, C.
WOOD, A.

The Musgrave Spinning Co., Ltd.

AITKEN, H.
ALLEN, R.
ARKWRIGHT, W. C.
ARMSTRONG, R.
ASHWORTH, J.
ASPINALL, E.
ASPINALL, J.
AUSTIN, A. J. W.
BAILEY, A.
BARLOW, E.
BARLOW, J.
BARLOW, T.
BARNES, R.
BARTON, J. H.
BEETON, R.
BENTLEY, W. W.
BERRY, S.
BIBBY, N.
BIBBY, W. H.
BLUNDELL, J.
BOOTH, J.
BOOTH, P.
BOLTON, W.
BOSTOCK, T.
BOWLING, H.
BRADLEY, A.
BRADLEY, J.
BRIDGE, W.
BROMLEY, R.
BROMLEY, W.
BROWN, J. H.
BROWN, R.
BURNS, J. B.
CALVERT, J.
CARDWELL, B.
CARSON, J.
CHAPPELL, J. W.
COLEMAN, J.
COXON, J.
CROOK, J.
CROWTHER, W.
DAVIES, G.
DENNING, W.
DEVENPORT, J.
DEWHURST, J. R.
DIER, J. A.
DORNING, P.
DUCKWORTH, H.
DUCKWORTH, W.
DUCKWORTH, W.
ECKERSLEY, W.
ENTWISTLE, H. H.
ENTWISTLE, J.
ENTWISTLE, R.
FAIRHURST, J.
FAIRHURST, T. R.
FEARNLEY, A.
FIELDING, I.
FISHER, W. R.
FLANNAGHAN, M.
FOSTER, G. H.
FOSTER, R.
FRANCE, J.
GANDY, J. A.
GILL, T. P.
GILLETT, W.
GLENN, F.
GREEN, R.
GREENHALGH, A.
GREENHALGH, R.
GREENHOUGH, E.
GREENWOOD, C.
GREGORY, J.
GREGSON, T.
GRIME, A.
HALL, E.
HAMER, W.
HARGREAVES, W.
HASLAM, J.
HASLAM, J. L.
HASLAM, T.
HEAP, F.
HEYWOOD, A.
HEYWOOD, H.
HILL, H.
HILTON, E.
HINCKLEY, F. E.
HINDLE, T.
HODGSON, T.
HODKINSON, P.
HOLDEN, W. D.
HOLLOWAY, H.
HOPE, C.
HOPE, F.
HOWARTH, F.
HOWARTH, R.
HOWARTH, T.
HOWARTH, T.
HULL, H.
HULME, T.
INCH, E.
JOBSON, S.
JOHNSON, D.
JONES, F.
JONES, S.
KERSHAW, J.
LAWRENCE, P. S.
LEACH, J. E.
LEVER, F.
LEYLAND, W. B.
McCANN, W. L.
McDERMOTT, J.
McGARRY, T.
McINTYRE, R.
McMILLAN, R.
MAKINSON, W.
MARRINER, J.
MARTIN, C.
MARSDEN, H.
MASON, A.
MILLS, R.
MIDDLETON, F.
MINION, T.
MORRIS, J. P. H.
MORRIS, T.
MORRIS, W.
MONKS, H.
NICKEL, J.
NOLAN, J. T.
OPENSHAW, T.
ORRELL, W.
OWEN, J. W.
PARKER, J.
PARKER, I.
PARKINSON, C.
PARKINSON, C.
PARKINSON, J.
PARSONS, A. G.
PARTINGTON, J.
PEARCE, R. H.
PERRY, T.
PETERS, M.
PILKINGTON, A.
PILKINGTON, D.
PILKINGTON, G.
PILKINGTON, W.
PLUMBLEY, W.
PRICE, H.
QUINN, J.
RATCLIFFE, A.
RAY, W.
RIDINGS, W.
RIGBY, J. R.
RIGBY, J. R.
ROBERTS, J. H.
ROBERTS, R.
ROTHWELL, T.
ROTHWELL, T.
ROWLES, T.
SCOWCROFT, W.
SEWART, J.
SEWELL, W.
SHAW, A.
SHAW, J. B.
SHAW, W. H.
SHIPLEY, W. S.
SHUTTLEWORTH, H.
SIMM, S.
SKINNER, H.
SKELTON, G.
SLACK, J.
SMETHURST, S.
SMITH, C. E.
SMITHSON, H.
STANLEY, W. H.
STEWART, C.
SWARBRICK, J. W.
SYKES, E.
TATE, F.
TATLEY, P.
TAYLOR, R.
THOMASSON, E.
THOMASSON, E.
THOMASSON, F.
THOMASSON, P.
THOMASSON, P.
THOMASSON, W. E.
THORNLEY, E.
THURSTON, R. J.
TURNER, J.
TYRER, T.
VERNON, J.
WADDELOVE, O.
WAIN, J.
WALMSLEY, G.
WARBURTON, F.
WASSALL, A.
WHITWORTH, A.
WHITWORTH, A.
WHITTLE, W.
WHITEHEAD, C.
WILCOX, J.
WILLIAMS, A.
WILLIAMS, T.
WILSON, J. R.
WOOD, E.
WOOD, F.
WOOD, H. H.
WOOD, J.
WOOD, W.
WOODCOCK, C.
WRIGHT, B.
YATES, A.
YATES, W.

Thos. Oliver and Sons (Bollington), Ltd.

ARNOLD, A.
ARNOLD, W.
BARTON, A.
BARTON, W.
BRADLEY, J. T.
BROGDEN, A.
BROOKES, A.
BROSTER, T.
BUNTING, H.
BUNTING, J. T.
CHADWICK, F.
CLARKE, W.
CLAYTON, J.
DAVIES, A.
EGERTON, W.
EYRES, A.
GLEAVE, H.
GOODWIN, J.
GOODWIN, S.
GOODWIN, T.
HAIGH, L.
HEATH, B.
HOUGH, A.
JACKSON, W.
KAY, F.
LEIGH, A.
LEIGH, A.
NEEDHAM, H.
SNAPE, A.
SNAPE, J.
SNAPE, H.
SNAPE, H.
SNAPE, W., Junr.
STUBBS, H. D.
THOMPSON, C.
VICKERS, J.
WALKER, C., Junr.
WALKER, J.
WALTON, P.
WHITEHURST, P.
WHITEHURST, W.

Bamford Mills.

BLAND, G.
BOTTOMLEY, I.
BRADLEY, L.
BRADWELL, W.
BURROWS, G.
*CROOKES, J.
CROOKES, J.
DIXON, T.
ELLIOTT, A.
HALL, J.
HALL, J. H.
JENNINGS, L.
MIDDLETON, A.
PALMER, D.
PALMER, J.
PEARSON, T.
ROLLEY, J.
SHIRL, B.
SIDEBOTTAM, H.
WALKER, G.
WALKER, M.
WELBURN, J.

Ormrod, Hardcastle and Co., Ltd.

BAMFORD, J.
BENTLEY, W.
BRINDLE, J.
BROWN, J.
CARSON, J.
CLIFF, W. H.
DANDY, J.
DRAPER, W.
FRANCE, W.
GARNER, T.
GARNER, W.
GETHINGS, J.
GREENHALGH, H.
GRIMSHAW, W.
HALLIWELL, J.
HAUGHTON, H.
HEYES, T.
HILSLEY, W.
HILTON, S.
HUNTING, W.
HUTCHINSON, F.
KNOWLES, W.
LEE, A.
LYON, J.
MARLAND, J.
MATHER, H.
MELLING, A.
MORRIS, H.
MURPHY, E.
NOBLE, J.
PASQUILL, T.
PASQUILL, W.
RIDGELEY, F.
RODGERS, J.
SHAW, T.
SMETHURST, J.
SMITH, J.
STOTT, E. C.
STOTT, W.
UNSWORTH, S.
WALKER, J. T.
WALLER, E.
WALLER, F. J.
WALLER, J.
WOODS, T.

Isaac Pearson, Ltd.

ANDREWS, H.
BAILEY, H.
BAINES, E.
BARRATT, S.
BOSWELL, G. A.
BROWN, I.
BURGESS, E.
BURGESS, T.
CALVERT, B.
CARSON, J.
CHAPPELL, J. W.
CLEWS, J
COLLIER, J.
CONNOR, G.
COOPER, W.
DAKIN, J. W.
DEAN, T.
DERBYSHIRE, W.
DIMELOW, H.
DOXEY, W.
FLYNN, J. W.
FORSHAW, C. H.
GILL, J. H.
HARGREAVES, E.
HEAPY, H.
HEAVYSIDE, W.
HILLER, F. W.
HOLLAND, A.
HUGHES, H.
KEARNS, M.
NIXON, W.
PEARSON, S.
PEAT, A. J.
PERKINS, W.
PRICE, W.
ROYLANCE, A.
SHENTON, H.
SHRIGLEY, A. E.
STOKES, J.
WADE, A.
WELCH, G.
WELLINGTON, F.
WILLANS, J.
WILSON, W.
WOOD, J. A.
WRIGHT, A.
WRIGHT, J. T.
WYLDE, S. H.

E. Peat, Son and Co., Ltd.

EAGLES, R.
THRESHER, C.
TOMLINSON, G.

Reddish Spinning Company.

ADSHEAD, J.
ANSTALL, W.
BINGHAM, A.
BOOTH, W. R.
BRAMWELL, J. A.
BROWN, A.
BROWN, D. H.
BROWN, W.
CAPSTICK, W.
CATTERALL, P. H.
CROFTS, W.
DAWSON, E.

The Fine Cotton Spinners' and Doublers' Association, Limited.—Con.

ECKERSLEY, T.
FIRTH, J.
HOLLAND, C. H.
HIBBERT, W.
HOOLEY, A.
HOOLEY, F.
HOOLEY, H.
INGHAM, J.
KIRKMAN, H.
LEIGH, G. E.
LITTLER, J. T.
LYNCH, J.
MARSH, W. H.
MAYERS, B. L.
OLDHAM, W. E.
PARTINGTON, F.
PLANT, A.
THRASHER, W. A.
WHITE, T.

Thomas Rivett, Ltd.

BARDSLEY, S.
BENFOLD, W.
BRADSHAW, W.
BRINDLEY, J. J.
BROWN, R.
CHEETHAM, F.
CLAYTON, T.
HANRAHAN, T.
ELLIOT, J.
FORSHAW, J.
GARRETT, F.
GIBBINS, F. J.
GOSLING, J. E.
HAYLEY, J. W.
HOLLAND, J.
HOLLOWAY, J.
INGHAM, D.
LEACH, G.
LEWIS, H.
LIDGETT, F.
McEVOY, G. H.
McEVOY, M.
PEARSON, A.
PEARSON, J. H.
RAWLINSON, B.
ROYLANCE, C.
STUBBS, J. W.
SYKES, H.
TETLOW, W.
THORNBER, W. J.
TICKLE, J. H.
WALLACE, W.
WHITE, J. W.
WILSON, G.
WRIGHT, A.
WRIGHT, F.
WYCHE, A.

Shaw, Jardine and Co., Ltd.

ALLEN, W.
ALLISON, A.
ARTHURS, E.
BLACKBURN, G.
BOWDON, H.
BOWDON, W. H.
CATTERALL, P.
CURRAN, T.
DENNY, J.
GREENHALGH, C.
GRIME, D.
GRINDROD, H.
HELSBY, J.
HILTON, H.
HOLIDAY, J.
HOWARD, S.
KAY, J. H.
KNIGHT, H.
LEE, J.
LEYLAND, B.
MAKIN, J.
MAKIN, R.
MOORES, E.
MORAN, W.
MOUNFIELD, E.
MYLOTT, J.
NORMOYLE, J.
OLIVER, A.
ORMSTON, R.
PEMBERTON, J.
ROTHWELL, R.
SMITH, A.
SNOW, J.
WHITE, J.

George Swindells and Son, Limited.

ASHLEY, J.
BANN, E.
BARROW, A.
BARTON, R.
BASSETT, T.
BEARD, H.
BERRY, A.
BERRY, W. A.
BRADLEY, J.
BROWN, J.
BURTON, D.
BUTTERWORTH, F.
CAVENEY, L.
CLAYTON, W.
DANIELS, E.
DUFFIELD, G.
GASKELL, W. B.
GEE, L.
GIBBON, R.
GOODWIN, E.
GOODWIN, J.
GOULD, A.
GRATTON, J.
HANDFORTH, J.
HARDING, J.
HARROP, F. H.
HEATHCOTE, A. E.
HUNT, A.
INGHAM, W.
INGLEY, H.
JACKSON, A.
KING, B.
KING, O.
KIRKHAM, H.
LEIGH, T.
LOMAS, C.
MAYERS, F.
MAYERS, H.
MOORES, O.
MOSS, W.
NOLAN, T.
PAGE, H.
PERKIN, C.
POTTS, G.
POTTS, W.
QUINN, R.
RATCLIFFE, W.
STUBBS, P.
WAINWRIGHT, A.
WAINWRIGHT, A. E.
WALTON, F.
WARBURTON, R.
WHEELTON, H.
WOOD, H.
WRIGHT, F.
WRIGHT, J.
WYATT, S.

Thomas Taylor and Sons, Limited.

ALDRED, F.
ALLSOP, H.
ALLSOP, J.
ALLSOP, J.
ATHERTON, J.
BARLOW, F.
BARLOW, T.
BARON, H.
BARTON, J. W.
BOOTH, J.
COURTNEY, A.
DILWORTH, W.
FLANAGAN, W.
GOATER, C.
GREGORY, T.
HALL, J.
HALL, T.
HAMER, T.
HIGGINSON, J.
HOLT, J.
HULME, J.
HULME, W.
ISHERWOOD, G.
MARSH, A.
MAYOH, C.
MORT, W.
MULLINEAUX, W.
PENDLEBURY, J.
SHIPWAY, H.
SMEDLEY, W.
WARD, S.
WOOD, S.

J. L. Thackeray and Son, Ltd.

BARBER, A.
BIBBY, W.
EDWARDS, J.
GORLEY, E.
KIRK, C. C.
LEE, C.
MADEN, J. E.
MOORE, R.
SHREWSBURY, J.
VOCE, J.

John Towle and Co., Ltd.

BURTON, F.
GARDINER, G.
KINGHAM, H. E.
MADELEY, J.

J. Towlson and Co., Ltd.

BINGHAM, B. B.
TOWLSON, L. A.

The Fine Cotton Spinners' and Doublers' Association, Limited.—Con.

The Tutbury Mill Co., Ltd.

BRINDLEY, S.
BROWN, A.
BULLOCK, F.
CLARKE, A.
COPE, T.
FAIRBANKS, G.
HOOLEY, A.
HOOLEY, G.
HOWARD, J.
KEMP, S.
LAMBURN, S.
MORLEY, A.
MORLEY, E.
PEGG, W.
PHILLIPS, N.
SHAW, H.
SHIPLEY, J.
TORTOISHELL, W.
TWIGG, W.
WALKER, R.
WOOD, F.
WOOD, G. A.

J. and G. Walthew, Ltd.

ASHTON, L.
ASHTON, R.
BOUCKLEY, H.
BURNS, J.
CHADWICK, C. E.
COLLIER, J. W. H.
COOPER, H.
COUPS, S.
CROFT, T.
FARROW, D.
GRANT, A.
GREAVES, A.
HEARDMAN, T.
JACKSON, F.
KELLY, J.
KENNEDY, G.
KING, W.
MERCER, C.
MURRAY, A.
OWEN, J. W.
OWEN, T. H.
REDFERN, A. H.
REYNOLDS, E.
REYNOLDS, F.
REYNOLDS, F.
RIDGWAY, A. H.
RIGBY, J.
ROWBOTTOM, C.
SMITH, G.
SWAIN, J. T.
TURNER, F.
WAINWRIGHT, G. H.
WAINWRIGHT, J.
WRIGHT, J.

Wolfenden and Son, Ltd. (Bolton).

Columbia Mill.

AINSWORTH, J.
ASPINALL, C.
BLACKBURN, E.
BOND, J.
CARROLL, W.
DOOLEY, T. H.
MANN, R. T.
McCANN, A.
PARKINSON, W.
PILKINGTON, J.
PILKINGTON, R.
RIGBY, T.
ROBINSON, S.
SAGAR, B.
SHARPLES, F.
WOOD, H.
WOODS, N.
YATES, W. V.

Marsh Fold Mill.

BARON, W. J.
BARTON, J.
CROOK, J.
HUTCHINSON, D.
MARSH, W.
SIMM, E. P.
TAYLOR, R.
TAYLOR, R. B.
WITTER, J.

Asia Mill.

ARMSTRONG, P.
ASPDEN, J.
BALDWIN, J.
BATSON, J.
BROOKS, A.
BROOKS, E.
BROOKS, J. B.
BURNS, A.
CATTERALL, H.
CHATBURN, W.
CLOUGH, J.
ELLWOOD, J. T.
EVA, J.
HINDLEY, J.
LONGWORTH, T.
MAKIN, N.
MANUELL, W. T.
NICHOLSON, J. P.
SEWELL, W. H.
TICKLE, G. H.
TONGE, H.
TOPP, J. W.
WARBURTON, T.
WARBURTON, W.
WHITWORTH, W.
WOODWARD, F.
YATES, J.

The Woodeaves Co., Limited.

McDONNA, W.
STANDRING, A.
WEATHERALL, J.
WILCOX, J.

C. Wright and Co., Limited.

ANDERTON, E.
ASPINALL, J.
BAKER, C.
BAKER, J.
BOARDMAN, J.
CALDWELL, A.
CALDWELL, R.
CHARLTON, F.
COUSINS, H.
CRIPPEN, H.
DARBYSHIRE, J.
DUNCAN, J.
ECKERSLEY, J.
FOULDS, E.
GERRARD, W.
GREENWOOD, J.
GRUNDY, J.
HAMER, R.
HAMPSON, J.
HEYWOOD, J.
HEYWOOD, J.
HILTON, T.
HILTON, T.
HINDLEY, J.
HORROCKS, R.
HOWCROFT, J.
HUNTER, E.
JACKSON, T.
KNIGHT, J.
LYON, C.
MATHER, J.
MERCER, G.
MERCER, W.
PARRY, R.
ROWNTREE, J.
SHARPLES, R.
SMITH, J.
THORP, F.
WALKER, T.
WHITTAKER, A.
WORRALL, H.

Felber, Jucker and Co., Ltd.
(See p. 521 in Roll of Honour.)

JUCKER, E. F., Governing Director
DICKINSON, E. F.
HOTTON, F.
KIRKHAM, R. H.
LEAH, P. B.
MARSDEN, F. A.
MILNE, W.
McDONALD, A.
PARKER, A.

Finlay, Campbell and Co., Ltd.
(See p. 520 in Roll of Honour.)

CAMPBELL, R. G.
CAHILL, J. H.
LUPTON, C. L.
DAVIES, J.
WILKES, E.
HUDSON, W.
MARSH, E.
WARWICK, W.
LEE, A.
MARSDEN, A.

Finnigans Ltd.

(See p. 515 in Roll of Honour.)

BIRD, T.	†FISHER, A. C.	OWEN, L.
BOAM, G.	GEDDES, A.	PHILLIPS, H.
BUNYAN, P.	GELDARD, L.	PUGH, A. P.
BURBERRY, F.	GILL, J.	†PEARCH, S. H.
BYRNE, R.	GONNE, C. R.	REID, H.
†BROWN, T.	GOODWIN, H.	ROBERTS, W.
CHAPMAN, E.	GRANEY, W.	ROGERS, W. C.
COLERIDGE. F. W.	GREEN, A.	ROLES, G.
COLLINS, A.	GREEN, R.	†REED, J.
CROFT, F. A.	GURLING, J. E.	†SHUFFLEBOTTOM, A.
CROSS, A.	HARVEY, E.	
CUMMINS, P.	HASTINGS, L.	†SMITH, R.
CUTTING, A.	HOLT, R.	SANDERSON, J. W.
COLEMAN, F.	HOOPER, B.	SCOTT, R. M.
DAVIES, E.	†HOBBS, J. G.	SEARLE, W.
DELL, E.	†HOOK, H.	SEYMOUR, L. C.
DOWNES, H.	KNIGHT, H. H.	SHADBOLT, W.
DOWNHAM, G.	KIRKBRIDE, R.	SLADE, H.
DUNCALF, D.	†KELLY, P.	SULLIVAN, D.
ELLIS, C.	†KNIGHT, F. W.	SCHNEIDER, H. S.
EVANS, A.	LAWLER, J.	TERRY, T.
FENNEMORE, E.	LEEDHAM, W.	†TAYLOR, S.
FINNIGAN, W., Jr.	MARSLAND, J.	WHITTAKER, A.
(Director.)	MASKELL, H. C.	WILKINSON, S.
FINNIGAN, H.	McBREARTY, R.	WILLIAMS, C.
(Director.)	MOONEY, T.	WILSON, G.
FINNIGAN, B.	MORRIS, J.	WILSON, W.
(Director.)	MURRAY, J. I.	†WESTON, W.
FURNEAUX, J. D.	MURRAY, H.	†WOODCOCK, A. R.
GARRAWAY, F.	O'ROURKE, J.	YOUNG, F.

I. Frankenburg and Sons, Ltd.

(See p. 516 in Roll of Honour.)

ALDCROFT, L.	HAMPSON, W.	THORP, W.
ASHWORTH, T.	HUXLEY, W.	TURNER, F.
ABRAHAMS, S.	HILL, T. C.	THOMPSON, G.
AARONS, I.	HUBBARD, C. E.	THOMPSON, D.
ALDCROFT, A.	HUBBARD, A. L.	THOMPSON, A.
BRADSHAW, A.	HOLLAND, T.	VERBLOSKI, H.
BUTLER, E.	IRVING, J.	WARD, P. S.
BOWKER, W. R.	JOHNSON, J.	WILLIAMS, H.
BOARDMAN, H.	JOHNSON, J.	WILLIAMSON, R.
BALL, G.	O'KEEFE, P.	WHITELEY, W.
BERRY, J. A.	KAY, T.	WILSON, R.
BOWERS, J. E.	LENNON, W. E.	YATES, W.
BOARDMAN, H.	LISTER, A. E.	†ALLCOCK, J.
BIRD, J.	LEE, T.	†BETTERIDGE, F.
BOARDMAN, W.	LEVI, J.	†BILLING, W.
CHADWICK, J.	LUNN, J.	†BARNES, C.
COVENTRY, B.	LITTLER, A.	†COLEMAN, J.
COOTES, G.	LAZARUS, L.	†DAVIES, S.
DAVIS, J.	MORRIS, W. G.	†CALLAGHAN, J.
DOWNEY, L.	MAKIN, J. T.	†EDWARDS, J.
DORER, J.	MATTHEWS, E.	†EASTWOOD, J. H.
DAWES, A. H.	MURRAY, W.	†FINK J.
DUGGAN, T.	MOORES, W. H.	†HUBBARD, F.
DARBY, S.	MAKIN, H.	†HAROLD, A.
DEANE, G.	MARSH, J.	†HAWTHORNE, M.
ENSTONE, J.	OLDHAM, M. A.	†HOLT, J.
EDWARDS, J. R.	PARKER, H.	†HACKIN, J.
EDWARDS, W.	PULMAN, H.	†KENNEDY, T.
EASTWOOD, J.	PROCTOR, J.	†MORRIS, S. J.
EDWARDS, J.	POVAH, W.	†MONKS, W.
EATON, C. H.	POTTS, E.	†McINNES, S.
EDWARDS, T.	RIDINGS, J.	†NUTTALL, J.
FRANKENBURG, M.	ROBINSON, W.	†PRAX, D. L.
	ROBERTS, T.	†POWIS, P.
FINK, S.	ROSENBLOOM, I.	†PERCY, A. E.
FLETCHER, J.	ROSENBERG, L.	†ROE, F.
FOWLER, W.	ROYLE, E. W.	†RYAN, M.
GARNER, A.	RUEBEN, S.	†RYAN, M.
GARNER, T.	RYAN, J.	†SHORROCKS, P.
GLEESON, J.	SHUKER, W. S.	†SMITH, H.
GETTINS, J. J.	SWANN, W.	†SMITH, W.
GREEN, E.	SCHOFIELD, W. E.	†SAVAGE, W.
GUY, A.	SCAMMELL, A. G.	†THORPE, W.
GLASSBERG, R.	SWEANEY, D.	†TIGHE, T.
GUY, F.	SPENCE, T.	†THOMAS, H.
GATTENBY, W.	SMITH, W. J.	†TOMLINSON, T.
HUGGINS, C.	SALMON, H.	†THOMPSON, P.
HAWTHORNE, A. A.	SPARROW, E.	†VERBLOSKI, C.
HARROP, E.	STANSFIELD, G.	†WALSH, J.
HAMILTON, G.	TAYLOR, P. A.	†WORTHINGTON, R.
HEBBLETHWAITE, J. J.	TOOHEY, J.	
	TOMLINSON, H.	†YOUILL, J.

† Rejected.

H. T. Gaddum and Co.

(See p. 525 in Roll of Honour.)

BUCKLEY, A. D.	HARDYMAN, A. C.	ROBERTS, A.
GILLHAM, A.	HARRISON, A.	SMITH, L. G. T.

Gatley, Vickers and Co.

(See p. 677 in Roll of Honour.)

GATLEY, H. J.	JARMAN, G.	DAVIES, A.
VICKERS, E. M.	SWINNERTON, J.	STAPLETON, T.
ARMSTRONG, H. T.	HEYWOOD, A.	HYDE, R.
BRISTOW, W. G.	SKELLHORN, W.	REEVES, J.
MURRAY, G.	STEELE, J.	HARRISON, J.
JAMIESON, W.	KENYON, J.	HULME, E.
HEYWOOD, J. J.	SUTTON, G.	JARVIS, A.
GILLIGAN, F.	RIGBY, A.	LLOYD, F.
LORD, S.	MUSCROFT, J.	DANIELS, G.
HUGES, E.	LEVIS, T.	ROBINSON, F.
DODD, W.	MOBEY, J.	SINCLAIR, G.
FALLON, F.	BURGESS, G.	BRADBURY, A.
ROGERSON, H.	GRUNDY, J.	ASHWORTH, E.
OLIVER, J.	WHYATT, T.	YOUNG, H.
HARRISON, J.	GROGAN, J.	

Richard Goodair, Ltd.

(See p. 523 in Roll of Honour.)

ALDCROFT, F.	†GREENHOUGH, A.	†PIMLOTT, J.
ADAMS, F. G.	HARTLEY, S.	†PAGE, W.
ACKROYD, F.	HAWKINS, W.	†PETTIGREW, J.
ASHWORTH, F.	HODKINSON, W.	PARKER, R.
BIRBECK, W.	HEWIS, H.	PILKINGTON, E.
BISHOP, E.	†HACKNEY, J.	†REECE, G.
†BROWNHILL, J.	†JOHNSON, J.	STEWART, W.
CLUBB, W. F.	JOHNSON, L.	STANDFAST, S.
CLARKE, M.	LAING, J.	SHERLOCK, W. R.
COCKER, E.	LANTSBERRY, H.	†STEWARD, G.
CARRINGTON, W.	†LEA, R. W.	†SIMPSON, H.
COOPER, W.	LINDSAY, R.	SCHOLES, H.
DUNN, T.	LAND, W.	TRENBATH, W. F.
DICKINSON, W. E.	NEWSOME, G.	WOLFENDEN, W.
ELLIOTT, H.	†OWEN, T.	WIGHTMAN, T.
FOLEY, E.	PARTINGTON, H. E.	WILLOUGHBY, A.
†FORRESTER, A.		WHITELEY, H.

Springfield Mills, Preston.

ATKINSON, J.	HOLT, W.	NIGHTINGALE, D.
ATHERTON, W.	HOTHERSALL, W.	PROCTOR, J.
BEARDSWORTH, J. B.	HETHERINGTON, J.	PITCHER, T.
CARDESS, J.	HARRIS, J.	RAWCLIFFE, E.
CRANGLE, E.	HALL, W.	SPENCER, H.
EASTHAM, E.	KIRKBY, R.	THOMPSON, S.
FAZAKERLEY, T.	LEE, F.	THOMPSON, S.
FLETCHER, W.	MONCRIEFF, W.	WOTHINGTON, R.
HARRIS, A.	NICKSON, J.	WILKINSON, G.
		WOODS, L.

G. W. Goodwin and Son.

(See p. 522 in Roll of Honour.)

Works.

ALSTON, R. A.	JONES, W.	ROBINSON, A.
BRADBURN, J.	LEVIS, J. W.	ROBINSON, J. A.
CALDWELL, J.	LOCKETT, W.	RYAN, J.
CASH, S.	LONG, E.	SHAW, W.
CHORLEY, Z.	LONGSTAFF, J.	TARRANT, J.
COOPER, A.	McAVOY, J. T.	THOMAS, J.
CUNNINGHAM, S.	MILLS, J.	THOMSON, A.
DANIELS, W. H.	POPE, R. L.	TURNER, J. H.
GOODWIN, J.	RAMSDEN, B.	WETHERALL, C.
HARFORD, J.	RIDGWAY, F. M.	WILKINSON, W.
HUGHES, J.	RIDGWAY, H. W.	
HUGHES, R. C.	RIGBY, R.	

Offices.

FOSTER, A.	MORRIS, H.	TONGE, F. F.
HEYWOOD, J.		

G. Gottschalck and Co.

(See p. 521 in Roll of Honour.)

ANDERTON, A.	MEANOCK, G.	WILLIAMSON, J. H.
BRIERLEY, A.	PROST, B.	
HAWLEY, A.	WILLIS, H.	

† Rejected.

Greg Bros. and Co.
(See p. 525 in Roll of Honour.)

ENRIGHT, H. A.	MOSS, E. A.	FORSTER, I. E.
THOMAS, F.	ROBERTS, T. W.	RICHARDSON, W.
CARPENTER, E. A.	PETTINGALE, G.	

Goldschmidt, Hahlo and Co.
(See p. 524 in Roll of Honour.)

SUMMERSGILL, F

Groves and Whitnall, Ltd.
(See p. 678 in Roll of Honour.)

AITKEN, C.	DAVIES, A.	LLOYD, E.
BARBOUR, A.	DAGNALL, G. H.	MITTON, A.
BALL, F. E.	DEAN, HUGH.	MAHONY, T.
BRADSHAW, R. L.	EVANS, W. F.	MANNING, F.
BANKS, F. W.	EDMUNDS, E.	NOBLE, H.
BOLLAND, A.	FULLER, G. W.	NEWTON, A.
BROUGHTON, J.	FORREST, P.	PYATT, T.
BRANNAN, J.	FRITH, A.	PLUNKETT, E.
BOWERMAN, P.	FILDES, G.	PROVOST, H.
BELL, J.	GOODWIN, C. E.	QUAYLE, J.
BARRY, J.	HUMPHREYS, H.	RATCLIFFE, F.
CORRY, A.	HYDE, T.	SYKES, T.
CHORLTON, E.	HAMMOND, T.	VENABLES, W.
COOPER, T.	HAMPSON, C.	VERITY, J.
CHORLTON, T.	HOWARD, W.	WATSON, W.
CLEWORTH, J.	HOLMES, G. W.	WEBB, W. H.
CLEWORTH, T.	JONES, J. B.	WILKINS, A.
CHADWICK, E.	JACKMAN, J.	WATSON, T.
DOCKRAY, P. S.	LEWIS, H.	WHITAKER, R.

Hall, Higham and Co.
(See p. 526 in Roll of Honour.)

BANCROFT, H.	HOOSON, J. W.	SINGLETON, W.
BENTLEY, A.	HOULT, P. W.	†SPILSBURY, A. N.
‡BELL, J. H.	INSKIP, G.	STANLEY, D.
†BOWDEN, F.	JENNINGS, J.	†STEPHENS, E. J.
†BURGESS, J.	JOHNSON, A. A.	STOWER, C. J.
*CADE, W. T.	†JOHNSON, C.	STUBBS, H.
CAMPBELL, H.	†JOHNSON, J. W. S.	†THOMAS, J. W.
†CHALLINER, W.	JONES, W.	THOMASON, J. W.
COHEN, L.	LEECH, W. H.	THORNTON, T.
†COTTLE, A.	LUKE, J.	TRAVIS, W. H.
†DIXON, F. A.	†MATHARS, O.	WATSON, G.
†EYRES, W.	†McHUGH, W.	WEBSTER, W.
†FELTON, T. P.	NUTTALL, W.	WILLIAMS, G.
†FITZGERALD, J.	†ORDISH, H.	WILLIAMS, W. D.
HAGGERSTONE, A.	PRIESTLEY, N. V.	WILLIAMSON, F.
†HALL, A.	POLLITT, F.	WILLS, J.
†HALL, A.	†SCOTT, F. L.	†WOLSTENHOLME, A. P.
HELSBY, S.	SHARP, S.	

Hall and Pickles.
(See p. 527 in Roll of Honour.)

BEBBINGTON, J. F	HUGHES, W. R.	MOORE, R.
BRISTOWE, G.	HALLIWELL, H.	MONEYPENNY, W.
BOLAND, D.	HAMAND, W.	*MOORE, H. H.
BEAVIS, J. W.	HARROP, W.	*MOOTZ, A. G.
CORRIE, R. E.	HENDERSON, J.	NEILSON, G. K.
CAMERON, M.	KAIN, J. H.	PARKER, E.
CLARKE, W.	KYDD, A.	SHERRATT, F. A.
EYRES, W.	*LANE, W.	SIMPSON, H.
FENTON, H.	LAWTON, J.	WAYGOOD, E. S.
FARRAR, T. S	LEE, S.	WILD, R.
GOODYER, C. B.	LEMMON, F.	WATSON, W. H.
GARNER, S. N.	MILLS, F. H.	WATKINS, J.
GOLDSTRAW, J.	MASON, C.	WILKES, A.
GREGORY, A. W.	*MARRIOTT, T.	*WHITTLE, C.
HALL, E. B.	MACE, C. F. L.	

M. Hertz and Co., Ltd.
(See p. 532 in Roll of Honour.)

BRIMBLE, J.	†HILL, A.	†PHILIPS, F.
BROCKLEHURST, H.	*JACKSON, A. G.	*PORTER, J.
CARR, J	†LEARY, A.	POYNTER, H.
*COOKE, J.	LEE, F.	†ROSCOE, E.
†GOLIGHTLY, B. W.	LOMAS, A.	SEQUEIRA, W. C.
GRINDROD, H.	McCLELLAND, W.	SMITH, J. F.
*HARROLD, F.	MONKS, F.	STANSFIELD, H. J.
	†PETTY, H.	†WALKER, E.

* Serving with the Colours. † Rejected.
‡ Since accepted for immediate service.

Haugk, von Zabern and Co.
(See p. 679 in Roll of Honour.)

MATHER, F.	†LANCASTER, H.

Heyn, Franc and Co.
(See p. 533 in Roll of Honour.)

ALSOP, G.	GREENHALGH, J. H.	PARISH, M. J.
AXON, E.		PEWTER, F. R.
BINNS, E.	HARROP, C.	RICHARDSON, J.
CLARKE, F.	GAVIN, G.	ROSTRON, N. E.
CROSS, G.	KEMP, A.	RUTHERFORD, R.
DAVIES, A.	KEMP, J.	STEMBRIDGE, L.
DONNAN, J.	MASSEY, A.	SUTCLIFFE, A.
DRUMMOND, W.	MOUNTAIN, P.	WAINE, S.
ELLIOTT, A. R.	OGDEN, A.	WILLIAMS, F. H.
EVANS, C.		

Heynssen, Martienssen and Co.
(See p. 680 in Roll of Honour.)

†KAY, MAX, M. (Partner)	GREENHOW, H.	POLE, A.
BEWSEY, J. R.	HARRISON, C. E.	SIMISTER, A.
BUCKLEY, J.	HOYES, F.	†SLACK, J.
CARTER, A. G.	JOHNSON, S.	TAYLOR, F. W.
†FLETCHER, E.	†LOMAS, C.	WIGNALL, P.
	MORRISEY, H.	WOOD, F.

Thos. G. Hill and Co., Ltd.
(See p. 681 in Roll of Honour.)

OWEN, H.	BROWN, J. W.	POLLARD, A.
AGNEW, W.	†ELLISON, F.	†DAVIS, G.
WOOD, C. J.	COX, J.	†WORRALL, R.
SLACK, H.	CHADWICK, J.	†GASKELL, W.
HUNT, F. J.	OGDEN, J.	
NUTTALL, W.	†BROOKE, J. A.	

Hiltermann Brothers.
(See p. 544 in Roll of Honour.)

CATON, J.	OGGIER, S. L.	†KNOOP, N. B.
CRITCHLEY, F.	POOLE, J. H.	†TITTERINGTON, J. R.
KELSEY, G. H.	TWITTEY, H.	
MILNE, H.	†CRAWFORD, J.	

S. Hinrichsen and Co.
(See p. 679 in Roll of Honour.)

FOOTE, J. A.	MARTIN, H.	GOODFELLOW, E.
*LAWSON, E.	TAYLOR, H. O.	

Hogg and Mitchell.
(See p. 538 in Roll of Honour.)

BEATTY, J.	McCOLL, E. C.	†BLADON, F.
BLAIR, D. J.	NIELD, E.	†BRADLEY, J.
DONAGHEY, B.	NIXON, C.	†BRADSHAW, P.
ELY, W. O.	NUTTALL, H.	†PLANK, E.
GORDON, A.	SPELMAN, M.	†RUSSELL, F. H.
GAMBLE, G.	WALLACE, A.	†ROBINSON, H.
LEE, J.*	RUSSELL, C.	
MELIA, P.	†BAYVEL, A. M.	

Hollins Mill Co., Ltd.
(See p. 534 in Roll of Honour.)

ADSHEAD, W.	HEYWOOD, W.	SULLIVAN, C.
BUCKLEY, J.	JACKSON, F.	SWAINE, A.
BARNSHAW, W.	JOHNSON, F.	TETLOW, P.
CORNER, G.	JOHNSON, J.	WHEELTON, N. H.
CRAWFORD, H.	JOHNSON, J. T.	WALSH, T.
GEE, F.	MANNING, J.	WITHINGTON, S.
GORDON, D.	OGDEN, W.	WHYATT, R.
HUGHES, E.	SEDDON, J.	YARWOOD, F.
HEYWOOD, W.	SMITH, J.	YATES, J.
HACKING, W.	SMITH, W.	

* Serving with the colours. † Rejected.

Horrockses, Crewdson and Co., Ltd.

(See p. 539 in Roll of Honour.)

ARMITT, C.	EAVES, W.	MILLER, A.
*ARNOLD, L.	FRANCIS, C.	MASON, W.
AXON, A.	HOLDEN, J.	*MILLER, H.
BIRCHALL, T.	HOUGH, A.	NORTH, D. H.
*BOWDEN, C.	HOLT, F.	*O'RYAN, F.
BUTTERWORTH, S., Junr.	HUTTON, F.	OGDEN, W.
	HAND, F. N.	PENNIALL, H. S.
BROWN, A.	HOWARD, T.	ROBINSON, F.
BENNETT, E. A.	HAWES, S.	REDFERN, H. B.
BLAKEWAY, J.	IRLAM, M.	RICHARDS, J.
CURRIE, J. G.	JONES, E. A.	SCHOFIELD, R.
CATTELL, G.	MOORE, T.	WILSON, C.
COLLIER, R. S. G.	McKNIGHT, A.	WOOD, E.
DUNN, S.	McNAMARA, E.	WATSON, T. H.
ETCHELLS, E.	MITTON, S.	YEARDLEY, J.

Richard Howarth and Company, Limited.

(See p. 529 in Roll of Honour.)

35, Dale Street.

AICKMANN, F.	HALL, H. J.	TODMAN, A.
ARNOLD, H. E.	HUMPHREYS, R. O.	VICKERS, A.
BATESON, T.	JOHNSON, J. V.	WEBSTER, W. E.
BEDDOW, S.	KINGSMILL, J.	WHITHAM, J. W.
BOLTON, J.	LINDSAY, E.	YOUNG, D.
BOSTON, H.	McNICOL, J. R.	†BLAKELEY, J.
BROADMEADOW, C	McHUGH, F.	†GROVES, J.
CLAYTON, P.	MURPHY, W.	†HOUSE, T.
COLLINGE, E. O.	NEWLAND, F. G.	†JOHNSON, S.
COLLINSON, C. R.	OLIVER, W.	†MOTTERSHEAD, H.
CRABTREE, B.	PACE, A.	
CROMPTON, R.	PICKUP, J.	†RICHARDSON, G. K.
EDWARDS, A. L.	SHEPHERD, W.	
FERNLEY, J.	SMITH, P.	†TUNSTALL, A.
FORD, W.	STIMPSON, B.	†TURNER, F.
GARDNER, C.	SUDLOW, E.	†WOOD, W. A.
HADDON, R. T.	TAYLOR, A.	
HAGUE, W. A.	TIMPERLEY, A.	

From the Mills, Salford.

MORRALL, P.	BRAITHWAITE, H.	STILLMAN, A.
CAVENEY, J.	BRISTOL, H.	STEVENS, S.
JORDAN, P.	CATTERALL, W.	†BAKEWELL, C.
BOWKER, G.	JENKINS, W.	†SUTTON, J.
McCORMICK, H.	ROBERTS, G.	†BUXTON, H.
BAIRD, J.	HAILES, A.	†HAYNES, A.
TILLISON, W.	HANSON, T.	†BAKEWELL, W.
SMITH, W.	CATTERALL, W.	†CHAPMAN, A.
CHAPMAN, J.	COLLINSON, H.	†WAKEFIELD, C.
WHELAN, J.	NUTTALL, A.	†WARD, H.
TILLEY, J.	SUTCLIFFE, J.	†WHALLEY, W.
MULLHOLLAND, A.	POPE, R.	†BLACKLEY, W.
HANSON, T.	SOMERS, R.	†LIGHTFOOT, J.
CRAWLEY, G.	JONES, W. R.	†SCHOFIED, W.
WHITTAKER, W.	TORR, L.	†CHAMBERS, E.
HENRY, J.	SUMMERSALL, H.	†CUNLIFFE, H.
HENRY, J.	ASHALL, H.	†HIGHAM, J.
ROBERTS, E.	BOTWOOD, J.	†WHALLEY, W. A.
TAYLOR, F.	HOWARTH, W.	†BERRY, M.
HOOLEY, R.	MORRELL, J.	†CATTERALL, T.
GORTON, W.	HEROD, J. W.	†SCHOFIELD, J.
ROBERTS, T.	SIMPSON, R.	†DOWNEY, T.
DUNNETT, C.	SIMPSON, J.	†HARPER, E.
CLEWS, J.	MARKHAM, F.	†EDWARDS, T.
DAVENPORT, P.	ROSCOE, T.	†BROOKES, J.
TAYLOR, J.	CHAPMAN, —.	†BLAKELY, C.
WOOD, R. J.	CAWSON, H.	†INGHAM, W.
LEACH, J.	HOOLEY, J.	†MOORE, A.
MILLINGTON, F.	ROWLEY, F.	†LEAMAN, H.
RIGBY, J.	CLAYTON, W.	†ROOK, A.
JONES, W.	DAVIES, J. H.	†JOHNSON, S.
SLATER, T.	McNEA, R.	†PIMLEY, F.
GOODLIFFE, W.	ROOK, W.	†OAKS, W.
WALLWORK, T.	MEE, R.	†BOWERS, H.
CHAPMAN, J.	DALY, A.	†MOSS, S.
WHITBY, F.	HUME, W.	†BARKER, G.
BANKS, W.	ROYLE, H.	†WARBURTON, W.
RIGBY, H.	THOMPSON, G.	†THOMPSON, W.
SHALLCROSS, T.	HAMINGWAY, W.	†WARD, J.
JAMES, E.	SLATER, A.	†CROSBIE, C.
CASSIDY, J.	SLATER, W.	†HOLDEN, R.
SPENCER, J.	GREATOREX, H.	
	PHILLIPS, F.	

* Serving with the Colours.   † Rejected.

Joshua Hoyle and Sons, Ltd.

(See p. 540 in Roll of Honour.)

KELLY, J.	SMITH, W. J.	KEEVNEY, E.
WORTHINGTON, P.	HALL, J. R.	HARDMAN, J.
PEARSON, L.	THOMPSON, R.	

Hough, Hoseason and Co.

(See p. 545 in Roll of Honour.)

TINNISWOOD, J.	MOORE, P.	GRADWELL, W.
WILSON, P.	STEVEN, G. H.	DOWD, J.
BOAM, E.	EWING, J. G.	BRIGGS, J.
GARNER, A.	HEALEY, A. J.	
CLAYTON, E.	SHAW, B.	

Sydney Hudson, Ltd.

(See p. 542 in Roll of Honour.)

BATE, H.	DOWNING, C.	STUBBS, J. H.
BOWKER, A.	SEDDON, J.	TILDSLEY, E.
BOWKER, H.	SMITH, W.	YATES, J. W.
BRIERLEY, J. H. V.	STREET, A.	
BRITNOR, B. A.	†STUBBINGS, W.	

Alfred Hulme, Ltd.

(See p. 545 in Roll of Honour.)

Directors { HULME, A., Jr.
          { LEES, A. W., Manager & Secretary.

WILLIAMS, S.	ROWLES, J.	ROWLES, W.

James F. Hutton and Co., Ltd.

(See p. 543 in Roll of Honour.)

HUMPHREYS, H. C	IRLAM, E.	SUMMERSGILL, H.
GRIMSHAW, W.	SMITH, C.	

Three others offered their services, but were not accepted.

Irwell and Eastern Rubber Co., Ltd.

(See p. 546 in Roll of Honour.)

ADSHEAD, F.	MAYBURY, A.	†DAVIES, G.
BECK, G.	OWEN, G.	†EVANS, W.
BLAIR, J.	ROBINSON, W.	†ELLIS, A.
BRIGHT, W.	REARDON, D.	†EDWARDS, C.
BRACEWELL, W.	RUSH, A.	†GRADWELL, J.
BURKE, T.	ROBINSON, H.	†HILL, W.
BUNTING, J.	RICE, J.	†HARTLEY, R.
BADROCK, W.	SAXTON, E.	†HUNT, W.
BIRTWISTLE, J.	SMITH, C. W.	†HOOD, J.
COOPER, A.	SLATER, J.	†HOWELLS, T.
CONNOLLY, J. W.	SUTCLIFFE, J.	†HUGHES, W.
CORNER, J.	SCHOLES, G.	†KAVANAH, B.
CLOUGH, E.	TOY, S.	†KNOTTMAN, J.
CUMPSTY, G.	TOWNTROW, S.	†MATHER, A.
CRAWFORD, W.	WHITE, H.	†MORAN, T.
DAVIES, T.	WRIGHT, P.	†MORGAN, R.
DUNWORTH, J. L.	WILLIAMS, F.	†MALONEY, J.
EVANS, R.	WINTER, B.	†OWEN, C.
FELL, R.	WROE, C.	†POWELL, A.
FLETCHER, A. W	WARBURTON, R.	†PAILIN, G.
FRASER, M.	†ALLEN, A.	†ROSTRON, J.
FORSHAW, E.	†BLAIR, J.	†RUMBELOW, T.
GOODWIN, A.	†BOOTH, W.	†ROUTLEDGE, W.
GLEAVE, G.	†BLANCHARD, S.	†SHERWIN, R.
GRIMSHAW, J.	†CHARD, F.	†STRATFORD, W.
GREEN, H.	†CUNNINGHAM, E.	†TAYLOR, G.
INGHAM, A.	†CLARKSON, J	†WRIGHT, R.
KIRKHAM, W.	†COOKE, A.	†WROE, J.
LOWE, F.	†DAVIES, F.	†WILLIAMSON, G.
MORRIS, C.	†DAVIES, J. W.	
MATTHEWS, G.	†DONIGAN, T.	

Jabez Johnson, Hodgkinson and Pearson, Ltd.

(See p. 552 in Roll of Honour.)

Manchester Warehouse.

PEARSON, W. J., Managing Director.	HOWE, W.	RAYNER, J.
	HUNT, R.	RODGERS, W.
FOSTER, W.	LATHAM, E.	WALKER, J.
HARDY, J. S.	MELLOR, W.	YOUNG, G.
HARPER, F.	MORRIS, A.	

† Rejected.

Jabez Johnson, Hodgkinson and Pearson, Ltd.—Con.

Moor Mills.

BURY, J.
JUMP, R. W.
GREGORY, W.
OPENSHAW, P.
EDGERLEY, H.
PARKINSON, R.
MONKS, A.
WALLWORK, A.
HESFORD, W.
SMITH, W.
TAYLOR, J.
JOHNSON, J.
WARBURTON, G. J.
CUMPSTEY, A.
WHAITE, J.
HODGES, W. G.
WHITEHEAD, W. H.
MORRIS, F.
SKILLEN, J.
JONES, J. J.
ALLEN, T.
MARSDEN, T.
FISHER, W.
HENSOR, F.
TAYLOR, P.
TAYLOR, W.
HOWARTH, J.
MEADS, V.
McCLELLAND, F.
WOOD, R.
RALPH, J.
JEVOUS, E.
BARNES, H.
EAMES, J.
JOLLEY, R.
SCHOFIELD, G. W.
TERRY, T.
SMITH, J. J.
ENTWISTLE, S.
BOARDMAN, A.
HOWARTH, J.

Victoria Mills.

CRAIG, N.
FARAGHER, P. S.
MATHER, J.
MORRIS, H.
NUTTALL, E.
FIELDING, J.
OBERSBY, J.
BRIGGS, T.
STANTON, M.
HURST, J.
SKILLON, J.
POWNALL, W.
MILLS, C.
GOODLAD, J.

Ainsworth Mills.

LINGARD, J.
GREAVES, C.
CRANK, J.
LINGARD, J. A.
HEALD, F.
HILL, A.
POLLITT, H.
ROTHWELL, W.
COUGHLIN, N.
HOLDEN, F.
ODDIE, T.
LOMAX, J.
OPENSHAW, J.
DAVIES, G.
HOLT, R.
SEDDON, W.
OLIVE, J.
BENNISON, T.
OLIVE, E.
MORRIS, J.
BROOKS, W.
NUTTALL, J.
HASLAM, H.

Richard Johnson, Clapham and Morris, Ltd.

(See p. 550 in Roll of Honour.)

Manchester and Liverpool Offices.

BARRETT, F.
BELLAS, W.
BISHOP, T.
BARWICK, L.
BERGIN, T.
*CARMICHAEL, A.
CROSSLEY, S.
CAMERON, C.
DILLON, G.
DEMEL, L.
ELLIS, J. H.
GARSIDE, J.
GREENLEAVES, F.
GRENVILLE, J.
HASLAM, W. E.
HAIGH H.
HICKEY, H.
HARVEY, T. W.
JACKSON, W. E.
JONES, G. W.
LEWIS, J. A.
LAWTON, F.
LIGHT, B.
LLOYD, W. E.
MILNER, F.
McKENZIE, P.
PEEL, S. C.
POLLOCK, N.
PRICE, J.
*ROEBUCK, E.
REDFERN, F.
REDFERN, H.
ROBERTS, T.
SMITH, W. E.
SYMOND, T.
SMITH, N.
THOMAS, A.
TAYLOR, H. H.
WHEELER, T.
WEILD, D.
WHARTON, J.
YATES, G.

Moston Works.

ASHCROFT, A. E.
ATKINS, G.
ASHTON, J. H.
AMBREY, H.
BOWDEN, J.
BROADHURST, F.
BERRY, H.
BAINES, S.
BENTON, P.
BISHOP, W.
BYRNE, W.
BAULK, J.
BARLOW, C.
BARRETT, J.
BRANDWOOD, H.
*BEECH, A. S.
BANKS, V.
COWLEY, J.
CARROL, W.
CAMPBELL, B.
CLARKE, F.
DANIELS, J.
FITZGERALD, J.
FORD, E.
FINCH, J.
FARROW, J.
FINCH, H.
FLETCHER, W.
FIRSTBROOK S.
FIRSTBROOK, T.
FAULKNER, F.
FOWLEY, H.
GALLEY, C.
GEMMELL, F.
GALLAGHER, A.
HEYWOOD, D.
HERON, P.
HARRIS, T.
HAYES, E.
HENSON, F.
HARKER, G.
HOLMES, W.
JONES, E.
JONES, F. M.
JACKSON, A.
JOHNSON, J. E.
KING, J.
LILLEY, J.
LIGHTFOOT, W.
LEES, F.
LEE, J.
LEWIS, A.
MASSEY, F.
MAKIN, W.
MOORES, F.
MATTHEWS, A.
MOORHOUSE, E.
NEWALL, G.
PLANT, W.
PEACH, J.
PLANT, H.
PEAK, J. F.
PHILLIPS, J. W.
PHILLIPS, J.
RENSHAW, H.
RENNISON, A.
STONES, P.
SAXON, E.
SALT, W.
SCALES, G.
SMITH, A.
SMITH, H.
STOCKTON, W.
THOMAS, F.
THOMAS, H.
THORPE, J.
TALBOT, A.
WRIGHT, H.
WHITTLE, J.
WILLIAMS, S.
WATSON, J.
WHITHAM, W.
WALLWORK, R.
WHITEHEAD, J.
WALLWORK, J.
WILKINS, E.
WHYMENT, W.
YOUNG, R.

Jones Brothers, Ltd.

(See p. 554 in Roll of Honour.)

BRIMELOW, J. H.
COOKSON, H. L.
DODD, H. P.
DE THIER, A. N.
EDDISFORD, H. A.
FEARN, R.
HILTON, R.
KAIN, H. J.
LOCKE, E.
MARSDEN, G. D.
MELLON, T.
NADEN, J.
NEWLANDS, A. C.
THOMAS, E.
WALL, E.
WINFIELD, W.
WRAY, S. W.
BANNISTER, J.
FENN, T.
PIMLOTT, J.
BALL, R.
BIRCHALL, W.
BACKHOUSE, W.
ENTWISTLE, A.
GREEN, J. H.
HARTLEY, B. H.
HILL, W.
PRIESTLEY, J.
SHAW, G.
SEPHTON, J.
SMITH, J.
TOONE, G.
WEBB, C.
BURT, J. W.
SLADE, H.
MITCHELL, D.
HILTON, S. C.
HENSON, W. E.
SNOW, A. A.

W. W. Jones, Dooly and Co.

(See p. 555 in Roll of Honour.)

HASLEHURST, J.
CLARK, A.
GOODWIN, J. P.
SLATER, J.
TOMLINSON, R.
*WETHERALL, F.
*NOLAN, P.
*BURROWS, R.

Kay and Lee, Ltd.

(See p. 682 in Roll of Honour.)

†ADAMSON, W.
ATKINS, F.
†BAILEY, F.
BANHAM, T.
BENNETT, H.
BROWN, T.
†BOWES, A. P.
COPELAND, J.
CROSSLEY, J.
†DAVIES, W.
†DUFFIN, T.
FLETCHER, W.
GIBBONS, W.
GOLDSBY, R.
GRAY, T.
†HEYWOOD, T.
HICKS, W.
HIGGINBOTTOM, T.
†HUNT, W.
HOLMES, R.
†JACKSON, E. A.
JUDGE, A.
LEE, STANLEY.
LEE, SIDNEY.
†MELVILLE, G. A.
OATES, J.
PRITCHARD, R.
PRITCHARD, A.
†ROBERTS, O. W.
ROBERTSHAW, G.
SHORE, T. C.
SMITH, G.
TOYNE, C.
VICKERS, W.
†WALKER, W. A.
WALKER, C.

Kendal, Milne and Co.

(See p. 556 in Roll of Honour.)

ALLEN, J.
ARCHER, T.
ARROWSMITH, J. E.
ASHWORTH, F.
BANCROFT, T.
BARRETT, F.
BARTON, S.
BIRCHALL, G.
BLOOMFIELD, C. E.
CHAPMAN, A.
COOPER, G.
CULLEY, J.
DAWSON, F.
DONE, F.
DUNN, J.
FLETCHER, H.
HAWKINS, J.
HEADLEY, H. C.
HEAPE, E.
HIGGINS, W.
HILTON, W.
HIRST, E.
HOWARD, G.
IRVING, J.
JEFFERY, E.
JOHNSON, F.
MELLOR, T.
LEWTHWAITE, A. E.
MEADOWCROFT, J. F.
O'CONNOR, T.
PARKE, W.
PARKIN, T.
PERRIN, J. E.
RAGGETT, J.
REAVY, R.
ROBERTSHAW, W.
ROYSTON, P.
SCHOFIELD, T.
SCHRIER, F.
SCOTT, S.
SIMPSON, C. L.
SINGLETON, R.
SKINNER, J.
SMITH, J.
STANTON, S.
STEPHENSON, H.
TAYLOR, J.
THOMPSON, G.
TORKINGTON, J. E.
WALKER, T.
WHALLEY, C.
WILLIAMS, F. O.
WILSON, J.
†ADSHEAD, T.
†DERBYSHIRE, F.
†EASTHAM, T.
†EVANS, T.
†GARNER, A.
†GILBERT, A. T.
†HEYWOOD, P.
†HILLWIG, W.
†LOWE, C.
†MANSFIELD, H.
†MILLS, H.
†PYLE, J.
†SEATON, C.
†SHINDLER, C.
†SKEENS, A. F.
†SMITH, H.
†SMITH, W.
†TAYLOR, J.
†THOMPSON E. J.
†THOMPSON, G. E.
†TOMBS, C.
†TREVOR, W.
†VIGGARS, A.
†WAKEFIELD, L. M.
†WALTON, T.
†WARD, A.
†WILD, N.
†WILLIAMS, E.

Kidsons, Taylor and Co.

(See p. 684 in Roll of Honour.)

KIDSON, L. D.
KIDSON, H., Junr.
†TAYLOR, H.
†BLAYNEY, J. H.
DEACON, S. W.
†HAMPTON, G. H.
†LEFTON, L. C.
†MATTHEWS, E. M.
†ROBERTS, E.
STEWART, C.
†TOWERS, H.
WARBURTON, E. D.
WILDE, H.

I. Kriegsfeld.

(See p. 683 in Roll of Honour.)

ALDRED, J.
BARNFIELD, L.
BERNSTEIN, D.
HIND, F. W.
SHELMERDINE, W.
WALTON, H. E.
PRICE, H.
ROTHWELL, J.

* Serving with the Colours.   † Rejected.

Langworthy Bros. and Co., Ltd.
(See p. 557 in Roll of Honour.)

*BOARDMAN, W.	WILTSHAW, W.	WELLS, J.
*CUMMINGS, J. J.	HESTIN, J.	DAWSON, W.
*GOLBORN, J.	HESTIN, S.	YATES, A.
*HARRISON, F.	OGDEN, H.	ODDIE, W.
*SIMPSON, F.	BROWN, A.	WALSH, E.
*WELSH, A.	BURTON, F.	HALL, J.
*ECKERSLEY, F.	ASHTON, W.	BROGAN, J.
HARPER, E.	STOCKLEY, J.	MAHON, —
WHITTAKER, J. H.	WILKINSON, W.	HALL, G.
SPENCER, J.	MOTT, J.	SWINDELLS, F.
BAINES, J.	ORMEROD, W.	KNOTT, T.
JOHNSON, J.	BUTLER, W.	PHELAN, M.
BARLOW, J.	GILLULEY, J.	NUTTALL, W.
WRIGHT, F.	PHELAN, J.	BOSCOE, W.
SHERIN, T.	DALE, H.	STUBBS, T.
ANDERSON, J.	SAVILLE, J.	BLACK, A.
ELLIS, W.	MORGAN, W.	BRADE, W.
CHIDLAW, J.	CROWE, J.	WRAY, A.
HAND, W.	McGEE, E.	HULTON, A.
HUNT, F.	SPEED, A.	STEVENSON, C.
THOMPSON, J.	ROWE, R.	ALLEN, G.
PARKER, R.	HOWARTH, F.	PENNINGTON, R.
OLGARD, H.	ROWE, J.	HESFORD, W.
MAYALL, J.	BANNISTER, J.	KILVERT, J.
WOOLFENDEN, J. T.	WRIGHT, F.	WALTON, J.
	LIVESAY, R.	TURNER, P.
MAKIN, R.	HILL, W.	PENDLEBURY, J.
CLARK, J.	WRIGLEY, F.	

R. J. Lea, Ltd.
(See p. 563 in Roll of Honour.)

§COWCROFT, J.	NORRIS, N.	WALKER, F. J.
HOLGATE, W.	GRAYSON, R.	BLACK, D. H.
BAILEY, J. D.	WAGSTAFF, J.	LITTLE, W. J.
FENNING, E.	BUCK, W. H.	PANTER, A. L.
WHITE, A. R.	ARNOLD, C. J.	MOODYCLIFFE, N.
PENNEY, J.	KERSHAW, J.	NEEDHAM, H.
KESTERTON, W.	THWAITE, W.	HARPER, T.
EAGLAND, H.	NEIL, H.	POWELL, W.
ACARNLEY, T.	ALLEN, G.	KNOX, C.
DAWES, W.	BRUCE, G. A. F.	WOOD, H.
GODDARD, J. H. A.	LEIGH, E. A.	

George Leek and Sons, Ltd.
(See p. 684 in Roll of Honour.)

LEEK, T. W.	TURTON, T.	HORROCKS, A.
ROBSON, S.	EVANS, R.	MATHEWS, A.
RYDER, S.	BARTON, W.	COOKE, W. A.
DALE, H.	RATCLIFFE, G.	LEEK, J. E.
PARKER, A.	ALLEN, J.	GOULBURN, J.
FARR, A.	HARDY, F.	

George Lenthall and Sons.
(See p. 561 in Roll of Honour.)

LENTHALL, W.	EARNSHAW, A.	ISHERWOOD, A.
COWAN, H. C.	EVANS, H.	HUDDART, W.
ROBERTS, E.	WOOD, J.	SIMPSON, T.
WADE, R.	JOHNSON, F. W.	PICKUP, S.
WHITTAKER, H.	PLATT, F. G.	

Levinstein Limited.
(See p. 560 in Roll of Honour.)

HURST, H. G.	PARTINGTON, C.	LOUGHREY, J.
ELLIS, C. S.	OULTRAM, G.	D'ARCY, T.
PARKINSON, W.	WHIPP, J.	LEWISS, W.
WRIGLEY, W.	WOOD, A.	JEHU, R.
BIRCH, A. C.	MOTTRAM, C.	HORSFALL, P.
MIDDLETON, H.	LOWE, H.	BALL, T. H.
CRANE, G.	WHITEHEAD, J.	STALLARD, R.
BRISBANE, C. H.	MARCROFT, H.	BAMFORD, H.
SPEAT, W.	WILDING, H.	COOK, J.
DOVE, W. N.	LYON, R.	BEAGAN, P.
COOPER, E. H.	BENTLEY, H.	ASHTON, JOHN.
STOTT, G.	MARCROFT, F.	ASHTON, JAMES.
LAY, J. W.	BURTON, J.	GREAVES, J. W.
WORMELL, W.	BAXENDALE, G.	NORMAN, W.
BAMFORD, H.	WHITEHEAD, J.	SIMPSON, T.
POLLITT, H.	RUTLEDGE, R.	ALDCROFT, A.
FLYNN, W.	GREENHALGH, K.	METCALFE, H.
BANNISTER, W.	MONOGHAN, J.	COOPER, D.

* Serving with the colours.

Levinstein Limited.—Con.

GOODWIN, H.	WARD, T.	SAXON, N.
NORRIS, E. W.	WOOD, E.	SHEPHERD, T.
DELAHUNTY, P. V.	CURLEY, J.	YATES, J.
KENYON, C.	WARD, J.	TATTERSALL, E.
JOHNSON, A.	THOMPSON, H.	ASHTON, T.
SPURR, L. D.	CRANE, M. (Jnr.).	JONES, T.
JACKSON, H.	BALL, G.	HARTLEY, S.
WHINYATES, L.	INGLESANT, J.	PARTINGTON, D.
STARKIE, J.	NEWTON, B.	SUMMERSGILL, H.
BUTTERWORTH, A.	KELLY, A.	TAYLOR, J.
	HEBDEN, C.	WARHURST, J.
HORNER, T.	ELLISON, T.	ANCELL, J. R.
CRONSHAW, C. J.	THORNLEY, F.	GREEN, T.
T.	CROWDER, H. G.	CROSSLEY, F.
ROBERTSHAW, G. F.	HOLDEN, H.	DANIELS, J.
	HAYES, J.	COTTON, E.
LIVESLEY, B.	McMULLEN, F.	CROWTHER, H.
MILLS, H.	KEEBLE, E. C.	KENDRICK, E.
LAMBERT, J.	HILTON, F.	JACKSON, J.
KERSHAW, F.	SMITH, J.	TONGE, T.
ARNOLD, W.	MINGHAM, A.	WILKINSON, A.
BAXTER, J.	YESFORD, F.	HADFIELD, A.
SANDFORD, J.	CLAYTON, E.	ELLIS, J.
HYDE, E.	WARBURTON, J.	FARADAY, G.
NORBURY, J.	WILKES, J.	McGEE, T.
WOOD, J.	BRADLEY, H.	GOODWIN, W.
ELLERSHAW, J.	SAUL, R.	WESTON, T.
PRICE, J.	McGARRIGALE, R.	MORGAN, T. O.
HYNES, W.	SPENCER, H.	LLOYD, A.
WEYMAN, C.	HOWARTH, E. G.	ORMROD, —
LEAVER, J.	JOHNSON, S.	COLLINS, F.
PARKER, W.	WOLFENDEN, R.	FOX, J.
PARTINGTON, H.	BROWN, E.	PEARSON, H.
CONNOR, C.	WOOD, D.	WHITELEGG, F.
PARKINSON, W.		

John T. Lewis and Sons, Ltd.
(See p. 561 in Roll of Honour.)

DEAN, T.	WYATT, W.	†JOHNSON, S.
GREGORY, R. D.	†ASHWORTH, R.	†PARKER, J. W.
GREENHALGH, J.	†ASHDOWN, W. W.	†THOMAS, W.
HOOLEY, J. P.	†HACKETT, A.	†WALKER, P.
O'CONNELL, G. S.	†HAUGHTON, T.	†WALKDEN, T.
SALTER, G.		

J. and E. Lichtenstein, Ltd.
(See p. 685 in Roll of Honour.)

BLOOM, L.	†LEE, H.	†PETERS, J.
CARMICHAEL, T.	MARKS, H.	RAISMAN, M.
CLULOW, H. W.	MASTERS, F.	†ROBINSON, C.
HASTINGS, J.	McLENNAN, W.	VAUGHAN, S.
†HYMAN, A.	MORLEY, E.	
†JACOBSON, L.	†PAYMAN, W.	

Julius Liepmann and Co's Succrs.
(See p. 562 in Roll of Honour.)

EGERTON, W.	HARPER, S. H.	TICKELPENNY, E.
EVANS, E. E.		

J. Liotard and Sestier.
(See p. 562 in Roll of Honour.)

*LYONS, S.	GUDGEON, T.	NEWBOULD, H.
*KIRK, J.	GODDARD, F.	SCOTT, W.
BAMFORD, J.	HADFIELD, J.	WROE, I.
ETTENFELD, F.	LEECH, F.	

Thomas Livesey and Son, Ltd.
(See p. 685 in Roll of Honour.)

AINSWORTH, J.	MITCHELL, H. A.	WILKINSON, H.
DUCKWORTH, L.	SEDGWICK, J.	
HOLDEN, J.	WILKINSON, G. E.	

Sam Luke.
(See p. 564 in Roll of Honour.)

FITZMAURICE, J. V.	LUKE, F.	ROWE, C.
	LUKE, J. N.	STANSFIELD, F.

* Serving with the Colours. † Rejected.

Lowthian, Drake and Co.

(See p. 564 in Roll of Honour.)

FENTON, J. H.	O'CONNELL, E.	STONE, J.
GRINDROD, W. E.	HINDSON, J.	JONES, L. W.
SLATER, S.	KEMP, T.	HUCKBODY, T.
MASSEY, R.	HALLIWELL, L.	EASTWOOD, E.
*WILD, S.	LUCAS, E.	ROUTLEDGE, A.
FAIRLIE, B. J.	*OLDHAM, J.	GRADWELL, C.
SALT, J.	BARTON, W.	DENHOLM, J.
GUEST, H.	ROYLE, F.	

Manchester Corporation.

(See p. 404a in Roll of Honour.)

City Architect's Office.

BARKER, F.	DILEY, A.	WHITTAKER, F. E.
CARLTON, J.	WHITEHEAD, W.	

Rivers Department.

ARDERN, E.	GORDON, G. H.	MARSLAND, J.
BALL, C. H.	GRAVES, F.	McGAGH, J. H.
BOARDMAN, W.	GREEN, F.	OWEN, J.
BRODERICK, G.	GREEN, H.	OWEN, T.
BROWN, C. J.	HANCOCK, J.	PENNINGTON, H.
BROWN, J.	HEWITT, S.	PORTHOUSE, W.
BUTLER, J.	HOLLINSHEAD, P.	TURNER, G.
COLLIER, S.	JONES, T.	

Sanitary Department.

WARRINGTON, J.	OWEN, H.	†PRIESTLEY, I
WORSLEY, A. H.	WINTERBOTTOM, W.	†ANDREW, P.
BROWN, A.	WOOD, A.	†BOOTH, A. E.
BOWKER, R.	BURN, R.	†HOLDEN, W. A.
THOMASON, H.	SCHOFIELD, A. J.	†HAMPTON, H. S.
CAPPER, S. T.	GARTSIDE, J.	†CHERRY, J. G.
ASHWORTH, A.	HOLLINSON, G.	†HEMMING, E. C.
WHITTAKER, E. E.	HIBBERT, J.	†STARK, W.
DRYLAND, H.	WILLIAMS, F.	†ILLINGWORTH, L.
BRADSHAW, A.	HIGHAM, W.	†PARTINGTON, T.
WALLIS, F.	PIPER, H.	†KELLY, E.
ADCOCK, G.	PILKINGTON, J.	†HOLT, J.
VOLP, J. F.	CONNOR, E. J.	†WORTHINGTON, S
HINCHLIFFE, A.	WARING, G.	†GREENWOOD, W.
VEYSEY, J. W.	STALKER, L.	†JONES, H.
TOLSON, R.	WATTS, J. W.	†DAVIES, J.
DOOLEY, E.	FALLOWS, J.	†INGHAM, L.
LINFOOT, T. A.	BENTHAM, C. J.	†BURGESS, S. H.
COOPER, E.	THOMAS, L. O.	†TONKIN, A. E.
GRIFFITHS, J.	KEWLEY, A.	†POWNALL, J. H. A.
HARRISON, J.	†CROSIER, T.	†FAWLEY, W.
NORRIS, J.	†WOOD, E.	†BERESFORD, J. E.
ROWLAND, A.	†ARMYTAGE, E. G.	†DAVIES, A. H.
TISSINGTON, J.		†RICHARDS, J.

Treasurer's Office.

BRAY, J. E.	DOWNING, F. H.	TAYLOR, A. E.
STAFFORD, T.	COWLING, E. G.	CATTER, L.
MOSS, C. A.	NAYLOR, T.	PRIME, L.
IBBETSON, J. A.	ELLISON, H.	BUCKLEY, F.
FREEMAN, T.	FRITH, M.	DYSON, J.
ASHWORTH, H.	WILLIAMS, S.	HALL, A.
WALLACE, H.	JOHNSON, E.	WALKER, A. S.

Weights and Measures Office.

COLE, G. B.	BOWMAN, J.	WHELAN, P.
DAWSON, T. C.	FISHER, E.	
ALLEN, W.	GRINSTED, W.	

City Art Gallery.

THORP, J. W.	TURNER, J. W.

Heaton Hall Branch Gallery.

DARLINGTON, J.

Queen's Park Branch Gallery.

CLULOW, T. W.

Markets Department.

ASHTON, A.	DELVES, W.	GOOCH, A.
BALLARD, H.	DIXON, I.	GRAVILL, R. E.
BARLOW, A.	DORAN, J.	GREGORY, W. H.
CHADWICK, A.	EGERTON, H.	GRIFFIN, J.
COLLINS, J.	FELL, J.	HEAPEY, E.
COTTON, W.	FLETCHER, J.	JAMES, R. F.

* Serving with the Colours. † Rejected.

Manchester Corporation.—Con.

JONES, T.	MILLS, W.	TOWLSON, J. E.
KIRKHAM, J. W.	RILEY, S. H.	WARD, J.
LYONS, M.	SANGSTER, J.	WHARF, A.
MEGAW, J.	TORBITT, T.	

Paving, Sewering and Highways Department.

ASTLES, J.	GREENHALGH, G.	OATES, C.
BERRY, J. R.	GREENHALGH, H.	OWEN, B.
BOSWORTH, H.	GRIFFITHS, W.	PARKES, W. H.
BRADBURY, J.	GRUNDY, H.	PLATT, J.
BROOKS, F. S.	HANDLEY, R.	QUINLAN, A. F.
BROOKS, J. W.	HARDMAN, G.	RAMSBOTTOM, T.
BURROWS, L.	HASLAM, R. H.	ROBINSON, D.
BUTTON, W. P.	HATTON, E.	ROPER, H.
CARTER, R.	HINDS, E.	ROSE, E.
CHADWICK, H.	HOLDSWORTH, W. H.	RUTLEDGE, E.
CLOWES, W.		SETTLE, A.
COLEMAN, B.	HOLLAND, J.	SIDEBOTTOM, S.
COOP, T. W.	HOYLE, A.	SMITH, J. W.
COPLEY, A.	JACKSON, H.	SQUIRES, J.
CURRAN, J. T.	JONES, R.	STANWORTH, G.
DALE, J. A.	KIRKHAM, T.	STEWART, E.
DEAN, F. W.	LEAVERSUCH, J. W.	STOPFORD, A.
DEAN, F. W.		SWINDELLS, H. C.
DEAN, H.	LEIGH, W.	SYER, J. R.
DENMAN, J.	LEONARD, C.	TAYLOR, R.
DICKENSON, W.	LEWIS, J. T.	THOMPSON, G. C.
DUGGAN, E.	LLOYD, W. J.	THOMPSON, J.
EATON, H.	LOMAX, J. G.	TOMLINSON, F. W.
EDWARDS, G. R.	MACKAY, H.	TRAVIS, J.
EGAN, M.	MARTIN, W. P.	TRAVIS, W.
ETCHES, T.	McAULEY, J.	VERNON, J. T.
ETCHES, W.	McINTYRE, T.	WARD, J. T.
FAZACKERLEY, W.	MASKELL, F.	WATKIN, W. A.
GAMBLE, E.	MAXFIELD, W.	WHITEHURST, A.
GARFIELD, J. S.	MEEK, J. H.	WHITEHURST, T.
GARRY, P.	MILLER, F. C.	WILES, J. W.
GILL, F. W.	MORRIS, R.	WILLCOX, W. H.
GOODWIN, J.	MOTTRAM, I. E.	WOOD, D.
GRIFFIN, J.	MURPHY, P. J.	

Stationery, etc., Department.

ALLMAN, W.	MITTON, A.

Baths and Wash-Houses Department.

HOLDEN, G.	WILLIAMS, R. H.	SMITH, J. W.
LANE, A.	BLAGBROUGH, W. J.	BISHOP, A.
LEE, C. J.		McKEIVOR, L.
LEACH, W. H.	MAHER, T.	DICKENSON, H.
LANE, T.	PATE, L. A.	KAY, W.
MUSGROVE, S. S.	LOWTH, C.	PRINCE, T.
SMITH, W.	HUMPHREYS, G.	SMITH, G.
ROTHWELL, A.	MOWATT, S. B.	PRINCE, C. H.
TYERS, J. H.	JACOB, A. E.	STEARNE, T.
TILSTON, T.	CARTER, J.	PENDER, A.
AINSCOW, T.	ROYLE, H.	BROWN, J.
ACKERLEY, W.	MUSGROVE, S.	FRANCIS, W
BAKER, R.	CHARLESWORTH, S.	COTTON, G.
DAVIES, J. H.		BOARDMAN, G.
GLEDHILL, C. H.	DAVIES, T. H.	NORVAL, J.
GLEDHILL, J. H.	PUGH, J.	PRIEST, J.
CALVERLEY, L.	MAYCOCK, C.	PILLING, T.
CRESWELL, A. E.	WRENSHALL, F.	TEASDALE, A.
KAY, S.	MORRISSEY, D.	ELLIS, T.
MARLAND, J.	CORDT, T. H.	BRICKLES, F.
BEAVER, A. E.	MAHER, A.	BOSTOCK, W.
ROWORTH, L.	BEIRNE, P.	EVERTON, A.
CORDT, J. P.	CURRELL, N.	SUTTON, A.

Town Clerk's Department.

BOOTH, W.	WHITLEY, D. A.	LITTLE, C. M.
ETCHELLS, T.	BALDWIN, A. E.	HALL TAYLOR, F.
PROUDLOVE, A.		

Parks and Cemeteries Department.

WOOD, N.	WEBB, J.	FREEMAN, T.
THOMPSON, G.	MASSEY, A.	MASSEY, E.
WILKINSON, T.	MACE, R. A.	PATERSON, G.
FOSTER, A.	MILLS, H.	WILSON, F.
EDWARDS, H.	HILTON, M.	LEATHER, T. P.
DAVIES, O.	KNIGHT, A.	WILSON, T.
DOD, E.	HILTON, S.	HULME, G.
SHERWIN, J.	TAYLOR, C. W.	BECKINGHAM, G.
ROBERTSON, T.	BALL, S.	HOLDEN, G.
HEWITT, G.	GAMMON, W. J.	REDFERN, J.
POTTS, P.	BOTTOMLEY, O.	ROGGIS, A.
BROWNHILL, L.	CHEMBERS, H.	WILKINSON, J. W.
PRIDDING, T.	KEOGAN, J.	OWEN, J.
ROYLE, W.	BEESLEY, G.	MILLATT, H.
DARBYSHIRE, J.	SANSON, H.	

Manchester Education Committee.
(See p. 404 b in Roll of Honour.)

Administrative Staff.

ALLEN, P.
ALLINSON, J.
ANDREW, G. H.
BEDFORD, C. A.
BENTLEY, J. A.
BERRY, J.
BESWICK, E.
BRACEWELL, R. E.
BRADSHAW, A.
BREZ, J. B.
BROWN, J.
BURKE, J. F.
BYROM, G. F.
CLEGG, W. A.
COBBOLD, J. H.
COOPER, H. J.
DODD, R.
DUNKS, A.
DUNNING, J.
FLOCKTON, H.
FOSTER, J. R.
HARDING, E. C
HARRISON, G.
HEALEY, T.
HEWETSON, L.
HILTON, A. C.
HINSLEY, H.
HOBSON, M.
HORNE, A.
JACKSON, J.
LEIGH, J.
NEWTON, F.
PARKER, R. A.
PARRY, D. J.
PRATT, J. A.
PRICE, H.
PRIESTLEY, J. A.
READY, N.
RHODES, F.
RICHARDS, P.
RICHMOND, G.
RISHWORTH, W. G. B.
ROBERTS, C.
ROBERTS, E. C.
SILCOCK, A.
SMITH, J. E.
SMITH, M. M.
STAFFORD, W.
TAYLOR, W.
TORBITT, J. H.
WALTON, E.
WEBB, G.
WHITELEGGE, J. B.

Teaching Staff.

ANDERSON, H.
ASHWORTH, F.
ASTLE, S.
ATKINSON, H.
BAILEY, H.
BALL, E. J.
BAMFORD, J. R.
BANKS, T.
BARBER, A. H.
BARKER, F.
BARLOW, A.
BATEMAN, J.
BAXTER, J.
BEAUMONT, H. W.
BERRY, J. R.
BILLINGTON, E.
BILLINGTON, H. C.
BOALER, C.
BOARDMAN, H.
BOOTH, J. S.
BOUGHEY, J.
BRAMWELL, F.
BRASIER, J.
BRIGGS, A. J. B.
BRODERICK, P. C.
BROWN, H. S.
BURKE, N.
BUTLIN, W.
CHANDLER, H.
CLARKSON, F.
CLAYTON, J. A.
CLEGG, E.
COATES, J. T.
COLECLOUGH, H. T.
COOP, A. E.
COOPER, C. W.
CORNEY, E.
CRITCHLOW, R. S.
CROPPER, J.
CROSS, E.
CROSS, E. W.
CROWTHER, G. F.
DANIELS, G.
DAVIES, J. H.
DAVIES, J. W.
DAVISON, L. E.
DEACON, F. W.
DEARDEN, F.
DEIGHTON, S
DERBYSHIRE, H. E.
DEWAR, D.
DIGGERY, W.
DOWNIE, A.
DOYLE, F. J.
DUDDLE, R. S.
DUNNING, J. E.
ECCLES, T.
ECKERSLEY, W.
EDWARDS, I. L.
ELLIS, O. C.
EWING, W. P.
FAIRBOURN, W. W.
FLAXMAN, F.
FOX, R. Y. C.
FROEHLICH, W.
FULLER, R. H.
FULTON, R. B.
GAHAN, R.
GAHAN, J. P.
GANDY, A. E.
GARNER, R.
GERRARD, P.
GERRARD, T.
GERRARD, T.
GIDDINGS, A. J
GLICKMAN, D.
GOODWIN, G. H
GREEN, J.
HALL, J.
HALL, R. C.
HARWOOD, H. T.
HEALD, E. J.
HEATHCOTE, H. R.
HERDSON, W. J.
HERON, W. C.
HEWITT, J. E.
HEYWOOD, T.
HIBBERT, S.
HILL, H.
HILYER, J.
HINCHCLIFFE, J.
HINDLEY, J. P.
HOLLAND, G.
HOLLIDAY, R.
HOLMES, F. D.
HOPE, H.
HOUGH, J. W.
HUDSON, A. H.
HUGHES, C.
HUGHES, P.
JACKSON, H.
JACKSON, R.
JOHNSON, E. W.
JOHNSON, H.
JONES, W. J.
JORDAN, S. B.
JUBB, J. B.
KELLY, B. J.
KELLY, J.
KENNEDY, J.
KNOX, J. R.
LAKIN, H.
LALLY, J.
LANTSBERRY, G.
LEAVER, C. W.
LEE, A. F. L. A.
LEWIS, A.
LOMAS, H.
LOVETT, F. J.
MADDRELL, R.
MARKHAM, E.
MARTINDALE, L.
MASSEY, H.
MATHER, E.
MATTHIEU, J.
MAXWELL, J. H.
MAY, W. G.
McKAIG, P.
McMANN, J. A.
MIDGLEY, H.
MILSOM, J. C.
MOLONEY, R.
MOOREHEAD, T. P.
MORGAN, W.
MORGAN-LEWIS, J. D.
MOSELEY, F.
MURRAY, J.
MURRELL, T.
NELSON, G. A.
NEWIS, H. T.
OGDEN, F.
ORCHARDSON, T.
OSBALDESTON, W. G.
PARKER, J. O.
PARKINSON, H.
PATCHETT, J. L.
PORTER, H.
PRINGLE, T.
RICHARDSON, R.
RILEY, F.
RILEY, L.
ROBERTS, E.
ROBERTS, F.
ROBINSON, J. O.
RUTTER, W. P.
SALT, A. E.
SARGENT, S. R.
SAUNSBERRY, R
SCHOLES, B.
SEDDON, W.
SEDGWICK, J.
SEYMOUR, R.
SHERRINGTON, P.
SILVANUS, E. M.
SILVERSTONE, M.
SLOANE, M.
SMETHURST, R.
SMITH, F. N.
SMITH, G. D.
SMITH, H.
SMITH, S. W.
STEPHENS, J. A.
SUDREN, R.
TATTERSAL, R.
TAYLOR, G. A.
THOMPSON, J. K.
TRUEBLOOD, R. P.
VARLEY, G. P.
WAITE, H. H.
WALKER, E. T.
WALLWORK, R. E.
WALMSLEY, W.
WALSH, G.
WARBURTON, H.
WATSON, C.
WATTS, H. P.
WHITE, H.
WHITE, R.
WHITTAKER, V. A.
WHITTAKER, G.
WILLIAMS, G.
WILSON, C. W.
WILSON, E.
WILSON, G. F.
WILSON, J. T.
WORSLEY, J.
WRAGG, J. R.
WRIGHT, T.
WYCH, J.

The Manchester Ship Canal Company.
(See p. 404 d in Roll of Honour.)

ABRAMS, J.
ABLE, F.
ABBOTT, W. A.
ACKERLEY, T.
ACTON, A.
ACTON, G.
ADAMS, A. E.
ADAMS, F.
ADAMS, J. A.
ADAMS, W. T.
ADDI, J.
ADDY, F.
ADDY, M.
ADSHEAD, H.
AGNEW, A.
AGNEW, P.
AINSBY, A.
AINSWORTH, A.
AINSWORTH, L.
AINSWORTH, R.
AINSWORTH, T. J.
ALCOCK, A.
ALDCROFT, J.
ALEXANDER, W.
ALLCOCK, J. H.
ALLEN, E. A.
ALLEN, H.
ALLEN, W. H.
ALLISON, J.
ALPORT, B.
ANCELL, L.
ANCHORS, C.
ANDERTON, F.
ANDREW, R. A.
ANDREWS, A.
ANDREWS, H.
ANDREWS, W.
ANGELL, C. H.
ANKERS, R.
ANTROBUS, H.
ANTROBUS, S.
APPLETON, H.
APPLEYARD, T.
ARDEN, J. E.
ARDERN, H.
ARMITAGE, S.
ARNOTT, T.
ARROWSMITH, H.
ARROWSMITH, L.
ARSTALL, J.
ARSTALL, J.
ARSTALL, J.
ASHCROFT, H.
ASHLEY, W.
ASHTON, E. J.
ASHTON, J.
ASHURST, T. W.
ASPINALL, R.
ASTLEY, C.
ASTON, C. F.
ATHERTON, C. E.
ATKINS, S.
ATKINSON, G. W.
ATKINSON, H.
ATKINSON, R.
ATKINSON, W. A.
ATTENBOROUGH, J.
ATTEWELL, E.
ATTREE, C. B.
ATTREE, W. G.
AUSTIN, H.
AVERY, S.
AXON, J. H.
AYTON, W. H.
BAGGOLEY, A.
BAGSHAW, T.
BAGULEY, J.
BAILEY, J.
BAILEY, J.
BAISON, R.
BAKER, P.
BAKER, W. R.
BALL, L.
BALL, S.
BALL, W.
BALMER, J.
BAMFORD, J.
BAMFORD, R.
BANKS, E.
BANKS, L.
BANNER, G.
BANNER, G. A.
BANNER, R. A.
BANNISTER, H.
BANNISTER, H.
BARBER, F.
BARBER, J.
BARBER, W.
BARBER, W.
BARKER, W. A.
BARLOW, H.
BARLOW, R.
BARLOW, W. H.
BARNES, A.
BARNES, E.
BARNES, S.
BARNETT, T.
BARON, A. J.
BARTON, C.
BARTON, J.
BARTON, J. J.
BASNETT, L.
BASSNETT, T.
BATE, A.
BATE, W.
BATE, W.
BATES, W.
BATTERSBY, —
BATTERSBY, H.
BAWN, T.
BAXTER, G.
BAXTER, R.
BAYLEY, T.
BAZLEY, A. E.
BEARD, C.
BEARD, E.
BEAUMONT, W.
BEBBINGTON, A.
BEBBINGTON, J. A.
BEBBINGTON, O.
BEBBINGTON, T.
BEBBINGTON, W.
BEIGHTON, R. A.
BELL, E.
BELL, H.
BELL, S.
BELLFIELD, A.
BELLINGHAM, W.
BENNION, R.
BENSON, A.
BENSON, W.
BENT, S.
BERESFORD, R.
BESSELL, W.
BESTLEY, A.
BESWICK, J.
BESWICK, T.
BETLEY, W.
BEVAN, D. W.
BEVAN, J. W.
BILLAM, H. T.
BILSBORROW, J.
BIRCH, F. A.
BIRCHALL, A.
BIRCHALL, T. P.
BIRLEY, H.
BLACKLEY, G. W.
BLAINEY, A.
BLAINEY, W.
BLAKEMORE, W
BLANCHARD, A.
BLASE, C.
BLEAKLEY, M. L.
BLINKHORN, A.
BLINSTON, J.
BLOMLEY, F.
BLONDON, J.
BLUHM, H.
BLYTHE, E.
BOALER, C.
BOARDMAN, C.
BOLTON, J.
BOLTON, J. E.
BOLTON, J. T.
BOND, F.
BONSALL, H.
BOOTH, A.
BOOTH, W.
BOOTHBY, B. H.
BOULTON, R.
BOURNE, J. C.
BOWRING, E.
BOYD, T.
BOYLE, M.
BRACKEN, M.
BRADBURN, S.
BRADBURN, W.
BRADLEY, G.
BRADLEY, J.
BRADSHAW, C. R.
BRADBURN, E.
BRAMHALL, E.
BRAMWELL, J. W.
BRASYENDALE, T.
BRATT, C.
BRAZENDALE, E.
BRAZENDALE, G.
BRAZENDALE, H.
BRAZENDALE, J.
BREEZE, J.
BRENNAN, M.
BRETTLE, H.
BRICE, J. T.
BRITTAIN, E.
BRITTAIN, S. D.
BROAD, S. G.
BROADBENT, W.
BROCKLEHURST, T.
BROCKLEHURST, T.
BROGDEN, J.
BROOK, T. H.
BROOK, T. W.
BROOKES, H.
BROOKS, J. J.
BROOME, J.
BROOME, J. J.
BROTHERTON, H.
BROUGH, L.
BROUGHTON, A. E.
BROWN, C. W.
BROWN, F.
BROWN, G.
BROWN, G.
BROWN, H.
BROWN, J.
BROWN, J. W.
BROWN, T.
BROWN, T.
BROWNHILL, A.
BROWNLOW, A.
BRUCE, W. J.
BRYAN, G.
BUCHANAN, J. T.
BUCKINGHAM, H.
BUCKLE, G. E.
BUCKLE, O.
BUCKLE, W.
BUCKLEY, W.
BUCKLETON, H.
BURBRIDGE, S.
BURGESS, T.
BURGESS, W.
BURK, W.
BURKE, J.
BURLEY, H.
BURNELL, J. O.
BURNS, J.
BURNS, P.
BURROWS, A. C.
BURROWS, F. B.
BUSTIN, F. R.
BUTLER, W. J.
BUTTERWORTH, J.
BUTTERWORTH, T.
BUTTERY, V. A.
BUXTON, T.
BYRNE, G.
BYRNE, M.
CAFFERY, J.
CAFFREY, P. E.
CALDWELL, J.
CALVERT, F.
CALLAM, P.
CAMERON, H.
CAMPBELL, P. A.
CAMPBELL, W. G.

The Manchester Ship Canal Company.—Con.

CAMPION, J. R.
CANAVAN, T.
CANDIBLE, J.
CANNING, J. H.
CARDUS, F.
CARNEY, J.
CARPENTER, J.
CARR, J. W.
CARR, W. H.
CARREW, G.
CARROL, D.
CARROLL, D.
CARROLL, M.
CARROLL, T. W.
CARTER, G. H.
CARTER, J. P.
CARTER, J.
CARTEY, A.
CARTWRIGHT, F.
CARTWRIGHT, W.
CASEY, J.
CASEY, M.
CASH, A.
CASKEY, J.
CASSIN, E.
CAVANAGH, T.
CAVANAGH, W.
CAWLEY, T.
CAWLEY, W. H.
CHADWICK, A. P.
CHALLINOR, J.
CHAMBERS, C.
CHAPMAN, A.
CHAPMAN, F.
CHAPMAN, H.
CHAPMAN, J.
CHAPMAN, W. C.
CHAPPELL, J. M.
CHARLESWORTH, W. H.
CHEETHAM, J.
CHEW, E.
CHORLTON, R.
CHRISTIAN, A. E.
CIRNEY, M.
CLARE, A.
CLARE, C.
CLARE, F. C.
CLARE, H.
CLARE, J.
CLARE, P.
CLARE, T.
CLARK, W. C.
CLARKE, F.
CLARKE, J.
CLARKE, J.
CLARKE, J. A.
CLARKE, J. J.
CLARKE, N.
CLARKE, T. M.
CLAYDON, T. A.
CLAYPOLE, A.
CLAYS, J.
CLAYTON, J.
CLAYTON, R.
CLEGG, A.
CLIFTON, E.
CLIFTON, W. H.
CLITHEROE, W.
COAKLEY, T.
COALS, C.
COATES, A.
COATES, T.
COLCLOUGH, J.
COLE, E. R.
COLES, J. W.
COLGAN, W. J.
COLLINGE, F.
COLLINS, A. E.
COLLINS, J.
COLLIS, W.
COLTER, A.
COLVILLE, B.
CONDON, M.
CONDRON, M.
CONNORTON, J.
CONSTANTINE, W.
COOK, A.
COOK, F.
COOK, T.
COOK, W.
COOKE, F.
COOKE, H.
COOKE, P.
COOKE, J.
COONEY, J.
COOPER, A.
CORNELIUS, D. P.
CORNER, J. A.
COSTELLO, J.
COTTON, J.
COUGHLAN, D.
COULTON, H.
COUSINS, A. F.
COWBURN, J. A.
COWELL, J.
COX, H. G.
COX, T.
COX, W.
COXON, C.
COY, P. J.
CRABB, W.
CRAGG, W.
CRAWSHAW, J.
CROASDALE, F.
CRITCHLEY, A.
CRITCHLOW, E.
CROMWELL, O.
CROSS, G.
CROSSLEY, A.
CROSSLEY, G.
CROSSLEY, W D.
CRUDDOS, J.
CULLEN, W.
CUNNINGHAM, J. T.
CURRAN, L.
CURTIS, A. R.
CUTTING, R. W.
DAINTON, W.
DALBY, E. T. G.
DALE, J.
DANIELS, J.
DANIELS, W.
DARBYSHIRE, W. A.
DARLINGTON, W.
DARLINGTON, W.
DARWELL, A.
DAVENPORT, F. H.
DAVENPORT, R.
DAVIDSON, S. A.
DAVIES, A.
DAVIES, A.
DAVIES, C. H.
DAVIES, E.
DAVIES, E.
DAVIES, E.
DAVIES, H.
DAVIES, H.
DAVIES, H.
DAVIES, I.
DAVIES, J.
DAVIES, J.
DAVIES, J.
DAVIES, J. H.
DAVIES, S.
DAVIES, W.
DAVIES, W.
DAVIES, W.
DAVIS, A. H.
DAVISON, H.
DAWSON, A.
DAWSON, G.
DAWSON, J.
DAWSON, W.
DAY, L.
DEAHAN, W. G.
DEAKIN, S.
DEAN, J.
DEAN, J. H.
DEIGHTON, W.
DELANEY, G.
DEMPSEY, P.
DENNIS, C. J.
DENTITH, F.
DEPLEDGE, H.
DERBYSHIRE, F.
DEVALL, J.
DEVINE, W. H.
DEWHURST, T.
DICKENS, J.
DICKINSON, J.
DICKINSON, J R.
DICKSON, T. E.
DIGGORY, A.
DINGWALL, A.
DIXON, A.
DIXON, E.
DIXON, F.
DIXON, H.
DIXON, J.
DIXON, J. F.
DIXON, T.
DOBSON, J.
DOBSON, J. J.
DOBSON, T.
DODD, A. R.
DODD, F.
DODD, J.
DODD, J.
DOE, R. H.
DOGGETT, W.
DOHERTY, J.
DOLAN, R.
DONE, F.
DONE, R.
DONOHUE, J.
DONOHUE, W.
DORAN, T.
DORE, J.
DORMAN, W.
DOVE, A. E.
DOWD, J.
DOWD, T.
DOWLING, H.
DOWLING, H. W.
DOYLE, E.
DOYLE, J.
DOYLE, J.
DRAKE, O.
DRAPER, P. J.
DRAYSON, C.
DRUDGE, W.
DUFF, W.
DUGDALE, A.
DUGDALE, G.
DUGDALE, H.
DUKES, F. J.
DUKES, S.
DUMBAVAND, A
DUMBAVAND, H.
DUMBELL, J.
DUNBABIN, B.
DUNN, H.
DUTES, W.
DUTSON, W.
DUTTON, E.
DUTTON, J.
DUTTON, T.
DUTTON, W.
DUTTON, W.
DYER, F. W.
DYKES, R.
DYSON, S.
EARNSHAW, W
EATON, S.
ECCLESTONE, T.
ECKERSLEY, A. E.
EDGE, F.
EDGE, T. H.
EDWARDS, F.
EDWARDS, G.
EDWARDS, G.
EDWARDS, T. R.
EGAN, H.
EGERTON, A.
EGERTON, T.
ELLABY, J.
ELLIOTT, F.
ELLIOTT, J. H.
ELLIS, A.
ELLIS, A.
ELLIS, B.
ELLIS, P. S.
ELLIS, T.
ELLIS, W. H.
ELLIS, W. S.
ELLSE, E. B.
ELWELL, I.
EMERY, G.
EMSLEY, T.
ENNIS, P.
EVANS, C.
EVANS, H.

The Manchester Ship Canal Company.—Con.

EVANS, J.
EVANS, R.
EVANS, W.
FAGA, N.
FAGAN, J.
FAGAN, T.
FAIRBROTHER, H. H.
FAIRHURST, F. C.
FALDING, G.
FALLOWS, A.
FARMER, W.
FARNWORTH, S.
FARR, H.
FARRAND, S.
FARRELL, J.
FARRELL, W. J.
FARRELLE, E. J.
FARRELLY, J.
FAULKNER, E.
FAULKNER, F.
FAULKNER, J.
FAULKNER, J.
FAULKNER, J. R.
FAULKNER, T. A.
FAWKES, A. G.
FEARHEAD, F.
FEARNLEY, J.
FEE, J.
FERGUSON, W.
FEWSTER, C.
FIELD, A. J.
FIELDHOUSE, W.
FIELDING, C.
FIELDING, F.
FIELDING, H.
FIELDING, I.
FIRTH, C. A.
FIRTH, E.
FISH, J.
FISH, W.
FISHER, O.
FITZPATRICK, T.
FLANAGAN, E.
FLANAGAN, P.
FLANNAGAN, W.
FLEMING, T.
FLETCHER, A.
FLETCHER, J.
FLETCHER, W.
FLINT, H. E.
FLINT, J. R.
FLYNN, J.
FLYNN, T.
FORREST, W. P.
FORSTER, T. A.
FORSTER, W.
FOSTER, T. C.
FOSTER, W.
FOWLES, D.
FOWLKES, T.
FOXTON, F.
FRADLEY, A.
FRANCE, P.
FRANCIS, M.
FRANKLAND, W.
FRAY, W.
FRENCH, J. T.
FROST, F.
FRYER, F.
FULLER, T. H.
GALLAGHER, J.
GALVIN, J.
GANDY, R.
GARNER, J.
GARRATT, F.
GARRETT, T.
GARRITY, M.
GARTON, J.
GARVEY, J.
GATLEY, B.
GATLEY, F.
GATLEY, J.
GAUNT, R. G.
GEARY, S.
GEE, W.
GERAGHTY, J.
GERRARD, H.
GERRARD, T.
GIBSON, R.
GILBERT, T.
GILBERTS, W.
GILES, W.
GILL, W.
GILLARD, W. T
GILMOUR, T.
GLAZZARD, S.
GOEDHART, M.
GOLDSTRAW, F.
GOLDSWORTHY, E.
GOODALL, H.
GOODE, J.
GOODE, J.
GOODFELLOW, G.
GOODIER, J.
GOODIER, J. W.
GORDON, D.
GORE, W.
GORRAN, W.
GOSLING, F.
GOTHARD, R.
GOUGH, G.
GOUGH, E.
GOULD, J.
GRAHAM, J.
GRAHAM, J.
GRANT, D.
GRANT, J.
GRANT, R.
GRAVES, W. H.
GRAY, J.
GREATHEAD, J
GREEB, C. F.
GREEN, A. J.
GREEN, E.
GREEN, H.
GREEN, J.
GREEN, W.
GREEN, W.
GREEN, W. H.
GREEN, W. J.
GREEN, W.
GREENWAY, —
GREENWOOD, A.
GREENWOOD B.
GREENWOOD, F.
GREENWOOD, H.
GREENWOOD, W. H.
GREGORY, E.
GREGORY, W.
GREGSON, T.
GRESTY, A.
GRESTY, R.
GRIFFIN, W.
GRIFFITHS, O. C.
GRIFFITHS, R
GRIFFITHS, S.
GRIFFITHS, T. H.
GRIFFITHS, W.
GRIMES, E.
GRIMES, R.
GRINDOD, W. T.
GROGAN, R.
GROOCOCK, T. L.
GROOME, F.
GROOME, J. B.
GROST, A.
GROST, W.
GRUBB, H
GRUNDY, T. W.
GUARD, A.
GUARD, J.
GUARD, S.
GUEST, F.
GUEST, G.
GUEST, G. E.
GUEST, O.
HACKETT, J.
HACKNEY, W. J
HADDOCK, S.
HAGUE, J.
HAILWOOD, L.
HALL, A.
HALL, R.
HALL, R. S.
HALL, T.
HALL, W.
HALLSWORTH, W.
HALSALL, H.
HAMBLETT, W.
HAMBY, J.
HAMER, A.
HAMER, J.
HAMILTON, A.
HAMILTON, R. A.
HAMILTON, V. A
HAMNETT, W.
HAMPSON, A
HAMPSON, F.
HAMPSON, T.
HAMPSON, W.
HAMPTON, W
HAND, W. H.
HANDLEY, J. W.
HANKEY, H.
HARDLEY, H.
HARDLEY, P.
HARDLEY, W.
HARDY, J. B.
HARDY, T. W.
HARGREAVES, A.
HARGREAVES, J.
HARGREAVES, T. E.
HARGREAVES, W
HARRINGTON, S.
HARRINGTON, T.
HARRIS, E.
HARRIS, H.
HARRIS, J.
HARRISON, A.
HARRISON, A.
HARRISON, D.
HARRISON, E.
HARRISON, G.
HARRISON, G. H
HARRISON, S.
HARRISON, W.
HARRISON, W.
HARROP, A.
HARROP, J. A.
HARROWER, T.
HARTLEY, J.
HARVEY, T.
HARWOOD, F.
HASLAM, G. R.
HASLAM, R.
HASLAM, R. E.
HASTINGS, A. J.
HATTERSLEY, J. W.
HATTON, R.
HATTON, W.
HAYES, E.
HAYES, J.
HAYES, J. L.
HAYES, R.
HAYES, R.
HAYES, W.
HAYGARTH, T.
HAYMER, J. H.
HAYWARD, C. B.
HAZELLS, H.
HEADON, W.
HEALEY, C. J.
HEALEY, R.
HEATH, E.
HEATH, G. H.
HEATH, J.
HEATH, W.
HEATON, L.
HEAWORD, J. W.
HEFFERSON, C.
HELSBY, C.
HENDERSON, A.
HENRY, C. A.
HENSHALL, C.
HENSHALL, G. K.
HENSHALL, J. T.
HERD, E.
HERNE, F.
HESKETH, E.
HESKETH, N.
HEWITT, A.
HEWITT, C.
HEWITT, T.
HEY, J. H.
HEYWOOD, W.
HICKEY, D.
HICKSON, T.
HIGGINS, A.
HIGGINS, D.
HIGGINS, D.
HIGGINS, J.

The Manchester Ship Canal Company.—Con.

HIGGINS, P.
HIGGINS, T.
HIGGINS, W.
HIGGINSON, A. V.
HIGGINSON, H.
HIGGINSON, J.
HIGGINSON, W. H.
HIGHAM, S.
HIGHFIELD, W.
HIGHTON, R.
HILL, A. W.
HILL, E.
HILL, H.
HILL, J. H.
HILL, M.
HILTON, E.
HILTON, E.
HILTON, H.
HILTON, J. B
HINDLEY, R.
HINES, W.
HOBSON, C.H.
HOCKENHULL, P.
HODGKISS, T.
HODSON, F.
HODSON, J.
HODSON, J.
HOLCROFT, T.
HOLDEN, J. E.
HOLIDAY, G.
HOLLAND, J. F.
HOLLAND, L.
HOLLINS, S. V.
HOLLINSHEAD, J. H.
HOLLOWAY, H.
HOLLOWS, A.
HOLMES, J.
HOLMES, J.
HOLROYD, J.
HOLT, A.
HOLT, A.
HOLT, A. P.
HOLT, F.
HOLT, F.
HOLT, G. W.
HOLT, H.
HOLT, H.
HOLT, T.
HOMER, H.
HOMES, J.
HOOPER, G.
HOOSEMAN, P.
HOPKINS, G. W.
HOPKINSON, T.
HOPLEY, J.
HOPWOOD, E.
HORNBY, W.
HORNER, F. S.
HORNER, H.
HORNER, R. D.
HOROBIN, H. H.
HORROCKS, A.
HORSFALL, C.
HORSFALL, E.
HORSFIELD, W.
HORTON, G.
HORTON, J.
HOUGH, A.
HOUGHTON, A
HOUGHTON, E.
HOUGHTON, G. A.
HOUGHTON, H.
HOUGHTON, J.
HOUGHTON, T.
HOWARD, A. W.
HOWARD, C.
HOWARD, H.
HOWARTH, J.
HOWARTH, R. H.
HOWE, A.
HOWES, J.
HOWROYD, F. O.
HOXWORTH, J.
HOXWORTH, R.
HUCKETT, J. J.
HUCKETT, T.
HUGHES, A.
HUGHES, A.
HUGHES, C.
HUGHES, F.

HUGHES, F.
HUGHES, H.
HUGHES, H.
HUGHES, J.
HUGHES, J.
HUGHES, P.
HUGHES, R.
HUGHES, R.
HUGHES, R.
HUGHES, R.
HUGHES, S.
HULME, P. T.
HULME, W.
HULSE, W.
HUMPHRIES, W.
HUNT, W. E.
HUNT, S.
HUNTER, J. W.
HURRELL, W. H. A.
HURST, F.
HUSBAND, F.
HUSBAND, J.
HUSSEY, J.
HUSSEY, R.
HUTCHINSON, C. E.
HUTSON, T.
HUXTABLE, J.
IGO, J.
IKIN, J.
ILLIDGE, H.
IMRIE, J. R.
INCE, A.
INCE, J. H.
INGE, H.
INGLESFIELD, J
IRELAND, W.
ISHERWOOD, C.
JACKSON, A.
JACKSON, G. R.
JACKSON, H.
JACKSON, H. A.
JACKSON, J.
JACKSON, J.
JACKSON, J.
JACKSON, J. F.
JACKSON, R.
JACKSON, S.
JACKSON, U.
JACKSON, W.
JACKSON, W. H.
JACOB, H. O.
JAMES, A. H.
JAMES, C.
JAMES, F.
JAMESON, W.
JAMIESON, J.
JARVEY, F.
JEFFES, T.
JEFFREY, W.
JEFFS, C. S.
JEFFS, G. W.
JENART, C.
JENKINS, E. J.
JENKINS, W.
JENKINS, W.
JENKINSON, A.
JENKINSON, C.
JENNINGS, A.
JEZARD, W.
JILLETT, D.
JOHNSON, D.
JOHNSON, E.
JOHNSON, E.
JOHNSON, J. A.
JOHNSON, W.
JOHNSON, W. L.
JOHNSTONE, F. A.
JOLLEY, C.
JOLLEY, F. J.
JOLLEY, R.
JOLLY, F.
JONES, A.
JONES, A. L.
JONES, B. V.
JONES, C. H.
JONES, C. W.
JONES, E.
JONES, E.

JONES, E.
JONES, E.
JONES, E. H.
JONES, G.
JONES, H.
JONES, H.
JONES, H.
JONES, H.
JONES, H.
JONES, H. J.
JONES, H. S.
JONES, H. V.
JONES, H. W.
JONES, J.
JONES, J.
JONES, J.
JONES, L. W.
JONES, R.
JONES, R.
JONES, R.
JONES, R.
JONES, W.
JONES, W.
JONES, W.
JONES, W.
JONES, W.
JONES, W. A.
JORDAN, V. W
JOYCE, J.
KABERRY, L.
KAY, B.
KAY, J.
KAY, R. V.
KEARSLEY, F.
KEARSLEY, J.
KEEN, A. F.
KEEN, W.
KEENAN, J.
KELLY, E.
KELLY, F. R.
KELLY, H.
KELLY, J. P.
KELSALL, W.
KENNEDY, C.
KENNEDY, C.
KENNEDY, J.
KENNEY, H.
KENNY, C.
KENNY, T.
KENT, P. A.
KENWRIGHT, H.
KENYON, A. S.
KENYON, F.
KENYON, J. R.
KERNAN, W. J.
KILKENNY, J.
KILWEX, P.
KING, P.
KING, T. W.
KIRK, C.
KIRK, G.
KIRKMAN, J.
KIRKMAN, S.
KIRWIN, A.
KORTENS, P.
LACE, W. C.
LAMB, G.
LAMB, H.
LAMBERT, E.
LAMBERT, H.
LAMBERT, J.
LAMEY, J. W.
LAMEY, W.
LANCASTER, J.
LANG, P.
LANGTON, E. L.
LATCHFORD, O.
LATCHFORD, P.
LATHAM, J. W.
LATHAM, T.
LAVATT, F.
LAWRENCE, E. E.
LAYLAND, J. H.
LEACH, E.
LEACH, F.
LEACH, S. T.
LEADSTONE, B.
LEADSTONE, J. J.
LEATHER, T.
LEATHWOOD, W.
LECK, F.
LEE, G.

The Manchester Ship Canal Company.—Con.

LEE, G. H.
LEECH, B.
LEES, J.
LEIGH, J. H.
LEIGH, S.
LENIHAM, J.
LENIHAM, P.
LEONARD, E.
LEONARD, T.
LEPTS, L. C.
LETT, J. B.
LEVIS, A.
LEVIS, T.
LEWIS, A.
LEWIS, A.
LEWIS, D.
LEWIS, J.
LEWISS, C.
LIEVESLEY, T.
LIGHTFOOT, A.
LIGHTFOOT, J.
LINDEY, R.
LINDICT, J.
LINDSAY, J.
LINLEY, W. H
LIPTON, M.
LISTER, H.
LITLER, W.
LITTLEHALES, J. T.
LITTLER, J.
LITTLER, J. H
LIVERLEY, J.
LLOYD, D.
LLOYD, D. L.
LLOYD, E.
LLOYD, E.
LLOYD, E.
LLOYD, G.
LLOYD, G. R.
LLOYD, J.
LLOYD, J.
LLOYD, R.
LOAN, J.
LOCKETT, J.
LOGAN, P.
LONGSDEN, T.
LOOMES, A.
LOOMES, T. H.
LORD, C.
LORD, J.
LOUGHREY, J.
LOSEBY, H.
LOVATT, A.
LOVELL, E. B.
LOVELL, L. G.
LOWE, P.
LOWE, W.
LOWNDES, W.
LOWRY, J. A.
LOWRY, T.
LUCAS, A. B.
LUDGATE, W.
LYE, J.
LYNCH, A.
LYNCH, A.
LYTHE, W.
LYTHGOE, A.
LYTHGOE, G.
LYTHGOE, S.
McCABE, M.
McCALDON, A. L.
McCASLIN, C.
McCLELLARD, R.
McCOMAS, C. H.
McCONNELL, B.
McCONNELL, T.
McCOY, S.
McCULLOUGH, W. A.
McDERMOTT, B.
McDONALD, A.
McEVOY, P. J.
McFARLAND, H.
McGLONE, W.
McGOWAN, J.
McGUIRE, J.
McHALE, F.
McINNES, J.
McKENZIE, W.
McKEON, R.
McLOUGHLIN, M.

McMAHON, J.
McMILLAN, G.
McMORTON, G
McMULLEN, G.
McMURDOE, —
McNABB, S.
McNALLY, A.
McNALLY, T.
McNEILL, T.
McNULTY, M.
McWILLIAMS, W.
MACKAY, J.
MACKENZIE, F. C.
MACKENZIE, J.
MACLEOD, N.
MADDEN, G.
MADDOCK, G.
MADDOCK, T.
MADDOCKS, J. W.
MAGEE. W. H.
MAHON, J.
MAHONEY, G. W.
MAKIN, J.
MALVERN, A.
MALVERN, D.
MANCHESTER, J. W.
MANLEY, S.
MANSELL, H.
MARCHANT, A.
MARCHANT, T.
MARLEY, J.
MARSH, J.
MARSH, H.
MARSH, R. H.
MARSH, T.
MARSHALL, A. E.
MARSHALL, G.
MARTIN, G.
MARTIN, H. J.
MARTIN, J. C.
MARTIN, W.
MASKEW, H.
MASKEW, W.
MASSEY, D.
MASSEY, J.
MASSEY, T.
MATHER, W.
MATHERS, G.
MATHERS, W.
MATTHEWSON, J.
MALTRAVERS, C.
MEALAND, E. E
MEANWELL, J. E.
MELLOR, F. B.
MELLOR, H.
MELLOR, J.
MELLOR, J. A.
MELLOR, R.
MELTON, A.
MERCER, E.
MERCER, T.
MEREDITH, F.
MEREDITH, G. L.
MERRICK, T.
METCALF, W.
METCALF, W. J.
MIDGELEY, W.
MILES, J.
MILLER, J.
MILLER, J.
MILLER, W.
MILLICAN, W.
MILLING, T. W.
MILLINGTON, G.
MILLINGTON, T.
MILLINGTON, T. H.
MILLISH, G.
MILLS, C.
MILLS, E.
MILLS, E. T.
MILLS, J.
MILLS, J. R.
MILLS, P. W.
MINNOCK, T.
MINSHALL, P.
MINSHULL, W.
MITCHELL, H.
MOLLART, A.
MOLLART, E.

MOLLOY, M.
MOLYNEUX, A.
MOLYNEUX, F.
MONAGHAN, T.
MONCRIEFF, F
MONKS, G.
MONKS, J.
MONROE, E.
MOONEY, T. E.
MOORE, H.
MOORES, W. J.
MORAN, J.
MORGAN, A.
MORGAN, D. J.
MORGAN, J.
MORGAN, J. T.
MORLEY, L.
MORLEY, W.
MORRALL, W.
MORRELL, A.
MORRIS, J.
MORRIS, H.
MORRIS, P.
MORRIS, T.
MORTIMORE, H
MORTON, E.
MORTON, T.
MORTON, W.
MOSELEY, H. R.
MOSS, W.
MOULTON, A.
MOULTON, G.
MULLANEY, J.
MULLINEUX, J.
MURDOCK, J.
MURPHY, C.
MURPHY, J.
MURPHY, J.
MURPHY, J. F.
MURPHY, T.
MURPHY, W.
MURRAY, R.
NAYLOR, W. E
NEAFSEY, M.
NEAFSEY, T.
NEARY, J. S.
NEILDON, S.
NEILL, W.
NELSON, R.
NELSON, R. W.
NELSON, W.
NEWLOVE J.
NEWTON, A.
NEWTON, J.
NICHOLL, C.
NICHOLLS, S.
NICHOLLS, T.
NICHOLLS, T.
NICKSON, J. W.
NIGHTINGALE, J.
NIXON, H.
NIXON, J.
NIXON, J.
NOBLE, R.
NORMAN, G.
NORRY, H.
NORTH, S.
NUTTALL, H.
NUTTALL, Z.
OATES, C.
OFFICER, J. W.
OGDEN, A. E.
OGDEN, E.
OGDEN, J.
OGDEN, T.
OGDEN, W.
O'HAGAN, T.
OLDHAM, J.
OLIVER, A.
O'NEILL, E.
ONION, F.
ORMSON, J.
ORMSON, W.
OSBORNE, W.
OSTERFIELD, F. J.
OSTERFIELD, J. W.
OSWALD, J.
OWEN, E.
OWEN, H.
OWEN, H.
OWEN, J.

The Manchester Ship Canal Company.—Con.

OWEN, J.
OWEN, J.
OWEN, J. H.
OWEN, J. W.
OWEN, W.
OWEN, W. E.
OXLEY, A.
PAGE, H.
PAGE, J.
PANTIN, S.
PARKER, G.
PARKER, R.
PARKER, S.
PARKER, V.
PARKER, W.
PARKES, W.
PARKINSON, F.
PARKINSON, W.
PARNELL, G. B.
PARR, A.
PARR, G.
PARRY, H.
PARSONS, J.
PASS, J. H.
PATERSON, H. S.
PATRICK, H.
PAULEY, E. H.
PEACOCK, E.
PEACOCK, J.
PEACOCK, P.
PEACOCK, P.
PEACOCK, W.
PEARCE, E.
PEARCE, H.
PEARCE, R.
PEARCE, T. G.
PEARSON, G.
PEARSON, H.
PEARSON, W.
PENDLEBURY, J.
PEMBERTON, T. F.
PENNINGTON J.
PENNY, G.
PERCIVAL, R. W.
PERCIVAL, W. H
PERROTT, G.
PETERS, R. J.
PETERSON, G.
PHILLIPS, H. D.
PICKER, S.
PICKFORD, J.
PICKSTOCK, S.
PILKINGTON, F.
PILSBURY, F.
PITTAM, C.
PLANT, S.
PLATT, S.
PLIMMER, G.
PLUMMER, A.
PLUMMER, F. A.
PLUMMER, S.
PLUMMER, S.
POLLARD, G. H.
POLLARD, H.
POLLARD, W. C.
POLLITT, J.
POLLITT, J. W.
POLLITT, W.
POLLITT, W. H
POOLE, E. J.
POOLE, R.
PORTER, J. H.
PORTER, J. J.
POSTLE, W.
POSTON, G.
POTTER, C. H.
POTTS, A.
POTTS, S. A.
POTTS, T.
POVEY, A. J.
POVEY, J.
POWELL, G. H.
POWELL, R.
POWELL, T.
PRESCOTT, E.
PRESCOTT, T.
PRESCOTT, W.
PRESTON, J.
PRESTON, N.
PRESTON, W.
PRICE, C.

PRICE, G. W.
PRICE, L.
PRIESTLEY, G. E.
PRINCE, E.
PRINCE, W.
PRITCHARD R.
PROVOST, J. H.
PUGH, P.
PURCELL, H.
PURKISS, W. H.
PURVES, R. A.
PYE, J.
QUENNELL, P.
RACLE, L. C.
RADFORD, J.
RAFERTY, J.
RAFFERTY, J.
RAFFERTY, P.
RAINS, H.
RAINS, W.
RAISIN, H.
RANDS, G.
RANDS, W. H.
RATCLIFFE, W.
RAWLINSON, W.
RAWLINSON, W. S.
RAVENSCROFT, E. C.
RAVENSCROFT, T.
RAY, W.
RAYNOR, D.
REDMOND, A.
REDWOOD, J.
REECE, G.
REECE, J. O.
REES, W. A.
REID, T.
RENSHAW, F. N.
RENSHAW, G.
RENSHAW, M.
RENTON, A. N.
REYNOLDS, N.
REYNOLDS, R.
REYNOLDS, W.
REYNOLDS, W.
RHODES, R.
RICHARDS, A.
RICHARDS, E.
RICHARDS, G. J.
RICHARDSON, A.
RICHARDSON, L.
RICHARDSON, T.
RICHARDSON, W. H.
RICHARDSON, W. J.
RICHMOND, G.
RICHMOND, A.
RIDGARD, E.
RIDGARD, R.
RIDGEWAY, W. H.
RIGBY, F.
RIGBY, J.
RIGBY, P.
RIGBY, R.
RIGBY, W.
RIGBY, W.
RILEY, A.
RILEY, A.
RILEY, G.
RILEY, G.
RILEY, J.
RILEY, P.
RIMMER, F.
ROACH, W. H.
ROBERTS, D.
ROBERTS, E.
ROBERTS, F.
ROBERTS, J.
ROBERTS, J. C.
ROBERTS, G. H.
ROBERTS, O.
ROBINSON, A.
ROBINSON, C.
ROBINSON, G.
ROBINSON, G. U.
ROBINSON, G. J.
ROBINSON, G. J.
ROBINSON, G. R.
ROBINSON, H. R.
ROBINSON, J.

ROBINSON, J.
ROBINSON, T.
ROBINSON, W.
ROBINSON, W. J.
ROCHE, T.
ROCKETT, H. E.
ROGERS, C.
ROGERS, H.
ROGERS, J.
ROGERS, J.
ROGERS, N.
ROGERS, W.
ROGERSON, A.
ROGERSON, J.
ROGERSON, J. W.
ROLES, W.
ROSCOE, G.
ROSCOE, J.
ROSE, J.
ROSE, J. W.
ROSE, W.
ROSSI, F.
ROTHERHAM, J.
ROTHWELL, C.
ROUGHSEDGE, F.
ROUGHSEDGE, S. G.
ROWE, C.
ROWBOTTOM, T.
ROWLANDS, J.
ROWLANDS, J.
ROWLANDS, J. T.
ROWLES, G.
ROWLINSON, S.
ROYCROFT, T.
ROYLE, J.
ROYLE, S.
ROYLE, S.
ROYLE, W.
ROYLE, W.
RUANE, J.
RUNON, J.
RUSHTON, C. F.
RUSHTON, F.
RUSHTON, H.
RUSHTON, R. H.
RUSSELL, A.
RUTTER, C.
RYAN, J.
RYAN, T.
RYCROFT, H.
RYCROFT, W.
RYDER, A.
SADDLER, G.
SADLER, J.
SADLER, J. H.
SADLER, J. T.
SALMON, S.
SALTHOUSE, H.
SANDERS, T. A.
SANDYS, A. E.
SANT, H.
SAPPLE, H.
SARGESON, T.
SAUNDERS, J.
SAUNDERS, J.
SAVAGE, T.
SCHOFIELD, F. C.
SCHOFIELD, K. B.
SCHOFIELD, T.
SCOTT, H.
SCOTT, J.
SCOTT, W.
SCRAGG, P. J.
SCROXTON, C.
SEAL, T.
SEDDON, O.
SEDGWICK, A.
SELBY, A.
SEFTON, H.
SEVILLE, A. E.
SEVILLE, F.
SEXTON, J. E.
SEXTON, W.
SHAKESHAFT, H.
SHARDLOW, A. C.
SHARPE, S.
SHAW, A. E.
SHAW, C.
SHAW, G.
SHAW, H.

The Manchester Ship Canal Company.—Con.

SHAW, H.
SHAW, J.
SHAW, J.
SHAW, J.
SHAW, P.
SHAW, T.
SHAW, T.
SHAW, T. J.
SHAW, W.
SHAW, W.
SHAWCROSS, A.
SHAWCROSS, F.
SHAWCROSS, N.
SHEA, M.
SHEARWOOD, H.
SHELDON, J.
SHEPHERD, A.
SHEPHERD, J.
SHEPHERD, T.
SHERIDAN, J.
SHERLOCK, T.
SHERLOCK, W.
SHERRATT, A.
SHERWIN, J.
SHINGLER, A.
SHINGLER, R. C.
SHINGLER, S.
SHOELRIDGE, E.
SHONE, F.
SHUFFLEBOTTOM, F.
SHUFFLEBOTTOM, J.
SHUTTLEWORTH, J.
SIDDALL, A.
SIDDALL, S.
SIDDLE, J.
SIDLEY, G.
SIMCOCK, J.
SIMMONDS, —
SIMPSON W.
SINNOTT, J.
SKELTON, E.
SKELTON, R.
SKINNER, F.
SLADE, W.
SLATER, C.
SMEDLEY, G. S.
SMETHAM, J. W.
SMIDDY, A.
SMITH, A.
SMITH, A.
SMITH, A.
SMITH, C. F.
SMITH, D.
SMITH, E.
SMITH, E. N.
SMITH, H.
SMITH, H. G.
SMITH, H. J.
SMITH, J.
SMITH, J.
SMITH, J. A.
SMITH, J. J.
SMITH, J. W.
SMITH, R. J.
SMITH, S.
SMITH, S. O.
SMITH, T. A.
SMITH, W.
SMITH, W.
SMITH, W. G.
SMITH, W. H.
SMITH, W. H.
SMITH, W. H.
SMITHAM, H.
SNELSON, G.
SOMNER, J.
SOUTHWOOD, E.
SOUTHWOOD, R.
SOUTHWOOD, W.
SOUTHWOOD, W. D.
SPEED, S.
SPENCER, F.
SPILLANE, H.
SPITTLE, H. S.
SQUIRES, S.
STABLER, S. J.
STAINSBY, G.

STANNER, F.
STANWAY, P.
STAPLEY, G.
STATE, A. E.
STATHAM, J.
STEEL, A.
STEELE, J. A.
STEVENSON, J. A.
STEWART, T. J.
STEWART, W.
STIMSON, J.
STOREY, J.
STREETS, A.
STREETS, A.
STREETS, T. H.
STREETS, W.
STRETCH, A.
STRETCH, R.
STRINGFELLOW, F.
STRYANE, P.
STUBBS, J. H.
STUBBS, P.
SUNLEY, C.
SUTCLIFFE, H.
SUTCLIFFE, H.
SUTCLIFFE, H.
SUTTON, F.
SWAINBANK, J.
SWINDELLS, T.
SYKES, G.
SYKES, W. H.
TAPP, O. H.
TAYLOR, A. E.
TAYLOR, C. H.
TAYLOR, E.
TAYLOR, E.
TAYLOR, E. A.
TAYLOR, F.
TAYLOR, F.
TAYLOR, G.
TAYLOR, H.
TAYLOR, J.
TAYLOR, J.
TAYLOR, J.
TAYLOR, J. A.
TAYLOR, J. C.
TAYLOR, J. H.
TAYLOR, L.
TAYLOR, M.
TAYLOR, O.
TAYLOR, P.
TAYLOR, R. T.
TEASDALE, J.
THEOBOLD, G.
THOMAS, H. W.
THOMAS, W.
THOMASON, J.
THOMPSON, G. F.
THOMPSON, H. E.
THOMPSON, J.
THOMPSON, J.
THOMPSON, W.
THORNDIKE, G.
THORNDIKE G. W.
THORNE, C. A.
THORNE, T.
THORNLEY, C. E.
THORNTON, A. E.
THORNTON, W.
THORPE, R.
THOW, D.
THREADGOLD, J. H
TICKLE, H.
TIERNEY, J.
TILDESLEY, W.
TODD, R.
TOFT, H.
TOFT, J.
TOMLIN, G.
TOMLIN, S.
TOMLINSON, W.
TOMLINSON, W.
TONGE, W.
TONKS, T. W.
TOOZE, S.
TOULMIN, W.
TOWNLEY, T.

TOWSE, F.
TRAVIS, J.
TRAVIS, P.
TRICK, W. H.
TRIGG, E. E.
TRIMBLE, C.
TROTT, A. E.
TROTT, J. T.
TRUE, G. J.
TURNER, A.
TURNER, D. R
TURNER, H.
TURNER, S.
TURNER, S.
TURNER, S.
TURNER, W.
TWIGG, E.
TYLER, G.
UNSWORTH, J.
UNSWORTH, R.
VALLELY, L.
VANN, T. A.
VAUGHAN, D.
VENABLES, W
VERE, E.
VINCENT, H.
VINTON, C.
VERITY, R.
VITTY, J.
WADSWORTH, H. T.
WAGSTAFF, E.
WAKEFIELD, E.
WAKEFIELD, J.
WAKEFIELD, P.
WAKEFIELD, T. H.
WALKER, A.
WALKER, A.
WALKER, A. H.
WALKER, D.
WALKER, E. W.
WALKER, F.
WALKER, F.
WALKER, H. R.
WALKER, J.
WALKER, J. W.
WALKER, L.
WALKER, S.
WALKER, W. H.
WALKER, W. H
WALKER, W. H.
WALKER, W. W.
WALLIS, E.
WALLWORK, G
WALSH, J. W. J.
WALTERS, T.
WALTON, R.
WALTON, T.
WALTON, W.
WARBURTON, J.
WARD, F.
WARD, R.
WARDLE, J.
WARHAM, O. H.
WARREN, J.
WARREN, W.
WARRINGTON, A.
WARRINGTON, H.
WASHBAND, S.
WASP, J.
WATERWORTH, J. H.
WATERWORTH, P.
WATERWORTH, R.
WATKIN, F. K.
WATKINS, T. H.
WATSON, J.
WATSON, T.
WAY, C. R.
WAY, F. W.
WEBB, T. H.
WEBBERLEY, R.
WEBSTER, A.
WEEDALL, G. L.
WEEKS, C.
WELLS, E.
WELSBY, W.
WEST, W.
WESTON, J. B.
WHALLEY, A.

35

The Manchester Ship Canal Company.—Con.

WHALLEY, F.	WILLIAMS, E. T.	WOODHOUSE, W.
WHALLEY, F.	WILLIAMS, F.	WOODS, B.
WHISTON, J.	WILLIAMS, G. L.	WOODS, C.
WHITBY, G.	WILLIAMS, G. L.	WOODS, F.
WHITBY, H. M.	WILLIAMS, H.	WOODS, G.
WHITE, C.	WILLIAMS, J.	WOODS, I.
WHITE, H.	WILLIAMS, J.	WOODS, J.
WHITE, J. H.	WILLIAMS, J.	WOODS, S.
WHITE, R.	WILLIAMS, J. G.	WOODS, W.
WHITEHEAD, T.	WILLIAMS, J. S.	WOODWARD, E.
WHITELEGG, W.	WILLIAMS, W.	WOODWARD, T.
WHITELEY, J.	WILLIAMSON, A.	WOODWARD, W.
WHITELEY, S.	WILLIAMSON, B.	WOODYETT, B.
WHITFIELD, F.	WILSON, A.	WOOTTON, T.
WHITFIELD, G.	WILSON, A. B.	WORRALL, J.
WHITFIELD, H.	WILSON, C. H.	WORRALL, T. W.
WHITTAKER, T.	WILSON, C. M	WORTHINGTON, H.
WHITTLE, J.	WILSON, J.	WORTHINGTON, H.
WHITTLE, J.	WILSON, J. A.	WORTHINGTON, S.
WHITTLE, P.	WILSON, J. R.	WRIGHT, C.
WHORK, T.	WILSON, S.	WRIGHT, F.
WHYTE, M.	WILSON, S. M.	WRIGHT, H.
WILDE. G.	WILSON, T.	WRIGHT, J.
WILDE G. A.	WILTON, H.	WRIGHT, J.
WILDING, E.	WINGFIELD, H.	WRIGHT, S.
WILDING, E.	WINSTANLEY, P.	WRIGLEY, W.
WILDING, J.	WINTERBURN, W.	WRIGLEY, W.
WILDING, J.	WINTOUR, R.	WROE, C. O.
WILDING, R.	WISHART, R.	WROE, T.
WILDING, R.	WITHINGTON, A.	WILDE, W. H.
WILKES, A.	WOLFENDEN, H.	WYNNE, H.
WILKES, J. H.	WOLSTENCROFT, T.	YARWOOD, R.
WILKINSON, A.		YATES, E.
WILKINSON, E.	WOMACK, F.	YATES, H.
WILKINSON, F.	WOOD, A.	YATES, J.
WILKINSON, J.	WOOD, N.	YATES, J.
WILKINSON, S.	WOOD, P. N.	YATES, J. A.
WILLCOCK, J.	WOOD, R. H.	YATES, W.
WILLIAMS, A.	WOOD, P. H.	YORK, A.
WILLIAMS, A.	WOOD, W.	YORKE, W.
WILLIAMS, C.	WOOD, W. W.	YOUNG, C. H.
WILLIAMS, C.	WOODHOUSE, D. P.	YOUNG, R.

Chas. Macintosh and Co., Ltd.

(See p. 566 in Roll of Honour.)

ALDCROFT, J.	BRADBURN, A.	COBLEY, A.
ANDERTON, F.	BLADES, W.	CLULOW, H.
ASHLEY W. H.	BARLOW, J.	CUMMINS, G.
ARMSTRONG, W.	BROWN, J.	CREWE, E. J.
ARRAND, R.	BLAKELEY, H.	CLEARY, T.
ANDERSON, T.	BROOKS, H.	CROMPTON, G.
*ALLEN, E.	BRADBURY, C.	*DALE, S.
ALLEN, H.	BERRY C.	DAWSON, F.
ALLEN, J.	BEARDWOOD, D.	DAVANPORT, H.
ACHESON, J. E.	BELL, J.	*DREW, J.
AVISON, J.	BRIGGS, J.	DUNNING, A.
AITKEN, J.	BLAKE, E.	DANIELS, J.
ASHWORTH, H.	BRADLEY, H. W.	DUFFIELD, J.
BOOTH, R.	BROWN, J.	DUTTON, T. G.
*BELL, G.	BURKE, J. T.	DAVENPORT, W.
BELL, H.	CORNOFSKY, D.	DEMPSTER, W.
*BENNETT, A.	CHISNELL, L.	DOLAN, W.
BERRY, E.	*CHISWELL, F.	DULSON, T.
BROWN, J. T.	COSGROVE, J.	DULSON, P.
BARROW, J.	CASSIDY, P. E.	DUCK, W.
BLAIR, W.	CORCORAN, H.	DIXON, H.
BROWN J.	CASSERLEY, T.	DABER, H.
BERRY, W.	COLE, C.	DENT, F.
BOOTE, G.	COOKSON, E.	DUFFY, J.
BROMLEY, A.	COLLINSON, E.	ENGLISH, T.
BROSTER, W.	CHISNELL, T.	EYRES, W.
BRAMLEY, J. W.	CHAPMAN, R.	ELSEY, —
BURNS J.	CONDUIT, W.	EPHRAIM, L.
BOOTH, F.	CONRIE, A.	EVERS, G.
BIRTWISTLE, W.	CRONE, T.	EATON, C.
BRADY A.	CROSBIE, R. B.	FISHER, W.
BARRATT, C.	COLLINS, C.	FODEN, S.
BELL, A.	CAVANAGH, H.	*FANING, T.
BOARDMAN, F.	CARTER, C. F.	FANNING, T.
BELL, J.	COOKSON, A. V.	FLETCHER, E.
BROOKS, H.	CARTWRIGHT, A.	FLETCHER, A.
BROSTER, R.	COLLINGS, E.	FOLEY, F.
BELL, G.	CLODE, H.	FAIRCHILD, A.
BELL, H.	CARPENTER, E.	FIELDING, E.
BROWN, L.	CAVANAGH, J.	FOGG, G.
BOARDMAN, F.	CARROLL, P.	FENTON, W. S.
BOND, J.	CHETHAM, R.	FLINT, H.
BURKE, P.	CAMPBELL, A.	FOLEY, J.

* Serving with the Colours.

Chas. Macintosh and Co., Ltd.—Con.

FIELDING, A.	*LAWSON, J.	PEARSON, —
FURNESS, G.	*LOCKETT, H.	PARSONS, W.
FAULKNER, R.	LAMIN, G.	PRICE, —
FELDON, C. R.	LOWE, G.	PLATFORD, W. H.
FISHER, J.	LOMAS, W.	PEERS, J.
FIDLER, J.	LEWIS, S.	PEGG, J.
FLEMING, C.	LOVETT, N.	PARKINGTON, T. A.
GIBSON, A.	LANCASTER, G.	PRITCHARD, J. H.
*GILLESPIE, A.	LEDWIDGE, M.	PRITCHARD, C. F
GRIMSLEY, W.	LAWRANCE, J.	POOLFORD, J.
GRESTY, J.	LLOYD, G.	PENDLEBURY, J.
GLANCEY, S.	LEATHER, F.	PILLING, E.
GARNER, J.	LINFOOT, T.	PATON, R.
GREGORY, T.	LAWTON, H.	PARRY, T.
GRAHAM, J.	LINGARD, E.	PURCELL, W.
GRIFFITHS, F. A.	LEATHER, T.	PEACH W.
GREGORY, J. C.	LONGMIRE, J. H.	QUINN, H.
GREEN, S.	LORD, G.	QUINN, W.
GASKILL, W.	LAWTON, T.	*RHODES, H.
GREENWOOD, C.	LEAH, J.	ROGERS, E.
GOODING, R.	LLOYD, W.	ROOKE, F.
GRANT, J.	LANE, J.	ROBINSON, W.
GLYNN, W.	LYONS, V.	RUSSELL, J.
GERRISH, H.	LAWLESS, W.	RENFREW, T.
GARSIDE, F.	LUCY, J.	RICHARDSON, H.
GROTE, F.	LOUGHHEAD, W. D.	RENSHAW, T.
GERRISH, J.		READ, G.
GIBBONS, W.	*MacNULTY, A.	RATCLIFF, —
GUNN, W.	MOORE, J.	RHATTIGAN, —
GRAY, T.	*MEIKLE, J.	RICHARDS, J.
GROUNDS, F.	MEE C.	ROWLANDS, A.
GLYNN, W.	MITCHELL, H.	RHODES, W.
*HATTON, T.	MUTCH, W.	READETT, J.
*HATFIELD, T. A.	MASON, L. F.	ROBSON, W.
(killed in action).	MAHER, J.	ROBERTS, T.
HORTON, R.	MORRALL, G.	RUSSELL, E.
HOPE, H.	MOSS, J.	RYAN, J.
HADDON, H.	MOONEY, M.	RICHARDSON, J.
HOWARD, E.	McGOWAN, J.	RICHARDSON, J.
HEALY, J.	MURDOCK, E.	ROE, A.
HARRISON, F.	McMILLAN, A.	RUSSELL, J.
HESKETH, R.	MAYOR, A.	RICHARDSON, E.
HIGHAM, J.	McVICAR, M.	RUSSELL, F.
HORTON, W.	MATTHEWS, J.	ROGERS, C.
HUGHES, A. S.	MURRAY, S.	RAYNER, J.
HAMMOND, W. A.	MOFFATT, W. S. G.	RAMSDEN, C.
HOLLAND, A.	MURRAY, S.	REILEY, B.
HADFIELD, W.	MARSHALL, W.	ROYLE, F.
HENSON, W.	McNAULTY, J.	ROYLE, H.
HOYLE, J.	McELHINNEY, J.	RIDGWAY, F.
HOLMES, R.	MOULD H.G.	ROBINSON A.
HUGHES, A.	MARTINSCROFT, P	RHODES, H.
HEALD, E.	MINES, W.	REGAN, T.
HARRISON, J.	McWILLIAMS, W.	ROBINSON, S.
HAMPSON, H.	MITCHELL, J.	*SAUL, G.
HURST, S.	MERIDITH, J.	*STRICKLAND, F.
HIGHAM, F.	MANNION, P.	STREET A.
HASTINGS, G.	MARKHAM, C.	SQUIRES, —
HOLLAND, W.	MELLOR, J.	SINCLAIR, A
HAMPSON, C. H.	McKINLEY, T.	SYDENHAM, W.
HAND J.	MORRIS, J.	SIMPSON, R.
HILL, W.	MORGAN, W.	SPRAGUE, F.
HEALD, G.	MANNION, J.	SUMNER, W.
HOLMES, E.	MORRIS, H.	SUMMERFIELD, —
HALTON, P. A.	MIZEN, R.	SHAW, J.
HAIGH, J.	MORLEY, R.	STRATTON, J.
HARDMAN, R.	MORLEY, J.	SIMPSON, J. E. P.
HODGKINSON, W.	MASSEY, W.	SMITH, S. C.
HUMPHRIES, F. J.	MANION, T.	SMITHIES, H.
HOLDEN, J. T.	MAHER, J. W.	SINGLETON, W.
HALKYARD, J. W. T.	McINTYRE, J.	SMITH, T. E.
*INGHAM, R.	MASTERSON, M. E.	SIMPSON, J.
JESSAMY, S. R.	MORGAN, J.	STANDISH, A.
JORDAN, C.	NESBITT, G.	SMITH, T. E.
JONES, E.	NEWTON, C.	SAXON, G.
JONES, E.	NIXON, J.	STEPHENSON, W
JOHNSON, J.	O'GARA, P.	SCHOFIELD, E.
JONES, W.	OWEN, R. T.	SMITH C.
JONES, H.	OWEN, G.	SAUL, G.
JONES A. B.	ORGAN, E.	SHUFFLEBOTHAM J.
JOHNSON, W.	OWEN, E.	SWENNEY, E.
JONES, W. V.	OATES, J.	SMITH, G.
JOHNSON, C.	O'CONNOR, M.	SULLIVAN, M.
KILLIN, W.	*PARKER, T. A.	STANSTREET, R.
KENYON, W.	PERRIS, J.	SEDDON, C. E.
KILGRASS, A.	PARKINSON, G.	SCHOFIELD, T.
*KIRK, J. W.	PERCIVAL, W.	SHUFFLEBOTTOM, A. J.
KITCHEN, C. D.	PEARSON, W.	TAYLOR L.
KENYON, L.	PEARSON, E.	TRANTER, W.
KERRY, S.	POOLE W.	
*LANNON, J.	PICKERING, A.	
	PARGETER, W.	

* Now serving with the Colours.

Chas. Macintosh and Co., Ltd.—Con.

TILEY, A.	†COETRUP, J.	†MULLEN, C.
TILEY, R.	†CARY, R.	†MULLEN, R.
TAYLOR, J.	†CALLAGHAM, J.	†McGRATH, B.
THORNLEY, A.	†CARROLL, W.	†MOLLAND, E.
THOMAS, W. E.	†COCHRAN, D.	†METCALFE, A.
TANNER, B.	†CLARKE, S.	†MYERS S.
TYSON, H. W.	†CLOWES, L.	†MILLS, A.
TODD, T.	†COLE, J.	†MOOR, C.
THOMAS, C.	†COLWELL, W.	†McLAUGHLIN, T.
TODD, L.	†CATLIN, J.	†MYCOCK, F.
TERRIS, J.	†COX, R.	†MITCHELL, R.
THOMPSON, H.	†COWBURN, J.	†MEAD, W.
THORPE, J.	†CORRIS, W.	†McDONALD, T.
TOWNEND, G.	†CRAMPTON, H. W.	†McGUIRE, N.
THOMPSON, G.	†COULSON, H. A.	†MANN, J.
TOMLIN, S.	†DAY, C.	†MACK, J.
TAYLOR, A.	†DALE, H.	†MACK, J.
THACKER, T.	†DUTTON, J.	†McKINLEY, C.
TOWNEND, G.	†DUNCAN, J.	†MORTON, W.
VICKERS, —	†DUNN, C. F.	†MAHONEY, T.
*WADE, G.	†DAVIES, G.	†McLEAN, J.
*WALKER, W.	†DUFFY, C.	†McKERION, T. J.
WARBURTON, A.	†DALEY, W.	†MORETON, J.
WESTON, S. E.	†DOWLING, J. T.	†McDERMOTT, J.
WILSON, E.	†EASTWOOD, F.	†MONTAGUE, A.
WAYWELL, F.	†EVANS, T.	†NIELD, H.
WHITING, T.	†EDMUNDSON, J. S.	†NIELD, F.
WATSON, F.	†ESCOTT, H. T.	†OAKDEN, G.
WALKER, H.	†FINNIGA, P.	†OLDFIELD, F.
WALTERS, L. J.	†FLETCHER, E.	†PRICE, C. M.
WILSON, A.	†FELLOWS, A.	†POOLE, A.
WILLIAMS, W.	†FEENEY, W.	†PETERS, A. E.
WATSON, H.	†FITTON, J.	†PARKINSON, J.
WATERFIELD, E.	†FIDDLER, T.	†PHAIR, R.
WILLIAMS, W.	†FITZSIMMONS, R.	†PAGET, H.
WILKINSON, J.	†FODEN, P.	†PURCELL, P.
WARING, J. E.	†GEE, A.	†QUITTY, J.
WALKER, W. A.	†GREEN, A.	†RAWSON, J.
WALLACE, W.	†GORTON, T.	†RATHBURN, J.
WARBURTON, A.	†GREEN, R.	†ROBINSON, J.
WRIGHT, H.	†GRIEVE, S.	†RICHARDSON, E.
WRAY, J.	†GROGAN, J.	†RAE, R.
WELHAM, F.	†GODDARD, J.	†RANKIN, N. J.
WINSTON, H.	†GRACE, J.	†RICHARDS, J.
WHITTLE, J.	†GODFORD, D.	†ROBERTS, S. R.
WRAY, J.	†GRANT, J. W.	†RIDGWAY, E.
WADE, G.	†GWYNNETH, F.	†ROGERS, T.
WINTER, W.	†GOULDING, W.	†RUAN, G.
WORSEMAN, F.	†GREENWOOD, H.	†REILLY, W.
WILSON, A.	†GOULDEN, C.	†RHODES, J.
WALLACE, A. W.	†HAYWOOD, J.	†RIGBY, T.
WRIGHT, P. H.	†HORRIDGE, W.	†RATCLIFFE, A.
YEARSLEY, B.	†HADDON, J.	†REGAN, T.
†ATHERTON, J.	†HUGHES, H.	†ROBINSON, R. J.
†ASHWORTH, C. H.	†HIBBERT, J.	†RILEY, P.
†ALLCOCK, J.	†HOPE, A.	†RIGBY, F.
†ATKINSON, F.	†HARRIS, —	†STONELEY, A.
†ALDRED, F.	†HARTLEY, H.	†SMITH, R.
†BROWN, A.	†HAMMOND, G.	†SMITH, —
†BOLT, W.	†HOLLIDAY, T.	†SPENCER, G.
†BURGESS, F.	†HEAPS, E.	†SHAW, G. H.
†BESWICK, F.	†HIBBERT, J.	†SINGLETON, W.
†BROWN, —	†HELSBY, J.	†STANLEY, J.
†BRAMMER, W.	†HOLT, J.	†STANDRING, C.
†BEILBY, J.	†HAND, P.	†SEAL, J.
†BARROW, A.	†HARNEY, J.	†SUMNER, J.
†BECKETT, J.	†HARRISON, W.	†SHUFFLEBOTTOM, J.
†BERRY, J.	†HIGGINS, J.	†SIMS, A.
†BACON, T.	†JOHNSON, G.	†SCHOLES, W.
†BOOTH, J.	†JAMIESON, E.	†SHAW, H.
†BURRELL, C.	†JONES, E.	†STEVENSON, J.
†BEESTON, W.	†JERVIS, J.	†SMITH, A.
†BOWERS, E.	†JENKINS, W.	†THOMAS, F.
†BOLTON, W.	†KINSEY, H.	†TURNER, W.
†BECKETT, W.	†KAY, L.	†TODD, J.
†BUTCHER, S.	†KAY, J.	†THOMPSON, H.
†BRADY, B.	†KENT, H.	†THREADER, A
†BOYD, W.	†KELLY, J.	†THOMPSON, J.
†BRETT, M.	†KNAGG, E.	†TAYLOR, J. R.
†BROWN, W.	†KELLY, M.	†UNWIN, H.
†CLAY, R. C.	†LEIGH, A.	†WELLS, A.
†CHEETHAM, A.	†LOMAS, G.	†WILSON, T.
†CARROLL, A.	†LITTLE, J.	†WILLCOCK, F.
†CHILTON, C.	†LIMB, W.	†WRIGHT, J. E.
†CLAQUE, R.	†LEACH, J.	†WYKE, J.
†CORFIELD, J.	†LOMAS, F.	†WEAVER, W.
†COBEY, J.	†LAWTON, A.	†WELLS, S.
†CAREY, R.	†LEE, F.	†WALLIS, W.
†COOPER, A.	†LANNON, P.	†WALKDEN, H.
†CAIN, F.	†LAWSON, J.	†WOOD, H.
†COOPER, C.	†LINSTEAD, C. P.	

* Serving with the Colours.   † Rejected.

Chas. Macintosh and Co., Ltd.—Con.

†WOOD, J.	†WARD, J.	†WOODBRIDGE, W.
†WORSLEY, W.	†WORSLEY, F.	†WATSON, A.
†WHITTAKER, S. J.	†WILLIAMS, E.	†WOLSTENHOLME, R. G.
†WOOD, F.	†WALKER, V.	†WAKEFIELD, S.
†WILSON, W.	†WALKER, R. P.	
†WILLIAMS, T. E.	†WADE, H.	

Mabbott and Company, Limited.

(See p. 565 in Roll of Honour.)

EDGE, A.	DOWNES, W.	EMSALL, W.
SIDEBOTHAM, E.	WHITTINGHAM, C. W.	RIGBY, J. H.
GARLICK, A.		ELLAM, S. R.
SLACK, S.	JACKSON, J.	HALL, H.
DOHERTY, H.	PRICE, F. F.	JORDAN, J. B.
WHITTAKER, J.	PARKINSON, H.	HINDLE, E.
ELLERBY, T.	WRIGLEY, F.	SWAIN P.
MILLS, G.	GUY, A. H.	DOHERTY, E.
BANKS, T.	PUGH, J. E.	SNOW, H.
SCOTCHFORD, A.	WYNNE, M.	SMITH, A. J. R.

Henry Marchington.

(See p. 686 in Roll of Honour.)

WILKINSON, H.	WHITLEY, S.	†DANIELS, W. A.
JOHNSON, C. A.	BERRY, J.	†ASHWORTH, G.

Manchester Liners, Ltd.

(See p. 578 in Roll of Honour.)

POOLE, H. J.	WILSON, F. W.	CLARK, J.
CLARKE, H. G.	TURNER, M. W.	JOHNSTONE, J. B.
VOSE, J. R.	KIRKWOOD, W.	DARLINGTON, R. C.
PITCHFORD, L. B.	SUTCLIFFE, A. C.	
THOMAS, D. S.	DOLAN, F. A.	DAVIES, D. E.

Mason, Scheidler and Co., Ltd.

(See p. 578 in Roll of Honour.)

BAKER, A.	DAVIDSON, W.	MARTIN, W.
BARLOW, C. E.	ENTWISTLE, B.	OVERALL, T.
BEELEY, A.	EVATT, G. E.	TAYLOR, C.
CALVERT, E.	GIBBONS, V.	TAYLOR, W.
CHAPMAN, H.	IZON, J. J.	WOODWARD, T.

Arthur McDougall, Ltd.

(See p. 579 in Roll of Honour.)

McDOUGALL, C., Managing Director.	GRUNDY, W. H.	LEAR, T. W.
	GREEN, J.	CRESSWELL, W.
HEY, H.	EGAN, J.	HASLAM, T.
HARTLEY, W.	EDWARDS, J.	HOLLINGSWORTH, J.
MOORE, B.	PEERS, S.	
WOODS, J.	EDWARDS, R.	CLARE, J. T.

Seymour Mead and Co.

(See p. 569 in Roll of Honour.)

ARDERN, J.	CLAYTON, A.	DONOGHUE, M.
ATKIN, G.	COWHAM, N.	DAWSON, W.
ATKINSON, R.	COOKSON, A.	DUTTON, L.
ABBOT, L. J.	CALVERT, J.	EASTAUGH, J.
AMPHLETT, A.	CADDICK, F.	FELL, G.
ABRAHAM, E.	CHISWELL, G.	FORSTER, R.
BELL, P.	COMPTON, S.	FORD, H. D.
BOON, N.	CLARKE, J.	FELL, A.
BARNETT, J.	CUNLIFFE, T.	GARRETT, P.
BREEZE, C.	CRAVEN, A.	GALLAGHER, T.
BANCROFT, N.	CLARKE, I.	GRENSIDE, W.
BEST, J.	COTTRELL, F.	GARROD, G. E.
BACON, A.	COOPER, H.	GODWIN, F. W.
BELL, W.	CHAPMAN, G.	GREALY, C.
BLANEY, R.	CASTLEDINE, F.	GROOM, H. W.
BOWLES, C.	DRAPER, R.	GRIFFITHS, J.
BRAGG, W.	DURNELL, H.	GARLICK, E.
BROCKBANK, J.	DEAKIN, T.	HIGGINS, A.
BURNETT, W.	DEAN, J.	HITCHINS, S.
COURTNEY, C.	DAVIES, L.	HILDITCH, W.
CUNNINGHAM, H.	DANIELS, F.	HAMNETT, A.
CLEMENTS, B.	DAVENPORT, E.	HOLDING, W.

† Rejected.

Seymour Mead and Co.—Con.

HOLMES, L.	MARRIOTT, A.	SMITH, P.
HAYTON, J.	MORRIS, R.	SOWERSBY, H.
HAUGHTON, H.	MARSLAND, L.	STORER, P.
HOLDSWORTH, J.	MILNER, G.	SUTCLIFFE, E.
HAMMERSLEY, P.	MADEN, W.	SCHOFIELD, W.
HILLIERS, W.	MORGAN, A.	SEARLE, A.
HOLT, J.	MASON, J.	STOKES, G.
HARRISON, G.	MASSEY, P.	SELBRIDGE, G.
HALLAM, P.	MILLINGTON, W.	SARGENT, C.
HARDMAN, W.	MATHER, J.	SHUTTLEWORTH, E.
HOLROYD, A.	MAWBY, E.	
HARGREAVES, W.	MARK, C.	SHARPE, T.
HOCKNALL, G.	MILES, H.	SOUTHERN, R.
HANCOCK, J.	NICHOLLS, F.	SAUNDERS, T.
HOLLAND, H.	NIXON, J.	SYKES, E.
HANDLEY, R.	NORTON, J.	SMITHSON, W.
HAMNETT, W.	NEWTON, E.	STREET, J.
HUNTINGTON, H.	OATES, R.	STUBBS, D.
HARRISON, E.	ORMROD, H.	SMITH, F.
HORSLEY, A.	PARTINGTON, J.	STORER, J.
HUGHES, P.	PANNIFER, E.	TAYLOR, A. J.
JONES, T.	PRIDHAM, W.	THOMPSON, J.
JONES, H.	PICKEN, B.	TASKER, A.
JORDAN, T.	POTTS, J.	THOMAS, E. A.
JONES, D.	PICKSTONE, R.	THOMPSON, A.
JONES, W.	RICKARDS, R.	TALBOT, F.
JONES, E.	RYDER, G.	VAUGHAN, R.
KITCHENER, J.	REDGROVE, J.	WEEKS, A.
KEVITT, C.	ROBERTS, D.	WITTY, J.
KILSHAW, A.	ROBERTS, E.	WILDMAN, C.
KILGOUR, W.	RADFORD, F.	WRIGLEY, W.
LAWTON, J.	ROBINSON, T.	WARD, S.
LEWIS, T.	REED, F.	WIGNALL, J.
LILLEY, W.	RICHARDSON, A.	WRIGHT, J.
LONGSTAFFE, W.	ROTHWELL, R.	WRIGHT, A.
LAWRENCE, W.	ROBINSON, A.	WILSON, P. C.
LINDSAY, T.	REDFEARN, H.	WEST, W.
LOWE, A.	RAMSDEN, J.	YOUNGS, S.
LLOYD, E.	ROYLE, A.	YATES, R.
LLOYD, R.	ROGERS, R.	

Merttens and Co., Ltd.

(See p. 579 in Roll of Honour.)

DUNN, G. E.	GRAINGER, J. W.	POIRETTE, A.
FLETCHER, J. H.	*JAMES, T. R.	*ROBINSON, F.
*FIELDING, F. J.	KEATE, A. M.	

Middleton, Jones and Co., Ltd.

(See p. 570a in Roll of Honour.)

BURNETT, F.	CHARLTON, G.	STOPFORD, J. P.
POTTS, T.	DALTON, R.	COOPER, J.
DAY, A.	ACTON, J.	HOLLAND, J.
LOCKWOOD, J. E	JONES, J.	LAYDEN, A.
JOHNSON, T.	HAMMEN, C.	HUGHES, H.
DARCY, J.	HOLLAND, A.	HAMPSON, L.

David Midgley and Sons, Ltd.

(See p. 571 in Roll of Honour.)

ALLEN, O.	GREGORY, G.	MORAN, D.
ASHWORTH, W. C.	GRIMSHAW, H.	PIRRIE, J. R.
BARLOW, P.	HAWKER, A. H.	PRIDEAUX, E. P.
BIRTLES, D. W.	HAYES, F.	RICHARDSON, A. R.
BROOKS, A.	HOFF, T.	RICHARDSON, T.
CLOUGH, J.	HOTHERSALL, S.	ROBERTS, E.
CORDWELL, W.	JONES, A.	SMITH, G.
DICKINSON, J. L	LANCASHIRE, C. E.	STEVENSON, H.
FISH, H.	LANE, R.	TAYLOR, E.
FLETCHER, A.	McADOREY, S.	WOOD, S. P. L.
GAYTHORPE, T. H.	McGRATH, J.	
GENT, T. H.	MONKHOUSE, T.	

James Moorhouse and Son, Ltd.

(See p. 572 in Roll of Honour.)

MOORHOUSE, H. H.	CLARKSON, J.	HEALD, W.
MOORHOUSE, W. E.	LOVETT, T.	SHELDRAKE, T.
	HALL, W., junr.	HARDMAN, T.
MOORHOUSE, J. D.	MOORHOUSE, F.	ALTHAM, C.
RILEY, A. T.	PILKINGTON, W. H.	REID, H.
NUTTER, R.		

* Now serving with the Colours.

Morreau, Spiegelberg and Co.

(See p. 573 in Roll of Honour.)

BROWN, J.	STEELE, W.	GREAVES, A.
POWELL, G. M.	MORRIS, J.	BARLOW, A.
BLACKBURN, J. T.	MATHER, J.	BOARDMAN, J.
MORTON, A.	MOFFATT, A.	KENYON, R.
BLACKER, G. O.	DOOLEY, E.	BRITNOR, C.
EAGLES, A.	DONLAN, J. M.	ETCHES, R.
HIND, W.	OLLIER, F. B.	BROWNE, E. D.
HART, J. E.	ROBINSON, J. B.	WILLSHAW, C.
JORDAN, A.	DICKINSON, J. M.	PARKER, R.
SCHOFIELD, F.	TATTERSALL, R.	BROOKES, H.
HARRISON, S. H.	MASON, A.	LOVELL, G.
WOOD, E.		

Morris and Jones, Ltd.

(See p. 574 in Roll of Honour.)

BLOMLEY, J.	KENNISON, J. A.	SALTER, A.
BROADHEAD, C.	LUNN, W.	SAIT, T. E.
COURTIS, F.	MORRISON, J.	TAYLOR, E.
DAVIES, I.	NUNN, A. A. W.	THOMAS, E. W.
†DAVIES, J. B.	OWEN, J. B.	THORLEY, S.
†DENT, L.	OWEN, J.	WILKINSON, G. A.
EVANS, D. G.	OWEN, W.	WILLIAMS, R. H.
†EVANS, H. T.	†PLATT, F. K.	WILLIAMS, E.
ELLIS, J. H.	ROTHWELL, J.	†WILLIAMS, J.
GOUGH, E.	REES, H.	WILLIAMS, R.
GWILT, E. C.	ROBERTS, W. H.	WILLIAMS, R.
HAMER, A.	†ROBERTS, A.	WILLIAMS, J. T.
JOBLING, J. R.	RANDLES, S. D.	WATSON, W.
JONES, O.	STUBBS, C. G.	
JONES, R.	STANDISH, T.	

David Moseley and Sons.

(See p. 575 in Roll of Honour.)

ACKERLEY, H.	FODEN, W. T.	NIELD, S.
BAGSHAW, A. F.	FORD, P.	O'SHEA, J.
BARNES, T.	FORD, W. T.	PARRY, J.
BARTON, H.	GIBBON, L.	POLLARD, T.
BENNETT, R.	GLEDHILL, R.	POOLE, J.
BESWICK, G.	GRIFFITH, K.	ROACH, J.
BEYNORE, R.	HARCOURT, W.	ROBERTS, D. E.
BOSTOCK, A. E.	BARRETT, J.	RYDER, S. J.
BOWDON, T.	HARROP, J.	SCOTT, J. T.
BOWTELL, T. G.	HAWLEY, J.	*SELLS, W.
BRADLEY, J.	HOLMES, A.	SHAW, H.
BROMLEY, J.	HOPE, J.	SHONE, L.
BROWN, H.	HOFFMAN, A.	SIMPSON, H. S.
CARR, W.	HULMES, T.	STOPFORD, A.
CATTERALL, E. M.	HUNTER, C.	STOPFORD, J. W.
CLEMENTS, A.	HUNTER, C.	SULLIVAN, L.
CONNOR, C.	INGHAM, J.	TOWNSEND, R.
COPE, F.	IRELAND, H. A.	WALMSLEY, J.
COSGROVE, F.	JOHNSON, M.	WARNE, W. J.
COX, C.	JOHNSON, F.	WARNE, W.
CRONSHAW, W.	JONES, A.	WHALAN, W.
CRYNES, F.	JOYNT, J.	WHITTAKER, A.
DEVANEY, A.	KELLY, J.	WILLIAMS, W. T.
EDWARDS, W. H.	KENYON, H.	WILSON, F.
ELLAM, R. W.	LOMAS, C.	WILTON, A.
ELLIS, G.	MARLBOROUGH, C. R.	WOLSTENCROFT, J.
ELLIS, J.	MOLLOY, L.	WRIGHT, H.
ETCHELLS, G.	MONAGHAN, T.	YEARDLEY, C.
FIELDING, H.	MOSS, H.	*YEARDSLEY, C.
FIELDING, W.		
FITZGERALD, G.		

N. P. Nathan's Sons.

(See p. 580 in Roll of Honour.)

JONES, H.	COWELL, E.	†ORANGE, A. G.
GRADWELL, R.	PAGE, H.	†RYAN, J.
EVANS, T.	GREENWOOD, W.	†WILD, J.
KAY, C.	SIMPSON, E. H.	†WIGHTMAN, D.
SIMPSON, O.	†MILLS, C.	†GLYNN, J.
VAUGHAN, J.	†ROONEY, G.	†GORDON, J.
HALL, H.	†TOMLINSON, C.	†SKADE, E.
PAGE, W. C.	†LINDSAY, W.	

The "Oak Tree" Hosiery Co., Ltd.

(See p. 581 in Roll of Honour.)

HARGREAVES, E. R.	TONGE, T. H.	FOZZARD, N.
GROVE, A.	HURST, H.	HOLLAND, H.
SHARPLES, R.	BALE, B. T.	WARD, A.

* Serving with the Colours.   † Rejected.

James E. Ogden and Sons, Ltd.
(See p. 689 in Roll of Honour.)

CHAPMAN, J. R.	OGDEN, C. R.	OGDEN, J. E.
TIMPERLEY, T.	KAY, A.	†WATSON, E. J.
POWELL, C. R.	GRAY, G.	†SHAWCROSS, W.
	LANG, E.	†BRUCKSHAW, A.

Wm. O'Hanlon and Co., Ltd.
(See p. 582 in Roll of Honour.)

O'HANLON, H. D.	SHEPPARD, G.	WALKER, W. A.
COWHAM, P. B.	WOLSTENCROFT, J. R.	MARTIN, E.
TREES, J. F.		SPROSTON, C.
RAMSBOTHAM, A.	CLARKE, J. K.	HEPWORTH, C. E
MEREDITH, A.	CHADDERTON, T.	STRINGER, A.
HOLLAND, J.	GODDARD, P.	SHAW, J.
JEVONS, J.	HOLT, T.	MATTHEWS, C. H.
BONNER, J.	HARRISON, G.	SHELDON, A.

G. B. Ollivant & Co. Ltd.
(See p. 689 in Roll of Honour.)

BARLOW, H.	*TAYLOR, W. H.	†PIERCE, H. T.
DEAN, A.	HOPE, J. L.	†LUNT, H. B.
*DIVER, C.	SMITH, W. S.	
NIXON, A.	†MOUNTAIN, T.	

Geo. Owen and Co.
(See p. 583 in Roll of Honour.)

OWEN, N. R.	BRESLANE, J. F.	†RYLE, A.
FERGUSON, J.	†KNIGHT, J. W.	†NAYLOR, A.
PERKINS, W. R.	NOAR, H. W.	†TAYLOR, G.
BROWN, E.	CRAIG, W. C.	†LEACH, W.
FACER, G. H.	WILDE, J.	
MASSEY, J.	†HARRISON, C. H.	

Oxendale and Co.
(See p. 583 in Roll of Honour.)

BROWN, C. C.	EVANS, G. H.	SMITH, S. W.
CARPENTER, E.	JEFFRIES, F. J.	TREHEARNE, R.
CLARKSON, W.	MADDOCKS, E.	
DALE, J.	POTTER, J.	

Paulsen, Koedt and Co.
(See p. 690 in Roll of Honour.)

CHAMPION, J. E. (Manager).

Peel, Watson and Co., Ltd.
(See p. 585 in Roll of Honour.)

BOOTH, S.	HUNTBACH, T. W.	REDFERN, B.
BARLOW, J. A.	HOLMES, W. B.	REYNOLDS, E. R.
*BROOKS, E.	JONES, C.	SMITH, H.
*BURROWS, T.	JONES, J.	SOUTHWORTH, E.
BUDDEN, C. A.	JACKSON, J. A.	SHARPLES, A.
CHAPPELL, A.	MANGNALL, C.	TARR, R.
CLARKE, J. H.	*POOLE, T.	UNSWORTH, G. C.
GUEST, E.	PIKE, L.	
HESLOP, A.	POOK, J.	

The Premier Waterproof and Rubber Co., Ltd.
(See p. 591 in Roll of Honour.)

GOODALL, E.	CROSSLEY, W.	PHILLIPS, F.
HOLLAND, J.	CARR, G.	EATON, G.
THEOBALD, A.	McNAUGHTON, W.	TURNER, W.
LANCASTER, J.	ALLEN, J.	RISK, J.
HUNT, G.	STONHEUR, W.	COHEN, J.
WOODRUFF, J.	GAFFNEY, M.	KRAUS, A.
MACINTOSH, A.	POLLARD, N.	THEOBALD, J.
PARSONAGE, W.	THORPE, J.	CHURCH, J.
DAVISON, J.	GOODWIN, A.	WRIGHT, S.
STOREY, S.	POWER, S.	ROTHWELL, W.
TAYLOR, J.	HENTHORN, H.	LUPTON, E.
FORSHAW, F.	BRIGGS, J.	LINTON, F.
FORSHAW, W.	KELLY, J.	GRAHAM, J.
HOWARTH, J.	DICKENS, C.	HANNEY, W.
PATTERSON, H.	QUINN, E.	WORRALL, W.
ARTINGSTALL, A.	AHERN, J.	WHELAN, H.
RYAN, T.	BRIGGS, H.	WHELAN, W.
SMITH, J.	DRINKWATER, E.	ROBINSON, A.
HYNES, D.	SLATER, J.	BRAYFORD, D.
DUNNE, T.	PROPHET, W.	SPILMAN, H.
BRADLEY, T.	SPRUCE, H.	WOOD, J.
O'DONNELL, J.	COHEN, H.	CARNEY, W.
POOLE, S.	SIMLOVITCH, S.	CONNOLLY, J.
BROARDMAN, G.	GLASSBERG, J.	CAMPBELL, A.
DIXON, W.	PHILLIPS, R.	HENN, J.
BEYNON, D.	BOARDMAN, T.	ROBERTS, W.
MOLLOY, P.	COCKILL, C.	HAYES, C.
FITZGERALD, J.	LANE, C.	

* Serving with the Colours. † Rejected.

J. and N. Philips and Co., Ltd.
(See p. 586 in Roll of Honour.)

KOCHY, F.	MATHER, H.	PAYNE, F.
CHADWICK, C.	WILLCOCK, C.	BOARDMAN, A.
LAPIERRE, G.	BARRINGER, R. S.	FLANNAGAN, F.
WATSON, J. L.	OLDHAM, W.	PARKE, H. F.
HEWITT, T. A.	DAVIDSON, J. R.	NUTTALL, J.
BOOTH, J. R.	PARRY, R.	ALLEN, T.
DOUGLAS, A. R.	GOODISON, H.	WILKINSON, J. H.
PODMORE, J. W.	FEARON, J.	BAGULEY, W.
GRIFFITHS, W.	STRATFORD, G.	VOYCE, G.
BENSON, A.	GAZE, J. W.	JONES, R.
BEARDSALL, A.	DOLAN, C. H.	EVANS, A.
PORTER, J.	WHINCUP, H.	WILSON, E.
CRAW, W. M.	TAYLOR, F.	ROBINSON, J.
GRIERSON, G. F.	CHAPMAN, H. E.	ELGAR, E.
SMETHURST, T.	LINDLEY, A.	†WORTHINGTON, E
CROMPTON, H.	HOLT, F. P.	†EDWARDS, C.
ROBINSON, G. P.	MAYNARD, A.	†CLERY, R.
HILLMER, C.	BURNS, H. B.	†KIRKMAN, P.
MORGAN, W. H.	HULME, W. S.	†DIXON, R. B.
MARSH, S.	LEIGH, H.	†BAIRD, A.
HOWARD, T.	WYNN, J.	†NORTH, R.
GRAVELL, H.	SYKES, F. O.	†JONES, E. T.
CORDEY, C. W.	STOCKDALE, H.	†WILLCOCKS, W. J.
ALDRED, S.	HEPBURN, J. J.	†SCRAGG, J.
TOWNEND, W. A.	THOMPSON, G.	†PARTON, W. G.
KNEEN, J. C.	LOMAS, H.	†COOPER, F.
ECCLES, C.	ARNFIELD, L.	†YATES, P.
SPEIRS, H.	WILSON, J. A.	†BELL, H.
STRINGER, A. H.	HOWARTH, J.	†CHADWICK, H. P.
COOPER, W.	BENTON, T. J.	†HUGHES, T. R.
HOLDEN, A. H.	BEATSON, R.	†LINDLEY, J.
WILLIAMS, G.	TAYLOR, C.	†BULLOUGH, W.
KEMP, F.	CRAWSHAW, E.	†CROSSLEY, H.
BOARDMAN, T.	BAKER, A.	†GARNETT, W.
WARD, T. F.	TOPPING, J.	†ATKINSON, A.
POWELL, J.	GRIFFITHS, J. J.	†DOWNS, H.
SHENTON, T. W.	TOYNE, H.	†EARLE, W. H.
JACKSON, R. E.	SPENCE, C. B.	†ROYLE, R.
HILTON, F. C.	SUMNER, J.	†CRETNEY, C.
PRIESTNER, C.	HILDITCH, T. E.	†CANNON, E. C.
BROTHERTON, F.	DANIEL, J. F.	†AVERY, J.
JACKSON, H. D.	DODD, J.	†HARRISON, H. E.
HICKLIN, E. W.	WADKIN, F.	†MATHER, H.
PROSSER, G. H.	CROLEY, J.	†HAMER, G.
HOMER, W.	SMITH, G.	†MILLS, F.
ISHERWOOD, H.	LINDSAY, A.	†ROUTLEDGE, J.
ROSE, J.	THORP, F. T.	†GLENNIE, F.
BULLIVANT, G. F.	STALEY, W. H.	†SMITH, L.
HOPE, G. H.	WHITEHURST, B.	†PAGE, J.
JACKSON, H.	PARKER, S. K	†STUBBS, J. G.
ALDCROFT, W.	PEEL, W.	†WHITNALL, A.
TIDESWELL, A. L.	DAKIN, H.	†BURTON, A.
RUSSELL, J. D.	PRESTON, F. L.	†WEBSTER, P.
DUESBURY, T. E.	PENDLEBURY, J.	†RIDGE, E. G.
HALLWOOD, F.	HANDS, J. A.	†BOND, F.
MASON, T.	THORNTON, R. J.	†GRAY, J.
BUCKLER, F.	THOMPSON, H.	†JEFFREY, T.
BROSTER, J. O.	HOWARD, J. H.	†BUTTERWORTH, H
SIMISTER, L.	CORNTHWAITE, T.	†GIBBON, B.
BRIGGS, H.	HULME, A.	†WAINE W. E.
EDMONDSON, N.	CONNELL, J.	†POWELL, L.
INGHAM, A.	FAIRWEATHER, W. J.	†ROBERTS, J. O.
ASHTON, H.		†DOLAN, J. P.
GREENWOOD, A. S.	EGERTON, J.	†NEILL, J.
POWER, A. J.	MOLYNEUX, F.	†SANDBACH, G.
RAWLING, W.	HOLT, J.	†MORRIS, H.
GUDGER, B.	HUGHES, T.	†DELVE, R.
PROUDLOVE, C. C.	CHAPPEL, G.	†GOSLING, A.
KRETSCHMER, P.	ROWBOTTOM, F.	†SPENCE, J.
HALL, J. W.	BENTLEY, H.	†STATHAM, H.
WALKER, W.	WHITNALL, C.	†WILLIAMS, W. A.
BARRIE, W. H.	DUESBURY, F.	†SMITH, H.
SOMERSET, G. W.	TOOLE, A. R.	†IKIN, J. E.
HORSEY, R. V.	COX, W.	†SIMPSON, W. E.
ASHTON, F. W.	HOUGHTON, G. H.	†LEIGHTON, A. G.
ENTWISTLE, R.	BOLTON, G. W.	†RATCLIFFE, R. L.
FRITH, W. S.	THORNTON, W.	†MACHIN, A. M.
BENT, W.	DALY, E.	†GREAVES, H.
FIELDING, J.	JONES, H. C.	

Pickard and Daine.

*Private F. W. BERRY, joined 8th Batt. Rifle Brigade, Sept., 1914.

*Private B. S. F. PICKARD, joined 18th City Battalion, Sept., 1914; obtained Commission in 3rd Batt. Connaught Rangers April, 1915. Subsequently attached to 1st Garrison Battalion Royal Irish Regiment.

* Serving with the Colours. † Rejected.

Paterson, Zochonis and Co., Ltd.
(See p. 690 in Roll of Honour.)

FLETCHER, G. E.	GOODE, S.	EVANS, F.
BYWATER, J. C.	BOSTOCK, J. A.	WILSON, A.
BLACK, H.	LEES, F. J.	

Ralli Brothers.
(See p. 592 in Roll of Honour.)

BARDSLEY, J.	HAYHURST, A.	TOOTILL, T.
BARROW, R.	HAYHURST, S.	VASEY, R.
BAYLEY, V.	JONES, W.	WALSH, P.
BELL, J.	KELSEY, J.	WHALLEY, W.
BIRDSALL, F. A.	KING, E.	WHITEHEAD, H. S.
BRAMALL, D.	LLOYD, E.	WILSON, F. C.
BRENNAN, J.	MARSDEN, F.	WILDE, J.
BROWNHILL, W.	MORT, J.	WOOD, A.
CAVANAGH, E.	MOTTERSHEAD, S.	YATES, W.
CHILTON, N.	MOULTON, F.	†BAILEY, G.
CREES, J.	NODEN, J.	†BROOKS, S.
DAVIES, A. G. P.	PARRY, W.	†COLLINSON, J. H.
DEMETRIADI, G. C.	PEARSON, F.	†CONDRON, J.
DEMETRIADI, A. C.	PICKARD, J. S.	†GILES, J. P.
DIGAN, H.	POTTAGE, F.	†GOWENLOCK, W.
ECCLES, J.	ROWLAND, T. V.	†GREEN, T.
EDWARDS, A.	SIMPSON, C.	†MORRISON, G.
FLINT, A.	SMITH, F.	†PRESCOTT, J.
FLINT, F.	SMITH, W. H.	†PHILLIPS, A.
FRASER, T.	STANLEY, J.	†TIPPETTS, A.
GREENHALGH, W.	STREET, S.	†TOMMINS, J. B.
GUILDFORD, C.	TAYLOR, A.	†VENABLES, J.
HAYDOCK, F.	TAYLOR, J.	†WHITE. F.

Refuge Assurance Company, Ltd.
(See p. 596 in Roll of Honour.)

AITKIN, A.	HACKER, J. H.	RACE, J. A.
ALDCROFT, R. D.	HALL, A.	RADCLIFFE, B.
ANDERSON, C.	HALL, E.	ROBINSON, F.
ASHTON, A.	HALLAM, F. A	ROWSON, P.
AUCHTERLONIE, C.	HARRISON, T.	SANDERS, A.
	HAWTHORNE, W.	SEEL, T.
BAGULEY, A. J.	HAYNES, C.	SMALLSHAW, R. W.
BAINES, J.	HEATH, J.	SMITH, A.
BARBER, W. F.	HENRYS, W.	SMITH, H.
BARKER, A.	HIGSON, E. G.	SMITH, R.
BASS, F. N.	HIGSON, H.	SMITH, W.
BATTERSBY, R.	HORNER, B.	PROCTOR.
BEELEY, F. S.	JEPSON, S.	STIRRUP, G.
BEELEY, T. C.	JOHNSON, S.	STOTT, W.
BENNETT, R.	JUMP, G.	SUTTON, B. J.
BOTTERILL, R.	LEACH. J	THOMAS, G.
BRADSHAW, G.	LEWIS, R.	TURNER, T.
BRIDGE, N.	LITTLEFAIR, J. T.	WALLIS, H. A.
BURNS, J. M.	LOWE, J.	WALKER, W.
BYRNE, J.	MATTHEWS, A.	WALTON, W. T.
BYRNE, W.	McCRACKEN, J.	WARD, W.
CHAPMAN. H.	MELL, A.	WEDGE, C.
COOPER, R.	METCALFE, C. F.	WILSON, C.
CROOK, J. G.	MOORES, E. M.	WHITTAKER, A. B.
DAVIES, F.	MORRIS, W. E.	WHITTAKER, W. G.
DAVIES, J. J.	O'REILLY, M. P.	WILLIAMS, W.
ENTWISTLE, E.	PEPWORTH, C. A.	WILLIS, F.
FARDELL, G.	PEPWORTH, F.	WILKINSON, A. W.
GANLEY, W.	PRESTON, H.	WOOD, C. E.
GARDNER, F.	QUARMBY, A.	WOODHOUSE, D. A.

Ritchie and Eason.
(See p. 696 in Roll of Honour.)

EASON, W. H.	PARTINGTON, T.	FIRTH, J.
WHEATLEY, R.	MULLINEUX, W.	†CRITCHLOW, RD.
SMITH, G.	SMITH, W.	†POWIS, A.
ASHWORTH, J.	PRIESTLEY, F.	

George Robinson and Co.
(See p. 598 in Roll of Honour.)

ROBINSON, N. O.	INGHAM, D.	SHARP, F.
RODIER, J. H.	INGHAM, E.	SMITH, R.
ALLEN, W. R.	IRVING, W.	TAGGART, C. S.
BENNETT, M. A.	JOHNSON, T. C. W.	TIPPING, E.
BESWICK, T.	JOHNSON, J.	WADSWORTH, L.
BRISTOL, B.	LORD, E.	WHITLOW, F.
CAMERON, G. A.	LOWE, F.	WHITEHEAD, N.
DANIEL, J. E.	McKILL, W.	WILLIAMS, A. J.
DIXON, T.	MERCER, W.	WILLIAMS, A.
FOSTER, H.	ROLES, H.	WRIGHT, W.
GARTSIDE, R. W.	ROWAN, E.	
HICKS, T.	ROYLANCE, A.	

In addition 26 Employees failed to pass the Medical Test.

† Rejected.

Redpath, Brown and Co., Ltd.
(See p. 692 in Roll of Honour.)

COWAN, A. W.	NICOL, W.	WINDSOR, F.
CHADWICK, G. E.	BENTLEY, W.	GERRITTY, P. J.
RICHARDSON, A.	CROMPTON, W.	JONES, E.
WALTON, P.	DICKSON, W.	GREEN, J. W.
MOIR, A. W.	GOSNAY, W.	JONES, H.
OLIVE, J.	TATTERSALL, A.	O'CONNELL, M.
JONES, G.	BELL, G.	ROBERTS, W.
LOWE, A.	HOY, J.	RICHARDS, A. J.
HEWITSON, H.	MILLINGTON, T.	WILLIAMS, J. E.
KAY, W.	DAVIES, W.	ASTBURY, F. W.
JONES, M. H.	PULLEIN, W.	OLIVE, W.
TAYLOR, T.	MILLINGTON, A.	McLEOD, J.
TAYLOR, R.	EVANS, F.	FYSH, A.
HASLAM, A.	ATKISS, B.	FOSTER, J. C.
LANE, E.	MILLINGTON, J.	DAVIES, T.
RUSSELL, G.	DIXON, A.	CRAWFORD, A.
OSBORNE, A. E.	WARHURST, J.	SWINDELLS, J. H.
DEAKIN, H.	HILL, H.	JACKSON, J. T.
RICHARDSON, J.	EAVES, H.	BOWYER, R.
WILSON, J.	DRINKWATER, J.	ROBINSON, T.
WILSON, F.	AINSWORTH, T.	ROWAN, J.
FOSTER, W.	MARSDEN, G.	BOWDEN, W.
EVANS, A.	SAVILE, J.	GIBBONS, T.
ROBERTS, A.	SHAW, W.	SHAW, W. F.
DRINKWATER, W.	DAVIES, W. T.	WILCOXEN, J. C.
BROADBENT, W.	CARTMELL, J.	JONES, R. W.
DRINKWATER, E.	CRIPPS, E.	BURLEY, A.
CLARK, A.	FISHER, C.	LAMB, W.
CONWELL, R.	TAYLOR, W.	AINSWORTH, F.
BOYES, J.	STANTON, S.	CAUSER, G.
WILSON, P.	BARBER, L.	HEALEY, T.
BUCHANAN, J.	FIRTH, W.	GOCKELEN, F. H.
JONES, R.	SMITH, H.	CONWELL, E.
HUNT, G.	JOHNSON, E.	HENRY, J.
HAIGH, G.	WALTON, J.	ALDRIDGE, A.
REDFERN, J.	MOORCROFT, V. T.	SOUTH, E.
RICHARDSON, H.	DUTSON, P.	ELSTON, A.
PENRICE, H.	WRIGHT, S.	SWALLOW, A.
VERNON, W.	WHAWELL, G.	HELLIWELL, J.
GRACE, A.	BAILEY, E.	NEWSOME, J. W.
LOUGHLIN, W.	JONES, T. H.	FAIRCLOUGH, E.
DICKINSON, J.	MINSHULL, J.	GARDNER, R.
PATERSON, T.	STOCKWELL, T.	BATEMAN, G.
HUGHES, H. M.	DAVIES, O. S.	HARVEY, H.
MACMILLAN, J.		

Reiss Bros.
(See p. 593 in Roll of Honour.)

STUBBS, W.	TATE, D.	†KERSHAW, H.
WILLIAMS, C. S.	BRAMLEY, H.	†SEFTON, N.
ELLIS, V.	TAYLOR, W.	†ROGERSON, S.
MARSDEN, J.	ALDRED, H.	†WHITEHILL, A.
BOARDMAN, M.	POOLE, W.	†HOUSLEY, H.
LIGHTFOOT, J.	†BAZLEY, E.	†VAYRO, R.
HINDLEY, J.	†CHAPMAN, E.	†JOHNSON, J.
THORNTON, W.	†GREENHALGH, W. E.	†OPENSHAW, —
WHITNEY, A.	†HARROP, A.	†LEGGE, F.
WHYATT, F.		†HARDY, J.
OGDEN, W.		

J. F. and H. Roberts, Ltd.
(See p. 599 in Roll of Honour.)

ALEXANDER, A.	GIBSON, A.	THOMPSON, E.
BARTON, E.	HAMPSON, W.	VEVERS, F.
BARBER, A. H.	HULLEY, B.	WILKINSON, J.
BREAKELL, A. E.	HORTON, T.	WIGGAN, A.
BRADSHAW, H.	HAYNES, W. E.	WADE, A.
BOFFEY, F.	HIBBITTS, W. J.	WILSON, F.
BROOKES, F.	JOHNSON, J.	WALSH, J. R.
BUTTERS, G.	KNOTT, G. H.	†BUCKLEY, F.
BELL, C. F.	LEATHERBARROW	†CORDWELL, R.
BATES, H.	LEDIARD, A.	†CORDOCK, H.
BRAZIER, F. A.	MATHER, R.	†COOKE, E.
COATES, T.	MORRIS, G.	†GILL, E.
CHADFIELD, H.	McLEOD, J. A.	†GREENWOOD, R.
CARTER, J. F.	McEWEN, C. D.	†JOHNSON, J.
CHADWICK, J.	NAYLOR, M. J.	†KNIGHT, A. K.
CROFT, T.	OLDHAM, J.	†LAMBERT, J.
DAWSON, T.	OLDHAM, WM.	†LIVESEY, F.
DAVIES, S. W.	OWEN, J.	†MERRICK, A. E.
DOGGETT, W.	PIERCE, N.	†McKENZIE, J.
DOXEY, G.	POTTS, H.	†ORCHARD, E.
ETCHELLS, E.	PLATT, E.	†PAIGE, S. J.
ELLIS, A.	POWELL, G. S.	†PORTWOOD, W.
FORRESTER, —	PARKER, R.	†ROBINSON, H.
FOLEY, M.	RODEN, A.	†SIMMONDS, L.
FRANCE, M.	ROBERTS, F.	†THORP, G.
FISH, P. C.	ROOK, G.	†WILLIAMS, F.
FLINT, E.	SAVAGE, F.	†WALKER, R. A.
GOULD, S.	SANDERSON, F.	†WARBURTON, J.
GEORGE, W. B.	SMITH, W. A.	
GREENWOOD, J. P.	SMITH, W.	

† Rejected.

Rose, Hewitt and Co.
(See p. 600 in Roll of Honour.)

HEWITT, O.
NALL, P.
DRABBLE, R.
ROGERS, J.
GURLEY, H. W.
ROBERTS, C.
HARDWICK, G.
PRICE, H.
SCHOFIELD, G.
MONTGOMERY, W.
PRUNIER, P.
HARDMAN, F.

Mill, Skipton.

HEWITT, F.
ROBERTS, G. W.
LANCASTER, H.
BREAKILL, T.
MITCHELL, H.
SWIRE, T.
GARNETT, A.
FURNESS, F.
PIKE, L.
MACRAE, G.
BAKER, J. T.

E. Rothwell and Sons.
(See p. 601 in Roll of Honour.)

*ROTHWELL, A.
*ROTHWELL, V.
*AINSWORTH, E.
*WADSWORTH, S.
*YATES, T.
*WORSLEY, T.
*CLOUGH, H.
*LEA, W.
*MATHER, F.
*MELLING, W.
WALKER, A.
*ROBERTS, E. G.
*BROOME, H.
*WORDEN, R.
BUCKLEY, J.
ROYLE, R.
*COOPER, J.
FARNWORTH, T.
MORRIS, W.
CAWTHORNE, J.
CARTLEDGE, W. H.
MONAGHAN, H.
SCOWCROFT, F.
BALDWIN, H.
SMYTHE, F. C.
HANCOCK, F.
TURNER, W. M.
RICHARDSON, A.
JONES, O. M.
PARKER, J. V.
COOK, H.
GREGORY, C.
ROYLE, J.
ASHBURNER, J.
GREENHALGH, J.
*MULLINEUX, H.
COUCILL, J. T.
PENNINGTON, S.
HARDMAN, W.
WILLIAMSON, A.
BROOKES, J.
HADFIELD, S. J.
HADFIELD, A. L.
CORSIE, W. A. C.

Royce Limited.
(See p. 691 in Roll of Honour.)

ALDRED, E.
ANDERSON, A. W.
ANLEZARK, T.
ASHTONHURST, W.
BAILEY, P. N.
BAGSHAW, J.
BARKER, M.
BARNETT, J. H.
BAYLEY, W.
BERRY, J.
BLACKSHAW, H.
BOOTH, W. S.
BRADSHAW, D.
BRENNAN, J.
BRERETON, G.
BROADBENT, H.
BULLOCK, P.
BUTTERWORTH, A.
CAPPER, F.
CHALLINOR, H.
CHILTON, F. E.
CONNOR, J. J.
CONSTANTINE, W. E.
CORBISHLEY, J. H.
CRABTREE, J. H.
CRAVEN, J. E.
CROSS, J. E.
CROSS, S. J.
CROWTHER, J.
DAVIES, R. M.
DAVIS, J. H.
DALZIEL, J.
DUNN, P.
DUNNING, C. J.
EDMONDSON, H.
FAWCETT, H.
FLOOD, W.
FROST, W.
GADD, H.
GEE, F.
GOODWIN, E.
GRAY, G.
GREEN, T. H.
GRIEVE, J. H.
HACKIN, J.
HALL, F.
HALLAM, A.
HAWORTH, C.
HEVER, L. F.
HEYWOOD, J.
HIGTON, A.
HOLMES, G.
HOPKINS, H.
HOPWOOD, J.
HOUGH, J.
HUDGHTON, G.
ILLINGWORTH, T. I.
JACKSON, W.
JONES, B.
JONES, G.
KERSHAW, S. A.
LARGE, G.
LEECH, G.
LEIGH, B.
LIDBETTER, J.
LINDSEY, G.
MADDOCKS, R.
MARTIN, F.
MATTERSON, W. C. M.
MATTHEWS, R.
MAYES, F.
McCULLOCH, D. N.
McLEAN, J.
MOLYNEUX, T.
MORRISON, W.
MURRAY, J.
NELSON, W.
NUTTALL, J.
NEWTON, A.
OWEN, J. F.
PAGE, J.
PALMER, H.
PRICE, A.
PRICE, E. A.
RAMSEY, W.
ROUTLEDGE, J.
RUDDY, T.
ROYLE, J.
SHARPLES, F.
SHAW, T.
SMITH, C.
SMITH, G.
SMITH, L.
SMITH, W.
SNAITH, W.
SPACKMAN, H.
SPANN, R.
STAINSBY, H.
TAYLOR, E.
TAYLOR, W. H.
TEGGART, E.
THOMPSON, F.
TOBIN, J.
TOMLINSON, A.
TOWNLEY, W. J. D.
TURNER, W. B.
WAINWRIGHT, F.
WALKER, F.
WALLWORK, R.
WASEY, T.
WHISKER, W.
WHITEHEAD, E. J.
WHITTAKER, W.
WINSTANLEY, S. W.
WOOD, W.
YATES, J.
YOUNGE, W. H.

Rylands and Sons, Ltd.
(See p. 602 in Roll of Honour.)
New High Street.

ANDREW, F.
ATACK, T.
ARMSTRONG, R. H.
ANDREW, A. E.
ALDERSON, H. S.
AYRES, E.
ATKINSON, P.
ARDRON, W.
AINSCOW, J.
ANDERSON, W. M.
ALTY, J.
ALDRIDGE, S.
AINSWORTH, C.
ASHTON, W. H.
BEACH, H.
BEEDON, W.
BURTON, A.
BARDISBANIAN, P.
BAMFORD, S.
BARDSLEY, J.
BYRNE, J. H.
BORLAND, R.
BROWN, J. J.
BARROWCLOUGH, E.
BOWEN, E. C.
BURNS, J.
BAYLISS, W. F.
BENNETT, S.
BROWNE, J. W.
BAIRD, J. H.
BROWN, J.
BEECH, W.

* Serving with the colours.

Rylands and Sons, Ltd.—Con.

BEESLEY, G. H.
BALL, H.
BURTON, S.
BARRATT, T. W.
BUTLER, F.
BOYD, G. H.
BARRATT, H.
BARNES, S.
BOOTH, G. H.
BELLAMY, C. F.
BILLSDEN, G.
BLINKHORN, A.
BOWDEN, R.
BULLMAN, L. G.
BARLOW, J.
BOWDEN, H.
BENNETT, J.
BROADY, T.
BARNES, H.
BAGULEY, W. H.
BOWYER, G.
BOSTOCK, P.
BERWICK, P.
BROWN, A.
BOYLAN, T.
BARRETT, A. H.
BUCHAN, T.
CALDWELL, H. B.
CHAMBERLAIN, W. H.
CHATBURN, A.
CUNDY, L. G.
CLARKSON, A.
CLOUGH, J.
COLLINGWOOD, S.
CONNOR, J.
CONNELL, J. H.
COMPTON, E.
CHAPMAN, T. A.
CREIGHTON, J. S.
COLLEY, H.
COTTIER, J. H.
COX, G. S.
COOPER, S.
COWARD, D.
COLLINSON, E. H.
CRAWLEY, G. H.
CARPMEAL, J.
CARR, F.
CHAPMAN, I.
CLARE, P.
CROWTHER, W.
COOKE, S.
CHAPMAN, J.
CATTE, G. W.
CRITCHLOW, A.
CURTIS, C.
CATERALL, F.
CONNEL, A.
CUMMINGS, A.
CLARKE, W. E.
COWBURN, J. H.
COTTERILL, F.
CROOK, J.
CROSS, W. H.
CUDDY, R.
DACE, W.
DAWSON, A.
DONNELLY, J.
DAVIES, F.
DUROSE, T.
DAWSON, T.
DAVENPORT, J.
DAVIES, H.
DENT, C.
DOLAN, G. E.
DIXON, W.
DARWELL, H. O.
DAVIES, J. H.
DEVENPORT, C.
DITCHFIELD, A.
DANIELS, T.
DONELLY, R.
EDGE, W. R.
ELLSE, W.
ECCLES, E. W.
ELLISON, H.
EVANS, H.
ENGLISH, A. C.
ENTWISTLE, E.
FINNIGAN, L.
FINNIGAN, J.
FALSHAW, T. L.
FLETCHER, W. J.
FALLOWS, W.
FARAGHER, T.
FREEMAN, W. C.
FARDELL, O.
FINAN, J.
FARNSWORTH, J.
FREY, G.
FOLLOWS, F. A.
GLEDHILL, J. W.
GARFORTH, J.
GRACE, J.
GREGORY, W.
GILSON, F.
GLOVER, F. T.
GARNER, F. W.
GREEN, H.
GREENLEES, S.
GEE, A. W.
GARDINER, B.
GREEN, W.
HIBBERT, A.
HOWARD, R. C.
HILTON, J.
HOOD, T. T.
HARGREAVES, A.
HOLT, W. H.
HAYNES, W.
HUGHES, J. P.
HOLLAND, J.
HANSON, A.
HARGREAVES, F.
HALLSWORTH, T.
HILTON, H.
HOBSON, B.
HOLYLAND, C. E.
HINCE, S.
HOWELL, L.
HAMER, H.
HILL, T.
HYDE, A.
HILTON, W.
HEATON, J.
HARRISON, J.
HUGHES, J. E.
HUGHES, W.
HUTTON, A. E.
HANDS, T. G.
HAMPSON, A.
HANSON, T. H.
HUSSEY, S.
HULME, J.
HYDE, H.
HEYWOOD, T.
HUMPHREY, W. S.
HOPKINS, J. G.
HUNT, W.
HOUGHTON, P.
HOWARD, A. E.
HOLLOWS, J. H.
HARGREAVES, P.
HARRISON, M.
HULTON, W.
HILTON, H.
HALLAM, W.
HEMMINGS, E.
HOARE, A.
HINDLE, H.
HARGREAVES, W.
HIRST, A. E.
HADFIELD, C.
HOLLINGWORTH, W.
HAWORTH, J. H.
INGRAM, J. C.
IRELAND, T. E.
JERVIS, A.
JACKSON, W. H.
JACKSON, W.
JONES, T. A.
JONES, W.
JONES, T. M.
JONES, T. R.
JONES, G.
JOHNSON, S.
JAMES, J.
JACKSON, H.
KETTLE, T.
KERNAHAN, S.
KNOWLES, V. J.
KERFOOT, F.
KINSEY, W.
LOMAS, L.
LORD, W. B.
LAWSON, G.
LLOYD, J. L.
LITCHFIELD, A. W.
LYTHE, A.
LILLEY, H.
LAST, E.
LAWLER, H.
LORD, J. F.
LEE, W.
LONGSON, G.
MORTON, T.
MARSH, A.
MARSDEN, F.
MELLOR, A.
MELLOR, J.
MILLINGTON, H.
MOSS, S.
McCANN, W.
McCLELLAND, G.
McMORINE, P. A.
MEGSON, W. D.
MARS, F.
McBURNEY, A. C.
MOLYNEUX, S.
MERRICK, S.
MURPHY, J.
MORGAN, P.
MAYSON, J. H. W.
McKENNA, J. A.
MILLWARD, A.
MAGINNIS, F.
MANSELL, E. B.
MILLWARD, J.
McDONALD, F.
MARTIN, J.
MAYO, A.
MASON, F.
MOSS, R.
MULLHALL, D.
MORREY, W.
MOORES, F.
McBURNEY, W. C.
NEWTON, H.
NEW, W. W.
NEWELL, H.
NEWSTEAD, J. E.
NOBLE, W. H.
NEWTON, W.
NICHOLSON, F. R.
NEEDHAM, J.
OGDEN, B.
OWEN, R.
O'BRIEN, J.
OGDEN, J.
OVENS, J.
OGDEN, A. E.
PARRY, E. H.
PLANT, T.
PAINTER, E.
PRESTON, E.
PHILLIPS, W. J.
PROCTOR, W.
PROPHET, H.
PALMER, H.
PEPLOE, C. R.
PENDLETON, J.
PAUL, C.
PINDER, F.
PRINCE, T.
PRESTON, H.
POVALL, W.
PLATT, H.
PODMORE, J.
PONTEFRACT, A. E.
PARKES, R. B.
PAIKIN, H.
PARKES, G.
PRICE, H.
PRICE, C.
POVAH, F. S.
PLANT, E. O.
PRITCHARD, Z.
POYSER, J. H.
PUGH, W.
PICKFORD, W. A.
RICHARDSON, A.
ROTHWELL, W. G.
ROYLE, L.
ROGERSON, S.
ROSEWARNE, J.

Rylands and Sons, Ltd.—Con.

RICHARDSON, H.
RAYNER, F.
ROTHWELL, L.
REYNOLDS, F.
ROBINSON, W.
ROBINSON, C.
REDGRAVE, H. W.
RICHARDS, J.
ROGERS, M. C.
RUSHTON, W.
REID, F.
RATCLIFFE, C.
ROGERSON, J.
ROSTRON, T. S.
SMITH, C.
SINGLETON F. D.
SMITH, W.
SUTTERBY, P. C.
SHAW, A.
SHAW, R. G.
SWEENEY, J.
SANDHAM, E. L.
SPROWSON, W.
SCHOLES, H.
SCOTT, C. H.
SMITH, W. E.
SNAPE, H. B.
SOUTHWARD, J.
SMITH, T.
SEDDON, W.
SYKES, H.
SOWDEN, R.
STOCKTON, J.
STICKLER, F. W.
SMALL, J.
SCALES, T.
STAFFORD, W.
STRINGER, R.
SCHOLES, J. H.
SMITH, A. B.
STANTON, E.
SMITH, W.
SILLK, T. F.
SLACK, A. B.
SMITH, W. R.
SAMPEY, T. J.
SHERLOCK, F.
TILSLEY, V. W.
TAYLOR, A.
TODD, C. E.
TAYLOR, W.
TURNER, A. S.
TETLOW, J. E.
TURNER, G. G. S.
TAYLOR, W. H.
TURNER, F.
TONGUE, J. N.
THOMPSON, W.
TAYLOR, E.
TOMLINSON, J. H.
TOOTHILL, S. A. R.
TIMMINS, R.
TURNER, W. J.
TAYLOR, J. W.
THATCHER, F.
TAYLOR, W.
THOMPSON, W.
UNSWORTH, S. F.
UNDERHILL, S.
VALANTINE, D.
VERNON, G.
VICKERS, J. W.
WORSENCROFT, J. W.
WALSHE, N. R.
WOOD, F.
WILKINSON, H.
WARBURTON, J.
WHITTAKER, E.
WILLIAMS, J. E. G.
WILDE, W.
WOODS, J. H.
WALL, R. E.
WOOD, A.
WRIGHT, A.
WRIGLEY, J.
WOOD, E.
WALHAUSER, E. C.
WILKINSON, F.
WORTHINGTON, E. M.
WILBURN, F.
WRIGHT, R.
WHIPP, T. E.
WILLIAMS, R. R.
WHITTAKER, J. A.
WILSON, J. C.
WHITFIELD, J.
WILLIAMS, G.
WOOD, W. H.
WHELAN, A.
WILLIAMS, H.
WILLIAMS, H. E.
WALKER, Q.
WILKINSON, A.
WALKER, S.
WILLIAMS, G.
WYATT, E.
WILSON, F.
WARD, C. S.
WORTH, J.
WILLIAMSON, J. L.
WORTHINGTON, J.
WHITTER, T. F.
WHITTAKER, A.
WATERHOUSE, R.
WILCOCK, G. E.
WATERS, W. G.
WHITEHURST, W.
YATES, W. H.

Liverpool.

ANDERSON, W.
APPLEBY, S.
BARNES, P.
BYRNE, E. P.
BAINBRIDGE, J.
BOLTON, G.
CASHEN, H. V.
CRAIG, R.
DAVIES, E. W.
DAWSON, S.
DONNELLY, W.
DENNIS, H. A.
FLETCHER, R.
FARAM, A. J.
FOSTER, A. J.
GATHERCOLE, J
GREGOR, J. T.
GOUGH, J. S.
GARDNER, W. C.
GIBBON, J.
HORSWELL, S.
JONES, E. L.
JONES, R. E.
JONES, A.
JONES, R. L.
KIRBY, J.
KENNY, E. A.
LEAVEY, F.
LOMAX, H.
MINSHULL, E.
MACKNEY, W. O.
MOUSIR, F. W.
MORRIS, W. R.
MORGAN, C.
MONTAGU, W.
NEALE, W.
OWEN, F. M.
PARR, I.
PARSONS, J
POTTER, H. M.
POPE, A.
ROBERTS, G. A.
ROBERTS, W.
ROBERTS, E. M.
ROFF, W. J.
ROWLANDS, F.
SNELLING, H.
SHARP, A.
SHAW, H. W.
SMITH, A. H.
THACKWRAY, M.
WALLACE, S. M.
WHITE, H.
WILSON, H. G.
WILLIAMS, R. B.
YARROW, G. D.

100, Portland Street.

GREGSON, J. W.
HARRISON, J. R.
HOLLYWOOD, J.
LAUDER, T.
OWEN, W. J.
PHILLIPS, T.
ROUND, A.
ROYLE, J.
SALMON, C.
SULLIVAN, J.
TUCKER, J. W.
WILLIAMSON, C. W.

Heapey.

AINSWORTH, R.
ASTLEY, R.
ADSHEAD, T.
ADAMS, J.
ASHTON, B.
BENNISON, W.
BOLTON, P.
BARLOW, O.
BILLINGTON, J.
BERRY, J.
BOLTON, T. H.
BRADSHAW, J.
BOOCOCK, A.
CLIFFE, H.
CLIFFE, J.
CLOUGH, R.
COLLINSON, J.
CULLEN, P.
ELLISON, F.
ELLISON, J. A.
ELLISON, R.
FOWLER, F.
FINCH, T.
FARNWORTH, W.
GRIME, F.
GRIME, H.
HEATON, R. E.
HOUGHTON, J.
IRELAND, J.
JOLLY, T.
JOYCE, J.
KETTLE, M.
KAY, D.
KIRBY, J.
LIVESEY, C.
LIVESEY, W.
LIVESEY, A. H.
LOWE, H.
MILLER, W.
MARSDEN, A.
MANGNALL, E
NORRIS, W.
ODDIE, H.
OWENS, T.
PILKINGTON, R.
RIGBY, R.
READ, J.
RIGBY, W.
RIDING, W.
RIDING, W.
SCOTT, H.
SANDIFORD, G.
SOUTHWORTH, J.
SLATER, H.
SEDDON, J.
SPIERS, F.
SIMMS, H.
TYRER, J.
TYRER, T.
VAUSE, W.
WARBURTON, R.
WIGGLESWORTH, J.
WALSH, T.
WIGNALL, J. H.
WHITWAM, A.
WESTHEAD, T.
WHITTAKER, D.

Chorley.

ADAMS, T. H.
ATHERTON, A.
BAMBER, J.
COPPOCK, G.
CATTERALL, G.
CLUBB, W.
CRITCHLEY, H.
EVANS, T.
FADDEN, J. J.
GERRARD, J.
GRIFFITHS, H.
GASKELL, J.
HODGKINSON, R.
HUSTINGS, T.
HODGKINSON, H.
HATCH, T.
MORGAN, W. E.
MITTON, A.
MELLOR, R.
PLATT, P.
SOLLOWAY, T.
STATHAM, T. V.
TAYLOR, W.
TAYLOR, F.
TOOTELL, J.
WRIGHT, R.
WILSON, W.
WRIGHT, W. J.
WARING, T.
WILDING, F.

Wigan.

ASHTON, J.
ATHERTON, P.
BROWN, J. W.
BEESLEY, J. T.
BEESLEY, A. J.
CARTER, J.
DAWBER, J.
DUNN, J.
FAIRHURST, J. W.
FOSTER, H.
GRINDLEY, A. L.
HODKINSON, C. L.
HUNT, G.
HESKETH, W.
JONES, J.
LANCASTER, J.
LEARY, J.
ROUND, R.
WADE, T. R.
WINSTANLEY, P.
WINSTANLEY, G.
WATSON, T. H.

Gorton.

BRADLEY, W. B.
CLEMENTS, J.
GRAHAM, E.
KILBURN, W.
McHALE, P.
NICHOLAS, H.
STAFFORD, I.
SUTTON, T.
STOPFORD, C.
SUMNER, G.
WRIGHT, H.
WILCOX, A.

Dacca Twist Co.

BROCKLEHURST, E.
CROFT, A.
EMERSON, W.
MIDDLETON, G.
RALPHS, H.
ROYLE, J.
WHYATT, A.

Swinton.

BURTON, A.
BOLESWORTH, G.
BOLESWORTH, W. E.
BOARDMAN, H.
CASS, V.
CASH, T.
COLLIER, J.
COOPER, R.
FISH, T.
GORTON, E.
HASTLE, J.
HASTLE, H.
HODGKINSON, T.
JOHNSON, A.
KENYON, W.
LOMAS, F.
MASON, H.
PAYNE, H.
ROYLE, E.
RICHARDSON, B.
STANLEY, A.
SEDDON, F.
SHARPLES, J.
SHARPLES, H.
WALTON, R.

Longford Works.

ADAMS, T.
ASHWORTH, A.
ASHTON, J.
BROWN, F.
CAPPER, C.
CUMMING, J.
COLTON, W.
CLUNIE, J.
CLARK, W.
FAIRCLOUGH, L.
FELL, J.
FOSTER, A.
FINGLETON, W.
GRONNOW, A.
HALL, W.
HOLGATE, J.
HALL, R.
KIRK, J.
MARA, W.
MILLS, R.
McBURNEY, D.
NORCROSS, I.
PAYNE, H.
PEAKE, H.
PATERSON, A.
PORTER, A.
SHERLOCK, R.
SHEPHERD, W.
STUBBS, J.
SHERRATT, T.
SILWOOD, B.
TANT, C.
VALENTINE, H.
WRIGHT, J.
WILLIAMSON, H.
WANSTON, W.

G. B. Street Stables.

BROOKS, J. N.
GREEN, H.
HAMLETT, E. W.
HOLLAND, S.
NODEN, W.
NICHOLSON, R.
OPENSHAW, D.
PENDLETON, J.
PRIEST, J. J.
PRICE, T.
THORLEY, W.
VALENTINE, J. T.

C. E. Samuels and Co.
(See p. 699 in Roll of Honour.)

LAWRENCE, F. A.
TAYLOR, A. G.
WHITAKER, E. J.
WILKINSON, T. H.

Schill Brothers, Ltd.
(See p. 608 in Roll of Honour.)

CHEETHAM, G. T.
CLEMMET, L.
COATES, H.
FIELDEN, J. H.
HALL, G.
HOLT, A.
LINDSAY, R.
MARSDEN, C. L.
SCHOLES, A.

Robert Scott and Co.
(See p. 610 in Roll of Honour.)

SCHOFIELD, J.
McCORMACK, J. A.
JACKSON, S. W.
BRASH, H.
PATERSON, L.
GROVE, W.
BRADBURY, H.
DOHERTY, J.

G. I. Sidebottom and Co.
(See p. 698 in Roll of Honour.)

SIDEBOTTOM, G. B.
STROUD, G. S.
FITTON, W. F.
BAKER, A.
DALLEY, J.
FARAGHER, F.
HACKETT, G. A.
HILLS, D.
McMAHON, J.

Scottish Widows' Fund Life Assurance Society.
(See p. 606 in Roll of Honour.)

SPENCE, J. F. D.   DODKINS, P. H.

The Shrewsbury and Challiner Tyre Co., Ltd.
(See p. 712 in Roll of Honour.)

Staff.
SHANKLAND, H.   IRVING, W.   BELL, A. F.
PROCTOR, N. G.   CHAPMAN, W.
GRAINGER, A.   DEWHURST, A.

Works.
QUINN, H.   BROCKLEHURST, H.   BROOKS, J.
HALL, R.   GIRVIN, J.
BATES, H.   BLOOMER, F.   MEADOWCROFT, A.
FIELDING, R.   ALSTON, G.
FRYER, C.   HARDMAN, P.   BILLINGTON, H.
LANG, J.   RATCLIFFE, G. A.   FOXTON, J.
MASSEY, A.   PARRY, F.   SHARKEY, F.
GREENALL, H.   KIND, J.   FOSTER, W.
GRIMSHAW, J.   RANDALL, T.   BAGSHAW, R.
BROWN, R.   WILSON, H.   POLLITT, J.
WRIGHT, J. W.   RAWLINSON, J.   FARNLEY, R.
PURDY, R. J.   BUTLER, H.   LATHWOOD, A. E.
BARLOW, W.   FLETCHER, F.   LATHAM, H.
McKENZIE, W.   DUTTON, E.   PEARSON, W.
ELPHICK, F.   MITCHELL, T.   HARDMAN, R. L.
DUTTON, B.   WARD, G.   TIERNEY, D. G.
READ, J.   COLLINS, H.   LUNT, F.
PAULDEN, A.   MEE, T.   CADMAN, F.
PICKFORD, J.   MELLOR, W.   ARMSTRONG, H.
HOLLAND, A.   MALPAS, S.   HARROP, W.
HALL, H.   BRIERLEY, R.   CANAVAN, D.
TOPPING, H.   WILLIAMSON, C.   ANDERSON, J.
MARTIN, C.   MADDOX, G. H.   BULLOCK, A.
DALEY, B.   MAHONEY, R.   HUNT, T.
LOMAX, P.   YATES, D.   TOMKINSON, S.
IRWIN, H.   CARSON, L.   CLOHERTY, J.
HOLLAND, H.   BAXENDALE, C.   ROBERTS, H.
ADAMS, S.   JONES, A.   BRENNAN, J.
STANSFIELD, A. E.   KEELING, E.   HUGHES, R.
DEAN, G.   BIGGINS, E.   CILGRAIN, P.
LANG, R.   BUCKLER, E.   BROOKS, F. W.
SKELLY, J.   BEEMAN, C. H.   BILLINGHAM, C.
MOLLOY, W.   ECKFORD, J.   ROGERS, A.
SIMISTER, J.   WOLFENDEN, R.   THOMPSON, J. W.

Simon, Son and Co.
(See p. 610 in Roll of Honour.)

BLAND, H.   SMITH, R. C.   †HARGREAVES, C. G.
RILEY, W. H.   DENNISON, C. W.
GREENWOOD, H.   HAWKES, F.   †BROOME, A.

Henry Simon, Ltd.
(See p. 611 in Roll of Honour.)

SIMON, E. D.   NUTTALL, G. A.   BOULTON, B. D.
*WILLIAMS, L.   WALLWORK, H.   BARKER, H. W.
WILLIAMS, C.   HELLIWELL, L.   ATHERTON, H.
WALDER, H.   ANDERSON, G. M.   RAINS, S. A.
PERRY, F.   BENTHAM, C.   CHAPMAN, J.
DAVIES, F.   WEBSTER, W.   PALMER, C.
KININMONTH, P.   WHEELER, J. G.   SIMPSON, A. G.
   *BARNES, C.   LOCKLEY, G.
NEILL, H.   MILBURN, A.   *HOLT, J. V.
SMITH, J. S.   SCHOFIELD, J. H.   *WILD, W. J.
FISH, H.   BURTON, H.   LEDGER, C.
GUTTERIDGE, J.   ISHERWOOD, A.

Simpson and Godlee, Ltd.
(See p. 612 in Roll of Honour.)

MARRISON, B. W.   YOUDE, T.   BAXENDALE, C.
ALLEN, A.   BOON, J.   DONNELLY, E.
ALLCOCK, I.   COWAN, R.   GIBSON, A.
GLADWELL, L. V.   STOCKDALE, A.   SLACK, W.
ADIN, J. H.   WALKDEN, C.   CLEMENTS, J.
HUDSON, A.   CLARKE, P.   BROWN, H. V.
HETHERINGTON, T.   PASK, N.   HARRINGTON, A.
   McCULLOCH, J.   GOLDING, J.
BLACK, V.   STANHOPE, T. B.   SAYWELL, A.
KIERNAN, A. A.   GEE, H.   WILKINSON, A.
CONBOY, W.   BARR, W.   WOOD, A.
MORRIS, J.   PARTINGTON, W.   COHEN, M.
REYNOLDS, J.   GODDARD, A.
WALLWORK, A.   WESTON, J. W.

Sivewright, Bacon and Co.
(See p. 614 in Roll of Honour.)

BACON, W. H.   LORD, H.   WOOD, W.
BUTLER, H. A.   SHAW, H.

* Since Enlisted.   † Rejected.

Henry and Leigh Slater, Ltd.
(See p. 615 in Roll of Honour.)

ARNOLD, H.   FURNESS, J.   OPENSHAW, T. E.
ARTHUR, A.   FURNESS, T.   SHELDON, S.
BANN, R. E.   GASKELL, A.   SLATER, C. F. L.
BASS, A.   HALL, H.   SLATER, H. S. L.
BENNETT, A.   HALLIWELL, E.   STEWART, N.
BURY, H.   HARRISON, J. A.   STRINGER, F.
BRINKLOW, A.   HODGKINSON, P.   TINSLEY, F.
BROADHEAD, W.   HOLYOAKE, T. H.   WEAVER, E.
BROWN, A.   KERSHAW, W. T.   WHEELTON, A.
BURGESS, H.   LOMAS, H.   WHISTON, A.
BUTT, A.   MAYERS, H.   WHISTON, C.
CAMPBELL, E.   MERVYN, A. S.   WHITEHURST, W.
CLARKE, H.   MOTTRAM, E. J.   WILDGOOSE, J.
COE, A.   NEWHAM, O.   WILLISON, F. H.
CROSIER, G.   NEWTON, H.   WOOD, R.
DUFFIELD, W.   NICHOLLS, F.   WOOLLEY, C. L.
FAULKNER, S.   OLDFIELD, J.   WRIGHT, S.

Joshua Smith, Limited.
(See p. 618 in Roll of Honour.)

ANDERSON, W.   HORSFALL, F.   PARKER, A.
CADMAN, O.   MARSHALL, W.   SLOAN, F.
DAVIES, A.   NICHOLLS, P.   THOMPSON, H.

Smith and Coventry, Ltd.
(See p. 617 in Roll of Honour.)

ATHERTON, J.   GOSS, C.   PORTER, R.
ANDERSON, W. M.   GRIFFITHS, T.   PONTIFRACT, A.
AVERNS, R. E.   GREENHOUGH, W.   PAYLOR, C.
ARMSTRONG, G.   GROSSIT, R.   PASK, A.
AUSTIN, J.   GRIFFITHS, W.   POWELL, J.
ANNABLE, E.   HORROCKS, H.   PEARSON, G.
ASHALL, W.   HOGG, J.   PARKER, R.
ANDERSON, F.   HIGHCOCK, F.   QUINN, C.
BALSHAW, E. P.   HATTON, E.   RICHARDSON, A.
BARLOW, J.   HIGSON, J. A.   RIGBY, A.
BROWN, W. H.   HAMPTON, T. J.   ROBINSON, J.
BROWN, A.   HAMPSON, W.   ROBINSON, W.
BECKETT, A.   HARDY, H.   RATCLIFFE, J.
BOWERS, E.   HAWORTH, A.   RIDINGS, A.
BOTTOMLEY, H.   JONES, J.   RILEY, A.
BECKETT, H.   JACKSON, W. S.   ROYLE, W.
BRIDGE, W.   JEFFERS, H.   RALPHS, W.
BACON, A.   JOHNSON, J.   SHAWCROSS, H. F.
BAKER, H.   JORDAN, S.   SMITH, J.
BROWN, H.   LAW, W.   STANTON, G.
CARTER, W.   LOCKWOOD, R.   STEVENSON, E.
CHAPMAN, J.   LERESCH, C. H.   SMITH, S. A.
COOK, W.   LOCKETT, J. H.   SPLAINE, J.
CARSLAKE, G.   LAMBERT, M.   SHARPLES, F.
CARNEY, J.   LEE, G. H.   STEELE, W. D.
CLAYPOLE, C.   LOWE, J.   STANSFIELD, F.
COXHILL, T. J.   LEE, R.   SHARPLES, A.
CURRIE, J.   LEAH, H.   STACEY, E. A.
DAVIES, J.   McMAHON, B.   TAYLOR, J.
DUTTON, J.   McLOUGHLIN, J.   THOMAS, F.
DAY, L.   MARSDEN, W.   TAYLOR, J.
EDWARDS, J.   MARSDEN, F.   TOMLINSON, C.
ECCLES, G.   McDERMOTT, L.   TIBBS, A.
EGGLESTON, T.   MARR, A.   TOOLE, R.
ELLAMS, A.   MAIN, A.   TURNER, H.
EPWORTH, A.   MERRICK, A.   VALELLEY, P.
ECCLES, S.   McCARTHY, J.   VICKERS, H.
ENTWISTLE, A.   MORGAN, J.   WORTH, C.
ECCLES, T.   NICHOLLS, S.   WHEAWILL, R.
EDWARDS, W.   NEAL, W.   WORSLEY, J.
FARRAR, G. F.   NICHOLSON, T.   WAUGH, J.
FORREST, J.   OAKES, P. E.   WILKINSON, J. W.
FORD, H.   OWEN, T.   WARD, A.
FISHER, E.   OWEN, R.   WHARTON, J.
GLEAVE, A.   PEEL, W.   WHARTON, L.
GOODWIN, J.   POWELL, B.   WILLIAMS, L.
GALLAGHER, J.   PRICE, A.   YOUNG, P.

J. T. Smith & J. T. Jones, Ltd.
(See p. 616 in Roll of Honour.)

ALBISON, J.   FIRBY, C.   ROBINSON, G.
BURLEY, A.   FARRELL, E.   RAMPLEY, H. R.
BAXTER, C.   HIBBERT, R.   RACKETT, W. J.
BARRETT, J.   JACK, H.   SIMISTER, E.
BOYLAN, F.   JACKSON, R.   TENNANT, E. R.
BERRY, J.   KIRK, E.   TOMLINSON, R.
BIELBY, P.   KINGSTON, G.   TONGE, R.
BARKER, W. R.   LOMAS, W.   WILKINSON, A.
COLLIER, T. H.   MARLOR, R.   WILSON, F.
DAWES, A.   PRIGG, G.   WINTER, J.
DALTON, T.   PARKIN, H. C.   WELCH, S.
EVANS, J.   PEERS, L.   WINDSOR, T.

The Southern Cotton Oil Co. of Great Britain, Ltd.
(See p. 620 in Roll of Honour.)

BARRY, J. C.	HARDY, L. J.	MONKS, E.
BARON, H.	HARRIS, G.	O'NEILL, J.
BOLLINGTON, R.	HESSIAN, J.	ROOMES, A.
BRADBURN, C.	HULL, A. A.	SEED, J. F.
DANNETT, H.	JENKINSON, J.	STEVENS, W. E.
GALWEY, J. J.	JONES, J. M.	STEWART, F.
GREENHALGH, J.	LUCAS, T.	TORRANCE, R. T.
HARDY, W. E. J	MARQUIS, C.	

Sparrow, Hardwick and Co.
(See p. 622 in Roll of Honour.)

SPARROW, A. C. G.	HARRIS, J.	†BLEACKLEY, E. E.
HORN, W. T.	ILLSTON, W. R.	†BAGSHAW, A.
PLOWRIGHT, H.	JONES, G.	†BURKE, S.
GEMMELL, A.	JONES, T.	†COLE, G.
BUTTERWORTH, B.	MAGAW, R.	†COOKSON, E.
ATKINSON, T.	NAIRN, J. G.	†CHARTRES, R.
ATKINSON, A.	SACKVILLE, F. E.	†DODGSON, M.
ASHWORTH, R.	SHILSTON, F.	†DUNN, J. E.
ADAMS, H.	SIMPSON, J. A.	†FOULKES, E. W.
BLACKIE, A. J.	SAMS, T.	†GREGORY, F.
BARLOW, E.	THOMASON, F.	†HOLLAND, W.
BURROWS, L. H.	TAYLOR, W.	†HARDWICK, F.
CROSS, J.	TYSON, J.	†HESKETH, S.
CATHCART, P.	TYSON, J. C.	†LATHAM, Z.
CLARE, C.	TAYLOR, H.	†PITT, W.
COTTERALL, J. S.	OSBORNE, T.	†ROBERTS, J. W.
CARTER, J. W.	WHITE, C. G.	†SPINKS, H. E.
DAVY, A.	WALLER, J. H.	†TILSLEY, C.
DAVIS, H.	FOULDES, F.	†WILSON, J. M. C.
VEVERS, H.	LONGDEN, F.	†WOOD, J.
FIRTH, J.	WILSON, W.	†WILD, A.
GRIFFITHS, G. T.	KELLY, A. T.	†LOWTHER, A.
GREEN, A. E.	PLANT, C.	†SCALES, J.
HAXBY, E.	CURRIE, A.	†WOODWARD, H.
HILL, W. H.	BUXTON, E.	†KAY, G.
HOLDEN, P.	FOTHERGILL, —	†MALLAN, H. E.
HOPE, E.	†SABIN, F.	†LATHAM, A. E.
HULME, S.	†BLAGBROUGH, C.	†WHITE, L.
HORROCKS, F.	†APTHOMAS, R.	

Hugh Stevenson and Sons, Ltd.
(See p. 626 in Roll of Honour.)

MAYERS, A. W.	BUSH, H.	WARRELL, A.
KEAY, C.	HATTON, F.	BEECHEY, J.
PERRINS, C. H.	BLATHERWICK, T.	BETTS, F.
DRONSFIELD, F.	POOLE, T.	DOBSON, J.
CONN, E.	TOOLE, E.	EDWARDS, W.
MARCUS, D.	SOWDON, B.	BROWN, W.
PROCTOR, J. H.	CHEETHAM, C.	SULLIVAN, J.
ATKINSON, J.	HULSTON, T.	CROOKS, A.
MACKINNON, C.	KENYON, G.	EDWARDS, H.
MARSH, F.	NORRIS, M.	THOMPSON, H.
HATTON, A.	WILKINS, J.	JORDAN, D.
ROBINSON, JOHN.	CLARK, W.	JORDAN, C.
ROBINSON, JOE.	HOOPER, T.	ROBINSON-NIXON, J.
SHEERIN, J.	STENNING, H.	BIRD, C.
STEVENSON, J.	SHIELDS, T.	STALLARD, H.
JAMIESON, A.	BROWN, A.	COOK, H.
HIBBERT, C.	THOMPSON, A.	BEITH, A.
GOLDSTONE, H.	SKINNER, W.	SMEATON, A.
ROBINSON, A.	WAIN, H.	BROWN, D.
AMES, J.	STRONG, A.	McGLASHAN, J.
DUTTON, E.	WILLIAMS, W.	STRACHAN, T.
FORD, T.	FOOT, G.	McCALLUM, J.
MASON, H.	CRIBB, H.	BLAIR, W. J.
COLLINS, J.	HOOPER, E.	TODD, A. H.
ALLSOPP, C.	COCKING, C.	SWADLING, G.
OWEN, S. W.	WILSON, W.	CLIFTON, G.
PICKERSGILL, W.	HILL, W.	BEVAN, C.
JARRETT, W.	BUCK, C.	BOLTON, G.
MAGILL, W.	WARRELL, W.	
ARCHIBALD, G.	DEAR, T.	
BARNES, R.	DALLASTON, J.	

Stadelbauer and Co.
(See p. 625 in Roll of Honour.)

PRESTWICH, H. (Partner)	FRASER, J.	MAYSON, H. W.
BARLOW, J. W.	HARDY, F.	PURDIE, R. S.
BAYLEY, H.	HART, F.	READING, S.
BLANKLEY, W.	HEWITT, A. E.	SURINGAR, W.
DARBYSHIRE, J.	HILTON, W.	SWANN, P.
DAVIES, R.	HORSFALL, J.	TURTON, C.
	JUMP, E. A.	

† Rejected.

Peter Spence and Sons, Ltd.
(See p. 624 in Roll of Honour.)

ABBOTT, G.	HARDY, S.	PARKINSON, J.
ADDY, J.	HAIGH, J. A.	PECK, W. A.
AISTROPE, G. W.	HALL, A.	PANTON, W.
AXUP, E. W.	HARRISON, J.	PICKERING, A.
BARNES, J.	HARRISON, R.	PHILLIPSON, T.
BAXTER, E.	HAYHURST, J.	POLLARD, J.
BAILEY, J.	HEMSWORTH, G.	PRIESTLEY, H.
BALL, R.	HEWITT, W.	RADCLIFFE, E.
BRIGGS, F. B.	HEWITT, J. A.	RADCLIFFE, J. N.
BROWN, F.	HICKEY, J. E.	REVELL, T.
BROWN, J.	HILL, W. A.	ROBINSON, F.
BOYLIN, E.	HOWELL, J.	REVELL, G.
BROOKE, G.	HUNTER, S.	RUSHTON, N.
BURNETT, T.	HEAPEY, J.	SCUTT, J. A.
BUTTRICK, P.	HEYWOOD, H.	SLATER, S.
CARROLL, J.	JACKSON, C. M.	SHERWOOD, A.
COOK, T.	JACKSON, W. L.	SHERWOOD, R.
COOK, H.	JACKSON, H. S.	SHERIFF, G.
COPE, B.	JOHNSON, T.	STAINFORTH, G.
COTTIER, F. C.	KING, H.	SWEETING, G. H.
COULT, W.	KITCHEN, T.	THOMPSON, D.
COOK, T.	KASSELL, H.	TOMKINS, J.
CRABTREE, E. D.	LATIMORE, J.	THORPE, H.
CRUICKSHANK, M.	LAWRINSON, A.	THORNHILL, G.
CUTHBERT, E.	LEAK, R. J.	TIGHE, W.
CURZON, A.	LEETHAM, R. J.	TILSTON, S.
DALTON, G.	LEIGHTON, J. W.	TOLAN, J.
DANIELSON, G.	LLEWELLYN, I. P.	TYAS, T.
DENBY, D.	LLEWELLYN, W. B.	VANSON, W.
DRAYTON, G. B.	LILLEY, G.	VICKERA, A.
DOUNTFIRE, G.	LOCKWOOD, J. C.	WARD, A. H.
DUNWELL, T.	LYNCH, C.	WARD, M.
EAGLES, C. H.	MAW, A.	WALKER, C. H.
ELLA, C. S.	MARSHALL, H.	WHITELEY, F.
ENRIGHT, T.	MARSHALL, J. W.	WESTON, F.
EVANS, J.	McNEILL, J.	WHITE, C. H.
FARRINGTON, L.	METCALF, A.	WHITE, H.
FAWCETT, G.	MIDDLETON, E.	WILDE, A. T.
FORSTER, W. H.	MILLS, S.	WILDE, J. W. T.
FIRTH, A.	MOORES, J.	WILSON, J.
FOX, C.	McGREGOR, A.	WILSON, H.
GALE, H.	NEW, W.	WRIGLEY, G.
GAWTRY, A.	NIGHTINGALE, J.	WOAD, T.
GREGG, R.	O'BRIEN, J. H.	WOODHAMS, F.
GARNER, B. V.	O'BRIEN, G.	WOFFENDEN, T. W.
GREEN, J. E.	OGDEN, R.	WOOLLAS, R.
GRIFFITHS, J.	O'NEILL, E.	YOUNG, P. J.
HAGUE, J. A.	OSBORNE, W.	
HALL, G.	PATTERSON, G. W.	

Robert Spencer and Nephews, Ltd.
(See p. 619 in Roll of Honour.)

BAYLEY, E. S.	DUNCLIFFE, W. H.	PERRIS, R.
CALVERT, R.	FALLOWS, S.	SIMPSON, J. W.
CLARE, J.	GALLEY, C.	WHEATLEY, A.
DENTON, F.	HOULTRAM, J. W.	WHITELEY, G.

Stewart, Thomson and Co., Ltd.
(See p. 628 in Roll of Honour.)

BOLTON, W. A. (Director).	DEAVILLE, F.	MARRIOTT, W.
BAGULEY, E. R.	FISHER, F.	MORETON, T.
BRODERICK, H.	FINNEY, J.	TOOLE, A.
HARPER, J.	GATELEY, J.	SMITH, D.
LOMAS, A. N.	GOODFELLOW, J.	WHITEHOUSE, J.
BARON, J.	HARVEY, G.	WHEELDON, H. J.
BAMFORD, J. J.	JONES, T.	YARWOOD, J.
CASWELL, H.	LESCURE, C.	CHADWICK, W.
COWPER, T.	MASSEY, E.	
	MARRIOTT, S.	

Sutcliffe and Bingham, Ltd.
(See p. 700 in Roll of Honour.)

CHEESMAN, G. W.	DUNKERLEY, F. W.	ELLIS, A.
COOPER, J. F.	FRASER, S.	RILEY, J.
YATES, J.	O'NEILL, A.	DOWNS, G.
CAINE, G. D.	FORD, E.	
LONGWORTH, J. H.	MIDDLETON, J.	

W. Sutcliffe and Son.
(See p. 700 in Roll of Honour.)

PAYTEN, A.	HACKNEY, A. J.	RENTON, H.
ROBINSON, C.	KILLIP, S.	ROBINSON, J.
BRADSHAW, J.	LAW, B.	SAGE, J.
CHAFER, F.	MURDOCH, R.	SHAW, W.
DUFFY, M.	NIXON, J.	THOMPSON, A.
GORTON, A. E.	OWEN, J.	

Louis Stott.

Lance-Corporal L. C. STOTT, 10789, D. Company, 18th Service Battalion Manchester Regiment.

Stott and Smith, Ltd.
(See p. 629 in Roll of Honour.)

Manchester Warehouse.

NEEDHAM, G.
JONES, S.
INNES, J.
SANDS, R.
HAWKINS, A.
POOLE, J.
TAYLOR, J. B.
WORTHINGTON, W.
O'HARE, F.
HAMPSON, H.
WILKINSON, F.
CHADDERTON, H.
LOMAS, J.
COLLIER, H.
WALKER, D.
SWINDELLS, A. R.
CROSSDALE, E.
ELTOFT, R. W.
BURLING, W.
WHITEHEAD, F.
SMITH, S. (London Office).
WHELAN, J. C.
BARLOW, H.
TURNER, J.
ROWEN, A.
BELL, R. D.
LEWIS, T.
DEER, W.

Empire Mill, Congleton.

MARSH, J. W.
DAVISON, H.
SPROSON, J.
BOON, A.
TOMLINSON, F.
BROWN, J.
BEFF, E.
CHARLESWORTH, H.
BROWN, H.
JOHNSON, W.
MARSH, H.
HULME, T.
SPARKS, F.
SPARKS, P.
SIMMS, H.
SCHLANK, J.
GREEN, G.
WOODCOCK, J.
CARTER, A.
BAYLEY, J.
KNIGHT, J.
REDFERN, A.
CLARKE, J.
CARSON, R.
POWELL, R.
OWEN, D.
OAKES, J.
BOOTH, H.
BROWN, E.
SPROSTON, J.
WORTHINGTON, J., Junr.
ROWE, S.
JOHNSON, P.
BAYLEY, A.
WILCOCK, A.
DAVIES, A.
BAYLEY, S.
HARDING, A.
CAMPBELL, T.
LOMAS, A.
LILLEY, G.
BROWN, A.
REDFERN, F.
DALE, W.
SHERRATT, E.
HILDITCH, A.
ROBINSON, J.
MINSHULL, G.
WILLIAMSON, A.
PYNE, J.
ANDREW, H.
CALLEY, S.
SKELLERN, T.
CHADDOCK, F.
REDFERN, F.
MELLOR, W.
WORTH, L.
TREACEY, W.
GREEN, J.
JOHNSON, J.
ROBINSON, H.
SHERRATT, A., Jun.
HARDING, J.
DALE, J.
CONWAY, L.
WOOD, F.

Joseph Stubbs, Ltd.
(See p. 630 in Roll of Honour.)

ARMSTRONG, T. W.
ALLOTT, J.
ACTON, —
ACTON, W.
BREEN, C. E.
BALLENTYNE, W.
BREEN, T. W.
BEESTON, G.
BOND, J.
BROOKS, A. E.
BENNETT, E.
BROWN, I.
BARNES, C. H.
BARRY, F. J.
BELLIS, A.
BURGESS, S.
BELL, W. W.
BOWDEN, F.
BENNETT, A.
BIRCH, G. W.
CANTY, S.
CONNOLLY, J. T.
CLOWES, F.
COFFEY, J.
COOKE, J. T.
CONLEY, R.
COLLINS, H.
CLAYTON, J.
CARR, B.
CUMBES, W.
COLLINS, J.
CUMMINGS, J.
CUMBERBIRCH, J.
CUCKOW, G.
DONBAVAND, J.
DENHOLME, G.
DONNELLY, J.
DAVIES, J.
DUTTON, J.
DONE, S.
DITCHFIELD, T.
DIXON, R.
DOBSON, C.
EDMUNDS, A.
EDWARDS, W.
ELSMORE, J.
EASTWOOD, F.
FARROW, G.
FRANCE, W. H.
FARRINGTON, J.
FAIRBANK, H.
FLETCHER, J.
FOXALL, J.
FAIRHURST, J. A.
GRIBBEN, W.
GLENNON, G.
GARFORTH, R.
GLENN, J.
GORMAN, F.
GILES, W. S.
GRUNDY, T.
GREEN, H.
GREGORY, J. (Ancoats Works.)
GREGORY, J. (Openshaw Works.)
GRIMSHAW, J.
GERRARD, G.
GREEN, W.
GRAY, G.
HORTON, J.
HOWARD, T.
HARRISON, A.
HUDSON, J.
HOPPE, B.
HATTON, W.
HARDING, E.
HALLIDAY, R.
HIGGINS, W.
HOLMES, J.
HALTON, W.
HUGHES, J.
HADSKISS, A.
HOLT, W.
HARDMAN, J.
HOLT, W.
HENDERSON, W.
HORNBY, D.
HYDE, C.
HURST, W.
HILL, J.
HOLT, H. E.
INSKIP, A.
IRVING, J.
JOHNSON, J. E.
JORDAN, J.
JACKSON, W.
JACKSON, A.
JONES, E.
JONES, C.
JOHNSON, S.
JONES, J. J.
JOHNSON, A.
KOYLE, J.
KIRKHAM, F.
KENT, W.
LEECH, R.
LOWE, J.
LOFTUS, H.
LACY, J.
LEIGHTON, J. R.
LEWIS, T. H.
LONGSON, R.
LIVINGSTONE, G.
LEES, E.
LEGGATT, J.
MORTON, W.
McCABE, T.
MITCHELL, W. J.
MARKHAM, W.
MULHOLLAND, W.
MILNER, A.
NEILL, J.
NOTON, B.
OSBORNE, T.
OAKES, W.
PHILLIPS, S.
PICKERING, J. H.
POTTER, J.
PLATT, H.
PRESCOTT, J.
PRINCE, J.
RUDD, W.
RICE, J. A.
RUTTER, E.
REVITT, J.
RILEY, S.

Joseph Stubbs, Ltd.—Con.

SKIFFINGTON, P.
SMITH, J.
SMITH, G. H.
SENIOR, G.
SHAW, J. W.
SWATKINS, J.
SMITH, C.
SEDDON, A.
SIMPSON, J.
STEELE, W.
STUBBS, G.
STUBBS, R. W.
SEDDON, J.
SHEPHERDSON, W.
SHEPHERDSON, H.
SHOTT, J.
STEELE, G.
SHARPLES, J.
SHIELDS, D.
SILCOCK, W.
SKEARY, J.
SHAW, F.
STEWART, J.
TILLEY, H.
TRELFA, J.
TILLEY, T.
TAYLOR, J. W.
THOMAS, D.
TRUEMAN, G.
TRIMM, H.
TILLEY, A.
TILLEY, J.
WOOD, J.
WILLIAMS, W.
WILKINSON, J. T.
WOLSTENHOME, A.
WALKER, F.
WRIGHT, T.
WADE, T.
WEBSTER, R.
WHITE, F.
WILLIAMS, E.
YATES, W.
YOUNGMAN, T.
YOUNG, W.

Tennants (Lancashire), Ltd.
(See p. 639 in Roll of Honour.)

SUTTON, G.
LEA, J.
BERRY, F.
TYSON, A.
STAFFORD, F.
MILLINGTON, W.
WARREN, J.
MILLWOOD, C.
LEONARD, C.
SCHOFIELD, A.
DUNN, D.
HALES, J.
CLARKE, J. W.
LATHAM, E.
CROMPTON, C.
WOOD, E.
CRYER, J.
GREEN, H.
KIERNAN, J. A.
HARRISON, J.
ARNOLD, J. S.
BERTENSHAW, J.
DOYLE, E.
BOSWELL, E.
BAILEY, J.
CASEMENT, J.
DENNY, D.
LOWRY, W.
COLEBOURNE, J. A.
FLYNN, J.
BARNES, R.
AKISTER, F.
SUMNALL, W.
HOWLES, J.
O'DONNELL, E.
GALLAGHER, B.
ROSE, A.
HOWLES, M.
GLEAVE, J. F.
MARSDEN, J.
EDWARDS, J.
SUDLOW, S.
YEARSLEY, C.
HAWKINS, J.
HALLIWELL, E.
TAYLOR, J.
PARK, T.
MARSHALL, J.
MORRIS, W.
NORTH, A.
JONES, E.
GODDARD, A.
WORTHINGTON, J.
BARKER, T.
LAMB, R.
CLAYSON, G.

Bertram Thomas.
(See p. 639 in Roll of Honour.)

ROYLE, E.
EWART, J. W.
RICHARDSON, J. H.
JACKSON, J.
SCOBLE, C.
WILSON, M. P.
WOOD, H.
ETHERIDGE, T. A.
ARMSTRONG, J.
PIGGOTT, G.
DAWSON, J. P.
MORRIS, F.
ELCOX, W. J.
FLETCHER, J.
COUCILL, C.
SCOBLE, E. G.
PAMPHILON, W.
BLACK, F.
BERRY, H.
REID, T.
WOOD, A.
TIMPERLEY, G.
WILLIAMS, J. H.
McKINSTRY, T.
JONES, J.
COUCILL, H.
HARRISON, O.
PARKER, C. F.
JONES, S.
CLEMINSON, H.
FLEMING, J.
BAXENDALE, A.
EDGE, A.
RENSHAW, W.
ROSS, F.
HIGHAM, J.
LOMAS, F.
ATTENBOROUGH, E.
HEMSLEY, W.
CAWLEY, J. M.
HOYE, F.
CROPP, J.
HENNIS, G.
TAGUE, G.
PARTINGTON, J.
COVER, G.
MARSH, E.
HILTON, J.
BARLOW, W.
AINSCOW, S.
†HEIL, A.
†RAMSDEN, T.
†MOCKRIDGE, F. F.
†HADDEN, F. W.
†RYAN, J.
†HOEY, G. A.
†SMETHURST, C.
†ALTHAM, T. A.

Thrutchley and Co., Ltd.
(See p. 702 in Roll of Honour.)

BODDY, A. G.
BYATT, A. L.
DILLON, C. H.
GRAVES, T.
HAYTER, W.
HONEYBALL, G. W.
HUMPHREYS, R.
LAVERACK, F. H.
LUSBY, H. E.
OLDHAM, E.
POTTS, L.
POWELL, A. A.
SHARMAN, G. O.
WILLIS, C.
WILLIAMS, A.

Henry Turnbull and Co.
(See p. 703 in Roll of Honour.)

TURNBULL, FRED
TURNBULL, G.
TURNBULL, FK.
WATTS, H.
THORP, C.
COCHRANE, W.
GRIERSON, R.
TROTMAN, J.
DAVIES, T.
GREEN, G.
FOWLER, L.
AINSCOW, F.
PLATT, W.
GARRETT, C.
DAVIS, J.

8 others offered their services, but were not passed by the doctor.

W. H. Tutton and Co., Ltd.
(See p. 702 in Roll of Honour.)

ARMSTRONG, G.
BROWN, M.
CAMPBELL, E.
GAUTBY, R. B.
GOODEN, S.
JACKSON, W.
JONES, W.
JACKSON, H.
LAMB, G.
LAVERACK, G. H.
NEWBURY, J. T.
NUTTALL, H.
PILKINGTON, J.
STANLEY, T.
VICKERS, W.
WILLIAMSON, W.

† Rejected.

Tootal Broadhurst Lee Company Limited.
(See p. 632 in Roll of Honour.)

ALLEN, T.
ALLISON, J. K.
ANDREW, E.
ARTINGSTALL, L. P.
ASHWORTH, A.
ATKINSON, W.
BAGNALL, G.
BAKER, J. W.
BARNES, J. H.
BARRETT, A.
BARTLEY, J.
(Ten Acres Mill).
BATTERSBY, J. H.
BEARDWOOD, E.
BEDALE, P.
BEECH, W.
BENTLEY, G.
BLAIR, H.
BLAIR, W.
BLAKELEY, G.
BLAND, T.
BLEACKLEY, A. V.
BOLTON, W.
BOOTH, H.
BOOTH, W.
BOWDEN, A.
(Ten Acres Mill).
BOWDEN, J.
BOWLES, F.
BOWYER, W.
BRADSHAW, A.
BRADSHAW, H. W.
BRADSHAW, J.
BRADBURY, A. J.
BRASH, E. G.
BRECKELL, W.
BRIDGE, G.
BRIDGE, J.
BRINDLEY, T.
BROWN, L.
(Ten Acres Mill).
BRUMMITT, A.
BRYDEN, W.
BULLOCK, N.
BURTON, F.
CAMPBELL, A.
CAMPBELL, S. A.
CAMPLING, H.
CARPENTER, A. H.
CARROLL, J.
CHAMBERLAIN, A.
(Ten Acres Mill).
CHAPMAN, A. B.
(Nottingham).
CHAPMAN, J. B.
(Nottingham).
CHORLTON, J.
CLAY, W. W.
COLLINS, G. A.
COLLIER, J.
COOK, F.
CONNOLLY, T.
CORFIELD, J. W.
(Ten Acres Mill).
CORRAN, A.
CORRAN, F.
CRAIG, J.
CRANE, H.
CROSSLEY, A.
CROWTHER, J.
DANDS, W.
DANN, W. W.
DAWSON, P.
(Ten Acres Mill).
DAVIDSON, S. J.
DAVIES, G.
DAVIES, S.
DAVIES, S. H.
DENBY, F.
DERBYSHIRE, F. W.
DIXON, R. W.
DOXEY, F.
(Ten Acres Mill).
DUNCAN, J.
DUNKERLEY, J.
ELLISON, C. K.
FARADAY, G.
FEATHERSTONE, E.
FIRTH, A.
FIRTH, J.
FLANAGAN, H.
FLETCHER, P.
(Glasgow).
FODEN, J.
FRIDAY, R. S.
GARNER, A.
GIBBONS, J.
GILBERT, R.
GILLISON, T. S.
GODDARD, L.
(Ten Acres Mill).
GOLDRICK, T.
(Ten Acres Mill).
GOUGH, J. R.
GRESTY, J. E.
GRIMSHAW, S.
HAGAN, E.
HAIGH, F. S.
(Leeds).
HARDMAN, G. R.
HARRIS, B.
HARRISON, L.
HARRISON, W.
HARTLEY, C.
(Ten Acres Mill).
HASLEHAM, G. A.
HAYES, A. W.
HESFORD, J.
HEWITT, H.
HEWITT, W. A.
HEYES, W.
HEYS, E.
HIGHAM, A.
HODGE, J.
HOLLAND, J.
(Ten Acres Mill).
HOLLAND, R.
HOPKINS, W.
HOPWOOD, W.
HORNER, A.
HORNER, J.
HORNER, W. E.
HOWCROFT, W.
INGHAM, J.
JACKSON, J.
JACKSON, W.
JONES, A. W.
(London).
KAY, J. T.
(Ten Acres Mill).
KELLY, R. M.
KENWORTHY, H.
KIRKHAM, E. A.
KIRKHAM, H.
KIRTON, C. H.
KNOWLES, C.
KYNASTON, F.
LAWSON, L. A.
LAWTON, J.
LEECH, F. W.
LEEMING, R.
(Ten Acres Mill).
LIDDLE, H.
LIGAT, J. M.
LIVEWELL, R.
(Ten Acres Mill).
LOVESEY, R.
LOWE, G.
LYNN, J. W.
MACKEY, D.
MACKIE, J.
(Glasgow).
MACKEY, J. C.
MADELEY, J. W.
MAHER, T. F.
MAHONEY, T.
MANLEY, E.
MATHER, P.
MAYOH, H.
MEADE, H. V.
MEREDITH, H.
MEREDITH, S.
MILNE, C. G.
MOORHOUSE, W.
MORING, C. P.
MORLEY, J.
MURBY, E. S.
NEWTON, G. F.
(Leeds).
NICHOLSON, C. L.
NIELD, W.
NORBURY, W.
NUTTALL, J.
OLIVER, R. S.
(Glasgow).
PARKS, W.
(Ten Acres Mill).
PARTINGTON, G. H.
PUGH, W.
RANSLEY, H.
RAYNER, E.
RILEY, E.
RILEY, W.
ROBERTS, J. S.
ROBINSON, J.
ROGERS, E. G.
ROGERS, H.
(Ten Acres Mill).
ROYLE, P.
(Ten Acres Mill).
SAMBROOK, H. J.
SANDERSON, J.
SCALES, T.
SCOTT, S.
SEDDON, H.
SHACKLETON, T.
SHARPLES, H.
SHAW, H.
SHEFFIELD, W.
SHEPHERD, F. H.
(Nottingham).
SHEPHERD, W.
SHERRY, F.
SHORROCK, A. G.
SHORROCK, H.
SIDEBOTTOM, S.
SIMISTER, E.
SKELTON, N.
SLATER, T.
SMETHURST, W.
SMITH, A.
STALEY, J.
STABLES, F. O.
STAMP, F.
(Ten Acres Mill).
STANLEY, H.
(Ten Acres Mill).
STATHAM, A. D.
STEVENS, E.
STEVENS, G.
STUBBS, W.
SUTHERLAND, G.
SWINDELLS, T.
TAYLOR, J.
TAYLOR, T.
TAYLOR, T.
THOMAS, H.
THOMAS, J.
THOMAS, J. A.
THOMASSON, H.
(Ten Acres Mill).
TOOTILL, C.
TRACEY, L.
TRUEBODY, P.
TURNER, P.
WADE, A.
WAITE, H.
WALKER, J.
WAKEFIELD, H.
WAKELING, G.
(London).
WARREN, J.
WATSON, J. A.
WATSON, J. F.
WELLS, G. F.
WELLS, H.
WHATLEY, E.
WHITE, E.
(London).
WHITELEGG, T.
WHITMORE, E.
WHITTAKER, C.
WHITWORTH, A.
WILLIAMS, H.
WILLIAMSON, E. B.
WILLIS, W. B.
WOOD, F. T.
WOOD, H.
WOODAL, R.
(Ten Acres Mill).
WOODWARD, A.
WRIGHT, T.
WRIGHT, T.
(Ten Acres Mill).
YATES, R.

Tootal Broadhurst Lee Company Limited.—Con.
Bolton Mill.

ASPINALL, J.
AXON, J.
BAILEY, A.
BARRETT, J. W.
BETLEY, A.
BLACKBURN, A.
BOARDMAN, E.
BOARDMAN, J.
BRAYSHAW, T.
BRIDGE, W.
BROMLEY, E.
BROOKS, J.
BROUGHTON, H.
CARTWRIGHT, E.
CLEGG, J. W.
CLOUGH, J.
CLOUGH, S.
CROOK, F.
CROOK, J.
CROOK, W. A.
CUNDY, J. H.
DAVIS, T.
FARRAR, S.
FISHER, A.
FLETCHER, R.
FORREST, H.
FOSTER, H.
GRACE, H.
GRIMWOOD, R.
HALLIWELL, J.
HAMER, T.
HAMPSON, J. H.
HAMPSON, W.
HANLEY, J.
HARRISON, W.
HASLAM, B.
HASLAM, T.
HART, W.
HAYES, H.
HENDERSON, S.
HEWITSON, R.
HIGSON, H.
HIGSON, H.
HIGSON, S.
HILTON, A.
HOLLAND, J.
HORROCKS, T.
HOUGHTON, H.
HOWARTH, F.
HUNT, J.
ISHERWOOD, H.
JEVONS, J.
KAY, H.
KENNEDY, J.
KNOWLES, J.
LEE, E.
LEE, F.
LITHERLAND, T.
LIVESEY, P.
LONEY, W.
LORD, A.
MAKIN, A.
MARSH, J.
McGARRY, J.
MOORES, H.
MORRIS, F.
NORCLIFFE, J.
NUTTALL, W.
ORMSTON, J.
PARKINSON, R.
PARTINGTON, P.
PILLING, H.
PLATT, J.
POWIS, G.
POTTER, J.
ROBINSON, G.
RONALD, A.
RIDINGS, E.
RUTTER, H.
SAMSON, F.
SCHOFIELD, A.
SEED, J.
SHARP, F.
SHARP, F. I.
SHARP, J.
SHARPLES, W.
SHARPLES, J. W.
SHAW, W.
SMETHURST, L.
SMITH, A.
TAYLOR, J.
TAYLOR, J.
TONGE, R.
TOWERS, N.
TRAVIS, D.
TUNNAH, H.
WALCH, R.
WALKDEN, A.
WALKDEN, J.
WALMSLEY, J.
WARBURTON, H.
WATKINSON, E.
WELLS, A.
WHITEHEAD, G.
WILCOCK, R.
WILCOCKSON, H.
WILKINSON, W.
WILKINS, A.
WILLIAMS, E.
WINSTANLEY, J.
WOOD, I.
WOOD, J.
WOODFIN, W.
YATES, P.

Union Bank of Manchester, Ltd.
(See p. 640 in Roll of Honour.)

ALEXANDER, D.
ANDERTON, G. W. A.
ATKINS, A., Jnr.
ASHWORTH, H.
ASHWORTH, J.
ASKEW, J. E.
BANCROFT, F. J.
BANNISTER, R. C.
BAMFORD, C.
BARLOW, T. R.
BARWICK, E. W.
BERTENSHAW, J. H.
BLEASE, R.
BOEDO, L.
BOOTH, V. H.
BOOTH, W. B.
BOUCHER, G. A.
BIBBY, F. E.
BROWN, G. D.
BRADBURY, H.
BROADBENT, J. D.
BENTLEY, R. V.
CHAPMAN, H. C.
CHADWICK, S.
CHARLES, J. H.
CHRISTIAN, W. G. S.
CHURM, F. A.
CRYER, F. S.
DARBYSHIRE, A.
*DAVIES, R. B.
DEWHIRST, N. S.
DEAN, H. C.
DOBELL, J.
*DOIG, H. R.
*DOWNS, R. B.
EATON, A.
EDLESTON, W. E.
EDMONDSON, W. A.
ELLIS, J.
ESLICK, P. S.
EVANS, H. A.
FARR, C. C.
FOGG, L. A.
FRANCIS, A. W. C.
FOSTER, J.
FURNESS, B. B.
*FRYER, P.
GLOVER, C. S. P.
GRIFFITHS, J.
GRIFFITHS, J. V.
GRIME, J. A.
GOULDEN, W. F.
HALL, J. A.
HILES, C. E.
HINDE, P. B.
HINDLE, J. M.
HODGE, J. G.
*HOBSON, E.
HUNT, R. M.
HOWARD, R. R.
INCE, J. S.
*ISHERWOOD, J.
*JEANS, J. F.
JONES, E. W.
KELSALL, N.
KERSHAW, H.
*KERSHAW, M.
KNOX, W.
LANG, H. W.
LEAR, C. A. D.
LEVER, F.
LEWTAS, A.
LORD, E.
*LOWE, A.
LING, A. L.
MACFEE, G.
MELLOR, J. C.
MELLOR, J. H.
MILLINGTON, J. A.
*MILNES, J.
*MILNE, R.
MOORE, W. C.
MYATT, A. S.
PARRISH, J. H.
PARTINGTON, H.
PEAT, A.
*PEERMAN, C. H. V.
*PIMLOTT, P.
POTTS, E. C.
PROCTOR, E.
RAMSBOTTOM, G.
RICHARDSON, E.
RIGG, G. E.
ROBINSON, W. H.
ROGERS, R. M.
SARGENT, J. H.
SETTLE, R. H.
SEWELL, J.
SHINKFIELD, W.
SHUTT, W. A.
SMITH, H.
*SUGDEN, J.
SUTTON, J. R.
STOCKDALE, S. R. V.
*TAYLOR, B.
*TAYLOR, C. H.
THOMPSON, C. L. N.
THORNLEY, D.
TOMLINSON, G. W.
UNSWORTH, A. E.
WALLWORK, G. B.
WESTHEAD, J. J.
WHITEHEAD, J. E.

Forty-four failed to pass the Medical Test.

Union Mills Co.
(See p. 704 in Roll of Honour.)

BENTLEY, R.
BURKE, H.
BARKER, J.
TAYLOR, F.
WILCOX, H.

* Now on Active Service.

United Yeast Co., Ltd.
(See p. 643 in Roll of Honour.)

AITCHISON, C. G.
ALMOND, W.
ARBREY, T.
ARBREY, S.
ASHFORD, C.
BARNES, J.
BARTARD, S. E. G.
BAILEY, A.
BAWLES, J. B.
BAYLEY, J. J.
BEACH, S. A.
BEAUMONT, H.
BENSON, G.
BENNETT, J.
BETTY, A.
BLACKMORE, J.
BLOMLEY, F.
BLAIR, R.
BLACKETT, M.
BOYLE, F.
BOWLES, —
BOWDEN, A.
BOSSON, W.
BORTHWICK C.
BROWN, G.
BROOKMAN, W. H.
BRAMBLE, R. C.
BROWN, T. A.
BURTON, R.
BURROUGHS, H
BUNN, W. W.
BURGESS, H. J.
BYRNE, A.
CADMAN, C.
CALWAY, —
CABLE, W. J.
CASTLEMAN, E. D.
CHAFFE, W.
CHARNOCK, G
CHEETHAM, F.
CHETHAM, J.
CLARKE, G. H. B.
COOK, E. R.
COLLIER, T. A.
COLE, W. A.
COLDWELL, J.
COOPER, A. F.
CONDREN, M.
COTTLE, W.
COGGINS, O.
COLLINS, C. B.
CRESSWELL, H.
CROSS, J.
CURRY, A.
DERHAM, S.
DERVALT, A.
DEWHIRST, L.
DINGLISON, P.
DOBSON, J. G.
DONOHOE, G.
DRAPER, F. J
DUTSON, H. C.
ELGER, E.
ELLIS, E.
ELLIS, W.
ELLIS, C.
FARROW, B. E.
FAWCETT, W.
FARLEY, F. J.
FAIRMAN, F.
FELSTEAD, J. E.
FEARBY, W
FELSTEAD, G. P.
FISHER, A.
FLETT, D.
FLETCHER, W. J.
FOSTER, W.
FREESTONE, W.
FULLARD, F. W.
GAY, A. G.
GAPP, A. A.
GAWATT, T.
GALE, S. W.
GILL, W.
GIBSON, H.
GILLIBRAND, J. W.
GIMBLETT, T. J.
GOMMERSALL, W.
GOLDTHORPE, J.
GOLDTHORPE, A.
GOTT, G.
GOODALL, G.
GOWER, A.
GREENHALGH, H.
GREENWOOD, C.
GREEN, —
GREENWOOD, W.
HARVEY, B. W.
HARRISON, A.
HAWKES, H.
HAREN, D.
HARMSWORTH, E. J.
HANCOCK, W.
HALL, G. E.
HALL, J. W.
HARRIS, A. J.
HELLIWELL, G.
HOUGHTON, E.
HOLDEN, H.
HORE, J. E.
HORNER, W.
HONEY, S. H.
HOLLIS, E.
HULL, T.
HUNT, P. W. H.
HUGHES, D.
IZANT, W. P.
JARRETT, —
JEFFERIES, H.
JENKINS, J. R.
JOHNSTON, S.
JONES, S.
JONES, W. L
JONES, R.
JONES, R.
JONES, E.
JONES, O.
JONES, J.
JONES, J. T.
JURY, E.
KELLING, A. A.
KING, J.
KING, —
KIRK, P. W.
LEEMING, M.
LEES, W. R.
LINDSAY, R. T.
LOWE, T.
LYON, W.
LYNN, N. R.
LYNN, C.
LOVELL, J.
MACKLEY, F.
MACKENZIE, H. S.
MAITLAND, A.
MARTIN, G.
MAW, C.
McLEOD, J.
MEADOWS, W.
MITTON, H.
MILLS, E.
MINTY, F. W.
MOLE, J.
MULBURY, H.
MUNDY, F. G.
MUNNERLEY, A.
NEWBOULD, A.
NICHOLSON, J.
NORMAN, I.
NORTON, T.
NOWELL, H.
O'HARA, D.
OSMOND, R.
PACK, D.
PAINE, P.
PALMER, J.
PARKINSON, R.
PARKER, —
PARKINSON, H.
PEARCE, J. G.
PEARCE, A. G.
PERCEVAL, C.
PILE, F. W.
PLANT, A.
POOLE, C.
PURCHASE, F. W.
PRICE, J.
RABJOHNS, T. A. J.
RANKIN, J.
RAYNE, O.
RENSHAW, P.
RIDLEY, A.
RIDLEY, E.
RIDING, T.
RICHARDSON, G.
RICHARDS, J. F.
RICHARDSON, J
ROUT, F.
ROSE, J.
ROBINSON, F. W.
ROBINSON, H.
ROBERTSON, W.
ROBINSON, F.
RUTLAND, A. H.
RYTON, R. L.
SALMON, W.
SCOTT, J.
SEAL, W.
SHAW, W.
SHAW, H.
SHARRATT, H.
SHORE, E.
SHORE, A.
SLEAP, E. J.
SMITH, T.
SMITH, S. T.
SMITH, W. A. Y.
SOCKETT, R.
STODDARD, H. G
STOTT, D.
STURTEWAGEN, A.
SUN, J. C.
SYMES, C. M. C.
TAYLOR, R.
TAYLOR, T. W.
THOMAS, C. W.
THOMAS, O.
THOMPSON, C.
TOWNSEND, F.
TUCK, T. W.
TYAS, —
UNWIN, R.
VERVALT, C.
VERVALT, B.
VINCENT, A.
WATSON, H.
WALKER, J.
WARD, W. H.
WATTS, A. S.
WARD, A.
WATKIN, W. H.
WEIGHTMAN, F.
WHALE, R.
WHYAND, E. H.
WHITE, P.
WILLIAMS, R.
WILLIAMS, A.
WILLIAMS, W. G.
WICKETTS, —
WILKIN, N.
WOOLEY, S.
WOOD, J. G.
WYARD, C. H.
YOUNG, J. R.

Thomas Vickers and Sons.
(See p. 705 in Roll of Honour.)

HADFIELD, W.
HALL, J. A.
FORTUNE, R.
HACKSTON, T.
PARSLOW, G.
SUTHERS, T.
HEATHCOTE, J.
McDONALD, W.
SMITH, G.
CHADWICK, G.
WALSH, J.
CRONSHAW, J.
GREER, B.
†SHAW, G. A.

† Rejected.

S. and J. Watts and Co.
(See p. 644 in Roll of Honour.)

ASHWORTH, S.
APPLEBY, E.
ATTWOOD, A. J.
ANSTEE, E. H.
AUSTIN, J. W.
AUSTIN, J.
ALLEN, F.
ASTIN, R.
AINSWORTH, J.
ARROWSMITH, S. C.
ASPINALL, P.
ALDGATE, J.
ARDERN, A.
ASHWORTH, W.
APPLEDORE, H.
ANDREWS, G. H.
BRITLAND, J. W.
BAMFORTH, J. G.
BROWN, W.
BINNS, W. T.
BRUCE, W. A.
BRADBORN, B.
BRANDRAETH, W.
BARDSLEY, W.
BROWN, H.
BUTTERS, W. V.
BENSON, H.
BURGESS, A.
BARLOW, C. G. H.
BAILEY, J. L.
BRYCE, A.
BUBIER, L.
BOWN, E.
BROCKLEHURST, W.
BENNETT, W. B
BOYLE, W.
BRASSINGTON, B.
BURNS, T.
BURGESS, J. C.
BROOKS, S.
BARRETT, J. H.
BROOKS, C.
BARNETT, A. F
BUCK, H. W.
BESWICK, R.
BROWN, J.
BENNETT, J.
BERRELL, W. J.
BENNETT, E.
CLEMENTS, A.
CORLETT, F.
COOPER, S.
CRAIG, H.
CARVEL, J.
COLLING, J.
CLANCY, T. R.
CALDWELL, H.
COOPER, A. E.
CARR, J.
COWLEY, J. E.
CAMPBELL, S. A.
CRAVEN, C.
CHRISTY, S.
DAVIES, C. E.
DAVENPORT, H.
DAY, E.
DICKEN, S.
DANIELS, G. H.
DAWES, J.
DOWNS, S.
DERBYSHIRE, W.
DAVIES, T. J.
DAVIES, A.
DUTTON, F.
EVANS, A.
EDWARDS, T.
EACHUS, W.
ELLIOTT, J.
ELLERY, W. H.
FARNWORTH, W. H.
FOLEY, C.
FEIRN, W. C.
FENTON, F.
FOLEY, W.
FARMERY, A.
FREARSON, H.
FIDLER, A.
FORD, A.
GARNER, T.
GALSTON, F.
GRANGE, R.
GRIFFIN, J.
GILLING, R.
GREENWOOD, M. B.
GREGORY, W. E.
GOODLAD, W.
HAY, J.
HENLEY, M. J.
HAMNETT, F. W.
HARDMAN, E. H.
HOWARD, W.
HOLLAND, J. F.
HARNESS, H.
HEATON, J. S.
HETHERINGTON, J.
HOBDAY, D. B.
HEALEY, L. W.
HOCKENHALL, J.
HAMER, J.
HEMSLEY, J
HAMMOND, W. T
HAMPSON, E. J.
HAMNETT, J.
HUSSEY, W.
HAYTOCK, J.
HOUGHTON, G.
HOLROYD, J. N.
HEMMINGS, P.
HOOLEY, W.
JOHNSTON, C. H.
JACKMAN, N.
JONES, C. E.
JEPSON, J.
JONES, H. S.
JAMES, J.
JAMES, C.
JONES, W.
JONES, H.
JACKSON, J.
KNOWLES, R. K.
KENT, A.
KERWIN, J.
LANCASHIRE, S.
LEE, J.
LEES, F. W.
LANGFORD, A.
LEWIS, J.
LANCASTER, S.
LEVER, J. H.
LITTLEFAIR, W.
LEE, W.
LATHAM, F.
LEWTHWAITE, W. H.
McNALLY, S.
MARTIN, C.
MURRAY, T. H.
MURRAY, J.
MINSHALL, A.
MOSS, T.
McHUGH, A.
MOTTRAM, T.
MAXWELL, C.
MIDWOOD, J.
MARSDEN, H.
McDOWELL, A.
MOSS, H.
MURPHY, J.
MARSDEN, F.
MacMURRAY, H.
NEWMAN, A.
NUTTALL, S.
NIELSON, E.
OWEN, E. J.
OWEN, R. E.
OTTEWELL, R.
OSBALDISTON, R.
PAYTON, G.
PEDDER, S. H.
PARTINGTON, R.
PLATTS, H.
PEAT, J.
PROUD, T. M.
POWER, R. L.
PARTINGTON, W.
PARRY, J.
PROSSER, H. L.
PASQUILL, J.
PARDOE, W.
PERCIVAL, J.
PALFREYMAN, T. V.
RUSSELL, W.
ROBERTS, O. E.
RIDGWAY, J.
REDFERN, W.
RICHARDSON, G. H.
ROYLE, A. H.
RATCLIFFE, G. W.
RAYMENT, F. C.
RHODES, N.
RICKWOOD, F. W.
ROBINSON, H.
RAW, B.
ROWBOTHAM, H. S.
SCHOFIELD, A.
SCOTT, W.
SUMMERS, A.
SUDDABY, N.
SCARBORO, H.
SIMPSON, C.
SHAW, S.
SUTTON, C.
SIMMONDS, H.
SHAW, J.
SKERTCHLEY, E. G
SINGLETON, R.
SEWELL, F.
SMITH, J. E.
SAGER, J.
SUMNER, D.
SUTTON, S.
STOCKS, G.
SEVERS, G.
SUTTON, S.
TOWNLEY, H. G.
THORNLEY, J.
THORNLEY, L.
TAYLOR, E.
TAMSWELL, A. E.
TAYLOR, H.
TUSTIN, C.
TATTERSALL, S.
TARR, W.
THORNTON, C.
TRUIN, F.
TAYLOR, O.
THOMPSON, S.
WRIGHT, T. H.
WALKER, J.
WILD, T.
WRIGHT, W. E.
WILKINSON, H.
WAGSTAFF, A.
WOLSTENHOLME, C.
WILLIAMS, J. R.
WATTS, J.
WORSENCROFT, L.
WEEDALL, W.
WALSHE, J.
WESTMACOTT, E. A
WHATMOUGH, A.
WILLIE, J. A. W.
WATSON, F.
WOOD, H.
WOODALL, P.
WEAVER, C. H.
WRIGLEY, J. H.
WILLIAMS, J.
WEBBER, H.
WILLIAMS, H. R.
WILSON L.
WATTS, C.
YOUNG, M.
YATES, F.
YOUNG, J. H.
YOUNG, A.

H. White, Wilson and Co.
(See p. 654 in Roll of Honour.)

WILSON, H. W.
DODSON, E. S.
CRYER, W.

The Wallpaper Manufacturers, Ltd.
(See p. 706 in Roll of Honour.)

Lightbown Aspinall Branch.

SUGDEN, A. V., Director.
ALMOND, W. L.
ANCELL, F.
BALL, J.
BARDSLEY, T.
BASTOW, W.
BELL, R.
BESWICK, M.
BUCKLEY, J.
CASEY, D.
CASEY, J.
CARLEY, G.
COCKER, J. E.
COOK, J. T.
COUNCIL, A. W.
DEPONT, F.
DUNN, T.
ELLERBY, T.
FERREY, R.
FOSTER, R.
FRANCIS, G.
FURNISS, T.
GREAVES, A.
HAGAN, F.
HEAP, J.
HOLLAND, G.
HOUGHTON, T.
HOWARTH, T.
HOWARTH, W.
HUGHES, C.
JACQUES, J. H.
KERRY, T.
KERSHAW, C.
NASH, T.
OAKLEY, J.
POPE, A. J.
RATCLIFFE, J.
RAYNER, W.
ROGER, J.
ROWLSTONE, A.
SHEARER, P.
SMITH, F.
THOMPSON, J.
TILDSLEY, J.
WALKER, A.
WALKER, H. R.
WALSH, J.
WATSON, T.
WEEBER, J.

Walker Carver Branch.

CARNEY, T.
CARVER, W.
ECKERSALL, A.
FIEFIELD, J.
FROST, G.
GREGORY, F.
HODGE, F.
HOOSON, J.
HOLMES, S.
JARVIS, S.
JONES, H.
JONES, R.
MILLER, S.
MORRIS, N.
OPENSHAW, E.
PARDELL, T.
RILEY, R.
ROBERTS, T.
TAYLOR, S.
VICKERS, G.
WALKER, B.
WATTERS, H.
WELSH, J.
WORRALL, R.

Geo. Watson and Co.
68, Barton Arcade.

WATSON, G.
*ANDERSON, T.
*PRICHARD, S.
STOTHARD, J. E.
RAVENSCROFT, H.

James Wheeldon and Sons, Ltd.
(See p. 707 in Roll of Honour.)

BARNES, R.
BLYTHE, D.
BARROW, H.
COWSILL, F.
CLAXTON, W. E.
DEAN, W.
DUGDALE, G.
ERITH, J. A.
FEATHERSTONE, A.
FENNON, E.
FLETCHER, H.
FAIRFIELD, H.
GATTENBY, I.
HICKFORD, G. A.
HICKFORD, J.
HALES, H.
HALLAM, T. H.
JOHNSON, F.
LINNEY, W.
LUMLEY, A.
LEIGH, G. E.
NIELD, A.
REDFERN, F.
ROSE, H. A.
ROME, W.
STANTON, P.
SWAINE, H.
THORNLOW, H.
TINKER, J.
THOMPSON, J.
TREVENNING, E.
WILLIAMS, W.
WHEELDON, E. C.
WHEELDON, A. L.
WALLWORK, H.

Wilson, Knowles & Co.
(See p. 709 in Roll of Honour.)

*MAYSON, J.
†HALLIDAY, J.
†COOK, J.
BRAGG, A.
SWALLOW, L.
†COLLIER, N.
HOLMES, J. H.
GRIGSBY, H.
DARBYSHIRE, W.

J. D. Williams and Co.
(See p. 654 in Roll of Honour.)

BIRCHALL, H.
BOOTH, T.
BROMLEY, H.
BUTTERFIELD, W.
ERASMUS, H.
EVANS, A.
GLAISTER, H.
HALL, W.
HOLDSWORTH, M.
JACKSON, G.
JONES, E.
LOMAS, A.
MOUNFIELD, H.
PEMBERTON, J.
ROUSE, J.
ROOTHAM, H.
SEED, D. R.
SPENCER, J. G.
WILLIAMS, E. L.

Wilson, Bothamley and Son.
(See p. 652 in Roll of Honour.)

GREAVES, A.
KERSHAW, P.
MEEK, R. H.
OWEN, D.
PEARS, W.
WADE, H.
†BOWEN, W. T.
†CANNELL, F.
†FREEBORN, G. V.
†NUTTALL, B. C.
†PARRY, E.
†YEARSLEY, J. C.

Woodhouse, Hambly and Co.
(See p. 653 in Roll of Honour.)

BUTLER, F. W.
BROCKBANK, H.
ELLIOTT, S. J.
McCORMACK, A.
ELLIS, W.
FAULKNER, A.

* Serving with the Colours. † Rejected.

Whitworth and Mitchell, Ltd.
(See p. 708 in Roll of Honour.)

POUNDER, F.
PILLING, F. A.
HARRISON, W. J.
BUCKLEY, T. E.
RIDEHAUGH, J.
CHETHAM, H.
HORROBIN, A.
NUTTALL, J.
KENDREW, A.

Edward Wood and Co., Ltd.
(See p. 648 in Roll of Honour.)

ADDISON, J.
ASPREY, A.
ASHLEY, A.
ANDERSON, J.
ASHTON, J.
BAXENDALE, H.
BROWN, C.
BLACKBURN, R. H.
BARTON, R.
BROWN, A.
BROW, W.
BACKHOUSE, J. A.
BENNETT, P.
BUTLER, S.
BARBER, J.
BLACKBURN, A.
BELL, C.
BLOOD, R.
BRADLEY, W.
BUTLER, L.
BUNN, T.
BENNETT, F.
BOULTON, W.
BRIGGS, J.
CARRICK, S.
CUNNINGHAM, J.
COATES, W.
CHEMNEY, J.
CALF, J.
CROMBLEHOLME, T.
CAWSON, S.
CHANDLER, H.
COOPER, J.
COOPER, D.
CALLAGAN, W.
CHADWICK, B.
COTTERILL, L.
CUNNINGHAM, H.
CROSS, E. J.
DAFFERN, S.
DOWSON, R.
DEAKIN, J.
DEAN, A. W.
DUTTON, J.
DENSTON, P. W.
DODD, D.
EDWARDS, T. C.
FILER, W. G.
GRAHAM, R.
GRAHAM, A.
GORDON, T.
GILLIGAN, T.
GRIFFITHS, J.
GOODALL, J.
GOULD, F.
GARSIDE, A.
HAMPSON, H.
HAY, W.
HIGHAM, T.
HUDSON, H. T.
HASTIE T. L.
HEASON, H.
HOWARD, H.
HAYES, J.
HORNBUCKLE, R.
HOLLAND, W.
HORN, W.
HANKEY, E.
HAYES, J.
HICKTON, C.
HURST, R.
HOLLINS, F.
JONES, W.
JOYNSON, A.
JESSON, J.
KITCHEN, H.
KENYON, A.
KENEEN, A.
KENNING, B.
KEMPLAY, H.
LANCASHIRE, A. E.
LITTLE, A.
LOCHEAD, W.
LAMBOURNE, J.
LEWIS, H.
LISTER, J. W.
LEWIS, C.
LEA, T.
MORTON, W.
MIDGLEY, A.
McGILL, T.
McRAE, T.
MERITON, H. R.
McLEAN, R.
McCUDDEN, J.
NICHOLLS, G. W. N.
ORMESHER, E.
ORME, A.
O'NEILL, W.
O'REILLY, F.
OULTON, G.
PARKER, C.
POLLITT, J.
PARKIN, R.
PAYNE W.
PATRICK, W.
PALMER, T.
REE, P.
REYNOLDS, F.
ROTHWELL, W. E.
RIDING, J.
RYAN, J.
ROBERTS, C. A.
REILLY, W.
ROSEBERRY, E.
RUSSELL, G.
ROBINSON, H.
ROBINSON, W.
SMALLEY, W. G.
STRAWSON, R.
STEPHENS, R. J. H.
SLATER, E.
SEDDON, C. F.
STANYER, H.
SLATER, W.
SLATER, F. I.
SHALLCROSS, W.
SAVAGE, G.
SHAW, J.
THOMPSON, J.
TATTERSALL, H.
VERNON, W.
WARD, W. N.
WILSON, A. E.
WARREN, A. S.
WHITEFOOT, T.
WHITEFOOT, W.
WILSON, C.
WHITE, R.
WALSHE, F.
WOOD, A.
WAREHAM, H.
WARD, P.
WARD, N.
WILLIAMS, T.

James Woolley, Sons and Co., Ltd.
(See p. 650 in Roll of Honour.)

ALDRED, W.
BENNETT, J.
BIRCH, G. N.
BUTT, E.
CHADWICK, P.
COBURN, E.
CRAGG, B.
CROWLEY, W.
DAVIES, F.
DAWSON, T.
DIDRIDGE, A.
*DIXON, B.
EASTWOO, D.
FARROW, J.
FLOOD, J.
GOODWIN, C. E.
GREENHALGH, J.
GRESTY, A. V.
HARPER, V.
HEDLEY, R.
HENSON, R.
IRLAM, C.
JONES, T.
KIRBY, A.
LEWIS, T.
MACDONALD, B. G.
MARKHAM, A.
MARREN, G. W.
MOTTERSHEAD, G.
PARTINGON, R.
PARTINGTON, W.
PHILBIN, J.
POOLE, H.
ROBERTS, W.
ROBINSON, B.
SAYER, C.
SHAW, G.
*SIDDONS, W.
SIMMONS, W.
SMITH, W.
SPROSON, D.
THOMPSON, H.
*WALLIS, W.
WILKINSON, W.
WOOLLEY, P.
RAY, A.
WRAY, T.
†AINSWORTH, G.
†BUCKLEY, C.
†BUTLER, T.
†CARD, W.
†DODSON, A.
†FARTHING, R.
†FERN, S.
†FURPHY, S.
†HOGAN, J.
†HUTCHINSON, F.
†IRLAM, F.
†McLAREN, W. R.
†NICHOLSON, P.
†O'CONNOR, J. B.
†PROUD, H.
†ROLLINGS, G.
†SLATER, C.
†SMETHURST, G.
†SMITH, W.
†WARHURST, A.

Alfred Young and Co., Ltd.
(See p. 653 in Roll of Honour.)

HARRISON, W.
PROSSER, T. B.
BOWEN, S. W.
GILBY, B.
HURST, J. F.
LOMAS, K.

* Serving with the Colours. † Rejected.

Supplementary List of Names of Men who have Attested under the Group System.

J. H. Agnew & Brother.
(See p. 761 in Roll of Honour.)

W. WALKER.
E. H. LEESE.
F. INGHAM.
T. RICHARDSON.
†C. H. SMITH.
†C. N. HOLT.
D. LANGSDORFF.

The Associated Newspapers Limited.
("Daily Mail" and "Weekly Dispatch.")
Deansgate, Manchester.
(See p. 747 in Roll of Honour.)

AIREY, W.
ALLEN, A. P.
ALLEN, J.
BARR, J. F.
†BARRY, M. D.
BATES, H.
†BEANLAND, V. A. S.
BECKLEY, G. H.
BENCH, A.
†BIBBY, H.
†BOOTH, J.
†BRANSON, W. G.
BROWN, C.
BUGLASS, R. S. B.
CHESTER, G.
†CLARKE, A.
†CLAY, T. A.
COLLIER, J.
COOKE, W.
COOPER, A. E.
COSGROVE, G. E.
CUTLER, R. H.
DAVIES, C. H.
DAVIES, F.
†DEAN, H.
DENT, J. B.
DEWAR, W. J. W.
DOWLING, H.
DUNN, T. W.
DUXBURY, J. H.
†EDWARDS, C.
ETHERINGTON, G.
GIBSON, H. C.
†GIBSON, W. O.
†GODWIN, W. T.
GRAY, A.
†GREGORY, T.
GRESTY, F. W.
HALLARD, T. H.
†HALLAS, A.
HALLEY, W.
HEAP, T.
†HIBBS, H. E.
†HITCHEN, T.
HODGKINSON, H.
HUNTER, A.
HUTCHINSON, A.
JEFFERIES, T.
JENYON, C.
JUDGE, F. W.
†KENDAL, E.
LANCASTER, N.
†LANDELLS, W.
LAYBOURNE, J.
LAYFIELD, J.
†LEE, A. L.
LEE, A. R.
LEE, W.
MARSHALL, A. C.
†MAYCOCK, F.
MITCHELL, R. E.
MORRIS, J. W.
NAYLOR, A.
†NAYLOR, H. B.
OLDHAM, T.
†PARKER, H.
PARKER, H. J.
PARKES, S. M.
†PATTERSON, S. G.
†PEARSON, W.
PEDDAR, H.
†POTTER, F.
†POTTS, F.
PRESS, A. E.
RILEY, E. C.
†ROBERTS, J. E.
ROBERTS, R.
†SADLER, W. G.
†SIMPSON, A.
†SIMPSON, J.
†STEED, T.
SWEENEY, M.
WALKER, E. V.
†WALKER, G. H.
WALKER, R.
WHALE, J. R.
WHITTAKER, A.
WHITTAKER, W.
WIMPENNY, F.
YATES, J.

Henry Bond & Co. Ltd.
(See p. 762 in Roll of Honour.)

BOWERS, H.
†HARTLEY, A. C.
BERRY, E.
HOGG, A.
GRUNDY, F.
FLITCROFT, J.
†JONES, L.
LEVER, T.
LEVER, W.
MARTIN, S.
†BROWN, W.
†TAYLOR, A.
GLAZEBROOK, W.
†WILSON, R.
SOUTHWELL, F.
†COUPS, C.

James S. Blair and Son.
(See p. 749 in Roll of Honour.)

O'BRIEN, J.
HALIDAY, W. E.
ABRAMS, H.
GRIMES, W.
TWEMLOW, T. N.
MELLOR, T.
TAIT, A. G.
† GALLIMORE, A.
† HODGKINSON, D. R.
† MOORE, T.

John Ditchfield.
(See p. 730 in Roll of Honour).

DITCHFIELD, J., Jnr.
DAVENPORT, S. H.
NUTTALL, A.
COOKE, A.
YEOMANS, W.
JOYNSON, S.
PHILLIPS, W.
OSBORNE, E.
BLOOR, R.
WHITE, W.
THORLEY, W.
BARLOW, J.
SLOANE, J.
BARLOW, H.
BIRD, W.
BARLOW, F.
MARSDEN, H.
L. HARRISON.

† Rejected.

"The Daily News" Ltd.
Northern Edition,
Dale Street, Manchester.
(See p. 758 in Roll of Honour.)

AYLMER, J.
ASHWORTH, T.
ATKINS, J. H.
ATKINSON, E.
BANKS, F.
BAXTER, W.
BENT, T.
BENTHAM, R. W.
BETNEY, C.
BOND, J.
BOOTH, E.
BRAMWELL, S. B.
BROADHURST, C.
BROUGHTON, J.
BROWN, T.
CARTER, F. R.
CLARKE, A. H.
CLEMENTS, J. E.
COGHILL, J.
COOPER, G.
COOPER, H. E
COUPE, J.
CARWARDINE, C. E. T.
CREGAN, J.
CRICK, B. J.
DAVIES, W.
DELANEY, M.
DIXON, H.
EATON, J.
EGLAND, F. A
FARRELL, H.
FOSTER, C. M.
GAUNT, J. T.
GIBSON, W.
GRAY, J.
HARDMAN, J.
HARGRAVES, A.
HAWORTH, W.
HEFFERMAN, C. F.
HIAM, H. J.
HIGGINSON, L.
HOLDEN, A.
HOLLAND, J. R.
HOUGHTON, J.
HUGHES, S.
HUMPHREY, F. G.
HUNT, T. H.
JACKSON, S.
JENKINS, J. A.
JONES, J. H.
JONES, J. W
JONES, T. F.
KIRK, A.
LANCASHIRE, J. R.
LEATHERBARROW J.
LESTER, H.
LEWIS, A. G.
MATHER, W
MILLER, E. R. S.
MORRIS, J.
MOSS, F.
MYALL, R.
NAYLOR, W. W.
NEILD, A. J.
O'GRADY, C. S.
PEARSON, J.
PHILLIPS, J.
PIDGEON, A. G.
PIKE, J.
POLLARD, A.
PRATT, W.
RADCLIFF, W.
SAUNDERS, J. E.
SHERMAN, H.
SIEPEN, L.
SIMON, T. E.
SMITH, A.
SMITHIES, R. J.
SOMERVILLE, J.
STEAD, H.
SWINDELLS, S.
TAYLOR, J. H.
THOMAS, E A.
TREVELYAN, J. A.
TURNER, C. E.
VICKERS, H.
WADE, A. S.
WALLACH, G. C. L.
WARWICK, E.
WATTS, H.
WELCH, A.
WEST, T. E.
WEST, W.
WHALLEY, T.
WHITAKER, F.
WHITTAKER, A.
WILKES, J. T.
WILLIAMSON, C.
WILMAN, A.
WILSON, N.
WOOLEY, C.
WORRALL, A.
WOTHERSPOON, A
WRIGHT, M.

Falk, Stadelmann and Co., Ltd.
(See p. 753 in Roll of Honour).

BANNISTER, A. E.
BENSON, F.
BRICKCLIFFE, E.
CHILMAN, H. J.
FRIEZER, C. G.
LEE, P.
MAGUIRE, E.
SAWTELL, H.
SEGUST, W.
PORT, W. P.
YEARSLEY, J.

Fisher Renwick Manchester-London Steamers Limited.
(See p. 748 in Roll of Honour.)

Office.

†BAXTER, C.
†CALASCA, H.
CLAPHAM, E.
†CRUMLEY, A.
FISHER, G.
†HUMPHREYS, W. E.
JARMAIN, J.
KNIGHT, A. T.
MONTGOMERY, J. C.
LOWDON, I. L.
†ROCKETT, H.
TATE, S.
†VEY, T.
†WHITNEY, A. F.
†WEIDIG, W.

Wharf.

CASHIN, C. J.
†CASHIN, H.
CHAMBERS, W.
DEAN, A.
DEAN, J.
FLETCHER, R.
GOODWIN, A. J.
†HANNAFORD, L.
HARRISON, A.
†HAYES, H.
HEATHCOTE, J.
HOLT, J.
JACKSON, J. W.
†MILNER, M.
NICHOLAS, J.
PRESTON, H.
SIMPSON, W.
SIMS, J.
STEELE, J. E.
STOCK, W. G.
WILSON, W.

† Rejected.

William Graham & Co.
(See p. 712 in Roll of Honour).

ASHBROOK, A.
BONEHILL, H.
BRYANS, H.
BRUGH, D.
BILLING, H. H.
BIRCH, S.
BROUGHEY, P.
CREASEY, F.
COLEMAN, W.
DWYER, S.
EASTWOOD, W. J.
ELLIS, T.
FOULKES, A.
GEARY, W. H.
GARNER, H. E.
HEELIS, W. R.
HEYWOOD, W.
JENNINGS, J.
JONES, J. H.
KOORIE, J.
LEE, W.
MAXWELL, W.
McDONALD, J.
NOBLETT, W.
OPENSHAW, F. V.
ORANGE, J. H.
POSTLETHWAITE, T.
PROCTOR, F.
RAYNER, C.
RAYNOR, J.
ROBERTS, W. E.
ROYLE, S.
RILEY, H.
SHARP, F.
SNAITH, F.
SIMMS, H.
SYKES, A. H.
TAYLOR, JAMES
WATTS, C.
WARRINGTON, G. W.
WILLIAMSON, J.
WILLIAMS, H. O.
WOODHOUSE, T.
YOUNG, H. O. E.
YORKE, H.

Grandage & Co.
(See p. 752 in Roll of Honour).

GASH, GEORGE F.
ELSMORE, GEORGE.
OWENS, ALBERT E.
MUDDIMAN, H.

John Heywood Ltd.
(See p. 744 in Roll of Honour.)

REYNOLDS, —
SIMPSON, —
HALTON, G.
BROOKS, —
STUTTARD, —
TOWNLEY, —
BRAY, —
MORGAN, —
SEDDON, C.
SAYWARD, —
THOMPSON, —
MacCALLIN, J.
PEGG, —
WARD, —
LENNOX, —
KIRBY, —
HUTCHINSON, —
TWIGG, —
CONN, J.
SIMMONS, T.
TIGGINS, —
SIMONS, R.
AIMERSLEY, P.
ANDREWS, W.
LANE, E.
BANNISTER, F.
CAMMILE, G.
HOWARTH, E.
WHITESIDE, I.
BILLINGHAM, F.
JACKSON, A.
DORNING, F.
HANDLEY, A.
TAVERNOR, W.
VOCE, —
TOLLADY, L.
HADFIELD, W.
TRACEY, R.
KNOWLES, G. W.
WEBSTER, J.
BARKER, F.
GILBODY, C.
FORREST, —
NURSELL, —
COOKE, —
RILEY, J.
HARGREAVES, —
BRADLEY, —
BOURNE, —
HODKINSON, —
ORMROD, H.
WORTHINGTON, —
BISHOP, —
HUBAND, —
FRANKLIN, —
BROWN, —
MULLANOPHY, —
BULLEN, —
SHELLEY, —
LAMBIE, —
JONES, —
ORMEROD, G., Jr.
HORNER, —
MAXWELL, —
WOOTTON, —

E. H. Hollings & Sons.
(See p. 714 in Roll of Honour).

HOLLINGS, A. H.
HOLLINGS, H. S.
COOPER, T.
GRAY, J.
HIGGINGSON, J.
HILTON, T.
JAMES, F.
KIDALL, S. B.
KNOWLES L.
LOWE, S.
McEWEN, R.
PARSONAGE, W.
YOUNG, R. N.

E. Hulton and Co., Ltd.
(See p. 723 in Roll of Honour.)

Total attested	330
Rejected	132
Grand total ..	462

R. Johnson and Sons, Ltd.
(See p. 728 in Roll of Honour).

JOHNSON, ROBT.
BROWN, E.
BEVINS, A.
CARDWELL, R.
DITCHFIELD, P.
DUCKWORTH, H.
EVANS, F.
HOLIDAY, F.
COOP, W.
MOSS, E.
LOXLEY, T.
RICHARDS, H.

Lawton & Stevenson, Ltd.
(See p. 722 in Roll of Honour).

CHAPMAN, R.
WILLINGTON, T. H.
ALCOCK, E.

Ricardo Moller.
(See p. 753 in Roll of Honour.)

HALL, G.
HORROCKS, J. G.
PRIEST, A.
STEPHENSON, T.
MURRAY, J.

Manchester Stock Exchange.
(See p. 730 for Roll of Honour.)

ARMSTRONG, W. (Marsden, Close-Brooks & Robertson).
ARNOLD, NORMAN (A. & J. J. Arnold).
ABERDEIN, J. J. (Lawson & Ormrod).
ASHWORTH, J. D. (W. R. Ashworth & Sons).
†BARRATT, W. (Marsland & Smethurst).
BELL, G. (Illingworth & Agnew).
BELL, OLIVER (Bell, White & Hardy).
BRADBURN, H. (Fernyhough & Ashe).
BRIERLEY, E. (H. Cooke & Son).
†BUTTERWORTH, W. (A. Jones).
†BOND, E. (Secretary's Office, Stock Exchange).
CAMPBELL, L. M. (Coppock & Bratby).
†CHAPMAN, W. (R. A. Armitage & Son).
CLAYTON, F. (Fielding & Hayes).
†CLARK, S. (Oliver & Co.).
COPPOCK, C. E. (F. W. Staveacre & Co.).
†CROWDER, H. (F. F. Page & Co.).
COTTRILL, J. W. (Pilling & Co.).
†COWTAN, R. A. (Dimmock Bros. & Cowtan).
DANIELS, A. (Marsland & Smethurst).
DAVIES, A. (F. W. Staveacre & Co.).
DUKE, G. (Bell, White & Hardy).
DIXON F. (W. A. Arnold & Sons).
FITTON, S. (Lawson & Ormrod).
†FORD, H. (W. A. Arnold & Sons).
GEARY, J. (T. M. Davies).
GRIMDITCH, F. (W. A. Arnold & Sons).
†GRIME, T. (Charlton & Illingworth).
GASKELL, T. (P. H. & F. C. Mosley).
GAUKROGER, V. (Y. Gaukroger).
†HILL, W. (D. Q. Henriques & Co.).
HOLDEN, T. H. (Langston, Goode & Challinor).
HOLLOWS, S. (Kerr & Lowe).
HUNTER, G. (H. Cooke & Son).
HODGSON, J. W. (Ogden, Whitehead & Smale).
†HEYWOOD, J. (Dimmock Bros. & Cowtan).
HOWARTH, M. L. (Coppock & Bratby).
JARROTT, A. (Illingworth & Agnew).
†JONES, S. A. (A. & J. J. Arnold).
JOHNSON, G. A. (Secretary's Office, Stock Exchange).
KEIGHLEY, J. (C. W. Lambert).
LEYLAND, T. A. (Ogden, Whitehead & Smale).
LEATHER, C. M. (Kerr & Lowe).
LAMBERT, C. W. (C. W. Lambert).
LEIGH. J. (D. Q. Henriques & Co.).
MIDDLETON, A. H. (Lawson & Ormrod).
†MOSLEY, P. H. (P. H. & F. C. Mosley).
MOSLEY, F. C. (P. H. & F. C. Mosley).
McDOWALL, W. (Goodwin & Ambery).
MORT, R. (Fernyhough & Ashe).
NEWMAN, G. W. (Secretary's Office, Stock Exchange).
†NUTTALL, S. (D. Q. Henriques & Co.).
PICKWELL, J. F. (Secretary's Office, Stock Exchange).
†PAGE, B. (W. A. Arnold & Sons).
*ROBERTSON, G. ST. CLAIR (Marsden, Close-Brooks & Robertson).
ROWLANDS, J. (Lawson & Ormrod).
†ROWLEDGE, F. A. (H. Cooke & Son).
SCHOFIELD, A. (J. H. Lancashire & Co.).
SLATER, J. H. P. (T. M. Davies).
†SMITH, F. C. (J. Kay & Son).
SNOWBALL, H. (Pilling & Co..
SHORROCKS, W. (S. Bridgford).
SIDDALL, A. D. (J. Siddall & Son).
†SIDDALL, S. H. (J. Siddall & Son).
SHARPLES, S. D. (O. Yates).
SOUTH, R. (Charlton & Illingworth).
STAVEACRE, W. B. (F. W. Staveacre & Co.).
STOCKTON, A. (F. F. Page & Co.).
SWALE, G. E. (J. Swale & Son).
†SAUL, E. A. (D. Q. Henriques & Co.).
†TEASDALE, J. (Halliday, Blakeway & Teasdale).
TOWNSON, J. (J. E. Winder & Son).
TAYLOR, F. (F. W. Staveacre & Co.).
†TUDOR, F. A. (Marsden, Close Brooks & Robertson).
†VALENTINE, J. H. (O. Yates).
†WILKINSON, N. (Mewburn & Barker).
†WHITWORTH, E. (Railton, Sons & Leedham).
WILSON, G. A. (Lawson & Ormrod).
WILLS, P. (Lawson & Ormrod).
†WOODWARD, H. (Becker & Carington).
WRIGHT, G. E. (Becker & Carington).
YATES, O. (Oliver Yates).

* Exempted.   † Rejected.

J. Mandleberg and Co., Ltd.

(See p. 770 in Roll of Honour.)

EMERY, C.
BRACEGIRDLE, C.
BAYLDON, G.
TAYLOR, J.
ARMSTRONG, R.
COWSILL, C. F. R.
KAUFMAN, K.
KAUFMAN, F.
HYMAN, M.
DAVIS, S.
PAULDEN, G.
DAVIS, G.
MACKAY, A.
ROYLE, W. C.
KEEFE, W.
SINCOCK, S. A.
CROWTHER, W.
WAREING, E. D.
BAMFORD, T.
LONGWORTH, W.
SOBEY, T.
MAKINSON, W.
MATHER, T.
POLLITT, A.
GRAINGER, T.
FLETCHER, T. H.
GRUNDY, J.
HAIGH, A.
MAHER, D.
McMELLON, A.
NEWBY, W.
WILLIAMS, W.
BARNET, G.
LEE, H.
MOSELEY, C. A.
ILES, H. J.
MORRISEY, J.
ALLEN, J. T.
WEBB, H.
GREENWOOD, J.
BROWN, J. R.
SMITH, S.
THOMAS, G.
STAINTHORPE, F. W.
LAFFEY, B.
ROFFEY, A. H.
BEATON, N.
CRAGG, T. J.
HINCHLEY, J.
SCHOLES, F. S.
JONES, C. S.
LLOYD, J.
DODDS, J.
CAWLEY, H. S.
HARDMAN, J.
THOMPSON, W. C.
DOWLING, F.
MALCOLM, C. V.
HUDSON, F.
MORRIS, A. H.
REDFORD, J.
RIGBY, W. J.
GOLDSTONE, D.
BRICKMAN, I.
RANDELL, N.
COLE, F.
HOLT, F.
GASH, H.
LEIGH, H.
TINSDEALL, E.
MUSCOVITCH, J.
WALKER, S. H.
FITZPATRICK, J. G.
LORD, H.
DEY, A.
HISCOX, H.
DOWNES, F.
ARCHER, C. R.
TUTTIET, T.
PRICE, H.
DAVIDSON, C. F.
DRISCOLL, A.
HEY, S. H.
CROSS, E.
GREENWOOD, F.
CLAYFIELD, W.
JOHNSON, J.
PRINCE, J. E.
HARGREAVES, T.
KENT, T.
COLE, F.
FINNERTY, J.
CARDWELL, W.
BRIGGS, J.
GREENHALGH, A.
GREGORY, J.
BARNES, T. S.
IRELAND, J.
HOY, W. C.
BIRCHENOUGH, V.
HASSALL, J.
GLYNN, A.
GREENHALGH, F.
TOWNLEY, W.
JAMIESON, H. C.
MYLETT, B.
ORMEROD, J.
ANDERSON, F.
CAFFERY, J.
BLACKHURST, H.
GROCOTT, J.
PALMER, J.
RAY, H.
BELL, W.
CLEGG, J.
McFARLANE, G.
McALLISTER, J.
McCORQUODALE, J.
MOLYNEUX, H.
McKENNA, W.
ROBERTS, H. F.
FENTON, W. H.
CRAVEN, T. C.
ELLIOTT, J. H.
BARLOW, H.
HORROCKS, J. W.
DEAN, J. E.
GEE, W.
GRAHAM, J. F.
HEATON, J. L.
DAVIES, J. L.
GARSIDE, W.
GREENHALGH, A. S.
McDONALD, H.
TURNER, A.
ROSCOE, F.
EYRES, C.
BIRCHENOUGH, T.
VICKERS, R.
BRADBURY, G. A.
MILLER, R.
HOWARTH, F.
WEEKS, W.
CHRISTY, F.
JACKSON, S. C.
KAY, F.
FOSTER, W.
CHAPMAN, S.
WATSON, W.
CHAMBERLAIN, T.
BANHAM, A.
WHITESIDE, F.
COLLINS, R.
MOLYNEUX, J.
STOREY, C.
ARCHER, G.
WILCOX, J.
WRIGHT, W.
WILCOX, J.
McDONALD, H.
BALSHAW, H.
KELLY, J.
KELLY, F.
WHARTON, J.
RIDGWAY, W. C.
GEOHEGAN, J.
CLARKE, WM.
LAWTON, S.
HARDMAN, S.
WOOD, R. C.
HANLON, J.
AINLEY, H.
NEWBURY, A. J.
WOOD, G.
McFARLAND, G. R. B.
ALDERSLEY, R.
BANHAM, T.
CUNLIFFE, W. B.
PARKER, E. J.
GRESTY, T.
GEE, B.
GREENHALGH, J. E.

H. N. Morris and Co., Ltd.

(See p. 715 in Roll of Honour.)

H.M. FACTORY, GORTON.

Staff.

RUTLAND, E. M.
JELLY, A.
SCOTT, M. L.
AIREY, I. J.
D. F. S.
CHOATE, M. F. S.
DIXON, W. G.
JOHNSON, H. E.

Works.

HARVEY, E. A.
WILKINSON, E.
HUMPHREYS, R. H.
SEED, J. H.
PRICE, E. H.
PRICE, E.
LAKE, H.
TURNER, E.
HEWITT, A.
APPLEYARD, A.
JONES, J.
TAYLOR, T. R.
HURLEY, T. W.
WHITLOW, T.
JONES, J.
COUNTER, W.
BECKINGHAM, T. E.
HAWORTH, R.
INMAN, R.
WIER, S.
KIMSON, R.
PLATT, J.
SCOTT, G.
HORTOP, W. H.
McKENNA, J. (Soldier)
DALEY, J. E.
NELLIST, H.

H. N. Morris & Co. Ltd.—continued.

FARRAL, F.
ATKINS, R. W.
BERESFORD, C.
WALTERS, J.
WORSLEY, P. (Soldier.)
HOBBS, J. W.
COBB, J.
JONES, A.
McCARTAN, W. H.
BARNETT, W.
BICKERSTAFF, D.
EVANS, G.
JONES, J. C.
WINCKLE, W.
CAPPER, E.
BLENCOWE, C.
SOUTHWORTH, H.
TIFFIN, A. A.
DAWES, F.
GILL, J. R.
BUCKLEY, A.
WOOD, S.
TURNER, A.
TYSON, A.
KENDRICK, W.
BOOKER, J. E.
AMMIS, H.
WIGNALL, J.
REED, A.
HUCKLE, T.
MILLS, G.
TAYLOR, J.
SYKES, L.
RUMLEY, R.
NEWTON, T.
HOLLAND, J.
HEELEY, T.
HUDSON, L.
ROBINSON, J. W.
ARROWSMITH, A.
CATO, H.
JONES, T.
GOLDSTRAW, H.
HELLIER, J.
FEAY, E.
RAYNER, I.
RUSHTON, A. H.
BROAD, E.
BOOKCOCK, J. T.
WILD, E.
CROMPTON, T.
HAZELL, J.
KING, W.
SPEECHLEY, W.
SYVRET, R.
FLINT, J.
SIMPKIN, F.
BATES, P.
DOYLE, E.
WHITEHEAD, J.
WATERHOUSE, J.
RIGBY, T.
KNOTT, C.
MAPE, P.
SMITH, J. H.
JONES, H.
JOHNSON, H.
RILEY, G. E.
FLEVILL, B.
GREEN, J. T.
CAIN, J.
HOWELL, F.
McKENNA, J.
SWINDELLS, A.
MELLORS, H. J.
CLARK, J.
McCORMICK, J. J.
CAMPBELL, S.
AMES, J. E.
DEVINS, C.
EARLE, A.
LOCKWOOD, W. E.
MARLEY, J.
HOLLAND, W.
NICHOLS, W.
RIDER, H.
WALKER, G.
CAVANAGH, E.
GILL, L.
BANKS, J. E.
BRACEGIRDLE, J.
GREY, G. F.
DAWSON, A.
FANIE, F.
FRANCE, E. W.
CRANKSHAW, A.
CARROLL, J.
DAY, F.
McCARTHY, E.
LONG, T.
LEIGH, G. A.
NEEDHAM, W.
PEARSON, W.
STANLEY, J.
SOUTHERN, R. W.
SANDERS, J.
WILD, C.
FARNWORTH, A.
HEARD, S.
BRACEGIRDLE, H.
BURNS, J.
CREEME, M.
FRANCIS, G.
MARKIE, W. H.
WORRALL, J.
WORRALL, W.
HARDY, J.
PUGH, R.
HEALEY, J.
THOMPSON, T. B.
COTGREAVE, W.
COCKS, J.
HAYWOOD, W.
HOOLEY, T.
BARNES, F.
PARTINGTON, J.
GLOUSTON, W. A.
ALDRED, S.
CARPENTER, A.
ATHERTON, H. A.
KENNY, G.
NELSON, F. H.
MONKS, G.
CASTLE, W. J.
TANDY, J.
SIDDALL, A.
MALEY, J.
HOOPER, A.
FITTON, D.
POWER, T.
HILL, J.
CROOK, W.
ROBINSON, G.
BYWATER, J.
RILEY, J.
BUCKLEY, T.
WALKER, C.
HALL, D.
FOSTER, T.
HIGHAM, W. T.
EVANS, W.
DOYLE, M.
GODSALL, E.
NOLAN, T.
BRIERLY, T.
WOODHEAD, C.
DITCHFIELD, H.
LYCH, C. T.
CHILTON, T.
MULBERRY, G.
TEAR, J.
TAYLOR, S. P.
CUNNINGHAM, T.
RYDER, G. W.
SMITH, J.
ASH, A.
ASHTON, E.
COOKSON, J.
STOTT, J. W.
PARTINGTON, T.
FORD, J. R.
FLANAGAN, J.
FOSTER, J.
HOLDEN, T.
COCKS, T.
MOORE, W. H.
HOUGH, D.
PEARSON, R.
GREY, J.
HILL, G. W.
DAWSON, G.
TICKLE, W.
THORPE, W. H.
HAWKINS, R.
SCOTT, A.
STONIER, J.
DICKENS, J.
O'SHEA, J.
GIBSON, H.
MAWSON, G.
OPENSHAW, J.
BELL, T. W.
MARSHALL, E.
WOLSTENCROFT, H.
BURNS, J. H.
HAMILTON, F.
SMITH, J.
FERNLEY, J.
ANGUS, A.
IBBOTSON, J. H.
BAILEY, C.
LILLEY, J.
SAVITT, W. H.
PLANT, C. H.
ROBINSON, G.
JONES, A.
GRECIAN, F.
HAMILTON, W.
TORKINGTON, J.
GREY, R.
TATE, E.
BILLINGON, W.
LESTER, H.
BEARDMAN, H.
BUNTING, R.
BROWN, G.
HARDMAN, H.
ALLEN, J.
LYNHAM, W. H.
JONES, J.
TAYLOR, R.
AMERY, S.
TRAVIS, A.
OWEN, H.
HAMNELL, T.
STONER, G. A.
MOSEY, E.
FORD, T.
BAMBER, J. W.
MANNION, J.
TAYLOR, J.
MOSEY, T. A.
JOHNSON, J. W.
BEEDIE, A. M.
SHEPPARD, R.
TAYLOR, A.
HOLLAND, J.
WILLIAMSON, T. S.
CHILTON, G. E.
GRACE, C. W.
EVANS, R. H.
CONNOLLEY, M.
ATKINS, J. W.
COULSON, L.
ETCHELLS, G.

Denton Works.

SMYTHE, J. H.
COOPER, J.
HOWIE, J.
McHUGH, J.
SCHOFIELD, W. H.
TRACEY, E.
DUGDALE, J.
DUGDALE, G.
TURLEY, J.
THORNLEY, T.
NEWMAN, J.

Manchester Steam Users' Association.
(See p. 714 in Roll of Honour.)

ASHWORTH, S.	GOUGH, P. E.	KIRKWOOD, P. T.
BIRCH, A.	HOLT, B.	POULSON, S. M.
BROWN, W.	HAGUE, C. F.	RITCHIE, E. G.
BURDOCK, A.	HOUGH, T.	RENDELL, F. G.
CUNLIFFE, J.	HOWARTH, H.	SLATER, N.
CHAPMAN, F.	HARPER, J.	WILLIAMS, W. E.
CHRYSTAL, G.	IRELAND, J.	WAGSTAFFE, J. H.
DICKINSON, A.	JONES, H. A.	

Myrtle, Burt and Co.
(See p. 750 in Roll of Honour.)

OWEN, J. R.	GASKELL, J.	†MORRELL, G. H.
WAUGH, W. L.	†FALLOWS, W. S.	†BURROWS, JAS.
CUNNINGHAM, W. F.	†CROOM, E. R.	†DUNLOP, F.
DODD, W.		

H. D. Pochin and Co., Ltd.
Worsley Street, Salford, Manchester.
(See p. 742 in Roll of Honour.)

Head Office.
TAYLOR, D. T.　DODDS, E.　MOORES, E.
GORDON, H. C.

Salford Works.
PRICE, W.

Warrington Works.

HICKLING, A.	GALLAHER, P.	CLARE, J.
STEWART, W.	NOCK, H.	FISHER, H.
CAMPBELL, J. H.	GABRIEL, J. E.	BURKS, J.
BARLOW, T.	WARD, J.	WINCOTT, C. H.
FENTON, M.	DICKS, A.	KEARNEY, T.
WORRALL, W.	LEAH, T.	FLANAGAN, J.
COLLINS, J.	DALEY, T.	GLAVIN, J.
RYLANCE, J.	COLLINS, P.	PRICE, G.
GLEDHILL, J. E.	BROWN, W.	WATKINS, G.
SMITH, W. H.	HOLLOWELL, C.	TAYLOR, J.
LEE, J.	KEENAN, R.	SCULLY, E.
TAYLOR, T.		

Newcastle Works.

HELM, E.	McCORNICK, J.	BENNY, G.
WATSON, G.	RANKIN, J.	STAFFORD, G.
MERRIN, C.	WHYTE, T.	PATTERSON, H.
ARTHUR, F.	WATSON, R.	HOUGH, E. P.
BRIGGS, J.	MITCHINSON, T.	STIMPSON, W.

Bristol Works.

TOWLER, J.	MEADDOWS, G.	HELPS, W.
RODDICK, G.	MOGER, W.	RICKETTS, J.

Gothers Clay Mine.

MARTYN, P.	HAWKEN, T.	CROWLE, E.
TABB, J.	PHILLIPS, W.	BEST, R.
BEST, W., Jr.	HAWKEN, C.	CROWLE, H.
BRAGG, W.	THOMAS, H.	THOMAS, R.
OSBORNE, R.	BULLOCK, A.	STONEMAN, G.
KELLY, J.	KEY, J.	BAZLEY, T.
MARTYN, H.	TRUSCOTT, L.	POAD, E.
KESSELL, W.	DYER, H.	ROGERS, F.
MARTYN, W. J.	SNELL, R.	TABB, C.
RUNNALLS, J.	BEST, J.	BRAY, W.
BRAGG, T.	MARTYN, E.	CRADDOCK, A.
DOCKING, J.	SLOEMAN, D.	GILL, G.
LIDDICOAT, W.	DAVEY, S.	

Halviggan Clay Mine.

JOSLIN, C.	MARTYN, H.	BURTON, F.
RICHARDS, G.	HAWKE, E.	BEST, W.
RICHARDS, W.	MAY, W.	
KELLY, J.	MAY, S.	

Leswidden Clay Mine.
TREBILCOCK, J.　NICHOLLS, T.

Park Clay Mine.
WILTON, W., Sr.　PENGELLY, N.　WILTON, F.

Clay Mine Staff.
HOOPER, J. Y.

† Rejected.

F. Phillips & Company.
(See p. 709 in Roll of Honour).

DYSON, J. A.　HOLDEN, G.　WOLFENDEN, F. W.

Pugh, Davies and Co., Ltd.
(See p. 717 in Roll of Honour.)

ASTON, E.	GRAHAM, P.	SIZER, W.
ASHWORTH, H.	HUGHES, P. T.	SHEARMAN, R.
BALL, H.	HUGHES, J. P.	SMITH, H.
BEDFORD, J.	HUGHES, W. T.	SMITH, W.
BROADBENT, W. H.	HULME, J.	THOMAS, R.
BURNETT, F. L.	JOHNSTON, H.	VARTY, H. C.
COOPER, J. V.	JOHNSTON, H. W.	WASHINGTON, E.
CRADDOCK, A. E.	LAMPITT, W.	WHITING, W. W.
CROSS, F. E.	MOORES, J.	WILLIAMS, D. C.
DAVID, N.	MILNE, E.	WINTERTON, J. H.
DENISON, A.	OWEN, E.	
	RHODES, G.	

A. V. Roe and Co., Ltd.
(See p. 727 in Roll of Honour.)

Staff.

ALLEN, A.	HARRIS, T. H.	RILEY, S. B.
ANDERSON, A.	HILL, P.	ROE, A. V.
ANDERSON, R.	HORRAX, C.	ROE, H. V.
BAYNES, A. F.	JARRETT, E.	SARRATT, C.
BROADSMITH, H. E.	LAWTON, G.	SHIRES, E.
BURKHILL, J. R.	LOWTHER, J. H.	SIMS, A.
CHADWICK, R.	MARTIN, J. H.	SKIDMORE, J.
CONLON, R.	MARWOOD, F. S.	SQUIRE, S.
CROWTHER, H. A.	McKENNA, F.	SMITH, M.
EDIS, W. T.	MENZIES, D.	TAYLOR, C. R.
ELLIS, R.	MORLAND, J.	TAYLOR, J. W.
FARRER, J. W.	NELSON, D.	TRACEY, J. C.
FARRELL, F. P.	PARROTT, R. J.	VERNON, F. W.
FLETCHER, E.	PARTRIDGE, A. R.	WARWICK, H.
GRAINGER, G.	PRIESTLEY, G. A.	WARMISHAM, A.
GREENWOOD, E.	PRIDAY, E. A.	WEBSTER, G.
	RADCLIFFE, J. W.	

Employees.

GRAHAM, J.	PENROSE, C.	DOLLEY, J.
GEDDES, J. H.	KELLETT, E.	OGDEN, —
PERKINS, H.	SEDDON, R.	DENTON, H.
WINTER, W.	OLDROYD, T.	KEMP, N.
CUFFWRIGHT, W.	WRIGLEY, J.	CRITCHLEY, A.
ISHERWOOD, P.	SHORT, J.	FOULKES, —
PAXTON, R. W.	JENKINS, F. J.	GREAVES, A.
AIREY, B.	PITCHIE, D.	KAY, J.
THOMPSON, R. O.	HOWARD, J.	SMITH, J. A.
KNOWLES, H.	STEPHENSON, G.	BOARDMAN, F.
MAYSON, H.	ROPER, B.	DRINKWATER, J.
JOHNSON, A.	WOOD, H.	TAYLOR, J.
TAYLOR, J. L.	WALSH, E.	MACKENZIE, W.
BROADHEAD, C.	McGOWAN, R.	JOHNSON, J. R.
CLELLAND, J.	POLLITT, S.	DONOUGH, J.
WOODWARD, G. H.	WILLAN, R.	TUKE, A.
BLACKWELL, W.	GRIMSHAW, J.	JACKSON, J. C.
HALLAM, A.	BURKHILL, J. R.	HIGGINS, S.
TURNBULL, A.	RAWSTHORNE, W. R.	THORPE, H.
THORNTON, H.	WHITTAKER, J.	SHUTTLEWORTH, J.
GARSIDE, A.	COOPER, F.	SERWIN, W.
MONTEITH, A. A.	OWEN, W. H.	NEWTON, J.
BUTTERWORTH,	PICKERING, T.	CHEETHAM, J.
LEIGH, E. H.	HOLLAND, J.	BARNET, F.
GEE, G.	ROBINSON, R. W.	WADE, F.
POTTS, E.	LUTY, W.	WORRALL, W.
HIDDERLEY, R. F.	BARRATT, P.	WARD, F. H.
WALKER, L.	GREENHALGH, E.	HOPE, F.
LLOYD, H.	BAILEY, D.	HARRISON, E.
DOBSON, R. H.	FIELDING, G.	HARDY, J. E.
CASTLE, S.	TAYLOR, W. E.	BROUGHAM, J.
CLARKSON, M.	JONES, T.	FERGUSON, R.
KERSHAW, A.	SHAW, W. N.	ROBINSON, G.
WAIN, A.	MURPHY, T.	OLDFIELD, F.
COOPER, S.	NEWBERRY, A.	BOYD, W.
BROOKS, N.	ROBSON, A. T.	BOWDEN, J. H.
DARBYSHIRE, W. G.	BUNTING, S.	HOTERSALL, E.
BONE, H.	NIXON, J. H.	WILLIAMSON, J.
BENNETT, J.	HARPER, C.	WOODCOCK, Y. E.
FORD, J.	PLANT, J.	WRIGHT, J. L.
TOPHAM, T.	HILL, S.	STEVENSON, L. G.
	SCOFIELD, H.	SHAW, J. E.
	HAIGH, G.	ROWLAND, E.

A. V. Roe and Co., Ltd.—continued.

HARTLEY, T. J.
HUDSON, G. H.
WARBURTON, A.
HARDMAN, J.
POWELL, J. E.
BECKETT, G.
FINCH, A.
ROLLEY, A.
BROADBENT, C.
BROWN, A.
HIGGINS, M.
RADCLIFFE, H.
RUDDOCK, W.
MILLER, J.
WILLMOTT, H.
PROCTOR, H. C.
GARNER, J.
FOGG, H.
ANDERSON, R.
HULME, C.
SEDDON, T.
SMITH, R.
HARDY, A.
WITHERS, A. E.
HOFFMAN, A.
PIMLOTT, F.
SCHOFIELD, W.
SHOREHAM, S.
AINSWORTH, H.
COWLEY, J. E.
POLLARD, F. D.
WHALLEY, A.
DUTTON, W.
PARTINGTON, J. H.
ATKIN, F.
TURNER, G. C.
HILTON, A. F.
JONES, H. E.
DAVIES, A.
HEALEY, J.
HARRISON, H.
GARSIDE, J.
CHIPCHASE, A. E.
HEDLEY, W. J.
STANSFIELD, C. H.
CONWAY, J. E.
COOPE, E.
BOARDMAN, S.
BALL, W. D.
HOWARTH, C.
BOARDMAN, W.
HILTON, H.
TAYLOR, H.
MALONEY, J.
SHERRATT, F.
HORTON, H.
HOLDEN, F. B.
TATTERSALL, W. H.
MURPHY, J. J.
HOFFMANN, F.
GRADY, W.
DUNKERLEY, J.
NIGHTINGALE, R. H.
SNOWDEN, T. W.
CADMAN, A.
HORSFALL, F.
BROWNJOHN, —
LEMON, J. J.
KAY, W.
HALL, F.
LUCAS, B.
MORSE, W. R.
CLAYTON, H.
DOYLE, P.
MARTIN, M.
LEVIN, F.
CLEGG, A.
CAISLEY, T.
JONES, J. W.
MOSS, W.
BOARDMAN, J. A.
SIMPSON, B.
HILL, H. F.
PRINCE, T.
HATFIELD, G.
HOLT, T.
HAYES, H.
FIELDING, A.
BOARDMAN, J.
TAYLOR, E.
CONVEY, W.

ABBOTT, H.
PILLING, J.
ELLIS, W.
SOUTHWORTH, F. C.
O'CONNOR, J.
PARKER, J.
REDFERN, E.
VICKERS, J.
MAGUIRE, H.
MITCHELL, C.
PEDLEY, P.
McANULTY, E.
BULLOCK, A.
PEACOCK, J.
MILLING, W.
ATKINS, J.
BOARDMAN, A.
HARDY, I.
PICKLES, T. E.
HOPE, R.
WEBSTER, H.
RITCHIE, D.
SWINDELL, J. W.
EVANS, J. P.
SPEAKE, J.
ROCHE, W.
HENDRICK, J.
ANDERSON, J.
EVANT, J. E.
JACKSON, E.
BRADBURY, S.
SWELL, J.
NOBLE, A.
MORLEY, J. L.
HAYNES, W.
YOXHALL, J.
MAURICE, J. I.
STEVENSON, J.
GASCOIGNE, J. E.
BOWLES, W.
CLEASBY, J.
SHAW, E. V.
PEAKE, A. E.
BRITTAND, E.
LITTLEMORE, J. H.
HARDMAN, H.
CARR, T.
CUBBIN, T.
BURGESS, G.
HODGSON, H.
WARD, W. R.
SMITH, H.
SINKINSON, W.
SCHOFIELD, F.
HAMER, P.
PRICE, —
DUCKWORTH, H.
JOHNSON, R.
PINDER, O. B.
PLATT, F.
HOLT, A.
STODDART, F.
SLOAN, C. R.
SHAW, H.
WILDE, A.
HARRISS, F. M.
BOYLAN, M.
FOULKES, J.
BROWNHILL, W. R.
GILL, W.
HOLLAND, F.
HALLSWORTH, W.
WILLIAMS, A.
WHITEHOUSE, J. W.
BOCKING, P. H.
STARR, E.
BROOMHEAD, F.
KNIGHT, J.
SEARLETT, W.
SMITH, J.
HOTCHKISS, W.
CLIFFE, R.
SEWELL, J.
MERTON, G.
MANSFIELD, J.
STEVENSON, F.
CASHMERE, I. E.
KEMP, T.
CONNOR, G.
SCRAGG, G. W.

WOODWARD, T.
SCALES, W.
PAGE, J.
PEDLEY, J. H.
LYON, P.
FODEN, H.
BURGESS, G. E.
BARBER, —
WRIGHT, J.
HAWKINS, W.
FLETCHER, W.
BYWATER, D.
LEE, C.
HACKITT, C.
SCHOFIELD, A.
PEACOCK, T. W.
KIRKHAM, A.
ESCOTT, C. E.
TOMLINSON, A.
LOWES, J.
BOWER, G.
JOHNSON, J. W.
ALLEN, J.
THOMPSON, W.
MASON, W.
LITTLE, R.
MURRAY, T.
MOTTERSHEAD, D.
SHARP, W. H.
MILLS, S. H.
TAYLOR, J.
MERRYWEATHER, J.
HARWORTH, C.
BRIERLEY, A.
WITHERS, J.
HOLLAND, J.
BAXTER, G.
ROBINSON, A.
MOORES, T.
WILLIAMSON, W.
OWEN, H.
CHAMBERLAIN, J.
LEA, A.
HALLIWELL, P.
HOEY, J.
WOMERSLEY, W.
HAYTON, J.
HART, W.
WARD, J. E.
HOROBIN, —
HARDMAN, —
DOWNEY, —
JOHNSON, R.
BREEZE, T.
LEWELL, W.
MARSHALL, J.
HEALEY, T.
CURTIS, F.
BROMLEY, S.
FOSTER, R.
FROGETT, F.
McCABE, J.
WATSON, F.
WHITTINGHAM, R.
WALMSLEY, B.
JOHNSON, J.
WALTON, G.
CASTLEDINE, H.
CUNNINGHAM, E.
KERSHAW, P.
HAWKINS, A.
DAVIES, E.
EVANS, H. C.
DONEGAN, W. J.
DINSDALE, J. S.
STEVENSON, H. W.
PEARSON, F.
BARNES, B.
HUTCHINSON, W.
BROOKS, H.
ODELL, B.
HIGGINBOTTOM, A.
BRIGH, T. V.
REED, W. S.
TAPLIN, J. H.
CHEETHAM, W. H.
HARGREAVES, G. W.
COVERLEY, R.
PEARSON, R.

A. V. Roe and Co., Ltd.—continued.

EDGAR, A.
TOOTHILL, H.
PINDER, P.
WHATNOUGH, A.
PINDER, W. H.
JONES, A. E.
DUCKER, A.
BARON, W.
MEADOWCROFT, E.
WHEWELL, G.
HAYCOCK, A.
LUND, J. L.
REID, F.
MACARTHUR, D.
BURD, J.

HORROCKS, —
WETTON, G.
McANULTY, E.
CARTEY, A.
McLEAN, D.
ETCHELLS, J.
HOOKEY, I.
CHAPLIN, J.
CARROL, F.
HARRISON, H.
TIGHE, S.
NORRISS, E.
BOXSHALL, G.
STOTT BUCKLEY, J. R.
TAYLOR, L.

TAYLOR, S.
SMITH, F.
POUND, J.
SMITH, W. H.
BAKE, —
BARTLEY, —
COOPER, —
TAYLOR, T.
FRANKLAND, H.
*BOLAS, —
*BUCKLEY, W.
*COTTERELL, —
*SHERWELL, —
*SHARPLES, A.

E. D. Sassoon and Co.

(See p. 751 in Roll of Honour.)

ALCOCK, A.
AYKROYD, W. C.
CHADWICK, P.
PURNISH, G. W.
GILMOUR, B.
GLOVER, H.
GRIMSHAW, A.
HEWITT, E. J.
HOCKADAY, E.

JONES, H. S.
LONGBOTTOM, J. W.
MARSLAND, A. C.
MORRIS, R.
NICHOLSON, M.
PILKINGTON, J. E.
PULFORD, T. C.
ROYLE, H.
RUCKER, A.

SADLER, J.
SMETHURST, A.
STANSFIELD, N.
TAYLOR, J.
WALCH, W.
WHITEHEAD, T.
WRAGGE, G.
WRIGLEY, T.

Schmidt's Superheating Co. (1910), Ltd.

(See p. 720 in Roll of Honour.)

ACTON, S.
ASHMAN, A.
ASHURST, F.
BATES, C.
BIRMINGHAM, J.
BOLAND, D.
BRAY, H. P.
BROWN, A.
CAPPER, E.
CONSTANTINE, E. B.
COOK, H. H.
CULLEN, W. A.
DAWSON, W. R.
DRYBURGH, A. P.
EVANS, F. W.
FISH, S.
FLANAGAN, J.
FLETCHER, R.
FOWELL, J.

FREEMAN, A.
GODBEHEAR, T. H.
HARDMAN, A.
HARKIN, J.
HAWKINS, J.
HAWLEY, S. C.
HAYES, H.
IBBOTTSON, C.
JACKSON, S.
JONES, T.
JONES, W.
JONES, W. R.
KNIGHT, A.
LAWSON, I. C.
LEONARD, E.
LEWIS, A.
MACADAM, H.
MATTHEWS, H.
MELHUISH, H.

MESSENGER, G.
O'BRIEN, J.
OLIVER, C. H.
PIGRAM, W. J.
PRICE, E. A.
READ, J.
ROBINSON, N. C.
ROWBOTTOM, A.
ROYLE, W. H.
SIMPSON, G.
SKIDMORE, J. F.
SMITH, T. H.
SPEAKMAN, R.
STIRLING, J. H.
SUMMERS, H., Sen.
THORLEY, H.
THORLEY, J.
UNWIN, S.
WILD, J.
WRIGHT, H.

Sherratt & Hughes.

(See p. 718 in Roll of Honour).

BULLOCK, W.
*CHEETHAM, J.

*DOOLEY, T.
EATON, G. M.

*HOLLAND, T. B.
*TAYLOR, J

Smethurst & Holden Ltd.

(See p. 755 in Roll of Honour.)

AYKROYD, A. E.
BRASSINGTON, H.
BRASSINGTON, T.
HIGGINBOTTOM, E.

HIGGINBOTTOM, H.
HOWARTH, C. A.
LATHAM, A.
MOONEY, W. P.
MELLOR, W.

POWNALL, J.
MEARE, T.
MELLOR, E.
ROWBOTHAM, O.
SHEPHERD, A.

Steinthal & Co.

(See p. 751 in Roll of Honour.)

CARLISLE, J
DARWIN, C. R.
EDGE, C.
GOLDSTRAW, A.
HARRISON, H. K.

JAMES, T. P.
MORGAN, H.
OGDEN, C.
PLANT, A.
RICHARDS, G. R.

SNELSON, C. L.
TATTERSALL, J. E.
WHITTAKER, F.
ZIMMERN, W. H.

* Serving with the Colours.

Spurrier, Glazebrook and Co., Ltd.
(See p. 722 in Roll of Honour).

AUSTIN, G.	ROSE, W.	PURDIE, A.
NICHOLLS, E.	HOLIDAY, O.	CLAYTON, H. O.
NICHOLLS, J.	CARLTON, J.	HANKINSON, E. A.
PALMER, S.	WELSBY, A.	

Geo H. Walker & Son.
(See p. 729 in Roll of Honour).

BADDELEY, H.	HARRISON, J. H.	NAYLOR, F.
CREE, A.	HARRISON, G.	RUTTER, H.
CHADDERTON, A. C.	HILL, J.	SMITH, A.
DENTITH, A.	HILL, R.	TAYLOR, H. T.
FALKENSTEIN, G.	HOWSE, T. S.	THORNTON, A.
FIRTH, A.	HOYLE, J. H.	WOOD, L. E.
FISHER, A.	INGALL, A.	

Walker and Homfrays, Limited.
(See p. 646 in Roll of Honour).

ASHTON, J. W.	MILES, W.	BEAUMONT, D.
ASHELBY, G.	McCANNAH, J.	CUNLIFFE, A.
ANDREWS, F. E.	PRESTON, H.	LEE, H.
BALL, H.	FOULKES, J. V.	NODEN, J.
CAVANAGH, J.	SPARY, R.	OGG, J.
O'CONNELL, J.	BUNN, G.	TOON, W.
DIXON, G.	BATTERSBY, —.	WHITTAKER, T.
FENTON, H.	COOMBES, A.	WHITTAKER, C.
FODEN, A.	FOSTER, S.	*BURROUGHES, H.
GEMMELL, D.	FOSTER, R.	Junr.
GILLOW, H. P.	GLASSER, F.	*CALLAGHAN, C.
GARVIE, J.	BAILEY, —.	*COLTON, J. G.
GIBBONS, B.	HIGGINGBOTTOM, G.	*CONNIAN, J.
HICKEY, W.	LOMAX, —.	*DAVENHILL, H.
HEYS, J.	PINDER, S.	*GREENHALGH, J.
HAIGH, E.	RUSSELL, —.	*HAYES, F.
HOWELL, W.	WARBURTON, —.	*JACKSON, A.
HORSLEY, H.	CHEETHAM, F.	*OGDEN, A.
JONES, H.	FERN, W.	*SENIOR, J.
KAY, F.	IRELAND, G.	*TOWLER, E.
LAWTON, J.	JONES, C.	*TURNOCK, S.
MASON, E.	ROSE, J.	*VALENTINE, J.

H. Wallwork and Co., Ltd.
(See p. 760 in Roll of Honour.)

AINSWORTH, R.	BAND, W.	BUTLER, A.
ALLCOCK, G.	BOWKER, D.	BUTLER, J.
ALLEN, G.	BRADSHAW, G.	BUXTON, H.
AMBROSE, E.	BRAZIL, W.	CADMAN, T.
ANDREWS, A.	BRIGHT, F.	CANVIN, H.
ARMSTRONG, H.	BUCKLEY, W.	CARNELL, P.
ARTEGAN, H.	BURNS, H.	CARROL, J.
BAGSHAW, H. C.	BURNS, T.	CAVENEY, W.
BALL, B.	BURTON, F.	CHAISTY, R.

* Now serving with the Colours.

H. Wallwork and Co., Ltd.—continued.

CHAPMAN, C.	HOGG, W.	RAMSBOTTOM, E.
CHAPMAN, R. H.	HOLMES, R.	REILLY, J.
CHEETHAM, J.	HORNER, J.	RENNIE, A.
CHRIPPS, W. T.	HORTON, J.	RICHARDSON, W.
CLARKE, A.	HOWARD, W.	ROBERTS, C. W.
CLARK, J.	HOWELL, J.	ROBERTSON, F.
CLOUGH, L.	HOWARTH, J.	SAUNDERS, T.
CUNNINGHAM, J.	HUBBARD, W.	SAUNDERS, W.
DANSBY, C.	HUGHES, B.	SCHOFIELD, E.
DAY, J.	HUGHES, H. J.	SCOTT, J.
DAY, W.	HUMPHRIES, J.	SCOTT, J. R.
DONOHUE, T.	JOBSON, L.	SEDDON, T.
DONOVAN, M.	JOHNSON, A.	SHAW, J.
DUNN, E.	JONES, R.	SHERIFF, J.
ELLIS, W.	KINLOCK, W.	SIGSWORTH, S. R.
ELLIS, W.	LATHAM, R.	SMETHURST, S.
EMBREY, F.	LAWTON, R.	SMITH, H.
ENGLAND, T.	LEE, S.	SMITH, J. W.
EVANS, C. W.	LEECH, J.	SMYTHE, J.
EVANS, D.	LEES, H.	SNEYD, R.
FERN, A.	LINGARD, J.	SPENCER, G.
FERN, G. H.	LITTLEWOOD, C.	SPENCER, H.
FERN, J. W.	LIVESEY, W.	TAYLOR, F.
FERN, S.	LOWE, W.	TAYLOR, S.
FIELDHOUSE, H.	McCRANN, M.	TAYLOR, W.
FINNEY, W.	McCULLOCK, G.	THOMPSON, A.
FISHER, R.	McDONALD, F.	TINSLEY, G.
FITZSIMMONS, L.	McGOWAN, A.	TINSLEY, W.
FLYNN, B.	McKENNA, P.	TODHUNTER, J.
FLYNN, J.	MAJOR, J.	TOMLINSON, C.
FOWLER, J.	MARKEY, E.	TURNBULL, J.
FOX, H.	MATHEWS, G.	TURNER, C.
FOY, J.	MEEHAM, T.	TURNER, C.
GANLY, W.	MIDGLEY, J.	VINT, J. A.
GARTLEY, T.	MIDGLEY, W.	WALKER, J. W.
GREAVES, W.	MOORES, H.	WALLWORK, A. V.
GRIFFITHS, E.	MORAN, M.	WALLWORK, G. B.
GYVES, J.	MURPHY, P.	WALLWORK, R. N.
HALL, T.	MURRAY, L.	WALLWORK, S.
HANVEY, S.	NAYLOR, J.	WEBSTER, J.
HARRISON, A.	NAYLOR, W.	WEIR, J.
HARRISON, A. E.	NEWTON, H.	WHITE, F.
HARRISON, J.	NORTON, J. W.	WHITEHEAD, A.
HARRISON, J.	ORCHARD, P. T.	WILKINSON, J.
HARTLEY, J.	OUSBY, J.	WILLIAMS, D.
HATTON, T.	PAGE, M. E.	WILLIAMS, H.
HAYES, G.	PEARSON, J.	WILLIAMSON, H.
HAYES, R.	PEARSON, J.	WILSON, P.
HAZELHURST, H.	PHILLIPS, J.	WOLFE, H.
HENEBURY, A	PLATT, T.	WOLFENDEN, W.
HENEBURY, R.	POSTLEWAITHE, T.	WOLSTENHOLME, J. E.
HENRY, D.	POWELL, T.	WOODCOCK, W.
HEYWOOD, J.	POWER, B.	WOOLLEY, A.
HICKSON, J.	PRESTON, J.	
HOGG, H.		

Ph. Ziegler & Co.
(See p. 718 in Roll of Honour).

FLINN, W. L. (partner)	†BINGHAM, A.	†PRESTON, M.
	†HODKINSON, J.	

† Rejected.

www.ingramcontent.com/pod-product-compliance
Lightning Source LLC
Chambersburg PA
CBHW060301010526
44108CB00042B/2595